lonely planet

Thailand

Joe Cummings
Sandra Bao
Steven Martin
China Williams

LONELY PLANET PUBLICATIONS
Melbourne • Oakland • London • Paris

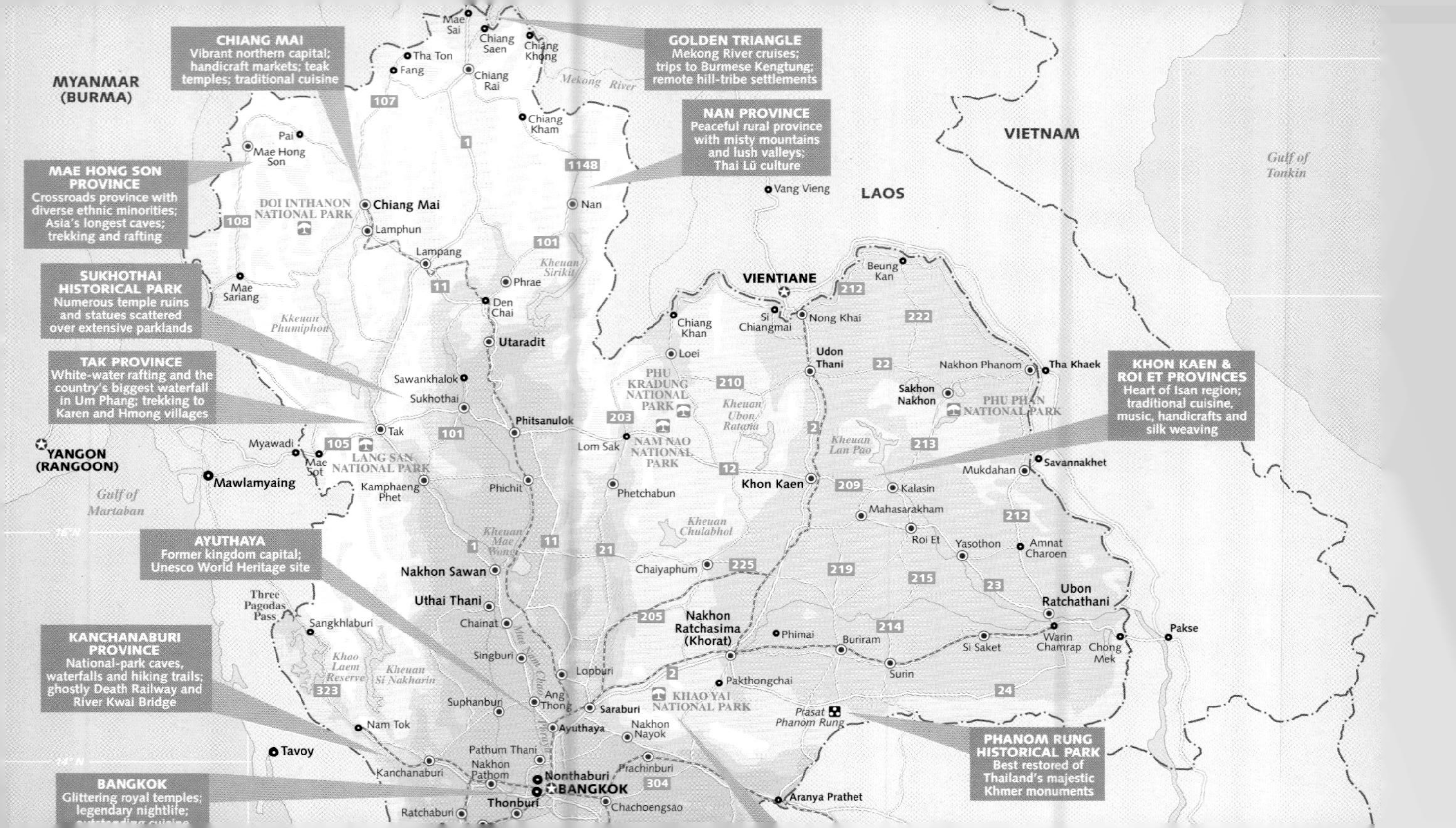

CHIANG MAI
Vibrant northern capital; handicraft markets; teak temples; traditional cuisine
GOLDEN TRIANGLE
Mekong River cruises; trips to Burmese Kengtung; remote hill-tribe settlements
NAN PROVINCE
Peaceful rural province with misty mountains and lush valleys; Thai Lü culture
MAE HONG SON PROVINCE
Crossroads province with diverse ethnic minorities; Asia's longest caves; trekking and rafting
SUKHOTHAI HISTORICAL PARK
Numerous temple ruins and statues scattered over extensive parklands
TAK PROVINCE
White-water rafting and the country's biggest waterfall in Um Phang; trekking to Karen and Hmong villages
KHON KAEN & ROI ET PROVINCES
Heart of Isan region; traditional cuisine, music, handicrafts and silk weaving
AYUTHAYA
Former kingdom capital; Unesco World Heritage site
KANCHANABURI PROVINCE
National-park caves, waterfalls and hiking trails; ghostly Death Railway and River Kwai Bridge
PHANOM RUNG HISTORICAL PARK
Best restored of Thailand's majestic Khmer monuments
BANGKOK
Glittering royal temples; legendary nightlife;
MYANMAR (BURMA)
VIETNAM
LAOS
Gulf of Tonkin
Gulf of Martaban
YANGON (RANGOON)
Mawlamyaing
Tavoy
VIENTIANE
Vang Vieng
Mae Sai
Chiang Saen
Chiang Khong
Tha Ton
Fang
Chiang Rai
Mekong River
Chiang Kham
Pai
Mae Hong Son
Chiang Mai
Lamphun
Nan
Lampang
Phrae
Den Chai
Mae Sariang
Utaradit
Sawankhalok
Sukhothai
Tak
Phitsanulok
Myawadi
Mae Sot
Kamphaeng Phet
Phichit
Nakhon Sawan
Uthai Thani
Chainat
Singburi
Lopburi
Ang Thong
Ayuthaya
Saraburi
Suphanburi
Nakhon Nayok
Pathum Thani
Nakhon Pathom
Nonthaburi
BANGKOK
Thonburi
Prachinburi
Chachoengsao
Ratchaburi
Kanchanaburi
Nam Tok
Sangkhlaburi
Three Pagodas Pass
Aranya Prathet
DOI INTHANON NATIONAL PARK
LANG SAN NATIONAL PARK
Kheuan Phumiphon
Kheuan Sirikit
Kheuan Mae Wong
Khao Laem Reserve
Kheuan Si Nakharin
Mae Nam Chao Phraya
Chiang Khan
Si Chiangmai
Nong Khai
Beung Kan
Loei
Udon Thani
PHU KRADUNG NATIONAL PARK
Kheuan Ubon Ratana
Lom Sak
NAM NAO NATIONAL PARK
Phetchabun
Khon Kaen
Kheuan Lan Pao
Kheuan Chulabhol
Chaiyaphum
Nakhon Ratchasima (Khorat)
Phimai
Pakthongchai
KHAO YAI NATIONAL PARK
Prasat Phanom Rung
Buriram
Surin
Si Saket
Kalasin
Mahasarakham
Roi Et
Yasothon
Amnat Charoen
Ubon Ratchathani
Warin Chamrap
Chong Mek
Pakse
Mukdahan
Savannakhet
Nakhon Phanom
Tha Khaek
Sakhon Nakhon
PHU PHAN NATIONAL PARK
107
1
1148
108
101
11
105
101
203
210
12
2
22
222
212
213
209
212
21
1
11
225
219
215
23
205
214
2
24
323
304
16°N
14°N

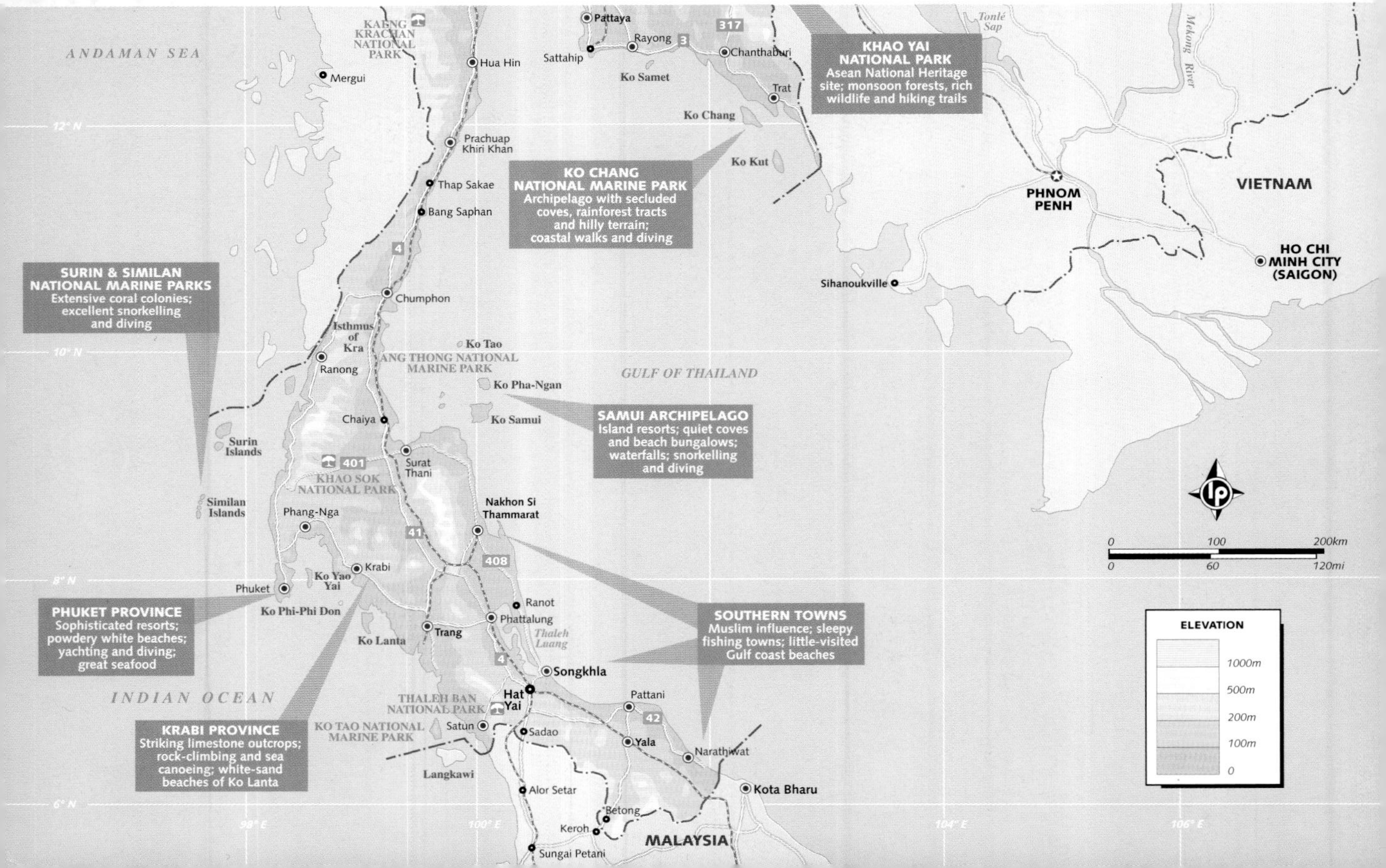

KHAO YAI NATIONAL PARK
Asean National Heritage site; monsoon forests, rich wildlife and hiking trails
KO CHANG NATIONAL MARINE PARK
Archipelago with secluded coves, rainforest tracts and hilly terrain; coastal walks and diving
SURIN & SIMILAN NATIONAL MARINE PARKS
Extensive coral colonies; excellent snorkelling and diving
SAMUI ARCHIPELAGO
Island resorts; quiet coves and beach bungalows; waterfalls; snorkelling and diving
PHUKET PROVINCE
Sophisticated resorts; powdery white beaches; yachting and diving; great seafood
SOUTHERN TOWNS
Muslim influence; sleepy fishing towns; little-visited Gulf coast beaches
KRABI PROVINCE
Striking limestone outcrops; rock-climbing and sea canoeing; white-sand beaches of Ko Lanta
ANDAMAN SEA
GULF OF THAILAND
INDIAN OCEAN
VIETNAM
MALAYSIA
PHNOM PENH
HO CHI MINH CITY (SAIGON)
Mekong River
Tonlé Sap
KAENG KRACHAN NATIONAL PARK
Mergui
Hua Hin
Pattaya
Sattahip
Rayong
Ko Samet
Chanthaburi
Trat
Ko Chang
Ko Kut
Sihanoukville
Prachuap Khiri Khan
Thap Sakae
Bang Saphan
Chumphon
Isthmus of Kra
Ranong
Ko Tao
ANG THONG NATIONAL MARINE PARK
Ko Pha-Ngan
Ko Samui
Chaiya
Surat Thani
KHAO SOK NATIONAL PARK
Surin Islands
Similan Islands
Phang-Nga
Nakhon Si Thammarat
Krabi
Ko Yao Yai
Phuket
Ko Phi-Phi Don
Ranot
Phattalung
Thaleh Luang
Trang
Ko Lanta
Songkhla
Hat Yai
THALEH BAN NATIONAL PARK
KO TAO NATIONAL MARINE PARK
Satun
Sadao
Pattani
Yala
Narathiwat
Kota Bharu
Langkawi
Alor Setar
Betong
Keroh
Sungai Petani
317
3
4
401
41
408
42
12° N
10° N
8° N
6° N
98° E
100° E
104° E
106° E
0
100
200km
60
120mi
ELEVATION
1000m
500m
200m
100m

Contents – Text

Contents – Maps

FACTS ABOUT THAILAND

GETTING AROUND

BANGKOK

CENTRAL THAILAND

SOUTHEASTERN THAILAND

CHIANG MAI PROVINCE

NORTHERN THAILAND

NORTHEASTERN THAILAND

UPPER SOUTHERN GULF

LOWER SOUTHERN GULF

ANDAMAN COAST

MAP LEGEND

METRIC CONVERSION

MAP INDEX

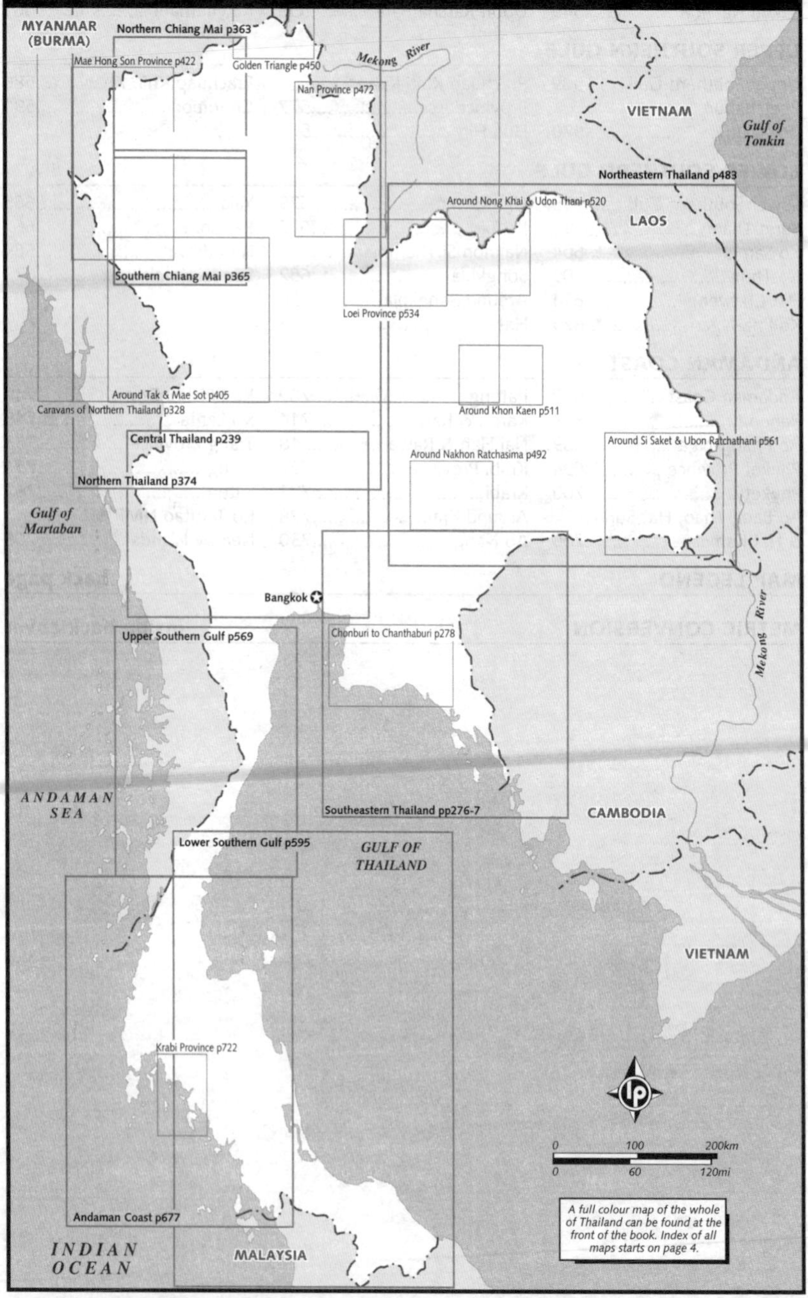

MYANMAR (BURMA)
Northern Chiang Mai p363
Mae Hong Son Province p422
Golden Triangle p450
Mekong River
Nan Province p472
VIETNAM
Gulf of Tonkin
Northeastern Thailand p483
Around Nong Khai & Udon Thani p520
LAOS
Southern Chiang Mai p365
Loei Province p534
Around Khon Kaen p511
Around Tak & Mae Sot p405
Caravans of Northern Thailand p328
Central Thailand p239
Around Si Saket & Ubon Ratchathani p561
Around Nakhon Ratchasima p492
Northern Thailand p374
Gulf of Martaban
Bangkok
Upper Southern Gulf p569
Chonburi to Chanthaburi p278
Mekong River
ANDAMAN SEA
Southeastern Thailand pp276-7
CAMBODIA
Lower Southern Gulf p595
GULF OF THAILAND
VIETNAM
Krabi Province p722
0 100 200km
0 60 120mi
Andaman Coast p677
INDIAN OCEAN
MALAYSIA
A full colour map of the whole of Thailand can be found at the front of the book. Index of all maps starts on page 4.

The Authors

Joe Cummings

Born in the subtropical port of New Orleans, Joe began travelling in Southeast Asia shortly after finishing university. Before writing became a full-time job, he played guitar in a succession of bands, volunteered for the Peace Corps, worked as a movie extra and taught English in Thailand, Malaysia, Taiwan and the USA. Along the way he earned an MA degree in Thai language and art history.

For Lonely Planet he has authored the Thai and Lao phrasebooks as well as *Bangkok*, *Thailand's Islands & Beaches*, *Laos* and *Myanmar*, and the pictorial book *Buddhist Stupas in Asia*. As a freelance journalist he has published articles in dozens of periodicals, including the *Ambassador*, *International Herald Tribune*, *Geographical*, *Guardian*, *Los Angeles Times*, *Observer*, *Outside*, *San Francisco Examiner*, *South China Morning Post* and the *Asian Wall Street Journal*.

Sandra Bao

Born to Chinese parents and raised in Buenos Aires, Argentina, Sandra reluctantly moved to the USA when she was nine. Despite her introduction to the country being a winter in Toledo, Ohio, she became a naturalised citizen and eventually wound up with a BA in psychology from UC Santa Cruz. Sandra has travelled extensively around the world, both before and after joining up with Lonely Planet, and now despairs at having to give up a healthy vegetable garden and promising rock-climbing career for her peripatetic lifestyle. She currently lives in Oakland with her husband, fellow Lonely Planet writer Ben Greensfelder. The two hope to someday acquire a Siamese cat.

Steven Martin

A native of southern California, Steven Martin has been living and travelling in Southeast Asia since 1981, and has written articles about the region for the *Associated Press*, *Agence France-Presse* and *Time*. Steven has also worked on Lonely Planet's *Thailand's Islands & Beaches* guidebook. He is currently based in Bangkok.

China Williams

Thailand doesn't know it, but China Williams is a kindred citizen. She adopted the country while teaching English in Surin, the northeast's elephant capital. Only her freckles and childlike speech marked her as a foreigner. Officially, she is a full-blooded American, having grown up in South Carolina and migrated from one coast to another. She is now temporarily stationed in the vacationlands of Maine with her husband, Matt. China has contributed to Lonely Planet's *Georgia & the Carolinas* and *New Orleans Condensed*.

FROM THE AUTHORS

Joe Cummings

Thanks to the following people in and out of Thailand who were of special assistance during this update: Lori Ashton, Avia Travel, Roy Chapin, Lynne Cummings, Suwannee Emon, Dennis Gillman, Andrew Forbes, Oliver Hargreave, David Henley, Peter Holmshaw, Julian & Pao, Brent & Karin Madison, Sombat Panarong, Ruengsang Sripaoraya and Theerada Suphaphong.

The Tourism Authority of Thailand and its employees throughout Thailand were, as usual, of considerable assistance. Thanks also to my co-authors China, Sandra and Steven, and to the hundreds of travellers who have taken time to write.

Sandra Bao

I have a whole lot of folks to thank for giving their time and energy in helping me make this a better book as well as a fun project. A hearty *khàwp khun kha* to Beau and Murphy in Songkhla; Thirdkiat Phenpapa and Somchay Khongkaew in Surat Thani; Nisa Srisanida, Panwilai Bunprasert, Jim Currie and Buffalo Bill in Hua Hin; Nong Vechiraya in Prachuap Khiri Khan; Chris Anderson, Mieke Ripken, Johan Van Den Berg and Heike on Ko Tao; Phillipa Warren, Sophawadee Creagh and Warren Burgart on Ko Pha-ngan; Natini Wongpuvarak in Narathiwat; Joel and Dang in Satun; Thip Ketrat in Trang; Larissa Webster on Ko Lanta; Eithne Shankar, Henrik Enevoldsen and Jacqui Cole in the Krabi area; Denis Weir on Ko Phi Phi; Gordon Fernandes on Phuket; Yuli Shrager on Ko Phayam; Nithi Wongprateep in Ban Kruit; and Oranut Petchsuda at the Berkeley Thai temple.

Special thanks also to my co-authors Joe Cummings, Steven Martin and China Williams, and to my husband Ben Greensfelder – without whose help I could not have finished this book (in time at least).

Steven Martin

Many thanks to Joe Cummings – it was good while it lasted! Thanks also to Boonpian Sirirat, Daniel Eaton, Dan Lovering, Mat Pennington and Thomas Crampton. Hearty thanks is also due to Craig Stuart and Susan Kim, Jeff Cranmer and Susie Park, Michael Carpenter and Winnie Park. Last but not least, a heartfelt thanks to the staff of the Whistling Swan in Stanhope, New Jersey.

China Williams

Millions of thanks to the kind strangers who gladly walked up four flights of stairs to show me a room that I had no intention of taking. And even more gratitude to the great staff at the Bangkok tourist information office and at TAT. Many thanks to Ajaan Bill for being a reliable beer companion, and to Sit, Alisa, Nongluck and Benjarong for remembering me after all these years and for becoming such successful adults. Special thanks to Terry Moore for being in the right place at the right time and for checking the sights that slipped through the cracks. Finally, thanks to Matt for picking me up at the airport in Maine with a winter coat.

This Book

The first eight editions of *Thailand* were authored by long-term Thailand resident Joe Cummings. For the 9th edition Joe shared the load with Steven Martin. This 10th edition of *Thailand* was written by coordinating author Joe Cummings (the front chapters, special sections and Chiang Mai and Northern Thailand chapters), and Steven Martin (Southeastern Thailand, Central Thailand and Northeastern Thailand chapters), Sandra Bao (Upper Southern Gulf, Lower Southern Gulf and Andaman Coast chapters) and China Williams (Bangkok chapter).

From the Publisher

This edition of *Thailand* was coordinated in Lonely Planet's Melbourne office by Victoria Harrison (editing and layout) and Jack Gavran (maps). Gina Tsarouhas took over from Victoria during layout. Kristin Odijk, Lara Morcombe, Cherry Prior, Sally Steward, Craig Kilburn, Meg Worby and Evan Jones assisted with editing and proofing. Yvonne Byron and Tamsin Wilson lent a helping hand during layout. Quentin Frayne edited the Language chapter. Helping out with the maps were Csanad Csutoros, Anthony Phelan, Barbara Benson, Tessa Rottiers, Valentina Kremenchutskaya, Amanda Sierp, Wayne Murphy, Andrew Smith, Jody Whiteoak and Corie Waddell.

Jane Thompson and Mary Neighbour wrote the brief for this edition, and Mary commissioned the book. Production was managed by Chris Love, Huw Fowles and Michelle Lewis.

The colour sections were designed by Sonya Brooke, and Vicki Beale took the book through layout; thanks also to Kate McDonald and Adriana Mammarella for layout checks. The cover was designed by Gerilyn Attebery.

Thanks to Nick Stebbing for his advice during production, to Chris LeeAck for sorting out map fonts, to Jane for checking the index, and to Bruce Evans for expert advice on all matters Thai and for proofing the Thai script throughout this book.

THANKS
Many thanks to the travellers who used the last edition and wrote to us with helpful hints, advice and interesting anecdotes. Your names appear in the back of this book.

Foreword

ABOUT LONELY PLANET GUIDEBOOKS

The story begins with a classic travel adventure: Tony and Maureen Wheeler's 1972 journey across Europe and Asia to Australia. There was no useful information about the overland trail then, so Tony and Maureen published the first Lonely Planet guidebook to meet a growing need.

From a kitchen table, Lonely Planet has grown to become the largest independent travel publisher in the world, with offices in Melbourne (Australia), Oakland (USA), London (UK) and Paris (France).

Today Lonely Planet guidebooks cover the globe. There is an ever-growing list of books and information in a variety of media. Some things haven't changed. The main aim is still to make it possible for adventurous travellers to get out there – to explore and better understand the world.

At Lonely Planet we believe travellers can make a positive contribution to the countries they visit – if they respect their host communities and spend their money wisely. Since 1986 a percentage of the income from each book has been donated to aid projects and human rights campaigns, and, more recently, to wildlife conservation.

Although inclusion in a guidebook usually implies a recommendation we cannot list every good place. Exclusion does not necessarily imply criticism. In fact there are a number of reasons why we might exclude a place – sometimes it is simply inappropriate to encourage an influx of travellers.

UPDATES & READER FEEDBACK

Things change – prices go up, schedules change, good places go bad and bad places go bankrupt. Nothing stays the same. So, if you find things better or worse, recently opened or long-since closed, please tell us and help make the next edition even more accurate and useful.

Lonely Planet thoroughly updates each guidebook as often as possible – usually every two years, although for some destinations the gap can be longer. Between editions, up-to-date information is available in our free, monthly email bulletin *Comet* (w www.lonelyplanet.com/newsletters). You can also check out the *Thorn Tree* bulletin board and *Postcards* section of our website, which carry unverified, but fascinating, reports from travellers.

Tell us about it! We genuinely value your feedback. A well-travelled team at Lonely Planet reads and acknowledges every email and letter we receive and ensures that every morsel of information finds its way to the relevant authors, editors and cartographers.

Everyone who writes to us will find their name listed in the next edition of the appropriate guidebook. The very best contributions will be rewarded with a free guidebook.

We may edit, reproduce and incorporate your comments in Lonely Planet products such as guidebooks, websites and digital products, so let us know if you don't want your comments reproduced or your name acknowledged.

How to contact Lonely Planet:
Online: e talk2us@lonelyplanet.com.au, w www.lonelyplanet.com
Australia: Locked Bag 1, Footscray, Victoria 3011
UK: 72-82 Rosebery Ave, London EC1R 4RW
USA: 150 Linden St, Oakland, CA 94607

Introduction

The Kingdom of Thailand draws more visitors than any other country in Southeast Asia with its virtually irresistible combination of breathtaking natural beauty, inspiring temples, the ruins of fabulous ancient kingdoms, renowned hospitality, and robust cuisine. From the stupa-studded mountains of Mae Hong Son to the verdant limestone islands of the Andaman Sea, from the pulse-pounding dance clubs of Bangkok to tranquil villages moored along the Mekong River, the country offers something for every type of traveller.

The spirit that sets Thailand apart might be at least partially due to the fact that, unlike its neighbours, it has never been colonised by a foreign power. Despite periodic invasions by the Burmese and the Khmers, and a brief occupation by the Japanese in WWII, the kingdom has never been externally controlled long enough to dampen the Thais' individualism. Whether this was a simple historical accident or whether the structure of Thai society itself is responsible for resisting European colonization remains a burning debate topic among scholars.

Of course Thailand, like other Asian countries, has been influenced by contact with foreign cultures. However the never-changing character of Thai culture has remained dominant, even in modern city life. Often depicted as fun-loving, happy-go-lucky folk (which indeed they often are), the Thais are also proud and strong, and have struggled for centuries to preserve their independence of spirit.

Those interested in Thailand's culture and history can enjoy its lively arts scene and wander around the remains of ancient cities. Blessed with a hugely diverse terrain, Thailand offers much to the outdoors enthusiast as well, from trekking in the north's picturesque mountains to chilling out on one of the many exotic islands in the south.

Meanwhile in Bangkok, a city moving at a frenetic pace, travellers can ride long-tail boats along the myriad canals, visit magnificently ornate temples, join the crowd at a Thai boxing match or shop in one of the many markets. All travellers will appreciate its tradition of friendliness and hospitality to strangers, as well as one of the world's most exciting cuisines. For those seeking a learning experience, Thailand offers a plethora of opportunities to study Thai massage, boxing and cooking, and Buddhist meditation.

Travelling around in this tropical country is comfortable, down-to-earth and exceptionally good value. The extensive rail, bus and air networks makes every place that is worth visiting, easily accessible. Many people find that whatever time they plan for a Thailand trip seems to fall short, given the country's multifaceted culture and the numerous things to go and do or see.

Whether in the tranquillity of a mountaintop temple, the curry-scented atmosphere of a riverside café, the raucous din of a festival procession, or in some other passing experience, somewhere, sometime, every visitor to Thailand intersects with a moment where the inexplicable heart of the Thai experience enters the soul. From that point onward, the most difficult part of being in the country is negotiating how much longer you can manage to stay, and how soon you will return.

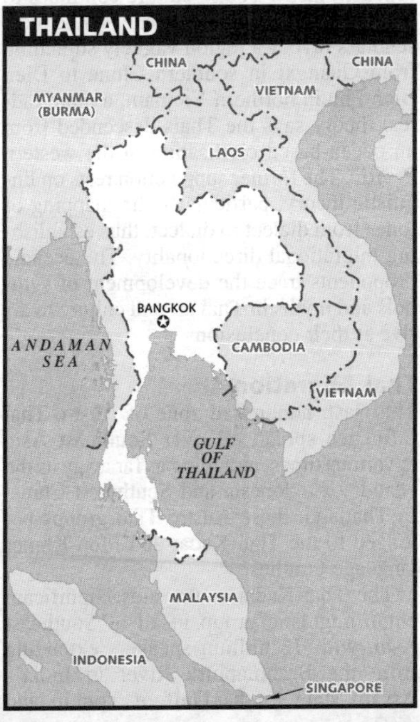

Facts about Thailand

HISTORY

Prehistory

Modern linguistic theory and archaeological evidence suggest that the first true agriculturists in the world, perhaps also the first metal workers, spoke an early form of Thai and lived in what we know today as Thailand. The Mekong River valley and Khorat Plateau in particular were inhabited as far back as 10,000 years ago, and rice was grown in the Ban Chiang and Ban Prasat areas of northeastern Thailand as early as 4000 BC (China, by contrast, was growing and consuming millet at the time). The Ban Chiang culture began bronze metallurgy before 3000 BC; the Middle East's Bronze Age arrived around 2800 BC, China's a thousand years later. Ban Chiang bronze works were stronger than their Mesopotamian or Chinese counterparts, mainly due to Ban Chiang's access to the abundant tin resources of the Thai-Malay Peninsula.

Given the nomadic nature of the early Thais, the exact origins of the Thai – or the broader Austro-Thai – culture continues to be a matter of academic debate. While most scholars favour a region vaguely stretching from Guangxi in southern China to Dien Bien Phu in northern Vietnam, a more radical theory says the Thais descended from an ocean-based civilisation in the western Pacific. The former supposition rests on linguistic theory, particularly the mapping of tones from dialect to dialect, thus establishing migrational directionality. The oceanic proponents trace the development of symbols and myths in Thai art and culture to arrive at their conclusions.

Thai Migration

This vast, nonunified zone of Austro-Thai influence spread all over Southeast Asia at various times, including as far away as the islands of Indonesia and Southwest China. In Thailand, these Austro-Thai groups belonged to the Thai-Kadai and Mon-Khmer language families.

The Thai-Kadai is the most significant ethno-linguistic group in all of Southeast Asia, with 72 million speakers extending from the Brahmaputra River in India's Assam state to the Gulf of Tonkin and China's Hainan Island. To the north, there are Thai-Kadai speakers well into the Chinese provinces of Yunnan and Guangxi, and to the south they are found as far as the northern Malaysian state of Kedah. In Thailand and Laos they are the majority populations, and in China, Vietnam and Myanmar (Burma) they are the largest minorities. The major Thai-Kadai groups are the Ahom (Assam), the Siamese (Thailand), the Black Thai or Thai Dam (Laos and Thailand), the Thai Yai or Shan (Myanmar and Thailand), the Thai Neua (Laos, Thailand and China), the Thai Lü (Laos, Thailand and China) and the Yuan (Laos and Thailand). All of these groups belong to the Thai half of Thai-Kadai; the Kadai groups are relatively small (less than a million) and include such comparatively obscure languages in southern China as Kelao, Lati, Laha, Laqua and Li.

A linguistic map of southern China, northeastern India and Southeast Asia clearly shows that the preferred zones of occupation by the Thai peoples have been river valleys, from the Red (Hong) River in the south of China and Vietnam to the Brahmaputra River in Assam, India. At one time there were two terminals for movement into what is now Thailand. The 'northern terminal' was in the Yuan Jiang and other river areas in China's modern-day Yunnan and Guangxi provinces, and the 'southern terminal' along central Thailand's Mae Nam Chao Phraya (Chao Phraya River). The human populations remain quite concentrated in these areas today, while areas between the two were merely intermediate relay points and have always been less populated.

The Mekong River valley between Thailand and Laos was one such intermediate migrational zone, as were river valleys along the Nan, Ping, Kok, Yom and Wang Rivers in northern Thailand, plus various river areas in Laos and also in the Shan State of Myanmar. As far as historians have been able to piece together from scant linguistic and anthropological evidence, significant numbers of Austro-Thai peoples in southern China or northern Vietnam probably began migrating southward and westward in small groups as early as the 8th

History Highlights

4000–3000 BC: Ban Chiang
Rice cultivation, pottery and one of the world's first known bronze-metallurgy cultures in what is now northeastern Thailand.

6th century AD: Spreading Settlement
Thriving agricultural communities and Theravada Buddhist beliefs are established in the south and central areas.

8th–10th centuries: Migration
'Thai-Kadai' peoples from northern Vietnam and southern China migrate into the Mekong River valley.

8th–12th centuries: Dvaravati Period
Lavo (Lopburi) and other non-Khmer Buddhist cultures flourish in central and eastern Thailand.

8th–13th centuries – Srivijaya Kingdom
The Srivijaya Empire controls much of southern Thailand, with a regional centre at Chaiya in Surat Thani Province.

9th–13th centuries: Khmer Empire
The spread of the Khmer Empire introduces Khmer influence in art, language and society, and leaves tokens of its architectural brilliance in northeastern Thailand.

13th–14th centuries: Sukhothai & Golden Age
Several Thai principalities unite to form what is considered to be the first Thai kingdom. King Ramkhamhaeng presides over a thriving 'Golden Age' of Thai culture.

1300 AD: Lanna Kingdom
Sukhothai joins Chiang Mai and Phayao to found the northern kingdom of La Na Thai.

14th-16th century: Ayuthaya Kingdom
The 400-year Ayuthaya Kingdom extends its influence east, eventually conquering Angkor in the 15th century. Ayuthaya is one of the greatest and wealthiest Asian cities.

16th century: Europeans
The Portuguese establish the first European mission in Ayuthaya, soon to be followed by the Dutch, English, Danish and French.

16th-18th century: Burmese Invasion
Ayuthaya's wealth attracts the attention of the Burmese, who attack in the mid-16th century and again in 1765, reducing the city to a devastated shell.

1769: King Taksin
Phraya Taksin, a general from the northern province of Tak, rallies the Thai forces and drives out the Burmese, appointing himself king at the new capital of Thonburi.

1782: Chakri Dynasty & Bangkok as Capital
King Taksin becomes deranged and Chao Phraya Chakri takes over as king, becoming Rama I, the first king of the current Chakri dynasty. He moves the site of the capital across the Mae Nam Chao Phraya to Bangkok.

1932: Constitutional Monarchy
Following a bloodless coup, Rama VII presides over a change from absolute monarchy to a constitutional monarchy.

1946: Democracy
Rama VIII dies of a gunshot wound and the present king, Rama IX, succeeds him. Thailand's first democratically elected government comes to power.

1947–1990s: The Military
The army stages a bloodless coup in 1947, setting a pattern of military involvement that is to dog Thai politics for the next four decades. Thai students demonstrate in 1973 and 1976 and are crushed by the military for their efforts. Many of them flee to the forests to join the People's Liberation Army of Thailand (granted amnesty in 1982). Since the 1992 Black May incident, military involvement in Thai politics seems to have had its day.

1997–2001: Economic Crash & Reform
After a decade of energetic economic growth, the Thai economy, fuelled largely by foreign loans, crashes when the national currency suffers precipitous deflation. Prime Minister Chuan Leekpai's government instigates unpopular austerity measures. In 2001 Thaksin Shinawatra is elected as prime minister on a platform of promises for sweeping economic reforms.

century AD – most certainly by the 10th century. These migrant Thais established local polities along traditional social schemata according to *meuang* (roughly 'principality' or 'city-state'), under the rule of chieftains or sovereigns called *jâo meuang*. Each *meuang* was based in a river valley or section of a valley. Some *meuang* were loosely collected under one *jâo meuang* or an alliance of several.

Wherever Thais met indigenous populations of Tibeto-Burmans and Mon-Khmers in the move south and westward (into what is now Myanmar, Thailand and Laos), they were somehow able to displace, assimilate or co-opt them without force. The most probable explanation for this relatively smooth assimilation is that there were already Thai peoples indigenous to the area. Current research on the development of Austro-Thai language and culture supports this idea.

Early Kingdoms

With no written records or chronologies it is difficult to say with certainty what kind of cultures existed among the *meuang* of Thailand before the middle of the first millennium AD. However, by the 6th century an important network of agricultural communities was thriving as far south as modern-day Pattani and Yala, and as far north and northeast as Lamphun and Muang Fa Daet (near Khon Kaen).

Theravada Buddhism was flourishing and may have entered the region during India's Ashoka period, in the 3rd or 2nd century BC, when Indian missionaries are said to have been sent to a land called Suvannabhumi (Land of Gold). Suvannabhumi most likely corresponds to a remarkably fertile area stretching from southern Myanmar, across central Thailand, to eastern Cambodia. Two different cities in Thailand's central river basin have long been called Suphanburi (City of Gold) and U Thong (Cradle of Gold).

Dvaravati This collection of *meuang* was given the Sanskrit name Dvaravati (literally 'Place of Gates'), the city of Krishna in the Indian epic poem *Mahabharata*. The French art historian Georges Coedès discovered the name on some coins that were excavated in the Nakhon Pathom area, which seems to have been the centre of Dvaravati culture. The Dvaravati period lasted until the 11th or 12th century AD and produced many works of art, including Buddha images (showing Indian Gupta influence), stucco reliefs on temple walls and in caves, architecture, exquisite terracotta heads, votive tablets and various sculptures.

Dvaravati may have been a cultural relay point for the Funan and Chenla cultures of ancient Laos and Cambodia to the northeast and east. The Chinese, through the travels of the famous pilgrim Xuan Zang, knew the area as Tuoluobodi, between Sriksetra (Myanmar) and Isanapura (Cambodia).

The ethnology of the Dvaravati peoples is a controversial topic, although the standard decree is that they were Mon-Khmer or Mon. In any event, the Dvaravati culture quickly declined in the 11th century under the political domination of the invading Khmers, who made their headquarters in Lopburi. The area around Lamphun, then called Hariphunchai, held out against the Khmers until the late 12th or early 13th century, as evidenced by the Dvaravati architecture of Wat Kukut in Lamphun.

Khmer Influence The Khmer conquests from the 7th to 11th centuries introduced Khmer art, language and religion as cultural influences. Some of the Sanskrit terms in the

Mon-Thai vocabulary entered the language during the Khmer period between the 11th and 13th centuries. Monuments from this period located in Kanchanaburi, Lopburi and many northeastern towns were constructed in the Khmer style and are comparable to architecture in Angkor.

Elements of Brahmanism, Theravada Buddhism and Mahayana Buddhism were intermixed as Lopburi became a religious centre, and some elements of each Buddhist school – along with Brahmanism – remain in Thai religious and court ceremonies.

Other Kingdoms While all this was taking place, a Thai state called Nan Chao (AD 650–1250) was flourishing in what later became Yunnan and Sichuan in China. Nan Chao maintained close relations with imperial China and the two neighbours enjoyed much cultural exchange. Although Thais from Nan Chao and other Thai settlements had long been migrating southward, settling in and around what is today Laos and northern Thailand, this migration increased when the Mongols, under Kublai Khan, conquered Nan Chao in 1253.

Meanwhile a number of Thais became mercenaries for the Khmer armies in the early 12th century, as depicted on the walls of Angkor Wat. The Khmers called the Thais 'Syam', possibly from the Sanskrit *shyama* meaning 'golden' or 'swarthy', and if so possibly in reference to the Thais' deeper skin colour. Whatever the meaning, this was how the Thai kingdom eventually came to be called Syam, or Sayam. In Myanmar and northwestern Thailand the pronunciation of Syam became 'Shan'. The English trader James Lancaster penned the first known English transliteration of the name as 'Siam' in 1592.

Meanwhile southern Thailand – the upper Malay peninsula – was under the control of the Srivijaya empire, the headquarters of which may have been in Palembang, Sumatra, between the 8th and 13th centuries. The regional centre for Srivijaya was Chaiya, near the modern town of Surat Thani. Remains of Srivijaya art can still be seen in Chaiya and its environs.

Sukhothai & Lan Na Thai Periods Several Thai principalities in the Mekong River valley united in the 13th and 14th centuries, when Thai princes wrested the lower north from the Khmers – whose Angkor government was declining fast – to create Sukhothai (Rising of Happiness). They later took Hariphunchai from the Mon to form Lan Na Thai (Million Thai Rice Fields).

In 1238 the Sukhothai kingdom declared its independence under King Si Intharathit and quickly expanded its sphere of influence,

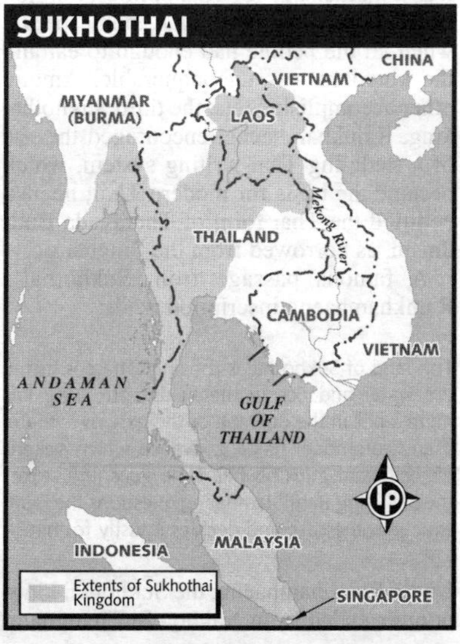

taking advantage not only of the declining Khmer power but the weakening Srivijaya domain in the south. Sukhothai is considered by the Thais to be the first true Thai kingdom. It was annexed by Ayuthaya in 1376, by which time a national identity of sorts had been forged.

Many Thais today have a sentimental, romantic view of the Sukhothai period, seeing it as a 'golden age' of Thai politics, religion and culture – an egalitarian, noble period when all the people had enough to eat and the kingdom was unconquerable. Among other accomplishments, the third Sukhothai king, Ramkhamhaeng, encouraged the use of a fledgling Thai writing system, which became the basis for modern Thai; he also codified the Thai form of Theravada Buddhism, as borrowed from the Singhalese.

A famous passage from Sukhothai's Ramkhamhaeng inscription reads:

> This land of Sukhothai is thriving. There is fish in the water and rice in the fields...The King has hung a bell in the opening of the gate over there; if any commoner has a grievance which sickens his belly and grips his heart, he goes and strikes the bell; King Ramkhamhaeng questions the man, examines the case and decides it justly for him.

Under Ramkhamhaeng, the Sukhothai kingdom extended from Nakhon Si Thammarat in the south to the upper Mekong River valley (Laos), and to Bago (Myanmar). For a short time (1448–86) the Sukhothai capital was moved to Phitsanulok.

Ramkhamhaeng also supported Phaya Mangrai of Chiang Mai, and Phaya Ngam Meuang of Phayao, two northern Thai *jâo meuang*, in the 1296 founding of Lan Na Thai, nowadays often known simply as 'Lanna'. Lanna extended across northern Thailand to include the *meuang* of Wiang Chan along the middle reaches of the Mekong River. In the 14th century, Wiang Chan was taken from Lanna by Chao Fa Ngum of Luang Prabang, who made it part of his Lan Xang (Million Elephants) kingdom. Wiang Chan later flourished as an independent kingdom for a short time during the mid-16th century and eventually became the capital of Laos in its royal, French (during which it got its more popular international spelling, 'Vientiane') and now socialist incarnations. After a period of dynastic decline, Lanna fell to the Burmese in 1558.

Ayuthaya Period

The Thai kings of Ayuthaya grew very powerful in the 14th and 15th centuries, taking over U Thong and Lopburi, former Khmer strongholds, and moving east in their conquests until Angkor was defeated in 1431. Even though the Khmers were their adversaries in battle, the Ayuthaya kings adopted large portions of Khmer court customs and language. One result of this acculturation was that the Thai monarch gained more absolute authority during the Ayuthaya period and assumed the title *devaraja* (god-king; *thewárâat* in Thai) as opposed to the *dhammaraja* (dharma-king; *thammárâat*) title used in Sukhothai.

Ayuthaya was one of the greatest and wealthiest cities in Asia, a thriving seaport envied not only by the Burmese but by the Europeans, who were in great awe of it. It has been said that London, at the time, was a mere village in comparison. The kingdom sustained an unbroken 400-year monarchical succession through 34 reigns, from King U Thong (r. 1350–69) to King Ekathat (r. 1758–67).

[Continued on page 17]

Thailand's Highlights

Thailand has many faces and exploring everything the country has to offer is a lifetime endeavour. Time and money constraints will compel most to decide – either in advance or as you go along – which parts you're going to see and which parts will have to be left out. In Thailand it usually pays to be a little under ambitious with your travel plans; don't try to see too much in too short an interval.

Most visitors are interested in islands and beaches, temple architecture, trekking, handicrafts and cuisine. While these are not necessarily mutually exclusive, it's hard to find one place that has them all! In Songkhla, for example, you'll find handicrafts and beaches, while many places in the northeast offer temple ruins and handicrafts.

Just soaking up the culture can be one of the highlights of travel in Thailand. You won't experience much culture if you travel around quickly or spend most of your time sitting around in guesthouse cafés or trekking with your own kind. At least once during your trip, try going to a small town well off the main circuit, stay at a local hotel and eat in Thai curry shops and noodle stands. It's not as easy as going with the crowd but you'll experience a lot more of the real Thailand.

Islands & Beaches

The coastline of Thailand boasts some of the finest islands and beaches in Asia.

Ko Chang Parts of this archipelago, near the Cambodian border, enjoy national marine-park status. So far high-profile development has been kept at bay by the island's distance from Bangkok and its

ANDREW MARSHALL & LEANNE WALKER

Title page: Ao Lo Dalam, Andaman Coast (Photograph by Dallas Stribley)

Inset: Painted umbrellas, Bo Sang (Umbrella Village), Chiang Mai Province (Photograph by Chris Mellor)

Bottom: Ko Chang (Elephant Island), Trat Province

KRAIG LIEB

mountainous geography. Although the main island is beginning to develop, outlying islands such as Ko Kut are still very quiet.

Prachuap Khiri Khan This province along the upper southern gulf coast offers sandy beaches along much of its length, from the well-touristed Hua Hin in the north to the little-known Thai resorts near Ao Manao and Bang Saphan. While there's not much in the way of diving here, the seafood is superb.

Ko Pha-Ngan Just north of Ko Samui in the gulf, Pha-Ngan remains the main backpackers' headquarters as the beach accommodation is the least expensive in the country. A few more-upmarket places have emerged, too. There is good snorkelling and diving in some parts of

BRETT SHEARER

Top & Bottom: Ko Pha-Ngan, Surat Thani Province

ANDREW LUBRAN

the island, but very little in the way of nightlife except at Hat Rin on the southeastern tip, which is famous for its full-moon parties.

Ko Samui Off the coast of Surat Thani, this is Thailand's third-largest island. It was once a haven for backpackers, but now it's mainly given over to mid-range hotels and guesthouses. The island is fast becoming a centre for **spas** and new-age **health centres**. Hat Chaweng remains one of the country's most scenic beaches despite being lined with up-market bungalows and tourist hotels.

Ko Tao This small island offers some of the best **diving** in the gulf and as a result, development here has outpaced Ko Pha-Ngan, to the south.

Ko Surin, Ko Similan & Ko Tarutao These Andaman Coast islands are separate national marine parks that are some of the best

RICHARD NEBESKY

Top: Ao Thong Ta Khian, Ko Samui, Surat Thani Province

Bottom: Hat Sai Ri, Ko Tao, Surat Thani Province

JULIET COOMBE

protected in Thailand. **Diving** and **snorkelling** here is a fantastic experience. It's possible to **camp** or stay overnight in park bungalows on these islands (except for one private island in Tarutao). It's best to visit outside the monsoon season between November and April.

Phuket Off the Andaman Coast, this is Thailand's largest island and was the first to develop a tourist industry. It has become a fairly sophisticated resort destination, albeit one with the highest number of 'green' hotel developments as well as some **national parks** that contain virgin rainforest. There is good **diving** at nearby islands and reefs and Ao Phang-Nga. The best Thai cuisine of any of the islands is found here.

Krabi This province, opposite Phuket on the Andaman Coast, offers a range of beaches and islands ringed with striking limestone formations. Because of the lack of provincial roads, many of Krabi's best mainland beaches, such as Hat Rai Leh, Hat Tham Phra Nang and Ao Mao, can only be reached by boat. Rock-climbing, snorkelling, diving, boating and beach camping can all be enjoyed here. Accommodation

Top: Phuket, Phuket Province

tends to book out between December and February, however it is mostly deserted during May, June, September and October.

Trang A largely undiscovered province, Trang is on the lower Andaman Coast. The islands and beaches aren't as pretty as neighbouring Krabi's, however there's good diving on the islands of Ko Ngai, Ko Muk and Ko Kradan. There's nowhere in Trang to rent diving gear, so unless you make arrangements through a dive operator, bring your own gear.

Songkhla, Pattani & Narathiwat These deep-south provinces on the lower Southern Gulf coast near Malaysia are lined with hundreds of kilometres of deserted beaches. It's best to visit outside the monsoon season, (November to March) as crosscurrents affect the clarity of the water.

KAREN TRIST

Bottom: Ko Phi-Phi, Krabi Province

JOHN ELK III

National Parks

Thailand is rich in national parks, boasting around 112 of them. Many more were in the pipeline before the 1997 economic crash. The latest trend is to link parks and wildlife reserves together into larger 'forest complexes', regional units with local community groups taking at least partial responsibility for conservation. Thailand's Western Forest Complex (Wefcom), for example, joins together nine national parks, six wildlife sanctuaries and two proposed national parks, covering 18,730 sq km.

Kaeng Krachan National Park Thailand's largest and least-explored park covers almost 3000 sq km of evergreen and mixed deciduous forests along the Myanmar border in Phetchaburi Province. Bisected by the Tenasserim Range, the park serves as a major watershed for upper-southern Thailand. Several streams and rivers feed the Kaeng Krachan Reservoir, the largest among them being the Mae Nam Phetburi and Mae Nam Panburi. For hikers and campers who venture into the interior, the **wildlife** – especially gibbons and hornbills – is superb. The best time to visit is between November and April.

Doi Inthanon National Park This 482-sq-km park near Chiang Mai surrounds Thailand's tallest mountain peak, Doi Inthanon. The misty upper slopes support a profusion of orchids, lichens, mosses and epiphytes as well as nearly 400 varieties of **bird** – more than any other habitat in Thailand. The park can be enjoyed year-round, though the summit is quite cold between November and February.

Khao Yai National Park Thailand's oldest and third-largest national park, is considered one of the best in the world in terms of its wildlife and the scope of its protection. The famous waterfall in the film *The Beach* (2000) is Khao Yai's Nam Tok Haew Suwat. This Asean National Heritage Site's 2172-sq-km area encompasses one of the largest intact monsoon forests in Southeast Asia, and is home to a sizable herd of **wild elephants**.

Top: Hat Tham Phra Nang, Krabi Province

There's park accommodation and hotels and guesthouses in nearby Pak Chong. It is best visited between October and June.

Nam Nao National Park Wide expanses of dry dipterocarp forest, bamboo groves and rolling sandstone hills make for excellent **hiking** in this park. There's plenty of **wildlife** as the park abuts Phu Khiaw Wildlife Sanctuary. Accommodation is very limited. It can be visited year-round, though the forest is at its lushest between May and November.

Phu Kradung National Park This flat-topped, bell-shaped mountain park is a favourite with Thais for its pine forests and **sweeping views**. The well-marked 9km ascent has benches and shelters along the way for hikers, and tents can be rented at the summit. **Wild elephants** are occasionally seen along the way. Phu Kradung is best visited between October and December, as ascents can be very difficult during the rainy season.

Khao Sok National Park Limestone crags, rainforests and jungle streams provide the perfect environment for some of Thailand's endangered species, including **tiger** and **clouded leopard** as well as two species of **rafflesia** (the world's largest flower). Treehouse-style accommodation protects the forest floor and means you experience one of Thailand's most important ecosystems. It is best visited between December and February.

Thaleh Ban National Park White meranti forest, waterfalls, limestone formations, a natural lake and varied bird life are found in this quiet 196-sq-km park, which straddles the Thai-Malaysian border. There's camping and bungalows and it's best visited between December and March.

Bottom left: Khao Sok National Park, Surat Thani Province

Bottom right: Nam Tok Haew Suwat, Khao Yai National Park, Nakhon Ratchasima Province

JOE CUMMINGS

JOHN ELK III

Temple Architecture

The former Thai capitals of Ayuthaya, Lopburi, Kamphaeng Phet, Sukhothai, Si Satchanalai and Chiang Mai offer a range of Buddhist temple architecture, most of it dating from the 11th to 17th centuries. The Thai government has developed several of these sites into historical parks, complete with museums and impressive restorations. For Khmer and Lao temple architecture, head to northeastern Thailand (called Isan by Thai people), where hundreds of Khmer ruins dating from the 8th to 13th centuries (including Angkor-period monuments) dot the countryside.

TOM COCKREM

Bottom: Wat Phra Si Sanphet, Ayuthaya Historical Park, Ayuthaya Province

GLENN BEANLAND

Ayuthaya Just an hour or two (depending on the traffic) north of Bangkok, this former royal capital harbours many 14th- to 18th-century **temple ruins** on an 'island' created by two rivers and a canal. Although the surrounding urban environment detracts a bit from the World Heritage–designated monuments, the Ayuthaya Historical Park is perfect for those with limited time.

Lopburi This central-Thai city is well worth a visit because it features a mix of Khmer and Thai **monuments**. The former palace of King Narai

JULIET COOMBE

Top: Wat Ratburana, Ayuthaya Historical Park, Ayuthaya Province

Bottom: Lopburi-style Buddha, Prang Sam Yot, Lopburi Province

GLENN BEANLAND

(17th century), whose chief adviser was the Greek adventurer Constantine Phaulkon, is particularly impressive.

Chiang Mai & Lampang These thoroughly northern-Thai cities feature many **older wooden temples** built in the Shan, Burmese and Lanna styles. **Wat Phra That Lampang Luang**, thought to be Thailand's oldest surviving wooden temple, makes for a fascinating side trip from Chiang Mai.

Top: Wat Chiang Man, Chiang Mai, Chiang Mai Province

Sukhothai & Si Satchanalai Both of these former royal cities in northern Thailand have been made into historical parks that feature **temple ruins** dating back to Thailand's 'Golden Age', the Sukhothai era from the 13th to 15th centuries. The two World Heritage parks are well

JULIET COOMBE

maintained; the one at Si Satchanalai has more of an off-the-beaten-track atmosphere because it is less visited.

Northeastern Thailand The most impressive sites are those at Prasat Hin Phimai and Prasat Hin Khao Phanom Rung (abbreviated to Phanom Rung), but don't neglect some of the smaller, out-of-the-way spots if you have the time and inclination. Dozens of famous **Lao temples** can be found along the banks of the Mekong River from Loei and Nong Khai Provinces to Ubon Ratchathani Province.

Top: Wat Mahathat, Sukhothai Historical Park, Sukhothai Province

Bottom: Temple ruins, Sukhothai Historical Park

SIMON BRACKEN

CHERYL CONLON

Museums

Thailand's Fine Arts Department maintains a good national-museum system with regional branches throughout the country. There are also a few idiosyncratic collections sponsored by other organisations, both public and private.

National Museum Housed in a former vice-regal palace in Bangkok, the country's most well-endowed museum features pottery, sculpture, furniture, clothing and musical instruments from Thailand and many other places in Southeast Asia. Phutthaisawan Chapel, a temple building on the grounds, contains some of the country's finest Buddhist mural paintings.

Chao Sam Phraya Museum & Palace Ayuthaya's 500-year history is the source of an extensive display of art and artefacts distributed among two separate national museums.

Nan National Museum Housed in a 1903-vintage former royal palace, this is the best place in Thailand to view art objects from the little-known Nan kingdom in the far north, including pieces of Lao and Thai Lü origin.

Phimai National Museum This very well-designed museum in the small town of Phimai contains exhibits of Khmer art from the Angkor period as well as the earlier Dvaravati-style art.

Ko Yo Folklore Museum Near Songkhla, this museum is sponsored by the Institute of Southern Thai Studies and displays an impressive array of southern-Thai religious and folk art.

Top: Temple carving, Chiang Mai, Chiang Mai Province

Handicrafts

Thailand's ethnic diversity means that a wide range of handicrafts is available for study or purchase throughout the country.

Chiang Mai As Northern Thailand's cultural capital and former crossroads for the historic caravan trade between China and Myanmar, Chiang Mai has served as the north's main handicrafts centre for over 200 years. Here you'll find virtually every type of craft produced in the region, as well as materials from Myanmar and Laos. Northern specialities include **silverware**, **woodcarving**, **painted umbrellas**, **hill-tribe crafts**, **leather**, **ceramics** and **antique furniture**.

JOHN HAY

Bottom: Thai-silk production

CHRIS MELLOR

Top: Traditional, painted umbrellas, Bo Sang (Umbrella Village), Chiang Mai Province

Nakhon Ratchasima & Surrounds The best selection of handmade cotton and silk textiles is found in the northeastern capitals of Nakhon Ratchasima (Khorat), Khon Kaen, Roi Et and Udon Thani. Visit some of these silk-weaving towns to experience Thai **weaving** techniques first-hand.

Ubon Ratchathani In Thailand's northeastern corner, this provincial capital offers a quality selection of crafts from nearby Cambodia and Laos, plus locally produced **silverware** and **ceramics**.

Nakhon Si Thammarat This provincial town on the coast of the lower-southern gulf is a busy centre for many indigenous handicrafts such as **nielloware**, **silverwork**, **shadow-play cutouts** and intricate **basketry**.

Songkhla & Surrounds For cotton **prints**, **sarongs** and **batik** (with Malay-Indonesian design influences), visit the southern provinces of Songkhla, Yala, Pattani and Narathiwat near the Malaysian border.

Cuisine

Thailand's topography and people vary immensely from north to south and east to west, and a corresponding set of culinary differences rides the coat-tails of this geographic and cultural variation from region to region. For more details on Thai cuisine see the special section 'Thai Cuisine'.

Bangkok & Central Thailand Try one or more of the well-known Thai curry triumvirate, *kaeng phèt* ('spicy curry' or red curry), *kaeng khĭaw-wăan* and *kaeng phá-naeng*, similar to *kaeng phèt* but thicker and creamier, and with the addition of kaffir lime leaves).

Bangkok and central Thailand also boast the best *kŭaytĭaw* (rice noodles) in the country: look for them in Bangkok's Chinatown and in the province of Chanthaburi.

JERRY ALEXANDER

Northern Thailand Don't go without trying Chiang Mai's famous *sâi ùa*, a dry, spicy pork sausage or *náam phrík nùm*, a spicy dip made with mashed green chillis. Throughout the north you'll find the delicious Yunnanese noodle speciality *khâo sawy* (egg noodles in a light curry broth).

Northeastern Thailand Although nowadays found all over the country, northern Thailand is the best place to savour the classic threesome of *kài yâang* (grilled herb-marinated chicken), *sôm tam* (spicy green papaya salad) and *khâo nĭaw* (sticky rice, a staple of the north and northeast).

Southern Thailand This is the place for chilli lovers to indulge themselves with Thailand's hottest curries. You may need to brace yourself for *kaeng tai plaa*, a very pungent and spicy curry made with fish innards, green beans, pickled bamboo shoots and potatoes. The more timid should stick to *kaeng lĕuang* (literally 'yellow curry'), a turmeric-hued fish curry cooked with green squash, pineapple, green beans and green papaya.

Stop off at one of Trang's Hokkien-style coffee shops for a cup of their the famously thick black *kopíi*.

FRANK CARTER

Top: Ingredients for Thai green curry

Bottom: Red and green chillies

[Continued from page 16]

By the early 16th century Ayuthaya was receiving European visitors and a Portuguese embassy was established in 1511. The Portuguese were followed by the Dutch in 1605, the English in 1612, the Danes in 1621 and the French in 1662. In the mid-16th century Ayuthaya and the independent kingdom of Lanna came under the control of the Burmese, but the Thais regained rule of both by the end of the century. In 1690 Londoner Engelbert Campfer proclaimed that 'Among the Asian nations, the Kingdom of Siam is the greatest. The magnificence of the Ayuthaya Court is incomparable.'

An exceptional episode unfolded in Ayuthaya when Constantine Phaulkon, a Greek, became a high official in Siam, under King Narai, from 1675 to 1688. He kept out the Dutch and the English but allowed the French to station 600 soldiers in the kingdom. Eventually the Thais, fearing a takeover, expelled the French and killed Phaulkon. Siam sealed itself from the West for 150 years following this experience with the *faràng* (a foreigner of European des-cent, from *faràngsèt,* meaning 'French').

The Burmese invaded Ayuthaya again in 1765 and the capital fell after two years of fighting. This time the invaders destroyed everything sacred to the Thais, including manuscripts, temples and religious sculpture. But the Burmese could not maintain a foothold in the kingdom, and Phraya Taksin, a half-Chinese, half-Thai general, made himself king in 1769, ruling from the new capital of Thonburi on the banks of the Mae Nam Chao Phraya, opposite Bangkok. The Thais regained control of the country and further united the provinces to the north with central Siam.

Taksin eventually came to regard himself as the next Buddha; his ministers, who did not approve of his religious fantasies, deposed and then executed him.

Rama I & the Solidification of Bangkok Power

One of Taksin's key generals, Chao Phraya Chakri, came to power and was crowned in 1782 as Phra Yot Fa. He moved the royal capital across the river to Bangkok and ruled as the first king of the Chakri dynasty. In 1809 his son, Loet La, took the throne and reigned until 1824. Both monarchs assumed the task of restoring the culture, which had been severely damaged by the Burmese decades earlier.

The third Chakri king, Phra Nang Klao (r. 1824–51), went beyond reviving tradition and developed trade with China, while increasing domestic agricultural production.

He also established a new royal title system, posthumously conferring 'Rama I' and 'Rama II' upon his two predecessors and taking the title 'Rama III' for himself. During Nang Klao's reign, American missionary James Low brought the first printing press to Siam and produced the country's first printed document in Thai script. Missionary Dan Bradley published the first Thai newspaper, the monthly *Bangkok Recorder*, from 1844 to 1845.

Rama IV & Reform Commonly known as King Mongkut (Phra Chom Klao to the Thais), Rama IV was a colourful and innovative Chakri king. He originally missed out on the throne in deference to his half-brother, Rama III, and lived as a Buddhist monk for 27 years. During his long monastic term he became adept in Sanskrit, Pali, Latin and English, studied Western sciences and adopted the strict discipline of local Mon monks. He kept an eye on the outside world and, when he took the throne in 1851, immediately courted diplomatic relations with a few European nations, taking care to evade colonisation.

In addition, he attempted to demythologise Thai religion by aligning Buddhist cosmology with modern science, and founded the Thammayut monastic sect, based on the strict discipline he had followed as a monk.

King Mongkut loosened Thai trade restrictions and many Western powers signed trade agreements with the monarch. He also sponsored Siam's second printing press and instituted educational reforms, developing a school system along European lines. Although the king courted the West, he did so with caution and warned his subjects: 'Whatever they have invented or done which we should know of and do, we can imitate and learn from them, but do not wholeheartedly believe in them.' Mongkut was the first monarch to show his face to Thai commoners in public.

Rama V & Modernisation Mongkut's son King Chulalongkorn (known to the Thais as Chula Chom Klao or Rama V; r. 1868–1910) continued his tradition of reform, especially in the legal and administrative realms. Educated by European tutors, Chulalongkorn abolished prostration before the king as well as slavery and corvée (state labour). Siam further benefited from relations with European nations and the USA: railways were built, a civil service was established and the legal code restructured. Although Siam still managed to avoid European colonisation, the king was compelled to concede territory to French Indochina (Laos in 1893 and Cambodia in 1907) and British Burma (three Malayan states in 1909) during his reign.

Rama V

Chulalongkorn's son, King Vajiravudh (Mongkut Klao or Rama VI; r. 1910–25), was educated in Britain and during his reign he introduced educational reforms including compulsory education. He further 'Westernised' the nation by conforming the Thai calendar to Western models. His reign was clouded by a top-down push for Thai nationalism that resulted in strong anti-Chinese sentiment.

Before Vajiravudh's reign, Thai parents gave each of their children a single, original name, with no surname to identify family origins. In 1909 a royal decree required the adoption of Thai surnames for all Thai citizens – a move designed to parallel the European system of family surnames and to weed out Chinese names.

In 1912 a group of Thai military officers unsuccessfully attempted to overthrow the monarchy, the first in a series of coup attempts that has continued. As a show of support for the Allies in WWI, Vajiravudh sent 1300 Thai troops to France in 1918.

Revolution

While Vajiravudh's brother, King Prajadhipok (Pokklao or Rama VII; r. 1925–35) ruled, a group of Thai students living in Paris became so enamoured of democratic ideology that in 1932 they mounted a successful coup d'etat against absolute monarchy in Siam. This bloodless revolution led to the development of a constitutional monarchy along British lines, with a mixed military-civilian group in power.

A royalist revolt in 1933 sought to reinstate absolute monarchy, but it failed and left Prajadhipok isolated from the royalist revolutionaries and the constitution-minded ministers. One of the king's last official acts was to outlaw polygamy in 1934, leaving behind the cultural underpinnings that now support Thai prostitution. For more explanation see the section on Prostitution later in this chapter.

In 1935 the king abdicated without naming a successor and retired to Britain. The cabinet promoted his nephew, 10-year-old Ananda Mahidol, to the throne as Rama VIII, although Ananda didn't return from school in Switzerland until 1945. Phibul Songkhram, a key military leader in the 1932 coup, maintained an effective position of power from 1938 until the end of WWII.

Under the influence of Phibul's government, the country's English name was officially changed in 1939 from Siam to Thailand – in Thai, 'pràthêt thai'. 'Pràthêt' is from the Sanskrit *pradesha* or 'country'. 'Thai' is considered to have the connotation of 'free', although in actual usage it refers to the Thai, Tai or T'ai peoples, who are found as far east as Tonkin, as far west as Assam, as far north as southern China, and as far south as northern Malaysia.

Ananda Mahidol came back to Thailand in 1945 but was shot dead in his bedroom under mysterious circumstances in 1946. Although there was apparently no physical evidence to suggest assassination, three of Ananda's attendants were arrested two years after his death and executed in 1954. No public charges were ever filed, and the consensus among historians today is that the attendants were 'sacrificed' to settle a karmic debt for allowing the king to die during their watch. His brother, Bhumibol Adulyadej, succeeded him as Rama IX. Nowadays no-one ever speaks or writes publicly about Ananda's death – whether it was a simple gun accident or a regicidal plot remains unclear.

WWII & Postwar Periods

During the Japanese invasion of Southeast Asia in 1941, the Phibul government sided with Japan and Phibul declared war on the USA and Britain in 1942. But Seni Pramoj, the Thai ambassador in Washington, refused to deliver the declaration. Phibul resigned in 1944 under pressure from the Thai underground resistance (known as Thai Seri), and after V-J Day in 1945, Seni became premier. Seni changed the English name of the country back to 'Siam' but kept Prathet Thai as the official Thai name.

In 1946 Seni was unseated in a general election and a democratic civilian group took power under Pridi Phanomyong, a law professor who had been instrumental in the 1932 revolution. Pridi's civilian government survived long enough to create the 1946 Constitution of the Thai Kingdom, only to be overthrown by Phibul, then field marshal, in 1947.

Using the death of Prajadhipok as a pretext, Phibul suspended the constitution and reinstated 'Thailand' as the country's official English name in 1949. Phibul's government took an extreme anticommunist stance, refused to recognise the newly declared People's Republic of China and became a loyal supporter of French and US foreign policy in Southeast Asia. Pridi, meanwhile, took up exile in China.

In 1951 power was wrested from Phibul by General Sarit Thanarat, who continued the tradition of military dictatorship. However, Phibul retained the actual title of premier until 1957 when Sarit finally had him exiled. Elections that same year forced Sarit to resign and go abroad for 'medical treatment'; he returned in 1958 to launch another coup. This time he abolished the constitution, dissolved the parliament and banned all political parties, maintaining effective power until he died of cirrhosis in 1963.

From 1964 to 1973 the Thai nation was ruled by the army officers Thanom Kittikachorn and Praphat Charusathien. During this time Thailand allowed the USA to establish several military bases within its borders in support of the US campaign in Vietnam.

Reacting to political repression, 10,000 Thai students publicly demanded a real constitution in June 1973. On 14 October of the same year the military brutally suppressed a large demonstration at Thammasat University in Bangkok, but King Bhumibol and General Krit Sivara, who sympathised with the students, refused to support further bloodshed, forcing Thanom and Praphat to leave Thailand. Oxford-educated Kukrit Pramoj took charge of a 14-party coalition government and steered a leftist agenda past a conservative parliament.

Among Kukrit's lasting achievements were a national minimum wage, the repeal of anticommunist laws and the ejection of US military forces from Thailand.

Polarisation

Kukrit's elected constitutional government ruled until 6 October 1976, when students demonstrated again, this time protesting against Thanom's return to Thailand as a monk. Thammasat University again became a battlefield as border-patrol police and right-wing, paramilitary civilian groups assaulted a group of 2000 students holding a sit-in. It is estimated that hundreds of students were killed and injured in the fracas, and more than a thousand were arrested. Using public disorder as an excuse, the military stepped in and installed a new right-wing government with Thanin Kraivichien as premier.

This bloody incident disillusioned many Thai students and older intellectuals not directly involved with the demonstrations. Numerous idealists 'dropped out' of Thai society and joined the People's Liberation Army of Thailand (PLAT), a group of armed communist insurgents based in the hills that had been active since the 1930s.

In October 1977 the military replaced Thanin with the more moderate General Kriangsak Chomanand in an effort to conciliate antigovernment factions. When this failed, the military-backed position changed hands again in 1980, leaving Prem Tinsulanonda at the helm. By this time PLAT had peaked with around 10,000 members. A 1981 coup attempt by the 'Young Turks' (a group of army officers who had graduated from the Chulachomklao Royal Military Academy together and styled themselves after a 1908 military movement at the heart of the Ottoman Empire) failed when Prem fled Bangkok for Khorat in the company of the royal family.

Stabilisation

Prem served as prime minister until 1988 and is credited with the political and economic stabilisation of Thailand in the post–Vietnam War years (only one coup attempt in the 1980s!). The major success of the Prem years was a complete dismantling of the Communist Party of Thailand (CPT) and PLAT through an effective combination of amnesty programs (which brought the students back from the forests) and military action. His administration is also considered to have been responsible for a gradual democratisation of Thailand that culminated in the 1988 election of his successor, retired general and businessman Chatichai Choonhavan. Prem continues to serve as a privy councillor and is an elder statesman *(rátthàbùrùt)* of the country.

It may be difficult for later arrivals to Thailand to appreciate the political distance Thailand covered in the 1980s. Under Prem, for example, a long-standing 1am curfew in Bangkok was lifted, and dissenting opinions were heard again in public.

Ever since 1932, every leading political figure in Thailand has needed the support of the Thai military to survive. Considering Thailand's geographic position during the Cold War years, it's not difficult to understand their influence. But as the threat of communist takeover (either from within or from nearby Indochinese states) diminished, the military gradually began loosening its hold on national politics.

Under Chatichai, Thailand enjoyed a brief period of unprecedented popular participation in government. Around 60% of Chatichai's cabinet members were former business executives rather than ex-military officers, as they were in the previous cabinet. Thailand entered a new era in which the country's double-digit economic boom ran concurrently with democratisation. Critics praised the political maturation of Thailand, even if they also grumbled that corruption seemed as rife as it ever was. By the end of the 1980s, however, certain high-ranking military officers had become increasingly dissatisfied, complaining that Thailand was being run by a plutocracy.

February 1991 Coup & its Aftermath

On 23 February 1991, in a move that shocked Thailand observers around the world, the military overthrew the Chatichai administration in a bloodless coup *(pàtìwát)* and handed power to the newly formed National Peace-Keeping Council (NPKC), headed by General Suchinda Kraprayoon. Although it was Thailand's 19th attempted coup and one of 10 successful coups since 1932, it was only the second coup to overthrow a democratically elected civilian government. The NPKC abolished the 1978 constitution and dissolved the parliament, charging Chatichai's civilian government with corruption and vote-buying. Rights of public assembly were curtailed but the press was only closed down for one day.

Following the coup, the NPKC appointed a hand-picked civilian prime minister, Anand Panyarachun, former ambassador to the USA, Germany, Canada and the United Nations (UN), to dispel public fears that the junta was planning a return to 100% military rule. Anand claimed to be his own man, but like his predecessors – elected or not – he was allowed the freedom to make his own decisions only insofar as they didn't affect the military. In spite of obvious constraints, many observers felt Anand's temporary premiership and cabinet were the best Thailand has ever had, either before or since.

In December 1991, Thailand's national assembly passed a new constitution that guaranteed a NPKC-biased parliament – 270 appointed senators in the upper house stacked against 360 elected representatives. Under this constitution, regardless of who was chosen as the next prime minister or which political parties filled the lower house, the government would remain largely in the hands of the military.

A general election in March 1992 ushered in a five-party coalition government with Narong Wongwan, whose Samakkhitham (Justice Unity) Party received the most votes, as premier. But amid US allegations that Narong was involved in Thailand's drug trade, the military exercised its constitutional prerogative and replaced Narong with (surprise, surprise) General Suchinda in April 1992.

In May 1992, several huge demonstrations demanding Suchinda's resignation – led by the charismatic Bangkok governor, Chamlong Srimuang – rocked Bangkok and larger provincial capitals. Chamlong won the 1992 Magsaysay Award (a humanitarian service award issued by a foundation in the Philippines) for his role in galvanising the public to reject Suchinda. After street confrontations between the protesters and the military near Bangkok's Democracy Monument resulted in nearly 50 deaths and hundreds of injuries, Suchinda resigned, having been premier for less than six weeks. Anand Panyarachun was reinstated as interim premier, winning praise for his fair and efficient administration.

Musical Chairs & a New Constitution

The September 1992 elections squeezed in veteran Democrat Party leader Chuan Leekpai, who helmed a four-party coalition government. A food vendor's son and native of Trang Province, the new premier didn't fit the usual mould since he was not a general, tycoon or academic. Although well regarded for his honesty and high morals, Chuan accomplished little in the areas of concern to the majority of Thais, most pointedly Bangkok traffic, national infrastructure and the undemocratic NPKC constitution.

After Chuan was unseated in a vote of no confidence, a new general election ushered in a seven-party coalition led by the Chart Thai (Thai Nationality) Party. At the helm was billionaire Banharn Silapa-archa, whom the press called a 'walking ATM'; they immediately attacked his tendency to appoint from a reservoir of rural politicians known to favour big business over social welfare. In September 1996 the Banharn government collapsed amid a spate of corruption scandals and a crisis of confidence.

The November national election, marked by electoral violence and accusations of vote buying, saw the former deputy prime minister and army commander Chavalit Yongchaiyudh, of the New Aspiration Party, secure premiership with a dubious mix of coalition partners.

In July 1997, following several months of warning signs that almost everyone in

Thailand and in the international community chose to ignore, the Thai currency fell into a deflationary tailspin and the national economy crashed and screeched to a virtual halt. See the Economy section later in this chapter for details.

Two months later the Thai parliament voted in a new constitution that guaranteed, at least on paper, more human and civil rights than had hitherto been codified in Thailand. As the first national charter to be prepared under civilian auspices, the 'people's constitution' fostered great hope in a population emotionally battered by the ongoing economic crisis.

Hope faded as Chavalit, living up to everyone's low expectations, failed to deal effectively with the economy and was forced to resign in November 1997. An election brought Chuan Leekpai back into office, where he did a reasonably decent job as an international public-relations man for the crisis.

A Fledgling Democracy

In January 2001, billionaire Thaksin Shinawatra was named prime minister after winning a landslide victory in compulsory nation-wide elections – the first in Thailand to be held under strict guidelines established by the 1997 constitution. Thaksin's party, Thai Rak Thai (Thais Love Thais) espouse a populist platform at perceivable odds with the man's enormous wealth and influence. Thaksin owns the country's only private radio station and his family owns Thailand's largest telecommunications company, which has lucrative coverage not only throughout Thailand but pending contracts with the governments of India and Myanmar as well. He has publicly stated his ambition to stay in office for four consecutive terms, or 16 years.

Meanwhile many Thai citizens, fed up with the government's slowness to right perceived wrongs in the countryside, continue to plague the administration with regular large-scale demonstrations. Most demonstrations plead for government relief from hardships caused by the shrinking economy, while some demand that the government dismantle World Bank or Asian Development projects, such as the Kheuan Pak Mun (Pak Mun Dam), that have been established without their consent. The government has promised land reform to help farmers, but these issues continue to smoulder, leaving observers to wonder if Thailand isn't heading for a period of unrest similar to that seen in the 1970s.

The Thaksin administration's main reaction so far has been to reject all criticism from within and outside Thailand as 'un-Thai'. In 2002 two *Far Eastern Economic Review* correspondents were nearly ejected from Thailand for reporting on business connections between Thaksin and the Crown Prince. Although in the end they were allowed to remain in the kingdom, the censorious action shocked many observers for whom Thailand was Southeast Asia's greatest bastion of press freedom.

Despite the current machinations of a fledgling democracy, some Thai sceptics will tell you that things never really change and that even democratically elected Thai governments may be mere short-lived deviations from the norm of military rule. The most hardened cynics hold the view that Thailand's 20th-century coups and counter-coups were a mere extension of the power plays of early Thai *jâo meuang*.

Optimists, on the other hand, claim that the military coup, as an instrument of change in Thailand, was only a minor detour on the country's road towards a more responsive and democratic national government. From this vantage point, Thai administrations of the new millennium appear to hold much promise. Without question, Thailand's revised and amended constitution strengthens the nation's future claim to democratic status and political stability.

GEOGRAPHY

Thailand has an area of 517,000 sq km: slightly smaller than the US state of Texas, or about the size of France. Its shape on the map has been likened to the head of an elephant, with its trunk extending down the Malay peninsula. The centre of Thailand, Bangkok, sits at about 14° north latitude – level with Madras, Manila, Guatemala and Khartoum.

The country's longest north–south distance is about 1860km, but its shape makes distances in any other direction 1000km or less. Because the north–south reach spans roughly 16 latitudinal degrees, Thailand has perhaps the most diverse climate in Southeast Asia. Twenty-three of its 76 provinces enjoy direct access to the sea and its potential for trade and livelihoods.

The topography varies from high mountains in the north (the southernmost extreme of ranges tumbling down from the Tibet Plateau) to limestone-encrusted tropical islands in the south that are part of the Malay Archipelago.

The rivers and tributaries of northern and central Thailand drain into the Gulf of Thailand via the Chao Phraya Delta near Bangkok; Mae Nam Mun and other northeastern waterways exit into the South China Sea via the Mekong River.

These broad geographic characteristics divide the country into four main zones. The fertile central region is dominated by Mae Nam Chao Phraya. The northeast, as the kingdom's poorest region (thanks to 'thin' soil plus occasional droughts and floods), is a plateau rising some 300m above the central plain. Northern Thailand is a region of mountains and fertile valleys, and the southern peninsula extends to the Malaysian border and is predominantly rainforest.

Extending from the east coast of the Malay peninsula to Vietnam, the Sunda Shelf separates the Gulf of Thailand from the South China Sea. On the opposite side of the peninsula, the Andaman Sea encompasses the Indian Ocean east of India's Andaman and Nicobar Islands. Thailand's Andaman Sea and Gulf of Thailand coastlines form 2710km of beaches, hard shores and wetlands. Hundreds of oceanic and continental islands lie offshore on both sides.

CLIMATE

Rainfall

Thailand's climate is ruled by monsoons that produce three seasons in northern, northeastern and central Thailand, and two seasons in southern Thailand. The three-season zone, which extends roughly from Thailand's northernmost reaches to Phetchaburi Province on the southern peninsula, experiences a 'dry and wet monsoon climate', with the southwest monsoon arriving around July and lasting into November (the 'rainy season'). This is followed by a dry, 'cool' period (the 'cool season') from November till mid-February, followed by much higher relative temperatures (the 'hot season') from March to June.

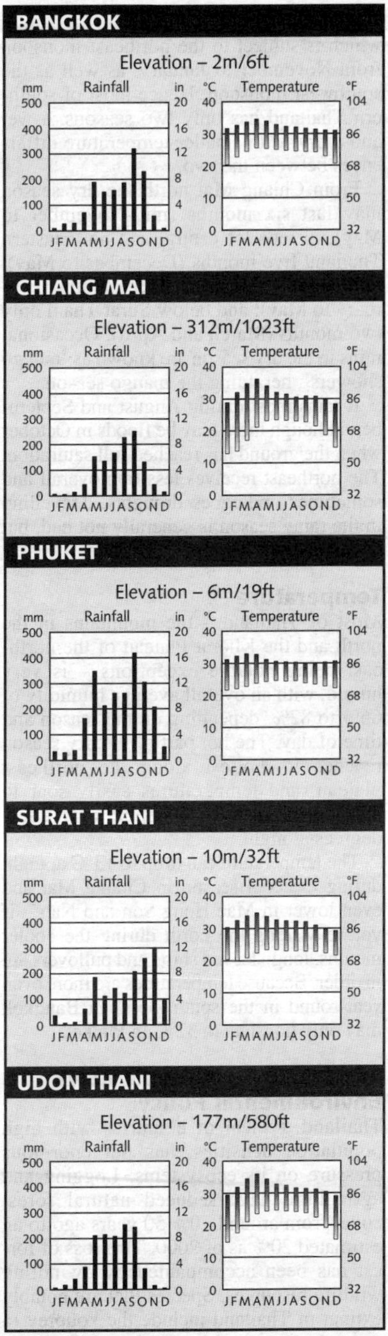

It rains more and longer in the south, which is subject to the northeast monsoon from November to January, as well as the southwest monsoon. Hence most of southern Thailand has only two seasons, a wet and a dry, with smaller temperature differences between the two.

From Chiang Mai north the dry season may last six months (mid-November to May); in most of central and northeastern Thailand five months (December to May); on the upper peninsula three months (February to May); and below Surat Thani only two months (March and April). Occasional rains in the dry season are known as 'mango showers', heralding the mango season.

It rains most during August and September, although there may be floods in October when the ground has reached full saturation. The northeast receives less rain overall and sometimes undergoes droughts. Travelling in the rainy season is generally not bad, but unpaved roads may be impassable.

Temperature

Most of Thailand – the mountains in the north and the Khorat Plateau of the northeast being notable exceptions – is very humid, with an overall average humidity of 66% to 82%, depending on the season and time of day. The hot part of the dry season reaches its hottest along the northeast plateau, and temperatures easily soar to 39°C in the daytime, dropping only a few degrees at night.

The temperature can drop to 13°C at night during the cool season in Chiang Mai and even lower in Mae Hong Son and Nan – if you're visiting the north during the cooler months, long-sleeved shirts and pullovers are in order. Because temperatures are more even year-round in the south, 35°C in Bangkok may only translate to 32°C in Phuket.

ECOLOGY & ENVIRONMENT

Environmental Policy

Thailand, typical of countries with high population densities, has put enormous pressure on its ecosystems. Logging and agriculture have reduced natural forest cover from around 70% 50 years ago to an estimated 20% as of 2000. This loss of forest has been accompanied by dwindling wildlife resources. Species that are notably extinct in Thailand include the kouprey (a type of wild cattle), Schomburgk's deer and the Javan rhino, but innumerable smaller species have also fallen by the wayside.

In response to environmental degradation the Thai government has created a large number of protected parks, reserves and sanctuaries since the 1970s, and has enacted legislation to protect specific plant and animal species. The government hopes to raise the total forest cover to 40% by the middle of this century. The latest World Conservation Monitoring Centre report (2000) from the United Nations Environment Programme (UNEP) confirms that Thailand has designated protected status for more forest cover than any other nation in South or Southeast Asia, both proportionately (30%) and in square kilometres (51,300 sq km).

In 1989 all logging was banned in Thailand following a disaster the year before in which hundreds of tonnes of cut timber washed down deforested slopes in Surat Thani Province, burying a number of villages and killing more than 100 people. It is now illegal to sell timber felled in the country, and all imported timber is theoretically accounted for before going on the market.

Thailand is a signatory to the UN Convention on International Trade in Endangered Species (Cites), and although Thailand has a better record than most of its neighbours, corruption hinders government attempts to shelter 'exotic' species from the illicit global wildlife trade. A crackdown on restaurants serving 'jungle food' *(aahăan pàa)* – exotic and often endangered wildlife species like barking deer, bear, pangolin, civet and gaur – has been fairly successful.

In any case wildlife experts agree that the greatest danger faced by Thai fauna is neither hunting nor the illegal wildlife trade but rather habitat loss – as is true for most of the rest of the world. If the forests, mangroves, marshes and grasslands are protected, they will in turn protect the animals.

The Royal Forest Department is under constant pressure to take immediate action in the areas where preservation laws have gone unenforced, especially coastal zones where illegal tourist accommodation has flourished. Their slowness to respond in the cases of Ko Phi-Phi and Ko Samet suggests corruption at the highest levels.

Forestry department efforts are also hampered by a lack of personnel and funds. The average ranger is paid less than 100B per day – some aren't paid at all but receive food and lodging – to take on armed poachers backed by the rich and powerful Chinese godfathers who control illicit timber and wildlife businesses.

Marine resources are also threatened by a lack of long-range conservation goals. The upper portion of the Gulf of Thailand, between Rayong and Prachuap Khiri Khan, was once one of the most fertile marine areas in the world. Now it is virtually dead due to overfishing and the release of mainland pollutants. Experts say it's not too late to rehabilitate the upper gulf by reducing pollution and the number of trawlers, and by restricting commercial fishing to certain zones. An effective ban on the harvest of mackerel *(plaa thuu)* in the spawning stages has brought stocks of this fish back from the brink of total depletion. The Bangkok Metropolitan Administration (BMA) is developing a system of sewage-treatment plants in the Chao Phraya Delta area with the intention of halting all large-scale dumping of sewage into Gulf waters, but similar action needs to be taken along the entire eastern seaboard, which has become Thailand's new industrial centre.

Tourism & the Environment

Conscious that the country's natural beauty is a major tourist attraction for both residents and foreigners, and that tourism is one of Thailand's major revenue earners, the government has stepped up efforts to protect wilderness areas and to add more acreage to the park system. In Khao Yai National Park, for example, all hotel and golf-course facilities have been removed in order to reduce human influence on the park environment. As a result of government and private sector pressure on the fishing industry, coral dynamiting has been all but eliminated in the Similan and Surin Islands, to preserve these areas for tourist visitation. As described in *National Parks of Thailand* by Gray, Piprell & Graham:

> A growing number of conservationists, development experts and government officials believe that boundary markers and even guns do little to halt encroachment. The surrounding communities must somehow be allowed to share in whatever economic benefits a park can offer. Some sanctuaries, like Huay Kha Khaeng, recruit employees from local villages. In Thaleh Noi Wildlife Preserve, local fishermen are hired to take visitors around the lake in their boats to view the rich bird life. Rangers at Laem Son National Park encourage local fishermen to take visitors to outlying islands rather than over-fish the sea. Phu Kradung National Park takes on several hundred locals as porters to carry hikers' gear up the mountain. Some have become so protective of their park that they will report violations of the regulations to the park rangers.

However, tourism has also made negative contributions. Eager to make fistfuls of cash, hotel developers and tour operators

Thai Environmentalism

One of the greatest victories by Thai environmentalists was the 1986 defeat of government plans to construct a hydroelectric facility across the Khwae Yai River. The dam was to be placed over a river section in the middle of Thung Yai Naresuan National Park, one of the largest and best preserved monsoon forest areas in Southeast Asia. It took four years of organised protest to halt the dam. Since this ground-breaking victory several other power projects have been halted through public protest. A coalition of farmers and environmentalists is currently working towards a dismantling of Kheuan Pak Mun (Pak Mun Dam).

On the other hand, there have been some great defeats, one of which was the construction of the Yadana gas pipeline from Myanmar's Gulf of Mottama to Ratchaburi Province through some of Thailand's most pristine monsoon woodlands. Environmental organisations are currently fighting tentative plans for a similar pipeline between Malaysia and Thailand.

More recently Thai environmentalists convinced the government to halt all plans to blast the Mekong River rapids (for navigational purposes) alongside Nong Khai Province, at least for the time being. Of more immediate threat is China's blasting of Mekong rapids along Chiang Rai Province without the consent of Thailand, Laos or any other country downriver.

have rushed to provide ecologically inappropriate services for visitors in sensitive areas. Ko Phi-Phi and Ko Samet are two national park islands notorious for overdevelopment and public land encroachment.

What can the average visitor to Thailand do to minimise the impact of tourism on the environment? We recommend the following:

- Don't buy coral or sea shells – it's illegal in Thailand to buy or sell either
- Avoid all restaurants serving 'exotic' wildlife species
- When using hired boats near coral reefs, insist that boat operators not lower anchor onto coral formations
- Refrain from purchasing or accepting drinking water offered in plastic bottles wherever possible. When there's a choice, request glass water bottles, which are recyclable in Thailand. The deposit is refundable when you return the bottle to any vendor who sells drinking water in glass bottles.
- In outdoor areas where rubbish has accumulated, consider organising an impromptu cleanup crew to collect plastic, Styrofoam and other non-biodegradables for delivery to a regular rubbish pick-up point
- Volunteer to collect (and later dispose of) rubbish when trekking or boating

An increasing number of guesthouses now offer drinking water from large, reusable plastic water containers, so that visitors may fill up their own canteens or water bottles.

Thais sensitive to Western paternalism are quick to point out that on a global scale the so-called 'developed' countries contribute far more environmental damage than does Thailand. For example, per capita greenhouse emissions for Australia, Canada and the USA average over five tonnes each, while countries that are members of the Association of Southeast Asian Nations (Asean) on average contribute less than one tenth that amount.

By expressing your desire to use environmentally friendly materials – and by taking direct action to avoid the use and indiscriminate disposal of plastic – you can provide an example of environmental consciousness not only for the Thais but for other international visitors.

Visitors may want to consider filing letters of complaint regarding any questionable environmental practices with the Tourism Authority of Thailand, Wildlife Fund Thailand and the Royal Forest Department at the following addresses. Markets selling endangered species should also be duly noted – consider enclosing photos to support your complaints.

Asian Society for Environmental Protection (☎ 0 2524 5363) CDG-SEAPO, Asian Institute of Technology, Bangkok 10501
Forest Protection Office (☎ 0 2579 3004, 0 2579 5266; ⓔ wildlifept@hotmail.com) Royal Forest Department, 61 Th Phahonyothin, Bangkhen, Bangkok 10900
Friends of Nature 670/437 Th Charansanitwong, Bangkok 10700
Network for Environmentally & Socially Sustainable Tourism Thailand (NESSThai; ⓔ beartai@bkk.loxinfo.co.th) PO Box 48, Krabi
Office of the National Environment Board 60/1 Soi Prachasamphan 4, Th Rama IV, Bangkok 10400
Project for Ecological Recovery 77/3 Soi Nomjit, Th Naret, Bangkok 10500
Tourism Authority of Thailand (TAT) 202 Th Ratchadaphisek, Huay Khwang, Bangkok 10310
Wildlife Fund Thailand (WFT; ☎ 0 2521 3435, fax 0 552 6083; ⓔ pisitnp@mozart.inet.co.th) 251/88–90 Th Phahonyothin, Bangkhen, Bangkok 10220
World Wide Fund for Nature (☎ 0 2524 6128; ⓦ www.wwfthai.org) WWF Program Office, Asian Institute of Technology, PO Box 4, Klong Luang, Pathum Thani 12120

FLORA & FAUNA

Unique in the region because its north–south axis extends some 1800km from mainland to peninsular Southeast Asia, Thailand provides potential habitats for an astounding variety of flora and fauna.

Flora

As in the rest of tropical Asia, most indigenous vegetation in Thailand is associated with two basic types of tropical forest: monsoon forest (with a distinct dry season of three months or more) and rainforest (where rain falls more than nine months per year). Forest cover varies by region from a high of 43% in the north to a low of 12% in the northeast. The most heavily forested province is Chiang Mai, followed by Kanchanaburi.

Monsoon forests amount to about a quarter of all natural forest cover in the country. They're marked by deciduous tree varieties, which shed their leaves during the dry season to conserve water. About half of all Thailand's forest cover consists of rainforests, all of it in southern Thailand, while a few zones support a mix of monsoon forest and rainforest vegetation. The remaining quarter of the country's forest cover consists of freshwater swamp forests in the delta regions; forested crags amid the karst topography of both the north and south; mangroves in the south; and pine forests at higher altitudes in the north.

The country's most famous flora includes an incredible array of fruit trees, bamboo (more species than any country outside China), tropical hardwoods and over 27,000 flowering species, including Thailand's national floral symbol, the orchid.

Fauna

As with plant life, variation in the animal kingdom closely affiliates with geographic and climatic differences. The indigenous fauna of Thailand's northern half is mostly of Indochinese origin while that of the south is generally Sundaic (ie, typical of peninsular Malaysia, Sumatra, Borneo and Java). The invisible dividing line between the two zoogeographical zones is across the Isthmus of Kra, about halfway down the southern peninsula. The large overlap area between zoogeographical and vegetative zones – from around Prachuap Khiri Khan on the southern peninsula to Uthai Thani in the lower north – means that much of Thailand is a potential habitat for plants and animals from both zones.

Thailand is particularly rich in bird life, with over 1000 recorded resident and migrating species – approximately 10% of the world's bird species. Insect species number some 6000, and the country's rich marine environment counts tens of thousands of species.

Indigenous mammals, mostly found in dwindling numbers within Thailand's national parks or wildlife sanctuaries, include tigers, leopards, elephants, Asiatic black bears, Malayan sun bears, gaur (Indian bison), banteng (wild cattle), serow (an Asiatic goat-antelope), sambar deer, barking deer, mouse deer, pangolin, gibbons, macaques, tapir, dolphins and dugongs (sea cows). Around 40 of Thailand's 300 mammal

Seub Nakasathien

One of the Thai environmental movement's biggest heroes to date is a man who spent much of his adult life trying to protect the kingdom's forests.

After graduating from Kasetsart University with two degrees in forestry, Seub Nakasathien began working for the Wildlife Conservation Division of the Royal Forestry Department (RFD) in the mid 1970s. Stationed at a small wildlife sanctuary in Chonburi Province, Seub made his first encounters with poachers, and earned the respect of both his peers and the criminals with his straightforward and fair treatment.

After going abroad to earn a master's degree in environmental conservation, Seub returned to Thailand and was promoted to the chief management position at Huay Kha Khaeng Wildlife Sanctuary in 1989. Here he once again came into contact with poachers as well as illegal loggers, and once again his efforts were met with measured success.

When the RFD granted a logging concession to a plywood company in some areas of Huay Kha Khaeng, Seub found himself in combat with the RFD itself. Frustrated with the way the department paid lip service towards conservation while collecting large sums of money from logging contracts, Seup appealed to Unesco to designate the Thung Yai – Huay Kha Khaeng Wildlife Sanctuary a World Heritage Site.

In September 1990 Seub donated his research gear to a wildlife centre, built a shrine dedicated to the spirits of park rangers who had given their lives to protect Huay Kha Khaeng and apparently committed suicide. Although the circumstances surrounding his death are unclear, Seup's commitment to Thailand's wildlife and ecology has become an inspiration for the environmental movement in Thailand and beyond.

For more information about Seub's life and legacy, and about a charitable fund created in his name, see W www.seub.or.th.

species, including clouded leopard, Malayan tapir, tiger, Irrawaddy dolphin, goral, jungle cat, dusky langur and pileated gibbon, are on the International Union for Conservation of Nature (IUCN) list of endangered species.

Around 200 to 300 wild tigers are thought to be hanging on in Khao Yai, Kaeng Krachan, Huay Kha Khaeng/Thung Yai Naresuan, Nam Nao, Thap Lan, Mae Wong and Khao Sok National Parks. Although tiger hunting and trapping is illegal, poachers continue to kill the cats for the lucrative overseas Chinese pharmaceutical market; among the Chinese, the ingestion of tiger penis and bone is thought to have curative effects.

Species of herpetofauna in Thailand number around 313 reptiles and 107 amphibians. These include four sea-turtle species along with numerous snake varieties, of which six are venomous: the common cobra (six subspecies), king cobra (hamadryad), banded krait (three species), Malayan viper, green viper and Russell's pit viper. Although the relatively rare king cobra can reach up to 6m in length, the nation's largest snake is the reticulated python, which can reach a whopping 10m. The country's many lizard species include two commonly seen in homes and older hotels or guesthouses, *túk-kae* (a large gecko) and *jîng-jòk* (a smaller house lizard), as well as larger species like the black jungle monitor.

National Parks, Reserves & Wildlife Sanctuaries

A system of wildlife sanctuaries was first provided for in the Wild Animals Reservation and Protection Act of 1960, followed by the National Parks Act of 1961, which established the kingdom's national park programme, with the setting up of Khao Yai National Park. Today the kingdom boasts 112 national parks, plus over a thousand 'nonhunting areas', wildlife sanctuaries, forest reserves, botanical gardens and arboretums. Nineteen of the national parks are marine parks that protect coastal, insular and open-sea areas. Altogether these cover over 13% of the country's land and sea area, which means Thailand has one of the highest percentages of protected areas of any nation in the world.

The majority of the parks, reserves and sanctuaries are well maintained by the

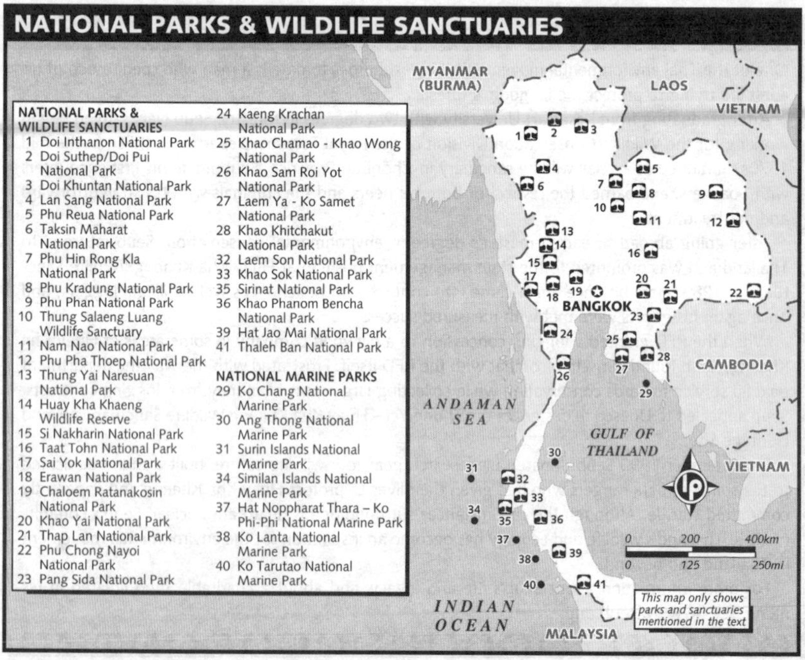

Royal Forest Department *(W www.forest.go.th/default_e.asp)*, but a few, notably Hat Noppharat Thara – Ko Phi-Phi National Marine Park, have allowed rampant tourism to threaten the natural environment. Poaching, illegal logging and shifting cultivation have also taken their toll on protected lands, but since 1990 the government has been cracking down on these issues with some success.

GOVERNMENT & POLITICS

Thailand (officially 'Kingdom of Thailand') has been an independent nation since AD 1238, and is the only country in South or Southeast Asia that was never colonised by a foreign power.

Since 1932, the political system has been a constitutional monarchy inspired by the British model but with a myriad of subtle differences. National polls elect the 500-member lower house (Sapha Phu Thaen Ratsadon or House of Representatives, with four-year terms) and prime minister. In Thailand the Senate is not as powerful as the House of Representatives; the latter legislates, while the Senate votes on constitutional changes. The king appoints all judges who sit on Thailand's supreme court *(săan diikaa)*.

Ten political parties field candidates in national elections, but only four receive the bulk of the votes: the Democrat, New Aspiration, National Development and Thai Nation Parties.

1997 Constitution

On 27 September 1997, the Thai parliament voted in a new charter, Thailand's 16th such document since 1932 and the first to be decreed by a civilian government. Known as the people's constitution *(rátthammánuun pràchaachon)* it puts mechanisms in place to monitor the conduct of elected officials and political candidates and to protect civil rights. In many ways the new charter constitutes a bloodless popular revolution, as prodemocracy groups had been fighting for more than 10 years to reform the constitution.

The document makes voting in elections compulsory, allows public access to information from state agencies, provides free public education for 12 years, permits communities to manage, maintain, and use local natural resources and forces parliament to consider new laws upon receipt of 50,000 or more signatures in a public referendum. It also establishes several watchdog entities, including the constitution court, administrative court, national anticorruption commission, national election commission and human rights commission to support the enforcement of the constitution.

Of course the latest charter is merely the start of a political reform process. Much now depends on the will of Thailand's political legislators to see that the charter guides new legislation – and that such legislation is enforced.

Administrative Divisions

Thailand is divided into 76 provinces *(jangwàt)*. Each province is further subdivided into districts *(amphoe)*, which are then apportioned into subdistricts *(kìng-amphoe)*, communes or groups of villages *(tambon)*, villages *(mùu-bâan)*, sanitation districts *(sùkhăaphíbaan)* and municipalities *(thêtsàbaan)*. Urban areas with more than 50,000 inhabitants and a population density of over 3000 per sq km are designated *nákhawn* ('nakhon'); those with populations of 10,000 to 50,000 with not less than 3000 per sq km are *meuang* ('muang' on Roman-script highway signs).

A provincial capital *(amphoe meuang)* takes the same name as the province of which it is capital, eg, 'amphoe meuang Chiang Mai' (often abbreviated as 'meuang Chiang Mai') means 'city of Chiang Mai, capital of Chiang Mai Province'.

Except for Krungthep Mahanakhon (Metropolitan Bangkok), provincial governors *(phûu wâa râatchákaan)* are appointed to their four-year terms by the Ministry of the Interior. Bangkok's governor and provincial assembly were elected for the first time in November 1985, when Chamlong Srimuang, a strict Buddhist and a former major general, won by a landslide. The mid-2000 elections saw tough-talking, 10-time former MP Samak Sundaravej take over as Bangkok governor.

District officers *(nai amphoe)* are also appointed by the Ministry of the Interior but are responsible to their provincial governors. Cities are headed by elected mayors *(naayók thêtsàmontrii)*, communes or groups of villages by elected commune heads *(kamnan)* and villages by elected village chiefs *(phûu yài bâan)*.

THAILAND'S PROVINCES

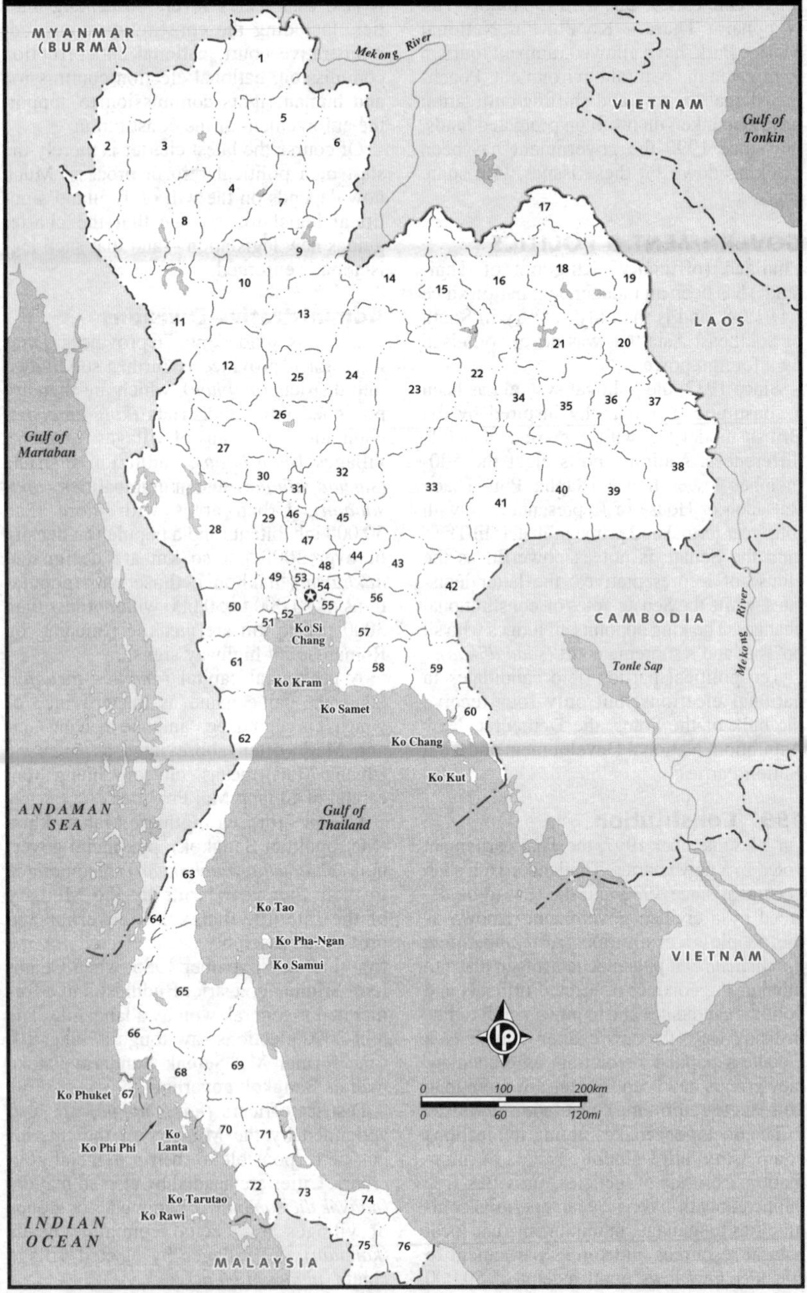

THAILAND'S PROVINCES

1	Chiang Rai	27	Uthai Thani	53	Nonthaburi
2	Mae Hong Son	28	Kanchanaburi	54	Bangkok
3	Chiang Mai	29	Suphanburi	55	Samut Prakan
4	Lampang	30	Chai Nat	56	Chachoengsao
5	Phayao	31	Singburi	57	Chonburi
6	Nan	32	Lopburi	58	Rayong
7	Phrae	33	Nakhon Ratchasima	59	Chanthaburi
8	Lamphun	34	Mahasarakham	60	Trat
9	Utaradit	35	Roi Et	61	Phetchaburi (Phetburi)
10	Sukhothai	36	Yasothon	62	Prachuap Khiri Khan
11	Tak	37	Amnat Charoen	63	Chumphon
12	Kamphaeng Phet	38	Ubon Ratchathani	64	Ranong
13	Phitsanulok	39	Si Saket	65	Surat Thani
14	Loei	40	Surin	66	Phang-Nga
15	Nong Bualamphu	41	Buriram	67	Phuket
16	Udon Thani	42	Sa Kaew	68	Krabi
17	Nong Khai	43	Prachinburi	69	Nakhon Si Thammarat
18	Sakon Nakhon	44	Nakhon Nayok	70	Trang
19	Nakhon Phanom	45	Saraburi	71	Phattalung
20	Mukdahan	46	Ang Thong	72	Satun
21	Kalasin	47	Ayuthaya	73	Songkhla
22	Khon Kaen	48	Pathum Thani	74	Pattani
23	Chaiyaphum	49	Nakhon Pathom	75	Yala
24	Phetchabun	50	Ratchaburi	76	Narathiwat
25	Phichit	51	Samut Songkhram		
26	Nakhon Sawan	52	Samut Sakhon		

Armed Forces & Police

Thailand spends less than 3% of its GDP on defence in a typical year. Armed services include the Royal Thai Army, Royal Thai Air Force and Royal Thai Navy under the Ministry of Defence, as well as the Royal Thai Police under the Ministry of the Interior. The latter department is divided into provincial police, metropolitan police, border patrol police and the central investigation bureau. Police corruption is common; recruits earn just US$150 a month on salary, so many take 'tea money' whenever they can.

Ever since the 1932 revolution, and particularly following WWII, the Thai military has had a substantial influence on the nation's political affairs. Generals have in fact commanded the premiership for 46 of the last 70 years. Following the demoralizing events of 1991–2, even the generals were admitting that the role of the military had to be reduced. Current conditions suggest that military coups are less likely to occur than at any time since 1932.

The Monarchy

His Majesty Bhumibol Adulyadej (pronounced 'phuumiphon adunyadet') is the ninth king of the Chakri dynasty (founded 1782) and the longest-reigning monarch in Thai history. His full name, including royal title, is Phrabatsomdet Boramintaramahaphumiphonadunyadet. Born in the USA in 1927, where his father Prince Mahidol was studying medicine at Harvard University, and schooled in both Bangkok and Switzerland, King Bhumibol was a nephew of Rama VII (King Prajadhipok) as well as the younger brother of Rama VIII (King Ananda Mahidol).

King Bhumibol ascended the throne in 1946 following the death of Rama VIII, who had reigned as king for only one year (see History earlier).

A jazz composer and saxophonist, His Majesty has had jam sessions with the likes of jazz greats Woody Herman and Benny Goodman, and his compositions (sounding like 1940s-style big band with bits of Thai melodic phrasing) are often played on Thai radio. He is fluent in English, French, German and Thai.

The king and Queen Sirikit have four children: Princess Ubol Ratana (born 1951), Crown Prince Maha Vajiralongkorn (1952), Princess Mahachakri Sirindhorn (1955) and Princess Chulabhorn (1957). A 15th-century royal decree means that the king's

The King & Who?

Many people who watch the musical *The King and I* or the two motion pictures on the same theme, *Anna and the King of Siam* (1946) or *Anna and the King* (1999), may believe they are watching the true story of Anna Leonowens, governess in the court of Siam during the reign of King Mongkut (Rama IV). The semi-comedic portrayals of the king, particularly those starring a shaven-headed Yul Brynner, so insulted the Thai people that the film has been banned from screenings in Thailand because of its historical and cultural distortions. In reality Anna Leon Owens, the author of the original book *The English Governess at the Siamese Court* (1870), not only misled the world as to the antics of the king but also as to her importance in the court, where she was employed not as a governess but as an English instructor. She also successfully concealed or distorted many events in her life prior to her five-year stay in Siam.

Courtesy of the students of Sriwittayapaknam School, Samut Prakan

senior son or full brother his heir apparent *(uparaja* or *ùpàràat)*. Thus Prince Maha Vajiralongkorn was officially designated as crown prince and heir when he reached 20 years of age in 1972.

Among the nation's soothsayers, it has long been prophesied that the Chakri dynasty will end with Rama IX. His Majesty's health has faltered in recent years, and most Thais are preparing themselves for the transfer of kingship to Prince Maha Vajiralongkorn.

Thailand's political system is officially a constitutional monarchy, but the Thai constitution stipulates that the king be 'enthroned in a position of revered worship' and not be exposed 'to any sort of accusation or action'. With or without legal writ, the vast majority of Thai citizens regard King Bhumibol as a sort of demigod, partly in deference to tradition but also because of his involvement in impressive public works.

In times of national political crisis, Thais have often looked to the king for leadership. Two attempted coups d'etat in the 1980s may have failed because they received tacit royal disapproval. By implication, the successful military coup of 1991 must have had palace approval, whether *post facto* or *a priori*.

Along with nationhood and religion, the monarchy is very highly regarded in Thai society – negative comment about the king or any member of the royal family is a social as well as legal taboo. See the Society & Conduct section later in this chapter.

ECONOMY

An 'Almost Dragon'

During the 1980s, Thailand maintained a steady GNP growth rate that by 1988 had reached 13% per annum. In the early and mid-1990s Thailand found itself on the threshold of attaining the exclusive rank of NIC – a newly industrialised country. Soon, economic experts said, Thailand would be joining Asia's 'little dragons', also known as the Four Dragons or Tigers – Hong Kong, Singapore, South Korea and Taiwan – in becoming a leader in the Pacific Rim economic boom.

In mid-1997 the 20-year boom went bust throughout Southeast and East Asia, with Thailand leading the way. The economies worst affected by the financial turmoil – Thailand, Indonesia, Malaysia, the Philippines and South Korea – displayed certain common pre-crisis characteristics, including wide current-account deficits, lack of government transparency, high levels of external debt and relatively low foreign-exchange reserves. For the most part the crisis stemmed from investor panic, with the rush to buy dollars to pay off debts creating a self-fulfilling collapse. Between 30 June and 31 October the baht depreciated roughly 40% against the US dollar, and dollar-backed external debt rose to 52.4% of the country's GDP.

Many banks and finance companies were forced to close in 1998, as the government made valiant efforts to restructure the economy and most especially the financial and property sectors. The International Monetary Fund (IMF) provided a US$17.2 billion rescue package in the form of short-term loans, with the stipulation that Thailand follow IMF's prescriptions for recapitalisation and restructuring.

Following the 1997 recession, the Thai economy shrank 10% in 1998, then grew 4% to 5% in 1999 and 2000, enabling Thailand to take an 'early exit' from the IMF's loan package in 2000. By the end of 2002, the economy was healthier than at any time since 1996. Despite positive indicators, however, the Thais are living in an era of self-imposed austerity and relatively high unemployment. Some observers have concluded that this forced cooling off is the best thing that could have happened to the overheated economy, giving the nation time to focus on infrastructure priorities and offering the Thai citizenry an opportunity to reassess cultural change.

The economic crisis has also precipitated a national discussion about Thailand's role in globalisation. Many want to cut all ties with the IMF and World Bank, and some are calling for stronger tariffs on foreign goods. Others acknowledge that the reason Thailand fell into this recession in the first place was because so many middle- and upper-class Thais – not to mention banks – refused to practise any self discipline with regard to credit.

Still, a long-term assessment of the journey the nation has travelled over the last three decades shows that, along with Malaysia and South Korea, no other country in the world has produced more rapid economic growth or seen such a dramatic reduction in poverty during that period. Per capita income levels in Thailand increased 19-fold in Thailand between 1963 and 1997. Even accounting for the baht devaluation, this means most Thais today are economically better off than they were in the 1960s.

In 2002, the minimum daily wage in Bangkok and surrounding provinces was 169B (US$3.93).

The Big Picture

Around one sixth of Thailand's exports are agricultural. The country ranks first in the world for rice and natural rubber, second in tapioca and fifth in coconut. Other important agricultural exports include sugar, maize, pineapple, cotton, jute, green beans, soya beans and palm oil. Processed food and beverages – especially canned shrimp, tuna and pineapple – also account for significant export earnings.

About half the Thai labour force is engaged in agriculture, followed by around 15% each in manufacturing, services and commerce. Manufactured goods have become an increasingly important source of foreign-exchange revenue, with textiles, cement, electronics, petrochemical products and car and truck manufacture leading the way. The country boasts substantial natural resources, including tin, petroleum and natural gas.

Since 1987, tourism has become a major earner of foreign exchange, occasionally outdistancing even Thailand's largest single export, textiles. The Thai government's economic strategy remains focused, however, on export-led growth through the continued development of textiles and other light industries such as electronics, backed by rich reserves of natural resources and a large, inexpensive labour force.

By 2000 raw average per capita income was around US$2000 per year; if measured using the purchasing-power parity method (which takes into account the price differences between countries), per capita incomes rises to US$6402. At the moment the economy is growing at a healthy rate of around 5% per annum. At the end of 2002 the inflation rate was a low 1.4% per annum. An estimated 20% of Thai citizens control over 60% of the wealth – most of these are residents of either Bangkok or Phuket.

POPULATION & PEOPLE

The population of Thailand is estimated at 62 million and is currently growing at a rate of 1% to 1.5% per annum, thanks to a vigorous nation-wide family-planning campaign.

Over a third of all Thais live in urban areas. Bangkok is by far the largest city in the kingdom, with a population of around six million in the city proper, or eight million including the adjacent provinces.

Ranking the nation's other cities by population depends on whether you look at the rather limited municipal districts *(thêtsà-baan)* or more realistic metropolitan districts *(meuang)*. Using the *meuang* measure, after Bangkok the five most-populated cities in descending order (not counting the densely populated 'suburb' provinces of Samut Prakan and Nonthaburi, which rank second and third if considered separately from Bangkok) are Udon Thani (pop 227,000), Nakhon Ratchasima (210,000), Hat Yai (191,000), Chonburi (188,000) and Chiang Mai (172,000). Most other towns in Thailand have populations below 100,000.

On the 2002 UN Human Development Index, Thailand received an overall ranking of 70, falling in the upper half of the UN-designated 'medium human development' range. The average life expectancy in Thailand is 70 years, the highest in mainland Southeast Asia. Thailand has a relatively youthful population; only about 12% are older than 50 years and 6% are aged over 65.

The Thai Majority

About 75% of citizens are ethnic Thais, who can be divided into four groups: Central Thais, or Siamese, of the Chao Phraya Delta (the most densely populated region of the country); Thai Lao of northeastern Thailand; Thai Pak Tai of southern Thailand; and northern Thais. Each group speaks its own Thai dialect and to a certain extent practises customs unique to its region. Politically and economically the Central Thais are the dominant group, although they barely outnumber the Thai Lao of the northeast.

Small minority groups who speak Thai dialects include the Lao Song (Phetchaburi and Ratchaburi); the Phuan (Chaiyaphum, Phetchaburi, Prachinburi); the Phu Thai (Sakon Nakhon, Nakhon Phanom, Mukdahan); the Shan (Mae Hong Son), the Thai Khorat or Suay (Khorat); the Thai Lü (Nan, Chiang Rai); the Thai-Malay (Satun, Trang, Krabi) and the Yaw (Nakhon Phanom, Sakon Nakhon).

The Chinese

People of Chinese ancestry, most of whom are second- or third-generation Hakka, Chao Zhou, Hainanese or Cantonese, make up 11% of the population. In northern Thailand there are also a substantial number of Hui – Chinese Muslims who emigrated from Yunnan to Thailand in the late 19th century to avoid religious and ethnic persecution during the Qing dynasty.

Ethnic Chinese in Thailand probably enjoy better relations with the majority of the population than they do in any other country in Southeast Asia, due partly to historical reasons and partly to the traditional Thai tolerance of other cultures – although there was a brief spell of anti-Chinese sentiment during the reign of Rama VI (1910–25). Rama V used Chinese businesspeople to infiltrate European trading houses, a move that helped defeat European colonial designs. Wealthy Chinese also introduced their daughters to the royal court as consorts, developing royal connections and adding a Chinese bloodline that extends to the current king.

Other Minorities

The second-largest ethnic minority living in Thailand are the Malays (3.5%), most of whom reside in the provinces of Songkhla, Yala, Pattani and Narathiwat. The remaining 10.5% of the population is divided among smaller non-Thai-speaking groups like the Vietnamese, Khmer, Mon, Semang (Sakai), Moken (*chao leh,* or sea gypsies), Htin, Mabri, Khamu and a variety of hill tribes.

A small number of Europeans and other non-Asians reside in Bangkok and the provinces, although their total numbers aren't recorded since few actually have official Thai immigrant status.

EDUCATION

Thailand's literacy rate runs at 95.5%, one of the highest rates in Southeast Asia. Free public schooling is compulsory for nine years. Although high value is placed on education as a way to achieve material success, at most levels the system itself tends to favour rote learning over independent thinking.

Thailand's public school system is organised around six years at the primary *(pràthǒm)* level, beginning at the age of six, followed by either three or six years of secondary *(máthǎyom)* education. The three-year course is for those planning to follow school with three to five years of trade school *(wí-chaa-chîip)*, while the six-year course *(máthǎyom)* is for students planning to continue at the tertiary *(ùdom)* level, ie, university. Less than nine years of formal education is the national norm.

Private and international schools for the foreign and local elite are found in Bangkok and Chiang Mai, and to a lesser extent in the other large provincial cities. The country boasts over 30 public and five private universities, as well as numerous trade schools and technical colleges.

A teaching certificate may be obtained after attending a two year, post-secondary programme at one of the many teachers colleges scattered throughout the country. Two of Thailand's universities, Thammasat and

Chulalongkorn, are considered to be among the top 50 in Asia.

ARTS

At the central point of Southeast Asia, Thailand's art scene has been influenced by many sources. As well as the arts of such native groups as the Mon and the Khmer, these include the great artistic traditions of India and China; the subtle renderings of Indo- and Sino-influenced art in neighbouring countries and the colonial and postcolonial cultural influx from Europe. In the more tightly connected modern world of aero- and cyberspace, there are influences from just about every other corner of the globe.

For information on Thai performing arts, see the special section 'Music, Theatre & Dance'.

Architecture

Considered the highest art form in traditional Thai society, architecture creates and adapts structures within which the people eat, sleep, work and worship. In addition to native Siamese styles, within Thailand's borders you'll find splendid examples from historical Khmer, Lao, Mon and northern Thai traditions.

Traditional Architecture Home and temple architecture traditionally followed relatively strict rules of design that dictated proportion, placement, materials and ornamentation. With the modernisation of Thailand in the 19th and 20th centuries, stylistic codification gave way first to European functionalism and then to stylistic innovation in more recent times.

The traditional Thai residential architecture consists either of single-room wooden houses raised on stilts or more elaborate structures of interlocking rooms with both indoor and shaded outdoor spaces, all supported at least 2m above the ground on stilts. Since originally all Thai settlements were founded along river or canal banks, the use of stilts protected the house and its inhabitants from flooding during the annual monsoon. Even in areas where flooding wasn't common, the Thais continued to raise their houses on stilts until relatively recently, using the space beneath the house as a cooking area, for tethering animals, or for parking their bicycles and motor vehicles. Teak has always been the material of choice for wooden structures, although with the shortage of teak in Thailand these days, few houses less than 50 years old are constructed of teak.

Rooflines in central, northern and southern Thailand are steeply pitched and often decorated at the corners or along the gables with motifs related to the *naga,* a mythical sea serpent, long believed to be a spiritual protector of Thai-speaking cultures throughout Asia. In southern Thailand bamboo and palm thatch have always been more common building materials than wood, and even today these renewable plant sources remain important construction elements.

In certain areas of the south you'll also see thick-walled structures of stuccoed brick – architecture that was introduced by Chinese, Portuguese, French and British settlements along the Malay Peninsula. In Thailand's four southernmost provinces, it's not unusual to come upon houses of entirely Malay design in which high masonry pediments or foundations, rather than wood stilts, lift the living areas well above the ground. Roofs of tile or thatch tend to be less steeply pitched, and hipped gables – almost entirely absent in traditional Thai architecture further north – are common in these Malay-influenced buildings.

What's a Wát? Technically speaking, a *wát* (from the Pali-Sanskrit *avasa* or 'dwelling for pupils and ascetics') is a Buddhist compound where men or women can be ordained as monks or nuns. Almost every village in Thailand has at least one wát, while in towns and cities they're quite numerous. Without an ordination area (designated by *sěmaa,* or stone markers), a monastic centre where monks or nuns reside is simply a *sǎmnák sǒng* (*sangha* residence). The latter are often established as meditation retreat facilities in forest areas, sometimes in conjunction with larger *wát pàa* (forest monasteries).

The typical wát compound in Thailand will contain at the very least an *uposatha* (*bòt* in central Thai, *sǐm* in northern and northeastern Thai), a consecrated chapel where monastic ordinations are held, and a *vihara* (*wíhǎan* in Thai), where important Buddha images are housed. Classic Thai *vihara* and *uposatha* architecture usually

Fire in the Lotus

Over the centuries, traditional Thai artists have taken the principle drama in Theravada Buddhism – the overcoming or taming of human passions via the practice of Buddhism – and made it an integral part of the artistic outcome. Buddhism offers a way to cool the passions through the practice of morality and mental development, an effect that if followed to conclusion will result in the extinguishing of that fire, the defeat of the existential angst produced by the human condition.

In its most simple artistic manifestation, the cooling effect of Buddhism is represented by the lotus *(padma)*, a motif seen throughout Thai Buddhist art, from such obvious examples as the lotus seat upon which Buddha figures sit to the less obvious lotus-bud shapes at the tip of classical Sukhothai *chedi* (stupa; monuments built to house a Buddha relic).

Less obvious still are the many shapes that combine the lotus bud motif with that of a flame to produce a symbol called *ka-nòk* – a peculiarly Thai innovation that brings human fire into contact with Buddhist cool. You can find this motif everywhere in Thai Buddhist art, and even in much traditional secular art, from the gold-leaf prints dotting lacquered temple walls to the unfurling tails of the *kinnari* (half human, half bird) and other mythical creatures painted into murals or standing in sculpted form on *wíhǎan* (temple hall) porticoes. Even the Buddha's *ùtsànít* – the flame atop the head, representing in this case both the burning out of the passions and enlightenment – in Thai sculpture often features aspects of the lotus bud.

Look closely at some of the most common prints found on traditional cotton *phâasîn*, the sarong once universally worn by Thai women and still worn by some in rural Thailand, and you'll see perhaps dozens of variations on this simple but highly evocative motif.

This juxtaposition and harmonisation of opposites says everything about the human side of Buddhism, the reality in which the coolness of the *padma*, or lotus, is in constant contention with the fire of *raga*, or passion.

involves a steeply pitched roof system tiled in green, gold and red, and often constructed in tiered series of three levels, representing the *tiratana* or triple gems, the Buddha (the Teacher), the Dhamma (Dharma in Sanskrit; the Teaching) and the Sangha (the fellowship of followers of the Teaching). Partial fourth and fifth tiers may also be included to shade porticoes at the front, rear or sides of the building. The front of the *wíhǎan/bòt*, at a minimum, will feature an open veranda; often the veranda will extend around the entire perimeter of the building.

Another classic component of temple architecture throughout the country is the presence of one or more *chedi* or *jedi* (from the Pali *cetiya*), also known by the more generic term 'stupa', a solid cone-shaped monument that pays tribute to the enduring stability of Buddhism. *Chedi* come in a myriad of styles, from simple inverted bowl-shaped designs imported from Sri Lanka to the more elaborate multi-sided *chedi* of northern Thailand, heir to the great Thai-Lao kingdoms of Lan Na and Lan Chang (Lan Xang). Many *chedi* are believed to contain 'relics' (pieces of bone) belonging to the historical Buddha. In northern and northeastern Thailand such *chedi* are known as *thâat*.

Other structures typically found in wát compounds include one or *sǎalaa* or open-sided shelters for community meetings and Dhamma lectures; a number of *kùtì* or monastic quarters; a *hǎw trai* or Tripitaka library where Buddhist scriptures are stored; a *hǎw klawng*, or drum tower (sometimes with a *hǎw rákhang*, or bell tower); various *chedi* or stupas (the smaller squarish stupas are *thâat kràdùk*, or bone reliquaries, where the ashes of deceased worshippers are interred); plus various ancillary buildings – such as schools or clinics – that differ from wát to wát according to local community needs. Many wát also have a *sǎan phǐi wát* or spirit house, for the temple's reigning earth spirit.

Historical Parks The Fine Arts Department, under the Ministry of Education, has developed nine key archaeological sites into well-cared-for historical parks *(ùtháyaan pràwàttìsàat)*: Ayuthaya Historical Park in Ayuthaya Province; Kamphaeng Phet

Historical Park in Kamphaeng Phet Province; Muang Singh Historical Park in Kanchanaburi Province; Phanom Rung Historical Park in Buriram Province; Phra Nakhon Khiri Historical Park in Phetchaburi Province; Prasat Hin Phimai Historical Park in Nakhon Ratchasima Province; Si Thep Historical Park in Phetchabun Province; and Sukhothai Historical Park and Si Satchanalai-Chaliang Historical Park in Sukhothai Province.

These parks are administered by the Fine Arts Department to guard against theft and vandalism. Unesco has declared the ruins at Ayuthaya, Kamphaeng Phet, Si Satchanalai-Chaliang and Sukhothai as World Heritage sites, which makes them eligible for UN funds and/or expertise in future restoration projects.

Contemporary Architecture Thai architects today are among the most daring in Southeast Asia, as even a short visit to Bangkok will confirm. Thais began mixing traditional Thai with European forms in the late 19th and early 20th centuries, as exemplified by Bangkok's Vimanmek Teak Mansion, the Author's Wing of the Oriental Hotel, the Chakri Mahaprasat next to Wat Phra Kaew, the Thai-Chinese Chamber of Commerce on Th Sathon Tai and any number of older residences and shophouses in Bangkok or provincial capitals throughout Thailand. This style is usually referred to as 'old Bangkok' or 'Ratanakosin'.

In the 1920s and '30s a simple Thai Deco style emerged, blending European Art Deco with functionalist restraint; surviving examples include the restored Chalermkrung Royal Theatre, the Royal Hotel, Ratchadamnoen Boxing Stadium, Hualamphong station, the main post office building and several buildings along Th Ratchadamnoen Klang. According to world Deco expert Carol Rosenstein, Bangkok possesses the richest trove of Art Deco in Southeast Asia, surpassing even former colonial capitals such as Hanoi, Jakarta, Kuala Lumpur and Singapore.

Buildings of mixed heritage in the north and northeast exhibit French and English influences, while those in the south typically show Portuguese influence. Shophouses throughout the country, whether 100 years or 100 days old, share the basic Chinese shophouse *(hâwng thǎew)* design where the ground floor is reserved for trading purposes while the upper floors contain offices or residences.

In the 1960s and '70s, the trend in modern Thai architecture, inspired by the European Bauhaus movement, moved towards a boring functionalism such that the average building looked like a giant egg carton turned on its side. The Thai aesthetic, so vibrant in the pre-WWII era, almost entirely disappeared in this characterless style of architecture.

When Thai architects finally began experimenting again during the building boom of the mid-1980s, the result was hi-tech designs like Sumet Jumsai's famous robot-shaped Bank of Asia on Th Sathon Tai in Bangkok. Few people seemed to find the space-age look endearing, but at least it was different. Another trend affixed gaudy Roman and Greek-style columns to rectangular Art Deco boxes in what was almost a parody of Western classical architecture.

More recently, a handful of rebellious architects has begun incorporating traditional Thai motifs – mixed with updated Western classics – in the design of new buildings. Rangsan Torsuwan, a graduate of Massachusetts Institute of Technology (MIT), introduced the neoclassic (or neo-Thai) style; the best example is the new Grand Hyatt Erawan in Bangkok. Another architect using traditional Thai architecture in modern functions is Pinyo Suwankiri, who has designed a number of Bangkok's government buildings.

For those with a general interest in Thai residential design, interior or exterior, William Warren's *Thai Style* (Asia Books), is a coffee-table tome with excellent photography by Luca Invernizzi Tettoni.

Sculpture

On an international scale, Thailand has probably distinguished itself more in traditional sculpture than in any other art form. Although the country hasn't produced any individually world-famous classical or modern sculptors, within the realm of Buddhist art, Thai work is quite well known and well appreciated internationally.

Traditional Sculpture Delicate clay and terracotta engravings found on cave walls and on votive tablets date as far back as the

6th century in Thailand, although if you count the bronze culture of Ban Chiang, sculptural endeavours began at least 4000 years ago.

Historically the most commonly sculpted materials have been wood, stone, ivory, clay and metal. Depending on the material, artisans use a variety of techniques (including carving, modelling, construction and casting) to achieve their designs.

Thailand's most famous sculptural output has been its bronze Buddha images, coveted the world over for their originality and grace. Nowadays historic bronzes have all but disappeared from the art market in Thailand. Most are zealously protected by temples, museums or private collectors.

Contemporary Sculpture Modern sculpture can be split into two camps, one imitating Western or Japanese trends, and the other reviving Thai themes but interpreting them in new ways. An example of the latter came along when artist Sakarin Kreu-On fashioned a huge, hollow Buddha head from a mixture of clay, mud, papier mâché, glue and turmeric. Entitled *Phawang Si Leuang* (Yellow Trance), the work was displayed lying on its side, nearly filling a small room, during a recent successful world tour.

Painting

As with sculpture, Thai painting traditions were mostly confined to religious art, in which the application of natural pigments to temple walls became the favoured medium. Always instructional in intent, such painted images ranged from the depiction of the *jataka* (stories of the Buddha's past lives) and scenes from the Indian Hindu epic *Ramayana,* to elaborate scenes detailing daily life in Thailand.

Traditional Thai Art Styles

Thai scholars categorise historical styles of Thai art as follows:

Mon Art (formerly Dvaravati, 6th to 11th centuries; and Hariphunchai, 11th to 13th centuries) Originating in central, northern and northeastern Thailand, Mon Art is an adaptation of Indian styles, principally Gupta

Khmer Art (7th to 13th centuries) Centred in central and northeastern Thailand, this style is characterised by classic and post-classic Khmer styles accompanying the spread of Khmer empires

Peninsular Art (formerly Srivijaya period) Centred on Chaiya and Nakhon Si Thammarat, this style exhibits Indian influence in the 3rd to 5th centuries, Mon and local influence in the 5th to 13th centuries and Khmer influence in the 11th to 14th centuries

Lanna (13th to 15th centuries) Centred in Chiang Mai, Chiang Rai, Phayao, Lamphun and Lampang, Lanna is influenced by Shan/Burmese and Lao traditions

Sukhothai (13th to 15th centuries) Centred in Sukhothai, Kamphaeng Phet and Phitsanulok, this style is unique to Thailand

Lopburi (10th to 13th centuries) This Central Thai style is characterised by a mix of Khmer, Pala and local styles

Suphanburi-Sangkhlaburi (formerly U Thong; 13th to 15th centuries) This Central Thai style, combining Mon, Khmer and local styles, was a prototype for the later Ayuthaya style

Ayuthaya A (1350–1488) This Central Thai style was characterised by Khmer influences which were gradually replaced by revived Sukhothai influences

Ayuthaya B (1488–1630) This style had characteristic ornamentation distinctive of the Ayuthaya style, with, for example, crowns and jewels on Buddha images.

Ayuthaya C (1630–1767) This style is characterised by a baroque stage and then decline

Ratanakosin (19th century to the present) This is the Bangkok style, which consisted of simpler designs and European influences

A good way to acquaint yourself with these styles is to visit the National Museum in Bangkok, where works from each era are on display. Then, as you travel upcountry and view old monuments and sculpture, you'll know what you're seeing, as well as what to look for.

National Museums

Thailand's **Fine Arts Department** (☎ *0 2222 3519; Th Na Phra That, Bangkok*) operates an excellent network of national museums in areas of the country known for historic art and archaeology. The museums typically offer a small exhibit of artefacts from around the country as well as more-extensive displays featuring works of local provenance. At present, visitors have a choice of 35 museums. Most national museums are open from 9am to 4pm Wednesday to Sunday; a few are open daily these same hours. Those most worth visiting (in provincial capitals unless otherwise stated) include the following.

provincial capital	museum
Ayuthaya	Chan Kasem Palace
	Chao Sam Phraya National Museum
Bangkok	National Museum
	National Royal Barges Museum
	Wat Benchamabophit National Museum
Chiang Mai	Chiang Mai National Museum
Chiang Rai	Chiang Saen National Museum (in Chiang Saen)
Kanchanaburi	Ban Kao Neolithic Museum (in Ban Kao)
Khon Kaen	Khon Kaen National Museum
Lamphun	Lamphun National Museum
Lopburi	Lopburi National Museum
Nakhon Pathom	Phra Pathom Chedi National Museum
Nakhon Ratchasima	Mahawirawong National Museum
	Phimai National Museum (in Phimai)
Nakhon Si Thammarat	Nakhon Si Thammarat National Museum
Nan	Nan National Museum
Songkhla	Matchimawat National Museum
	Songkhla National Museum
Sukhothai	Ramkhamhaeng National Museum
Surin	Surin National Museum
Sawankhalok	Sawanworanayok Museum
Surat Thani	Chaiya National Museum (in Chaiya)
Ubon Ratchathani	Ubon National Museum
Udon Thani	Ban Chiang National Museum (in Ban Chiang)

Lacking the durability of other art forms, pre-20th century religious painting is limited to very few surviving examples. However the study and application of mural painting techniques have been kept very much alive, and modern mural projects are undertaken somewhere within the country, practically every day of the year. Influenced by international styles, a uniquely Thai movement in secular painting is also flourishing.

Traditional Painting Except for the prehistoric and historic cave or rock-wall murals that have been found throughout the country, there's not much formal painting that predates the 18th century in Thailand. There were Presumably a great number of temple murals in Ayuthaya that were destroyed by the Burmese invasion of 1767. The earliest surviving temple examples are found at Ayuthaya's Wat Ratburana (1424), Wat Chong Nonsii in Bangkok (1657–1707) and Phetchaburi's Wat Yai Suwannaram (late 17th century).

Nineteenth-century religious painting has fared better; Ratanakosin-style temple art is in fact more highly esteemed for painting than for sculpture or architecture. Typical temple murals feature rich colours and lively detail. Some of the finest are found in Wat Phra Kaew's Wihan Buddhaisawan Chapel in Bangkok and at Wat Suwannaram in Thonburi.

Contemporary Painting The beginnings of Thailand's modern art movement are usually attributed to Italian artist Corrado Feroci, who was first invited to Thailand by Rama VI in 1924. Feroci's design of Bangkok's Democracy Monument was inspired by Italy's fascist art movement of the 1930s. He also created the bronze statue of Rama I that stands at the entry to Memorial Bridge and several monuments around the city. Feroci founded the country's first fine arts institute in 1933, a school that eventually developed into Silpakorn University, Thailand's premier training ground for artists. In gratitude, the Thai government gave Feroci the Thai name Silpa Bhirasri.

One of the most important modern movements in Thai art has been an updating of Buddhist themes, begun in the 1970s by painters Pichai Nirand, Thawan Duchanee and Prateung Emjaroen. The movement has grown stronger since their early efforts to combine modern Western schemata and Thai motifs, culminating most recently in the very successful 'Thai Spiritual Ties' exhibition, which toured Thailand and received rave reviews in 2002. The most important painters working in this 'neo-Thai' medium include Surasit Saokong, Songdej Thipthong, Monchai Kaosamang and Tawatchai Somkong.

Temple murals have regained the interest of a privileged few who receive handsome sums for painting the interior walls of well-endowed ordination halls. Chakrabhand Pasayakrit's postmodern murals at Wat Tritosathep Mahawarawihan, only half completed, are being hailed as a masterwork of Thai Buddhist art of any era.

See the Art Galleries section in the Bangkok chapter for more on contemporary art galleries in Thailand.

Literature

The written word has a long history in Thailand, dating back to the 11th or 12th century when the first Thai script was fashioned from an older Mon alphabet. The first known work of literature to be written in Thai is thought to have been composed by Sukhothai's Phaya Lithai in 1345. This was *Traiphum Phra Ruang*, a treatise that described the three realms of existence according to a Hindu-Buddhist cosmology. According to contemporary scholars, this work and its symbolism was and continues to be of considerable influence on Thailand's artistic and cultural universe.

Classic Literature The 30,000-line Phra Aphaimani, composed by poet Sunthorn Phu in the late 18th century, is Thailand's most famous classical literary work. Like many of its epic predecessors around the world, it tells the story of an exiled prince who must complete an odyssey of love and war before returning to his kingdom in victory.

But of all classical Thai literature, *Ramakian* is the most pervasive and influential in Thai culture. The Indian source, *Ramayana*, came to Thailand with the Khmers 900 years ago, first appearing as stone reliefs on Prasat Hin Phimai and other Angkor temples in the northeast. Eventually, however, the Thais developed their own version of the epic, which was first written down during the reign of Rama I. This version contained 60,000 stanzas and was a quarter longer than the Sanskrit original.

Although the main theme remains the same, the Thais embroidered the *Ramayana* by providing much more biographical detail on arch-villain Ravana (Dasakantha, called Thotsakan, or '10-necked' in the *Ramakian*) and his wife Montho. Hanuman, the monkey-god, differs substantially in the Thai version, in his flirtatious nature (in the Hindu version he follows a strict vow of chastity). One of the classic *Ramakian* reliefs at Bangkok's Wat Pho depicts Hanuman clasping a maiden's bared breast as if it were an apple.

Also passed on from Indian tradition are the many *jataka,* or life stories of the Buddha (*chaa-dòk* in Thai). Of the 547 jataka tales in the *Pali Tripitaka* (Buddhist canon), each one chronicling a different past life, most appear in Thailand almost word-for-word as they were first written down in Sri Lanka.

A group of 50 'extra' stories, based on Thai folk tales of the time, were added by Pali scholars in Chiang Mai 300 to 400 years ago. The most popular *jataka* in Thailand is one of the Pali originals known as the *Mahajati* or *Mahavessantara (Maha Wetsandon),* the story of the Buddha's penultimate life. Interior murals in the *bòt* (ordination chapels) of Thai wát typically depict this *jataka* and nine others: Temiya, Mahajanaka, Suvannasama, Nemiraja, Mahosatha, Bhuridatta, Candakumara, Narada and Vidhura.

Poetry During the Ayuthaya period, Thailand developed a classical poetic tradition based on five types of verse – *chăn, kàap, khlong, klawn* and *râi*. Each of these forms uses a set of complex, strict rules to regulate metre, rhyming patterns and number of syllables. Although all of these poetic systems use the Thai language, *chăn* and *kàap* are derived from Sanskrit verse forms from India, while *khlong*, *klawn* and *rai* are native forms. The Indian forms have all but disappeared from 21st-century use.

During the political upheavals of the 1970s, several Thai newspaper editors, most notably Kukrit Pramoj, composed lightly disguised political commentary in *klawn* verse. Modern Thai poets seldom use the classical forms, preferring to compose in blank verse or with song-style rhyming.

Contemporary Literature For a look at rural life in Thailand, the books of Pira Sudham are unparalleled. Sudham was born into a poor family in northeastern Thailand and has written *Siamese Drama, Monsoon Country* and *People of Esarn*. These books are not translations – Sudham writes in English in order to reach a worldwide audience.

In the Mirror is an excellent collection of translated modern Thai short stories from the 1960s and '70s. *The Lioness in Bloom* is an eye-opening collection of 11 short stories written by or about Thai women and translated by Susan Fulop Kepner.

Thai wunderkind SP Somtow has written and published more titles in English than any other Thai writer. Born in Bangkok, educated at Eton and Cambridge, and now a commuter between two 'cities of angels' – Los Angeles and Bangkok – Somtow's prodigious output includes a string of well-reviewed science fiction/fantasy/horror stories, including *Moon Dance, Darker Angels* and *The Vampire's Beautiful Daughter*. The most accessible Somtow novel, and the one most evocative of Thai culture, is *Jasmine Nights* (1995). Following a 12-year-old Thai boy's friendship with an African-American boy near Bangkok in the 1960s, this semi-autobiographical work blends Thai, Greek and African myth, American Civil War lore and a dollop of magic realism into a seamless whole.

Cinema

In 1927, Bangkok Film kicked off the domestic film industry with the launch of the first Thai-directed silent movie, *Chok Sorng Chan*. In Thailand, silent films proved to be more popular than talkies right into the 1960s, and as late as 1969 Thai studios were still producing them from 16mm stock. Perhaps partially influenced by India's famed *masala* (curry) movies – which gained a strong following in post-WWII Bangkok – film companies blended romance, comedy, melodrama, and adventure.

The arrival of 35mm movies in Thailand around this same time brought a proliferation of modern cinema halls and a surge in movie-making. During this era Thai films attracted more cinema-goers than *năng faràng* (movies from Europe and America), and today many Thais consider the '60s to be a golden age of Thai cinema. Over half of the approximately 75 films produced annually during this period starred the much-admired onscreen couple Mit Chaibancha and Petchara Chaowaraj.

Despite the founding of a government committee to promote Thai cinema in 1970, Thai film production in the 1970s and early '80s was mostly limited to inexpensive action or romance stories. Among notable exceptions, 1983's *Child of the Northeast (Luk Isan)*, based on a Thai novel of the same name, followed the ups and downs of a farming family living in drought-ridden Isan. *Luk Isan* became one of the first popular films to offer urban Thais an understanding of the hardships endured by many northeasterners, and initiated a social drama subgenre that continues to this day.

Butterfly and Flower (Peesua lae Dokmai), again drawn from a popular Thai novel of the time, highlighted the hardships faced by a boy forced by economic circumstance to smuggle rice across the Thai-Malaysian border. Aside from once again exposing Thai audiences to regional poverty, the 1985 movie broke new ground by portraying a Buddhist-Muslim romance. *Butterfly and Flower* delighted the Thai public when it earned a Best Film award at the 1986 East-west Film Festival in Honolulu.

Despite this budding acclaim, the Thai movie industry almost died during the 1980s and '90s, swamped by Hollywood extravaganzas and the boom era's taste for anything imported. From a 1970s peak of a couple hundred releases per year, the Thai output shrank to an average of only 10 films a year by 1997.

While the Southeast Asian economic crisis of that year threatened to further bludgeon the ailing industry, a lack of more substantial budgets coupled with the need to compete with foreign films brought about a new emphasis on quality rather than quantity. The current era sees a new generation of seriously good Thai directors, several of whom studied film abroad during Thailand's 1980s and early '90s boom period.

Recent directorial efforts have been so encouraging that Thai and foreign critics

Surfing Thai Cinema's New Wave

If you're seeking out the best of this new Thai cinema, start with the following six-pack, all A-grade flicks by most international standards. Most are available on video or DVD with English subtitles.

Mon Rak Transistor, directed by Pen-Ek Ratanaruang, is arguably the best Thai movie made so far, in both the sense that it feels very 'Thai'and is seamlessly directed, acted and filmed. The story follows the odyssey of a young *lûuk thûng* singer who tries to crack the big time in Bangkok and in the end realises, predictably, that there's no place like home.

Sixty-Nine (in Thailand, *Reuang Talok 69*), another Pen-Ek outing, is also tightly directed and features excellent acting. A Bangkok woman laid off from work during the 1997 crash finds a box of money outside her apartment door, takes it, and is pursued by Tarantino-esque thugs who want it back. A Thai friend who saw the movie commented, 'This is the first time I've heard Thai actors speaking like real Bangkok people.' It earned awards at the Berlin and Brooklyn film festivals.

Satree Lex (also called *Iron Ladies* in English; directed by Yongyoot Thongkongtoon) is based on the true story of a Lampang volleyball team, made up almost entirely of transvestites and transsexuals, that won a national (men's) volleyball championship. At home, this film became Thai cinema's second-largest grossing effort to date, and was also the first Thai film ever to hit the art-house cinemas in Europe and America in general release.

Nang Nak (directed by Nonzee Nimibutr) is the exquisite retelling of the Mae Nak Phrakhanong legend, in which the spirit of a woman who died during childbirth haunts the home of her husband. Featuring beautiful sets, and oozing with culture, the film became the largest-grossing film in Thai history when it was released in 1998, even beating *Titanic*. The film took best director, best art director, and best sound at the 1999 Asia-Pacific Film Festival.

Fah Talai Jones (directed by Wisit Sasanatieng), an intriguing avant-garde parody of quasi-cowboy Thai melodramas of the 1950s and '60s, has incredible use of colour, with every frame hand-tinted. It received honourable mention at Cannes (where it was quickly dubbed a 'cult hit') and took an award at the Vancouver Film Festival. Miramax distributed the film in the USA, where it was called *Tears of the Black Tiger*.

Mekong Full Moon Party (in Thailand, *Kham Deuan 11*; directed by Jira Malikul), a favourite on the 2002 festival circuit, and a blockbuster in Thailand as well, buries itself deep in the Thai cultural psyche, using the legend of Nong Khai's famous *naga* lights (see the Nong Khai section in the North-eastern Thailand chapter for details) as a springboard for juxtaposing folk beliefs, modern science and Thai Buddhism in a rural Isan community. Much of the dialogue is spoken in the Isan dialects, necessitating both Thai and English subtitles in places.

A close tie for sixth place is *Bangkok Dangerous*, in which a deaf, mute hit man discovers love too late. Directed by the Oxide brothers, Danny and Pang, who hail from Hong Kong but have made Thailand their cinematic home, the film earned honours at the Toronto Film Festival in 2000.

Don't bother with *Jan Dara*, a distant also-ran with bad acting, beautiful sets, clumsy soft porn and a thin plot that tries to cop a feel from Vietnam's *Scent of Green Papaya*. Meanwhile, the lavishly produced, royally sponsored *Suriyothai*, a ponderous retelling of the 1548 Battle of Hanthawaddy, flopped overseas and received muted reviews at home. Legendary American producer-director Francis Ford Coppola has agreed to re-edit the film to create a shorter, more internationally palatable version for general release.

alike speak of a current Thai 'new wave'. Avoiding the soap operatics of the past, the current crop of directors favour gritty realism, artistic innovation, and a strengthened Thai identity.

SOCIETY & CONDUCT

Traditional Culture

When outsiders speak of 'Thai culture' they're referring to behavioural modes rooted in the history of Tai migration throughout Southeast Asia, with many commonalities shared by the Lao people of neighbouring Laos, the Shan of northeastern Myanmar and the numerous tribal Tais found in isolated pockets from Dien Bien Phu (Vietnam), all the way to Assam (India). These modes are most prevalent in Thailand, the largest of the Tai homelands.

The Thais themselves don't really have a word that corresponds to the term 'culture'. The nearest equivalent, *wáthánátham*, emphasises fine arts and ceremonies. So if you ask Thais to define their culture, they'll often talk about architecture, food, dance, festivals and the like. Religion – obviously a big influence on culture as defined in the Western sense – is considered more or less separate from *wáthánátham*.

Although Thailand is the most 'modernised' of the existing Tai societies, the cultural underpinnings are evident in virtually every facet of everyday life. Those aspects that might be deemed 'Westernised' (eg, the wearing of trousers instead of a *phâakhamáa* (sarong), the presence of automobiles, cinemas and 7-Eleven stores) show how Thailand has adopted and adapted elements from other cultures. Nevertheless there are certain aspects of Thai society that virtually everyone recognises as cultural markers.

Sànùk

The Thai word *sànùk* means 'fun'. In Thailand anything worth doing – even work – should have an element of *sànùk*, otherwise it automatically becomes drudgery. This doesn't mean Thais don't want to work or strive, just that they tend to approach tasks with a sense of playfulness. Nothing condemns an activity more than the description *mâi sànùk* – 'not fun'. While you're in Thailand sit down beside a rice field and watch workers planting, transplanting or harvesting rice. That it's back-breaking labour is obvious, but participants generally inject the activity with lots of *sànùk* – flirtation between the sexes, singing, trading insults and cracking jokes. The same goes in an office or a bank, or other white-collar work situations – at least when the office in question is predominantly Thai. The famous Thai smile comes partially out of this desire to make *sànùk*.

Saving Face

Thais believe strongly in the concept of saving face, ie, avoiding confrontation and endeavouring not to embarrass yourself or other people (except when it's *sànùk* to do so). The ideal face-saver doesn't bring up negative topics in conversation, and when they notice stress in another's life, they usually won't say anything unless that person complains or asks for help. Laughing at minor accidents – like when someone trips and falls down – may seem callous to outsiders but it's really just an attempt to save face on behalf of the person undergoing the mishap. This is another source of the Thai smile – it's the best possible face for almost any situation.

When encounters take a turn for the worse, try to refrain from getting angry – it won't help matters, since losing your temper means a loss of face for everyone present. Talking loudly is perceived as rude by cultured Thais, whatever the situation. See the Conduct section that follows for more on the rewards for 'Thai-ness' – the pushy foreigner often gets served last.

Status & Obligation

All relationships in traditional Thai society – and virtually all relationships in the modern Thai milieu as well – are governed by connections between *phûu yài* ('big person' or senior) and *phûu náwy* ('little person' or junior). *Phûu náwy* are supposed to defer to *phûu yài* following simple lines of social rank defined by age, wealth, status and personal and political power. Some examples of 'automatic' *phûu yài* status include adults (vs children), bosses (vs employees), elder classmates (vs younger classmates), elder siblings (vs younger siblings), teachers (vs pupils), members of the military (vs civilians), Thais (vs non-Thais) and so on.

While this tendency towards social ranking is to some degree shared by many societies around the world, the Thai twist lies in the set of mutual obligations linking *phûu yài* to *phûu náwy*. *Phûu náwy* are supposed to show a degree of obedience and respect (together these concepts are covered by the single Thai term *kreng jai*) towards *phûu yài*, but in return *phûu yài* are obligated to care for or 'sponsor' the *phûu náwy* they have frequent contact with. In such relationships *phûu náwy* can, for example, ask *phûu yài* for favours involving money or job access. *Phûu yài* reaffirm their rank by granting requests when possible; to refuse would be to risk a loss of face and status.

Age is a large determinant where other factors are absent or weak. In such cases the terms *phîi* (elder sibling) and *náwng* (younger sibling) apply more than *phûu yài* and *phûu náwy*, although the intertwined obligations remain the same. Even people unrelated by blood quickly establish who's *phîi* and who's *náwng*. This is why one of the first questions Thais ask new acquaintances is 'How old are you?'.

When dining, touring or entertaining, the *phûu yài* always picks up the tab; if a group is involved, the person with the most social rank pays the bill for everyone, even if it empties his or her wallet. For a *phûu náwy* to try and pay would risk loss of face.

Money plays a large role in defining *phûu yài* status in most situations. A person who turned out to be successful in his or her post-school career would never think of allowing an ex-classmate of lesser success (even if they were once on an equal social footing) to pay the bill. Likewise a young, successful executive will pay an older person's way in spite of the age difference.

The implication is that whatever wealth you come into is to be shared, at least partially, with those less fortunate. This doesn't apply to strangers – the average Thai isn't big on charity – but always comes into play with friends and relatives.

Conduct

Personal power (*baará-mii*, sometimes mistranslated as 'charisma') also has a bearing on one's social status, and can be gained by cleaving as close as possible to the ideal 'Thai' behaviour. 'Thai-ness' is first and foremost defined, as might be expected, by the ability to speak Thai.

Other hallmarks of the Thai ideal, which has been heavily influenced by Thai Buddhism, include discretion in behaviour towards the opposite sex, modest dress, a neat and clean appearance, and modes of expression and comportment that value the quiet, subtle and indirect rather than the loud, obvious and direct.

The degree to which Thais can conform to these ideals matches the degree of respect they receive from most of their associates. Although high rank – based on age or civil, military or clerical roles – will exempt certain individuals from chastisement by their social 'inferiors', it doesn't exempt them from the way they are perceived by other Thais. This goes for foreigners as well, even though most first-time visitors can hardly be expected to speak idiomatic Thai. But if you do learn some Thai, and you do make an effort to respect Thai social ideals, you'll come closer to enjoying some of the perks awarded for Thai-ness.

Social Graces

Thais are tolerant of most kinds of behaviour as long as it doesn't insult the two sacred cows of monarchy and religion. For information on how to behave when visiting hill tribes in Thailand, see the special section 'Hill Tribes'.

King & Country The monarchy is held in considerable respect in Thailand and visitors should be respectful too – avoid disparaging remarks about anyone in the royal family. One of Thailand's more outspoken intellectuals, Sulak Sivaraksa, was arrested in the early 1980s for lese-majesty (treason) because of a passing reference to the king's fondness for yachting (referring to His Majesty as 'the skipper'), and again in 1991 when he referred to the royal family as 'ordinary people'. The penalty for lese-majesty is seven years' imprisonment.

While it's OK to criticise the Thai government and even Thai culture openly, it's considered a grave insult to Thai nationhood as well as to the monarchy not to stand when you hear the national or royal anthems. Radio and TV stations in Thailand broadcast the national anthem daily at 8am and 6pm; in towns and villages (even in some Bangkok neighbourhoods) this can be heard over public loudspeakers in the streets. The Thais stop whatever they're doing to stand during the anthem (except in Bangkok where nobody can hear anything above the street noise) and visitors are expected to do likewise. The royal anthem is played just before films are shown in public cinemas; again, the audience always stands until it's over.

Temple Etiquette Correct behaviour in temples entails several considerations, the most important of which is to dress neatly and to take your shoes off when you enter any building that contains a Buddha image. Buddha images are sacred objects, so don't pose in front of them for pictures and definitely do not clamber upon them.

Shorts or sleeveless shirts are considered improper dress for both men and women when visiting temples. Thai citizens wearing either would be turned away by monastic authorities, but except for the most sacred temples in the country (eg, Wat Phra Kaew in Bangkok and Wat Phra That Doi Suthep near Chiang Mai), Thais are often too polite to refuse entry to improperly clad foreigners. Some wát will offer trousers or long sarongs for rent so that tourists dressed in shorts may enter the compound.

Monks are not supposed to touch or be touched by women. If a woman wants to hand something to a monk, the object should be placed within reach of the monk or on the monk's 'receiving cloth', not handed directly to him. When sitting in a religious edifice, keep your feet pointed away from any Buddha images. The usual way to do this is to sit in the 'mermaid' pose in which your legs are folded to the side, with the feet pointing backwards.

Some larger wát in Bangkok charge entry fees. In other temples, a small donation is appropriate. Usually donation boxes are near the entry of the *bòt* (central sanctuary) or next to the central Buddha image at the rear.

Social Gestures & Attitudes Traditionally Thais greet each other with a prayer-like palms-together gesture known as a *wâi*. If someone *wâi*-s you, you should *wâi* back (unless *wâi*-ed by a child or serviceperson). Most urban Thais are familiar with the international-style handshake and will offer the same to a foreigner, although a *wâi* is always appreciated.

Thais are often addressed by their first name with the honorific *khun* or other title preceding it. Other formal terms of address include *naai* (Mr) and *naang* (Miss or Mrs). Friends often use nicknames or kinship terms like *phîi* (elder sibling), *náwng* (younger sibling), *mâe* (mother) or *lung* (uncle), depending on the age differential.

A smile and a cheery 'sàwàt-dii khráp/khâ' (the all-purpose Thai greeting) goes a long way towards calming the initial trepidation that locals may feel upon seeing a foreigner, whether in the city or the countryside.

When handing things to other people you should use both hands or your right hand only, never the left hand (reserved for toilet ablutions).

Books and other written materials are given a special status over other secular objects. Hence you shouldn't slide books or documents across a table or counter-top, and never place them on the floor – use a chair if table space isn't available.

Feet & Head The feet are the lowest part of the body (spiritually as well as physically) so don't point your feet at people or point at things with your feet. Don't prop your feet on chairs or tables while sitting. Never touch any part of someone else's body with your foot.

In the same context, the head is regarded as the highest part of the body, so don't touch Thais on the head (or ruffle their hair) either. If you touch someone's head accidentally, offer an immediate apology or you'll be perceived as very rude.

Don't sit on pillows meant as headrests, as this represents a variant of the taboo against head-touching. We once watched a young woman on Ko Samet bring a bed pillow from her bungalow to sit on while watching TV; the Thai staff got very upset and she didn't understand why.

Never step over someone, even on a crowded 3rd-class train where people are sitting or lying on the floor. Instead squeeze around them or ask them to move.

In rural areas and at temple fairs food is often eaten while seated on the floor; stepping over the food is a sure way to embarrass and offend your Thai hosts.

Shoes These should not be worn inside Thai people's homes, nor in some guesthouses and shops. If you see a pile of shoes at or near the entrance, you should remove your shoes before entry. Several Thais have confided in us that they can't believe how oblivious some foreigners seem to be of this simple and obvious custom. To them wearing shoes indoors is disgusting and the behaviour of those who ignore the custom is nothing short of boorish.

Dress & Nudity Shorts (except knee-length walking shorts), sleeveless shirts, tank tops (singlets) and other beach-style attire are not considered appropriate dress for anything other than sporting events. Such dress is especially counterproductive if worn to government offices (eg, when applying for a visa extension). The attitude of 'This is how I dress at home and no-one is going to stop me' gains nothing but contempt or disrespect from the Thais.

Sandals or slip-on shoes are OK for almost any but the most formal occasions. Short-sleeved shirts and blouses with capped sleeves likewise are quite acceptable.

Thais would never dream of going abroad and wearing dirty clothes, so they are often shocked to see Westerners travelling around Thailand in clothes that apparently haven't been washed in weeks. If you keep up with your laundry, you'll receive much better treatment wherever you go.

Bathing nude at beaches in Thailand is illegal. Topless bathing for females is frowned upon in most places except on heavily-touristed islands such as Phuket, Samui and Samet. According to Thailand's National Parks Act, any woman who goes topless on a national-park beach (eg, Ko Chang, Ko Phi-Phi, Ko Samet) is breaking the law.

Visiting Homes Thais can be very hospitable and it's not unusual to be invited home for a meal or a sociable drink. Even if your visit is very brief, you will be offered something – a glass of water, a cup of tea, a piece of fruit, a shot of rice liquor, or whatever they have on hand. You are expected to partake of whatever is offered, whether you're thirsty or hungry or not; to refuse at least a taste is considered impolite.

Treatment of Animals

In less-developed rural regions, particularly in the north and northeast, and among the hill tribes of Thailand, hunting remains a norm for obtaining animal protein.

Harder to understand, at least for some of us, is the capture of monkeys, birds and other animals from the jungle to be kept as pets – usually tied by a rope or chain to a tree, or confined to cages. Several non-governmental organisations (NGOs), such as the Phuket Gibbon Rehabilitation Centre, are working to educate the public as to the cruelty of such practices, and have initiated wildlife rescue and rehabilitation projects.

Thailand is a signatory to the UN Convention on International Trade in Endangered Species (Cites). Educational levels have risen to the point that many international watchdog groups, such as the World Wide Fund for Nature and Wildlife Conservation Society, receive much local support. An illicit trade in endangered and threatened wildlife continues but appears to be much smaller than it was even a decade ago.

For further comment on this topic, see the Ecology & Environment section earlier in this chapter.

Prostitution

Thais generally blame 19th-century Chinese immigrants for bringing prostitution to Thailand, while foreigners blame Indochina War–era soldiers, but in reality Thailand has a long-standing concubinary tradition inherited from India. Until the mid-20th century most men of wealth counted among their retinue at least one *sǒhphenii* (from the Sanskrit term for a woman trained in the *Kamasutra* and other amorous arts), a word which has come to mean 'prostitute' but which was once better translated as 'courtesan'. Seventeenth-century Ayuthaya, for example, had an official government office in charge of operating a corps of 600 concubines. Siam had no laws forbidding polygamy – or even a word for this Judaeo-Christian concept – till 1934.

In addition, the traditional Thai *mia yài mia nói* (major wife, minor wife) system made it socially permissible for a man to keep several mistresses – all Thai kings up to Rama IV had *mia nói* (or *sànǒm*, as the royal version was called), as did virtually any Thai male who could afford them until more recently. Even today talk of *mia nói* hardly raises an eyebrow in Thailand as the tradition lives on among wealthy businessmen, *jâo phâw* (organised-crime 'godfathers') and politicians.

The first private brothel district in Bangkok was established by Chinese immigrants in the Sampeng Lane area in the mid-19th century and today prostitution is now found in nearly every town and city in the kingdom. Ethnic Chinese still control most of the trade, although the prostitutes themselves come from almost every ethnic background.

Prostitution wasn't declared illegal until the 1950s. The numbers of women working as commercial sex workers (CSWs) increased immediately after prohibition. In the 1960s and '70s the Vietnam War brought unprecedented numbers of foreign soldiers to Bangkok and Pattaya on 'rest and recreation' (R&R) tours, creating a new class of prostitutes who catered to foreigners rather than Thais.

Estimates of the number of Thai residents directly involved in offering sex services vary wildly, depending on the source. Chulalongkorn University's Population Institute puts forth a reasoned estimate of 200,000 to 220,000, a figure now widely considered the most realistic. Although often portrayed as Asia's sex capital, according to international human development reports Thailand actually ranks well behind Taiwan, the Philippines and India (not to mention several Western countries) in its per-capita number of sex workers.

Less than 3% of all Thai CSWs work in the sorts of bars or massage parlours portrayed in the Western media. The remainder work in 'cafés', barbershops and brothels only rarely patronised by non-Thai clients. Experts say Thai-to-foreigner transactions represent less than 5% of the total. 'Pimps' as known in the West don't exist in this market, which is controlled by the women themselves. The average Patpong type 'bar girl' earns 6000B to 7000B per month (more than the average Thai civil servant) directly from the bar she works in. Fees for sexual services, which take place elsewhere, are negotiated between her and the customer and can be anything from 1000B to 2500B per assignation, none of which goes to a controller.

Most CSWs are uneducated and come from village areas. Many women return to their villages – some with a nest egg for their families, others with nothing – where surprisingly they are often treated with a measure of respect. Various Thai volunteer groups offer counselling to Thailand's CSWs – helping them to leave the industry or to educate them to the dangers of sexually transmitted infections, particularly AIDS. Thanks to such efforts, the latest surveys indicate that condom use among sex workers in Thailand averages 94%.

Legal Aspects Officially prostitution remains illegal, but the government has been either powerless or unwilling to enforce most laws forbidding the trade ever since it was first outlawed. In 1993, largely due to international pressure, Prime Minister Chuan Leekpai ordered a crackdown on CSWs under 18 years of age, an act that has had quantifiable results but has by no means banished under-18s from the trade.

Under current Thai law, a jail term of four to 20 years and/or a fine of 200,000B to 400,000B can be imposed on anyone caught having sex with prostitutes under 15 years of age (the age of consent in Thailand). If the child is under 13, the sentence can amount to life imprisonment. Many Western countries have also instituted extra-territorial legislation whereby citizens can be charged for child-prostitution offences committed abroad.

The sexual exploitation of children is a significant problem. If you see or suspect anything involving minors, please don't just ignore it; if you have any information (ie, the offender's name and nationality), speak to their embassy. The Thai government is encouraging people to assist in the eradication of child prostitution by reporting child sexual abuses to the relevant authorities. In this instance, travellers visiting Thailand can contact **End Child Prostitution and Traffic International** (*ECPAT;* ☎ *0 2215 3388;* ⓔ *ecpatbkk@ksc15.th.com;* ⓦ *www.ecpat.org; 328 Th Phayathai, Bangkok 10400*), a global network of organisations that works to stop child prostitution, child pornography and the traffic of children for sexual purposes.

RELIGION

Buddhism

Approximately 95% of the Thai citizenry are Theravada Buddhists. Thai scholars sometimes refer to the religion as Lankavamsa

(Singhalese lineage) Buddhism because Thailand originally received this form of Buddhism from Sri Lanka during the Sukhothai period. Prior to the arrival of Singhalese monks in the 13th century, an Indian form of Theravada existed at the kingdom of Dvaravati (6th to 10th centuries), while Mahayana Buddhism of the Tantric variety was known in pockets of the northeast under Khmer control in the 10th and 11th centuries.

Since the Sukhothai period (13th to 15th centuries), Thailand has maintained an unbroken canonical tradition and 'pure' ordination lineage, the only country among the Theravadin countries to have done so. Ironically, when the ordination lineage in Sri Lanka broke down during the 18th century under Dutch persecution, it was Thailand that restored the *sangha* (Buddhist monastic community) there. To this day the major sect in Sri Lanka is called Siamopalivamsa (Siam-Upali lineage, Upali being the name of the Siamese monk who led the expedition to Sri Lanka), or simply Siam Nikaya (Siamese sect).

Basically, the Theravada school of Buddhism is an earlier and, according to its followers, less corrupted form of Buddhism than the Mahayana schools found in East Asia or in the Himalayan lands. The Theravada (literally, Teaching of the Elders) school is also called the 'Southern' school since it took a southern route from India, its place of origin, through Southeast Asia (Sri Lanka, Myanmar, Thailand, Laos and Cambodia), while the 'Northern' school travelled north into Nepal, Tibet, China, Korea, Mongolia, Vietnam and Japan.

Theravada doctrine stresses the three principal aspects of existence: *dukkha* (stress, unsatisfactoriness, disease), *anicca* (impermanence, transience of all things) and *anatta* (insubstantiality or nonessentiality of reality – no permanent 'soul'). The truth of *anicca* reveals that no experience, no state of mind, no physical object lasts. Trying to hold onto experience, states of mind and objects that are constantly changing creates *dukkha*. *Anatta* is the understanding that there is no part of the changing world that we can point to and say 'This is me' or 'This is God' or 'This is the soul'.

These three concepts, when 'discovered' by Siddhartha Gautama in the 6th century BC, were in direct contrast to the Hindu belief in an eternal, blissful self *(paramatman)*. Hence Buddhism was originally a 'heresy' against India's Brahmanic religion. Gautama, an Indian prince-turned-ascetic, subjected himself to many years of severe austerity before he realised that this was not the way to reach the end of suffering. He turned his attention to investigating the arising and passing away of the mind and body in the present moment. Seeing that even the most blissful and refined states of mind were subject to decay, he abandoned all desire for what he now saw as unreliable and unsatisfying. He then became known as Buddha, 'the enlightened' or 'the awakened'. Gautama Buddha spoke of four noble truths that had the power to liberate any human being who could realise them. These four noble truths are:

1. The truth of *dukkha*: 'All forms of existence are subject to *dukkha*.'
2. The truth of the cause of *dukkha*: '*Dukkha* is caused by *tanha* (grasping).'
3. The truth of the cessation of *dukkha*: 'Eliminate the cause of *dukkha* (ie, grasping) and *dukkha* will cease to arise.'
4. The truth of the path: 'The Eightfold Path is the way to eliminate grasping/extinguish *dukkha*.'

The Eightfold Path (Atthangika-Magga) leading to the end of *dukkha* consists of:

1. Right understanding
2. Right mindedness (right thought)
3. Right speech
4. Right bodily conduct
5. Right livelihood
6. Right effort
7. Right attentiveness
8. Right concentration

These eight limbs belong to three different 'pillars' of practice: wisdom or *pañña* (path factors 1 and 2), morality or *sila* (3 to 5) and concentration or *samadhi* (6 to 8). The path is also called the 'Middle Way', since it avoids the extremes of both austerity and sensuality. Some Buddhists believe it is to be taken in successive stages, while others say the pillars and/or limbs are interdependent. Another key point is that the word 'right' can also be translated as 'complete' or 'full'.

[Continued on page 55]

Music, Theatre & Dance

RICHARD I'ANSON

Traditional dancer, Vimanmek Teak Mansion, Bangkok

JOE CUMMINGS

Lisu people celebrate New Year

RICHARD NEBESKY

Mural, Wat Phra Kaew, Bangkok

JOE CUMMINGS

Padaung woman

RICHARD I'ANSON

Musicians, Erawan Shrine, Bangkok

MUSIC

Throughout Thailand you'll find a diversity of musical genres and styles, from the serene court music that accompanies classical dance-drama to the chest-thumping house music played at Bangkok's hip discos and dance venues.

Traditional Music

Classical central-Thai music is spicy, like Thai food, and features an incredible array of textures and subtleties, hair-raising tempos and pastoral melodies.

The classical orchestra is called the *pìi-phâat* and can include as few as five players or more than 20. Among the more common instruments is the *pìi*, a woodwind instrument that has a reed mouthpiece; it is heard prominently at Thai-boxing matches. The *pìi* is a relative of a similar Indian instrument, while the *phin*, a stringed instrument that's plucked like a guitar, is considered native to Thailand. A bowed instrument, similar to those played in China and Japan, is aptly called the *saw*. The *ránâat èk* is a bamboo-keyed percussion instrument resembling the xylophone, while the *khlùi* is a wooden flute.

One of the more amazing Thai instruments is the *kháwng wong yài*, which consists of tuned gongs arranged in a semicircle. There are also several different kinds of drums, some played with the hands, some with sticks. The most important Thai percussion instrument is the *tà-phon* (or *thon*), a double-headed hand-drum that sets the tempo for the ensemble. Prior to a performance, the players make offerings of incense and flowers to the *tà-phon*, which is considered to be the 'conductor' of the music's spiritual content.

The *pìi-phâat* ensemble was originally developed to accompany classical dance-drama and shadow theatre but can be heard in straightforward performance these days, at temple fairs as well as concerts. One reason classical Thai music may sound strange to visitors is that it does not use the tempered scale. The standard Thai scale spans the eight-note octave but it is divided in seven full-tone intervals, with no semitones. Thai scales were first transcribed by the Thai-German composer Peter Feit (Phra Chen Duriyanga), who also composed Thailand's national anthem in 1932.

In the north and northeast there are several popular reed instruments with multiple bamboo pipes, which function basically like a mouth-organ. Chief among these is the *khaen*, which originated in Laos; when played by an adept musician it sounds like a rhythmic, churning steam organ.

Recommended books include *The Traditional Music of Thailand* by David Morton and *Thai Music* by Phra Chen Duriyanga (Peter Feit).

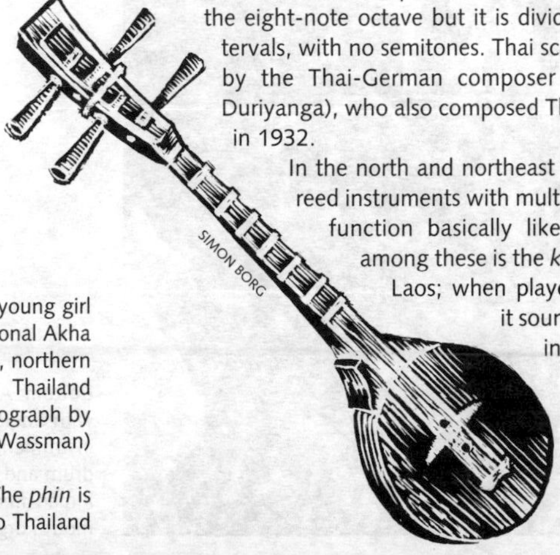

Title Page: A young girl in traditional Akha costume, northern Thailand (Photograph by Bill Wassman)

Bottom: The *phin* is native to Thailand

Thai Pop

Popular Thai music has borrowed much from Western music, particularly its instrumentation, but still retains a distinct flavour of its own. The best-selling of all modern musical genres in Thailand remains *lûuk thûng*, which translates as 'children of the fields'. As a social phenomena *lûuk thûng* dates back to the 1940s and is analogous to country-and-western music in the USA, ie, it's a genre that tends to appeal most to working-class Thais. Its subject matter almost always cleaves to tales of lost love, tragic early death and the dire circumstances of farmers who work day in, day out and at the end of the year still owe money to the bank.

Lûuk thûng song structures tend to be formulaic as well, though there are two basic styles: the original Suphanburi style, with lyrics in standard Thai; and an Ubon style that is sung in an Isan dialect. Thailand's most famous *lûuk thûng* singer, Pumpuang Duangjan, was given a royally sponsored cremation when she died in 1992 and a major shrine at Suphanburi's Wat Thapkradan receives a steady stream of worshippers.

Several popular magazines and TV programmes are dedicated to the promotion of the *lûuk thûng* industry, as well as a few Thai films. The Thai box-office hit *Mon Rak Transistor*, released in 2002, followed the tribulations of a young *lûuk thûng* singer trying to make it in Bangkok.

Lesser-known genres with regional followings include *phleng kham meuang*, guitar-based northern-Thai style folk-pop, and *măw lam*, based on the Lao-Isan *khaen*, a wind instrument devised of a double row of bamboo-like reeds fitted into a hardwood soundbox. For *phleng kham meuang*, look for CDs by Chiang Mai singer Soontaree Vechanont. Jintara Punlarp is the most famous artist performing *măw lam* at the moment.

JOE CUMMINGS

Bottom: A Lam band with traditional Isan instruments: a hand drum and the *khaen*, a reed-free bamboo mouth organ

Since the 1970s Thai music fans have shown a growing preference for a blend of Thai and international styles. A major musical revolution came along in the '70s when Caravan created a modern-Thai folk style known as *phleng phêua chii-wít* (songs for life). Songs of this nature have political and environmental topics rather than the usual love themes; during the authoritarian dictatorships of the '70s many of Caravan's songs were officially banned. Though the band dissolved in the early '80s, it re-forms for the occasional live concert.

Another durable example of this style, Carabao, took *phleng phêua chii-wít*, fused it with *lûuk thûng*, rock and heavy metal, and spawned a whole generation of imitators. *Phleng phêua chii-wít* remains a staple of the Thai music scene.

Thailand also has a less interesting but thriving pop industry centred on artists who have been chosen for their good lucks, mated with syrupy song arrangements. Currently singers who are *lûuk khreung* – half-Thai, half-Western – and sport English names are particularly popular, eg, Tata Young, Nicole Theriault and Bird Macintyre.

There's also a growing alternative movement, although as in the West, 'alternative' is for the most part simply a marketing category. Major alternative acts in Thailand at the moment include Modern Dog and Pru, along with punk metal ensemble Ebola and Thai rapper Joey Boy.

Jazz & World Music Influences

Yet another significant movement in modern Thai music is the fusion of international jazz with Thai classical and folk motifs. The leading exponent of this genre is the composer and instrumentalist Tewan Sapsanyakorn (also known as Tong Tewan), who plays soprano and alto sax, violin and *khlùi* with equal virtuosity. Tewan's compositions are often based on Thai melodies but the improvisations and rhythms are drawn from such diverse jazz sources such as Sonny Rollins and Jean-Luc Ponty.

Thai instrumentation within world-music settings is also a speciality of Todd Lavelle and Nupap Savantrachas, each of whom scored hits in Thailand during the late 1990s. Fong Nam, a Thai orchestra led by an American composer, Bruce Gaston, performs an inspiring blend of Western and Thai classical motifs.

THEATRE & DANCE

Traditional Thai theatre consists of six genres: *khŏn*, formal masked classical dance-drama, depicting scenes from *Ramakian* (the Thai version of India's *Ramayana*) and originally performed only for the royal court; *lákhawn*, a general term covering several types of dance-drama (usually for nonroyal occasions) as well as Western theatre; *lí-keh* (likay), a partly improvised, often bawdy folk play featuring dancing, comedy, melodrama and music; *mánohraa*, the southern-Thai equivalent of *lí-keh*, but based on a 2000-year-old Indian story; *năng*, or shadow-puppet theatre, found only in southern Thailand; *lákhawn lék* or *hùn lŭang*, royal-puppet theatre; and *lákhawn phûut*, contemporary spoken theatre.

Monkeys & Demons

Khõn In all *khŏn* performances, four types of characters are represented – male humans, female humans, monkeys and demons. Monkey and demon figures are always masked with the elaborate head coverings often seen in tourist brochures. Despite the masks and make-up, all of the actors are male. Traditional *khŏn* is a very expensive production – the retinue of Ravana alone (the principal villain of the *Ramakian*) consists of over 100 demons, each with its own distinctive mask.

Perhaps because it was once limited to royal venues and hence never gained a popular following, the *khŏn* or Ramakian dance-drama tradition nearly died out in Thailand. Bangkok's **National Theatre** *(☎ 0 2224 1342; Th Chao Fa)* was once the only place where *khŏn* was regularly performed for the public; the renovated **Chalermkrung Royal Theatre** *(☎ 0 2222 0434; cnr Th Charoen Krung & Th Triphet)* now hosts occasional *khŏn* performances enhanced by laser graphics and hi-tech audio.

Scenes performed in traditional *khŏn* (and *lákhawn* performances – see later) come from the 'epic journey' tale of the *Ramayana*, with parallels in the Greek Odyssey and the myth of Jason and the Argonauts. The central story revolves around Prince Rama's search for his beloved Princess Sita, who has been abducted by the evil 10-headed demon Ravana and taken to the island of Lanka. Rama is assisted in his search and in the final battle against Ravana by a host of mythical half-animal, half-human characters including the monkey-god Hanuman. See Literature in the Facts about Thailand chapter for more on the differences between the Indian *Ramayana* and the Thai *Ramakian*.

Drama Through Dance

Lákhawn The more formal *lákhawn nai* (inner *lákhawn*, ie, performed inside the palace) was originally performed for the lower nobility by all-female ensembles; today it's a dying art, even more so than royal *khŏn*. In addition to scenes from the *Ramakian*, *lákhawn nai* performances may include traditional Thai folk tales; whatever the story, text is always sung.

Lákhawn nâwk (outer *lákhawn*, ie, performed outside the palace) deals exclusively with folk tales and features a mix of sung and spoken text, sometimes with improvisation. Both male and female performers are permitted. Like *khŏn* and *lákhawn nai*, performances are becoming increasingly rare.

More common these days is the less refined *lákhawn chaatrii*, a fast-paced, costumed dance-drama usually performed at rural temple festivals or at shrines (commissioned by a shrine devotee whose wish was granted by the shrine deity). *Chaatrii* stories have been influenced by the older *mánohraa* theatre of southern Thailand (see later).

A variation on *chaatrii* that has evolved specifically for shrine worship, *lákhawn kâe bon*, involves an ensemble of around 20 members, including musicians. At an important shrine such as Bangkok's Lak Meuang, four different *kâe bon* troupes may alternate performances, each for a week at a time, as each performance lasts from 9am till 3pm and there is usually a long list of worshippers waiting to hire them.

Melodrama & Slapstick

Lí-keh In rural Thailand you might be lucky enough to come across the gaudy, raucous *lí-keh*. This theatrical art form is thought to have descended from drama-rituals that were brought to southern Thailand by Arab and Malay traders. The first native public performance in central Thailand came about when a group of Thai Muslims staged a *lí-keh* for Rama V in Bangkok during the funeral commemoration of Queen Sunantha. *Lí-keh* grew very popular under Rama VI, peaked in the early 20th century and has been fading slowly since the 1960s.

Most often performed at Buddhist festivals by troupes of travelling performers, *lí-keh* presents a colourful mixture of folk and classical music, outrageous costumes, melodrama, slapstick comedy, sexual innuendo and up-to-date commentary on Thai politics and society. Westerners – even those who speak fluent Thai – are often left behind by the highly idiomatic, culture-specific language and gestures. Most *lí-keh* performances begin with the *àwk khàek*, a prelude in which an actor dressed in Malay costume takes the stage to pay homage to the troupe's teacher and to narrate a brief summary of the play to the audience. For true *lí-keh* aficionados, the coming of a renowned troupe is a bigger occasion than the release of a new *Mission: Impossible* sequel at the local cinema.

Kidnappings & Rescues

Mánohraa Also known simply as *nora*, *mánohraa* is southern Thailand's equivalent of *lí-keh* and is the oldest surviving Thai dance-drama. The basic story line bears some similarities to the *Ramayana*. In this case the protagonist, Prince Suthon (Sudhana in Pali), sets off to rescue the kidnapped Mánohraa, a *kinnárii*, or woman-bird princess. As in *lí-keh*, performers add impromptu comic rhymed commentary – famed *nora* masters sometimes compete at local festivals to determine who's the best rapper.

Bottom: Shadow puppets are made from cow or buffalo hide

Shadows & Shapes

Năng Shadow-puppet theatre – in which two-dimensional figures are manipulated between a cloth screen and a light source at night-time performances – has been a Southeast Asian tradition for perhaps five centuries. Originally brought to the Malay Peninsula by Middle Eastern traders, the technique eventually spread to all parts of mainland and peninsular Southeast Asia; in Thailand it is mostly found in the south. As in Malaysia and Indonesia, shadow puppets in Thailand are carved from dried buffalo or cow hides (known as *năng* in Thai).

SIMON BORG

Two distinct shadow-play traditions survive in Thailand. The most common, *năng tàlung*, is named after Phattalung Province, where it developed around Malay models. Like their Malay-Indonesian counterparts, Thai shadow puppets represent an array of characters from classical and folk drama, principally the *Ramakian* and *Phra Aphaimani* in Thailand. A single puppetmaster manipulates the cutouts, which are bound to the ends of buffalo-horn handles. *Năng tàlung* is still occasionally seen at temple festivals in the south, mostly in Songkhla and Nakhon Si Thammarat Provinces. Performances are also held period-ically for tour groups or visiting dignitaries from Bangkok.

The second tradition, *năng yài* (literally, big hide), uses much larger cutouts, each bound to two wooden poles held by a puppetmaster; several masters may participate in a single performance. *Năng yài* is rarely performed nowadays because of the lack of trained *năng* masters and the expense of the shadow puppets. Most *năng yài* that are made today are sold to interior designers or tourists; a well-crafted hide puppet may cost as much as 5000B.

In 1994, in order to celebrate the king's 50th year on the throne, the Fine Arts Department initiated a project to restore the original 180-year-old set of *năng yài* figures used by the Thai royal court. The project required the refurbishing of 352 puppets along with the creation of 100 new ones to complete the royal set, known as Phra Nakhon Wai (City-Shaking) – a tribute to the impact they had on audiences nearly two centuries ago. In addition to the occasional performance in Nakhon Si Thammarat or Bangkok, *năng yài* can be seen at Wat Khanon in Ratchaburi Province, where *năng yài* master Khru Chalat is passing the art along to younger men.

Royal Marionettes

Lákhawn lék Also known as *hùn lŭang* (royal puppets), *lákhawn lék* (little theatre), like *khŏn*, was once reserved for court performances. Metre-high marionettes made of *khòi* paper and wire, wearing elaborate costumes modelled on those of the *khŏn*, are used to convey similar themes, music and dance movements.

Two puppetmasters are required to manipulate each *hùn lŭang* – including arms, legs, hands, even fingers and eyes – by means of wires attached to long poles. Stories are drawn from Thai folk tales, particularly *Phra Aphaimani*, and occasionally from the *Ramakian*.

Hùn lŭang is no longer performed, as the performance techniques and puppet-making skills have been lost. The *hùn lŭang* puppets themselves are highly collectable; the Bangkok National Museum has only one example in its collection. Surviving examples of a smaller, 30cm court version called *hùn lék* (little puppets) are occasionally used in live performances; only one puppeteer is required for each marionette in *hùn lék*.

Another Thai puppet theatre, *hùn kràbàwk* (cylinder puppets), is based on popular Hainanese puppet shows. It uses 30cm hand puppets that are carved from wood, and they are viewed from the waist up. These marionettes are still being crafted and used in performances.

Contemporary Theatre

Lákhawn phûut Known in the West as live contemporary theatre, *lákhawn phûut* (speaking theatre) is enjoyed by a very small, mainly elite audience in Bangkok only. Virtually the entire scene, such as it is, centres around two venues, Patravadi Theatre and Bangkok Playhouse.

Buddha's Words

The Buddha taught his disciples:

When you see, just see.
When you hear, just hear.
When you smell, just smell.
When you touch, just touch.
When you know, just know.

[Continued from page 48]

The ultimate end of Theravada Buddhism is *nibbana* (in Sanskrit, nirvana), which literally means the 'blowing out' or extinction of all grasping and thus of all suffering *(dukkha)*. Effectively, it is also an end to the cycle of rebirths (both moment-to-moment and life-to-life) that is existence.

In reality, most Thai Buddhists aim for rebirth in a 'better' existence rather than the supramundane goal of *nibbana*. By feeding monks, giving donations to temples and performing regular worship at the local wát they hope to improve their lot, acquiring enough merit (Pali *puñña;* Thai *bun*) to prevent or at least reduce their number of rebirths. Making merit *(tham bun)* is an important social and religious activity in Thailand. The concept of rebirth is almost universally accepted in Thailand, even by non-Buddhists, and the Buddhist theory of karma is well expressed in the Thai proverb 'tham dii, dâi dii; tham chûa, dâi chûa' ('good actions bring good results; bad actions bring bad results').

All the Tiratana (Triple Gems) revered by Thai Buddhists – the Buddha, the Dhamma (the teachings) and the Sangha (the Buddhist community) – are quite visible in Thailand. The Buddha, in his myriad sculptural forms, is found on a high shelf in the lowliest roadside restaurants as well as in the lounges of expensive Bangkok hotels. The Dhamma is chanted morning and evening in every wát and taught to every Thai citizen in primary school. The Sangha is seen everywhere in the presence of orange-robed monks, especially in the early morning hours when they perform their alms rounds, in what has almost become a travel-guide cliche in motion.

Thai Buddhism has no particular 'Sabbath' or day of the week when Thais are supposed to make temple visits. Nor is there anything corresponding to a liturgy or mass over which a priest presides. Instead, Thai Buddhists visit the wát whenever they feel like it, most often on *wan phrá* (literally, excellent days), which occur every 7th or 8th day depending on phases of the moon. On such visits typical activities include: the traditional offering of lotus buds, incense and candles at various altars and bone reliquaries around the wát compound; the offering of food to the temple *sangha* (monks, nuns and lay residents – monks always eat first); meditating (individually or ingroups); listening to monks chanting *suttas* or Buddhist discourse; and attending a *thêt* or Dhamma talk by the abbot or some other respected teacher. Visitors may also seek counsel from individual monks or nuns regarding new or ongoing life problems.

An illustration from the 17th-century *Du Royaume De Siam*, by Simon de la Loubère.

Spirit Houses

Many Thai houses or buildings have spirit houses *(sǎan phĭi wát)*, which are places for the spirits of the site *(phrá phuum)* to live in. Without this vital structure you're likely to have the spirits living in the house with you, which can cause all sorts of trouble. An average spirit house looks rather like a birdhouse-sized Thai temple mounted on a pedestal. A big hotel may have a shrine covering 100 sq metres or more.

How do you ensure that the spirits take up residence in your spirit house rather than in the main house with you? Mainly by making the spirit house a more auspicious place to live in than the main building, through daily offerings of food, flowers, candles and incense. The spirit house should also have a prominent location and should not be shaded by the main house. Thus its position has to be planned from the very beginning and the house installed with due ceremony. If your own house is improved or enlarged, the spirit house should be as well. The local *phâw khruu* or *mâe khruu* ('father teacher' or 'mother teacher') usually presides over the initial installation as well as later improvements.

The interior of a spirit house is usually decorated with ceramic or plastic figurines representing the property's guardian spirits. The most important figurine, the *jâo thîi* (place lord), embodies a *phrá phuum* who reigns over a specific part of the property. Larger or more elaborate spirit houses may also contain figurines that serve as family, retainers or servants for these resident spirits. Thai believers purchase these figurines – as well as the bowls, dishes and other accoutrements for making daily offerings – at rural temples or, in larger cities, at supermarkets and department stores.

An abandoned or damaged spirit house can't simply be tossed aside like a broken appliance, left to rot or dismantled for firewood. Instead, it should be deposited against the base of a sacred banyan tree or in the corner of a sympathetic wát where benevolent spirits will watch over it.

Monks Socially, every Thai male is expected to become a monk (in Pali, *bhikkhu;* in Thai, *phrá* or *phrá phíksù*) for a short period in his life, optimally between the time he finishes school and the time he starts a career or marries. Men or boys under 20 years of age may enter the *sangha* as novices (in Pali, *samanera;* in Thai, *nen*) – this is not unusual since a family earns great merit when one of its sons 'takes robe and bowl'. Traditionally, the length of time spent in the wát is three months, during the Buddhist lent *(phansǎa),* which begins in July and coincides with the rainy season. However, nowadays men may spend as little as a week to accrue merit as monks. There are about 32,000 monasteries in Thailand and 460,000 monks; many of these monks are ordained for a lifetime. Of these a large percentage become scholars and teachers, while some specialise in healing and/or folk magic.

The Sangha is divided into two sects: the Mahanikai (Great Society) and the Thammayut (from the Pali *dhammayutika* or '*dharma*-adhering'). The latter is a minority sect (the ratio being one Thammayut to 35 Mahanikai) begun by King Mongkut and patterned after an early Mon form of monastic discipline that he had practised as a monk. Members of both sects must adhere to 227 monastic vows or precepts as laid out in the Vinaya Pitaka – Buddhist scriptures dealing with monastic discipline. Overall discipline for Thammayut monks, however, is generally stricter. For example, they eat only once a day – before noon – and must eat only what is in their alms bowl, whereas most Mahanikais eat twice before noon and may accept side dishes. Thammayut monks are expected to attain proficiency in meditation as well as Buddhist scholarship or scripture study; the Mahanikai monks typically 'specialise' in one or the other. Other factors may supersede sectarian divisions when it comes to disciplinary disparities. Monks who live in the city, for example, usually emphasise study of the Buddhist scriptures, while those living in the forest tend to emphasise meditation.

Nuns At one time the Theravada Buddhist world had a separate Buddhist monastic lineage for females. The female monks were called *bhikkhuni* and observed more vows than monks did – 311 precepts as opposed to the 227 followed by monks. The *bhikkhuni sangha* travelled from its birthplace in India to Sri Lanka around two centuries after the

Buddha's lifetime, taken there by the daughter of King Ashoka, Sanghamitta Theri. However, the tradition died out there following the Hindu Chola invasion in the 13th century. Monks from Siam later travelled to Sri Lanka to restore the male *sangha*, but because there were no ordained *bhikkhuni* in Thailand at the time, Sri Lanka's *bhikkhuni sangha* was never restored.

In Thailand, the modern equivalent is the *mâe chii* (Thai for 'nun', literally, mother priest) – women who live the monastic life as *atthasila* (eight-precept) nuns. They are largely outnumbered by male monastics (by 46 to 1). Thai nuns shave their heads, wear white robes and take vows in an ordination procedure similar to that of the monks. Generally speaking, nunhood in Thailand isn't considered as 'prestigious' as monkhood. The average Thai Buddhist makes a great show of offering new robes and household items to the monks at the local wát but pays much less attention to the nuns. This is mainly due to the fact that nuns generally don't perform ceremonies on behalf of lay people, so there is often less incentive for self-interested lay people to make offerings to them. Furthermore, many Thais equate the number of precepts observed with the total merit achieved; hence nunhood is seen as less 'meritorious' than monkhood since *mâe chii* keep only eight precepts.

This difference in prestige represents social Buddhism, however, and is not how those with a serious interest in Buddhist practice regard the *mâe chii*. Nuns engage in the same fundamental eremitic activities (meditation and Dhamma study) as monks do, activities that are the core of monastic life. The reality is that wát that draw sizable contingents of *mâe chii* are highly respected, since women don't choose temples for reasons of clerical status. When more than a few nuns reside at one temple, it's usually a sign that the teachings there are particularly strong. The Institute of Thai Mâe Chii, headquartered at Wat Bowonniwet since 1962, publishes a quarterly journal (Thai only) devoted to the activities of Thai Buddhist nuns.

Further Information If you wish to find out more about Buddhism you can contact the **World Fellowship of Buddhists** (*☎ 0 2661 1284–90; Ⓦ www.wfb-hq.org; 616 Soi 24, Th Sukhumvit, Bangkok*). Senior *faràng* (Western) monks hold English-language Dhamma/meditation classes here on the first Sunday of each month from noon to 6pm; all are welcome. If you're only interested in the meditation part of the monthly programme, you can arrive as late as 1.30pm; the meditation begins at 2pm sharp.

A Buddhist bookshop across the street from the north entrance to Wat Bowonniwet in Bangkok sells a variety of English-language books on Buddhism. **Asia Books** (*☎ 0 2252 7277; Soi 15, 221 Th Sukhumvit, Bangkok*) also carries a good selection of Buddhist literature.

For more information on studying meditation in Thailand, see the Meditation Courses sections in both the Facts for the Visitor and Bangkok chapters.

Thailand's First Female Buddhist Novitiation

Over the last 20 years or so a small movement to restore the *bhikkhuni* (female monk) *sangha* in Thailand has arisen. During this time, several Thai women have been ordained in Taiwan or India, where the Mahayana tradition has maintained a *bhikkhuni* lineage, then returned to Thailand to practise as full *bhikkhuni*.

In 1998 the Theravada *bhikkhuni* lineage was restored in Sri Lanka and in 2002 Ven Bhikkhuni Saddha Sumana travelled to Thailand to ordain a 56-year-old Thai *mâe chii* as a 10-precept *samanera* (novice) at a nunnery called Watra Songtham Kalayani in Nakhon Pathom Province. Eventually Dhammarakhita Samaneri, as the new novice has been named by her preceptor, will seek full *bhikkhuni* ordination in the Sri Lankan tradition.

Many of the women at Songtham Kalayani are Mahayana-ordained nuns, a status the Bangkok clerical establishment doesn't officially recognise. The centre can't legally be called a *wát* (*watra* simply means 'practice' in Sanskrit) for this reason. Yet the Thai *sangha* has yet to issue a ruling as to whether they will recognize the Dhammarakhita's novitiation.

Recommended books about Buddhism include:

Buddhism Explained by Phra Khantipalo
Buddhism, Imperialism, and War by Trevor Ling
Good, Evil & Beyond: Kamma in the Buddha's Teaching by PA Payutto
Heartwood from the Bo Tree by Buddhadasa Bhikku
In This Very Life: The Liberation Teachings of the Buddha by Sayadaw U Pandita
Living Dharma by Jack Kornfield
The Long View: An Excursion into Buddhist Perspectives by Suratano Bhikku (T Magness)
The Mind and the Way by Ajahn Sumedho
Phra Farang: An English Monk in Thailand by Phra Peter Pannapadipo
A Still Forest Pool: the Teaching of Ajahn Chah at Wat Pah Pong compiled by Jack Kornfield & Paul Breiter
Thai Women in Buddhism by Chatsumarn Kabilsingh
Things as They Are by Ajahn Maha Boowa Nyanasampanno
What the Buddha Never Taught by Timothy Ward
What the Buddha Taught by Walpola Rahula
World Conqueror and World Renouncer by Stanley Tambiah

The **Barre Center for Buddhist Studies** *(Lockwood Rd, Barre, MA 01005, USA)* has good publications on Theravada Buddhism.

On the Internet, an excellent source is Access to Insight: Readings in Theravada Buddhism (www.accesstoinsight.org), from which you can freely download many publications (including many English translations from the Pali canon), all cross-indexed by subject, title, author, proper names and even Buddhist similes. Two other recommended Internet sites with lots of material on Theravada Buddhism as well as links to other sites include DharmaNet International (www.dharmanet.org) and Buddha Net (www.buddhanet.net).

Other Religions

A small percentage of Thais and most of the Malays in the south, (which amounts to about 4% of the total population), are followers of Islam. Half a percent of the population – primarily missionised hill tribes and Vietnamese immigrants – profess Christian beliefs, while the remaining half percent are Confucianists, Taoists, Mahayana Buddhists and Hindus. Mosques (in the south) and Chinese temples are both common enough that you will probably come across some while travelling throughout Thailand. Before entering any temple, sanctuary or mosque you must always remove your shoes, and in a mosque your head must be covered.

Facts for the Visitor

SUGGESTED ITINERARIES

With the exception of the upper southern peninsula, from Phetchaburi to Surat Thani, Thailand's asymmetric shape doesn't lend itself to simple linear north–south or east–west routes. Depending on your interests and available time you might pick from the following circuits or combine parts of several to create your own travel route.

These itineraries assume you want to see as much of the country as possible within a given interval. Another approach is to spend more time in a few places rather than less time in many. You might decide to spend a full two weeks or even more just exploring the north. If you're into Isan (northeastern) culture, a month spent in the towns and cities along the Mekong River could be very rewarding. And, of course, some people choose to hole up on a beach or island for their entire stay.

Most visitors begin their journey in Bangkok. Depending on how much time you have available, you might want to save Bangkok until after you've seen other parts of the country. That way it won't seem quite so overwhelming as it can be on first arriving. You'll also understand more about the Thai character after travelling around the country.

See the special section 'Thailand's Highlights' for a listing and brief discussion of some of the country's more outstanding attractions.

One Week

Temples & Gulf Beaches For a short Thailand sampler, start with a two-day taste of Bangkok's heavily gilded temples and urban intensity, then flee towards the former royal capital of Ayuthaya to take in the 400-year-old temple and palace ruins, right in the centre of the city. A day in Ayuthaya is enough for most people with limited time. Transit back through Bangkok and head southeast to Ko Samet, off the eastern coast of the Gulf of Thailand, for two or three nights on this all-season island before saying farewell to Thailand. Substitute Hat Jomtien, near Pattaya, for Samet if your tastes run towards international hotels rather than simple beach bungalows.

Floating Markets, River Kwai & Lopburi From Bangkok get an early morning start for one of the floating markets southwest of the city – Damnoen Saduak is the most well known but there are several others in the vicinity. Spend the night in Nakhon Pathom and take in the world's tallest Buddhist monument, Phra Pathom Chedi. Continue on to Kanchanaburi by bus or train to see the world-famous 'bridge over the River Kwai' and experience a fairly typical provincial Thai town. Return to Bangkok via Suphanburi and Lopburi, passing through the country's 'rice bowl' and stopping for a night in Lopburi to catch the Khmer and Thai temple ruins there.

Two Weeks

Northern Thailand After completing a one-week circuit, take an overnight train (or fly) to Chiang Mai. Shop till you flop at the Chiang Mai Night Bazaar, sample the excellent cuisine of northern Thailand, and decide whether to move northwest to Mae Hong Son or northeast to Nan. Both areas have mountains and national parks that can be trekked, and hill-tribe populations.

Northeastern Thailand Start with one of the central Thailand circuits, then take a train to Nakhon Ratchasima (Khorat) and visit the nearby Angkor-period ruins at Phimai. If you want to see more Khmer architectural splendour, make a short journey to the Phanom Rung Historical Park in Buriram Province.

Finish with a journey along the Mekong River – from Chiang Khan to Si Chiangmai if you prefer small towns and villages, or from Nakhon Phanom to Ubon Ratchathani if you like cities.

Bangkok to the Malaysian Border After you've had your fill of Bangkok (three or four days does the trick for most people who have two weeks to spend) start your roll down the Malay Peninsula with a two-night, one-day stopover in Phetchaburi, a city of venerable late-Ayuthaya-period temples and a hill-top royal palace.

After Phetchaburi, take your pick of the beaches at Cha-am, Hua Hin or in the vicinity of Prachuap Khiri Khan – places where middle-class Thais go for vacation. You can visit Khao Sam Roi Yot National Park, which is good for coastal and hillside hiking.

For some serious beach time, zero in on one or more of the three major islands off the coast of Chumphon and Surat Thani Provinces – Ko Tao, Ko Pha-Ngan and Ko Samui – depending on your tastes (see Islands & Beaches in the special section 'Thailand's Highlights').

If you're ready for a little culture, sail back to the mainland and visit Chaiya (featuring Srivijaya-era ruins and a world-famous meditation monastery) or Songkhla (featuring Sino-Portuguese architecture and a national museum).

Follow with a night or two in Hat Yai to sample some of Thailand's best Chinese food outside Bangkok and to shop for southern-Thai or Malay textiles. For your entry into Malaysia, take the east–coast route via Narathiwat for the best natural scenery, or the west coast if you're in a rush to reach Penang or Kuala Lumpur.

One Month

Temples, Trekking & Beaches In a month you can sample many of Thailand's major highlights. Spend a few days in Bangkok (or leave it until last) then take a slow ride north with two-night stopovers in Lopburi, Phitsanulok and Sukhothai to take in some of Thailand's most historic temple architecture, ancient as well as modern. From Sukhothai head southwest to Mae Sot, nestled in a zone of Karen and Burmese influence, and explore the less-than-beaten path – with waterfalls, trekking, rafting and working elephants – stretching from Um Phang to Mae Sariang. Continue north from Mae Sariang along the Mae Hong Son loop to Tha Ton on the Mae Kok (Kok River), and either boat down the river to Chiang Rai or take a ride on a *săwng-thăew* (pick-up truck) through the mountains on the Myanmar border to the Yunnanese settlement of Mae Salong.

With roughly a week left in your itinerary, choose an island or beach along the upper Gulf of Thailand coast (Pattaya, Ko Samet, Ko Chang or Hua Hin) if you want to get there quickly via Bangkok; or pick from either the Andaman Coast (Phuket, Khao Lak, Krabi, Trang) or the lower Gulf coast (Ko Samui, Ko Pha-Ngan, Ko Tao) if you don't mind a longer trip by air, road or rail. If you like your beaches untrammelled it might be worth the extra effort to visit one of the national marine parks off the Andaman Coast – Ko Tarutao, Ko Similan or Ko Surin.

If you have time while in the south, make a side trip to Khao Sok National Park, one of Thailand's most important refuges for tigers and rainforest.

North by Northeast If beaches don't matter much to you, go for a major intake of culture and nature by starting with the Lopburi–Mae Salong route described earlier. From Mae Salong continue eastward to Nan and Phrae, two of the north's less-travelled provinces, then segue into Loei Province for the Mekong River loop from Chiang Khan to Ubon.

If there's time at the end of the latter, head into the interior to visit Prasat Hin Phimai and Phanom Rung Historical Parks. The more adventurous can substitute a whirl along the Cambodian border from Ubon to Aranya Prathet via Surin and Si Saket – provinces that are home to a number of smaller and lesser-known Khmer temple sites. If you find that temple trekking has paled by this point, go hiking in Khao Yai National Park, one of Thailand's largest and oldest protected areas.

Two Months

In two months you can combine two or three itineraries to link the best sights of southern, northern, northeastern and central Thailand.

PLANNING

When to Go

The best overall time for visiting most of Thailand falls between November and March – during these months it rains least and is not so hot. Remember that temperatures are more even in the south, so southern Thailand is good for respite when the rest of Thailand is miserably hot (April to June). The north is best from mid-November to early December or in February when it begins warming up again. If you're spending time in Bangkok, be prepared to roast in April and do some flood-water wading in October – probably the two worst months, weather-wise, for visiting the capital.

The peak seasons are August, November, December, February and March, with secondary peak months in January and July. If your main objective is to avoid crowds and to take advantage of discounted rooms and low-season rates, you should consider travelling during the least crowded months (April, May, June, September and October), On the other hand it's not difficult to leave the crowds behind, even during peak months, if you simply avoid some of the most popular destinations (eg, Chiang Mai and all islands and beaches).

Maps

Lonely Planet publishes the 1:1,000,000-scale *Thailand, Vietnam, Laos & Cambodia Road Atlas*. This atlas features over 80 pages of detailed maps, including close-ups of popular destinations and city maps. It has topographic shading, handy trip maps, distance charts and a complete geographic index. The atlas is readily available at many Bangkok bookshops as well as overseas.

The Roads Association of Thailand publishes a good large-format, 48-page, bilingual road atlas called *Thailand Highway Map*. The atlas, which is updated every year, has cut the Highway Department maps to a more manageable size and includes dozens of city maps. It also gives driving distances and lots of travel and sightseeing information. Beware of inferior knock-offs. A big advantage of the *Thailand Highway Map* is that the town and city names are printed in Thai as well as Roman script.

The Lonely Planet atlas or *Thailand Highway Map* is more than adequate for most people. Do-it-yourself trekkers, or anyone with a keen interest in geography, may find sheet maps issued by the Thai military to be helpful. These maps are available in several scales, complete with elevations, contour lines, place names (in Thai and Roman script) and roadways. Most trekkers find the 1:250,000-scale maps are perfectly adequate: there are 52 separate sheets costing 60B each. Four (Mae Hong Son, Mae Chan, Tavoy and Salavan) of the 52 aren't available to the public because of ongoing border disputes with Myanmar and Laos – the Thai army doesn't want to be accused of propagating incorrect borders. These maps can be purchased at the **Thai Army Map Department** *(Krom Phaen Thi Thahan; ☎ 0 2222 8844; Th Kanlayana Maitri, Bangkok)*, sometimes referred to as the Royal Survey Department, opposite the Interior Ministry on the western side of Th Ratchini in Ko Ratanakosin, very near Wat Ratchabophit.

City Maps Lonely Planet's *Bangkok* map is printed on durable laminated paper and is a handy reference for getting your bearings in the big city. See the individual city sections for information on other city maps.

What to Bring

Bring as little as possible – one medium-sized shoulder bag, duffel bag or backpack should do. Pack lightweight clothes, unless you're going to be in the north in the cool season, in which case you should have a pullover. Natural fibres can be cool and comfortable, except when they get soaked with sweat or rain, in which case they quickly become heavy and block air flow. Some of the lightweight synthetics breathe better than natural fibres, draw sweat away rather than holding it in, and may be more suitable for the beach or mid-rainy season.

Most Thai women don't use tampons, and thus they can be difficult to find in Thailand. If you're coming for a relatively short interval, it's best to bring your own. Sanitary napkins are widely available from minimarts and supermarkets throughout Thailand.

Pick up a sarong – either a *phâakhamáa* (short Thai-style men's sarong) or a *phâasîn* (a longer sarong for women) – to wear in your room, on the beach or when bathing outdoors. These can be bought at any local market (different patterns and colours can be found in different parts of the country) and the vendors will show you how to tie them. It's a very handy item: it can be used to sleep on or as a light bedspread (many Thai guesthouses do not supply top sheets or bedspreads); as a makeshift 'shopping bag'; as a turban or scarf to keep off the sun and absorb perspiration; as a towel; as a small hammock and as a device with which to climb coconut palms – to name just a few functions.

An unsewn sarong is not proper street attire. Women can have sarongs sewn into a 'tube' suitable for everyday wear as a skirt. Hooks and eyes may be added to the waistline for ease of keeping the sarong on, or you can learn to tie them in the traditional way.

Also consider taking include the following:

- slip-on shoes or sandals – besides being cooler than lace-ups, they are easily removed before entering a Thai home or temple
- small torch (flashlight)
- compass
- cigarette lighter for lighting candles and mosquito coils
- foam earplugs for noisy nights
- universal sink plug, a few plastic clothes pegs and 3m of plastic cord (or plastic hangers) for hanging wet clothes out to dry
- snorkel and mask if you plan to dive (see Diving & Snorkelling in the Activities section later in this chapter)

TOURIST OFFICES

The **Tourism Authority of Thailand** *(TAT; ☎ 0 2250 5500, fax 0 2250 5511; e center@tat.or.th; w www.tat.or.th; 1600 Th Phetburi Tat Mai, Makkasan, Rachathewi, Bangkok 10310)*, a government-operated tourist information and promotion service, was founded in 1960 and is attached to the prime minister's office. It maintains 22 offices within the country and 16 overseas.

The quality of the printed information that TAT produces is second to none among Southeast Asian countries, with pamphlets on sightseeing, accommodation and transportation. Its staff is huge and the main office in Bangkok occupies its own building.

Tourist Offices in Thailand

You'll find TAT information counters in the international and domestic terminals of Bangkok's Don Muang Airport, at the Chatuchak Weekend Market and on Th Khao San in Bangkok.

See the relevant destination chapters for the contact details of TAT offices around Thailand.

Tourist Offices Abroad

TAT's international offices include the following.

Australia (☎ 02-9247 7549, fax 9251 2465, e info@thailand.net.au) Level 2, 75 Pitt Street, Sydney, NSW 2000
France (☎ 01-53 53 47 00, fax 45 63 78 88, e tatpar@wanadoo.fr) 90 Avenue des Champs Elysées, 75008 Paris
Germany (☎ 069-138 1390, e info@thailandtourismus.de) Bethmannstrasse 58, D-60311 Frankfurt/Main
UK (☎ 020-7925 2511, fax 020-7925 2512, e info@tat-uk.demon.co.uk) 3rd Floor, Brook House, 98-99 Jermyn St, London SW1Y 6EE
USA (☎ 323-461 9814, fax 461 9834, e tatla@ix.netcom.com) 611 North Larchmont Blvd, 1st floor, Los Angeles, CA 90004
(☎ 1 800-THAILAND, 212-219 4655, fax 219 4697, e tatny@aol.com) 304 Park Avenue South, 8th Floor, New York, NY 10010 (temporary office)

You'll also find overseas TAT offices in the following cities: Kuala Lumpur, Singapore, Hong Kong, Taipei, Seoul, Tokyo, Osaka, Fukuoka, Stockholm and Rome. Check TAT's website for contact information.

VISAS & DOCUMENTS

Passports

Entry into Thailand requires a passport valid for at least six months from the time of entry. If your passport will expire while you're in Thailand, obtain a new one before arrival.

Visas

Whichever type of visa you have, be sure to check your passport immediately after stamping. Overworked officials sometimes stamp it for 30 days, even though you hold a longer visa; if you point out the error before you've left the immigration area at your port of entry, officials will make the necessary corrections. If you don't notice this until you've left the port of entry, go to Bangkok and plead your case at the **Immigration Bureau** *(☎ 0 2287 3101; Soi Suan Phlu, Th Sathon Tai)*.

Once a visa is issued, it must be used (ie, you must enter Thailand) within 90 days. The Royal Thai Ministry of Foreign Affairs enumerates its visa policies at its website w www.mfa.go.th/web/12.php.

Tourist Visa Exemptions The Thai government allows people of 57 different nationalities, including most European countries, Australia, New Zealand and the USA, to enter the country for tourism purposes without a visa for 30 days at no charge.

Citizens of Brazil, Korea and Peru may enter Thailand without a visa, in accordance with inter-governmental agreements, for a maximum stay of 90 days for purposes of tourism or temporary business only.

Tourist Visas If you plan to stay in Thailand more than a month, you should apply for the 60-day Tourist Visa. This visa costs US$15. One passport photo must accompany all applications. You can buy more than one Tourist Visa at a time, each for US$15, and thus extend your stay in multiples of two months for a maximum of eight months in one passport. This works out less expensive, and keeps you in the country longer, than buying extensions.

Non-Immigrant Visas Good for 90 days, the Non-Immigrant Visa must be applied for in your home country, costs US$20 and is not difficult to obtain if you can offer a good reason for your visit. Business, study, retirement and extended family visits are among the purposes considered valid. If you want to stay longer than six months, this is the one to get.

The Non-Immigrant Business Visa (usually abbreviated by Thai immigration officials as 'non-B') allows unlimited entries to Thailand for one year. The only hitch is that you must leave the country at least once every 90 days to keep the visa valid.

Visa Extensions & Renewals Sixty-day Tourist Visas may be extended by up to 30 days at the discretion of Thai immigration authorities. Apply at the Bangkok **Immigration Bureau** *(☎ 0 2287 3101; Soi Suan Phlu, Th Sathon Tai)* or at any immigration office in the country – every province that borders a neighbouring country has at least one. The usual fee for extending a Tourist Visa is 500B. Bring along one photo and one copy each of the photo and visa pages of your passport. Normally only one 30-day extension is granted.

The 30-day, no-visa stay can be extended for seven to 10 days (depending on the immigration office) for 500B. You can also leave the country and return immediately to obtain another 30-day stay. There is no limit on the number of times you can do this, nor is there a minimum interval you must spend outside the country.

Extension of the 15-day, on-arrival Transit Visa is only allowed if you hold a passport from a country that has no Thai embassy.

If you overstay your visa, the usual penalty is a fine of 200B for each extra day, with a 20,000B limit; fines can be paid at any official exit point or in advance at the **Investigation Unit** *(☎ 0 2287 3101–10; Immigration Bureau, Room 416, 4th floor, Old Bldg, Soi Suan Phlu, Th Sathon Tai, Bangkok)*.

Extending a Non-Immigrant Visa very much depends on how the officials feel about you – if they like you then they will extend it. Other than the 500B extension fee, money doesn't usually come into it; a neat appearance and polite behaviour count for more. Typically, you must collect a number of signatures and go through various interviews, which may result in a 'provisional' extension. You may then have to report to a local immigration office every 10 to 14 days for the next three months until the actual extension comes through.

Retirees 50 years of age or older may extend the 90-day Non-Immigrant Visa by one year at a time. To do this you will need to bring the following documents to the immigration bureau: a copy of your passport, one photo, a 500B extension fee and proof of your financial status or pension. The requirement for the latter is that foreigners must show proof of an income of not less than 800,000B per year (or 65,000B per month for extensions of less than a year).

Tax Clearance

Anyone who receives income while they are in Thailand must obtain a tax clearance certificate from the **Revenue Department** *(☎ 0 2281 5777, 0 2282 9899; Th Chakkapong, Bangkok)* before being permitted to leave the country. The Bangkok office is not far from the Democracy Monument and there are offices in every provincial capital.

Onward Tickets

Thai immigration does not seem very concerned that you arrive with proof of onward travel. Legally speaking, all holders of Tourist Visas or the no-visa 30-day stay permit are *supposed* to carry such proof. In all our years of frequent travel in and out of the kingdom, our onward travel documents haven't been checked a single time.

Travel Insurance

A travel insurance policy to cover theft, loss and medical problems is a good idea. Some policies offer lower and higher medical-expense options. There is a wide variety of policies available, so check the small print.

Some policies specifically exclude 'dangerous activities', which can include scuba diving, motorcycling or even trekking. A locally acquired motorcycle licence is not valid under some policies.

You may prefer a policy which pays doctors or hospitals directly rather than you having to pay on the spot and claim later. If you have to claim later make sure you keep all documentation. Some policies ask you to call back (reverse charges) to a centre in your home country where an immediate assessment of your problem is made.

Check that the policy covers ambulances or an emergency flight home.

Driving Licence & Permits

An International Driving Permit is necessary for any visitor who intends to drive a motorised vehicle while in Thailand. These are usually available from motoring organisations in your home country. If you'd like to obtain a Thai driving licence, see the Driving Permits section of the Getting Around chapter for details.

Hostel Cards

Hostelling International (*HI;* 🅦 *www.tyha.org*) issues a membership card that allows you to stay at Thailand's member hostels. Without such a card or the purchase of a temporary membership (from any member hostel worldwide) you won't be admitted. See the Accommodation section later in this chapter for more information.

Student Cards

International Student Identity Cards (ISIC) can be used as identification to qualify for the student discount at some museums in Thailand (although these are rare). It's probably not worth getting just for a visit to Thailand, but if you already have one, or plan to use one elsewhere in Asia, then bring it along.

Copies

All important documents (passport data page and visa page, credit cards, travel insurance policy, air/bus/train tickets, driving licence etc) should be photocopied before you leave home. Leave a copy with someone at home and keep another with you, separate from the originals.

You can also store details of your vital travel documents in Lonely Planet's free online Travel Vault. See International Phonecards in Post & Communications later in this chapter.

EMBASSIES & CONSULATES

Thai Embassies & Consulates

To apply for a visa, contact the Royal Thai embassy (or consulate) in any of the following countries. In many cases if you apply in person, you may receive a Tourist or Non-Immigrant Visa on the day of application; by mail it generally takes anywhere from two to six weeks.

Australia (☎ 02-6273 1149, 6273 2937) 111 Empire Circuit, Yarralumla, Canberra, ACT 2600
Consulate in Adelaide: (☎ 08-8232 7474) Level 1, 72 Flinders St, Adelaide 5000
Consulate in Brisbane: (☎ 07-3846 7771) 87 Annerley Road, South Brisbane, Qld 4102
Consulate in Melbourne: (☎ 03-9533 9100) Suite 301, 566 St Kilda Rd, Melbourne Vic 3004
Consulate in Perth: (☎ 09-9221 3237) 4th floor, Durack Centre, 263 Adelaide Tce, Perth WA 6000
Consulate in Sydney: (☎ 02-9241 2542/3) Level I, 131 Macquarie St, Sydney NSW 2000

Cambodia (☎ 023-363 869–71) 196 MV Preah Nordom Blvd, Sangkat Tonle Bassa, Khan Chamkar Mon, Phnom Penh

Canada (☎ 613-722 4444) 180 Island Park Drive, Ottawa, ON K1Y OA2
Consulate: (☎ 604-687 1143) 1040 Burrard St, Vancouver, BC V6Z 2R9

France (☎ 01-56 26 50 50) 8 Rue Greuze, 75116 Paris

Germany (☎ 030-794810) Lepsuisstrasse 64-66, 12163 Berlin
Consulate in Frankfurt: (☎ 069-698680) 109 Kennedyalle, 60596 Frankfurt
Consulate in Munich: (☎ 089-1689788) Prinzenstrasse 13, 80639 Munchen

Laos (☎ 21-214581–3) Th Phonkheng, Vientiane Poste 128
Consulate: (☎ 41-212445) No 26, Ban Xayamongkhon, Th Kouvoravong, Savannakhet

Malaysia (☎ 03-2148 8222) 206 Jalan Ampang, Kuala Lumpur
Consulate in Kelantan: (☎ 09-744 5266) 4426 Jalan Pengkalan Chepa, 15400 Kota Bharu, Kelantan
Consulate in Penang: (☎ 04-226 8029) No 1 Jalan Tunku Abdul Rahman, 10350 Penang

Myanmar (Burma; ☎ 01-512017, 512018) 437 Pyay Road, 8 Ward, Kamayut township, Yangon

UK & Northern Ireland (☎ 020-7589 0173, 7589 2944) 29-30 Queen's Gate, London SW7 5JB
USA (☎ 202-944 3608) 1024 Wisconsin Ave NW, Washington, DC 20007
Consulate in Illinois: (☎ 312-664 3129) 700 N Rush St, Chicago, Illinois 60611
Consulate in Los Angeles: (☎ 323-962 9574-77) 611 N Larchmont Blvd, 2nd floor, Los Angeles, CA 90004
Consulate in New York: (☎ 212-754 1770, 754 1896) 351 East 52nd St, New York, NY 10022
Vietnam (☎ 08-932 7637) 77 Tran Quoc Thao St, District 3, Ho Chi Minh City
Consulate: (☎ 04-823 5092–94) 63–65 Hoang Dieu St, Hanoi

Embassies & Consulates in Thailand

Bangkok is a good place to collect visas for onward travel, and most countries have diplomatic representation there. The visa sections of most embassies and consulates are open from around 8.30am to 11.30am weekdays only (call first to be sure, as some are open only two or three days a week).

Countries with diplomatic representation in Bangkok include the following.

Australia (Thanon Silom map; ☎ 0 2287 2680) 37 Th Sathon Tai
Cambodia (☎ 0 2254 6630) 185 Th Ratchadamri, Lumphini
Canada (Thanon Silom map; ☎ 0 2636 0540) 15th floor, Abdulrahim Bldg, 990 Th Phra Ram IV
China (Greater Bangkok map; ☎ 0 2245 7043) 57 Th Ratchadaphisek
France (Thanon Silom map; ☎ 0 2266 8250–6) 35 Soi 36, Th Charoen Krung.
Consular Section: (Thanon Silom map; ☎ 0 2287 2585–7) 29 Th Sathon Tai
Germany (Thanon Silom map; ☎ 0 2287 9000) 9 Th Sathon Tai
India (☎ 0 2258 0300–6) 46 Soi Prasanmit (Soi 23), Th Sukhumvit
Indonesia (Siam Square & Pratunam map; ☎ 0 2252 3135) 600–602 Th Phetburi
Laos (Greater Bangkok map; ☎ 0 2539 6667) 520/1–3 Th Pracha Uthit, end of Soi 39, Th Ramkhamhaeng
Nepal (Greater Bangkok map; ☎ 0 2391 7240) 189 Soi Phuengsuk (Soi 17), Th Sukhumvit
New Zealand (Siam Square & Pratunam map; ☎ 0 2254 2530; 93 Th Withayu
Malaysia (Thanon Silom map; ☎ 0 2679 2190–9) 33–35 Th Sathon Tai
Myanmar (Thanon Silom map; Burma; ☎ 0 2233 2237, 0 2234 4698) 132 Th Sathon Neua
Sri Lanka (☎ 0 2261 1934–5) 13th fl, Ocean Tower II Bldg, 75/6 Soi 19, Th Sukhumvit
UK & Northern Ireland (Siam Square & Pratunam map; ☎ 0 2253 0191–9) 1031 Th Withayu
USA (Central Bangkok map; ☎ 0 2205 4000) 120-22 Th Withayu
Vietnam (Siam Square & Pratunam map; ☎ 0 2251 5836–8) 83/1 Th Withayu

CUSTOMS

Like most countries, Thailand prohibits the importation of illegal drugs, firearms and ammunition (unless registered in advance with the Police Department), and pornographic media. A reasonable amount of clothing for personal use, toiletries and professional instruments are allowed in duty-free, as are one still or one movie/video camera with five rolls of still film or three rolls of movie film or videotape. Up to 200 cigarettes can be brought into the country without paying duty, or other smoking materials to a total of up to 250g. One litre of wine or spirits is allowed in duty-free.

Electronic goods such as personal stereos, calculators and computers can be a problem if the customs officials have reason to believe you're bringing them in for resale. As long as you don't carry more than one of each, you should be OK.

For information on importing or exporting currency, see the Money section later in this chapter.

Antiques & Art

Upon leaving Thailand you must obtain an export licence from the Fine Arts Department for any antiques or objects of art you want to take with you. If in doubt whether you have either, visit one of the offices below for inspection and possible licensing.

Thailand has special regulations for taking a Buddha or other deity image (or any part thereof) out of the country. These require not only a licence from the Fine Arts Department but a permit from the Ministry of Commerce as well. The one exception to this are the small Buddha images *(phrá khrêuang)* that are meant to be worn on a chain around the neck; these may be exported without a licence as long as the reported purpose is religious.

An application can be made by submitting two front-view photos of the object (no more than five objects to a photo) and a photocopy of your passport, along with the object in question. These are accepted at the following four locations only.

Office of Archaeology and National Museums (☎ 0 2628 5032) 81/1 Th Si Ayuthaya, Thewet, Dusit, Bangkok
Chiang Mai National Museum (☎ 0 5322 1308) Th Superhighway, Chiang Mai
Songkhla National Museum (☎ 0 7431 1728) 13/1 Th Jana, Songkhla
Thalang National Museum (☎ 0 7631 1426) Tambon Si Sunthon, Amphoe Thalang, Phuket

You will need to allow three to five days for the application and inspection process to be completed.

Temporary Vehicle Importation

Passenger vehicles (eg, car, van, truck or motorcycle) can be brought into Thailand for tourist purposes for up to six months. Docu-ments needed for the crossing are a valid International Driving Permit, passport, vehicle registration papers (in the case of a borrowed or hired vehicle, authorisation from the owner) and a cash or bank guarantee equal to the value of the vehicle plus 20%. For entry through Khlong Toey Port or Bangkok International Airport, this means a letter of bank credit; for overland crossings via Malaysia a 'self-guarantee' filled in at the border is sufficient.

MONEY

Currency

The basic unit of Thai currency is the baht *(bàat)*. There are 100 satang *(sàtàang)* in one baht; coins include 25-satang and 50-satang pieces and baht in 1B, 5B and 10B coins. Older coins exhibit Thai numerals only, while newer coins have Thai and Arabic numerals. Twenty-five satang equals one *sàlĕung* in colloquial Thai, but the latter term is rarely used anymore since ongoing inflation makes purchases of less than 1B almost obsolete.

Paper currency comes in denominations of 10B (brown), 20B (green), 50B (blue), 100B (red), 500B (purple) and 1000B (beige). A 10,000B bill was on the way when the 1997 economic crash came, and has been put on hold for the time being. Ten-baht bills are being phased out in favour of the 10B coin and have become rather uncommon. Fortunately for newcomers to Thailand, numerals are printed in their Western as well as Thai forms. Notes are also scaled according to the amount; the larger the denomination, the larger the note. Large denominations – 500B and especially 1000B bills – can be hard to change in small towns, but banks will always change them.

Exchange Rates

The following are the exchange rates at the time of writing.

country	unit		baht
Australia	A$1	=	25.9B
Canada	C$1	=	29.2B
European Union	€1	=	48.9B
Hong Kong	HK$1	=	5.5B
Japan	¥100	=	36.4B
New Zealand	NZ$1	=	23.8B
Singapore	S$1	=	24.3B
UK	UK£1	=	67.8B
USA	US$1	=	42.9B

Prior to June 1997 the baht was pegged to a basket of currencies heavily weighted towards the US dollar, and for over 20 years its value hardly varied from 20B to 26B per US$1. A year after flotation, the baht had slipped approximately 30% against the US dollar. Over the last two years exchange rates have stabilised, but there's always the chance the Thai currency will go for another roller coaster ride. Hence it's a good idea to stay abreast of exchange rates during your stay in Thailand – changing currencies at the right time could extend your budget significantly. Exchange rates are printed in the *Bangkok Post* and the *Nation* every day, or you can walk into any Thai bank and ask to see a daily rate sheet.

Exchanging Money

There is no black market in Thailand for exchanging baht, so there's no reason to import any Thai currency. The banks or legal moneychangers offer the best exchange rates within the country. For buying baht, US dollars are the most readily acceptable currency and travellers cheques get better rates than cash. Since banks charge 23B commission and duty for each travellers cheque cashed, you will save on commissions, if you use larger cheque denominations (eg, a US$50 cheque will only cost 23B to cash, while five US$10 cheques will cost 115B). British pounds are second to the US dollar in general acceptability.

Note that you can't exchange Malaysian ringgit, Indonesian rupiah, Nepali rupees, Cambodian riel, Lao kip, Vietnamese dong or Myanmar kyat with Thai baht at banks, although some moneychangers along Th Charoen Krung and Th Silom in Bangkok carry these currencies. The latter can in fact be good places to buy these currencies, if you're going to any of those countries. The bank rates are comparable with black-market rates in countries where there's a discrepancy between the 'official' and free-market currency values.

Visa and MasterCard credit-card holders can get cash advances through branches of the Kasikornbank, Bangkok Bank and Siam Commercial Bank (and also at the night-time exchange windows in touristy spots like Banglamphu, Chiang Mai, Ko Samui and so on).

American Express (AmEx) card holders can also get advances, but only in travellers cheques. The AmEx agent in Bangkok is **SEA Tours** (☎ *0 2216 5759, 0 2273 0022; Suite 88-92, Payathai Plaza, 8th floor, 128 Th Phayathai, Bangkok*).

Banking Hours In the provinces banks are generally open 8.30am to 3.30pm, weekdays, while in Bangkok bank hours are from 10am to 4pm weekdays. Several banks have special foreign-exchange offices in tourist areas that are open longer hours (8.30am to 8pm) and every day of the week. All banks are closed on public holidays.

Exchange Control Legally, any traveller arriving in Thailand must have at least the following amounts of money in cash, travellers cheques, bank draft or letter of credit, according to visa category: Non-Immigrant Visa, US$500 per person or US$1000 per family; Tourist Visa, US$250 per person or US$500 per family; Transit Visa or no visa, US$125 per person or US$250 per family. Your funds may be checked by authorities if you arrive on a one-way ticket or if you look as if you're at 'the end of the road'.

There is no limit to the amount of Thai or foreign currency you may bring into the country. Upon leaving Thailand, you're permitted to take no more than 50,000B per person without special authorisation; exportation of foreign currencies is unrestricted. An exception is made if you're going to Cambodia, Laos, Malaysia, Myanmar or Vietnam, where the limit is 500,000B.

It's legal to open a foreign-currency account at any commercial bank in Thailand. As long as the funds originate from abroad, there are no restrictions on their maintenance or withdrawal.

ATMs & Debit/Credit Cards ATM and debit cards issued by a bank in your own country can be used at several Thai banks to withdraw cash (in Thai baht only) directly from your cheque or savings account back home, thus avoiding all commissions and finance charges. You can use MasterCard debit cards to buy baht at foreign exchange booths or desks at either the Bangkok Bank or Siam Commercial Bank. Visa debit cards can buy cash through the Kasikornbank exchange services.

These cards can also be used at most Thai ATMs. Many travellers now use debit or ATM cards in lieu of travellers cheques because they're quicker and more convenient, although it's a good idea to bring along an emergency travellers-cheque fund in case you lose your card.

Credit cards as well as debit cards can be used for purchases at many shops, hotels and restaurants. The most commonly accepted cards are Visa and MasterCard, followed by AmEx and Japan Card Bureau (JCB).

It's against Thai law to pass on to the customer the 3% to 5% merchant fee charged by banks, but almost all merchants in Thailand do it anyway. The only exception seems to be hotels (although even a few hotels will hit you with a credit-card surcharge). If you don't agree to the surcharge they'll simply refuse to accept your card. Begging and pleading or pointing out the law doesn't seem to help.

The best way to get around the illegal surcharge is to politely ask that the credit-card receipt be itemised with cost of product or service and the surcharge listed separately. Then when you pay your bill, photocopy all receipts showing the surcharge and request a 'charge back'. Not all banks in all countries will offer such refunds – banks in the UK, for example, refuse to issue such refunds, while those in the USA usually will.

To report a lost or stolen credit/debit card, call the following telephone hotlines in Bangkok: **AmEx** *(☎ 0 2273 5050, 0 2273 5544)*; **MasterCard** *(☎ 001 800 11 887 0663)*; **Visa** *(☎ 001 800 441 3485)*. See Dangers & Annoyances later in this chapter for important warnings on credit-card theft and fraud.

International Money Transfers Justifiably claiming to be 'the fastest way to send money worldwide', **Western Union** *(☎ 0 2254 7000; Central Department Store, 1027 Th Ploenchit)* has offices at Central and Robinson department stores around the city, in Hat Yai and Chiang Mai, as well as at the Bank of Ayudhya and Bank of Asia.

If you have a bank account in Thailand or your home bank has a branch in Bangkok, you can have money wired direct via a telegraphic transfer. This costs a bit more than having a cheque sent; telegraphic transfers take anywhere from two days to a week to arrive. International banks with branches in Bangkok include Bank of America, Bank of Tokyo, Banque Indosuez, Banque Nationale de Paris, Citibank, Deutsche Bank, Hongkong Bank, Chase Manhattan Bank, Merrill Lynch International Bank, Sakura Bank, Standard Chartered Bank, United Malayan Bank and many others.

Security

Give some thought in advance as to how you're going to carry your financial media – whether travellers cheques, cash, credit and debit cards, or some combination of these. Many travellers favour pouches that can be worn hidden beneath clothing. Hip-pocket wallets are easy marks for thieves. Pickpockets work markets and crowded buses throughout the country, so it pays to keep your money concealed.

It's a good idea not to keep all your money in one place; keep an 'emergency' stash well concealed in a piece of luggage separate from other money.

Costs

Food and accommodation outside Bangkok are generally quite inexpensive and even in Bangkok they are fairly cheap, especially considering the value compared to other countries in South and Southeast Asia. Since the 1997 baht devaluation, prices have dropped even lower, at least in relation to hard currencies.

Those on a budget should be able to get by on 300B per day outside Bangkok, if they really watch expenses, eg by sharing rooms with other travellers. This estimate includes basic food, guesthouse accommodation, nonalcoholic beverages and local transport, but not film, souvenirs, tours, long-distance transport or vehicle hire. Add another 60B to 85B per day for every large beer (30B to 55B for small bottles) you drink.

Expenses vary, of course, from place to place; where there are high concentrations of budget travellers, for example, food tends to be more expensive and accommodation cheaper. With experience, you can travel in Thailand for even less money if you live like a Thai of modest means and learn to speak the language.

Travellers with more money to spend will find that for around 400B to 500B per day, life can be quite comfortable; cleaner and quieter accommodation is easier to find once you pass the 200B-a-night zone in room rates. Of course, a 100B guesthouse room with a mattress on the floor and responsive management is better than a poorly-maintained 500B room with air-con that won't turn off and a noisy all-night card game next door.

In Bangkok there's almost no limit to the amount you *could* spend, but if you avoid the tourist ghettos and ride the public bus system you can get by on slightly more than you would spend in the provinces. Where you stay in Bangkok is of concern, as accommodation is generally more expensive than it is in rural areas. If you can do without air-con, accommodation can be found in Bangkok for as little as 75B per person. The noise, heat and pollution in Bangkok may drive many budget travellers to seek more comfort than they might otherwise need in the countryside; 400B per day in Bangkok is the absolute minimum for air-con.

If you can spend 1000B a day for accommodation, you'll be able to stay in the best rural accommodation Thailand has, which usually means air-con, hot water, TV and telephone. Those seeking international-class accommodation and food will spend at least

1500B to 2000B a day for a room with all the modern amenities – IDD phone, 24-hour hot water and air-con, carpeting, swimming pool, fitness centre and all-night room service. Such hotels are found only in the major cities and resort areas.

Bangkok is the typical 'primate city' cited by sociologists, meaning that most goods produced by the country as a whole end up in Bangkok, so it's usually as cheap to eat in Bangkok as anywhere else in Thailand. The exception is international food: Bangkok has more than anywhere else in the kingdom but charges the most for it. International fast-food chains – which Thailand has plenty of – in particular can be real budget-busters. Eat only Thai and Chinese food if you're trying to spend little.

Tipping & Bargaining

Tipping is not the normal practice in Thailand, although they're getting used to it in expensive hotels and restaurants – elsewhere don't bother. The exception is loose change left from a large restaurant bill; for example if a meal costs 288B and you pay with a 500B note, some Thais and foreign residents will leave the 12B coin change on the change tray. It's not so much a tip as a way of saying 'I'm not so money-grubbing as to grab every last baht'. On the other hand change from a 50B note for a 44B bill will usually not be left behind.

Anything bought in a market should be bargained for; prices in department stores and most nontourist shops are fixed. Sometimes accommodation rates can be bargained down. One may need to bargain hard in heavily touristed areas since the one-week, all air-con type of visitor often pays whatever is asked, creating an artificial price zone between the local and tourist market that the budgeter must deal with.

On the other hand the Thais aren't *always* trying to rip you off, so use some discretion when going for the bone on a price. There's a fine line between bargaining and niggling; getting hot under the collar about 5B makes both the seller and the buyer lose face. Likewise a frown is a poor bargaining tool. More specific suggestions concerning costs can be found in the Accommodation and Shopping sections of this chapter.

The cost of transportation between cities and within them is very reasonable; again, bargaining (when hiring a vehicle) can save you a lot of baht. See the rental section in the Getting Around chapter for more details on hiring a vehicle.

Value-Added Tax

Thailand has a 7% value-added tax (VAT). The tax applies only to certain goods and services but unfortunately no-one seems to know what's subject to VAT and what's not, so the whole situation can be rather confusing. Legally the tax is supposed to be applied to a retailer's cost for the product. For example, if a merchant's wholesale price is 100B for an item that retails at 200B, the maximum adjusted retail including VAT should be 207B, not 214B. But this rarely stops Thai merchants from adding 'VAT' surcharges to their sales.

Visitors to Thailand who hold valid tourist visas (and have been in the country for less than 180 days in the calendar year) and who depart Thailand by air may apply for a VAT refund on purchases made at certain designated shops and department stores. Fill out a VAT refund application at the airport and present it to customs officers along with the purchased goods and relevant receipts.

Other Consumer Taxes

Tourist hotels will usually add a 10% hotel tax, and sometimes an 8% to 10% service charge as well, to your room bill.

POST & COMMUNICATIONS

Thailand has a very efficient postal service and local postage is very cheap.

Bangkok has a **main post office** *(Th Charoen Krung; open 8am-8pm Mon-Fri, 8am-1pm Sat, Sun & holidays)*. A 24-hour international telecommunications service (with telephone, fax, telex and telegram) is located in a separate building to the right and slightly in front of the main post-office building. The street is also called New Rd.

The **AmEx office** *(☎ 0 2273 5544; SP Bldg, 388 Th Phahonyothin; open 8.30am-5pm Mon-Fri)* will also take mail on behalf of AmEx card holders but won't accept courier packets that require your signature.

Outside Bangkok, the typical provincial main post office is open from 8.30am to 4.30pm weekdays and 9am to noon on Saturday. Larger main post offices in provincial capitals may also be open for a half-day on Sunday.

Postal Rates

International air-mail letters cost 14B to 19B for 10g or less, postcards 12B to 15B and aerograms a flat 15B.

International express-mail service (EMS) ranges from 310B to 2050B for documents, from 460B to 2400B for parcels. Within Thailand, this service costs only 25B in addition to regular postage.

Shipping parcels internationally is cheapest by surface (takes up to two months) and most expensive by air (one to two weeks, depending on the destination). Economy SAL (for Sea, Air, Land) uses a combination of surface and air-mail modes and costs somewhere in between.

Most provincial post offices sell do-it-yourself packing boxes, and some will pack your parcels for you for a small fee.

Receiving Mail

Thailand's poste restante service is generally very reliable, though with email these days few tourists use it anymore. When you receive mail, you must show ID; sign your name; and write your passport number, the number of the letter and date of delivery in the book provided.

As with many Asian countries, confusion at poste restante offices is most likely to arise over first names and family names. Ask people who are writing to you to print your family name clearly and to underline it. If you're certain a letter should be waiting for you and it cannot be found, it's always wise to check that it hasn't been filed under your first name. Mail can be sent to poste restante at almost any post office in Thailand.

Couriers

Several companies in Thailand offer courier services. The main ones, headquartered in Bangkok, include the following.

DHL Worldwide (☎ 0 2658 8000) 22nd floor, Grand Amarin Tower, 1550 Th Phetburi Tat Mai
Federal Express (☎ 0 2367 3222) 8th floor, Green Tower, Th Phra Ram IV
UPS (☎ 0 2712 3300) 16/1 Soi 44/1, Th Sukhumvit

Telephone

The telephone system in Thailand, operated by the government-subsidised Telephone Organization of Thailand (TOT) under the Communications Authority of Thailand (CAT), is quite efficient. From Bangkok you can usually direct-dial most major centres with little difficulty.

The telephone country code for Thailand is ☎ 66. When dialling Thailand from outside the country, you must first dial whatever international access code is necessary (eg, from the USA dial ☎ 011 first for all international calls), followed by ☎ 66 and then the phone number in Thailand. All Thai phone numbers listed in this book are preceded by ☎ 0, but you only need to include the zero when dialling numbers within Thailand.

Main post-office telephone centres in most provincial capitals are open from 7am to 11pm daily; the smaller provincial phone offices may be open from 8am to either 8pm or 10pm. Bangkok's international CAT phone office, now called the **Public Telecommunications Service Center** *(Th Charoen Krung)*, at the main post office, is open 24 hours.

International Calls To direct-dial an international number (other than those in Malaysia and Laos) from a private phone, simply dial ☎ 001 before the number you're calling. For operator-assisted international calls, dial ☎ 100.

Home Country Direct service is available at Bangkok's main post office, at airports in Bangkok, Chiang Mai, Phuket, Hat Yai and Surat Thani, at post office CAT centres in Bangkok, Hat Yai, Phuket, Chiang Mai, Surat Thani, Pattaya, Hua Hin and Kanchanaburi. Home Country Direct phones offer easy one-button connection with international operators in some 40 countries around the world. You can also direct-dial Home Country Direct access numbers from any private phone (from most hotel phones it won't work) in Thailand.

Hotels generally add surcharges (sometimes as much as 50% over and above the CAT rate) for international long-distance calls; it's always cheaper to call abroad from a CAT telephone office. These offices are almost always attached to a city's main post office, often on the building's 2nd floor, around the side or just behind the main post office.

The procedure for making an international long-distance call *(thorásàp ráwàang pràthêt)*, once you've found the proper office and window, begins with filling out a form with details of the call. Except for reverse-charge calls, you must estimate in advance the time you'll be on the phone and pay a deposit equal to the time/distance rate. There is always a minimum three-minute charge, which is refunded if your call doesn't go through. Usually, only cash or international phone credit cards are acceptable for payment at CAT offices; some provincial CAT offices also accept AmEx and a few take Visa and MasterCard.

If the call doesn't go through you must pay a 30B service charge anyway – unless you're calling reverse charges *(kèp plai thaang)*. For reverse-charge calls it's the opposite, ie, you pay the 30B charge only if the call goes through. Depending on where you're calling, reimbursing someone later for a reverse-charge call to your home country may be less expensive than paying CAT/TOT charges – it pays to compare rates at the source and destination.

Private long-distance telephone offices exist in most towns, but sometimes only for calls within Thailand. Often these offices are just a desk or a couple of booths in the rear of a retail shop. They typically collect a 10B surcharge for long-distance domestic calls and 50B for international calls, and accept cash only.

Whichever type of phone service you use, the least expensive time of day to make calls is from midnight to 5am (30% discount on standard rates), followed by 9pm to midnight or 5am to 7am (20% discount). You pay full price from 7am to 9pm (this rate is reduced by 20% on Sunday). Some sample rates for a one-minute call during the daytime include: Africa 45B, Asia 40B, Australia 22B, Europe 36B, USA 22B. After one minute you're charged 10% of the original one-minute rate for every six seconds you remain connected.

If you're calling from a private phone, you must dial the international access code ☎ 001 before dialling the country code, area code and phone number you wish to reach.

A new CAT service called eFONE allows you to place a call from any private phone via Internet Protocol Network and thereby reducing the normal phone charges by 20% to 30%. To take advantage of the programme, after dialling the regular international access code, add the eFONE code ☎ 809 before the rest of the number.

Malaysia & Laos CAT does not offer long-distance service to Laos or Malaysia. To call these countries you must go through TOT. To call Laos you can direct dial ☎ 007 and country code ☎ 856, followed by the area code and number you want to reach. Malaysia can be dialled direct by prefixing the code ☎ 09 to the Malaysian number (including area code).

International Phonecards A CAT-issued, prepaid international phonecard, called ThaiCard, comes in 300B and 500B denominations and allows calls to many countries at standard CAT rates. You can use the ThaiCard codes from either end, for example calling the UK from Thailand or calling Thailand from the UK.

Lenso phonecards allow you to make international phone calls from yellow Lenso International Cardphone, wall phones found in airports, shopping centres and found out the front of some post offices. Cards come in two denominations, 250B and 500B, and are sold in convenience stores and some supermarkets. You can also use most major credit cards with Lenso phones and dial AT&T direct-access numbers (though rates are high).

Lonely Planet's ekno global communication service provides low-cost international calls – for local calls you're usually better off with a local phonecard. ekno also offers free messaging services, email, travel information and an online travel vault, where you can securely store all your important documents. You can join online at 🅆 www.ekno.lonelyplanet.com, where you will find the local-access numbers for the 24-hour customer-service centre. Once you have joined, always check the ekno website for the latest access numbers for each country and updates on new features.

Internet Phone Of course the cheapest way to call internationally is via the Internet. Some Internet calls – such as from Thailand to the USA – are free, while others are much cheaper than regular phone calls. Many Internet cafés in Thailand are set up to allow Internet phone calls. Most charge only the regular per-minute or per-hour fees they charge for any other kind of Internet access, if the call itself is a free call, as in the previous example. A few charge extra for Internet phone calls, and of course if the call isn't free you will pay for both Internet time and the call – but this is still often less expensive than using CAT.

CAT itself is getting in on the act by offering the PhoneNet card, which comes in 1000B denominations and allows you to call overseas via Voice over Internet Protocol for a 21% to 40% savings over regular rates. The difference with PhoneNet is that you can call from any phone, ie, you don't call from a computer. They're available from any CAT office.

Domestic Calls In most destinations there are three kinds of public pay phones in Thailand – 'red', 'blue' and 'green'. The red phones are for local city calls, the blue phones are for both local and long-distance calls (within Thailand) and the green ones are for use with phonecards.

All Thai phone numbers listed in this book are preceded by ☎ 0, which must be included when dialling numbers within Thailand.

Local calls from pay phones cost 1B for 164 seconds (add more coins for more time). Local calls from private phones cost 3B, with no time limit. Some hotels and guesthouses feature private pay phones that cost 5B per call. Long-distance rates within the country vary from 3B to 12B per minute, depending on the distance.

Card phones are available at most Thai airports as well as major shopping centres and other public areas throughout urban Thailand. Phonecards come in 25B, 50B, 100B, 200B and 240B denominations, all roughly the same size as a credit card; they can be purchased at any TOT office or 7-Eleven. At airports you can usually buy them from the airport information counter or at gift shops.

Cellular Phones TOT authorises the use of private cell phones tuned to GSM networks. If you bring your own mobile phone, roaming is not usually a problem, though it can be quite expensive.

Two cellular operators in Thailand, Orange and DTAC, will allow you to use their SIM cards in an imported phone, as long as your phone isn't SIM-locked. Rates depend on the calling plan you choose but are typically around 3B per minute anywhere in Thailand. Mobile-phone shops that sell such cards can easily be found in most shopping centres in Bangkok and in various smaller shops around the country.

Major hotels in Bangkok can arrange the rental of handsets and SIM cards for 150B to 250B a day depending on how many days you need them, with call rates of 6B to 12B a minute.

In Bangkok and Chiang Mai we've seen sidewalk tables where you can make cell phone calls anywhere in Thailand for 2B to 5B per minute. The vendors are able to do this by repeatedly taking advantage of special promotions on new cell phone accounts.

Fax

Telephone offices in main post offices throughout the country offer fax services as well as phone services. There's no need to bring your own paper, as post offices supply their own forms. A few TOT offices also offer fax services. International faxes typically cost 100B to 130B for the first page, and 70B to 100B per page for the remaining pages, depending on the size of the paper and the destination.

Larger hotels with business centres offer the same telecommunication services but always at higher rates.

Email & Internet Access

Thailand is more advanced in the cybernautic world than any other country in Southeast Asia at the moment and rates continue to drop from year to year. Many guesthouses and bars and cafés in Bangkok, Chiang Mai, Ko Samui and Phuket now offer email and Internet at house terminals. For the visitor who only needs to log on once in a while, these are a less expensive alternative to getting your own account – and it certainly beats lugging around a laptop. The going rate is 1B or 2B per on- and offline minute, although we've seen a few places where slower connections are available at a half-baht per minute.

Internet centres are plentiful in any town with a population over 50,000. For that reason we don't list cybercafés in this guide, except for towns where they're a rarity, or where the services offered are especially extensive.

If you're travelling with a laptop, temporary Internet accounts are available from several Thai ISPs. One of the better ones is WebNet, offered by **Loxinfo** (W *www.loxinfo.co.th*). You can buy a block of 30 hours (380B), or 63 hours (750B), good for up to one year.

DIGITAL RESOURCES

A growing number of online entities offer information on Thailand. Many of these websites are commercial sites established by tour operators or hotels. The ratio of commercial to noncommercial sites is liable to increase.

Consider starting with the Lonely Planet website W www.lonelyplanet.com. Here you'll find succinct summaries on travelling to most places on earth, postcards from other travellers and the Thorn Tree bulletin board, where you can ask questions before you go or dispense advice when you get back. You can also find travel news and updates to this edition, and the subwwway section links you to the most useful travel resources elsewhere on the Web. Go to W www.lonelyplanet.com.au/dest/sea/thai.htm for a direct link to Thailand-related material.

Other useful websites include:

Asia Travel Perhaps the best of the many commercial sites with travel-booking capabilities. W www.asiatravel.com/thailand.html

Bangkok Post Contains the entire newspaper (except for ads) daily, and archives of stories for several years. W www.bangkokpost.com

The Nation Another good source of local news, although the archive is much less comprehensive. W www.nationmultimedia.com

Mahidol University A very useful website that's searchable by keyword. W www.mahidol.ac.th/Thailand

National Electronics & Computer Technology Center (Nectec) Contains links on everything from a list of all Thai embassies and consulates abroad and details of visa requirements to weather updates. W www.nectec.or.th

Greenpeace Southeast Asia This branch of Greenpeace is headquartered in Bangkok, and its website carries lots of up-to-date news about environmental issues in Thailand. W www.greenpeacesoutheastasia.org

Tourism Authority of Thailand Contains a province guide, up-to-date press releases, tourism statistics, TAT contact information and planning hints. W www.tat.or.th or W www.tourismthailand.org

Thai Students Online Providing relief from the usual ad-studded pages, students at Sriwittayapaknam School in Samut Prakan Province maintain a complex of highly informative Web pages to form what is the largest non-commercial website in Thailand. W www.thaistudents.com

BOOKS

Thailand boasts the largest selection of English-language books and bookshops in Southeast Asia. The principal chains are Asia Books, Bookazine and DK Book House; each has branches in half a dozen locations around Bangkok and DK also has branches in larger tourist destinations like Chiang Mai, Ko Samui and Phuket. Some larger tourist hotels also have bookshops with English-language books and periodicals.

See the destination chapters for more details.

Lonely Planet

Aside from this guidebook, other Lonely Planet publications of interest to anyone visiting Thailand include the *Thai phrasebook*, the *Hill Tribes phrasebook* and the *Thailand, Vietnam, Laos & Cambodia Road Atlas*. Lonely Planet's *Chiang Mai & Northern Thailand* covers all the provinces of the north with more detail than you'll find in this country guide. *Thailand's Islands & Beaches* goes into more detail on the kingdom's coastal and marine destinations, while the *Bangkok* city guide presents more-extensive information on Bangkok in a smaller and more portable form. *Diving & Snorkeling Thailand* is chock-a-block full of colour photos and essential diving information. *Bangkok Condensed* is a compact guide that's ideal for short-stay visitors. *World Food Thailand* is a unique culinary guide that takes you to the heart of the kingdom's culture.

Travel Writing

The earliest Western literature of note on Thailand, Guy Tachard's *A Relation of the Voyage to Siam*, recounts, with little literary flair, a 1680s French expedition through parts of the country. Shortly after, Simon de la Loubére's 1693 *New Historical Relation of the Kingdom of Siam* chronicled the French mission to the Ayuthaya court in great detail. Maurice Collis novelised this period with a focus on the unusual political relationship between King Narai and his Greek minister, Constantine Phaulkon, in *Siamese White*.

Frank Vincent's *The Land of the White Elephant*, first published in 1873, is a very readable account of an American merchant's travels in Siam. Carl Bock's illustrated *Temples and Elephants* covered similar territory in 1884. Tachard, Loubére, Collis, Vincent and Bock have all been republished by Bangkok publisher White Lotus and are readily available in bookshops in Bangkok, Chiang Mai and Phuket.

Anna Leonowens wrote *The English Governess at the Siamese Court* in 1870. Its largely unauthentic descriptions of Siamese life (see the boxed text 'The King & Who?' in the Facts about Thailand chapter) were later transformed into three Hollywood movies and a Broadway musical.

Joseph Conrad evoked Thailand in several of his pre-WWII novels and short stories, most notably in *The Secret Sharer* (1920s) and *Falk: A Reminiscence*. More detail from this era can be found in *Teak Wallah*, by Reginald Campbell, a Briton who worked as a teak inspector in northern Thailand.

Pierre Boulle's post-WWII novel *The Bridge on the River Kwai* dramatised the construction and destruction of the Death Railway Bridge in Kanchanaburi Province. In 1957 it was made into an Academy Award–winning motion picture that remains the most internationally famous film about Thailand.

Charles Nicholls' semifictional *Borderlines* (1992) takes the reader on a voyage to the Thai-Myanmar border in the company of a colourful group of travellers. Along the way the author weaves cultural insights into the storyline – it's more than just a beach read.

Summer reading is exactly what you can expect from Alex Garland's 1997 novel *The Beach*, a tale of island-hopping backpackers trying to carve out their own private paradise in a Thai national marine park. A film based on the novel and starring Leo DiCaprio was released in 2000 and although critical reviews were savage, cinema earnings topped US$200 million.

Nicholls, Pico Iyer, Robert Anson Hall and several other well-known and not-so-well-known authors have contributed travel essays of varying style to 1994's *Travelers' Tales Thailand*. Some savvy travel tips are sprinkled throughout the text.

A more serious collection of literature is available in *Traveller's Literary Companion: Southeast Asia*, edited by Alastair Dingwall. The Thailand chapter, edited by scholar Thomas John Hudak, is packed with hard-to-find information on the history of literature in Thailand and includes extracts from various works by Thai and foreign authors.

History & Politics

Georges Coedès' classic pre-WWII work on Southeast Asian history, *The Indianised States of Southeast Asia*, contains groundbreaking historical material on early Thai history, as does WAR Wood's *A History of Siam*, published in the same era. One of the more readable general histories written in the latter half of the 20th century is David Wyatt's *Thailand: A Short History* (Trasvin Publications, Chiang Mai).

At first glance *Siam Mapped: A History of the Geo-Body of a Nation* by Thongchai Winichakul appears to be a simple history of the mapping of Thailand. But a thorough reading will uncover a profound and very well-researched study of Thai notions of identity and sovereignty within the context of Southeast Asian history and European involvement in the region.

Concentrating on post-revolutionary Thailand, *The Balancing Act: A History of Modern Thailand* (Asia Books, 1991), by Joseph Wright Jr, starts with the 1932 revolution and ends with the coup of February 1991. Wright's semi-academic chronicle concludes that certain 'natural laws' – endemic to the culture – govern the continuous circulation of elites. Although the book is packed with detail, such deep-structure theorising brings to mind the way Anglo scholars, until very recently, identified all French political trends as 'Bonapartiste'. Wright's most convincing thesis is that, despite the 1932 revolution, democracy has never gained a firm foothold in Thai society.

Thailand's role in the international narcotics trade is covered thoroughly in Alfred McCoy's *The Politics of Heroin in Southeast Asia*. *Chasing the Dragon: Into the*

Heart of the Golden Triangle, by Christopher R Cox, contains some decent writing and interesting news titbits as it traces a journalist's path to Khun Sa's former Ho Mong headquarters near the Thai-Myanmar border.

Although it's fiction, former Prime Minister Kukrit Pramoj's 1961 *Red Bamboo* vividly portrays and predicts the conflict between the Thai communist movement and the establishment during the 1960s and '70s. His book *Si Phaendin: Four Reigns* (1981), the most widely read novel ever published in Thailand, covers the late 19th and 20th centuries. Both of these novels are available in English-language versions.

Axel Aylwen's novel *The Falcon of Siam* and its sequel *The Falcon Takes Wing* are not up to Kukrit's literary standards but nonetheless capture the feel and historical detail of 17th-century Siam; Aylwen obviously read Collis, Loubére and Tachard closely (see the Travel Writing section earlier).

Although it's tough to find, *The Devil's Discus* (Cassell & Co, 1964) by Rayne Kruger focuses on the mysterious death of Rama VIII. The book is banned in Thailand for its police-blotter style analysis of a taboo topic.

Natural History

Complete with sketches, photos and maps, *The Mammals of Thailand* (Association for the Conservation of Wildlife, 1988), by Boonsong Lekagul & Jeffrey McNeely, remains the classic on Thai wildlife in spite of a few out-of-date references (it was first published in 1977). Bird lovers should seek out the *Guide to the Birds of Thailand* (Saha Kharn Bhaet, 1991), by Boonsong Lekagul & Phillip Round, for the comprehensive descriptions of Thailand's numerous avian species.

Detailed summaries of Thailand's national parks, along with an objective assessment of current park conditions, are available in *National Parks of Thailand* (Communication Resources, Bangkok) by Gray, Piprell & Graham.

The Siam Society's *Culture & Environment in Thailand* is a collection of scholarly papers (by Thai and foreign authors) that were delivered at a 1988 symposium on the relationship between Thai culture and the natural world; topics range from the oceanic origins of the Thai race, and nature motifs in Thai art, to attitudes that are evolving in Thailand towards the environment.

Culture & Society

Naga: Cultural Origins in Siam & the Western Pacific by Sumet Jumsai (Chalermnit Press/DD Books, 1997) is an inspired piece of speculative theory on the supposed oceanic origins of Thai people and culture. The late R Buckminster Fuller collaborated with author, architect and Cambridge lecturer Sumet in prose and carefully collected illustrations, how Thai myths, symbols and architecture stem from an earlier phase in Asian-Western Pacific history when most of the peoples of the region inhabited islands and lived largely seafaring lives. In particular, the *naga* or sea-dragon motif was common to Thailand and other mainland Southeast Asian civilisations. The proposed confrontation between 'water-based' Thai culture and 'land-based' Khmer (and later Western) culture is fascinating and of intrinsic value whether or not the oceanic-origin theory is accurate.

Letters from Thailand by Botan (translated by Susan Fulop Kepner) and Carol Hollinger's *Mai Pen Rai Means Never Mind* can also be recommended for their insights into traditional Thai culture. *Working with the Thais* by Henry Holmes and Suchada Tangtongtavy covers just about everything you might need to know before entering into a serious work situation in Thailand.

Jack Reynolds' *A Woman of Bangkok* (1950s, republished in 1985), the well-written and poignant story of a young Englishman's descent into the world of Thai brothels, remains the best novel yet published with this theme. Expat writer Christopher G Moore covers the Thai underworld in his 1990s novels *A Killing Smile, Spirit House, A Bewitching Smile* and a raft of others, which are largely set in the go-go bar scene. His description of Bangkok's sleazy Thermae Coffee House (called 'Zeno' in *A Killing Smile*) is the closest literature comes to evoking the behaviours to which these places cater.

Sex and Borders: Gender, National Identity and Prostitution Policy in Thailand by Leslie Ann Jeffrey, 2002, is a detailed academic study of commercial sex workers in

Thailand, and suggests that prostitution is empowering work for women who grow up in Thailand with few other employment possibilities. Decrying Western media sensationalism that presents Bangkok's brothels as icons of Third World exploitation, Jeffrey observes that Thailand's sex workers have begun to demand not pity but rights as workers in the global economy.

For information on books about Buddhism and how it is practised in Thailand, see the Further Information section of Religion in the Facts about Thailand chapter.

Hill Tribes

For more-detailed information on hill tribes, look for a copy of *The Hill Tribes of Northern Thailand* by Gordon Young (Monograph No l, The Siam Society). Young was born of third-generation Christian missionaries among the Lahu people, spoke several tribal dialects and was even an honorary Lahu chieftain with the highest Lahu title, the Supreme Hunter. The monograph covers 16 tribes, including descriptions, photographs, tables and maps.

Peoples of the Golden Triangle, by Elaine & Paul Lewis, is also very good, very photo-oriented and expensive. Lonely Planet's *Hill Tribes phrasebook* has descriptions of Thailand's major hill tribes and phrases in several hill-tribe languages.

The Hill Tribes of Thailand, published by the Tribal Research Institute at Chiang Mai University, also contains sound advice for trekkers but the hill-tribe information is rather skimpy.

Teak House, a Thai publishing house, does a series of book-length monographs devoted to a few of the ethnic groups found in Thailand, including *The Haw: Traders of the Golden Triangle* (Andrew Forbes & David Henley), *The Akha: Guardians of the Forest* (Jim Goodman) and *The Khon Muang: People & Principalities of North Thailand* (Andrew Forbes & David Henley).

Food & Shopping

Lonely Planet's compact *World Food: Thailand* enables food-conscious visitors, as well as residents, to appreciate the full range of Thai cuisine by providing explanations of the cooking methods, an extensive menu glossary and lots of cultural and historical background.

Kasma Loha-unchit's stylish *It Rains Fishes: Legends, Traditions and the Joys of Thai Cooking* brings together Thai culinary lore, cooking techniques and recipes tailored to the American kitchen. Kasma's *Dancing Shrimp* focuses on Thai seafood, with special emphasis on authenticity.

Among the explosion of Thai cookbooks that have appeared in recent years, one of the best remains *Thai Cooking* (formerly *The Original Thai Cookbook*) by Jennifer Brennan. Although *Thailand the Beautiful Cookbook* by Panurat Poladitmontri is expensive and unwieldy, its huge, coffee table–style format contains excellent photography and authentic recipes.

Three small books in the Periplus Nature Guide series, *Tropical Herbs & Spices of Thailand, Tropical Fruits of Thailand* and *Tropical Vegetables of Thailand* make good additions to anyone's library.

Although it's a bit out of date, John Hoskins' 1988 *Buyer's Guide to Thai Gems & Jewellery* is a must for anyone contemplating a foray into Thailand's gem market. *Arts and Crafts of Thailand,* written by William Warren and photographed by Luca Invernizzi Tettoni, makes a useful primer for delving into the world of Thailand's handicrafts.

FILMS

A number of classic international films have used Thailand either as a subject or as a location – more often the latter. Nowadays location shooting in Thailand has become something of a boom industry as Thailand's jungles, rice fields and islands find themselves backdrops for all manner of scripts set in 'exotic' tropical countries. See Cinema in the Facts About Thailand chapter.

Jungles & Kingdoms

The first film to come out of Thailand for foreign audiences was *Chang Sang Chorn,* a 1927 silent picture shot entirely in Nan Province (then still a semi-independent principality with Siamese protection). Produced by American film impresarios Copper & Schoedsack – who later produced several major Hollywood hits – *Chang* contains some of the best jungle and wildlife sequences filmed in Asia to date.

Later came *Anna and the King of Siam,* a 1946 US production (filmed on Hollywood sets) starring Rex Harrison. It was based on the book *The English Governess at the Siamese Court* by Anna Leonowens, who taught English to Rama IV's children in the 19th century. Although the movie opened to very mixed reviews, screenwriter Arthur Miller was honoured with an Academy Award. A 1956 musical remake, *The King and I,* grew from a very successful Broadway stage production starring Yul Brynner (who earned an Oscar for the film). Most recently Jodie Foster starred in *Anna and the King,* which caused quite a stir when the Thai government refused permission to film the movie in Thailand on the grounds that the script contained historical and cultural distortions. Instead the studios used Malaysia as a backdrop (and non-Thai actors speaking Thai badly), and the US$75 million film opened in 1999 to flat reviews. All three films, as well as the musical, are banned in Thailand because they are seen to compromise the dignity of the monarchy.

Probably the most famous movie associated with Thailand is *The Bridge on the River Kwai,* a 1957 Academy Award-winning production stemming from Pierre Boulle's book of the same name and starring Alec Guinness. Although based on WWII events in Thailand, much of the film was shot on location in Sri Lanka (then Ceylon).

Another early film of some notoriety was 1962's *The Ugly American,* a Marlon Brando vehicle based on the novel by William J Lederer. In this muddled picture Thailand stands in for the fictional Southeast Asian nation of Sarkan. Part-time Thai politician and academic Kukrit Pramoj enjoyed a substantial film role as the fake nation's prime minister. Kukrit went on to become Thailand's prime minister in 1974.

Bond, Sex, Martial Arts & Vietnam

The Man with the Golden Gun, a pedestrian 1974 James Bond movie starring Roger Moore and Christopher Lee, brought the karst islands of Ao Phang-Nga to international attention for the first time. A year later the French soft-porn movie *Emmanuelle* ('Much hazy, soft-focus coupling in downtown Bangkok', wrote the *Illustrated London News*) added to the myth of Thailand as sexual idyll and set an all-time box office record in France.

Virtually every film produced with a Vietnam War theme has been shot either in the Philippines or in Thailand, with the latter ahead by a long shot as the location of choice due to relative logistical ease. The first Vietnam-themed movie to use Thailand as a location was *The Deer Hunter,* which starred Robert De Niro and relative newcomer Meryl Streep; it won five Oscars in 1978, including Best Picture and Best Director.

Jean-Claude Van Damme's *The Kickboxer* brought Thai boxing to the big screen with a bit more class than the average martial arts flick; more than a few foreign pugilists have packed their bags for Bangkok after viewing the movie's exotic mix of ring violence and Thai Buddhist atmospherics.

Twenty-three years after his first visit, James Bond returned to Thailand for the filming of 1997's *Tomorrow Never Dies*.

Backpacker Mayhem

Two notorious films released in 1999 and 2000 directly addressed the travel scene in Thailand. Both managed to make Thailand look sinister and dangerous, at least for those who play with drugs. Claire Danes and Kate Beckinsale portray two young Americans imprisoned in Bangkok for trying to smuggle drugs to Hong Kong in *Brokedown Palace* (1999). Based on a true story in which the convicted Australian pair received a relatively light 33-year sentence for a crime that usually warrants execution in Thailand, the movie fed on the same travel paranoia as 1978's *Midnight Express*. Location filming took place in the Philippines.

Trainspotting's Danny Boyle directed Leonardo DiCaprio in a film adaptation of Alex Garland's novel *The Beach* (see Books earlier), which was released in early 2000 to mixed reviews. Boyle did a decent job of depicting the backpacker scene in Thailand, but he and the producers were later criticised for making alterations to a beach on Ko Phi-Phi Leh.

NEWSPAPERS

Thailand's 1997 constitution guarantees freedom of the press, although the Royal Police Department reserves the power to suspend publishing licences for national security reasons. Newspaper editors nevertheless exercise self-censorship in certain realms, particularly with regard to the monarchy. These issues aside, Thailand is widely considered to have the freest print media in Southeast Asia. The nation's reputation for press freedom, however, was temporarily dented in 2002 when two Western journalists were nearly expelled for writing about the Thai king's public criticism of billionaire prime minister, Thaksin Shinawatra.

Two English-language newspapers are published daily in Thailand and distributed in most provincial capitals throughout the country – the *Bangkok Post* in the morning and the *Nation* in the afternoon. The *Post,* Thailand's first English-language daily (since 1946), has a mixed Thai and foreign staff and tends to feature more international reporting than the *Nation,* which is more 'Thai' in outlook and has the edge in regional coverage.

The Singapore edition of the *International Herald Tribune* is widely available in Bangkok, Chiang Mai and heavily touristed areas like Pattaya and Phuket.

The best Thai-language journalism is found in the daily *Matichon* (a weekly version is also available, and quite good). Many Thais read the English-language dailies as they consider them better news sources. There's also a Thai-language version of the popular *Bangkok Post.*

MAGAZINES

English-language magazine publishing has faltered with the economic slowdown in Thailand and several mags failed after 1997. Published by Bangkok expats *Farang* aims itself squarely at the backpacker market with coverage of Thailand's travel and party scene.

The monthly *Gavroche* offers news and feature stories on Thailand for the Francophone community.

Many popular magazines from the UK, USA, Australia and Europe – particularly those concerned with computer technology, cars, fashion, music and business – are available in bookshops that specialise in English-language publications (see the Books section earlier).

RADIO & TV

Thailand has more than 400 radio stations, almost all of them government-owned and operated. Some of the Bangkok FM stations feature some surprisingly good music programmes with British, Thai and American DJs. Looking for *lûuk thûng* music? Station Luk Thung 90 FM broadcasts classic and new *lûuk thûng* styles (see the special section 'Music, Theatre & Dance'). For Thai alternative music, tune into 'Fat Radio' 104.5 FM.

The BBC World Service, Radio Canada, Radio Japan, Radio New Zealand, Singapore Broadcasting Company and Voice of America (VOA) all have English- and Thai-language broadcasts over short-wave radio. The frequencies and schedules, which change hourly, are listed in the *Post* and the *Nation.*

Radio France Internationale and Deutsche Welle broadcast short-wave programmes in French and German respectively. Deutsche Welle also broadcasts 50 minutes of English programming three times daily.

Thailand has five VHF TV networks based in Bangkok, all but one government-operated. The single private network, ITV, is owned by the current prime minister, so even this one cleaves to the government line politically. All telecast a mixture of news, music, documentaries and dramatic series.

Cable & Satellite TV

UBC (W *www.ubctv.com)* is the only cable TV company in Thailand. It carries six English-language movie channels (censored for offensive language, nudity and violence), four sports channels, imported TV series, three music channels (MTV Asia, Channel V and VH1), CNN International, CNBC, NHK, BBC World Service Television, the Discovery Channel and all the standard Thai networks. You can access further information on UBC's website or in the Bangkok dailies.

Thailand has its own ThaiCom 1 and 2 as uplinks for AsiaSat and as carriers for the standard Thai networks as well as Thai Sky (TST). The latter includes five channels offering news and documentaries, Thai music videos and Thai variety programmes. Other satellites tracked by dishes in Thailand include China's Apstar 1 and Apstar 2. Additional transmissions from these and from Vietnam, Myanmar and Malaysia are available with a satellite dish.

PHOTOGRAPHY & VIDEO

Film & Equipment

Print film is fairly inexpensive and widely available throughout Thailand. Japanese print film costs around 100B per 36 exposures, US print film a bit more. Fujichrome slide films cost around 265B per roll, Kodak Ektachrome 200B to 270B. Slide film can be hard to find outside Bangkok and Chiang Mai, so be sure to stock up before heading out to rural areas. Blank video cassettes of all sizes are readily available in the major cities.

Processing

Film processing is generally quite good in the larger cities in Thailand and also quite inexpensive. Dependable E6 processing is available at several labs in Bangkok but is untrustworthy elsewhere. Kodachrome must be sent out of the country for processing, so it can take up to two weeks to get it back.

Professionals will find a number of labs in Bangkok that offer same-day pick-up and delivery at no extra cost within the city. **IQ Lab** *(☎ 0 2266 4080; 160/5 ITF Bldg, Th Silom, Bangkok • ☎ 0 2714 0644; 9/33-34 Soi 63, Th Sukhumvit, Bangkok)*, actually off Silom on Th Chong Nonsi, near the Chong Nonsi BTS station, offers the widest range of services, with all types of processing (except for Kodachrome), slide duping, scanning and custom printing.

Technical Tips

Pack some silica gel with your camera to prevent mould growing on the inside of your lenses. A polarising filter could be useful to cut down on tropical glare at certain times of day. Tripods are a must for shooting interiors in natural light.

For more tips, pick up a copy of *Travel Photography: A Guide to Taking Better Pictures*. Written by internationally renowned travel photographer, Richard I'Anson, it's full colour throughout and designed to take on the road.

Photographing People

In some of the regularly visited areas hill-tribe people expect money if you photograph them, while certain hill tribes will not allow you to point a camera at them. Use discretion when photographing villagers anywhere in Thailand as a camera can be a very intimidating instrument. You may feel better leaving your camera behind when visiting certain areas.

Airport Security

The X-ray baggage-inspection machines at Thailand's airports are all deemed film safe. Nevertheless if you're travelling with high-speed film (ISO 400 or above) you may want to have your film hand-inspected rather than X-rayed. Security inspectors are usually happy to comply. Packing your film in see-through plastic bags generally speeds up the hand inspection process. Some photographers pack their film in lead-lined bags to ward off potentially harmful rays.

TIME

Thailand's time zone is seven hours ahead of GMT/UTC (London). Thus, when it's noon in Bangkok, it's 9pm the previous day in Los Angeles – except during daylight saving time (DST), when it's 10pm; midnight in New York (DST 1am); 5am (the same day) in London; 6am in Paris; 1pm in Perth; and 3pm in Sydney (DST 4pm).

The official year in Thailand is reckoned from 543 BC, the beginning of the Buddhist Era (BE), so that AD 2003 is BE 2546.

ELECTRICITY

The electric current in Thailand is 220V, 50 cycles. Electrical wall outlets are a hybrid arrangement that accept both round, two-pole as well as flat, two-bladed terminals. A few accept the round-pole variety only, but this has become increasingly rare. Any electrical supply shop will carry adapters for any international plug shape, as well as voltage converters.

WEIGHTS & MEASURES

Dimensions and weight are usually expressed using the metric system in Thailand. The exception is land measure, which is often quoted using the traditional Thai measures of *waa, ngaan* and *râi*. Older people who live in the provinces will occasionally use the traditional Thai system of weights and measures in speech, as will boat-builders, carpenters and other craftspeople when talking about their work. The following table of conversions may come in handy on such occasions.

Thai units		metric conversion
1 tàraang waa	=	4 sq m
1 ngaan	=	400 sq m
1 râi	=	1600 sq m
1 bàat	=	15g
1 tàleung or tamleung (4 bàat)	=	60g
1 châng (20 tàleung)	=	1.2kg
1 hàap (50 châng)	=	60kg
1 níu	=	about 2cm (or 1 inch)
1 khêup (12 níu)	=	25cm
1 sàwk (2 khêup)	=	50cm
1 waa (4 sàwk)	=	2m
1 sên (20 waa)	=	40m
1 yôht (400 sên)	=	16km

LAUNDRY

Virtually every hotel in Thailand offers a laundry service. Charges are generally geared to room rates. Cheapest of all are public laundries, where you pay by the kilogram.

Many hotels and guesthouses have laundry areas where you can wash your clothes at no charge; sometimes there's even a hanging area for drying. In accommodation where there is no laundry, DIY-types can wash their clothes in the sink and hang clothes out to dry in their rooms – don't forget to pack some cord and a few pegs for hanging up your washing. Laundry detergent is readily available in convenience stores and supermarkets.

Laundries that advertise dry-cleaning often don't really dry-clean (they just boil everything!) or they do it badly. A few luxury hotels have dependable dry-cleaning services.

TOILETS

As in many other Asian countries, the 'squat toilet' is the norm except in hotels and guesthouses geared towards tourists and international business travellers. These sit more-or-less flush with the surface of the floor, with two footpads on either side. For travellers who have never used a squat toilet it takes a bit of getting used to.

If there's no mechanical flush, toilet-users scoop water from an adjacent bucket or tank with a plastic bowl and use it to clean their nether regions while still squatting over the toilet. A few extra scoops of water must be poured into the toilet basin to flush waste into the septic system.

More rustic yet are toilets in rural areas, which may simply consist of a few planks over a hole in the ground.

Even in places where sit-down toilets are installed, the plumbing may not be designed to take toilet paper. In such cases the usual washing bucket will be standing nearby or there will be a waste basket where you're supposed to place used toilet paper.

HEALTH

Travel health depends on your predeparture preparations, your daily health care while travelling and how you handle any medical problem that does develop. While the potential dangers can seem quite frightening, in reality few travellers experience anything more than an upset stomach.

Predeparture planning

Immunisations Plan ahead for getting your vaccinations: Some of them require more than one injection, and certain vaccinations should not be given together. Note that some vaccinations should not be given during pregnancy or to people with allergies – discuss with your doctor.

Although there is no risk of yellow fever in Thailand, you will need proof of vaccination if you're coming from a yellow fever-infected area (sub-Saharan Africa and parts of South America).

It is recommended you seek medical advice at least six weeks before travel. Be aware that there is often a greater risk of disease with children and during pregnancy.

If you want immunisations while in Thailand, they are available from a number of sources, including both public hospitals and private clinics. Bangkok is your best bet in terms of finding less-common or more-expensive vaccines. Discuss your requirements with your doctor, but vaccinations you should consider having for Thailand include diphtheria, polio, hepatitis A and B, rabies and Japanese B encephalitis.

Malaria Medication Antimalarial drugs do not prevent you from being infected but kill the malaria parasites during a stage in their development and significantly reduce the risk of becoming very ill or dying. Expert advice on medication should be sought,

RYAN FOX

Wat Pho, Bangkok

RICHARD NEBESKY

Garlands, Samut Songkhram

DENNIS JOHNSON

Wat Pho, Bangkok

RICHARD I'ANSON

Wat Phra Kaew (Temple of the Emerald Buddha), Bangkok

RICHARD I'ANSON

Monk, Nakhom Pathom

CHRIS MELLOR

Damnoen Saduak Floating Market, Bangkok

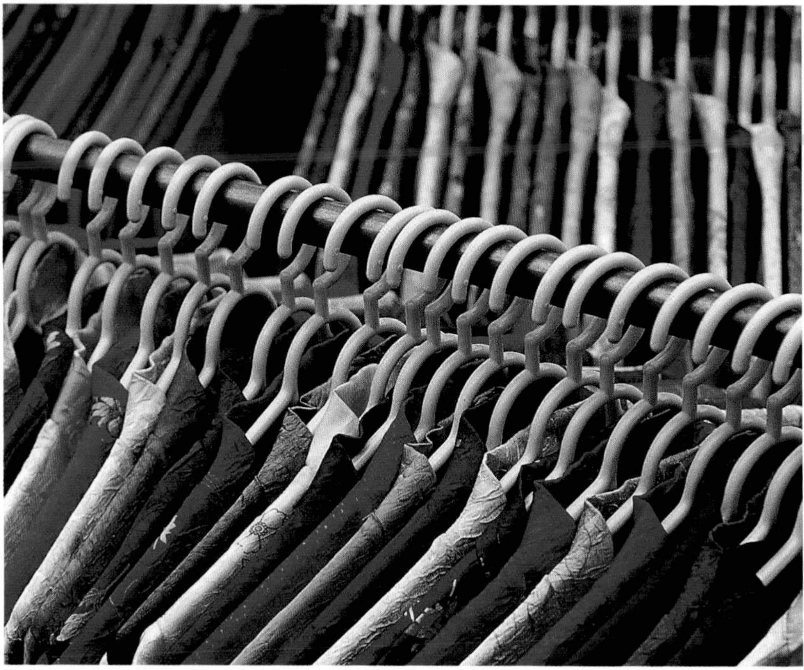

RICHARD I'ANSON

Modern Thai clothing, Phahurat Market, Bangkok

as there are many factors to consider, including the area to be visited, the risk of exposure to malaria-carrying mosquitoes, the side-effects of medication, your medical history and whether you are a child or an adult or pregnant. Travellers to isolated areas in high risk countries may like to carry a treatment dose of medication for use if symptoms occur. See Malaria under Insect-Borne Diseases later in this chapter for information on the prevalence of malaria in Thailand.

Medical Kit Check List

Following is a list of items you should consider including in your medical kit – consult your pharmacist for brands that are available in your country.

- ☐ **Aspirin or paracetamol (acetaminophen in the USA)** – for pain or fever
- ☐ **Antihistamine*** – for allergies, eg, hay fever; to ease the itch from insect bites or stings; and to prevent motion sickness
- ☐ **Cold and flu tablets*, throat lozenges* and nasal decongestant**
- ☐ **Multivitamins*** – consider for long trips, when dietary vitamin intake may be inadequate
- ☐ **Antibiotics** – consider including these if you're travelling well off the beaten track; see your doctor, as they must be prescribed, and carry the prescription with you
- ☐ **Loperamide* or diphenoxylate** – 'blockers' for diarrhoea
- ☐ **Prochlorperazine or metaclopramide** – for nausea and vomiting
- ☐ **Rehydration mixture*** – to prevent dehydration, which may occur, eg, during bouts of diarrhoea; particularly important when travelling with children
- ☐ **Insect repellent*, sunscreen*, lip balm* and eye drops***
- ☐ **Calamine lotion, sting relief spray or aloe vera** – to ease irritation from sunburn and insect bites or stings
- ☐ **Antifungal cream or powder** – for fungal skin infections and thrush
- ☐ **Antiseptic* (such as povidone-iodine)** – for cuts and grazes
- ☐ **Bandages*, Band-Aids (plasters)* and other wound dressings**
- ☐ **Water purification tablets or iodine**
- ☐ **Scissors*, tweezers and a thermometer** – note that mercury thermometers are prohibited by airlines

* Easily available in Thailand

Health Insurance Make sure that you have adequate health insurance. See Travel Insurance in the Visas & Documents section earlier in this chapter for details.

Travel Health Guides Lonely Planet's *Healthy Travel Asia & India* is a handy pocket size and packed with useful information including planning, emergency first aid, immunisation and disease information and what to do if you get sick on the road. Its *Travel with Children*, by Cathy Lanigan, includes advice on travel health for younger children.

Guide to Healthy Living in Thailand, published jointly by the Thai Red Cross Society and US embassy, is available in Bangkok from the **Snake Farm** (☎ *0 2252 0161; Queen Saovabha Memorial Institute, Th Phra Ram IV)* for 100B. This booklet is rich in practical health advice on safe eating, child care, tropical heat, immunisations and local hospitals. It contains wise titbits with a literary flair, including 'Bangkok is a stopping point for many travellers and restless souls. Acute psychiatric emergencies, including alcohol and drug abuse, are, unfortunately, not rare' and 'Bangkok's traffic poses a far greater danger than snakes and tropical diseases combined'.

There are also a number of excellent travel health sites on the Internet. Lonely Planet's website, w www.lonelyplanet.com has links to the World Health Organization and the US Centers for Disease Control and Prevention.

Other Preparations Make sure you're healthy *before* you start travelling. If you are going on a long trip make sure your teeth are OK. If you wear glasses take a spare pair and your prescription.

If you require a particular medication, take an adequate supply as it may not be available in Thailand. Take part of the packaging showing the generic name rather than the brand, which will make getting replacements easier. To avoid any problems it's a good idea to have a legible prescription or letter from your doctor to show that you legally use the medication.

Basic Rules

Food Beware of ice cream that is sold in the street or anywhere it might have melted and been refrozen; if there's any doubt (eg, a power cut in the last day or two), steer well clear. Raw or undercooked shellfish such as mussels, oysters and clams should be avoided as well as undercooked meat, particularly in the form of mince.

If a place looks clean and well run and the vendor also looks clean and healthy, then the food is probably safe. In general, places that are packed with travellers or locals will be fine, while empty restaurants are questionable. The food in busy restaurants is cooked and eaten quite quickly.

Water The number-one rule is *be careful of the water* and especially ice. If you don't know for certain that the water is safe, you should assume the worst – although *all* water served in restaurants or to guests in a restaurant, office or home in Thailand will be purified. It's not necessary to ask for bottled water unless you prefer it. Reputable brands of Thai bottled water or soft drinks are generally fine, although in some places bottles may be refilled with tap water. Only use water from containers with a serrated seal – not tops or corks. Try to purchase glass water bottles, however, as these are recyclable (unlike the plastic disposable ones).

Fruit juices are made with purified water and are safe to drink. Milk in Thailand is always pasteurised.

Ice is generally produced from purified water under hygienic conditions and is therefore theoretically safe. The rule of thumb is that if it's chipped ice, it probably came from an ice block (which may not have been handled well) but if it's ice cubes or 'tubes', it was delivered from the ice factory in sealed plastic.

Water Purification In Thailand, virtually no-one bothers with filters, tablets or iodine since bottled water is so cheap and readily available. However, if you are stuck without bottled water, the simplest way of purifying water is to boil it thoroughly. Vigorous boiling should be satisfactory; however, at high altitude water boils at a lower temperature, so germs are less likely to be killed. Boil it for longer in these environments.

If you plan to do any long camping trips, consider purchasing a 'total' water filter, which removes all parasites, bacteria and viruses and makes water safe to drink. If you cannot filter water in this way, it should be treated chemically. Chlorine tablets will kill many pathogens, but not some parasites like giardia and amoebic cysts. Iodine is more effective than chlorine at purifying water and is available in tablet form. Follow the directions carefully and remember that too much iodine can be harmful.

Medical Problems & Treatment

Self-diagnosis and treatment can be risky, so you should always seek medical help. Although there are drug dosages in this section, they are for emergency use only. Correct diagnosis is vital. An embassy, consulate or five-star hotel can usually recommend a local doctor or clinic.

In Thailand medicine is generally available over the counter and the price will be much cheaper than in the West. However, be careful when buying drugs, particularly where the expiry date may have passed or correct storage conditions may not have been followed.

Antibiotics should ideally be administered only under medical supervision. Take only the recommended dose at the prescribed intervals and use the whole course, even if the illness seems to be cured earlier. Stop immediately if there are any serious reactions and don't use the antibiotic at all if you are unsure that you have the correct one. Some people are allergic to commonly prescribed antibiotics such as penicillin; carry this information (eg, on a bracelet) when travelling.

Hospitals & Clinics

Thailand's most technically advanced hospitals are in Bangkok. In the north, Chiang Mai has the best medical care; in the northeast it's Udon Thani; and in the south it's Hat Yai and Phuket. Elsewhere in the country, every provincial capital has at least one hospital (of varying quality) as well as several public and private clinics. The best emergency health care can usually be found at military hospitals *(rohng pháyaabaan tháhăan)*; they will usually treat foreigners in an emergency.

See information on local medical services for further information on specific hospitals, clinics and other health-care facilities.

Environmental Hazards

Air Pollution Pollution is something you'll become very aware of in Thailand, especially in Bangkok, where heat, dust and motor fumes combine to form a powerful brew of potentially toxic air. Air pollution can be a health hazard, especially if you suffer from lung diseases such as asthma. It can also aggravate coughs, colds and sinus problems and cause eye irritation or even infections. Consider avoiding badly polluted areas if you think they may jeopardise your health, especially if you have asthma, or invest in an air filter.

Heat Exhaustion Dehydration and salt deficiency can cause heat exhaustion. Take time to acclimatise to high temperatures, drink sufficient liquids and do not do anything too physically demanding.

Salt deficiency is characterised by fatigue, lethargy, headaches, giddiness and muscle cramps; salt tablets may help, but adding extra salt to your food is better.

Anhidrotic heat exhaustion is a rare form of heat exhaustion caused by an inability to sweat. It tends to affect people who have been in a hot climate for some time, rather than newcomers. It can progress to heatstroke. Treatment involves removal to a cooler climate.

Heatstroke This is a serious, occasionally fatal, condition that occurs when the body's heat-regulating mechanism breaks down and the body temperature rises to dangerous levels. Long, continuous periods of exposure to high temperatures and insufficient fluids can leave you vulnerable to heatstroke.

The symptoms are feeling unwell, not sweating very much (or at all) and a high body temperature (39° to 41°C, or 102° to 106°F). Where sweating has ceased, the skin becomes flushed and red. Severe, throbbing headaches and lack of coordination will also occur and the sufferer may be confused or aggressive. Eventually the victim will become delirious or convulse. Hospitalisation is essential, but in the interim get victims out of the sun; remove their clothing; cover them with a wet sheet or towel and then fan continually. Give fluids if they are conscious.

Prickly Heat This itchy rash is caused by excessive perspiration trapped under the skin. It usually strikes people who have just arrived in a hot climate. Keep cool, bathe often, dry the skin and use a mild talcum, and resort to an air-con environment all help.

Sunburn In the tropics you can get sunburnt surprisingly quickly, even through cloud cover. Use a sunscreen, a hat and a barrier cream for your nose and lips. Calamine lotion and aloe vera are good for mild sunburn. Protect your eyes with good-quality sunglasses, particularly if you're near water or sand.

Infectious Diseases

Diarrhoea Simple things like a change of water, food or climate can all cause a mild bout of diarrhoea, but a few rushed toilet trips with no other symptoms is not indicative of a major problem.

Dehydration is the main danger with any diarrhoea, particularly in children or the elderly, in whom dehydration can occur quite quickly. Under all circumstances *fluid replacement* (at least equal to the volume being lost) is the most important thing to remember. Weak black tea with a little sugar, soda water, or soft drinks allowed to go flat and diluted 50% with clean water are all good.

In the case of severe diarrhoea a rehydrating solution is preferable as it will replace the minerals and salts that have been lost. Commercially available oral rehydration salts (ORS) are very useful; add them to boiled or bottled water. In an emergency you can make up a solution of six teaspoons of sugar and a half teaspoon of salt to a litre of boiled or bottled water.

You need to drink at least the same volume of fluid that you are losing in bowel movements and vomiting. Urine is the best guide to the adequacy of replacement – if you have small amounts of concentrated urine, you need to drink more. Keep drinking small amounts often. Stick to a bland diet as you recover.

Gut-paralysing drugs such as loperamide diphenoxylate can be used to bring relief from the symptoms, although they do not actually cure the problem. Only use these drugs if you do not have access to toilets, eg, if you *must* travel. For children under 12 years old these drugs are not recommended.

Do not use these drugs if the person has a high fever or is severely dehydrated.

In certain situations antibiotics may be required: diarrhoea with blood or mucus (dysentery), any diarrhoea with fever, profuse watery diarrhoea, persistent diarrhoea not improving after 48 hours and severe diarrhoea. These suggest a more serious cause of diarrhoea and in these situations gut-paralysing drugs should be avoided.

In these situations, a stool test may be necessary to diagnose what bug is causing your diarrhoea, so you should seek medical help urgently. Where this is not possible the recommended drugs for bacterial diarrhoea (the most likely cause of severe diarrhoea in travellers) are norfloxacin (400mg twice daily for three days) or ciprofloxacin (500mg twice daily for five days). These are not recommended for children or pregnant women. The drug of choice for children would be co-trimoxazole, with the dosage dependent on the child's weight. A five-day course should be given. Ampicillin or amoxycillin may be given in pregnancy, but medical care is necessary.

Another cause of persistent diarrhoea in travellers in Thailand, although quite rare, is amoebic dysentery. Caused by the protozoan *Entamoeba histolytica*, amoebic dysentery is characterised by a gradual onset of low-grade diarrhoea, often with blood and mucus. Cramping, abdominal pain and vomiting are less likely than in other types of diarrhoea, and fever may not be present. Amoebic dysentery will persist until treated and can recur and cause other health problems.

You should seek medical advice, if you think you have amoebic dysentery, but where this is not possible, tinidazole (2g single dose) or metronidazole (250mg of metronidazole three times daily for five to 10 days) are the recommended drugs.

Fungal Infections These occur more commonly in hot weather and are usually found on the scalp, between the toes (athlete's foot) or fingers, in the groin and on the body (ringworm). You get ringworm (which is a fungal infection, not a worm) from infected animals or other people. Moisture encourages these infections.

To prevent fungal infections wear loose, comfortable clothes, avoid artificial fibres, wash frequently and dry yourself carefully. If you do get an infection, wash the infected area at least daily with a disinfectant or medicated soap and water, and rinse and dry well. Apply an antifungal cream or powder like tolnaftate. Try to expose the infected area to air or sunlight as much as possible and wash all towels and underwear in hot water, change them often and let them dry in the sun.

Hepatitis This is a general term for inflammation of the liver. It is a common disease worldwide. There are several different viruses that cause hepatitis, and they differ in the way that they are transmitted. The symptoms are similar in all forms of the illness, and include fever, chills, headache, fatigue, feelings of weakness and aches and pains, followed by loss of appetite, nausea, vomiting, abdominal pain, dark urine, light-coloured faeces, jaundiced (yellow) skin and yellowing of the whites of the eyes. People who have had hepatitis should avoid alcohol for some time after the illness, as the liver needs time to recover.

The most common form, hepatitis A, is transmitted by contaminated food and drinking water. You should seek medical advice, but there is not much you can do apart from resting, drinking lots of fluids, eating lightly and avoiding fatty foods. Hepatitis E is transmitted in the same way as hepatitis A; it can be particularly serious in pregnant women.

There are almost 300 million chronic carriers of hepatitis B in the world. It is spread through contact with infected blood, blood products or body fluids, for example through sexual contact, unsterilised needles and blood transfusions, or contact with blood via small breaks in the skin. Other risk situations include having a shave, tattoo or body piercing with contaminated equipment. The symptoms of hepatitis B may be more severe than type A and the disease can lead to long-term problems such as chronic liver damage, liver cancer or a long-term carrier state. Hepatitis C and D are spread in the same way as hepatitis B and can also lead to long-term complications.

There are vaccines against hepatitis A and B, but there are currently none against the other types of hepatitis. Following the basic rules about food and water (hepatitis A and E) and avoiding risk situations (hepatitis

B, C and D) are very important preventative measures.

HIV & AIDS Infection with the human immunodeficiency virus (HIV) may lead to acquired immune deficiency syndrome (AIDS), which is a fatal disease. Any exposure to blood, blood products or body fluids may put the individual at risk. The disease is often transmitted through sexual contact or dirty needles – tattooing, vaccinations, acupuncture and body piercing can potentially be as dangerous as intravenous drug use, if the equipment is not clean.

In Thailand transmission is predominantly through heterosexual sexual activity (over 80%). The second most common source of HIV infection comes from drug users sharing needles (about 6%).

HIV/AIDS can also be spread through infected blood transfusions, although this risk is virtually nil in Thailand due to vigorous blood-screening procedures.

If you do need an injection, ask to see the syringe being unwrapped in front of you, or take a needle and syringe pack with you.

Intestinal Worms These parasites are most common in rural areas. Different worms have different ways of infecting people. Some may be ingested in food such as undercooked meat (eg, tapeworms) and some enter through your skin (hookworms). Infestations may not show up for some time. Although they are generally not serious, if they're left untreated some can cause severe health problems later. Consider having a stool test when you return home to check for these and determine the appropriate treatment.

Opisthorchiasis Southeast Asian liver flukes *(Opisthorchis viverrini,* in Thai *pháyâat bai mái)* are occasionally present in freshwater fish and when ingested can cause a liver condition known as opisthorchiasis. The main risk comes from eating raw or undercooked fish. In particular travellers should avoid eating *plaa ráa* (sometimes called *paa daek* in northeastern Thailand), an unpasteurised fermented fish used as an accompaniment for rice in the northeast. *Plaa ráa* is not commonly served in restaurants, but is common in rural areas of the northeast, where it's considered a great delicacy. The Thai government is currently trying to discourage northeasterners from eating *plaa ráa* and other uncooked fish products.

The intensity of symptoms depends very much on how many of the flukes get into your body. At low levels, there are virtually no symptoms at all; at higher levels, general fatigue, a low-grade fever and swollen or tender liver (or general abdominal pain) are the usual symptoms, along with worms or worm eggs in the faeces. People suspected of having liver flukes should have a stool sample analysed by a doctor or clinic. The usual medication is 25mg per kilogram of body weight of praziquantel three times daily after meals for two days.

Schistosomiasis Also known as bilharzia, this disease is transmitted by minute worms *(Schistosoma mekongi,* in Thai *pháyâat bai mái).* They infect certain varieties of freshwater snails found in rivers, streams, lakes and particularly behind dams. The worms multiply and are eventually discharged into the water.

The worm enters through the skin and attaches itself to your intestines or bladder. The first symptom may be a general feeling of being unwell, or a tingling and sometimes a light rash around the area where it entered. Weeks later a high fever may develop. Once the disease is established abdominal pain and blood in the urine are other signs. The infection often causes no symptoms until the disease is well established (several months to years after exposure) and damage to internal organs irreversible.

The overall risk of this disease is quite low, but it's highest in the southern reaches of the Mekong River and in the lakes of northeastern Thailand – avoid swimming and bathing in these waterways.

These flukes are endemic to villages around Sakon Nakhon Province's Nong Han, the largest natural lake in Thailand. Don't swim in this lake! A less common way to contract liver flukes is through swimming in rivers. The only other known contaminated area is in the southern reaches of the Mekong River.

A blood test is a reliable way to diagnose bilharzia, but the test will not show positive until a number of weeks after exposure. Treatment is the same as for intestinal worms, see above.

Sexually Transmitted Infections (STIs)

HIV/AIDS and hepatitis B can be transmitted through sexual contact – see the relevant sections earlier for more details. Other STIs include gonorrhoea, herpes and syphilis; sores, blisters or rashes around the genitals and discharges or pain when urinating are common symptoms. In some STIs, such as wart virus and chlamydia, symptoms may be less marked or not observed at all, especially in women. Syphilis symptoms eventually disappear completely but the disease continues and can cause severe problems in later years. Gonorrhoea and syphilis are treated with antibiotics. Different sexually transmitted infections each require specific antibiotics.

While abstinence from sexual contact is the only 100% effective prevention, using condoms *(thǔng yaang ànaamai)* is also effective. Good-quality latex condoms are distributed free by offices of the Ministry of Public Health (MPH) throughout the country; one of the better commercial brands available in Thailand is Durex.

Insect-Borne Diseases

Malaria This serious and potentially fatal disease is spread by mosquito bites. Malaria risk exists throughout the year in rural Thailand, especially in forested and hilly areas. Thailand's high-risk areas include northern Kanchanaburi Province (especially Thung Yai Naresuan National Park) and parts of Trat Province along the Cambodian border (including Ko Chang).

According to the US Centers for Disease Control (CDC) and Thailand's Ministry of Public Health, there's virtually no risk of malaria in urban areas or in other main tourist areas (eg, Bangkok, Phuket, Pattaya and Chiang Mai).

If you are travelling in endemic areas it is extremely important to avoid mosquito bites and to take tablets to prevent the onset of this disease. Symptoms range from fever, chills and sweating, headache, diarrhoea and abdominal pains to a vague feeling of ill-health. Seek medical help immediately if malaria is suspected. Without treatment malaria can rapidly become more serious and can be fatal.

Every medical clinic or hospital in Thailand can easily test for malaria and treat the disease. If for some reason medical care is not available, certain malaria tablets can be used for treatment. If you took antimalarial tablets before contracting malaria, you'll need to use a different malaria tablet for treatment as obviously the first one didn't work.

Travellers are advised to prevent mosquito bites at all times. The main messages are:

- Wear light-coloured clothing
- Wear long trousers and long-sleeved shirts
- Use mosquito repellents containing the compound DEET on exposed areas (prolonged overuse of DEET may be harmful, especially to children, but its use is considered preferable to being bitten by disease-transmitting mosquitoes)
- Avoid perfumes or aftershave
- Use a mosquito net impregnated with mosquito repellent (permethrin) – it may be worth taking your own
- Impregnate clothes with permethrin, which effectively deters mosquitoes and other insects

Dengue Fever This viral disease is transmitted by mosquitoes and is fast becoming one of the top public-health problems in the tropical world. In Thailand there is only a small risk to travellers except during epidemics, which are usually seasonal (during and just after the rainy season).

Signs and symptoms of dengue fever include a sudden onset of high fever, headache, joint and muscle pains (hence its old name, 'breakbone fever') and nausea and vomiting. A rash of small red spots appears three to four days after the onset of fever. Dengue is commonly mistaken for other infectious diseases, including influenza.

Minor bleeding such as nose bleeds may occur in the course of the illness, but this does not necessarily mean that you have progressed to the potentially fatal dengue haemorrhagic fever (DHF). This is a severe illness, characterised by heavy bleeding, which is thought to be a result of a second infection due to a different strain (there are four major strains) and usually affects residents of the country rather than travellers. Recovery even from simple dengue fever may be prolonged, with tiredness lasting for several weeks.

You should seek medical attention as soon as possible if you think you may be infected. A blood test can exclude malaria and indicate the possibility of dengue fever. There is no specific treatment for dengue.

Aspirin should be avoided, as it increases the risk of haemorrhaging. There is no vaccine against dengue fever. The *Aedes aegypti* mosquito, which transmits the dengue virus, is most active during the day, unlike the malaria mosquito, and is found mainly in urban areas in and around human dwellings. The best prevention is to avoid mosquito bites by covering up, using insect repellents containing the compound DEET and mosquito nets.

In 2000 Thailand's Mahidol University announced the development of a vaccine for all serotypes of dengue. The new vaccine began human trials late that year, and if successful the vaccine could be available by 2004.

Japanese B Encephalitis Mosquitoes transmit this viral infection of the brain. Most cases occur in rural areas as the virus exists in pigs and wading birds. Symptoms include fever, headache and alteration in consciousness. Hospitalisation is needed for correct diagnosis and treatment. There is a high mortality rate among those who have symptoms; of those who survive, many are intellectually disabled.

Cuts, Bites & Stings

Cuts & Scratches Wash well and treat any cut with an antiseptic such as povidone-iodine. Where possible avoid bandages and Band-Aids, which can keep wounds wet. Coral cuts are notoriously slow to heal and if they are not adequately cleaned, small pieces of coral can become embedded in the wound.

Bedbugs & Lice Bedbugs live in various places, but particularly in dirty mattresses and bedding, evidenced by spots of blood on bedclothes or on the wall. Bedbugs leave itchy bites in neat rows. Calamine lotion or a sting-relief spray may help.

All lice cause itching and discomfort. They make themselves at home in your hair (head lice), clothing (body lice) or pubic hair (crabs). You catch lice through direct contact with infected people or by sharing combs, clothing and the like. Treatment (powder, gel or shampoo depending on the type) will kill the lice and infected clothing should then be washed in very hot, soapy water and left in the sun to dry.

Bites & Stings Bee and wasp stings are usually painful rather than dangerous. Calamine lotion or a sting-relief spray are good and ice packs will reduce the pain and swelling. However, in people who are allergic to stings, severe breathing difficulties may occur and require urgent medical care.

There are some spiders with dangerous bites but antivenins are usually available in local hospitals. Scorpions often shelter in shoes or clothing, and their stings are notoriously painful. No varieties in Thailand carry fatal venom.

There are various fish and other sea creatures whose sting or bite are dangerous, or that are dangerous to eat – be sure to seek local advice.

Jellyfish Avoid any contact with these sea creatures, which have stinging tentacles – seek local advice. Dousing in vinegar will deactivate any stingers that have not 'fired'. Calamine lotion, antihistamines and analgesics may reduce the reaction and relieve the pain.

Leeches These may be present in damp forest conditions in Thailand; they attach themselves to your skin to suck your blood. Trekkers often get them on their legs or in their boots. Salt or a lighted cigarette end will make them fall off and an insect repellent may keep them away. Do not pull them off, as the bite is then more likely to become infected. Clean and apply pressure if the point of attachment is bleeding.

Snakes To minimise your chances of being bitten always wear boots, socks and long trousers when walking through undergrowth where snakes may be present. Don't put your hands into holes and crevices, and be careful when collecting firewood.

Snake bites do not cause instantaneous death and antivenins are usually available. Immediately wrap the bitten limb tightly, as you would for a sprained ankle, and then attach a splint to immobilise it. Keep the victim still and seek medical help, if possible with the dead snake for identification. Don't attempt to catch the snake if there is a possibility of being bitten again. Tourniquets and sucking out the poison are now comprehensively discredited.

Snakebite antivenin is available at hospitals throughout Thailand as well as in pharmacies in larger towns and cities.

Less Common Diseases

The following diseases pose a small risk to travellers in Thailand, and so they are only mentioned here in passing. Be sure to seek medical advice if you think you may have any of these diseases.

Rabies This fatal viral infection is found in many countries, including Thailand. Many animals (eg, dogs, cats, bats and monkeys) can be infected and it is their saliva that is infectious. Any bite, scratch or even lick from an animal should be cleaned promptly and thoroughly. Scrub with soap and running water, and then apply alcohol or iodine solution. Seek medical help immediately to receive a course of injections.

Traditional Thai Medicine

In villages and rural areas many Thais still practise forms of traditional healing that were codified in Thailand over 500 years ago. Clinics and healers specialising in traditional Thai medicine can also be found in urban areas, although modern, international therapies tend to predominate in cities. Some Thai doctors offer a blend of international medicine and indigenous medical systems.

Traditional Thai medical theory features many parallels with India's Ayurvedic healing tradition as well as Chinese medicine. In practice, however, Thai diagnostic and therapeutic techniques may differ significantly.

Obviously influenced to some degree by these traditions, Thai medicine has in turn been the predominant influence on traditional medicine in Cambodia and Laos.

Most Thai medicine practised today is based on two surviving medical texts from the Ayuthaya era, the *Scripture of Diseases* and the *Pharmacopoeia* of King Narai. Presumably many more texts were available before the Burmese sacked Ayuthaya in 1767 and destroyed the kingdom's national archives. A coexisting oral tradition passed down from healer to healer conforms to the surviving texts; other *materia medica* developed in the Ratanakosin (or old Bangkok) era are founded on both these texts and the oral tradition.

Like medical practitioners elsewhere in the world, traditional Thai physicians perform diagnoses by evaluating the pulse, heartbeat, skin colour/texture, body temperature, abnormal physical symptoms and bodily excretions (eg, blood, urine, faeces) of their patients. Unlike orthodox Western doctors, Thai healers favour a holistic approach that encompasses external, internal and psycho-spiritual conditions. Thus, once diagnosed, patients may be prescribed and issued treatments from among three broad therapeutic categories.

Massage

The most internationally famous type of Thai medical therapy is *ráksăa thaang nûat* (massage treatment). The extensive and highly refined Thai massage system combines characteristics of massage (stroking and kneading the muscles), chiropractic (manipulating skeletal parts) and acupressure (applying deep, consistent pressure to specific nerves, tendons or ligaments) in order to balance the functions of the four body elements *(thâat tháng sìi)*. These four elements are earth (*din* – solid parts of the body, including skeleton, muscles, blood vessels, tendons and ligaments); water (*nám* – blood and bodily secretions); fire (*fai* – digestion and metabolism); and air (*lom* – respiration and circulation).

From the Ayuthaya period until the early 20th century, the Thai Ministry of Public Health included an official massage division *(phànàek mǎw nûat)*. Under the influence of international medicine and modern hospital development, responsibility for the national propagation and maintenance of Thai massage was eventually transferred to Wat Pho in Bangkok, where it remains today. Traditional massage therapy has persisted mostly in the provinces, however, and has enjoyed a resurgence of popularity throughout the country.

Within the traditional Thai medical context, a massage therapist (*mǎw nûat;* literally, massage doctor) usually applies Thai massage together with pharmacological and/or psycho-spiritual treatments as prescribed for a specific medical problem.

Typhus This disease is spread by ticks, mites or lice. It begins with fever, chills, headache and muscle pains, followed by a body rash a few days later. There is often a large painful sore at the site of the bite and nearby lymph nodes are swollen and painful. Typhus can be treated under medical supervision. Seek local advice on areas where ticks pose a danger and always check your skin carefully for ticks after walking in tropical forests. An insect repellent can help, and those walking in tick-infested areas should consider wearing boots and trousers impregnated with benzyl benzoate and dibutylphthalate.

WOMEN TRAVELLERS

Attitudes towards Women

In rural areas female family members typically inherit the land and throughout Thailand they tend to control the family finances.

Traditional Thai Medicine

Nowadays many Thais also use massage as a tool for relaxation and disease prevention, rather than just for specific medical problems. Massage associated with Bangkok's Turkish baths *(àap òp nûat)* is for the most part performed for recreational or entertainment purposes only (or as an adjunct to prostitution); the techniques used are loosely based on traditional Thai massage.

For problems affecting the nerves rather than the muscular or skeletal structures, many Thais resort to *nûat jàp sên* (nerve-touch massage), a Chinese-style massage technique that works with the body's nerve meridians, much like acupuncture.

Herbal Medicines

Traditional pharmacological therapy employs prescribed herbs from among 700 plant varieties (plus a limited number of animal sources), which are infused, boiled, powdered or otherwise rendered into a consumable form. Common household medicines *(yaa klaang bâan)* include the root and stem of *bawráphét* (*Tinospora rumphii,* a type of wood climber) for fever reduction; *râak cháa-phluu* (Piper roots) for stomach ailments; and various *yaa hǎwm* (fragrant medicines) used as balms for muscle pain or headaches. These medicines are readily available over the counter at traditional medicine shops and, to a lesser extent, in modern Thai pharmacies.

More complex remedies called *yaa tamráp lŭang* (royally approved medicine) are prepared and administered only by herbalists skilled in diagnosis, as the mixture and dosage must be adjusted for each patient. One of the most well known is *chanthá-liilaa*, a powerful remedy for respiratory infections and influenza-induced fevers.

As in the Chinese tradition, many Thai herbs find their way into regional cuisine with the intent of enhancing health as well as taste. *Phrík thai* (black pepper; *Piper nigrum*), *bai kà-phrao* (holy basil) and *bai maeng lák* (a variety of basil) are common curry ingredients that have proven antacid and carminative (antiflatulent) properties. Thais eat soups containing *mará* (bitter melon) – a known febrifuge – to bring down a fever.

Psycho-Spiritual Healing

A third aspect of traditional Thai medicine called *ráksăa thaang nai* (inner healing) or *kâe kam kào* (literally, 'old karma repair') includes various types of meditation or visualisation practised by the patient, as well as shamanistic rituals performed by qualified healers. These strategies represent the psycho-spiritual side of Thai medical therapy, and like massage are usually practised along with other types of treatment. With the increasing acceptance of meditation, hypnosis and biofeedback in international medicine, anthropologists nowadays are less inclined to classify such metaphysical therapy as 'magico-religious', accepting them instead as potentially useful adjunct therapies.

Psycho-spiritual techniques are most commonly reserved for medical conditions with no apparent physical cause or for which other therapies have proved unsuccessful. They are also occasionally used as preventive measures, as in the *bai sĭi* ceremony of northeastern Thailand and Laos. This ceremony, marked by the tying of string loops around a subject's wrists, is intended to bind the 32 *khwăn* or personal guardian spirits – each associated with a specific organ – to the individual. The ritual is often performed before a person departs on a major journey.

Women constitute 55% of all enrolments in secondary and tertiary schools and about 45% of Thailand's workforce, outranking both China and the USA in both categories. In fields such as economics, academia and health services, women hold a majority of the administrative positions; 80% of the country's dentists, for example, are female.

So much for the good news. The bad news is that although women generally fare well in education, the labour force and in rural land inheritance, their cultural standing is a bit less than that of men. An oft-repeated Thai saying reminds us that men form the front legs of the elephant, women the hind legs (at least they're pulling equal weight). Parts of some Buddhist temples may be off-limits to women, and when hanging laundry, the custom is always to place female underwear lower than men's!

Safety Precautions

Around 40% of all foreign visitors to Thailand are women, a ratio higher than the worldwide average and ahead of most other Asian countries. This ratio continues to grow, with the overall increase for women visitors climbing faster than that for men every year since 1993.

Everyday incidents of sexual harassment are much less common in Thailand than in India, Indonesia or Malaysia and this may give a false sense of security. Over the past decade, several foreign women have been attacked while travelling alone in remote areas, and in 2000 a British woman was murdered at a guesthouse in Chiang Mai. Such incidents, however, are extremely rare.

If you're a woman travelling alone, try to pair up with other travellers when travelling at night or in remote areas. Make sure hotel and guesthouse rooms are secure at night – if they're not, demand another room or move to another hotel or guesthouse.

When in the company of single Thai males, do keep an eye on your food and drink. We've received a couple of reports from women who alleged they had been drugged and raped by Thai trekking guides in Chiang Mai.

See Dangers & Annoyances later in this chapter for more information and advice on safe travel.

GAY & LESBIAN TRAVELLERS

Thai culture is relatively tolerant of homosexuality, both male and female. The nation has no laws that discriminate against homosexuals and there is a fairly prominent gay and lesbian scene in Bangkok. With regard to dress or mannerism, lesbians and gays are generally accepted without comment. However public displays of affection – whether heterosexual or homosexual – are frowned upon.

According to Utopia gay and lesbian centre, 'Thai lesbians prefer to call themselves *tom* (for tomboy) or *dee* (for lady), as the term 'lesbian', in Thailand, suggests pornographic videos produced for straight men. *Tom* and *dee*, by contrast, are fairly accepted and integrated categories for Thai women, roughly corresponding to the Western terms 'butch' and 'femme'. The usual Thai role terms for men are *gay king* and *gay queen*.

Organisations & Publications

Utopia (*w www.utopia-asia.com*), once a gay and lesbian centre consisting of a guesthouse, bar, café and gallery, is now mostly a Web presence with lots of Thailand information. Utopia also runs Thailand tours (*☎ 0 2238 3227; Lobby, Tarntawan Place Hotel, Th Surawong*).

Anjaree Group (*☎/fax 0 2668 2185; w www.anjaree.org; PO Box 322, Ratchadamnoen, Bangkok 10200*), is Thailand's premier (and only) lesbian society. Anjaree sponsors various group activities and produces a Thai-only newsletter.

Gay men may be interested in the services of the **Long Yang Club** (*☎/fax 0 2679 7727; w www.longyangclub.com; PO Box 1077, Silom Post Office, Bangkok 10504*), a 'multicultural social group for male-oriented men who want to meet outside the gay scene', with branches in London, Amsterdam, Toronto, Canberra, Ottawa and Vancouver.

The 'Pink Page' of the monthly tourist rag *Guide to Bangkok* usually stays abreast of events. *Pink Ink* (w www.khsnet.com/pinkink), a Web-only publication by and for Bangkok's English-speaking gay and lesbian community, is another useful resource.

DISABLED TRAVELLERS

Thailand presents one large, ongoing obstacle course for the mobility impaired. With its high curbs, uneven sidewalks and non-stop traffic, Bangkok can be particularly difficult – many streets must be crossed via pedestrian bridges flanked with steep stairways, while buses and boats don't stop long enough for even the mildly disabled. Rarely are there any ramps or other access points for wheelchairs.

Hyatt International, Novotel, Sheraton, Holiday Inn and Westin are the only hotel chains we know of in the country that make consistent design efforts to provide disabled access for each of their properties. In other accommodation options you're pretty much left to your own resources, although in many cases hotel staff can help where architecture fails.

For wheelchair travellers, any trip to Thailand will require a good deal of advance planning; fortunately a growing network of information sources can put you in touch with those who have wheeled through Thailand before.

There is no better source of information than someone who's done it. A reader wrote with the following tips:

The difficulties you mention in your book are all there. However, travel in the streets is still possible, and enjoyable, providing you have a strong, ambulatory companion. Some obstacles may require two carriers; Thais are by nature helpful and could generally be counted on for assistance.

- Don't feel you have to rely on organised tours to see the sights – these often leave early mornings at times inconvenient to disabled people. It is far more convenient (and often cheaper) to take a taxi or hired car. It's also far more enjoyable as there is no feeling of holding others up.
- A *túk-túk* is far easier to get in and out of. It's better equipped to carry two people and a wheelchair than a taxi. Even the pedicabs can hang a wheelchair on the back of the carriage.
- Be ready to try anything – in spite of my worries, riding an elephant proved quite easy.

Organisations

Three international organisations with information on mobility-impaired travel are listed here.

Access Foundation (☎ 516-887 5798) PO Box 356, Malverne, NY 11565, USA

Mobility International USA (☎ 541-343 1284, ⓔ info@miusa.org, Ⓦ www.miusa.org) PO Box 10767, Eugene, OR 97440, USA

Society for the Advancement of Travelers with Handicaps (SATH; ☎ 212-447 7284, ⓔ sathtravel@aol.com, Ⓦ www.sath.org) 347 Fifth Ave, Suite 610, New York, NY 11242, USA

The book *Exotic Destinations for Wheelchair Travelers* by Ed Hansen & Bruce Gordon (Full Data, San Francisco) contains a useful chapter on seven locations in Thailand. Others books of value include *Holidays and Travel Abroad – A Guide for Disabled People* (Radar, London) and *Able to Travel* (Rough Guides, London, New York).

Accessible Journeys (*☎ 610-521 0339; Ⓦ www.disabilitytravel.com; 35 West Sellers Ave, Ridley Park, Pennsylvania, USA*), specialises in organising group travel for the mobility impaired. Occasionally the agency offers Thailand trips.

SENIOR TRAVELLERS

Seniors discounts aren't generally available, but the Thais more than make up for this with the respect they show for the elderly. In Thai culture status comes with age; there isn't as heavy an emphasis on youth as there is in the Western world. Deference for age manifests itself in the way Thais will go out of their way to help older people in and out of taxis or with luggage, and – usually but not always – in serving them first in shops and post offices.

Nonetheless, some cultural spheres are for the young. In particular, cross-generational entertainment is less common than in Western countries. There is a strict stratification among discos and nightclubs, for example, according to age group. One place will cater to teenagers, another to people in their early 20s, one for late 20s and 30s, yet another for those in their 40s and 50s, and once you've reached 60 you're considered too old to go clubbing! An exception to this rule is entertainment at the more traditional venues, such as *wát* (temple) fairs and events, at which young and old will dance and eat together.

TRAVEL WITH CHILDREN

Like many places in Southeast Asia, travelling with children in Thailand can be a lot of fun as long as you come well prepared with the right attitude, equipment and the usual parental patience. Lonely Planet's *Travel with Children* by Cathy Lanigan contains useful advice on how to cope with kids on the road and what to bring along to make things go more smoothly, with special attention paid to travel in developing countries.

Thais love children and in many instances will shower attention on your offspring, who will find ready playmates among their Thai counterparts and a temporary nanny service at practically every stop.

For the most part parents needn't worry too much about health concerns, although it pays to lay down a few ground rules (such as regular hand washing) to head off potential medical problems. Children especially should be warned not to play with animals as rabies is relatively common in Thailand. All the usual health precautions apply (see the Health section earlier for details).

DANGERS & ANNOYANCES

Although Thailand is in no way a dangerous country to visit, it's always wise to be a little cautious, particularly if you're travelling alone. Solo travellers should take special care on arrival at Bangkok International Airport, particularly at night. Only take taxis from the airport's Public Taxi Queue or take the public bus.

All travelers should ensure their rooms are securely locked and bolted at night. Inspect cheap rooms with thin walls in case there are strategic peepholes.

Take caution when leaving valuables in hotel safes. Many travellers have reported unpleasant experiences leaving valuables in Chiang Mai guesthouses while trekking. Make sure you obtain an itemised receipt for property left with hotels or guesthouses – note the exact quantity of travellers cheques and all other valuables.

When you're on the road, keep zippered luggage secured with small locks, especially

Scams

Thais can be so friendly and laid-back that some visitors are lulled into a false sense of security that makes them vulnerable to scams of all kinds. Scammers tend to haunt the areas where first-time tourists go, such as Bangkok's Grand Palace and Wat Pho area. Though you could come across them anywhere in Thailand, the overwhelming majority of scams take place in Bangkok, with Chiang Mai a very distant second.

Most scams begin the same way: a friendly Thai male (or, on rare occasions, a female) approaches a lone visitor – usually newly arrived – and strikes up a conversation. Sometimes the con man says he's a university student, other times he may claim to work for the World Bank or a similarly distinguished organisation (some even carry cellular phones). If you're on the way to Wat Pho or Jim Thompson's House, for example, he may tell you it's closed for a holiday. Eventually the conversation works its way around to the subject of the scam – the better con artists can actually make it seem like you initiated the topic.

The most common scam involves gems. The victims find themselves invited to a gem and jewellery shop – your new-found friend is picking up some merchandise for himself and you're just along for the ride. Somewhere along the way he usually claims to have a connection, often a relative, in your home country (what a coincidence!) with whom he has a regular gem export-import business. One way or another, victims are convinced (usually they convince themselves) that they can turn a profit by arranging a gem purchase and reselling the merchandise at home. After all, the jewellery shop just happens to be offering a generous discount today – it's a government or religious holiday, or perhaps it's the shop's 10th anniversary, or maybe they've just taken a liking to you!

There is a seemingly infinite number of variations on the gem scam, almost all of which end up with the victim making a purchase of small, low-quality sapphires and posting them to their home countries. Once you return home, of course, the cheap sapphires turn out to be worth much less than you paid for them (perhaps one-tenth to one-half).

Many have invested and lost virtually all their savings; some admit they had been scammed even after reading warnings in this guidebook or those posted by the Tourism Authority of Thailand (TAT) around Bangkok.

Even if you were somehow able to return your purchase to the gem shop in question, chances are slim-to-none they'd give a full refund. The con artist who brings the mark into the shop gets a commission of 10% to 50% per sale – the shop takes the rest.

while travelling on buses and trains. Several readers' letters have recounted tales of thefts from their bags or backpacks during long overnight bus trips, particularly on routes between Bangkok and Chiang Mai or Ko Samui.

Credit Cards

On return to their home countries, some visitors have received huge credit-card bills for purchases (usually jewellery) charged to their cards in Bangkok while the cards had, supposedly, been secure in the hotel or guesthouse safe. You might consider taking your credit cards with you if you go trekking – if the cards are stolen on the trail at least the bandits aren't likely to be able to use them. There are organised gangs in Bangkok specialising in arranging stolen credit-card purchases – and in some cases these gangs pay dodgy foreigners to fake the signatures on the credit cards.

When making credit-card purchases, don't let vendors take your credit card out of your sight to run it through the machine. Unscrupulous merchants have been known to rub off three or four or more receipts with one purchase: after the customer leaves the shop, they use the one legitimate receipt as a model to forge your signature on the blanks, then fill in astronomical 'purchases'. Sometimes they wait several weeks – even months – between submitting each charge receipt to the bank, so that you can't remember whether you'd been billed at the same vendor more than once.

Drugging

In bars and on trains and buses beware of friendly strangers offering gifts such as

Scams

The Thai police are usually no help whatsoever, believing that merchants are entitled to whatever price they can get. The main victimisers are a handful of shops who get protection from certain high-ranking government officials. These officials put pressure on police not to prosecute or to take as little action as possible. Even TAT's tourist police have never been able to prosecute a Thai jeweller, even in cases of blatant, recurring gem fraud. (For information on initiatives to protect consumers, see Jewellery in the Shopping section later in this chapter).

Card games are another way to separate suckers from their money. A friendly stranger approaches the lone traveller on the street, strikes up a conversation and then invites them to the house or apartment of his sister (or brother-in-law etc) for a drink or meal. After a bit of socialising a friend or relative of the con arrives on the scene; it just so happens a little high-stakes card game is planned for later that day. Like the gem scam, the card-game scam has many variations, but eventually the victim is shown some cheating tactics to use with help from the 'dealer', some practice sessions take place and finally the game gets under way with several high rollers at the table. The mark is allowed to win a few hands first, then somehow loses a few, gets bankrolled by one of the friendly Thais, and then loses the Thai's money. Suddenly your new-found buddies aren't so friendly any more – they want the money you lost. Sometimes the con pretends to be dismayed by it all. Sooner or later you end up cashing in most or all of your travellers cheques or making a costly visit to an ATM. Again the police won't take any action because gambling is illegal in Thailand – you've actually broken the law.

Other minor scams involve *túk-túk* drivers, hotel employees and bar girls who take new arrivals on city tours; these almost always end up in high-pressure sales situations at silk, jewellery or handicraft shops. In this case the victim's greed isn't the ruling motivation – it's simply a matter of weak sales resistance.

Follow TAT's number-one suggestion to tourists: Disregard all offers of free shopping or sightseeing help from strangers – they invariably take a commission from your purchases. We would add: beware of deals that seem too good to be true – they're usually neither good nor true. You might also try lying whenever a stranger asks how long you've been in Thailand – if it's only been three days, say three weeks! Or save your Bangkok sightseeing until after you've been up north. The con artists rarely prey on anyone except new arrivals.

Contact the **Tourist Police** (*☎ 1155, 0 2255 2964; 29/1 Soi Lang Suan, Th Ploenchit, Bangkok*) if you have any problems with consumer fraud.

cigarettes, drinks, cookies or sweets (candy). Several travellers have reported waking up sometime later with a headache, only to find that their valuables have disappeared.

Male travellers have also encountered drugged food or drink from friendly Thai women in bars and from prostitutes in their own hotel rooms. Female visitors have encountered the same with young Thai men, albeit less frequently. Conclusion: don't accept gifts from strangers.

Assault

Robbery of travellers by force is very rare in Thailand, but it does happen. Isolated incidences of armed robbery have tended to occur along the Thai-Myanmar and Thai-Cambodian borders and on remote islands. In February 2000, armed bandits robbed an Australian couple camping illegally in Doi Ang Khang National Park, near the Myanmar border. The couple tried to resist and, during the ensuing scuffle, one of them was shot and killed.

The safest practice in remote areas is not to go out alone at night and, if trekking in northern Thailand, always walk in groups.

Touts

Touting (grabbing newcomers in the street or in train stations, bus terminals or airports to sell them a service) is a longtime tradition in Asia, and while Thailand doesn't have as many touts as, say, India, it has its share. In the popular tourist spots it seems like everyone – young boys waving fliers, túk-túk drivers, *săamláw* (three-wheeled vehicle) drivers, schoolgirls – is touting something, usually hotels or guesthouses. For the most part they're completely harmless and sometimes they can be very informative. But take anything a tout says with two large grains of salt. Since touts work on commission and get paid just for delivering you to a guesthouse or hotel (whether you check in or not), they'll say anything to get you to the door.

Often the better (most honest and reliable) hotels and guesthouses refuse to pay tout commissions – so the average tout will try to steer you away from such places. Hence don't believe them if they tell you the hotel or guesthouse you're looking for is closed, full, dirty or 'bad'. Sometimes (rarely) they're right but most times it's just a ruse to get you to a place that pays more commission.

Always have a look yourself before checking into a place recommended by a tout. Túk-túk and săamláw drivers often offer free or low-cost rides to the place they're touting. If you have another place you're interested in, you might agree to go with a driver only if he or she promises to deliver you to your first choice after you've had a look at the place being touted. If drivers refuse, chances are it's because they know your first choice is a better one.

This type of commission work isn't limited to low-budget guesthouses. Travel agents at Bangkok International Airport and Hualamphong railway station are notorious for talking newly arrived tourists into staying at badly located, overpriced hotels.

However one reader had this to say on the subject of touts:

> After reading your book's general chapters I was expecting a much worse situation. Compared to travelling in countries like Morocco, Tunisia, Turkey etc, I think travelling in Thailand is relatively easy and hassle-free. When people in Thailand tout something usually saying 'No' once – or twice – persuades them that you are not interested. In some countries you have to invest much more energy to get rid of people trying to sell.

Bus Touts Watch out for touts wearing (presumably fake) TAT or tourist information badges at Hualamphong train station. They have been known to coerce travellers into buying tickets for private bus rides, saying the train is 'full' or 'takes too long'. Often the promised bus service turns out to be substandard and may take longer than the equivalent train ride due to the frequent changing of vehicles. You may be offered a 24-seat VIP 'sleeper' bus to Chiang Mai, for example, and end up stuffed into a minivan all the way. Such touts are 'bounty hunters' who receive a set fee for every tourist they deliver to the bus companies. Avoid the travel agencies (many of which bear 'TAT' or even 'Lonely Planet' signs) just outside the train station for the same reason.

Border Areas

A little extra caution should be exercised along Thailand's borders with Myanmar and Malaysia. The Myanmar border between

Um Phang and Mae Sariang occasionally receives shelling from Burmese troops in pursuit of Karen or Mon rebels. Karen rebels are trying to maintain an independent nation called Kawthoolei along the border with Thailand. The risks of catching a piece of shrapnel are substantially lower if you keep several kilometres between yourself and the Thai-Myanmar border in this area – fighting can break out at any time. Mae Sot itself is quite safe these days, although you can still occasionally hear mortar fire in the distance.

The presence of Shan and Wa armies along the Myanmar-Thai border in northern Mae Hong Son makes this area dangerous if you attempt to travel near amphetamine- and opium-trade border crossings; obviously these are not signposted, so take care anywhere along the border in this area. As many as 8000 Shan fighters, split among four armies, are still active in the area bordering Mae Sai south to Mae Hong Son.

There is also the potential for hostilities breaking out between Myanmar government troops and the Thai army over a disputed Thai-Myanmar border section near Doi Lang, southwest of Mae Sai in Mae Ai district. The territory under dispute amounts to 32 sq km; at the moment the two sides are trying to work things out peaceably according to the 1894 Siam-Britain Treaty, which both countries recognise. The problem is that British mapping at that time made geographical naming errors that unintentionally seemed to favour the Burmese side. It is likely that Burmese and Thai troops will remain poised for action on either side of the border until the matter is resolved.

Four of Thailand's southernmost provinces (Songkhla, Yala, Pattani and Narathiwat) go through hot and cold periods that involve the Pattani United Liberation Organisation (PULO), a small armed group allegedly dedicated to forming a separate Muslim state. The PULO is known to receive support from the Kumpulan Mujahideen Malaysia (KMM), a radical Islamic group in Malaysia.

In 2002 a series of 13 attacks or bombings took place in these provinces, primarily in Pattani and Songkhla. Most attacks were on military posts or police posts. The Thai government claims such incidents were motivated by banditry or gang rivalry, since no group stepped forward to take credit.

Following the bombing of Bali nightclubs in 2002, the Thai government tightened security and immigration at all its borders and international airports.

Drugs

Opium, heroin, amphetamines, hallucinogens and marijuana are widely used in Thailand, but it is illegal to buy, sell or possess these drugs in any quantity. The possession of opium for consumption, but not sale, is legal among hill tribes.

In the south, especially on the rainy islands in the Gulf of Thailand, magic mushrooms (*hèt khîi khwai,* 'buffalo-shit mushrooms', or *hèt mao,* 'drunk mushrooms'), which contain the hallucinogen psilocybin, are sometimes sold to or gathered by foreigners. Usie or possession of such mushrooms is now illegal and a risky proposition as well, as the dosage is always uncertain. We've heard confirmed stories of a foreigner who swam to his death off Ko Pha-Ngan after a 'special' mushroom omelette, and there have been other confirmed casualties as well. If you must indulge, watch the dosage carefully.

Bai kràthâwm (a leaf of the *Mitragyna speciosa* tree), was once used by workers and students as a natural stimulant, but after it was criminalised in 1943, both groups turned to amphetamines.

Yaa bâa (literally 'crazy drug'), or amphetamine tablets, are imported in large quantities from Wa-controlled areas of northeastern Myanmar and sold inexpensively in Thailand. The quality is low and dosages erratic. This is another illegal drug to be extremely careful of. The Thai Senate is considering legalising *bai krathâwm* to combat amphetamine abuse.

The enforcement of Thai drug laws is arbitrary – the only way not to risk getting caught is to avoid the drug scene entirely. Every year perhaps dozens of visiting foreigners are arrested in Thailand for drug use or trafficking and end up doing time in Thai prisons. A smaller but significant number die of heroin overdoses.

Ko Pha-Ngan is one of Thailand's leading centres for recreational drug use, and the Thai police have begun to take notice there as well. Particularly on days leading up to Hat Rin's famous monthly full-moon rave, police often set up inspection points on the road between Thong Sala and Hat Rin. Every vehicle, including bicycles and motorcycles, is stopped and the passengers and vehicles thoroughly searched.

The legal penalties for drug offences are stiff: if you're caught using marijuana, mushrooms or LSD, you face a fine of 10,000B plus one year in prison, while for heroin or amphetamines, the penalty for use can be anywhere from six months' to 10 years' imprisonment, plus a fine of 5000B to 10,000B. The going rate for bribing one's way out of a small pot bust is 50,000B.

Drug smuggling – defined as attempting to cross a border with drugs in your possession – carries considerably higher penalties, including execution.

LEGAL MATTERS

In general Thai police don't hassle foreigners, especially tourists. If anything they generally go out of their way not to arrest a foreigner breaking minor traffic laws, instead taking the approach that a friendly warning will suffice.

One major exception is drugs, which most Thai police view as either a social scourge against which it's their duty to enforce the letter of the law, or an opportunity to make untaxed income via bribes. Small-time offenders are sometimes offered the chance to pay their way out of an arrest, while traffickers usually go to jail.

If you are arrested for any offence, the police will allow you the opportunity to make a phone call to your embassy or consulate in Thailand, if you have one, or to a friend or relative if not. There's a whole set of legal codes governing the length of time and manner in which you can be detained before being charged or put on trial, but a lot of discretion is left to the police. In the case of foreigners the police are more likely to bend these codes in your favour. However, as with police worldwide, if you don't show respect you will make matters worse.

Thai law does not presume an indicted detainee to be either 'guilty' or 'innocent' but rather a 'suspect', whose guilt or innocence will be decided in court. Trials are usually speedy.

Tourist Police Hotline

The tourist police can also be very helpful in cases of arrest. Although they typically have no jurisdiction over the kinds of cases handled by regular cops, they may be able to help with translation or with contacting your embassy.

The best way to deal with most serious hassles regarding ripoffs or thefts is to contact the tourist police, who are used to dealing with foreigners, rather than the regular Thai police. The tourist police maintain a hotline – dial ☎ 1155 from any phone in Thailand. You can call this number 24 hours a day to lodge complaints or to request assistance with regards to personal safety. You can also call this number between 8.30am and 4.30pm daily to request travel information.

Visiting Someone in Prison

If you know someone serving a prison sentence in Bangkok or elsewhere, and would like to visit that person, the normal procedure is to visit the prisoner's Bangkok embassy first. Tell the consular staff the name of the prisoner you would like to visit, and ask to receive a letter from the embassy requesting you be permitted to see that prisoner. The embassy can also provide directions to the prison where the person is being held and let you know what the visiting hours are. Ordinarily there are only a couple of days a week when you are permitted to visit. For the latest information on visitation policies, contact your embassy in Bangkok.

Over the last couple of years visiting imprisoned foreigners in Bangkok has become something of a fad. Note that the Thai corrections system does not accept the Western notion that prisoners should receive random visitors. Some prisoners, likewise, don't like being viewed as an 'animal in a cage', as one prisoner recently lamented in *Farang* magazine.

BUSINESS HOURS

Most government offices are open from 8.30am to 4.30pm weekdays, but often close from noon to 1pm for lunch. Businesses usually operate between 8.30am and 5pm weekdays and sometimes on Saturday morning. Larger shops usually open from 10am to 6.30pm or 7pm but smaller shops may open earlier and close later.

Note that all government offices and banks are closed on public holidays.

PUBLIC HOLIDAYS & SPECIAL EVENTS

The number and frequency of festivals and fairs in Thailand is incredible – there always seems to be something going on, especially during the cool season between November and February.

The exact dates for festivals may vary from year to year, either because of the lunar calendar, which isn't quite in sync with the solar calendar – or because local authorities have decided to change festival dates. The TAT (see Tourist Offices earlier for contact information) publishes an up-to-date *Major Events & Festivals* calendar each year that is useful for anyone planning to attend a particular event.

January

New Year's Day Public holiday, 1 January, in deference to the Western calendar.

That Phanom Festival An annual week-long homage to the northeast's most sacred Buddhist stupa (Phra That Phanom) in Nakhon Phanom Province. Pilgrims from all over the country, as well as from Laos, attend.

February

Chiang Mai Flower Festival Colourful floats and parades exhibit Chiang Mai's cultivated flora.

Magha Puja *(maakhá buuchaa)* Held on the full moon of the third lunar month to commemorate Buddha preaching to 1250 enlightened monks who came to hear him 'without prior summons'. A public holiday throughout the country, it culminates with a candle-lit walk around the main chapel *(wian tian)* at every wát.

Phra Nakhon Khiri Diamond Festival This is a week-long celebration of Phetchaburi's history and architecture focused on Phra Nakhon Khiri Historical Park (also known as Khao Wang), a hill topped by a former royal palace overlooking the city. It features a sound-and-light show on Khao Wang; the temples are festooned with lights and presentations of Thai classical dance-drama.

Late February–Early March

Chinese New Year Called *trùt jiin* in Thai, Chinese populations all over Thailand celebrate their lunar New Year (the date shifts from year to year) with a week of house-cleaning, lion dances and fireworks. The most impressive festivities take place in the Chinese-dominated province capital of Nakhon Sawan.

March

Asean Barred Ground Dove Festival This is a large dove-singing contest that attracts dove-lovers from all over Thailand, Malaysia, Singapore and Indonesia. It's held in the first week of March in Yala

Bangkok International Jewellery Fair Held in several large Bangkok hotels, this is Thailand's most important annual gem and jewellery trade show. It runs concurrently with the Department of Export Promotion's Gems & Jewellery Fair.

Phanom Rung Festival A newly established festival to commemorate restoration work in the Phanom Rung Historical Park, an impressive Angkor-style temple complex in Buriram Province. It involves a daytime procession up Phanom Rung Hill and spectacular sound-and-light shows at night. It takes place on the last week of the month – be prepared for very hot weather.

April

Chakri Day Public holiday, 6 April. Commemorating the founder of the Chakri dynasty, Rama I.

Songkran Held from 13 to 15 April, this is the celebration of the lunar New Year. Buddha images are 'bathed', monks and elders receive the respect of younger Thais by the sprinkling of water over their hands, and a lot of water is generously tossed about for fun. Songkran generally gives everyone a chance to release their frustrations and literally cool off during the peak of the hot season. Hide out in your room or expect to be soaked; the latter is a lot more fun.

May

International Labour Day Public holiday, 1 May.

Coronation Day Public holiday, 5 May. The king and queen preside at a ceremony at Wat Phra Kaew, commemorating their 1950 coronation.

Visakha Puja *(wísăakhà buuchaa)* A public holiday that falls on the 15th day of the waxing moon in the 6th lunar month, this day commemorates the date of the Buddha's birth, enlightenment and *parinibbana*, or passing away. Activities are centred around the wát, with candle-lit processions, much chanting and sermonising.

Mid-May–Mid-June

Phi Ta Khon Festival One of the wildest in Thailand, this is an animist-Buddhist celebration held in Loei's Dan Sai district (nowadays also in other places around Loei Province) in which revellers dress in garish 'spirit' costumes, wear painted masks and brandish carved wooden phalli. The festival commemorates a Buddhist legend in which a host of spirits *(phĭi)* appeared to greet the Buddha-to-be upon his return to his home town, during his penultimate birth.

Rocket Festival (Bun Bang Fai) In the northeast, villagers craft large skyrockets of bamboo, which they then fire into the sky to bring rain for rice fields. This festival is best celebrated in the town of Yasothon, but is also good in Ubon Ratchathani and Nong Khai.

Royal Ploughing Ceremony To kick off the official rice-planting season, the king participates in this ancient Brahman ritual at Sanam Luang (the large field across from Wat Phra Kaew) in Bangkok. Thousands of Thais gather to watch, and traffic in this part of the city comes to a standstill.

Mid- to late July

Asalha Puja *(àsǎanhà buuchaa)* This festival commemorates the Buddha's first sermon.

Candle Festival Khao Phansa (see following) is celebrated in the northeast by parading huge carved candles on floats in the streets. This festival is best celebrated in Ubon Ratchathani.

Khao Phansa *(khâo phansǎa)* A public holiday and the beginning of Buddhist 'lent', this is the traditional time of year for young men to enter the monkhood for the rainy season and for all monks to station themselves in a monastery for the three months. It's a good time to observe a Buddhist ordination.

August

Queen's Birthday This public holiday is celebrated on 12 August. In Bangkok, Th Ratchadamnoen Klang and the Grand Palace are festooned with coloured lights.

Mid-September

Thailand International Swan-Boat Races These take place on the Mae Nam Chao Phraya (Chao Phraya River) in Bangkok near Saphan Phra Ram IX (Rama IX Bridge).

Last Week of September

Narathiwat Fair An annual week-long festival celebrating local culture in Narathiwat Province with boat races, dove-singing contests, handicraft displays, traditional southern Thai music and dance. The king and queen almost always attend.

Late September–Early October

Vegetarian Festival A nine-day celebration in Trang and Phuket during which devout Chinese Buddhists eat only vegetarian food. There are various ceremonies at Chinese temples and merit-making processions that bring to mind Hindu Thaipusam in its exhibition of self-mortification. Smaller towns in the south such as Krabi and Phang-Nga also celebrate the vegie fest on a smaller scale.

Mid-October–Mid-November

Kathin *(thâwt kàthǐn)* A month at the end of the Buddhist lent during which new monastic robes and requisites are offered to the Sangha (monastic community). In Nan Province longboat races are held on Mae Nan (Nan River).

October

Chulalongkorn Day Public holiday, 23 October. This holiday is in commemoration of King Chulalongkorn (Rama V).

November

Loi Krathong On the proper full-moon night, small lotus-shaped baskets or boats made of banana leaves containing flowers, incense, candles and a coin are floated on Thai rivers, lakes and canals. This is a peculiarly Thai festival that probably originated in Sukhothai and is best celebrated in the north. In Chiang Mai, where the festival is called Yi Peng, residents also launch paper hot-air balloons into the sky. At the Sukhothai Historical Park there is an impressive sound-and-light show held at this time.

Surin Annual Elephant Roundup Held on the third weekend of November, Thailand's biggest elephant show is popular with tourists. If you have ever had the desire to see a lot of elephants in one place, then here's your chance.

Late November–Early December

River Khwae Bridge Week There are sound-and-light shows every night at the Death Railway Bridge in Kanchanaburi. Events include historical exhibitions and vintage-train rides on the infamous railway.

December

King's Birthday Public holiday, 5 December. This holiday is celebrated with some fervour in Bangkok. As with the queen's birthday, it features lots of lights and other decorations along Th Ratchadamnoen Klang. Some people erect temporary shrines to the king outside their homes or businesses.

Constitution Day Public holiday, 10 December. This day commemorates the establishment of the constitutional monarchy in 1932.

ACTIVITIES

Cycling

Details on pedalling your way around Thailand and bicycle hire can be found in the Getting Around chapter.

Trekking

Wilderness walking or trekking is one of northern Thailand's biggest draws. Typical trekking programmes run for four or five days (although it is possible to arrange everything from one- to 10-day treks). They feature daily walks through forested mountain areas coupled with overnight stays in hill-tribe villages to satisfy both ethno- and eco-tourism urges. See the Trekking sections in the Northern Thailand chapter for more detail.

Other trekking opportunities are available in Thailand's larger national parks (including Doi Phu Kha, Kaeng Krachan, Khao Sam Roi Yot, Khao Sok, Khao Yai, Phu Reua and Thap Lan), where park rangers may be hired as guides and cooks for a few days at a time. Rates are reasonable. For more information, see the respective park entries in the destination chapters.

Diving & Snorkelling

Thailand's two coastlines and countless islands are popular among divers for their mild waters and colourful marine life. The biggest diving centre – in terms of the number of participants, but not the number of dive operations – is still Pattaya, simply because it's less than two hours' drive from Bangkok. There are several islands with reefs just a short boat ride from Pattaya and the town is packed with dive shops.

Phuket is the second-biggest jumping-off point (or the biggest if you count dive operations) and has the advantage of offering the largest variety of places to choose from. This includes small offshore islands less than an hour away; also nearby are Ao Phang-Nga (a one- to two-hour boat ride), with its unusual rock formations and clear green waters, and the world-famous Similan and Surin Islands in the Andaman Sea (about four hours away by fast boat). Reef dives in the Andaman are particularly rewarding – some 210 hard corals and 108 reef fish have so far been catalogued in this under-studied marine zone, where probably thousands more species of reef organisms live.

Over the last decade or so dive operations have multiplied on the palmy islands of Ko Samui, Ko Pha-Ngan and Ko Tao, in the Gulf of Thailand off Surat Thani. Chumphon Province, just north of Surat Thani, is another worthwhile area where there are a dozen or so islands with undisturbed reefs. Newer frontiers include the so-called Burma Banks (northwest of Ko Surin), Khao Lak and islands off the coast of Krabi and Trang provinces.

All of these places, with the possible exception of the Burma Banks, have areas that are suitable for snorkelling as well as scuba diving, since many reefs are covered by water no deeper than 2m.

Masks, fins and snorkels are readily available for rent not only at dive centres but also through guesthouses in beach areas. If you're particular about the quality and condition of the equipment you use, however, you might be better off bringing your own mask and snorkel – some of the stuff for rent is second-rate. People with large heads may have difficulty finding masks that fit, since most of the masks are made, or imported, for Thai people.

Most dive shops also offer basic instruction and NAUI or PADI qualification for first-timers – PADI is by far the most prevalent. The average four-day, full-certification course costs around 10,000B, including all instruction, equipment and several open-water dives. Shorter, less expensive 'resort' courses are also available.

It's a good idea to shop around the dive companies, not just to compare prices but to suss out the types of instruction, the condition of the equipment and the personalities of the instructors. German and English are the most common languages of instruction, but French and Italian courses are also available. See the relevant destination sections of this book for the names and locations of established diving centres.

When to Dive Generally speaking, the Gulf of Thailand has a year-round dive season, although tropical storms sometimes blow out the visibility temporarily. On the Andaman Coast the best diving conditions occur between December and April; from May to November monsoon conditions prevail. Whale sharks and manta rays in the offshore Andaman (eg, Similan and Surin Island groups) are a major bonus during planktonic blooms in March and April.

Safety Due to the overall lack of medical facilities for diving injuries, great caution should be exercised when diving in Thailand. Recompression chambers are located at three permanent facilities:

Apakorn Kiatiwong Naval Hospital (☎ 0 3860 1185) Sattahip, Chonburi, 26km east of Pattaya; urgent care available 24 hrs

Somdej Phra Pinklao Naval Hospital (☎ 0 2460 0000–19 ext 341, 0 2460 1105) Department of Underwater & Aviation Medicine, Th Taksin, Thonburi, Bangkok; open 24 hrs

Sub-aquatic Safety Service (SSS; ☎ 0 7634 2518, 0 1606 1869, fax 0 7634 2519) Hat Patong, Phuket

Lonely Planet's richly illustrated *Diving & Snorkeling Thailand*, written by resident diving instructors, is full of vital diving information.

Windsurfing

The best combination of rental facilities and wind conditions are found on Pattaya and Jomtien beaches in Chonburi Province, on Ko Samet, on the west coast of Phuket and on Hat Chaweng on Ko Samui. To a lesser extent you'll also find rental equipment on Hat Khao Lak (north of Phuket), Ko Pha-Ngan, Ko Tao and Ko Chang.

The windsurfing gear rented at Thai resorts is generally not the most complete and up-to-date. For the novice windsurfer this probably won't matter, but hot-doggers may be disappointed in the selection. Wetsuits aren't necessary in Thailand's year-round tropical climate.

If you have your own equipment you can set out anywhere you find a coastal breeze. If you're looking for something undiscovered, you might check out the cape running north from Narathiwat's provincial capital in southern Thailand. In general the windy months on the Gulf of Thailand are from

Responsible Diving

The popularity of diving is placing immense pressure on many sites. Please consider the following tips when diving and help preserve the ecology and beauty of reefs.

- Do not use anchors on the reef, and take care not to ground boats on coral. Encourage dive operators and regulatory bodies to establish permanent moorings at popular dive sites.
- Avoid touching living marine organisms with your body or dragging computer consoles and gauges across the reef. Polyps can be damaged by even the gentlest contact. Never stand on corals, even if they look solid and robust. If you must secure yourself to the reef, only hold fast to exposed rock or dead coral.
- Be conscious of your fins. Even without contact the surge from heavy fin strokes near the reef can damage delicate organisms. When treading water in shallow reef areas, take care not to kick up clouds of sand. Settling sand can easily smother the delicate organisms of the reef.
- Practise and maintain proper buoyancy control. Major damage can be done by divers descending too fast and colliding with the reef. Make sure you are correctly weighted and that your weight belt is positioned so that you stay horizontal.
- If you have not dived for a while, have a practice dive in a pool before taking to the reef. Be aware that buoyancy can change over the period of an extended trip: initially you may breathe harder and need more weighting; a few days later you may breathe more easily and need less weight.
- Take great care in underwater caves. Spend as little time within them as possible as your air bubbles may be caught within the roof and thereby leave previously submerged organisms high and dry. Taking turns to inspect the interior of a small cave will lessen the chances of damaging contact.
- Resist the temptation to collect or buy corals or shells. Aside from the ecological damage, taking home marine souvenirs depletes the beauty of a site and spoils the enjoyment of others.
- The same goes for marine archaeological sites (mainly shipwrecks). Respect their integrity; they may even be protected from looting by law.
- Ensure that you take home all your rubbish, and any litter you may find as well. Plastics in particular are a serious threat to marine life. Turtles will mistake plastic for jellyfish and eat it.
- Resist the temptation to feed fish. You may disturb their normal eating habits, encourage aggressive behaviour or feed them food that is detrimental to their health.
- Minimise your disturbance of marine animals. In particular, do not ride on the backs of turtles as this causes them great anxiety.

mid-February to April. On the Andaman Sea side of the Thai-Malay peninsula winds are strongest from September to December.

Surfing

This sport has never really taken off in Thailand, not least because there don't seem to be any sizeable, annually dependable breaks (write to us if you find any). Phuket's west coast occasionally kicks up some surfable waves during the southwest monsoon season (May to November). We have also seen some fair surf action on the west coast of Ko Chang during the same time of year, and on the east coast of Ko Samet during the dry season (November to February). We'd be willing to bet there's decent surf on Ko Chang's east coast during these months.

Bigger surf is usually found on Laem Singh and Hat Surin. Coastal areas of Trang Province are historically reputed to receive large waves during the southwest monsoon, but we've never heard of anyone surfing there. Low-quality boards can be rented in Pattaya and on Phuket's Patong Beach, where there's average surf.

Paddling

Touring the islands and coastal limestone formations around Phuket and Ao Phang-Nga by inflatable canoe has become an increasingly popular activity over the last five years. Typical tours seek out half-submerged caves called *hong* (*hâwng,* Thai for 'room'), timing their excursions so that they can paddle into the caverns at low tide. Several outfits in Phuket and Krabi offer equipment and guides. *Faràng* (Western) outfitters claim to have 'discovered' the *hong*, but local fishermen have known about them for hundreds of years. Several islands with partially submerged caves in Ao Phang-Nga have carried the name Ko Hong (Room Island) for at least the last half-century.

You might consider bringing your own craft. Inflatable or folding kayaks are easier to transport, but hard-shell kayaks track better. In Thailand's tropical waters an open-top or open-deck kayak – whether hard-shell, folding or inflatable – is more comfortable and practical than the closed-deck type with a spray skirt and other sealing paraphernalia, which will only transform your kayak into a floating sauna.

River & Canal Excursions

Boat travel is possible along Thailand's major rivers and canals through the extensive public boat system and aboard a small number of tourist boat services. So far regular leisure boating has only been introduced to lower Mae Nam Chao Phraya and a few rivers in northern Thailand. A variety of watercraft are available, from air-con tourist boats along the Mae Nam Chao Phraya around Bangkok, to rustic bamboo rafts on the Mae Kok and sturdy white-water kayaks on the Mae Pai and Mae Klong.

The Mekong River, considered perilous until the late 1980s due to regional hostilities, has enormous potential. During the last six years or so short-distance boat trips have been offered in Chiang Rai, Loei and Nong Khai provinces, and in early 1994 an experimental tour service between Chiang Saen and China was inaugurated (so far the route has yet to be regularised). Central Thailand's vast network of canals, centred on the Chao Phraya Delta and fanning out for hundreds of kilometres in all directions, offers numerous boating opportunities. However, the motorised boat traffic along these waterways has meant that very few foreign visitors have tried canoeing or kayaking this grid. For the adventurous traveller the potential is huge, as by public and chartered long-tail boats you can piece together canal journeys of several days' duration.

Anyone seeking inspiration for some long-distance river paddling need look no further than Steve Van Beek's *Slithering South*, an exhilarating chronicle of the author's 58-day voyage from the headwaters of Mae Ping to the mouth of Mae Nam Chao Praya.

For more information on river and canal travel possibilities, see the relevant destination chapters.

LANGUAGE COURSES

Several language schools in Bangkok and Chiang Mai offer courses in Thai language. Tuition fees average around 250B per hour. Some places will let you trade English lessons for Thai lessons.

Recommended schools in Bangkok include the following.

AUA Language Center (☎ 0 2252 8170) 179 Th Ratchadamri. American University Alumni (AUA) runs one of the largest English-language teaching institutes in the world, so this is a good place to meet Thai students. AUA-produced books are stodgy and outdated, but many teachers make their own – better – instructional materials. *Paw hòk* (6th grade primary-school level, essential for working in the government school system) courses are available.

Chulalongkorn University (☎ 0 2218 4888, fax 0 2218 4877, ⓔ tkongkar@chula.ac.th) Intensive Thai Office/Faculty of Arts, Chulalongkorn University, Th Phayathai. Offers a 100-hour programme consisting of three basic, three intermediate, and three advanced courses, each lasting five weeks.

Nisa Thai Language School (☎ 0 2286 9323) YMCA Collins House, 27 Th Sathon Tai. Like AUA, Nisa offers a course in preparing for the *paw hòk* examination along with all the usual levels. There is a second branch (☎ 0 2671 3359) at 32/14-6 Th Yen Akat.

Siri Pattana Thai Language School (☎ 0 2286 1936) YWCA, 13 Th Sathon Tai. Offers Thai language lessons as well as preparation for the *paw hòk* exam.

Union Language School (☎ 0 2252 8170) Christ Church Thailand Bldg, 109 Th Surawong. Generally recognised as having the best and most rigorous course (many missionaries study here), Union employs a balance of structure-oriented and communication-oriented methodologies in 80-hour, four-week modules. Private tuition is also available.

THAI STUDIES

Chulalongkorn University *(☎ 0 2218 3393, fax 0 2218 3926; ⓔ surapeepan.c@chula.ac.th; Perspectives on Thailand, Continuing Education Center, 5th floor, Vidhyabhathan Bldg, 12 Soi Chulalongkorn, Chulalongkorn University, Bangkok 10330)*, the most prestigious university in Thailand, offers a two-week intensive Thai studies course called Perspectives on Thailand. The 60-hour programme includes classes in Thai culture, economics, history, politics, religion, art, geography, language, trade and current events. Classes are offered once a year in July only. Students who have taken the course say they have found the quality of instruction excellent. The cost for this programme excluding airfare, meals and lodging is US$950 per person. A fee for optional on-campus accommodation is US$200.

Chulalongkorn also offers a two-year master's degree programme in Thai Studies in which participants have the opportunity to study and analyse a considerable body of knowledge under the supervision of recognised Thai experts in the field. The language of instruction is English, and tuition and registration fees total 46,000B per semester. Contact **Thai Studies Section** *(Faculty of Arts, Chulalongkorn University, Bangkok 10330)* for further information. Nondegree students may enrol in courses offered in the Thai Studies programme at a cost of 15,000B, plus a registration fee of 11,000B.

MEDITATION COURSES

Thailand has long been a popular place for Western students of Buddhism, particularly those interested in Buddhist meditation.

Two basic meditation systems are taught, *samatha* and *vipassana*. *Samatha* aims to calm the mind and develop refined states of concentration, similar to other traditions of meditation or contemplation found in most of the world's religions.

Unique to Buddhism, particularly Theravada and to a lesser extent Tibetan Buddhism, is a system of meditation known as *vipassana* (in Thai, *wípàtsànaa*) a Pali word that roughly translates as 'insight'. Foreigners who come to Thailand to study *vipassana* can choose from dozens of temples and meditation centres *(sǎmnák wípàtsànaa)* specialising in these teachings. Teaching methods vary but the general emphasis is on observing mind-body processes from moment to moment. Thai language is usually the medium of instruction but several places also provide instruction in English. Some centres and monasteries teach both *vipassana* and *samatha* methods, others specialise in one or the other.

Contact details for some of the more popular meditation-oriented temples and centres are given in the destination chapters. Instruction and accommodation are free of charge at temples, although donations are expected.

Short-term students will find that the two-month Tourist Visa is ample for most courses of study. Long-term students may want to consider getting a three- or six-month Non-Immigrant Visa (see Visas & Documents earlier in this chapter). A few Westerners are ordained as monks or nuns in order to take full advantage of the monastic environment. Monks and nuns are generally (but not always) allowed to stay in Thailand as long as they remain in robes.

Places where English-language instruction is usually available include the following.

Boonkanjanaram Meditation Centre (☎ 0 3823 1865) Hat Jomtien, Pattaya, Chonburi
International Buddhist Meditation Centre (☎ 0 2623 6326, afternoons only) Wat Mahathat, Th Maharat, Tha Phra Chan, Bangkok
International Buddhist Meditation Centre (☎ 0 2240 3700 ext 1480, 0 2511 0439, fax 0 2512 6083) Nakhon Pathom
Sathira Dhammasathan (☎ 0 2510697; ⓔ savika@loxinfo.co.th) Soi Watcharaphon, Th Ramintha, Bangkok
Sorn-Thawee Meditation Centre (☎ 0 3854 1405) Bangkla, Chachoengsao
Thailand Vipassana Centre (☎ 0 2216 4772, fax 0 2215 3408) Pathumwan, Bangkok
Wat Asokaram (☎ 0 2395 0003) Bang Na-Trat Highway (32km south of Bangkok), Samut Prakan
Wat Khao Tham, Ko Pha-Ngan, Surat Thani
Wat Phra That Chom Thong (☎ 0 5336 2067) 157 Ban Luang Chom Thong, Chiang Mai
Wat Suan Mokkhaphalaram (fax 0 7639 1851, Attn: SMI) Chaiya, Surat Thani
Wat Tapotaram (Wat Ram Poeng; ☎ 0 5327 8620) Chiang Mai
Wiwekasom Vipassana Centre (☎ 0 3828 3766) Ban Suan, Chonburi
World Fellowship of Buddhists (☎ 0 2661 1284) Benjasiri Park, next to The Emporium, Soi 24, Th Sukhumvit, Bangkok

The International Buddhist Meditation Centre at Wat Mahathat also sponsors weekends at rural locations in Pathum Thani, Nakhon Ratchasima and Phetchabun provinces.

Before visiting one of these centres, it's a good idea to call or write first to make sure space and instruction are available. Some places require that you wear white clothes when staying overnight. For even a brief visit, wear clean and neat clothing (ie, long trousers or skirt and sleeves that cover the shoulders).

For a detailed look at *vipassana* study in Thailand, including visa and ordination procedures, read *A Guide to Buddhist Monasteries & Meditation Centres in Thailand* (available from the World Fellowship of Buddhists in Bangkok or online at ⓦ www.dharmanet.org/thai_94.html).

Useful reading material includes Jack Kornfield's *Living Dharma,* which contains short biographies and descriptions of the teaching methods of 12 well-known Theravada teachers, including six Thais. Serious meditators will want to study *The Path of Purification (Visuddhi Magga),* a classic commentary that reveals every detail of canonical Buddhist practice and includes a Pali-English glossary defining all the tricky terms (*kasina, jhana, nimitta, vipaka* and so on). These books are available from bookshops in Bangkok.

MARTIAL ARTS COURSES

Many Westerners have trained in Thailand, but few last more than a week or two in a Thai camp – and fewer still have gone on to compete on Thailand's pro circuit.

Thai Boxing

Training in *muay thai* takes place at dozens of boxing camps around the country. Most centres are reluctant to take on foreign trainees, except in special cases where the applicant can prove a willingness to conform *totally* to the training system, the diet and the rustic accommodation. Most important is the ability to learn the Thai language. Rates vary from US$50 to US$250 per week, including food and accommodation, depending on room choice (fan versus air-con etc) and experience with foreigners. Here are some camps that do take *faràng*.

Fairtex Muay Thai (*☎ 0 2757 5148; ⓦ www.fairtexbkk.com; 99/5 Mu 3, Soi Buthamanuson, Th Thaeparak, Bangpli, Samut Prakan*), a popular, long-running camp that accepts foreign students (women as well as men) is a good choice for newcomers interested in training at a traditional *muay thai* camp.

Jitti's Gym Thai Boxing & Homestay (*Sor Vorapin; ☎ 0 2282 3551; 13 Soi Krasab, Th Chakraphong*), in west Banglamphu, also specialises in training foreign students of both genders.

Muay Thai Institute (*☎ 0 2992 0096; ⓦ www.muaythaiinstitute.com; 336/932 Th Prachatipat, Pathumthani, Rangsit*), associated with the respected World Muay Thai Council, is located inside the Rangsit Muay Thai Stadium, north of Bangkok International Airport. The institute offers three main study programmes: three basic courses of 10 days each plus a 90-day 'professional' course; three 15-day courses for instructors; and three 15-day courses for referees and judges. All text books are available in English, and there is accommodation on site. Many experts would be sceptical that *muay thai* could be learned in such relatively short intervals, but the school's credentials are 100% Thai.

Lanna Muay Thai (*☎/fax 0 5389 2102;* Ⓦ *www.lannamuaythai.com; 64/1 Soi 1 (Soi Chang Kian), Th Huay Kaew, Chiang Mai 50300*) and **Patong Boxing Club** (*☎ 0 1978 9352, fax 0 7629 2189; 59/4 Mu 4, Th Na Nai, Patong Beach, Phuket*) specialise in training foreigners. Be forewarned, however. The training is gruelling and features full-contact sparring, unlike tae kwon do, kenpo, kung fu and other East Asian martial arts.

In Ubon Ratchathani two rustic camps accept foreigners: **Phaw Meuang Ubon** (*☎ 0 4524 2399; 78/1 Th Sri Narong*); and **Sit U-Meuang Ubon** (*☎ 0 1967 3495; Wing 21, Ubon*).

The website Ⓦ www.muaythai.com contains loads of information including the addresses of training camps.

THAI MASSAGE COURSES

Described by some as a 'brutally pleasant experience', this ancient form of healing was first documented in the West by the French liaison to the Thai Royal Court in Ayuthaya in 1690, who wrote: 'When any person is sick in Siam he causes his whole body to be moulded by one who is skilful herein, who gets upon the body of the sick person and tramples him under his feet.'

Unlike in most Western massage methodologies, such as Swedish and Californian techniques, Thai massage does not directly seek to relax the body through a kneading of the body with palms and fingers. Instead a multipronged approach uses the hands, thumbs, fingers, elbows, forearms, knees and feet, and is applied to the traditional pressure points along the various *sên* or meridians (the human body is thought to have 72,000 of these, of which 10 are crucial).

The client's body is also pulled, twisted and manipulated in ways that have been described as 'passive yoga'. The objective is to distribute energies evenly throughout the nervous system so as to create a harmony of physical energy flows. The muscular-skeletal system is also manipulated in ways that can be compared to modern physiotherapy and chiropractic.

Thailand offers ample opportunities to study its unique tradition of massage therapy. Wat Pho in Bangkok is considered the master source for all Thai massage pedagogy, although the northern provinces boast a 'softer' version. See the Traditional Massage sections in the Bangkok and Northern Thailand chapters for more information.

COOKING COURSES

More and more travellers are coming to Thailand just to learn how to cook. Many foreign chefs seek out recipe inspirations for East-West fusion cuisine. You, too, can amaze your friends back home after attending a course in Thai cuisine at one of the following places.

The Boathouse (☎ 0 7633 0015–7, fax 0 7633 0561, Ⓔ info@theboathousephuket.com) Kata Yai Beach, Phuket

Chiang Mai Thai Cookery School (☎ 0 5320 6388, fax 0 5320 6387, Ⓔ nabnian@loxinfo.co.th) 1-3 Th Moon Muang

Modern Housewife Centre (☎ 0 2279 2834) 45/6-7 Th Sethsiri, Bangkok

Oriental Hotel Cooking School (☎ 0 2659 9000, Ⓔ orbkk_bsc@mohg.com) Soi Oriental, Th Charoen Krung, Bangkok. This school features a plush five-day course under the direction of well-known star chef Chali (Charlie) Amatyakul.

Siam Chiang Mai Cookery School (☎ 0 5327 1169, fax 0 5320 8950) 5/2 Soi 1, Th Loi Khraw.

Thai House (☎ 0 2903 9611, 0 2997 5161, fax 0 2903 9354, Ⓔ pip_thaihouse@hotmail.com) Amphoe Bang Yai, Nonthaburi. This is a popular residential cooking course about 40 minutes north of Bangkok by boat. The programme includes all meals, four nights' accommodation and transfer to and from Bangkok.

UFM Food Centre (☎ 0 2259 0620–33) 593/29-39 Soi 33/1, Th Sukhumvit, Bangkok. This is the most serious and thorough cooking school in Thailand, with a multilayered curriculum. Most classes are offered in Thai and you will need at least four people for an English-language class.

WORK

Thailand's steady economic growth has provided a variety of work opportunities for foreigners, although in general it's not as easy to find a job as in the more developed countries. The one exception is English teaching; as in the rest of East and Southeast Asia, there is a high demand for English speakers to provide instruction. This is not due to a shortage of qualified Thai teachers with a good grasp of English grammar, but rather a desire to have native-speaker models in the classroom.

Teaching English

Those with academic credentials, such as teaching certificates or degrees in English as a second language (ESL) or English as a foreign language (EFL), get first crack at the better-paying jobs at universities and international schools. But there are perhaps hundreds of private language-teaching schools that hire teachers who don't have credentials, by the hour, throughout the country.

Private tutoring is also a possibility in the larger cities such as Bangkok, Chiang Mai, Hat Yai, Khon Kaen, Lampang, Phitsanulok, Phuket and Songkhla. International oil companies pay the highest salaries for English instructors but are also quite picky.

Start with the English-language *Yellow Pages of the Greater Bangkok Metropolitan Telephone Directory,* which contains many rural and Bangkok listings. Check all the usual headings, such as Schools, Universities, Language Schools (there are over 75 listings in Bangkok alone).

A website maintained by an EFL teacher in Bangkok, w www.ajarn.com, has tips on where to find teaching jobs and how to deal with Thai classrooms, as well as current job listings.

Volunteer & Other Positions

Voluntary and paid positions with organisations that provide charitable services in education, development or public health are available for those with the right educational and/or experiential backgrounds. Contact **Voluntary Service Overseas** *(VSO; ☎ 020-8780 7200; w www.vso.org.uk)* in London; **VSO Canada** *(☎ 613-234 1364; w www.vsocan.com)* in Ottawa; **Overseas Service Bureau** *(OSB; ☎ 03-9279 1788)* in Melbourne; **Volunteer Service Abroad** *(☎ 04-472 5759; w www.vsa.org.nz)* in Wellington, New Zealand; or **US Peace Corps** *(☎ 800-424 8580; w www.peacecorps.gov)*, in Washington, DC.

The UN supports a number of ongoing projects in the country. In Bangkok interested people can try contacting the **United Nations Development Programme** *(☎ 0 2288 2129; w http:surf.undp.or.th)*; **World Food Program** *(☎ 0 2655 4115; e wfpbkk.unescap@un.org)*; **World Health Organization** *(☎ 0 2282 9700; w w3.whosea.org)*; **Food and Agriculture Organization** *(☎ 0 2697 4000; w www.fao.or.th)*; **Unicef** *(☎ 0 2356 9499; e thailandao@unicef.org)*; or **Unesco** *(☎ 0 2391 0577; w www.unescobkk.org)*.

Mon, Karen and Burmese refugee camps along the Thailand-Myanmar border can use volunteer help. Since none of the camps are officially sanctioned by the Thai government, few of the big NGOs or multilateral organisations are involved here. This means the level of overall support is low but the need for volunteers is definitely there. If this interests you, travel to the relevant areas (primarily Sangkhlaburi and Mae Sot) and ask around for the 'unofficial' camp locations.

Work Permits

All employment in Thailand requires a Thai work permit. Thai law defines work as 'exerting one's physical energy or employing one's knowledge, whether or not for wages or other benefits', and therefore, theoretically, even volunteer work requires a permit.

Certain jobs, including architecture, civil engineering and clerical or secretarial services, are closed to foreigners by royal decree. You may wish to contact your local Thai embassy or consulate for the latest information on employment in Thailand.

Work permits should be obtained through an employer, who may file for the permit before you enter Thailand. The permit itself is not issued until you enter Thailand on a valid Non-Immigrant Visa.

For information about work permits, contact any Thai embassy abroad or **Consular Services** *(w www.thaiembdc.org)*.

ACCOMMODATION

Places to stay in Thailand are abundant, varied and very reasonably priced.

However, a word of warning about touts: don't believe them if they say a place is closed, full, dirty or crooked. Sometimes they're right but most times it's just a ruse to get you to a place that pays them more commission. (See Dangers & Annoyances earlier for more about touts.)

Fire

If you're concerned about hotel fire safety, always check the fire exits at Thai hotels to make sure they're open and functioning. In 1997 the 17-storey Royal Jomtien Resort Hotel in Pattaya burned down, taking with it the lives of 80 people. The hotel had no sprinkler system and the fire exits were chained shut. In the wake of the fire, regulations were supposedly tightened up around the country, but we've seen hotels in various locations that also chain or otherwise block off fire exits – to keep guests from skipping the room bill and to block potential thieves.

National Park Camping & Accommodation

Thailand has 112 national parks and nine historical parks. All but 10 of the national parks have bungalows for rent that sleep as many as 10 people for rates of 500B to 1500B, depending on the park and the size of the bungalow. During the low seasons you can often get a room in one of these park bungalows for 100B per person. A few of the historical parks have bungalows with rates comparable to those in the national parks, mostly for use by visiting archaeologists.

Camping is allowed in all but four of the national parks (Doi Suthep/Doi Pui in Chiang Mai Province, Hat Jao Mai in Trang Province, Nam Tok Phliu in Chanthaburi Province and Thap Lan in Prachinburi Province) for only 5B to 20B per person per night. Some parks hire out tents (50B to 100B a night), but always check the condition of the tents before agreeing to rent. It's a good idea to take your own sleeping bag or mat, and other basic camping gear. You should also take a torch (flashlight), rain gear, insect repellent, a water container and a small medical kit. A few parks also have *reuan thǎew* (longhouses) where rooms are around 150B to 300B for two people.

Advance bookings for accommodation are advisable at the more popular parks, especially on holidays and weekends. Most parks charge an entry fee to visit (adults 200B, children 14 and under 100B). Be sure to save your receipt for the duration of your stay. You may be asked by a ranger to show proof of having paid.

Temple Lodgings

If you are a Buddhist, or are able to behave like one, you may be able to stay overnight in some temples for a small donation. Facilities are very basic, however, and early rising is expected. Temple lodgings are usually for men only, unless the wát has a place for lay women to stay. Neat, clean dress and a basic knowledge of Thai etiquette are mandatory. See Meditation Courses earlier for information on wát in Thailand that will accommodate long-term lay students.

Hostels

There is a Thai branch of **Hostelling International** (*☎ 0 2282 0950, fax 0 2628 7416, Ⓦ www.tyha.org; 25/2 Th Phitsanulok, Sisao Thewet, Dusit, Bangkok 10300*), formerly International Youth Hostel Federation, with member hostels in Bangkok, Ayuthaya, Chiang Mai, Kanchanaburi, Lopburi, Phimai, Phitsanulok and Rayong. There have been others in Chiang Rai, Ko Phi-Phi and Nan but at the time of writing these were closed. Thai youth hostels range in price from around 80B for a dorm bed to 280/350B per air-con single/double room. Generally speaking only HI card holders are accepted as guests in Thai hostels. Membership costs 300B per year or 50B for a one-night membership.

Guesthouses

Guesthouses are generally the cheapest accommodation in Thailand and are found in wherever travellers go throughout central, northern and southern Thailand; they are spreading slowly to the east and northeast as well. Guesthouses vary quite a bit in terms of the facilities on offer, which also influences prices. Generally rock-bottom is 50B to 80B per person, while more average rates run 120B to 200B. Some are especially good value, while others are only good for a night at most! Many serve food, although there tends to be a bland sameness to meals in guesthouses wherever you are in Thailand.

YMCAs & YWCAs

A YMCA or YWCA costs quite a bit more than a guesthouse or hostel, and sometimes more than a local hotel, but they are generally good value. There are Ys in Bangkok (the YMCA here under renovation at the time of writing), Chiang Mai and Chiang Rai.

Resorts

In most countries 'resort' refers to hotels that offer substantial recreational facilities (eg, tennis, golf, swimming, sailing) in addition to accommodation and dining. In Thai hotel lingo, however, the term simply efers to any hotel that isn't located in an ırban area. Hence a few thatched beach ıuts or a cluster of bungalows in a forest nay be called a 'resort'. Several places in Thailand fully deserve the resort title under ıny definition – but it will pay for you to ook into the facilities before making a eservation.

Chinese-Thai Hotels

The standard Thai hotels, often run by Chinese-Thai families, are the easiest accommodation to come by and generally ıave reasonable rates (average 150B to 200B for rooms without bath or air-con, 180B to 250B with fan and bath, 250B to 500B with air-con). These may be located on the main street of the town or near bus ınd train stations.

The most economical hotels are those vithout air-con; typical rooms are clean and nclude a double bed and a ceiling fan. Some have attached Thai-style bathrooms this will cost a little more). Rates may or nay not be posted; if not, they may be ncreased for *faràng*, so it is worthwhile argaining.

It's best to have a look around before greeing to check in, to make sure the room s clean, that the fan and lights work and so n. If there's a problem, request another oom or a discount. If possible, always hoose a room off the street and away from he front lounge to cut down on noise.

For a room without air-con, ask for a *âwng thammádaa* (ordinary room) or *âwng phát lom* (room with fan). A room vith air-con is *hâwng ae*. Sometimes *faràng* sking for air-con are automatically offered 'VIP' room, which usually comes with air-on, hot water, fridge and TV and is about wice the price of a regular air-con room, ie, 00B to 1000B.

Some Chinese-Thai hotels may double as rothels; the perpetual traffic in and out can e a bit noisy but is generally bearable. Unccompanied males may be asked if they vant female companionship when checking nto inexpensive hotels. Even certain middle-lass (by Thai standards) hotels are reserved or the 'salesman' crowd, meaning travelling hai businessmen, who frequently expect extra night-time services. Foreign women are usually left alone.

The cheapest hotels may have names posted in Thai and Chinese only, but with experience you will be able to identify them. Many of these hotels have restaurants downstairs; if they don't, there are usually restaurants and noodle shops nearby.

Tourist, Business & Luxury Hotels

These are found in Bangkok, Chiang Mai, Chiang Rai, Hat Yai, Kanchanaburi, Ko Pha-Ngan, Ko Samui, Pattaya, Phuket, Songkhla and a sprinkling of large provincial capitals such as Khon Kaen, Nakhon Ratchasima (Khorat), Phitsanulok, Ubon Ratchathani, Udon Thani and Yala. Prices start at around 600B outside Bangkok and Chiang Mai and proceed to 2000B or more – genuine tourist-class hotels in Bangkok start at 1000B or so and go to 2500B for standard rooms, and up to 5000B or 10,000B for a suite. These will all have air-con, TV, Western-style showers and baths, toilets, IDD phones and restaurants. Added to room charges will be a 7% government tax (VAT), and most of these hotels will include an additional service charge of 8% to 10%.

In addition to the international hotel chains of the Accor, Hilton, Holiday Inn, Hyatt, Sheraton and Westin, Thailand has several respectable home-grown chains, including Amari, Dusit and Royal Garden.

Discounts of 30% to 50% for hotels costing 1000B or more per night can easily be obtained through many Thai travel agencies. Several top-end hotels offer discounts of up to 60% for reservations made via the Internet. In the arrival halls of both the international and domestic terminals at Bangkok Airport, the Thai Hotels Association (THA) desk can also arrange discounts. If you are holding Thai International Airways (THAI) tickets, or flew in with THAI, the airlines can arrange substantial discounts.

FOOD

From pulse-pounding Bangkok to tranquil villages moored along the Mekong River, Thai cooks concoct a seemingly endless variety of dishes, whether from old court recipes, the latest in Euro-Thai fusion or simple fare guided by seasonal and regional necessity. For more information see the special sections 'Thai Cuisine' and 'Thailand's Highlights'.

DRINKS

Non-alcoholic Drinks

Fruit Juices & Shakes The incredible variety of fruit found in Thailand means a corresponding availability of nutritious juices and shakes. The all-purpose term for fruit juice is *náam phǒn-lá-mái*. Put *náam* (water or juice) together with the name of any fruit, from *náam mánao* (lime juice) to *náam taeng moh* (watermelon juice).

When a blender or extractor is used, fruit juices may be called *náam khán,* or squeezed juice (eg, *náam sàppàrót khán* – pineapple juice; *náam sôm khán* – orange juice). When mixed in a blender with ice the result is *náam pon* (literally, mixed juice) as in *náam málákaw pon,* a papaya smoothie or shake. Night markets will often have vendors specialising in juices and shakes.

Thais prefer to drink most fruit juices with a little salt mixed in. Unless a vendor is used to serving *faràng*, your drink will come slightly salted. If you prefer unsalted fruit juices, specify *mâi sài kleua* (without salt).

Sugar-cane juice *(náam âwy)* is a Thai favourite and a very refreshing accompaniment to curry-and-rice plates. Many small restaurants or food stalls that don't offer any other juices will have a supply of freshly squeezed *náam âwy* on hand. For the same made from sugar-palm sap, ask for *náam taan sòt*.

Coffee Instant coffee has made deep inroads into the Thai coffee culture at the expense of freshly ground coffee. Typical Thai restaurants, especially those in hotels, guesthouses and other tourist-oriented establishments, will serve instant coffee with packets of artificial, non-dairy creamer on the side. Upmarket hotels and coffee shops sometimes also offer filtered and espresso coffees at premium prices.

Traditionally, coffee in Thailand is locally grown (mostly in the hilly areas of northern and southern Thailand), roasted by wholesalers, ground by vendors and filtered just before serving. Thai-grown coffee may not be as full and rich-tasting as gourmet Sumatran, Jamaican or Kona beans but it's still considerably tastier than instant coffee.

Some restaurants or vendors with the proper accoutrements for making traditional filtered coffee will keep a supply of Nescafé just for foreigners (or moneyed Thais, since instant always costs a few baht more per cup than filtered). To get real Thai coffee ask for *kaafae thǔng* (literally, bag coffee) or *kaafae tôm* (boiled coffee), which refers to the traditional method of preparing a cup of coffee by filtering hot water through a bag-shaped cloth filter. Thailand's best coffee of this sort is served in Hokkien-style cafés in the southern provinces. Elsewhere throughout Thailand, the outdoor morning markets are the best places to find *kaafae thǔng*.

The usual *kaafae thǔng* is served mixed with sugar and sweetened condensed milk – if you want black coffee, say 'kaafae dam'; if you don't want sugar, be sure to specify 'mâi sài náam-taan'.

In more international venues, where Italian-style automatic coffee machines pump out the black brew, it's often referred to as *kaafae sòt (*fresh coffee) to distance the stuff from both instant coffee and Thai-style coffee.

Tea Both Indian-style (black) and Chinese-style (green or semi-cured) teas are commonly served in restaurants in Thailand. The latter predominates in Chinese restaurants and is also the usual ingredient in *náam chaa,* the weak, often lukewarm tea-water traditionally served in Thai restaur-ants for free. The aluminium teapots you find on every table in some restaurants are filled with *náam chaa*; ask for a plain glass *(kâew plào)* and you can drink as much of this stuff as you like at no charge. For iced *náam chaa* ask for a glass of ice (usually 1B) and pour your own; for fresh, undiluted Chinese tea, ask for *chaa jiin*.

Black tea, both the imported and Thai-grown kind, is usually available in the same restaurants or food stalls that serve real coffee. An order of *chaa ráwn* (hot tea) almost always results in a cup (or glass) of black tea with sugar and condensed milk. As with coffee you must specify when ordering whether you want the tea with or without milk and sugar.

Water Whether boiled or filtered, water that has been purified for drinking purposes is simply called *náam dèum* (drinking water). *All* water offered to customers in restaurants or to guests in an office or home will be purified, so you needn't fret about the safety of taking a sip (see the Health section earlier in this chapter). In restaurants you can ask for *náam plào* (plain water), which is always either boiled or taken from a purified source; it's served by the glass at no charge or you can order by the bottle. A bottle of carbonated water (soda) costs about the same as a bottle of plain purified water but the bottles are smaller.

Alcoholic Drinks

Drinking in Thailand can be quite expensive compared with other travel costs. The Thai government has placed increasingly heavy taxes on liquor and beer, so that now nearly half the price you pay for a large beer is tax. One large bottle (630mL) of Singha beer costs more than half the minimum daily wage of a Bangkok worker.

Beer Only a few brands of beer *(bia)* are readily available all over Thailand. Advertised with such slogans as 'pràthêht rao, bia rao' (Our Land, Our Beer), the Singha label is considered the quintessential 'Thai' beer by foreigners and locals alike. Pronounced 'sǐng', it's a strong, hoppy-tasting brew thought by many to be one of the best beers brewed in Asia. The rated alcohol content is a heady 6% and it's available in 630mL and 355mL bottles as well as 330mL cans.

Boon Rawd Breweries, makers of Singha, also produce a lighter (4.5% alcohol), blander beer called Singha Gold which only comes in small bottles and cans. Better is Singha's canned 5% 'draught beer' *(bia sòt)*. True Singha draught (6%), from fresh 30L kegs available only at bars or direct from Boon Rawd, is by far the best way to enjoy this classic beer.

Kloster, similarly inspired by German brewing recipes, is a notch smoother and lighter with an alcohol content of 4.7% and generally costs about 5B or 10B more per bottle. Kloster claims only about 5% of Thailand's beer consumption. Boon Rawd bought Kloster from Belgian giant Interbrew in 2002, so very soon we may see more Kloster around the country. Like Singha, it's available in cans and bottles.

Carlsberg, jointly owned by Danish and Thai interests, waded into the market in the early 1990s and has proved to be a strong contender. As elsewhere in Southeast Asia, Carlsberg used an aggressive promotion campaign, and when test marketing found that Thais considered it too weak, the company adjusted its recipe to come closer to Singha's 6% alcohol content. In its first two years of business, Carlsberg managed to grab around 25% of the Thai market. Like Kloster, it has a smoother flavour than Singha. Carlsberg is also available on tap in some bars, but for the most part only in Bangkok.

As the beer wars heated up, Singha retaliated with advertisements suggesting that drinking Danish beer was unpatriotic! Carlsberg responded by creating Beer Chang, which matches the hoppy taste of Singha but tops the alcohol content up to 7%. Although the concept, in name, may appear similar to Carlsberg Elephant as sold in Europe (since in Thai *cháang* means 'elephant'), Beer Chang uses an entirely different recipe and label design.

Beer Chang has managed to capture around 70% of the Thai market, partially because it retails at a significantly lower price than Singha and thus offers more bang per baht. Carlsberg also hired pop superstar Add Carabao to tout Beer Chang as the ultimate Thai beer in a series of TV ads.

Predictably, the next offensive in the war was launched with the marketing of Boon Rawd's cheaper brand, Leo. Sporting a black and red leopard label, Leo costs only slightly more than Chang but is similarly high in alcohol. To differentiate the new product from the flavour of the competition, Boon Rawd gave Leo a maltier taste.

Although still available in supermarkets, Leo failed to take off in bars and restaurants, so in their latest effort Boon Rawd has come up with the 'Thai Beer' and hired two superstar Thai boxers to appear in associated ads. With its bluntly nationalistic name, 6.5% ABV and lower price, Thai Beer clearly has its sites set on Beer Chang.

Dutch giant Heineken comes fourth after Beer Chang, Singha and Carlsberg in sales. Other Thailand-produced, European-brand beers you'll find in larger cities include a stout-like Black Beer (formerly Black Tiger), malty-sweet Mittweida and Amstel lager.

Singapore's Tiger brand will be testing Thailand's market in 2003.

Spirits Rice whisky is a big favourite in Thailand and is more affordable than beer for the average Thai. It has a sharp, sweet taste not unlike rum, with an alcoholic content of 35%. The most famous brand is Mekong (pronounced 'mâe khŏng'). In rural areas you'll find several other labels including Kwangthong, Hong Thong, Hong Ngoen, Hong Yok and Hong Tho. Mekong costs around 120B for a large bottle *(klom)* or 60B for the flask-sized bottle *(baen)*. The Hong brands are less expensive.

One company in Thailand produces a true rum, ie, a distilled liquor made from sugar cane, called Sang Som. Alcohol content is 40% and the stock is supposedly aged. Sang Som costs several baht more than the rice whiskies, but for those who find Mekong and the like unpalatable, it is an alternative worth trying.

More expensive Thai whiskies that are produced from barley and appeal to the can't-afford-Johnnie-Walker-yet set include Blue Eagle, 100 Pipers and Spey Royal, each with 40% alcohol content. These come dressed up in shiny boxes, much like the expensive imported whiskies that they imitate.

Other Liquor A cheaper alternative is *lâo khăo* (white liquor), of which there are two broad categories: legal and bootleg. The legal kind is generally made from sticky rice and is produced for regional consumption. Like Mekong and its competitors, it is 35% alcohol, but sells for around 60B per *klom,* or roughly half the price. The taste is sweet and raw and much more aromatic than the amber stuff – no amount of mixer will disguise the distinctive taste.

The illegal kinds are made from various agricultural products including sugar palm sap, coconut milk, sugar cane, taro and rice. Alcohol content may vary from as little as 10% or 12% to as much as 95%. Generally this *lâo thèuan* ('jungle liquor') is weaker in the south and stronger in the north and northeast. This is the drink of choice for many Thais who can't afford the heavy government liquor taxes; prices vary but 10B to 20B worth of the stronger concoctions will intoxicate three or four people. These types of home-brew or moonshine are generally taken straight with pure water as a chaser. In smaller towns, almost all of the garage-type restaurants (except, of course, Muslim restaurants) keep some under the counter for sale. Sometimes roots and herbs are added to jungle liquor to enhance flavour and colour.

Herbal liquors are somewhat fashionable throughout the country and can be found at roadside vendors, small pubs and in a few guesthouses. These liquors are made by soaking various herbs, roots, seeds, fruit and bark in *lâo khăo* to produce a range of concoctions called *lâo yaa dawng*. Many of these preparations are purported to have specific health-enhancing qualities. Some of them taste fabulous and others are rank.

Wine Thais are becoming increasingly interested in wine-drinking, but still manage only a minuscule average consumption of one glass per capita per year. Wines that are imported from France, Italy, the USA, Australia, Chile and other countries are available in restaurants and wine shops, but a 340% government tax makes them out of reach for most of us – or at the very least a poor bargain. If the government drops the tax, wine could become very fashionable in Thailand.

Various enterprises have attempted to produce wine in Thailand, most often with disastrous results. However successful wines have been produced by wineries in Loei and Phetchabun, namely Chateau de Loei (near Phu Reua in Loei Province) and Peak Eagle Winery (Khao Kho, Phetchabun Province). Both wineries make French-style wines from cabernet, syrah, chenin blanc and other grapes well known to wine tipplers around the world. Prices range from 350B to 400B per bottle.

Over 400 producers in 52 provinces also legally produce sticky-rice wine, known as *săa-thoh*. This somewhat milky beverage, typically 8% or 9% ABV, has a sweet-sour taste that goes well with Thai cuisine, especially Isan dishes. It's very cheap at around 30B per 630mL bottle. New legislation in Thailand recently made it legal for home brewers to make any alcoholic beverage they choose, as long as the alcohol content stays below 30%.

ENTERTAINMENT

Bars & Kaa-feh

Thai bars tend to follow a few major themes. Urban sophistication announced by gleaming chrome, blue lighting and abstract art is the latest trend to hit Bangkok and larger cities. This type tends to attract young Thais who fancy themselves as 'inter' (meaning international) as well as older Thais, 'tuppies' (Thai yuppies).

Once popular all over Thailand, but now relegated mostly to small towns, the 'old-west' style patterns itself after Thai fantasies of the 19th-century American West – lots of wood and cowboy paraphernalia. Another style is the 'Thai classic' pub, typically decorated with old black-and-white photos of Thai kings Rama VI and Rama VII, along with Thai antiques from northern and central Thailand.

On the Wild Side The go-go bars seen in lurid photos published by the Western media are limited to a few areas in Bangkok, Chiang Mai, Pattaya and Phuket's Patong Beach. These are bars in which girls typically wear swimsuits or other scant apparel. In some bars they dance to recorded music on a narrow raised stage. For obvious reasons, these places predominantly attract male customers. In Bangkok, Pattaya and Chiang Mai, gay men's go-go bars are also popular.

The *kaa-feh* (café) is an old-fashioned Thai nightclub, where Thai men consort with hostesses. These are the Thai counterparts of *faràng* go-go bars, except girls wear skimpy dresses and take turns singing songs in front of a live band. Small groups of men sit at tables ogling the girls while putting away prodigious amounts of whisky. For the price of a few house drinks – despite the name, no one drinks coffee in these places – the men can invite one of the singers to sit at their table for a while. Some of the singers work double shifts as part-time mistresses; others limit their services to singing and pouring drinks.

Closing Times All bars and clubs that don't feature live music or dancing are required to close by 1am except in designated 'tourist zones' like Pattaya and Hat Patong in Phuket, where the legal closing time is 2am. Places with live music may stay open till 2am, although in northern Thailand the local police often force live music bars to close at 1am.

Dance Clubs

Dance clubs are popular in larger cities, but outside Bangkok they're mostly attached to tourist or luxury hotels. The main clientele is Thai, although foreigners are welcome. Some provincial clubs employ female staff as professional dance partners for male entertainment, but dance clubs are generally considered fairly respectable nightspots for couples.

International DJ culture has arrived with a flourish in Bangkok, where dance clubs are now much like their counterparts in other large cities around the world. Local as well as visiting foreign 'superstars' spin hip-hop, drum 'n' bass, rap, house, trance, techno and whatever trends are sweeping the globe. Most Bangkok dance clubs collect a cover charge that includes a free drink or two, while rural clubs are generally free.

Thai law permits dance clubs to stay open till 2am.

Cafés & Coffee Shops

Western-style cafés, featuring a variety of espresso and coffee drinks, comfortable seating, and a selection of newspapers or magazines, are becoming increasingly popular in Bangkok, Chiang Mai and tourist areas.

Although they are fast disappearing, traditional Hokkien-style coffee shops *(ráan kaa-fae)* where thick, black, filtered coffee served in simple, casual surroundings can still be found in the Chinese quarters of southern Thai provincial capitals, and in certain Bangkok quarters. Frequented mostly by older Thai and Chinese men, they offer a place to read the newspaper, sip coffee and gossip about neighbours and politics.

Cinemas

Movie theatres are found in towns and cities throughout the country. Typical cinema programmes include US and European shoot-em-ups mixed with Thai comedies and romances. Violent action pictures are always a big draw; as a rule of thumb, the smaller the town, the more violent the films.

English-language films are only shown with their original soundtracks in a handful of theatres in Bangkok, Chiang Mai and Hat Yai; elsewhere all foreign films are dubbed in Thai. Ticket prices average 80B to 100B.

Every film in Thailand begins with the royal anthem, accompanied by pictures of the royal family projected onto the big screen. All viewers are expected to stand during the royal anthem.

SPECTATOR SPORTS

Thai Boxing

Almost anything goes in this martial sport, both in the ring and in the stands. If you don't mind the violence (in the ring), a Thai boxing match is worth attending for the pure spectacle – the wild musical accompaniment, the ceremonial beginning of each match and the frenzied betting throughout the stadium.

Thai boxing is also telecast on Channel 7 from noon to 2pm every Saturday afternoon, which explains the quiet streets at these times.

Rules & Forms Bouts are limited to five three-minute rounds separated with two-minute breaks. Contestants wear international-style gloves and trunks (always either red or blue) and their bare feet – no shoes are worn – are taped.

There are 16 weight divisions, ranging from miniflyweight to heavyweight, with the best fighters said to be in the welterweight division. As in international-style boxing, matches take place on a 7.3-sq-metre canvas-covered floor with rope retainers supported by four padded posts, rather than in the traditional dirt circle.

All surfaces of the body are still considered fair targets and any part of the body, except the head, may be used to strike an opponent. Common blows include high kicks to the neck, elbow thrusts to the face and head, knee hooks to the ribs and low crescent kicks to the calf. A contestant may even grasp an opponent's head between his hands and pull it down to meet an upward knee thrust. Punching is considered the weakest of all blows and kicking merely a way to 'soften up' one's opponent; knee and elbow strikes are decisive in most matches.

A Thai boxer's training and his relationship with his trainer are highly ritualised. When a boxer is considered ready for the ring, he is given a new name, with the name of the training camp as his surname.

A *ram muay* (boxing dance) precedes every match. This ceremony usually lasts about five minutes and expresses obeisance to the fighter's guru *(khruu)*, as well as to

History of *Muay Thai*

Most of what is known about the early history of Thai boxing comes from Burmese accounts of warfare between Myanmar and Thailand during the 15th and 16th centuries. The earliest reference (AD 1411) mentions a ferocious style of unarmed combat that decided the fate of Thai kings. A later description tells how Nai Khanom Tom, Thailand's first famous boxer and a prisoner of war in Burma, gained his freedom by roundly defeating a dozen Burmese warriors before the Burmese court.

King Naresuan the Great (r. 1590–1605) was supposed to have been a top-notch boxer himself, and he made *muay thai* a required part of military training. Later, another Thai king, Phra Chao Seua (the 'Tiger King') further promoted Thai boxing as a national sport by encouraging prize fights and the development of training camps in the early 18th century. There are accounts of massive wagers and bouts to the death during this time. Phra Chao Seua himself is said to have been an incognito participant in many of the matches. Combatants' fists were wrapped in thick horsehide for maximum impact with minimum knuckle damage. They also used cotton soaked in glue and ground glass and, later, hemp. Tree bark and seashells were used to protect the groin from lethal kicks.

The high incidence of death and physical injury led the Thai government to institute a ban on *muay thai* in the 1920s, but in the '30s it was revived under a set of regulations based on the international Queensberry rules.

No-one trained in any other martial art has been able to defeat a ranking Thai *nák muay* (fighter trained in *muay thai*) and many martial art aficionados consider the Thai style the ultimate in hand-to-hand fighting. On one famous occasion, Hong Kong's top five kung fu masters were all dispatched by knock-out in less than 6½ minutes.

the guardian spirit of Thai boxing. The complex series of gestures and movements is performed to the ringside musical accompaniment of Thai oboe *(pìi)* and percussion. Each boxer works out his own dance, in conjunction with his trainer and in accordance with the style of his particular camp.

Fighters wear sacred headbands and armbands into the ring for good luck and divine protection. The headband is removed after the *ram muay*, but the armband, which contains a small Buddha image, is worn throughout the match. After the bout begins, the fighters continue to bob and weave in rhythm, until the action begins to heat up. The musicians continue to play and the volume and tempo rise and fall along with the events in the ring.

Coloured belts denoting training ranks, such as those issued by karate schools, do not exist in Thai boxing. As one well-known trainer said, 'The only belts Thai boxers are concerned with are the Lumphini Stadium and the Ratchadamnoen Stadium championship belts.' Lumphini and Ratchadamnoen, both in Bangkok, are Thailand's two main Thai boxing venues.

As Thai boxing has become more popular among Westerners (as both spectators and participants), increasing numbers of bouts are staged for tourists in places like Pattaya, Phuket and Ko Samui. In these, the action may be genuine but amateurish, and the judging way below par. Nonetheless, with around 60,000 full-time boxers in Thailand, authentic matches are held frequently at the major Bangkok stadiums and in the provinces, and are easily sought out.

Several Thai boxers have gone on to win world championships in international-style boxing. Khaosai Galaxy, the greatest Asian boxer of all time, chalked up 19 World Boxing Association (WBA) bantamweight championships in a row before retiring undefeated in December 1991. At any given time Thailand typically claims five concurrent international boxing champions, usually in the bantamweight and flyweight categories.

In some areas of the country pre-1920s versions of *muay thai* still exists. In northeastern Thailand *muay boraan* is a highly ritualised form that resembles *taijiquan* (t'ai chi) or classical dance. In pockets of southern Thailand, fighters practising *muay kàtchii* still bind their hands in hemp, and a more localised southern style in Chaiya known as *muay chaiyaa* uses the elbows and forearms to good advantage. Each year around the lunar New Year (Songkran) in April, near the town of Mae Sot on the Thai-Myanmar border, a top Thai fighter challenges a Burmese fighter of similar class from the other side of the Mae Nam Moei (Moei River) to a no-holds barred, hemp-fisted battle that ends only after one of the opponents wipes blood from his body. For more on *muay thai* see Martial Arts Courses earlier.

Kràbìi-Kràbawng

Another traditional martial art still practised in Thailand is *kràbìi-kràbawng*. This tradition focuses on hand-held weapons, in particular the *kràbìi* (sword), *phlawng* (quarter-staff), *ngáo* (halberd), *dàap sǎwng meu* (a pair of swords held in each hand) and *mái sun-sàwk* (a pair of clubs). Although for most Thais *kràbìi-kràbawng* is a ritual artefact to be displayed during festivals or at tourist venues, the art is still solemnly taught according to a 400-year-old tradition handed down from Ayuthaya's Wat Phutthaisawan. The king's elite bodyguards are trained in *kràbìi-kràbawng*; many Thai cultural observers perceive it as a 'purer' tradition than *muay thai*.

Like *muay thai* of more than 70 years ago, modern *kràbìi-kràbawng* matches are held within a marked circle, beginning with a *wâi khruu* ceremony and accompanied throughout by a musical ensemble. Thai-boxing techniques and judo-like throws are employed in conjunction with weapons techniques. Although sharpened weapons are used, the contestants refrain from striking their opponents – the winner is decided on the basis of stamina and the technical skill displayed. Although an injured fighter may surrender, injuries do not automatically stop a match.

Takraw

Sometimes called Siamese football in old English texts, takraw *(tàkrâw)* refers to games in which a woven rattan ball about 12cm in diameter is kicked around. The rattan (or sometimes plastic) ball itself is called a *lûuk tàkrâw*. Popular in several neighbouring countries, takraw was introduced to the Southeast Asian Games by Thailand, and international championships tend to alternate between the Thais and Malaysians. The traditional way to play takraw in Thailand is for players to stand in a circle (the size depending on the number of players) and simply try to keep the ball airborne by kicking it soccer-style. Points are scored for style, difficulty and variety of kicking manoeuvres.

A popular variation on *takraw* – and the one used in intramural or international competitions – is played like volleyball, with a net, but with only the feet and head permitted to touch the ball. It's amazing to see the players perform aerial pirouettes, spiking the ball over the net with their feet. Another variation has players kicking the ball into a hoop 4.5m above the ground – basketball with feet, and no backboard!

SHOPPING

Many bargains await you in Thailand if you have the luggage space to carry them back. Always haggle to get the best price, except in department stores. And don't go shopping in the company of touts, tour guides or friendly strangers as they will inevitably – no matter what they say – take a commission on anything you buy, thus driving prices up.

Textiles

In Thailand, fabric is possibly the best all-round buy. Thai silk is considered the best in the world – the coarse weave and soft texture of the silk means it is more easily dyed than harder, smoother silks, resulting in brighter colours and a unique lustre. Silk can be purchased cheaply in the north and northeast where it is made or, more easily, in Bangkok. Excellent, reasonably priced tailor shops can make your choice of fabric into almost any pattern. A Thai-silk suit should cost around 4500B to 6500B. Chinese silk is available at about half the cost – 'washed' Chinese silk makes inexpensive, comfortable shirts or blouses.

Cottons are also a good deal – common items like the *phâakhamáa* (cotton sarongs) and the *phâasîn* (the slightly larger female equivalent) make great tablecloths and curtains. Good ready-made cotton shirts are available, such as the *mâw hâwm* (Thai work shirt) and the *kúay hâeng* (Chinese-style shirt). See the sections on Pasang and Hat Siaw in the Northern Thailand chapter and Ko Yo in the Lower Southern Gulf chapter for places to see cotton weaving.

Cotton weaving has also become very popular in the northeast and there are fabulous finds in Nong Khai, Roi Et, Khon Kaen and Mahasarakham. The *mǎwn khwǎan,* a hard, triangle-shaped pillow made in the northeast, makes a good souvenir and comes in many sizes. The northeast is also famous for *mát-mìi* cloth – thick cotton or silk fabric woven from tie-dyed threads – similar to Indonesia's ikat fabrics.

In the north you can also find Lanna-style textiles based on intricate Thai Daeng, Thai Dam and Thai Lü patterns from Nan, Laos and China's Xishuangbanna.

Fairly nice batik *(paa-té)* is available in the south in patterns that are more similar to the batik found in Malaysia than in Indonesia.

Clothing

Tailor-made and ready-to-wear clothes are relatively inexpensive. If you're not particular about style you could pick up an entire wardrobe of travelling clothes at one of Bangkok's many street markets (eg, Pratunam) for what you'd pay for one designer shirt in New York, Paris or Milan.

You're more likely to get a good fit if you resort to a tailor but be wary of the quickie 24-hour tailor shops; the clothing is often made of inferior fabric or the poor tailoring means the arms start falling off after three weeks wear. It's best to ask Thai or longtime foreign residents for a recommendation and then go for two or three fittings.

Shoulder Bags

Thai shoulder bags *(yâam)* come in many varieties, some woven by hill tribes, others by the northern Thai cottage industry. The best are made by the Lahu hill tribes, whom the Thais call Musoe. The weaving is more skilful and the bags tend to last longer than those made by other tribes. For an extra-large *yâam*, the Karen-made bag is a good choice, and is easy to find in the Mae Sot and Mae Hong Son areas. These days many hill tribes are copying patterns from tribes other than their own.

Overall, Chiang Mai has the best selection of standard shoulder bags, but Bangkok has the best prices – try the Indian district,

Pahurat, for these as well as anything else made of cloth. Roi Et and Mahasarakham in the northeast are also good hunting grounds for locally made shoulder bags. Prices range from 70B for a cheaply made bag to 200B for something special.

Antiques

Real antiques cannot be taken out of Thailand without a permit. No Buddha image, new or old, may be exported without the permission of the Fine Arts Department. See Customs earlier in this chapter for more information on the export of art objects and antiques.

Chinese and Thai antiques are sold in two areas of Bangkok's Chinatown: Wang Burapha (the streets that have Chinese 'gates' over the entrance) and Nakhon Kasem. Some antiques (and many fakes) are sold at the Weekend Market in Chatuchak Park, and also at the River City complex in Bangkok. Merchandise in the tourist antique shops are, predictably, fantastically overpriced. Value-wise, northern Thailand has become the best source of Thai antiques – prices are about half what you'd typically pay in Bangkok.

Jewellery

Thailand is the world's largest exporter of gems and ornaments, rivalled only by India and Sri Lanka. The International Colorstones Association (ICA) relocated from Los Angeles to Bangkok's Charn Issara Tower several years ago, and the World Federation of Diamond Bourses (WFDB) has established a Bourse in Bangkok – two events that recognise Thailand as the world trade-and-production centre for precious stones.

Although rough-stone sources in Thailand have decreased dramatically, stones are now imported from Australia, Sri Lanka and other countries to be cut, polished and traded. Native stones, such as sapphires, make up only about 25% of business. At least 40% of all gem-related exports consist of diamond products, all of which are imported rough and then finished in Thailand by expert gem-cutters, mostly in Bangkok. One of the results of this remarkable growth – in Thailand the gem trade has increased roughly 10% every year for the last two decades – is that the prices are rising rapidly.

If you know what you are doing you can make some really good buys in both unset gems and finished jewellery. Gold ornaments are sold at a good rate as labour costs are low. The best bargains in gems are jade, rubies and sapphires.

Buy from reputable dealers only, preferably members of the Jewel Fest Club, a guarantee programme established by TAT and the Thai Gem and Jewellery Traders Association (TGJTA). When you purchase an item of jewellery from a shop that is identified as a member of the Jewel Fest Club, a certificate detailing your purchase will be issued. This guarantees a refund, less 10%, if you return the merchandise to the point of sale within 30 days. A refund less 20% is guaranteed if the items are returned after 30 days but within 45 days of purchase. You can obtain a list of members direct from **Jewel Fest Club** *(☎ 0 2235 3039, 0 2267 5233–7)* or from TAT.

The biggest centres in Thailand for gem stones native to Thailand, neighbouring Myanmar and Cambodia, are Kanchanaburi, Mae Sot, Mae Sai and Chanthaburi. These are the areas where Bangkok dealers go to buy their stones.

The Asian Institute of Gemological Sciences *(☎ 0 2267 4315, fax 0 2267 4320; Jewelry Trade Center, South Tower, 11th floor, 919/1 Th Silom)*, offers month-long and one-day short courses in gemology as well as tours of gem mines. You can bring gems here for inspection but the staff don't assess value, only authenticity and grading.

John Hoskins' book *Buyer's Guide to Thai Gems & Jewellery,* available at Bangkok bookshops, is a useful introduction to Thai gems.

Warning Be wary of special 'deals' that are offered for one day only or that set you up as a 'courier' in which you're promised big money. Many travellers end up losing big. Shop around and *don't be hasty*. Remember, there's no such thing as a 'government sale' or 'factory price' at a gem or jewellery shop; the Thai government does not own or manage any gem or jewellery shops.

See the boxed text 'Scams' earlier in this chapter for a detailed warning on gem fraud.

Hill-Tribe Crafts

Interesting embroidery, clothing, bags (see Shoulder Bags earlier in this section) and jewellery from the northern provinces can be bought in Bangkok at **Narayan Phand** *(Th Lan Luang)*, at branches of the **Queen's Hillcrafts Foundation**, and at various tourist shops around town.

In Chiang Mai there are many shops selling handicrafts along Th Tha Phae and Th Loi Khraw, and there is a shop sponsored by missionaries near Prince Royal College. It's worth shopping around for the best prices and bargaining. The all-round best buys of northern hill-tribe crafts are at the Chiang Mai Night Bazaar – if you know how to bargain and don't mind wading through lots of junk.

Lacquerware

Good lacquerware, a lot of which is made in Myanmar and sold along the northern Myanmar border, can be found in Thailand. Try Mae Sot, Mae Sariang and Mae Sai for the best buys.

Today's styles originated in 11th-century Chiang Mai. In 1558 Myanmar's King Bayinnaung captured a number of Chiang Mai lacquer artisans and brought them to Bago in central Myanmar to establish the tradition of incised lacquerware. Lacquer (not to be confused with *lac*, which comes from an insect), comes from the *Melanorrhea usitata* tree and in its most basic form is mixed with paddy-husk ash to form a light, flexible, waterproof coating over bamboo frames.

To make a lacquerware object, a bamboo frame is first woven. If the item is top quality, only the frame is bamboo and horse or donkey hairs will be wound round it. With lower-quality lacquerware, the whole object is made from bamboo. The lacquer is then coated over the framework and allowed to dry. After several days it is sanded down with ash from rice husks, and another coating of lacquer is applied. A high-quality item may have seven layers of lacquer.

The lacquerware is engraved and painted, then polished to remove the paint from everywhere except in the engravings. Multicoloured lacquerware is produced by repeated applications. From start to finish it can take five or six months to produce a high-quality piece of lacquerware, which may have as many as five colours. Flexibility is one characteristic of good lacquerware: a top-quality bowl can have its rim squeezed together until the sides meet without suffering damage. The quality and precision of the engraving is another thing to look for.

Lacquerware is made into bowls, trays, plates, boxes, containers, cups, vases and many other everyday items. Octagonal folding tables are also popular.

Nielloware

This art came from Europe via Nakhon Si Thammarat and has been cultivated in Thailand for over 700 years. Engraved silver is inlaid with niello – an alloy of lead, silver, copper and sulphur – to form striking black-and-silver jewellery designs. Nielloware is one of Thailand's best buys.

Ceramics

Many kinds of hand-thrown pottery, old and new, are available throughout the kingdom. The best-known ceramics are the greenish Thai celadon products from the Sukhothai-Si Satchanalai area, and central Thailand's *benjarong* or 'five-colour' style. The latter is based on Chinese patterns while the former is a Thai original that has been imitated throughout China and Southeast Asia. Rough, unglazed pottery from the north and northeast can also be very appealing. For international styles, the many ceramic factories of Lampang are the best places to look for bargains.

Other Crafts

Under the queen's Supplementary Occupations & Related Techniques (Support) foundation, a number of regional crafts from around Thailand have been successfully revived. *Málaeng tháp* collages and sculptures are made by the artful cutting and assembling of the metallic, multicoloured wings and carapaces of female wood-boring beetles (*Sternocera aequisignata)*, harvested after they die at the end of their reproductive cycle between July and September. Hailing mostly from the north and northeast, they can nonetheless be found in craft shops all over Thailand.

For 'Damascene ware' *(khraam)*, gold and silver wire is hammered into a cross-hatched steel surface to create exquisitely patterned bowls and boxes. Look for them in the more upmarket department stores and craft shops of Bangkok.

Yaan líphao is a type of intricately woven basket made from a hardy grass in southern Thailand. Ever since the queen and other female members of the royal family began carrying delicate *yaan líphao* purses, they have been a Thai fashion staple. Basketry of this type is most easily found in the southern provincial capitals, or in Bangkok shops that specialise in regional handicrafts.

Furniture

Rattan and hardwood furniture items are often good buys and can be made to order. Bangkok and Chiang Mai have the best selection. With the ongoing success of teak farming and recycling, teak furniture has once again become a bargain in Thailand if you find the right places. Asian rosewood is also a good buy.

Fake or Pirated Goods

In Bangkok, Chiang Mai and other tourist centres there is black-market street trade in fake designer goods, particularly Benetton pants and sweaters; DKNY shirts; Lacoste (crocodile) and Ralph Lauren polo shirts; NBA-franchise T-shirts; Levi's jeans; Reebok sneakers; and Rolex, Dunhill and Cartier watches. No-one pretends they're the real thing, at least not the vendors. Western companies are applying heavy pressure on Asian governments to get this stuff off the street, but so far have had little success. Experts claim around one-fourth of all trademarked goods sold in Thailand are counterfeit or pirated and that trademark owners lose 25B for every 100B spent on their products in this country.

In some cases foreign-name brands are produced under licence in Thailand and represent good value. A pair of legally produced Levi's 518s (low-rise, lycra-woven, flared bottoms), for example, typically costs US$10 from a Thai street vendor, and US$35 to US$45 in the company's home town of San Francisco! Careful examination of the product usually reveals tell-tale characteristics that confirm or deny its authenticity.

Unlicensed CDs and DVDs are another illegal bargain in Thailand. These discs are 'pirated', ie, no royalties are paid to the copyright owners. Average prices are from 100B per audio CD, 150B to 200B per DVD. The sale of pirated discs is for the most part limited to Bangkok, Chiang Mai and beach resort areas. Licensed CDs and DVDs are also available, although the selection is much poorer and the cost much higher.

Department Stores

Thailand's two big department-store chains, **Robinson** and **Central**, offer reasonably priced clothing, electronics and homewares at several branches throughout Bangkok as well as in other larger cities. Smaller, local department stores are also commonly found in provincial capitals, and will carry a modest selection of inexpensive ready-made clothing, cosmetics, homewares and so on.

Getting There & Away

AIR

Airports

Thailand has six international airports, one each in Bangkok, Chiang Mai, Phuket, Samui, Sukhothai and Hat Yai. Chiang Rai is designated as 'international', but at the time of writing it did not actually field any international flights.

A district directly north of Bangkok known as Don Muang has been the main hub for air traffic in and out of Thailand since 1931. Today it's home to Bangkok International Airport, the busiest airport in Southeast Asia in terms of scheduled arrivals and departures.

A second airport at Nong Ngu Hao (located 20km east of Bangkok), Suvarnabhumi International, is intended to replace the one at Don Muang in October 2005.

For information on arrival and departure procedures in Bangkok, as well as details on getting to and from the airport, see the Getting There & Away section of the Bangkok chapter.

Bangkok International Airport The two international terminals at Bangkok International Airport are among the most modern and convenient in Asia. Immigration procedures can be slow going during peak arrival times (11pm to midnight). Baggage claim is usually very efficient.

Warning

The information in this chapter is particularly vulnerable to change: Prices for international travel are volatile, routes are introduced and cancelled, schedules change, special deals come and go, and rules and visa requirements are amended. You should check directly with the airline or a travel agent to make sure you understand how a fare (and ticket you may buy) works and be aware of the security requirements for international travel.

The upshot of this is that you should get opinions, quotes and advice from as many airlines and travel agents as possible before you part with your hard-earned cash. The details given in this chapter should be regarded as pointers and are not a substitute for your own careful, up-to-date research.

Touts

Beware of airport touts – this means anyone trying to steer you away from the public taxi queue outside or asking where you plan to stay while you're in Bangkok. A legion of touts – some in what appear to be airport or airline uniforms – are always waiting in the arrival area, and will begin their badgering as soon as you clear customs. Posing as helpful tourist information agents, their main objective is to get commissions from overpriced taxi rides or hotel rooms. If you're foolish enough to mention the hotel or guesthouse you plan to stay at, chances are they'll tell you it's full and that you must go to another hotel (which will pay them a commission, though they may deny it). Sometimes they'll show you a nice collection of photos; don't get sucked in, as these touted hotels are often substandard and badly located.

The customs area has a green lane for passengers with nothing to declare – just walk through if you're one of these, and hand your customs form to one of the clerks by the exit. Baggage trolleys are free for use inside the terminal.

Currency Exchange The foreign-currency booths (Thai Military Bank, Bangkok Bank, Krung Thai Bank) on the ground floor of the arrival hall and in the departure lounge of both terminals give a good rate of exchange, so there's no need to wait till you're in the city centre to change money. These banks also have ATMs in the arrival and departure halls.

Post & Communications There is a 24-hour post office with a Home Country Direct phone service (see the Facts for the Visitor chapter for details of this service) in the departure hall (3rd floor) of Terminal 1. There's another 24-hour post office in the departure lounge; a third one, in the arrival hall, is open from 9am to 5pm weekdays.

The Communications Authority of Thailand (CAT) operates the 24-hour Telecommunications Center on the 2nd floor of

Terminal 2, where international phone calls may be arranged in a variety of ways, including by credit card, collect (reverse charges) and Home Country Direct. The telecommunications centre also offers three computer terminals rigged for quick email and Internet access.

Left Luggage & Day Rooms There are 24 left-luggage facilities in the departure halls of both terminals. In the transit lounge of Terminal 1, clean **day rooms** (*☎ 0 2535 3710–24*) with washing and toilet facilities can be rented for US$86 a double per eight hours. Less expensive rooms without bathrooms are available for US$31 per four-hour block.

Hotel Reservations The hotel reservation desks operated by the Thai Hotels Association (THA) at the back of the arrival hall in each terminal offer a selection of accommodation options in the city, but only above the guesthouse price range (roughly 900B and above). THA staff can often arrange room rates well below normal walk-in rates.

There are usually one or two other desks in the arrival hall offering similar services, but THA seems to be the most reliable.

Shopping There are several newsstands and souvenir shops in the arrival and departure areas of each terminal. Duty-free shopping is available in the departure lounge as well.

The domestic terminal has a much better book and magazine selection. If you have enough time to walk across the footbridge from Terminal 1 to the Amari Airport Hotel, you will find an even better bookshop in the hotel's shopping arcade (south of reception).

Facilities near the Airport If you leave the airport-building area and cross the pedestrian bridge over the expressway (just north of the passenger terminal), you'll find yourself in the district of Don Muang, where there are all sorts of shops, a market, lots of small restaurants and food stalls, and even a *wát* (temple), all within 100m or so of the airport terminal buildings.

Amari Airport Hotel (*☎ 0 2566 1020–1*) is a luxurious and modern hotel that has its own air-conditioning, enclosed footbridge from Terminal 1 and 'special ministay' daytime rates (8am to 6pm) for stays of up to three hours. For additional information on overnight accommodation in the Don Muang area, see Places to Stay, airport area, in the Bangkok chapter. The Amari also has a selection of decent restaurants serving Italian, Japanese and Thai food.

Other International Airports Travellers heading for southern or northern Thailand can skip Bangkok altogether by flying directly to these areas. Thai Airways International (THAI) has regular flights to Phuket and Hat Yai from Singapore; to Phuket from Kuala Lumpur and Singapore; and to Chiang Mai from Singapore, Kuala Lumpur, Hong Kong, Beijing, Kunming, Yangon, Mandalay and Vientiane.

Bangkok Airways fields flights between Sukhothai and Luang Prabang, between Ko Samui and Singapore, and between Chiang Mai and Jinghong.

The Chiang Rai International Airport only services flights to and from Bangkok, but THAI hopes to establish international routes, to and from other Asian capitals, over the next few years.

Airlines

The national carrier THAI dominates inbound and outbound air traffic, but around 80 other international airlines fly in and out of Bangkok.

Bangkok Airways flies between Bangkok and Phnom Penh (Cambodia), Siem Reap (Cambodia), Luang Prabang (Laos), Jinghong (China) and Xi'an (China).

See the Getting There & Away section of the Bangkok chapter for the Bangkok offices of all the international airlines, and see the Getting Around chapter for a list of domestic airline offices in Thailand.

Tickets

With a bit of research – ringing travel agents, checking Internet sites, perusing the travel ads in newspapers – you can usually get yourself a good travel deal. Start early, as some of the cheapest tickets need to be bought well in advance and popular flights can sell out.

Full-time students and people under 26 years of age (under 30 in some countries) have access to some better deals than other travellers. You have to show a document proving your date of birth or a valid International Student Identity Card (ISIC) when buying your ticket and boarding the plane.

Generally, there is nothing to be gained by buying a ticket directly from the airline (except for tickets purchased on the Web). Discounted tickets are released to selected travel agents and specialist discount agencies and these are usually the cheapest deals going.

Tickets can also be purchased cheaply on the Internet and many airlines offer excellent fares to Web surfers. They may sell seats by auction or simply cut prices to reflect the reduced cost of electronic selling.

Many travel agencies around the world have websites, which can make the Internet a quick and easy way to compare prices. There is also an increasing number of online agents that operate only on the Internet.

Online ticket sales work well if you are doing a simple one-way or return trip on specified dates. However, online fare generators are no substitute for a travel agent who knows all about special deals, has strategies for avoiding layovers and can offer advice on everything from which airline has the best vegetarian food to the best travel insurance to bundle with your ticket.

You may find the cheapest flights are advertised by obscure agencies. Most such firms are honest and solvent, but there are some rogue fly-by-night outfits around. Paying by credit card generally offers protection, as most card issuers provide refunds if you can prove you didn't get what you paid for. Agents who accept only cash should hand over the tickets straight away and not tell you to 'come back tomorrow'. After you've made a booking or paid your deposit, call the airline and confirm that the booking was made.

If you purchase a ticket and later want to make changes to your route or get a refund, you need to contact the original travel agent. Airlines issue refunds only to the purchaser of a ticket – usually the travel agent who bought the ticket on your behalf. Many travellers change their routes halfway through their trips, so think carefully before you buy a ticket that is not easily refunded or changed.

Booking flights in and out of Bangkok during the high season (December to March) can be difficult. For air travel during these months you should make your bookings as far in advance as possible.

Also, be sure to reconfirm return or ongoing tickets when you arrive in Thailand (THAI claims this isn't necessary with its tickets). Failure to reconfirm can mean losing your reservation.

Bangkok is one of the cheapest cities in the world to fly out of, due to the Thai government's loose restrictions on air fares and the high level of competition between airlines and travel agencies. The result is that with a little shopping around you can come up with some real bargains. If you can find a cheap one-way ticket to Bangkok, take it, because you are virtually guaranteed to find one of equal or lesser cost for the return trip once you get there.

Fares listed in this chapter should serve as a guideline.

Special Deals Full-time students and people under 26 have access to better deals than other travellers. The better deals may not always be cheaper fares but can include more flexibility to change flights and/or routes. You have to show a document proving your

Second-Hand Tickets

You'll occasionally see advertisements on youth hostel bulletin boards and sometimes in newspapers for 'second-hand tickets'. That is, somebody purchased a return ticket or a ticket with multiple stopovers and now wants to sell the unused portion of the ticket.

The prices offered look very attractive indeed. Unfortunately, these tickets, if used for international travel, are usually worthless, as the name on the ticket must match the name on the passport of the person checking in. Some people reason that the seller of the ticket can check you in with his or her passport, and then give you the boarding pass – wrong again! Usually the immigration people want to see your boarding pass, and if it doesn't match the name in your passport, then you won't be able to board your flight.

If you purchase a ticket and then change your name, be sure you have documents such as your old passport to prove that the old you and the new you are the same person.

date of birth or a valid International Student Identity Card (ISIC) when buying your ticket and boarding the plane. There are plenty of places around the world where nonstudents can get fake student cards, but if you get caught using a fake card you could have your ticket confiscated.

Most airlines offer frequentflyer deals that can earn you a free air ticket or other goodies. To qualify, you have to accumulate sufficient mileage with the same airline or airline alliance. Many airlines have 'blackout periods', or times when you cannot fly for free on your frequent-flier points (Christmas and Chinese New Year, for example). The worst thing about frequent-flier programmes is that they tend to lock you into one airline, and that airline may not always have the cheapest fares or most convenient flight schedule.

Travellers with Special Needs

Most international airlines can cater to people with special needs – travellers with disabilities, people with young children and even children travelling alone.

Travellers with special dietary preferences (vegetarian, kosher etc) can request appropriate meals with advance notice. If you are travelling in a wheelchair, most international airports can provide an escort from check-in desk to plane where needed, and ramps, lifts, toilets and telephones are generally available.

Airlines usually allow babies up to two years of age to fly for 10% of the adult fare, although a few may allow them free of charge. Reputable international airlines usually provide nappies (diapers), tissues, talcum and all the other paraphernalia needed to keep babies clean, dry and half-happy. For children between the ages of two and 12, the fare on international flights is usually 50% of the regular fare or 67% of a discounted fare.

Departure Tax

All passengers leaving Thailand on international flights are charged a departure tax (officially called an 'airport service charge') of 500B, which is not included in the price of air tickets, but paid at the check-in counter. Only baht is accepted. Be sure to have enough baht left over at the end of your trip to pay this tax – otherwise you'll have to revisit one of the currency-exchange booths.

The USA

The *New York Times, LA Times, Chicago Tribune* and *San Francisco Examiner* all have weekly travel sections in which you'll find any number of travel agency ads. STA Travel has offices in major cities nationwide.

It's cheaper to fly to Bangkok from West Coast cities than from the East Coast. You can get some great deals through the many bucket shops (which discount tickets by taking a cut in commissions) and consolidators (agencies that buy airline seats in bulk) operating in Los Angeles and San Francisco. Through agencies such as these a return (round-trip) air fare to Bangkok from any of 10 West Coast cities starts at around US$750, with occasional specials (especially in May and September) of just US$600. If you're flying from the East Coast, add US$150 to US$200 to these fares.

One of the most reliable discounters is **Avia Travel** (*☎ 800-950 AVIA, 510-558 2150, fax 558 2158; Ⓦ www.aviatravel.com; Suite E, 1029 Solano Ave, Albany CA 94706*), which specialises in custom-designed round-the-world fares, eg, San Francisco/Los Angeles–Bangkok–Rome/Paris/London–San Francisco/Los Angeles for US$1135, as well as Circle Pacific fares such as Los Angeles–Tokyo–Taipei–Singapore–Bangkok–Hong Kong–Los Angeles for US$1100. The agency sets aside a portion of its profits for Volunteers in Asia, a nonprofit organisation that sends volunteers to work in Southeast Asia.

While airlines can rarely match the prices of the discounters, they are worth checking, if only to get benchmark prices to use for comparison. Tickets bought directly from the airlines may also have fewer restrictions and/or less strict cancellation policies than those bought from discounters.

The airlines that generally offer the lowest fares from the USA include China Airlines, CP Air, EVA Airways, Korean Air and THAI. Each has a budget and/or 'super Apex' fare that costs around US$900 to US$1500 return from Los Angeles, San Francisco or Seattle, depending on the season. Add US$150 to US$200 for departure from the East Coast. Korean Air occasionally runs special fares for US$600 to US$750 return between San Francisco or Los Angeles and Bangkok. Several of these airlines also fly out of New York, Dallas, Chicago and Atlanta – add another US$150 to US$250 to their lowest fares.

EVA Airways (Taiwan) offers the 'Evergreen Deluxe' class between the USA and Bangkok, via Taipei, which has business class-sized seats and personal movie screens for about the same cost as regular economy fares on most other airlines.

Canada

Travel CUTS (*w www.travelcuts.com*) has offices in all major cities. The *Globe & Mail* and the *Vancouver Sun* carry travel-agency ads.

Canadian Pacific flies from Vancouver to Bangkok for around C$1100 to C$1500 return for advance-purchase excursion fares. Travellers living in eastern Canada will usually find the best deals out of New York or San Francisco – add on fares for travel from Toronto or Montreal (see The USA section earlier).

Australia

STA Travel (*☎ 1300 360 960; w www.statravel.com.au*) has offices in all major cities and on many university campuses. **Flight Centre** (*☎ 131 600; w www.flightcentre.com.au*) has dozens of offices throughout Australia. Alternatively, you'll find advertisements for many small, independent travel agents in the weekend editions of most of the major newspapers.

From the east coast of Australia, THAI and Qantas have direct flights to Bangkok ranging from around A$995 in the low season to A$1350 in the high season. Garuda Indonesia, Singapore Airlines, Philippine Airlines and Malaysia Airlines also have frequent flights and some good fare deals, with stopovers, to Bangkok.

New Zealand

The *New Zealand Herald* has a travel section in which travel agents advertise fares. **Flight Centre** (*☎ 09-309 6171; National Bank Towers cnr Queen & Darby Sts, Auckland*) has branches throughout the country. **STA Travel** (*☎ 09-309 0458; w www.statravel.com.au; 10 High St, Auckland*) also has offices in Hamilton, Palmerston North, Wellington, Christchurch and Dunedin.

Air New Zealand and THAI both have direct flights from Auckland to Bangkok. Return low-season fares start from around NZ$1300; a return ticket in the high season starts from around NZ$1500. Qantas, Malaysian Airlines and Garuda International also have flights to Bangkok, with stopovers.

The UK & Continental Europe

Discount air travel is big business in London and London-to-Bangkok is arguably the most competitive air route in the world. Typical discounted air fares along this route range from UK£350 to UK£450 return. You may have to call around to get these fares, or better yet check the ads that appear in the travel pages of the weekend broadsheet newspapers, in *Time Out*, the *Evening Standard* or in the free magazine *TNT*.

For students or travellers under 26, **STA Travel** is popular in the UK. It operates branches throughout the country and although it caters especially to young people and students, it sells tickets to all travellers.

Other recommended travel agencies for all age groups include the following.

Bridge the World (☎ 020-7734 7447, w www.b-t-w.co.uk) 4 Regent Place, London W1
Flightbookers (☎ 020-7757 2000, w www.ebookers.com) 177–178 Tottenham Court Rd, London W1
Trailfinders (☎ 020-7938 3939, w www.trailfinders.co.uk) 194 Kensington High St, London W8
Travel Bag (☎ 020-7287 5158, w www.travelbag.co.uk) 52 Regent St, London W1B 5DX

At least two dozen airlines fly between the two capitals, although only three of them – British Airways, Qantas and THAI – fly nonstop. If you insist on a nonstop flight, you will probably have to pay between UK£500 and UK£800 return for the privilege (or around UK£100 less if you are a student or under 26). A one-way ticket is usually only slightly cheaper than a return ticket.

Gulf Air does a Paris–Bangkok–Paris flight via Tashkent for €569. Other cheap return flights are with Malaysia Airlines from Amsterdam (€518, via Kuala Lumpur); with Emirates Air from Munich (€711), Stockholm (5519kr) and Zurich (Sfr897); and with Finnair from Berlin (€723).

Asia

There are regular flights to Bangkok International Airport from every major city in Asia and most airlines offer about the same fares for intra-Asia flights. Below is a list of common one-way intra-Asia fares from Bangkok. Return tickets are usually double the one-way fare, although occasionally airlines run special discounts of up to 25% for such tickets. For fares in the reverse direction, convert to local currency.

from	approx one-way fare
Calcutta	6758B
Denpasar	8070B
Ho Chi Minh City	5230B
Hong Kong	6540B
Kathmandu	9460B
Phnom Penh	5580B
Seoul	13,950B
Singapore	3360B
Taipei	11,250B
Tokyo	14,390B
Yangon	4230B

Although other Asian centres are now competitive with Bangkok, it's still a good place for shopping around for discounted airline tickets, especially with the baht trading low against most hard currencies.

Travellers should note, however, that some Bangkok travel agencies have a shocking reputation. Taking money and then delaying or not coming through with the tickets, as well as providing tickets with limited validity periods or severe usage restrictions, are all part of the racket. There are a large number of perfectly honest agents, but beware of the rogues.

A good Internet source for discounted fares out of Bangkok is Ⓦ www.bangkoktickets.com.

LAND & RIVER

Malaysia

Road You can cross the west-coast border between Malaysia and Thailand by taking a bus to one side and another bus from the other, the most obvious direct route being between Alor Setar and Hat Yai. This is the route used by taxis and buses but there's a 1km stretch of no-man's land between the Thai border control at Sadao (also known as Dan Nok) and the Malaysian border control at Changlun.

It's much easier to go to Padang Besar, where the train line crosses the border. Here you can get a bus right up to the border, walk across and take another bus or taxi on the other side. On either side you'll most likely be mobbed by taxi and motorcycle drivers wanting to take you to immigration. It's better to walk over the railway bridge into Thailand, and then ignore the touts until you get to the 'official' Thai taxis, which will take you all the way to Hat Yai, with a stop at the immigration office (2.5km from the border), for around 50B. The immigration and customs office and bus-and-train station complex make the whole transition smoother.

A daily bus runs between Alor Setar, Hat Yai and Kota Bharu.

There's also a border crossing at Keroh (Betong on the Thai side), right in the middle between the east and west coasts.

See the Sungai Kolok section in the Lower Southern Gulf chapter for information on crossing the border on the east coast.

Train Riding the rails from Singapore to Bangkok via Butterworth, Malaysia, is a great way to travel to Thailand – as long as you don't count on making a smooth change between the Keretapi Tanah Melayu (KTM) and State Railway of Thailand (SRT) trains. The Thai train almost always leaves on time; the Malaysian train rarely arrives on time. Unfortunately the Thai train leaves Padang Besar even if the Malaysian railway express from Kuala Lumpur (or the 2nd-class connection from Butterworth) is late. To be on the safe side, purchase the Malaysian and Thai portions of your ticket with departures on consecutive days and plan a Butterworth/Penang stopover. If you want to try it straight through, KTM train No 36 leaves Butterworth at 1.10pm and the Thai connection arrives at Bangkok the following day at 11.10am.

Bangkok–Butterworth/Penang The daily special express No 35 leaves from Bangkok's Hualamphong station at 2.20pm, arriving in Hat Yai at 6.45am the next day and terminating at Padang Besar at 7.50am. Everyone disembarks at Padang Besar, proceeds through immigration, then boards the 2nd-class KTM train No 99 arriving in

Butterworth at 11.55pm Malaysian time (one hour ahead of Thai time).

The fare to Padang Besar is 767B for 1st class, 360B for 2nd class, plus an 80B special-express charge and 250B for air-con. There is no 3rd-class seating on this train.

For a sleeping berth in 2nd class, add 130B for an upper berth, 200B for a lower. In 1st class it's 520B per person.

Bangkok–Kuala Lumpur & Singapore To get to Kuala Lumpur, make the Thai and Malaysian rail connections to Butterworth as described earlier, changing to an express or limited express at Butterworth. There are early morning, noon and evening services to Kuala Lumpur, and the trip takes six to seven hours.

There are daily services between Kuala Lumpur and Singapore – early morning, early afternoon and evening – which take six to eight hours, depending on what type of train you take.

The information offices at the train terminals in Butterworth (☎ 0 4334 7962) and Kuala Lumpur (☎ 0 3274 7435) can provide information about schedules, fares and seat availability on the Malaysian and Singaporean services.

Laos

Road The 1174m Thai–Lao Friendship Bridge spans a section of the Mekong River between Ban Jommani (near Nong Khai, Thailand) and Tha Na Leng (near Vientiane, Laos) and is the main transportation gateway between the two countries. A parallel rail bridge is planned to extend the Bangkok–Nong Khai railway into Vientiane, although a construction schedule has yet to be announced.

Construction of a second Mekong bridge is about to begin. When it opens in 2005 it will span the Mekong at Mukdahan (opposite Savannakhet) to create a land link between Thailand and Vietnam. The Asian Development Bank's much vaunted title for this development project is 'the Thailand–Lao PDR–Vietnam East–West Corridor'. A similar plan for Nakhon Phanom (opposite Laos' Tha Khaek) is still undergoing a feasibility study.

Another bridge was planned to span the river between Thailand's Chiang Khong and Laos' Huay Xai by 1998, but the project was abandoned in 1997 after the drastic drop in the value of the baht. If it ever resumes development, the bridge will link Thailand with China by a road through Bokeo and Luang Nam Tha Provinces in Laos – it is part of an ambitious transport project known as 'Chiang Rai–Kunming Road'.

A land crossing from Pakse (Champasak Province) in Laos to Chong Mek in Thailand's Ubon Ratchathani Province is open to foreign visitors with valid Lao visas. If you're travelling in the opposite direction, from Thailand to Laos you can receive a visa on arrival. See Chong Mek & the Emerald Triangle in the Northeastern Thailand chapter.

Ferry It's legal for non-Thais to cross the Mekong River by ferry between Thailand and Laos at the following points: Nakhon Phanom (opposite Tha Khaek), Chiang Khong (opposite Huay Xai) and Mukdahan (opposite Savannakhet).

International Border Crossings

These are border points where Thai customs and immigration posts allow foreigners to cross to or from neighbouring countries.

Thailand	Malaysia
Betong	Keroh
Padang Besar	Kaki Bukit
Sadao	Changlun
Sungai Kolok	Rantau Panjang
Thailand	**Laos**
Chiang Khong	Huay Xai
Chong Mek	Pakse
Mukdahan	Savannakhet
Nakhon Phanom	Tha Khaek
Nong Khai	Vientiane
Thailand	**Cambodia**
Aranya Prathet	Poipet
Hat Lek	Koh Kong
Thailand	**Myanmar**
Mae Sai	Tachileik
Mae Sot	Myawadi*
Ranong	Kawthoung
Three Pagodas Pass	Payathonzu*

*Entry permitted for day trips only

Thais are permitted to cross at all of the above checkpoints plus at least a half-dozen others in Thailand's Loei and Nong Khai Provinces, including Chiang Saen, Ban Khok Phai, Ban Nong Pheu, Ban Pak Huay, Beung Kan, Chiang Khan and Pak Chom. For the most part these checkpoints are good only for day crossings (by Thai and Lao only). In the future one or more of these may become available for entry by foreign visitors as well.

Myanmar

Road Several border crossings between Thailand and Myanmar are open to day-trippers or for short excursions in the vicinity. As yet none of these links up with routes to Yangon or Mandalay or other cities of any size. Nor are you permitted to enter Thailand by land from Myanmar, except at Mae Sai.

Mae Sai–Tachileik This crossing features an infamous bridge, Lo Hsing-han's former 'Golden Triangle' passageway for opium and heroin, spans the Mae Sai (Sai River) between Thailand's northernmost town and the border boom town of Tachileik (called Thakhilek by the Thai, Shan and Khün peoples). Border permits for up to two weeks may be obtained from the Burmese immigration facility, at the border, for excursions to Tachileik and beyond as far north as Kengtung and Mengla. You can also use this border as a way to renew your Thai visa if you happen to be in northern Thailand.

On occasion – most recently for six months in 2002 – this border crossing has been closed due to fighting between Shan insurgent armies and the Burmese; or other regional disturbances. At the time of writing the crossing was open.

Rumour has it that an overland route going all the way to China via Kengtung will soon open here, but so far Mengla is the end of the line. The road continuing west from Kengtung to Taunggyi is in usable condition, although this runs through the opium-poppy harvesting area of the Golden Triangle, a common site for Shan army clashes with the Burmese military, and is definitely off-limits to non-Burmese. It's 163km from Tachileik to Kengtung, and another 450km from Kengtung to Taunggyi.

Mae Sot–Myawadi This crossing begins a route from Myawadi to Mawlamyaing (Moulmein) via Kawkareik. It's a rough road that has long been off limits to foreigners due to Mon and Karen insurgent activity in the area. There are regular buses from Tak to Mae Sot in Tak Province. Politics sometimes closes this crossing for a few weeks or months at a time. At the moment the bridge that crosses the Mae Moei between Myawadi and Mae Sot (actually 6km from Mae Sot proper) is open to all comers.

Foreigners may cross from Mae Sot to Myawadi only for the day – the area beyond Myawadi is off limits. The Myanmar government has plans to open the road from Myawadi all the way to Pa-an in the Kayin State, and Thai groups have sometimes had permission to travel by chartered bus all the way to Yangon. See Mae Sot in the Northern Thailand chapter for details.

Three Pagodas Pass A gateway for various invading armies and an important smuggling route for many centuries, this is one of the most interesting and accessible of the border-crossing points. The settlement on the Burmese side, called Payathonzu (Three Pagodas), is open on-and-off to foreign tourists for day trips. Travellers have been allowed to go as far as a dozen or so kilometres inside Myanmar from this point, but the roads are so bad that almost no-one makes it even that far. See Around Kanchanaburi in the Central Thailand chapter for details.

Prachuap Khiri Khan Not only is there a road over the Mawdaung Pass between Ban Huay Yang and Tanintharyi, there is a major business smuggling timber in from Myanmar. Myanmar's Mon and Karen ethnic groups, rather than the Burmese government, carry on most of this illicit timber trade. The 'toll gate', formerly controlled by Karen guerrillas from the Karen National Union/Karen National Liberation Army, is now once again controlled by Myanmar forces. If you can find a local who knows the area well, it's possible to visit near the border crossing of Dan Singkhon.

Cambodia

Road It's legal to cross between Cambodia and Thailand at Aranya Prathet, opposite the Cambodian town of Poipet. If you're coming from Cambodia by road, you don't need a Thai visa (or rather you will be granted a free 30-day Tourist Visa on arrival), but in the reverse direction you will need a Cambodian visa, available at the border for US$20.

The border is open from 8am to 6pm daily. You have to take a taxi or *moto* (Cambodian for motorcycle) a further 4km from the crossing to reach Aranya Prathet itself, from where there are regular buses and trains onward to Bangkok and other points in northeastern Thailand. See Aranya Prathet in the Southeastern Thailand chapter for more details.

China

Road The governments of Thailand, Laos, China and Myanmar have agreed to the construction of a four-nation ring road through all four countries. The western half of the loop will proceed from Mae Sai in Thailand to Jinghong in China, via Myanmar's Tachileik, Kengtung and Mengla (near Dalau on the China-Myanmar border); while the eastern half will extend from Chiang Khong in Thailand to Jinghong via Huay Xai in Laos (opposite Chiang Khong) and Boten (on the Yunnanese border south of Jinghong) in Laos.

The stretch between Tachileik and Dalau is still under construction (some sections towards the Chinese border are complete) but it's possible to arrange trips as far as Kengtung in Myanmar's Shan State (see Mae Sai in the Northern Thailand chapter for details). A road between Huay Xai and Boten already exists (built by the Chinese in the '60s and '70s) but needs upgrading. Once the roads are built and the visa formalities have been worked out, this loop will provide alternative travel connections between China and Southeast Asia, in much the same way as the Karakoram Hwy has forged new links between China and South Asia. It's difficult to predict when all the logistical variables will be settled, but progress so far points to a cleared path by 2006.

The eastern half of this loop, from Boten to Huay Xai, Laos, and across to Chiang Khong, Thailand, can be done relatively easily now, although roads between Boten and Huay Xai are a little rough.

Exit Stamps

Whenever you leave Thailand via land, river or sea, make sure you get your passport stamped with a proper exit stamp from Thai immigration. At some Thai border crossings, stamping may be lax. If you were to re-enter Thailand and the immigration police noticed you didn't have an exit stamp from your previous visit, you could find yourself in a detention centre or jail for days, even weeks, before the case was sorted out.

Boat An express boat runs along the Mekong River between Sop Ruak in Chiang Rai Province, and China's Yunnan Province. For the moment, permission for such travel is restricted to very infrequent private tour groups, but it's reasonable to assume that a scheduled public service may become available. The boat trip takes six hours – considerably quicker than any current road route. However it's only navigable all the way to China during the rainy season and in the period immediately after.

Future Rail Possibilities

At a 1995 summit meeting in Bangkok, representatives of the Association of Southeast Asian Nations (Asean) proposed the completion of a regional rail network linking Singapore with China via Malaysia, Thailand, Laos, Cambodia and Vietnam. In all but Laos and Cambodia, rail beds for such a circuit already exist. The plans called for the extension of a rail line across the Mekong River from Thailand to Laos via the existing Thai–Lao Friendship Bridge. If completed this line may some day connect with a proposed north–south line from Vientiane to Savannakhet in Laos and then with a west–east line from Savannakhet to Dong Ha.

A 1998 joint-venture agreement between the Lao government and a company called Lao Railways Transportation purports to establish a railway line along the middle of the Friendship Bridge. After a feasibility study was completed the line, which would reportedly extend to Vientiane and Luang Prabang, was supposed to have become operational in four years. Like most other transport projects in Laos, however, it will probably take much longer – if it ever happens at all.

Another rail link undergoing a feasibility study is a spur eastward from Udon Thani, across the Mekong to Tha Khaek, Lao PDR, and across Laos to connect with the Ho Chi Minh City–Hanoi railway in Vietnam.

SEA

Malaysia

There are several ways of travelling between Thailand's southern peninsula and Malaysia by sea. The simplest is to take a long-tail boat between Satun, right down in the southwestern corner of Thailand, and Kuala Perlis. The cost is about RM5, or 50B, and boats cross fairly regularly. You can also take a ferry from Satun to the Malaysian island of Langkawi. There are immigration posts at both ports so you can make the crossing quite officially. From Satun you can take a bus to Hat Yai and then arrange transport to other points in the south. It's possible to bypass Hat Yai altogether by heading directly for Phuket or Krabi via Trang.

All foreign-registered vessels, skippers and crew must check in with the relevant Thai authorities as soon as possible after entering Thai waters. Although major ports throughout Thailand offer port check-ins, most leisure boating visitors check in at Phuket, Krabi, Samui, Pranburi or Pattaya. Because Phuket's Ao Chalong pier brings customs, immigration, and harbourmaster services together in one building, Phuket is the most popular check-in point nationwide.

Before departing Thailand by boat, you must also check out with immigration, customs and harbourmaster. Check-in and check-out fees can vary from port to port, but typically one pays 300B per boat plus 10B per passenger for immigration fees upon arrival, plus 100B each to customs and harbourmaster upon departure. Vessels caught without harbour clearance may be fined up to 5000B.

Myanmar

You can travel by boat between Kawthoung in Myanmar's Tanintharyi Division and the port of Ranong in Thailand via the Gulf of Martaban and Pakchan Estuary. Exiting Myanmar from Kawthaung is legal, and you don't need a visa to enter Thailand for a stay of 30 days or less. In the reverse direction you don't need a Myanmar visa for a day trip, though you'll need one if you plan to stay overnight or to continue farther north.

Cambodia

Travellers can sometimes travel by sea to Cambodia via Hat Lek. For more details see Hat Lek to Cambodia in the Southeastern Thailand chapter.

Getting Around

AIR

Domestic Airlines

Five domestic carriers, Thai Airways International (THAI), Bangkok Airways, Air Andaman, PB Air and Phuket Airlines fly in and out of 28 domestic airports around the country.

The accompanying 'Air Fares & Railways' map shows some of the fares on more popular routes. Note that through fares are generally less than the combination fares – Chiang Rai to Bangkok, for example, is less than the addition of Chiang Rai–Chiang Mai and Chiang Mai–Bangkok fares.

THAI *(☎ 0 2513 0121; 89 Th Viphavadi Rangsit)* operates domestic air services to many provincial capitals, and maintains offices in over 25 provincial cities; see the destination chapters for details.

Bangkok Airways *(☎ 0 2229 3434, reservations ☎ 0 2229 3456; 60 Queen Sirikit National Convention Centre, Th Ratchadaphisek Mai, Bangkok)* has flights along three main routes: Bangkok–Sukhothai–Chiang Mai; Bangkok–Ko Samui–Phuket; and Bangkok–Hua Hin–Ko Samui.

Air Andaman *(☎ 0 2229 9555; Sirinrat Bldg, 16th floor, 3388/56 Th Phra Ram IV, Bangkok)* has flights to Buriram, Nakhon Ratchasima, Phrae, Nan, Mae Sot, Narathiwat and Chumphon from Bangkok; plus Phitsanulok, Nan, Mae Sot and Chiang Rai from Chiang Mai.

PB Air *(☎ 0 2261 0220; 17th floor, UBC II Bldg, 591 Soi 33, Th Sukhumvit, Bangkok)*, until recently a charter-only airline, now has flights between Bangkok and Krabi, Lampang, Roi Et, Sakhon Nakhon, Nakhon Phanom and Nakhon Si Thammarat.

Phuket Airlines *(☎ 0 2679 8999; Lumpini Tower Bldg, 34B floor, 1168/102 Th Phra Ram IV, Thungmahamek, Sathon. Bangkok)* offers domestic flights only from Bangkok to Ranong, Krabi and Phuket at the moment.

Bangkok International Airport

The domestic terminal stands a few hundred metres south of the international ones. Facilities include a post and telephone office on the ground floor, a snack bar in the departure lounge and a restaurant on the 2nd floor. THAI operates a free shuttle bus between the international and domestic terminals every 15 minutes between 6am and 11.20pm.

See Getting Around in the Bangkok chapter for information on transport to/from the airport.

BUS

Government Bus

The Thai government subsidises an excellent bus system operated by the Borisat Khon Song (*bàw-rí-sàt khŏn sòng*, literally, 'transportation company'), usually abbreviated to Baw Khaw Saw. Every city and town in Thailand linked by bus transportation has a Baw Khaw Saw station, even if it's just a patch of dirt by the side of the road.

Depending on where you're going, you'll find from one to five classes of bus service. The cheapest and slowest are the ordinary buses *(rót thammádaa)* that stop in every little town and for every waving hand along the highway. For some destinations – such as smaller towns – these orange-painted buses are your only choice, but at least they leave frequently. The government also runs faster, more comfortable but less frequent air-con buses called *rót ae* (air bus), *rót pràp aakàat* (air-con bus) or *rót thua* (tour bus); these are painted with blue markings. If these are going to your destination, they are your very best choice since they don't cost that much more than the ordinary stop-in-every-town buses.

The service on the government air-con buses is usually quite good and includes beverage service and video. On longer routes (eg, Bangkok–Chiang Mai, Bangkok–Nong Khai), the air-con buses even distribute claim checks (receipt dockets) for your baggage. Longer routes may also offer two classes of air-con buses, 2nd class and 1st class; the latter have toilets. 'VIP buses' have fewer seats (30 to 34 instead of 44; some routes have Super VIP, with only 24 seats) so that each seat reclines more. Sometimes these are called *rót nawn* or sleepers. For small- to medium-sized people they are more comfortable, but if you're bigger you may find yourself squashed when the person in front of you leans back.

Occasionally you'll get a government air-con bus in which the air-con is broken or

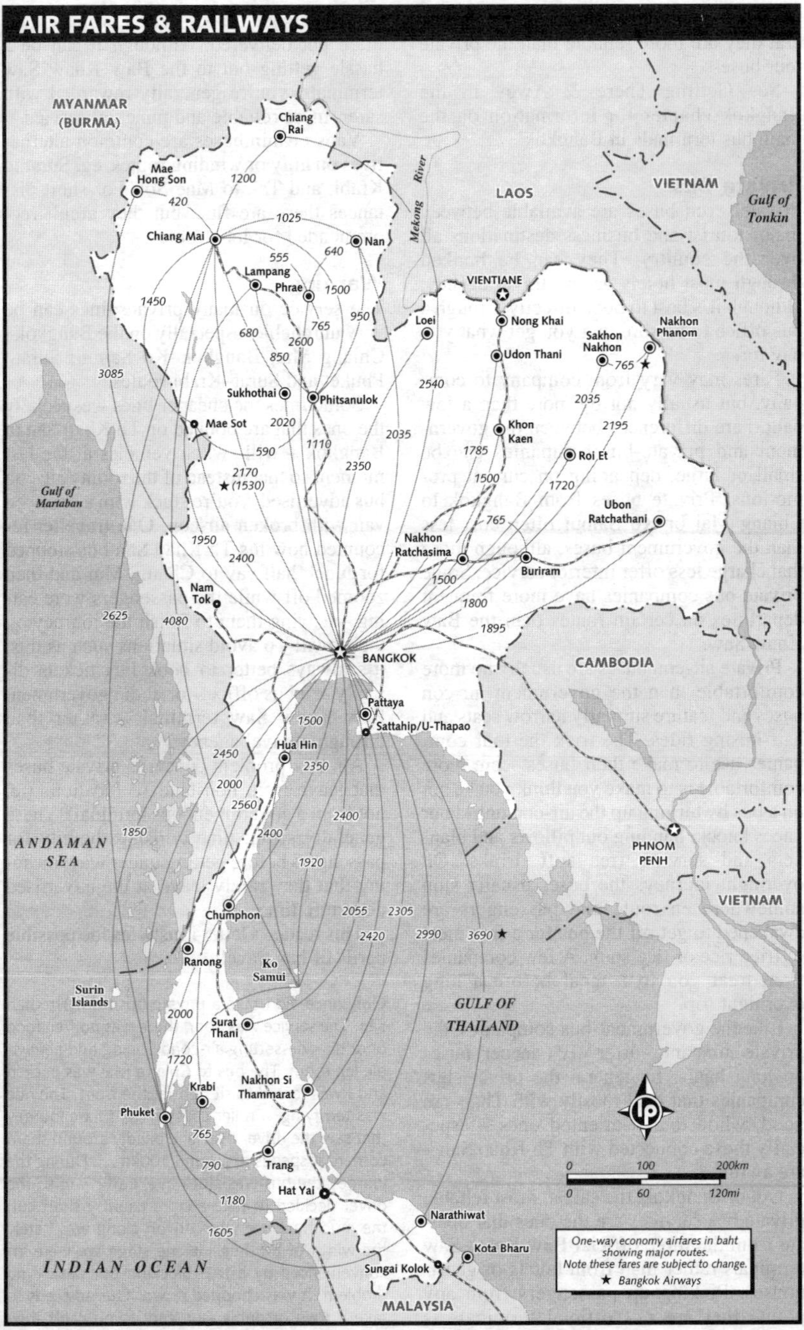
AIR FARES & RAILWAYS
MYANMAR (BURMA)
LAOS
VIETNAM
Gulf of Tonkin
Mekong River
VIENTIANE
CAMBODIA
PHNOM PENH
VIETNAM
Gulf of Martaban
ANDAMAN SEA
GULF OF THAILAND
INDIAN OCEAN
MALAYSIA
Chiang Rai
Mae Hong Son
Chiang Mai
Nan
Lampang
Phrae
Loei
Nong Khai
Udon Thani
Sakhon Nakhon
Nakhon Phanom
Sukhothai
Phitsanulok
Mae Sot
Khon Kaen
Roi Et
Ubon Ratchathani
Nakhon Ratchasima
Buriram
Nam Tok
BANGKOK
Pattaya
Sattahip/U-Thapao
Hua Hin
Chumphon
Ranong
Ko Samui
Surin Islands
Surat Thani
Nakhon Si Thammarat
Krabi
Phuket
Trang
Hat Yai
Narathiwat
Kota Bharu
Sungai Kolok
1200
420
1025
555
640
1450
1500
950
680
765
2600
850
3085
2540
2035
765
2195
2020
1110
2035
590
2350
1785
2170
★ (1530)
1500
1720
765
1950
2400
1500
1800
1895
2625
4080
1500
2450
2350
2000
2560
2400
2400
1850
1920
2055
2305
2420
2990
3690 ★
2000
1720
765
790
1180
1605
0 100 200km
0 60 120mi
One-way economy airfares in baht showing major routes.
Note these fares are subject to change.
★ Bangkok Airways

the seats are not up to standard, but in general they are more reliable than the private tour buses.

See Getting There & Away in the Bangkok chapter for information on the main bus terminals in Bangkok.

Private Bus

Privately run buses are available between major tourist and business destinations all over the country. They can be booked through most hotels or any travel agency, although it's best to book directly through a bus office to be sure that you get what you pay for.

Fares may vary from company to company, but usually not by more than a few baht. Fare differences between the government and private-bus companies can be small or large, depending on current promotions. Private buses from Bangkok to Chiang Mai or Ko Samui often cost less than the government buses, although those that charge less offer inferior service. Some private bus companies have more frequent departures on certain routes than the Baw Khaw Saw.

Private air-con buses are usually no more comfortable than the government air-con buses and feature similarly narrow seats and hair-raising rides. The trick the tour companies use to make their buses seem more comfortable is to make you think you're not on a bus by turning up the air-con until your knees knock, handing out pillows and blankets and serving free soft drinks. On overnight journeys the buses usually stop somewhere en route and passengers are awakened to get off the bus for a free meal of fried rice or rice soup. A few companies even treat you to a meal before a long overnight trip.

Like the government-bus companies, the private companies offer VIP (sleeper) buses on long hauls. In general the private bus companies that deal mostly with Thais are good, while tourist-oriented ones – especially those connected with Th Khao San – are awful.

Out of Bangkok, the safest, most reliable private bus services are the ones that operate from the three official Baw Khaw Saw terminals rather than from hotels or guesthouses. Picking up passengers from any points that are not official terminals is actually illegal, and services promised are often not delivered. Although it can be a hassle getting out to the Baw Khaw Saw terminals, you're generally rewarded with safer, more reliable and punctual service.

Vans or minibuses are common alternatives on hilly or winding routes, eg, Surat to Krabi, and Tak to Mae Sot. For short distances these are fine, but they aren't recommended for long routes.

Warning

The service on many private lines can be very unreliable, especially on the Bangkok–Chiang Mai, Bangkok–Ko Samui, Surat–Phuket and Surat–Krabi routes.

Sometimes the cheaper lines – especially the ones that are booked on Th Khao San in Bangkok – will switch vehicles at the last moment so that instead of the roomy air-con bus advertised, you're stuck with a cramped van with broken air-con. One traveller recounted how his Th Khao San bus stopped for lunch halfway to Chiang Mai and then zoomed off while the passengers were eating – leaving them to finish the journey on their own! To avoid situations such as this, it's always better to book bus tickets directly at a bus office – or at the government Baw Khaw Saw terminal – rather than through a travel agency.

Another problem concerns private buses that leave from nonstandard locations (ie, not from a government bus terminal). These generally spend time cruising the city for passengers before getting under way, meaning that they rarely leave at the advertised departure time.

This reader's letter illustrates the possible perils of bus travel:

> Only once did I take a private bus from Th Khao San. The service was poor; there was no free food or drink, one-setting air-conditioning and negligible leg room. The bus to Chiang Mai was packed and I was forced to sit right at the front. The ride was terrifying, a roller coaster nightmare journey that saw the driver overtake blindly around sharp corners at speeds of around 100km/h. During the journey the bus was stuck in a traffic jam so the driver decided to take a cross-country short cut; the mud track we were driven along was barely the width of the bus. At one stage we were inconvenienced by a tree blocking our path – no problem. It was chopped down. Our advice is to take a train or public bus and if you can't then

make sure you sit at the back of the bus. The public bus journeys we took were far superior: two free meals, plenty of leg room and drivers who had at least a modicum of respect for human life.

Safety Statistically, private buses meet with more accidents than government air-con buses. Turnovers on tight corners and head-on collisions with trucks are probably due to the inexperience of the drivers on a particular route. Private buses licensed to operate from government bus terminals, however, are usually much better than those operating 'pirate routes' from tourist centres such as Th Khao San or Hat Patong in Phuket.

Keep an eye on your bags when riding buses – pilfering by stealth is still the most popular form of robbery in Thailand, though again the risks are not that great – just be aware. Most pilfering seems to take place on the private bus runs between Bangkok and Chiang Mai or Ko Samui, especially on buses booked on Th Khao San. Keep zippered bags locked and well secured.

TRAIN

The government railway network, the **State Railway of Thailand** *(SRT; w www.srt.or.th)*, is, on the whole, very well run. It isn't possible to take the train everywhere in Thailand, but often it is by far the best public transport. If you travel 3rd class, it is often the cheapest way to cover a long distance; by 2nd class it's about the same as a private tour bus but much safer and more comfortable. Trains take a bit longer than chartered buses on the same journey but are worth the extra travel time, on overnight trips especially.

The trains offer many advantages: there is more room to move and stretch out (even in 3rd class) than there is on even the best buses. The windows are big and, if you choose non-air-con, they're usually left open, so that there is no glass between you and the scenery (good for taking photos) and more to see. The scenery itself is always better along the train routes than along highways – the trains regularly pass small villages, farmland, old temples etc. The pitch and roll of the railway carriages is much easier on the bones, muscles and nervous system than the quick stops and starts, the harrowing turns and the pothole jolts endured on buses.

Rail Routes

Four main rail lines cover 4500km along the northern, southern, northeastern and eastern routes. There are several side routes, notably between Nakhon Pathom and Nam Tok (stopping in Kanchanaburi) in the western central region, and between Tung Song and Kantang (stopping in Trang) in the south. The southern line splits at Hat Yai: one route goes to Sungai Kolok on the Malaysian east-coast border, via Yala; and the other goes to Padang Besar in the west, also on the Malaysian border.

A Bangkok–Pattaya spur has not been as popular as expected but is still running. There is talk that a southern spur may be extended from Khiriratnikhom to Phuket, establishing a rail link between Surat Thani and Phuket. A spur from Den Chai to Chiang Rai in the north has also been under discussion, though nothing concrete has happened yet. The SRT may also renovate the Japanese line between Nam Tok and Sangkhlaburi in Kanchanaburi Province that was built with the forced labour of prisoners of war (POWs) and coolies during WWII. All of these projects are currently described on the SRT website, but the 1997 economic crash appears to have slowed progress beyond feasibility studies.

Bangkok Terminals Most long-distance trains originate from Bangkok's Hualamphong station. Before a railway bridge was constructed across the Mae Nam Chao Phraya (Chao Phraya River) in 1932, all southbound trains left from Bangkok Noi, the main station in Thonburi. Today this station services commuter and short-line trains to Kanchanaburi/Nam Tok, Suphanburi, Ratchaburi and Nakhon Pathom. (You could also reach Ratchaburi and Nakhon Pathom by train from Hualamphong). Thonburi's Wong Wian Yai station, running services to Samut Songkhram, is rarely used.

Classes

The SRT operates passenger trains in three classes – 1st, 2nd and 3rd – but each class may vary considerably depending on whether you're on an ordinary, rapid or express train.

3rd Class A typical 3rd-class carriage consists of two rows of bench seats divided into facing pairs. Each bench seat is designed to seat two or three passengers, but on a crowded rural line nobody seems to care about design considerations. On a rapid train, 3rd-class seats are padded and reasonably comfortable for shorter trips. On ordinary 3rd-class-only trains in the east and northeast, seats are sometimes made of hard wooden slats, and are not recommended for more than a couple of hours at a time. Express trains do not carry 3rd-class carriages at all. Commuter trains in the Bangkok area are all 3rd class and the carriages resemble modern subway or rapid-transit trains, with plastic seats and ceiling hand-straps for standing passengers.

2nd Class The seating arrangements in a 2nd-class carriage are similar to those on a bus, with pairs of padded seats, usually recliners, all facing towards the front of the train. The seats convert into two fold-down berths, one over the other. Curtains provide a modicum of privacy and the berths are fairly comfortable, with fresh linen for every trip. A toilet stall and washbasins are located at one end of the carriage.

Second-class carriages are found only on rapid and express trains; some routes offer air-con 2nd class as well as ordinary 2nd class.

1st Class Each private cabin in a 1st-class carriage has individually controlled air-con (older trains also have an electric fan), a washbasin and mirror, a small table and long bench seats that convert into beds. Drinking water and soap are provided free of charge. First-class carriages are available only on rapid, express and special-express trains.

Costs

There is a 60B surcharge for express trains *(rót dùan)* and 40B for rapid trains *(rót rew)*. These trains are somewhat faster than the ordinary trains, as they make fewer stops. Some 2nd- and 3rd-class services are air-con, in which case there is a 70B surcharge (note that there are no 3rd-class carriages on either rapid or express trains). For the special-express trains *(rót dùan phísèt)* that run between Bangkok and Padang Besar and between Bangkok and Chiang Mai there is an 80B surcharge (or 120B if a meal is included).

The charge for 2nd-class sleeping berths is 100B for an upper berth and 150B for a lower berth (or 130B and 200B, respectively, on a special express). The difference between upper and lower is that there is a window next to the lower berth and a little more head room. The upper berth is still comfortable enough. For 2nd-class sleepers with air-con add 250/320B per upper/lower ticket. No sleepers are available in 3rd class.

Air-con really isn't necessary on night trains, as a steady breeze circulates through the train and cools things down quickly. In fact the air-con in 2nd class can become uncomfortably cold at night and cannot be regulated by passengers; for this reason we recommend choosing non-air-con.

All 1st-class cabins come with individually controlled air-con. For a two-bed cabin the surcharge is 520B per person. Single 1st-class cabins are no longer available, so if you're travelling alone you may be paired with another rail passenger, although the SRT takes great care not to mix genders.

You can figure on a 500km journey costing around 200B in 2nd class (not including the surcharges for the rapid and express services), roughly twice that in 1st class and less than half in 3rd. Surprisingly, basic fares have changed only slightly over the last decade, although supplementary charges have increased steadily. Currently the government continues to subsidise train travel, particularly 3rd class, to some extent. However, there has been some talk of privatisation – which would, of course, ring the death knell for the high standards of this railway system, as it has in most other formerly rail-faring countries of the world.

Train Passes The SRT issues a couple of train passes that may save on fares if you plan to use the trains extensively within a relatively short interval. These passes are only available in Thailand, and may be purchased at Hualamphong train station.

The cost for 20 days of unlimited 2nd- or 3rd-class rail travel (blue pass) is 1100B, or 2000B including all supplementary charges; children aged four to 12 pay half the adult fare. Supplementary charges include all extra charges for rapid, express, special express and air-con. Passes must be validated at a local station before boarding the first train. The price of the pass includes seat reservations that, if required, can be made at any SRT ticket office. The pass is valid until midnight on the last day of the pass, although if the journey is commenced before midnight on the last day of validity, the passenger can use the pass until that train reaches its destination.

Do the passes represent a true saving over buying individual train tickets? The answer is 'yes' but only if you can average more than 110km by rail per day for 20 days (ie, 2200km in total). In addition, on less crowded routes where there are plenty of available 2nd-class seats the passes save time that might otherwise be spent at ticket windows, but for high-demand routes (eg, from Bangkok to Chiang Mai or Hat Yai) you'll still need to make reservations.

Bookings

The disadvantage of travelling by rail, in addition to the booking time factor mentioned earlier, is that trains can be difficult to book. This is especially true around holiday time, eg, the middle of April approaching the Songkran Festival, as many Thais prefer the train. Trains out of Bangkok should be booked as far in advance as possible – a minimum of a week for popular routes such as the northern line to Chiang Mai and the southern line to Hat Yai, especially if you want a sleeper. For the northeastern and eastern lines a few days will suffice. Mid-week departures are always easier to book than weekends; during some months of the year you can easily book a sleeper even one day before departure, as long as it's on a Tuesday, Wednesday or Thursday.

Advance bookings may be made one to 60 days before your intended date of departure. If you want to book tickets in advance, go to Hualamphong station in Bangkok, walk through the front of the station house and go straight to the back right-hand corner where a sign says 'Advance Booking' (open from 8.30am to 4pm daily). The other ticket windows, lined up in front of the platforms, are for same-day purchases, mostly 3rd class. From 5am to 8.30am and from 4pm to 11pm, advance bookings can also be made at windows Nos 2 to 11.

Reservations are computerised in the Advance Booking office, and you simply take a queue number and wait until your number appears on one of the electronic marquees. You can only pay in cash (baht) here.

Booking trains back to Bangkok is generally not as difficult as booking trains out of Bangkok; however, at some stations it can be quite difficult (eg, buying a ticket from Surat Thani to Bangkok).

Tickets between any station in Thailand can be purchased at **Hualamphong station** *(☎ 0 2223 3762, 0 2225 6964, 0 2224 7788, 0 2225 0300 ext 5200 03)*. You can also make advance bookings at Don Muang station (across from Bangkok International Airport) and at the Advance Booking offices at train stations in the larger cities. Advance reservations can be made by phone from anywhere in Thailand. Throughout Thailand SRT ticket offices are *generally* open from 8.30am to 6pm on weekdays, and 8.30am to noon on weekends and public holidays. Train tickets can also be purchased at certain travel agencies in Bangkok. It is much simpler to book trains through these agencies than to book them at the station; however, they usually add a surcharge (50B to 100B) to the ticket price.

Train Information

Accurate, up-to-date information on train travel is available at the Rail Travel Aids counter in Hualamphong station. There you can pick up timetables, and ask questions about fares and scheduling – one person behind the counter usually speaks a little English. There are two types of timetable available: four condensed English timetables with fares, schedules and routes for rapid, express and special express trains on the four trunk lines; and four Thai timetables for each trunk line, with side lines as well. These latter timetables give fares and schedules for all trains – ordinary, rapid and express. The English timetables only display a couple of the ordinary routes; eg, they don't show the wealth of ordinary trains that go to Ayuthaya and as far north as Phitsanulok.

Eating Facilities

Meal service is available in dining carriages and at your seat in 2nd- and 1st-class carriages. Menus change as frequently as the SRT changes catering services. For a while there were two menus, a 'special food' menu with 'special' prices (generally given to tourists) and a cheaper, more extensive menu. Nowadays all the meals seem a bit overpriced (75B to 200B on average) by Thai standards.

Several readers have written to complain about being overcharged by meal servers on the trains. If you do purchase food on board, be sure to check the prices on the menu rather than trusting server quotes. Also check the bill carefully to make sure you haven't been overcharged.

Station Services

If you have any questions or problems other than bookings, there is a special **tourist service** *(☎ 0 2282 8773)*.

You'll find all train stations in Thailand have baggage-storage services (sometimes called the 'cloak room'). The rates and hours of operation vary from station to station. At Hualamphong station the hours are 4am to 10.30pm daily and left luggage costs 10B per day per piece for up to five days, after which it goes up to 15B per day. Hualamphong station also has a 10B shower service in the rest rooms.

Hualamphong Station is jammed with modern coffee shops and a coupon-style cafeteria. All stations in the provincial capitals have restaurants or cafeterias as well as various snack vendors. Although Hat Yai station is the only one with a hotel attached, there are usually hotels within walking distance of major stations.

Hualamphong station has a couple of travel agencies where other kinds of transport can be booked, but beware of touts who try to drag you there, saying the trains are fully booked when they aren't. Avoid the travel agencies outside the station, which have very poor reputations. Near the front of the station, at one end of the foyer, **Mail Boxes Etc** *(MBE; open 7.30am-7.30pm Mon-Fri, 9am-4pm Sat, 9am-8pm Sun)* provides mailing, courier and packing services.

CAR & MOTORCYCLE

Roadways

Thailand has over 170,000km of roadways, of which around 18,000km are classified 'national highways' (both two lane and four lane), which means they're generally well maintained. Route numberings are fairly consistent: some of the major highways have two numbers, one under the national system and another under the optimistic 'Asia Highway' system that indicates highway links with neighbouring countries. Route 105 to Mae Sot on the Myanmar border, for example, is also called Asia 1, while Hwy 2 from Bangkok to Nong Khai is Asia 12. For the time being, the only border regularly crossed by noncommercial vehicles are the Thai-Malaysian and Thai-Lao borders.

Kilometre markers are placed at regular intervals along most larger roadways, but place names are usually printed on them in Thai script only. Highway signs in both Thai and Roman script, which show the destinations and the distances, are becoming increasingly common.

Road Rules

Thais drive on the left-hand side of the road – most of the time. Other than that seemingly just about anything goes, in spite of road signs and speed limits – the Thais are notorious scofflaws when it comes to driving. Like many places in Asia, every two-lane road has an invisible third lane in the middle that all drivers feel free to use at any time. Passing on hills and curves is common – as long as you've got the proper Buddhist altar on the dashboard, what could happen?

The main rule to be aware of is that right of way belongs to the bigger vehicle; this is not what it says in the Thai traffic law, but it's the reality. Maximum speed limits are 50km/h on urban roads, 100km/h on most highways – but on any given stretch of highway you'll see vehicles travelling as slowly as 30km/h or as fast as 150km/h. Speed traps are common along Hwy 4 in the south and Hwy 2 in the northeast.

Indicators are often used to warn passing drivers about oncoming traffic. A flashing left indicator means it's OK to pass, while a right indicator means that someone's approaching from the other direction.

The principal hazard to driving in Thailand, besides the general disregard for traffic laws, is having to contend with so many different types of vehicles on the same road – bullock carts, 18-wheelers, bicycles, *túk-túk* (motorised pedicab) and customised racing bikes. This danger is often compounded by the lack of running lights. In village areas the vehicular traffic is lighter but you have to contend with stray chickens, dogs, water

Road Distances (km)

	Aranya Prathet	Ayuthaya	Bangkok	Chiang Mai	Chiang Rai	Chumphon	Hat Yai	Hua Hin	Khon Kaen	Mae Hong Son	Mae Sai	Mukdahan	Nakhon Ratchasima	Nakhon Sawan	Nong Khai	Phitsanulok	Phuket	Sungai Kolok	Surat Thani	Tak	Trat	Ubon Ratchathani
Ubon Ratchathani																						---
Trat																					---	729
Tak																				---	727	707
Surat Thani																			---	1066	965	1072
Sungai Kolok																		---	688	1694	1593	1700
Phuket																	---	761	286	1264	1163	1270
Phitsanulok																---	1227	1657	1029	146	690	572
Nong Khai															---	411	1466	1896	1268	557	883	443
Nakhon Sawan														---	546	135	1092	1522	894	172	555	535
Nakhon Ratchasima													---	372	359	435	1107	1357	909	544	524	163
Mukdahan												---	320	692	347	608	1427	1857	1229	754	886	157
Mae Sai											---	1155	982	682	958	547	1774	2204	1576	528	1237	1119
Mae Hong Son										---	474	1142	969	604	945	578	1696	2126	1498	432	1397	1106
Khon Kaen									---	829	842	313	193	408	166	295	1300	1730	1102	441	717	277
Hua Hin								---	633	1029	1107	760	440	425	799	560	667	1097	469	597	496	603
Hat Yai							---	810	1443	1839	1917	1570	1250	1235	1609	1370	474	287	401	1407	1306	1413
Chumphon						---	555	269	902	1298	1376	1029	709	694	1068	829	412	842	214	866	765	872
Chiang Rai					---	1308	1849	1039	774	406	68	1087	914	614	890	479	1706	2136	1508	460	1169	1051
Chiang Mai				---	191	1138	1679	869	604	225	259	917	744	444	720	309	1536	1966	1338	280	999	881
Bangkok			---	686	856	452	993	183	450	846	924	577	257	242	616	377	250	1280	652	414	313	420
Ayuthaya		---	79	607	777	531	1072	262	397	767	845	524	204	163	563	298	929	1359	731	335	392	367
Aranya Prathet	---	246	275	844	1014	727	1268	458	432	1013	1082	601	239	409	598	535	1125	1555	927	581	285	444

buffaloes and goats. Once you get used to the challenge, driving in Thailand is very entertaining.

Checkpoints

Military checkpoints are common along highways throughout northern and northeastern Thailand, especially in border areas. Always slow down for a checkpoint – often the sentries will wave you through without an inspection, but occasionally you will be stopped and briefly questioned. Use common sense and don't act belligerently or you're likely to be detained longer than you'd like.

Rental

Cars, jeeps and vans can be rented in Bangkok, Chiang Mai, Cha-am, Chiang Rai, Mae Hong Son, Pattaya, Phuket, Ko Samui, Hat Yai, Khorat and Udon Thani. Check with travel agencies or large hotels for rental locations. A Japanese sedan (eg, Toyota Corolla) typically costs from around 1000B to 1500B per day; minivans (eg, Toyota Hi-Ace, Nissan Urvan) go for around 1800B to 2500B a day. International rental companies tend to charge significantly more; Avis, for example, rents the Honda 1.5 City for 2400B a day (13,810B weekly), the larger Toyota 1.6 Corolla Altis for 4000B a day (23,200B weekly) and the 4WD Jeep Cherokee for 5000B per day (28,770B weekly).

The best deals are usually on 4WD Suzuki Caribians, which can be rented for as low as 800B per day with no per-kilometre fees for long-term rentals during low-season months (May to June, September to October), 1000B to 1500B at other times. Unless you absolutely want the cheapest vehicle, you might be better off with a larger vehicle; Caribians are notoriously hard to handle at speeds above 90km/h and tend to crumple dangerously in collisions. Cars with automatic shift are uncommon. Drivers can usually be hired with a rental for an additional 300B to 400B per day.

It is advisable always to verify that a vehicle is insured for liability before signing a rental contract; you should also ask to see the dated insurance documents. If you have an accident while driving an uninsured vehicle you're in for some major hassles.

Motorcycles can be rented in major towns and many smaller tourist centres such as Krabi, Ko Pha-Ngan, Ko Samui, Mae Sai, Nong Khai and Pai.

Daily rentals average around 200B a day for a 100cc step-through (eg, Honda Dream, Suzuki Crystal). As there is a glut of motorcycles of this type for rent in Chiang Mai, Phuket and Ko Samui these days, they can be rented in these areas for as little as 150B per day (or as low as 100B per day long-term or off-season). On the other hand you'll pay up to 500B a day for a good 250cc dirt bike, possibly less in low seasons (May to June and September to October). A substantial deposit is usually required to rent a car; motorcycle rental usually requires that you leave your passport.

The motorcycle industry in Thailand stopped assembling dirt bikes a number of years ago, so many of the rental bikes of this type are getting on in years. When they're well maintained they're fine; when they're not so well maintained they can leave you stranded, or worse.

Driving Permits

Short-term visitors who wish to drive vehicles (including motorcycles) in Thailand need an International Driving Permit. Long-term visitors can apply for a Thai driver's licence at the **Police Registration Division** *(PRD; ☎ 0 2513 0051–5; Th Phahonyothin, Bangkok)*, which also has offices in provincial capitals. If you present a valid foreign driver's licence at the PRD you'll probably only have to take a written test; other requirements include a medical certificate and two passport-sized colour photos. The forms are in Thai only, so you may also need an interpreter. Some PRDs request an affidavit of residence, obtainable from your country's embassy in Thailand upon presentation of proof that you reside in Thailand (eg, a presenting a utility bill in your name).

Fuel & Oil

Modern petrol (gasoline) stations with electric pumps are in plentiful supply all over Thailand, wherever there are paved roads. In more remote off-road areas petrol *(bensin* or *náam-man rót yon)* is usually available at small roadside or village stands – typically just a couple of ancient hand-operated pumps fastened to petrol barrels. The Thai phrase for 'motor oil' is *náam-man khrêuang*.

At the time of writing, regular (*thammá-daa,* usually 91 octane) petrol costs about 15B per litre, while super (*phísèht,* which is 94 to 95 octane) costs a bit more. Diesel *(dii-soen)* fuel is available at most pumps for around 12B per litre. All fuel in Thailand is unleaded.

Motorcycle Touring

Motorcycle travel has become a popular way to get around Thailand, especially in the north. Dozens of places along the guest-house circuit, including many guesthouses themselves, have set up shop with no more than a couple of motorbikes for rent (see Rental earlier for more details). It is also possible to buy a new or used motorbike and sell it before you leave the country. A used 125cc bike can be purchased for as low as 20,000B to 25,000B; you'll pay up to 60,000B for a reconditioned Honda MTX or AX-1, and more for the newer and more reliable Honda Degree or Yamaha TTR 250.

The legal maximum size for motorcycle manufacture in Thailand is 150cc, though in reality few bikes on the road exceed 125cc. Anything over 150cc must be imported, which means the addition of up to 600% in import duties. The odd rental shop specialises in bigger motorbikes (average 200cc to 500cc) – some were imported by foreign residents and later sold on the local market, but most came into the country as 'parts' and were discreetly assembled, and licensed under the table.

A number of used Japanese dirt bikes are available, especially in northern Thailand. The 250cc, four-stroke, water-cooled Honda AX-1 and Yamaha TTR combine the qualities of both touring and off-road machines, and feature economical fuel consumption. If you're looking for a more narrowly defined dirt bike, check out the Yamaha Serow.

While motorcycle touring is undoubtedly one of the best ways to see Thailand, it is also undoubtedly one of the easiest ways to cut your travels short, permanently. You can also run up very large repair and/or hospital bills in the blink of an eye. However, with proper safety precautions and driving conduct adapted to local standards, you can see parts of Thailand inaccessible by other modes of transport and still make it home in one piece. Some guidelines to keep in mind:

- If you've never driven a motorcycle before, stick to the smaller 100cc step-through bikes with automatic clutches. If you're an experienced rider but have never done off-road driving, take it slowly the first few days.
- Always check a machine over thoroughly before you take it out. Look at the tyres to see if they still have tread, look for oil leaks and test the brakes. You may be held liable for any problems that weren't duly noted before your departure. Newer bikes cost more than clunkers, but are generally safer and more reliable. Street bikes are more comfortable and ride more smoothly on paved roads than dirt bikes; it's silly to rent an expensive dirt bike if most of your riding is going to be along decent roads. A two-stroke bike suitable for off-roading generally uses twice the fuel of a four-stroke bike with the same engine size, thus lowering your cruising range in areas where roadside pumps are scarce.
- Wear protective clothing and a helmet (required by law in 17 provinces – most rental places can provide them). Without a helmet, a minor slide on gravel can leave you with concussion. Long pants, long-sleeved shirts and shoes are highly recommended as protection against sunburn and as a second skin if you fall. If your helmet doesn't have a visor, wear goggles, glasses or sunglasses to keep bugs, dust and other debris out of your eyes. Gloves are also a good idea, to prevent blisters due to holding on to the twist-grips for long periods of time. It is practically suicidal to ride on Thailand's highways without taking these minimum precautions for protecting your body.
- For distances of over 100km or so, take along an extra supply of motor oil, and if riding a two-stroke machine carry two-stroke engine oil. On long trips, oil burns fast.
- You should never ride alone in remote areas, especially at night. There have been incidents where foreigners have been shot or harassed while riding alone, mostly in remote rural areas. When riding in pairs or groups, stay spread out so you'll have room to manoeuvre or brake suddenly if necessary.
- Distribute whatever weight you're carrying on the bike as evenly as possible across the frame. Too much weight at the back of the bike makes the front end harder to control and prone to rising up suddenly on bumps and inclines.
- Get insurance with the motorcycle if at all possible. The more reputable motorcycle-rental places insure all their bikes; some will do it for an extra charge. Without insurance you're responsible for anything that happens to the bike. If an accident results in a total loss, or if the bike is somehow lost or stolen, you can be out at

least 25,000B. To be absolutely clear about your liability, ask for a written estimate of the replacement cost for a similar bike – take photos as a guarantee. Some agencies will only accept the replacement cost of a new bike. Health insurance is also a good idea – get it before you leave home and check the conditions with regard to motorcycle riding.

Golden Triangle Rider (w www.gt-rider.com) is an excellent website for detailed, up-to-date information on motorcycle touring in Thailand. See Organised Tours later for details of motorcycle tours.

BICYCLE

Just about anywhere outside Bangkok, bicycles are the ideal form of local transport because they're cheap, nonpolluting and keep you moving slowly enough to see everything. Bicycles can be hired in many locations; guesthouses often have a few for rent at only 30B to 50B per day. Carefully note the condition of the bike before hiring; if it breaks down you are responsible and parts can be very expensive.

Many visitors are bringing their own touring bicycles to Thailand these days. For the most part, drivers are courteous and move over for bicycles. Most roads are sealed, with roomy shoulders. Grades in most parts of the country are moderate; exceptions include the far north, especially Mae Hong Son and Nan Provinces, where you'll need iron thighs. There is plenty of opportunity for dirt-road and off-road pedalling, especially in the north, so a sturdy mountain bike would make a good alternative to a touring rig. Favoured touring routes include the two-lane roads along the Mekong River in the north and the northeast – the terrain is mostly flat and the river scenery is inspiring.

One note of caution: Before you leave home, go over your bike with a fine-toothed comb and fill your repair kit with every imaginable spare part. As with cars and motorbikes, you won't necessarily be able to buy that crucial gismo for your machine when it breaks down somewhere in the back of beyond as the sun sets. In addition to this, it is advisable to bring a helmet, reflective clothing and plenty of insurance.

No special permits are needed for bringing a bicycle into the country, although it may be registered by customs – which means if you don't leave the country with your bicycle, you'll have to pay a huge customs duty. Most larger cities have bike shops – there are several in Bangkok and Chiang Mai – but they often stock only a few Japanese or locally made parts.

You can take bicycles on the train for a little less than the equivalent of one 3rd-class fare. Buses often don't charge (if they do, it will be something nominal); on the ordinary buses they'll place your bike on the roof, and on air-con buses it will be put in the cargo hold.

The 2500-member **Thailand Cycling Club** (*☎ 0 2612 5510; w www.thaibike.org; 849/53 Soi 6 Chulalongkorn, Bangkok*), established in 1959, serves as an information clearing house on biking tours and cycle clubs around the country. One of the best shops for cycling gear in Thailand is the centrally located **Probike** (*☎ 0 2253 3384, fax 0 2254 1077; 237/1 Soi Sarasin, Bangkok*) opposite Lumphini Park.

HITCHING

Hitchhiking is never entirely safe in any country in the world, and we don't recommend it. Travellers who decide to hitch should understand that there's a small but serious risk. However, many people do choose to hitch, and the advice that follows should help to make the journey as fast and safe as possible.

People have mixed success with hitching in Thailand; sometimes it's great and at other times no-one wants to pick you up. It seems easiest in the more touristy areas of the north and south, and most difficult in the central and northeastern regions where tourists are a relatively rare sight. To stand on a road and try to flag every vehicle that passes by is, to the Thais, something only an uneducated village dweller would do.

If you're prepared to face this perception, the first step is to use the correct gesture used for flagging a ride – the thumb-out gesture isn't recognised by the average Thai. When Thais want a ride they stretch one arm out with the hand open, palm fa-cing down, and move the hand up and down. This is the same gesture used to flag a taxi or bus, which is why some drivers will stop and point to a bus stop if one is nearby.

In general, hitching isn't worth the hassle as ordinary (no air-con) buses are frequent and fares are cheap. However, there's no need to stand at a bus station – all you have to do is stand on any road going in your direction and flag down a passing bus or *sǎwngthǎew* (pick-up truck).

The exception is in areas where there isn't any bus service, though in such places there's not likely to be very much private vehicle traffic either. If you do manage to get a ride, it's customary to offer food or cigarettes to the driver if you have any.

BOAT

There is plenty of water in Thailand and you'll probably have opportunities to get out on it sometime during your trip. The true Thai river transport is the long-tail boat *(reua hǎang yao)*, so-called because the propeller is mounted at the end of a long drive shaft extending from the engine. The engine, which can be anything from a small marine engine to a large car engine, is mounted on gimbals and the whole unit is swivelled to steer the boat. Long-tail boats can travel at a phenomenal speed.

Between the mainland and islands in the Gulf of Thailand or Andaman Sea, all sorts of larger ocean-going craft are used. The standard is an all-purpose wooden boat, 8m to 10m long, with a large inboard engine, a wheelhouse and a simple roof to shelter passengers and cargo. Faster, more expensive hovercraft or jetfoils are sometimes available in tourist areas.

LOCAL TRANSPORT

The Getting Around entry in the Bangkok chapter has more information on local transport.

Bus

Bangkok has an extensive city bus system. Only two provincial capitals that we know of, Phitsanulok and Ubon Ratchathani, also run buses with established routes. In these cities, fares are usually from 4B to 8B. For other places, you must rely on sǎwngthǎew, túk-túk or *sǎamláw* (three-wheeled pedicabs).

Taxi

Many regional centres have taxi services, but although there may well be meters, they're never used. Establishing the fare before departure is essential. Try to get an idea from a third party as to what the fare should be and be prepared to bargain. In general, fares are reasonably low.

See the relevant destination chapters for more information on taxis.

Sǎamláw & Túk-Túk

Sǎamláw means 'three wheels', and that's just what they are – three-wheeled vehicles. There are two types of sǎamláw – motorised and nonmotorised.

You'll find motorised sǎamláw throughout the country. They're small utility vehicles, powered by horrendously noisy two-stroke engines (usually LPG-powered) – if the noise and vibration doesn't get you, the fumes will. Tourists commonly know motor sǎamláw as túk-túk, because of the noise they make. Among themselves, the Thais still call these sǎamláw – the term túk-túk is strictly foreigner talk but it's what most Thais use when speaking to Western tourists.

The nonmotorised sǎamláw, ie, the bicycle rickshaw or pedicab, is similar to what you may see in other parts of Asia. There are no bicycle sǎamláw in Bangkok but you will find them elsewhere in the country.

With either form of sǎamláw the fare must be established, by bargaining if necessary, before departure.

Readers interested in pedicab lore and design may want to have a look at Lonely Planet's hardcover pictorial book, *Chasing Rickshaws*, by Lonely Planet founder Tony Wheeler.

Sǎwngthǎew

A sǎwngthǎew (literally, 'two rows') is a small pick-up truck with two rows of bench seats down both sides of the truck bed. They sometimes operate on fixed routes, just like buses, but they may also run a share-taxi type of service or even be booked individually just like a regular taxi. Sǎwngthǎew are often colour-coded, so that red ones, for example, go to one destination or group of destinations while blue ones go to another.

Motorcycle Taxi

Many cities in Thailand also have *mawtoesai ráp jâang*, 100cc to 125cc motorcycles that can be hired, with a driver, for short distances. They're not very suitable if you're carrying more than a backpack or small suitcase, but if you're empty-handed they can't be beat for quick transport over short distances. In addition to the lack of space for luggage, motorcycle taxis also suffer from lack of shelter from rain or sun. Although most drivers around the country drive at safe, sane speeds, the kamikaze drivers of Bangkok are a major exception.

In most cities you'll find motorcycle taxis clustered near street intersections, rather than cruising the streets looking for fares. Fares tend to run from 10B to 30B, depending on distance. Some motorcycle taxis specialise in regular, short routes, eg, from one end of a long street to another. In such cases the fare is usually a fixed 10B.

ORGANISED TOURS

Many operators around the world can arrange guided tours of Thailand. Most of them simply serve as brokers for tour companies based in Thailand; they buy their trips from a wholesaler and resell them under various names in travel markets overseas. Hence, one is much like another and you might as well arrange a tour in Thailand at a lower cost – there are so many available. Two of the largest tour wholesalers in Bangkok are: **World Travel Service** *(☎ 0 2233 5900, fax 0 2236 7169; W www.wts.co.th; 1053 Th Charoen Krung)* and **Diethelm Travel** *(☎ 0 2255 9150, fax 0 2256 0248; e dto@dto.co.th; Kian Gwan Building II, 140/1 Th Withayu, Bangkok)*. A smaller one that's particularly good with innovative itineraries and custom designs is **Asian Trails** *(☎ 0 2658 6090, fax 2658 6099; W www.asiantrails.net, 15th floor, Mercury Tower, 540 Th Ploenchit, Lumphini, Bangkok)*.

Motorcycle tours of northern Thailand (with extensions into Laos and Southwest China) can be organised by **Siam Bike Tour** *(e davidfl@chmai.loxinfo.co.th)*.

Overseas Companies

The better overseas tour companies build their own Thailand itineraries from scratch and choose their local suppliers based on which ones best serve these itineraries. Of these, several specialise in adventure and/or ecological tours. **Asia Transpacific Journeys** *(☎ 800-642 2742, 303-443 6789, fax 443 7078; W www.southeastasia.com; 3055 Center Green Dr, Boulder, CO 80301, USA)*, for example, offers trips across a broad spectrum of Thai destinations and activities, from northern Thailand trekking to sea canoeing in the Phuket Sea, plus tour options that focus exclusively on northeastern Thailand. The average trip runs 14 to 17 days.

Ms Kasma Loha-Unchit *(☎/fax 510-655 8900; W www.thaifoodandtravel.com; PO Box 21165, Oakland, CA 94620, USA)*, a Thai woman living in California, offers personalised, 19- to 28-day 'cultural immersion' tours of Thailand.

The following list of companies are also recommended.

Club Aventure (☎ 514-527 0999, fax 527 3999, W www.clubaventure.com) 757 ave du Mont-Royal Est, Montreal, QUE H2J 1W8, Canada

Exodus (☎ 020-8673 0859, fax 8673 0779, W www.exodustravels.co.uk) 9 Weir Rd, London SW12 OLT, UK

Intrepid Travel (☎ 03-9473 2626, fax 9419 4426, W www.intrepidtravel.com) 11–13 Spring St, Fitzroy, Vic 3065, Australia

Mountain Travel Sobek (☎ 800-227 2384, 510-527 8100, fax 525 7710, W www.mtsobek.com) 6420 Fairmount Ave, Berkeley, CA 94530, USA

Bangkok

The very epitome of the modern, steamy Asian metropolis, Bangkok (560 sq km, population six million plus) is a worthy subject for any urban connoisseur. Between canyons of concrete skyscrapers, speeding vehicles roar through space enacting a human-scaled version of nuclear fission. The noise is deafening, the pollution asphyxiating and the heat stifling; and then there are the floods. But conquering a man-made jungle is the modern version of bush-whacking. Once you hack through the 12-lane highways and the throngs of people, you'll find a small village, napping in the narrow lanes with an unmistakable *khwaam pen thai* ('Thai-ness').

The capital of Thailand was established at Bangkok in 1782 by the first king of the Chakri dynasty, Rama I. The name Bangkok comes from Bang Makok, meaning 'Place of Olive Plums', and refers to the original site, which is only a very small part of what is today called Bangkok by foreigners. The official Thai name for the city is quite a tongue twister:

Krungthep mahanakhon amonratanakosin mahintara ayuthaya mahadilok popnopparat ratchathani burirom udomratchaniwet mahasathan amonpiman avatansathit sakkathattiya witsanukamprasit

The 1989 album *Fak Thong* (Pumpkin) by rock duo Asanee-Wasan contained the hit 'Krung Thep Mahanakhon', a big-sound raver consisting of Bangkok's full name chanted over a hypnotic rhythm. Roughly translated, the name means 'Great City of Angels, Repository of Divine Gems, Great Land Unconquerable, Grand and Prominent Realm, Royal and Delightful Capital City Full of Nine Noble Gems, Highest Royal Dwelling and Grand Palace, Divine Shelter and Living Place of Reincarnated Spirits'.

Fortunately this is shortened to Krung Thep (City of Angels) in everyday usage. Metropolitan Krung Thep includes Thonburi, the older part of the city (and predecessor to Bangkok as the capital). In many ways, it's the most exciting and dynamic city in Southeast Asia, with, for example, the region's largest foreign media correspondent base.

Highlights

- Meditate on the exquisite Emerald Buddha, colourful mosaics and glittering spires at Wat Phra Kaew
- Explore Vimanmek Teak Mansion, one of the world's largest golden teak buildings
- Catch a performance of classical dance-drama at the Chalermkrung Royal Theatre
- Take a river taxi (a kinder commute) along the mighty Mae Nam Chao Phraya
- Take in a bout of Thai boxing at Lumphini or Ratchadamnoen stadiums
- Get lost among the temples, bazaars, shophouses and alleys of the Chinese & Indian market districts
- Catch the cool breeze and bird's-eye view from the elevated Skytrain
- Take a trip to Muang Boran, Samut Prakan's ancient city and an introduction to Thailand's architectural treasures

There are museums, temples, historic sites and other vestiges of traditional Thai culture right alongside all the trappings of a modern metropolis – an endless variety of international restaurants, cultural and social events, movies in several languages, discos and even modern-art galleries. As William Warren, the dean of expat authors in Thailand, has said, 'The gift Bangkok offers me is the assurance I will never be bored'.

ORIENTATION

The eastern side of Mae Nam Chao Phraya (Chao Phraya River), Bangkok proper, can be divided in two by the main north–south railway. The portion between the river and the railway is old Bangkok (often called Ko Ratanakosin), where most of the older temples and the original palace are located, as well as the Chinese and Indian districts. The part of the city east of the railway, which is many times larger than the old districts, is 'new' Bangkok. It can be divided again into the business and tourist district wedged between Th Charoen Krung (New Rd) and Th Phra Ram IV, and the sprawling business, residential and tourist district stretching along Th Sukhumvit and Th Phetburi Tat Mai.

This leaves the hard-to-classify areas below Th Sathon Tai (South Sathon Rd, which includes Khlong Toey, Bangkok's main port), and the area above Th Phra Ram IV between the railway and Th Withayu (Wireless Rd), which comprises an infinite variety of businesses, several cinemas, civil-service offices, the shopping area of Siam Square, Chulalongkorn University and the National Stadium. The areas along the eastern bank of Mae Nam Chao Phraya are experiencing a surge of redevelopment and many new buildings, particularly condos, are going up.

On the opposite (western) side of the river is Thonburi, which was Thailand's capital for 15 years, before Bangkok was founded. Few tourists ever set foot on the Thonburi side except to visit Wat Arun, the Temple of Dawn. Fàng thon (Thonburi Bank), as it's often called by Thais, seems an age away from the glittering high-rises on the river's eastern bank, although it isn't immune to developments like condos and traffic.

Bangkok Addresses

Any city as large and unplanned as Bangkok can be tough to get around. Street names often seem unpronounceable to begin with, compounded by the inconsistency of Romanised Thai spellings. For example, the street often spelt as Rajadamri is pronounced Ratchadamri (with the appropriate tones), or abbreviated as Rat'damri. The 'v' in Sukhumvit is pronounced with a 'w'. The most popular location for foreign embassies

Bangkok city seal

is known as both Wireless Rd and Th Withayu (*wítháyú* is Thai for radio).

Many street addresses show a string of numbers divided by slashes and dashes; for example, 48/3-5 Soi 1, Th Sukhumvit. This is because undeveloped property in Bangkok was originally bought and sold in lots. The number before the slash refers to the original lot number; the numbers following the slash indicate buildings (or entrances to buildings) constructed within that lot. The pre-slash numbers appear in the order in which they were added to city plans, while the post-slash numbers are arbitrarily assigned by developers. As a result, you'll find the numbers along a given street don't always run consecutively.

The Thai word *thànŏn* means road, street or avenue. Hence Ratchadamnoen Rd (sometimes referred to as Ratchadamnoen Ave) is always called Th Ratchadamnoen in Thai.

A *soi* is a small street or lane that runs off a larger street. So, the address referred to as 48/3-5 Soi 1, Th Sukhumvit, will be located off Th Sukhumvit on Soi 1. Alternative ways of writing the same address include 48/3-5 Th Sukhumvit Soi 1, or even just 48/3-5 Sukhumvit 1. Some Bangkok *soi* have become so large that they can be referred to both as *thànŏn* and *soi*, eg, Soi Sarasin/Th Sarasin and Soi Asoke/Th Asoke.

Smaller than a *soi* is a *tràwk* (usually spelt *trok*) or alley. Well-known alleys in Bangkok include Chinatown's Trok Itsaranuphap and Banglamphu's Trok Rong Mai.

Taxi to Nowhere

In most large cities, the taxi drivers are usually seasoned navigators familiar with every out-of-the-way neighbourhood or street. This is not the case in Bangkok where, if you succeed in correctly pronouncing your destination, the taxi driver might still stare blankly at your map. To ensure that you'll be able to return home, grab your hotel's business card, which will have directions in Thai.

Maps

A map is essential for finding your way around Bangkok, and there are lots of maps competing for your attention. Apart from Lonely Planet's *Bangkok* city map (printed on durable laminated paper), there are more detailed locally produced maps. A bus map is necessary if you want to use the fairly economical bus system. One of the most popular, because it is cheap and clearly shows all the bus routes (and some walking tours), is the *Tour 'n' Guide Map to Bangkok Thailand,* often referred to by travellers as the 'blue map' because of its monotonous aqua colour. The map costs 40B and, although it's regularly updated, some bus routes will inevitably be wrong, so take care. The coated paper on which it is printed resists stains – another plus.

Other clones include Bangkok Guide's *Bangkok Bus Map*, which has lots of sightseeing tips but tends to tear with strenuous use, and *Latest Tour's Map to Bangkok & Thailand.*

The Tourism Authority of Thailand (TAT) publishes and distributes the free *City Map of Bangkok,* a folded sheet map on coated paper with bus routes, all the major hotels, the latest expressways, sightseeing, hospitals, embassies and more – it's very useful, though a bit hard to read due to the small print. Separate inset maps of Ko Ratanakosin (labelled 'Ratchadamnoen Klang Ave Area'), Th Silom, Khlong Saen Saep, Th Sukhumvit and Th Phra Ram I are very helpful. You can pick up the map at the airport TAT desk or at any Bangkok TAT office.

The long-running, oft-imitated and never-equalled *Nancy Chandler's Map of Bangkok* costs 140B and contains a whole host of information on out-of-the-way places, including lots of stuff on where to buy unusual things around the city. The six different water-coloured panels (Greater Bangkok, Chinatown, Th Sukhumvit, Chatuchak Weekend Market, Central Shopping Area and Markets of Central Bangkok) are all drawn, written and laid out by hand. The 21st edition, published in 2002, includes a handy categorised index booklet.

Another contender on the market, Groovy Map's *Bangkok by Day Map 'n' Guide* (100B) combines an up-to-date bus map, the usual sightseeing features, and a short selection of restaurant and bar reviews, on decent coated paper. It covers a smaller area (only central Bangkok) and lacks street detail; only the main avenues and a handful of *wát* (temples) are labelled. More successful is Groovy Map's *Bangkok by Night Map 'n' Guide* (100B), which shares the same basic map features as the 'day map', but without any bus routes and many more recommendations for restaurant, bar and night-time entertainment venues.

A detailed map covering a large portion of the city is *Bangkok Map,* a 188-page hardcover street atlas put out by the Agency for Real Estate Affairs, a private company specialising in real-estate surveys of the city. Each page features a colour-coded street grid showing various office and apartment buildings, hotels, restaurants and even many nightclubs. This atlas is available from most bookshops in Bangkok that carry English-language books.

INFORMATION

Tourist Offices

The Tourism Authority of Thailand (TAT) produces the usual selection of colourful brochures, but is also one of the best tourist offices in Asia for putting out useful hard facts. Many of its staff speak English.

TAT's new **main office** *(☎ 0 2250 5500, fax 0 2250 5511; W www.tourismthailand.org; 1606 Th Phetburi Mai, 4th floor; open 8.30am-4.30pm daily)* can be reached on air-con bus No 512, microbus No 10 and ordinary bus Nos 11, 38, 58, 60, 72, 99 and 113. The main office is also a 10-minute walk from the Nana Skytrain station, via Sukhumvit Soi 3 (Nana).

TAT also has a desk in the arrivals area of both **Terminal 1** *(☎ 0 2504 2701; open*

GREATER BANGKOK

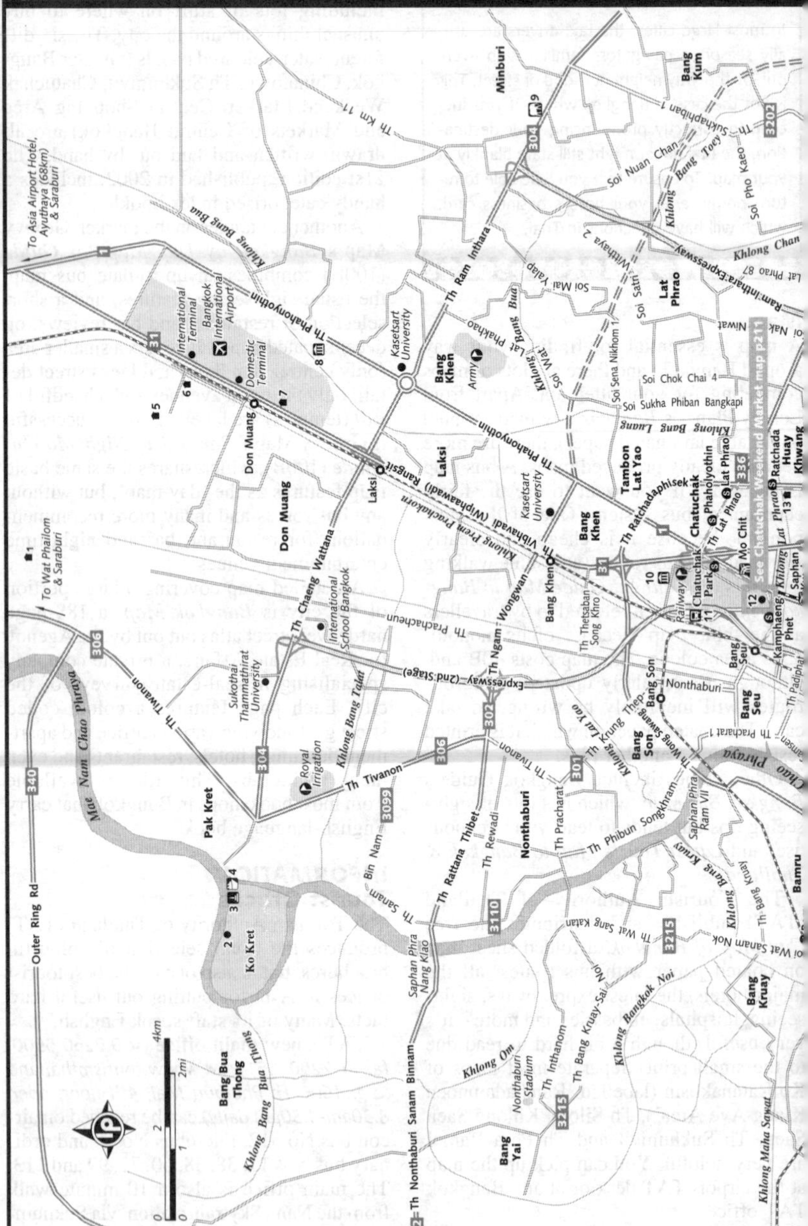

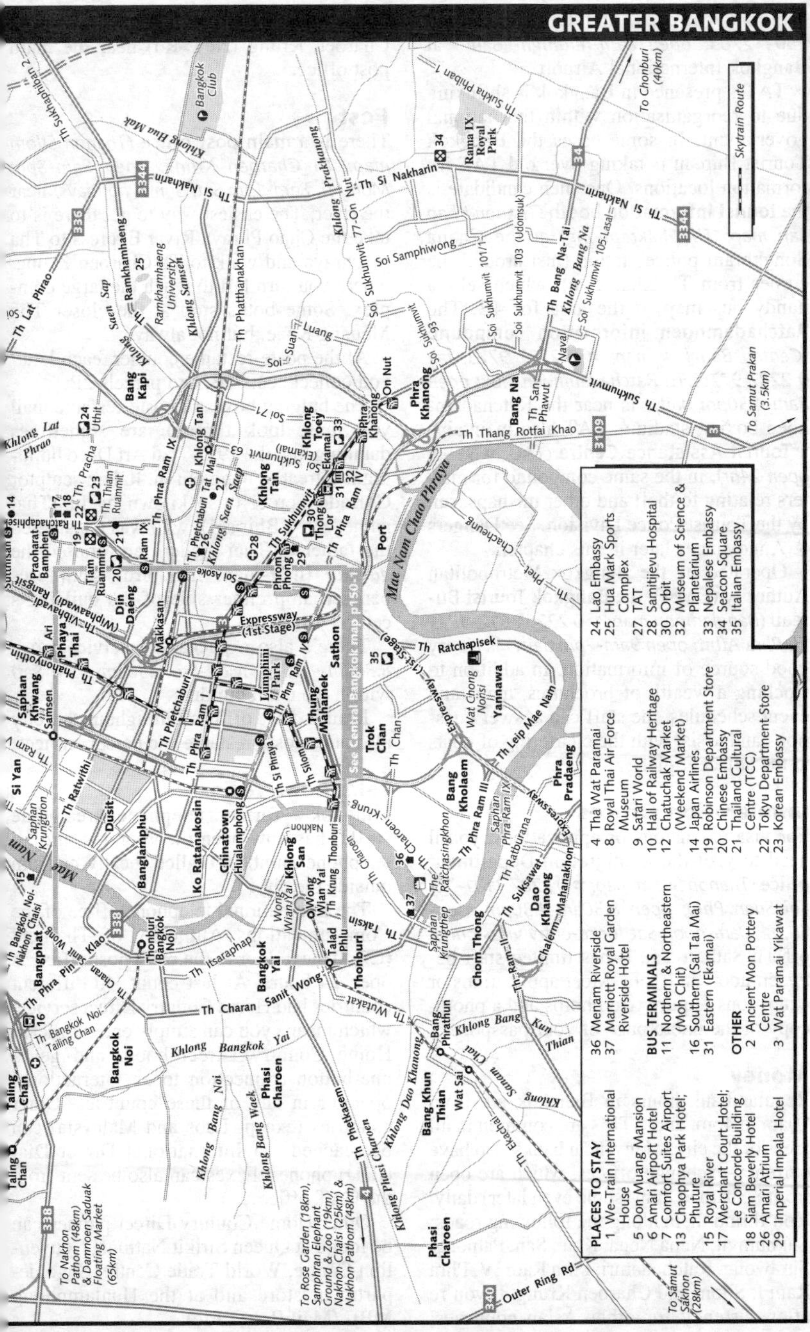
GREATER BANGKOK
Skytrain Route
See Central Bangkok map p150-1
PLACES TO STAY
1 We-Train International House
5 Don Muang Mansion
6 Amari Airport Hotel
7 Comfort Suites Airport
13 Chaophya Park Hotel; Phuture
15 Royal River
17 Merchant Court Hotel; Le Concorde Building
18 Siam Beverly Hotel
26 Amari Atrium
29 Imperial Impala Hotel
36 Menam Riverside
37 Marriott Royal Garden Riverside Hotel
BUS TERMINALS
11 Northern & Northeastern (Moh Chit)
16 Southern (Sai Tai Mai)
31 Eastern (Ekamai)
OTHER
2 Ancient Mon Pottery Centre
3 Wat Paramai Yikawat
4 Tha Wat Paramai
8 Royal Thai Air Force Museum
9 Safari World
10 Hall of Railway Heritage
12 Chatuchak Market (Weekend Market)
14 Japan Airlines
19 Robinson Department Store
20 Chinese Embassy
21 Thailand Cultural Centre (TCC)
22 Tokyu Department Store
23 Korean Embassy
24 Lao Embassy
25 Hua Mark Sports Complex
27 TAT
28 Samitivej Hospital
30 Orbit
32 Museum of Science & Planetarium
33 Nepalese Embassy
34 Seacon Square
35 Italian Embassy
To Nakhon Pathom (48km) & Damnoen Saduak Floating Market (65km)
To Rose Garden (18km), Samphran Elephant Ground & Zoo (19km), Nakhon Chaisi (25km) & Nakhon Pathom (48km)
To Samut Sakhon (28km)
To Samut Prakan (3.5km)
To Chonburi (40km)
Mae Nam Chao Phraya
Outer Ring Rd

8am-midnight daily) and **Terminal 2** *(☎ 0 2504 2703; open 8am-midnight daily)* at Bangkok International Airport.

TAT's presence in Bangkok is shrinking due to reorganisation within the national government. In some cases the Bangkok Tourist Bureau is taking over old TAT information locations. One such candidate is the **tourist information booth** *(Thanon Khao San map; Th Chakraphong)* at the Chana Songkhram police station (just around the corner from Th Khao San), which sells a handy bus map of the area for 4B. The **Ratchadamnoen information compound** *(Central Bangkok map; ☎ 0 2282 9773, fax 0 2282 9775; Th Ratchadamnoen Nok; open 8am-4.30pm daily)* is near the Ratchadamnoen boxing stadium. TAT also maintains a **Tourist Assistance Centre** *(TAC; ☎ 1155; open 24hr)*, in the same compound for matters relating to theft and other mishaps, run by the Tourist Police Division. See Dangers & Annoyances later in this chapter.

Operated by the Bangkok Metropolitan Authority (BMA), the **Bangkok Tourist Bureau** *(Banglamphu map; ☎ 0 2225 7612; 17/1 Th Phra Athit; open 9am-7pm daily)* is a very good source of information. In addition to stocking a wealth of brochures, maps and event schedules, the staff can answer questions and assist with the chartering of boats at the adjacent pier.

Immigration Offices

For visa extensions or applications, you'll need to visit the **Immigration Department office** *(Thanon Silom map; ☎ 0 2287 3101–10; Soi Suan Phlu; open 8.30am-4.30pm Mon-Fri, 8.30am-noon Sat for re-entry visas only)*, off Th Sathon Tai. It has limited staff between noon and 1pm. Most applications or extensions require two photos and a photocopy of the photo page of your passport.

Money

Regular bank hours in Bangkok are from 10am to 4pm, and ATMs are common in all areas of the city. Many Thai banks also have currency-exchange offices, which are open from 8.30am to 8pm (some even later) daily. You'll find them along the following roads: Sukhumvit, Nana Neua, Khao San, Patpong, Surawong, Ratchadamri, Phra Ram IV, Phra Ram I, Silom and Charoen Krung. If you're after currency for other Asian countries, check with the moneychangers along Th Charoen Krung (New Rd) near the main post office.

Post

There is a **main post office** *(Thanon Silom map; Th Charoen Krung; open 8am-8pm Mon-Fri, 8am-1pm Sat, Sun & holidays)* near the river. The easiest way to get there is to take the Chao Phraya River Express to Tha Si Phraya and walk to Th Charoen Krung, where you turn left to reach the large complex. Some boats stop at the closer Tha Meuang Khee, but not always.

At the poste-restante counter, each letter you collect costs 1B, and parcels 2B.

The bulging boxes of poste-restante mail you must look through are sometimes daunting, but the 1927 Thai Art Deco building is a treat to hang out in. Italian sculptor Corrado Feroci (also known by his Thai name, Silpa Bhirasri), who was considered the father of Thai modern art, crafted the *garuda* (half-man, half-bird) sculptures perched atop either side of the building's central tower.

There's also a **packaging service** *(open 8.30am-4.30pm Mon-Fri, 8.30am-noon Sat)* within the main building.

Branch post offices throughout the city also offer poste-restante and parcel services.

Telephone & Fax

Bangkok's former telephone area code (☎ 02) has now been incorporated into all telephone numbers dialled locally or from outside the city.

The international telephone office of the Communications Authority of Thailand (CAT), next door to the main post office, is open 24 hours. At last count, 40 different countries had Home Country Direct service, which means you can simply enter a vacant Home Country Direct booth and get a one-button connection to an international operator in any of these countries. Other countries (except Laos and Malaysia) can be reached via International Direct Dial (IDD) phones. Faxes can also be sent from the CAT office.

Other Home Country Direct phones can be found at Queen Sirikit National Convention Centre, World Trade Centre, Sogo department store and at the Hualamphong MBE (Mail Boxes Etc).

You can also make long-distance calls and send faxes at the **Telephone Organization of Thailand** *(TOT; Siam Square & Pratunam map; Th Ploenchit)*, but this office only accepts cash and reverse-charge calls are not allowed. Calls to Laos and Malaysia can only be made from TOT offices or private phones. For long-termers, an English version of Bangkok's *Yellow Pages* is available from this office for 30B.

Email & Internet Access

Internet users can check their email or skim the Net at the dozens of Internet cafés, bars and centres throughout the city. Rates vary depending on the concentration and affluence of Net-heads; around Siam Square usage costs about 25B for 15 minutes; Th Sukhumvit and Silom areas cost around 50B for 15 minutes. Th Khao San and its environs plunges to 1B per minute; connections tend to be slow and are frequently lost mid-click.

There's not much point in recommending one place over another as they're all struggling to keep up with their competitors, and hence the equipment and functionality changes from month to month. Some places are little more than one terminal set up in the corner of a *ráan cham* (sundries shop), while the better spots offer scanner and printer services for additional charges.

Digital Resources

The website ⓦ www.bangkok.thailandtoday.com posts a solid collection of information on shopping, nightlife, dining and sightseeing, with an emphasis on the river and Ko Ratanakosin area.

Travel Agencies

Bangkok is packed with travel agencies of every description. Around Th Khao San alone there are over a dozen places where you can book bus and air tickets; some are reliable and offer unbelievably low prices, but you should exercise caution because there are always a few bad apples in the bunch. In the past five years at least two agencies on Th Khao San closed shop and absconded with payments from dozens of tourists, who never received their tickets. The bad agencies change their names frequently, so ask other travellers for advice. Wherever possible, try to see the tickets before you hand over any of your money.

You can also verify that a travel agency has a TAT licence at ⓦ www.tat.or.th/tbgr/cgi-bin/tour_e.pl.

STA Travel *(Thanon Silom map; ☎ 0 2233 2582; Wall Street Tower, 33/70 Th Surawong)* maintains reliable offices that specialise in discounted yet flexible air tickets. Another reliable, long-running agency is **Viang Travel** *(Banglamphu map; ☎ 0 2280 3537; Trang Hotel, 99/8 Th Wisut Kasat)*.

If you are heading to Europe and need a Eurail Pass, **Dits Travel** *(☎ 0 2627 3350; 93/1 Th Withayu)* is authorised to issue them.

Guidebooks

Lonely Planet's *Bangkok* covers all of the information in this chapter along with extra details concerning business services in the city, and excursions to nearby provinces. For weekenders, pick up a copy of Lonely Planet's *Bangkok Condensed*. *Vivre à Bangkok*, published by Une Équipe de Bénévoles Bangkok Accueil for La Communautée Francophone en Thaïlande, is a thick spiral-bound book that covers all the usual territory with special attention to French speakers – including, for example, a list of travel agents who speak French. It's available in Bangkok bookshops where foreign-language books are sold, such as Asia Books (see Bookshops).

Newspapers & Magazines

The *Nation* and the *Bangkok Post* contain useful articles and listings of events, especially in the papers' Friday or weekend supplements.

The tears and fears of the backpacker community have been given an irreverent voice in the free monthly *Farang* magazine. In previous editions the magazine has profiled new bars in 'undiscovered' areas beyond Th Khao San. Available at bookshops and some newsstands, the French-language magazine *Gavroche* is a good source for news and views.

Bookshops

Bangkok has probably the best selection of bookshops in Southeast Asia.

Asia Books *(Thanon Sukhumvit map; ☎ 0 2252 7277; Soi 15, 221 Th Sukhumvit)* lives up to its name by having Bangkok's best and largest selections of English-language titles on Asia. It has several other large branches at Landmark Plaza, Soi 3 and Soi 4, Th Sukhumvit; 2nd floor, Peninsula Plaza, Th Ratchadamri; 3rd floor, World Trade Centre, Th Ploenchit; 4th floor Siam Discovery Centre, Th Phra Ram I; 3rd floor, Thaniya Plaza, Th Silom; Times Square, Th Sukhumvit; and Emporium complex, Th Sukhumvit.

DK Book House *(☎ 0 2251 6335, 0 2251 1467, 0 2250 1262; 244-246 Soi 2, Th Phra Ram I, Siam Square)* is good for textbooks. There is also a branch on Th Sukhumvit, across from the Ambassador City complex (excellent for fiction titles); and in the Mahboonkrong shopping centre opposite Siam Square.

There are two English-language bookshops in the Siam Square complex (see the Siam Square & Pratunam map), **Book Chest** *(Soi 2)* and **Odeon Store** *(Soi 1)*. In The Emporium shopping centre, **Kinokuniya** *(Thanon Sukhumvit map; Soi 24, Th Sukhumvit)* is also quite good, not only for Japanese-language materials but for English-language books.

Teck Heng Bookstore *(☎ 0 2234 1836; 1326 Th Charoen Krung)*, between the lanes leading to Shangri-La and Oriental Hotels, is one of the better independent bookshops in this neighbourhood. It carries up-to-date books on Southeast Asia and the owner is very helpful.

Suksit Siam *(☎ 0 2225 9531; 113-115 Th Fuang Nakhon)*, opposite Wat Ratchabophit, specialises in books on Thai politics, especially those representing the views of outspoken social critic Sulak Sivaraksa and the progressive Santi Pracha Dhamma Institute next door. The shop also has a number of mainstream titles.

Shaman Books *(Thanon Khao San map; ☎ 0 2629 0418; 71 Th Khao San)* carries a good mixture of new and used guidebooks, maps, novels and books on spirituality in several languages. Much smaller, but with an attached outdoor café, is **Banana Leaf Books & Café** *(Thanon Khao San map)*, off the northwestern end of Th Khao San. **Aporia Books**, on the east side of Th Tanao almost opposite the eastern entrance to Th Khao San, also offers an extensive selection of new and used books.

Elite Used Books *(Thanon Sukhumvit map; 593/5 Th Sukhumvit west of Soi 33/1; open 10am-8pm)*, near Villa supermarket, carries a decent selection of used titles in foreign languages, including English, Chinese, French, German and Swedish.

The **Chatuchak Weekend Market** in Chatuchak Park is also a source of used, often out-of-print books in several languages. On Th Khao San in Banglamphu, there are at least three street vendors specialising in used paperback novels and guidebooks, including many Lonely Planet titles.

Libraries

Besides offering an abundance of reading material, Bangkok's libraries make a peaceful escape from the heat and noise.

In a class all of its own, the **Neilson Hays Library** *(Thanon Silom map; ☎ 0 2233 1731; 195 Th Surawong; open 9.30am-4pm Tues-Sat, 9.30am-2pm Sun)*, next to the British Club, is a historical monument as well as a good, all-purpose lending library. Built in 1921 by Dr Heyward Hays as a memorial to his wife, the classic colonial-style edifice is operated by the 100-year-old Bangkok Library Association and is the oldest English-language library in Thailand. It has well over 20,000 volumes, including a good selection of children's books and titles on Thailand. The periodical section offers a few Thai magazines.

Although the building has only one aircon reading room, the ancient ceiling fans do a good job of keeping the others cool. The library's Rotunda Gallery hosts monthly art exhibitions and also the occasional art sale. Free parking for members is available at the library's small car park near the corner of Th Surawong and Th Naret.

The National Library *(Central Bangkok map; ☎ 0 2281 5212; Th Samsen)* is an impressive institution with a huge collection of Thai material dating back several centuries, as well as smaller numbers of foreign-language books. Membership is free. Two places, **The Siam Society** *(Thanon Sukhumvit map; 131 Soi Asoke, Th Sukhumvit)* and the **National Museum** *(Ko Ratanakosin map; Th Na Phra That)* also have an English-language collection on the history, art and culture of Thailand.

Although you won't be permitted to borrow books unless you're enrolled, the library at **Chulalongkorn University** (south of Siam Square) is a good place to hang out – quiet and air-conditioned.

The **Foreign Correspondents Club of Thailand** (see Cultural Centres following) has a small selection of books on Southeast Asian affairs, as well as current copies of the *International Herald Tribune* and other periodicals. Nonmembers are welcome to browse as long as they buy something at the bar or restaurant.

Cultural Centres

Various Thai and foreign associations organise cultural events that can be good places to meet Bangkok residents and Thais with an international outlook. Some of the more active organisations include the following.

Alliance Française (Thanon Silom map; ☎ 0 2213 2122, 0 2286 3841, W www.alliance-francaise.or.th) 29 Th Sathon Tai
American University Alumni (Central Bangkok map; AUA; ☎ 0 2252 4021) 179 Th Ratchadamri
British Council (Siam Square & Pratunam map; ☎ 0 2652 5480, fax 0 2253 5311, W www.britishcouncil.or.th) Siam Square, 254 Soi Chulalongkorn 64, Th Phra Ram I
Foreign Correspondents Club of Thailand (Siam Square & Pratunam map; FCCT; ☎ 0 2652 0580, 0 2254 8165, fax 0 2652 0582, W www.fccthai.com) Penthouse, Maneeya Center, 518/5 Th Ploenchit
Goethe Institut (Central Bangkok map; Thai-German Cultural Centre; ☎ 0 2287 0942, W www.goethe.de/bangkok) 18/1 Soi Goethe, between Th Sathon Tai and Soi Ngam Duphli
Thailand Cultural Centre (Greater Bangkok map; TCC; ☎ 0 2245 7742, W www.thaiculturalcenter.com) Th Ratchadaphisek, Huay Khwang

Medical Services

Bangkok has three university research hospitals, 12 public and private hospitals, and hundreds of medical clinics. The Australian, US and UK embassies usually keep up-to-date lists of the doctors who can speak English; for doctors who speak other languages, contact the relevant embassy.

Several shop-front clinics in the Th Ploenchit area specialise in lab tests for sexually transmitted diseases. Bangkok General Hospital is considered by many to have the most sophisticated HIV blood-testing programme. Bangkok's better hospitals include the following insitutions.

Bangkok Adventist (Mission) Hospital (Central Bangkok map; ☎ 0 2281 1422, 0 2282 1100) 430 Th Phitsanulok
Bangkok Christian Hospital (Thanon Silom map; ☎ 0 2233 6981–9) 124 Th Silom
Bangkok General Hospital (Greater Bangkok map; ☎ 0 2318 0066) 2 Soi 47, Th Phetburi Tat Mai
Bangkok Nursing Home (☎ 0 2632 0540–87) 9 Th Convent
Bumrungrad Hospital (Siam Square & Pratunam map; ☎ 0 2667 1000) 33 Soi 3, Th Sukhumvit
Chao Phraya Hospital (☎ 0 2884 7140) 113/44 Th Pinklao Nakhon-Chaisi, Bangkok Noi
Mahesak Hospital (Thanon Silom map; ☎ 0 2635 7123) 46/7-9 Th Mahesak
Phayathai Hospital (☎ 0 2245 2620) 364/1 Th Si Ayuthaya
Samitivej Hospital (Greater Bangkok map; ☎ 0 2381 6728, 0 2381 6831) 133 Soi 49, Th Sukhumvit
St Louis Hospital (Thanon Silom map; ☎ 0 2675 5000) 215 Th Sathon Tai

There are plenty of Chinese doctors and herbal dispensaries in Bangkok's Sampeng district, near Th Ratchawong, Th Charoen Krung, Th Yaowarat and Th Songwat, including the Art Deco **Pow Tai Dispensary** *(572-574 Th Charoen Krung)*. Readers have recommended the shopfront clinics in Banglamphu for minor medical problems, such as travellers diarrhoea or food poisoning. **Lumpoo Polyclinic** *(Banglamphu map; ☎ 0 2281 2922; 58 Th Samsen; open 7am-10pm)* and **Nana Clinic** *(Banglamphu map; ☎ 0 2280 1818; 62 Th Samsen; open 8am-9pm)* both have English-speaking doctors and are a short walk or inexpensive taxi ride from Th Khao San.

For urgent eye care, try the **Rutnin Eye Hospital** *(☎ 0 2258 0442; 80/1 Soi Asoke)*.

Emergency

All of the hospitals listed previously offer 24-hour service. Bangkok does not have an emergency phone system staffed by English-speaking operators. Between 8am and midnight, your best bet for English-speaking assistance is the **Tourist Assistance Centre** *(☎ 0 2281 5051, 0 2282 8129)*, or call the **tourist police** *(☎ 1155; open 24hr)*.

All in all there are some 500 English-speaking tourist-police officers stationed in tourist areas – their kiosks, cars and uniforms are clearly marked. If you have any problems related to criminal activity, try

CENTRAL BANGKOK

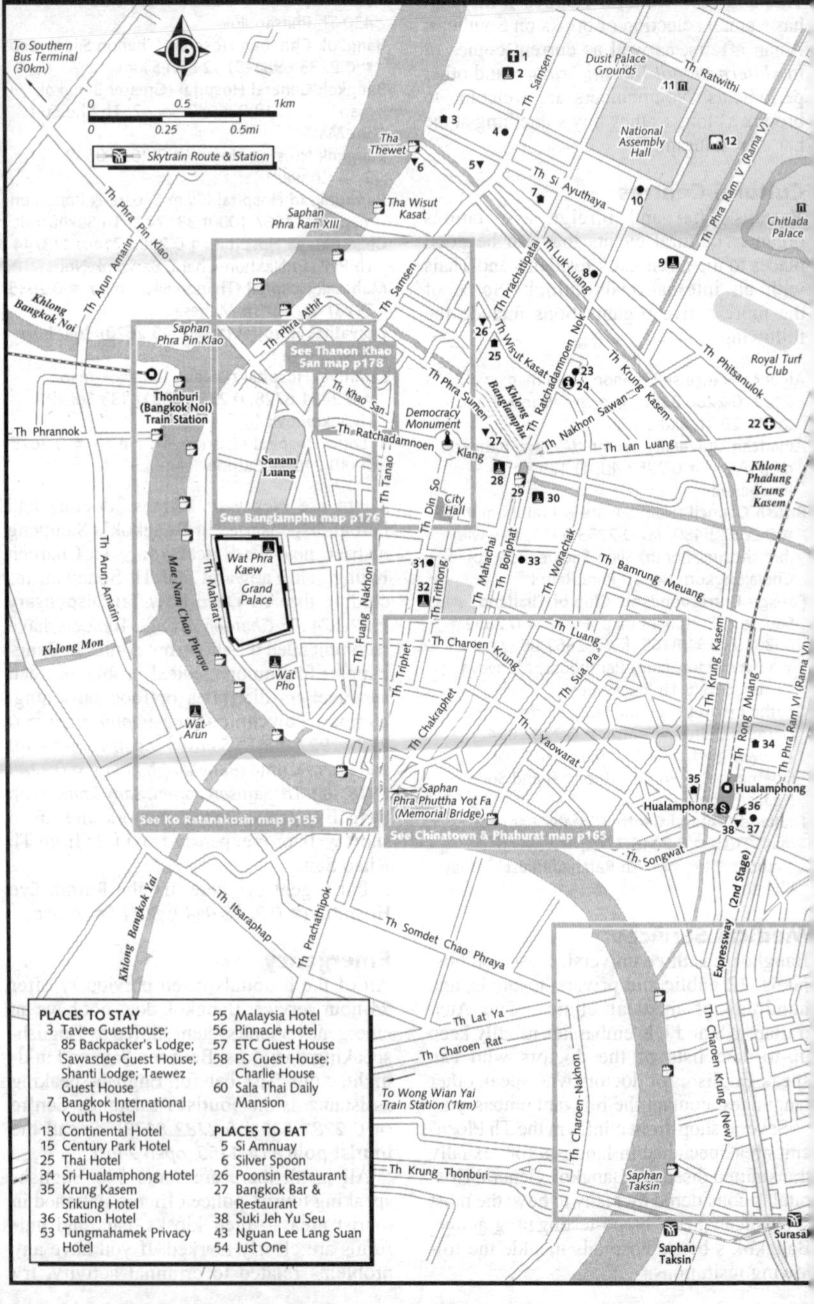

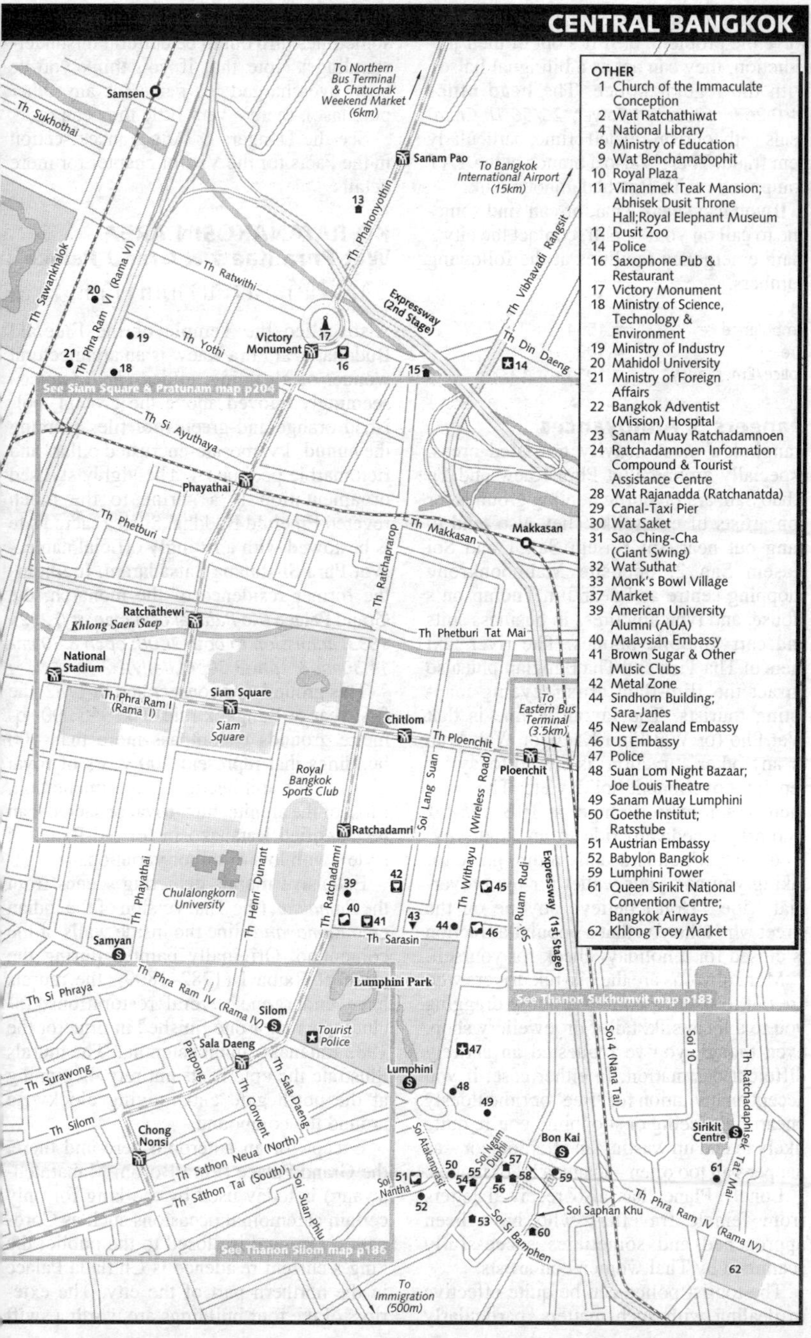
CENTRAL BANGKOK
OTHER
1 Church of the Immaculate Conception
2 Wat Ratchathiwat
4 National Library
8 Ministry of Education
9 Wat Benchamabophit
10 Royal Plaza
11 Vimanmek Teak Mansion; Abhisek Dusit Throne Hall;Royal Elephant Museum
12 Dusit Zoo
14 Police
16 Saxophone Pub & Restaurant
17 Victory Monument
18 Ministry of Science, Technology & Environment
19 Ministry of Industry
20 Mahidol University
21 Ministry of Foreign Affairs
22 Bangkok Adventist (Mission) Hospital
23 Sanam Muay Ratchadamnoen
24 Ratchadamnoen Information Compound & Tourist Assistance Centre
28 Wat Rajanadda (Ratchanatda)
29 Canal-Taxi Pier
30 Wat Saket
31 Sao Ching-Cha (Giant Swing)
32 Wat Suthat
33 Monk's Bowl Village
37 Market
39 American University Alumni (AUA)
40 Malaysian Embassy
41 Brown Sugar & Other Music Clubs
42 Metal Zone
44 Sindhorn Building; Sara-Janes
45 New Zealand Embassy
46 US Embassy
47 Police
48 Suan Lom Night Bazaar; Joe Louis Theatre
49 Sanam Muay Lumphini
50 Goethe Institut; Ratsstube
51 Austrian Embassy
52 Babylon Bangkok
59 Lumphini Tower
61 Queen Sirikit National Convention Centre; Bangkok Airways
62 Khlong Toey Market
To Northern Bus Terminal & Chatuchak Weekend Market (6km)
Samsen
Th Sukhothai
Sanam Pao
To Bangkok International Airport (15km)
Th Phahonyothin
Th Sawankhalok
Th Phra Ram VI (Rama VI)
Th Ratwithi
Expressway (2nd Stage)
Th Vibhavadi Rangsit
Th Yothi
Victory Monument
Th Din Daeng
See Siam Square & Pratunam map p204
Th Si Ayuthaya
Phayathai
Th Phetburi
Th Makkasan
Makkasan
Th Ratchaprarop
Ratchathewi
Khlong Saen Saep
Th Phetburi Tat Mai
National Stadium
Th Phra Ram I (Rama I)
Siam Square
Chitlom
Th Ploenchit
To Eastern Bus Terminal (3.5km)
Ploenchit
Royal Bangkok Sports Club
Soi Lang Suan
Th Withayu (Wireless Road)
Ratchadamri
Th Phayathai
Th Henri Dunant
Th Ratchadamri
Chulalongkorn University
Soi Ruam Rudi
Expressway (1st Stage)
Th Sarasin
Samyan
Lumphini Park
See Thanon Sukhumvit map p183
Th Si Phraya
Th Phra Ram IV (Rama IV)
Silom
Tourist Police
Sala Daeng
Patpong
Th Sala Daeng
Th Convent
Th Surawong
Lumphini
Soi 4 (Nana Tai)
Soi 10
Th Ratchadaphisek Tat Mai
Th Silom
Chong Nonsi
Th Sathon Neua (North)
Th Sathon Tai (South)
Soi Suan Phlu
Soi Atakanprasit
Soi Ngam Duphli
Bon Kai
Sirikit Centre
Soi Nantha
Soi Saphan Khu
Soi Si Bamphen
Th Phra Ram IV (Rama IV)
See Thanon Silom map p186
To Immigration (500m)

contacting them first. When officers can't solve the problem, or if it's out of their jurisdiction, they can act as a bilingual liaison with the regular police. The **head office** *(☎ 0 2678 6800; TPI Tower, 26/56 Th Chan)* deals with tourism-related crime, particularly gem fraud. There's also a branch at the TAT compound on Th Ratchadamnoen Nok.

If you can speak Thai, or can find someone to call on your behalf, contact the city's main emergency facilities at the following numbers.

Ambulance	☎ 1554
Fire	☎ 199
Police/Emergency	☎ 191 or ☎ 123

Dangers & Annoyances

Bangkok's most heavily touristed areas, especially around Wat Phra Kaew and Th Khao San, are favourite hunting grounds for con artists of every ilk. They also tend to hang out near Soi Kasem San 1 and Soi Kasem San 2, opposite Mahboonkrong shopping centre and near Jim Thompson's House, and typically dress in business suits and carry mobile phones. The river taxi piers of Tha Tien and Tha Banglamphu also attract the flim-flam artists eyeing map-toting tourists. The favourite line is that Wat Pho (or Wat Phra Kaew or Wat Arun or any other attraction) is closed today for repairs, government holiday etc. They will then graciously arrange a 10B *túk-túk* (motorised pedicab) ride to an 'undiscovered' wát, which is usually a thin guise for taking you and your wallet for the proverbial 'ride'. Don't believe anyone on the street who tells you that a popular attraction is closed for a holiday; check for yourself.

More obvious are the túk-túk drivers who are out to make a commission by dragging you to a local silk, tailor or jewellery shop, even though you've requested an entirely different destination. In either case, if you accept an invitation for 'free' or ridiculously cheap sightseeing or shopping, you're quite likely to end up wasting an afternoon or – as happens all too often – losing a lot of money.

Lonely Planet has also received letters from female travellers who have been approached and sometimes successfully scammed by Thai women con artists.

The tourist police can be quite effective in dealing with such matters, particularly 'unethical' business practices – which sometimes turn out to be cultural misunderstandings. Note that if you think you've been overcharged for gems (or any other purchase), there's very little they can do.

See the Dangers & Annoyances section in the Facts for the Visitor chapter for more details.

KO RATANAKOSIN AREA

Wat Phra Kaew & Grand Palace

วัดพระแก้ว/พระบรมมหาราชวัง

Also called the Temple of the Emerald Buddha, Wat Phra Kaew is an architectural wonder of gleaming, gilded *chedi* (stupas) seemingly buoyed above the ground, polished orange-and-green roof tiles piercing the humid sky, mosaic-encrusted pillars and rich marble pediments. The highly stylised ornamentation is a shrine to the much revered Emerald Buddha. Such a sacred site is bestowed with a fittingly official name – Wat Phra Si Ratana Satsadaram. It adjoins the former residence of the monarch, the Grand Palace *(Ko Ratanakosin map; ☎ 0 2224 1833; admission to both 200B; open 8.30am-11.30am & 1pm-3.30pm daily)*.

This ground was consecrated in 1782, the first year of Bangkok rule. The 945,000-sq-metre grounds encompass more than 100 buildings that represent 200 years of royal history and architectural experimentation. Most of the architecture, royal or sacred, can be classified Ratanakosin (or old-Bangkok style), with lots of minor variations.

Extensive murals depicting scenes from the *Ramakian* (the Thai version of the Indian epic *Ramayana*) line the inside walls of the compound. Originally painted during the reign of Rama I (1782–1809), the murals have undergone several restorations, including a major one finished in time for the 1982 Ratanakosin bicentennial. The murals illustrate the epic in its entirety, beginning at the north gate and moving clockwise around the compound.

Except for an anteroom here and there, the Grand Palace (Phra Borom Maharatchawang) is today used by the king for only certain ceremonial occasions such as Coronation Day and is closed to the public; the king's current residence is Chitlada Palace in the northern part of the city. The exteriors of the four buildings are worth a swift

Travels of the Emerald Buddha

The so-called Emerald Buddha, or Phra Kaew Morakot, is not made of emerald but probably jasper quartz or perhaps nephrite jade. It stands 60cm to 75cm high, depending on how it is measured. It's not known for certain where the image originated or who sculpted it, but it first appeared on record in 15th-century Chiang Rai. It is said to have been covered with plaster and gold leaf and placed in Chiang Rai's own Wat Phra Kaew (Temple of the Jewel Image). The image supposedly lost its plaster covering in a fall. It next appeared in Lampang, where it enjoyed a 32-year stay (again at a Wat Phra Kaew) until it was brought to Wat Chedi Luang in Chiang Mai.

In the mid-16th century Laotian invaders took the image from Chiang Mai to Luang Prabang in Laos. Later it was moved to Wiang Chan (Vientiane). When Thailand's King Taksin waged war against Laos 200 years later, the image was taken back to the Thai capital of Thonburi by General Chakri, who later succeeded Taksin as Rama I, the founder of the Chakri dynasty.

Rama I had the Emerald Buddha moved to the new Thai capital in Bangkok and had two royal robes made for it, one to be worn in the hot season and one for the rainy season. Rama III added another to the wardrobe, to be worn in the cool season. Three new robes were made in 1996 in honour of the King's Golden Jubilee and are still solemnly changed at the beginning of each season by the king himself. The huge *bòt* (central sanctuary) at Wat Phra Kaew, in which it is displayed, was built expressly for the purpose of housing the diminutive image.

perusal for their royal bombast. The intrigue and rituals that occurred within the walls of this once cloistered community are relatively silent to the modern visitor. A fictionalised version is told in the trilogy *Four Reigns*, by Kukrit Pramoj, which tells the story of a young girl named Ploi, growing up in the Royal City.

Borombhiman Hall (eastern end), a French-inspired structure that served as a residence for Rama VI, is occasionally used to house visiting foreign dignitaries. In April 1981 General San Chitpatima used it as headquarters for an attempted coup. The building to the west is **Amarindra Hall**, originally a hall of justice but used today for coronation ceremonies.

The largest of the palace buildings is the **Chakri Mahaprasat**, literally 'Great Hall of Chakri' but usually translated as 'Grand Palace Hall'. Built in 1882 by British architects using Thai labour, the exterior shows a peculiar blend of Italian Renaissance and traditional Thai architecture. This is a style often referred to as *faràng sài chá-daa* (Westerner in a Thai crown) because each wing is topped by a *mondòp* – a heavily ornamented spire representing a Thai adaptation of the Hindu *mandapa* (shrine). The tallest of the *mondòp*, in the centre, contains the ashes of Chakri kings; the flanking *mondòp* enshrine the ashes of Chakri princes. Thai kings traditionally housed their huge harems in the inner palace area, which was guarded by combat-trained female sentries.

Last, from east to west, is the Ratanakosin-style **Dusit Hall**, which initially served as a venue for royal audiences and later as a royal funerary hall.

The admission fee includes entry to the **Royal Thai Decorations & Coins Pavilion** (on the same grounds) and to both Vimanmek (billed as 'the world's largest golden-teak mansion') and Abhisek Dusit Throne Hall, near the Dusit Zoo (both are covered later in this chapter). A two-hour, self-guided audio-cassette tour is available for 100B. Real live guides depart roughly every half-hour.

Since wát are sacred places to Thai Buddhists, this one particularly so because of its royal associations, visitors should dress and behave decently. If you wear shorts or a sleeveless shirt you may be refused admission; sarongs and baggy pants are often available on loan at the entry area. For walking in the courtyard areas, you must wear closed shoes – thongs aren't permitted. As at any temple compound, shoes should be removed before entering the main chapel *(bòt)* or sanctuaries *(wíhăan)*.

The most economical way of reaching Wat Phra Kaew and the Grand Palace is by air-con bus No 508 or 512 or ordinary bus Nos 6, 9 and 32. You can also take the Chao Phraya River Express, disembarking at Tha Chang.

Wat Pho

วัดโพธิ์(วัดพระเชตุพน)

The oldest and largest wát in Bangkok, Wat Pho *(Ko Ratanakosin map; Wat Phra Chetuphon; ☎ 0 2221 9911; admission 20B; open 8am-5pm daily)* features the largest reclining Buddha and the largest collection of Buddha images in Thailand, and was the earliest centre for public education. As a temple site it dates back to the 16th century, but its current history really begins in 1781 with the complete rebuilding of the original monastery.

The grounds are divided in two by narrow Th Chetuphon, with each section surrounded by huge whitewashed walls. The most interesting part is the northern compound, which includes a very large *bòt*, enclosed by a gallery of Buddha images and

Ratanakosin Temples & River Walking Tour

This walk covers the area of Ko Ratanakosin (Ratanakosin Island), which rests in a bend of the river in the middle of Bangkok and contains some of the city's most historic architecture and prestigious universities. (See the Ko Ratanakosin map.) The river bank in this area is dotted with piers and markets, worthwhile attractions in themselves. Despite its name, Ko Ratanakosin is not an island at all, though in the days when Bangkok was known as the 'Venice of the East', Khlong Banglamphu and Khlong Ong Ang – two lengthy adjoining canals that run parallel to the river to the east – were probably large enough for the area to seem like an island.

This walk (one to three hours depending on your pace) begins at Tha Tien, a pier on the Chao Phraya River Express route. From the pier walk out to the main road and turn right onto Th Maharat, then left onto Th Chetuphon and enter **Wat Pho** through the second portico. Officially named Wat Phra Chetuphon, this is Bangkok's oldest temple and is famous for its reclining Buddha and massage school, the oldest in Thailand. The temple's affiliated massage school is located outside of the grounds in a small lane, a few blocks from Tha Tien; Thai massage isn't as relaxing as you might imagine, but the technique will silence your nagging feet.

Exit the temple through the same portico and turn left towards Th Sanamchai, turn left again and follow the street past the stark fortress-like wall of the Grand Palace. At the intersection of Th Ratchadamnoen Nai and Th Lak Meuang, opposite the southern end of Sanam Luang, you'll find **Lak Meuang**. By tradition, every city in Thailand must have a foundation stone that embodies the city spirit *(phîi meuang)* and from which intercity distances are measured. This is Bangkok's most important site of animistic worship; believers throng the area day and night.

From Lak Meuang, follow Th Na Phra Lan towards the river and the entrance to the famed **Grand Palace** and **Wat Phra Kaew**. The Grand Palace has been supplanted by Chitlada Palace as the primary residence of the royal family, but it is still used for ceremonial occasions. Wat Phra Kaew is a gleaming example of Bangkok temple architecture at its most baroque.

After wandering around the palace and temple grounds, exit via the same doorway and turn left towards the river again. On the right-hand side you'll pass the entrance to **Silpakorn University**, Thailand's premier university for fine-arts studies. Originally founded as the School of Fine Arts, by Italian artist Corrado Feroci, the university campus includes part of an old palace built for Rama I. A small bookshop inside the gate, and to the left, sells English-language books on Thai art.

If you've had enough walking and túk-túk offers, turn left at Th Maharat to catch an air-con city bus (No 508 or No 512). Also nearby is **Tha Chang**, another express-boat stop, from where you can be whisked away.

Still with us? Then turn right at Th Maharat (past the Siam City Bank on the corner) and almost immediately you'll see vendor tables along the street. Here they're selling cheap amulets representing various Hindu and Buddhist deities. If you're interested in religious amulets, you can get better-quality ones a bit farther north along Th Maharat in the **amulet market** on the small lanes between the road and the river. Opposite the amulet market on Th Maharat is **Wat Mahathat**, another of Bangkok's older temples and the headquarters for the Mahanikai sect, Thailand's largest monastic sect.

four *wíhăan*, four large *chedi* commemorating the first three Chakri kings (Rama III has two *chedi*), 91 smaller *chedi*, an old *Tripitaka* (Buddhist scriptures) library, a sermon hall, a large *wíhăan* that houses the reclining Buddha and a school building for classes in Abhidhamma (Buddhist philosophy), plus several less important structures. The temple is currently undergoing renovations.

If you're hungry by now, you're in luck. For an immediate air-con treatment backtrack down Th Maharat to Trok Thawiphon (the Roman-script sign reads 'Thawephon'), just past the amulet market towards Tha Maharat, which is now a private pier. This driveway leads to an **S&P Bakery & Restaurant**, a ubiquitous but reliable chain. There's also a warren of smaller food vendors lining the lanes along the river. The food here is very good and extremely inexpensive – to order, just point.

Looking for something with more lounging possibilities? Follow Th Maharat to Th Phra Chan, near **Thammasat University**, known for its law and political science faculties; it was also the site of the bloody October 1976 demonstrations, when hundreds of Thai students were killed or wounded by the military. Turn left to reach Tha Phra Chan, a cross-river pier where you can catch a 2B ride to Tha Wang Lang on the Thonburi side. **Supatra River House** and **Krua Rakhang Thong** have great food and views, but cater to different budgets (see Places to Eat later in this chapter for details).

Now that you're on the river, you're on a virtual expressway (with a few boat changes) to more sights. To avoid temple-overload, consider visiting the **Royal Barges National Museum**, which is to the north and accessible by catching a boat to Tha Rot Fai. From the pier, the museum is a 15-minute walk (see Royal Barges National Museum later for directions).

If your meal came with views of **Wat Arun**, fill the rest of your day with a closer look at its striking *prang* – a tall Khmer-style pagoda. From Tha Wang Lang catch a southern-bound boat to Tha Tien, where you'll change to an adjacent pier to catch a cross-river ferry to the foot of the temple.

KO RATANAKOSIN

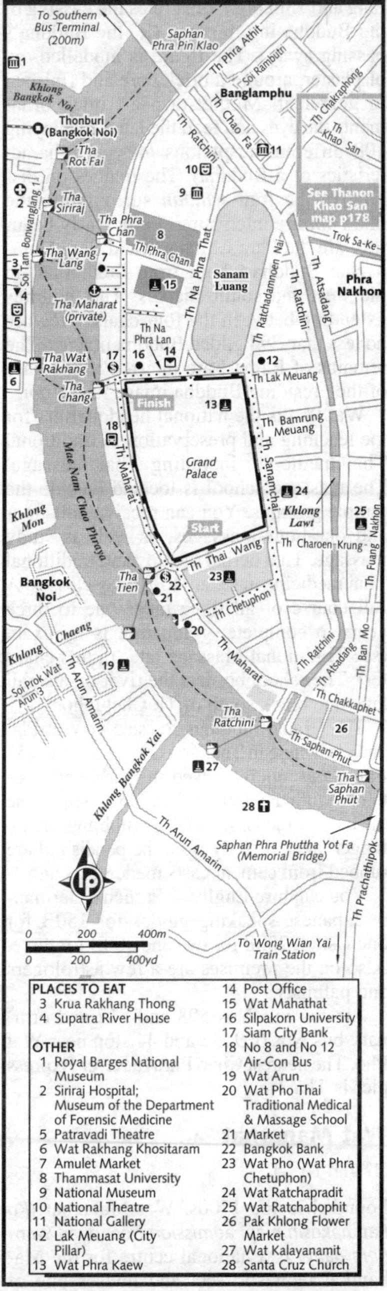

PLACES TO EAT
3 Krua Rakhang Thong
4 Supatra River House

OTHER
1 Royal Barges National Museum
2 Siriraj Hospital; Museum of the Department of Forensic Medicine
5 Patravadi Theatre
6 Wat Rakhang Khositaram
7 Amulet Market
8 Thammasat University
9 National Museum
10 National Theatre
11 National Gallery
12 Lak Meuang (City Pillar)
13 Wat Phra Kaew
14 Post Office
15 Wat Mahathat
16 Silpakorn University
17 Siam City Bank
18 No 8 and No 12 Air-Con Bus
19 Wat Arun
20 Wat Pho Thai Traditional Medical & Massage School
21 Market
22 Bangkok Bank
23 Wat Pho (Wat Phra Chetuphon)
24 Wat Ratchapradit
25 Wat Ratchabophit
26 Pak Khlong Flower Market
27 Wat Kalayanamit
28 Santa Cruz Church

The tremendous **reclining Buddha**, 46m long and 15m high, illustrates the passing of the Buddha into nirvana (ie, the Buddha's passing away). The figure is modelled out of plaster, around a brick core and finished in gold leaf. Mother-of-pearl inlay ornaments the eyes and feet, the latter displaying 108 different auspicious *láksànà* (characteristics of a Buddha). The images on display in the four *wíhǎan* surrounding the main *bòt* are interesting. Particularly beautiful are the Phra Chinnarat and Phra Chinnachai Buddhas, both from Sukhothai, in the west and south chapels. The galleries extending between the four chapels feature no less than 394 gilded Buddha images. The remains of Rama I are interred in the base of the presiding Buddha image in the *bòt*.

Wat Pho is the national headquarters for the teaching and preservation of traditional Thai medicine, including Thai massage. The massage school is located outside the temple grounds. You can receive half-hour and one-hour massages, as well as study massage, Thai herbal therapy and traditional Thai medicine in seven- to 10-day classes. A full course of all three takes one to three years to complete; graduation is by exam (see Traditional Massage later in this chapter). The school borders the river on a small lane one block south of Th Chetuphon.

The temple rubbings for sale at Wat Pho and elsewhere in Thailand come from the 152 *Ramakian* reliefs, carved in marble and obtained from the ruins of Ayuthaya, which line the base of the large *bòt*. The rubbings are no longer taken directly from the panels but are rubbed from cement casts made years ago.

You can hire English-, French-, German- or Japanese-speaking guides for 150B for one visitor, 200B for two and 300B for three. Also on the premises are a few astrologers and palmists.

Air-con bus Nos 508 and 512 and ordinary bus Nos 6, 9, 32 and 44 stop near Wat Pho. The nearest Chao Phraya River Express pier is Tha Tien.

Wat Mahathat

วัดมหาธาตุ

Founded in the 1700s, Wat Mahathat *(Ko Ratanakosin map; admission free; open 9am-5pm daily)* is a national centre for the Mahanikai monastic sect and houses one of Bangkok's two Buddhist universities, **Mahathat Rajavidyalaya**. The university is the most important place of Buddhist learning in mainland Southeast Asia today.

Wat Mahathat and the surrounding area have developed into an informal Thai cultural centre of sorts, though this may not be obvious at first glance. A daily **open-air market** features traditional Thai herbal medicine, and out on the street you'll find a string of shops selling herbal cures and offering Thai massage. On weekends, a large **produce market** held on the temple grounds brings people from all over Bangkok and beyond. Opposite the main entrance on the other side of Th Maharat is a large religious **amulet market**.

The monastery's International Buddhist Meditation Centre offers **meditation instruction** in English on the second Saturday of every month, from 2pm to 6pm in the Dhamma Vicaya Hall. Those interested in more intensive instruction should contact the monks in Section 5 of the temple.

Wat Mahathat is on the western side of Sanam Luang. Air-con bus Nos 508 and 512 both pass by it, and the nearest Chao Phraya River Express pier is Tha Chang.

Wat Arun

วัดอรุณฯ

This striking temple *(Ko Ratanakosin map; Temple of Dawn; ☎ 0 2466 3167; admission 20B; open 8.30am-5.30pm daily)*, named after the Indian god of dawn, Aruna, looms on the Thonburi side of Mae Nam Chao Phraya as if it were carved from granite, but a closer inspection reveals that intricate mosaic tiles cover the imposing structures. The present wát was built on the site of 17th-century Wat Jaeng, which served as the palace and royal temple of King Taksin when Thonburi was the Thai capital; hence, it was the last home of the Emerald Buddha before Rama I brought it across the river to Wat Phra Kaew.

The 82m *prang* (Khmer-style tower) was constructed during the first half of the 19th century by Rama II and Rama III. The unique design elongates the typical Khmer *prang* into a distinctly Thai shape. Its brick core has a plaster covering embedded with a mosaic of broken, multihued Chinese porcelain, a common temple ornamentation in the early Ratanakosin period, when Chinese ships calling at Bangkok used tonnes of old porcelain as ballast. Steep stairs reach a lookout point about halfway up the *prang* from where there are fine views of Thonburi and the river. During certain festivals, hundreds of lights illuminate the outline of the *prang* at night.

Also worth a look is the interior of the *bòt*. The main Buddha image is said to have been designed by Rama II himself. The murals date to the reign of Rama V; particularly impressive is one that depicts Prince Siddhartha encountering examples of birth, old age, sickness and death outside his palace walls, an experience that led him to abandon the worldly life. The ashes of Rama II are interred in the base of the presiding Buddha image.

Between the *prang* and the cross-river ferry pier is a huge sacred banyan tree. Scattered around the periphery are simple wooden cut-outs of Thai dancers luring visitors to snap a picture of their mugs imposed on to the figures. A fairly innocuous scam is at work here: after the camera has clicked, a hawker emerges to collect a fee of 40B, although no charge is posted in front of the figures.

To reach Wat Arun from the Bangkok side, catch a cross-river ferry from Tha Tien at Th Thai Wang. Crossings are frequent and cost only 2B.

Lak Meuang (City Pillar)

ศาลหลักเมือง

The City Pillar is across the street from the eastern wall of Wat Phra Kaew, at the southern end of Sanam Luang. This shrine encloses a wooden pillar erected by Rama I in 1782 to represent the founding of the new Bangkok capital city, and a shorter companion was added under Rama IV. Rama V built the sheltering pavilion.

The taller pillar originated from a *chaiyápréuk* (*Cassia laburnum* or 'tree of victory') that was cut down in effigy, following the Burmese sacking of Ayuthaya in 1767. Through a series of Buddhist-animist rituals, the felling of the tree empowered the Thais to defeat the Burmese in a series of battles. Thus it was considered an especially talismanic choice to mark the founding of the new royal capital. Two metres of the pillar's 4.7m total length are buried in the ground.

The spirit of the pillar – Phra Sayam Thewathirat (Venerable Siam Deity of the State) – is considered the city's guardian deity and receives the daily supplications of countless worshippers. Some of these worshippers commission classical Thai dancers to perform *lákhon kâe bon* (propitiatory dances) at the shrine between 11am and 4pm daily. The offerings include severed pigs' heads with sticks of incense sprouting from their foreheads.

Sanam Luang

สนามหลวง

Sanam Luang (Royal Field), just north of Wat Phra Kaew, is the traditional site for royal cremations, and for the annual Ploughing Ceremony in which the king officially initiates the rice-growing season. The most recent ceremonial cremation took place here in March 1996, when the king presided over funeral rites for his mother. Before that the most recent Sanam Luang cremations were held in 1976, without official sanction, for Thai students killed in the demonstrations of that year. A statue of Mae Thorani, the earth goddess (borrowed from Hindu mythology's Dharani), stands in a white pavilion at the northern end of the field. Erected in the late 19th century by King Chulalongkorn, the statue was originally attached to a well that provided drinking water to the public.

Before 1982, Bangkok's famous Weekend Market was regularly held at Sanam Luang (it's now at Chatuchak Park). Nowadays the large field is mostly used as a picnic and recreational area. A large kite competition is held here during the kite-flying season (mid-February to April).

Sanam Luang is a hub for several bus lines, including Nos 30, 32, 47 and 53.

National Museum

พิพิธภัณฑสถานแห่งชาติ

On the western side of Sanam Luang, the National Museum *(Ko Ratanakosin map; ☎ 0 2224 1370; Th Na Phra That; admission 40B; open 9am-4pm Wed-Sun)* is the largest museum in Southeast Asia and an excellent place to learn about Thai art. All periods

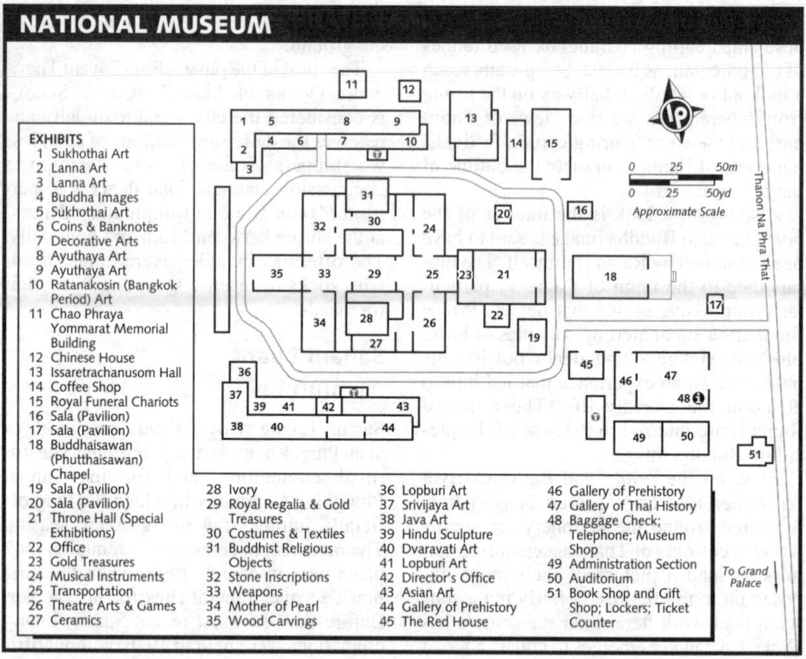

and styles are represented from Dvaravati to Ratanakosin, and English-language literature is available. Room 23 contains a well-maintained collection of traditional musical instruments from Thailand, Laos, Cambodia and Indonesia. Other permanent exhibits include ceramics, clothing and textiles, woodcarving, regalia and weaponry.

The museum buildings were built in 1782 as the palace of Rama I's viceroy, Prince Wang Na. Rama V turned it into a museum in 1884.

In addition to the exhibition halls, there is the restored **Buddhaisawan (Phutthaisawan) Chapel**. Inside the chapel (built in 1795) are some well-preserved original murals and one of the country's most revered Buddha images, Phra Phut Sihing. Legend says the image came from Sri Lanka, but art historians attribute it to 13th-century Sukhothai.

Free English-language tours of the museum are given by volunteers on Wednesday (Buddhism) and Thursday (Thai art, religion and culture). These guided tours are excellent. The tours are also conducted in German (Thursday), French (Wednesday) and Japanese (Wednesday). All tours start from the ticket pavilion at 9.30am.

The museum is serviced by bus Nos 30, 32, 47 and 53.

Royal Barges National Museum
เรือพระที่นั่ง

The royal barges are long, fantastically ornamented boats used in ceremonial processions on the river. The largest is 50m long and requires a rowing crew of 50 men, plus seven umbrella bearers, two helmsmen and two navigators, as well as a flagman, rhythm-keeper and chanter.

The barges are kept in **sheds** *(Ko Ratanakosin map; ☎ 0 2424 0004; admission 30B; open 9am-5pm daily)*, on the Thonburi side of the river. The sheds are next to Khlong Bangkok Noi, near Saphan Phra Pin Klao (Phra Pin Klao Bridge). *Suphannahong,* the king's personal barge, is the most important of the boats. Made from a single piece of timber, it's the largest dugout in the world. The name means 'Golden Swan', and a huge swan head has been carved into the bow of the barge. Lesser barges feature bows carved into other Hindu-Buddhist mythological shapes such as *naga* (mythical sea serpent) and *garuda* (Vishnu's bird mount).

One of the best times to see the fleet in action on the river is during *kàthĭn*, the royal ceremony where robes are presented to monks, at the end of *phansăa* (the Buddhist Rains Retreat, ending with an October or November full moon) when new robes are offered to the monastic contingent.

You must pay an additional 100B if you want to take photos.

The easiest way to get to the museum is by the cross-river ferry from Tha Phra Chan to Tha Rot Fai (the Roman-script sign says 'Railroad Station'). The museum is just across the canal from the train station but the closest bridge is the elevated highway. Walk along the street parallel to the railway tracks past the fruit market until you come to a set of stairs that leads to the elevated highway over the canal. Once on the other side, signs will direct you through a labyrinth of concrete walkways that pass a poor housing area and eventually lead to the barge sheds. You can also get there by long-tail boat during a one-hour tour (600B). Boats can be chartered from any pier on the Bangkok side of the river, or you can join a guided tour (780B) with **Chao Phraya Express Boat** *(☎ 0 2623 6001)*.

CENTRAL BANGKOK AREA

Wat Benchamabophit

วัดเบญจมบพิตร(วัดเบญฯ)

Made of white Carrara marble, Wat Ben *(Central Bangkok map; Marble Temple; cnr Th Si Ayuthaya & Th Phra Ram V; admission 20B; open 8am-5.30pm daily)* was built in the late 19th century under Chulalongkorn (Rama V). The large cruciform *bòt* is a prime example of modern Thai wát architecture in Thailand. The base of the central Buddha image, a copy of Phitsanulok's Phra Phuttha Chinnarat, contains the ashes of Rama V. The courtyard behind the *bòt* exhibits 53 Buddha images (33 originals and 20 copies) representing famous figures and styles from all over Thailand and other Buddhist countries – an education in itself if you are interested in Buddhist iconography.

Wat Ben is diagonally opposite Chitlada Palace. Bus Nos 503 (air-con) and 72 stop nearby.

Garuda

Wat Saket

วัดสระเกศ

Even if you're wát-ed out, you should break your Beer Chang routine with a brisk walk to Wat Saket *(Central Bangkok map; between Th Worachak & Th Boriphat; ☎ 0 2223 4561; admission to Golden Mount 10B; open 8am-5pm daily)*. Like all worthy summits, the temple's Golden Mount (Phu Khao Thong), which is visible from Th Ratchadamnoen and situated on the western side of the grounds, plays a good game of optical illusion, appearing closer than its real location. Serpentine steps wind through an artificial hill shaded by gnarled trees, some of which are signed in English, and past graves of ghostly looking residents. This artificial hill was created when a large *chedi*, under construction by Rama III, collapsed because the soft soil beneath would not support it. The resulting mud-and-brick hill was left to sprout weeds until Rama IV built a small *chedi* on its crest.

At the peak, you'll find what Frank Vincent, a well-travelled American writer, described in his 1871 ascent in *The Land of the White Elephant:*

> From the summit…may be obtained a fine view of the city of Bangkok and its surroundings; though this is hardly a correct statement, for you see very few of the dwelling-houses of the city; here and there a wát, the river with its shipping, the palace of the King, and a waving sea of cocoa-nut and betel-nut palms, is about all that distinctly appears. The general appearance of Bangkok is that of a large, primitive village, situated in and mostly concealed by a virgin forest of almost impenetrable density.

King Chulalongkorn later added to the structure and housed a Buddha relic from India (given to him by the British government) in the *chedi*. The concrete walls were added during WWII to prevent the hill from eroding. Every year in November there is a big festival on the grounds of Wat Saket, which includes a candle-lit procession up the Golden Mount.

Generally, admission to Wat Saket is free except for the final approach to the summit of the Golden Mount. The temple is within walking distance of the Democracy Monument; air-con bus Nos 511 and 512 pass nearby.

Wat Rajanadda
วัดราชนัดดา

Across Th Mahachai from Wat Saket, Wat Rajanadda (Ratchanatda) dates from the mid-19th century. It was built under Rama III and is an unusual specimen, possibly influenced by Burmese models.

The wát has a well-known market selling Buddhist amulets or magic charms *(phrá phim)* in all sizes, shapes and styles. The amulets not only feature images of the Buddha, but also famous Thai monks and Indian deities. Full Buddha images are also for sale. Wat Rajanadda is an expensive place to purchase a charm, but a good place to look.

Democracy Monument
อนุสาวรีย์ประชาธิปไตย

This large, Art Deco monument – four highly stylised angel wings arranged in a circle at the intersection of Th Ratchadamnoen Klang, Th Din So and Th Prachatipatai – was erected in 1932 to commemorate Thailand's momentous transformation from absolute to constitutional monarchy. Italian artist Corrado Feroci designed the monument and buried 75 cannonballs in its base to signify the year BE 2475 (AD 1932). Before immigrating to Thailand to become the nation's 'father of modern art', Feroci designed monuments for Italian dictator Benito Mussolini.

In recent years 'The Demo' has become a favourite spot for public demonstrations, most notably during the antimilitary, prodemocratic protests of 1992.

Vimanmek Teak Mansion
พระที่นั่งวิมานเมฆ

Originally constructed on Ko Si Chang in 1868 and moved to the present site in the Dusit Palace grounds in 1910, this beautiful L-shaped, three-storey mansion *(Central Bangkok map; Phra Thi Nang Wimanmek; ☎ 0 2628 6300; admission 100B, free with Grand Palace ticket; open 9.30am-3.15pm daily)* contains 81 rooms, halls and anterooms, and is said to be the world's largest golden teak building. The staircases, octagonal rooms and lattice walls are nothing short of magnificent, but in spite of this, the mansion retains a surprisingly serene and intimate atmosphere.

Vimanmek was the first permanent building on the Dusit Palace grounds. It served as Rama V's residence in the early 1900s, was closed in 1935 and reopened in 1982 for the Ratanakosin bicentennial. The interior of the mansion contains various personal effects of the king, and a treasure trove of early Ratanakosin art objects and antiques.

English-language tours are held every half-hour between 9.30am and 3pm. The tours cover around 30 rooms and last an hour. Smaller adjacent buildings display historic photography that documents the Chakri dynasty.

Vimanmek is towards the northern end of the grounds, which also contains Abhisek Dusit Throne Hall, Royal Elephant Museum, landscaped gardens and a stage for traditional dancing shows (at 10.30am and 2pm). As this is royal property, visitors wearing shorts or sleeveless shirts will be refused entry.

Bus Nos 70, 72 and 510 will drop you at Th U-Thong Nai, Th Si Ayuthaya and Th Ratwithi respectively.

Abhisek Dusit Throne Hall
พระที่นั่งอภิเศกดุสิต

Originally built as a throne hall for King Rama V in 1904, this smaller structure *(Central Bangkok map: admission 50B, free with Grand Palace ticket; open 9.30am-4pm daily)* is typical of the finer architecture of the era. Victorian-influenced 'gingerbread' architecture and Moorish porticoes blend to create a striking and distinctly Thai exterior. The hall houses an excellent display of regional handiwork crafted by members of the Promotion of Supplementary Occupations & Related Techniques (Support) foundation, an organisation sponsored by Queen Sirikit. Among the exhibits are cotton and silk, *málaeng tháp* (collages made from metallic, multicoloured beetle wings), damascene and nielloware, and basketry.

There is a souvenir shop on the premises. As at Wat Phra Kaew and Vimanmek, visitors must be properly dressed. See Vimanmek Teak Mansion earlier for directions to Abhisek Dusit Throne Hall.

Royal Elephant Museum
พิพิธภัณฑ์ช้างต้น

In the Dusit Palace grounds, along with the Vimanmek Teak Mansion and Abhisek Dusit Throne Hall, two large stables that once housed three 'white' elephants – animals whose auspicious albinism automatically made them crown property – are now a museum. One of the structures contains artefacts and photos outlining the importance of elephants in Thai history and explaining their various rankings according to physical characteristics. The second stable holds a sculptural representation of a living royal white elephant (now kept at the Chitlada Palace, home to the current Thai king). Draped in royal vestments, the statue is more or less treated as a shrine by the visiting Thai public.

Admission to the Royal Elephant Museum is free with admission to Vimanmek Teak Mansion and Abhisek Dusit Throne Hall.

Dusit Zoo
สวนสัตว์ดุสิต(เขาดิน)

The collection of animals at Bangkok's 19-hectare Dusit Zoo *(Central Bangkok map; Suan Sat Dusit; adult/child 30/5B; open 9am-6pm daily)* includes more than 300 mammals, 200 reptiles and 800 birds, including relatively rare indigenous species such as banteng, gaur, serow and some rhinoceros.

Originally a private botanic garden for Rama V, it was converted into a zoo in 1938 and is now one of the premier zoological facilities in Southeast Asia. The shady grounds feature trees labelled in English, Thai and Latin, plus a lake in the centre with paddle boats for hire. There's also a small children's playground.

If nothing else, the zoo is a nice place to get away from the noise of the city and observe how Thai people amuse themselves – mainly by eating. There are a couple of

Rama V Cult

Although seemingly entrenched in the culture, the veneration of Rama V (r. 1868–1910; also known as King Chulalongkorn or, to the Thais, Phra Chula Chom Klao) dates as far back as 1991 and is particularly strong in Bangkok (and other large urban centres) with middle-class Thais who have careers in commerce.

In Bangkok the most visible devotional activities are focused on a bronze statue of Rama V standing in Royal Plaza, opposite the southeastern corner of the Vimanmek Teak Mansion and Abihisek Dusit Throne Hall compound from where the venerated king once ruled the kingdom. Although originally intended as mere historical commemoration, the statue has quite literally become a religious shrine, where every Tuesday evening thousands of Bangkok residents come to offer candles, flowers (predominantly pink roses), incense and bottles of whisky.

No single event occurred to ignite the Rama V movement; rather, its growth can be traced to a series of events beginning with the 1991 military coup – which caused the intelligentsia to once again lose faith in the constitutional monarchy – on top of the 1990–2 economic recession. Along with the worsening traffic, declining economy and a host of other problems, these events brought about an unfocused, general mistrust of modern politics, technology and affluence among many Thais, who began looking for a new spiritual outlet with some historical relevancy. They seized on Rama V, who without the help of a parliament or the military had brought Thai nationalism to the fore, while fending off European colonisation. He is also considered a champion of the common person for his abolition of slavery and corvée (the requirement that every citizen be available for state labour when called).

restaurants by the lake that serve a range of delicious, inexpensive Thai food.

A small circus performs on weekends and holidays between 11am and 2pm. Sunday can be a bit crowded – if you want the zoo mostly to yourself, go on a weekday.

The zoo is in the Dusit district, between Chitlada Palace and the National Assembly Hall; the main entrance is off Th Ratwithi. Buses that pass the entrance include air-con No 510 and ordinary Nos 18, 28 and 70.

Lumphini Park

สวนลุมพินี

Named after the Buddha's birthplace in Nepal, this is Bangkok's largest and most popular park. It is bordered by Th Phra Ram IV to the south, Th Sarasin to the north, Th Withayu to the east and Th Ratchadamri to the west, with entrance gates on all sides. A large artificial lake in the centre is surrounded by broad, well-tended lawns, wooded areas and walking paths – in other words, it's the best way to escape Bangkok without leaving town.

One of the best times to visit the park is in the morning before 7am when the air is fresh (well, relatively so for Bangkok) and legions of Chinese are practising *taijiquan* (t'ai chi). Also in the morning, vendors set up tables to dispense fresh snake blood and bile, considered health tonics by many Thais and Chinese. Rowing boats and paddle boats can be rented at the lake for 30B per half-hour. A weight lifting area in one section becomes a miniature 'muscle beach' on weekends. Other facilities include a snack bar, an asphalt jogging track, several areas with tables and benches for picnics, and a couple of tables where women serve Chinese tea.

During the kite-flying season (mid-February to April), Lumphini becomes a favoured flight zone; kites *(wâo)* can be purchased in the park during these months.

You can get to Lumphini Park via the Skytrain at Ratchadamri station or bus No 47.

Queen Saovabha Memorial Institute (Snake Farm)

สถานเสาวภา

At this Red Cross research institute *(Thanon Silom map; ☎ 0 2252 0161; Th Phra Ram IV; admission 70B; open 8.30am-11.30am & 1pm-4pm Mon-Fri, 8.30am-noon Sat & Sun)*, formerly known as the Pasteur Institute, venomous snakes (the common cobra, king cobra, banded krait, Malayan pit viper, green pit viper and Russell's viper) are milked daily at 11am and 2.30pm weekdays and 11am on weekends to make antivenin, which are distributed throughout the country.

When the institute was founded in 1923 it was only the second of its kind in the world (the first was in Brazil). The milking sessions have become a major tourist attraction. Unlike other 'snake farms' in Bangkok, this is a serious herpetological research facility; a very informative half-hour slide show on snakes is presented before the milking sessions. This will be boring to some, fascinating to others. Feeding is at 3pm. The institute is near Th Henri Dunant.

A booklet entitled *Guide to Healthy Living in Thailand*, published jointly by the Thai Red Cross and the US embassy, is available here for 100B. You can also get common vaccinations against such diseases as cholera, typhoid, tetanus, polio, encephalitis, meningitis, rabies, small pox, and hepatitis A and B. If you are bitten by a strange animal, this is a good place to come for antirabies serum; bring the animal, dead or alive, if possible.

There is also an anonymous STD clinic on the grounds of the institute. To get here, take bus No 47.

Monk's Bowl Village & Sao Ching-Cha

บ้านบาตรและเสาชิงช้า

This is the only one remaining of three such villages established in Bangkok by Rama I for the purpose of handcrafting bowls *(bàat)*. The black bowls, used by Thai monks to receive food alms from faithful Buddhists every morning, are still made here in the traditional manner. Due to the expense of purchasing a handmade bowl, the 'village' has been reduced to a single alley in a district known as Ban Baht *(bâan bàat)* or Monk's Bowl Village. About half a dozen families still hammer the bowls together from eight separate pieces of steel representing, they say, the eight spokes of the Wheel of Dharma (which symbolise Buddhism's Eightfold Path). The joints are fused in a wood fire with bits of copper, and the bowl is polished and coated with several layers of black lacquer. A typical output is one bowl per day.

To find the village, head south along Th Boriphat, past Th Bamrung Meuang, then turn left into Soi Baan Baht. The artisans who fashion the bowls are not always at work, so it's largely a matter of luck as to whether you'll see them in action. At any of the houses that make the bowls, you can purchase a fine-quality alms bowl from 600B to 800B.

At nearby Sao Ching-Cha (Giant Swing) a spectacular Brahman festival in honour of the Hindu god Shiva used to take place each year until it was stopped during the reign of Rama VII. Participants would swing in ever-higher arcs in an effort to reach a bag of gold suspended from a 15m bamboo pole – many died trying. The Giant Swing is about 500m south of the Democracy Monument. Nearby shops on Th Bamrung Meuang sell monks' robes and bowls are for sale.

Air-con bus No 508 travels Th Bamrung Meuang.

CHINATOWN & PHAHURAT

Chinatown

เยาวราช(สำเพ็ง)

Bangkok's Chinatown (Sampeng), off Th Yaowarat and Th Ratchawong, comprises a confusing and crowded array of jewellery, hardware, wholesale food, automotive and fabric shops, as well as dozens of other small businesses. It's a great place to shop as goods here are cheaper than almost anywhere else in Bangkok and the Chinese proprietors like to bargain, especially along Sampeng Lane (Soi Wanit 1).

Chinese and Thai antiques of varying age and authenticity are available in the so-called Thieves' Market (Nakhon Kasem), but it's better for browsing than buying these days. See the Shopping section later for more details.

During the annual Vegetarian Festival, celebrated fervently by Thai Chinese for the first nine days of the ninth lunar month (September to October), Bangkok's Chinatown becomes a virtual orgy of vegetarian food. The festivities are centred around **Wat Mangkon Kamalawat** *(Neng Noi Yee; Th Charoen Krung)*, one of Chinatown's largest temples. All along Th Charoen Krung in this vicinity, as well as on Th Yaowarat to the south, restaurants offer different vegetarian dishes.

A Chinese population was moved here from Bang Kok (today's Ko Ratanakosin) by the royal government in 1782 to make room for the new capital. A census in the area taken exactly 100 years later found 245 opium dens, 154 pawnshops, 69 gambling establishments and 26 brothels. Pawnshops, along with myriad gold shops, remain a popular Chinatown business, while the other three vices have gone underground; brothels continue to exist under the guise of 'tea halls' *(rohng chaa)*, back-street heroin dealers have replaced the opium dens and illicit card games convene in the private upstairs rooms of certain restaurants. Several Chinese-language newspapers are printed and distributed in the district.

At the southeastern edge of Chinatown stands **Hualamphong station**, built by Dutch architects and engineers just before WWI. One of the city's earliest and best examples of the movement towards Thai Art Deco, its vaulted iron roof and neoclassical portico demonstrate engineering that was state of the art in its time, while the patterned, two-toned skylights exemplify pure de Stijl–style Dutch modernism.

Examples of Thai Art Deco from the 1920s and '30s can be found along Chinatown's main streets, particularly Th Yaowarat. Vertical towers over the main entrances are often surmounted with Deco-style sculptures – a replica of the Eiffel Tower, a lion, an elephant, a Moorish dome. Atop one commercial building on Th Songwat near Tha Ratchawong is a rusting model of a WWII vintage Japanese Zero warplane, undoubtedly placed there by the Japanese during their brief 1941 occupation of Bangkok; in style and proportion it fits the surrounding Thai Deco elements.

Ordinary bus No 53 does a long circuitous route through Chinatown, Phahurat and Banglamphu; it's a good greatest-hits ride, but won't get you anywhere in a hurry.

Phahurat

พาหุรัด

At the edge of Chinatown, around the intersection of Th Phahurat and Th Chakraphet (Chakkaphet), is a small but thriving Indian

Walking Tour – Chinatown & Phahurat

Chinatown is packed – every inch of it is used to make a living. From the fresh-food market festooned with freshly killed carcasses to the plastic beeping-toy stores, commerce never rests. This walking tour plunges you into the crowded claustrophobic alleys lined with vendors selling more variety than the modern shopping centres. At points you'll be shocked, disgusted and thoroughly amazed – just come prepared for crowds and smells.

This tour should last about an hour. When combined with visits to other Chinatown markets, including Nakhon Kasem, Saphan Han Market, Phahurat Market and the flower market of Pak Khlong, you can evaporate a whole day.

Start at **Tha Ratchawong**, along the banks of Mae Nam Chao Phraya reached via river taxi. Walk along **Th Ratchawong**, the main street leading away from the pier. Here are some of the more established vendors selling wholesale products you've seen in smaller quantities at other markets. Turn right at Sampeng Lane (Soi Wanit 1); you won't be able to see a street sign here because the corner is packed with stalls, but you'll know it by the queue of people slowly shuffling into the alley. You have now entered the shopping fun house, where the sky is completely obscured and bargains lie in ambush – that is if you really want 500 Hello Kitty pens.

After about 100m, Sampeng Lane crosses Th Mangkon. On either side of the intersection are two of Bangkok's oldest commercial buildings, a **Bangkok Bank** and the venerable **Tang To Kang** gold shop, which are both over 100 years old. The exteriors of the buildings are classic early Ratanakosin (or Bangkok), showing lots of European influence; the interiors are heavy with hardwood panelling. Good luck spotting these as you squeeze against your neighbour to allow a pushcart of mangoes to pass.

Continue walking another 60m or so to Trok Itsaranuphap, where you take a left onto a wider lane past rows of vendors selling huge bags of fried pork skins, dried fish and other delicacies. Down the lane on your right is **Talat Kao** (Old Market) – the entrance is ornamented in Chinese style. This market section off Trok Itsaranuphap has been operating continuously for over 200 years. All manner and size of freshwater and saltwater fish and shellfish alive and filleted are displayed here – or as sometimes is the case, half alive and half filleted.

If you remain on Trok Itsaranuphap, continue to **Th Yaowarat**, a main Chinatown thoroughfare. This section of Th Yaowarat is lined with large and small gold shops; for price and selection, this is probably the best place in Thailand to purchase a gold chain (sold by the *bàat*, a unit of weight equal to 15g). To cross the road, shadow a few savvy Thai shoppers possessing that innate Bangkok ability to dodge traffic.

Trok Itsaranuphap continues now in the guise of 'Soi 16', according to the street sign. This section is lined with vendors purveying cleaned chickens, freshly plucked ducks, scaled fish, unnaturally coloured vats of pickled food, prepackaged snacks – hungry yet? **Hong Kong Noodle** and **Hong Kong Tim Sum**, on the left, do a rollicking business from appetites aroused by the sight of such raw ingredients.

Cross the next major intersection, Th Charoen Krung, and continue for another 20m for **Wat Mangkon Kamalawat** (Neng Noi Yee) on your left, one of Chinatown's largest and liveliest temples; the name means Dragon Lotus Temple. Along this stretch of Th Charoen Krung, the shops sell fruit, cakes, incense and ritual burning paper for offering at the temple. Inscriptions at the temple's entrance are in Chinese and Tibetan, while the labyrinthine interior features a succession of Buddhist, Taoist and Confucian altars. At almost any time of day or night this temple is packed with worshippers lighting incense, filling the ever-burning altar lamps with oil and praying to their ancestors.

Work your way back to Trok Itsaranuphap, which has now changed its name to Soi 21, and continue past religious stalls and Chinese altars to Th Yommarat Sukhum. Turn right onto Th Phlap Phlachai and follow the bend in the road into the blazing hot sun, past more religious shops until you are back on Th Charoen Krung, where this walking tour ends – fittingly beside a coffin shop.

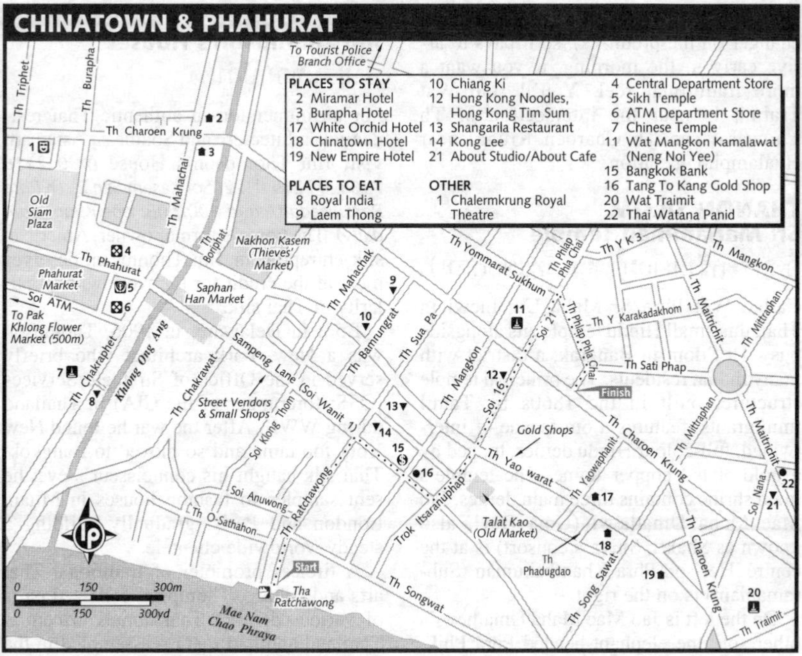

district, generally called Phahurat. Here dozens of Indian-owned shops sell all kinds of fabric and clothes. The selection is unbelievable, and Thai shoulder bags *(yâam)* sold here are the cheapest in Bangkok, perhaps in Thailand.

Behind the more obvious shopfronts along these streets, in the 'bowels' of the blocks, is a seemingly endless Indian bazaar selling not only fabric but household items, food and other necessities. **Th Chakraphet** is well known for its Indian restaurants and shops selling Indian sweets. One of the best eateries in the area is the Royal India, which serves north-Indian cuisine and is justly famous for its tasty selection of Indian breads (see Places to Eat later).

In an alley off Th Chakraphet, there's a **Sikh Temple** (Sri Gurusingh Sabha). Basically it's a large hall, somewhat reminiscent of a mosque interior, devoted to the worship of the Guru Granth Sahib, the 16th-century Sikh holy book, which is itself considered to be a 'living' guru and the last of the religion's 10 great teachers. Reportedly the temple is the second-largest Sikh temple outside of India. Visitors are welcome, but they must remove their shoes. If you arrive on a Sikh festival day you can partake of the *langar* (communal Sikh meal served in the temple).

Wat Traimit
วัดไตรมิตร

The attraction at Wat Traimit *(Temple of the Golden Buddha; ☎ 0 2623 1226; admission 20B; open 9am-5pm daily)* is, of course, the impressive 3m-tall, 5.5-tonne, solid-gold Buddha image, which gleams like no other gold artefact we've ever seen.

Sculpted in the graceful Sukhothai style, the image was 'discovered' some 40 years ago beneath a stucco or plaster exterior, which fell from a crane while being moved to a new building within the temple compound. It has been theorised that the covering was added to protect it from 'marauding hordes', either during the late Sukhothai period or later in the Ayuthaya period when the city was under siege by the Burmese. The temple itself is said to date from the early 13th century.

The golden image can be seen every day. Nowadays lots of camera-toting tour groups haunt the place (there's even a money-changer on the premises), so it pays to arrive early in the morning, if you want a more traditional feel. You'll find Wat Traimit is near the intersection of Th Yaowarat and Th Charoen Krung, near Hualamphong station.

THANON SILOM

Sri Mariamman Temple

วัดพระศรีมหาอุมาเทวี(วัดแขกสีลม)

Called Wat Phra Si Maha Umathewi in Thai, this small Hindu temple sits alongside busy Th Silom in Bangrak, a district with many Indian residents. The principal temple structure, built in the 1860s by Tamil immigrants, features a 6m facade of intertwined, full-colour Hindu deities, topped by a gold-plated copper dome. The temple's main shrine contains three main deities, Jao Mae Maha Umathewi (Uma Devi, also known as Shakti, Shiva's consort) is at the centre. Her son Phra Khanthakuman (Subramaniam) is on the right.

On the left is Jao Mae Maha Umathewi's other son, the elephant-headed Phra Phikkhanet (Ganesh). Along the left interior wall sit rows of Shivas, Vishnus and other Hindu deities, as well as a few Buddhas, so that just about any non-Muslim, non-Judaeo-Christian Asian can worship here – Thai and Chinese devotees come to pray along with Indians. Bright yellow marigold garlands are sold at the entrance for this purpose.

An interesting ritual takes place in the temple at noon on most days, when a priest brings out a tray carrying an oil lamp, coloured powders and holy water. He sprinkles the water on the hands of worshippers, who in turn pass their hands through the lamp flame for purification. They then dip their fingers in the coloured powder and daub prayer marks on their foreheads. On Friday at around 11.30am, *prasada* (blessed vegetarian food) is offered to devotees.

Thais call this temple Wat Khaek – *khàek* is a colloquial expression for people of Indian descent. The literal translation is 'guest', an obvious euphemism for a group of people you don't particularly want as permanent residents; hence most Indians living permanently in Thailand don't appreciate the term.

SIAM SQUARE & PRATUNAM

Jim Thompson's House

บ้านจิมทอมป์สัน

For an immersion in authentic Thai residential architecture and Southeast Asian art, visit Jim Thompson's House *(☎ 0 2216 7368, 0 2215 0122; Soi Kasem San 2, Th Phra Ram I; adult/child 100/50B; open 9am-5pm daily)*. The home's former owner, American silk entrepreneur Jim Thompson, deserves most of the credit for the worldwide popularity of Thai silk.

Born in Delaware, in 1906, Thompson was a New York architect who briefly served in the Office of Strategic Services (OSS; forerunner of the CIA) in Thailand during WWII. After the war he found New York too tame and so moved to Bangkok. Thai silk caught his connoisseur's eye; he sent samples to fashion houses in Milan, London and Paris, gradually building a steady worldwide clientele.

A tireless promoter of traditional Thai arts and culture, Thompson collected parts of various derelict Thai homes in central Thailand and had them reassembled in the current location in 1959. Although for the most part assembled in typical Thai style, one striking departure from tradition is the way each wall has its exterior side facing the house's interior, thus exposing the wall's bracing system.

While out for an afternoon walk in the Cameron Highlands of western Malaysia in 1967, Thompson disappeared and has never been heard from since. That same year his sister was murdered in the USA, fuelling various conspiracy theories to explain the disappearance. Was it communist spies? Business rivals? Or a man-eating tiger? The most recent theory – for which there is apparently some hard evidence – has it that the silk magnate was accidentally run over by a Malaysian truck driver who hid his remains.

The Legendary American – The Remarkable Career & Strange Disappearance of Jim Thompson (Houghton Mifflin, 1970), by William Warren, is an excellent book on Thompson, his career, residence and intriguing disappearance. In Thailand, it has been republished as *Jim Thompson: The Legendary American of Thailand* (Jim Thompson Thai Silk Co, Bangkok).

His small but splendid Asian art collection and his personal belongings are on display in the main house. The Jim Thompson Foundation has a table at the front where you can buy prints of old Siam maps and Siamese horoscopes in postcard and poster form.

The admission fee goes to Bangkok's School for the Blind. The *khlawng* (canal) at the end of the lane is one of Bangkok's most lively. Beware of well-dressed touts, who will tell you Thompson's house is closed – it's just a ruse to earn a hefty commission from you.

Take the Skytrain to the National Stadium station or the canal taxi to Tha Ratchathewi. From Banglamphu take bus Nos 15 and 47.

Wang Suan Phakkat

วังสวนผักกาด

This collection of five traditional wooden Thai houses was once the residence of Princess Chumbon of Nakhon Sawan and before that a lettuce farm, thus the name 'Lettuce Farm Palace' *(☎ 0 2245 4934; Th Si Ayuthaya; admission 100B; open 9am-4pm daily)*. Within the stilt buildings are displays of art, antiques and furnishings. The landscaped grounds are a peaceful oasis complete with ducks and swans, and a semi-enclosed garden.

The diminutive **Lacquer Pavilion**, at the back of the complex, dates from the Ayuthaya period and features gold-leaf *jataka* (stories of the Buddha's past lives) and *Ramayana* murals as well as scenes from daily Ayuthaya life; the building originally sat in a monastery compound on Mae Nam Chao Phraya, just south of Ayuthaya. Larger residential structures at the front of the complex contain displays of Khmer-style Hindu and Buddhist art, Ban Chiang ceramics and a very interesting collection of historic Buddhas, including a beautiful late U Thong–style image.

The palace is between Th Phayathai and Th Ratchaprarop and is within walking distance from Phayathai Skytrain station.

Other Attractions

Bangkok Doll Factory & Museum *(☎ 0 2245 3008; 85 Soi Ratchataphan/Soi Mo Leng; admission free; open 8am-5pm Mon-Sat)*, off Th Ratchaprarop in the Pratunam district, houses a colourful selection of traditional Thai dolls, both new and antique. Dolls are also available for purchase.

Next to the Grand Hyatt Erawan Hotel is **Erawan Shrine** *(San Phra Phrom; cnr Th Ratchadamri & Th Ploenchit)*, which was originally built to ward off bad luck during the construction of the first Erawan Hotel (torn down to make way for the Grand Hyatt Erawan some years ago). The four-headed deity at the centre of the shrine is Brahma (Phra Phrom in Thai), the Hindu god of creation. Apparently the developers of the original Erawan (named after Airvata, Indra's three-headed elephant mount) first erected a typical Thai spirit house but decided to replace it with the more impressive Brahman shrine after several serious mishaps delayed the hotel construction. Worshippers who have a wish granted may return to the shrine to commission the musicians and dancers, who are always on hand for an impromptu performance.

Since the success of the Erawan Shrine, several other flashy Brahman shrines have been erected around the city next to large hotels and office buildings. Next to the World Trade Centre on Th Ploenchit is a **large shrine** containing a standing Brahma, a rather unusual posture for Thai Brahmas. Next to Amarin Plaza, near the Chit Lom Skytrain station, is a sizeable **Indra Shrine**.

THANON SUKHUMVIT
Siam Society & Ban Kamthieng

สยามสมาคม/บ้านคำเที่ยง

The Siam Society *(131 Soi Asoke, Th Sukhumvit)* is the publisher of the renowned *Journal of the Siam Society* and its members are valiant preservers of traditional Thai culture. A reference library is open to visitors and Siam Society monographs are for sale. Almost anything you'd want to know about Thailand (outside the political sphere, since the society is sponsored by the royal family) can be researched here. An ethnological museum of sorts exhibiting Thai folk art is located on the Siam Society grounds in the northern-style Ban Kamthieng *(Kamthieng House; ☎ 0 2661 6470; open 9am-5pm Tues-Sat)*. It seems to be under permanent renovation, and as a result the usual 100B entry charge has been waived.

GREATER BANGKOK

Rama IX Royal Park

สวนหลวงร.9

Opened in 1987 to commemorate King Bhumibol's 60th birthday, Bangkok's newest green area *(sŭan lŭang raw kâo)* covers 81 hectares and includes a water park and botanic gardens *(admission 10B; open 5am-6pm daily)*. Since its opening, the latter has developed into a significant horticultural research centre. A **museum** (☎ *0 2328 1385)*, with an exhibition on the life of the king, occupies the centre of the park. Take bus No 2, 23 or 25 to Soi Udomsuk (Soi 103), off Th Sukhumvit in Phrakhanong district, then a green minibus to the park. Alternatively, you can take air-con bus No 145 from the Weekend Market, getting off at the first intersection after the two large shopping malls, Seacon Square and Seri Centre. Turn left and catch either an orange minibus or *sǎwngthǎew* (also written songthaew) for the remaining 10-minute ride.

Wat Phailom

วัดไผ่ล้อม

Outside Bangkok, on the eastern bank of Mae Nam Chao Phraya in Pathum Thani Province, this old, wooden Mon wát is noted for the tens of thousands of open-billed storks *(Anastomus oscitans)* that nest in bamboo groves opposite it, from December to June. Temple architecture buffs will note the Ayuthaya-style *bòt*, backed by a Mon *chedi*.

The temple is 51km from the centre of Bangkok in Pathum Thani's Sam Kok district. Take a Pathum Thani-bound bus (12B) from Bangkok's Northern bus terminal and cross the river by ferry to the wát grounds.

Bus No 33 from Sanam Luang goes all the way to Phailom and back. The Chao Phraya River Express tours from Tha Maharat to Bang Pa-In each Sunday also make a stop at Wat Phailom – see River & Canal Trips later in this chapter.

OTHER TEMPLES

Wat Bowonniwet (also spelt 'Bovornnives' and shortened to Wat Bowon), on Th Phra Sumen in Banglamphu (see the Banglamphu map), is the national headquarters for the Thammayut monastic sect. King Mongkut, founder of this minority sect, began a royal tradition by residing here as a monk – in fact he was the abbot of Wat Bowon for several years. King Bhumibol and Crown Prince Vajiralongkorn, as well as several other males in the royal family, have been temporarily ordained as monks here. The temple was founded in 1826, when it was known as Wat Mai.

Bangkok's second Buddhist university, Mahamakut University, is housed at Wat Bowon. India, Nepal and Sri Lanka all send selected monks to study here. Across the street from the main entrance to the wát are an English-language Buddhist bookshop and a Thai herbal clinic. Because of its royal status, visitors should be particularly careful to dress properly for admittance to this wát – no shorts or sleeveless shirts.

Marked by its enormous, modern 32m standing Buddha, **Wat Intharawihan** borders Th Wisut Kasat, at the northern edge of Banglamphu (see the Banglamphu map later). Check out the hollowed-out air-con stupa with a lifelike image of Luang Phaw Toh, a famous monk. Entry to Wat In is by donation.

Wat Suthat (see the Central Bangkok map), begun by Rama I and completed by Rama II and Rama III, boasts a *wíhǎan* with gilded bronze Buddha images (including Phra Si Sakyamuni, one of the largest surviving Sukhothai bronzes) and colourful *jataka* murals. Wat Suthat holds a special place in the Thai religion because of its association with Brahman priests who perform important annual ceremonies, such as the Royal Ploughing Ceremony in May. These priests perform rites at two Hindu shrines near the wát – the Thewa Sathaan (Deva Sthan) across the street to the northwest and the smaller Saan Jao Phitsanu (Vishnu Shrine) to the east. The former contains images of Shiva and Ganesh, while the latter is dedicated to Vishnu. The wát holds the rank of Rachavoramahavihan, the highest royal-temple grade; the ashes of Rama VIII (Ananda Mahidol, the current king's deceased older brother) are contained in the base of the main Buddha image in Suthat's *wíhǎan*.

Wat Chong Nonsi, off Th Ratchadaphisek near the Bangkok side of the river (see the Greater Bangkok map), contains notable *jataka* murals painted between 1657 and 1707. It is the only surviving Ayuthaya-era temple in which both the murals and architecture are of the same period with no renovations. As a single, 'pure' architectural and painting unit, it's considered quite important for the study of late Ayuthaya art; the painting style is similar to that found in the Phetchaburi Province monasteries of Wat Yai Suwannaram and Wat Ko Kaew Sutharam.

There are also numerous temples on the Thonburi side of the river (see the Ko Ratanakosin map) that are less visited. These include **Wat Kalayanamit**, with its towering Buddha statue, and, outside, the biggest bronze bell in Thailand; **Wat Pho Bang-O**, with its carved gables and Rama III-era murals; **Wat Chaloem Phrakiat**, a temple with tiled gables; and **Wat Thawng Nophakhun**, with its Chinese-influenced *uposatha* (or *bòt*). **Wat Yannawa**, on the Bangkok bank of the river near Tha Sathon, was built during Rama II's reign and features a building resembling a Chinese junk.

HISTORIC CHURCHES

Several Catholic churches were founded in Bangkok from the 17th to 19th centuries. Worth seeing is the **Holy Rosary Church** (Talat Noi), near the River City shopping complex (see the Thanon Silom map). It is also known in Thai as Wat Kalawan, from the Portuguese 'Calvario'. Originally built in 1787 by the Portuguese, the Holy Rosary was rebuilt by Vietnamese and Cambodian Catholics in the late 19th century, hence the French inscriptions beneath the stations of the cross. This old church has a splendid set of Romanesque stained-glass windows, gilded ceilings and a Christ statue that is carried through the streets during Easter celebrations. The alley leading to the church is lined with old Bangkok shophouse architecture.

Church of the Immaculate Conception near Saphan Krungthon north of Thewet (see the Central Bangkok map) was also founded by the Portuguese and later taken over by Cambodians fleeing civil war. The present building is an 1837 reconstruction on the church's 1674 site. One of the original church buildings survives and is now used as a museum housing holy relics. Another Portuguese-built church is 1913 vintage **Santa Cruz** (Wat Kuti Jin) on the Thonburi side of Mae Nam Chao Phraya (see the Ko Ratanakosin map), near Saphan Phra Phuttha Yot Fa (Memorial Bridge), usually called Saphan Phut by Thais. The architecture shows Chinese influence, hence the Thai name, which means 'Chinese monastic residence'.

Christ Church *(Thanon Silom map; 11 Th Convent)*, next to the Bangkok Nursing Home, was established as English Chapel in 1864. The current Gothic-style structure, opened in 1904, features thick walls and a tiled roof braced with teak beams; the carved teak ceiling fans date to 1919.

OTHER MUSEUMS

Museum of the Department of Forensic Medicine *(Ko Ratanakosin map; Th Phrannok; admission free; open 9am-4pm Mon-Fri)* is the ground floor of the Forensic Medicine Building in the Siriraj Hospital, near the Thonburi (Bangkok Noi) train station. It is the most famous of 10 medical museums on the hospital premises. Among the grisly displays are the preserved bodies of famous Thai murderers.

Military aircraft aficionados shouldn't miss the **Royal Thai Air Force Museum** *(Greater Bangkok map; Th Phahonyothin; free admission for groups; open 8.30am-4.30pm daily)*, near Wing 6 of the airport at Don Muang. Among the world-class collection of historic aircraft is the only existing Japanese Tachikawa Trainer, along with a Spitfire and several Nieuports and Breguets.

Bangkok also has a **Museum of Science & Planetarium** *(Greater Bangkok map; ☎ 0 2392 1773)*, which are both on Th Sukhumvit between Soi 40 and Soi 42.

ART GALLERIES

The **National Gallery** *(Ko Ratanakosin map; ☎ 0 2282 8525, 0 2281 2224; Th Chao Fa; admission 30B; open 9am-4pm Wed-Sun)*, housed in an early Ratanakosin-era building opposite the National Theatre, displays traditional and contemporary art, mostly by artists who receive government support. The general consensus is that it's not Thailand's best, but the gallery is worth a visit for die-hard art fans or if you're in the vicinity and want to escape the crowds.

Silpakorn University *(Ko Ratanakosin map; open 8am-7pm Mon-Fri, 8am-4pm Sat,*

Sun & holidays), opposite the Grand Palace, is Bangkok's fine arts university and its gallery exhibits the work of students.

Bangkok's latest trend in public art consumption is the 'gallery pub', an effort to place art in a social context rather than leaving it to sterile galleries and museums. **About Studio/About Cafe** *(Chinatown & Phahurat map; ☎ 0 2623 1742; 418 Th Maitrichit)* is the best of the several venues that attempt to combine gallery space with social space. Hours are erratic; despite what may be posted on the front door, figure on finding the place open roughly from 7pm to midnight. You can reach it on bus Nos 25, 53 and 73. Taxis have a terrible time finding the place, but the nearby publishing company, Thai Watana Panid, might be a helpful landmark.

Bangkok's foreign cultural centres hold regular exhibits of foreign and local artists; check the daily newspapers or the monthly bulletins issued by the AUA, Alliance Française, the British Council and the Goethe Institut (see Cultural Centres in the Information section earlier).

Several of Bangkok's luxury hotels display top-quality contemporary art in their lobbies and other public areas. The **Grand Hyatt Erawan** *(Siam Square & Pratunam map; cnr Th Ratchadamri & Th Ploenchit)* and the **Landmark Hotel** *(Thanon Sukhumvit map; Th Sukhumvit)* have the best collections of contemporary art in the city. The Erawan alone has nearly 2000 works exhibited on a rotating basis.

The **Neilson Hays Library** *(Thanon Silom map; 193 Th Surawong)* occasionally hosts small exhibitions in its Rotunda Gallery.

TRADITIONAL MASSAGE

Massage as a healing art is a centuries-old tradition in Thailand. One of the best places to experience a traditional massage, also called 'ancient' massage, is at **Wat Pho Thai Traditional Medical & Massage School** *(Ko Ratanakosin map; ☎ 0 2221 3686; ⓔ wat pottm@netscape.net)*. Massages here cost 250B per hour or 150B for half an hour.

For those interested in studying massage, the temple also offers two 30-hour courses – one on general Thai massage, the other on massage therapy – that you attend for three hours per day for 10 days, or two hours per day for 15 days. Tuition is 7000B (3600B for Thais). A 15-hour foot massage course costs 3600B. For those so inclined there are also longer one- to three-year programmes that combine Thai herbal medicine with massage for a full curriculum in Thai traditional medicine. Some knowledge of Thai will ease the communication barrier in all of these courses. The school is outside the temple compound in a nicely restored old Bangkok shophouse on Th Sanam Chai, opposite the temple's western wall.

There is a strip of Thai herbal medicine shops, next to Wat Mahathat, offering good massage for a mere 150B an hour.

A more commercial area for Thai massage, as well as Thai herbal saunas, is Th Surawong near the infamous Th Patpong. Here you'll find **Marble House** *(Thanon Silom map; ☎ 0 2235 3519; 37/18-19 Soi Surawong Plaza, Th Surawong)*; **Vejakorn** *(☎ 0 2237 5576; 37/25 Soi Surawong Plaza, Th Surawong)*; and **Eve House** *(☎ 0 2266 3846; 18/1 Th Surawong)*, opposite Soi Thaniya. **Arima Onsen** *(☎ 0 2235 2142; 37/10-11 Soi Surawong Plaza)* specialises in Japanese-style massage and reflexology. All of these places charge about 330B for two hours.

Near Th Sukhumvit you can find traditional Thai massage at **Buathip Thai Massage** *(Thanon Sukhumvit map; ☎ 0 2255 1045; 4/13 Soi 5, Th Sukhumvit)* and at **Winwan** *(☎ 0 2251 7467)* between Soi 1 and Soi 3, off Th Sukhumvit.

Fees for traditional Thai massage should be no more than 300B per hour, although some places have a 1½ hour minimum. Not every place advertising traditional or ancient massage offers a really good one; sometimes the only thing 'ancient' about the pummelling is the age of the masseuse or masseur. Thai massage aficionados say that the best massages are given by blind masseurs (available at Marble House). Beware of any massage centre that has TVs in the massage rooms, as this often means the massage staff pay more attention to soap operas than to giving a good massage.

Most hotels also provide a legitimate massage service either through their health clubs or as part of room service.

RIVER TRIPS

In 1855 British envoy Sir John Bowring wrote, 'The highways of Bangkok are not streets or roads but the river and the canals. Boats are the universal means of conveyance and communication'. The wheeled motor vehicle has long since become Bangkok's conveyance of choice, but fortunately it hasn't yet become universal. A vast network of canals and river tributaries surrounding Bangkok still carry a motley fleet of watercraft, from paddled canoes to rice barges. In these areas many homes, trading houses and temples remain oriented towards life on the water and provide a fascinating glimpse into the past, when Thais still considered themselves *jâo náam* (water lords).

Mae Nam Chao Phraya

You can observe urban river life from the water for several hours for only 10B to 15B by boarding a **Chao Phraya River Express** *(☎ 0 2623 6001, fax 0 2225 3002)* boat at any pier and taking it in either direction to its final stop. The terminus for most northbound boats is Nonthaburi and for most southbound boats is Tha Sathon (also called Central Pier), near the Saphan Taksin Skytrain station. By catching a boat with a green flag (from a green-flag serviced pier), you can go as far north as Pak Kret or as far south as Wat Ratchasingkhon (around 25B). Standard boats run about every 15 minutes throughout the day, and express boats run during morning and evening rush hours. See the Getting Around section for more information and the Chao Phraya River Express & Thonburi Canals map for locations of the piers.

Tours along the river to sites such as the Royal Barges National Museum, Wat Phra Kaew and Grand Palace and Wat Arun can be arranged at most river piers, especially Tha Chang. It usually costs 500B for a boat for one hour, excluding admission. These sites, however, are easily accessible via public transport.

Khlong Bangkok Noi

Another good boat trip is through Bangkok Noi canal, just across the river in the area known as Thonburi. The further up the canal you go, the better the scenery, with teak houses on stilts, old wát and plenty of greenery.

Stop off at **Wat Suwannaram** to view 19th-century *jataka* murals painted by two of early Bangkok's foremost religious muralists. Art historians consider these the best surviving temple paintings in Bangkok.

Long-tail boats leave from Tha Chang (next to Silpakorn University) for Bang Yai (a district in Nonthaburi) for 60B return (8am to 3pm, Monday to Friday); there is also a regular canal taxi that delivers residents to their homes in Bangkok Noi, but sightseers are discouraged from using this boat.

Other Thonburi Canals

Trips along **Khlong Bangkok Yai** pass Wat Intharam, where a *chedi* contains the ashes of Thonburi's King Taksin, who was assassinated in 1782. Fine gold-and-black lacquerwork adorning the main *bòt* doors depicts the mythical *naariiphŏn* tree, which bears fruit that's shaped like beautiful maidens. Durian plantations line picturesque **Khlong Om**, which loops back to the river from Khlong Bangkok Noi. **Khlong Mon**, between Bangkok Noi and Bangkok Yai, offers more typical canal scenery, including orchid farms.

The usual price for hiring a long-tail boat to explore these canals is around 600B for one hour and 800B to 900B for two hours. Shop around at the different piers for a competitive price and clarify that the quote is for the duration of the trip, regardless of number of people. Make sure the price is agreed upon before climbing aboard – you can't bargain in the middle of the river.

Tha Chang usually has the largest selection of boats, but most piers offer boat hire. Don't forget to check in at less popular piers, like Tha Ratchawong, if other operators are too aggressive. Avoid touts who offer to 'arrange' a tour for you, in exchange for a commission from the boat driver.

Those interested in seeing Bangkok's deep-water port can hire long-tail boats to Khlong Toey or as far downriver as Pak Nam, which means 'river mouth' in Thai. It's about two hours each way by boat, or a bit quicker if you take a bus or taxi one way.

Ko Kret

เกาะเกร็ด

This island in the middle of Mae Nam Chao Phraya, at Bangkok's northern edge, is home to one of Thailand's oldest Mon settlements. The Mon, who between the 6th and

CHAO PHRAYA RIVER EXPRESS & THONBURI CANALS

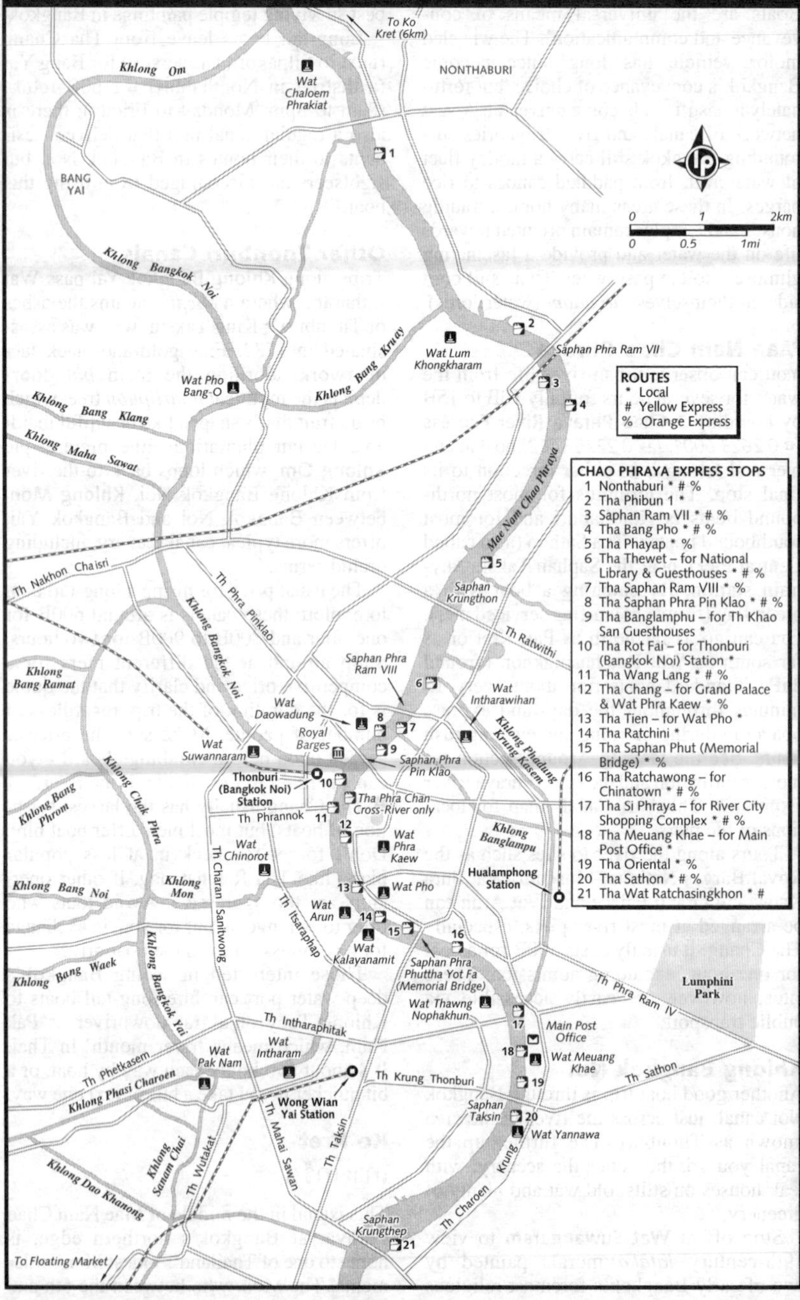

10th centuries AD were the dominant culture in central Thailand, are skilled potters. Ko Kret remains one of the oldest and largest sources of earthenware in the region. An exhibit of local pottery can be seen at the island's Ancient Mon Pottery Centre; there are also plenty of opportunities to watch the locals making it. A Mon Buddhist temple called **Wat Paramai Yikawat**, also known simply as 'Wat Mon', contains a Mon-style marble Buddha.

If you have time to kill in Pak Kret town, you can get a good, low-cost massage at the **School for the Blind**, which has a training programme in massage therapy. You may also want to check the progress of the new **health resort**, being built on the island, which will feature yoga, meditation and other well-being classes.

Once upon a time Ko Kret could be reached by ordinary river taxi, but this is no longer the case. Current transport options are far from affordable and take the fun out of 'doing it yourself'. Most visitors hire a boat from any pier along the river (prices range from 600B to 800B depending on the duration) or join the Sunday tours through Chao Phraya River Express. The tour departs from Tha Maharat (see the Ko Ratanakosin map) at 9am and takes in the Ancient Mon Pottery House, Ban Khanom Thai (to watch Thai sweets being made) and Wat Chaloem Phrakiat. The tour returns to Tha Maharat at 3pm and costs 250/150B per adult/child.

Dinner Cruises

A dozen or more companies in Bangkok run regular dinner cruises along Mae Nam Chao Phraya. The less expensive, more casual boats allow you to order as little or as much as you want from moderately priced menus; a modest charge of 120B per person is added to the bill for the cruise. It's a fine way to dine outdoors when the weather is hot – away from city traffic and cooled by a river breeze. Several of the dinner boats cruise under the well-lit Saphan Phra Ram IX, the longest single-span cable-suspension bridge in the world. This engineering marvel supports the elevated expressway joining Bangkok's Th Tok district (see the Greater Bangkok map) with Thonburi's Ratburana district. For more information contact **Khanap Nam Restaurant** *(☎ 0 2424 8453)* or **Riverside Bangkok** *(☎ 0 2434 0090)*.

Loy Nava *(☎ 0 2437 4932, 0 2437 7329)* offers a more swanky dinner cruise for a set price of 1150B, but beer and liquor cost extra. It operates from 6pm to 8pm and 8pm to 10pm nightly, or by appointment.

The **Marriott Royal Garden Riverside Hotel** *(Greater Bangkok map; ☎ 0 2476 0021)* offers a three-hour dinner cruise aboard the *Manohra* for 1400B plus tax and service (excluding drinks). Before its regular three-hour 7.30pm dinner cruise, the *Manohra* sails at 5pm from the Marriott Royal Garden Riverside Hotel for an hour-long sunset cocktail cruise. Boarding costs 500B plus tax and service (about 589B), which includes one drink and a light snack. A free river taxi operates between Tha River City and the hotel's pier at 4pm, just in time for the 5pm cruise departure.

Bang Pa-In & Ayuthaya Cruises

All-day or overnight trips take a northern course from Bangkok to the former royal capital of Ayuthaya and/or to the nearby summer palace of Bang Pa-In. To ruin-weary travellers, the river journey might broaden the historical centre's appeal.

The **Chao Phraya River Express Boat** *(☎ 0 2623 6001, fax 0 2225 3002)* does a reasonably priced tour (350/250B adult/child) to Bang Pa-In and other attractions on Sunday only. The tour price does not include lunch or admission fees, and the boat leaves Tha Maharat (see the Ko Ratanakosin map) at 8am and returns at 6pm.

Mit Chao Phraya Express Boat Co *(☎ 0 2225 6179)* offers a similarly priced trip from Tha Chang to Bang Pa-In from 8am to 5pm on Sunday.

The **Oriental Hotel** *(☎ 0 2266 9316)* runs cruises, in the luxurious all air-con *Oriental Queen*, to Bang Pa-In and then buses to Ayuthaya; it leaves at 8am daily from Tha Oriental and returns at 5pm. The *Oriental Queen* cruise costs 1600B, including lunch and a guided tour. **Horizon Cruise** *(☎ 0 2236 777 ext 1204)*, from the Shangri-La Hotel, runs a similar programme.

For a real indulgence, climb aboard a restored 50-year-old teak rice barge decorated with antiques and Persian carpets – the nautical equivalent of the *Eastern & Oriental Express* train. The *Mekhala* and the *Manohra 2* can sleep four to 10 passengers and typically leave in the afternoon, whether starting out from Bangkok or returning from Ayuthaya. In the evening they anchor at a wát, where a candle-lit dinner is served. The next morning passengers offer food to the monks from the wát, and then the barge moves on to Bang Pa-In. After a tour of the Summer Palace, a long-tail boat takes passengers on a tour of the ruins of Ayuthaya. At present, four Ayuthaya cruises per week are scheduled. The cost for the two-day cruise varies from US$500 to US$600 per person depending on which barge is used. For details contact the **Marriott Royal Garden** *(☎ 0 2476 0021)* for the *Manohra 2*, or the **Menam Riverside Hotel** *(☎ 0 2256 7168)* for the *Mekhala*.

THEME & AMUSEMENT PARKS

Just outside Bangkok are a host of artificial tourist attractions that provide either the see-the-whole-country-in-an-hour theme or the standard Western-style amusement park. It's often worth booking tickets through travel agencies, if their packages include round-trip transport.

Thirty-two kilometres west of Bangkok, on the way to Nakhon Pathom, the **Rose Garden Country Resort** *(☎ 0 2253 0295, 0 2295 3261; admission 10B; resort & rose garden open 8am-6pm daily, cultural village 10.30am-5pm daily)* encompasses a faux Thai 'cultural village' (with demos of handicrafts, dancing, traditional ceremonies and martial arts), swimming pools, tennis courts, a 3-hectare lake, elephant rides and a golf course. The 24-hectare garden area boasts 20,000 rose bushes. Tickets for the 2.45pm performances in the cultural village cost 220B. Shuttle buses run between the resort and major Bangkok hotels. There is also a hotel on the premises, should you like the place so much you want to spend the night.

Just 1km north is the 9-hectare **Samphran Elephant Ground & Zoo** *(☎ 0 2284 1873; adult/child 250/150B; open 8am-5.30pm daily)*, where you can see elephant 'roundups' and crocodile shows; a number of other animals can also be observed in zoo-like conditions. There are crocodile wrestling, elephant and magic shows in the afternoon.

Safari World *(Greater Bangkok map; ☎ 0 2518 1000; 99 Th Ramindra 1; adult/child 700/450B combo for Safari & Marine Park; open 9am-5pm daily)* is a 69-hectare wildlife park said to be the largest 'open zoo' in the world. It's divided into two portions, the drive-through Safari Park and the walk-through Marine Park. The 5km Safari Park drive (in air-con coaches or your own vehicle) intersects eight habitats with an assortment of giraffes, lions, zebras, rhinos, monkeys, elephants, orang-utans, and other African and Asian animals. A Panda House displays rare white pandas, and the Marine Park focuses on trained dolphin performances. It's 45km east of central Bangkok; for public transport catch a No 26 bus from the Victory Monument to Minburi, then a săwngthăew to the park. A taxi costs about 300B and can be arranged at most hotels.

Two attractions, **Ancient City** and the **Crocodile Farm**, in nearby Samut Prakan Province are often included on lists of popular Bangkok sights. See Samut Prakan in the Around Bangkok section later for more details.

SPORTS FACILITIES

The first and grandest of the city's sports facilities is the **Royal Bangkok Sports Club** (RBSC; see the Central Bangkok map), between Th Henri Dunant and Th Ratchadamri (the green oval marked 'Turf' on the Bangkok bus maps). Facilities include a horse-racing track, polo grounds (located off Th Withayu), a swimming pool, sauna, squash and tennis courts (both hard and grass), and an 18-hole golf course. There's a waiting list for membership, so the only way you're likely to frolic at this prestigious club is to be invited there by a lucky RBSC member.

Membership at the **British Club** *(Thanon Silom map; ☎ 0 2234 0247; 189 Th Surawong)* is open to citizens of Australia, Canada, New Zealand and the UK, or to others by invitation; membership fees are very costly. Among the sports facilities are a pool, golf driving range, and squash and tennis courts.

The least expensive swimming facility in Bangkok is the one operated by the Department of Physical Education at the **National Stadium** *(Siam Square & Pratunam map; ☎ 0 2215 1535; Th Phra Ram I)*, next to Mahboonkrong shopping centre. Membership costs just 300B per year plus 25B per hour.

The top-class **Clark Hatch Physical Fitness Centres** with weight machines, pool, tennis, squash, aerobics, sauna and massage, can be found at Century Park, Amari Atrium and Amari Watergate Hotels, and in Thaniya Plaza and Charn Issara Tower II; nonhotel guests are welcome.

Sports clubs that are open to the public include the following.

Central Tennis Court (☎ 0 2213 1909) 13/1 Soi Atakanprasit, Th Sathon Tai; tennis

Diana Women's Club (☎ 0 2279 1943) 33 Soi 2, Th Phahonyothin

Fitness First (Thanon Sukhumvit map; ☎ 0 2237 0777) 138 Th Sukhumvit, The Landmark Bangkok, 4th floor, between Soi 4 & 6; yoga, Pilates and boxing classes

Kanpaibun Tennis Court (☎ 0 2391 8784, 0 2392 1832) 10 Soi 40, Th Sukhumvit; tennis

Kaithip Swimming Pool (☎ 0 2331 3842) 140 Soi 56, Th Sukhumvit; tennis, badminton, swimming

Soi Klang Racquet Club (☎ 0 2391 0963) 8 Soi 49, Th Sukhumvit; squash, tennis, racquetball, swimming, aerobics

The Bangkok Gym (Thanon Sukhumvit map; ☎ 0 2255 2440) 9th floor, Delta Grand Pacific Hotel, 259 Soi 19, Th Sukhumvit; weights, sauna, swimming, aerobics

MEDITATION COURSES

Although at times Bangkok may seem like the most un-Buddhist place on earth, there are several places where foreigners can learn about Theravada Buddhist meditation. For more information about meditation centres or teachers with English skills in Bangkok and beyond, contact the **International Buddhist Meditation Centre** *(☎ 0 2511 0439)* or the **World Fellowship of Buddhists** *(Thanon Sukhumvit map; WFB; ☎ 0 2661 1284, fax 0 2661 0555; Soi 24, Th Sukhumvit)*, at the back of Benjasiri Park, next to The Emporium. It is a clearing house for information on Theravada Buddhism as well as dialogue between various schools of Buddhism. The centre hosts meditation classes (usually led by English-speaking monks from Wat Pa Nanachat, Ubon Ratchathani) from 2pm to 6pm on the first Sunday of every month. Donations are accepted; it also sells a booklet (50B) for meditation centres throughout Thailand.

Wat Mahathat *(Ko Ratanakosin map; ☎ 0 2222 6011)*, an 18th-century wát, provides daily meditation instruction at Section 5, a meditation hall near the monks' residences. Some of the Thai monks here speak English, and there are often Western monks or long-term residents available to interpret. There is also a Saturday session for foreigners at Wat Mahathat's **Dhamma Vicaya Hall** *(☎ 0 2222 2835)*. Instruction is based on the Mahasi Sayadaw system of developing the *satipatthana* (foundations of mindfulness). Air-con bus Nos 508 and 512 both pass near the wát; the nearest Chao Phraya River Express pier is Tha Maharat.

Wat Pak Nam *(☎ 0 2467 0811)*, where hundreds of monks and nuns reside during the Buddhist Rains Retreat *(phansăa)*, has hosted many foreigners (especially Japanese) over the years. The meditation teacher, speaks some English and there are usually people around who can interpret. The emphasis is on developing concentration through *nimitta* (acquired mental images) in order to attain *jhana* (state of 'absorption'). A small English library is available. Wat Pak Nam is on Th Thoet Thai, Phasi Charoen, Thonburi. To get there take bus No 504, 509 or 103. The wát can also be reached by chartered long-tail boat from Tha Chang or Tha Saphan Phut along the river and Thonburi canals.

OTHER COURSES

For more information about cooking, language, martial arts and meditation courses in Bangkok, see Activities in the Facts for the Visitor chapter.

PLACES TO STAY – BUDGET

Bangkok has perhaps the best variety and quality of budget places to stay of any Asian capital, which is one of the reasons why it's such a popular destination for roving world travellers. Because of the wide distribution of places, you might first narrow your choices by deciding which part of the city you want to be in – the upscale business sections of Th Sukhumvit and Th Silom, the backpackers ghetto of Th Khao San and the surrounding area of Banglamphu, the centrally located Siam Square area, boisterous Chinatown or the old travellers centre around Soi Ngam Duphli off Th Phra Ram IV.

Banglamphu and Chinatown (around Hualamphong station) are the cheapest districts for eating and sleeping. These neighbourhoods are also less urbanised than other areas, meaning that the mangy dogs far outnumber the skyscrapers.

The Siam Square area is centrally located and on both Skytrain lines; air-con walkways from the Skytrain stations to the district's popular shopping malls are suggestive of a future where going outside is an antiquated necessity. Th Sukhumvit and Th Silom-Surawong are major business areas with nonexistent budget-hotel options and the constant hustle and bustle of commerce. The Sukhumvit area tends to attract sex tourists visiting the nearby go-go bars.

In Bangkok, budget accommodation can cost anywhere between 80B and 600B per night.

Banglamphu

If you're on a tight budget, head for the grande dame of shoestring travel, Th Khao San in the neighbourhood of Banglamphu. Ordinary bus Nos 3, 15, 30, 39, 44, 47, 53, 59 and 79 and air-con bus Nos 511 and 512 will get you there. The Airport Bus (route A-2) also stops nearby. The Skytrain does not extend to Banglamphu, but the new subway under construction will. The best way to reach Banglamphu via the Skytrain is to take a Silom line train all the way to its southwestern terminus at Saphan Taksin, then take a Chao Phraya River Express boat north along the river and get off at Tha Banglamphu.

Rates in Banglamphu are the lowest in Bangkok and, although some places are barely adequate (bedbugs can be a problem), a few are excellent value, if you can afford just a bit more. At the budget end,

BANGLAMPHU

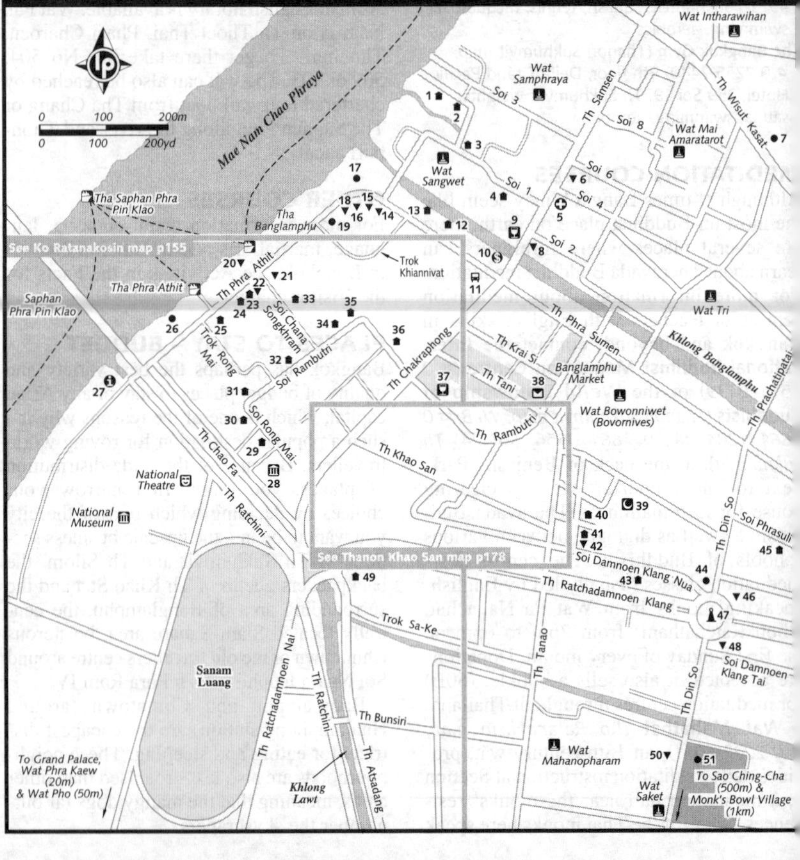

rooms are quite small and the dividing walls are thin. If there are windows, they usually open onto interior hallways. Bathrooms are usually down the hall or out the back; mattresses may be on the floor. Stepping up the price scale, rooms are a smidge bigger with sturdier dividing walls and air-con; pay even more for a private bathroom and hot shower. Some of these guesthouses have small cafés with limited menus.

The least expensive rooms are 100/150B for singles/doubles, though these are hard to come by due to the hordes seeking them out. More common are the 150/180B rooms. Occasionally, triple rooms are available for as low as 180B and dorm beds for 90B.

Most of the year, it pays to visit several guesthouses before making a decision, but in the high season (December to February), take the first vacant bed you come across. The best time of day to find a vacancy is from 9am to 10am.

In the early 1980s, when we first stumbled onto Th Khao San, there were only two Chinese-Thai hotels, the Nith Jaroen Suk (now called Nith Charoen Hotel) and the Sri Phranakhon (now the Khao San Palace Hotel). Today there are close to 100 guesthouses in the immediate vicinity (hundreds more off Th Khao San), far too many to list here. The guesthouses along Th Khao San tend to be cubicles in modern shophouses, while those in Banglamphu's quieter lanes and alleys are often housed in old homes, some of them with a lot of character. There is also a whole new generation of multistorey hotels, many of them good value.

At the cheaper places it's not worth calling ahead, since the staff will only hold a room for you if you pay in advance. For places that *may* take phone reservations we've included phone numbers. The following places to stay can be found on the Thanon Khao San map.

Thanon Khao San Many of the places on or just off Th Khao San are very similar to one another – small rooms with shared toilet and shower down the hall. **Prakorp's House & Restaurant** *(singles/doubles 90/180B)* provides a nice break from Khao San's concrete warrens with simple rooms in a teak house. It is also lauded as having the best guesthouse coffee on Th Khao San. **Grand Guest House**, **Lek Guest House** and **Lucky Beer & Guest House** are in the 150B to 250B range. Some rooms are permanently scarred with the lame graffiti of copycat travellers. **Chada Guest House** *(singles/doubles 180/200B)* has small clean crypts. **Classic Inn** *(singles/doubles with fan 250/300B, with air-con & bath 390/450B)* has decent rooms with upgradeable amenities, such as hot water and TV, if you are starved for creature comforts. **CH I Guest House** *(singles/doubles 200/250B)* has reliable basic rooms, but don't expect any handholding from the hardboiled owners.

BANGLAMPHU

PLACES TO STAY

1 Home & Garden Guest House
2 River House
3 Bamboo Guest House
4 Villa Guest House
12 Gipsy Guest House
13 PS Guest House
23 Pra Arthit Mansion
24 New Merry V
25 Peachy Guest House
29 Chai's House
30 Baan Sabai
31 Sawasdee Krungthep Inn
32 Bella Bella House
33 New Siam Guest House
34 Merry V Guest House
35 My House
36 Sawasdee House; Bangkok Bar
40 Central Guest House
41 Srinthip Guest House
43 Sweety Guest House
45 Prasuri Guest House
49 Royal Hotel

PLACES TO EAT

6 Phon Sawan
8 Jeh Hoy
14 Kuay Tiaw Mae
15 Joy Luck Club
16 Roti-Mataba
18 Khrua Nopparat
20 Ton Pho
21 Saffron Bakery
22 Raan Kin Deum
42 Vegetarian Restaurants
46 Vijit (VR)
48 Methavalai Sorn Daeng
50 Arawy

OTHER

5 Nana Clinic; Lumpoo Polyclinic
7 Viang Travel
9 Ad Here the 13th
10 Siam Commercial Bank
11 Bus Stop for No 53
17 Phra Sumen Fort
19 108
26 Unicef
27 Bangkok Tourist Bureau
28 National Gallery; National Film Archives
37 Salvador Dali
38 Post Office
39 Mosque
44 McDonald's
47 Democracy Monument
51 Municipal Hall

THANON KHAO SAN

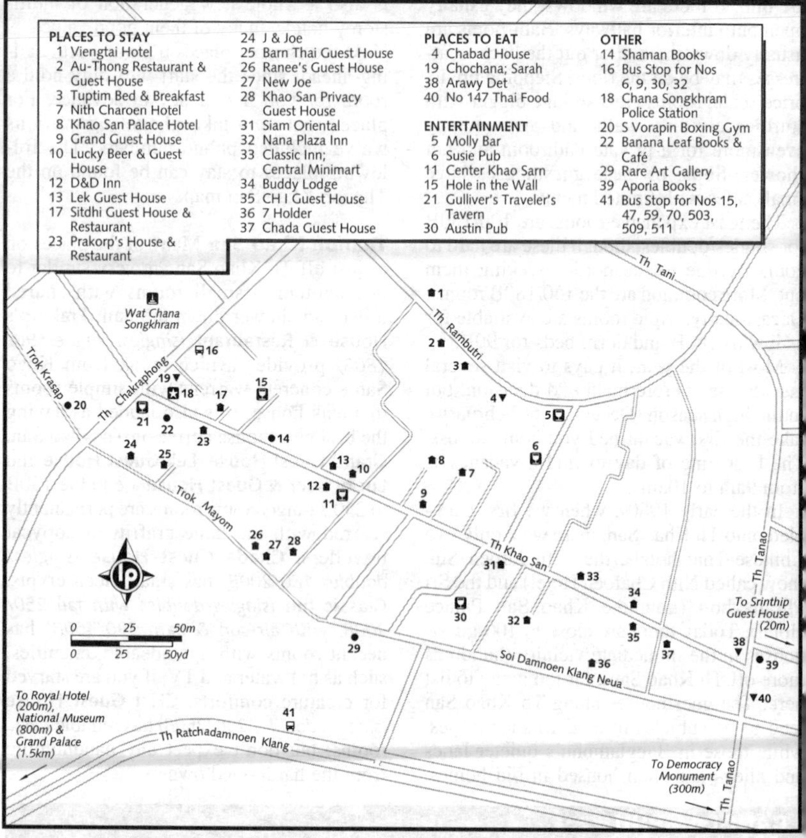

Khao San Palace Hotel *(Khao San Palace Inn; ☎ 0 2282 0578; 139 Th Khao San; rooms with fan 280-350B, with air-con 400-480B, deluxe 730B)*, down an alley, is a friendly, slightly more upmarket place. It is well kept; rooms have private bath, and air-con rooms have TV and hot water.

Nith Charoen Hotel *(☎ 0 2281 9872; rooms with fan 360B)*, has rooms with private bath. **Nana Plaza Inn** *(☎ 0 2281 6402; singles/doubles 500/700B)*, is a large, hotel-like enterprise, built around a popular **sushi restaurant**, and offers no-frills rooms with air-con, private bath and hot water. **D&D Inn** *(singles/doubles 450/600B)* has similar perks.

Siam Oriental *(☎ 0 2629 0312; 190 Th Khao San; singles with fan 280B, quads with air-con 680B)* has a variety of rooms, most with private bath, of varying sizes and amenities. There's also a lift – a big plus in this neighbourhood.

Parallel to Th Khao San but much quieter is Trok Mayom, an alley reserved for mostly pedestrian traffic. **J & Joe** *(☎ 0 2281 2949, 0 2281 1198; singles/doubles/triples 100/180/230B)* is a sprawling old teak complex with areas for hanging out; it's often full and a little noisy. **New Joe** *(☎ 0 2281 2948, fax 0 2281 5547; rooms with bath 250B, air-con 500B)* is a rather modern-looking place set off Trok Mayom, with an **outdoor café**. Some rooms can sleep up to four people; it also has email and fax services. **Barn Thai Guest House** *(☎ 0 2281 9041; singles 200/300B, doubles with bath 400B)* is a converted wooden house, which is in a tiny alley off

Trok Mayom. A good option for quiet solo travellers, it's kept clean and the front gate is locked at midnight. Bathroom sinks are in the outside courtyard.

Khao San Privacy Guest House *(Privacy Guest House; singles/doubles with fan 180/280B, doubles with air-con 400B)*, up Trok Mayom near Barn Thai, has decent-sized rooms with shared squat toilets. Nearby is **Ranee's Guest House** *(singles/doubles without bath 120/200B)*, which has an extensive **vegetarian menu**, and **7 Holder** *(rooms 150-250B)*, which caters to Japanese travellers and even has Japanese fonts on its Internet-café computers.

Walking west along Th Rambutri you'll come to two adjacent guesthouses in old restored wooden buildings with cheery paint jobs. **Au-Thong Restaurant & Guest House** *(☎ 0 2629 2172; ⓔ au_thong@hotmail.com; 78 Th Rambutri; singles with fan/air-con 200/300B, doubles with fan/air-con 300/400B)* has a few simple rooms with shared toilet and shower. The **garden restaurant** at the front (and small air-con dining room inside the old house) breaks the mould for guesthouse fare. **Tuptim Bed & Breakfast** *(☎ 0 2629 1535, fax 0 2629 1540; ⓔ info@tuptimb-b.com; 82 Th Rambutri; singles with fan 250B, singles/doubles with air-con 399/550B)* looks similar but the emphasis is on the rooms rather than the food. Air-con rooms have shared gender-segregated toilets and hot-water showers; there are also rooms for up to four people.

West Banglamphu A different-flavoured backpacker enclave has developed on the lanes west of Th Chakraphong and Th Phra Sumen towards Mae Nam Chao Phraya. Room prices are a little higher than on Th Khao San, and former wage-slave travellers prefer their Beer Chang unaccompanied by the latest Ibiza techno mix. This area is within walking distance to Tha Banglamphu where you can catch express boats to major historical sites. The following places to stay can be found on the Banglamphu map.

Sawasdee House *(☎ 0 2281 8138, fax 0 2629 0994; 147 Soi Rambutri; singles 180-250B, doubles 350-400B, with air-con 550B)*, west of Th Chakraphong, is a cheerfully decorated multistorey hotel with a busy downstairs **restaurant** and **bar**. Single rooms are very small but doubles have a little more wiggle room.

Merry V Guest House *(☎ 0 2282 9267; Soi Rambutri; rooms 140-350B)* is a popular and friendly place, just around the bend; the bathrooms won't encourage lingering though. **My House** *(☎ 0 2282 9263; singles/doubles 120/200B, with bath 160/300B, rooms with air-con 500B)*, on the same lane, has a nice Thai-style sitting area and reasonable rooms.

Bella Bella House *(☎ 0 2629 3090; singles/doubles 170/240B, with bath 300B, doubles with air-con 390B)*, just past the soi that leads to New Siam Guest House, is a five-storey building with a sheltered rooftop area and probably ranks as the best of the crew. **Sawasdee Krungthep Inn** *(☎/fax 0 2629 0072; rooms 290-500B)*, a few doors away, is part of the Sawasdee empire, which has four other properties in Banglamphu. **Baan Sabai** *(☎ 0 2629 1599, fax 0 2629 1595; singles/doubles 170/270B, doubles with air-con 450B)* resembles an old Bangkok-style building and is aptly named for its relaxed atmosphere.

Chai's House *(singles/doubles/triples 150/250/350B, doubles with air-con 350B)* is a family-run place with clean shared bathrooms. It's quiet and security-conscious, with a sitting area out the front. If you're heading south from Baan Sabai, swing a right on to the neighbouring soi to get there.

New Siam Guest House *(☎ 0 2282 4554, fax 0 2281 7461; rooms with fan 340B, with bath 450B, with air-con 550B)* is a four-storey place with quiet and clean rooms. It seems well organised and is almost always full.

Towards the river, Th Phra Athit is another accommodation strip. **Peachy Guest House** *(☎ 0 2281 6471; dorm beds 80B, singles/doubles 100/160B, doubles with air-con & private bath 350B)* has a range of options; rooms facing the street are serenaded by the buzz of traffic. **New Merry V** *(rooms with/without bath 250/120B, with air-con 380B)*, next door, has comfortable rooms with private hot-water showers.

East Banglamphu The following places can be found on the Banglamphu map. There are several guesthouses clustered in the alleys east of Th Tanao. In general, the rooms are bigger and quieter here than at the places around Th Khao San.

Central Guest House *(☎ 0 2282 0667; Trok Bowonrangsi; singles/doubles/triples 100/130/160B)* has rooms that are clean and simple. Look for the rather inconspicuous signs.

Srinthip *(singles & doubles from 150B)* is an old wooden house further south, off Trok Bowonrangsi. The entrance is grotty, but the rooms are OK. Safety might not be paramount here; on a recent visit, no-one was manning the front desk and we wandered around the entire place unnoticed.

Sweety Guest House *(☎ 0 2281 6756; singles 80-100B, doubles 120-200B, with air-con 350B)*, around the corner from Srinthip, on a small road parallel to Th Ratchadamnoen Klang, has small windowless singles, larger doubles and air-con rooms. It has a roof terrace for hanging laundry.

If you follow Trok Mayom straight through, away from Th Tanao, you'll reach Th Din So. Cross Th Din So, walk north from the roundabout into a neighbourhood of Chinese storefronts. Follow the sign for **Prasuri Guest House** *(☎/fax 0 2280 1428; singles/doubles/triples with fan 220/250/330B, with air-con 350/380/450B)* down Soi Phrasuli, off Th Din So. Instead of the usual crowd of sunburned Europeans, it's dining room is crowded with Thai students on lunch break. Despite the din of secondary-school gossiping, the rooms are quiet, clean and all have private bathroom.

North Banglamphu The following places to stay can be found on the Banglamphu map. Towards the river end of Th Phra Sumen, **PS Guest House** *(☎ 0 2282 3932; Th Phra Sumen; singles/doubles/triples 130/190/250B)* is on the south side of Khlong Banglamphu. Its rooms are light and airy, and have shared facilities. There's a **restaurant** downstairs, and upstairs is a small seating area that overlooks the canal.

Gipsy Guest House *(singles/doubles 200/250B)*, next door, is like stepping into an MC Escher painting; stairs wind through a hallway sized for Lilliputians to dimly lit rooms. An interior courtyard and seating area opens only slightly to the sun, to reveal the neighbouring canal. Note, only the rooms on the canal side have windows opening onto the outside.

There is a great neighbourhood where you can get a little more bang for less baht, off Th Samsen, north of Khlong Banglamphu. Down the residential lanes, these small family-owned guesthouses are in convenient proximity to the Tha Saphan Ram VIII. **Villa Guest House** *(☎ 0 2281 7009; Soi 1; rooms 250-500B)* is a leafy old teak house with 10 rooms (all with shared bath) and real furniture; it's perfect for reclusive solo travellers and is often full, so call ahead. **Bamboo Guest House** *(☎ 0 2282 3412; singles/doubles/family 150/120/330B)* gets mixed reviews but families like the fenced-in front area to keep children from wandering out into the street.

On Soi 3 Samsen (also known as Soi Wat Samphraya), there are three neighbouring guesthouses offering small rooms with shared bath for 120B to 150B. **River House** *(☎ 0 2280 0876)* is the best of the bunch. **Clean & Calm Guest House** is popular with African visitors waiting for visas; the bathroom has an earthenware basin for bathing. Note that Soi 3 zigzags left, then right, before reaching these three guesthouses, a good walk from Th Samsen.

Thewet & National Library Area

Thewet, the district north of Banglamphu near the National Library, is another travellers enclave, especially for families and the over-30 crowd. It is a lovely leafy area but during the rainy season it is prone to flooding.

Ordinary bus Nos 3, 16, 30, 31, 32, 33, 53, 64 and 90 and air-con bus No 506 stop at Th Si Ayuthaya, while travelling along Th Samsen. Air-con bus No 510 from the airport also passes close to the area along Th Ratwithi to the north, before crossing Saphan Krungthon. Chao Phraya River Express boats stop at Tha Thewet (the Roman-script sign reads 'Tha Thewes') on Th Krung Kasem, which intersects Th Samsen; turn left there and cross the canal to reach the guesthouse area.

The following places to stay can be found on the Central Bangkok map.

On two parallel lanes on the river side of the intersection of Th Samsen and Th Si Ayuthaya, you'll find several guesthouses run by various members of the same extended family: **Tavee Guest House** *(☎ 0 2280 1447)*; **Sawasdee Guest House** *(☎ 0 2282 5349)*; and **85 Backpacker's Lodge** *(☎ 0 2282 3231)*. All are well kept, fairly quiet and singles/doubles with fan cost from 200/350B and doubles with air-con for around 400B. The Sawasdee also offers dorm beds from 70B to 100B. **Shanti Lodge** *(☎ 0 2281 2497; rooms with fan & shared/private bath 300/400B, with air-con 450B)* has stylish rooms, but travellers complain that the staff are rude. **Taewez Guest House** *(☎ 0 2280 8856; singles 150B, rooms with fan/air-con 200/300B)* is presently the best of the bunch, with friendly staff, a roomy **café** with Internet facilities and no-frills concrete rooms.

East of Th Samsen, **Bangkok International Youth Hostel** *(☎ 0 2281 0361, fax 0 2628 7416; e bangkok@tyha.org; 25/2 Th Phitsanulok; dorm beds with fan/air-con 70/120B, singles/doubles with fan 200/250B, singles/doubles with air-con 280/350B)* has rooms with private hot-water bath. There's a **cafeteria** downstairs. The hostel no longer accepts nonmembers as guests. Annual Hostelling International membership costs 300B; nonmembers pay an extra 50B as a temporary membership fee. For each temporary membership fee paid, you receive a 'welcome stamp', six of which entitle you to a one-year membership.

Soi Ngam Duphli Area

This area, off Th Phra Ram IV, is where budget travellers used to come on their first trip to Bangkok back in the 1970s and early '80s. With a couple of notable exceptions, most of the places here are not especially cheap and the area oozes seediness; it is also clogged by cars and motorcycles with few or no sidewalks. The Banglamphu area has better-value accommodation but some travellers still prefer Soi Ngam Duphli, because it has less of a 'scene'. Several countries maintain embassies on nearby Th Sathon, so it's also a convenient location for those with visa/passport business at these embassies. The following places to stay can be found on the Central Bangkok map.

Soi Ngam Duphli runs off Th Phra Ram IV, near the Th Sathon Tai roundabout, and within walking distance of verdant Lumphini Park and the Th Silom business district. Ordinary bus Nos 13, 14, 74, 109, 115 and 116 and air-con bus No 507 all pass by Soi Ngam Duphli, along Th Phra Ram IV. The nearest Skytrain station is Sala Daeng, on Th Silom.

The **ETC Guest House** *(☎ 0 2286 9424, fax 0 2287 1478; singles/doubles with fan 140/180B, with air-con & bath 220/280B)* is at the northern end of Soi Ngam Duphli and is a multistorey building with a travel agency downstairs. The rooms are small and emulate that timeless skid-row aesthetic. Rates include a breakfast of cereal, fruit, toast and coffee or tea.

Tungmahamek Privacy Hotel *(☎ 0 2286 2339, 0 2286 8811; doubles with air-con & bath 370B)* has spacious rooms. Many short-term residents enjoy the 'privacy' aspect of the hotel and might not be the best neighbours, although everything seemed on the level during a recent visit.

Turn left (southeast) into Soi Si Bamphen, and then turn left at the second lane on the left. Take the first right and you'll end up in a cul-de-sac with guesthouses of varying quality. **Sala Thai Daily Mansion** *(☎ 0 2287 1436; rooms 200-350B)*, at the end of the alley, has large, clean rooms, all with shared bathroom. A sitting area with TV on the 3rd floor makes for a pleasant gathering place, and there is a breezy rooftop terrace. The owner speaks English and her design background is evident in the tasteful furnishings. Many repeat or long-term guests fill the rooms here.

Nearby are **Charlie House** (see Places to Stay – Mid Range) and **PS Guesthouse** *(☎ 0 2679 8823; fax 0 2679 8823; singles/doubles with fan 190/230B, with air-con 250/280B)*, which would be a great little budget nook if the bathrooms met a scrub brush.

Chinatown & Hualamphong Station

The hotels around Hualamphong train station are dirt cheap and can provide you with simple shelter before you escape Bangkok. Within the centre of Chinatown, comfortable rooms with loads of amenities cost 500B to 800B, an unheard of occurrence in other districts. This area is central but difficult to get in and out of (unless travelling by boat) because of a steady supply of traffic. Ordinary bus Nos 53, 25 and 73 and air-con bus Nos 501 and 507 travel the main thoroughfares of Th Yaowarat and Th Charoen Krung. The closest river pier is Tha Ratchawong at the foot of Th Ratchawong.

Watch your pockets and bags around the Hualamphong area, both on the street and on the bus. The cream of the 'razor artists' operate here as train passengers make good pickings.

New Empire Hotel *(Chinatown & Phahurat map; ☎ 0 2234 6990–6, fax 0 2234 6997; 572 Th Yaowarat; singles/doubles with air-con 580/650B)* is a short walk from Wat Traimit. Air-con rooms come with hot water, and there are some more expensive ones for up to 800B. Rooms with exterior windows are a bit noisy, but it's in a great location. The New Empire is a favourite among Chinese Thais from southern Thailand.

Other Chinatown hotels of this calibre can be found along Th Yaowarat, Th Chakraphet and Th Ratchawong. **Burapha Hotel** *(Chinatown & Phahurat map; ☎ 0 2221 3545–9, fax 0 2226 1723; cnr Th Mahachai & Th Charoen Krung; rooms 550-600B)*, on the edge of Chinatown, is a notch better than the Empire.

River View Guest House *(Thanon Silom map; ☎ 0 2234 5429, 0 2235 8501, fax 0 2237 5428; ⓔ riverview@mailcity.com; 768 Soi Phanurangsi, Th Songwat; rooms with fan 450B, with air-con 690B)* is just north of River City Shopping Complex, south of Chinatown – and straddles the budget and mid-range divide. The building is in a neighbourhood filled with small machine shops. To get there, turn right from the corner of Th Si Phraya (facing the River City shopping complex), take the fourth left, then the first right. Rooms are large and have fan and private bath, or air-con and hot water. As the name suggests, many rooms have a view of the river; the view from the 8th floor **restaurant** is superb. If you call from the River City complex, someone from the guesthouse will pick you up. It's not far from Tha Si Phraya.

River City Guest House *(Thanon Silom map; ☎ 0 2235 1429, fax 0 2237 3127; 11/4-5 Soi 24, Th Charoen Krung; twins with air-con 500B)* is closer to the River City shopping complex and easier to find. Its decent rooms have clean bathrooms with tub and hot water, TV, fridge and phone. There's a **Chinese restaurant** downstairs (the management speaks better Mandarin than Thai).

Sri Hualamphong Hotel *(Central Bangkok map; 445 Th Rong Muang; rooms 200B)*, along the eastern side of the railway line, is a very long-running and atmospheric spot with a grand ornamented staircase and terrace sitting area; rooms are simple padlocked partitions.

Station Hotel *(Central Bangkok map; rooms with fan/air-con 300/400B)*, behind the market and towards the front of the train station, has rooms with attached bath.

Krung Kasem Srikung Hotel *(Central Bangkok map; ☎ 0 2225 0132, fax 0 2225 4705; 1860 Th Krung Kasem; rooms 550B)*, southwest of the station, costs more but is quieter and more secure. Clean, sizeable rooms have air-con and hot water. There's a small **coffee shop** downstairs.

Siam Square & Pratunam

Several upper-budget places with air-con and hot-water shower can be found in this central area, connected to other parts of the city via the Skytrain and the Khlong Saen Saep canal taxi. There aren't a lot of cultural sights nearby, but the area is perfect for those who have been away from civilisation for a while and need bookshops, cinemas and shopping malls. The only drawback is that the nightlife closes down with the shopping malls. The following places to stay can be found on the Siam Square & Pratunam map.

Soi Kasem San 1 has all the traveller support systems and budget options amid an active Thai community; it is off Th Phra Ram I near Jim Thompson's House and the National Stadium. **Muangphol Mansion** *(Muangphon Mansion; ☎ 0 2215 0033, fax 0 2216 8053; cnr Soi Kasem San 1 & Th Phra Ram I; rooms 500/450B with/without TV & fridge)* is an eight-storey place that's in need of renovation but remains relatively popular.

Pranee Building *(☎ 0 2216 3181, fax 0 2215 0364; rooms with fan/air-con 300/450B)*, on Soi Kasem San 1 near the intersection with Phra Ram 1, is an apartment-style place, behind the Muangphol, that offers long-term rentals at a 10% discount. The bathrooms could benefit from a good bleaching.

White Lodge *(☎ 0 2216 8867, fax 0 2216 8228; 36/8 Soi Kasem San 1; rooms 400B)* is further down the lane. It offers clean if somewhat small rooms; those on the 1st floor open directly onto a noisy hallway. There's a pleasant **terrace café** out the front. **Wendy House** *(☎ 0 2216 2436, fax 0 2216 8053; singles/doubles 400/450B, rooms with fridges 550B)*, next door, is a three-storey place sporting a fresh coat of paint with small but clean rooms that have air-con, hot-water shower and TV.

A-One Inn *(☎ 0 2215 3029, fax 0 2216 4771; 25/13-15 Soi Kasem San 1; doubles/triples 480/680B)* is a friendly place that gets a lot of return business. It has fair-sized air-con doubles with bathroom, hot water and TV, and spacious triples. The maze-like **Bed & Breakfast Inn** *(☎ 0 2215 3004; singles/doubles 380/480B)* has air-con rooms that are substantially smaller than those at the A-One Inn, but the rates include a European breakfast.

Thanon Sukhumvit

Staying in this area puts you in the newest part of Bangkok and seemingly light-years away from old Bangkok. Taxis take longer to get here because of the one-way streets and omnipresent traffic. On the other hand, the Skytrain runs all the way from the start of Th Sukhumvit at Th Ploenchit to well beyond the Eastern bus terminal and connects the area to Th Silom, Siam Square and the river. The majority of hotels in this area are mid-range, but there are some budget options. The area has a lot of international bars and restaurants as well as the city's most thriving go-go scene. These places are on the Thanon Sukhumvit map.

The Atlanta *(☎ 0 2252 1650, 0 2252 6069, fax 0 2656 8123; 78 Soi 2, Th Sukhumvit; singles with fan 330B, with air-con 450B, suites 500B, add 120B for each additional person)* is the oldest, most centrally located and truly budget hotel in the area. Founded in the 1950s by Dr Max Henn, a former secretary to the Maharajah of Bikaner and proprietor of Bangkok's first international pharmacy, the Atlanta doesn't look like much from the outside, but the lobby, used as backdrops for Bangkok fashion shoots, retains its early '60s chic. The subdued diner features a heavily annotated menu (itself a crash course in Thai cuisine), a selection of European newspapers, a sound system playing Thai, classical and jazz (including an hour of King Bhumibol's compositions beginning at noon), and evening video selections that include film classics with Thailand themes (eg, *Chang*, *Bridge on the River Kwai*). The letter-writing desks, in the lobby area, each with its own light and fan, and the 1954 swimming pool (the first

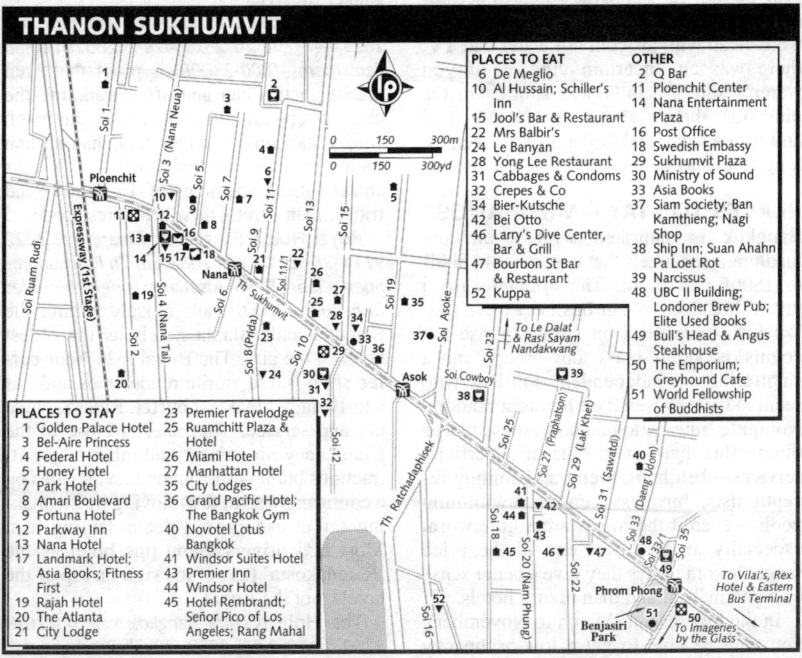

hotel pool in Thailand) in the courtyard, round out the offerings at this Bangkok institution.

The cheapest rooms fall into the 'bare bones' category, and the small air-con suites have two single beds and a small antechamber; the large air-con suite can sleep up to four. Rooms aren't aging as well the time-capsuled lobby. Monthly stays are discounted by 10%, if paid in advance. The Atlanta is the only hotel in the neighbourhood that openly forbids sex tourists. It is about a 15-minute walk from the Nana Skytrain station.

Golden Palace Hotel *(☎ 0 2252 5115, fax 0 2254 1538; 15 Soi 1, Th Sukhumvit; rooms from 550B)* is another strong budget contender, despite its institutional facade. The rooms are a decent size with air-con and private bathroom, and the swimming pool is clean enough to enjoy a dip. The hotel is a five-minute walk to the Ploenchit Skytrain station.

Miami Hotel *(☎ 0 2253 0369, fax 0 2253 1266; e miamihtl@asiaaccess.net.th; 2 Soi 13, Th Sukhumvit; singles/doubles 550/600B)* dates back to the 1960s and '70s Vietnam War period. Its standards seem to seesaw every three years or so. Although the rooms were clean with air-con, hot water and TV, there was an uncertain vibe, as if you weren't sure the milk was spoilt. On the plus side, there's a small swimming pool and **coffee shop**, and discounts are given for long-term stays.

PLACES TO STAY – MID-RANGE

Bangkok is saturated with small and medium-sized hotels that cost roughly 600B to 1800B per night. The clientele are a mixed bunch of Asian business travellers, Western journalists on slim expense accounts, economy-class tour groups and a smattering of independent tourists who seem to have chosen their hotels at random. Not quite 'international class', these places often offer their guests lots of superficial services – bell hops, pretty and smiling receptionists, business centres, swimming pools – even if the rooms are a little worn, especially at the lower end of the price range. In some ways they give a better sense of being in Thailand than luxury hotels.

In the low season (March to November), you may be able to get a low-occupancy discount. Many hotels in this category can also be booked through the Internet, travel agencies or airport hotel desks for 20% to 40% less than the rates listed here. Some hotels also charge a 7% tax.

Banglamphu

Viengtai Hotel *(Thanon Khao San map; ☎ 0 2280 5434, fax 0 2281 8153; W www.viengtai.co.th; 42 Th Rambutri; singles/doubles 1650/1850B)* used to be the most popular Banglamphu hotel before Th Khao San was 'discovered'. Over the last decade or so the Viengtai has continually renovated until it now sits solidly in the mid-price range of Bangkok hotels and even attracts Thai families. There are standard rooms in the six-storey old wing, and deluxe rooms in the remodelled nine-storey wing; breakfast is included. There is a swimming pool on the 3rd floor.

Pra Arthit Mansion *(Banglamphu map; ☎ 0 2230 0747, fax 0 2280 0742; 22 Th Phra Athit; rooms 600-900B)*, just a few steps from Tha Banglamphu, has high-powered Western-style bathrooms and comfortable beds for a little break from the ascetic backpacker lifestyle.

Buddy Lodge *(Thanon Khao San map; ☎ 0 2629 4477, fax 0 2629 4744; 265 Th Khao San; rooms 1800-2300B)* is proof that even tourist ghettos can gentrify. Straddling the mid- to top-end divide, this boutique hotel, smack dab on Th Khao San, has stylish rooms accented with traditional Thai designs and the usual amenities of TV, phone and fridge. Don't fret – there's no dress code.

Royal Hotel *(Banglamphu map; ☎ 0 2222 9111–26, fax 0 2224 2083; cnr Th Ratchadamnoen Klang & Th Atsadang; singles/doubles from 960/1300B)* trails closely behind the Oriental and Atlanta hotels as the oldest hotel in the city. The Royal's 24-hour **coffee shop** is a favourite rendezvous and has a tasty daily breakfast buffet. Rates include tax and service. The hotel is close to the Democracy Monument and other major attractions but it is surrounded on all sides by a confusing web of fast-moving traffic making a foot excursion a death-defying feat. Most taxi drivers know this hotel as the 'Ratanakosin' (as per the sign on top of the hotel), not the Royal.

Thai Hotel *(Central Bangkok map; ☎ 0 2629 2100, fax 0 2280 1299; 78 Th Prachatipatai;*

singles/doubles 950/1250B) is another mid-range place in the area.

Chinatown & Phahurat

There are a few mid-range options along Chinatown's main thoroughfares. The following places to stay can be found on the Chinatown & Phahurat map.

The **Chinatown Hotel** *(☎ 0 2225 0230, fax 0 2226 1295; w www.chinatownhotel.co.th; 526 Th Yaowarat; rooms 1000-1800B)* and the **Miramar Hotel** *(☎ 0 2226 3579, fax 0 2225 4994; 777 Th Mahachai; rooms 750-1800B)* are both solid choices for affordable comfort. The **White Orchid Hotel** *(☎ 0 2226 0026, fax 0 2255 6403; 409-421 Th Yaowarat; rooms from 900B)*, which is diagonally opposite the Chinatown Hotel, offers travellers nicer accommodation.

Soi Ngam Duphli Area

Malaysia Hotel *(Central Bangkok map; ☎ 0 2679 7127, fax 0 2287 1457; e malaysia@ksc15.th.com; 54 Soi Ngam Duphli; singles/doubles 588/668B, with TV & fridge 638/738B)* was once Bangkok's most-famous budget-travellers hotel. Nowadays it has 120 standard air-con, hot-water rooms, some with TV and fridge. All rates include tax and service charges. The six-storey hotel has a small swimming pool that may be used by nonguests for 50B per day.

Since the 1970s, the Malaysia has made a conscious effort to distance itself from the backpackers' market; for a while it seemed to be catering directly to the lonely male hired-sex market, although this wasn't apparent during a daytime visit; perhaps the freaks come out at night.

Pinnacle Hotel *(Central Bangkok map; ☎ 0 2287 0111, fax 0 2287 3420; e pinhl@loxinfo.co.th; 17 Soi Ngam Duphli, Th Phra Ram IV; rooms 1500B)* is a surprisingly nice hotel for the area with a gracious lobby and rooms with clean baths; rates include breakfast. There's also a fitness centre with sauna, steam room and outdoor rooftop Jacuzzi.

Charlie House *(Central Bangkok map; ☎ 0 2679 8330, fax 0 2679 7308; 1034/36-37 Soi Saphan Khu, Th Phra Ram IV; singles/doubles with air-con 750/900B)*, between Lumphini Tower and Soi Ngam Duphli, is a small nonsmoking hotel with carpeted rooms with hot showers. The beds bow worse than the back of the fabled old grey mare.

Thanon Silom

The **YWCA Hostel** *(☎ 0 2679 1280; w www.ywcabangkok.com; 13 Th Sathon Tai; singles/doubles 700/1000B)* includes breakfast in its rates. To get there from Th Sathon Tai, take the small driveway next to the Bangkok International Building and Sukhothai Hotel.

Sathorn Inn *(☎ 0 2637 8338, fax 0 2237 6668; 37 Soi 9/Suksavitthaya, Th Silom; rooms 700-900B)* is a clean modern hotel conveniently located on a little lane just spitting distance from Chong Nonsi Skytrain station. The rooms show signs of ageing, but the location and amenities of air-con, TV and phone make it worthwhile. Note that Soi 9 is also known as Seuksa Withaya.

New Fuji *(☎ 0 2234 5364, fax 0 2233 8274; 299-310 Th Surawong; rooms 750-1100B)* is a classic mid-range hotel with friendly staff and a 24-hour **bar** and **restaurant**.

Manohra Hotel *(☎ 0 2234 5070, fax 0 2237 7662; 412 Th Surawong; singles/doubles 1200/1400B)*, across the street, is a larger business hotel with simple rooms and lots of '*waii*-ing' staff.

Silom Village Inn *(☎ 0 2635 6810, fax 0 2635 6817; e silom-village-inn@thai.com; 286 Th Silom; rooms from 1800B)* is part of the Silom Village Trade Centre, a small collection of craft and art shops that form a mini-resort. Guests frequently grab a drink in the open-air pavilion to watch TV or passers-by. All rooms come with the usual upper mid-range amenities and discounts of up to 50% are often available.

Silom Golden Inn *(☎ 0 2238 2663, fax 0 2238 2667; e silom_golden_inn@thaimail.com; 41/4 Soi 19, Th Silom; rooms from 850B)* is a five-storey hotel with 60 tired air-con rooms sporting all the usual amenities. The rates are phenomenally cheap for the area and include breakfast, but the neglected fish tank in the lobby and abandoned furniture in the halls suggest a downward descent. Monthly and weekly rates are available.

Bangkok Christian Guest House *(☎ 0 2233 6303, fax 0 2237 1742; e bcgh@loxinfo.co.th; 123 Sala Daeng Soi 2, Th Convent; rooms 704-2222B)*, was undergoing drastic renovations at the time of writing – contact the guesthouse to see if it is open when you plan to visit.

Intown Residence *(☎ 0 2233 3596, fax 0 2236 6886; 1086/6 Th Charoen Krung; singles 600-700B, doubles 700-800B)*, between Th

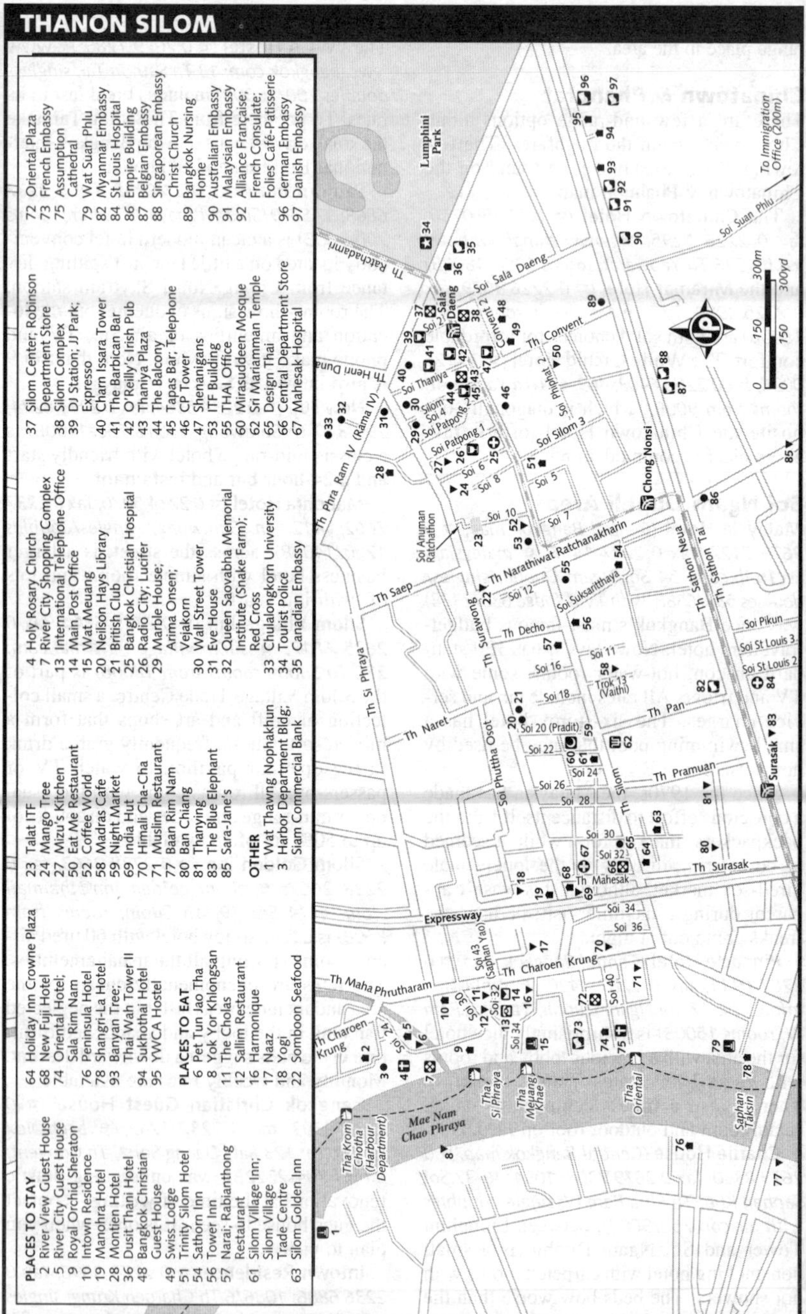
THANON SILOM
PLACES TO STAY
2 River View Guest House
5 River City Guest House
9 Royal Orchid Sheraton
10 Intown Residence
19 Manohra Hotel
28 Montien Hotel
36 Dusit Thani Hotel
48 Bangkok Christian Guest House
49 Swiss Lodge
51 Trinity Silom Hotel
54 Sathorn Inn
56 Tower Inn
57 Narai; Rabianthong Restaurant
61 Silom Village Inn; Silom Village Trade Centre
63 Silom Golden Inn
64 Holiday Inn Crowne Plaza
68 New Fuji Hotel
74 Oriental Hotel; Sala Rim Nam
76 Peninsula Hotel
78 Shangri-La Hotel
93 Banyan Tree; Thai Wah Tower II
94 Sukhothai Hotel
95 YWCA Hostel
PLACES TO EAT
6 Pet Tun Jao Tha
8 Yok Yor Khlongsan
11 The Cholas
12 Sallim Restaurant
16 Harmonique
17 Naaz
18 Yogi
22 Somboon Seafood
23 Talat ITF
24 Mango Tree
27 Mizu's Kitchen
50 Eat Me Restaurant
52 Coffee World
58 Madras Cafe
59 Night Market
69 India Hut
70 Himali Cha-Cha
71 Muslim Restaurant
77 Baan Rim Nam
80 Ban Chiang
81 Thanying
83 The Blue Elephant
85 Sara-Jane's
OTHER
1 Wat Thawng Nophakhun
3 Harbor Department Bldg; Siam Commercial Bank
4 Holy Rosary Church
7 River City Shopping Complex
13 International Telephone Office
14 Main Post Office
15 Wat Meuang
20 Neilson Hays Library
21 British Club
25 Bangkok Christian Hospital
26 Radio City; Lucifer
29 Marble House; Arima Onsen; Vejakorn
30 Wall Street Tower
31 Eve House
32 Queen Saovabha Memorial Institute (Snake Farm); Red Cross
33 Chulalongkorn University
34 Tourist Police
35 Canadian Embassy
37 Silom Center; Robinson Department Store
38 Silom Complex
39 DJ Station; JJ Park; Expresso
40 Charn Issara Tower
41 The Barbican Bar
42 O'Reilly's Irish Pub
43 Thaniya Plaza
44 The Balcony
45 Tapas Bar; Telephone
46 CP Tower
47 Shenanigans
53 ITF Building
55 THAI Office
60 Mirasuddeen Mosque
62 Sri Mariamman Temple
65 Design Thai
66 Central Department Store
67 Mahesak Hospital
72 Oriental Plaza
73 French Embassy
75 Assumption Cathedral
79 Wat Suan Phlu
82 Myanmar Embassy
84 St Louis Hospital
86 Empire Building
87 Belgian Embassy
88 Singaporean Embassy
Christ Church
89 Bangkok Nursing Home
90 Australian Embassy
91 Malaysian Embassy
92 Alliance Française; French Consulate; Folies Café-Patisserie
96 German Embassy
97 Danish Embassy

Si Phraya and Soi 30, is a clean, modern place; rooms have TV, air-con and phone, and rates include breakfast. There's a respectable **coffee shop** and a Thai-Chinese **restaurant**. Monthly rates are also available from 13,000B.

Siam Square & Pratunam

Unless otherwise indicated, the following places to stay can be found on the Siam Square & Pratunam map.

Reno Hotel (*☎ 0 2215 0026, fax 0 2215 3430; 40 Soi Kasem San 1; standard doubles 890B*) is a veteran from the Vietnam War days, when a number of hotels, named after US cities, opened in Bangkok. It has a pool and rates include breakfast. There is also a spiffy downstairs **restaurant** that attracts a well-scrubbed crowd of locals.

Jim's Lodge (*☎ 0 2255 3100, fax 0 2253 8492; ⓔ jimslodge@yahoo.com; 125/7 Soi Ruam Rudi; standard singles/doubles 1100/1200B, superior singles/doubles 1300/1400B*) provides clean rooms with TV, fridge, air-con and carpeting in a six-storey building.

Siam Orchid Inn (*☎ 0 2251 4417, fax 0 2255 3144; ⓔ siam_orchidinn@hotmail.com; rooms around 1100B*) offers well-appointed rooms and rates include breakfast. It is set off Ratchadamri opposite the World Trade Centre; follow the entrance to the Narayana Phand car park to reach the hotel.

Opera Hotel (*☎ 0 2252 4031, fax 0 2253 5360; 16 Soi Somprasong 1/Soi 11 Phetburi, Th Phetburi; doubles 590-740B*) is quiet and has air-con doubles with hot water. It also has a swimming pool and **coffee shop**.

Borarn House (*☎ 0 2253 2252, fax 0 2253 3639; 487/48 Soi Wattanasin, Th Ratchaprarop; singles/doubles 850/950B*) is tricky to find, tucked deep into a neighbourhood of maze-like lanes, where daily life extends from the open-style living rooms to the ever-narrowing streets. It's best to call for directions to the hotel. Rooms in this Thai-style apartment building have air-con and TV.

Florida Hotel (*☎ 0 2247 0990, fax 0 2247 7419; 43 Phayathai Square, Th Phayathai; singles/doubles with air-con 1200/1400B*) is another Vietnam War–era place.

Just north of Siam Square, in the Victory Monument area, are several hotels. **Century Park Hotel** (*Central Bangkok map; ☎ 0 2246 7800, fax 0 2246 7197; ⓔ century@samart.co.th; 9 Th Ratchaprarop; rooms from 2500B*) is a busy, semi-plush place, where rooms are readily discounted by 50%. **Continental Hotel** (*Central Bangkok map; ☎ 0 2278 1385, fax 0 2271 3547; 971/16 Th Phahonyothin; singles/doubles from 2500B*) is similar to Century Park, and discounts to 1200B are available.

Thanon Sukhumvit

Stick to the lower-numbered lanes to save cross-town travel time. Many of the Th Sukhumvit hotels in this price range were built for soldiers on leave from the Vietnam War. Some made the transition to a more-traditional tourist clientele with style and grace, while others continue to have a slightly rough image. The following places to stay can be found on the Thanon Sukhumvit map.

The cluster of high-rise hotels on Soi 3 and Soi 4 mostly cater to male tourists and their Thai 'friends' from the Nana Entertainment Plaza (NEP) on Soi 4 (Soi Nana Tai), but these hotels are also conveniently close to the Nana Skytrain station. **Parkway Inn** (*☎ 0 2255 3711, fax 0 2254 2180; Soi 4, 132 Th Sukhumvit; rooms 990B*), near the Landmark Hotel, is a small American-style inn with big beds, modern bathrooms and 24-hour Thai massage; the rooms may be slightly noisy.

Fortuna Hotel (*☎ 0 2251 5121, fax 0 2253 6282; 19 Soi 5; rooms 1000-2000B*) is in the Little Arabia district and attracts a lot of male Japanese tourists. This older hotel offers decent rooms with all the mod cons.

Premier Travelodge (*☎ 0 2251 3031, fax 0 2253 3195; ⓔ premierlodge@yahoo.com; 170-170/1 Soi 8, Th Sukhumvit; rooms 700B*) is a small, friendly hotel with lots of amenities, but the rooms are a little musty smelling; reservations are recommended.

Federal Hotel (*☎/fax 0 2253 5332; 27 Soi 11, Th Sukhumvit; rooms 675-960B*) has ground-level rooms, which occasionally flood in the rainy season and aren't worth the price, so be sure to get one of the larger, older upstairs rooms. The small pool and American-style **coffee shop** are the main attractions. The Nana Skytrain station is about a 10-minute walk away.

Manhattan (*☎ 0 2255 0166, fax 0 2255 3481; ⓦ www.hotelmanhattan.com; 13 Soi 15, Th Sukhumvit; singles/doubles 1400/1600B*) has good-sized and fairly well-kept rooms that are as sterile as those at American chain hotels; rates include breakfast.

Ruamchitt Plaza & Hotel *(☎ 0 2254 0205, fax 0 2253 2406; e ruamjit@comnet3.ksc.net.th; Soi 15, 199 Th Sukhumvit; singles/doubles with air-con from 1150/1350B)* has rooms with carpet, fridge and TV; amenities include a rooftop pool and attached shopping arcade. In the basement of the arcade is the **Thermae Coffee House**, an infamous after-hours venue for Thai sex workers.

Royal Asia Lodge *(☎ 0 2251 5514; fax 0 2253 2554; w www.royalasialodge.com; 91 Soi 8, Th Sukhumvit; rooms from 1200B)*, at the end of a peaceful residential lane, has quiet, comfortable rooms that are well removed from the area's constant hustle and bustle. A free shuttle service provides transport to Th Sukhumvit.

There are two spiffy **City Lodge** *(☎ 0 2253 7705, fax 0 2255 4667; Soi 9 • ☎ 0 2254 4783, fax 0 2255 7340; Soi 19; w www.amari.com; rooms with air-con 1350-2300B)* hotels popular among middle-class business travellers and small tour groups. Rooms include telephone, minibar, TV and video.

Honey Hotel *(☎ 0 2253 0646, fax 0 2254 4716; 31 Soi 19, Th Sukhumvit; standard singles/doubles 800/1000B, larger singles/doubles 900/1800B)* is a former Vietnam War–era place with a loyal clientele and clean good-sized rooms. **Rex Hotel** *(☎ 0 2259 0106, fax 0 2258 6635; 762/1 Soi 32, Th Sukhumvit; singles/doubles 800/1000B)* is another holdover from the Vietnam War.

Premier Inn *(☎ 0 2261 0401, fax 0 2261 0414; 9/1 Soi 20, Th Sukhumvit; rooms 800-1200B)* is opposite the Windsor Hotel (see Places to Stay – Top End). It offers rooms and suites with hot water and satellite TV, but the new facade is beginning to show its age; rates include breakfast. The nearest Skytrain station is Phrom Phong.

Airport Area

Finding decent, moderately priced accommodation near the airport area is difficult. Most charge nearly twice as much as comparable hotels in the city. **Don Muang Mansion** *(Greater Bangkok map; ☎ 0 2566 3064; 118/7 Th Soranakom, Don Muang; rooms 1000-1200B)* has small air-con rooms that are a steal for the airport area, but would cost considerably less in Bangkok. It's possible to negotiate a lower rate of 800B.

Comfort Suites Airport *(Greater Bangkok map; ☎ 0 2552 8921–9, fax 0 2552 8920; 88/117 Viphavadi Rangsit Hwy; rooms 2500-2600B)* is better value if you can spend more. It is about five minutes south of the airport by car. Large rooms come with all the amenities (satellite TV, air-con, hot-water bathroom and shower) and are cheaper (1400B) if you book through a travel agent or the Internet. Best of all, the hotel provides a free shuttle to/from the airport. The only negative is that you can hear the planes landing and taking off until around 1am.

We-Train International House *(Greater Bangkok map; ☎ 0 2929 2222, 0 2929 2301, fax 0 2929 2300; e we-train@linethai.co.th, w www.we-train.linethai.co.th; 501/1 Mu 3, Th Dechatungkha, Sikan, Don Muang; dorm beds 140B, rooms 580B)* is a well-run place, where you can stay for quite a bit less. To these rates add the usual 10% service charge but no tax since it's operated by a nonprofit women's group (but male guests are welcome). Facilities include a pool, Thai massage, laundry service, coffee shop and beauty salon. One major drawback is its distance from the airport. If you don't have a lot of luggage, walk across the airport pedestrian bridge to reach the Amari Airport Hotel, then get a taxi – it's much cheaper this way because you avoid the high taxi-desk fees. There are usually no taxis near the guesthouse to get back to the airport or continue on to Bangkok, but transportation can be arranged on request for 200B one way to Bangkok, or 70B to/from the Amari Airport Hotel. There's a helpful map and directions on the hotel's website.

PLACES TO STAY – TOP END

Bangkok has all sorts of hotels that are of an international standard, from the straightforward packages to some of Asia's classics.

Although there's no specific area for top-end hotels, you'll find quite a few around Siam Square, along Th Surawong, Th Silom and on the river, while many of the slightly less expensive places are scattered along Th Sukhumvit.

A few top-end places quote prices in US dollars (a holdover from the 1997 devaluation of the baht), while others raised the baht prices to bring exchange levels back in line with 1996 prices.

Even so, you should still be able to negotiate discounts of up to 40% during the low season (anytime except from December to March and from July to August). Booking through a travel agency almost always means lower rates, or try asking for a hotel's 'corporate' discount. Several top-end hotels offer discounts of up to 60% when you make your reservation via the Internet. Thai Airways International (THAI) can also arrange substantial discounts for its passengers.

The hotels in this category will add a 10% service charge plus 7% tax to hotel bills.

On the River

Oriental Hotel *(Thanon Silom map; ☎ 0 2236 0400, 0 2236 0420, fax 0 2236 1937; W www.madarin-oriental.com; 48 Th Oriental; rooms from US$300)*, right on Mae Nam Chao Phraya, is one of the most famous hotels in Asia – right up there with Raffles in Singapore or the Peninsula in Hong Kong. This 124-year-old hotel is also rated as one of the very best hotels in the world and is just about the most expensive in Bangkok. Once you've stayed here the staff will remember your name, what you like to eat for breakfast, even what type of flowers you'd prefer in your room.

Nowadays the Oriental Hotel is looking more modern and less classic – the original Author's Wing is dwarfed by the Tower (built in 1958) and River (1976) wings. Authors who have stayed here and had suites named after them include Joseph Conrad, W Somerset Maugham, Noel Coward, Graham Greene, John le Carré, James Michener, Gore Vidal and Barbara Cartland. Suites are as much as 10 times the room prices. It's worth wandering in, if only to see the lobby (no shorts, sleeveless shirts or sandals allowed). Apart from the usual luxury recreational facilities, the Oriental also has a Thai Cooking School and a Thai Culture Programme. Even if the Oriental is well beyond your means, stop by for an evening drink on the riverside terrace.

Shangri-La Hotel *(Thanon Silom map; ☎ 0 2236 7777, fax 0 2236 8579; W www.shangri-la.com; 89 Soi Wat Suan Phlu, Th Charoen Krung; singles/doubles from US$190/210)* is another luxury gem along the river. Facilities and services are of a very high standard. The capacious lounge areas off the main lobby have a less formal and more relaxed feel than those at the Oriental, and are a favourite rendezvous spot even for nonhotel guests. As an added bonus for guests, the hotel can arrange a 15-minute helicopter service from Bangkok International Airport to the hotel rooftop, for around 17,000B per trip (minimum of three persons; an additional three people costs 3500B each).

Marriott Royal Garden Riverside Hotel *(Greater Bangkok map; ☎ 0 2476 0021, fax 0 2476 1120; e marriottrgr@minornet.com; 257/1-3 Th Charoen Nakhon; rooms from US$150)*, near Saphan Krungthep, is on the Thonburi side of the river. This tastefully appointed hotel is highly valued for its serene atmosphere and expansive, airy public areas. The grounds encompass a large swimming pool, lush gardens, two lighted tennis courts and a world-class health club.

Royal Orchid Sheraton *(Thanon Silom map; ROS; ☎ 0 2266 0123, fax 0 2236 8320; W www.sheraton.com/royalorchid; 2 Soi Captain Bush, rooms from US$210)*, also on the river (near River City Shopping Complex), is known for crisp, efficient service; its business centre is open 24 hours.

Menam Riverside *(Greater Bangkok map; ☎ 0 2688 1000, fax 0 2291 9400; e menamhtl@mozart.inet.co.th; 2074 Th Charoen Krung; rooms from 2400B)* towers over the river.

Royal River *(Greater Bangkok map; ☎ 0 2433 0300, fax 0 2433 5880; 670/805 Th Charan Sanitwong, Thonburi; rooms 2300-3000B)* receives lots of tour groups.

Peninsula Hotel *(Thanon Silom map; ☎ 0 2861 2888, fax 0 2861 1112; e pbk@peninsula.com; 333 Th Charoen Nakhon; rooms from US$260, suites from US$400)* is a luxurious tower hotel on the west bank of the river. A complimentary shuttle transports guests to/from points along the river.

Siam Square & Pratunam

The following places to stay can be found on the Siam Square & Pratunam map.

Regent Bangkok *(☎ 0 2251 6127, fax 0 2251 5390; 155 Th Ratchadamri; rooms from US$200)* is a plush hotel that some claim tops the Oriental in overall quality. This is particularly true for business travellers because of the Regent's efficient business centre and central location; local calls are free at the Regent, probably the only luxury hotel in the city to offer this courtesy. It also offers (for around 2000B an hour) an 'office on wheels', which is a hi-tech, multipassenger van equipped with computers, cell phones, fax machines, TVs and videos, and swivelling leather seats so that small conferences can be held while crossing town.

Hilton International Bangkok *(☎ 0 2253 0123, fax 0 2253 6509; ⓔ bkkhitwsal@hilton.com; 2 Th Withayu; rooms from 8640B)* is another top executive choice. The expansive and secluded grounds are a major plus, and a dip in the tropically landscaped pool is an instant elixir for jet lag.

Grand Hyatt Erawan *(☎ 0 2254 1234, fax 0 2254 6308; cnr Th Ratchadamri & Th Ploenchit; standard rooms from 11,520B)* was built on the site of the original Erawan Hotel with obvious ambitions to become one of the city's top-ranked hotels. The neo-Thai architecture has been well executed; inside is an impressive collection of contemporary Thai art. Adding to the elite atmosphere, the rooms at the rear of the hotel overlook the prestigious Bangkok Royal Sports Club racetrack. It vies with the Regent Bangkok or the Novotel Bangkok on Siam Square for being in the best location for transport and shopping.

Amari Watergate *(☎ 0 2653 9000, fax 0 2653 9045; ⓔ watergate@amari.com; 847 Th Phetburi; singles/doubles US$184/200)* is a 34-storey hotel right in the centre of Bangkok's busiest district, near the Th Ratchaprarop intersection. The neoclassical interior design blends Thai and European motifs, guest rooms are large, and facilities include a 900-sq-metre fitness centre, an American-style pub, and highly rated Cantonese and Italian restaurants. The 8th-storey pool catches breezes and views unimaginable from street level. Tour groups check in via a separate floor and lobby.

Other Amari hotels in central Bangkok include the **Amari Atrium** *(Greater Bangkok map; ☎ 0 2718 2000, fax 0 2718 2002; ⓔ atrium@amari.com; Th Phetburi Tat Mai; singles/doubles from US$134/142)*, east of Soi Asoke, and the **Amari Boulevard** *(Thanon Sukhumvit map; ☎ 0 2255 2930, fax 0 2255 2950; ⓔ boulevard@amari.com; 2 Soi 5, Th Sukhumvit)*. There's also an Amari Airport Hotel – see the Airport Area section later for details.

Novotel Bangkok on Siam Square *(☎ 0 2255 6888, fax 0 2255 1824; Soi 6, Siam Square; rooms from 5100B)* is another hotel that's extremely well located for business or leisure. Just steps away from Bangkok's major shopping district, as well as the Siam Skytrain station, the Novotel boasts a full business centre, **bakery**, pool and various **restaurants**.

Le Meridien President Hotel *(☎ 0 2656 0444, fax 0 2656 0555; ⓔ information@lemeridien-bangkok.com; 971 Th Ploenchit; rooms & suites from 8200B)* and its more modern sister, **Le Royal Meridien**, in the heart of the Th Ploenchit shopping area and near the Chit Lom Skytrain station, offers 758 well-appointed rooms and suites. Amenities include two pools, a health club, business centre, bookshop, tobacconist, and 10 **restaurants** and **bars**.

Asia Hotel *(☎ 0 2215 0808, fax 0 2215 4360; ⓦ www.asiahotel.co.th; 296 Th Phayathai; rooms from 3200B)* is a huge place with faux fancy decor. It's in a good location and the rooms are large, but it is often packed to the gills with tour groups and convention attendees. **Indra Regent** *(☎ 0 2208 0033, fax 0 2208 0388; ⓦ www.indrahotel.com; 120/126 Th Ratchaprarop; rooms from 2000B)* is similar to the Asia.

Siam City Hotel *(☎ 0 2247 0123, fax 0 2247 0178; ⓦ www.siamhotels.com; 477 Th Si Ayuthaya; rooms 4500B)* is independently owned and operated. Large, well-maintained rooms come with all the amenities. The **restaurants** here are highly regarded by Thai businesspeople.

Holiday Mansion Hotel *(☎ 0 2255 0099, fax 0 2253 0130; ⓔ hmtel@ksc.th.com; 53 Th Withayu; rooms with air-con 2000B)*, next to Home Pro Plus on busy Th Withayu, a little north of Th Ploenchit, is a simple but well-run place. It has good-sized rooms with the standard amenities and breakfast. There is also a pool, business centre and 24-hour **coffee shop**. It's only a three-minute walk from the Ploenchit Skytrain station. Rates can drop as low as 500B during the low season.

Thanon Silom

The following places to stay can be found on the Thanon Silom map.

Sukhothai Hotel *(☎ 0 2287 0222; fax 0 2287 4980; ⓔ reservations@sukhothai.com; ⓦ www.sukhothai.com; 13/3 Th Sathon Tai;*

superior/deluxe rooms US$260/310) features a minimalist Asian decor, including an inner courtyard with lily ponds and *chedi* styled after Thailand's ancient capital; the same architect and interior designer created Phuket's landmark Amanpuri. Apart from superior and deluxe rooms, there are also more-expensive suites.

Banyan Tree *(☎ 0 2679 1200, fax 0 2679 1199; W www.banyantree.com; Th Sathon Tai; rooms from US$170)* is an ultra-modern hotel with business suites in the lower two and top 28 floors of the Thai Wah Tower II, which dominates Th Sathon Tai. Huge rooms feature separate work and sleep areas, two-line speaker phones with data ports and two TV sets, along with all the other amenities expected of lodgings at this rate. The spa and fitness centre – the biggest such hotel facility in Bangkok – spans four floors.

Two of the top hotels in the district are the very Thai **Montien** *(☎ 0 2233 7060, fax 0 2236 5218; e bangkok@montien.com; 54 Th Surawong; rooms from 6500B)* and the great **Dusit Thani** *(☎ 0 2236 9999, fax 0 2236 6400; W www.dusit.com; 946 Th Phra Ram IV; rooms from US$190)*. Both offer significant discounts via the Internet.

There are many hotels that have similar amenities but are cheaper because of their location or smaller staff-to-guest ratios. In the Th Silom and Th Surawong area, these include **Narai** *(☎ 0 2237 0100, fax 0 2236 7161; W www.narai.com; 222 Th Silom; rooms from 3500B)* and **Holiday Inn Crowne Plaza** *(☎ 0 2238 4300, fax 0 2238 5289; W www crowneplaza.com; 981 Th Silom; rooms from US$165)*.

Swiss Lodge *(☎ 0 2233 5345, fax 0 2236 9425; W www.swisslodge.com; 3 Th Convent; singles/doubles 3375/3760B, includes breakfast)* has only 57 rooms, so the management is able to pay close attention to service details, such as offering cold towels whenever you enter the lobby from outside. Data ports and soundproof windows further enhance the attraction for people doing business.

Trinity Silom Hotel *(☎ 0 2231 5333, fax 0 2231 5417; 150 Soi 5, Th Silom; rooms 1450-2500B)*, at the far end of the lane, is another top-end hotel. **Tower Inn** *(☎ 0 2237 8300-4, fax 0 2237 8286; W www.towerinnbangkok com; 533 Th Silom; rooms from 2700B)* is a multistorey hotel with large, renovated rooms and many repeat business travellers. Also on the premises are a pool, gym and **restaurant**.

Thanon Sukhumvit

Hotel Rembrandt *(☎ 0 2261 7100, fax 0 2261 7017; W www.rembrandtbkk.com; 19 Soi 18, Th Sukhumvit; rooms 4200-5550B)* is tastefully decorated with large rooms as well as serviced apartments. Facilities include a swimming pool and the best Mexican restaurant in Bangkok, **Señor Pico's of Los Angeles**. Another advantage is its proximity to the Queen Sirikit National Convention Centre, off Soi 16. The hotel is between the Asoke and Phrom Phong Skytrain stations.

Landmark *(☎ 0 2254 0404, fax 0 2253 4259; W www.landmarkbangkok.com; 138 Th Sukhumvit; rooms from 5600B)* has well-appointed rooms and its business centre is one of the hotel's strong points; the heavy traffic along this stretch of Th Sukhumvit is not. It's about halfway between Ploenchit and Nana Skytrain stations.

Grand Pacific Hotel *(☎ 0 2651 1000, fax 0 2255 2441; W www.grandpacifichotel.com; Th Sukhumvit between Soi 17-19; rooms from 6500B)* is between Soi 17 and Soi 19, and easy to reach from either Th Sukhumvit or Th Phetburi; there's a nearby pedestrian bridge across Th Sukhumvit. The hotel caters mainly to Japanese businesspeople, but its rates drop on weekends; it is attached to Robinson department store and also bears the distinction of having the highest karaoke lounge in the city.

Windsor Hotel *(☎ 0 2258 0160, fax 0 2258 1491; 8-10 Soi 20, Th Sukhumvit; singles/doubles 2000/2400B, superior singles/doubles 2400/2600B)* is a fairly deluxe place. Rates include a cooked-to-order breakfast. There's a 24-hour **coffee shop** on the premises. Hotel guests have the use of all amenities at the Windsor Suites Hotel next door. **Windsor Suites Hotel** *(☎ 0 2262 1234, fax 0 2262 1212; W www.windsorsuiteshotel.com; singles/doubles from 6000B/6500B)* features spacious suites (each with two TVs). A complimentary breakfast buffet is included. The nearest Skytrain station is Phrom Phong.

Bel-Aire Princess *(☎ 0 2253 4300, fax 0 2255 8850; e bela@dusit.com; 16 Soi 5, Th Sukhumvit; rooms from 2800B)*, **Park Hotel** *(☎ 0 2255 4300, fax 0 2255 4309; 6 Soi 7,*

Th Sukhumvit; rooms from 2000B) and the more expensive **Imperial Impala Hotel** *(Greater Bangkok map; ☎ 0 2259 0053, fax 0 2258 8747; W www.imperialhotels.com; 9 Soi 24, Th Sukhumvit; singles/doubles from 3500/4120B)* are all moderately expensive places in the this area.

Novotel Lotus Bangkok *(☎ 0 2261 0111, fax 0 2262 1700; W www.accorhotels.com; 1 Soi 33, Th Sukhumvit; rooms from 4600B)*, Accor's well-designed hotel, features plush rooms.

Ratchada

This entertainment and business district in the Huay Khwang neighbourhood of northeastern Bangkok features several flash hotels along Th Ratchadaphisek. The following places to stay can be found on the Greater Bangkok map.

Merchant Court at Le Concorde *(☎ 0 2694 222, fax 0 2694 2223; e info@merchantcourt.th.com; 202 Th Ratchadaphisek; singles/doubles from 5000/5500B)*, a well-appointed hotel managed by Singapore's Raffles International, occupies one of the two tower blocks of Le Concorde building. Rooms on floors set aside for executives offer two phone lines, ergonomically designed writing desk and chair, and optional personal computer and fax/printer. Nonsmoking floors are available. When the subway has been built, there will be a station right in front of this hotel.

Siam Beverly Hotel *(☎ 0 2275 4397, fax 0 2290 0170; 188 Th Ratchadaphisek; rooms from 1800B)*, next to the Le Concorde building and close to several upmarket entertainment centres, is fairly affordable and rates include breakfast. It's not spectacular but the service is friendly and the rooms have all the amenities.

Airport Area

Amari Airport Hotel *(Greater Bangkok map; ☎ 0 2566 1020, fax 0 2566 1941; e airport@amari.com; doubles from US$190)*, connected to the airport by an air-conditioned walkway, is obviously the closest hotel to Bangkok International Airport. The Amari offers nonsmoking rooms, a 'ladies' floor, rooms for disabled persons, and an executive floor with huge suites and 24-hour butler service. Discounts are rarely available since rooms are very much in demand; however, passengers who fly with THAI receive a 50% discount when they show their current boarding pass or ticket. Amari also offers 'ministay' rates for stays of up to three hours (US$20), including tax and service, provided the check-in time is between 8am and 6pm.

Asia Airport Hotel *(Greater Bangkok map; ☎ 0 2992 6999, fax 0 2532 3193; rooms from 2000B)* is north of the airport at the Km 28 marker. Rooms are comfortable, and discounts to 1200B or 1500B are often available. A shuttle service to the airport is provided.

PLACES TO EAT

No matter where you go in Bangkok, you're rarely more than 50m away from a restaurant or street vendor. The variety of places to eat is simply astounding and defeats all but the most tireless food samplers in their quest to say they've tried everything. As with places to stay, you can find something in every price range in most districts.

While Thai food may be sufficiently exotic, Bangkok offers an international menu prepared by its many immigrant communities. Chinatown is naturally a good area for Chinese food. In a corner of Chinatown, known as Phahurat, and around Th Silom, Indian residents keep themselves and the culinary traveller well fed in small closet-sized restaurants down narrow lanes. In the crowded bazaar-like area of Little Arabia, just off Th Sukhumvit, there is Muslim cuisine from every far flung corner of the region.

Western cuisine, ranging from Italian to American, is prepared in the haute fashion for power players or as pub grub to cure homesickness.

Vegetarians will certainly have eating challenges, but Bangkok's endless variety will ease the foraging. In addition to the vegie-speciality spots, Indian and Muslim restaurants frequently have vegie options, as do Chinese restaurants. During the vegetarian festival in October, the whole city goes mad for tofu, and stalls and restaurants indicate their nonmeat menu with yellow flags.

At the bottom of the price scale (but not the taste scale), there are plenty of vendor stands where you can buy a bowl of noodles or a plate of *râat khâo* (rice with curry poured over it) for 25B to 40B. A restaurant

Thanon Khao San, Bangkok

ANDREW LUBRAN

Young boy, Bangkok

KRAIG LIEB

Thanon Ratchaprarop, Pratunam, Bangkok

RICHARD I'ANSON

BILL WASSMAN

Chakri Mahaprasat (Grand Palace Hall), Bangkok

JOHN BORTHWICK

Hand-painted movie poster, Bangkok

RICHARD I'ANSON

Vimanmek Teak Mansion, Bangkok

CHRIS MELLOR

Guards, Grand Palace, Bangkok

meal at the lower end of the range should cost 100B or less per person; the bill increases as the ambience becomes more upmarket or if the ingredients are predominantly imports. Fine dining with an army of waiters and artful dishes with gourmet ingredients can peak at about 500B per person – a veritable steal compared to Western prices. An exception are the restaurants in top-end hotels, which feature prices on a par with, or just below, what you'd expect to pay at any flash hotel in the world.

Banglamphu & Ko Ratanakosin

This area, near the river and in the old part of the city, is one of the best for cheap eating establishments, but the quality isn't nearly as reliable. Recommending a restaurant on the tourist strip of Th Khao San, in most cases, is instant death to the quality of the food served there. Even street vendors, who are typically stalwarts, tend to let standards sag when they stake out claims near Th Khao San. Guesthouses do a brisk restaurant business, but their food is comparable to airline food – a necessary evil.

Unless otherwise indicated, the following places to eat can be found on the Banglamphu map.

Arawy Det *(Thanon Khao San map; cnr Th Khao San & Th Tanao)*, an old Hokkien-style noodle shop, has somehow managed to stay semi-authentic amid the cosmic swirl. If you want noodles or what the Thais are eating, just point. **No 147 Thai Food** *(Thanon Khao San map; Th Tanao)*, opposite the eastern end of Th Khao San, is also reasonably authentic. Also check out the **open-air restaurants** at the western end of Th Rambutri. Grilled fish and cold beer have found a happy outdoor home along Soi Rambutri.

Chabad House *(Thanon Khao San map; Th Rambutri; dishes 100-200B; open noon-9pm Sun-Thur, noon-4.30pm Fri)* is a Jewish place of worship and serves Israeli-style kosher food downstairs as part of its non-profit community outreach. **Chochana** (another sign reads 'Shoshana'), down an alley off Th Chakraphong, around the corner from Th Khao San, serves cheaper falafel-and-hummus plates. **Sarah**, right next door to Chochana, also serves Israeli dishes.

Roti-Mataba *(cnr Th Phra Athit & Th Phra Sumen; dishes 50-80B; open 7am-8pm Tues-Sun)* is a small shop near the river (opposite Phra Sumen Fort) that offers delicious *rotii* (fried Indian flatbread), *kaeng mátsàmàn* (Thai Muslim curry), chicken korma and chicken or vegetable *mátàbà* (a sort of stuffed Indian pancake), and has a bilingual menu. An upstairs air-con dining area and outdoor tables barely provides enough seating for its loyal fans.

Kuay Tiaw Mae, two doors down, might be the most stylish *kŭaytĭaw* (rice noodles) shop in the universe with wooden benches lining the walls and art hanging on the walls. The *kŭaytĭaw tôm yam* (rice noodles in a spicy lemongrass broth) with pork or tofu substitution keeps noodle fans reverently bowed.

Ton Pho *(no Roman-script sign; ☎ 0 2280 0452; Th Phra Athit; dishes 60-100B)*, at Tha Banglamphu, is another great spot, overlooking the muddy Mae Nam Chao Phraya, for traditional, authentic Thai.

Along Th Phra Athit, there are several small but up-and-coming Thai places with chic, casual decor, which create a neighbourhood café scene sometimes compared to High Street Kensington or Greenwich Village. The evenings usually host a solo singer and his weeping guitar, while university students share plates of food or plow through bottles of whiskey. By and large, the food is mediocre with poorly cooked rice as the worst offender. But these joints are still worth it for a beer and a few side dishes, or as an air-con break from street-side eating.

Khrua Nopparat *(Th Phra Athit; dishes 60-100B; open 10.30am-9.30pm daily)*, a notable exception, is plainly decorated with harsh fluorescent lighting, leaving more resources to go into the menu. The dishes are a little small, so don't shy away from the Thai tradition of over-ordering. Winners include the deep-fried shrimp or *phat phak kha-naa* (stir-fried Chinese greens).

Saffron Bakery *(Th Phra Athit)*, a bright and cheery place opposite the Food & Agriculture Organization, has good pastries and fresh coffee, but only a few tables.

Vijit *(dishes 70-200B)* and **Methavalai Sorn Daeng** *(dishes 70-200B)* are a couple of well-established Thai restaurants at the Democracy Monument circle roundabout on Th Ratchadamnoen Klang. Both have reasonable prices considering the quality of the food and air-con facilities. At lunchtime on weekdays they're crowded with local government office workers. Both stay open until 11pm or so, another plus.

Jeh Hoy *(Th Samsen; dishes 50-100B; open 6pm-midnight)* is an open-air restaurant that does a bustling business in Hokkien specials, such as *puu phàt phǒng kàrìi* (crab stir-fried with curry powder and egg). The restaurant is on the corner of Soi 2 and Th Samsen, just across the canal bridge from Th Khao San, and the staff can make awkward foreigners feel comfortable.

Bangkok Bar & Restaurant *(Central Bangkok map; ☎ 0 2281 6237; 591 Th Phra Sumen; dishes 150-300B; open 6pm-2am)*, not to be confused with a similarly named place on Soi Rambutri, overlooks Khlong Banglamphu in a classical Sino-Portuguese house. Dramatic lighting, sleek furniture and hip tunes mingle to make even the plastic-bottle filled canal seem magical. If you have something to celebrate, clean yourself up and strike a pose at one of the outdoor tables.

Si Amnuay *(Central Bangkok map; no Roman-script sign; dishes 30-50B)* is near the National Library and the cluster of guesthouses near Tha Thewet. This is a good, clean place for *kŭaytĭaw* or *khâo phat thaleh* (fried rice with seafood).

Poonsin Restaurant *(Central Bangkok map; 460 Th Wisut Kasat; dishes 50-150B)* is famous for its *pèt yâang* (grilled duck), which could transform duck-haters into devotees; the accompanying dipping sauce is sweet enough to find a home in a Dixieland kitchen. Poonsin's unadorned cafeteria-style restaurant fills up quickly with chatting families and sugar-spiked kids.

Vegetarian Many of the Th Khao San guesthouse cafés offer vegetarian dishes. To find the following out-of-the-way places, turn left on Th Tanao at the eastern end of Th Khao San, then cross the street and turn right down the first narrow alley, then left at Soi Wat Bowon. **Arawy** *(Banglamphu map; 152 Th Din So; open 7am-7pm daily; dishes 35B)*, the Roman-script sign reads 'Alloy', is opposite the Municipal Hall a few doors from a 7-Eleven store. This is one of the best Thai vegetarian restaurants in the city; a selection of prepared dishes makes it user-friendly, and the cook brings out the flavour of the vegies without the usual oil spill. This was one of Bangkok's first Thai vegetarian restaurants, inspired by the strict vegetarianism of Chamlong Srimuang, the ex-governor of Bangkok.

Phon Sawan *(Banglamphu map; 80 Th Samsen; dishes 35B)*, directly across from the Bangkok Bank, feeds Banglamphu expats tofu-based Thai-Chinese dishes, served on a bed of hearty *khâo klâwng* (unbleached rice). Once you pass Soi 4 on Th Samsen, keep an eye out for a handwritten 'Vegetarian Food' sign inside the simple shopfront.

For all-vegie menus at low prices, check out the string of **vegetarian restaurants** near Srinthip Guest House (see the Banglamphu map).

Thanon Silom

This area is at the heart of the financial district so it has a lot of pricey restaurants, along with cheaper ones that attract both office workers and the more flush with cash. Many restaurants are found along the main avenues but there's an even greater number tucked away in lanes and alleys. Soi Sala Daeng, near Sala Daeng Skytrain station off Th Convent, is a Thai gourmets' enclave with some regional interpretations of international cuisine. The river end of Th Silom and Th Surawong towards Th Charoen Krung (the Bangrak district) is a good hunting ground for Indian food.

Thai & Other Asian The **Soi Pradit (Soi 20) Night Market**, which assembles each evening off Th Silom in front of the municipal market pavilion, is good for cheap eats. During the day there are also a few **food vendors** in this lane, but much better daytime fare can be found amid the mass of food stalls purveying pots of curry and miles of noodles inside **Talat ITF** at the end of Soi 10.

Ban Chiang *(☎ 0 2266 6994; 14 Soi Si Wiang, Th Surasak; open lunch & dinner daily)* is a great place for traditional Thai and Isan (northeastern-Thai) fare. It is in a restored wooden house in a verdant setting, off Th Silom, west of Umathewi Temple.

Thanying *(☎ 0 2236 4361, 0 2235 0371; 10 Soi Si Wiang, Th Pramuan; dishes from 220B, set menu 500-600B; open noon-11pm daily)*, owned by a Thai movie star, has elegant Western decor and artfully arranged royal Thai cuisine. There's also a set menu for 500B to 600B. There's another **branch**

(Siam Square & Pratunam map; ☎ 0 2255 9838; open 11.30am-10.30pm daily) on the 6th floor of the World Trade Centre on Th Ploenchit.

Mango Tree *(☎ 0 2236 1681; 37 Soi 6/Than Tawan; dishes from 150B; open lunch & dinner daily)*, off Th Surawong, offers classic Thai cuisine and live traditional music surrounded by historical photos and antiques. Recommended dishes include *plaa sămlii dàet diaw* (half-dried, half-fried cotton fish with spicy mango salad) and *kài bai toei* (chicken baked in pandanus leaves).

A good one-stop eating place with a lot of variety is the Silom Village Trade Centre, an outdoor shopping complex at Soi 24. Although it's basically a tourist spot with higher than average prices, the restaurants are of high quality and plenty of Thais dine here as well. **Silom Village** *(☎ 0 2234 4448; dishes 150-400B)* is the centrepiece with a shaded pavilion, outdoor tables and a menu of fresh seafood, and Chinese and Japanese dishes. Also in the trade centre, **Silom Coffee Bar** makes a good choice for a quick and casual meal.

Somboon Seafood *(☎ 0 2233 3104; cnr Th Surawong & Th Narathiwat Ratchanakharin; open 4pm-11pm daily)* is a famous, reasonably priced seafood restaurant known for the best crab curry in town. Soy-steamed sea bass *(plaa kràphong nêung sii-íu)* is also a speciality.

Mizu's Kitchen *(Th Patpong 1; dishes 150B; open lunch only)* has a loyal Japanese and Thai following for its inexpensive Japanese food, including Japanese-style steak. The place self-consciously evokes an Italian trattoria with chequered tablecloths and a crooning Sinatra as background music.

Harmonique *(☎ 0 2237 8175; Soi 34, Th Charoen Krung; dishes 60-150B; open 11am-10pm Mon-Sat)*, around the corner from the main post office, is a tiny but refreshing oasis in this extremely busy, smog-filled section of town. European-managed and unobtrusive, the little shop serves Thai food, French and Chinese bread plus a variety of tea, fruit shakes and coffee on Hokkien-style marble-topped tables – a pleasant spot to read while quenching your thirst.

Sara-Jane's *(☎ 0 2676 3338; 55/21 Th Narathiwat Ratchanakharin)*, about 100m southeast off Th Sathon Tai, has the same fantastic Isan and Italian food as the original (see the Siam Square section later). This branch has an outdoor eating area and beer garden, as well as indoor air-con seating. It's not far from the Chong Nonsi Skytrain station, and you can easily cross busy Th Sathon.

The Blue Elephant *(☎ 0 2673 9352; 233 Th Sathon Tai; dishes 200-500B; open lunch & dinner)* got its start in Brussels more than two decades ago as an exotic outpost of royal-Thai cuisine. After spreading to other foreign city's, The Blue Elephant boldly chose Bangkok, the cuisine's birth mother, as its 9th location. Set in a refurbished Sino-Thai colonial building with service fit for royalty, this newcomer promises fine dining within striking distance of the city's luxury hotels. Skip the set meals and choose wisely from the extensive menu of modernised ancient dishes – which range from idiot to savant. The salmon *lâap* (salad with mint leaves) and mesquitish *phàk bûng fai daeng* (stir-fried greens) are divine, while the Muslim (Matsaman) lamb curry is too sweet. The Blue Elephant is near St Louis Hospital at the Surasak Skytrain station.

Indian, Muslim & Burmese Towards the western end of Th Silom and Th Surawong, in an area known as Bangrak, Indian eateries begin to appear. Unlike most Indian restaurants in Bangkok, the menus in Bangrak tend to steer clear of the usual, boring predilection for north-Indian Moghul-style cuisine.

Madras Cafe *(☎ 0 2235 2128; 31/10-11 Trok 13, Th Silom; dishes 40-60B; open 9am-10pm daily)*, near the end of the lane, offers home-style south-Indian food (*dosa*, *idli*, *vada* etc). The owners also run a **guesthouse**, which attracts visiting Indians who are happy to wave a new face into the café.

Between Th Silom and Th Surawong, near Sri Mariamman Temple, **street vendors** sometimes sell Indian and Muslim snacks.

India Hut *(☎ 0 2635 7876; Th Surawong; dishes 90-250B; open lunch & dinner)*, opposite the Manohra Hotel, specialises in Nawabi (Lucknow) cuisine. The vegetarian samosa, and fresh prawns cooked with ginger, are particularly good.

Himali Cha-Cha *(☎ 0 2235 1569; Soi 47/1, Th Charoen Krung; dishes 135-215B; open lunch & dinner)* features north-Indian cuisine (vegie and meat options) at slightly higher prices. The founder, Cha-Cha, worked as a chef for India's last Viceroy; his son has taken over the kitchen here.

The Cholas *(dishes 50-80B)*, a small air-con place downstairs in the Woodlands Inn (off Soi 32, Th Charoen Krung), just north of the main post office, serves decent, no-fuss north-Indian food.

Sallim Restaurant *(Soi 32, Th Charoen Krung; dishes 50-70B)*, an open-air place around the corner from Woodlands, is even cheaper, with north-Indian, Malay and Thai-Muslim dishes – it's usually packed.

Naaz *(Soi 43 (Soi Saphan Yao); dishes 50-70B; open 7.30am-10.30pm daily)*, pronounced 'Naat' in Thai, is often cited as having the richest *khâo mòk kài* (chicken biryani) in the city. The milk tea is also very good, and daily specials include chicken masala and mutton korma. For dessert, the speciality of the house is *firni,* a Middle Eastern pudding spiced with coconut, almonds, cardamom and saffron.

Yogi *(Soi Phuttha Osot)* is a very simple and inexpensive, all-vegetarian Indian restaurant. Finding it is a little tricky since an expressway bisected the original approach from Th Charoen Krung. Now the best way to reach it is by walking north from Th Surawong along a lane opposite Th Mahesak and the New Fuji Hotel, then turn left at Soi Phuttha Osot. It's a little way down on the left – just have faith that you'll find it.

Muslim Restaurant *(1356 Th Charoen Krung; dishes under 40B)*, near the intersection of Th Charoen Krung and Th Silom, has been feeding various Lonely Planet authors for over 20 years. The faded walls and stainless steel tables don't make for the best decor, but an assortment of curries and rotis are displayed in a clean glass case for easy pointing and eye-catching allure. Masjid Mirasuddeen is a mosque on Soi 20 (Soi Pradit), off Th Silom, so **Muslim-food vendors** are common in that area.

Rabianthong Restaurant *(☎ 0 2237 0100; Th Silom; set lunch/dinner 270/290B)*, in the mezzanine area of Narai Hotel, offers a very good vegetarian section in its luncheon buffet on *wan phrá* (full-, half- and new-moon days).

European & American If you crave Western food, a variety of restaurants can be found on and around Th Patpong 1 and Patpong 2, a short walk from the Sala Daeng Skytrain station.

O'Reilly's Irish Pub *(☎ 0 2632 7515; 62/1-2 Th Silom; open 11am-2am daily)*, at the entrance to Thaniya Plaza (corner of Th Silom and Soi Thaniya), promotes itself as 'Thairish' – a Thai-Irish hybrid pub and features a lunch buffet and an evening happy hour. **Irish Xchange** *(☎ 0 2266 7160; 1-4 Sivadon Bldg, Th Convent; open lunch & dinner daily)* serves a lunch buffet (270B) from Monday to Friday, plus other international food daily. A **lunch-time vendor** sells a Muslim variation of *khâo mòk kài* in front of the pub.

Eat Me Restaurant *(☎ 0 2238 0931; Soi Phiphat 2, off Th Convent; dishes 130-280B; open 6pm-1am daily)* heralds the city's phoenix-like resurrection from the late, great economic crash. An international menu leaning towards Italy is perused amid chic, minimalist decor by a quick-draw cell-phone crowd. The works of modern Thai artists enjoy bimonthly exposure, and a weekend jazz band fills the spaces in between.

Folies Café-Patisserie *(29 Th Sathon Tai; open 11am-2pm)*, at the Alliance Française, serves inexpensive to moderately priced French dishes.

Coffee World, on the northern side of Th Silom, near the mouth of Soi 10, serves a variety of coffee, tea, Italian soda, sandwiches and pastries in a large, clean, California-style café. Foreign magazines and newspapers are on hand for a read.

Siam Square

This shopping area is interspersed with several low- and medium-priced restaurants as well as American fast-food franchises. Soi Lang Suan, off Th Ploenchit near Chit Lom Skytrain station, has a variety of dinner options. Unless otherwise indicated, the following places to stay can be found on the Siam Square & Pratunam map.

Thai & Other Asian Despite its Western name, **Sara-Jane's** *(☎ 0 2650 9992; Sindhorn Bldg, 130-132 Th Withayu; dishes 35-175B; open 11am-10.30pm)* serves very good Isan and Italian food in a casual air-con dining room, towards the back of the Sindhorn Building. There's another branch on Th Narathiwat Ratchanakharin (see the previous Thanon Silom section).

Khao Man Kai Siam *(Siam Chicken; 280 Th Phra Ram I; dishes 35-50B)*, on the Siam Square side of Th Phra Ram I and in the shadow of the Siam Skytrain station, is slick and sterile, but still maintains the calling card of a traditional *khâo man kài* (boiled chicken over rice with a lemongrass broth served on the side) shop – dangling chicken carcasses in front of the kitchen.

If you're staying on or nearby Soi Kasem San 1, you don't have to suck motorcycle fumes crossing Th Phra Ram I and Th Phayathai, to find something to eat. Besides the typical hotel coffee shops found on the lane, there are also two very good and inexpensive **curry-and-rice vendors** with tables along the east side of the soi. There is no need to worry about your lack of fluency in Thai, the staff are used to the 'point-and-serve' system. At the Th Phra Ram I entrance to Pranee Building hotel is a simple **restaurant** feeding local students; the menu has been poetically translated into English, including everyone's favourite 'fired rice and vegetables'.

The **World Trade Centre** *(cnr Th Ploenchit & Th Ratchadmri; Chit Lom Skytrain station)* has branches of several well-known restaurants, including **Vijit** (traditional Thai), **Lai Lai Suki** and **Chao Sua** (two sumptuous Chinese banquet-style places). There are also two **food centres** on the 6th floor serving standard Thai and Chinese dishes, which are only a little more expensive than the usual Bangkok food centres.

Whole Earth Restaurant *(☎ 0 2252 5574; 93/3 Soi Lang Suan; dishes 100-200B; open 11.30am-2pm & 5.30pm-11pm daily)* is a good Thai vegetarian restaurant with service to match. The upstairs room features low tables with floor cushions. Nonvegetarian dishes are also served.

Nguan Lee Lang Suan *(Central Bangkok map; cnr Soi Lang Suan & Th Sarasin)* is a semi-outdoor place specialising in Chinese-style seafood and *kài lâo daeng* (chicken steamed in Chinese herbs).

Le Lys *(☎ 0 2652 2401; 75 Sub-Soi 3, Soi Lang Suan; dishes 80-200B; open 11am-10.30pm daily)* offers a soothing respite from Bangkok's traffic and the pressures of formality. Tucked into a breezy colonial house surrounded by a garden, Le Lys prepares superb Thai dishes, such as *kaeng phèt mǔu yâang bai chà-om* (roast pork curry with acacia leaves), easily chosen from a menu accompanied by appetising photos. Some diners snack and drink in between sets of *la patenque* (French lawn bowling) in the restaurant's backyard.

International & Fusion Local chain **S&P Restaurant & Bakery** *(Soi 11; dishes 45-75B)* does an extensive menu of Thai specialities with a few Chinese, Japanese, European and vegetarian dishes, plus bakery items, coffee drinks and ice cream.

Hard Rock Cafe *(Soi 11, Siam Square; open until 2am daily)*, the Bangkok branch of the London anchor, serves good American and Thai food that's easily washed down with the evening's two-for-one beer specials. Look for the túk-túk captioned 'God is my co-pilot' coming out of the building's facade. The café stays open a bit later than many Siam Square eateries.

On both sides of Th Phra Ram I, in Siam Square and Siam Center, you'll find a battery of American **fast-food franchises**, which have recently added adaptations of Thai dishes to their menus. Prices are close to what you would pay in the West. Siam Center, Siam Discovery Center and MBK contain a bevy of good, moderately priced **coffee shops** and Western-food **restaurants**, which are often crowded with young Thais. Don't miss the 7th-floor **food centre** at MBK, where you'll also find a trippy, techno bowling alley, which feels like stepping into a video game.

Well-heeled bilinguals enjoy the high art of Thai service at neighbouring restaurants in the Mercury Tower. **Fabb Fashion Cafe** *(☎ 0 2658 6200; 540 Th Ploenchit; dishes 390-520B; open 11am-midnight daily)* serves Thai-Italian fusion in a swank dining room, with an evening jazz band. **Auberge DAB** *(☎ 0 2658 6222; dishes 400-15750B, set menu 950B)* is all French, with pan-fried duck liver in raspberry dressing, poached oysters wrapped in spinach leaves with champagne sauce and roast pigeon among the offerings.

Pan Pan Capri *(☎ 0 2252 7104; 45 Soi Lang Suan; dishes 120-190B; open dinner nightly)* is Italian-owned and popular for its wood-fired pizza (takeaway orders accepted), pasta, salads, gelato (the best in Thailand) and pastries. A low-calorie vegetarian menu is available on request. The dishes aren't as good as mama used to make but it scratches the tomato-and-garlic itch just fine.

Thanon Sukhumvit

This avenue, stretching east all the way to the city limits, has hundreds of Thai, Chinese and Western restaurants. The quality of the international fare, especially Middle Eastern cuisine, tends to exceed that of the local cuisine.

The following places to eat can be found on the Thanon Sukhumvit map.

Thai & Other Asian Near Asia Books, **Yong Lee Restaurant** *(no Roman-script sign; Soi 15, Th Sukhumvit; open lunch & dinner)* is a little grungy, but has excellent Thai and Chinese food at very reasonable prices, and is a long-time favourite among both Thai and faràng residents. There is another branch between Soi 35 and Soi 37, further down Th Sukhumvit.

Le Dalat *(☎ 0 2258 4192, 0 2260 1849; 47/1 Soi 23 • ☎ 0 2661 7967; 14 Soi 23; dishes from 200B; open 11.30am-2.30pm & 6pm-10pm daily)* has the most celebrated Vietnamese cuisine in the city. A house speciality is *năem neuang,* which is grilled meatballs that you place on steamed rice-flour wrappers, then add chunks of garlic, chilli, ginger, star fruit and mango along with a tamarind sauce, and finally wrap the whole thing into a lettuce bundle before popping it into your mouth.

Cabbages & Condoms *(☎ 0 2229 4610; Soi 12, Th Sukhumvit; dishes 150-200B; open 11am-10pm daily)*, about 50m from Th Sukhumvit next to the Population and Community Development Association (PDA) headquarters, uses familiar vegetables, such as celery and tomatoes, to create sufficiently complex flavours for those 'wading' into Thai food. Dishes like *yam wun sên* (mung-bean noodle salad) provide a source of raw vegetables that might otherwise go unfilled in this salad-less country. Instead of after-dinner mints, diners get packaged condoms; all proceeds go towards sex-education and AIDS-prevention programmes in Thailand.

For a shot of the LA blonde wood-and-metal look, try the enormously trendy **Greyhound Cafe** *(2nd floor, The Emporium, Soi 24, Th Sukhumvit; dishes 100-200B)*. The hybrid menu emphasises updated Thai cuisine after a sojourn in southern Europe.

Kuppa *(☎ 0 2663 0495; 39 Soi 16, Th Sukhumvit; dishes 150B lunch, 400B dinner; open 10.30am-11.30pm daily)* is Miami Beach meets Bangkok, with sleek reflecting pools and modern rattan furniture attracting a fashionable bunch – particularly for late breakfasts. Real salads (no iceberg here) and US grain–fed beef are some of the menu standouts.

Hua Lamphong Food Station *(☎ 0 2661 3538; 92/1 Soi 34, Th Sukhumvit)*, nowhere near Bangkok's main railway station despite the name, is so well hidden that your arrival is like a journey to the provinces. Decorated with country Thai furnishings, it serves delicious Isan and northern-Thai food, and has traditional music nightly from 8pm to 10pm. From Th Sukhumvit, take a motorcycle taxi to the restaurant, which is too hard to find on foot.

Vientian Kitchen *(☎ 0 2258 6171; 8 Soi 36, Th Sukhumvit; dishes 120-200B; open 11am-midnight)*, near the beginning of the lane, is easier to find than Hua Lamphong, if your dinner venture fails. You'll find all the Isan and Laos 'soul-food' standards, such as *lâap* with duck lips, fried frog and deep-fried chicken innards. Smothered in chilli peppers, you'll swear it was chicken-breast meat. For the less daring, there are plenty of middle-of-the-road options, too. The closest Skytrain station is Thong Lor.

Indian & Muslim In front of the Swiss Park Hotel, **Mrs Balbir's** *(☎ 0 2651 0498; 155/18 Soi 11/1; dishes 150-220B, buffet lunch 150B; open Tues-Sun noon-10.30pm daily)* serves both vegetarian and nonvegetarian Indian food (mostly north Indian) to a predominately tourist crowd; don't write off the food though, the missus still knows her stuff. Mrs Balbir has been teaching Indian and Thai cooking for many years, and has her own Indian grocery service as well. On the first Wednesday of every month, she offers a **walking tour** of Little India (550B).

Just off of Th Sukhumvit and Soi 3 (Soi Nana Neua), there is a winding maze of cramped sub-lanes known as Little Arabia, where the number of Middle Eastern and African residents make Thais seem like foreigners. **Al-Hussain** *(dishes 50-120B)* is an open-air café on the corner of Soi 3/5; there's also an indoor air-con dining area. A steam table holds a range of vegetarian, chicken, mutton and fish curries, along with *dahl* (curried lentils), *aloo gobi* (spicy potatoes and cauliflower), *naan* (bread) and rice. **Schiller's Inn**, across the same lane, is a slightly pricier indoor place that provides hookahs for Middle Eastern gentlemen, who while away the afternoon smoking in front of the restaurant. Similar places nearby include **Mehmaan**, **Akbar's**, **Al Hamra**, **Ali** and **Shaharazad**.

Rang Mahal *(☎ 0 2261 7100; Soi 18; entrees 150-230B, set vegetarian/nonvegetarian lunch 350/370B; open lunch & dinner daily)* is an elegant rooftop restaurant in the Hotel Rembrandt, offering north- and south-Indian 'royal cuisine' with overly attentive service and stunning cityscape views. In addition to the regular menu, there are two set menus. On Sunday the restaurant puts on a sumptuous **Indian buffet** *(adult/child 510/295B)* between 11am and 2pm. An open-air observation platform on the same floor is reason enough for a visit.

International Cuisine Down the same lane as Cabbages & Condoms, **Crepes & Co** *(☎ 0 2653 3990; 18/1 Soi 12, Th Sukhumvit; dishes 140-280B, open 9am-midnight daily)* is a cute cottage creperie that serves crepes of all kinds. European-style breakfasts and a nice selection of Mediterranean dishes are also sailed onto garden-view tables.

Jool's Bar & Restaurant *(☎ 0 2252 6413; Soi 4/Soi Nana Tai)*, just past Nana Entertainment Plaza, generously feeds homesick Brits solid and liquid sustenance. **Ship Inn**, on the western side of Soi 23 just around the corner from Soi Cowboy, is a small but authentic-style British pub with food and libation.

Bei Otto *(☎ 0 2262 0892; 1 Soi 20, Th Sukhumvit)* is one of the most popular German restaurants in town and has a comfortable bar. Attached are a bakery, deli and butcher shop.

Bier-Kutsche *(☎ 0 2252 5776; 4 Soi 15, Th Sukhumvit; dishes 120-200B; open breakfast, lunch & dinner daily)* serves large portions of German and Austrian food; there are recent German-language newspapers on hand and an attached open-air bar.

Bourbon St Bar & Restaurant *(☎ 0 2259 0328; Soi 22; dishes 200-400B; open breakfast, lunch & dinner daily)*, behind Mambo Cabaret, introduces Bangkok to Louisiana's revered mudbug – the crayfish. If New Orleanians ever left their fair city, they would find a suitable menu emphasising Cajun and Creole cooking, with some Mexican dishes thrown in for good measure; some nights there is also free live music.

Larry's Dive Center, Bar & Grill *(☎ 0 2663 4563; ⓔ bangkok@larrysdive.com; Soi 22; dishes 95-175B)*, in a bright-yellow two-storey building, serves American and Tex-Mex fare amid kitsch sand-floor-and-potted-palms decor. The fake newspaper menu ('largest circulation of any newspaper on Soi 22') lists stuffed potato skins, salads, quesadillas, nachos, chilli, spicy chicken wings and Larry's food guarantee: 'Served in 30 minutes, or it's cold.' There's an attached dive shop, should you get the urge to go snorkelling in a nearby canal.

Le Banyan *(☎ 0 2253 5556; 59 Soi 8, Th Sukhumvit; dishes 390-450B; open 6.30pm-9.30pm Mon-Sat)*, which is in a charming early Ratanakosin-style house surrounded by a lush garden, is one of the top French restaurants in the city and probably the best that isn't associated with a luxury hotel. The French-managed kitchen covers the territory from *ragout d'escargot* (snail stew) to *maigret de canard avec foie gras* (duck breast with duck liver). It has a superb wine list. The restaurant is further down the lane than you would expect; keep an eye out for the artistically trimmed bamboo hedge.

De Meglio *(☎ 0 2651 3838; Soi 11; dishes 160-400B)* is an elegant but comfortable Italian restaurant with a creative, seasonal menu, including a tasty selection of vegetarian entrees. Affordable set menus fill the breakfast, lunch and dinner needs.

Señor Pico's of Los Angeles *(☎ 0 2261 7100; 2nd floor, Hotel Rembrandt, Soi 18, Th Sukhumvit; dishes 250-500B; open dinner nightly)* offers the city's best Mexican food and reasonably authentic Tex-Mex cuisine, including the usual suspects like fajitas, *carnitas* (spiced-pork tortilla) and nachos. Live Latin music is the norm most evenings and the dress code prohibits sleeveless shirts or sandals.

Chinatown, Hualamphong & Phahurat

Some of Bangkok's best Chinese and Indian food is found in these adjacent districts, but because few tourists stay in this part of town (for good reason – it's simply too congested) they rarely make any eating forays into the area. A few old Chinese restaurants have moved from Chinatown to locations with less traffic, but many places are still hanging on to their venerable Chinatown addresses, where the atmosphere is still a part of the eating experience.

Most specialise in southern Chinese cuisine, particularly that of coastal Guangdong and Fujian Provinces. This means seafood, rice noodles and dumplings are often the best choices. Unless otherwise indicated, these places to eat can be found on the Chinatown & Phahurat map.

Large, banquet-style Chinese places are mostly found along Th Yaowarat and Th Charoen Krung, and include **Laem Thong** *(38 Th Bamrungrat)*, just off Th Charoen Krung, and **Shangarila Restaurant**, near the corner of Th Yaowarat and Th Ratchawong. Each has an extensive menu, including good-quality dim sum (220B to 500B) before lunch time.

The best noodle and dumpling shops are hidden away on smaller lanes and alleys. **Chiang Ki** *(54 Soi Bamrungrat)* is a funky place where the 100B *khâo tôm plaa* (rice soup with fish) belies the casual surroundings – no place does it better. **Kong Lee** *(137/141 Th Ratchawong)* has a very loyal clientele for its *bà-mìi hâeng* (dry-fried wheat noodles) – again reportedly the best in Bangkok.

Hong Kong Noodles *(136/Trok Itsaranuphap, Th Charoen Krung)*, deep in the heart of a vendor-lined soi, does a busy trade in steaming bowls of roast duck noodles; if you can find a seat, it has a nice vista of the ensuing commerce. Next door is its sister restaurant **Hong Kong Tim Sum**, for dim sum and steamed pork buns on the go.

Pet Tun Jao Tha *(Thanon Silom map; no Roman-script sign; 945 Soi Wanit 2)* is another great noodle place, on the southeastern edge of Chinatown, opposite the Harbour Department building. The restaurant's name means 'Harbour Department Stewed Duck'; the speciality is *kŭaytĭaw* served with duck or goose, which is either roasted or stewed.

All-night **food hawkers** set up along Th Yaowarat at the Th Ratchawong intersection, opposite Yaowarat Market and near the Cathay department store; this is the least expensive place to dine out in Chinatown.

Suki Jeh Yu Jing *(Central Bangkok map; Th Phra Ram IV; open 6am-10pm daily)*, a Chinese restaurant just 70m from Hualamphong station, serves excellent, if a bit pricey, vegetarian food in a clean, air-con atmosphere. The fruit shakes are particularly well made; this is a great place to fortify yourself with food and drink while waiting for a train. The service can be slow, so leave plenty of time to make your train departure. The Roman-script sign reads 'Vegetarian'.

Over in Phahurat, the Indian fabric district, most places serve north-Indian cuisine, which is heavily influenced by Moghul or Persian flavours and spices. **Royal India** *(☎ 0 2221 6565, 392/1 Th Chakraphet; dishes under 80B)* qualifies as one of the best north-Indian restaurants in town. Follow the signs off Th Chakraphet into a concrete alley. Royal India also has a branch on Th Khao San in Banglamphu, but it's not as good. The lane before Royal India has a handful of other **Indian restaurants**, should you be thwarted by a full dining room.

ATM department store *(Th Chakraphet)*, near the pedestrian bridge, has a food centre on the top floor that features cheap and tasty Indian food. Alongside the ATM building, on Soi ATM, are several small **teahouses** that serve very inexpensive Indian and Nepali food, including lots of fresh chapati and strong milk tea. At a shop called Pandey's you can buy Indian spices and cooking ware. In the afternoons a Sikh man sets up a **pushcart** on the corner of Soi ATM and Th Chakraphet, and sells vegetarian samosa, often cited as the best in Bangkok.

Wedged between the western edge of Chinatown and the northern edge of Phahurat, the three-storey **Old Siam Plaza** shopping centre houses a number of Thai, Chinese and Japanese restaurants. The most economical places are on the 3rd floor, where a **food centre** serves relatively inexpensive meals from 10am to 5pm.

During the annual Vegetarian Festival (which is in September/October and centred around Wat Mangkon Kamalawat on Th Charoen Krung), Bangkok's Chinatown becomes a virtual orgy of vegetarian Thai and Chinese cuisine. The restaurants and noodle shops in the area offer hundreds of different dishes. The temporary **food stalls** set up along Soi Vanit 2 off Soi 20, Th Charoen Krung, offer the most generous spreads.

Soi Ngam Duphli

Just One *(Central Bangkok map; ☎ 0 2679 7932; 58 Soi 1, Th Sathon Tai)*, an outdoor Thai place opposite Tungmahamek Privacy Hotel and beside the Malaysia Hotel, is a popular lunch spot.

There's a cafeteria-style **food centre** *(Central Bangkok map; Th Phra Ram IV, open 7am-2pm)* on the 11th floor of Lumphini Tower. Opposite, on the same road, is a warren of **food vendors** with cheap eats.

Ratsstube *(Central Bangkok map; ☎ 0 2287 2822; Goethe Institut, Soi Goethe, Soi Atakanprasit; open 11am-2.30pm & 5.30pm-10pm Mon-Fri, 11am-10pm Sat & Sun)*, in the Thai-German Cultural Centre, is another restaurant in this area worth mentioning. Home-made sausages and set meals for around 150B attract a large and steady clientele. The softly lit Euro-Asian decor borders on rococo.

River Restaurants & Dinner Cruises

River restaurants come in all shapes and prices, but all share the cool evening breezes and a knack for extraordinary seafood dishes, from cultured to comfort.

Baan Rim Nam *(Thanon Silom map; ☎ 0 2860 4500; 723 Th Charoen Nakhon)*, across the river from Bangkok, has an open-air pavilion to dine amid the bright lights of the Shangri-La and Oriental Hotels. Take a cross-river ferry (2B), from the end of the lane in front of the Shangri-La Hotel, to the wooden pier on the Thonburi shore. Wind through the narrow lanes until you come to a main road (Th Charoen Nakhon), then turn left. Near a large shopping centre, follow the signs for the restaurant. The ferry runs until around 2am.

Supatra River House *(Ko Ratanakosin map; ☎ 0 2411 0305; 266 Soi Wat Rakhang, Thonburi; dinner 200-400B; lunch 130-150B; open daily)* is modern elegance in a traditional Thai-style house. The restaurant is perfectly situated in a crook in the river to afford views of Wat Phra Kaew and Wat Arun – most stunning at night when both temples are illuminated. Highly recommended is anything in the seafood category, where the kitchen particularly excels. Dinner can be followed with a theatre performance at the restaurant's affiliated stage, Patravadi Theatre. A free ferry service is available from Tha Mahathat to the restaurant; reservations are recommended.

Krua Rakhang Thong *(Ko Ratanakosin map; dishes under 150B)* is the trailer-park neighbour to well-manicured Supatra River House, with similar (and cheaper) river views. It serves excellent Thai food, including a good selection of vegetarian dishes. Particularly good is the *sôm-tam yâwt má-phráo àwn* (spicy salad) made with coconut shoots. A small outdoor section upstairs has a few tables, including one or two with the famous dual-temple view. The restaurant is a lovely walk from Tha Wang Lang (reached from the Bangkok side by a cross-river ferry at Tha Chang); from the pier turn left at the first through street past the market crowded with vegie sellers and vendors glued to the same TV soap operas. The Roman-script sign at the entrance reads 'River View'.

Yok Yor Khlongsan *(Thanon Silom map: ☎ 0 2437 1121; dishes 100-200B)* is a floating restaurant opposite River City shopping complex on the Thonburi side of the river. It runs inexpensive evening dinner cruises (8pm to 10pm) – you order from the regular menu and pay a nominal 70B charge for the boat service.

Silver Spoon *(Central Bangkok map; Th Krung Kasem; dishes 70-200B)*, next door to Tha Thewet, has a magnificent view of the elegant Saphan Phra Ram XIII (King Rama XIII Bridge). Dining is casual and relaxed, and the satisfying dishes won't hurt that shrinking wallet.

There are a number of companies that run dinner cruises. Prices cost 120B to 1200B per person depending on how far the boats go and whether dinner is included in the fare. For more information, see River Trips earlier in this chapter.

Hotel Restaurants

Many of Bangkok's luxury hotels provide memorable – if expensive – eating experiences. With Western cuisine, particularly, the quality usually far exceeds anything found in Bangkok's independent restaurants. Some of the city's best Chinese restaurants are also located in hotels.

If you're on a budget, check to see if a lunch buffet is available on weekdays; these are usually the best deals, ranging from 300B to 600B per person. Dinner entrees do a quick ascent to 700B to 1500B for a main dish. Also check the *Bangkok Post* and the *Nation* for weekly specials presented by visiting chefs from far-flung corners of the globe – Morocco, Mexico City, Montreal, no matter how obscure, they've probably done the Bangkok hotel circuit.

Lunch usually runs from 11.30am to 2pm, and dinner from 5pm to 10pm. Reservations are recommended, and business casual (long sleeves, closed-toe shoes) will probably suffice, at least for daytime dining. The lunch buffets are popular business rendezvous points where the Western-style suits outnumber the leisure set.

The Oriental Hotel (see the Thanon Silom map) has six restaurants, all managed by world-class chefs, and buffet lunches are offered at several of these. The hotel's **China House** (*☎ 0 2236 0400 ext 3378*), set in a charming restored private residence opposite the hotel's main wing, has one of the best Chinese kitchens in Bangkok, with an emphasis on Cantonese cooking. The lunch-time dim sum is superb and a bargain by luxury hotel standards. The Oriental's **Lord Jim's** (*☎ 0 2236 0400 ext 3202*) is designed to imitate the interior of a 19th-century Asian steamer, with a view of the river; the menu focuses on seafood (lunch buffet available).

Bai Yun (*☎ 0 2679 1200*), on the 60th floor of the Banyan Tree (see the Thanon Silom map), specialises in nouvelle Cantonese – an East-West fusion.

Chinatown (*☎ 0 2236 9999 ext 2299*), in Dusit Thani (see the Thanon Silom map), focuses on Chao Zhou (Chiu Chau) cuisine as well as Cantonese. Dim sum, drunken chicken and shark's fin soup are just a few of the delicacies on the lunch-buffet menu. The Dusit also has the highly reputed **Mayflower**, with pricey Cantonese cuisine, and the Vietnamese **Thien Duong**.

Jade Garden (*☎ 0 2233 7060*), at the Montien Hotel (see the Thanon Silom map), offers hotel dim sum almost as good as that at the Dusit Thani or Oriental hotels – but at less than a third of the price. Although not quite as fancy in presentation, the food is nonetheless impressive.

For French food, the leading contenders are **Ma Maison** (*☎ 0 2253 0123*) at the Hilton International (see the Siam Square & Pratunam map), **Le Normandie** (*☎ 0 2236 0400 ext 3380*) at the Oriental Hotel and **Regent Grill** (*☎ 0 2251 6127*) at the Regent Bangkok (see the Siam Square & Pratunam map).

Grappino Italian Restaurant (*☎ 0 2653 9000*) is a very posh and formal restaurant in the Amari Watergate (see the Siam Square & Pratunam map) and offers one of the best Italian dining experiences in the city. All pasta and bread is prepared fresh on the premises daily, and the small but hi-tech wine cellar is one of Bangkok's best – the grappa selection is unmatched.

Biscotti (*☎ 0 2255 5443*), in the Regent Bangkok, is of a similar quality – or perhaps better – than Grappino's, and is probably the busiest Italian restaurant in the city. It serves inventive dishes for relatively reasonable prices, considering the location and the high quality of the cooking.

Angelini's (*☎ 0 2236 7777 ext 1766*), in the Shangri-La Hotel (see the Thanon Silom map), is more relaxed and serves fine Italian cuisine in some of Bangkok's most impressively chic decor. An array of upmarket grappa are available at the sleek bar, where a live pop band plays mood music.

Colonnade Restaurant (*☎ 0 2287 0222*) is Sukhothai Hotel's minimalist restaurant (see the Thanon Silom map), which lays out a huge Sunday brunch with made-to-order lobster bisque. A jazz trio supplies background music.

ENTERTAINMENT

Bangkok's entertainment scene goes well beyond its naughty-nightlife image, a hangover from the days when the City of Angels was an R&R stop for GIs serving in Vietnam in the 1960s and early '70s.

Today, Bangkok offers a heady assortment of entertainment venues, nightclubs, bars, cafés and clubs appealing to every sort of taste. Many specialise in live music – rock, country and western, Thai pop, jazz and rhythm and blues. Bangkok is prone to trends, such as salsa clubs and brew pubs, which are short-lived firework displays that leave town without a trace.

All bars and clubs are supposed to close at 1am or 2am (the latter closing time is for places with dance floors and/or live music); in most cases this is enforced by stone-faced policemen who usher out the dazed customers.

Parts of Banglamphu near the tourist strip of Th Khao San are one big outdoor party, where small stalls set up tables and chairs for a night of Beer Chang drinking. Surprisingly, even Th Khao San attracts a lot of young Thais who come to shop, get fake dreadlocks or swill beer with the Westerners. A more local scene can be found on weekends at the restaurant-bars along Th Phra Athit (see the Banglamphu map); these places feature live music (see Places to Eat previously).

Th Sukhumvit has a lot of diversity in its nightlife: there are a handful of expat bars and trendy clubs, and every short-lived trend makes a run on the street. The city's ever present go-go scene has two outposts: Soi Cowboy and Nana.

Th Silom has a lot of contrasting night crawlers. The infamous go-go district of Patpong is off Th Silom, as well as a late-night souvenir market, low-key English-style pubs and yuppie bars for unwinding office workers.

To get an idea of what's available, check the entertainment listings in the daily *Bangkok Post* and the *Nation*. Possibilities include classical music performances, rock concerts, videotheque dancing, Asian music and theatre ensembles on tour, art shows and dinner theatre.

Pubs & Bars

Trendy with locals these days are bars that strive for a sophisticated atmosphere, with good service, drinks and music. The Thais often call them pubs but they bear little resemblance to a traditional English pub. Some are 'theme' bars, conceived around a particular aesthetic, and most serve imported liquor and house cocktails, which despite the various names all taste like Tom Collins.

Center Khao Sarn *(Thanon Khao San map; Th Khao San)* has a front-row view of the street's spectacle as well as pool tables. **Gulliver's Traveler's Tavern** *(Thanon Khao San map; cnr Th Khao San & Th Chakraphong)* is a lot like your local sports bar. A central bar is flanked by pool tables, sports shows on TV and single men contemplating the shape of their beer bottles. **Hole in the Wall** *(Thanon Khao San map)*, on a short dead-end lane, affords a cheap refuge from Khao San's inundation of fisherman pants and pierced navels. It's an on-and-off-again place (often closed during slow months).

Susie Pub and its sister pub, **Austin Pub**, attract a lot of Thai university students celebrating birthdays. Both are beautiful bars, but the music tends to gravitate towards too-sweet Western pop music. Venture further down the lane past Austin Pub, to find open-air beer stalls blasting Bob Marley and techno. An odd neighbour to this clique is the **Rare Art Gallery**, which features local photographers working in black-and-white.

Salvador Dali *(Banglamphu map; Th Rambutri)*, tucked away amid a row of noodle stands, is a comfortable, two-storey air-con bar with a more intimate, speakeasy feel that tiptoes past the official closing time. An outdoor **beer stand**, with lots of drunken socialising, sets up nearby. Further east on Th Rambutri is **Molly Bar** *(Thanon Khao San map)*, a lively bar with outdoor tables, where beach bums decompress for the flight home.

Bangkok Bar *(Banglamphu map; 149 Soi Rambutri)*, next door to Sawasdee House, is a slick newcomer to the ratty backpacker zone. Smooth samba beats waft like incense over the bar's cosy corners, where Western-Thai couples sip fairy-juice cocktails.

Three low-key, British-style taverns can be found off Th Sukhumvit. Owner, Big Dave, sits at the helm of **Jool's** *(Thanon Sukhumvit map; Soi 4)*, near Nana Entertainment Plaza, steering the sinking ship through the district's commercial 'friendliness'. With a ring of the captain's bell, indicating a free round, the mood shifts to a

Bangkok Goes Smoke-free

Does your smoker's cough seem to be getting worse in Bangkok? If you've begun to suspect those cheap Thai cigarettes instead of the pollution, the Thai government has beaten you to the ashtray. In November 2002, most air-con buildings were declared smoke-free. The list includes such obvious places as school buses, fitness and shopping centres and libraries. But wait, even air-con bars (although enforcement is nonexistent) and restaurants are covered by the ban. The list-makers also threw in public piers, telephone booths and beauty parlours. Now if the government could only do something about those diesel-smoking buses, clean air could be a new Bangkok attraction.

good-times drinking club. **Bull's Head & Angus Steakhouse** *(Thanon Sukhumvit map; Soi 33/1, Th Sukhumvit)* is a beautiful galleried bar that's well suited to imagining foggy London nights; infrequent comedy shows here make light of the expat life. **Ship Inn** *(9/1 Soi 23; open 9am-midnight)*, just around the corner from Soi Cowboy, attracts a quiet drinking crowd. The bar is as well stocked as a ship captain's quarters.

Suan Ahahn Pa Loet Rot *(Thanon Sukhumvit map; ☎ 0 2258 5070; Soi 33/1)*, two doors closer to Th Sukhumvit, offers a similar kind of escapism but it's more for displaced Thais. On its patio, shaded by the hair-like tendrils of an ancient banyan tree, tipplers are temporarily transported to the Thai countryside. Even the squat toilets are authentic.

Cheap Charlie's *(Thanon Sukhumvit map; Soi 11, Th Sukhumvit)* is a well-hidden beer stall on a sub-lane off Soi 11, past De Meglio's Italian restaurant. Look for the 'Sabai Sabai Massage' sign and a crowd of foreigners standing around drinking beers cloaked in koozies (stubby holders). Decorated country-Thai style, this wooden stall started out selling cigarettes, graduated to beer and now has a faithful following of neighbourhood characters.

Londoner Brew Pub *(Thanon Sukhumvit map; ☎ 0 2261 0238; Soi 33, Th Sukhumvit, open 11am-1am)*, in the basement of the UBC II Building, brews its own beers and ales and runs a bevy of promotions to entertain the swillers. Quiz nights, daily happy hours and promotions for foreign-language

SIAM SQUARE & PRATUNAM

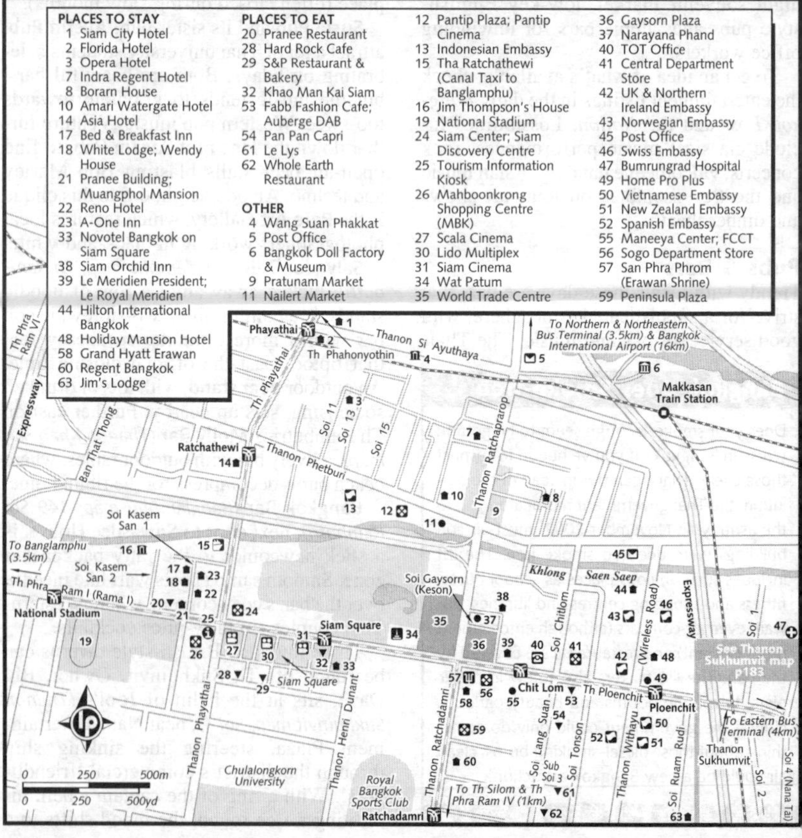

teachers bring in the crowds. Football matches and rock bands complete the bar's weekly engagements.

Irish Xchange *(Thanon Silom map; ☎ 0 2266 7160; 1-4 Sivadon Bldg, Th Convent)*, just around the corner from Th Silom, is one of the few places in Bangkok that serves draught Guinness. The interior wooden panels, glass mirrors and bench seating were all custom-made and imported from Ireland. Bands of varying quality play from Tuesday to Saturday, and the place is often packed from 6pm until closing.

O'Reilly's Irish Pub *(Thanon Silom map; ☎ 0 2632 7515; 62/1-2 Th Silom; open from 11am daily)*, at the entrance to Thaniya Plaza (corner of Th Silom and Soi Thaniya), draws a slow pint of Guinness or Kilkenny in a comparatively low-key setting that resembles an old camera shop. Early drinkers will like O'Reilly's opening time. Both pubs feature daily happy hours when their otherwise pricey beers are temporarily discounted.

The Barbican Bar *(Thanon Silom map; 9 Soi Thaniya)*, in the same block as massage parlours for Japanese businessmen, is a straight-laced upmarket bar, where office crews come for happy hour and stay until closing time.

Hard Rock Cafe *(Siam Square & Pratunam map; ☎ 0 2254 0830; Soi 11, Siam Square)* has a guitar-shaped bar and features the full range of cocktails and a small assortment of local and imported beers. The crowd is an ever-changing assortment of Thais, expats and tourists. From 10pm onwards there's also live music.

Hotel bars are a hot commodity in this skyscraper city. For slick aerial views, the place to go is the 84-storey **Baiyoke Sky Hotel** *(Th Ratchaprarop, Pratunam)*, the tallest building in Thailand. On the 77th floor there's an **observation deck** *(open 24hr)*, or you can check out the cityscape while dining in one of the **restaurants** on the 78th and 76th floors. **Compass Rose** *(Thanon Silom map; Th Sathon Tai; open 11.30am-1am)*, a bar on the 59th floor of the Banyan Tree, is also sky high.

One half of the **Regent Hotel** lobby is devoted to cigar smokers, with Dominican and Cuban brands available from the hotel's humidor; the Regent claims the largest selection of single-malt whiskies in Asia.

La Casa del Habano *(Thanon Silom map; Oriental Hotel)* offers around 25 brands of Cuban cigars from US$3 to US$120 each, with a tiny lounge equipped with a select list of fine cognacs, port and single-malt whiskies. Other hotel cigar lounges include **Cigar Cafe** *(Siam Square & Pratunam map; Hilton International)*, **Siam Havana** *(Thanon Silom map; Dusit Thani)* and **Club 54** *(Thanon Silom map; Montien Hotel)*.

Live Music

Bangkok's live-music scene has expanded rapidly over the past decade or so. Most bands, with varying success, are tributes to Western music; but even if the accent isn't Mick Jagger, a familiar tune can work wonders on a world wanderer.

Saxophone Pub & Restaurant *(Central Bangkok map; ☎ 0 2246 5472; 3/8 Th Phayathai; shows 9.30pm)* is a Bangkok institution for reggae, rhythm and blues, jazz and blues. Reminiscent of a German beer cellar, it is a comfortable venue with seats encircling the band or perched in the 2nd-floor alcoves. On Sunday there's an open jam session. The bar-restaurant serves surprisingly good food. From the Skytrain station's elevated walkway, descend the stairs near the night market.

Not to be overlooked is the strip of music bars along Th Sarasin, including the small jazz club **Brown Sugar** *(Central Bangkok map)*.

Ad Here the 13th *(Banglamphu map; 13 Th Samsen)*, next door to Khlong Banglamphu, is a cramped neighbourhood joint with a soulful house band that plays blues at 10pm nightly. It does a version of 'Me and Bobby McGee' that will make you swear Janice Joplin has been reincarnated. Everyone knows each other, so don't be shy about mingling.

Concept CM2, a multi-themed complex in the basement of the Novotel Bangkok on Siam Square, hosts a rotation of Western bands and Thai recording artists interspersed with DJ dance music.

Radio City *(Thanon Silom map; ☎ 0 2266 4567; Soi Patpong 1)*, next to the Madrid Restaurant, has a talented house band that performs oldies from the 1960s, '70s and '80s. Occasionally Thai Elvis and Tom Jones impersonators who perform here really get the crowd going. Come late with a sufficient amount of social lubrication to enjoy the vacation-land cheesiness of the place.

Dance Fever *(☎ 0 2247 4295; 71 Th Ratchadaphisek)*, a large club in the burgeoning 'Ratchada' entertainment district, features a state-of-the-art sound and lighting system, giant video screens, a bar and restaurant. International bands such as Bush and Blur have played here.

Metal Zone *(Central Bangkok map; ☎ 0 2255 1913; Soi Lang Suan)* offers Thai heavy metal – with plenty of hair throwing and lip jutting – nightly. Along with the dungeons-and-dragons decor is a regular line-up of bands authentically producing everything from thrash to Gothic to speed metal, Ozzy squeal to Axel rasp, even a few convoluted Helmet tunes. The volume level is perfect – loud enough for chest compression, but not so loud as to extract blood from the ears. **Rock Pub** *(☎ 0 2208 9664; Th Phayathai)*, opposite the Asia Hotel, is similar to Metal Zone.

Hard Rock Cafe *(Soi 11, Siam Square)* features live rock music, including some big names, most evenings from around 10pm to 12.30am.

Witch's Tavern *(☎ 0 2391 9791; 306/1 Soi 55, Th Sukhumvit)* is a spacious bar with leather couches and chairs arranged in clusters like in a hotel lobby. Jazz and folk bands start up around 8.30pm. At 10.30pm the house cover band takes over the stage, accepting requests from the audience; romantic ballads get the biggest round of applause from the mainly Thai crowd.

Imageries By The Glass *(2 Soi 24, Th Sukhumvit)*, owned by Jirapan Ansvananada, a Thai composer-musician, boasts a huge sound board and closed-circuit TV for its stage shows, which welcome local as well as foreign bands of all genres. This is a classic Thai nightclub with very polished bands verging towards canned.

The Oriental's famous **Bamboo Bar** has live lounge jazz nightly in an elegant atmosphere. The Sukhothai Hotel's **Colonnade** offers jazz from Tuesday to Saturday.

Discos & Dance Clubs

Bangkok is famous for its hi-tech discos that feature mega-watt sound systems, giant video screens and the latest in light-show technology. The clientele for these dance palaces is mostly young moneyed Thais experimenting with lifestyles of conspicuous affluence, plus the occasional Bangkok celebrity and a sprinkling of bloodshot-eyed expats.

Cover charges are standard: around 400B on weeknights and around 600B on weekends, including three complimentary drinks. Prices and the number of complimentary drinks will vary depending on how well you're dressed. Most places don't begin filling up until after 11pm.

Phuture *(Greater Bangkok map; Th Ratchadaphisek)*, attached to the north side of the Chaophya Park Hotel, once enjoyed the fickle title of the 'best' disco. **Ministry of Sound** *(Thanon Sukhumvit map; ☎ 0 2229 5850; 2 Soi 12, Th Sukhumvit)*, a recent arrival from Britain, devotes several floors to local and luminary DJs including a well-publicised visit from veteran Paul Oakenfold. Glam night, old skool and various shades of electronica are spotlighted throughout the week.

Narcissus *(Thanon Sukhumvit map; ☎ 0 2258 2549; 112 Soi 23, Th Sukhumvit)* is a more exclusive, hi-tech place frequented by well-heeled Thais and Thai celebrities. **Orbit** *(Greater Bangkok map; ☎ 0 2261 3991; Soi 26, Th Sukhumvit; admission 500B)*, formerly known as Taurus, flexes some serious money muscle with half of Thailand's Mercedes Benz fleet parked out the front.

Q Bar *(Thanon Sukhumvit map; ☎ 0 2252 3274; Soi 11, Th Sukhumvit)*, a Ho Chi Minh City refugee, is *soooo* New York circa five minutes ago. Black lights and neon are the only navigational tools through this minimalist two-storey club of glowing cocktails (including absinthe) and spike heels. DJs drive a groovy beat from hip-hop to Latin, and everyone has their own dance moves, some of which are straight off a Nana stage. To find it, take Soi 11 all the way to the end and hang a left; it will be a short jog over from there. The dress code calls for no sandals and no shorts.

A string of small dance clubs on Soi 2 and Soi 4 (Soi Jaruwan), both parallel to Soi Patpong 1 and 2, off Th Silom, attracts a mixed clubbing crowd. The dance clubs on Soi 2 swing towards a predominantly gay crowd, but have become more integrated as word got around about the great dance scene. Most places collect cover charges of around 100B to 300B depending on the night of the week; the smaller ones are free. Things don't get started here until relatively late – around midnight. **Lucifer** *(Thanon Silom map; Patpong 1)*, upstairs from Radio City (see Live Music previously), has become one of the most popular techno/rave dance clubs in town. **DJ Station** on Soi 2 and **Tapas Bar** on Soi 4 are good places to start the night.

Go-Go Bars

Bangkok's infamous go-go bars are a serious business that typically cater to men only, whether straight or gay. They come in blocked-off districts concentrated on Soi Cowboy between Soi 21/Asoke and Soi 23 off Th Sukhumvit; in the Nana Entertainment Plaza, on Soi 4/Nana Tai off Th Sukhumvit; and in the world-famous Patpong area, between Th Silom and Th Surawong.

Patpong has calmed down a lot over the years and now draws more sightseers than flesh-seekers. These days it has evolved into an open-air market where commerce has shifted from erotica to fake designer watches and exotic foodstuffs. There are still a handful of 35 or 40 go-go bars, mainly concentrated on Soi Patpong 2, but you are likely to see more *kàthoey* (transvestites) on Th Khao San than in the pick-up bars. Most downstairs clubs, with names like **King's Castle** and **Pussy Galore**, feature go-go dancing where women and couples are welcome; the real raunch is kept behind closed doors. Avoid bars touting 'free' sex shows as there are usually hidden charges and when you try to ditch the outrageous bill the doors are suddenly blocked by muscled bouncers. An exception is **Supergirls**, infamous for its sex-on-a-flying motorcycle show. The 2am closing law is strictly enforced on Soi Patpong 1 and 2.

The gay men's equivalent can be found on nearby Soi Thaniya, Soi Pratuchai and Soi Anuman Ratchathon, where go-go bars feature in-your-face names like **Golden Cock** plus the cryptic **Super Lex Matsuda**. Along with male go-go dancers and 'bar boys', several bars feature live sex shows, which are generally much better choreographed than the hetero equivalents on Patpong.

A more direct legacy of the Vietnam War days is **Soi Cowboy**, a single lane strip of 25 to 30 bars off Th Sukhumvit, between Soi 21 and Soi 23. By and large it's seedier than Th Patpong, and you will see fewer women and couples in the crowd.

Nana Entertainment Plaza, off Soi 4 (Soi Nana Tai), Th Sukhumvit, is a three-storey complex with around 20 bars that have surged in popularity among resident and visiting oglers over the last five or more years. NEP comes complete with its own guesthouses in the same complex, used almost exclusively by female bar workers for illicit assignations. The 'female' staff at **Casanova** consists entirely of Thai transvestites and transsexuals – this is a favourite stop for foreigners visiting Bangkok for sex re-assignment surgery.

Asian tourists – primarily Japanese, Taiwanese and Hong Kong males – flock to the Ratchada entertainment strip (part of Huay Khwang district) along wide Th Ratchadaphisek, between Th Phra Ram IX and Th Lat Phrao. Lit up like Las Vegas, this stretch of neon boasts huge male-oriented massage-snooker-and-karaoke and go-go emporiums such as **Caesar's Sauna** and **Emmanuelle** – far grander in scale and more expensive than anything in Patpong.

Gay & Lesbian Venues

Utopia, a clearing house for the Southeast Asian gay community, has gone cyber with an online events and entertainment website (W www.utopia-asia.com). Visit its site for the latest and greatest news. **Anjaree** *(☎ 0 2477 1776)* is a lesbian resource group that organises social events and community outreach programmes.

Soi Patpong 2 and Silom Soi 4 (see the Thanon Silom map) has the highest concentration of gay clubs in the city. **DJ Station** and **JJ Park** are just some of many clubs that pack narrow Soi Patong 2 with late-night energy. DJ Station also boasts *kàthoey* cabaret. Chill out at **Expresso** beside the waterfall wall for a birds-eye view of the pretty boys. On Silom Soi 4 **Telephone**, Bangkok's oldest gay bar, has a telephone by which patrons can get to know each other. Across the street, **The Balcony** has prime people-watching tables. There's a cluster of seedier gay bars around Soi Anuman Ratchathon, off Soi Tantawan, which joins Th Surawong opposite the Ramada Hotel – the gay equivalent of Th Patpong (see Go-Go Bars previously).

Babylon Bangkok *(Central Bangkok map; ☎ 0 2213 2108; 50 Soi Atakanprasit, Th Sathon Tai; open 5am-11pm daily)* is a four-storey gay sauna that has been described as one of the Top 10 gay men's saunas in the world. Facilities include a bar, roof garden, gym, massage room, steam and dry saunas, and spa baths. The spacious, well-hidden complex also has accommodation.

Vega *(☎ 0 2258 8273, 0 2662 6471; Soi 39, Th Sukhumvit)* is a lesbian-owned casual pub-restaurant that also features live music and dancing, while upstairs there's karaoke. On Friday and Saturday nights local lesbian celebrities sometimes stop by.

There is also a strong lesbian presence at Th Silom nightspots such as Telephone and The Balcony, as well as Th Phra Athit bars such as Hemlock and Indy.

At the following bars, the crowd swings more towards straight than gay, but sometimes dilution is a welcome diversion. **Number 53** *(Soi 53, Th Sukhumvit)* is a bar-café owned by a famous TV make-up artist. **Kitchenette** *(☎ 0 2381 0861; 1st floor, Dutchess Plaza, 289 Soi 55, Th Sukhumvit) is a* café with live music on weekends.

Cabaret

Transvestite *(kàthoey)* cabarets are big in Bangkok. **Calypso Cabaret** *(☎ 0 2261 6355, 0 2216 8937; 296 Th Phayathai; tickets 700B)*, in the Asia Hotel (see the Siam Square & Pratunam map), has the largest transvestite troupe in town, with nightly shows at 8.15pm and 9.45pm. Tickets include one drink.

Although the audience at cabarets is almost 100% tourists, the shows are very good and include plenty of Thai and Asian themes as well as the usual Broadway camp.

Several of Bangkok's gay bars feature short drag shows between dance sets.

Massage Parlours

It's well known that virtually all of the city's dozens of *àap òp nûat* or 'bathe-steam-massage' (sometimes referred to as 'Turkish bath') parlours also deal in prostitution; less well known is the fact that many (but by no means all) of the women working in the parlours are bonded labour – they are not necessarily there by choice.

All but the most insensitive of males will be saddened by the sight of 50 girls/women behind a glass wall with numbers pinned to their dresses. Often the bank of masseuses is divided into sections according to skill and/or appearance. Most expensive is the 'superstar' section, in which the women try to approximate the look of fashion models or actresses. A smaller section is reserved for women who are actually good at giving massages, and who offer nothing extra. Virtually all massage parlours of this sort insist on condom use, if services extend beyond the massage.

Cinemas

Get out of the smog and heat at one of the city's hi-tech cinemas. For the royal treatment, opt for the VIP tickets (300B), with reclining seats, table service and spotless bathrooms – you'll deserve this before the cattle-car class flight back home. Regular seats cost 100B to 150B. All movies screened in Thai cinemas are preceded by the Thai royal anthem and everyone is expected to stand respectfully for its duration.

Hollywood movies released in Thailand are usually about six months behind the US openings. Home-grown talent feeds the cinemas with a steady diet of Thai movies, which are typically subtitled in English. Reviews and screening times of local and international movies appear in the *Nation* and the *Bangkok Post*.

Foreign films are often altered before distribution by Thailand's film censors; usually this involves obscuring nude sequences, although gun fights are sometimes also edited out.

Film buffs may prefer the weekly or twice-weekly offerings at Bangkok's foreign cultural clubs. French and German films screened at the cultural clubs are almost always subtitled in English. Admission is sometimes free, sometimes from 30B to 40B. For contact details, see the Cultural Centres section earlier in this chapter.

At the following cinemas, English movies are subtitled rather than dubbed in Thai. Grand EGV and United Artists have the most state-of-the-art sound and projection facilities.

Grand EGV (Siam Square & Pratunam map; ☎ 0 2812 9999) Siam Discovery Centre
Hollywood Theatre (☎ 0 2208 9194) Hollywood Street Centre, Th Phetburi
Indra (☎ 0 2251 6230) Th Ratchaprarop

Lido Cinema (Siam Square & Pratunam map; ☎ 0 2252 6498) Siam Square, Th Phra Ram I
MacKenna (☎ 0 2252 6215) 17/2 Th Phayathai
Major Cineplex (☎ 0 2714 2828) Soi 63, Th Sukhumvit
Micromack (☎ 0 2251 6215) Ground floor, MacKenna Theatre, Th Phayathai
Pantip (Siam Square & Pratunam map; ☎ 0 2251 2390) Pantip Plaza, Th Phetburi Tat Mai
Scala Cinema (Siam Square & Pratunam map; ☎ 0 2251 2861) Siam Square, Soi 1, Th Phra Ram I
SF Cinema City (Siam Square & Pratunam map; ☎ 0 2611 6444) Mahboonkrong shopping centre, Th Phra Ram I
Siam Cinema (Siam Square & Pratunam map; ☎ 0 2251 1735) Siam Square, Th Phra Ram I
United Artists (Thanon Sukhumvit map; ☎ 0 2664 8771) 6th floor, The Emporium, Th Sukhumvit
United Artists (☎ 0 2673 6060–88) 7th & 8th floors, Central Plaza, Th Ratchada-Phra Ram III
Warner (☎ 0 2234 3700–9) 119 Th Mahesak
World Trade 1, 2, 3 (Siam Square & Pratunam map; ☎ 0 2255 9500) 6th floor, World Trade Centre, cnr Th Ploenchit & Th Ratchadamri
World Trade 4, 5 (Siam Square & Pratunam map; ☎ 0 2255 9500) Basement floor, World Trade Centre, cnr Th Ploenchit & Th Ratchadamri

Video Rental

Video rental is popular in Bangkok; not only is it cheaper than a cinema ticket, but many movies are available on video that aren't approved for theatre distribution by Thailand's film censors. The average rental is 20B to 50B. Th Sukhumvit has the highest concentration of video shops; the better ones are found in the residential area between Soi 39 and Soi 55. **Blockbuster** has branches in the city's wealthier areas, especially off Th Sukhumvit, Th Ploenchit and Th Lat Phrao. **Mangpong** *(Thanon Silom map; Silom Complex, Th Silom)* is the Thai version of Blockbuster. **Silver Bell** *(☎ 0 2236 2845–51; 113/1-2 Surawong Centre, Th Surawong)* rents TVs and VCRs (both PAL and NTSC).

Theatre & Dance

A Thai Art Deco building at the edge of the Chinatown-Phahurat district, **Chalermkrung Royal Theatre** *(Chinatown & Phahurat map; Sala Chaloem Krung; ☎ 0 2222 0434; cnr Th Charoen Krung & Th Triphet)* provides a striking venue for *khŏn* performance (masked dance-drama based on stories from the *Ramakian*; see the 'Music Theatre & Dance' special section) in Thailand. When it opened in 1933, the royalty-funded Chalermkrung was the largest and most modern theatre in Asia, with state-of-the-art film-projection technology and the first chilled-water air-con system in the region. Prince Samaichaloem, a former student of the École des Beaux-Arts in Paris, designed the hexagonal building.

The theatre's 1993 renovations added a 80,000-watt audio system, combined with computer-generated laser graphics, which enable the 170-member dance troupe to present a technologically enhanced version of traditional *khŏn*. Although the special effects are reasonably impressive, the excellent costumes, set design, dancing and music are reason enough to attend.

Khŏn performances last about two hours plus intermission. Other Thai performing arts and film festivals may also be scheduled at the theatre. Check the local newspapers for current performance schedules. For ticket reservations, call the number listed or visit the box office personally. The theatre requests that patrons dress respectfully, which means no shorts, tank tops or sandals. Bring a wrap or long-sleeved shirt in case the air-con is running full blast.

The Chalermkrung Royal Theatre is adjacent to the Old Siam Plaza complex. Air-con bus No 508 and ordinary bus Nos 48 and 73 pass the theatre (going west on Th Charoen Krung). You can also comfortably walk to the theatre from the western terminus of the Saen Saep canal ferry. Taxi drivers may know the theatre by its original name, Sala Chaloem Krung, which is spelt out in Thai in the lighted sign located on the front of the building.

National Theatre *(Ko Ratanakosin map; ☎ 0 2224 1342; Th Chao Fa; admission 20-200B)*, near Saphan Phra Pin Klao, holds Thailand's most traditional *lákhon* and *khŏn* performances. The theatre has regular performances on the last Friday and Saturday of each month. Seeing a *khŏn* performance here is highly recommended.

A range of dance performances from classical to modern, Thai to Western are also held at the **Thailand Cultural Centre** *(Greater Bangkok map; ☎ 0 2245 7742; Th Ratchadaphisek)* and at the **College of Dramatic**

Arts *(☎ 0 2224 1391)*, which is near the National Theatre.

Patravadi Theatre *(Ko Ratanakosin map; ☎ 0 2412 8287; 69/1 Soi Wat Rakhang; tickets 300-500B)*, next to Supatra River House in Thonburi, is Bangkok's only open-air theatre. Led by Patravadi Mejudhon, a famous Thai actress, the troupe's performances blend traditional Thai dance and themes with modern choreography, music and costumes. Attendees often have dinner at the affiliated Supatra House before the 7.30pm performances on Friday, Saturday and Sunday. A free shuttle picks up patrons at Tha Mahathat, near Silpakorn University; reservations are recommended.

Dinner Theatre Many tourists view performances put on solely for their benefit at one of the Thai classical-dance dinner theatres in the city. The admission prices at these venues costs 200B to 500B per person and includes a 'typical' Thai dinner (often toned down for Western palates), a couple of selected dance performances and a martial arts display.

The historic Oriental Hotel (see the Thanon Silom map) has its own dinner theatre, the **Sala Rim Nam** *(☎ 0 2437 2918, 0 2437 3080)*. The admission price is well above average (1600B) but so is the food, the performance and the Thai-pavilion decor (teak, marble and bronze). Call for reservations and starting times.

Other dinner theatres include **Baan Thai Restaurant** *(☎ 0 2258 5403; 7 Soi 32, Th Sukhumvit)*; **Maneeya Lotus Room** *(☎ 0 2282 6312; 518/5 Th Ploenchit)*; **Piman Thai Theatre Restaurant** *(☎ 0 2258 7866; 46 Soi 49, Th Sukhumvit)*; and **Suwannahong Restaurant** *(☎ 0 2245 4448, 0 2245 3747; Th Si Ayuthaya)*.

Puppet Theatre The ancient art of Thai puppetry has been rescued by Sakorn Yangkhiawsod, who is known more popularly as Joe Louis. His creations are controlled by three manipulators and can strike many human-like poses. Modelled after the characters in the *Ramakian*, the puppets perform in the **Joe Louis Theatre** *(Central Bangkok map; Suan Lum Night Bazaar)* at 7.30pm nightly.

Shrine Dancing Free performances of traditional *lákhon kâe bon* can be seen daily at the **Lak Meuang and Erawan Shrines** (see the Siam Square & Pratunam map), if you happen to arrive when a performance troupe has been commissioned by a worshipper. Although many of the dance movements are the same as those seen in traditional *lákhon*, these relatively crude performances are specially choreographed for ritual purposes, and don't represent true classical dance forms. But it is colourful – the dancers wear full costume and are accompanied by live music – so it's worth stopping to watch.

Thai Boxing

Muay thai can be seen at two boxing stadiums, **Sanam Muay Lumphini** *(Central Bangkok map; Th Phra Ram IV; 6pm Tues & Fri, 5pm Sat)*, near Lumphini Park, and **Sanam Muay Ratchadamnoen** *(Central Bangkok map; Th Ratchadamnoen Nok; 6pm Mon, Wed & Sun, 5pm & 9pm Thur)* not far from the Democracy Monument. The cheapest seats are 500B for the outer circle, 800B for the middle circle and 1500B for ringside. This is for 12 fights of five rounds each; the last three are the headliner events.

Aficionados say the best-matched bouts are reserved for Tuesday night at Lumphini and Thursday night at Ratchadamnoen.

The **restaurants** on the northern side of Ratchadamnoen stadium are well known for their delicious *kài yâang* (grilled chicken) and other Isan dishes. Ratchadamnoen stadium can be reached via air-con bus No 503 and ordinary bus No 70. Lumphini stadium can be reached via ordinary bus No 47.

Warning Touts often try to steer tourists into buying more expensive seats claiming that all other seats are sold out. Ignore them and look for the appropriate ticket windows. Don't believe anyone who says seats are sold out, unless you hear it directly from a vendor at a window. There are official attendants who are quite helpful and will give you an English schedule of fights and explain the pricing structure; it is still wise, however, not to buy tickets from touts.

SHOPPING

Regular visitors to Asia know that, in many ways, Bangkok beats Hong Kong and Singapore for good deals on handicrafts, textiles, gems, jewellery, art and antiques – nowhere else will you find the same quality, prices and selection. The difficulty is finding the good spots, as the city's intense urban tangle makes orientation sometimes difficult. *Nancy Chandler's Map of Bangkok* makes a very good shopping companion, with annotations on all sorts of small, out-of-the-way shopping venues and markets *(tàlàat)*.

Be sure to read the Shopping section in the Facts for the Visitor chapter before setting out on a spree. Amid all the bargains are a number of cleverly disguised rip-off schemes – *caveat emptor*!

Markets

Phenomenal bargains can be found at the city's endless variety of markets. Most are an odd assortment of plastic toys, household goods and polyester clothes in Asian sizes mixed with knock-off designer watches and bags. Even more interesting are the food markets, where food-savvy Thais forage for brightly coloured tapioca desserts, spicy curries and fruit that look like medieval torture devices.

Weekend Market Also known as Chatuchak Market *(Talat Nat Jatujak; Greater Bangkok & Chatuchak Market maps; 8am-6pm Sat & Sun)* this is the behemoth of Thai markets. On weekends 15,000 stalls cater to an estimated 200,000 visitors a day. Everything is sold here, from live chickens and snakes to opium pipes and herbal remedies. Thai clothing such as sarongs for men *(phâakhamáa)* and women *(phâasîn),* Chinese pants *(kaang keng jiin)* and blue, cotton farmer's shirts *(sêua mâw hâwm)* are good buys. You'll also find musical instruments, hill-tribe crafts, religious amulets, antiques, flowers, clothes imported from India and Nepal, camping gear and military surplus. The best bargains are household goods such as pots and pans, dishes and drinking glasses. If you're moving to Thailand for an extended period, pick up stuff here for your kitchen. Don't forget to try out your bargaining skills.

There is an information centre, a couple of banks with ATMs and foreign-exchange booths at the Chatuchak Park offices, near the northern end of the market's Soi 1, Soi 2 and Soi 3. Schematic maps and toilets are conveniently located throughout the market. Plan to spend a full day, as there's plenty to see, do and buy.

The main part of the Weekend Market is open from around 8am to 6pm on weekends, although some places may stay open as late as 8pm. There are a few vendors out on weekday mornings and a daily vegetable, plant and flower market opposite the market's southern side. One section of the latter, known as the Aw Taw Kaw Market, sells organically grown fruit and vegetables.

The Weekend Market is in the northern part of the city, next to Chatuchak Park, and near the Northern bus terminal. Air-con bus Nos 502, 503, 509, 510, 512 and 513, and ordinary bus No 77 and a dozen others stop at the market. The Skytrain runs direct to Moh Chit station, which stands almost in front of the market.

CHATUCHAK WEEKEND MARKET

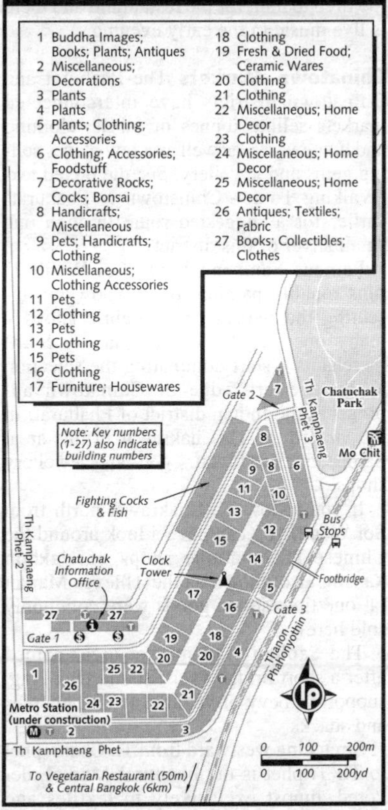

Operated by the Asoke Foundation, the **vegetarian restaurant** near the Weekend Market is one of Bangkok's oldest. It's open only on weekends from 8am to noon and is an adventure to find. If you're successful, then this is a real treasure. Take the footbridge across Th Kamphaeng Phet, away from the market, and towards the southern end of Th Phahonyothin. Take the first right onto a through street, and walk past nightclubs and bars into what looks like a car park. Head to your right, and you'll see a new block of buildings selling bulk food stuff; you're getting closer because these are organic wholesalers (smell that 'health-food store' scent?). The restaurant is at the end of this strip. Prices are ridiculously low (around 10B per dish) and you buy tickets at the front desk.

There is plenty of interesting and tasty food for sale within the market, if you're too tired to hunt for the restaurant, and there is live music in the early evening.

Chinatown Markets The Phahurat and Chinatown districts have interconnected markets selling tonnes of fabric, clothing and homewares, as well as a few places selling gems and jewellery. See the boxed text 'Walking Tour – Chinatown & Phahurat' earlier for a suggested route through one small sliver of this district.

Famous Sampeng Lane (Soi Wanit 1) runs roughly parallel to Th Yaowarat, bisecting the two districts. Fabric shops – many operated by Indian (mostly Sikh) merchants – start dominating the selection as the western edge of Chinatown approaches the Indian district of Phahurat. In the vicinity of Th Chakrawat in this area, Sampeng Lane favours gem and jewellery shops.

If you follow Th Chakrawat north from Soi Wanit, you can have a look around the Chinese-Thai antique shops of **Nakhon Kasem**, also known as the Thieves Market (at one time stolen goods were commonly sold here).

The **Saphan Han** market area, named after a short bridge over Khlong Ong Ang, supports a bevy of vendors selling noodles and snacks.

Stretching westward from Th Chakraphet to Th Triphet is the **Phahurat Market**, devoted almost exclusively to textiles and clothing. Th Phahurat itself runs parallel to, and just north of, the market.

If you're ready to escape the market hustle and bustle, you can catch city buses on Th Chakraphet (heading north and then east to the Siam Square and Pratunam areas) or along Th Phahurat (heading west and then north along Th Tri Thong to the Banglamphu district). Or walk to the river and catch a Chao Phraya River Express boat from Tha Saphan Phut, which is just to the northwest of Phra Phuttha Yot Fa (Memorial) Bridge.

Other Markets The **Nailert Market** *(Nai Loet Market; Siam Square & Pratunam map; Th Phetburi, Pratunam, open 8am-6pm daily)* is opposite the Amari Watergate Hotel. It was opened as a central alternative to Chatuchak Market. The array of goods is similar. Nearby **Pratunam Market** *(Siam Square & Pratunam map; cnr Th Phetburi & Th Ratchaprarop; open 8am-6pm daily)* gets very crowded, but has great deals in new, cheap clothing. You won't see it from the street – look for one of the unmarked entrances that lead behind the main shopfronts.

Under the expressway in the Khlong Toey district is the **Khlong Toey Market** *(Central Bangkok map; cnr Th Phra Ram IV & Th Narong)*, possibly the cheapest all-purpose market in Bangkok (it's best on Wednesday). South of the Khlong Toey Market, closer to the port, is the similar **Penang Market**, so called because a lot of the goods 'drop off' cargo boats from Penang (and Singapore, Hong Kong etc).

The huge **Banglamphu Market** spreads several blocks over Th Chakraphong, Th Phra Sumen, Th Tanao and Th Rambutri, a short walk from the guesthouse area of Th Khao San. The Banglamphu Market area is probably the most comprehensive shopping district in the city as it encompasses everything from street vendors to upmarket department stores.

Soi Lalaisap *(Soi 5, Th Silom; open 8am-6pm daily)*, also known as the 'money-melting street', has a number of vendors selling all sorts of cheap clothing, watches and homewares during the day.

The **Wong Wian Yai Market** in Thonburi, next to the large roundabout directly southwest of Saphan Phra Phuttha Yot Fa, is another all-purpose market.

Flower Markets The city's largest wholesale flower source is **Pak Khlong** *(Ko Ratanakosin map; open 8am-6pm daily)*, near the river and the mouth of Khlong Lawt, between Th Atsadang and Saphan Phra Phuttha Yot Fa. The colourful displays of baby roses, delicate orchids and button carnations are endless and so inexpensive that even a cement-cell dweller on Th Khao San could afford a bouquet. Pak Khlong is also a big market for vegetables.

You'll find a good selection of tropical flowers and plants is available at the **Thewet Market** *(Th Krung Kasem; open 8am-6pm daily)*, which is northwest of Banglamphu near Tha Thewet. **Talat Phahonyothin** *(Phahonyothin Market; open 8am-6pm daily)* is the newest and largest plant market, and is opposite the southern side of Chatuchak Market, near the Northern bus terminal off Th Phahonyothin.

Tourist Markets The main guesthouse strip in Banglamphu, Th Khao San, has itself become a shopping bazaar offering cheap audio tapes, used books, jewellery, beads, clothing, Thai 'axe pillows', T-shirts, tattoos, body piercing and just about any other product or service.

At night Patpong Soi 1 and Soi 2 fill up with vendors selling cheap tourist junk, inexpensive clothing, fake watches – you name it. Along both sides of Th Sukhumvit between Soi 1 and Soi 5, there are also lots of street vendors selling similar items.

Department Stores & Shopping Centres

Bangkok may be crowded and polluted, but its department stores are modern oases of order. By no accident, the Skytrain stations often have shaded walkways delivering passengers directly in to nearby stores, never having to set foot on ground level. **Central Department Store** *(W www.central.co.th)* is generally regarded as the all-round best for quality and selection, with 13 branches in Bangkok, including the flagship store on Th Ploenchit, near Chit Lom Skytrain station (see the Siam Square & Pratunam map). In addition to designer clothes, Western cosmetics, fabrics, furniture, handicrafts and an attached supermarket, the store offers free alterations to all clothing purchases and free delivery to Bangkok hotels.

Peninsula Plaza *(Siam Square & Pratunam map; Th Ratchadamri)* has a more exclusive selection of shops – many of which also have branches at River City and Oriental Plaza – and a good-sized branch of Asia Books.

The eight floors of the **World Trade Centre** *(WTC; Siam Square & Pratunam map; cnr Th Ploenchit & Th Ratchadamri)* seem to go on and on. The main focus is the Zen department store, which has clothing shops reminiscent of Hong Kong's high-end boutiques. On the 8th floor is Bangkok's premier antidote to the tropics, the World Ice Skating Center. If you're looking for kids clothing or toys, ABC Babyland on the 2nd floor has just about everything.

Siam Square *(Siam Square & Pratunam map; Th Phra Ram I)*, near Th Phayathai, is a network of some 12 lanes lined with shops selling mid-price designer clothes, books, sporting goods and antiques. On the opposite side of Th Phra Ram I, the four-storey **Siam Center** was Thailand's first shopping centre (built in 1976). It features designer and brand-label clothing shops – Benetton, Quicksilver, Chaps, Esprit and Lacoste to name a few – as well as coffee shops, travel agencies, banks and airline offices. Next door, and connected by an enclosed pedestrian bridge, **Siam Discovery Center** contains yet more designer stores, plus a branch of Asia Books, stylish homeware shops and several large restaurants.

Mahboonkrong *(MBK; Siam Square & Pratunam map)* shopping centre is loved by teenagers; it has many small, inexpensive stalls and shops selling cell-phone accessories, cheap T-shirts, wallets, handbags, in addition to Diesel shoes, Paul Frank accessories and the middle-class Tokyu department store. The Travel Mart on the 3rd floor stocks a reasonable supply of travel gear and camping equipment – not the highest quality but useful in a pinch.

North of Siam Square, **Pantip Plaza** *(Siam Square & Pratunam map; Th Phetburi)* specialises in computer equipment and software.

Anchored by Central Department Store, the six-storey **Silom Complex** *(Thanon Silom map; Sala Daeng Skytrain station)* remains one of the city's busiest shopping centres. Also on the same street is the upscale **Thaniya Plaza**, with good-quality clothing boutiques, bookshops, jewellery shops and more.

Old Siam Plaza, bounded by Th Charoen Krung, Th Burapha, Th Phahurat and Th Triphet (see the Chinatown & Phahurat map), is the most significant development ever in this area. Along with the renovation and reopening of the adjacent Chalermkrung Royal Theatre, this old Bangkok-style shopping centre represents a minor renaissance for an otherwise shabby and congested district. Most of the shops purvey Thai-style goods and services; one whole side is devoted to gun dealers, another to gem and jewellery shops, the rest to Thai handicrafts, furniture, restaurants and coffee shops.

Gaysorn Plaza *(Siam Square & Pratunam map; Th Ploenchit)* has been transformed into a *haute couture* catwalk, with spiralling staircases and all white halls. In addition to top-name designers, there are several shops on the top floor specialising in furniture and home furnishings, both antique and contemporary Thai.

Emporium *(Thanon Sukhumvit map; between Soi 22 & Soi 24, Th Sukhumvit)* has six floors of what's-hot as well as popular eateries and escalators full of stylish shoppers. Prada, Miu Miu and Chanel even share space with a bookstore **Kinokuniya**. It is also so conveniently located that you can do a shot of retail therapy before the Sunday afternoon meditation sessions at nearby World Fellowship of Buddhists.

Sogo *(494 Th Ploenchit)*, a Japanese department store, is the proud host of the **Thai Craft Museum Shop**, formerly located in Gaysorn Plaza. In addition to its clothing stores, the supermarket gets rave reviews for interesting Japanese imports.

Antiques

Real Thai antiques are rare and costly. Most Bangkok antique shops keep a few authentic pieces for collectors, along with lots of pseudo-antiques or traditionally crafted items that look like antiques. The majority of shop operators are quite candid about what's really old and what isn't. Many shops specialise in decorative items for the home.

Reliable antique shops (using the word 'antique' loosely) can be found at **Silom Village Trade Centre** *(Thanon Silom map; Soi 24; Th Silom)*, which has a few inexpensive antique and handicraft shops, such as **Artisan's** *(☎ 0 2237 4456)*.

Nagi Shop *(☎ 0 2661 6480; 131 Soi 21/Asoke, Th Sukhumvit; open 9am-5pm Tues-Sat)*, next door to the Siam Society, is an odd collection of antiques from across Asia. Amid the treasures, equally as old Westerners can often be found discussing bygone colonial days.

River City shopping complex (see the Thanon Silom map) contains a number of high-quality art and antique shops on its 3rd and 4th floors. **Acala** *(shop 312)* is a gallery of unusual Tibetan and Chinese artefacts. **Old Maps & Prints** *(☎ 0 2237 0077 ext 432; shop 432)* has one of the best selections of one-of-a-kind, rare maps and illustrations with a focus on Asia. **Oriental Plaza** *(Thanon Silom map; Soi Oriental, Th Charoen Krung)* also has several good, if pricey, antique shops.

Triphum *(☎ 0 2656 1795; 2nd floor, Grayson Plaza; Th Ploenchit)* features tasteful Southeast Asian art.

Upmarket handicrafts are sold in the **Thai Craft Village**, on the ground floor of Le Royal Meridien (see the Siam Square & Pratunam map).

Bronzeware

Thailand has the oldest bronze-working tradition in the world and there are several factories in Bangkok producing bronze sculpture and cutlery. Two factories that sell direct to the public (and where you may also be able to observe the process) are **Siam Bronze Factory** *(☎ 0 2234 9436; 1250 Th Charoen Krung)*, between Soi 36 and Soi 38, and **Somkij Bronze** *(☎ 0 2251 0891; 1194 Th Phetburi Tat Mai)*. Make sure any items you buy are silicon-coated, otherwise they'll tarnish. To see the casting process for Buddha images, go to the **Buddha Casting Foundry** *(Th Phrannok, Thonburi)* next to Wat Wiset Khan; take a river ferry from Tha Phra Chan on the Bangkok side to reach the start of Th Phrannok.

Many vendors at Wat Mahathat's Sunday market sell old and new bronzeware – it is imperative to haggle.

Photography Supplies & Processing

For a wide range of camera models and brands, try **Sunny Camera** *(☎ 0 2235 2123, 0 2233 8378; 1267/1 Th Charoen Krung • ☎ 0 2236 8627; 144/23 Th Silom • ☎ 0 2217*

9293, 3rd floor Mahboonkrong shopping centre). On the northwestern corner of Soi 12, **Niks** *(Thanon Silom map; ☎ 0 2235 2929; 166 Th Silom)* sells all types of professional equipment, and services Nikon, Mamiya and Rollei. **Central Department Store** *(Th Ploenchit)* has a good camera section with surprisingly reasonable prices.

Film prices in Bangkok are generally lower than anywhere else in Asia, including Hong Kong. Both slide and print film are widely available, although the highest concentration of photo shops can be found along Th Silom and Th Surawong. In Mahboonkrong shopping centre, **FotoFile** on the ground floor has the best selection of slide films.

Quick, professional-quality processing of most film types is available at **Image Quality Lab** *(IQ Lab; ☎ 0 2266 4080; IF Silom Palace Bldg, Th Silom • ☎ 0 2714 0644; 9/33 Thana Arcade, Soi 63, Th Sukhumvit)* and **Eastbourne Professional Color Laboratories** *(☎ 0 2664 8515; 622 Soi 24/Kasem, Th Sukhumvit)*.

Gems & Jewellery

Recommending specific shops is tricky, since one coloured stone looks as good as another to the average eye – the risk of a rip-off is much greater than for most other shopping items. Before heading out on a gem-buying spree, read Dangers & Annoyances in the Facts for the Visitor chapter, and remember that the term 'precious' stone describes the item's beauty as well as the *price*.

One shop that's been a long-time favourite with Bangkok expats for service and value in set jewellery is **Johnny's Gems** *(☎ 0 2224 4065; 199 Th Fuang Nakhon)*, off Th Charoen Krung. Another dependable place specialising in unset stones is **Lambert Holding** *(☎ 0 2236 4343; Soi 17, 807 Th Silom)*.

Handicrafts

Bangkok has excellent buys in Thai handicrafts, although for northern hill-tribe crafts, you might do better in Chiang Mai. **Narayana Phand** *(Siam Square & Pratunam map; ☎ 0 2252 4670; Th Ratchadamri)* is a bit on the touristy side but has a large selection and good marked prices – no haggling is necessary. The **Central Department Store** *(Siam Square & Pratunam map; Th Ploenchit)* has a large Thai handicrafts section with marked prices.

International School Bangkok *(ISB; Greater Bangkok map; ☎ 0 2583 5401; 39/7 Soi Nichadathani Samakhi)* puts on a large charity sale of Thai handicrafts every sixth Saturday or so (except during ISB's summer holiday, from June to August). Sometimes you can find pieces here that are unavailable elsewhere. At other times it's not very interesting; it all depends on what it's able to collect during the year. ISB is north of the city, towards the airport, and inside the Nichada Thani townhouse complex.

Perhaps the most interesting places to shop for handicrafts are the smaller, independent handicraft shops, each with its own style and character. Quality is high at **Rasi Sayam** *(☎ 0 2258 4195; 32 Soi 23, Th Sukhumvit)*. Many of the numerous items sold here, including wall hangings and pottery, are made specifically for this shop.

Another good shop for pottery, as well as lacquerware and especially fabrics, is **Vilai's** *(☎ 0 2391 6106; 731/1 Soi 55/Thong Lor, Th Sukhumvit)*.

Nandakwang *(☎ 0 2258 1962; 108/3 Soi 23/Soi Prasanmit, Th Sukhumvit)* is a branch of a factory shop of the same name in Pasang, northern Thailand. Nandakwang specialises in high-quality woven cotton clothing and linen (tablecloths, napkins etc).

Lao Song Handicrafts *(☎ 0 2261 6627; 2/56 Soi 41, Th Sukhumvit)* is a nonprofit shop that sells village handicrafts to promote cottage industries.

Khŏn masks of intricately formed wire and papier-mâché can be purchased at **Padung Cheep** *(Th Chakraphong)*, just south of the Th Khao San intersection.

For quality Thai celadon, check **Thai Celadon** *(☎ 0 2229 4383; 8/6-8 Th Ratchadaphisek Tat Mai)*. Inexpensive places to pick up new Thai pottery of all shapes and sizes at wholesale prices include **United Siam Overseas** *(☎ 0 2721 6320)* and **Siamese Merchandise** *(☎ 0 2333 0680)*, both on Soi On Nut, off Soi 77, Th Sukhumvit. Overseas shipping can be arranged.

Thai Arts & Crafts Museum *(4th floor, Sogo Department Store, Th Ploenchit)* isn't technically a museum, but why be so literal with all the pieces of celadon and nielloware bowls, baskets and other handicrafts (see the Siam Square & Pratunam map.)

Taekee Taekon *(Banglamphu map; 118 Th Phra Athit)* has a beautiful selection of Thai textiles from the main silk-producing regions of the country.

Design Thai *(Thanon Silom map; ☎ 0 2235 1553; 304 Th Silom)* has a lovely assortment of subdued Thai silks and cottons as well as Italian-designed ties and small silk gifts.

Diving Supplies

Larry's Dive Center, Bar & Grill *(☎ 0 2663 4563; ⓔ bangkok@larrysdive.com; Soi 22; dishes 95-175B; open 9am-5pm daily)* stocks all manner of diving and snorkelling gear. There's a restaurant and bar attached, so you can eat while your air tanks are filled.

Tailors

Bangkok abounds in places where you can have clothing designed, cut and sewn by hand. Workmanship ranges from shoddy to excellent, so it pays to ask around before committing yourself. Shirts and trousers can be turned around in 48 hours or less with only one fitting. But no matter what a tailor may tell you, it takes more than one or two fittings to create a good suit, and most reputable tailors will ask for two to five sittings. A well-made suit that will escort you back into the hallowed halls of Western commerce will need to be entrusted to the more expensive and reputable tailors in the city's luxury hotels, such as the Peninsula Plaza, Landmark, Oriental and Shangri-La hotels. The same goes for women's formal wear.

Discount tailors are particularly good at copying your favourite piece of casual clothing. Shirts costing upwards of US$100 at home can be made for not much more than a tenth of the price. The one area where you need to be most careful is in fabric selection. If possible, bring fabric from home, especially if you want 100% cotton. Most of the so-called 'cotton' offered by Bangkok tailors is actually a blend of cotton and synthetic; more than a few tailors will actually try to pass off full polyester or Dacron as cotton. Good-quality silk, on the other hand, is plentiful. Tailor-made silk shirts should cost no more than US$20, depending on the type of silk (Chinese silk is cheaper than Thai).

Virtually every tailor working in Bangkok is of Indian or Chinese descent. Generally speaking the best shops are those found along the outer reaches of Th Sukhumvit (out beyond Soi 20 or so) and on or off Th Charoen Krung. Th Silom also has some good tailors. The worst tailor shops tend to be those in tourist-oriented shopping areas in inner Th Sukhumvit, Th Khao San, the River City shopping complex and other shopping malls. 'Great deals', like four shirts, two suits, a kimono and a safari suit all in one package, almost always turn out to be of inferior materials and workmanship.

Avoid any tailor shop suggested by a stranger you meet on the street, as these usually pay high commissions to the 'stranger', thus driving the cost of the work far beyond its normal value. Tailoring scams have become almost as notorious as gem scams in Bangkok.

GETTING THERE & AWAY

Air

Bangkok is a major centre for international flights throughout Asia. International and domestic flights arrive and depart from Bangkok International Airport at Don Muang, 25km outside the city. A new international airport is under construction at Nong Ngu Hao (20km east of Bangkok in the Bang Phli district) and is scheduled to open some time in 2005; upon completion Don Muang will handle only domestic and cargo flights.

Bangkok is also a major centre for buying discounted airline tickets, but be warned that its travel-agency business has a few crooked operators. Domestic flights operated by THAI and Bangkok Airways also leave from Bangkok. The following airline companies have offices in Bangkok.

Aeroflot (☎ 0 22541 1180–2) Regent House, Th Ratchadamri
Air France (☎ 0 2635 1199, reservations ☎ 0 2635 1191) 20th floor, Vorawat Bldg, 849 Th Silom
Air India (☎ 0 2254 3280–2) 12th floor, One Pacific Place, 140 Th Sukhumvit
Air New Zealand (Central Bangkok map; ☎ 0 2254 8440) 14th floor, Sindhorn Bldg, 130-132 Th Withayu
Alitalia (☎ 0 2634 1800–9) 3rd floor, SP Tower 3, Unit 15A, 88 Th Silom
All Nippon Airways (Thanon Silom map; ANA; ☎ 0 2238 5121) 2nd floor, CP Tower, 313 Th Silom

American Airlines (☎ 0 2263 0225) 11th floor, Ploenchit Tower, Th Ploenchit
Asiana Airlines (Thanon Sukhumvit map; ☎ 0 2656 8610) 18th floor, Ploenchit Center, Soi 2 Sukhumvit
Bangkok Airways (Central Bangkok map; ☎ 0 2229 3434, 0 2253 4014) Queen Sirikit National Convention Centre, 60 Th Ratchadaphisek Tat Mai
Biman Bangladesh Airlines (☎ 0 2235 7643–4) Chongkolnee Bldg, 56 Th Surawong
British Airways (☎ 0 2636 1700) 990 Th Phra Ram IV
Canadian Airlines International (Central Bangkok map; ☎ 0 2253 0263) 14th floor, Sindhorn Bldg, 130-132 Th Withayu
Cathay Pacific Airways (☎ 0 2263 0606) 11th floor, Ploenchit Tower, 898 Th Ploenchit
China Airlines (☎ 0 2253 4242) 4th floor, Peninsula Plaza, 153 Th Ratchadamri
China Southern Airlines (☎ 0 2266 5688) 491/35-37 Silom Plaza, Th Silom
Delta Air Lines (☎ 0 2237 6847–9) 7th floor, Patpong Bldg, 1 Th Surawong
Druk Air (Greater Bangkok map; ☎ 0 2535 1960) Room 3237, Central Block, Bangkok International Airport
Egypt Air (Thanon Silom map; ☎ 0 2231 0504–8) 3rd floor, CP Tower, 313 Th Silom
El Al Israel Airlines (☎ 0 2671 6145, 0 2249 8818) 14th floor, Manorom Bldg, 3354/47 Th Phra Ram IV
EVA Airways (☎ 0 2240 0890) 2nd floor, Green Tower, 3656/4-5 Th Phra Ram IV
Finnair (☎ 0 2535 1234) 6th floor, Vorawat Bldg, 849 Th Silom
Garuda Indonesia (Central Bangkok map; ☎ 0 2679 7370–2) 27th floor, Lumphini Tower, 1168/77 Th Phra Ram IV
Gulf Air (Siam Square & Pratunam map; ☎ 0 2254 7931–4) 12th floor, Maneeya Center Bldg, 518/5 Th Ploenchit
Japan Airlines (Greater Bangkok map; JAL; ☎ 0 2692 51851) JAL Bldg, 254/1 Th Ratchadaphisek
KLM-Royal Dutch Airlines (☎ 0 2679 1100 ext 2) 19th floor, Thai Wah Tower II, 21/133-4 Th Sathon Tai
Korean Air (☎ 0 2267 0990) 9th floor, Kongboonma Bldg, 699 Th Silom
Kuwait Airways (☎ 0 2523 6993) 12th floor, RS Tower, 121/50-51 Th Ratchadaphisek
Lao Aviation (☎ 0 2237 6982) Ground floor, Silom Plaza, 491/17 Th Silom
Lauda Air (☎ 0 2267 0873–9) 18th floor, room 1802, Wall Street Tower, Th Surawong
LOT Polish Airlines (☎ 0 2233 0347–8) 485/11-12 Th Silom
LTU International Airways (☎ 0 2267 1235–7) 11th floor, Bangkok Gem & Jewelry Tower, 322 Th Surawong
Lufthansa Airlines (☎ 0 2264 2400) 18th floor, Q House, Asoke Bldg, 66 Soi 21, Th Sukhumvit
Malaysia Airlines (☎ 0 2263 0520–32, reservations ☎ 0 2263 0565–71) 20th floor, Ploenchit Tower, 898 Th Ploenchit
Myanmar Airways International (☎ 0 2630 0334–8) 23rd floor, Jewelry Trade Center Bldg, 919/298 Th Silom
Northwest Airlines (Siam Square & Pratunam map; ☎ 0 2254 0771) 4th floor, Peninsula Plaza, 153 Th Ratchadamri
Pakistan International Airlines (PIA; ☎ 0 2236 4475) 2nd floor, Chongkolnee Bldg, 56 Th Surawong
Qantas Airways (☎ 0 2636 1747) 14th floor, Abdulrahim Place, 990 Th Phra Ram IV
Royal Air Cambodge (☎ 0 2653 2261; reservations ☎ 0 2653 2261–6) 20th floor, Ploenchit Tower, Th Ploenchit
Royal Brunei Airlines (Thanon Silom map; ☎ 0 2233 0056) 4th floor, Charn Issara Tower, 942/135 Th Phra Ram IV
Royal Jordanian (Thanon Silom map; ☎ 0 2638 2960) 4th floor, CP Tower, 313 Th Silom
Royal Nepal Airlines (☎ 0 2216 5691–5) 9th floor, Phayathai Plaza Bldg, 128 Th Phayathai
Scandinavian Airlines (SAS; ☎ 0 2260 0444) 8th floor, Glas Haus Bldg, 1 Soi 25, Th Sukhumvit
Singapore Airlines (Thanon Silom map; SIA; ☎ 0 2236 0440) 12th floor, Silom Center, 2 Th Silom
South African Airways (☎ 0 2635 1413–4) 20th floor, Vorawat Bldg, 849 Th Silom
Swissair (☎ 0 2636 2150) 21st floor, Abdulrahim Place, 990 Th Phra Ram IV
Tarom (☎ 0 2253 1681) 89/12 Bangkok Bazaar, Th Ratchadamri
Thai Airways International (THAI; head office ☎ 0 2513 0121, reservations ☎ 0 2280 0060) 89 Th Viphavadi Rangsit; (Thanon Silom map; ☎ 0 2234 3100–19) 485 Th Silom; (☎ 0 2288 0060, 0 2280 0110) 6 Th Lan Luang; (☎ 0 2215 2020–1) Asia Hotel, 296 Th Phayathai; (Siam Square & Pratunam map; ☎ 0 2535 2081–2, 0 2523 6121) Bangkok International Airport, Don Muang; (☎ 0 2223 9746–8) 3rd floor, Room 310-311, Grand China Bldg, 215 Th Yaowarat
United Airlines (Central Bangkok map; ☎ 0 2996 7752) 14th floor, Sindhorn Bldg, 130-132 Th Withayu
Vietnam Airlines (Thanon Sukhumvit map; ☎ 0 2656 9056–8) 7th floor, Ploenchit Center Bldg, Soi 2, Th Sukhumvit

Bus

Bangkok is the centre for bus services that fan out all over the kingdom.

There are three main public-bus terminals. The **Northern & Northeastern bus terminal** *(☎ 0 2527 8055 for Northern routes; ☎ 0 2936 2841 for Northeastern routes; Th Kamphaeng Phet)* is just north of Chatuchak Park. It's also commonly called the **Moh Chit station** *(sàthǎanii mǎw chít)*, or, since it has moved to an air-con building on the other side of the highway a little further north, it's sometimes referred to as 'New' Moh Chit *(mǎw chít mài)*. Buses depart from here for northern and northeastern destinations like Chiang Mai and Nakhon Ratchasima (Khorat), as well as places closer to Bangkok such as Ayuthaya and Lopburi. Buses to Aranya Prathet also go from here, not from the Eastern bus terminal as you might expect. Air-con city bus Nos 510, 512 and 523, along with ordinary bus Nos 3, 49, 77 and others all pass the terminal. The Mo Chit Skytrain station is also within walking distance of the bus terminal.

The **Eastern bus terminal** *(☎ 0 2391 2504; Soi 40/Soi Ekamai, Th Sukhumvit)*, the departure point for buses to Pattaya, Rayong, Chanthaburi and other points east, is a long way out along Th Sukhumvit, opposite Soi 63. Most folks call it **Ekamai station** *(sàthǎanii èk-kàmai)*. Air-con bus Nos 501, 508, 511 and 513 all pass this station, and the Skytrain stops at its own Ekamai station in front of Soi 40.

The **Southern bus terminal** *(☎ 0 2435 1200, 434 7192)*, for buses south to Phuket, Surat Thani and closer centres to the west like Nakhon Pathom and Kanchanaburi, has one Thonburi location for both ordinary and air-con buses at the intersection of Hwy 338 (Th Nakhon Chaisi) and Th Phra Pinklao. This station is known in Thai as *sathǎanii khon sòng sǎai tâi* (Southern transport terminal), often shortened to *sǎai tâai mài* (new southern route). A convenient way to reach the station is by air-con bus Nos 503, 507 and 511 and ordinary city bus Nos 30, 124 and 127.

When travelling on night buses take care of your belongings. Some of the long-distance buses leaving from Bangkok now issue receipts for luggage stored under the bus, but valuables are still best kept on your person or within reach.

Allow an hour to reach the Northern bus terminal from Banglamphu or anywhere along the river, and more than an hour to reach the Southern bus terminal. The Eastern bus terminal takes 30 to 45 minutes under most traffic conditions. During gridlock, eg, Friday afternoons before a holiday, it can take up to three hours to get across town to the terminals by public transport; this is greatly reduced if travelling solely by Skytrain.

Private Bus The more reputable and licensed private-tour buses leave from the public-bus terminals. Some private bus companies arrange pick-ups at Th Khao San and other guesthouse areas – note, these pick-ups are illegal since it's against municipal law to carry passengers within the city limits, except en route to/from an official terminal. This is why the curtains on these buses are sometimes closed when picking up passengers.

Although fares tend to be lower on private buses, the incidence of reported theft is far greater than on the government buses. They are also generally – but not always – less reliable, promising services (eg, air-con or VIP seats) that they don't deliver. For safer, more reliable and more punctual service, stick to buses that leave from the official public terminals.

For details on bus fares to/from other towns and cities in Thailand, see the Getting There & Away sections in the relevant destination chapters.

Train

Bangkok is the terminus for the main trunk rail services to the south, north, northeast and east. There are two principal train stations. The big **Hualamphong station** *(☎ 1690; advance booking ☎ 0 2220 4567; general information ☎ 0 2621 8701; Th Phra Ram IV)* handles services to the north, northeast and some of the southern services.

There is a TAT-licensed travel agency in the mezzanine level of the station.

Across the river, **Thonburi station** *(Bangkok Noi)* handles a few services to the south. If you're heading down to southern Thailand, make sure you know which station your train departs from. See the Train section in the Getting Around chapter for further details.

GETTING AROUND

Getting around Bangkok may be difficult at first for the uninitiated but once you're familiar with the bus system the whole city is accessible. The main obstacle is the traffic, which moves at a snail's pace during much of the day. This means advance planning is a must when you are attending scheduled events or arranging appointments.

If you can travel by river, canal or Skytrain from one point to another (ie, avoid the roads), it's always the best choice.

To/From the Airport

At Bangkok International Airport there's a choice of transport modes from the airport to the city, costing 3.50B and 300B.

Skytrain and subway service will connect the new international airport (in Bang Phli district) to central Bangkok.

Airport Bus A 21-seat airport-express bus service operates from Bangkok International Airport to three different Bangkok districts for 100B per person. Buses run every 30 minutes from 6am to 12.30am. A map showing the designated stops is available at the airport; buses on each route make approximately six stops in each direction. This service means you can avoid haggling with taxi drivers over fares and forgo the slow pace of the regular bus routes.

The Airport Bus counter is around 200m to the left (with your back to Terminal 1) of the left-most terminal exit. The routes are:

A-1 To the Silom business district via Pratunam and Th Ratchadamri, stopping at big hotels like the Century, Indra, Grand Hyatt Erawan, Regent Bangkok and Dusit Thani.

A-2 To Banglamphu via Th Phayathai, Th Lan Luang, Th Ratchadamnoen Klang, Th Tanao, Th Phra Athit and Sanam Luang; this is the best route for the Victory Monument, Siam Square, Democracy Monument or Banglamphu/Th Khao San areas. In Banglamphu, it stops opposite the Food & Agriculture Organization headquarters on Th Phra Athit.

A-3 To Th Sukhumvit, including Ekamai station (for buses east to Pattaya and Trat) and Soi 55 (Soi Thong Lor). Hotel stops include the Ambassador and the Delta Grand Pacific.

Public Bus Cheapest of all are the public buses to Bangkok; these stop on the highway in front of the airport. There are two non-air-con bus routes and four air-con routes; take note, however, that the non-air-con buses no longer accept passengers carrying luggage.

Air-con bus No 29 costs 16B and plies one of the most useful, all-purpose routes from the airport into the city as it goes to the Siam Square and Hualamphong areas. After entering the city limits via Th Phahonyothin, (which turns into Th Phayathai), the bus passes Th Phetburi, (get off to change buses for Banglamphu), then Th Phra Ram I at Siam Square and Mahboonkrong shopping centre (for buses out to Th Sukhumvit, or to walk to Soi Kasem San 1 for various lodgings) and finally turns right on Th Phra Ram IV to go to the Hualamphong district (where the main train station is located). You'll want to go the opposite way on Th Phra Ram IV for the Soi Ngam Duphli lodging area. Bus No 29 runs 24 hours.

Air-con bus No 513 also goes to Bangkok from the airport, coming down Th Phahonyothin (like No 29), turning left at the Victory Monument to Th Ratchaprarop, then south to Th Ploenchit, where it travels east along Th Sukhumvit all the way to Bang Na. This is definitely the bus to catch if you're heading for the Th Sukhumvit area. It costs 16B and operates from 4.30am to 9pm.

Air-con bus No 504 costs 16B and operates from 4.10am to 8.30pm. It begins with a route parallel to that of bus No 29 bus – down Th Viphavadi Rangsit to Th Ratchaprarop and Th Ratchadamri (Pratunam district), crossing Th Phetburi, Th Phra Ram I, Th Ploenchit and Th Phra Ram IV, then down Th Silom and left on Th Charoen Krung to Thonburi.

Air-con bus No 510 goes from the airport all the way to the Southern bus terminal in Thonburi for 16B and operates from 4.10am to 9.30pm.

Ordinary bus No 59 (no luggage allowed) costs only 3.50B (5B from 10pm to 6am) and operates 24 hours – it zigzags through to Banglamphu (Democracy Monument area) from the airport, a trip that can take up to 1¾ hours or more in traffic. Ordinary bus No 29 costs 3.50B, or 5B from 11pm to 5am, and operates 24 hours.

Terminal Shuttle The airport authority runs free air-con shuttle buses between the international and domestic terminals, so if you're just going between these buildings, you can jump on any bus that comes along. In addition, THAI runs shuttles between different points within the airport complex; inquire about this service at the information desks in Terminals 1 and 2.

Train You can also get into Bangkok from the airport by train. Inside Terminal 1 follow the signs for trains to Bangkok; you'll cross the highway via the pedestrian bridge, which leads to Don Muang train station. Buy tickets from the booth on the airport side of the tracks. The 3rd-class fare from Don Muang to Bangkok is only 5B to 10B on the ordinary and commuter trains. Rapid or express train tickets cost 55B and 75B each respectively.

Trains run frequently between 4.40am and 9.45pm, and it takes from 45 minutes to one hour to reach Hualamphong, the main station in central Bangkok. In the opposite direction trains depart between 6.40am and 10pm. Once you arrive at Hualamphong station, walk out of the main entrance and turn left. Bus No 53 to Banglamphu runs along the street directly in front of you (the street that runs parallel to the train tracks); there's usually a gang of motorcycle and túk-túk drivers conveniently hanging out near the bus stop.

Some travellers disembark from the airport and catch trains northward from Don Muang train station to Ayuthaya, Sukhothai, Khorat or other points in the north or northeast, thus avoiding Bangkok altogether.

Taxi The Department of Land Transport has stepped in to police the airport taxi service, and for the moment, at least, there seems to be substantially fewer hassles with airport taxi drivers than in previous years. During the past two years we've had no problems at all getting regular metered taxis.

Metered taxis waiting near the arrival area of the airport are supposed to be regulated by the airport. Ignore all the touts waiting in the arrival hall and buy a taxi ticket from the public taxi booth near the kerb outside the hall. Fares differ according to destination; fares to most destinations in central Bangkok cost 200B to 300B.

On top of the fare, airport taxis are permitted to collect a 50B airport surcharge. You must also reimburse drivers for any toll charges paid, if they take the tollway into the city (20B to 50B), which almost always saves time.

If you end up taking a flat-rate taxi, the driver should pay all toll charges. Two, three, or even four passengers (if they don't have much luggage) can split the fare.

Sometimes unscrupulous drivers will approach you before you reach the taxi booth and try to sell you a ticket for 350B or 400B – ignore them and head for the kerb queue. Touts from the old taxi mafia that used to prowl the arrival area are still around and may approach you with fares of around 200B. Their taxis have white-and-black plates and are not licensed to carry passengers, hence you have less legal recourse in the event of an incident than if you take a licensed taxi (yellow-and-black plates). Robberies have reportedly occurred in these taxis.

A few drivers still try to renegotiate the fare once you're inside a metered taxi. The occasional driver will refuse to use his meter and quote a flat rate of 300B to 400B; however, this is rarer than it used to be. Passengers now receive a bilingual Taxi-Meter Information sheet, issued by the Department of Land Transport, which indicates the name of the driver, the taxi licence number, the date and the time. A phone number for registering complaints against the driver is listed on this sheet, so if you have a problem you should call and report the driver. The passenger – *not* the driver – is supposed to keep this sheet. The driver may want to glance at the sheet to read your destination, but you should receive it back immediately.

Metered taxis, flagged down on the highway in front of the airport (turn left from the arrival hall), are even cheaper since they don't have to pay the 50B airport surcharge. When the queue at the public-taxi desk is particularly long, it's sometimes faster to go upstairs or walk out to the highway and flag one down.

Three companies maintain counters at the airport offering airport limousine service, which is really just a glorified air-con taxi. **THAI Limousine** (*☎ 0 2535 2803*), **Airport Associate Limousine** (*☎ 0 2535 5905, 0 2535 5361*) and **Prapirab Limousine** (*☎ 0 2535 1894*) all have a starting rate of 650B to destinations in central Bangkok, more than double the usual meter-taxi fare. The main advantage is not having to wait in the public-taxi queue.

Buses to Pattaya THAI operates direct air-con buses to Pattaya from the airport daily at 9am, noon and 7pm; the fare is 200B one way. Private sedans cost 1500B to 2500B per trip.

Bus

You can save a lot of money in Bangkok by sticking to the **Bangkok Metropolitan Transit Authority** *(BMTA; w www.bmta/mot.go.th)* public buses, which cost 5B for any journey under 10km on the ordinary white-and-blue buses, or 3.50B on the red buses or smaller green buses. Smaller 'baht buses' plying the lanes are painted red and maroon, and cost 2B each.

Cream-and-blue air-con buses are available for 8B for the first 8km, and increase by 2B increments up to 20B to 24B, depending on the distance travelled. Orange Euro 2 air-con buses cost 12B for any distance, while white-and-pink air-con buses cost 25B to 30B. The air-con buses are not only cooler, but are usually less crowded (all bets are off during rush hours).

Most bus lines run from 5am to 11pm, except for the all-night cream-and-red ordinary buses, which run from 10pm to 5am on some routes and cost 5B. Buddhist monks and novices ride for free.

One air-con service that's never overcrowded is the Microbus – it stops taking passengers once every seat is filled. The fare is a flat rate of 25B – you deposit the money in a box at the front of the bus (exact change only). These buses are pink and white. A couple of useful Microbus lines include the No 6, which starts on Th Si Phraya (near the River City shopping complex) and proceeds to the Siam Square area, then out to Th Sukhumvit; and the No 8, which runs between the Victory Monument area and Banglamphu district.

Safety Be careful with your belongings while riding Bangkok buses. The place you are most likely to be 'touched' is on the crowded ordinary buses. Razor artists abound, particularly on buses in the Hualamphong station area. These dexterous thieves specialise in slashing your backpack, shoulder bag or even your trouser pockets with a sharp razor and slipping your valuables out unnoticed. Hold your bag in front of you, under your attention and carry money in a front shirt pocket, preferably (as the Thais do) maintaining a tactile and visual sensitivity to these areas if the bus is packed shoulder to shoulder.

Skytrain

The Skytrain elevated-rail network is perfect for those wanting to escape the often horrendous traffic jams on Bangkok's streets. So far two lines have been built by the **Bangkok Mass Transit System Skytrain** *(BTS; ☎ 0 2617 7300; w www.bts.co.th)*, known to the Thais simply as *rót fai fáa* (sky train).

One line starts from the Mo Chit station in the north, next to the Northern and North-eastern bus terminal as well as Chatuchak Park, and ends at the On Nut station, near Soi 81, Th Sukhumvit. Often referred to as 'the Sukhumvit line', work has begun to extended this line 9km further southeast to Samut Prakan. There is also talk of extending this line as far as the international airport under construction in Nong Ngu Hao.

The second line (the 'Silom line') runs from the National Stadium east to Siam Square and soon after makes an abrupt turn to the southwest, continuing above Th Ratchadamri, down Th Silom to Th Narathiwat Ratchanakharin, then out Th Sathon until it terminates next to the foot of Saphan Taksin on the banks of Mae Nam Chao Phraya. Work has begun to extend this line a further 2km over the river into Thonburi and possibly as far as Wong Wian train station.

Although the Skytrain has yet to make a sizeable dent in Bangkok traffic, it's estimated that on an average day there are 40,000 fewer cars on the road than before the train's 1999 launch, and that a large number of city residents have switched from the crowded air-con buses of BMTA, which has lowered the number of buses on the road at any one time, perhaps making a very small contribution to improving city air.

Another advantage to the Skytrain is that it offers a pleasant semi-bird's-eye view of the city, allowing glimpses of greenery and historic architecture not visible at street level due.

Riding the Skytrain Trains run frequently from 6am to midnight along both lines. If you've ever ridden a modern light rail system that used ticket cards with magnetic stripes, you'll have no trouble figuring out the simple Skytrain system. You can change between the two lines at the double-height Siam station (also known as 'Central Station'), in front of Siam Square and Siam Center. Free maps of the system are available at all Skytrain station ticket booths. All trains are air-conditioned, often heavily so.

From your point of departure, fares vary from 10B to 40B depending on which of the 23 current stations you plan to disembark from. Ticket machines at each station accept 5B and 10B coins only. If you don't have correct change, buy your ticket from staffed ticket booths at Skytrain stations. You can also buy tickets in 100B increments from all station ticket booths, and at branches of Siam Commercial Bank, Black Canyon Coffee shops and Watsons drug stores. Fares are posted inside every station.

If you're not sure where you're going, ticket staff at each station offer helpful advice even though their English may be limited.

Subway

Since 1998, the **Metropolitan Rapid Transit Authority** *(MRTA)* has been building the city's first-ever subway. The 18-station line is designed to link Hualamphong near the river with Bang Seu in the north via the Queen Sirikit National Convention Centre. The line intersects Skytrain routes at two points – near the Asoke Skytrain station and the Mo Chit Skytrain station. The subway (*rót fai tâi din*) should be up and running 2004.

Taxi

Metered taxis *(tháeksii miitôe)* were introduced in Bangkok in 1993, and now far outnumber the old nonmetered taxis. The ones with meters have signs on top reading 'Taxi Meter', the others 'Taxi Thai' or just 'Taxi'. Fares for metered taxis are always lower than those for nonmetered; however, they can be a little harder to flag down during peak hours. Demand often outstrips supply between 8am and 9am, 6pm and 7pm, and also late at night when bars are closing (1am to 2am). Because metered-taxi drivers use rented vehicles and must return them at the end of their shifts, they sometimes won't take longer fares as quitting time nears.

Metered taxis charge 35B at flag fall for the first 2km, then 4.50B for the next 10km, 5B for 13km to 20km, and 5.50B for any distance over 20km, but only when the taxi travels at 6km/h or more; at speeds under 6km/h, a surcharge of 1.25B per minute kicks in. Freeway tolls – 20B to 40B depending where you start – must be paid by the passenger. A 24-hour 'phone-a-taxi' service **Siam Taxi** *(☎ 0 2377 1771)* is available for an extra 20B.

For certain longer routes it can be very difficult to find a taxi driver who's willing to use the meter. One such instance is going from the Southern bus terminal across the river to Bangkok proper – most drivers ask for a flat 350B but will settle for 250B. For those times when you're forced to use a nonmetered taxi, you'll have to negotiate the fare. Fares to most places within central Bangkok cost 60B to 80B, and you should add 10B or 20B if it's during peak hour or after midnight. For trips to the airport the nonmetered drivers charge 200B to 300B.

You can hire a taxi all day for around 1000B or 1500B, depending on how much driving is involved.

Túk-Túk

In heavy traffic, túk-túk are usually faster than taxis since they're able to weave between cars and trucks. On the down side, they have no air-con, so you have to breathe all that lead-soaked air (at its thickest in the middle of Bangkok's wide avenues), and they're also more dangerous since they can easily flip over, when braking into a fast curve. The typical túk-túk fare nowadays offers no savings over a metered taxi – around 40B for a short hop (eg, Siam Square to Soi 2 Sukhumvit).

Túk-túk drivers tend to speak less English than taxi drivers, so many new arrivals have a hard time communicating their destinations. Although some travellers have complained about túk-túk drivers deliberately taking them to the wrong destination (to collect commissions from certain restaurants, gem shops or silk shops), others never seem to have a problem with túk-túk, and swear by them. Beware of túk-túk drivers who offer to take you on a sightseeing tour for

Túk-Túk Wars

In 18th-century Bangkok, residents got around on foot, by canal or in human-drawn rickshaws, called *rót chék* or 'Chinese vehicles'. During the early 20th century, the rickshaw gave way to the three-wheeled pedicab *(săamláw)*, which then added inexpensive Japanese two-stroke engines after WWII to become the onomatopoeic túk-túk.

These small three-wheeled taxicabs sound like power saws gone berserk and commonly leave trails of blue smoke whenever they rev up, despite the fact they run on LP gas, a cleaner fuel than diesel or petrol. Objecting Bangkokians have been trying for years to enact a ban on túk-túk. More than a decade ago the city forbade the further production of any new three-wheeled taxis, but every time we go to Bangkok we see hordes of brand-new ones. It's a moral dilemma because túk-túk drivers are usually poor northeasterners, who can't afford to rent the quieter, less polluting Japanese vehicles.

10B or 20B – it's a touting scheme designed to pressure you into purchasing overpriced goods.

Motorcycle Taxi

As passengers become more desperate in their attempts to beat rush-hour gridlock, motorcycle taxis have moved from the lanes to the main avenues. Fares for a motorcycle taxi are about the same as túk-túk except during heavy traffic, when they may cost a bit more.

Riding on the back of a speeding motorcycle taxi is even more hair-raising than riding in a túk-túk. Keep your legs tucked in – the drivers are used to carrying passengers with shorter legs than those of the average Westerner and they pass perilously close to other vehicles while weaving in and out of traffic. Even if you're not in a hurry, catching a motorcycle taxi through traffic is a close approximation to an extreme sport.

Car & Motorcycle

Cars and motorcycles are easily rented in Bangkok, if you can afford them and have steel nerves. Rates start at around 1500B per day or 9000B per week for a small car (much less for a motorcycle), excluding insurance. For long-term rentals you can usually arrange a discount of up to 35%. An International Driving Permit and passport are required for all rentals.

For long, cross-country trips, you might consider buying a new or used motorcycle and reselling it when you leave – this can end up being cheaper than renting, especially if you buy a good used bike. See the Getting Around chapter for more details.

The following car-rental companies are located in Bangkok.

Avis Rent-A-Car (☎ 0 2255 5300–4, fax 0 2253 3734) 2/12 Th Withayu; (☎ 0 2535 4052) Bangkok International Airport; (☎ 0 2254 1234) Grand Hyatt Erawan Hotel; (☎ 0 2253 0444) Le Meridien President Hotel

Budget Car Rental (☎ 0 2203 0250, fax 0 2203 0249) 19/23 Bldg A, Royal City Avenue, Th Phetburi Tat Mai

Grand Car Rent (☎ 0 2248 2991) 233-5 Th Asoke-Din Daeng

Highway Car Rent (☎ 0 2266 9393) 1018/5 Th Phra Ram IV

Lumpinee Car Rent (☎ 0 2255 1966, 0 2255 3482) 167/4 Th Withayu

National Car Rental (☎ 0 2928 1525) Amari Airport Hotel; (☎ 0 2722 8487) 727 Th Si Nakharin
Petchburee Car Rent (☎ 0 2319 7255) 2371 Th Phetburi Tat Mai
Sathorn Car Rent (☎ 0 2633 8888) 6/8-9 Th Sathon Neua

There are more rental agencies along Th Withayu and Th Phetburi Tat Mai. Some also rent motorcycles, but you're better off renting or leasing a bike at a place that specialises in motorcycles, like **Chusak Yont Shop** *(☎ 0 2251 9225, 1400 Th Phetburi Tat Mai)*.

Boat

Bangkok was once called the 'Venice of the East', but much of the original canal system has been filled in for road construction. Larger canals, especially on the Thonburi side, remain important commercial arteries but many of the smaller canals are hopelessly polluted and survive only as drains. Still there is plenty of transport along and across Mae Nam Chao Phraya and up adjoining canals. River transport is one of the nicest ways to get around Bangkok as well as, quite often, being much faster than any road-based alternatives. For a start, you get quite a different view of the city; secondly, it's much less of a hassle than tangling with the polluted, noisy and traffic-crowded Bangkok streets.

Along Mae Nam Chao Phraya, the **Chao Phraya River Express** *(☎ 0 2623 6001–3)* operates from Wat Ratchasingkhon, in south-central Bangkok, northwards to Nonthaburi Province. There are three boat lines: two express lines (indicated by yellow or orange flags) and the local line (without a flag).

Express boats stop at certain piers during morning and evening (usually 6am to 9am and 3pm to 7pm) and cost 10B to 25B, depending on the destination.

Local boats stop at all piers from 6am to 7.40pm, and cost 6B to 10B.

For travellers staying in Banglamphu (near Th Khao San), the closest pier *(tha)* is Tha Banglamphu on Th Phra Athit. See the Chao Phraya River Express & Thonburi Canals map for other piers close to the Grand Palace and Wat Phra Kaew (Tha Chang), Wat Pho (Tha Tien) and Chinatown (Tha Ratchawong).

Bangkok Metropolitan Authority operates two lengthy and useful canal routes: Khlong Saen Saep (Banglamphu to Bang Kapi) and Khlong Phasi Charoen in Thonburi (Kaset Bang Khae port to Saphan Phra Ram I). Although the canal boats can be crowded, the service is generally much faster than either a taxi or bus. Along Th Sukhumvit, however, the Skytrain is generally preferable.

The Khlong Saen Saep canal service is one of the most useful for most visitors. This one provides a quicker alternative to road transport between the river and eastern Bangkok (ie, Siam Square, outer Sukhumvit and Bang Kapi). The boat from Banglamphu to the Ramkhamhaeng University area, for example, costs 10B and takes only 40 minutes. A bus would take at least an hour under Bangkok's normal traffic conditions. The main detraction from this route is the seriously polluted canal – passengers typically hold newspapers over their clothes and faces to prevent being splashed by the stinking black water. Not the best choice of transport if you're dressed for a formal occasion.

Most visitors, however, use the Khlong Saen Saep canal taxi to get to Siam Square (6B); the boat stops at Tha Ratchathewi by the bridge next to the Asia Hotel (see the Siam Square & Pratunam map). It is really easy to miss this stop, so let the person sitting next to you know that you want '**see**-yahm **sa**-quare' (Thai for Siam Square). The canal-taxi pier in Banglamphu is near Wat Saket and the Democracy Monument (see the Central Bangkok map).

Walking

At first glance, Bangkok doesn't seem like a great town for walking – its main avenues are so choked with traffic that the noise and thick air will probably drive you indoors. However, quiet spots, where walks are rewarding, do exist (eg, Lumphini Park or neighbourhoods off the main streets). And certain places are much more conveniently seen on foot, particularly the older sections of town along Mae Nam Chao Phraya where the roads are so narrow and twisting that bus lines don't go there.

For walking tours, see the boxed texts 'Walking Tour – Chinatown & Phahurat' and 'Ratanakosin Temples & River Walking Tour' earlier in this chapter.

[Continued on page 230]

Thai Cuisine

RICHARD I'ANSON

PETER HINES

JULIET COOMBE

KAREN TRIST

JULIET COOMBE

JULIET COOMBE

PAUL BEINSSEN

RICHARD I'ANSON

Clockwise from top left: orange chillies; grilled mackerel; tropical fruit; steamed seafood; lychees; grilled squid; Thai curry; sour and spicy soup, *tom yam kung*

Standing at the crossroads of India, China and Oceania, Thailand has adapted cooking techniques and ingredients from all three of these major spheres of influence as well as from the culinary kits carried by passing traders and empire-builders from the Middle East and southern Europe. Over the centuries, indigenous rudiments fused with imported elements to produce a distinctive native cuisine, instantly recognisable to any discerning palate. Today Thai food has become so globally appreciated that many gourmands rank it alongside the cuisines of France, Italy and China in perceived excellence and scope.

As with other well-developed world cuisines, it can be divided into several regional variations. It's also possible to distinguish between high and low cuisine – or in Thai terms 'royal' and 'common' cooking – a historical distinction that's made between recipes reserved for court palates and those enjoyed by commoners. Nowadays court recipes may mingle with ordinary ones in the same restaurants, such as Bangkok's Thanying, which specialises in the former. However, the overall spirit of the cuisine – and a majority of the ingredients – are shared across all classes and regions.

Ingredients

Some people take to the food in Thailand immediately while others don't; Thai dishes can be pungent and spicy – lots of garlic and chillies are used, especially *phrík khîi nŭu* (literally, mouse-shit peppers; these are the small torpedo-shaped devils that can be pushed aside if you are timid about red-hot curries). Almost all Thai food is cooked with fresh ingredients, particularly herbs. Plenty of lime juice, lemon grass and fresh coriander leaf are added to give the food its characteristic tang, and fish sauce (*náam plaa*, generally made from anchovies) or shrimp paste *(kà-pì)* to make it salty.

Other common seasonings include galanga root *(khàa)*, black pepper, three kinds of basil, ground peanuts (more often a condiment), tamarind juice *(náam mákhăam)*, ginger *(khĭng)* and coconut milk *(kà-thí)*. Thai people eat a lot of what could be called Chinese food (there has always been a large Chinese migrant population in Thailand), which is generally, but not always, less spicy.

Rice *(khâo)* is eaten with most meals; 'to eat' in Thai is literally 'eat rice' or *kin khâo*. Thais can be very picky about their rice, insisting on the right temperature and cooking times. Ordinary white rice is called *khâo jâo* and there are many varieties and grades. The finest-quality Thai rice is known as *khâo hăwm málí*, or jasmine-scented rice, for its sweet, inviting smell when cooked. In the north and northeast 'sticky' or glutinous rice *(khâo nĭaw)* is common.

Where to Eat

Many smaller restaurants and food stalls do not have menus, so it is worthwhile memorising a standard repertoire of dishes. Most provinces have their own local specialities in addition to the standards and you might try asking for 'whatever is good', allowing the proprietors to

itle page & inset: Fresh food, Pak Khlong market, Bangkok (Photograph by Jerry Alexander)

choose for you. Of course, you might get stuck with a large bill this way, but with a little practice in Thai social relations you may also get some very pleasing results.

The most economical places to eat – and the most dependable – are noodle shops *(ráan kŭaytĭaw)*, curry-and-rice shops *(ráan khâo kaeng)* and night markets *(tàlàat tôh rûng)*. Most towns and villages have at least one night market and several noodle and/or curry shops. While the night markets in Chiang Mai have a slight reputation for over-charging (especially for large parties), this is usually not the case in Thailand. It helps if you speak Thai as much as possible. Curry shops are generally open for breakfast and lunch only, and are a very cheap source of nutritious food. Another common food venue in larger cities is the *ráan khâo tôm* (literally, boiled-rice shop), a type of Chinese-Thai restaurant that offers not just boiled rice soups *(khâo tôm)* but an assortment of *aahăan taam sàng* (food made to order). In the better places, cooks pride themselves in being able to fix any Thai or Chinese dish you name. One attraction of the *ráan khâo tôm* is that they tend to stay open late – some are even open 24 hours.

Sponsored by the Shell oil company, Thai food critic Thanad Sri bestows the Shell Chuan Chim award upon his favourite dishes at restaurants around Thailand. Look out for the outline of a green bowl next to the familiar Shell symbol, which is usually displayed outside the restaurant. It's not a foolproof guarantee; some restaurants hang onto their signs long after the kitchen has lowered its standards.

Ordering

Except for 'rice plates' and noodle dishes, Thai meals are usually ordered family-style – two or more people order together, sharing different dishes. Traditionally, the party orders one of each kind of dish, eg, one of chicken, one soup etc. One dish is generally large enough for two people. One or two extras may be ordered for a large party. If you come to eat at a Thai restaurant alone and order one of these 'entrees', you had better be hungry or know enough Thai to order a small portion. Eating alone is not really very acceptable socially; Thais generally consider it unusual – but then as a *faràng* (Westerner) you're an exception anyway.

Using the Right Tool for the Job

If you're not offered chopsticks, don't ask for them. When Westerners ask for chopsticks to eat Thai food, it only puzzles the restaurant proprietors. For white rice, use the fork and spoon provided (fork in the left hand, spoon in the right, or the reverse for left-handers). An even more embarrassing act is trying to eat sticky rice (popular in northern and northeastern Thailand) with chopsticks. Use your right hand instead, picking up clumps of sticky rice with your fingers.

Chopsticks are reserved for eating Chinese-style food from bowls (eg, noodles) or for eating in all-Chinese restaurants. In either case you will be supplied with chopsticks without having to ask. Unlike their counterparts in many Western countries, restaurateurs in Thailand won't assume that you don't know how to use them.

A cheaper alternative is to order dishes 'over rice' *(râat khâo)*. Curry *(kaeng)* over rice is called *khâo kaeng;* in a standard curry shop *khâo kaeng* is only about 15B or 20B a plate.

Another category of Thai food is called *kàp klâem* – dishes meant to be eaten while drinking alcoholic beverages. On some menus these are translated as 'snacks' or 'appetisers'. Typical *kàp klâem* include *thùa thâwt* (fried peanuts), *kài sǎam yàang* (literally, three kinds of chicken; a plate of chopped ginger, peanuts, 'mouse-shit' peppers and bits of lime – to be mixed and eaten by hand) and various kinds of *yam*, Thai-style salads made with lots of chillies and lime juice.

Vegetarian

Those visitors who wish to avoid eating meat and seafood can be accommodated with some effort. Vegetarian restaurants are increasing in number throughout the country, thanks largely to Bangkok's ex-governor, Chamlong Srimuang, whose strict vegetarianism has inspired a nonprofit chain of vegetarian restaurants *(ráan aahǎan mangsàwírát)* in Bangkok and several provincial capitals. Many of these are sponsored by the Asoke Foundation, an ascetic (some would say heretic) Theravada Buddhist sect that finds justification for vegetarianism in the Buddhist sutras. Look for the green sign out the front of shops (depicting large Thai numerals) – each restaurant is numbered according to the order in which it was established. The food at these restaurants is usually served buffet-style and is very inexpensive – typically from 7B to 15B per dish. Most are open only from 7am or 8am until noon, and a few as late as 2pm. At an Asoke lecture we attended in Chiang Mai last year, a spokesperson for the foundation said their objective is to *lose* money at these restaurants.

Other easy, though less widespread, venues for vegetarian meals include Indian restaurants, which usually feature a vegetarian section on the menu. Currently these are most prevalent in Bangkok, Chiang Mai, Pattaya and Phuket's Hat Patong. Chinese restaurants are also a good bet since many Chinese Buddhists eat vegetarian food during Buddhist festivals, especially in southern Thailand.

JERRY ALEXANDER

Bottom: Night-market food stall, Bangkok

More often than not, however, visiting vegetarians are left to their own devices at the average Thai restaurant. In Thai the magic words are *phŏm kin jeh* (for men) or *dì-chăn kin jeh* (women). Like other Thai phrases, it's important to get the tones right – the key word, *jeh*, should equate with the English 'jay' without the 'y'. Loosely translated this phrase means 'I eat only vegetarian food'. It might also be necessary to follow with the explanation *phŏm/dì-chăn kin tàe phàk* (I eat only vegetables). Don't worry – this won't be misinterpreted as 'no rice, herbs or fruit'.

In Thai culture, brown or unpolished rice *(khâo klâwng)* was traditionally reserved for prisoners, but nowadays it's occasionally available in vegetarian restaurants.

Those interested in tapping into the Thai vegetarian movement can phone the **Vegetarian Society of Bangkok** *(☎ 0 2272 4282)* for information on the group's activities. The society usually meets monthly to share a vegetarian feast, swap recipes and discuss the whys and wherefores of vegetarianism. In 1999 the World Vegetarian Congress convened in Chiang Mai.

Condiments

As shakers of salt and pepper are to many European tables, the saucer of *phrík náam plaa* – a simple concoction of sliced fresh red and green chillies floating in fish sauce – is a standard condiment found on nearly every Thai table.

Sometimes also called *náam plaa phrík* – the word order is unimportant – this sauce is spooned onto your food whenever you feel the need for more saltiness, and for an extra kick that goes far beyond that of black pepper. Those who are timid about the chillies in *phrík náam plaa* should scoop up the sauce, avoiding the sliced chillies, and spoon it onto their food as needed. Of course the fish sauce absorbs some heat from the chillies, but there's a huge degree of difference.

To accompany seafood, the flavour or *phrík náam plaa* can expanded with the addition of minced garlic, lime juice and a little sugar. With fried or grilled chicken you may get a small dish of *náam jîm kài* (chicken dipping sauce), a mixture of red chilli flakes, honey (or sugar) and rice vinegar, or, especially in the northeast, a thicker sauce made with dried roasted chillies.

With noodles you'll also receive jars of ground red peppers *(phrík pòn)*, vinegar with sliced chillies *(náam sôm phrík)*, sugar and possibly ground peanuts *(thùa pòn)*. Egg and oyster dishes come with a spicy orange-red sauce called *náam phrík sĭi raachaa* (from Si Racha in Chonburi Province, of course). Soy sauce *(náam sii-íw)* can be requested, though this is normally used as a condiment for Chinese food only.

Street Food

An entire culinary subculture revolves around the *rót khĕn* or pushcart, and street vendors purvey practically every single dish from the Thai kitchen. Big cities, small towns, even villages feature meals-on-wheels, an institution that perfectly suits the Thai penchant for enjoying a snack anytime, anywhere.

Street-Food Hygiene

We've eaten hundreds of meals cooked by street vendors in Thailand, and as far as we know have yet to encounter ill effect. Nonetheless, we do take some precautions. The first is we avoid eating cooked vendor food that isn't either refrigerator cold or stove hot. If you don't see it cooked in front of you, don't eat it. Sausages or barbecued meats that have been sitting out all afternoon could be particularly troublesome.

Second, avoid vendor stands where standards are clearly well below average. In Bangkok and other large cities, the competition usually drives substandard vendors out of business, but in small and medium-sized towns that's not necessarily the case. If the cook looks unclean or unhealthy, or if the food cabinets have more than a few flies, keep on walking.

Prices at vendor stalls tend to be very low, and are kept that way by low overheads. Almost anything edible, from bird's nest soup to Italian espresso to hamburgers, is available from a street vendor somewhere in Thailand; however, there are certain dishes that come recommended.

One is *jóhk*, a thick rice porridge served with thin slivers of fresh ginger and rough meatballs made of ground pork *(jóhk mǔu)* or, less frequently, chicken *(jóhk kài)*. If you ask, the cook will toss in a raw egg just before serving. Stir the steaming hot porridge well, and the egg will cook itself in a minute or so.

Noodles are another vendor zone you should feel free to enter with the expectation that you'll be very satisfied. *Kǔaytǐaw phàt thai*, thin rice noodles stir-fried with egg, tofu and dried shrimp, is one noodle dish that can be especially superior from the right vendor; it's not uncommon to see Thais standing in line in front of a sidewalk *kǔaytǐaw phàt thai* vendor in the early evening.

After the sun goes down one of the most popular vendor dishes throughout the country is the Indian Muslim roti or *roh-tii*. In their simplest form, *roh-tiis* are quickly fried on a griddle, drizzled with sweetened condensed milk and granulated sugar and then rolled into a piece of paper in an attempt to keep the customer's hands clean (it never works). Bananas, chocolate, egg and many other fillings may also be added, depending on how elaborate the vendor stand is.

PAUL BEINSSEN

Bottom: Food stall

[Continued from page 224]

Around Bangkok

If you can negotiate Bangkok's traffic jams, there are a couple of sights not far from the capital that make interesting day trips. The giant stupa at Nakhon Pathom, the floating markets and the Ancient City are all worth seeing, and are all within an hour or so of town.

NAKHON PATHOM

อ.เมืองนครปฐม

postcode 73000 • pop 46,400

Only 56km west of Bangkok, Nakhon Pathom is often referred to by Thais as the oldest city in Thailand – the name, in fact, is derived from the Pali 'Nagara Pathama', meaning 'First City'. At one time it functioned as the centre of the Dvaravati kingdom, a loose collection of Mon city states that flourished between the 6th and 11th centuries AD in Mae Nam Chao Phraya valley. Some historians speculate that the area may have been inhabited before India's Asokan period (3rd century BC), as there is a theory that Buddhist missionaries from India visited Nakhon Pathom at that time. Although one could point out that other areas of Thailand were inhabited earlier, Nakhon Pathom may very well be the longest continually inhabited place within the country's current borders.

Today's Nakhon Pathom is a typical provincial Thai city whose only visible link to its glorious past is the famous Phra Pathom Chedi.

Phra Pathom Chedi

พระปฐมเจดีย์

The Phra Pathom Chedi, rising to 127m, is the tallest Buddhist monument in the world. The original monument, buried within the massive orange-glazed dome, was erected in the early 6th century by Theravada Buddhists of Dvaravati (possibly at the same time as Myanmar's famous Shwedagon stupa), but in the early 11th century the Khmer king, Suriyavarman I of Angkor, conquered the city and built a Brahman

AROUND BANGKOK

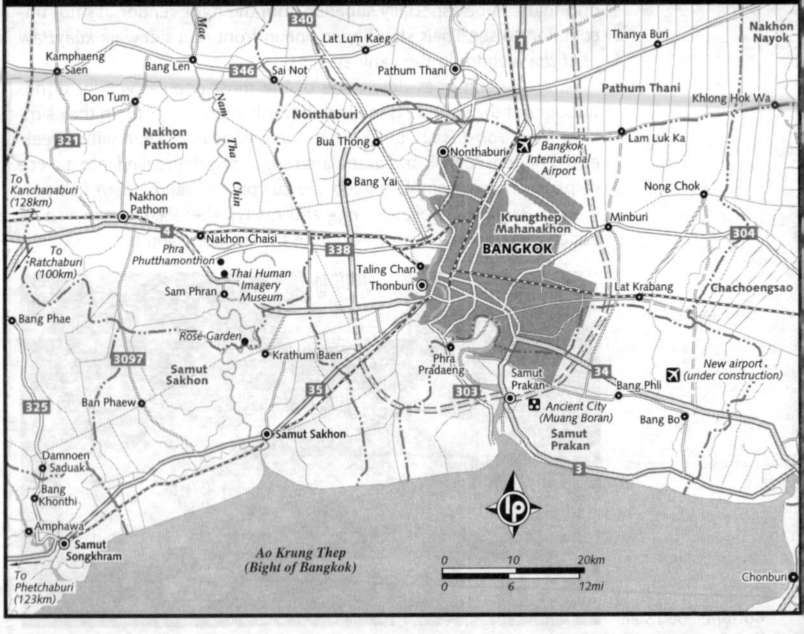

prang over the sanctuary. The Burmese of Bagan, under King Anawrahta, sacked the city in 1057 and the *prang* lay in ruins until King Mongkut had it restored in 1860. The king built a larger *chedi* over the remains according to Buddhist tradition, adding four *wíhăan*, a *bòt*, a replica of the original *chedi*, *săalaa* (meeting hall) and assorted *prang*, and other embellishments. There is even a Chinese temple attached to the outer walls of the *chedi*, next to which outdoor *lí-keh* (Thai folk dance-drama) is sometimes performed.

On the eastern side of the monument, in the *bòt*, is a Dvaravati-style Buddha seated in a European pose similar to the one in Wat Phra Meru in Ayuthaya. It may, in fact, have come from there.

The wát surrounding the *chedi* enjoys the kingdom's highest temple rank, Ratchavoramahavihan; it's one of only six temples so honoured in Thailand. King Rama VI's ashes are interred in the base of the Sukhothai-era Phra Ruang Rochanarit, a large standing Buddha image in the wát's northern *wíhăan*. Also of interest are the many examples of Chinese sculpture carved from a greenish stone that came to Thailand as ballast in the bottom of 19th-century Chinese junks.

Located opposite the *bòt* is a **museum** *(admission 20B; open 9am-4pm Wed-Sun)*, which contains some interesting Dvaravati sculpture.

Other Attractions

Besides the *chedi*, the other highlights of the town are **Silpakorn University**, west of the *chedi* off Phetkasem Hwy, and **Sanam Chan**, adjacent to the university. Sanam Chan, formerly the grounds of Rama VI's palace, is a pleasant park with a canal passing through it.

The somewhat run-down palace still stands in the park, but entry to the palace is not permitted.

Southeast of the city towards Bangkok, between the districts of Nakhon Chaisi and Sam Phran, stands **Phra Phutthamonthon**. This Sukhothai-style standing Buddha, at 40.7m, is reportedly the world's tallest; it's surrounded by a 400-hectare landscaped park that contains sculptures representing the major stages in the Buddha's life (eg, a 6m-high Dharma wheel, carved from a single slab of granite). The Buddha statue, which is particularly beautiful, was designed by Corrado Feroci.

All Bangkok to Nakhon Pathom buses pass the access road to the park; from there you can walk, hitch or flag one of the frequent săwngthăew into the park itself. From Nakhon Pathom you can take a white-and-purple Salaya bus; the stop is on Th Tesa across from the post office.

The **Thai Human Imagery Museum** *(☎ 0 3433 2607; admission 200B; open 9am-5.30pm Mon-Fri, 8.30am-6pm Sat & Sun)*, at Km 31 on Th Pinklao–Nakhon Chaisi (the highway to Bangkok), contains an exhibition of lifelike resin sculptures. A group of Thai artists reportedly spent 10 years studying their subjects and creating the figures, which fall into four categories: famous Buddhist monks of Thailand; former kings of the Chakri dynasty; Thai lifestyles; and chess playing. The museum is near Phra Putthamonthon park, and an inexpensive motorcycle taxi can deliver you between the two places.

Places to Eat

Nakhon Pathom has an excellent **market** along the road between the train station and Phra Pathom Chedi; its *khâo lăam* (sticky rice and coconut steamed in a bamboo joint) is reputed to be the best in Thailand. There are many good, inexpensive food vendors and restaurants in this area.

An old standby on Th Thesa, east of the *chedi*, is the inexpensive Chinese **Tang Ha-Seng** *(no Roman-script sign)*; there are two branches, one at No 71/2-3 and another at No 59/1-2.

Ratchaphreuk *(no Roman-script sign; Th Ratchadamnoen)*, near Soi 5 directly west of Phra Pathom Chedi, offers a pleasant Thai *săalaa* setting with good, medium-priced Thai food. If you catch this place on a slow day, your only dining companions will be members of Kiss, the Beatles and other rock stars adorning the walls.

Getting There & Away

Bus Air-con bus Nos 997 and 83 leave from the Southern bus terminal (Thonburi, Bangkok) for Nakhon Pathom throughout the day (34B, one hour). To return to Bangkok, catch one of the idling buses from Th Phayaphan on the canal side of the road a block from the train station.

The locations of bus stops in Nakhon Pathom seem to change regularly.

At the time of writing, buses to Kanchanaburi (No 81) were leaving throughout the day from Th Khwa Phra, south of Phra Pathom Chedi, near the police station.

Buses to Damnoen Saduak floating market (bus No 78; for more information see the Damnoen Saduak Floating Market section) and to Phetchaburi (bus No 73) leave from the same stop, departing about every 30 minutes.

Local buses going to Phra Phutthamonthon (see Other Attractions earlier in this section) stop on Th Tesa, at the shelter across the street from the post office. You can also wave down Samut Sakhon–bound buses (No 402; 25B) at this stop.

Train Ordinary trains (3rd class only) leave Thonburi (Bangkok Noi) station for Nakhon Pathom at 7.35am and 1.45pm (14B, approximately 1¼ hours). Express trains (90B to 120B, two hours) from Nakhon Pathom return to Thonburi at 4pm and Hualamphong station in Bangkok at 6.45pm.

DAMNOEN SADUAK FLOATING MARKET

ตลาดน้ำดำเนินสะดวก

Wooden canoes laden with multicoloured fruits and vegetables, paddled by Thai women wearing indigo-hued clothes and wide-brimmed straw hats – this quintessential picture of Thailand might have wooed you to this country, but this image is over 20 years old and is more a piece of history than a current snapshot. An updated version would show rows and rows of souvenir stands lining the canals, and boatloads of tourists glued to their cameras. The floating fruit vendors are still there, but the piles of exotic colours have diminished to a few lacklustre, overpriced bunches of bananas.

So should you scratch the famous floating market *(tàlàat náam)* off of your list? Not so fast – despite its decay, the floating market can still be fun, if you catch it early.

The best advice is to arrive in Damnoen Saduak the night before, stay at the conveniently located Noknoi Hotel (see Places to Stay following) and get up around 7am or 8am to see the market. By 9am the package tours from Bangkok arrive, draining what little authenticity is left. It is almost impossible to beat the tours if you leave that morning from Bangkok, especially on a weekday.

Talat Ton Khem, which is over 100 years old, is the town's only remaining market – regardless of what the operators tell you. Minor markets, such as **Talat Hia Kui** and **Talat Khun Phitak**, once offered more local exposure to the tradition, but those have since disappeared.

You can hire a boat from any pier that lines Th Sukhaphiban 1, which is the land route to the floating market area. The going rate is 150B per person per hour.

Beyond the market, the residential canals are quite peaceful and can be explored by hiring a boat for a longer duration. South of the floating market are several small family businesses that welcome tourists; these include a Thai candy maker, a pomelo farm and a knife crafter. Damnoen Saduak's enthusiastic tourist office can arrange transport to these sites for a two- to three-hour tour (around 500B for the boat). The tourist office can also arrange homestays and canal trips. For more on floating markets, see its entry under Samut Songkhram later.

Places to Stay Clean and quiet, **Noknoi** *(Little Bird; ☎ 0 3225 4382; rooms with fan/air-con 170/300B)* is about a 15-minute walk from the floating market.

Ban Sukchoke Resort *(☎ 0 3225 4301; rooms 800-1400B)* offers comfortable bungalows set over the canal. There is also a small house that sleeps 10 people. Ban Sukchoke is 1.5km northwest of Damnoen Saduak's market area.

Getting There & Away Damnoen Saduak is in Ratchaburi Province between Nakhon Pathom and Samut Songkhram. Air-con bus Nos 78 and 996 go direct from Bangkok's Southern bus terminal to Damnoen Saduak (52B, two hours) every 20 minutes from 6.30am. The ladies in the red dresses will scoop you up at the Southern bus terminal and deposit you on the right bus.

Most buses will drop you off at a pier along Khlong Hia Kui or Khlong Damnoen Saduak where you can hire a boat directly to the floating market. The regular bus stop is in town just across the bridge. A yellow sǎwngthǎew (5B) does a frequent loop

DAMNOEN SADUAK FLOATING MARKET

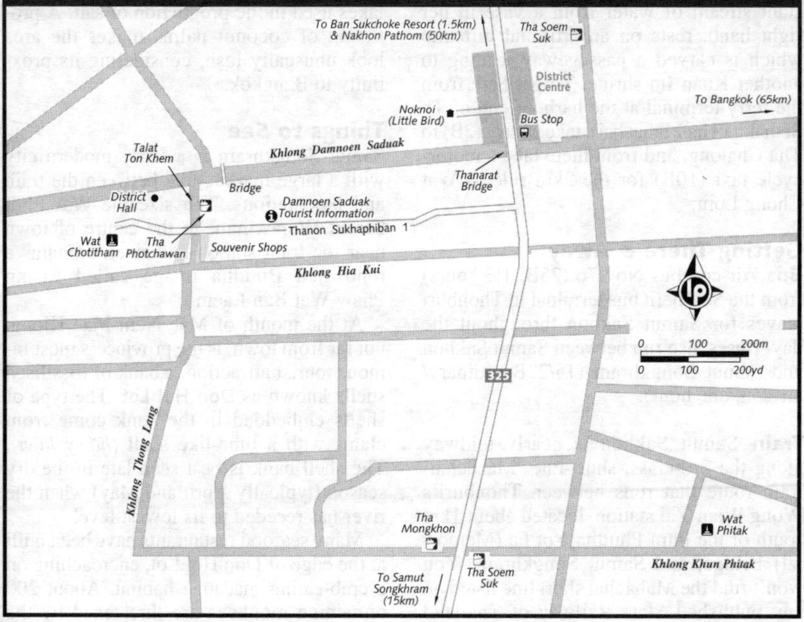

between the floating market and the bus stop in town.

The scenery between Damnoen Saduak and Samut Songkhram is a worthwhile excursion. See the Samut Songkhram section later in this chapter for more information.

SAMUT SAKHON

สมุทรสาคร

postcode 74000 • pop 57,500

Twenty-eight kilometres southwest of Bangkok, Samut Sakhon is popularly known as Mahachai because it straddles the confluence of Mae Nam Tha Chin and Khlong Mahachai. Just a few kilometres from the Gulf of Thailand, this busy port features a lively market area and a pleasant breezy park around the crumbling walls of **Wichian Chodok Fort**. A few rusty cannon pointing towards the river testify to the fort's original purpose of guarding the mouth of Mae Nam Tha Chin from foreign invaders. Before the arrival of European traders in the 17th century, the town was known as Tha Jin (Chinese pier) because of the large number of Chinese junks that called here.

Samut Sakhon set a macabre world record in December 1997 when the skeletal remains of 21,347 unclaimed road-accident victims (many from Bangkok) were cremated in a specially built electric crematorium at the edge of town. The cremation of the corpses, which had been collected over 11 years by the Paw Tek Teung Foundation (a Chinese benevolent society dedicated to this purpose), took seven days of constant burning to complete.

A few kilometres west of Samut Sakhon, along Hwy 35, is the Ayuthaya-period **Wat Yai Chom Prasat**, which is known for the finely carved wooden doors on its *bòt*. You can easily identify the wát by the tall Buddha figure standing at the front. To get here from Samut Sakhon, take an orange westbound bus (10B) heading towards Samut Songkhram from the bus station; the wát is only a 10-minute ride from the edge of town.

The Jao Mae Kuan Im Shrine at **Wat Chong Lom** is a 9m-high fountain in the shape of the Mahayana Buddhist Goddess of Mercy, and is popular with tour groups from Hong Kong, Taiwan and Singapore.

The colourful image, which pours a constant stream of water from a vase in her right hand, rests on an artificial hill into which is carved a passageway leading to another Kuan Im shrine. To get here from the ferry terminal at the harbour end of Th Sethakit (Tha Mahachai), take a ferry (2B) to Tha Chalong, and from there take a motorcycle taxi (10B) for the 2km ride to Wat Chong Lom.

Getting There & Away

Bus Air-con bus No 976 (25B, 1½ hours) from the Southern bus terminal in Thonburi leaves for Samut Sakhon throughout the day. Buses also run between Samut Sakhon and Samut Songkhram (15/22B ordinary/air-con, one hour).

Train Samut Sakhon is nearly midway along the 3rd-class, short-line 'Mahachai' train route that runs between Thonburi's Wong Wian Yai station, located about 1km south of the Phra Phuttha Yot Fa (Memorial) Bridge, and Samut Songkhram. You won't find the Mahachai short line listed on any published State Railway of Thailand (SRT) schedule, whether in English or Thai, as it's strictly a local proposition.

The fare to/from either Thonburi or Samut Songkhram is 10B; there are departures at 7.30am, 10.10am, 1.30pm and 4.40pm heading south, and at similar times heading north from Samut Sakhon.

Getting Around

Săamláw and motorcycle taxis around town cost 20B to 30B, depending on the distance.

SAMUT SONGKHRAM

สมุทรสงคราม

postcode 75000 • pop 35,000

Wedged between Ratchaburi, Samut Sakhon and Phetchaburi, 416-sq-km Samut Songkhram is Thailand's smallest province. Commonly known as 'Mae Klong', the capital lies along a sharp bend in Mae Nam Mae Klong, 74km southwest of Bangkok and just a few kilometres from the Gulf of Thailand. Due to flat topography and abundant water sources, the area surrounding the capital is well suited for the steady irrigation needed to grow guavas, lychees and grapes. Along the highway from Thonburi, visitors will pass a string of artificial sea lakes used in the production of salt. A profusion of coconut palms makes the area look unusually lush, considering its proximity to Bangkok.

Things to See

Samut Songkhram is a fairly modern city with a large market area between the train and bus stations. The sizeable **Wat Phet Samut Worawihan**, in the centre of town near the train station and river, contains a renowned Buddha image called Luang Phaw Wat Ban Laem.

At the mouth of Mae Nam Mae Klong, not far from town, is the province's most famous tourist attraction, a bank of fossilised shells known as **Don Hoi Lot**. The type of shells embedded in the bank come from clams with a tube-like shell *(hǎwy làwt)*. The shell bank is best seen late in the dry season (typically April and May) when the river has receded to its lowest level.

Many seafood restaurants have been built at the edge of Don Hoi Lot, encroaching on a crab-eating macaque habitat. About 200 remaining monkeys are threatened by the development. To get to Don Hoi Lot you can hop on a sǎwngthǎew (10B, 15 minutes) in front of Somdet Phra Phuttalertla Hospital at the intersection of Th Prasitwatthana and Th Thamnimit. Or you can charter a boat from Tha Talat Mae Klong, a scenic journey that takes about 45 minutes.

Wat Satthatham, 500m along the road to Don Hoi Lot, is notable for its *bòt* constructed of golden teak and decorated with 60 million baht worth of mother-of-pearl inlay. The inlay covers the temple's interior and depicts scenes from *jataka* murals above the windows and the *Ramakian* (the Thai version of the Indian classic, *Ramayana*) below.

Some of the most picturesque countryside this close to Bangkok lies along Rte 325 between Damnoen Saduak and Samut Songkhram. Coconut plantations interspersed with small wooden houses line the road and add to the tropical-pastoral atmosphere. You can take an ordinary bus (10B) heading in either direction or get off along the way to visit Ban Benjarong or the Orchid Farm.

Ban Benjarong *(☎ 0 3475 1322)* is a small factory in a modern house that produces top-quality *benjarong*, the traditional five-coloured Thai ceramics. Here you can watch craftsmen painting the intricate arabesques and ornate floral patterns for which benjarong is known. This isn't the glossy stuff you see at Chatuchak Market in Bangkok, but the real thing; prices start at about 1000B. A **showroom** *(open 8am-10.30pm daily)* displays the many styles produced here.

Another local attraction is the **Orchid Farm**, which is 4km north of Samut Songkhram on the road to Damnoen Saduak. Despite its commercial and tourism functions, it is really quite impressive for the colour of its orchids.

Only a 10-minute walk from Talat Nam Amphawa is **King Buddhalertla Naphalai Memorial Park** *(open 9am-6pm daily)*, where there's a **museum** *(admission 10B; open 9am-4pm Wed-Sun)* dedicated to King Rama II, a native of Amphawa district. The museum is housed in traditional central-Thai houses set on two hectares and contains a library of rare Thai books, antiques from early 19th-century Siam and an exhibition of dolls depicting four of Rama II's theatrical works (*Inao, Mani Phichai*, a version of the *Ramakian* and *Sang Thong)*. Behind the houses is a lush botanic garden and beyond that, a drama school. To get there from Talat Nam Amphawa, walk over the bridge and follow the road through the gardens of Wat Amphawan Chetiyaram.

Floating Markets Samut Songkhram Province is crisscrossed with canals intersecting the lazy bends of Mae Nam Mae Klong, creating the perfect environment for traditional Thai floating markets. Three of the better ones are held in Amphawa district, about 7km northwest of Samut Songkhram city via Mae Nam Mae Klong. **Talat Nam Amphawa** convenes in front of Wat Amphawan from 6am to 8am daily, but is best on weekends. The other two operate only on weekends and on six days a month following the traditional lunar calendar. **Bang Noi floating market** takes place in nearby Bang Noi from 6am to 11am on the third, eighth and 13th days of both the waxing and waning moons, while the **Tha Kha floating market** occurs on the second, seventh and 12th days of the waxing and waning moons. The latter convenes along an open, breezy canal lined with greenery and older wooden houses – well worth seeking out.

For most travellers it's easiest to visit on the weekends, but if you want to try to catch the floating market on one of the traditional lunar dates (and thus avoid the crowds), a little detective work is required. First acquire a Thai calendar, available for a few baht from homeware markets, that show which days of the solar month coincide with this lunar schedule.

These floating markets can be visited by chartered long-tail boat from Ta Talat Mae Klong for highly negotiable rates ranging from 250B for an hour to 500B for all morning. Pretend that you're not really interested in going and the rate might drop.

Getting There & Away

Bus Taxis and buses park at the intersection of Th Ratchayat Raksa and Th Prasitphatthana. Buses from Bangkok's Southern bus terminal to Damnoen Saduak also stop here, but some buses from Bangkok may drop you off on the main highway, from where you can either walk or take a săamláw or a săwngthăew (5B). Ordinary buses to Bangkok's Mo Chit station (44B) and air-con buses to the Southern bus terminal (40B) depart from the bus stop near the market. There are also many daily buses to Samut Sakhon (15/22B ordinary/air-con, one hour).

Train Samut Songkhram is the southernmost terminus of a 70km railway that originates at Wong Wian Yai station (Thonburi). There is a 3rd-class train to/from Bangkok (20B, one hour, four daily); see Getting There & Away under the Samut Sakhon section earlier for Bangkok departure times. From Samut Songkhram trains depart at 6.20am, 9am, 11.30am and 3.30pm. The train station is a five-minute walk from the bus station, where Th Kasem Sukhum terminates at Th Prasitphatthana, near the river.

SAMUT PRAKAN

สมุทรปราการ

postcode 10270 • pop 73,600

This small province lies at the mouth of Mae Nam Chao Phraya where it empties into the Gulf of Thailand. The city's name means 'Ocean Wall', a reference to **Phra Chula Jawm Klao Fort**, built around 1893, 7km south of the provincial hall. Today it's one of Thailand's most densely populated provincial capitals, with over 70,000 people packed into 7.3 sq km.

The province's two major attractions, Ancient City and the Crocodile Farm & Zoo, are popular day trips from Bangkok. In fact, Samut Prakan is best visited as a day trip – overnight it differs little from spending the night in Bangkok.

Ancient City
เมืองโบราณ

Thailand isn't all squat concrete buildings, dusty roads and screaming motorcycles. Billed as the largest open-air museum in the world, the Ancient City *(Muang Boran; ☎ 0 2323 9253; adult/child 50/20B; open 8am-5pm daily)* covers more than 80 hectares of peaceful countryside littered with 109 scaled-down facsimiles of many of the kingdom's most famous monuments. The grounds have been shaped to replicate Thailand's general geographical outline, with the monuments placed accordingly.

Visions of Las Vegas and its corny replicas of world treasures may spring to mind, but the Ancient City is architecturally sophisticated – a preservation site for classical buildings and art forms. For students of architecture or those who want an introduction to Thai architecture, it's worth a day's visit. It's also a good place for long, undistracted walks or bicycle rides (50B rental), as it's usually quiet and never crowded.

Some might recognise the monuments of Ancient City, as they're frequently used as a backdrop for *jàk-jàk wong-wong,* the camp, made-for-TV renditions of classical Thai legends that go to air alongside cartoons on Saturday morning.

The **Ancient City Co** *(☎ 0 2226 1936, fax 0 2226 1227)* publishes a lavish bilingual periodical devoted to Thai art and architecture called *Muang Boran*. The journal is edited by some of Thailand's leading art historians.

There's lots of open space for picnics if you want to pick up some food from the market in central Samut Prakan, or you can enjoy a leisurely meal of *sômtam* in an open-air pavilion catching cool breezes and listening to the rhythm of the mortar and pestle mixing your dish's ingredients.

The Ancient City is 33km from Bangkok along the Old Sukhumvit Hwy, outside central Samut Prakan. From Samut Prakan take a green minibus No 36 (6B), which passes the entrance to the Ancient City. Nervous types should sit on the left side of the bus to watch for the 'Muang Boran' sign. To return to town, cross the main highway and catch a white No 36 săwngthăew (5B), which can also drop you off at the road leading to the Crocodile Farm.

Samut Prakan Crocodile Farm & Zoo
ฟาร์มจระเข้สมุทรปราการ

In the same area as the Ancient City is Samut Prakan Crocodile Farm & Zoo *(☎ 0 2387 0020; adult/child 300/200B; open 7am-6pm daily)*, where you can even see crocodile wrestling! There are over 30,000 crocs here (including the largest known Siamese croc, a boy named Yai who's 6m long and weighs 1114kg), as well as elephants, monkeys and snakes.

The farm has trained-animal shows – including croc wrestling every hour from 9am to 11am and 1pm to 4pm daily. Elephant shows take place at 9.30am and 11.30am, while the reptiles usually get their dinner between 4pm and 5pm.

Items made from crocodile hide that are certified by the Convention on International Trade in Endangered Species (Cites) – handbags, belts, shoes – are available from the farm's gift shop.

From central Samut Prakan, you can reach the crocodile farm by taking the blue No S61 săwngthăew; this will go directly to the gate. If you are coming from the Ancient City, catch a white No 36 săwngthăew (5B) to the farm's access road and then a motorcycle taxi (10B) to the entrance.

Other Attractions

The Ayuthaya-era **Phra Samut Chedi**, popularly known as Phra Chedi Klang Nam (Chedi in the Middle of the River) for its original location on an island in Mae Nam Chao Phraya, now sits on the river bank in front of the Provincial Hall. Beginning on the fifth day of the waning moon in the 11th lunar month each year (usually in October), the *chedi* is the site of a nine-day festival with lots of food, music and lights.

Samut Prakan Province is commonly referred to as Meuang Pak Nam. The crowded port area of the city, **Pak Nam**, may smell overpowering to visitors but to residents the smell of fish is their bread and butter. Motorcycle taxi drivers mend fishing nets while waiting for a fare; vendors shoo flies from crates of iced ocean dwellers.

Getting There & Away

Ordinary bus No 25 (3.50B) and air-con bus Nos 507, 508 and 511 (16B) ply regular routes between central Bangkok and Pak Nam (central Samut Prakan). The trip can take up to two hours, depending on traffic. If the traffic is horrendous, consider catching the Skytrain's Sukhumvit line to On Nut station and then catching the aforementioned buses on the road heading out of Bangkok. You can also catch the Skytrain at On Nut heading back to Bangkok. From On Nut to Siam station, it takes 15 minutes and costs 35B.

Getting Around

The bus station is on Th Srisamut in front of the harbour and the market. Make a note of where the Bangkok bus drops you off because Samut Prakan has very few street signs in Roman script. Săwngthăew and minibuses to the town's attractions are usually parked nearby; see those sections for specific transportation details.

Central Thailand

Central Thailand is often overlooked by travellers who land in Bangkok and then make a beeline for the beaches to the south or the mountains in the north. While the region may be upstaged by Thailand's sprawling capital city, it is in these surrounding provinces that you will meet the easygoing people who were once known as the Siamese.

Ayuthaya and Lopburi are long-settled and relatively rural provinces where you'll find some of Thailand's most impressive Buddhist and Hindu ruins, some dating back to when all of central Thailand was a far-flung outpost of the Angkorian Empire of the ancient Khmer.

Kanchanaburi is a wild and mountainous province that once acted as a natural barrier to Myanmar (Burma) to the west. The province is best known for the infamous Death Railway, but it is also home to some of Thailand's most spectacular and pristine national parks.

The people of central Thailand share a common dialect that is considered 'standard' Thai simply because Bangkok, the seat of power, happens to be in the region. High concentrations of Chinese are found in the cities of the central provinces since this is where a large number of Chinese immigrants started out as farmers and merchants. Significant numbers of Mon and Karen live in Kanchanaburi, and pockets of Lao and Phuan – the descendents of war captives who were forcibly resettled following Thai raids into Laos over the centuries – can be found in all three provinces.

Highlights

- Visit the ancient ruins of Ayuthaya, former capital of Siam and Unesco World Heritage site
- See Kanchanaburi's infamous Death Railway and bridge, along with museums and cemeteries memorialising those fallen during WWII
- Marvel at the juxtaposition of ancient stone temples and modern architecture in the long-inhabited city of Lopburi
- Get a taste of Myanmar and shop for bargains at Three Pagodas Pass in Kanchanaburi province

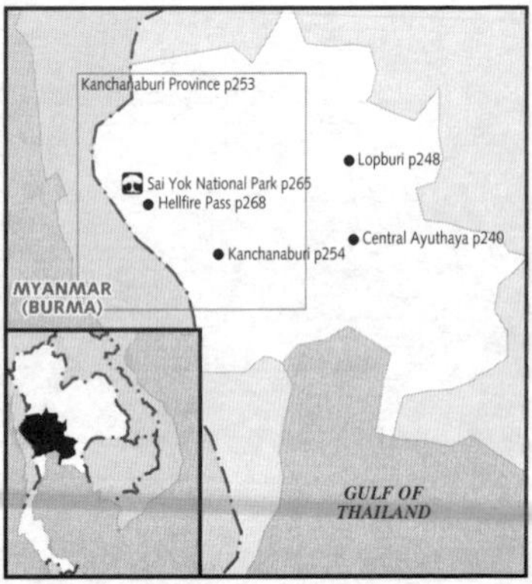

Ayuthaya Province

AYUTHAYA

พระนครศรีอยุธยา

postcode 13000 • pop 78,200

Approximately 86km north of Bangkok, Ayuthaya served as the Siamese royal capital from 1350 to 1767. Prior to 1350, when the capital moved here from U Thong, it was a Khmer outpost. The city was named after Ayodhya (Sanskrit for 'unassailable' or 'undefeatable'), the home of Rama in the Indian epic *Ramayana*. Its full Thai name is Phra Nakhon Si Ayuthaya (Sacred City of Ayodhya).

Although the Sukhothai period is often referred to as Thailand's 'golden age', in many ways the Ayuthaya era was the kingdom's true historical apex – at least in terms of sovereignty, which extended well into present-day Laos, Cambodia and Myanmar, dynastic endurance (over 400 years) and world recognition. Thirty-three kings of various Siamese dynasties reigned in Ayuthaya until it was conquered by the Burmese. During its heyday, Thai culture and international commerce flourished in the kingdom and Ayuthaya was courted by Dutch, Portuguese, French, English, Chinese and Japanese merchants. Ayuthaya's population

had reached one million by the end of the 17th century – virtually all foreign visitors claimed it to be the most illustrious city they had ever seen.

Ayuthaya's close proximity to Bangkok makes it a convenient way to see some ruins and get some history, though the sheer size of the old city means that many of the sites are scattered over a wide area and difficult to visit without a vehicle. Especially during the hot or rainy seasons, many visitors find their enthusiasm for ruins is soon conquered by the heat and humidity. If you have limited time or find the weather too much to handle, consider going north to Lopburi where the ruins are concentrated in a much smaller area and are easily visited on foot.

Orientation & Information

The present-day city is located at the confluence of three rivers: Mae Nam Chao Phraya, Mae Nam Pa Sak and the smaller Mae Nam Lopburi. A wide canal joins them and makes a complete circle around the town. Long-tail boats can be rented from the boat landing across from Chan Kasem Palace for a tour around the river; several of the old *wát* (temple) ruins (Wat Phanan Choeng, Wat Phutthaisawan, Wat Kasatthirat and Wat Chai Wattanaram) may be glimpsed from the canal, along with picturesque views of river life.

Tourist Offices The **Tourist Authority of Thailand** *(TAT; ☎ 0 3524 6078, 1672; Th Si Sanphet; open 8am-4.30pm daily)* recently moved its visitors centre into the renovated municipal building right next door to the main TAT office. The floors above the visitors centre contain interactive displays of life in old Ayuthaya. The **tourist-police office** *(☎ 0 3524 1446, emergency ☎ 1155)* is nearby, next to the old TAT office.

Post & Communications The **main post office** *(Th U Thong; open 8.30am-4.30pm Mon-Fri, 9am-noon Sat)* has an **international telephone service** *(open 8am-8pm daily)* upstairs. There's also a small **branch post office** in the TAT visitors centre.

Ayuthaya Historical Park

A Unesco World Heritage site, Ayuthaya's historic temples are scattered throughout

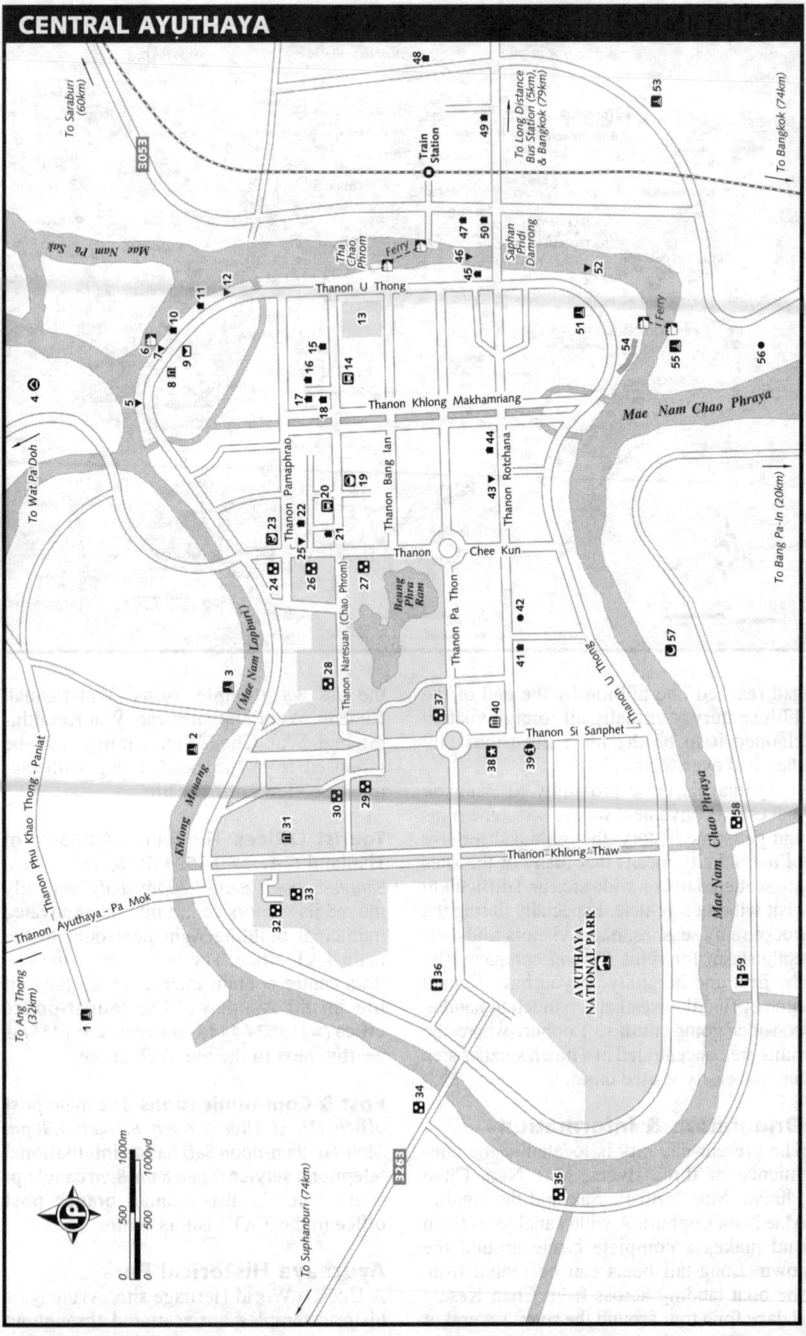
CENTRAL AYUTHAYA
To Saraburi (60km)
3053
Train Station
To Long Distance Bus Station (5km), & Bangkok (79km)
To Bangkok (74km)
Mae Nam Pa Sak
Tha Chao Phrom
Ferry
Saphan Pridi Damrong
Thanon U Thong
Thanon Khlong Makhamriang
Mae Nam Chao Phraya
To Wat Pa Doh
Thanon Pamaphrao
Thanon Bang Ian
Thanon Rotchana
Thanon Chee Kun
To Bang Pa-In (20km)
Beung Phra Ram
Thanon Naresuan (Chao Phrom)
Thanon Pa Thon
(Mae Nam Lopburi)
Khlong Meuang
Thanon Si Sanphet
Thanon Phu Khao Thong - Paniat
Thanon Khlong Thaw
Thanon Ayuthaya - Pa Mok
To Ang Thong (32km)
AYUTHAYA NATIONAL PARK
Mae Nam Chao Phraya
3263
To Suphanburi (74km)
0 500 1000m
0 500 1000yd

CENTRAL AYUTHAYA

PLACES TO STAY

10 U-Thong Hotel
11 Cathay Hotel
15 Ayothaya Hotel
16 Tony's Place
17 Ayuthaya Guest House; Toto Guest House; BJ1 Guest House; PU Guest House
18 TMT Guest House
21 New BJ Guest House
22 PS Guest House
41 Suan Luang (Royal Garden) Hotel
44 Wieng Fa Hotel
45 Baan Khun Phra
47 Tevaraj Tanrin Hotel
48 Ayuthaya Grand Hotel
49 U-Thong Inn
50 Krungsri River Hotel

PLACES TO EAT

5 Hua Raw Night Market
7 Night Market
12 Chainam
13 Chao Phrom Market
25 Malakor
43 Moradok-Thai
46 Floating Restaurants
52 Phae Krung Kao

OTHER

1 Phu Khao Thong Temple (Golden Mount Chedi)
2 Wat Phra Meru
3 Wat Kuti Thong
4 Elephant Kraal
6 Pier (Boat Landing)
8 Chan Kasem Palace; Chantharakasem National Museum
9 Main Post Office
14 Main Bus Station
19 Air-Con Minivans to Bangkok
20 Air-Con Buses to Bangkok
23 Chinese Shrine
24 Wat Suwannawat
26 Wat Ratburana
27 Wat Phra Mahathat
28 Wat Thammikarat
29 Wat Mongkhon Bophit
30 Wat Phra Si Sanphet
31 Old Royal Palace
32 Wat Chetharam
33 Wat Lokaya Sutha
34 Wat Kasatthirat
35 Wat Chai Wattanaram
36 Queen Suriyothai Memorial Pagoda
37 Wat Phra Ram
38 Tourist Police
39 City Hall; TAT Office
40 Chao Sam Phraya National Museum
42 Ayuthaya Historical Study Centre
51 Wat Suwan Dararam
53 Wat Yai Chai Mongkhon
54 Phom Phet Fortress
55 Wat Phanan Choeng
56 Ayuthaya Historical Study Centre (Annexe)
57 Mosque
58 Wat Phutthaisawan
59 St Joseph's Cathedral

this once magnificent city, and along the encircling rivers. Several of the more central ruins – Wat Phra Si Sanphet, Wat Mongkhon Bophit, Wat Na Phra Meru, Wat Thammikarat, Wat Ratburana and Wat Phra Mahathat – can be visited on foot, although you would be wise to avoid the hottest part of the day (11am to 4pm). Or you could add more temples and ruins to your itinerary by touring the city on a rented bicycle. An ideal transport combination for visitors who want to see everything would be to hire a bicycle for the central temples and charter a longtail boat to take a tour of the outlying ruins along the river. See under Getting Around in the Ayuthaya section in this chapter for details on modes and rates of transport. At many of the ruins a 20B to 30B admission fee is collected from 8am to 6.30pm.

Wat Phra Si Sanphet This was the largest temple *(admission 30B)* in Ayuthaya in its time and it was used as the royal temple/palace for several Ayuthaya kings. Built in the 14th century, the compound once contained a 16m-high standing Buddha covered with 250kg of gold, which was melted down by the Burmese conquerors. It is mainly known for the line of three large *chedi* (stupas) erected in the quintessential Ayuthaya style, which has come to be identified with Thai art more than any other single style.

What's Wat in Ayuthaya?

Wat Phra Si Sanphet
วัดพระศรีสรรเพชญ์

Wat Mongkhon Bophit
วัดมงคลบพิตร

Wat Phra Mahathat
วัดพระมหาธาตุ

Wat Ratburana
วัดราชบูรณะ

Wat Thammikarat
วัดธรรมิกราช

Wat Phanan Choeng
วัดพนัญเชิง

Wat Na Phra Meru (Phra Mehn)
วัดหน้าพระเมรุ

Wat Yai Chai Mongkhon
วัดใหญ่ชัยมงคล

Wat Mongkhon Bophit This monastery, near Wat Phra Si Sanphet, contains one of Thailand's largest Buddha images, a 15th-century bronze casting. The present *wíhăan* (Buddhist image sanctuary) was built in 1956.

Wat Phra Mahathat This wát *(admission 30B; open 8am-6.30pm daily)*, on the corner of Th Chee Kun and Th Naresuan (Chao Phrom), dates back to the 14th century and was built during the reign of King Ramesuan. Despite extensive damage – not much was left standing after the Burmese hordes had finished – the Khmer-style tower is still impressive: it was one of the first built in the capital. One of the most photographed sites in Ayuthaya is a Buddha head around which tree roots have grown.

Wat Ratburana The Ratburana *(Ratchaburana; admission 30B; open 8am-6.30pm daily)* ruins are the counterpart to Wat Phra Mahathat across the road; the *chedi*, however, contain murals of the early Ayuthaya period and are not quite as dilapidated.

Wat Thammikarat To the east of the royal palace grounds, inside the river loop, Wat Thammikarat features overgrown *chedi* ruins and lion sculptures.

Wat Phanan Choeng Southeast of town on Mae Nam Chao Phraya, this wát was built before Ayuthaya became a Siamese capital. It's not known who built the temple, but it appears to have been constructed in the early 14th century so it's possibly Khmer. The main *wíhăan* contains a 19m-high sitting

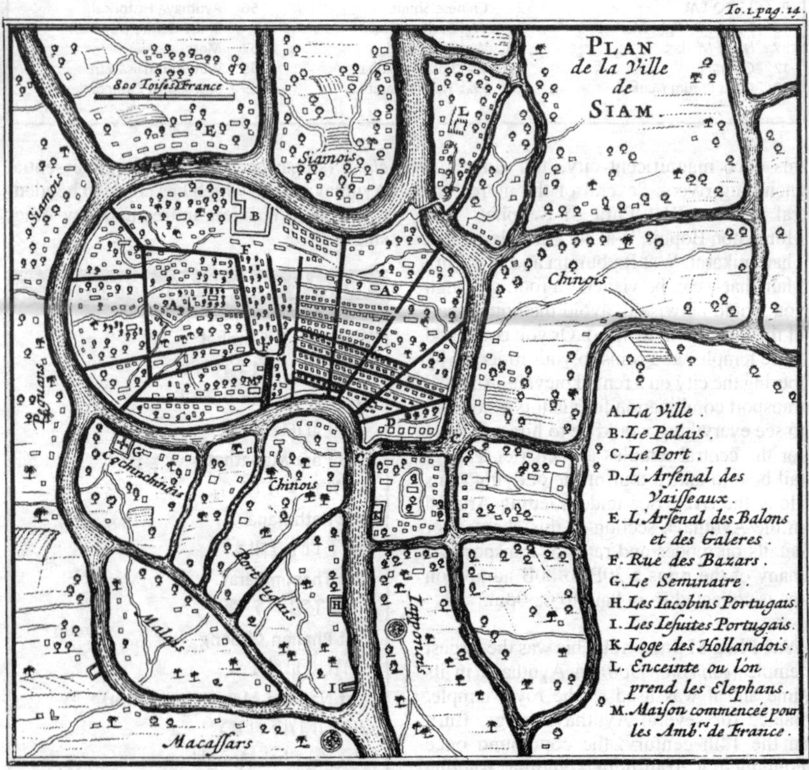

This map of Ayuthaya was published in 1691 in *Du Royaume De Siam*, which recounts the experiences of French envoy Simon de la Loubère. Ayuthaya began receiving European visitors in the early 16th century.

Buddha image that is named after Sam Po, a Chinese explorer who visited Ayuthaya in 1407, and is highly revered by Thai-Chinese. On weekends the wát is crowded with Buddhist pilgrims from Bangkok who pay for lengths of saffron-coloured cloth to be ritually draped over the image's shoulder.

The easiest way to get to Wat Phanan Choeng is by ferry from the pier near Phom Phet fortress, inside the southeast corner of the city centre. For a few extra baht you can take a bicycle with you on the boat.

Wat Na Phra Meru (Phra Mehn) North of the old royal palace grounds is a bridge that can be crossed to arrive at Wat Na Phra Meru *(admission 20B)*. This temple is notable because it escaped destruction from the Burmese in 1767, though it has required restoration over the years. The main *bòt* (central sanctuary) was built in 1546 and features fortress-like walls and pillars. During the Burmese invasion, Myanmar's Chao Along Phaya chose this site from which to fire a cannon at the palace; the cannon exploded and the king was fatally injured, thus ending the sacking of Ayuthaya.

The *bòt* interior contains an impressive carved wooden ceiling and a splendid Ayuthaya-era, crowned sitting Buddha, 6m high. Inside a smaller *wíhăan* behind the *bòt* is a green-stone Buddha from Sri Lanka in a European pose (sitting in a chair). It is said to be 1300 years old. The walls of the *wíhăan* show traces of 18th- or 19th-century murals.

Wat Yai Chai Mongkhon Wat Yai *(admission 20B)*, as the locals call it, is southeast of the town proper, but can be reached by *túk-túk* (motorised *săamláw*, or three-wheeled pedicab) for 30B. It's a quiet, old place that was once a famous meditation wát, built in 1357 by King U Thong. The compound contains a very large *chedi* from which the wát takes its popular name (*yài* means 'big'), and a large reclining Buddha. There are monks and a community of Buddhist nuns residing here.

Other Temples

Just north of Wat Ratburana, to the west of a colourful Chinese shrine, are the smaller ruins of **Wat Suwannawat**. The 400-year-old brick remains of eight *chedi*, a *bòt* and a *wíhăan* are arranged in a circle – a typical early Ayuthaya layout.

The ruined Ayuthaya-style tower and *chedi* of **Wat Chai Wattanaram** (admission 20B), on the western bank of Mae Nam Chao Phraya southwest of the city centre, have been restored. These ruins can be reached by boat or by bicycle via a nearby bridge. If you go by road, you'll pass **Wat Kasatthirat** on the way.

A short boat ride north along Mae Nam Lopburi will bring you to modern **Wat Pa Doh**. In front of the *bòt*, a unique, Sukhothai-style, walking Buddha image strides over a narrow arch, symbolising the crossing from *samsara* to nirvana.

National Museums

There are two museums; the main one is the **Chao Sam Phraya National Museum** *(admission 30B; open 9am-4pm Wed-Sun)*, which is near the intersection of Th Rotchana (the city centre's main street, connecting with the highway to Bangkok) and Th Si Sanphet, near the centre of town. It features a basic roundup of Thai Buddhist sculpture with an emphasis on Ayuthaya pieces. A selection of books on Thai art and archaeology is on sale at the ticket kiosk.

The second museum building, **Chantharakasem National Museum** *(Chan Kasem Palace or Phra Ratchawang Chan Kasem; admission 30B; open 9am-4pm Wed-Sun)*, is a museum piece in itself, built by the 17th king of Ayuthaya, Maha Thammaracha, for his son Prince Naresuan, who later became one of Ayuthaya's greatest kings. Among the exhibits is a collection of gold treasures from Wat Phra Mahathat and Wat Ratburana. Chan Kasem Palace is in the northeast corner of town, near the river.

Ayuthaya Historical Study Centre

ศูนย์ศึกษาประวัติศาสตร์อยุธยา

Funded by the Japanese government, the US$6.8 million Ayuthaya Historical Study Centre *(☎ 0 3524 5124; combined admission adult/student 100/50B; open 9am-4.30pm Mon-Fri, 9am-5pm Sat & Sun)* has two buildings: The main one is on Th Rotchana near the Chao Sam Phraya National Museum, and the annexe is just south of Wat Phanan Choeng on the south bank of the Mae Nam Pa Sak and Mae Nam Chao Phraya junction,

CENTRAL THAILAND

in a district that housed a Japanese community during Ayuthaya's heyday. The hi-tech exhibit area in the main building covers five aspects of Ayuthaya's history: city development, port, administration, lifestyles and traditions. The annexe contains an exhibit on foreign relations with Ayuthaya.

Elephant Kraal
เพนียดคล้องช้าง

This is a restored version of the wooden stockade once used for the annual roundup of wild elephants. A huge fence of teak logs planted at 45-degree angles kept the elephants in; the king had a special raised pavilion from which to observe the thrilling event.

Places to Stay – Budget

Hostels & Guesthouses There are several budget guesthouses in Ayuthaya to choose from, most in a small area on Th Naresuan. As elsewhere in Thailand, sǎamláw (also written samlor) and túk-túk drivers will tell you anything to steer you towards guesthouses that pay commissions.

Baan Khun Phra (*☎ 0 3524 1978; 48/2 Th U Thong; dorm beds 150B, singles/doubles 250/350B*), formerly known as Reuan Doem, is an 80-year-old teak house almost directly across the river from the train station. This is the most atmospheric place to stay in Ayuthaya. Besides rooms, there are beds in a four-bed dorm. Rooms come with ceiling fans and shared bathroom. The place was recently given a tasteful renovation and is decorated with the friendly owner's antique collection. A very good **restaurant** extends from the river side of the house.

Tony's Place (*☎ 0 3525 2578; 12/18 Th Naresuan; fan rooms 160-250B, air-con 350B*) is a two-storey house surrounded by trees on a street with a number of guesthouses. Relatively new and very friendly, this place has a good **restaurant** and bar with pool table. Without a doubt this is the most amiable and best value accommodation on this street, and it shows: Tony's Place is quite popular.

PS Guest House (*single/double rooms with fan 100/150B, air-con 300B*) is a two-storey house on a back road parallel to Th Naresuan and off Th Chee Kun.

PU Guest House (*☎ 0 3525 1213; 20/1 Soi Thaw Kaw Saw; rooms 140B*) doesn't offer a very friendly reception.

TMT Guest House (*☎ 0 3525 1474; rooms with/without bath 400/200B*), around the corner from PU Guest House, has small but clean rooms.

The following four places are run by the same extended family. **Ayuthaya Guest House**, near Tony's Place, comes with a warning: the owner is abusive, even violent, towards guests and we don't recommend you stay here. **Toto Guest House** (*☎ 0 3525 1468; beds in dorm 100B, rooms with fan 350B, with air-con 500B*) is next door to (and managed by) the Ayuthaya Guest House. **BJ1 Guest House** (*☎ 0 3525 1526; singles/doubles 100/160B*), with fan rooms, is next to Toto. It's rather run down and dreary. **New BJ Guest House** (*☎ 0 3524 4046; 19/29 Th Naresuan; dorm beds 80B, singles/doubles 120/150B*) offers fan rooms and dorm beds. There was a 'for sale' sign at the front when we visited so it might not be around by the time you read this.

Hotels Two standard Thai-Chinese–style hotels at the junction of Mae Nam Lopburi and Mae Nam Pa Sak have been accommodating Ayuthaya visitors for over two decades now, and it shows. Both places are pretty run down. **U-Thong Hotel** (*☎ 0 3525 1136; Th U Thong; singles/doubles with fan 300/370B, with air-con 380/450B*), near Hua Raw Night Market and Chan Kasem Palace, has adequate rooms with fan or with air-con, TV and hot-water shower. Check the air-con rooms before agreeing to one as some of the machines are on their last legs. **Cathay Hotel** (*☎ 0 3525 1562; 36/5-6 Th U Thong; singles/twins with fan 150/270B, rooms with air-con 300B*), a little southeast of the U-Thong Hotel, has rather dirty rooms with fan, and some with air-con. Both hotels back up to the river. The U-Thong is the better choice, but not by much.

Places to Stay – Mid-Range & Top End

Wieng Fa Hotel (*☎ 0 3524 3252; 1/8 Th Rotchana; rooms 400-500B*) is a friendly, cosy, two-storey place with clean, relatively quiet rooms around a garden courtyard. All rooms come with TV, fridge and air-con; English is spoken.

Suan Luang Hotel (*Royal Garden; ☎/fax 0 3524 5527; rooms 500-600B, rooms with 6 beds 1500B*) is a five-storey hotel beside the

Ayuthaya Historical Study Centre. This place has decent air-con rooms with fridge and TV as well as a couple of six-bed air-con rooms. All rooms have bathroom and TV.

Ayothaya Hotel *(☎ 0 3523 2855, fax 251018; 12 Soi 2, Th Thetsaban; rooms 1100-3500B)*, formerly the Sri Smai Hotel and just off Th Naresuan, is a more upmarket place where rooms have air-con, bathroom, fridge and cable TV. There is also a swimming pool.

U-Thong Inn *(☎ 0 3524 2236, fax 0 3524 2235; Th Rotchana; old-/new-wing rooms 1000/1500-2500B)* is moving towards the top end, and offers comfortable air-con rooms in the old wing, while in the newer wing rooms have separate sitting areas. The new wing is better value. Facilities include a pool, sauna and massage room. Discounts of up to 50% are given in the low season. It's past the turn-off for the train station.

Ayuthaya Grand Hotel *(☎ 0 3533 5483, fax 0 3533 5492; 55/5 Th Rotchana; rooms high season 1300-1800B, low season 1000-1200B)* is a six-storey hotel out beyond U-Thong Inn, and features rooms with all the mod cons.

Krungsri River Hotel *(☎ 0 3524 4333, fax 0 3524 3777; 27/2 Th Rotchana; single/double rooms 1600/1800B, suites 5000-10,000B)* is a nine-storey hotel and Ayuthaya's flashiest digs, with decked-out rooms and suites. Facilities include a bar/coffee house, Chinese restaurant, beer garden, fitness centre, pool, bowling alley and snooker club.

Tevaraj Tanrin Hotel *(☎ 0 3523 4873, fax 0 3524 4139; 91 Th Rotchana; singles/doubles from 900/1200B)* is a 102-room hotel next door to the Krungsri, and has similar rooms with river views; rates include breakfast. It has a floating restaurant on a converted rice barge.

Places to Eat

The most dependable and least expensive places to eat are the **Hua Raw Night Market**, on the river near Chan Kasem Palace, and the **Chao Phrom Market**, opposite the ferry piers along the eastern side of the island. The stalls at the former offer a good variety of Thai-Chinese and Muslim dishes. **Chainam** is a restaurant near Chan Kasem Palace near the Cathay Hotel. It has tables on the river and a bilingual menu – on which dishes spelled out in English cost about 30% more than on the Thai menu. If you have a problem with this, try practising your Thai and order from the similar places nearby.

Malakor *(Th Chee Kun; dishes 35-50B)*, opposite Wat Ratburana, is located in a two-storey wooden house with a charming view of the temple and has good, cheap Thai dishes, plus an excellent selection of coffees.

Moradok-Thai *(☎ 0 3524 3342; Th Rotchana; dishes 60-120B)* is one of several restaurants that can be found on Th Rotchana. It's a Thai food establishment that is very popular with Thai tourists. There is a selection of wines. It's a good place to soak up the air-con after touring the ruins.

There are four **floating restaurants** on Mae Nam Pa Sak, three on either side of Saphan Pridi Damrong (Pridi Damrong Bridge) on the west bank, and one on the east bank north of the bridge. **Phae Krung Kao** *(open 10am-2am daily)*, on the southern side of the bridge on the west bank – has the better reputation of these floating restaurants. **Ruenpae**, north of the bridge on the west bank, is similar. **Baan Khun Phra** *(☎ 0 3524 1978; 48/2 Th U Thong)* is an eatery on the river behind the guesthouse of the same name; it is also quite good and has the most intimate atmosphere of the riverside places.

The restaurant at **Tony's Place** (see Places to Stay earlier in this section) is the best of the guesthouse eateries. In the evening video movies are shown.

Getting There & Away

Bus Ordinary buses run between the Northern and Northeastern bus terminals in Bangkok and Ayuthaya's main bus terminal on Th Naresuan (39B, two hours) every 20 minutes between 5am and 7pm. Air-con buses operate along the same route every 20 minutes from 5.40am to 7.20pm (64B); the trip takes 1½ hours when traffic north of Bangkok is light, two hours otherwise. Near the Ayuthaya bus terminal is a minivan service to Bangkok that runs every 20 minutes from 5am to 5pm for 45B. It drops off passengers at Bangkok's Victory Monument.

If you're arriving by bus from some place other than Bangkok or cities nearby, you may be dropped off at the long-distance bus terminal, 5km east of Saphan Pridi Damrong at the Hwy 32 junction.

Săwngthăew (pick-up trucks used as buses or taxis; also written songthaew) to/from

Bang Pa-In leave from the main bus terminal on Th Naresuan and cost 10B; Bang Pa-In is about 45 minutes away.

Train The trains to Ayuthaya leave Hualamphong station in Bangkok every hour or so between 4.20am and 10.10pm. The 3rd-class fare is 15B (1½ hours); it's hardly worth taking a more expensive class for this short trip. Train schedules are available from the information booth at Hualamphong station.

From Ayuthaya's train station, the quickest way to reach the old city is to walk west to the river, where you can take a short ferry ride across for 2B.

Upon arrival at Bangkok International Airport, savvy repeat visitors to Thailand sometimes choose to board a northbound train direct to Ayuthaya rather than head south into the Bangkok maelstrom. This only works if you arrive by air during the day or early evening, as the last train to Ayuthaya leaves Bangkok's Hualamphong train station at 10pm. There are frequent 3rd-class trains throughout the day between Don Muang station (opposite Bangkok International Airport) and Ayuthaya.

Boat There are no scheduled or chartered boat services that run between Bangkok and Ayuthaya.

Several hotels in Bangkok operate luxury cruises to Bang Pa-In with side trips by bus to Ayuthaya for around 1600B to 1900B per person, including a lavish luncheon. Longer two-day trips in converted rice barges start at 6200B. See River Trips in the Bangkok chapter for more details.

Getting Around

Săwngthăew and shared túk-túk ply the main city roads for 5B to 10B per person depending on distance. A túk-túk from the train station to any point in old Ayuthaya should cost around 30B; on the island itself figure no more than 20B per trip.

For touring the ruins, your most economical and ecological option is to rent a bicycle from one of the guesthouses (about 30B to 50B a day). You can hire a săamláw, túk-túk or săwngthăew by the hour or by the day to explore the ruins, but the prices are quite high by Thai standards (200B per hour for anything with a motor in it, 500B all day when things are slow). Many drivers ask upwards of 700B for a day's worth of sightseeing – it would be much less expensive simply to take separate rides from site to site.

It's also interesting to hire a boat from Tha Chan Kasem to do a semicircular tour of the island and see some of the less accessible ruins. A long-tail boat that will take up to eight people can be hired for 500B for a two- to three-hour trip with stops at Wat Phutthaisawan, Wat Phanan Choeng and Wat Chai Wattanaram.

From Ayuthaya's train station, the quickest way to reach the old city is to walk west to the river, where you can take a short ferry ride across for 2B.

AROUND AYUTHAYA

Bang Pa-In

บางปะอิน

Twenty kilometres south of Ayuthaya is Bang Pa-In, which has a curious collection of palace buildings *(admission 100B; open 8.30am-3.30pm daily)* in a wide variety of architectural styles. It's a nice boat trip from Bangkok if you're taking one of the cruise tours, although in itself it's not particularly noteworthy.

The postcard stereotype here is a pretty little **Thai pavilion** in the centre of a small lake by the palace entrance. Inside the palace grounds, the Chinese-style **Wehat Chamrun Palace** and the **Withun Thatsana** building, which looks like a lighthouse with balconies, are the only buildings open to visitors. The latter was built to give a fine view over gardens and lakes. There are various other buildings, towers and memorials in the grounds plus an interesting topiary garden where the bushes have been trimmed into the shape of a small herd of elephants.

Wat Niwet Thamaprawat, across the river and south from the palace grounds, is an unusual wát that looks much more like a miniature Gothic Christian church than anything from Thailand. Like Bang Pa-In, it was built by Rama V (Chulalongkorn). You get to the wát by crossing the river in a small trolley-like cable car. The crossing is free.

Getting There & Away Bang Pa-In can be reached by minibus – it's really a large săwngthăew – (10B, 45 minutes), which departs around the corner from Ayuthaya's Chao Phrom Market on Th Naresuan. From

Bangkok there are buses every half-hour or so from the Northern and Northeastern bus terminal (ordinary 29B, air-con 44B; one hour). You can also reach Bang Pa-In by train from Bangkok (3rd class 12B, one hour).

The **Chao Phraya River Express Boat Co** (*☎ 0 2222 5330*) does a tour every Sunday from Tha Maharat in Bangkok. The tour makes stops at Bang Pa-In and Bang Sai Royal Folk Arts & Crafts Centre. It leaves Bangkok at 8am and returns around 6pm. The fare of 350B per person does not include the entrance fee to the Bang Pa-In complex (100B) or the Bang Sai Royal Folk Arts & Crafts Centre (100B). For more expensive river cruises to Bang Pa-In, which include tours of old Ayuthaya, see River Trips in the Bangkok chapter.

Bang Sai Royal Folk Arts & Crafts Centre

ศูนย์ศิลปาชีพบางไทร

This 115-hectare facility (*☎ 0 3536 6092; admission 100B; open 8.30am-5pm Mon-Fri, 8.30am-7pm Sat & Sun*), in Beung Yai, Bang Sai district, is an important training centre for artisans. Under the auspices of Queen Sirikit's Promotion of Supplementary Occupations & Related Techniques (Support) Foundation, handicraft experts teach craft techniques to novices while at the same time demonstrating them for visitors.

The centre has craft demonstrations daily except Monday; call for more information.

The **Loi Krathong festival** here is considered one of the more traditional versions in central Thailand (no firecrackers allowed).

Lopburi Province

LOPBURI

อ.เมืองลพบุรี

postcode 15000 • pop 55,600

The town of Lopburi, 154km north of Bangkok, has been inhabited since at least the Dvaravati period (6th to 11th centuries AD), when it was called Lavo. Nearly all traces of Lavo culture were erased by Khmer and Thai inhabitants following the 10th century, but the Lopburi National Museum has many Dvaravati artefacts. Ruins and statuary in Lopburi span a remarkable 12 centuries.

The Angkor empire was extended to include Lavo in the 10th century, when the Prang Khaek (Shiva Shrine), San Phra Kan (Kala Shrine) and Prang Sam Yot (Three Spired Shrine) were built, as well as the impressive tower at Wat Phra Si Ratana Mahathat.

Power over Lopburi was wrested from the Khmers in the 13th century as the Sukhothai kingdom to the north grew stronger, but the Khmer cultural influence remained to some extent throughout the Ayuthaya period. King Narai fortified Lopburi in the mid-17th century to serve as a second capital when the kingdom of Ayuthaya was threatened by a Dutch naval blockade. His palace in Lopburi was built in 1665 and he died there in 1688.

For the visitor Lopburi is of interest for its fine juxtaposition of ancient brick ruins and not-so-ancient shophouses, hotels and restaurants. It's one of the few cities in Thailand that actually feels as old as it is. The town also boasts a resident troop of monkeys that keeps things lively.

Orientation & Information

The new town of Lopburi dates to around 1940. It is some distance east of the old fortified town and is centred on two large roundabouts. There is really nothing of interest in the new section, so try to stay at a hotel in the old town if you're interested in the palace and temple ruins. All the historical sites in Lopburi can be visited on foot in a day or two.

There's a **TAT office** (*☎ 0 3642 2768–9; Th Phraya Kamjat*) opposite the White House Garden Restaurant. The staff distribute the usual brochures and can be helpful with advice about your visit.

The **Communications Authority of Thailand** (*CAT; Th Phra Narai Maharat; open 8am-6pm daily*) office is located next to the **post office**, towards the new city. CAT has a Home Country Direct phone.

Phra Narai Ratchaniwet

พระนารายณ์ราชนิเวศน์

King Narai's palace (*open 7.30am-5.30pm daily*), is probably the best place to begin a tour of Lopburi. After King Narai's death in 1688 the palace was used only by King Phetracha (King Narai's successor) for his

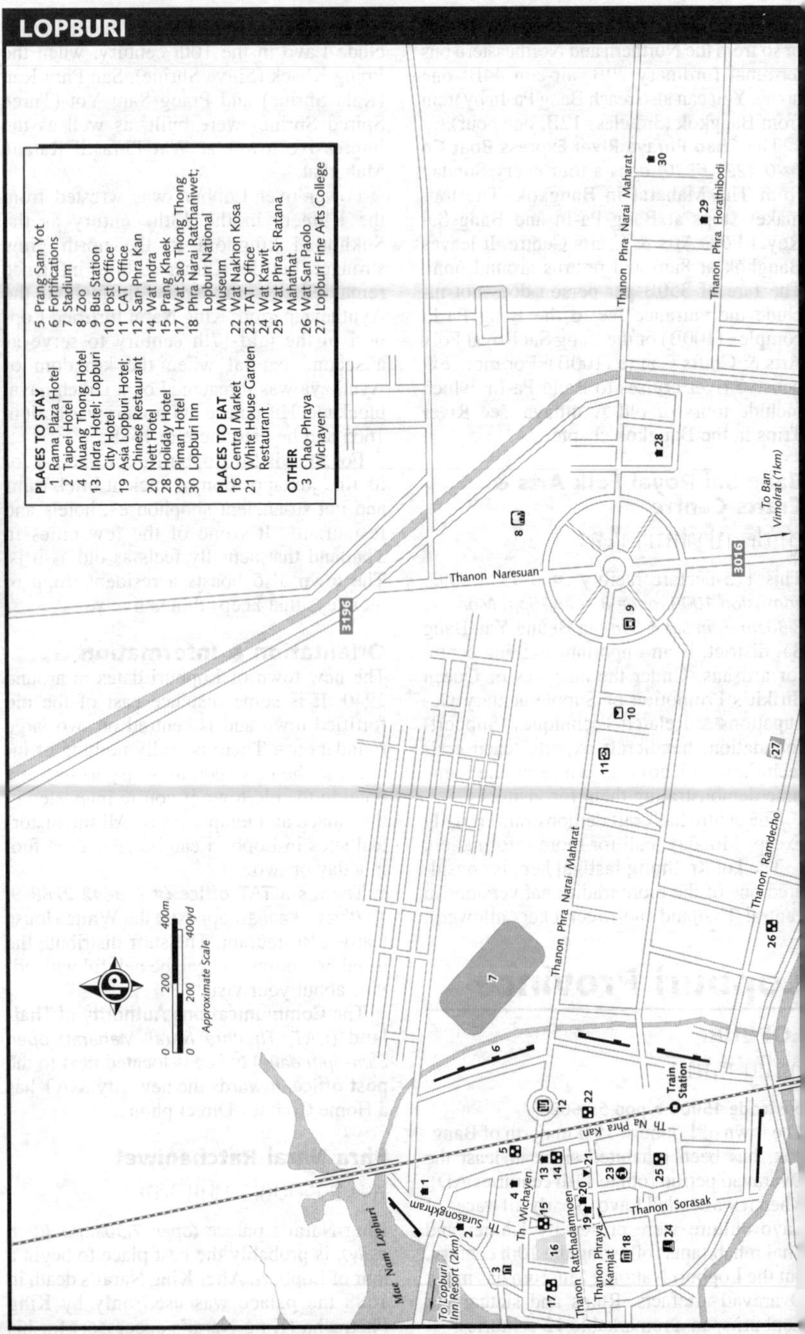
LOPBURI
PLACES TO STAY
1 Rama Plaza Hotel
2 Taipei Hotel
4 Muang Thong Hotel
13 Indra Hotel; Lopburi City Hotel
19 Asia Lopburi Hotel; Chinese Restaurant
20 Nett Hotel
28 Holiday Hotel
29 Piman Hotel
30 Lopburi Inn
PLACES TO EAT
16 Central Market
21 White House Garden Restaurant
OTHER
3 Chao Phraya Wichayen
5 Prang Sam Yot
6 Fortifications
7 Stadium
8 Zoo
9 Bus Station
10 Post Office
11 CAT Office
12 San Phra Kan
14 Wat Indra
15 Prang Khaek
17 Wat Sao Thong Thong
18 Phra Narai Ratchaniwet; Lopburi National Museum
22 Wat Nakhon Kosa
23 TAT Office
24 Wat Kawit
25 Wat Phra Si Ratana Mahathat
26 Wat San Paolo
27 Lopburi Fine Arts College
0 200 400m
0 200 400yd
Approximate Scale
Thanon Naresuan
3196
3016
Thanon Phra Narai Maharat
Thanon Phra Horahibodi
To Ban Vimolrat (1km)
Thanon Ramdecho
Train Station
Th Na Phra Kan
Thanon Sorasak
Thanon Phraya Kamjat
Thanon Ratchadamnoen
Th Wichayen
Th Surasongkhram
Mae Nam Lopburi
To Lopburi Inn Resort (2km)

coronation ceremony and was then abandoned until King Mongkut ordered restoration in the mid-19th century.

It took 12 years to build the palace (1665–77) and French architects contributed to the design. Khmer influence was still strong in central Thailand at that time so it's not surprising that the palace exhibits an unusual blend of Khmer and European styles.

The main gate into the palace, **Pratu Phayakkha**, is off Th Sorasak, opposite the Asia Lopburi Hotel. The grounds are well kept, planted with trees and shrubbery, and serve as a kind of town park for local children and young lovers.

Immediately on the left as you enter are the remains of the king's elephant stables, with the palace reservoir in the foreground. In the quadrangle to the left is the royal reception hall and the **Phra Chao Hao**, which probably served as a *wíhǎan* for a valued Buddha image. Passing through more stables, you come to the southwest quadrangle with the **Suttha Sawan** pavilion in the centre. The northwest quadrangle contains many ruins, including what were once an audience hall, various *sǎalaa* (open-sided covered meeting halls or resting places) and residential quarters for the king's harem.

The **Lopburi National Museum** *(admission 30B; open 8.30am-noon & 1pm-4pm Wed-Sun)* is located here in three separate buildings. Two of these house an excellent collection of Lopburi-period sculpture and an assortment of Khmer, Dvaravati, U Thong and Ayuthaya art. The third building features traditional farm implements and dioramas of farm life. *A Guide to Ancient Monuments in Lopburi* by MC Subhadradis Diskul, Thailand's leading art historian, may be available from the counter on the 2nd floor of the museum.

In mid-February the Phra Narai Ratchaniwet is the focus of the three-day **King Narai Festival**, which includes the exhibition and sale of locally woven textiles, and *lákhon ling* (traditional drama performed by monkeys).

Wat Phra Si Ratana Mahathat
วัดพระศรีรัตนมหาธาตุ

Directly across from the train station, this large 12th-century Khmer wát *(admission 30B)* has been restored by the Fine Arts

Monkey Trouble

More than any other place in Thailand, Lopburi is a city besieged by monkeys. The city's original troop of monkeys (actually a type of macaque) inhabits the San Phra Kan (Kala Shrine) during the day and then crosses the street in the evening to roost in the halls of Prang Sam Yot. At some time in the past, the band split into two factions. The splinter troop, lead by a half-blind dominant male, gave up the sanctity of the shrine for the temptations of the city. These renegades can be seen making nuisances of themselves by swinging from shop fronts and smearing excrement on the windshields of parked cars. Many human residents of the old city have been forced to attach special monkey foils to their television antennas, lest simian antics spoil TV reception. Some locals even swear that the city-dwelling monkeys have been known to board trains for other provinces, returning to Lopburi once their wanderlust is spent.

Like Thailand's legions of stray dogs, Lopburi's monkey population survives in part due to Buddhist discouragement of killing animals. Moreover, many locals say that Lopburi's monkeys are the 'children' of the Hindu god Kala and that to harm one would bring on misfortune. For the most part, however, the inhabitants of Lopburi seem to agree that the monkeys' delinquent behaviour is outweighed by the tourist dollars that they bring in. In late November Lopburi holds a feast for the monkeys at Prang Sam Yot to thank them for their contribution to the prosperity of Lopburi. Buffet tables are meticulously laid out with peanuts, cabbage, watermelon, bananas, pumpkin, pineapple, boiled eggs and cucumbers; the latter two items are monkey favourites, causing plenty of spats. Thousands of Thais turn out to watch the spectacle.

While monkeys frolicking on stone temples make for great photo opportunities, visitors to Lopburi should keep in mind that these are wild animals whose natural fear of humans has diminished over time. Monkeys have been known to attack humans, especially would-be photographers who use food to lure monkeys into the range of their camera lenses.

Department. During Lopburi's heyday this was the town's largest monastery, a fact clearly shown on a map drawn by French cartographers in 1687. A tall laterite tower still stands and features a few intact lintels and some ornate stucco. There is also a large *wíhăan* added by King Narai. Several *chedi* (stupas) and smaller towers dot the grounds.

Wat Nakhon Kosa
วัดนครโกษา

This wát is just north of the train station, near San Phra Kan. It was built by the Khmers in the 12th century and may originally have been a Hindu shrine. U Thong and Lopburi images found at the temple and now in the Lopburi National Museum are thought to have been added later. There's not much left of this wát, although the foliage growing on the brick ruins is an interesting sight. However, half-hearted attempts to restore it with modern materials and motifs detract from the overall effect. A recent excavation has uncovered a larger base below the monument.

Prang Khaek
ปรางค์แขก

Situated on a triangular slice of land bordered by Th Wichayen to the north, Prang Khaek was recently restored by the Fine Arts Department and features towers with Khmer-style brickwork. The structure is thought to have originally been a temple to the Hindu god Shiva and dates back to the 11th century.

Wat Indra & Wat Racha
วัดอินทราและวัดราชา

Wat Indra *(Th Ratchadamnoen)* is near the corner of Th Na Phra Kan. Practically nothing is known of its history and it's now merely a brick foundation. Wat Racha, off Th Phraya Kamjat, is another pile of bricks with little-known history.

Wat San Paolo
วัดสันเปาโล

A partial brick and stucco tower off Th Ramdecho east of the train station is all that's left of a Jesuit church founded by the Portuguese during King Narai's reign. A contingent of 12 French priests came to run the church in 1687. An octagonal, three-storey, celestial observatory was also erected here, though it is unclear under whose direction it was built.

Wat Sao Thong Thong
วัดเสาธงทอง

This wát is northwest of the palace centre, behind the central market. The buildings here are in pretty poor shape. The *wíhăan* and large seated Buddha are from the Ayuthaya period; King Narai restored the *wíhăan* (changing its windows to an incongruous but intriguing Gothic style) so it could be used as a Christian chapel. Niches along the inside walls contain Lopburi-style Buddhas with *naga* (serpent) protectors.

Chao Phraya Wichayen
บ้านวิชชาเยนทร์

King Narai built this Thai-European **palace** *(admission 30B)* as a residence for foreign ambassadors, of whom the Greek Constantine Phaulkon was the most famous. Phaulkon became one of King Narai's advisers and was eventually a royal minister. In 1688, as Narai lay dying, Phaulkon was assassinated by Luang Sorasak, who wanted power for himself. The palace is across the street and northeast of Wat Sao Thong Thong.

San Phra Kan
ศาลพระกาฬ

To the north of Wat Nakhon Kosa, near the train tracks, is the unimpressive San Phra Kan *(Kala Shrine; open 5am-7pm daily)*, which contains a crude gold-leaf-laden image of Kala, the Hindu god of time and death. A virtual sea of monkeys surrounds the shrine, falling out of the tamarind trees and scurrying along the steps leading to the sanctuary. They are getting fat on hand-outs and can be nasty with visitors. A reader wrote to say he was bitten by a monkey and had to receive rabies injections.

Prang Sam Yot
ปรางค์สามยอด

Opposite the San Phra Kan, near the Muang Thong Hotel, this shrine *(admission 30B;*

open 8am-6pm daily) represents classic Khmer-Lopburi style and is another Hindu-turned-Buddhist temple. Originally, the three towers symbolised the Hindu Trimurti of Shiva, Vishnu and Brahma. Now two of them contain ruined Lopburi-style Buddha images. Some Khmer lintels can still be made out, and some appear unfinished.

A rather uninteresting U Thong-Ayuthaya imitation Buddha image sits in the brick sanctuary in front of the linked towers. At the back, facing the Muang Thong Hotel, are a couple of crudely restored images, probably once Lopburi style. The grounds allotted to Prang Sam Yot are rather small and are virtually surrounded by modern buildings. The best view of the monument would probably be from one of the upper floors of the Muang Thong. The monument is lit up at night.

Places to Stay

Old Lopburi It's possible to visit Lopburi as a day trip en route to the north, but if you want to stay overnight there are a number of hotels in the older part of the city you can try. **Asia Lopburi Hotel** *(☎ /fax 0 3661 8893; cnr Th Sorasak & Th Phraya Kamjat; singles/doubles with fan 200/240B, rooms with air-con 300B, with TV 350B)*, overlooking Phra Narai Ratchaniwet, is clean, comfortable and was recently renovated. It has two Chinese **restaurants**. Ask for a room off the street if traffic noise is bothersome.

Nett Hotel *(☎ 0 3641 1738; 17/1-2 Th Ratchadamnoen; singles/doubles with fan 160/280B, with air-con 300/400B)* is on a lane between Th Ratchadamnoen and Th Phraya Kamjat, parallel to Th Sorasak. Clean and quiet rooms have bathrooms but are not as good value as at the Asia Lopburi Hotel.

Muang Thong Hotel *(☎ 0 3641 1036; 1/1-11 Th Prang Sam Yot; single/double rooms 140/300B)* across from Prang Sam Yot, has noisy and not-so-clean rooms with fan and bathroom. Double rooms are actually one large and one small bed. If only this place would get a makeover that took advantage of its excellent view of the temple!

Taipei Hotel *(☎ 0 3641 1524; 24/6-7 Th Surasongkhram; singles with fan 140-200B, doubles with fan 170-260B singles/doubles with air-con 290/350B)*, north of the palace area, is better than Muang Thong. Clean rooms come with private bathroom while the more expensive fan rooms and all air-con rooms have TV.

Rama Plaza Hotel *(☎ 0 3641 1663; rooms with fan 200B, with air-con 250B)*, further north on Th Surasongkhram, offers medium-price rooms with bathroom. It's taken a dive since we last visited – some rooms are better than others so have a look first.

Indra Hotel *(☎ 0 3641 1261; Th Na Phra Kan; singles & doubles with fan 140-200B, with air-con from 250B)*, across from Wat Nakhon Kosa, has clean, spacious rooms with bathroom. The more expensive fan rooms have TV. **Lopburi City Hotel** *(☎ 0 3641 1245; doubles with air-con 250B)*, next door to the Indra, is a modern building with small air-con rooms, all with TV and fridge.

New Lopburi If you get stuck in the new part of town for some reason, you can choose from **Piman Hotel** *(☎ 0 3641 2507; Soi Ekathot, Th Phra Horathibodi)*, **Holiday Hotel** *(☎ 0 3641 1343; Soi Suriyothai 2, Th Phra Narai Maharat)*, or **Lopburi Inn** *(☎ 0 3641 2300, fax 0 3641 1917; 28/8 Th Phra Narai Maharat; rooms 500-1200B)*. The first two are mostly middle-class, short-time places with rates around 350B to 400B a night. The Lopburi Inn features very nice rooms with all the amenities and includes breakfast.

Ban Vimolrat *(Lopburi Youth Hostel; ☎ 0 3661 3731; 5/19 Mu 3, Th Naresuan; doubles with fan/air-con 150/350B)*, a 10B motorcycle taxi ride south along Th Naresuan (Rte 3016) from new Lopburi's western traffic circle, is a relatively new hostel with shared bathroom. Large furnished double rooms come with a TV, fridge, desk and a small balcony. There's also one four-bed room with fan for 320B. Lopburi train station, Phra Narai Ratchaniwet and Prang Sam Yot ruins will cost 60B in a túk-túk from the youth hostel.

Lopburi Inn Resort *(☎ 0 3642 0777; 144 Tambon Tha Sala; singles/doubles 800/900B, suites 1200B)* is at the top end and rooms come with all the modern amenities – including a fitness centre and swimming pool. Breakfast is included with the price of the room.

Places to Eat

Several **Chinese restaurants** operate along Th Na Phra Kan, parallel to the railway, especially near the Indra Hotel. The food is good but a bit overpriced.

Restaurants on the side streets of Th Ratchadamnoen and Th Phraya Kamjat can be better value. **Chinese-Thai restaurant** *(Th Sorasak; dishes 20-40B)*, next to the Asia Lopburi Hotel and across from the main gate to Phra Narai Ratchaniwet, is a good stand-by.

There are also plenty of cheap **curry vendors** down the alleys and along the smaller streets in old Lopburi.

White House Garden Restaurant *(Th Phraya Kamjat; dishes 40-100B)*, a couple of blocks east of the Asia Lopburi Hotel, is one of the more pleasant spots for a Thai meal in the old city.

The **central market**, off Th Ratchadamnoen and Th Surasongkhram (just north of the palace), is a great place to pick up *kài thâwt* or *kài yâang* (fried or roast chicken) with sticky rice, *hàw mòk* (fish and coconut curry steamed in banana leaves), *klûay khàek* (Indian-style fried bananas), a wide selection of fruit, satay, *khâo krìap* (crispy rice cakes), *thâwt man plaa* (fried fish cakes) and other delights.

Sala Mangsawirat *(Vegetarian Pavilion; dishes 15-30B; open 9am-2pm daily)*, in the heart of the market, is an inexpensive – but in this case not very appetising – Thai vegie food place; like most Thai vegetarian restaurants, it's only open short hours.

In the evenings a **night market** sets up along Th Na Phra Kan.

Getting There & Away

Bus From Ayuthaya buses leave for Lopburi every 10 minutes or, if you're coming from Bangkok, about every 20 minutes (from 5.30am to 8.30pm) from the Northern and Northeastern bus terminal (62B ordinary, 85B for air-con, three hours); it's about half that price from Ayuthaya.

Lopburi can also be reached from the west via Kanchanaburi or Suphanburi. If you're coming from Kanchanaburi, take a local, orange bus (no air-con) to Suphanburi (2½ hours); there's great scenery all the way. In Suphanburi, get off the bus in the town's main street, Th Malaimaen, signed in English, at the intersection that has an English sign pointing to Sri Prachan. From here you can catch a direct bus to Lopburi (40B, three hours).

If you happen to miss the direct bus, you can also hopscotch to Lopburi by catching a bus first to Singburi or Ang Thong, across the river from Lopburi. The scenery is even better between Suphanburi and Singburi (2½ hours) – you'll pass many old, traditional Thai wooden houses (late Ayuthaya style), countless cool rice paddies and small wát of all descriptions. Finally, at the Singburi bus station, catch one of the frequent buses to Lopburi (45 minutes). The Singburi bus makes a stop in front of Prang Sam Yot in old Lopburi – if you get off here, you won't have to backtrack from the new city. An alternative to the Suphanburi to Singburi route is to take a bus to Ang Thong and then a share taxi or bus to Lopburi. This is a little faster but not quite as scenic.

From the northeast, Lopburi can be reached via Khorat (Nakhon Ratchasima) aboard air-con buses for 85B.

Train Ordinary trains depart from Bangkok's Hualamphong station, heading north, at 7am and 8.40am, and take only 20 to 30 minutes longer to reach Lopburi than the rapid or express. These ordinary trains are 3rd class only. Rapid trains leave Bangkok at 6.20am and 2.55pm, 7pm, 8.10pm and 10pm (2½ hours). Only one express train (No 9) stops in Lopburi, leaving Bangkok at 8.30am (2nd-class seats only). Fares are 64B in 2nd class and 28B in 3rd class, not including surcharges for rapid or express trains.

There are also regular trains from Ayuthaya to Lopburi (13B in 3rd class, one hour).

Getting Around

Săwngthăew run along Th Wichayen and Th Phra Narai Maharat between the old and new towns for 5B per passenger; there is also a system of city buses (5B). Săamláw will go anywhere in the old town for 30B.

Kanchanaburi Province

The town of Kanchanaburi was originally established by Rama I as a first line of defence against the Burmese, who might use the old invasion route through the Three Pagodas Pass on the Thailand-Myanmar

border. It's still a popular smuggling route into Myanmar today.

During WWII the Japanese used Allied prisoners of war (POWs) to build the infamous Death Railway along this same invasion route, from Mae Nam Khwae Noi to the pass. Thousands of prisoners died as a result of brutal treatment by their captors, their experiences chronicled by Pierre Boulle in his book *The Bridge On the River Kwai* and popularised by the movie of the same name. The bridge is still there (still in use, in fact) and so are the graves of the Allied soldiers.

West and northwest of Kanchanaburi city are several of Thailand's largest waterfalls and most extensive wildlife sanctuaries. Most of the province, in fact, remains sparsely populated and wild.

KANCHANABURI

อ.เมืองกาญจนบุรี

postcode 71000 • pop 53,700

Kanchanaburi lies 130km west of Bangkok in the slightly elevated valley of Mae Nam Mae Klong amid hills and sugar-cane plantations. The weather here is slightly cooler than in Bangkok and the evenings can be especially pleasant by contrast. Meuang Kan, Kan'buri, or just Kan (as the locals call it) has begun receiving larger numbers of Western visitors in recent years. In years past most tourists were Asians on package tours. Visitors of all stripes will find Kanchanaburi a pleasant town with plenty to do and a convenient springboard for treks into the province's lush forests.

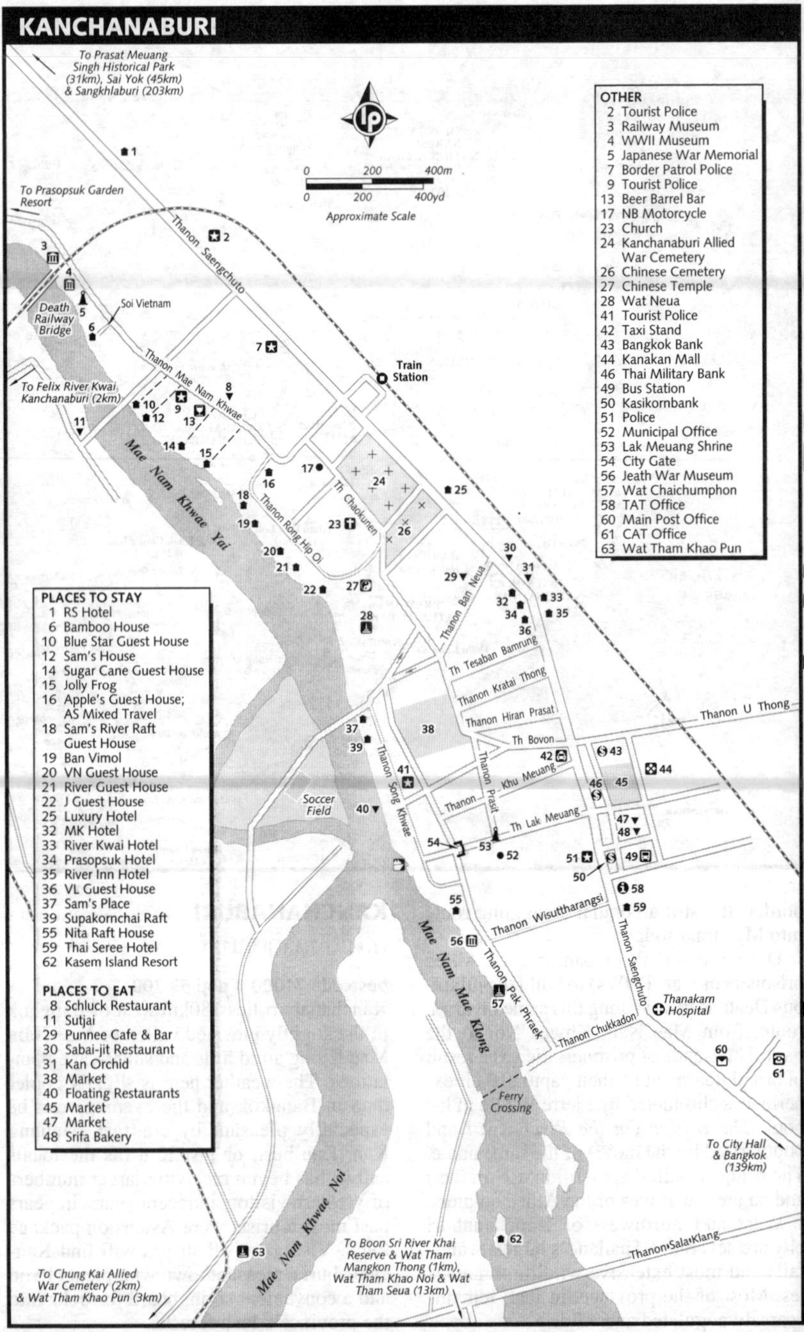
KANCHANABURI
To Prasat Meuang Singh Historical Park (31km), Sai Yok (45km) & Sangkhlaburi (203km)
To Prasopsuk Garden Resort
To Felix River Kwai Kanchanaburi (2km)
0 200 400m
0 200 400yd
Approximate Scale
Death Railway Bridge
Soi Vietnam
Thanon Saengchuto
Thanon Mae Nam Khwae
Train Station
Mae Nam Khwae Yai
Thanon Rong Hip Oi
Th Chaokunen
Thanon Ban Neua
Th Tesaban Bamrung
Thanon Kratai Thong
Thanon Hiran Prasat
Th Bovon
Thanon U Thong
Thanon Khu Meuang
Thanon Prasit
Th Lak Meuang
Thanon Song Khwae
Soccer Field
Thanon Wisutthararangsi
Thanon Pak Phraek
Thanon Saengchuto
Thanon Chukkadon
Thanakarn Hospital
Mae Nam Mae Klong
Ferry Crossing
Mae Nam Khwae Noi
Thanon Sala Klang
To City Hall & Bangkok (139km)
To Boon Sri River Khai Reserve & Wat Tham Mangkon Thong (1km), Wat Tham Khao Noi & Wat Tham Seua (13km)
To Chung Kai Allied War Cemetery (2km) & Wat Tham Khao Pun (3km)
OTHER
2 Tourist Police
3 Railway Museum
4 WWII Museum
5 Japanese War Memorial
7 Border Patrol Police
9 Tourist Police
13 Beer Barrel Bar
17 NB Motorcycle
23 Church
24 Kanchanaburi Allied War Cemetery
26 Chinese Cemetery
27 Chinese Temple
28 Wat Neua
41 Tourist Police
42 Taxi Stand
43 Bangkok Bank
44 Kanakan Mall
46 Thai Military Bank
49 Bus Station
50 Kasikornbank
51 Police
52 Municipal Office
53 Lak Meuang Shrine
54 City Gate
56 Jeath War Museum
57 Wat Chaichumphon
58 TAT Office
60 Main Post Office
61 CAT Office
63 Wat Tham Khao Pun
PLACES TO STAY
1 RS Hotel
6 Bamboo House
10 Blue Star Guest House
12 Sam's House
14 Sugar Cane Guest House
15 Jolly Frog
16 Apple's Guest House; AS Mixed Travel
18 Sam's River Raft Guest House
19 Ban Vimol
20 VN Guest House
21 River Guest House
22 J Guest House
25 Luxury Hotel
32 MK Hotel
33 River Kwai Hotel
34 Prasopsuk Hotel
35 River Inn Hotel
36 VL Guest House
37 Sam's Place
39 Supakornchai Raft
55 Nita Raft House
59 Thai Seree Hotel
62 Kasem Island Resort
PLACES TO EAT
8 Schluck Restaurant
11 Sutjai
29 Punnee Cafe & Bar
30 Sabai-jit Restaurant
31 Kan Orchid
38 Market
40 Floating Restaurants
45 Market
47 Market
48 Srifa Bakery

Mae Nam Mae Klong is a focus for much weekend and holiday activity among the Thais – it's a popular destination for students from Bangkok. A number of floating discos – party boats that go up and down the river – are host to nightly music and revelry that reverberate off the river and give the riverside places of accommodation an acoustic pummeling. If you don't like noise, don't stay on this part of the river!

You may notice the fish-shaped street signs in Meuang Kan – they represent *plaa yîisòk,* the most common food fish in Mae Nam Mae Klong and its tributaries.

Information

Tourist Offices The **TAT office** *(☎ 0 3451 1200, 0 1239 0767; Th Saengchuto; open 8.30am-4.30pm daily)* is right before the police station as you enter town from Bangkok. A free map of the town and province is available, as well as comprehensive information on accommodation and transport. The **tourist police** *(☎ 0 3451 2668, emergency ☎ 1155)* has an office at the northern end of Th Saengchuto. There is a smaller office on Th Mae Nam Khwae near Sam's House, as well as a third one on Th Song Khwae. Any problems with criminal occurrences or accidents should be reported to the tourist police.

Money The major Thai banks are represented and offer foreign-exchange services and ATMs (automated teller machines). The highest concentration of banks is found on and off Th Saengchuto near the market and the bus terminal.

AS Mixed Travel *(☎ 0 3451 2017; 52 Soi Rong Hip Oi)*, next to Apple's Guest House, and **Punnee Cafe & Bar** *(☎/fax 0 3451 3503; Th Ban Neua)* both have a money-changing service that's useful on weekends and holidays. A small **exchange booth** *(open 10.30am-3.30pm)* is located at the Death Railway Bridge.

Post & Communications The **main post office** *(Th Saengchuto; open 8.30am-4.30pm Mon-Fri, 9am-2pm Sat)* is around the corner from the CAT office, which has an **international telephone service** *(open 7am-10pm daily)*, and a Home Country Direct phone located outside and available 24 hours a day. There are also numerous private shops along Th Mae Nam Khwae offering long-distance calls.

Medical Services On Th Saengchuto near the junction of Th Chukkadon, **Thanakarn Hospital** *(☎ 0 3462 2358)* is the best equipped to handle foreign visitors.

Death Railway Bridge

สะพานข้ามแม่น้ำแคว

The so-called 'Bridge On the River Kwai', or Saphan Mae Nam Khwae, looks quite ordinary but it is the story behind the bridge that is dramatic. It spans Mae Nam Khwae Yai, a tributary (Khwae Yai literally translates as 'large tributary') of Mae Nam Mae Klong, which is 3km from Kanchanaburi's Lak Meuang shrine (*làk meuang*, town pillar/phallus). The materials for the bridge were brought from Java by the Imperial Japanese Army during its occupation of Thailand. In 1945 the bridge was bombed several times and was only rebuilt after the war – the curved portions of the bridge are original. The first version of the bridge, completed in February 1943, was all wood. In April of the same year a second bridge of steel was constructed.

It is estimated that 16,000 Prisoners of War (POWs) died while building the Death Railway to Myanmar, of which the bridge was only a small part. The strategic objective of the railway was to secure an alternative supply route for the Japanese conquest of Myanmar and other Asian countries to the west. Construction of the railway began on 16 September 1942 at existing stations in Thanbyuzayat, Myanmar, and Nong Pladuk, Thailand. Japanese engineers at the time estimated that it would take five years to link Thailand and Myanmar by rail, but the Japanese army forced the POWs to complete the 415km, 1m-gauge railway (of which roughly two-thirds ran through Thailand) in 16 months. Much of the railway was built in difficult terrain that required high bridges and deep mountain cuttings. The rails were finally joined 37km south of Three Pagodas Pass; a Japanese brothel train inaugurated the line. The Death Railway Bridge was in use for 20 months before the Allies bombed it in 1945. Only one POW is known to have escaped, a Briton who took refuge among pro-British Karen guerrillas.

Although the number of POWs who died during the Japanese occupation is horrifying, the figures for the labourers, many from Thailand, Myanmar, Malaysia and Indonesia, are even worse. It is thought that 90,000 to 100,000 coolies died in the area.

Today little remains of the original railway as the rails were torn up by Thailand following WWII. Many of these rails were used to build the primitive sun shelters found at rural railway stations – look closely and you may notice these at some of the smaller railway stations in Thailand's northeast.

Train enthusiasts may enjoy getting a close up look at the old locomotives used during WWII that are parked on display near the bridge. Every year during the first week of December there is a nightly **sound-and-light show** at the bridge, commemorating the Allied attack on the Death Railway in 1945. It's a big scene, with the sounds of bombers and explosions, fantastic bursts of light, and more. The town gets a lot of Thai tourists during this week, so book early if you want to witness this spectacle.

Getting There & Away The best way to get to the bridge from town is to catch a săwngthăew along Th Saengchuto heading north. Regular săwngthăew are 10B and stop at the bridge. A motorcycle taxi will cost 20B to 30B. You can also take a train from the train station to the bridge for 2B.

Allied War Cemeteries
สุสานทหารสงครามโลกครั้งที่2

There are two cemeteries containing the remains of Allied POWs who died in captivity during WWII: one is in the north of town off Th Saengchuto, just before the train station, and the other is across Mae Nam Mae Klong in the west of town and a few kilometres down Mae Nam Khwae Noi (Little Tributary River).

The Kanchanaburi Allied War Cemetery, well cared for with green lawns and healthy flowers, is usually a cool spot on a hot Kanchanaburi day. It's only a 15-minute walk from the River Kwai Hotel or you can catch a săwngthăew or orange minibus (No 2) anywhere along Th Saengchuto going north – the fare is 5B. Jump off at the English sign in front of the cemetery on the left, or ask to be let off at the *sùsăan* (cemetery). Just before the cemetery on the same side of the road there is a very colourful **Chinese cemetery** with burial mounds and inscribed tombstones.

The easiest way to get to the Chung Kai Allied War Cemetery is to rent a bicycle or motorbike and ride there yourself. Cross the Saphan Wat Neua and then another smaller bridge just past the soccer field before continuing southwest about 3km. Follow the curving road through a wooded area until you reach the cemetery on your left. Like the more visited cemetery north of town, the Chung Kai burial plaques carry names, military insignia and short epitaphs for Dutch, British, French and Australian soldiers. This cemetery sees fewer tourists than the Kanchanaburi Allied War Cemetery but is just as well kept.

About 1km southwest of the Chung Kai cemetery is a dirt path that leads to **Wat Tham Khao Pun**, one of Kanchanaburi's many cave temples. This wát became notorious in late 1995 when a drug-addicted monk living at the wát murdered a British tourist and disposed of her corpse in a nearby sinkhole. The monk was defrocked and sentenced to death (commuted to life imprisonment without parole by the king in 1996). During WWII the cave complex was used by the Japanese to store weapons and equipment, and some of the smaller chambers are said to have been used to imprison and torture POWs. Despite the gruesome history, the caves are filled with images of the Buddha, Hindu deities and Thai kings, and attract a trickle of pilgrims from around Thailand. The cave complex is fairly extensive and more interesting than similar caves at Wat Tham Seua.

Jeath War Museum
พิพิธภัณฑ์สงคราม

This odd museum *(Th Wisuttharangsi; admission 30B; open 8.30am-6pm daily)*, next to Wat Chaichumphon (Wat Tai) is worth visiting just to sit on the cool banks of Mae Nam Mae Klong. Phra Maha Tomson Tongproh, a Thai monk who devotes much energy to promoting the museum, speaks some English and can answer questions about the exhibits, as well as supply information about what to see around Kanchanaburi and how best to get there. The

RYAN FOX

Ayuthaya Historical Park

LEE FOSTER

Buddha figures, Ayuthaya Historical Park

STAEVEN VALLAK

Ayuthaya Historical Park, Ayuthaya Province

BILL WASSMAN

Saphan Mae Nam Khwae ('bridge on the Kwai River'), Kanchanaburi Province

BILL WASSMAN

Wooden bridge, Kanchanaburi Province

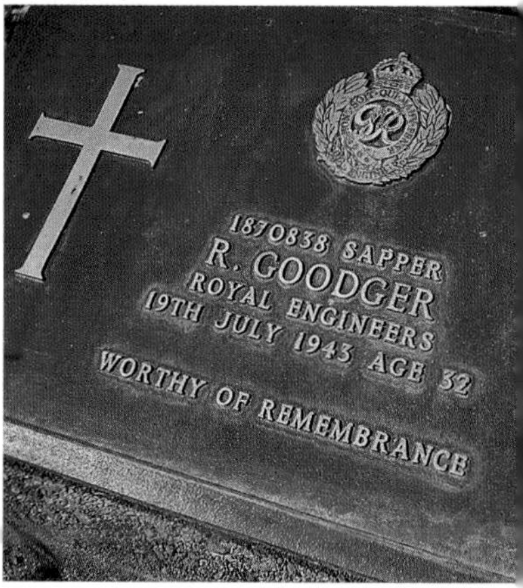

DENNIS JOHNSON

Kanchanaburi Allied War Cemetery

BILL WASSMAN

Young Mon women, Kanchanaburi Province

museum is a replica of the bamboo-*atap* huts used to house Allied POWs during the occupation. The long huts contain various photographs taken during the war, drawings and paintings by POWs, maps, weapons and other war memorabilia. The acronym Jeath represents the meeting of Japan, England, Australia/America, Thailand and Holland at Kanchanaburi during WWII.

The war museum is at the west end of Th Wisuttharangsi (Visutrangsi), not far from the TAT office. The common Thai name for this museum is *phíphítháphan sǒngkhraam wát tâi*.

WWII Museum

พิพิธภัณฑ์สงครามโลกครั้งที่2

A monument to kitsch, this somewhat garish museum *(Art Gallery & War Museum; admission 30B; open 9am-6pm daily)*, just south of the famous Death Railway Bridge, looks like a Chinese temple on the outside. The larger, more lavishly built of the two buildings has nothing to do with WWII and little to do with art unless you include the garish murals throughout. The bottom floor contains Burmese-style alabaster Buddhas and a *phrá khrêuang* (sacred amulets) display. Upper floors exhibit Thai weaponry from the Ayuthaya period, ceramics and brightly painted portraits of all the kings in Thai history. On the 5th and uppermost floor – above the royal portraits (flirting with lese-majesty) – is the history of the Chinese family who built the museum, complete with a huge portrait of the family's original patriarch in China.

A smaller building opposite contains WWII relics, including photos and sketches made during the POW period and a display of Japanese and Allied weapons. Along the front of this building stand life-size sculptures of historical figures associated with the war, including Churchill, MacArthur, Hitler, Einstein, de Gaulle and Hirohito. The English captions are sometimes unintentionally amusing or disturbing – a reference to the atomic bomb dropped on Hiroshima, for example, reads 'Almost the entire city was destroyed in a jiffy'. Even more odd is a diorama of the famous bridge being bombed. During the war, the Japanese forced POWs to stand on the bridge in an unsuccessful attempt to deter allied bombing, and this is depicted in the diorama with life-sized, papier-mache POWs, emaciated and dressed in loincloths (a few of which are askew, revealing some anatomically bizarre details).

A sign in front of the museum announces 'Jeath' in an effort to confuse visitors. Don't fall for it, the original Jeath War Museum is still where it's always been.

Lak Meuang (City Pillar)

ศาลหลักเมือง

Like many other older Thai cities, Kanchanaburi has a *làk meuang* enclosed in a shrine at what was originally the town centre. Kanchanaburi's Lak Meuang shrine is appropriately located on Th Lak Meuang, which intersects with Th Saengchuto two blocks north of the TAT office.

The bulbous-tipped pillar is covered with gold leaf and is much worshipped. Unlike Bangkok's Lak Meuang you can get as close to this pillar as you like – no curtain.

Within sight of the pillar, towards the river, stands Kanchanaburi's original **city gate**.

Wat Tham Mangkon Thong

วัดถ้ำมังกรทอง

The Cave Temple of the Golden Dragon has long been an attraction because of the 'floating nun' – a *mâe chii* (Thai Buddhist nun) who meditated while floating on her back in a pool of water. The old nun finally passed away, but a disciple continues the tradition – sort of. Despite what her predecessor was known for, the current floating nun doesn't meditate but instead strikes Buddha-like poses based on traditional mudra (ritual hand movements). It's very popular with Chinese and Korean tour groups. The spectacle takes place in a tank surrounded by bleachers and a high wall – a mini coliseum especially built for the purpose. Just in case you thought the nun was doing this for spiritual reasons, a sign informs visitors that the nun doesn't float for less than 200B. If a tour group of 20 or more people is here for the show, you're in luck – you only have to pay 10B. Is it worth it? In our opinion yes, but only if you happen to be here when a tour group is around. Watching the Asian tourists' reactions to the floating nun's poses is more engaging than watching the nun go through her routine – with each new pose there's a frenzy of camera flashes. Most tour groups hit this temple in the evening around 5pm.

A long and steep series of steps with dragon-sculpted handrails leads up the craggy mountainside behind the main *bòt* to a complex of limestone caves. Follow the string of light bulbs through the front cave and you'll come out above the wát with a view of the valley and mountains below. One section of the cave requires crawling or duck-walking, so wear appropriate clothing and shoes – the cave floor can be slippery.

Another cave wát is off this same road about 1km to 2km from Wat Tham Mangkon Thong towards the pier. It can be seen on a limestone outcrop back from the road some 500m or so. The name is **Wat Tham Khao Laem**. The cave is less impressive than that at Wat Tham Mangkon Thong, but there are some interesting old temple buildings on the grounds.

Getting There & Away It's necessary to have your own bike or motorcycle to get out here. Heading southeast down Th Saengchuto from the TAT office, turn right on Th Sala Klang (just opposite the City Hall). Cross the bridge (locally called Saphan Sala Klang) and continue for another kilometre. The road can be dusty in the dry season but at least it's flat.

Wat Tham Seua & Wat Tham Khao Noi

วัดถ้ำเสือและวัดถ้ำเขาน้อย

These large, hill-top monasteries about 15km southeast of Kanchanaburi are important local pilgrimage spots, especially for Chinese Buddhists. Wat Tham Khao Noi (Little Hill Cave Monastery) is a Chinese temple monastery similar in size and style to Penang's Kek Lok Si. Adjacent is the half-Thai, half-Chinese–style Wat Tham Seua (Tiger Cave Monastery). Both are built on a ridge over a series of small caves. Wat Tham Khao Noi isn't much of a climb, since it's on the side of the slope. Seeing Wat Tham Seua means climbing either a steep set of *naga* stairs or a meandering set of steps past the cave entrance.

A climb to the top is rewarded with views of Mae Nam Khwae on one side, rice fields on the other. Wat Tham Seua features a huge sitting Buddha facing the river, with a conveyor belt that carries money offerings to a huge alms bowl in the image's lap. The easier set of steps to the right of the temple's *naga* stairs leads to a cave and passes an aviary with peacocks and other exotic birds. The cave has the usual assortment of Buddha images.

Getting There & Away By public transport, you can take a bus (5B) to Tha Meuang (12km southeast of Kanchanaburi), then a motorcycle taxi (30B) from near Tha Meuang Hospital directly to the temples.

If you're travelling by motorcycle or bicycle, take the right fork of the highway when you reach Tha Meuang, turn right past the hospital onto a road along the canal and then across the Kheuan Meuang (City Dam). From here to Wat Tham Seua and Wat Khao Noi is another 4km. Once you cross the dam, turn right down the other side of the river and follow this road 1.4km, then turn left towards the pagodas, which can be seen easily from here. The network of roads leading to the base of the hill offers several route possibilities – just keep an eye on the pagodas and you'll be able to make the appropriate turns.

By bicycle, you can avoid taking the highway by using back roads along the river. Follow Th Pak Phraek in Kanchanaburi southeast and cross the bridge towards Wat Tham Mangkon Thong, then turn left on the other side and follow the gravel road parallel to the river. Eventually (after about 14km) you'll see the Kheuan Meuang up ahead – at this point you should start looking for the hill-top pagodas on your right. This makes a good day trip by bicycle – the road is flat all the way and avoids the high-speed traffic on the highway. You can break your journey at Ban Tham, a village along the way with its own minor cave wát.

Boat Trips

Rafts Several small-time enterprises offer raft trips up and down Mae Nam Mae Klong and its various tributaries. The typical raft is a large affair with a two-storey shelter that will carry 15 to 20 people. The average rental cost per raft is 1500B for half a day and 3500B for an overnight trip, divided among as many people as you can fit on the boat. Such a trip would include stops at **Hat Tha Aw** (Tha Aw Beach), Wat Tham Mangkon Thong, Tham Khao Pun and the Chung Kai Allied War Cemetery, plus all meals and one night's accommodation on the raft. Alcoholic beverages are usually extra. Bargaining can be fruitful as there are said to be over 500 rafts available in the city.

Inquire at any guesthouse or the TAT office about raft trips.

Long-Tail Boats One way to see the same river sights at a lower cost is to hire a long-tail boat instead of a raft. Long-tail boats cost around 500B per hour and can take up to six passengers. For 1000B a group could take a two-hour long-tail boat trip to the Jeath War Museum, Wat Tham Khao Pun, Chung Kai Allied War Cemetery and the Death Railway Bridge. Boats can be hired from the boat pier off Th Chukkadon or at the Jeath War Museum.

Trekking

Several companies and guesthouses in town offer treks into Kanchanaburi's hinterland. One-day or overnight treks to Karen villages often include elephant rides and a journey down the river on a bamboo raft. Trips to caves, waterfalls and the province's other sights can also be arranged. Take care when choosing a trek. Many companies and guesthouses offer treks for as little as 300B per person, but if enough people don't sign up for the trek, it gets cancelled at the last minute. **AS Mixed Travel** *(☎ 0 3451 2017)*, next to Apple's Guest House, is locally owned and reliable. Prices are a bit more than at other agencies but the quality of the treks is high. Prices per person range from 400B to 890B for one-day treks, more for overnight treks. The same company also offers one- and two-day **cycling** tours and three-day combination cycling/trekking programmes. Bicycles and helmets are provided and a support vehicle is always on hand in case of emergencies.

Cooking Courses

The restaurant at **Apple's Guest House** *(☎ 0 3451 2017; W www.applenoi-kanchanaburi.com)*, known for its excellent Thai food, offers highly recommended, one-day Thai cooking courses for 700B per person. Groups are usually limited to eight people so it's a good idea to book a couple of days in advance.

Places to Stay – Budget

Kanchanaburi has numerous places to stay in every price range but especially in the guesthouse category. Those along the river can be a little noisy on weekends and holidays due to the floating disco traffic, which can go on all night, so choose your accommodation carefully; there are even karaoke rafts now! A local commission of guesthouse owners has attempting to enact a ban on the floating discos for years, so far to no avail.

The popularity of floating accommodation has seen a profusion of 'raft rooms' added to the choice of accommodation at riverfront guesthouses. These are essentially rooms constructed on a platform that rests on steel pontoons. Some guesthouses try to cut their expenses by pumping river water into the bathrooms – not a healthy situation if you consider that waste water and sewage are dumped directly into the river. A few guesthouses have gone to great trouble to hide their elicit plumbing from guests; at other establishments the setup is in plain view. If you are in doubt, before agreeing to take a room simply fill the bathroom sink with water. It will be readily apparent if the water came from the river or not.

Săamláw drivers get a 50B to 100B commission for each foreign traveller they bring to guesthouses from the bus or train station (on top of what they charge you for the ride), so don't believe everything they say with regard to 'full', 'dirty' or 'closed' – see for yourself. Some guesthouses will provide free transport from the bus or train station if you call.

On the River At the junction of Mae Nam Mae Klong and Mae Nam Khwae Noi, **Nita Raft House** *(☎ 0 3451 4521; 27/1 Th Pak Phraek; singles & doubles 80B, doubles with fan 120B, with shower 180B)* has older rooms with mosquito nets or doubles with fan and/or private shower. It's basic but quite well run, although you should heed the warning about floating discos on weekends and holidays. You can get good information on the local sights and activities here.

Sam's Place *(☎ 0 3451 3971; 7/3 Th Song Khwae; singles & doubles with fan 150B, with air-con 300-350B)* is near some floating

CENTRAL THAILAND

restaurants. Rooms here have private bathroom and the raft has a small **coffee shop**. A drawback to Sam's is that it's within range of the floating discos.

Supakornchai Raft *(☎ 0 3451 2055; 7/4 Th Song Khwae; singles with fan 150-200B, doubles with fan 300B, singles & doubles with air-con 300-350B)* is right next to Sam's Place and is similar. Raft rooms have a bathroom and either one or two large beds. Little English is spoken here.

Two places a little closer to the city centre are the **River Guest House** *(☎ 0 3451 2491; 42 Soi Rong Hip Oi 2, Th Mae Nam Khwae)* and the nearby **J Guest House** *(☎ 0 3462 0307)*. Both are located in a hyacinth-choked lagoon and have raft singles/doubles with shared bathroom for 80B to 100B/100B to 150B. They're both rather basic but not lacking in character.

VN Guest House *(☎ 0 3451 4082; 44 Soi Rong Hip Oi 2, Th Mae Nam Khwae; singles/doubles 60/80B, with bath 100/150B, with air-con 200/300B)*, just upriver, has small, basic raft rooms, some with bathroom and air-con. All are close to the train station and tend to get booked out in the high season.

Ban Vimol *(☎ 0 3451 4831; 48/5 Soi Rong Hip Oi 2, Th Mae Nam Khwae; fan rooms 150B, air-con 600B)* is just upriver from the VN Guest House and offers tastefully decorated bamboo accommodation with fan and private bathroom. The more expensive air-con rooms are closest to the river. **Sam's River Raft Guest House** *(Th Rong Hip Oi 2; rooms with fan/air-con 250/350B)*, a bit further north on the river, has raft rooms with private bathroom. There is also a restaurant and sunbathing platform.

Apple's Guest House *(☎ 0 3451 2017; W www.applenoi-kanchanaburi.com; single/twin bungalows 200/250B)*, under a huge mango tree near the intersection of Th Mae Nam Khwae and Th Rong Hip Oi, offers one- or two-bed bungalows. All have clean toilet and shower, fan and screened doors to allow for better ventilation. The guesthouse restaurant gets rave reviews and one-day Thai cooking courses are offered (see Cooking Courses earlier in the Kanchanaburi section). The guesthouse is locally owned and very friendly.

Jolly Frog *(☎ 0 3451 4579; 28 Soi China; doubles with fan 200B, four-bed rooms with fan 400B)*, north along Th Mae Nam Khwae, is a comparatively huge 'bamboo motel' that is popular with those who are counting every baht – it's one of the cheapest places in town. Beware of the gauntlet of fly-by-night businesses (trekking, massage and tattooing) that have sprouted up around the entrance to the Jolly Frog.

Sugar Cane Guest House *(☎ 0 3462 4520, 22 Soi Pakistan, Th Mae Nam Khwae; raft doubles 400-550B, bungalow doubles 150-250B)*, about 100m upriver, has comfortable rooms on a raft with a wide veranda as well as bungalows and a riverside **restaurant**. Raft rooms are all doubles with private bathroom, and cost varies depending on the size of the room and whether or not it has air-con; bungalow doubles have private bathroom. The management is friendly and helpful.

Sam's House *(☎ 0 3451 5956; W www.samsguesthouse.com; Th Mae Nam Khwae; rooms with fan from 150-250B, with air-con up to 450B)*, near the bridge that crosses over to Sutjai Restaurant, has raft rooms, rooms in an L-shaped stone building and bungalows; rooms have private bathroom, some with hot water. As at the original Sam's Place, there is a terrace **restaurant**.

Blue Star Guest House *(☎ 0 3451 2161; Th Mae Nam Khwae; rooms 150-300B, with air-con 380B)*, near Sam's House, has A-frame bungalows, all with private bathroom. There are a couple of imaginatively constructed tree-house rooms for 300B. Discounts are offered for long-term stays. There is also an open-air **restaurant** on the premises.

Bamboo House *(☎ 0 3462 4470; 3-5 Soi Vietnam, Th Mae Nam Khwae; rooms with fan 200-300B, with air-con 500B)*, on the river a few hundred metres before the Japanese war memorial is a suitable choice if you want to stay out near the Death Railway Bridge (and away from the floating discos). The place is locally owned and well kept, the owners are very friendly and the setting is peaceful.

In Town Across the street from the River Kwai Hotel, **VL Guest House** *(☎ 0 3451 3546; rooms with fan 250B, with air-con 350-400B)*, a three-storey hotel, has clean, spacious singles and doubles with TV and hot-water shower. It has a small dining area downstairs.

Prasopsuk Hotel *(☎ 0 3451 1777; Th Saengchuto; singles/doubles with fan 200/300B, with air-con 300/400B)* is similar to the VL Guest

House next door. Rooms have bath and TV. Air-con singles (not the doubles) also come with phone. A **restaurant** on the premises serves inexpensive Thai dishes.

River Inn Hotel *(☎ 0 3462 1056; Th Saengchuto; rooms from 360B)*, south of the River Kwai Hotel, has decent air-con rooms with TV and hot-water shower. At this price it's good value.

Sri Muang Kan *(☎ 0 3451 1609; 313/1-3 Th Saengchuto; rooms with fan/air-con 190/370B)*, at the northern end of Th Saengchuto, has clean singles and doubles with bathroom. It's a bit of a short-time place: rooms are also rented by the hour. **Thai Seree Hotel** *(☎ 0 3451 1128; Th Saengchuto; rooms with fan 150B, singles & doubles with air-con 300B)*, at the southern end of the same road near the TAT office, has adequate rooms with fan and others with air-con. It's also involved in the short-time trade.

Luxury Hotel *(☎ 0 3451 1168; 284/1-5 Th Saengchuto; singles/doubles 600/700B)* is a bungalow-style place a couple of blocks north of the River Kwai Hotel and not as centrally located. All rooms have air-con, TV and hot-water shower.

Places to Stay – Top End

On the River On an island in the middle of Mae Nam Mae Klong, **Kasem Island Resort** *(☎ 0 3451 3359 • in Bangkok ☎ 0 2255 3604; rooms with fan/air-con 750/1250B)* sits about 200m from Th Chukkadon. The tastefully designed, thatched cottages and house rafts are cool, clean and quiet. There are facilities for swimming, fishing and rafting as well as an outdoor bar and restaurant. The resort has an office and parking lot near Th Chukkadon, where you can arrange for a free shuttle boat to the island; shuttle service stops at 10pm.

North of the Death Railway Bridge are several river resorts of varying quality, most featuring standard wooden bungalows for about 1000B. **Prasopsuk Garden Resort** *(☎ 0 3451 3215; doubles 1000B, bungalows with two bedrooms 1200B, bungalows for 10 people 4000B)* is a 50-room place, about 2km before the turn-off for Rte 323. It has townhouse doubles and bungalows of varying size, all air-conditioned. Its clientele is mainly Thai and it can get noisy at night, when the karaoke starts up.

Boon Sri River Kwai Resort *(☎ 0 3451 5143; rooms 400-800B)* on the river, opposite Wat Tham Mangkon Thong to the south, offers more of the same, though it's a bit of a short-time place for the local players.

Felix River Kwai Kanchanaburi *(☎ 0 3451 5061, fax 0 3451 5095; rooms 2000-2200B)* is a luxurious place that sits on the western bank of the river, about 2km north of the new one-lane bridge. The more expensive rooms have a view of the river. The very nicely landscaped grounds include two swimming pools. Spacious rooms and suites have IDD phones, cable TV, fridge and personal safe.

In Town Kanchanaburi's original 1st-class hotel is the **River Kwai Hotel** *(☎ 0 3451 3348; 284/3-16 Th Saengchuto; rooms from 900B)*, offering semideluxe rooms with air-con, hot-water shower, fridge, telephone and TV. Facilities include a coffee shop, karaoke bar, disco and swimming pool. Breakfast is included in the room rates.

MK Hotel *(☎ 0 3462 1143-4; Th Saengchuto; rooms with air-con 300-600B)* is a multistorey, 52-room hotel opposite the River Kwai Hotel. The base rate will get you a two-bed room and for 100B more you can add either TV or hot-water shower. Rooms with all the amenities are available for the top rate (or 500B with breakfast).

RS Hotel *(☎ 0 3462 5128; 264 Th Saengchuto; rooms 700-2400B)*, north of the train station, has large rooms and all the expected amenities. There's also a swimming pool.

Places to Eat

The greatest proliferation of inexpensive restaurants in Kanchanaburi is along Th Saengchuto near the River Kwai Hotel. From here south, to where Th U Thong crosses Th Saengchuto, are many good Chinese, Thai and Isan-style restaurants. As elsewhere in Thailand, the best are generally the most crowded.

Kan Orchid *(Th Saengchuto; dishes 40-80B)*, an eatery next to the River Kwai Hotel, has a good selection of Thai food and also offers reasonably priced sandwiches, baked goods and ice cream.

The restaurant at **Apple's Guest House** (see Places to Stay – Budget earlier for details) continues to go way above and beyond normal guesthouse fare. Both the *kaeng mátsàmàn* (Muslim-style curry) and *phàt thai* (fried noodles) are highly recommended. Apple also does what is perhaps the best banana pancake in Thailand.

Good, cheap eating places can be found in the **markets** along Th Prasit and between Th U Thong and Th Lak Meuang east of Th Saengchuto. In the evenings, a sizable **night market** convenes along Th Saengchuto near the Th Lak Meuang intersection.

Sabai-jit Restaurant *(Th Saengchuto; dishes 40-80B)*, north of the River Kwai Hotel, has an English menu. Beer and Mekong whisky are sold here at quite competitive prices and the food is consistently good. Other Thai and Chinese dishes are served apart from those listed on the English menu. If you see something not listed that you'd like, point.

Punnee Cafe & Bar *(☎ 0 3451 3503; Th Ban Neua; dishes 40-80B)* serves Thai and European food according to expat tastes and advertises the coldest beer in town. Lots of information on Kanchanaburi is available here; there are also used paperback books for sale or trade.

Schluck Restaurant *(Th Mae Nam Khwae; dishes 80-140B)* offers good steaks and other Western food, and is open evenings from 6pm to 1am. **Pizza Company** *(☎ 1112)* delivers and is located on Th Saengchuto.

Down on the river there are several large floating restaurants where the quality of the food varies but it's hard not to enjoy the atmosphere. Most of them cater to Thais out for a night of drinking and snacking, so if you go, don't expect Western food or large portions – but if you know what to order, you could have a very nice meal here. Recommended is **Mae Nam** *(Th Song Khwae)*. Across from the floating restaurants, along the road, are several restaurants that are just as good but less expensive; the best on this row is **Jukkru** (no Roman-script sign – look for blue tables and chairs). **Sutjai** is a garden-style place on the western bank of the river next to the one-lane bridge. Although it's a little out of the way, it is one of the better riverside restaurants in town.

There are also **food vendors** on both sides of Th Song Khwae along the river near the new tourist-police office, where you can buy inexpensive takeaways and picnic on mats along the riverbank. This is a festive and prosperous town and people seem to eat out a lot.

One bakery handles most of the pastry and bread business. **Srifa Bakery**, on the northern side of the bus station, is a modern place that has everything from Singapore-style curry puffs to French-style pastries.

Entertainment

A crop of bars, complete with videos, pool tables and prostitutes, have sprouted up along Th Mae Nam Khwae. Many of the establishments seem to be run by Westerners (one brazenly advertises 'Get Shit Faced on a Shoestring') so they may not survive the government's ongoing crackdown. Keep in mind that this type of business is relatively new to the local scene and many guesthouses will not allow their guests to bring prostitutes back to their rooms.

Beer Barrel Bar *(Th Mae Nam Khwae)*, 100m north of Sugar Cane Guest House, is a well presented outdoor beer garden under a huge banyan tree.

Getting There & Away

Bus Ordinary buses leave Bangkok for Kanchanaburi from the Southern bus station in Thonburi every 15 minutes from 4am to 6.30pm daily (48B, three hours). Buses back to Bangkok leave Kanchanaburi between the same hours. Air-con (2nd class) buses cost 62B and leave at similar intervals.

First-class air-con buses leave Bangkok's Southern bus station every 15 minutes from 5am to 7pm (79B). Air-con buses only take about two hours to reach Bangkok. The first bus out is at 4am; the last one to Bangkok leaves at 7pm.

Buses to Kanchanaburi leave frequently throughout the day from nearby Nakhon Pathom (28B, 1½ hours). For travellers heading south, Nakhon Pathom makes a good connecting point – this way you avoid having to go back to Bangkok. Other frequent direct bus services are available to/from Ratchaburi (No 461, 36B, 2½ hours) and Suphanburi (No 411, 35B, 2½ to three hours).

Train Ordinary trains leave Thonburi (Bangkok Noi) station at 7.35am and 1.45pm, arriving at 10.51am and 4.31pm. Only 3rd-class seats are available (25B). Trains return to Bangkok (Bangkok Noi station, Thonburi) from Kanchanaburi at 7.26am and 2.50pm, arriving at 10.25am and 5.40pm.

Ordinary train tickets to Kanchanaburi can be booked on the day of departure only.

Officially these trains leave from the recently renovated old Bangkok Noi station on the western bank of the Mae Nam Chao Phraya. In actuality the trains leave from a temporary station that is about 1km away, but the government runs a free sǎwngthǎew from the old Bangkok Noi station to the temporary one. Tickets are still purchased at the old station. Whether or not this situation is temporary is unclear. Travelling by train is slower than going by bus, but the scenery is much more interesting. Sadly, passenger use on this line has dropped dramatically over the past few years, and as usage drops, so too does reliability. Late arrivals are very common.

Three trains daily depart from Kanchanaburi station for the Death Railway Bridge (see Getting Around later in this section). The same trains go on to the end of the line at Nam Tok (two hours), which is near Nam Tok Sai Yok (Sai Yok Falls). The trains depart from the bridge at 6.18am and 10.59am, and 4.39pm for Nam Tok Sai Yok; the fare is the same (17B). The 6.18am trains do not run on weekends and holidays. Nam Tok is 8km from Nam Tok Khao Pang and 18km from Hellfire Pass and the Mae Nam Khwae village. Coming back from Nam Tok, there are trains at 5.25am and 1pm and 3.15pm.

Tourist Trains The SRT runs a special tourist train *(☎ 0 3456 1052)* from Bangkok's Hualamphong station at around 6.30am, returning at 7.55pm, on weekends and holidays. The return fare is 200B for air-con, 100B for fan. It typically includes a stop in Nakhon Pathom to see the Phra Pathom Chedi, a stop at the Death Railway Bridge, a minibus to Prasat Meuang Singh Historical Park (see Around Kanchanaburi later in this chapter for details) for a short tour, a walk along an elevated 'Death Railway' bridge (no longer in use), a three-hour stop at the river for lunch and a bat cave visit, before returning to Bangkok with a one-hour stopover at one of the war cemeteries. This itinerary is subject to change so it's suggested you call first and buy tickets at least one day in advance.

On weekends and holidays a **steam train** runs between Kanchanaburi and Wang Pho (10.25am departure, 2pm return, with a 90-minute stopover at the waterfall) for 100B one way, 150B return. These tickets should be booked in advance, although it's worth trying on the day even if you're told it's full. The SRT changes the tour itinerary and price from time to time.

Share Taxi & Minivan You can also take a share taxi from Th Saengchuto to Bangkok for 70B per person. Taxis leave throughout the day whenever five passengers accumulate at the taxi stand. These taxis will make drops at Th Khao San or in the Phahurat district. Kanchanaburi guesthouses also arrange daily minivans to Bangkok for 100B per person. Passengers are dropped at Th Khao San but they really pack them in – if you have long legs or lots of gear, you might want to think twice.

Getting Around

Unless you're in the mood to be thoroughly fleeced, don't even consider letting a sǎamláw driver show you around – the asking price for an hour-long tour is 500B. The town is not large, so getting around on foot or bicycle is easy. A sǎamláw or motorcycle taxi from the bus or train stations to the river area and most guesthouses should cost from 20B to 30B. Sǎwngthǎew run up and down Th Saengchuto and Th Pak Phraek for 10B per passenger.

Motorcycles can be rented at some guesthouses, or at one of the many shops along Th Mae Nam Khwae. These places tend to come and go though, and it's difficult to recommend one. One that is reliable is **NB Motorcycle** *(☎ 0 3451 1087)* on Th Chaokunen near the Kanchanaburi Allied War Cemetery. Their rates are 150/200B for a 100/125cc bike per day.

If possible, it's best to rent a bicycle from the place where you're staying. Prices range from 80B to 100B per day.

You can take the train from the Kanchanaburi station out to the Death Railway Bridge, a three-minute ride (2B). There are three trains per day at 6.11am (No 485), 10.51am (No 257) and 4.31pm (No 259).

The river ferry across Mae Nam Mae Klong costs 5B per person. Sometimes there's an extra few baht charge for bikes (motor or push) taken on the ferry, although usually it's included in the 5B fare.

AROUND KANCHANABURI

Most of the interesting places around Kanchanaburi are to the north and west of the capital, heading towards Three Pagodas Pass. Many guesthouses and tour agencies in the provincial capital can arrange two-day trips to Three Pagodas Pass, with stops at Hellfire Pass, various waterfalls and hot springs, and a night in Sangkhlaburi.

Kanchanaburi Province has seven major waterfalls, all northwest of Kanchanaburi. They are Erawan, Pha Lan, Trai Trang, Khao Pang, Sai Yok, Pha That and Huay Khamin. Of these, the three most worth visiting – if you're looking for grandeur and swimming potential – are Erawan, Sai Yok and Huay Khamin. Nam Tok Erawan is the easiest to get to from Kanchanaburi, while Sai Yok and Huay Khamin are best visited only if you are able to spend the night near the falls.

Any of these waterfalls could be visited by motorcycle. Many places around town will rent out motorbikes (see under Getting Around earlier in the Kanchanaburi section).

Tiger Temple (Wat Seua)

วัดเสือ

This is one of those places that sounds great when first described: a Buddhist temple in the middle of the jungle where wild tigers roam about free and easy, frolicking with the saffron-robed Buddhist monks. It began when a monk accepted two tiger cubs that had supposedly survived an attempt to have them stuffed and mounted. Then another tiger cub arrived, then three more (it's not uncommon in Thailand for people to give abandoned pets or orphaned wild animals to Buddhist monasteries). The word got out and the media ate it up, and soon tourists were flocking to see the exotic mix of tigers and monks. Not surprisingly things eventually began to sour. At last count the temple had eight tigers and at least one tourist has been seriously mauled. The monks have been ordered not to allow visitors to pet the animals and to keep the tigers caged (visitors pay 100B to get in and must sign a waiver releasing the monks of liability if anyone is scratched, bitten or worse).

At the time of writing, the show was still going on and some tour operators in Kanchanaburi were actively promoting visits to the temple. More responsible operators confided to us that they didn't think playing with tigers was such a good idea. We agree. If the so-called Tiger Temple is still in operation when you read this, we don't recommend you visit.

Erawan National Park

อุทยานแห่งชาติเอราวัณ

This 550-sq-km park *(200B; open 8am-4pm daily)* is the most visited national park in Thailand and one of the most beautiful.

Once in the park, you'll have to walk 2km from the trail entrance to the end of seven levels of **waterfalls** (the first level is reached 700m from the visitors centre), which feed into Mae Nam Khwae Yai. The trails weave in and out of the numerous pools and falls, sometimes running alongside the water, sometimes leading across footbridges. Wear good walking shoes or sneakers. Also, bring a bathing suit as several of the pools beneath the waterfalls are great for swimming. The uppermost fall is said to resemble Airvata (Erawan in Thai), the three-headed elephant of Hindu mythology.

The waterfalls here, as elsewhere in Kanchanaburi, are best visited during the rainy season or in the first two months of the cool season, when the pools are full and the waterfalls most impressive. The peak crowds at Erawan come in mid-April around the time of the **Songkran festival** (when there's not much water); weekends can also be crowded.

Two limestone caves in the park worth visiting are **Tham Phra That** (12km northwest of the visitors centre via a rough road) and **Tham Wang Badan** (west). **Thung Na Dam** appears 28km before Erawan.

Places to Stay & Eat Official park **bungalows** *(Bangkok ☎ 0 2579 7223)* that sleep up to 15 people cost from 250B to 1000B per night. The park staff can also make arrangements for you to sleep in unofficial housing from 50B to 100B per person, or you can pitch a tent for 5B. **Erawan Resort Guest House** *(☎ 0 1907 8210; bungalows 200-1000B)*, off the highway before the park entrance, has small, solid bungalows, with attached bathroom, on the river. **Pha Daeng Resort** *(☎ 0 3451 3909; rooms & bungalows 500-2700B)*, further towards Kanchanaburi along the same road as Erawan Resort, near the 46km marker, has a variety of air-con rooms and bungalows.

There are **food stalls** near the park entrance and at the bus station, outside the park. To cut down on rubbish, food is not allowed beyond the second level of the falls.

Getting There & Away The first bus to Erawan leaves the Kanchanaburi bus station at 8am (26B, one hour). Ask for 'rót thammádaa pai náam tòk eh-raawan' (ordinary bus going to Nam Tok Erawan). Take this first bus, as you need a full day to appreciate Erawan. The last bus back to Kanchanaburi leaves Erawan at 5.20pm.

Nam Tok Huay Khamin
น้ำตกห้วยขมิ้น

Part of little-visited **Si Nakharin National Park**, Huay Khamin (Turmeric Stream) has what are probably Kanchanaburi Province's most powerful waterfalls. The pools under the waterfalls are large and deep and this is an excellent place for swimming. Explorations further afield in the park can be rewarding for self-contained campers. Elephants and other wildlife are not uncommon.

Getting There & Away Getting to Huay Khamin can be difficult. The 45km road from the Erawan falls is in bad condition and takes at least two hours by motorcycle or rugged 4WD (you must bring your own transport). The falls can also be reached by a similarly rugged – and much longer – dirt road from Rte 323 north of Thong Pha Phum.

An alternative is to charter a boat at Tha Reua Khun Phaen, a pier on the southeastern shore of Si Nakharin Reservoir (Kheuan Si Nakharin) in the village of Mongkrathae. The price varies – according to your bargaining skills and the mood of the boat pilots – from 1200B to 3500B; this need not be as expensive as it sounds if you bring a group (boats can hold up to 20 people). A good price for a long-tail boat with five to 10 people would be 1500B return. If you can afford it, boat is a much better option than road.

Sai Yok National Park
อุทยานแห่งชาติไทรโยค

About 100km northwest of Kanchanaburi, scenic **Nam Tok Sai Yok Yai** and **Nam Tok Sai Yok Noi** are part of 500-sq-km Sai Yok National Park *(admission 200B)*. In addition to the park's waterfalls, other attractions include the limestone caves of **Tham Sai Yok, Tham Kaew** and **Tham Phra**, the remains of a **Death Railway bridge** and **Japanese cooking stoves** (actually little more than piles of brick), and a network of clear streams that bubble up from **springs** in the park. There are established footpaths and trails between the falls, caves, railway bridge and a **bat cave**. One particular cave is full of bats and people come to watch clouds of them stream out of it at dusk.

It was at Sai Yok National Park that the famous Russian-roulette scenes in the 1978 movie *The Deer Hunter* were filmed. The area is well known for overnight raft trips that leave from here along Mae Nam Khwae Noi; the waterfalls empty directly into the river. The trips are not cheap, but those who have gone say they're worth the money.

Nam Tok Sai Yok Noi is higher than Nam Tok Sai Yok Yai, but the volume of falling water is greater at the latter. Sai Yok Yai is more set up for visitors and hence

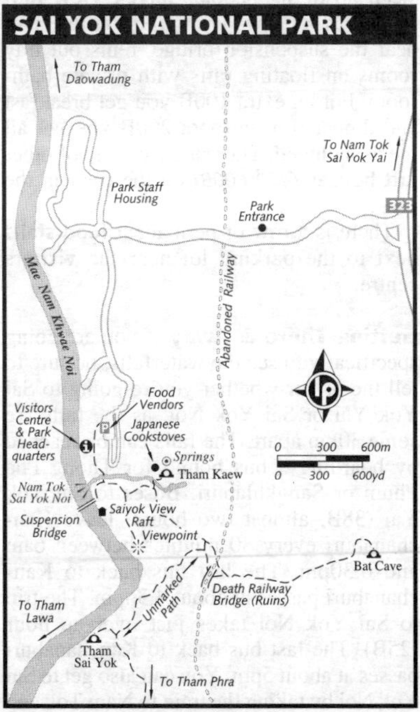

gets bus loads of Thai tourists. Sai Yok Noi is more relaxing.

The eight-room **Tham Daowadung**, one of Thailand's prettiest limestone caves, is further north in the park while Tham Lawa is in the park's far southwestern corner; both are best visited by taking boat trips to an access point along Mae Nam Khwae Noi, then hiking in. **Hin Dat Hot Springs** *(admission 5B)* is 40 minutes north of Tham Daowadung by boat. The *bàw náam ráwn* (hot springs) have been upgraded recently and now have changing rooms and bathrooms. The hot springs are no longer looked after by the monks at the nearby Buddhist monastery, so women are now welcome.

Notable wildlife in the park includes Kitti's hog-nosed bats (the world's smallest mammal), regal crabs, barking deer, blue pittas, wreathed hornbills, gibbons, Malayan porcupines, slow loris and serow. There are also wild elephants that occasionally cross over from Myanmar.

Places to Stay & Eat Forestry department **bungalows** *(☎ 0 2579 5734; 500-1000B)* are available at Sai Yok National Park; they sleep up to six people. **Saiyok View Raft** *(☎ 0 3451 4194; rooms 500B)*, on the river near the suspension bridge, rents out tidy rooms on floating rafts with private bathroom. For an extra 100B you get breakfast and dinner; for an extra 200B you get all meals included. There are a couple of other **raft houses** *(400-600B)* on the river in the park.

There is a row of permanent **food stalls** next to the parking lot near the visitors centre.

Getting There & Away If you are going specifically to see the waterfalls, be sure to tell the driver whether you're going to Sai Yok Yai or Sai Yok Noi, as the falls are some 30km apart. The falls can be reached by boarding a bus bound for Thong Pha Phum or Sangkhlaburi. Buses to Sai Yok Yai (38B, almost two hours) leave Kanchanaburi every 30 minutes between 6am and 6.30pm. The last bus back to Kanchanaburi passes at about 4.30pm. The trip to Sai Yok Noi takes just over an hour (25B). The last bus back to Kanchanaburi passes at about 5pm. You can also get to Sai Yok Noi by taking the train to Nam Tok and then hiring a săwngthăew for half a day to take you to Sai Yok Noi and back to the Nam Tok station. This should cost no more than 400B, but the isolation of this end-of-the-line train station has made some săwngthăew drivers greedy. Unless you're really a train nut, it's probably better to do this trip by bus from Kanchanaburi.

Prasat Meuang Singh Historical Park
อุทยานประวัติศาสตร์ปราสาทเมืองสิงห์

Approximately 43km from Kanchanaburi are the remains of an important 13th-century Khmer outpost of the Angkor empire called Meuang Singh *(admission 40B; open 8am-5pm daily)*. Located on a bend in Mae Nam Khwae Noi, the recently restored city ruins cover 73.6 hectares and were declared a historical park under the administration of the Fine Arts Department in 1987. Originally this location may have been chosen by the Khmers as a relay point for trade along Mae Nam Khwae Noi.

All the Meuang Singh shrines are constructed of laterite bricks and are situated in a huge grassy compound surrounded by layers of laterite ramparts. Sections of the ramparts show seven additional layers of earthen walls, suggesting cosmological symbolism in the city plan. Evidence of a sophisticated water system has also been discovered amid the ramparts and moats.

The town encompasses four groups of ruins, although only two groups have been excavated and are visible. In the centre of the complex is the principal shrine, **Prasat Meuang Singh**, which faces east (towards Angkor). Walls surrounding the shrine have gates in each of the cardinal directions. A reproduction of a sculpture of Avalokitesvara stands on the inside of the northern wall and establishes Meuang Singh as a Mahayana Buddhist centre. The original is in the National Museum in Bangkok. Inside the main prang is a reproduction of a sculpture of Prajnaparamita, another Mahayana Buddhist deity.

To the northeast of the main *prasat* are the remains of a smaller **shrine** whose original contents and purpose are unknown. Near the main entrance to the complex at the north gate is a small **museum**, which contains various sculptures of Mahayana Buddhist deities and stucco decorations, most of which are reproductions.

Clear evidence that this area was inhabited before the arrival of the Khmers can be seen in another small **museum** to the south of the complex next to the river. The roof shelters two human skeletons arranged in a prehistoric burial site and a detailed explanation of the findings, which included an ornate bronze spoon. A more complete exhibit of local Neolithic remains is at the Ban Kao Neolithic Museum.

Ban Kao Neolithic Museum

พิพิธภัณฑ์บ้านเก่ายุคหิน

During the construction of the Death Railway along Mae Nam Khwae Noi, a Dutch POW named Van Heekeren uncovered Neolithic remains in the village of Ban Kao (Old Town), about 7km southeast of Meuang Singh. After WWII, a Thai-Danish team retraced Van Heekeren's discovery, concluding that Ban Kao is a major Neolithic burial site. Archaeological evidence suggests it may have been inhabited 10,000 years ago.

A small but well-designed museum *(admission 30B; open 8am-4.30pm Wed-Sun)*, displaying 3000- to 4000-year-old artefacts from the excavation of Ban Kao, has been established near the site. Objects are labelled and include a good variety of early pottery and other utensils, as well as human skeletons.

Places to Stay & Eat Bungalows and raft houses are available for rent at **Ban Rai Rim Kwai** *(☎ 0 3465 4077; 333 Mu 2; rooms 1200-2400B)*, 3.5km from the Ban Kao (Tha Kilen) train station, which has a small restaurant. There are other small eateries within walking distance.

Getting There & Away Meuang Singh and Ban Kao are best reached by train from Kanchanaburi via Ban Kao (Tha Kilen) station, which is only 1km south of Meuang Singh. Walk west towards the river and follow the signs to Meuang Singh. Trains leave Kanchanaburi for Tha Kilen (10B, one hour) at 6.11am and 10.51am and 4.31pm daily.

To get to Ban Kao, you may have to walk or hitch 6km south along the road that follows Mae Nam Khwae Noi, although the occasional săwngthăew passes along this road, too. Motorcycle taxis are sometimes available at Tha Kilen station for around 30B for the journey to either Ban Kao or Prasat Meuang Singh.

It's possible to get from Kanchanaburi to Meuang Singh and back in one day by catching the 6.11am train there and the 4.30pm train back.

If you have your own transport, Ban Kao and/or Meuang Singh would make convenient rest stops on the way to Hellfire Pass or Sangkhlaburi.

Coming from the Erawan National Park area, there's no need to backtrack all the way to Kanchanaburi before heading north on Rte 323. A paved road heads west from Rte 3199 at the 25km marker, then proceeds 16km to meet Rte 323 between the 37km and 38km markers – thus cutting half a day's travel from the old loop. This winding, scenic, lightly trafficked short cut is tremendous for cycling.

Chaloem Ratanakosin National Park (Tham Than Lot)

อุทยานแห่งชาติเฉลิมรัตนโกสินทร์ (ถ้ำธารลอด)

Chaloem Ratanakosin National Park *(Tham Than Lot; admission 200B)*, a 59-sq-km park 97km north of Kanchanaburi, is of interest to speleologists because of two caves, **Tham Than Lot Yai** and **Tham Than Lot Noi**, and to naturalists for its waterfalls and natural forests. Three waterfalls – **Trai Trang**, **Than Ngun** and **Than Thong** – are within easy hiking distance of the bungalows and camp ground. **Bungalows** *(Bangkok ☎ 0 2579 5734; 500-1000B)* sleep 10 to 12 people. Pitch your own tent for 5B per person.

Getting There & Away Take a bus from Kanchanaburi to Ban Nong Preu (20B, two to three hours) and then catch a săwngthăew to the park. Most visitors arrive by car, jeep or motorcycle.

Hellfire Pass

ช่องเขาขาด

The Australian-Thai Chamber of Commerce completed the Hellfire Pass Memorial project in 1998. The purpose of the project is to honour the Allied POWs and

CENTRAL THAILAND

HELLFIRE PASS

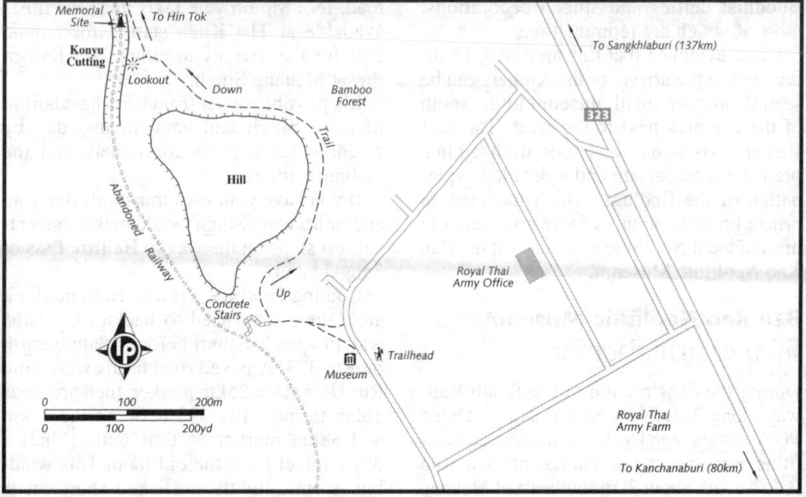

Asian conscripts who died while constructing some of the most difficult stretches of the Burma-Thailand Death Railway, 80km northwest of Kanchanaburi. 'Hellfire Pass' was the name the POWs gave to the largest of a 1000m series of mountain cuttings through soil and solid rock, which were accomplished with minimal equipment (3.5kg hammers, picks, shovels, steel tap drills, cane baskets for removing dirt and rock, and dynamite for blasting).

The original crew of 400 Australian POWs was later augmented with 600 additional Australian and British prisoners, who worked round the clock in 16- to 18-hour shifts for 12 weeks. The prisoners called it Hellfire Pass because of the way the largest cutting at Konyu looked at night by torch light. By the time the cuttings were finished 70% of the POW crew had died and were buried in the nearby Konyu Cemetery.

The memorial consists of a marked trail that follows the railway remains through the 110m Konyu cutting, then winds up and around the pass and continues through the jungle as far as Compressor cutting (about a three-hour walk). At the far end of Konyu cutting is a memorial plaque fastened to solid stone, commemorating the deaths of the Allied prisoners. There are actually seven cuttings spread over 3.5km – four smaller cuttings and three larger ones.

The Australian-Thai Chamber of Commerce has also cleared a path to the Hin Tok trestle bridge, northwest of the Konyu cutting. This bridge was called the 'Pack of Cards' by the prisoners because it collapsed three times during construction. Eventually some of the track may be restored to exhibit rolling stock from the WWII era. A **museum** *(donations accepted)* at the Hellfire Pass trailhead contains artefacts from the era and a short documentary film featuring reminiscences of survivors, which is screened continuously. The museum charges no admission but donations are greatly appreciated.

Getting There & Away Access to Hellfire Pass is via the Royal Thai Army (RTA) farm on Rte 323, between Kanchanaburi and Thong Pha Phum. Proceeding northwest along Rte 323, the farm is 80km from Kanchanaburi, 18km from the Nam Tok train terminus. The entrance to the memorial is well marked.

Once you arrive at the museum, follow the ramp from its entrance down to the trailhead. A fork in the trail gives hikers the option of taking a 500m trail through a bamboo forest or down a concrete stairway directly to the railway. If you can spare the time (about one hour), taking the 'bamboo trail' is more rewarding as it affords an initial view of the cutting from a lookout point above it. From Konyu cutting, follow the railway south to the concrete stairway that leads back up to the museum, or continue along the railway in a northwesterly direction through four cuttings and over six trestle bridges. This latter hike is only recommended if you arrive early and are up to walking for a few hours. After returning to the museum, you can cool off while watching the short documentary.

Any bus from Kanchanaburi to Thong Pha Phum or Sangkhlaburi will pass the RTA farm, but you'll have to let the bus crew know where you want to get off – tell them *châwng khăo khàat* (Hellfire Pass). If you're driving, look for the English signs announcing Hellfire Pass on Rte 323.

KANCHANABURI TO THREE PAGODAS PASS

Three Pagodas Pass (Phra Chedi Sam Ong) was one of the terminals of the Death Railway in WWII, and for centuries has been a major relay point for Thai-Burmese trade. Until 1989, when the Myanmar government took control of the Myanmar side of the border from insurgent armies, it was a place that the TAT and the Thai government would rather you'd forget about (much like Mae Salong in the north some years ago), but since then it's been promoted as a tourist destination. There's really not much to see at the pass – the attraction lies in the journey itself and the impressive scenery along the way.

It's an all-day journey and will require you to spend at least one night in Sangkhlaburi, which is an interesting off-the-track destination in itself. The distance between Kanchanaburi and Sangkhlaburi alone is about 200km, so if you take a motorcycle it is imperative that you fill up before you leave Kanchanaburi and stop for petrol again in Thong Pha Phum, the last town before Sangkhlaburi. By bicycle this would be a very challenging route, but it has been done.

The paved highway used to end in Thong Pha Phum, but now the roads from Thong Pha Phum to Sangkhlaburi and from Sangkhlaburi to Three Pagodas Pass are also paved. The best time to go is in the cooler months of January and February. During the rainy season nearly the whole of Sangkhlaburi district is under water, making travel difficult.

The road between Kanchanaburi and Thong Pha Phum passes through mostly flat terrain interrupted by the odd limestone outcrop. This is sugar-cane country, and if you're travelling by bicycle or motorcycle during harvest you'll have to contend with huge cane trucks, which strew pieces of cane and dust in their wake – take extra care. Cassava is also cultivated but the cassava trucks aren't such a nuisance.

The road between Thong Pha Phum and Sangkhlaburi is one of the most beautiful in Thailand. It winds through mountains of limestone and along the huge Kheuan Khao Laem, a hydroelectric dam near Thong Pha Phum. North of Thong Pha Phum is a major teak reforestation project. In spite of the fact that the road surface is in good condition during the dry season, steep grades and sharp curves make this a fairly dangerous journey, especially the last 25km or so before Sangkhlaburi.

For several years there has been talk of rebuilding the train connection between Nam Tok and Sangkhlaburi, using the old Japanese rail bed. If it ever happens (don't hold your breath), this will be a spectacular train trip.

Thong Pha Phum
ทองผาภูมิ

Surrounded by scenic karst topography, the area around the small town of Thong Pha Phum is slowly changing from a simple way station along Rte 323 to a destination in itself. Many of its inhabitants – mainly Mon or Burmese – originally congregated here to work on the construction of the Kheuan Khao Laem.

Mae Nam Khwae Noi runs along the east side of town, and it's possible to **raft** down river as far as Sai Yok or even all the way to Kanchanaburi. There are some interesting **walks** and **day trips** in the area. You can, for example, ford the river over a footbridge close to town to climb a prominent limestone cliff topped by a wát.

Further afield are **Nam Tok Dai Chong Thong** (35km north via Rte 323), **Nam Tok Kroeng Krawia** (33km north), **Nam Tok Pha That** (30km south at the Km 105 marker) and **Hin Dat Hot Springs** (32km south at the

CENTRAL THAILAND

Km 107 marker). All are easily accessible from the highway.

More difficult to find, discovered in 1995 by a forest monk, is **Tung Nang Khruan**, a nine-level cascade about 15km north of Thong Pha Phum and about 5km off the road to Sangkhlaburi. You'll need a guide from nearby Ban Tung Nang Khruan and sturdy legs to find it. Eventually a sign-posted road to the falls will probably be constructed; ask in Thong Pha Phum if you're interested in checking it out.

Places to Stay & Eat On the left-hand side of the town's main street off the highway, **Som Jainuk Bungalow** *(☎ 0 3459 9067; 29/10 Mu 1; rooms with fan/air-con 120/400B)* has basic but clean rooms with fan and bathroom around a shaded courtyard. A newer, all air-con building offers large, comfortable rooms with hot-water showers. The same owner has raft rooms on the lake for 500B to 3000B. **Sa Boonyong Bungalows** *(☎ 0 3459 9441; rooms with fan/air-con 180/300B, with TV 400B)* has rooms with fan similar to those at Som Jainuk, plus air-con rooms. Since it's a bit further off the street it tends to be quieter.

Ban Chaidaen Phuphaphum Hotel *(☎ 0 3459 9035; rooms 500B)*, out on the highway, has upmarket rooms with satellite TV, fridge and other amenities.

Green World Hot Spring Resort & Golf Club *(☎ 0 3459 9210 • Bangkok ☎ 0 2539 4613; rooms 800-1100B)*, 33km south of town near the 108km marker, is a huge resort with posh rooms.

Just beyond the dam west of town are eleven rustic lakeside **resorts**. However, it's mostly a Thai scene, with thatched bungalows and raft houses in the 500B to 2000B range. As Thais usually come in big groups (college students are the main clientele here) the rooms are typically huge and devoid of furniture so that up to twenty can share sleeping quarters. If business is slow you may be able to have a big room to yourself for 200B to 300B.

In typical Mon style, several shops and vendors along the main street proffer curry in long rows of pots; instead of two or three curry choices more typical of Thai vendors, the Mon vendors lay out eight or more – all delicious. The best variety is at a shop called **Roi Maw** (Hundred Pots); a branch of the same shop can be found in a relatively new shophouse on the highway just south of town.

A small **night market** convenes near the centre of town each evening with the usual rice and noodle dishes. **Saep-i-li**, a riverside restaurant near the highway bridge, serves good Isan food but it's more set up for drinking and snacking.

Getting There & Away Ordinary buses (No 8203) leave the Kanchanaburi bus station for Thong Pha Phum every half-hour from 6am until 6.30pm (54B, about three hours). Air-con buses and minivans to Sangkhlaburi also stop in Thong Pha Phum for about half the regular fare from Kanchanaburi to Sangkhlaburi – see the Sangkhlaburi Getting There & Away section for details.

Sangkhlaburi
อำเภอสังขละบุรี

postcode 71240 • pop 10,300

This small but important Kanchanaburi outpost is inhabited by a mixture of Burmese, Karen, Mon and Thai people, but is mostly Karen and Mon. You'll find very little English spoken out this way – in fact, you may hear as much Burmese, Karen and Mon as Thai. There is also a small and relatively unknown population of Lao here.

What this means for visitors is a chance to get a taste of Myanmar without having to go there. A large Mon settlement across the lake from Sankhlaburi is a wonderful place to spend an afternoon, taking in sights (sarong-clad villagers etc) that are typical of Myanmar but very uncommon in Thailand.

The distance between Kanchanaburi and Sangkhlaburi is about 227km. From Thong Pha Phum to Sangkhlaburi it's 74km.

Information For foreign-exchange services head to **Siam Commercial Bank**, in the city centre near the market, and **Phornphalin Hotel** *(both open 8.30am-3.30pm)*.

Things to See & Do Sangkhlaburi sits at the edge of the huge Kheuan Khao Laem. The town was created after the dam flooded out an older village near the confluence of the three rivers that now feed the reservoir. There's not much to do in town except explore the small **markets** for Burmese handicrafts such as checked cotton blankets, *longyi* (Burmese sarongs) and cheroots. The town comes alive on Mon National Day, celebrated during the last week of July.

Thailand's longest wooden bridge leads over a section of the lake near town to a friendly **Mon settlement** of traditional Mon-style wooden homes connected by dirt paths. A market in the village purveys goods smuggled from Myanmar, China and India; there are also a few food vendors with pots of rich Mon curry. On weekends cockfights are held around the village – to find one just listen for the enthusiastic cheers of the spectators. The village can be reached in five or 10 minutes by boat, or by walking or by cycling over the bridge.

Wat Wang Wiwekaram Also called Wat Mon since most of the monks here are Mon, this monastery is about 3km north of the town on the edge of the reservoir. A tall and revered stupa, Chedi Luang Phaw Uttama, is the centrepiece of the wát. Constructed in the style of the Mahabodhi stupa in Bodhgaya, India, the *chedi* is topped by 400 *bàat* (about 6kg) of gold. An earlier *chedi* is located some distance behind the tall one and is 300 to 400 years old. From the edge of the monastery grounds is a view of the tremendous lake and the three rivers that feed into it.

A new section of the Mon temple built across the road features a flashy, multi-roofed *wíhăan* with stainless-steel–plated pillars, heavy carved wooden doors and marble banisters. It's surrounded by a carp-filled moat. Local rumour has it that it was built from profits made selling weapons and other supplies to the Mon and Karen armies; the wildest stories even claim that a huge weapons cache is stashed beneath the *wíhăan*. A more likely source of support for the wát was the black-market tax collected by the Mon rebel soldiers on all goods smuggled through their territory.

A Burmese **handicrafts market** convenes at the wát daily from mid-morning until sunset. The selection of wares is as good if not better than what's on offer at Three Pagodas Pass.

Kheuan Khao Laem This huge lake was formed when a dam was constructed across Mae Nam Khwae Noi near Thong Pha Phum in 1983. The lake submerged an entire village at the confluence of the Khwae Noi, Ranti and Sangkhalia Rivers. The spires of the village's **Wat Sam Prasop** (Three Junction Temple) can be seen protruding from the lake in the dry season.

Canoes can be rented for exploring the lake, or for longer trips you can hire a long-tail boat and pilot. **Lake boating** is a tranquil pastime, best early in the morning with mist and bird life; early evening is also good for bird-watching. At one time a sprawling Mon refugee camp was accessible from the lake but it was recently moved inland. Since relations between Thailand and Myanmar became strained after a series of hostage-taking incidents in late 1999/early 2000, the district's Mon refugee camps have been off limits to visitors.

A branch meditation centre of Kanchanaburi's Sunyataram Forest Monastery is found on the lake's **Ko Kaew Sunyataram** (Sunyataram Jewel Isle). Permission to visit must be obtained from the Sunyataram Forest Monastery, 42km before Sangkhlaburi.

P Guest House (see Places to Stay following) can arrange bamboo-raft or long-tail boat trips on the lake (one of the most popular is a journey by raft along Mae Nam Sangkhalia), elephant riding and jungle trekking for 850B.

Day trips to nearby waterfalls are also a possibility. The rates depend on how many people are on the trip, but they tend to be very reasonable.

Places to Stay Sangkhlaburi's one hotel is **Phornphalin Hotel** *(☎ 0 3459 5039; rooms with fan/air-con 200/500B)* and it is on the southern edge of town near an army camp and the central market. Air-con rooms have bathroom with hot water, TV and fridge. The rooms are fairly clean and comfortable.

P Guest House *(☎ 0 3459 5061; rooms 200B)* is down on the lake behind the town. It has bungalows with verandas that have been placed along a slope overlooking the lake; all rooms have a fan and shared bathing facilities. This place does packages (850B) that include rafting on the lake and elephant riding, as well as a room for one night. If you stay longer the price of the room drops to 100B per night. If you show up and aren't interested in a tour, you'll likely be shown the door, unless business is really slow, in which case you may be able to get a room for 200B. The guesthouse is about 1.2km from the bus stop in town.

Burmese Inn *(☎/fax 0 3459 5146; rooms with/without bath 120/80B, larger rooms with bath 250-500B)* is perched in a lagoon with views of the wooden bridge that crosses to the Mon village, about 800m south from the Sangkhlaburi bus station. On offer are thatched-roof bungalows with shared bathroom, bungalows with private bathroom and fan, and larger rooms, including one with a TV. A major downside is the amazingly surly staff. A motorcycle taxi from the bus stop in Sangkhlaburi to either guesthouse costs 10B.

A handful of 'resorts' along the shore of the lake come and go with each season. These resorts are oriented towards Thai tourists more than Westerners.

Places to Eat There's a decent restaurant downstairs at **Phornphalin Hotel** and it features an extensive English menu. **Rung Arun** restaurant, opposite the Phornphalin, also serves good Thai-Chinese food (dishes 30B to 60B); there are three or four other places to eat down the street, serving similar fare. Both **Burmese Inn** and **P Guest House** offer food. The day market in the centre of town sometimes has a couple of vendor **stalls** offering Indian naan and curry.

Shopping Visitors interested in acquiring some Karen weaving should visit the gift shop operated by **Ban Unarak**, a home for abandoned children and destitute mothers. The gift shop is located on the road that runs between Burmese Inn and P Guest House.

Getting There & Away Ordinary bus No 8203 leaves the Kanchanaburi bus station for Sangkhlaburi (84B) at 6am, 8.40am, 10.20am and noon, and takes five to six hours, depending on how many mishaps occur on the Thong Pha Phum–Sangkhlaburi road. An air-con bus (151B) leaves at 9am and 1.30pm and takes four to five hours.

A minivan service from Kanchanaburi to Sangkhlaburi via Thong Pha Phum (120B, three hours) leaves six times daily, from 7.30am to 4.30pm. From Sangkhlaburi the vans depart from near the market seven times daily between 6.30am and 3.30pm. From either end it's usually best to reserve your seat a day in advance.

If you go by motorcycle or car you can count on about three hours to cover the 217km from Kanchanaburi to Sangkhlaburi, including three or four short rest stops. Alternatively, you can make it an all-day trip and stop off in Ban Kao, Meuang Singh and Hellfire Pass. Be warned, however, that this is not a trip for an inexperienced motorcycle rider. The Thong Pha Phum to Sangkhlaburi section of the journey (74km) requires sharp reflexes and previous experience on mountain roads. This is also not a motorcycle trip to do alone as stretches of the highway are practically deserted – it's tough to get help if you need it and easy to attract the attention of would-be bandits.

Three Pagodas Pass (Payathonzu)

ด่านเจดีย์สามองค์

The pagodas themselves are rather small, but it is the remote nature of this former black-market outpost that draws a trickle of visitors. Control of the Myanmar side of the border once vacillated between the Karen National Union and the Mon Liberation Front, since Three Pagodas (Chedi Sam Ong) was one of several 'toll gates' along the Thailand-Myanmar border where insurgent armies collected a 5% tax on all merchandise that passed. These ethnic groups used the funds to finance armed resistance against the Myanmar government. Now the border crossing and the town on the Myanmar side, Payathonzu, are controlled by the Myanmar government, although much of the long border between the two countries is not under government control.

The Karen people conduct a huge multimillion-dollar business in illegal mining and logging, the products of which are smuggled into Thailand by the truckload. Pressure for control of these border points has increased since the Thai government enacted a ban on all logging in Thailand in 1989, which has of course led to an increase in teak smuggling.

In late 1988 heavy fighting broke out between the Karen and the Mon for control of the 'toll gate' here. Since this is the only geographical location for hundreds of kilometres in either direction where a border crossing is convenient, this is where the Mon army (which has traditionally controlled this area) had customarily collected the 5% tax on smuggling. The Karen insurgents do the same at other points north along the Thailand-Myanmar border. Myanmar government pressure on the Karen further north led to a conflict between the Karen and the Mon over Three Pagodas trade and the village on the Myanmar side was virtually burnt to the ground.

The Myanmar government wrested control of the town in 1989 from both the Karen and Mon and have been firmly established at the ever since. It renamed the town Payathonzu (Three Pagodas) and filled it with shops catering to an odd mix of troops and tourists.

Depending on the political situation, foreigners are sometimes allowed to cross the border here for day trips but you must complete the necessary paperwork in Sangkhlaburi before coming to the border. Apply for a border pass by visiting the Sangkhlaburi immigration office (around the corner from the Phornphalin Hotel) and providing two passport-sized photos and one copy each of the photo and visa pages of your passport. Once your pass is in order, proceed to the border and pay US$10 on the Myanmar side. The crossing is open from 8.30am to 6pm. Unlike the border crossing at Mae Sai in Chiang Rai, this crossing is not an 'official' crossing, and your passport isn't actually stamped, so don't bother coming up here to get some more Thai visa time on your passport.

A true frontier town, Payathonzu has around a half dozen Burmese **teahouses** (a couple of them with *nam-bya* – the Burmese equivalent to Indian naan bread), one **cinema**, several mercantile **shops** with Burmese *longyi* (sarongs), cheroots, jade and clothes, and a few general souvenir shops with Mon-Karen-Burmese handicrafts. It is necessary to bargain; traders speak some English and also some Thai. In general the goods are well priced. A Buddhist temple, **Wat Suwankhiri**, can be seen on a bluff near the town.

A Myanmar military checkpoint at the edge of town usually bars all visitors from leaving the town limits.

Three Pagodas Pass hosts a large **Songkran Festival** in April, which is complete with hemp-fisted Thai-Burmese kick boxing, cockfights, and Karen, Thai, Burmese and Mon folk dancing.

Getting There & Away The 19km paved road to Three Pagodas Pass begins 4km before you reach Sangkhlaburi off Rte 323. At this intersection is a Thai police checkpoint where you may have to stop for minor interrogation, depending on recent events in the Three Pagodas Pass area. Along the way you'll pass a couple of villages inhabited by Mon or Karen people.

If you don't have your own wheels, sǎwngthǎew to Three Pagodas Pass (30B) leave about every hour between 6am and 6.40pm from a lot near Sangkhlaburi's central market. The last sǎwngthǎew back to Sangkhlaburi leaves Three Pagodas Pass at around 5pm or 6pm.

The border is only a short walk from the sǎwngthǎew stop in Three Pagodas Pass.

THUNG YAI NARESUAN & KHAO LAEM NATIONAL PARKS

อุทยานแห่งชาติทุ่งใหญ่นเรศวร/
อุทยานแห่งชาติเขาแหลม

Approximately 34km south of Sangkhlaburi between the 39km and 40km markers, you'll find a turn-off on the east side of the highway for the 3200-sq-km Thung Yai Naresuan National Park *(admission 200B)*, Thailand's largest protected land parcel. This rough dirt road leads to **Nam Tok Takien Thong**, where pools are suitable for swimming nearly year-round. There are at least two other tracks off the highway into the sanctuary, but to find anything of interest you really should go with a guide – check with the Burmese Inn or P Guest House in Sangkhlaburi. Thung Yai Naresuan is one of the last natural habitats in Thailand for the tiger, whose total numbers nationwide are estimated to be less than 500, perhaps no more than 250.

On the opposite side of the highway near the Thung Yai Naresuan turn-off is a paved road into the recently established Khao Laem National Park *(admission 200B)*. As yet there are no facilities to speak of, but presumably the park was created to protect the riverine habitats near the lake.

Tham Sukho is a large limestone cave shrine just off the highway at the 42km marker.

Southeastern Thailand

The provinces that comprise southeastern Thailand are culturally very similar, populated for the most part by central Thai speakers. To visitors this region of Thailand is known mainly for its beaches, which range from the wildly overdeveloped and overtouristed shores of Pattaya in Chonburi Province, to the near pristine islands south of Trat Province's Ko Chang. The reason for this lopsided development is due to the former's nearness to Bangkok, and the latter's proximity to western Cambodia which was, until just a few years ago, still enveloped in civil war. The demise of the Khmer Rouge and peace in Cambodia have given the green light to tourism and development along this long-neglected bit of Thai coast. Inland, the region gets very few visitors, with the exception of those on their way overland to Cambodia, which may be accessed via two border crossings: at Aranyaprathet in Sa Kaew Province, and at Hat Lek in Trat.

Highlights

- Check out Pattaya diving scene, some of the best in Thailand and within easy striking distance of Bangkok
- Spend a relaxing week on Ko Samet on palm-lined beaches and feasting on delicious seafood
- Explore the pristine beaches and coves of the Ko Chang archipelago in scenic and little-visited Trat Province
- Take the bawdy back door to Angkor via the casino town of Poipet and Sa Kaew's border town of Aranyaprathet

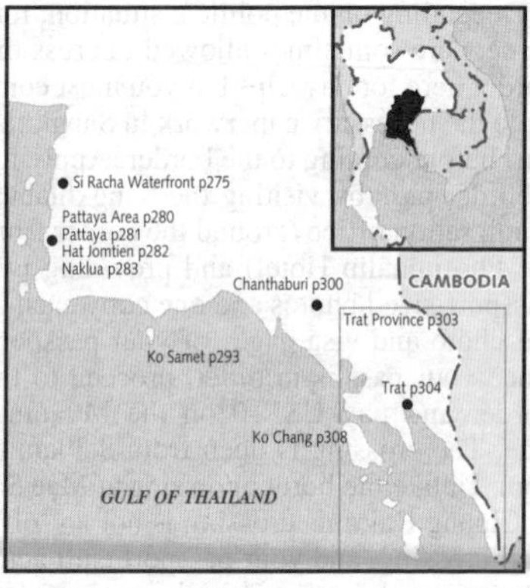

Chonburi Province

SI RACHA

ศรีราชา

postcode 20110 • pop 145,600

About 105km from Bangkok on the eastern coast of the Gulf of Thailand is the small town of Si Racha, home of the famous spicy sauce *náam phrík sĭi raachaa*. Some of Thailand's best seafood, especially the local oysters, is served here accompanied by helpings of this sauce.

On **Ko Loi**, a small rocky island connected to the mainland by a long jetty, stands a Thai-Chinese Buddhist temple. Further offshore lies larger Ko Si Chang, flanked by two smaller islands – Ko Kham Yai to the north and Ko Khang Kao to the south. As this grouping of islands provides a natural shelter from the wind and sea, it is used as a harbour by large incoming freighters. Smaller boats transport goods to the Chao Phraya delta some 50km away.

The motorised *săamláw* in this fishing town and on Ko Si Chang are unlike anywhere else in Thailand – huge motorcycles powered by auto engines, with the plush passenger seating at the rear.

Si Racha Tiger Farm

สวนเสือศรีราชา

The Si Racha Tiger Farm (*☎ 0 3829 6571; adult/child 300/150B; open 8am-6pm daily)* is an attraction covering 250 *râi* (40 hectares) off Rte 3241 about 9km southeast of town. The zoo combines a world-famous tiger-breeding facility with a crocodile farm, 'herbivores zone', scorpion farm and circus-like performances.

The complex is very popular with Asian package tourists who pay to be photographed posing with tiger cubs and iguanas, but if you are turned off by caged or performing animals (and insects), give this place a miss.

Animal shows on offer include a crocodile-wrestling show, chimpanzee show and even a 'Scorpion Queen' show (a woman who dances while handling large black scorpions). These take place throughout the day and cost 30/20B extra per adult/child. Telephone for further information.

Places to Stay

For most people the town of Si Racha is more of a transit point than an overnight stop. The best places to stay in Si Racha are the rambling wooden hotels built on piers over the waterfront.

Siriwatana Hotel *(☎ 0 3831 1037; 35 Th Jermjompol; rooms 160-200B, room for up to 5 people 300B)*, across from Th Tessaban 1 and the Bangkok Bank, is the cleanest of the lot and has the best service. There are rustic sitting areas with tables outside the rooms along the piers. Basic rooms have fan and shower. There's also a small restaurant. **Samchai** *(☎ 0 3831 1800; Soi 10; rooms 260B, with air-con 380-400B)*, across from Th Surasakdi 1, has reasonable rooms and some air-con rooms as well. All three are open and breezy, with outdoor tables where you can bring food in the evening from nearby markets.

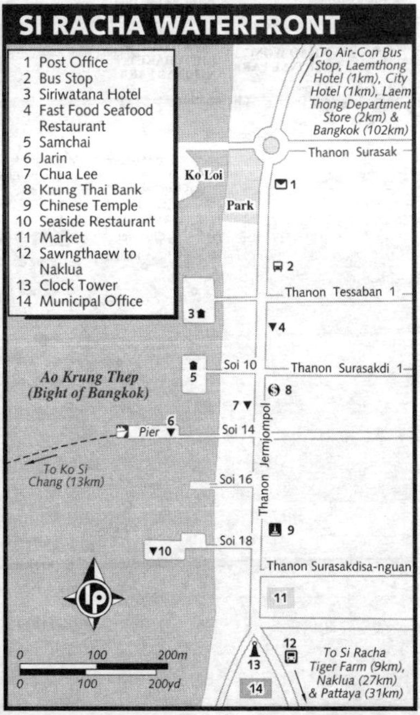

There are several top-end hotels in town. **Laemthong Hotel** *(☎/fax 0 3832 2886; doubles from 963B)*, a 20-storey hotel in the centre of town, just off Th Sukhumvit (Hwy 3), is one such place. Comfortable doubles come with all the amenities, including breakfast; facilities on the premises include a swimming pool and tennis courts.

City Hotel *(☎ 0 3832 2700, fax 0 3832 2739; 6/126 Th Sukhumvit; rooms from 2296B)* is a classy hotel that offers capacious rooms, and discounts of up to 40% are sometimes available. An escalator leads from the pavement to the 2nd-floor reception; facilities include a pub, coffee shop, fitness centre and business centre.

Places to Eat

There is plenty of good seafood in Si Racha, but you have to watch the prices. **Chua Lee** *(Th Jermjompol (Joemjomphon); dishes 80-260B)*, across from the Krung Thai Bank, is a Chinese-owned restaurant and the best known in town. The seafood is great but probably the most expensive in town.

Next door and across the street are several seafood places with similar fare at much more reasonable prices, such as the **Fast Food Seafood Restaurant** *(dishes 60-100B)* just south of Th Tessaban 1.

Jarin *(Tha Soi 14; dishes 50-80B)* has very good one-plate seafood dishes, especially *khâo hàw mòk thá-leh* (steamed seafood curry with rice) and *kŭaytĭaw phàt thai kûng sòt* (Thai-style rice noodles with fresh shrimp). It's a great restaurant in which to kill time while waiting for the next boat to Ko Si Chang; prices are low to moderate.

Seaside Restaurant *(Soi 18; dishes 120-180B)* is a large place at the end of the Soi 18 pier – now just about the best all-round seafood place in town for atmosphere, service and value. The full-colour bilingual menu includes a tasty grilled-seafood platter stacked with squid, mussels, shrimp and cockles.

The cheapest place to eat is in the **market** near the clock tower at the southern end of town. In the evenings the market offers everything from noodles to fresh seafood, while during the daytime it's a food and

SOUTHEASTERN THAILAND

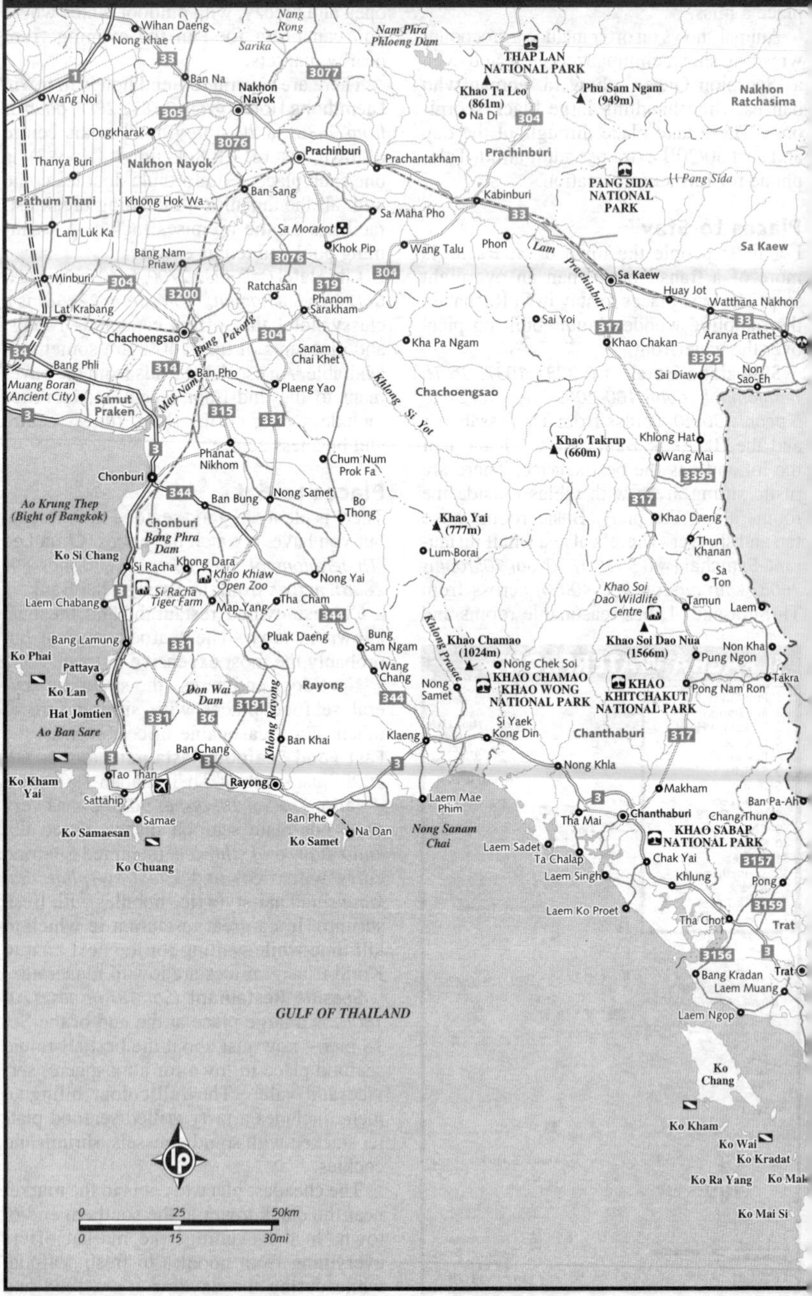

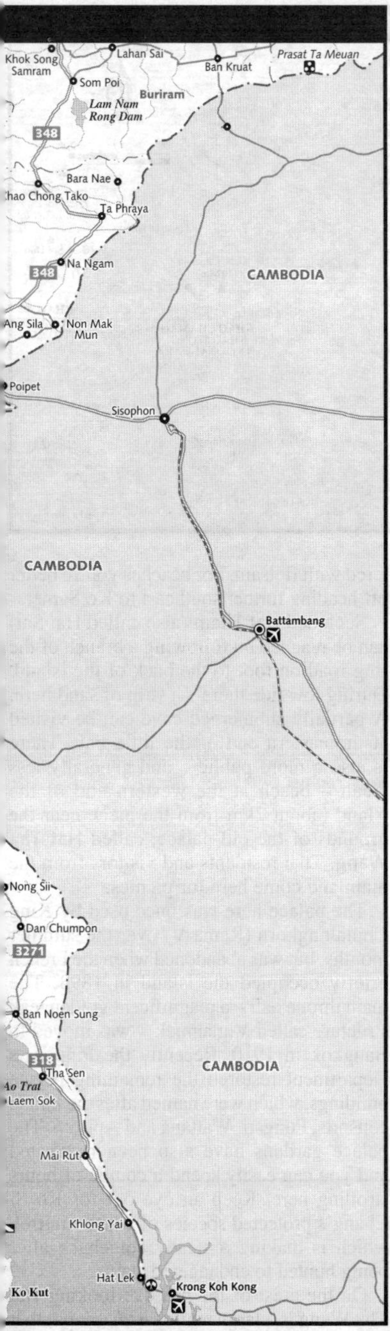

clothing market with some noodle and snack stands.

Outside town, off Th Sukhumvit (Hwy 3) on the way to Pattaya, there are a couple of good fresh-seafood places. At **Ao Udom**, a small fishing bay close to town in the same direction, you'll also find several open-air seafood eateries.

Getting There & Away

Buses to Si Racha leave the Eastern bus station in Bangkok every 30 minutes or so from 5am to 7pm (ordinary 48B, air-con 88B; about 1¾ hours). Ordinary direct buses stop near the pier for Ko Si Chang, but through buses and air-con buses stop on Th Sukhumvit (Hwy 3), near the Laemthong department store, from where there are *túk-túk* (motorised sǎamláw, or three-wheeled pedicab) to the pier.

You can also reach Si Racha by 3rd-class train (28B), although not many people come by this method. Train No 365 leaves Bangkok's Hualamphong station at 6.55am and arrives at Si Racha at 10.11am (about an hour slower – but a good deal more scenic – than the bus).

White *sǎwngthǎew* (pick-up trucks used as buses or taxis; also written songthaew) bound for Naklua (North Pattaya) leave from near the clock tower in Si Racha frequently throughout the day (15B, 30 minutes). Once you're in Naklua you can easily catch another sǎwngthǎew on to central Pattaya.

Boat services to Ko Si Chang leave from Tha Soi 14.

Getting Around

In Si Racha and on Ko Si Chang there are fleets of huge motorcycle taxis, many of which are powered by Nissan engines, that will take you anywhere in town or on the island for 20B to 30B.

KO SI CHANG

เกาะสีชัง

postcode 20120 • pop 4100

Ko Si Chang makes a nifty one- or two-day getaway from Bangkok. There is only one town on the island, facing the mainland; the rest of the tiny island has some history and is fun to explore. The small population is made up of fisherfolk, retired and working mariners and government workers who are

CHONBURI TO CHANTHABURI

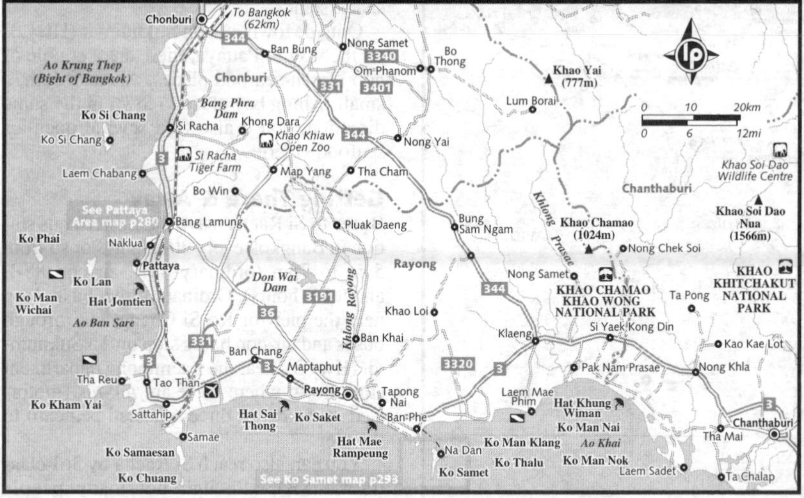

stationed with the customs office or with one of the aquaculture projects on the island.

Information

A branch of Kasikornbank in town – on the main road to the right as you walk up from the pier – does foreign exchange on weekdays.

Things to See & Do

A meditation hermitage, **Yai Phrik Vipassana Centre**, is ensconced in limestone caves and palm huts along the island's centre ridge. The hermit caves make an interesting visit but should be approached with respect – monks and *mâe chii* (nuns) from all over Thailand come here to take advantage of the peaceful environment for meditation. Be careful that you don't fall down a limestone shaft; some are almost completely covered with vines.

On the opposite side of the island, facing out to sea, are some beaches with decent swimming, though take care with the tide and the sea urchins. You shouldn't come here looking for perfect white sand and turquoise waters, as the island's proximity to shipping lanes and fishing grounds means its shores are less than tidy. Depending on sea currents and time of year, the shoreline can be relatively clean or cluttered with flotsam. For beaches you're better off heading further southeast to Ko Samet.

Secluded **Hat Tham** (also called Hat Sai) can be reached by following a branch of the ring road on foot to the back of the island. During low tide there's a strip of sand here. A partially submerged cave can be visited at the eastern end of the little bay. There is also a more public – and generally less clean – beach at the western end of the island (about 2km from the pier), near the grounds of the old palace, called **Hat Tha Wang**. Thai residents and visitors from the mainland come here for picnics.

The **palace** here was once used by King Chulalongkorn (Rama V) over the summer months, but was abandoned when the French briefly occupied the island in 1893. The main throne hall – a magnificent golden teak structure called Vimanmek – was moved to Bangkok in 1910. Recently the Fine Arts Department restored the remaining palace buildings, which were named after the king's consorts, Pongsri, Wattana and Apirom. The palace gardens have also been renovated and you can easily spend a couple of hours strolling here. Keep an eye out for Ko Si Chang's protected species of white squirrel, which is making a steady comeback after being hunted to endangered status.

On the crest of the hill overlooking Hat Tha Wang is a large white *chedi* (stupa) that contains **Wat Atsadangnimit**, a small consecrated chamber where King Chulalongkorn used to meditate. The unique Buddha image inside was fashioned 50 years ago by a local monk who now lives in the cave hermitage. Nearby you'll come to a stone outcrop wrapped in holy cloth. The locals call it 'Bell Rock' because if struck with a rock or heavy stick it rings like a bell.

Not far from Wat Atsadangnimit is a large limestone cave called **Tham Saowapha**, which appears to plunge deep into the island. If you have a torch, the cave might be worth exploring.

To the east of town, high on a hill overlooking the sea, is a large Chinese temple called **San Jao Phaw Khao Yai**. During Chinese New Year in February, the island is overrun with Chinese visitors from the mainland. This is one of Thailand's most interesting Chinese temples, with shrine caves, several different temple levels and a good view of Si Chang and the ocean. It's a long and steep climb from the road below.

Like most islands along Thailand's eastern seaboard, Ko Si Chang is best visited on weekdays; on weekends and holidays the island can get crowded.

Places to Stay

Si Phitsanu Bungalow *(☎ 0 3821 6034; rooms from 500B, 1-bedroom bungalows 800B, 2-bedroom 1500-1800B)* is near Hat Tham at the back of the island. It's easily the friendliest and most relaxing place on the island. There are rooms in a row house or you can get a comfortable bungalow overlooking the small bay. There's also a small restaurant and bicycles for rent. To reach this area from town, take the first right past the Tiewpai Park Resort, then follow the road past the Yai Phrik Vipassana Centre. A motorcycle sǎamláw will cost you 30B.

Tiewpai Park Resort *(Thiw Phai; ☎ 0 3821 6084; rooms with fan 400B, with air-con 600-750B)*, not far from the main piers, it recently underwent a renovation. Tiewpai has rooms with private shower, air-con and TV.

Benz Bungalow *(☎ 0 3821 6091; rooms with air-con 600B)*, out near the gate to Hat Tha Wang, offers clean rooms facing the sea in a basic hotel-style building or in one of its unique stone bungalows. Its two-bed rooms can comfortably sleep three.

Sichang View Resort *(☎ 0 3821 6210; rooms with fan 500B, with air-con 800-1400B)*, near the Chinese temple, has tidy apartment-style rooms on nicely landscaped grounds, and a good **restaurant**.

Sichang Palace *(☎ 0 3821 6276; rooms with pool/sea view 810/910B)* is a three-storey hotel in the middle of town on Th Atsadang, with clean, comfortable rooms either facing the swimming pool, or with sea views. During weekends the staff may add 100B to 200B to these prices.

Places to Eat

The town has several small restaurants, but nothing special, with all the Thai and Chinese standard dishes. Along the road that leads to the public beach (Hat Tha Wang) are a couple of rustic **seafood places**.

Sichang Palace and **Sichang View Resort** each have their own restaurants serving good seafood at medium-high prices. **Tiewpai Park Resort** offers reasonably priced Thai and Western food.

Getting There & Away

Boats to Ko Si Chang leave on an hourly basis from the pier in Si Racha at the end of Soi 14, Th Jermjompol. The fare is 30B each way; the first boat leaves at about 6am and the last at 7pm. The last boat back to Si Racha from Si Chang is at 6pm. As you approach Ko Si Chang by boat, check out the dozens of barges anchored in the island's lee. Their numbers have multiplied from year to year as shipping demands by Thailand's booming import and export business have increased.

Getting Around

There are fleets of huge motorcycle taxis that will take you anywhere on the island for 20B to 30B. You can also get a complete tour of the island for 150B per hour. Asking prices for any ride tend to be outrageous; the supply of taxis is plentiful, however, and you can usually get the local price after talking to several drivers.

PATTAYA

พัทยา

postcode 20260 • pop 79,200

Pattaya, 147km southeast of Bangkok, is Thailand's busiest beach resort, with over 12,000 rooms available in hotels, bungalows

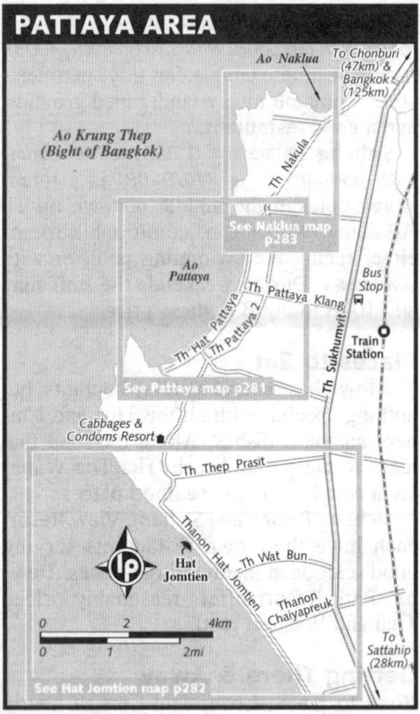

and guesthouses spread along Hat Pattaya and adjoining Naklua and Jomtien beaches. Hat Pattaya is the most active of the three beaches, a crowded crescent of sand where jet skis and powerboats slice the surf and parasails billow over the palms all day long. Sunburned visitors jam the beachfront road in rented jeeps and motorcycles.

According to TAT statistics, an average one-third of foreign tourists to Thailand visit Pattaya; in a typical November to March season Pattaya receives around a million visitors. Most of them are package tourists from Europe, Russia and the Middle East. Depending on their tastes, some visitors will find Pattaya lacking in culture as well as good taste, since much of the place seems designed to attract tourists interested in a prefabricated, Western-style beach vacation with almost no 'Thai' ingredients.

Hat Pattaya is also not that great (although it must have been at one time) and the town's biggest businesses – water sports and sex – have driven prices for food and accommodation beyond Bangkok levels. Compared with many other Thai resort areas, it's more money-oriented and less friendly.

Pattaya got its start as a resort when US GIs from a base in Nakhon Ratchasima began visiting the one-time fishing village in 1959. US navy men from nearby Sattahip added to the military influx during the Vietnam War years. Nowadays there are still plenty of sailors around, but of many nationalities. National and international convention-goers make up another large segment of the current market, along with Asian golfers seeking out the many local golf courses, including courses designed by names such as Robert Trent Jones and Jack Nicklaus.

Another thing the Pattaya area has going for it is diving centres. There are over a dozen nice islands off Pattaya's shore, although they can be expensive (compared with the rest of Thailand) to reach. If you're a snorkelling or scuba enthusiast, equipment can be booked at any of the several diving shops or diving schools at Hat Pattaya. Ko Lan, the most popular of the islands, even has places to stay. Of course, Pattaya is also acclaimed for its seafood, although it's generally way overpriced by national (but not international) standards.

Information

Tourist Offices The **TAT office** *(☎ 0 3842 8750; ⓔ tatpty@chonburi.ksc.co.th; open 8.30am-7.30pm daily)*, at the northwestern edge of King Rama IX Park, has piles of brochures, but otherwise it's not very helpful. There is a **tourist-police office** *(☎ 0 3842 9371, emergency ☎ 1155; Th Pattaya 2)*.

Immigration Offices There is an **immigration office** *(☎ 0 3842 9409; Th Pattaya Klang Soi 8; open 8.30am-4.30pm Mon-Fri)*.

Money There are banks with foreign-currency exchange windows all over Pattaya, so you won't have to walk far to find one. Nearly every bank in Pattaya has an ATM.

Post & Communications The **main post office** *(Soi 15; open 8.30am-4.30pm Mon-Fri, 9am-noon holidays)* is in South Pattaya.

The **CAT office** is located near the corner of Th Pattaya Tai and Th Pattaya 3. There are also several private long-distance phone offices in town: the best one is the **Overseas Cafe** *(open 9am-4am daily)*, near the intersection of Th Hat Pattaya and Th Pattaya Tai. Rates are among the lowest in town, and its opening hours allow you to take advantage of night-time discounts.

Newspapers & Magazines *Explore Pattaya*, a free monthly magazine distributed around town, contains information on current events, sightseeing and advertisements for hotel and restaurant specials. *What's On Pattaya* is a similar publication. *Pattaya Mail* (🅦 www.pattayamail.com), a weekly newspaper, publishes articles on political, economic and environmental developments in the area as well as the usual ads. It makes for some absorbing reading as Pattaya's famed social ills are well covered – much of the mayhem you'll read about here never makes it to the Bangkok papers. Not surprisingly given Pattaya's popularity with German-speakers, there is also a German-language newspaper, *Pattaya Blatt*.

Medical Services A 24-hour service is offered by **Pattaya Memorial Hospital** (*☎ 0 3842 9422–4, 3842 2741; Th Pattaya Klang*).

Apakorn Kiatiwong Naval Hospital (*☎ 0 3843 7171–2*), 26km southeast of Pattaya in Sattahip, has a fully operative decompression chamber; urgent care is available 24 hours. If it's really an emergency, you'll get to the hospital much faster if you go through one of Pattaya's dive shops. **Mermaid Dive Center** (*☎ 0 3823 2219*) is reliable.

Beaches

Curving around Ao Pattaya (Pattaya Bay), **Hat Pattaya** is a relatively scenic crescent

PATTAYA

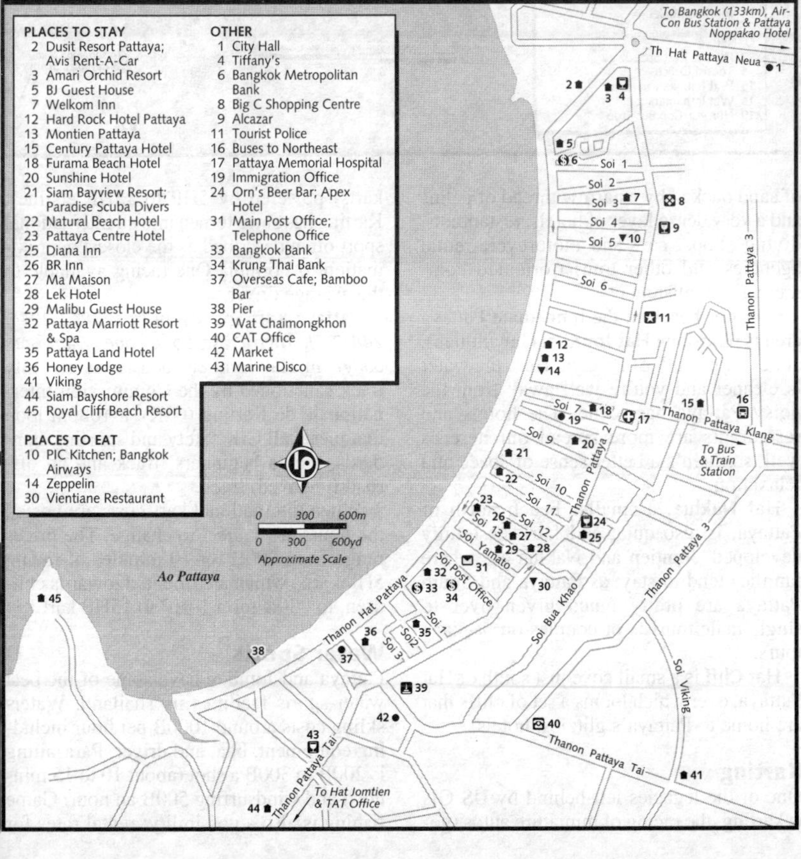

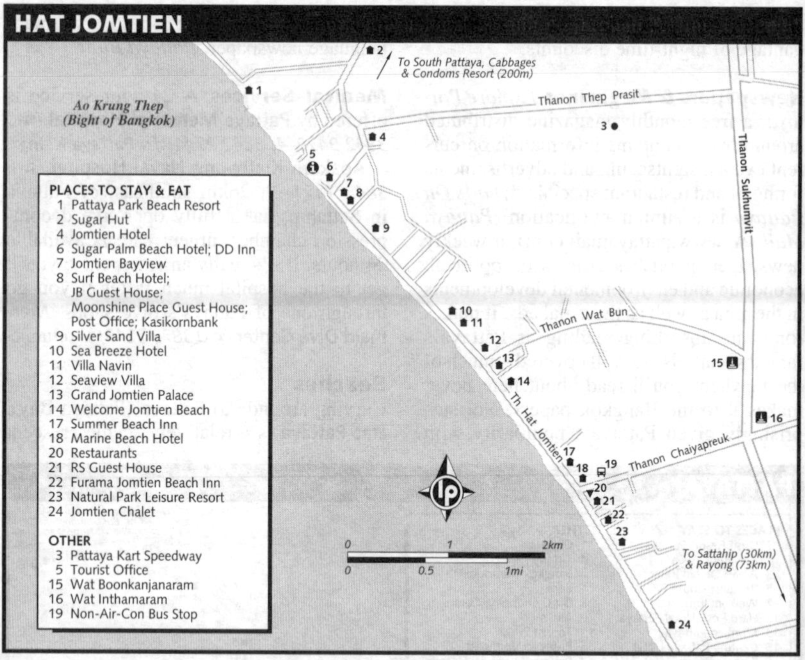

of sand backed by a narrow thread of palms and a very dense layer of hotels, restaurants, diving shops, car- and motorcycle-rental agencies and other tourist-oriented commercial establishments.

A better beach in the immediate Pattaya area is 6km-long **Hat Jomtien** (Jawmthian), about 2km south of Pattaya. Here the water is cleaner and you're well away from the noisy Pattaya bar scene. The hotels and restaurants are more spread out here as well, so there's a better sense of space and relaxation.

Hat Naklua, a smaller beach north of Pattaya, is also quiet and fairly tastefully developed. Jomtien and Naklua are where families tend to stay, as Pattaya and South Pattaya are pretty much given over to single male tourists or couples on package tours.

Hat Cliff is a small cove just south of Hat Pattaya, over which looms a set of cliffs that are home to Pattaya's glitziest hotels.

Karting

One of the legacies left behind by US GIs is karting, the racing of miniature autos (go-karts) powered by 5HP to 15HP engines. Karting has since turned into an international sport often described as the closest approximation to Formula One racing available to the average driver.

Pattaya Kart Speedway (*☎ 0 3842 2044; 248/2 Th Thep Prasit Soi 9; open 9am-6pm daily*), in Hat Jomtien, boasts Asia's only track sanctioned by the Commission Internationale de Karting (CIK), a 1080m loop that meets all CIK safety and sporting standards, plus a beginners' track and an off-road (unpaved) track.

When international kart races are hosted the hours are subject to change. The prices range from 200B for 10 minutes of racing 5HP karts, which are oriented towards children, to 250B for a 10HP to 15HP kart.

Water Sports

Pattaya and Jomtien have some of the best water-sports facilities in Thailand. Water-skiing costs around 1000B per hour including equipment, boat and driver. Parasailing is 200B to 300B a shot (about 10 to 15 minutes) and windsurfing 500B an hour. Game fishing is also a possibility; rental rates for boats, fishing guides and tackle are quite reasonable.

Hat Jomtien is the best spot for windsurfing, not least because you're a little less likely to run into parasailors or jet skiers. **Surf Beach Hotel** *(Th Hat Jomtien)* rents out equipment and offers instruction.

Scuba Diving Pattaya is the most convenient diving location to Bangkok, but it is far from the best locations that Thailand has to offer. In recent years the fish population has dwindled considerably and visibility is often poor due to heavy boat traffic. Although nearby Ko Lan, Ko Sak and Ko Krok are fine for beginners, accomplished divers may prefer the 'outer islands' of Ko Man Wichai and Ko Rin, which have more visibility. In most places you can expect 3m to 9m of visibility under good conditions, or in more remote sites 5m to 12m. Further southeast, the shipwrecks of *Petchburi Bremen* and *Hardeep* off Sattahip and Samae have created artificial reefs and are interesting dive sites.

Diving costs are quite reasonable: a two-dive excursion averages from 1900B to 2900B for boat, equipment, underwater guide and lunch. Snorkellers may join such day trips for 500B to 800B. For shipwrecks, the price goes up to 3000B to 3500B (depending on the season), and for an overnight trip with five to seven dives, figure up to 6000B per person. Full National Association of Underwater Instructors (NAUI) or Professional Association of Dive Instructors (PADI) certification, which takes three to four days, costs 9000B to 12,000B for all instruction and equipment.

Some shops do half-day group trips to nearby islands for as low as 500B to 800B per person, and to islands a bit further out from 650B; these prices include lunch, beverages, transport and dive master but not equipment rental beyond mask, fins and snorkel.

Average rental rates per day are: mask, fins and snorkel 200B to 250B; regulator 300B to 400B; buoyancy compensation device 250B to 400B; weight-belt 150B; tank 150B; wetsuit 300B; or full scuba outfit 1500B. Airfills typically cost 100B to 150B. To protect themselves from steep baht fluctuations, some diving operators quote only in US dollars – a reasonable strategy considering virtually all equipment must be imported.

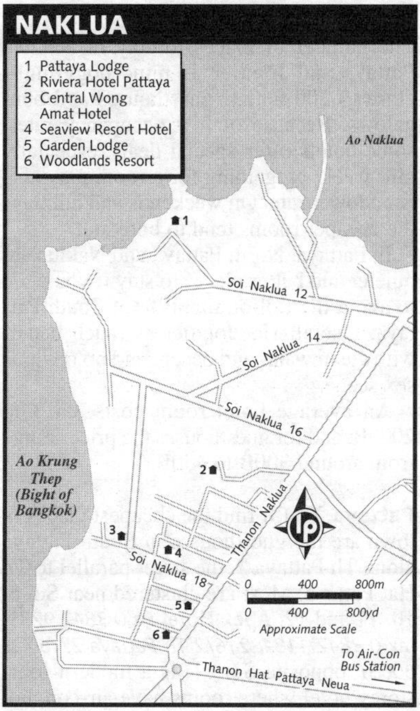

Pattaya shops advertise trips, and several Pattaya hotels also arrange excursions and equipment, including the following.

Aquanauts Diving (☎ 0 3836 1724) Th Hat Pattaya
Dave's Diver Den (☎ 0 3842 0411, fax 0 3836 0095) 190/11 Mu 9, Th Pattaya Klang
Mermaid Dive Center (☎ 0 3823 2219, fax 0 3823 2221) Soi White House, Hat Jomtien
Millennium Divers (☎ 0 3842 7185) Soi Pattaya Land 1, South Pattaya
Paradise Scuba Divers (☎ 0 3871 0567) Siam Bayview Resort
Seafari Sports Center (☎ 0 3842 9060, fax 0 3842 4708) Soi 5, North Pattaya

Other Sports

Other recreational activities available include bowling, snooker, archery, tennis, target shooting, golf and horse riding. Among the several gyms and fitness centres around town is Gold's Gym in South Pattaya's Julie Complex. Gold's has a second branch in North Pattaya just past Soi 1 on Th Naklua-Pattaya.

Places to Stay – Budget

The number of places to stay in Naklua, Pattaya and Jomtien is mind-boggling – close to 200 hotels, guesthouses and bungalows. Because of low occupancy rates, some hotels offer special deals, especially mid-week; bargaining for a room may also net a lower rate. On weekends and holidays the cheaper rooms tend to book out.

In Pattaya, North Pattaya and Naklua are quieter and better places to stay if you want to avoid the full-on nightlife of South Pattaya. Overall Hat Jomtien is much better, with clean water and beach, and no obvious sex scene.

An average hotel room costs 350B to 2000B, and for guesthouses the prices range from around 300B to 450B.

Pattaya You'll find the cheapest places in town are the guesthouses in South Pattaya along Th Pattaya 2, the street parallel to Th Hat Pattaya. Most are clustered near Soi 6, 10, 11 and 12. **Apex Hotel** (*☎ 0 3842 9233, fax 0 3842 1184; 216/2 Th Pattaya 2; rooms 500B*), opposite Soi 11, is a modern four-storey hotel where rooms have air-con, hot water, TV and fridge. There's also a pool on the premises.

Honey Lodge (*☎ 0 3842 9133, fax 0 3871 0185; 597/8 Mu 10, Th Pattaya Tai; rooms 500B*) has air-con rooms with hot water, fridge and phone. The staff are helpful and friendly. It also has a **restaurant** and pool.

Diana Inn (*☎ 0 3842 9675, fax 0 3842 4566; rooms 750B*), almost next door to the Apex, has large rooms with air-con and hot-water bath, plus a restaurant. Breakfast is included in the price of the room. There's also a swimming pool. Some of the rooms are bombarded by noise from the nightclub next door – and once you've checked in, moving rooms is out of the question. Choose carefully.

BR Inn (*☎ 0 3842 8229; singles & doubles 400B, triples 600B*), in a lane south of Soi 12, is a family-run place offering single and double rooms and an air-con room that sleeps three. All rooms have TV. **Malibu Guest House** (*☎ 0 3842 8667; Soi 13; rooms 300B*) is one of many guesthouses on Soi 13 that are in the 300B to 350B range, but rooms are usually cramped and without windows. Malibu is typical, with air-con and hot-water showers but nothing else. At least it's clean. **Ma Maison** (*☎ 0 3842 9318, fax 0 3842 6060; rooms 800B*) is an exception and offers chalet-style air-con rooms around a swimming pool, including breakfast; as the name suggests, it's French managed and there's a French **restaurant** on the premises. Advance reservations are highly recommended, as it's often booked out.

Viking (*☎ 0 3842 3164, fax 0 3842 5964; Soi Viking; rooms with fan/air-con 350/400B*), down in South Pattaya, has been a long-time favourite for its quiet rooms and pool. It's popular with long-termers and charges 3500B to 4000B per month. **Pattaya Land Hotel** (*☎ 0 3842 9569; 325/42-45 Soi 1, Th Pattaya Land; rooms with air-con 400B*) sits right smack in the middle of 'Boys Town' and has a gay go-go bar attached to it. Not surprisingly, the majority of the hotel's clientele didn't come for a night's sleep.

BJ Guest House (*☎ 0 3842 1147; Th Hat Pattaya; rooms 400B*) a three-storey hotel wedged between North and Central Pattaya, sits across from the beach and has air-con rooms with TV and fridge. There's also a decent restaurant.

Welkom Inn (*☎ 0 3842 2589, fax 0 3836 1193; Soi 3, Th Hat Pattaya; rooms 600-850B*) is a German-oriented place with air-con rooms. A large pool, Thai garden restaurant and Franco-Belgian restaurant with piano bar are pluses. There's also a small Internet café.

Hat Jomtien At Hat Jomtien, the budget category consists of several places around the mid-range Surf Beach Hotel at the northern end of the beach. **Moonshine Place Guest House** (*☎ 0 3823 1956; rooms 500B*) has rooms; the popular old-west-style **bar-restaurant** downstairs could make it noisy at night. Then again, you won't have to travel far for a cold beer.

DD Inn (*☎ 0 3823 2995; 410/50 Th Hat Jomtien; rooms with/without balcony 550/500B*) is also at the northern end of the beach (sometimes referred to separately as Hat Dong Tan or 'Sugar Palm Beach'). Clean air-con rooms have TV and some have a balcony. Discounts at this friendly establishment are given for long-term stays. **Sugar Palm Beach Hotel** (*☎ 0 3823 1386, fax 0 3823 1713; rooms 650B*) is almost next door and offers rooms with air-con, TV and refrigerator, in a small but well-kept beachfront property.

SOUTHEASTERN THAILAND

JB Guest House *(☎ 0 3823 1581; rooms with fan & cold bath 300B, with air-con, hot bath & TV 350B, with fridge & sea view 450B)*, near Sugar Palm, is very good value and has excellent rooms with a range of amenities. **Seaview Villa** *(Chom Thaleh; ☎ 0 3823 1070; Th Hat Jomtien; bungalows 1000-1800B)*, further south on Th Hat Jomtien, has nicely appointed bungalows, the more expensive with air-con and two rooms.

Villa Navin *(☎ 0 3823 1066, fax 0 3823 1318; 350 Mu 12, Th Hat Jomtien; rooms Mon-Thur 1500-2000B, Fri-Sun 2300-2700B; bungalows Mon-Thur 2700-3000B, Fri-Sun 3300-3500B)* is a friendly four-storey establishment with doubles and three-bedroom air-con bungalows. An outdoor **restaurant** specialises in seafood.

RS Guest House *(☎ 0 3823 1867; rooms with fan 350B, with air-con 400-600B)*, a tidy place that sits at the southern end of the beach near Th Chaiyapreuk, is one of the cheapest places to stay. Reasonable, smallish rooms all have hot-water showers and TV. The most expensive rooms are nearest the sea.

You can also find unnamed **rooms for rent** in 'condotels' along Hat Jomtien for about 200B to 400B a night with fan and 400B to 600B with air-con. These are little more than concrete cubes filled with box-like rooms, often lacking in ventilation and plumbing efficiency.

Jomtien Hotel *(☎ 0 3825 1606, fax 0 3825 1097; 403/74 Mu 12, Th Hat Jomtien; rooms with fan 200B, with air-con up to 1200B)*, at the northern end of Jomtien off the road leading to South Pattaya, stands well away from the beach. It's basically a low-end tourist hotel. The fan rooms look rather neglected but are cheap – they're only 2800B per month and are usually full during the high season. There is a small rectangular pool on the roof.

Pattaya Noppakao Hotel *(☎/fax 0 3837 0582; 10/17 Mu 6, Th Hat Pattaya Neua; rooms from 450B)*, next to the station for air-con buses to Bangkok, offers spacious, clean rooms with air-con, hot-water shower and satellite TV – good value for Pattaya. Breakfast is also included.

Places to Stay – *Mid-Range*

Pattaya Good mid-range places can be found in Naklua, North Pattaya and Jomtien. **Sunshine Hotel** *(☎ 0 3842 9247, fax 0 3842 1302; 217/1 Soi 8; rooms 600-980B)* is tucked away in Pattaya, and all rooms come with air-con, TV and fridge. Rooms in the newer building are more expensive, but the rooms in the original building are just as comfortable. The hotel also has a pool and a **restaurant** that stays open until midnight.

Natural Beach Hotel *(☎ 0 3871 0121; Soi 11; rooms 750B)* overlooks the beach and has good air-con rooms. This modern, breezy, two-storey hotel also contains a small restaurant.

Lek Hotel *(☎ 0 3842 5552, fax 0 3842 6629; cnr Th Pattaya 2 & Soi 13; rooms 560-960B)* is a high-rise that has decent air-con rooms with TV. The more expensive rooms are in a new addition to the building, where the rooms are a tad bigger.

Furama Beach Hotel *(☎ 0 3842 8580; 164 Mu 9, Th Pattaya Klang; rooms 600B)*, which is a couple of blocks back from the beach, is a worn but clean hotel with all the basic resort amenities. On the premises are a coffee shop (open until midnight), seafood restaurant and swimming pool.

Naklua A two-storey place built around a circular drive just off Th Naklua, **Garden Lodge** *(☎ 0 3842 9109, fax 0 3842 1221; rooms 750B)* features air-con rooms, plus a clean pool and good service.

Seaview Resort Hotel *(☎ 0 3842 4825; Soi 18, Th Naklua; rooms 750B)*, on a quiet lane off Th Naklua, is an L-shaped four-storey hotel with decent air-con rooms. Breakfast is included. **Pattaya Lodge** *(☎ 0 3822 5464; 6-person/9-person/12-person bungalows 2700/3300/3800B)*, further off Th Naklua right on the beach, is quieter and far from Pattaya's noise, pollution and bars. It may be preferred by families and small groups. Two-storey, air-con bungalows have two, three or four bedrooms. Discounts of 20% are given during the week.

Riviera Hotel Pattaya *(☎ 0 3822 5230, fax 0 3822 5764; 157/1 Soi Wat Pa Samphan, Th Naklua; rooms 350B, with fridge & TV from 450B)* stands between the road and the beach and has cosy, quiet air-con rooms, some with fridge and TV. The Riviera also boasts a large garden area and pool.

Hat Jomtien Peaceful Hat Jomtien has mostly mid-range condotel places with prices ranging from 500B to 800B.

Silver Sand Villa *(☎ 0 3823 1289, fax 0 3823 2498; rooms in old/new wing 800/1200B)*, set back from the main drag, has spacious double air-con hotel rooms in either the old or new wing. There are two swimming pools on the premises.

Jomtien Bayview *(☎ 0 3825 1889; rooms Mon-Thur 490B, Fri-Sun 590B)*, further north than Silver Sand, has air-con rooms with TV.

Surf Beach Hotel *(☎ 0 3823 1025–6; rooms 450B, with sea view 550B)*, next to the Kasikornbank, is a friendly and popular place with air-con rooms. All rooms come with TV and fridge.

Marine Beach Hotel *(☎ 0 3823 1129–31; 131/62 Th Hat Jomtien; rooms 600-1200B)* has air-con rooms with TV and fridge, but the staff make themselves scarce and you might have to remind them to clean the room now and again.

Sea Breeze Hotel *(☎ 0 3823 1056–8, fax 0 3823 1059; rooms 1000B)* is a well-run place with air-con, TV and fridge in every room. Breakfast is included with the room rate.

Summer Beach Inn *(☎ 0 3823 1777, fax 0 3823 1778; rooms 700B)*, near the Marine Beach Hotel, is a friendly, five-storey, good-value place with fairly new air-con rooms, that all include satellite TV and fridge.

Furama Jomtien Beach Inn *(☎ 0 3823 1545; Th Hat Jomtien; rooms with/without sea view 700/600B)* is a pink-walled hotel, south of Th Chaiyapreuk and is another good deal, with standard rooms with TV and air-con, and larger rooms. The Furama caters particularly to Japanese, Chinese and Korean package tourists.

Jomtien Chalet *(☎ 0 3823 1205–8; 57/1 Mu 1, Th Hat Jomtien; bungalows 1300-1800B)* offers simple, clean, air-con bungalows, or two rooms in an old refurbished railway car, one which sleeps two (1200B), and another which sleeps six (1800B). If you're coming to Pattaya and want some memorable accommodation, this is the place. A restaurant serves Thai and Western food.

Places to Stay – Top End

Pattaya is really a resort for package tourists and convention goers, so the vast majority of its accommodation is in this price bracket. All of the following hotels have air-con rooms and swimming pools (unless otherwise noted). In most cases the upper end of the price range represents suites, while the lower end are standard doubles. Many of the top-end hotels have reduced rates on standard singles and doubles, so it's worth asking if anything cheaper is available when requesting a rate quote. Rooms are also often cheaper when booked through a Bangkok travel agency, or via the Internet.

Pattaya In North Pattaya, **Dusit Resort Pattaya** *(☎ 0 3842 5611, fax 0 3842 8239 • in Bangkok ☎ 0 2236 0450; 240/2 Th Hat Pattaya Neua; rooms US$80-700)* is among the reigning monarchs of Pattaya luxury hotels. It has 500 rooms, two pools, tennis and squash courts, a health centre, a semiprivate beachfront and exceptional dim sum in the rooftop restaurant.

Amari Orchid Resort *(☎ 0 3842 8161, fax 0 3842 8165 • in Bangkok ☎ 0 2267 9708; e amorchid@loxinfo.co.th; rooms US$60-119)*, near the Dusit, is another excellent choice in this category. Its 234 rooms are set on four lush hectares in North Pattaya, with an Olympic-size swimming pool, two tennis courts, children's playground, mini-golf, garden chess and one of the best Italian restaurants in Pattaya. The Amari quotes only in US dollars: add 10% service charge and 7% value-added tax (VAT).

Pattaya Marriott Resort & Spa *(☎ 0 3841 2120, fax 0 3842 9926; 218/2-4 Mu 10, Th Hat Pattaya; rooms with garden/sea view 4100/4900B)* is one of Pattaya's most well-established resorts and was recently bought out by the Marriott group. The hotel sits on three hectares of palms in Central Pattaya and has lotus ponds and Thai-style pavilions. It's attached to a relatively new four-storey shopping centre as well as a Ripley's Believe It or Not Museum. Also on the premises are a fitness centre, two tennis courts, two cinemas and a pool.

Royal Cliff Beach Resort *(☎ 0 3825 0421–30, fax 0 3825 0522; Th Cliff; rooms with garden/sea view 6120/6826B)* is another older luxury property at the southern end of Pattaya. It is really three hotels in one: a central section for package tours and conventions, a family wing and the very up-market Royal Wing.

Hard Rock Hotel Pattaya *(☎ 0 3842 8759, fax 0 3842 1673; Th Hat Pattaya; rooms from US$105)*, once the down-at-the-heels Merlin Pattaya, this place was given a costly revamp

SOUTHEASTERN THAILAND

and is now one of the hipper places in the city. Rooms have all the expected amenities and are themed on rock and roll idols. Of course, there's a Hard Rock Cafe attached to the hotel.

Montien Pattaya (*☎ 0 3842 8155–6, fax 0 3842 3155; Th Hat Pattaya; rooms from 3756B*) is a long-established place that gets lots of German package tourists. Rooms are large and comfortable, and there's a swimming pool.

Moving south are yet more top-enders, varying little in amenities and services. Each of the following offers comfortable air-con rooms with phone, TV and fridge, plus other amenities on the premises such as a coffee shop or restaurant, travel agent and swimming pool.

Century Pattaya Hotel (*☎ 0 3842 7800, fax 0 3842 8069; 129/16 Th Pattaya Klang; rooms 800-1100B*) has rooms that vary in cost depending on the view. There's also a swimming pool here with bar service and a restaurant.

Pattaya Centre Hotel (*☎ 0 3842 5877, fax 0 3842 0491; Soi 12, Th Hat Pattaya; rooms from 1319B*) has dropped its rates and is starting to show wear, but if you don't mind the gaggles of package tourists in the lobby, it's fairly good value. Breakfast is included in the rates.

Siam Bayview Resort (*☎ 0 3842 3871, fax 0 3842 3879; 310/2 Th Hat Pattaya; rooms from 2100B*) is right in the thick of Central Pattaya, and has a pool, garden and terrace café. The resort's Bali Hai **restaurant** is quite good.

Siam Bayshore Resort (*☎ 0 3842 8678–81, fax 0 3842 8730; Th Pattaya Tai; rooms 4440B*) is a labyrinthine-like place, set at South Pattaya's quieter edge, and has rooms that are a cut above the standard. Breakfast is included and the rates drop 30% during the low season.

Cabbages & Condoms Resort (*C&C Resort; ☎ 0 3825 0035, fax 0 3825 0034; Th Phra Tamnak Soi 4; rooms 4355B*), as with the C&C restaurants around Thailand, puts all profits towards HIV/AIDS education and prevention. It's the brainchild of Thai MP Mechai Viravaidya (you'll sometimes see him staying here) and the standards of quality and service are high. There's a swimming pool and the resort has its own stretch of beach. Discounts of up to 900B are sometimes given on weekdays and during the low season.

Naklua On Hat Naklua, **Central Wong Amat Hotel** (*☎ 0 3842 6990, fax 0 3842 8599; 277-278 Mu 5, Th Naklua; rooms from 3310B*) is a very quiet 10-hectare resort. **Woodlands Resort** (*☎ 0 3842 1707, fax 0 3842 5663; 164/1 Th Naklua; rooms from 1800B*) is a smaller 80-room place oriented towards families, with a children's pool, playground and baby-sitting services. Room rates include breakfast.

Hat Jomtien One of the best places to stay in the entire Pattaya area is **Sugar Hut** (*☎ 0 3825 1686, fax 0 3825 1689; 391/18 Th Pattaya Tai; bungalows 8430B*), however, it's not even on the beach, but off the road connecting Pattaya and Hat Jomtien. Thirty-three Thai-style bungalows on stilts are thoughtfully scattered among 15 *râi* (2.4 hectares) of tropical gardens, complete with rabbits and birds, three swimming pools, a restaurant, a modern fitness centre and jogging track. The bungalows feature partially open bathrooms inspired perhaps by upmarket Balinese resorts. Each bungalow has a separate living room and two bedrooms. Breakfast is included. Discounts of up to 20% are given during the low season.

Pattaya Park Beach Resort (*☎ 0 3825 1201 fax 0 3825 1209 • in Bangkok ☎ 0 2511 0717; 345 Th Hat Jomtien; rooms from 1836B*) is a huge cement entertainment and hotel complex oriented towards package tourists or families, with such attractions as a tailor shop, huge 'fun complex', beer garden, diving shop and water park. If you're in need of a thrill, you can slide down a cable that stretches from the top of the Pattaya Park's 55-storey tower to the ground. The slide is open 10am to 10pm and costs 200B.

Grand Jomtien Palace (*☎ 0 3823 1405, fax 0 3823 1404 • in Bangkok ☎ 0 2271 3613; 356 Th Hat Jomtien; rooms 1210B, with sea view 1452B*) is a 14-storey place that is quite popu lar with German and Russian package tourists.

Welcome Jomtien Beach (*☎ 0 3823 2701–15, fax 0 3823 2716; rooms from 1050B*), near Grand Jomtien, also caters to package tourists.

Natural Park Leisure Resort (*☎ 0 3823 1561, fax 0 3823 1567; 412 Th Hat Jomtien;*

rooms Mon-Thur 950B, Fri-Sun 1200B) is a nicer low-rise hotel with an attractive free-form swimming pool.

Places to Eat

Most food in Pattaya is expensive. The front signs outside the many snack bars and restaurants in town reveal that *bratwurst mit brot* (sausage with bread) is far more readily available than *khâo phàt* (fried rice). Arabs and South Asians have been coming to Pattaya for many years now, so there are also plenty of Indian, Pakistani and Middle Eastern restaurants in town, some with fairly moderate prices. An influx of Russians, which began in the late 1990s, has inspired several restaurants to add Russian translations to their menus; more recently a few Russian cafés have been added to the scene.

Decent Thai food is available in shops along Pattaya's backstreet (Th Pattaya 2), away from the beach. The best seafood restaurants are in South Pattaya, where you pick out the sea creatures and are charged by their weight. Prices tend to be sky-high by Thai standards.

Savoey Seafood *(☎ 0 3842 8580–1; open until midnight daily)*, part of the Furama Beach Hotel in Central Pattaya, is one of the better places for fresh seafood without breaking the bank.

PIC Kitchen *(Soi 5; dishes 70-140B; open 8am-midnight daily)*, the second entrance on Soi 4, is one moderately priced yet well-appointed Pattaya restaurant. The Thai-style *sǎalaa* have low wooden tables and cushions for dining and the emphasis is on Thai food with a limited selection of Western dishes.

Vientiane Restaurant *(☎ 0 3841 1298; 485/18 Th Pattaya 2; lunch specials 30-50B, dishes 60-120B; open 11am-midnight daily)*, opposite Soi Yamato, is another interesting place to eat. The 503-item menu includes mostly Thai and Lao dishes, plus lunch specials.

La Gritta *(☎ 0 3842 8161; Th Hat Pattaya; dishes 180-300B; open 6pm-11pm daily)*, near the Amari Orchid Resort, is good for a splurge and does Italian-style seafood with some flair. Prices are moderate to expensive but there's a pianist to keep you entertained.

Moonshine Place Guest House *(Th Hat Jomtien; dishes 40-80B)* specialises in Mexican and southern-Thai food; you can also buy a picnic lunch here.

Zeppelin *(☎ 0 3842 0016; Th Hat Pattaya; dishes 120-280B; open noon-midnight daily)*, in the Nova Hotel, is one of many German restaurants found in Pattaya. The Royal Garden Plaza shopping centre, which is attached to Royal Garden Resort Pattaya, contains several **fast-food franchise restaurants**, as does the Big C shopping centre located on Th Pattaya 2.

On Hat Jomtien, opposite the bus station on the corner of Th Hat Jomtien and Th Chaiyapreuk, there are a few basic and cheap **restaurants** serving the usual Thai and Chinese dishes.

Entertainment

Eating, drinking and merry-making are the big pastimes once the sun goes down. Merry-making in Pattaya, aside from the professional sex scene, means everything from hanging out in a video bar to dancing all night at one of the discos in South Pattaya. Two transvestite palaces, **Alcazar** *(☎ 0 3842 9694; 78/14 Th Pattaya 2; admission 500-600B)* and **Tiffany's** *(☎ 0 3842 1701; Th Pattaya 2; admission 500-600B)*, have drag-queen shows; the Alcazar is the best and puts on three shows nightly at 6.30pm, 8pm and 9.30pm. **Marine Disco** *(Th Pattaya Tai)* is older but still popular.

One of the best things to do in the evening is to stroll down Th Hat Pattaya and check out the amazing variety of bars – there's one for every proclivity, including a couple of outdoor *muay thai* (Thai boxing) bars featuring local talent. Truly the 'garden of earthly delights', in the most Boschean sense, 'Pattaya Land', encompassing Soi 1, 2 and 3 in South Pattaya, is one of the most concentrated bar areas. The many gay bars on Soi 3 are announced by a sign reading 'Boys Town'.

With all the emphasis on sex-for-sale venues, there's precious little in the way of live music in Pattaya.

Bamboo Bar *(Th Pattaya Tai)*, situated near the intersection with Th Hat Pattaya, is one of the town's original nightspots and is one of the few places you can find live music. There are two bands each night (the second act, starting around midnight, is usually better). There are of course plenty of hostesses happy to keep you company, but no one minds if you just want to knock back a few drinks and take in the music.

FRANK CARTER

Ko Chang, Trat Province

SARA-JANE CLELAND

Pier, Ko Chang, Trat Province

ANDREW MARSHALL & LEANNE WALKER

Ko Chang, Trat Province

FRANK CARTER

Ao Kiu Na Nok, Ko Samet, Rayong Province

KRAIG LIEB

Ko Chang, Trat Province

FRANK CARTER

Ko Samet, Rayong Province

Pattaya Vice

Pattaya's notoriety for sex tourism revolves around a huge collection of discos, outdoor bars and transvestite cabarets comprising Pattaya's red-light district at the southern end of the beach. That part of South Pattaya known as 'the village' attracts a large number of prostitutes, including *kàthoey* (transvestites), who pose as female hookers and ply their trade among the droves of *faràng* (Western) sex tourists. There is also a prominent gay sex-for-sale scene in Pattaya. White prostitutes from as far away as Romania and Russia (favourites with male Asian sex tourists) and black male prostitutes from Nigeria (primarily servicing female sex tourists from Japan) can all be had in Pattaya. Talk about one-stop shopping! Of course, prostitution is just as illegal here as elsewhere in the country – which is to say, enforcement of the laws against it is cyclic at best.

Local authorities and travel agents have been trying to improve Pattaya's image for years, usually with media blitzes and glossy brochures. Of late, the strict enforcing of a 2am closing time for all entertainment venues has put a dent in the sex industry.

Orn's Beer Bar, next to the Apex Hotel, is a smaller place with live tunes. The quality of the music varies, but the place has a good feel to it, and if you feel you can do justice to a song, you might be able to take to the stage yourself.

Shenanigan's Pattaya (☎ *0 3871 0641; Th Pattaya 2; open 9am-2am daily)* brings Bangkok's popular Irish pub to Pattaya with all the usual trimmings, including Guinness on tap. It's not cheap, so have a look at the price list before you get too involved.

Getting There & Away

Air There are daily flights on **Bangkok Airways** (☎ *0 3841 2382; PIC Plaza, Soi 4, Th Pattaya 2)* between Ko Samui and U-Taphao airfield (about 30km south of Pattaya). The fare is 2650B one way to Ko Samui and 3000B in the reverse direction due to Ko Samui's higher departure tax. Children under 12 fly for half price.

Bus Air-con buses from Bangkok's Eastern bus station leave every 30 minutes from 4.30am to 7.30pm (84B, 2½ hours). Air-con buses to Pattaya are also available from Bangkok's Northern and Northeastern bus station for the same fare. In Pattaya the air-con **bus station** *(Th Pattaya Neua)* is near the intersection with Th Sukhumvit. Several hotels and travel agencies in Bangkok also run thrice-daily air-con tour buses to Pattaya for around 100B to 150B. Cramped minivans from Th Khao San typically cost 170B per person. These buses take around two hours in either direction. Once you reach the main Pattaya bus station, waiting red săwngthăew will take you to the main beach road for 20B per person.

From Si Racha you can grab a public bus on Th Sukhumvit to Pattaya for 12B.

There are also buses between Pattaya and several Northeastern towns, including Nakhon Ratchasima (223B air-con).

Pattaya has a separate bus stop for buses to the Northeast, near the intersection of Th Pattaya Klang and Th Pattaya 3.

Train The No 365 train goes from Bangkok's Hualamphong station to Pattaya (31B) via Chachoengsao at 6.55am, arriving at 10.37am daily. In the opposite direction train No 240 leaves Pattaya at 2.50pm and arrives at Hualamphong at 6.35pm. Although this is an hour longer than the typical bus ride from Bangkok, it beats biting your nails in traffic jams along the highway from Bang Na to Trat. The Pattaya train station is just north of the T-junction of Th Pattaya Klang and Th Sukhumvit.

Getting Around

To/From the Airport If you've just flown into Bangkok and need to get to Pattaya right away, there are airport minibuses that go directly to Pattaya (200B) at 9am, noon and 7pm daily. In the reverse direction, the THAI minibus (also 200B) leaves from next to the Gulf Siam Hotel in Pattaya at 6.30am, 2pm and 6.30pm. It usually takes around 2½ hours to reach the airport, though give yourself plenty of time as traffic can make this a four-hour journey. Some hotels in Pattaya also run their own buses to Bangkok for 200B to 300B one way.

Car & Motorcycle Jeeps can be hired for around 2000B per day, and cars start at 1200B (as low as 800B for a 4WD Suzuki

SOUTHEASTERN THAILAND

in the low season) depending on size and model; insurance and tax cost up to 160B more. All vehicle rentals in Pattaya are on a 24-hour basis.

Avis Rent-A-Car *(☎ 0 3836 1628, 0 3842 5611)* has an office at the Dusit Resort Pattaya, and is by far the most expensive option. Of course, if something goes wrong you don't have to worry about any hassles (like a formerly unseen disclaimer popping up in your insurance policy). Avis also offers a pick-up and drop-off service at your hotel.

Motorcycles cost 150B to 200B per day for an 80cc or 100cc; a 125cc to 150cc will cost 300B, and you'll even see a few 750cc to 1000cc machines for hire for 500B to 1000B. There are motorcycle hire places along Th Hat Pattaya and Th Pattaya 2. Pattaya is a good place to purchase a used motorcycle – check the rental shops.

Săwngthăew Locally called 'baht buses', săwngthăew cruise Hat Pattaya and Th Pattaya 2 frequently – just hop on and when you get out pay 10B anywhere between Naklua and South Pattaya, 20B as far as Jomtien. Don't ask the fare first as the driver may interpret this to mean you want to charter the vehicle. A chartered săwngthăew to Jomtien should be no more than 40B. It's usually easier to get a share săwngthăew from Jomtien to central Pattaya rather than vice versa.

Many readers have complained about having ridden the 10B săwngthăew with local passengers and then been charged a higher 'charter' price of 20B to 50B or more when they got off. In some instances drivers have threatened to beat *faràng* (Western) passengers when they wouldn't pay. It's little use complaining to the tourist police unless you can give them the licence-plate number of the offending driver's vehicle. A refund is highly unlikely but perhaps if the tourist police receive enough complaints, they'll take some action to reduce or eliminate the rip-offs.

Rayong Province

RAYONG & AROUND

อ.เมืองระยอง

postcode 21000 • pop 46,400

Rayong lies on the Gulf of Thailand coast 220km from Bangkok by the old highway (Hwy 3) or 185km on Hwy 36. The province produces fine fruit (especially durian and pineapple) and *náam plaa* (fish sauce). Rayong itself is not worth visiting, but nearby beaches are fair and Ko Samet is a favourite island getaway for Bangkok residents. Except for Ko Samet, this area has not received many foreign visitors, but it has been popular with Thai tourists for several years.

Estuarial beaches at **Laem Charoen** about 2km south of the provincial capital of Rayong, aren't that great, but there are some reasonable seafood restaurants. Better are the beaches near **Ban Phe**, a seaside town around 25km southeast of Rayong (this is also the departure point for Ko Samet). If sun and sand are what you've come to Rayong for, head straight for Ban Phe. Then pick out a beach or board a boat bound for Ko Samet.

Another much smaller island near Rayong is **Ko Saket**, which is a 20-minute boat ride from the beach of Hat Sai Thong (turn south off Hwy 3 at the 208km marker).

Suan Son (Pine Park), 5km further down the highway from Ban Phe, is a popular place for Thai picnickers and has white-sand beaches as well.

Suan Wang Kaew is 11km east of Ban Phe and has more beaches and rather expensive bungalows. **Ko Thalu**, across from Suan Wang Kaew, is said to be a good diving area – the proprietors of Suan Wang Kaew, a private park, can arrange boats and gear. Other resort areas along the Rayong coast include **Laem Mae Phim** and **Hat Sai Thong**. **Hat Mae Rampeung**, a 10km strip of sand between Ban Taphong and Ban Kon Ao (11km east of Rayong), is part of Laem Ya-Ko Samet National Park. See the Ko Samet section later in this chapter for more information.

Khao Chamao-Khao Wong National Park (admission 200B) is inland about 17km north of the 274km marker off Hwy 3. Although less than 85 sq km, the park – which actually overlaps into Chantaburi Province – is famous for limestone mountains, caves, high cliffs, dense forest and waterfalls. According to park officials, the park is sanctuary to populations of tigers, wild elephants and bears. To get here from Ban Phe take a săwngthăew to the 274km marker for 24B, and another săwngthăew to the park.

Cleared areas for camping are available, so you can pitch your own tent for 10B. There are also eight large bungalows that can sleep up to eight people each (800B per bungalow), though, as with most national park accommodation, these were built with visiting Thai students in mind and must be completely rented out, even if you show up alone.

Information

Tourist Offices There is an office of the **TAT** *(☎ 0 3865 5420; ⓔ tatry@infonews.co.th; 153/4 Th Sukhumvit)* near Rayong. The staff can provide maps and fairly up-to-date lists of accommodation and sights in Rayong and Chanthaburi Provinces.

Money Several banks along Rayong's main drag, Th Sukhumvit, have exchange services, including **Bangkok Bank, Kasikornbank** and **Bank of Ayudhuya**. Opening hours are 8.30am to 3.30pm Monday to Friday and 8.30am to noon Saturday. Besides Rayong, there are also banks with currency-exchange service in Ban Phe. Travellers heading for Ko Samet should know that there are no banks on the island, although currency exchange can be done at many of the larger places of accommodation, albeit at a rate slightly less than what you'd get at the bank.

Places to Stay & Eat

Rayong Should you somehow get caught overnight in Rayong, there are a few inexpensive hotels near the bus station off Th Sukhumvit.

Rayong City Hotel *(0 3861 4873; 11 Ratbamrung Soi 4; singles/doubles with air-con 500/700B)* is probably the best mid-range place in town. Rooms are large, clean and comfortable with TV and fridge, and there is a swimming pool on the premises. The management is quite helpful and friendly.

Rayong President Hotel *(☎ 0 3861 1307; rooms 500B)* is similar in amenities to the Rayong City Hotel. The hotel is located down a small side street, so it's quiet at night. From the bus station, cross to the other side of Th Sukhumvit, turn right and after about three minutes' walk you'll see a sign pointing down a side street to the hotel.

There are many other places along Th Sukhumvit with simple rooms with fan for 150B to rooms with air-con and hot water for 500B.

For cheap food, check the **market** near the Thetsabanteung cinema, or the string of **restaurants** and **noodle shops** on Th Taksin Maharat just south of Wat Lum Mahachaichumphon. If you have plenty of time, take a sǎwngthǎew (5B) south from Th Sukhumvit to the mouth of Mae Nam Rayong at Laem Charoen, where the well-established **Laem Charoen** and **Ocharos** (Ocha Rot) serve moderately priced seafood. Sǎwngthǎew (8B) from the bus station take you to a small wooden bridge that crosses Mae Nam Rayong onto a long spit of land. After crossing the bridge you can catch a motorcycle taxi (10B) that will take you to the restaurants.

Ban Phe There are several hotels in Ban Phe near the central market and within walking distance of the pier.

Queen *(☎ 0 3865 1018; rooms with/without bath 150/100B, with air-con 250B)* is up the lane from the pier, near the central market, and has a variety of rooms; the painted ladies on hand testify to its mainly short-time clientele, although it's basically an OK place. **Hotel Diamond Phe** *(☎ 0 3865 1826, fax 0 3865 1757; rooms with fan/air-con 300/500B)* is a six-storey place, also close to the pier. It has fan rooms with private bath and good-value air-con rooms with TV, hot-water shower and fridge.

Thale Thong restaurant, where the tour bus from Bangkok stops, has good Thai seafood dishes – especially recommended is the *kǔaytǐaw thá-leh* (seafood noodle soup). The shop across the street is a good place to stock up on food, mosquito coils and the like to take to Ko Samet. You'll most likely spend some time in this spot waiting for the boat to leave the nearby pier for Ko Samet or for the bus to arrive from Bangkok.

Getting There & Away

See Getting There & Away under Ko Samet later in this chapter for details on transport to and from Rayong.

Nearby Islands

Ko Man Klang and Ko Man Nok, along with Ko Man Nai to their immediate west, are part of Laem Ya-Ko Samet National Park. This official designation has not kept away all development, only moderated it. Ko Man Nai is home to the **Sea Turtle Preservation Sanctuary** *(☎ 0 3861 6096; open daily 9am-4pm)*. The island has been set aside as a breeding place for endangered sea turtles and has a small visitors centre that describes their life cycle. It is most easily visited on a tour arranged by one of the following places to stay.

Places to Stay Ko Man Klang and Ko Man Nok offer accommodation packages that include boat transport from the nearest pier along with four meals a day. These can be arranged only by phone in advance through Bangkok reservation numbers. **Ko Nok Island Resort** *(in Bangkok ☎ 0 2860 3025–6, fax 0 2860 3028; room package per person 2590B)* on Ko Man Nok, has a one-night, two-day package. The island is 15km off Pak Nam Prasae (53km east of Ban Phe).

Eight kilometres off Laem Mae Phim (27km east of Ban Phe) on Ko Man Klang, the **Raya Island Resort** *(in Bangkok ☎ 0 2316 6717; bungalows 1200B)* offers 15 bungalows (a one night and two days' stay costs 1400B per person), boat transport and four meals included. Tiny Ko Saket, a 15-minute boat ride from Hat Sai Thong, used to have accommodation, but it has been razed as the island is now being adapted for industrial purposes.

Getting There & Away Public transport to the pier departure points for the two small islands off Rayong can be arranged in Ban Phe. On weekends and holidays there may be share taxis (or sǎwngthǎew) out to the piers; otherwise you'll have to charter a vehicle from the market for 60B to 100B one way – be sure to make a pick-up appointment for your return.

KO SAMET

เกาะเสม็ด

This T-shaped island earned a permanent place in Thai literature when classical Thai poet Sunthorn Phu set part of his epic *Phra Aphaimani* on its shores. The story follows the travails of a prince exiled to an undersea kingdom ruled by a lovesick female giant. A mermaid aids the prince in his escape to Ko Samet, where he defeats the giant by playing a magic flute. Formerly Ko Kaew Phitsadan or 'Vast Jewel Isle' – a reference to the abundant white sand – this island became known as Ko Samet or 'Cajeput Isle' after the cajeput tree that grows in abundance here and is very highly valued as firewood throughout Southeast Asia. Locally, the *samet* tree has also been used in boat building.

In the early 1980s, the 13.1-sq-km Ko Samet began receiving its first visitors interested in more than cajeput trees and sand – young Thais in search of a retreat from city life. At that time there were only about 40 houses on the island, built by fisherfolk and Ban Phe locals. Rayong and Bangkok speculators saw the sudden interest in Ko Samet as a chance to cash in on an up-and-coming Phuket and began buying up land along the beaches. No-one bothered with the fact that Ko Samet, along with Laem Ya and other nearby islands, had been a national marine park since 1981.

When *faràng* started coming to Ko Samet in greater and greater numbers, the National Parks Division stepped in and built a visitors office on the island, ordered that all bungalows be moved back behind the tree line and started charging a 5B admission into the park.

This entry fee has since risen to 200B for foreigners (100B for children 14 and under), with separate park units at each beach in charge of fees collection. There are now more frequent boat services from Ban Phe and a much improved water situation. Ko Samet is a very dry island (which makes it an excellent place to visit during the rainy season). Before they started trucking water to the bungalows you had to bathe at often-muddy wells. Now most of the bungalows have proper Thai-style bathrooms and Ko Samet is a much more comfortable place to visit, although some would say that it has become overcrowded and expensive. This of course is due to its proximity to Bangkok. Accommodation on Ko Samui and Ko Pha-Ngan is better value overall, although of course these islands are much more expensive and time-consuming to reach from Bangkok.

In spite of the fact that the island is supposedly under the protection of the National Parks Division, Ko Samet – like Ko Phi Phi in Krabi and Ko Chang in Trat – has been developed. As often happens, as long as

KO SAMET

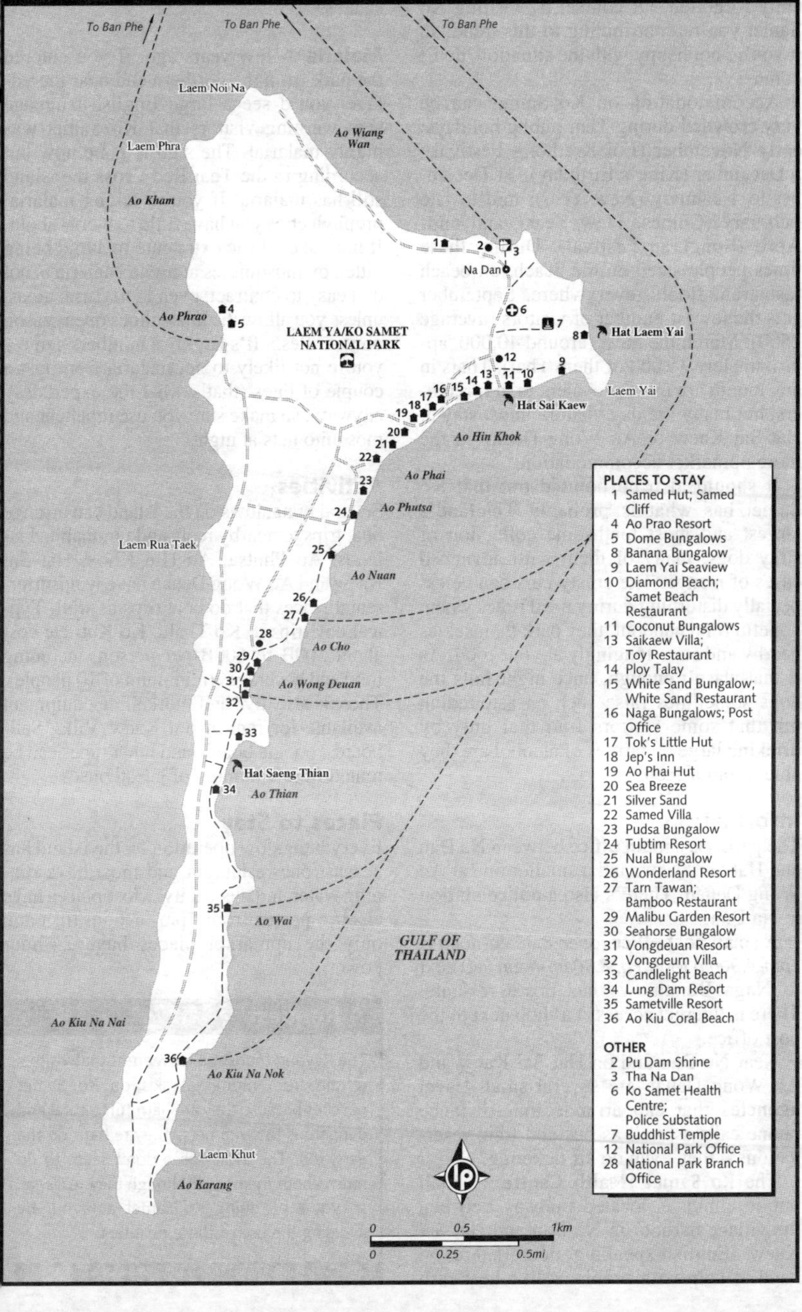
To Ban Phe
To Ban Phe
To Ban Phe
Laem Noi Na
Ao Wiang Wan
Laem Phra
Ao Kham
Na Dan
Ao Phrao
LAEM YA/KO SAMET NATIONAL PARK
Hat Laem Yai
Laem Yai
Hat Sai Kaew
Ao Hin Khok
Ao Phai
Ao Phutsa
Laem Rua Taek
Ao Nuan
Ao Cho
Ao Wong Deuan
Hat Saeng Thian
Ao Thian
Ao Wai
GULF OF THAILAND
Ao Kiu Na Nai
Ao Kiu Na Nok
Laem Khut
Ao Karang
PLACES TO STAY
1 Samed Hut; Samed Cliff
4 Ao Prao Resort
5 Dome Bungalows
8 Banana Bungalow
9 Laem Yai Seaview
10 Diamond Beach; Samet Beach Restaurant
11 Coconut Bungalows
13 Saikaew Villa; Toy Restaurant
14 Ploy Talay
15 White Sand Bungalow; White Sand Restaurant
16 Naga Bungalows; Post Office
17 Tok's Little Hut
18 Jep's Inn
19 Ao Phai Hut
20 Sea Breeze
21 Silver Sand
22 Samed Villa
23 Pudsa Bungalow
24 Tubtim Resort
25 Nual Bungalow
26 Wonderland Resort
27 Tarn Tawan; Bamboo Restaurant
29 Malibu Garden Resort
30 Seahorse Bungalow
31 Vongdeuan Resort
32 Vongdeurn Villa
33 Candlelight Beach
34 Lung Dam Resort
35 Sametville Resort
36 Ao Kiu Coral Beach
OTHER
2 Pu Dam Shrine
3 Tha Na Dan
6 Ko Samet Health Centre; Police Substation
7 Buddhist Temple
12 National Park Office
28 National Park Branch Office
0 0.5 1km
0 0.25 0.5mi

there is money to be made, laws are conveniently forgotten. Of course, by visiting Ko Samet you're contributing to this trend, so if you're not happy with the situation, don't come.

Accommodation on Ko Samet can be very crowded during Thai public holidays: early November (Loi Krathong Festival); 5 December (King's Birthday); 31 December to 1 January (New Year); mid to late February (Chinese New Year); and mid-April (Songkran Festival). During these times people sleep on the beach, on beach restaurant floors, everywhere. September gets the lowest number of visitors (average 2500); March the most (around 40,000, approximately 36,000 of them Thai). Thais in any month are more prevalent than foreigners, but many are day visitors; most stay at Hat Sai Kaew or Ao Wong Deuan in the more upmarket accommodation.

It should also be pointed out that Ko Samet has what is probably Thailand's largest and most loathsome collection of stray dogs, many of them with advanced cases of mange. The crusty curs can be especially disturbing during meal times when, hopeful for a handout, they park themselves nearby and stare longingly at your food. As if that wasn't enough, once night falls the dogs sometimes raise such an astounding din that some visitors find that only by drinking large quantities of alcohol are they able to fall asleep.

Information

The park has a **main office** between Na Dan and Hat Sai Kaew, and a smaller one at Ao Wong Deuan. There's also a **police station** in Na Dan.

A small **post office** *(open 8.30am-noon & 1pm-4.30pm Mon-Fri, 8.30am-noon Sat)* next to Naga Bungalows has poste restante. There is Internet access at a shop next to the post office.

Near Na Dan and on Hat Sai Kaew and Ao Wong Deuan are several small **travel agencies** that can arrange long-distance phone calls as well as bus and train reservations – they even do air ticketing.

The **Ko Samet Health Centre**, a small public clinic, is located midway between the village harbour in Na Dan and Hat Sai Kaew. English-speaking doctors are on hand to help with problems like heat rash or bites from poisonous sea creatures or snakes.

Malaria A few years ago, if you entered the park from the northern end near the village, you'd see a large English-language sign warning visitors that Ko Samet was highly malarial. The sign is gone now but according to the Thai Red Cross the island still has malaria. If you're taking malarial prophylactics you have little to worry about. If not, take a little extra care to avoid being bitten by mosquitoes at night. Malaria is not that easy to contract, even in malarial areas, unless you allow the mosquitoes open season on your flesh. It's largely a numbers game – you're not likely to get malaria from just a couple of bites (that's what the experts say anyway), so make sure you use repellent and mosquito nets at night.

Activities

Several bungalows on the island can arrange boat trips to nearby reefs and uninhabited islands. Ao Phutsa, Ao Hin Khok, Hat Sai Kaew and Ao Wong Deuan have windsurfer-rental places that do boat trips as well. Typical day trips to Ko Thalu, Ko Kuti etc cost about 500B to 600B per person, including food and beverages (minimum of 10 people). There is also dive and snorkelling equipment available for rent at Sai Kaew Villa. Sailboards, boogie boards and inner tubes can be rented from a number of guesthouses.

Places to Stay

Every bungalow operation on the island has at least one restaurant and most have running water and electricity. Most places have electric power from 5pm or 6pm till 6am; only the upmarket places have 24-hour power.

A Request

The Rayong tourist police request that visitors refrain from hiring jet skis on Ko Samet beaches because they are harmful to coral and dangerous to swimmers. They're hard on the ears, too. The local police don't seem to do much about them, even though they're illegal, so you'll be doing Ko Samet a favour by avoiding the use of these polluters.

Ko Samet seems to be gaining in popularity each year, and rising prices reflect this trend. Even places with the most basic accommodation facilities are asking 200B, with 300B to 400B being the norm during the high season. Bungalows with furniture and air-con start at 600B. Some places offer discounts for stays of four or more days, while on weekends and public holidays most will raise their rates to meet the demand – sometimes dramatically.

Some resorts, mostly around the Hat Sai Kaew area, have also been known to boot out foreigners without warning to make room for free-spending Thai groups during long weekends and holidays. For this same reason, almost no resort will take reservations over the phone. Unless you're there in person to hand over a cash deposit (typically two nights in advance), you can forget about any of these places actually honouring (or even making) reservations. It's strictly first come, first serve on Ko Samet.

Since this is a national park, camping is allowed, although there is only one designated camping area, near the visitors centre. Try to pitch a tent anywhere else and you'll likely be told it's not allowed. Don't even think of pitching a tent on a beach near one of the bungalow operations.

East Coast The two most developed (overdeveloped) beaches are Hat Sai Kaew and Ao Wong Deuan. All of the other spots are still rather peaceful.

Hat Sai Kaew Ko Samet's prettiest beach, 'Diamond Sand', is a kilometre or so long and 25m to 30m wide. The bungalows here happen to be the most commercial on the island, with video in the restaurants at night and lots of electric lights. They're all very similar and offer accommodation, from 400B (in the low season) for simple bungalows without bath, to 600B for one with fan and private bath, and as high as 2500B with air-con. Many reckon that even if you're not staying here, this is the place to head to once the sun goes down. In the evenings some of the bungalow operations move their bar/restaurants onto the beach, where you can sit on mats among rows of low tables adorned with twinkling oil lamps.

Coconut Bungalows *(bungalows with fan 500B, with air-con up to 1500B)* offers 30 bungalows with fan or with air-con, TV and fridge. Each bungalow has a small veranda and chairs.

Ploy Talay *(rooms with bath 500-1500B)* is another option. The pricier bungalows are newish and more comfortable than the cheaper ones.

White Sand Bungalow *(☎ 0 3864 4000–5; rooms with fan 500B, with air-con 1000B)* Concrete bungalows with fan and bath and not much else. Air-con bungalows are much more comfortable and come with TV and fridge. Electricity is on between 5pm and 9am. The restaurant here is long-running and good.

Laem Yai Seaview *(☎ 0 3865 1956; rooms with fan & bath 800B, with air-con 1200B)* has wooden bungalows with fan or air-con and attached bath but not much else in the way of amenities. Electricity is on from 6pm to 6am.

Saikaew Villa *(☎/fax 0 3865 1852; rooms with fan 700-1300B, with air-con & TV from 1650B)* is a huge complex off the beach. It's the top-end place near the prettiest part of the beach. Breakfast is included and the establishment boasts 24-hour power – try to get a room away from the noisy generators. Discounts for long-term stays are available. This is one of a couple of places on the island where you can use the Internet, but it's not cheap.

Ao Hin Khok The beach here is about half the size of Sai Kaew but just as pretty – the rocks that give the beach its name add a certain character. Ao Hin Khok is separated from Hat Sai Kaew by a rocky point surmounted by a mermaid statue. Ao Hin Khok and Ao Phai, the next inlet south, offer the advantage of having among the least expensive huts on the island along with reasonably priced restaurants serving good food.

Two of Samet's original bungalow operations still reign here – **Naga Bungalows** *(bungalows 300-700B)* and **Tok's Little Hut** *(bungalows from 300B)*. Naga offers basic but passable bungalows set on a hill overlooking the sea. It's one of the most popular places on the island due to its reasonably cheap bungalows and its restaurant, neither of which are anything special but the prices are right. There is also Internet access, a bar and a pool table. Bungalows at Tok's Little Hut have small verandas, as well as fan and bath, and vary in price depending on size and proximity to the generator.

Jep's Inn *(bungalows 450-600B)*, further down the road from Tok's, has nicely designed, clean bungalows with bath and fan. The restaurant here is also quite good, and there's a nice shaded dining area right at the edge of the beach.

Ao Phai Around the next headland is another shallow bay with a nice wide beach, although it can get fairly crowded.

Ao Phai Hut *(single/double bungalows with fan 500/600B, rooms with air-con 800-2000B)* at the northern end is friendly and has screened bungalows with bath and fan, and air-con bungalows (rates vary depending on size). Add 200B on weekends and holidays. Electricity is available from 5pm to 6am. The staff organise tours around the island and have an international telephone service, as well as basic postal services.

Sea Breeze *(bungalows with fan 500B, with air-con 600-1200B)* is the next place along with rather closely spaced bungalows, all with bath. Adjacent is a small shop and a bookshop that also has international phone and fax services. This place is often full and the staff seem quite put out by having to deal with guests.

Silver Sand *(bungalows with fan 400-500B, with air-con 700-800B)* has fan or air-con bungalows; all have attached bath and 24-hour electricity. This place can be noisy due to the close proximity of each of the bungalows.

Samed Villa *(bungalows from 600B, family bungalows up to 1200B)* has clean, screened, well-maintained tree-shaded bungalows with large verandas. Smaller units have private bath and larger bungalows are suitable for family accommodation. It has 24-hour electricity and quite good food, and some of the bungalows have great sea views.

Ao Phutsa Ao Phutsa, also known as Ao Thap Thim, has **Pudsa Bungalow** *(bungalows with fan & bath 400-600B)*. The better bungalows are close to the water, but have a look inside before agreeing to stay there as some are grungier than others.

Tubtim Resort *(bungalows with fan 500B, with air-con up to 1200B)*, at the southern end of the beach, has bungalows on a hillside. All bungalows have attached bath and are well kept. The restaurant is good and the whole operation is well run.

Ao Nuan If you blink, you'll miss this beach, which is one of the more secluded places to stay without having to go to the far south of the island.

Nual Bungalow *(Nuan; bungalows 250-400B)* offers bungalows with shared bath and intermittent electricity. Some are little more than bamboo huts. The food is quite good here and the eating area is set in an imaginatively arranged garden. It's a five-minute walk over the headland from Ao Phutsa.

Ao Cho A five-minute walk across the next headland from Ao Nuan, Ao Cho (Chaw) has its own pier and can be reached directly from Ban Phe. Although just north of crowded Ao Wong Deuan, it's fairly quiet here, although the beach is not among Samet's best.

Wonderland Resort *(bungalows 300-800B)* is at the northern end of the beach and has basic, rather scruffy huts and slightly better bungalows with shower and toilet (rates are higher on weekends and holidays). Not the best value for the price.

Tarn Tawan *(bungalows 600-800B)* has bungalows with fan and bath that could use a good scrub. The restaurant is little better, though it was full when we came through so perhaps the good food outweighs the cleanliness issue.

Ao Wong Deuan This once-gorgeous bay is now filled with speedboats and jet skis, and there's a lot of accommodation packed into a small area, making things a bit cramped. The crescent-shaped beach is still nice, but it is noisy and often crowded. **Vongdeuan Resort** *(☎ 0 3865 1777, fax 0 3865 1819; bungalows with fan 800B, with air-con 1100-1200B)* is the best of the lot. Bungalows come complete with running water and flush toilet, and electricity is on 24 hours.

Vongduern Villa *(bungalows 850-2500B)* is similar in amenities but all rooms have air-con.

Malibu Garden Resort *(bungalows with fan 800-1200B, with air-con 1500-2500B)* has well-built brick or wooden bungalows; the more-expensive rooms have TV. Breakfast is included and if you tire of the scene at the beach this place even has a swimming pool.

Seahorse Bungalow *(rooms & bungalows with fan 600B, with air-con 800-1000B)* has practically taken over the beachfront with two restaurants, a travel agency and bungalows with bath.

Three boats go back and forth between Ao Wong Deuan and Ban Phe – the *Malibu*, *Seahorse* and *Vongduern*.

Ao Thian From this point south things start to get much quieter. Better known by its English name Candlelight Beach, Ao Thian is quite scenic, with stretches of sand and rocky outcrops.

Candlelight Beach *(bungalows 500-900B)* is on the bay's northern end and has fan and bath bungalows that vary in price, depending on proximity to the beach. This long-runner has steadily gone up in price over the years, while the bungalows have hardly changed. However, the location is both scenic and tranquil.

Lung Dam Resort *(bungalows 500-600B)* formerly Lung Dam Hut, is at the southern end of the bay and has rustic bungalows with veranda and attached bath. During the high season the restaurant sets up on the beach for drinks under the stars. This place is a long-running favourite with repeat visitors to the island.

Other Bays You really have to be determined to get away from it all to go further south on the east coast of Ko Samet, but it can be well worth the effort. Lovely Ao Wai is about 1km from Ao Thian, but can be reached from Ban Phe by scheduled boat or by speedboat. Most seem to come by the latter.

Sametville Resort *(☎ 0 3865 1682; bungalows with fan 800-900B, with air-con 1500B)* is the only bungalow operation here. It's very private and offers a fine combination of upmarket accommodation and isolation. Two-bed bungalows have baths and either fan or air-con. Most bookings are done by phone, but you can try your luck by contacting someone at the Ban Phe piers.

A 20-minute walk over the rocky shore from Ao Wai, Ao Kiu Na Nok also had only one place to stay at the time of writing.

Ao Kiu Coral Beach *(☎ 0 3865 2561; tents 300B, huts 300-400B, bungalows 400-800B)* is friendly and clean. There are only two bamboo huts remaining, but there are better-equipped cement huts and tents that can be rented. The beach here is gorgeous, one of the nicest on the island. Another plus is that it's a mere five-minute walk to the western side of the island and a view of the sunset.

One boat a day is scheduled to come to this beach, but in reality most do it by speedboat and the 'scheduled' boat doesn't always make the trip.

West Coast Hat Ao Phrao is the only beach on the western side of the island, and it has nice sunset views. The name means Coconut Bay Beach, but for marketing reasons bungalow operators tend to use the cliched 'Paradise Beach' moniker. So far there are no jet skis on this side of the island, so it tends to be quieter than the island's east coast. Bungalow operators also do a good job of keeping the beach clean.

Ao Prao Resort *(☎ 0 3864 4101–9; rooms 3212B, bungalows 3033-10450B)*, at the northern end of the beach, has hotel-style rooms as well as air-con bungalows with large verandas surrounded by lush landscaping. Amenities include cable TV and hot water, attached bath and perhaps the best restaurant on the island. Ao Prao Divers at the resort offers diving, windsurfing, kayaking and boat trips.

Dome Bungalows *(☎ 0 3865 1377, fax 0 3865 2600; bungalows with fan 900B, with air-con 1200-1500B)*, in the middle of the beach, has nice fan and bath bungalows on the hillside. Breakfast is included in the rates. A pleasant restaurant on the premises features Thai and international dishes.

There is a daily boat between Ban Phe and Ao Phrao for 80B per person.

Na Dan & Around To the northwest of Ko Samet's main pier (Tha Na Dan) is a long beach called Ao Wiang Wan, where several rather characterless bungalows are set up in straight lines facing the mainland. Here you get neither sunrise nor sunset.

Samed Cliff *(singles/doubles with fan 800-900B, with air-con 1000-1500B)* is the best place and is shady and well laid-out. There's a small swimming pool and restaurant. All rooms have attached bath. **Samet Hut** *(bungalows with fan 700-900B, with air-con 1200B)* is located next to it and is quite similar.

It acts as a spillover for the popular Samed Cliff.

Between Na Dan and Hat Sai Kaew, along the northeastern corner of the island, are a couple of small beach bays with bungalow operations. Hardly anyone seems to stay here unless everything else is occupied.

Banana Bungalow *(☎ 0 3861 2231; bungalows 300-500B)* is a collection of small concrete or brick bungalows that are rather small and dank.

Places to Eat

All bungalows have restaurants offering mixed menus of Thai and traveller food; prices are typically 40B to 60B per dish. Fresh seafood is almost always available and costs around 60B to 150B per dish. Take a walk along the beaches of Ao Hin Khok and Ao Phai paying attention to the signs at different bungalows offering seafood barbecues, usually between 7pm and 9pm. These can be a good deal if you bring a big appetite. The pleasant **Bamboo Restaurant** *(dishes 30-60B)* at Ao Cho, behind Tarn Tawan, offers inexpensive but tasty food and good service. It's open for breakfast, lunch and dinner. **Naga Bungalows** *(dishes 30-60B)* on Ao Hin Khok has a very good bakery with all kinds of breads and cakes. Ao Wong Deuan has a cluster of restaurants and bars serving Western and Thai food that seem to change every season. At the southern tip of the beach the **Vongduern Villa** *(dishes 50-100B)* restaurant is a bit more expensive, but both the food and the location are quite nice.

On Hat Sai Kaew, the **White Sand Restaurant** has good seafood in the 100B range. For cheaper fare on this beach, try the popular **Toy Restaurant**, next to Saikaew Villa. **Samet Beach Restaurant**, next to Diamond Beach, has also been recommended for good food with reasonable prices and friendly staff.

Probably the most atmospheric eatery on the island is the fancy open-air terrace restaurant at **Ao Prao Resort** *(dishes 100-180B)* though the food is really just average.

Getting There & Away

Bus Many Th Khao San agencies in Bangkok provide transport to Ko Samet for 250B. This is more expensive than doing it on your own, and the minivans are usually packed to the gills and decidedly weak on air-con. One reader wrote in to complain that the driver of one of these vans chain-smoked the whole way down and refused to let anyone roll down the windows. On the other hand, it will save you a trip to the Eastern bus terminal.

For those who want the flexibility and economy of arranging their own travel, the way to go is to take an air-con bus from Bangkok's Eastern bus terminal to Rayong (120B) and then a săwngthăew to Ban Phe (15B). There are also non-air-con buses going direct to Ban Phe, but they take almost four hours, versus 2½ hours on the air-con bus. Both buses from Bangkok and săwngthăews from Rayong stop in Ban Phe in front of Saphan Nuan Tip.

Ordinary buses go to Chanthaburi from Rayong (55B, 2½ hours). To get one of these, you need to catch a motorcycle taxi (15B) to the bus stop on Th Sukhumvit (Hwy 3).

Minibuses to Bangkok's Th Khao San and Pattaya can be arranged through several of the guesthouses on Ko Samet or through travel agencies in Ban Phe near the 7-Eleven opposite the Saphan Nuan Thip pier. Minibuses to Bangkok leave twice daily (250B). Minibuses to Pattaya leave five times daily (150B).

Boat There are various ways to get to and from the island by boat.

To Ko Samet Saphan Nuan Tip (just opposite the 7-Eleven) is the pier that you'll get dropped off at if you take a bus or minivan from Bangkok. Another pier just to the west called Saphan Si Ban Phe, also services Ko Samet. Other piers are private or used by supply boats only. Ticket booths near both piers sell tickets for regularly scheduled passenger boats, and can also arrange passage by speedboat. What you choose depends on how much you want to spend and where you want to go. Regularly scheduled boats are slower, and passengers have to pay the 200B national park entrance fee upon arrival at Ko Samet. Ticket vendors may try to talk you into staying at one of their recommended 'resorts' on the island, saying that you can get a discount on the park entrance fee (or skip paying the fee altogether). In our experience, if you don't have a place to stay in mind, it's better to pay the full fee and take your chances looking around. If you already have a place of accommodation in mind and a large enough group (eight to 12 people), it can actually be cheaper to hire a speedboat (800B to 1200B, depending on which beach you go to and what time of day or night you hire it). Doing this usually saves you having to pay the 200B entrance fee.

Passenger boats to Ko Samet leave at regular intervals throughout the day starting around 8am and ending around 5pm. How frequently the boats depart depends on whether they have enough passengers or cargo to make the trip profitable. Obviously there will be more frequent trips in the high season (December to March). Still, there are always at least three or four boats a day going to Na Dan and Ao Wong Deuan.

Some travellers have reported being hassled by 'agents' who show them photo albums of bungalows on Ko Samet, claiming that they must book a bungalow for several days in order to get onto the island. This is false; ignore these touts and head straight for the boats. Report any problems with the touts to the TAT office in Rayong.

For Hat Sai Kaew, Ao Hin Khok, Ao Phai and Ao Phutsa, catch a boat to Na Dan; the fare is 40B. These generally leave as soon as there are at least 20 passengers. Ignore touts or ticket agents who claim the fare is 100B or more; simply buy a ticket from Saphan Nuan Tip ticket office, or you can even board the boat and buy the ticket there. From Na Dan you can either walk to these beaches (10 to 15 minutes) or take one of the trucks that go round the island.

The Saphan Nuan Tip ticket office also has boats to Ao Wong Deuan (50B one way), Ao Phrao (80B) and Ao Wai (80B).

The Saphan Sri Ban Phe ticket office sells tickets for Na Dan (40B) as well as Ao Wong Deuan (50B), Ao Wai (80B), Ao Kiu Na Nok (100B), Ao Phrao (80B), Ao Nuan and Ao Thian (50B). Again, go directly to the ticket office and ignore what touts tell you.

From Ko Samet Boats are scheduled to leave from Na Dan four times daily between 7am and 4pm, though it really depends on how many passengers show up. If there aren't enough passengers to make the run profitable, sit back and hope more passengers show up. The fare is 40B. Or you can hire a speedboat for 800B to 900B.

These days it is so easy to get boats back from the main beaches to Ban Phe that few tourists go to Na Dan to get a boat. There are four daily boats each from Ao Wong Deuan plus at least one daily boat from Ao Cho, Ao Wai, Ao Kiu Na Nok and Ao Phrao.

While waiting for a boat back to the mainland from Na Dan, you may notice a shrine not far from the pier. This *săan jâo phâw* is a spirit shrine to Pu Dam (Grandfather Black), a sage who once lived on the island. Worshippers offer statues of *reusĭi* (hermit sages), flowers, incense and fruit.

Getting Around

If you take the boat from Ban Phe to Na Dan, you can easily walk the distance to Hat Sai Kaew, Ao Phai or Ao Phutsa. A checkpoint and visitors centre here collects the 200B entrance fee. If you're going further down the island, or have a lot of luggage, you can take a săwngthăew, but the number of visitors using speedboats to go directly to the beach of their choice has meant that săwngthăews have become scarce and expensive.

Set fares for transport around the island from Na Dan are posted on a tree in the middle of a square in front of the Na Dan harbour, but nobody pays them any mind. If drivers don't have enough people to fill the vehicle, they either won't go, or passengers will have to pay up to 200B to 500B to charter the vehicle.

There are trails from Ao Wong Deuan all the way to the southern tip of the island, and a few cross-island trails as well. Near Sea Breeze bungalows in Ao Phai, the main road south to Ao Wong Deuan turns inland and heads down the middle of the island. A little further along the road from here is where the cross-island road to Ao Phrao on the west coast starts.

After Ao Phutsa, the remaining beaches south are separated from one another by fairly steep headlands. To get from one to the next, you have a choice of negotiating rocky paths over the hilly points or walking west to the main road that goes along the centre of the island, then cutting back on side roads to each beach.

Motorcycles can be rented from a number of bungalow operations on Hat Sai

Kaew, Ao Phai and Ao Phrao. Figure on about 500B per day or an hourly rate of 150B.

Chanthaburi Province

CHANTHABURI

อ.เมืองจันทบุรี

postcode 22000 • pop 89,000

Situated 330km from Bangkok, the 'City of the Moon' is a busy gem trading centre, particularly noted for sapphires and rubies from all over Southeast Asia and further afield. Chanthaburi (Chan'buri) is also renowned for tropical fruit (rambutan, durian, langsat and mangosteen) and rice noodles – Chanthaburi noodles are in fact exported all over the world.

A significant proportion of the local population comprises Vietnamese Christians who fled religious or political persecution in Vietnam years ago. The first wave arrived in the 19th century as refugees avoiding anti-Catholic persecution in Cochin China (southern Vietnam); the second came between the 1920s and 1940s, fleeing French rule; and the third wave arrived after the 1975 communist takeover of southern Vietnam. From 1893 to 1905, while negotiating with the Siamese over the borders for Laos and Cambodia, the French occupied the town.

Chanthaburi's most recent claim to fame arose in 1993 when 1500 tonnes of war material were found cached in 12 warehouses throughout the province. The arms were thought to have been destined for the Khmer Rouge communist rebels, who held parts of western Cambodia at the time. The allegations were never proven, but it is almost certain the arms were in the control of certain factions in the Thai military.

Things to See & Do

Vietnamese-French influence has resulted in Chanthaburi having some interesting shophouse architecture – particularly along the river. The French-style **cathedral** here is the largest in Thailand. A small missionary chapel was built on this site in 1711, but

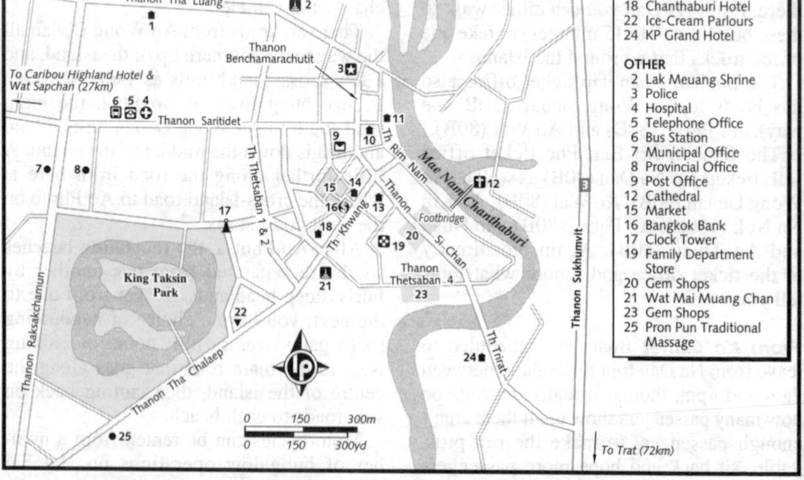

after undergoing four reconstructions between 1712 and 1906 (the last carried out by the French) the structure has changed into its current form.

The **gem dealers** in town are found mostly along Th Si Chan and along Trok Kachang and Th Thetsaban 4, off Th Si Chan in the southeast quarter. All day long buyers and sellers haggle over little piles of blue and red stones. During the first week of June every year there is a gem festival and Chanthaburi can get very crowded. Most of the gems bought and sold here come from places other than Chanthaburi – chiefly Cambodia, Vietnam, Myanmar and Australia. The sapphires and rubies can be very good buys if (and only if) you know what you're buying.

King Taksin Park is a large public park with gazebos and an artificial lake near the centre of town – nice for an evening stroll. A few kilometres north of town off Rte 3249 is **Khao Phloi Waen** (Sapphire-Ring Mountain), which is only 150m high but features a Sri Lankan-style *chedi* on top, built during the reign of Rama IV. Tunnels dug into the side of the hill were once gem-mining shafts.

Wat Khao Sukim, a fairly well-known meditation centre, is 16km north of Chanthaburi off Rte 3322. A **museum** on the *wát* (temple) grounds contains all manner of valuables donated to the temple, such as jade carvings, ceramics and antique furniture, as well as resin figures of some of Thailand's most-revered monks. Another meditation centre is at **Wat Sapchan**, 27km west of Chanthaburi in Tha Mai district; Wat Sapchan is a branch of Sunyataram Forest Monastery in Kanchanaburi.

Chanthaburi seems to have more than its fair share of massage parlours, most of which are found along Thanon Tha Chalaep. **Porn Pun Traditional Massage** *(☎ 0 3933 2286; 779-781 Thanon Tha Chalaep)* is said to do legitimate massage. There are plenty of others on this street but we can't vouch for them.

Places to Stay

Kasemsan I Hotel *(☎ 0 3931 2340; 98/1 Th Benchamarachutit; rooms with fan/air-con 280/350B)* is a three-storey place with large, clean rooms with private shower and toilet. As usual, rooms off the street are quieter than those on it, but it's the best deal in town and very convenient to the city centre.

Chantra Hotel *(☎ 0 3931 2310; Th Rim Nam; rooms 100-300B)*, down by the river at a nice spot on Th Rim Nam, is smaller than Kasemsan; the more expensive rooms have a river view. It's the cheapest place in town and rooms with windows on the river catch a breeze, but have a look at the room before you lay down your cash.

Chai Lee Hotel *(no Roman-script sign; ☎ 0 3931 3767; Th Khwang; singles/doubles with fan 200/230B, with air-con 330B)* has large, clean rooms, all with TV.

Chanthaburi Hotel *(☎ 0 3932 8077; Th Tha Chalaep; rooms with fan 170B, with air-con 300B)* is in the same area as Chai Lee and has rooms with bath. It's sort of a short-time place and can be noisy on weekends.

Muang Chan Hotel *(☎ 0 3932 1073; Th Si Chan; singles/doubles with fan 230/280B, with air-con 350/400B)* has a sign on the door that reads 'hotel', and is a friendly place with adequate rooms with bath and TV.

Kiatkachorn Hotel *(☎ 0 3931 1212; Th Tha Luang; rooms with fan/air-con 220/300B)* is out at the northern end of town, away from everything. All rooms have TV, phone and private baths. One 'VIP' room has fridge and hot water (350B).

KP Grand Hotel *(☎ 0 3932 3201–13, fax 0 3932 3214; 35/200-201 Th Trirat; rooms 900-3500B)* is where business travellers – at least those who are into buying gems – tend to stay. It's an 18-storey hotel where rooms come with amenities. Breakfast is included in the price of the room.

Caribou Highland Hotel *(☎ 0 3932 3431; Th Chawan Uthit; rooms 1000B, suites from 2200B)*, west of the town centre, is a six-storey hotel that offers the best accommodation in town – large air-con rooms with TV, IDD phone and fridge (often discounted to 700B including breakfast). One- and two-bedroom suites are also available (discounted to 1600B).

Places to Eat

For those famous Chanthaburi noodles, *kŭaytĭaw sên jan*, head for the Chinese-Vietnamese part of town along Mae Nam Chanthaburi and you'll see variations on the basic rice noodle theme, including delicious crab with fried noodles. **Chanthon Phochana**, next to the Kasemsan I Hotel is a popular

SOUTHEASTERN THAILAND

place with a good variety of Thai and Chinese dishes.

Sunflower *(Th Chawan Uthit; dishes 40-120B)*, located on the top floor of the Caribou Highland Hotel, is a clean, medium-priced restaurant and coffee shop serving Thai food and Western breakfasts.

Family department store *(Soi Sri Sakhon 1)*, off Th Si Chan, has a huge 2nd-floor food centre.

There are also a number of good **rice and noodle shops** just west of the department store. On the southeastern corner of King Taksin Park are a couple of outdoor **ice-cream parlours** that also serve a few standard Thai dishes.

Getting There & Away

From Bangkok, air-con buses cost 145B, regular buses 100B; from Rayong it's 50B. Ordinary buses go to Trat (30B, 1½ hours), as do share taxis (60B).

If you have your own set of wheels, take Rte 317 north to Sa Kaew, then Hwy 33 west to Kabinburi and Rte 304 north to Khorat. From Sa Kaew you can also head east and reach Aranya Prathet on the Thailand–Cambodia border after just 46km. Now that this border crossing is open you can take a share taxi from Poipet on the Cambodian side of the border to Siem Reap (near Angkor Wat).

AROUND CHANTHABURI

Two small national parks are within an hour's drive of Chanthaburi. Both are malarial, so take the usual precautions.

Khao Khitchakut National Park *(admission 200B)* is about 28km northeast of town off Rte 3249 and is known for Nam Tok Krathing. It's one of Thailand's smallest national parks (59 sq km) although the unprotected forest surrounding the park is much larger and is said to harbour herds of wild elephants. There's a series of trails to the falls nearest the park headquarters, but visitors are discouraged from going deeper into the forest without being accompanied by a ranger as a guide.

Just across the road from the **park headquarters** *(☎ 0 3943 1983)* there are **bungalows** *(per 7/12 people 600/1200B)* and **camping** *(10B, tents 50B)*. A very basic **restaurant** sells various snacks and a few rice dishes.

To get to Khao Khitchakut by public transport, take a săwngthăew from the northern side of the market (20B, 50 minutes). The săwngthăew stops 1.5km from the park headquarters on Rte 3249, from which point you'll have to walk.

Khao Sabap National Park *(admission 200B)* off Hwy 3 is only about 14km southeast of Chanthaburi and features the **Nam Tok Phliu**. There are three park **bungalows** *(8-10 people 600-800B)* near the **park headquarters** *(in Bangkok ☎ 0 2579 4842)* at Nam Tok Phliu. A simple food service is available.

To get to the park, catch a săwngthăew from the northern side of the market in Chanthaburi to the park entrance (25B, 30 minutes), or get out 2.5km from the park entrance on Th Sukhumvit (10B), from where you will have to walk (this is how you will have to depart if there are no taxis). Entry fees of 200B per person are collected at both parks (see under National Parks, Reserves & Wildlife Sanctuaries in the Facts about Thailand chapter).

Trat Province

About 400km from Bangkok, Trat Province borders Cambodia and, as in Chanthaburi, gem mining and gem trading are important occupations. *Tàlàat phloi* (gem markets) are open intermittently at the **Hua Thung** and **Khlong Yaw** markets in the Bo Rai district, about 40km north of Trat on Rte 3389. A smaller market is sometimes open all day in **Khao Saming** district only 20km northwest of Trat. There has been a drop in activity in the gem markets due to the dwindling supply of local gem stock. A sad by-product of gem mining has been the destruction of vast tracts of land – the topsoil is stripped away, leaving hectares of red-orange mud.

If the gem business doesn't interest you, another attraction is **Nam Tok Salak Tai** (15km northwest of Bo Rai). As Rte 318 goes east and then south from Trat on the way to Khlong Yai district, the province thins to a narrow sliver between the Gulf of Thailand and Cambodia. Along this sliver are a number of little-known beaches, including Hat Sai Si Ngoen, Hat Sai Kaew, Hat Thap Thim and Hat Ban Cheun. The latter two have accommodation.

TRAT PROVINCE

At the 70km marker, off Rte 318, is **Jut Chom Wiw** (Lookout Point), where you can get a panorama of the surrounding area, including Cambodia. Trat Province's southeasternmost point is at **Hat Lek**, which is also a jumping-off point for trips to the Cambodian coast. Although there are Thai military checkpoints between Trat and Hat Lek (two at last count), foreign tourists are no longer turned back. The border crossing is now open to all and, if you have a Cambodian visa, you will be allowed to visit Cambodia's Koh Kong and beyond.

TRAT & AROUND

อ.เมืองตราด

postcode 23000 • pop 20,700

The provincial capital of Trat has little to offer except as a jumping-off point for the Ko Chang island group or forays into outlying Cambodian markets. The locals are friendly, however, and there are certainly worse places to spend a few days. Note: Trat seems to have more markets for its size than almost any other town in Thailand, which is partly due to Cambodian coastal trade.

Information

There is no immigration office in Trat – you must go to the provincial offices in Khlong Yai or Laem Ngop for visa extensions or other immigration matters. Khlong Yai is where you have to go to have your passport stamped upon return from Cambodia.

Bangkok Bank and **Krung Thai Bank** on Th Sukhumvit have foreign-exchange windows open 8.30am to 3.30pm daily.

The **main post office** *(Th Tha Reua Jang; open 8.30am-4.30pm Mon-Fri, 9am-noon Sat & Sun)* is a long walk from the city centre. The **telecommunications office** *(open 7am-10pm daily)* is on the corner a few doors down from the post office and offers international phone and fax services.

Medical Services Rates of malaria infection are significantly higher in rural Trat (including Ko Chang) than for much of the rest of Thailand, so take the usual precautions. There is a malaria centre on the main road through Laem Ngop (20km southwest of Trat); here you can get the latest information on the disease. This office can also assist with the testing and treatment of malaria.

Wat Plai Khlong

วัดปลายคลอง

Wat Plai Khlong (Wat Bupharam), 2km west of the city centre, is over 200 years old and worth a visit if you're looking to kill an hour or so. Several of the wooden buildings date to the late Ayuthaya period, including the *wíhăan*, bell tower and *kùtì* (monk's quarters). The *wíhăan* contains a variety of sacred relics and Buddha images dating from the Ayuthaya period and earlier.

Trat is famous for *náam-man lĕuang* (yellow oil), a herb-infused liquid touted as a remedy for everything from arthritis to stomach upsets. It's produced by a resident, Mae Ang-Ki (Somthawin Pasananon), using a secret pharmaceutical recipe that has been handed down through her Chinese-Thai family for generations. The Thais say that if you leave Trat without a couple of bottles of Mae Ang-Ki's yellow oil, then you really haven't been to Trat. This stuff really works! Put a couple of drops on your palms, rub them together and take a good whiff: it's quite a rush! It's also great for aches and pains, and is available at all the pharmacies in town.

Further afield, **Ban Nam Chiaw** – about 8km from Trat – is a mostly Muslim village where hemispherical straw hats called *ngâwp*, the traditional Khmer rice-farmer's hat, are hand-woven.

Markets

Of Trat's several markets, the largest are the relatively new day market beneath the municipal shopping centre off Th Sukhumvit; the old day market off Th Tat Mai; and the day market next to the air-con bus office. The latter becomes a night market in the evening.

Places to Stay

Residang Guest House *(☎ 0 3953 0103; Th Thana Charoen; singles/doubles 80/120B)* is in a concrete three-storey building. Large rooms have fan and shared bath. Bicycles are rented for 50B per day to guests, 80B for non-guests.

NP Guest House *(☎ 0 3951 2270; 1-3 Soi Luang Aet; singles/doubles 60/100B)*, down a lane that is a southwest continuation of Th Tat Mai, is a short walk from the main day and night markets as well as local bus stops. It's basically an old wooden shophouse with a glassed-in downstairs; rooms have shared bath. Thai and Western food is available.

Friendly Guest House *(☎ 0 3952 4053; 106 Th Lak Meuang; singles/doubles 60/100B)* is aptly named. It feels more like a homestay than what you usually expect from a Thai guesthouse. Rooms are basic but clean, and bathrooms are shared.

Most of the hotels in Trat are along or just off Th Sukhumvit. **Trat Inn** *(☎ 0 3951 1028; 1-5 Th Sukhumvit; rooms 120-200B)* though housed in a run-down concrete shell, has a friendly Thai-speaking staff.

Trat Hotel *(Meuang Trat; ☎ 0 3951 1091; rooms with fan 250B, with air-con 370B)*, off Th Sukhumvit, is slightly more comfortable than Trat Inn, and has standard rooms with fan and some with air-con. This is the only hotel in town with a lift.

Ban Pu Resort *(☎/fax 0 3954 2355; bungalows 1200B)* is a famous seafood restaurant and crab farm standing adjacent to Suan Pu, 11km southeast of town at Ban Laem Hin. Large, well-appointed wooden bungalows

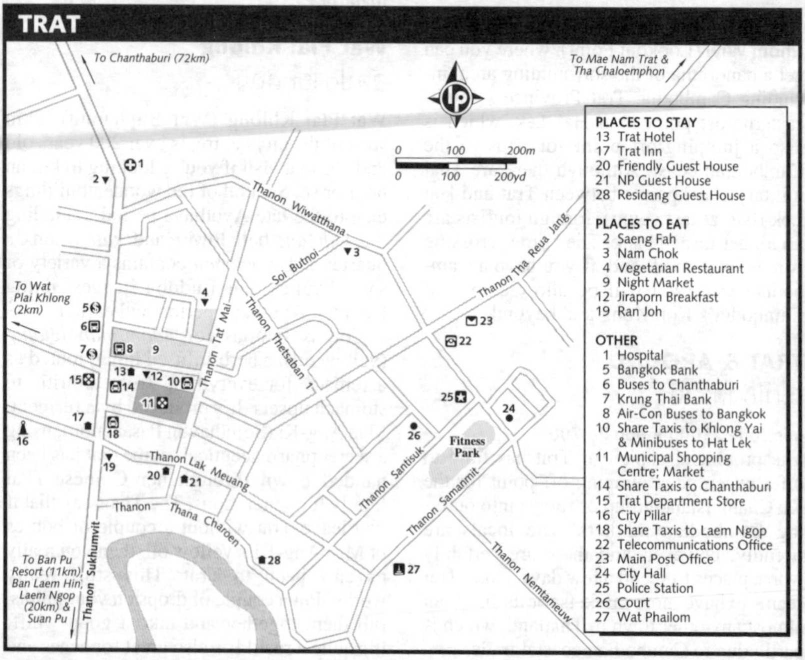

connected by a boardwalk surrounding a large crab pond have one-bedroom with two double beds or one king-size bed. There is a larger one-bedroom unit with six beds. All of these come with air-con, TV and a fridge. There are also deluxe VIP two-bedroom bungalows with TV, VCR and private karaoke room, and there's a health club on the premises. It's a 20B, 15-minute săwngthăew ride from town.

Places to Eat

With all the markets in Trat, you're hardly ever more than 50m away from something good to eat. The **indoor market** beneath the shopping centre has a food section with cheap, good noodle and rice dishes from early morning to early evening. Another good spot for a cheap breakfast is the ancient **coffee stand** in the old day market on Th Tat Mai.

In the evenings, there's a good **night market** next to the air-con bus station. On Mae Nam Trat in the northern part of town is another smaller but atmospheric **night market** – a good choice for long, leisurely meals. Trat is a great city for seafood, which is cheaper here than in Bangkok or in well-touristed cities around the country (it's not the international tourists who drive up the seafood prices but the Thais, who spend huge sums of money eating out).

Jiraporn Breakfast *(☎ 0 3951 1335; breakfasts 20-30B)* is one of the longest-running Thai-Chinese restaurants in town. It's a small café-style place a few doors up from the Trat Hotel where older regulars hang out over tea and coffee every morning. As the name implies, it's mostly a breakfast place. The main menu offerings are toast and eggs with ham, *jók* (rice gruel) and *khâo tôm* (rice soup), but it also serves fried rice or noodles.

Nam Chok *(no Roman-script sign; ☎ 0 3951 2389; cnr Soi Butnoi & Th Wiwatthana; dishes 30-40B)* is another local institution. You can get just about anything over rice here, but there's no English menu so you'll have to try out your Thai. **Ran Joh** *(no Roman-script sign; 90 Th Lak Meuang; open lunch only)* is a good find around lunchtime. It's the place diagonally opposite the Trat Inn, making *khànŏm bêuang* (a Khmer vegie crepe prepared in a wok). Ran Joh also serves other local specialities – it's very inexpensive.

Saeng Fah *(☎ 0 3951 1222; 157-159 Th Sukhumvit; dishes 30-100B)* is a good mid-range restaurant with air-con and a menu with Thai specialities. The food is good, and there are plenty of seafood dishes. Try the 'jellyfish soup' or 'bloody clam salad'. The staff also serve breakfast, when you might (or might not) want to try the house speciality – 'rice with curdled pig's blood'.

A **vegetarian restaurant**, down a lane behind the area where the night market is held, offers seven or eight pots of fresh vegie dishes daily from around 6am to 2pm, or until the food runs out. A plate of rice with your choice of toppings costs only 20B.

Suan Pu *(Crab Farm; ☎ 0 3954 2355; dishes 60-180B)* is the best place in the whole province for seafood. It's in Ban Laem Hin, on the way to Laem Sok, 11km southeast of town (a 20B săwngthăew ride one way). Tables are atmospherically arranged on wooden piers over Ao Meuang Trat. All seafood is served fresh; crab, raised on the premises, is of course the house speciality and prices are moderate to high (but still considerably cheaper than in Bangkok).

Getting There & Away

Bangkok For Trat, air-con buses (191B, five to six hours) or ordinary buses (119B, eight hours) leave from Bangkok's Eastern bus station.

Three bus companies operate a Trat to Bangkok service. **Sahamit-Cherdchai** *(Th Sukhumvit)* near the Trat Hotel and night market, has the best and most frequent (12 trips a day) air-con buses.

Chanthaburi Ordinary buses between Chanthaburi and Trat (35B, 1½ hours, 66km) leave every 30 minutes from 6am to 2.30pm and at 3.45pm, 4.20pm and 5.30pm.

You can also take the quicker share taxis that run between Trat and Chanthaburi (60B, 45 minutes). During the middle of the day, however, it may take up to an hour to gather the seven passengers necessary for a departure; try to schedule your departure from Trat to between 7am and 9am or 4pm and 6pm for the shortest wait.

Khlong Yai, Hat Lek & Bo Rai Săwngthăew and share taxis go to Khlong Yai (ordinary/chartered 35/400B, 45 minutes) and leave from the back of the municipal shopping centre market. Săwngthăew go from Khlong Yai to Hat Lek (ordinary/chartered 30/200B, 16km); motorcycle taxis also make this journey (50B). Săwngthăew go to Bo Rai (50B).

Direct minibuses from Trat to Hat Lek (100B, one hour) leave every half-hour from Th Sukhumvit in front of the municipal shopping centre market.

Getting Around

Săamláw around town should cost 10B per person. Small săwngthăew cost 5B per person on a share basis or 20B to 40B for the whole vehicle.

BEACHES

The sliver of Trat Province that extends southeastward along the Cambodian border is fringed by several Gulf of Thailand beaches. **Hat Sai Si Ngoen** (Silver Sand Beach) lies just north of the 41km marker off Hwy 3. Nearby, at the 42km marker, is **Hat Sai Kaew** (Crystal Sand Beach) and at the 48km marker, **Hat Thap Thim** (also known as Hat Lan); they're OK to walk along the water's edge or picnic in the shade of casuarina and eucalyptus trees. The only place of accommodation here is the **Sun Sapha Kachat Thai** *(Thai Red Cross; ☎ 0 3950 1015; rooms 700B)*, which has newly built and comfortable bungalows with all the usual amenities, as well as a restaurant.

The only other beach with accommodation is **Hat Ban Cheun**, a very long stretch of clean sand near the Km 63 marker. The 6km road that leads to the beach passes a defunct Cambodian refugee camp. There are the usual casuarina and eucalyptus trees, a small **restaurant** and basic **bungalows** *(200B)* set on swampy land behind the beach. Travellers have reported that the friendly family that runs the operation is quite accommodating.

LAEM NGOP

แหลมงอบ

Laem Ngop is where you have to go for ferries to Ko Chang (see Getting There & Away under Ko Chang National Marine Park later) and for visa extensions. **TAT** *(☎ 0 3959 7259; 100 Mu 1, Th Trat-Laem Ngop)* has an office here.

A **Kasikornbank** (between Chut Kaew Guest House and the pier) has an **exchange counter** *(open 8.30am-3.30pm Mon-Fri)*.

Places to Stay & Eat

There's usually no reason to stay here, since most boats to Ko Chang leave in the morning and early afternoon and it's only 20km from Trat. However, there are a couple of good accommodation choices. **Chut Kaew Guest House** *(☎ 0 3959 7088; rooms per person 80B)* is a five-minute walk from the harbour and on the right side. It is run by a nurse, teacher and university student – local, somewhat dated information (including hiking information for Ko Chang) is available in thick notebooks compiled by guests. Rooms come with fan and bamboo-thatch walls and are relatively clean; facilities are shared. Food and laundry services are also available.

Laem Ngop Inn *(☎ 0 3959 7044; bungalows with fan 300B, singles/doubles with air-con 450/600B)* is further up the road and down a side lane about 300m. The 31 clean, concrete bungalows (each with separate garage) come with fan, telephone and TV. Air-con rooms also have a fridge.

Near the pier in Laem Ngop are several rustic seafood places with views of the sea and islands. **Ruan Talay**, an inexpensive wooden place on stilts over the water, is one of the more popular spots with local Thais and Thai tourists.

Also good are **Kung Ruang Seafood**, **Tamnak Chang** and **Krua Rim Nam**, and all are moderately priced.

Getting There & Away

Share taxis to Laem Ngop (20B, 150B chartered) leave Trat from a stand on Th Sukhumvit next to the municipal shopping centre market. They depart regularly throughout the day, but after dark you will have to charter. Travel agents at Tha Laem Ngop arrange daily minibuses to Th Khao San in Bangkok (350B, five to six hours, one daily at 11am); Pattaya (350B, three hours, one daily at 1pm).

KHLONG YAI

คลองใหญ่

Khlong Yai consists of a cluster of older wooden buildings west of the highway, surrounded by modern structures on both sides of the highway. There's a large market in the centre of town, as well as the moderately priced Suksamlan Hotel and two banks with foreign-exchange services. Just south of town is a large shrimp farm.

Places to Stay

Suksamlan Hotel (*☎ 0 3958 1109; rooms with fan from 150B, singles/doubles with air-con 300/350B*) is an old-fashioned Thai-Chinese–style place on a street between the market and the highway. **Bang In Villa** (*☎ 0 3958 1401; rooms 150B, bungalows 250-300B*), out of town a bit off Hwy 3, has nicer bungalows than Suksamlan, but with less character, as well as cheaper rooms in a row building.

Getting There & Away

See Getting There & Away under Trat for information on public transport to Khlong Yai.

HAT LEK TO CAMBODIA

The small Thai border outpost of Hat Lek is the southernmost part on the Trat mainland. Untaxed goods travel back and forth between Cambodia and Thailand at this point; at the small market just before the border crossing itself, next to the pier for boats travelling to Cambodia.

Opposite Hat Lek on Cambodian turf (Sao Thong) there's a cockfighting arena and casino popular with residents from both sides of the border.

There are two military checkpoints along Hwy 3 between Trat town and Hat Lek. Depending on the political situation, drivers and passengers may be stopped and questioned.

Motorcycle and automobile taxis are available from Hat Lek across the border into Cambodia for 30B and 50B. There is accommodation on the island of Koh Kong in Cambodia, but little to keep you there. If you plan to continue farther, you can embark on a four-hour boat ride (US$15) to Sihanoukville. There is only one boat per day to Sihanoukville and it leaves at 8am, so if you don't get across the border early, you'll have to spend a night on Koh Kong. Basically, if you want to get from Trat to Sihanoukville in one day, you should be on the 6am minibus to Hat Lek and at the border with passport in hand as soon as it opens at 7am. This border crossing closes at 5pm.

A Cambodian visa on arrival is sometimes available at the border (US$20 and one passport photo is necessary), but you should check with the Cambodian embassy in Bangkok before heading out here. If you are going into Cambodia for a day trip, you might need to have a valid Thai visa on which you can return to Thailand. Nowadays Thailand grants most nationalities a one-month visa on arrival. If your nationality is not on the instant-visa list, you will find yourself stuck in Cambodia.

See Getting There & Away under Trat for transport information to Hat Lek.

KO CHANG NATIONAL MARINE PARK

อุทยานแห่งชาติเกาะช้าง

Forty-seven of the islands off Trat's coastline belong to a national park named after **Ko Chang** (Elephant Island), which at 492 sq km is the second-largest island in Thailand after Phuket. The entire park officially encompasses 192 sq km of land surface, and 458 sq km of sea. Ko Chang itself is about 70% undisturbed island rainforest – the best preserved in Thailand and perhaps in all Southeast Asia – with steep hills and cliffs reaching as high as the 744m-high Khao Jom Prasat.

Notable wildlife includes the stump-tailed macaque, small Indian civet, Javan mongoose, monitor lizard, water monitor, Burmese and reticulated pythons, king cobra, barking deer and wild pig. Avian species (61 resident species, plus 12 migratory species) include Pacific reef egret, nightjar, green imperial pigeon, white-winged tern, blue-winged pitta, hooded pitta and three hornbill species. An endemic amphibian, *Rana kohchang* (Ko Chang frog), is also found here.

Until rather recently there wasn't a single paved road on Ko Chang. Now a paved road nearly circles the island. In October 2001, the Thai government announced a grand plan to transform Ko Chang and neighbouring islands into a luxury resort for the rich in which, according to a government forestry official, 'Backpackers would not be welcomed'. Whether or not this was just a bit of hyperbole, wild speculation in land ensued and there has been a visible rush to build more accommodation. Just a few years ago, Ko Chang received around 75,000 visitors a year. The prediction for 2002 was 400,000 visitors. What all this means for the future of Ko Chang is unclear.

Other major islands in the park include Ko Kut and Ko Mak. Ko Chang is ringed with small bays and beaches, among them Ao Khlong Son, Hat Sai Khao, Ao Khlong Phrao, Hat Kaibae, Ao Bang Bao and Ao Salak Phet. Near each of these beaches and bays are small villages.

A combination of steep terrain and year-round streams creates several scenic waterfalls. A series of three falls along the stream of Khlong Mayom in the interior of the island, **Nam Tok Than Mayom** *(admission 200B)*, can be reached via Tha Than Mayom or Ban Dan Mai on the east coast. The waterfall closest to the shore can be climbed in about 45 minutes via a well-marked footpath. The view from the top is quite good and there are two inscribed stones bearing the initials of Rama VI and Rama VII nearby. The second waterfall is about 500m further east along Khlong Mayom and the third is about 3km from the first. At the third waterfall is another inscribed stone, this one with the initials of Rama V. At the lower levels are public picnic areas.

On **Ko Kut** you'll find beaches mostly along the western side, at Hat Tapho, Hat Khlong Chao and Hat Khlong Yai Ki. The water off some of these beaches is the most amazing shade of turquoise. A dirt road runs between Ban Khlong Hin Dam, the island's main village on the west coast, and

KO CHANG

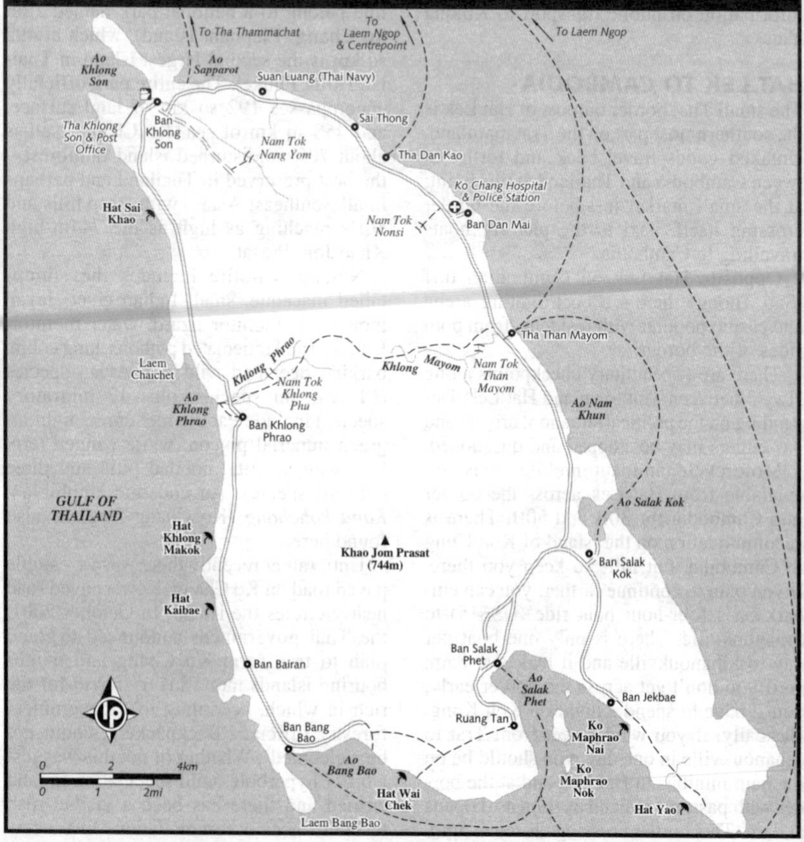

Ao Salat along the northeastern shore. Other villages on the island include Ban Ta Poi, Bang Ao Salat, Ban Laem Kluai, Bang Khlong Phrao and Ban Lak Uan. Nam Tok Tan Sanuk and Khlong Chao offer inland water diversions. The nearby small islands of **Ko Rang** and **Ko Rayang** have good coral in spots. Ko Kut can be reached from Khlong Yai on the mainland or from Ko Mak.

Ko Mak, the smallest of the three main islands, has a scenic beach along the northwest bay. Monsoon forest covers 30% of the island while coconut plantations take up another 60%. A few tractors or jeeps travel along the single paved road that leads from the pier to the main village. It is possible to rent motorcycles and organise diving trips from the resorts on the island.

Ko Wai has some of the best coral and is excellent for snorkelling and diving. The island has two bungalow operations. **Ko Kham** is also recommended for underwater explorations; accommodation is available. **Ko Lao Ya** has natural attributes similar to those at Ko Wai, with one rather expensive place to stay. The tiny **Ko Rang** archipelago, southwest of Ko Chang, is a primary nesting ground for the endangered hawksbill sea turtle.

Information

The park headquarters are divided into four units, found at Tha Than Mayom, Ban Khlong Son, Tha Khlong Plu and Ban Salak Phet. All offer roughly the equivalent information, but the Tha Than Mayom visitors centre features informative displays on park flora and fauna.

Entry fees are collected at any one of the four park headquarters. Be sure to keep your receipt as rangers may demand payment from visitors who don't have one. Admission is 200B.

Money There is no bank on Ko Chang, but moneychangers will change US dollars and travellers cheques at very unfavourable rates. Ask around at places of accommodation. Those at Hat Sai Khao and Hat Kaibae seem to have the best rates. The only **post office** is near the pier at Ban Khlong Son, where there is a telegram service but no international phone. On Hat Sai Khao and Hat Kaibae, a few places offer an **international telephone service** at very high rates.

Medical Services Located at Ban Dan Mai, **Ko Chang Hospital** can handle most minor emergencies. Another choice is the hospital at **Laem Ngop** on the mainland. There are health clinics at Ban Khlong Son, Hat Sai Khao and Hat Kaibae.

Legal Matters The local **police headquarters** is in Ban Dan Mai, as is the jail where visitors who are caught with drugs during periodic sweeps are detained before being shipped off to Bangkok.

Nudity and topless sunbathing are forbidden by law in Ko Chang National Marine Park; this includes all beaches on Ko Chang, Ko Kut, Ko Mak, Ko Kradat etc.

Diving & Snorkelling

Ko Chang and its vicinity is a new frontier compared with other marine locales in Thailand. With regard to climate and visibility, November to April is the best diving season. The better dive sites are at islets and seamounts off the southern tip of the island, stretching between Ko Chang and Ko Kut. In this area **Hin Luk Bat** and **Hin Lap** are both coral-encrusted seamounts with depths of around 18m to 20m. A few kilometres further south, the northern end of **Ko Rang Yai** gets scenic at 10m to 25m, while **Hin Phrai Nam** (between Ko Wai and Ko Rang) has coral and white-tip reef sharks visible to around 20m. A small islet near Ko Rang Yai's northern tip, **Ko Kra**, has good snorkelling in depths of 4m to 5m near the islet's southern end. The islets around Ko Rang are favoured nesting grounds for sea turtles – this is one of the better opportunities to see them in Thailand.

Southwest of Ao Salak Phet, reef-fringed **Ko Wai** features a good variety of colourful hard and soft corals at depths of 6m to 15m.

Near the mouth of Ao Salak Phet, at the southeastern tip of the island, lies a **Thai warship** wreck at a depth of 15m. The ship was supposedly sunk by the French in 1941 during a dispute over whether these islands belonged to Thailand or to the French colony of Cambodia. Thai historians claim there should be a second wreck nearby but divers have yet to report on it. This site should not be dived without a guide.

Dive Centres Next to Bamboo Bungalows at Hat Sai Khao, **Ko Chang Divers** specialises in PADI certification for novice divers. Prices for instruction in beginning and advanced diving range from 11,000B per person. Instruction material is available in English, French, German, Italian and Japanese. Dive trips typically include two dives with all guiding, transport, equipment and food, and cost 3000B. **SeaHorse Dive Centre**, located at the Kaibae Hut Resort at Hat Kaibae, has similar instruction ranging from 6500B to 8000B. All-inclusive dive trips cost 1200B to 1500B per person. **Eco-Divers**, located in the Chaichet Resort at Khlong Phrao, and at Moonlight Resort at Hat Sai Khao, offers diving instruction from 10,000B and dive trips for 6900B to 2800B.

You can also **hire boats** from Ko Chang's western beaches for around 1500B a day, but there's no guarantee the boat pilots will be able to locate dive sites.

Elephant Trekking

An elephant camp located near Ban Khlong Son has a small herd of elephants that formerly worked the teak forests on the mainland before a ban on logging went into effect. Visitors can watch the elephants being bathed by their mahouts and then hire them for treks into the forest. Treks cost 900B for 1½ hours or 450B for half-hour treks. If you're staying at one of the many places between Hat Sai Khao and Hat Kaibae, transportation to and from your place of hotel is included in the price. Most places of accommodation can arrange this for you if given a day's advance notice.

Walking on Ko Chang

The more interesting hikes are in the southern half of the island where there are fewer roads. At the northern end you can walk from Ban Khlong Son to Hat Sai Khao in about 1½ to two hours; from Hat Sai Khao to Ao Khlong Phrao in about two hours; and from Ao Khlong Phrao to Hat Kaibae in about two hours. All three are straightforward walks along the main road.

If you're looking for more of a grunt, just head for the interior – the steep, forested hills will have you sweating in no time. A footpath connects Ban Khlong Phrao on the west coast with Khlong Mayom on the east, but this all-day cross-island route shouldn't be undertaken without a local guide.

Don't try Ban Bang Bao to Ao Salak Phet unless you're an experienced tropical hiker with moderate orienteering skills – there are a lot of hills and many interconnecting trails. A Swede who hiked the perimeter of the island suggested that for this part of the island you carry a note in Thai reading 'I would like to go to Salak Phet. I like very much to walk in the jungle and have done it before. Please show me the start of this trail'.

If you don't get lost, this hike will take four to six hours; should you decide to attempt it, carry enough food and water for an overnight stay, just in case.

If you do get lost, climb the nearest hill and try to locate the sea or a stream to get a bearing on where you are. Following any stream will usually take you either to a village or to the sea. Then you can either follow the coast or ask directions. This advice is also good for hiking anywhere across the island, as it is very easy to get lost on the many intersecting, unmarked trails.

At the southeastern end of Ao Bang Bao, around a headland that leads to Ao Salak Phet, is a beautiful and secluded beach, **Hat Wai Chek**.

Other Activities

Some of the guesthouses at Hat Sai Khao and Hat Kaibae rent out kayaks, sailboards, masks and snorkels, and boogie boards. Mountain bikes can be rented for 150B per day at several places on the island, most of which are located at Hat Sai Khao and Hat Kaibae.

Several bungalow operations along Ko Chang's west coast beaches offer day trips to nearby islands for 150B to 1000B. Overnight trips can also be arranged and cost 1500B to 2000B per person.

Places to Stay

Ko Chang Many beach huts on the island have been open for years and others have just popped up, so standards vary quite a bit. Most of the older and simpler bungalow complexes have been upgraded and prices revised accordingly. A few close down during the rainy season (June to October), but as the island has become more popular, most places stay open and offer low season prices. During the rainy season, boats will usually only go as far as Ao Sapparot, Ban Dan Mai and Tha Than Mayom, from which visitors can continue on to the beaches by săwngthăew. Note that the surf further south along the east coast can be impassable during heavy rains.

West Coast As the island's better beaches are along the west coast, this is where most of the beach accommodation is. Most bungalows consist of one large bed (big enough to sleep two) plus a mosquito net, though the trend has been to replace the mosquito nets with screens on windows – a problem as doors are usually left wide open while rooms are being cleaned. If you want to avoid mosquito bites, it's best to bring your own net and repellent.

If you are staying longer than a few days some places will discount their rates, though this custom is fast fading with Ko Chang's rising popularity. Still, it doesn't hurt to ask. Most of the island now has electricity; if your bungalow isn't on the grid yet, kerosene or gas lanterns are usually provided.

At the northern tip of the island is the largest village, Ban Khlong Son, which has a network of piers at the mouth of the *khlawng* (canal; also written 'khlong'), a wát, a school, several noodle shops and a health clinic. **Premvadee Resort** *(☎ 0 3959 7032); bungalows with fan & bath 500-1500B, large bungalows 3500B)* is a bit south of the northern cape of Ao Khlong Son. It has roomy bungalows with fan and bath, and large two-room houses with bath and fan.

Aiyapura Resort *(☎ 0 3952 1656–60, fax 0 3952 1656; rooms from 5800B, bungalows from 7500B)* is the future of Ko Chang if Bangkok politicians and developers get their way, and it's nice – if you can afford it. Well-built and modern duplex bungalows, all with spacious verandas, are set in a coconut grove. There's also a hotel-style building with rooms. Just in case the beach isn't good enough for you, there's a huge swimming pool right next to it. The Aiyapura has a good albeit pricey restaurant as well as a poolside bar.

White Sand Beach Resort *(bungalows 200-250B, with bath & fan 500-700B)* is a nicely landscaped place at Hat Sai Khao, 5km away, and separated from other Hat Sai Khao bungalow developments by a couple of small rocky points. There are simple woven-bamboo bungalows as well as more solid wooden ones, all with attached bath.

Rock Sand Bungalow *(bungalows 150B, with bath & fan 350-450B, with air-con 900B)*, next south, is a more isolated spot and has rustic wooden huts on a rocky outcrop surrounded by beach; nicer huts cost a little more. There's a neat two-storey restaurant-bar.

KC Resort *(bungalows with fan/air-con 1000/1600B)* has undergone recent renovations and now offers tasteful bungalows, all with attached hot-water shower and fridge. The restaurant does a good seafood barbecue nightly during the high season.

Yakah Bungalows *(bungalows 300-500B)* has clean bamboo huts with spacious verandas and there are swings for children and a well-stocked library. **Aranee's Resort** *(rooms 300B)*, across the road from Yakah, offers rooms in a wooden hotel-style building with bath and fan. Aranee's offers international call and currency exchange services.

Further south along Hat Sai Khao is a string of huts that have gradually gone upmarket (and up in price) over the past few years. A host of newcomers have sprouted up, making this beach Ko Chang's most populated. **Tantawan** *(bungalows with fan & bath 500-1300B)* offers brick bungalows with fan and bath. **Bamboo Bungalows** *(bungalows 250B, with bath & fan 500-800B)*, near Tantawan, has simple bamboo-and-thatch huts with shared facilities. Ko Chang Divers is located here. The Tiger's Den Bar just opposite is also a good diversion.

Cookie Bungalow *(bungalows with fan 500-700B, with air-con 800-1200B)* is well run by friendly staff and has comfortable bungalows with bath. Cookie also has a large and popular beachside restaurant. **Mac Bungalow** *(bungalows with fan 700B, with air-con 1500-2000B)* has the more expensive air-con bungalows nearest the beach. Its minimart is a plus.

Sabay Beach Bungalow *(bungalows with bath & fan 500B)* is on the beach south of Cookie, and features typical fan bungalows. During our visit, new bungalows were being built that will have air-con and, when completed, will cost about 1500B.

Koh Chang Lagoon Resort *(bungalows with fan 900B, with air-con 1600-2000B)* offers fan and bath bungalows near the beach and air-con units set back further from the beach. **Apple** *(huts with fan & bath 350-450B)* offers huts with fan and bath. On our last visit we were told that Apple's huts would soon become an upmarket resort – a shame if true. This was once the island's best Thai-Rasta scene, with long nights of Bob Marley tunes played at bong-rattling volume.

Best Garden Beach Resort *(☎ 0 3952 9632; bungalows 2000-6800B)* has well-designed bungalows, all with attached hot-water bath, TV and air-con. Large bungalows with two beds and a loft that sleep up to six are the most expensive, and are set nearest the beach. The semi-outdoor restaurant does seafood barbecues in the evenings. **Banpu Ko Chang Resort** *(in Trat ☎ 0 3954 2355; W www.banpuresort.com; rooms 2000B, bungalows 2500-3500B)* has both hotel accommodation and wooden bungalows set in an attractive garden that slopes down to the beach. The hotel rooms feature air-con, hot water and TV. Bungalows have the same amenities. There's also a swimming pool. This place is often packed out with Thai tourists on the weekends as it is geared for two-day packages.

Moonlight Resort *(bungalows with fan 600-700B, with air-con 1500B)* has typical bungalows with small verandas, all with attached bath. The price of the fan bungalows depends on their proximity to the beach.

Plaloma Cliff Resort *(rooms & bungalows with fan 700-1000B, with air-con 1500-2000B)* is south of Sunsai on the other side of a rocky headland, spread over a rocky cliff. This place has quiet, spacious stone-and-cement bungalows with private bath, as well as a large building with hotel-like rooms. The interspersed coconut palms and sea views are pluses.

About 4km south of Hat Sai Khao is Ao Khlong Phrao (Coconut Bay). It stretches south of Laem Chaichet and encompasses Khlong Phrao and the village of Ban Khlong Phrao.

Boutique Resort & Spa *(bungalows from 2000B)* is a new place with exotic-looking bungalows of palm thatch and wood, all with attached bath, air-con and TV. There's Thai massage available, as well as a sauna and Jacuzzi. Breakfast is included in the rates.

Chaichet Bungalows *(bungalows with fan/air-con 600/1200B)*, on the northern side of the canal, has bungalows strung out along Laem Chaichet, a gently curving cape. Although there's no beach to speak of, it's picturesque all the same.

Coconut Beach Bungalows *(wooden bungalows 600-700B, concrete bungalows 1600-2500B)*, near Ban Chaichet, south of Ao Khlong Phrao, has wooden bungalows and concrete bungalows, all with bath. The bungalows are well kept, if somewhat close together. The more expensive are nearest the beach.

Ko Chang Resort & Spa *(in Bangkok ☎ 0 2277 5256; bungalows 2000-2800B)* is a pricey place about a 10-minute walk further south along the beach. Upmarket bungalows include air-con, hot water and satellite TV. The majority of the guests are Thais on packages (about 4000B for three days and two nights). **Klong Plow Resort** *(bungalows with air-con 2200B)*, near Ko Chang Resort, has wooden bungalows around a lagoon. There's also a two-storey house that can accommodate 15 people.

KP Bungalows *(huts 150-200B, with bath 300-800B, family bungalows 1000-2000B)* is near Wat Ban Khlong Phrao. Here you'll find well-spaced basic thatched huts, larger ones with bath and two-room family bungalows.

Around another headland to the south are two beach areas separated by a canal – Hat Khlong Makok and Hat Kaibae (15km south of Khlong Son).

Magic Resort *(bungalows with fan 500B, with air-con 5500B)*, on Hat Khlong Makok, has A-frame bungalows with fan and concrete bungalows with private bath. Smaller bungalows sleep three persons, larger bungalows sleep up to five. Magic has a pier, telephone service and scuba diving. The owner has a private boat service from Laem Ngop so is able to funnel many passengers directly to this beach. Magic's best feature is its restaurant built over the bay.

Hat Kaibae is an area that has become quite developed, with a new pier and bungalows with electricity. Several of the old collections of huts have gone upscale, so there is some very comfortable accommodation to be found here. The downside, of course, is that prices continue to rise.

Chang Park Resort & Spa *(in Bangkok ☎ 0 2692 0121; bungalows 1600-4200B)* is the ritziest place on the beach. Bungalows are built in Thai style and have all the amenities. The most expensive bungalow

SOUTHEASTERN THAILAND

has its own Jacuzzi. There's a swimming pool and breakfast is included.

Coral Resort *(bungalows with fan 400-800B, singles/doubles with air-con 1500/1800B)* is a long line of well-built bungalows along the beach, most with private bath. The air-con rooms are comfortable and have satellite TV. A restaurant on the premises has an interesting menu that includes Thai and French dishes.

Kaibae Hut Resort *(bungalows with bath 300-500B, deluxe bungalow 2500B)*, also on the southern side of the *khlawng*, has a nicely laid-out restaurant and fair bungalows, plus a bit of a beach even at high tide. There is a large deluxe air-con bungalow (with TV, fridge and fan) that can fit up to eight people. It's quiet and has a security gate that's locked at night. SeaHorse Dive Centre offers dive trips and instruction during the dry season. **KB Bungalows** *(bungalows with fan 600-1000B, with air-con 1500B)* on a grassy bank above the beach is next south. Bungalows with bath and fan sleep two to four people. Air-con bungalows have one large bed. All have small verandas at the front.

KaiBae Beach Bungalow *(bungalows with fan 500B, with air-con 1500B)* has undergone some upgrading since our last visit. Bungalows are newish but a bit crowded together, and the staff aren't the friendliest. **Porn's** *(huts 150B, with bath & fan 300B)* is another 100m walk from KaiBae and offers basic huts. We were told during our visit that it would soon be upgraded. **Sea View Resort** *(☎ 0 3952 9022; hotel rooms 900-1200B, bungalows with fan/air-con 1500/3500B, bungalow for 10 people 5500B)* is a large place beyond Porn's with bungalows and hotel rooms. The grounds are lush and the bungalows well spaced. One large bungalow is suitable for an extended family, if you happen to be travelling with one. **Siam Bay Resort** *(bungalows with bath from 500B, concrete bungalows with air-con up to 600B)*, the last place on the beach, is secluded and friendly with huts, bungalows with private bath, and fancier concrete bungalows. At low tide you can walk out to Ko Man Nai opposite.

South of Hat Kaibae is another small stretch of beach, known as Hat Thanam, but called 'Lonely Beach' on the tourist brochures. It's becoming less and less lonely with each season, but there are some long-running gems here.

Tree House Lodge *(huts 100-180B)*, in a rocky area near a secluded white-sand beach, can be reached by a 30-minute walk along the path to Ao Bang Bao. Simple thatched huts are on stilts in a coconut grove. This is one of those lazy yet well-maintained places that one gets to and finds somewhat hard to leave. Let's hope it never goes upscale.

South Coast The south coast places used to close during the rainy season, from May to November, but felt like the edge of the world even during the high season. Nowadays places seem to be open year round, and there's a lot more going on than in the past.

Bang Bao Blue Wave *(huts 150B, with bath 200B, with fan & bath 230B)*, a friendly place on Ao Bang Bao, has huts with private bath. The generator electricity is on from 6pm to 10pm. The owner also has a boat for hire. **Bang Bao Resort** *(rooms 100B)* is an optimistically named place located on a pier over the water in the village of Ban Bang Bao. Simple rooms come with shared bath and there are good seafood restaurants nearby.

Salakpet Seafood Restaurant & Resort *(☎ 0 3952 1751; rooms with air-con 900-1800B)*, at the head of the road near the pier at Ao Salak Phet, has clean rooms built over the water with air-con. There are rooms that house two, four and six people. Most people who stay here are on two-day packages that include food. Prices of packages depend on the time of year.

Sang Aroon Bungalows & Restaurant *(bungalows 600B)* at Ban Jaekbae, which is a 20-minute boat ride across the bay, is another in the growing trend of 'package resorts'. Two-night, three-day packages are 2000B, including six meals and transport from Laem Ngop. If things are quiet, you may get away with renting just a room for 600B per night.

Tantawan Resort *(single/double huts 100/200B)* is right at the tip of the cape, and is a friendly place on a rocky outcrop. The beach is only a two-minute swim away. To get here take a boat from Ao Salak Phet (30B).

East Coast There are a couple of mediocre places to stay near the headquarters of the national park, in attractive surrounds, at Tha Than Mayom. **Koh Chang Cabana** *(rooms 500-600B, bungalows 1500-2500B)*, near the Dan Kao pier, is privately managed and rents out rooms with fan in a long row house or there are separate air-con bungalows. Tour groups are the main clientele here. **Than Mayom Bungalows** *(house 500B, house for 30 people 2200B)*, about 500m from the park offices, has a large and comfortable two-room house and a house that can accommodate 30 people.

If you have camping gear, it might be better to hike up and **camp** near Nam Tok Than Mayom.

Other Islands Ko Kut, Ko Mak, Ko Kradat, Ko Kham and Ko Wai are quieter and more secluded than Ko Chang, but transport can be a little tricky – although from December to April there are daily boats. Also, you can't just pick up and walk down the beach to another bungalow if you don't like the one you've landed at. Except at the package places, room rates overall are less expensive than on Ko Chang.

From May to November, it's a good idea to call in advance to make sure boat transportation is available. Most places of accommodation close down from June to September.

Ko Kut As on Ko Chang, the best beaches are found along the west coast, particularly at Hat Tapho. It is possible to visit the island on your own, but you will find it next to impossible to get accommodation without being on a package tour. These typically last two nights and three days and include accommodation, all meals, trips to waterfalls and snorkelling. You could always try getting a room as a walk-in, but the resorts are really not equipped to handle individual travellers, and so, if you can get them to agree to take you, you'll end up paying through the nose. The clientele are almost all Thai. The prices listed here are walk-in rates. Booking a package will bring the price down 30% to 40%. The bungalow operations on this island include **Ko Kut Sai Khao Resort** *(☎ 0 3951 1429; bungalows 3200B)*; **Kut Island Resort** *(in Bangkok ☎ 0 2374 3004, 0 2311 0639; bungalows 3950B)*; **Captain Hook Resort** *(in Bangkok ☎ 0 2966 1800; bungalows 3900B)*; **Peter Pan Resort** *(in Bangkok ☎ 0 2966 1800)*; **Ko Kut Cabana** *(☎ 0 3952 2955; bungalows 3900-4600B)*; and **Khlong Jaow Resort** *(☎ 0 3952 0337 • in Bangkok ☎ 0 2245 8523; bungalows 3200B)*. All of these places offer the usual amenities of a Thai-style 'resort'. All rooms have attached bath and air-con, and each resort has its own restaurant.

Ko Mak Like Ko Kut, many 'resorts' on Ko Mak are set up for package tourists, or upgrading their facilities to allow them to do so. It is difficult to get accommodation at these places without being on a package tour. These typically last two nights and three days and include accommodation, all meals, trips to waterfalls and snorkelling. Again, as with Ko Kut, you could always try getting a room as a walk-in, but the resorts are really not equipped to handle individual travellers, and you'll end up paying three times as much as if you'd booked a package. The clientele are almost all Thai, many of whom come for deep-sea fishing trips that can be booked here as well. The prices listed here for the more pricey places of accommodation are walk-in rates. Booking a package will bring the price down 30% to 40%.

The saving grace here is that there are still a few nonresorts that rent rooms the old fashioned way, with no strings attached. Though how long these will hold out remains to be seen.

Ko Mak Coco-Cape *(in Bangkok ☎ 0 2711 2058; bungalows 3400B)* has bamboo and thatch bungalows, some over the water and linked by wooden causeways. Each room is basically furnished with bed and mosquito net. Toilets and shower facilities are shared.

Ko Mak Resort *(in Bangkok ☎ 0 2319 6714–5; bungalows 500-1500B)*, on the western bay amid a coconut and rubber plantation, is a friendly place that has bungalows with fan and bath, some of them large and with two rooms. A windsurfing school on the beach offers courses and rents out equipment.

Ko Mak Fantasia Resort *(bungalows 250B)*, not far away from Ko Mak Resort, has concrete bungalows with private bath. **TK Huts** *(☎ 0 3952 1631; huts 100-150B, bungalows 300-350B)*, to the west, has basic huts with shared bath and bungalows, the more expensive with fan and bath are nearest the beach. The staff are friendly and helpful.

Ao Khao Resort *(huts 150B, bungalows 350-1000B)* offers comfortable bungalows with fan and private bath and smaller basic huts. Diving equipment and instruction are available from Lagona Divers located on the premises. **Lazy Days** *(huts 100-150B)* is an aptly named place near Ao Khao Resort, with tepees made from bamboo and palm fronds and larger huts. Facilities are shared and there is a small library.

Some of these places tend to close during the rainy season.

Ko Kradat Only open to people on a pre-arranged package tour, **Ko Kradat Resort** *(in Bangkok ☎ 0 2368 2675; bungalows 1800B)* has air-con bungalows with attached bath.

Ko Kham Run by a friendly ex-cop, **Ko Kham Resort** *(huts 120-150B, bungalows 700B)* offers bamboo bungalows and more upmarket huts. During the November to May high season you can get a boat here from Tha Laem Ngop.

Ko Wai The staff are friendly and the food is quite good at **Ko Wai Paradise** *(huts 150-250B, larger bungalows 1200B)*, which has simple wooden bungalows on the beach and one larger bungalow with two rooms and attached bath located behind the restaurant.

Places to Eat

Menus at all the bungalows on Ko Chang are pretty similar. On Hat Sai Khao, highest marks go to the kitchens at **Cookie Bungalow**. Several small **eateries** along the eastern side of the main road in Hat Sai Khao offer options, most of it travellers' fare and not bad, though these places seem to come and go with each season. **Ban Nuna Restaurant-Cafe**, is an upstairs place where you sit on cushions, and is good for Thai lunches and dinners, pizza and Western breakfasts.

White House Bakery, across the road from Sabai Beach Bungalow, offers a variety of baked goods, fruit shakes and plenty of information on island activities.

Salakpet Seafood Restaurant, at Ao Salak Phet, Ko Chang, serves the very best seafood on the island; prices are moderate. Also worth trying are the **seafood restaurants** on the pier at Ban Bang Bao.

At the end of a small pier at **Tha Than Mayom** is a very casual restaurant with rice and noodle dishes.

Getting There & Away

Ko Chang Take a sǎwngthǎew (20B, 25 minutes) from Trat to Laem Ngop on the coast, then a ferry to Ko Chang. There are now three piers serving Ko Chang – the main one at the end of the road from Trat, called Tha Laem Ngop; another 4km northwest of Laem Ngop called Tha Ko Chang Centrepoint (operated by Rooks Ko Chang Resort); and a newer one called Tha Thammachat at Ao Thammachat, further west of Laem Ngop.

Tha Laem Ngop is the best jumping-off point as there are boats to all the islands from here. Boats go to Tha Dan Kao on Ko Chang year-round; this is the boat most people take. During the high season – roughly December to April – boats depart hourly from 7am to 5pm (50B, one hour). The remainder of the year the schedule is reduced to about every two hours, although departures ultimately depend on weather, number of passengers and any number of other factors. You should check on fares in advance – sometimes the boat crews may overcharge *faràng*. At Tha Dan Kao, sǎwngthǎew will be waiting to take you to any of the various beaches along the west coast or to Ao Salak Phet.

Weather permitting, it may be possible to charter a boat directly to Hat Sai Khao, but you'd better have deep pockets. We were told it could be done for 4000B.

From Tha Ko Chang Centrepoint, there are eight boats to Ko Chang from 7am to 5.30pm daily (40B, 45 minutes). This is also a vehicle ferry, so this is the place to come if you're driving your own vehicle. Vehicles with four wheels cost 100B, motorcycles and bicycles are 70B. From Ko Chang this ferry makes eight trips to Tha Ko Chang Centrepoint between 8am and 6.30pm.

Another way to get to Ko Chang is via a vehicle ferry from Ao Thammachat. The ferry leaves six times daily (300B for a vehicle and driver, plus 60B per passenger or pedestrian, 30 minutes).

Ko Mak From November to May, boats to Ko Mak (170B, three to 3½ hours) leave from Tha Laem Ngop at 3pm daily, with additional departures at 10am on Monday, Thursday and Saturday. In the reverse direction the boats depart at 8am daily, with additional departures at 1pm on Wednesday, Friday and Sunday. During the rainy season the departure schedule is cut back to every other day – except in high surf when boats may be cancelled altogether for several days.

Ko Kut Most people get to Ko Kut from Ko Mak (150B). There are no direct boats from Laem Ngop to Ko Kut, but the 10am boat to Ko Mak (leaves Monday, Thursday and Saturday) carries on to Ko Kut after making a stop at Ko Mak and departing at 1pm. The cost is 170B and the trip takes three hours. Return boats from Ko Kut to Laem Ngop via Ko Mak leave on Friday and Saturday at noon.

If you want to charter a boat to Ko Kut from the mainland, the best place to do so is from Ban Khlong Son, about 2km south of Khlong Yai off Rte 318. A long-tail boat, capable of carrying up to 10 people, can be chartered here (1500B, one hour). During the rainy season these boats may suspend service.

Other Islands Daily boats to Ko Kham depart from Laem Ngop around 3pm (170B, three hours). From Ko Mak to Ko Kham, it's a short hop from the pier at Ko Mak Resort; boats leave at 10am and 1pm and 2pm daily (50B to 80B). A boat from Laem Ngop to Ko Wai leaves at 3pm and arrives at 5.30pm (120B). Both boats return the next day at around 8am.

Getting Around

Motorcycle Bungalow operators along the west coast charge 60B per hour or 400B per day for motorcycle hire; elsewhere on the island rental bikes are scarce. The owners claim they have to charge these rates because the island roads are so hard on the bikes.

Săwngthăew The săwngthăew meeting the boats at Tha Dan Kao charge 30B per person to Hat Sai Khao, Hat Kaibae and Ban Khlong Phrao on the west coast. Between Tha Dan Kao and Ban Salak Phet, the local price is only 30B per person, although tourists may be charged more.

Boat Charter trips to nearby islands average 500B to 800B for a half-day, or 1000B to 2000B all day, depending on the boat and distances covered. Ensure that the charter includes all 'user fees' for the islands – sometimes the boat operators demand 200B on top of the charter fee for 'using' the beach.

On the southern end of the island, you can charter a long-tail boat or fishing boat between Hat Kaibae and Ao Bang Bao for 1000B or around 150B per person shared by a boatful of passengers. Similar charters are available between Ao Bang Bao and Ao Salak Phet and Long Beach Bungalows on Hat Yao for around 150B.

Boat rides up Khlong Phrao to the falls cost 50B per person and can be arranged through most bungalows.

Prachinburi & Sa Kaew Provinces

Lying roughly halfway between Bangkok and the Cambodian border, the largely rural provinces of Prachinburi and Sa Kaew are peppered with many small Dvaravati and Khmer ruins. The latter province's name, in fact, means 'Jewel Pool', a reference to various Mon-Khmer reservoirs in the area. Little more than loose collections of laterite blocks, most will be of little interest to the casual visitor. The provincial capitals and larger towns lie next to the banks of Mae Nam Prachin – now paralleled by the eastern railway line and Hwy 33 – in the midst of a rice-growing region crossed by canals. The eastern districts of Prachinburi centred around *amphoe* Sa Kaew attained separate provincial status in January 1994.

NATIONAL PARKS

North of Prachinburi, Rte 3077 leads to Khao Yai National Park (see Nakhon Ratchasima Province in the Northeastern Thailand chapter). North and northeast of Kabinburi, along the southern escarpment of the Khorat Plateau, are the contiguous Thap Lan National Park and Pang Sida National Park. Together these parks encompass 3084 sq km, one of the largest protected natural areas in Thailand.

Thap Lan National Park *(adult/child 200/100B)* is well known as a habitat for the abundant *tôn laan* (talipot palm), the leaves of which were once used for Buddhist manuscripts. Wildlife seen in the park includes elephants, gaur, tigers, sambar, barking deer, palm civets, hornbills and gibbons. Lowland bird varieties are particularly well represented here. This area was an important refuge for Thailand's communist guerrillas during the 1960s and 1970s, and remnants of their camps can be seen along the streams Khlong Nam Brang and Khlong Sam Son.

Facilities in the park are minimal; anyone who would like to explore the interior should contact the rangers at park headquarters in Thap Lan village, Amphoe Na Di. The rangers can arrange for a tour of the park and provide camping permits.

There is no public transport to the park entrance, which is around 32km north of Kabinburi via Rte 304 (the road to Nakhon Ratchasima).

Pang Sida National Park, around 30km southeast of Thap Lan near Sa Kaew, is smaller but hillier than Thap Lan. Streams that cut through the park form several scenic waterfalls, including **Nam Tok Pang Sida** and **Nam Tok Na Pha Yai** near the park headquarters, and the more difficult to reach **Suan Man Suan Thong** and **Nam Tok Daeng Makha**.

National park entry fees are collected at each of these parks *(adult/child 200/100B)*.

SA MORAKOT & SA KAEW
สระมรกต/สระแก้ว

Southeast of Prachinburi provincial capital via Rtes 319 and 3070, in the village of Ban Sa Khoi (between Khok Pip and Sa Maha Pho on Rte 3070), is the Angkor-period Sa Morakot. Thai for 'Emerald Pool', this was an important Khmer reservoir during the reign of Angkor's Jayavarman VII. Original laterite-block sluices next to the dam, along with assorted *sěmaa* (boundary stones), *naga* sculptures, pedestals and a sandstone lingam, can still be seen here.

Water from this reservoir is considered sacred and has been used in Thai coronation ceremonies.

Sa Kaew (Jewel Pool), another historic reservoir site, is just south of Khok Pip off Rte 3070. This one features a Dvaravati-period laterite quarry with some surviving bas-relief on the walls.

There are a number of other Dvaravati and Angkor laterite foundations in the area.

ARANYA PRATHET
อรัญประเทศ

postcode 27120 • pop 56,700

This district next to the Thailand–Cambodia border has long been an important trade and transport centre. After the Khmer Rouge took over Cambodia in 1975, and again when the Vietnamese invaded Cambodia in 1979, Aranya Prathet became a major recipient of Cambodian refugees. Until 1997, random skirmishes between Khmer Rouge guerrillas and the Phnom Penh government continued to send Cambodian citizens scurrying over the border from time to time. Now with the Khmer Rouge gone, the area is considered safe and the border between Aranya Prathet and the Cambodian town of Poipet is fully open to all visitors. A Cambodian visa on arrival is sometimes available at the border (US$20 and one passport photo is necessary), but you should check with the Cambodian embassy in Bangkok before heading out here.

A crackdown on gambling in Phnom Penh has caused a glut of casinos to be built in Poipet. Six casinos are in operation now, mostly catering to Thais from Bangkok. The staggering contrast between the visiting high-rollers and the dirt-poor locals has created sights that are not easily forgotten.

Talat Rong Kleua This large market consisting of rows of warehouse-like sheds at the northern edge of town attracts a ragtag crowd of Cambodians who sell gems, textiles, basketry, brass and other handicrafts to the Thais. It's a fascinating spot to visit just to observe the steady stream of Cambodians crossing the border with huge hand-pulled carts piled high with market goods. Rickety rickshaws made of wood and bicycle tyres transport up to six passengers at a time between the market and the border crossing. There are several simple restaurants serving Thai food in the market.

Theft and banditry are common in the area, so take care with night travel. Although it's relatively safe to cross the border directly to Poipet, areas to the north and south of the district seat are heavily mined. You should also keep in mind that Poipet regularly experiences outbreaks of cholera and dengue fever, especially during the rainy season.

Places to Stay & Eat

Aran Garden 1 *(59/1-7 Th Rat Uthit; rooms 140-180B)* is an older, somewhat seedy central hotel with acceptable rooms with fan and bath. **Aran Garden 2** *(110 Th Rat Uthit; rooms with fan/air-con 200/400B)* is newer and larger and offers clean, quiet rooms.

Aran Park *(☎ 0 3723 2588, fax 0 3723 2115; rooms 720B)*, on the main highway leading into Aranya Prathet from the west, offers clean modern rooms with air-con, phone, satellite TV and fridge. **Inter Hotel** *(☎ 0 3723 1291, fax 0 3723 1848; rooms with fan/air-con 300/550B)* is tucked away in a quiet residential area near the town centre on Soi Ban Aran and is better-located than Aran Park (for anyone who wants to see the town on foot). Nice rooms have satellite TV and private bath have hot water.

Little Home Restaurant *(open 7.30am-9.30pm)*, an air-con place in the town centre, serves pizza, salads, sandwiches, ice cream and Thai and Chinese food. A block south-east of Little Home is a small **night market** with a cluster of food vendors.

Getting There & Away

Ordinary buses from Bangkok's Northern and Northeastern bus station to Aranya Prathet (102B, five hours) leave on an hourly basis from 5.30am to 4.30pm; air-con buses (196B) leave hourly from 5.30am to 10.30am and from noon to 5pm.

Trains on the 3rd-class-only eastern railway line between Bangkok and Aranya Prathet leave Bangkok's Hualamphong station twice daily at 5.55am and 1.05pm (48B, 5½ hours).

If you have your own wheels you could also reach Aranya Prathet from Chanthaburi Province to the south via Rte 317, or you could reach it from Buriram Province to the north via Rte 3068.

Border Crossing (Cambodia) The SRT train continues on for another half-hour east of Aran (as Aranya Prathet is commonly known) to the border for 5B. From Poipet on the Cambodian side you can take a pick-up truck to Siem Reap, for Angkor Wat, or to Sisophon. From Sisophon you can ride another pickup to Battambang, and from there it's possible to catch a train all the way to Phnom Penh.

Chiang Mai Province

Chiang Mai straddles the most important historical crossroads of northern Southeast Asia, a fertile region of mountains, valleys and rivers where peoples from China, Laos, Myanmar and Thailand have long traded goods and ideas in a fusion of cultures. This blend has been further enlivened by the presence of tribal societies – such as the Hmong-Mien, Thai Lü and Phuan – whose ethnic heritage knows no fixed political boundaries.

Outside of the provincial capital, Chiang Mai Province boasts more natural forest cover than any other province in the north. Cycling, hiking, bird watching and camping attract those interested in northern Thailand's natural surroundings, while visitors keen on learning more about the region's ethnic minorities can visit semi-remote villages on mountain slopes.

Highlights

- Follow the winding, cobblestone lanes of Chiang Mai to Thai cooking schools, crumbling stupas, semi-hidden bars and noodle stands
- Take an historical stroll through the atmospheric temple ruins of Chiang Mai's first capital, Wiang Kum Kam
- View a perfect example of 14th-century Lanna temple architecture at the large hall at Wat Phra Singh, containing one of Thailand's most sacred Buddha images
- Visit the Chiang Mai Night Bazaar and survey the ultimate souvenir stand, stretching for a half-dozen blocks and bringing together the good, the bad and the ugly
- Enjoy a traditional Thai massage or enrol in a course to become a thumb master yourself
- When the city heat gets too much, head for Doi Inthanon National Park

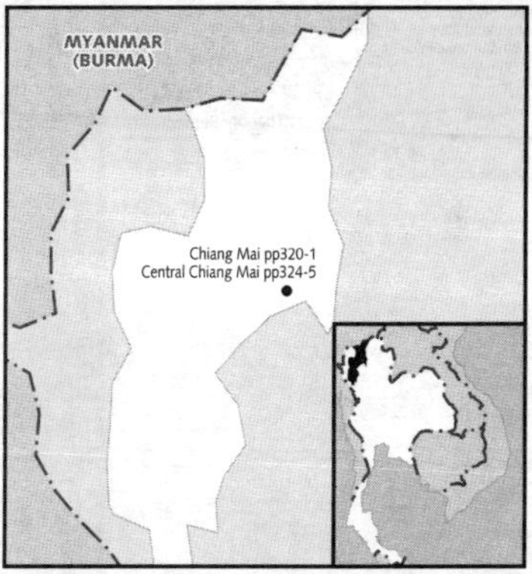

Chiang Mai

อ.เมืองเชียงใหม่

postcode 50000 • pop 160,000

One of the many questions Thais may ask a foreigner visiting Thailand is 'Have you been to Chiang Mai yet?', underscoring the feeling that Chiang Mai is a keystone of any journey to Thailand. Along with Sukhothai farther south, it was the first Southeast Asian state to make the historic transition from domination by Mon and Khmer cultures to a new era ruled by Thais. Although Thais idealise their beloved northern capital as a quaint, moated and walled city surrounded by mountains with legendary, mystical attributes, the truth is Chiang Mai has all but left that image behind to become a modern, cosmopolitan city exhibiting many of the hallmarks of contemporary world culture and technology.

More than 700km northwest of Bangkok, Chiang Mai has over 300 temples (121 within the *thêtsàbaan* or municipal limits) – almost as many as in Bangkok – a circumstance that makes it visually striking. Auspicious Doi Suthep rises 1676m above and behind the city, providing an ever-present reminder that this fast-developing centre is mountain-bound.

Many visitors stay in Chiang Mai longer than planned because of the high quality and low price of accommodation, food and shopping, the cool nights (compared with central Thailand), the international feel of the city and the friendliness of the people. With the increasing number of cultural and spiritual learning experiences available to visitors in Chiang Mai these days – Thai language, Thai

CHIANG MAI

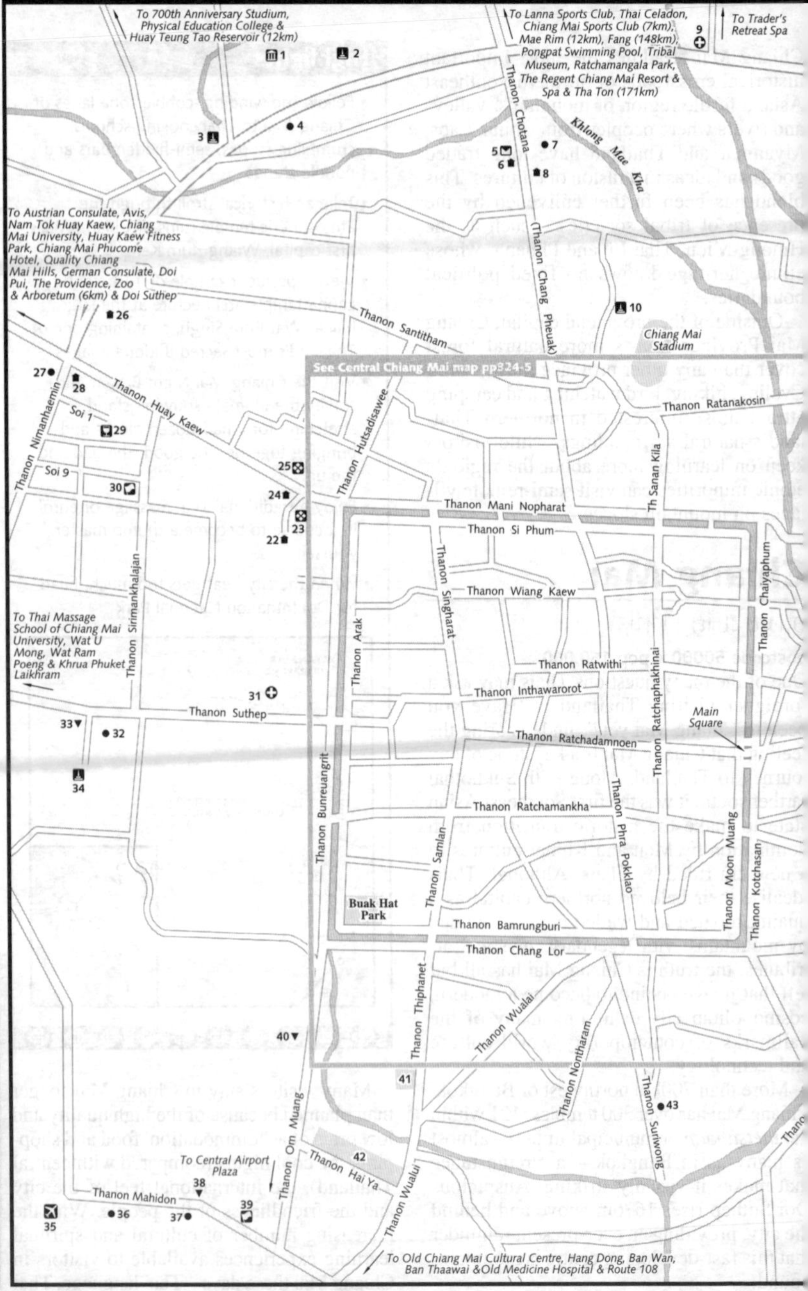
To 700th Anniversary Studium, Physical Education College & Huay Teung Tao Reservoir (12km)
To Lanna Sports Club, Thai Celadon, Chiang Mai Sports Club (7km), Mae Rim (12km), Fang (148km), Pongpat Swimming Pool, Tribal Museum, Ratchamangala Park, The Regent Chiang Mai Resort & Spa & Tha Ton (171km)
To Trader's Retreat Spa
Thanon Chotana
(Thanon Chang Pheuak)
Khlong Mae Kha
To Austrian Consulate, Avis, Nam Tok Huay Kaew, Chiang Mai University, Huay Kaew Fitness Park, Chiang Mai Phucome Hotel, Quality Chiang Mai Hills, German Consulate, Doi Pui, The Providence, Zoo & Arboretum (6km) & Doi Suthep
Thanon Santitham
Chiang Mai Stadium
See Central Chiang Mai map pp324-5
Thanon Nimanhaemin
Soi 1
Thanon Huay Kaew
Thanon Hutsadisawee
Thanon Ratanakosin
Soi 9
Th Sanan Kila
Thanon Mani Nopharat
Thanon Si Phum
Thanon Singharat
Thanon Sirimankhalajan
Thanon Wiang Kaew
Thanon Chaiyaphum
To Thai Massage School of Chiang Mai University, Wat U Mong, Wat Ram Poeng & Khrua Phuket Laikhram
Thanon Arak
Thanon Ratwithi
Thanon Inthawarorot
Thanon Suthep
Main Square
Thanon Ratchadamnoen
Thanon Ratchaphakhinai
Thanon Bunreuangrit
Thanon Phra Pokklao
Thanon Ratchamankha
Thanon Samlan
Thanon Moon Muang
Thanon Kotchasan
Buak Hat Park
Thanon Bamrungburi
Thanon Chang Lor
Thanon Thiphanet
Thanon Wualai
Thanon Nontharam
Thanon Suriwong
Thanon Om Muang
To Central Airport Plaza
Thanon Hai Ya
Thanon Wualui
Thanon Mahidon
To Old Chiang Mai Cultural Centre, Hang Dong, Ban Wan, Ban Thaawai &Old Medicine Hospital & Route 108

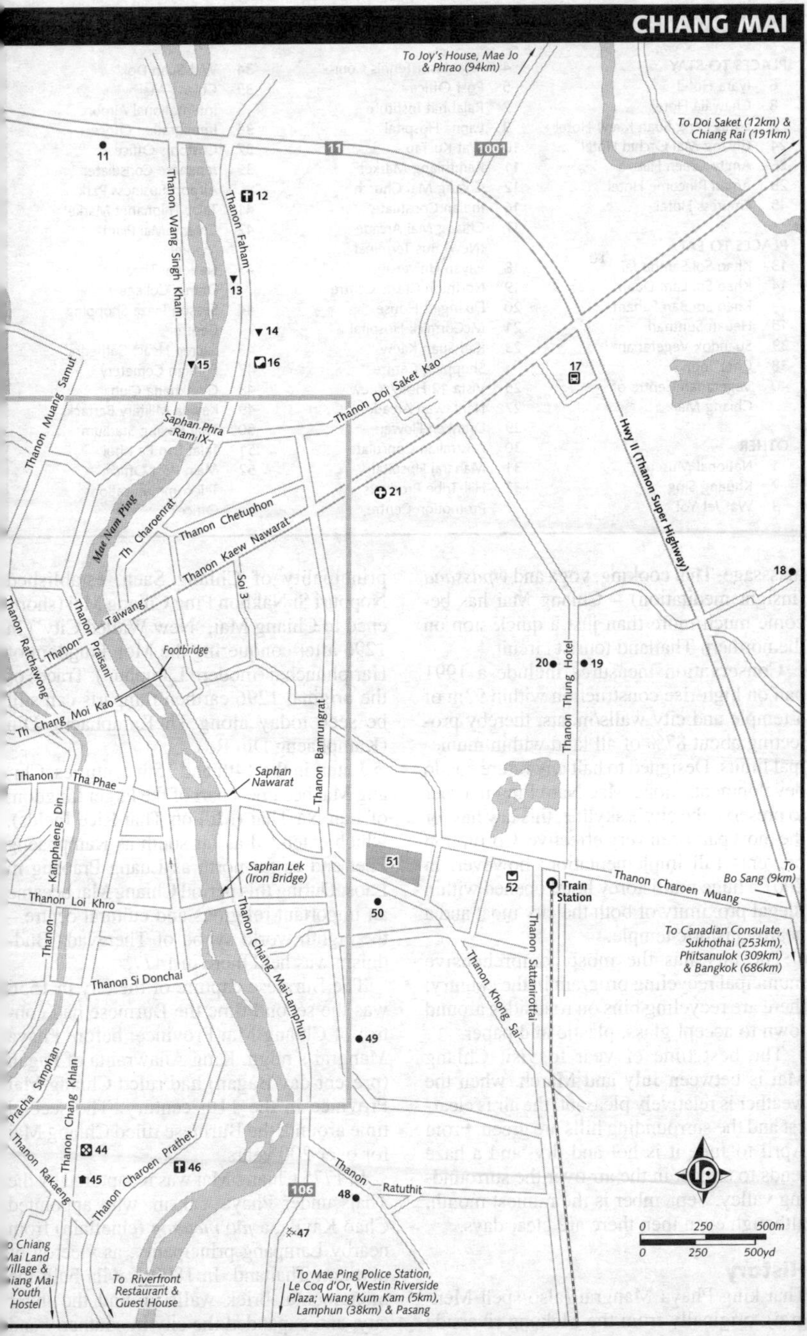
CHIANG MAI
To Joy's House, Mae Jo & Phrao (94km)
To Doi Saket (12km) & Chiang Rai (191km)
11
1001
Thanon Wang Singh Kham
Thanon Faham
Thanon Muang Samut
Thanon Doi Saket Kao
Saphan Phra Ram IX
Mae Nam Ping
Th Charoenrat
Thanon Chetuphon
Thanon Kaew Nawarat
Soi 3
Hwy 11 (Thanon Super Highway)
Thanon Ratchawong
Thanon Taiwang
Thanon Praisani
Footbridge
Th Chang Moi Kao
Thanon Tha Phae
Saphan Nawarat
Thanon Bamrungrat
Thanon Thung Hotel
Thanon Kamphaeng Din
Saphan Lek (Iron Bridge)
Thanon Loi Khro
Thanon Chiang Mai-Lamphun
Train Station
Thanon Charoen Muang
To Bo Sang (9km)
To Canadian Consulate, Sukhothai (253km), Phitsanulok (309km) & Bangkok (686km)
Thanon Sattanirottai
Thanon Khong Sai
Thanon Si Donchai
Pracha Samphan
Thanon Chang Khlan
Thanon Rakaeng
Thanon Charoen Prathet
Thanon Ratuthit
106
To Chiang Mai Land Village & Chiang Mai Youth Hostel
To Riverfront Restaurant & Guest House
To Mae Ping Police Station, Le Coq d'Or, Westin Riverside Plaza; Wiang Kum Kam (5km), Lamphun (38km) & Pasang
0 250 500m
0 250 500yd
11 12 13 14 15 16 17 18 19 20 21 44 45 46 47 48 49 50 51 52

CHIANG MAI

PLACES TO STAY
6 Iyara Hotel
8 Chawala Hotel
22 Lotus Pang Suan Kaew Hotel
24 Chiang Mai Orchid Hotel
26 Amity Green Hills
28 Amari Rincome Hotel
45 Empress Hotel

PLACES TO EAT
13 Khao Soi Samoe Jai
14 Khao Soi Lam Duan; Khao Soi Ban Faham
15 Heuan Sunthari
33 Suandok Vegetarian
38 Chez John
40 Vegetarian Centre of Chiang Mai

OTHER
1 National Museum
2 Khuang Sing
3 Wat Jet Yot
4 Anantasiri Tennis Courts
5 Post Office
7 Rajabhat Institute
9 Lanna Hospital
10 Wat Ku Tao
11 Kamthiang Market
12 Chiang Mai Church
16 Indian Consulate
17 Chiang Mai Arcade (New) Bus Terminal
18 Payap University
19 Northern Crafts Centre
20 Duangjitt House
21 McCormick Hospital
23 Kad Suan Kaew Shopping Centre
25 Vista 12 Huay Kaew
27 Nantawan Arcade
29 Drunken Flower
30 Australian Consulate
31 Maharaj Hospital
32 Hill-Tribe Products Promotion Centre
34 Wat Suan Dok
35 Chiang Mai International Airport
36 Immigration Office
37 Customs Office
39 Japanese Consulate; Airport Business Park
41 Talat Thiphanet Market
42 Chiang Mai Plant Market
43 National Theatre; Drama College
44 Season Plaza Shopping Centre
46 Sacred Heart Cathedral
47 Foreign Cemetery
48 Gymkhana Club
49 Kawila Military Barracks
50 Thai Boxing Stadium
51 Talat San Pa Khoi
52 Main Post Office; Telecommunications Office

masssage, Thai cooking, yoga and *vipassana* (insight meditation) – Chiang Mai has become much more than just a quick stop on the northern Thailand tourist circuit.

Conservation measures include a 1991 ban on high-rise construction within 93m of a temple and city walls/moats, thereby protecting about 87% of all land within municipal limits. Designed to halt any future condo developments along Mae Nam Ping in order to preserve the city's skyline, this law has for the most part been very effective. Corruption prevents full implementation; however, in 2001 a huge multistorey hotel opened within illegal proximity of both the city moat and a nearby historic temple.

The city has the most comprehensive municipal recycling program in the country; there are recycling bins on roadsides around town to accept glass, plastic and paper.

The best time of year to visit Chiang Mai is between July and March, when the weather is relatively pleasant, the air is clearest and the surrounding hills are green. From April to June it is hot and dry, and a haze tends to collect in the air over the surrounding valley. September is the rainiest month, although even then there are clear days.

History

Thai king Phaya Mangrai (also spelt Mengrai), originally from the Mekong riverside principality of Chiang Saen, established Nopburi Si Nakhon Ping Chiang Mai (shortened to Chiang Mai, 'New Walled City') in 1296 after conquering the Mon kingdom of Hariphunchai (modern Lamphun). Traces of the original 1296 earthen ramparts can still be seen today along Th Kamphaeng Din (Kamphaeng Din Rd).

Later, in the 14th and 15th centuries, Chiang Mai became a part of the larger kingdom of Lan Na Thai (Million Thai Rice Fields), which extended as far south as Kamphaeng Phet and as far north as Luang Prabang in Laos. During this period Chiang Mai became an important religious and cultural centre – the eighth world synod of Theravada Buddhism was held there in 1477.

The Burmese capture of the city in 1556 was the second time the Burmese had control of Chiang Mai Province: before Phaya Mangrai's reign, King Anawrahta of Pagan (present-day Bagan) had ruled Chiang Mai Province in the 11th century. The second time around, the Burmese ruled Chiang Mai for over 200 years.

In 1775 Chiang Mai was recaptured by the Thais under Phaya Taksin, who appointed Chao Kavila, a *jâo meuang* (chieftain) from nearby Lampang principality, as viceroy of northern Thailand. In 1800 Kavila built the monumental brick walls around the inner city, and expanded the city in southerly and easterly directions, establishing a river port at the end of what is today Th Tha Phae (*thâa phae* means 'raft pier').

Under Kavila, Chiang Mai became an important regional trade centre. Many of the later Shan- and Burmese-style temples seen around the city were built by wealthy teak merchants who emigrated from Burma during the late 19th century.

The completion of the northern railway to Chiang Mai in 1921 finally linked the north with central Thailand. In 1927 King Rama VII and Queen Rambaibani rode into the city at the head of an 84-elephant caravan, becoming the first central Thai monarchs to visit the north, and in 1933 Chiang Mai officially became a province of Siam.

Long before tourists began visiting the region, Chiang Mai was an important centre for handcrafted pottery, umbrellas, weaving, silverwork and woodcarving. By the mid-1960s tourism had replaced commercial trade as Chiang Mai's number one source of outside revenue

Orientation

The old city of Chiang Mai is a neat square bounded by moats and partial walls. Th Moon Muang (Mun Meuang), along the eastern moat, is the centre for inexpensive accommodation and places to eat. Th Tha Phae runs straight from the middle of this side and crosses Mae Nam Ping, where it changes into Th Charoen Muang.

The train station and the main post office are farther down Th Charoen Muang, a fair distance from the city centre. There are several bus terminals around Chiang Mai, so make sure you go to the right one.

Several of Chiang Mai's important temples are within the moat area, but there are others to the north and west. Doi Suthep rises up to the west of the city and its temples give you a fine view over the city.

Maps Finding your way around Chiang Mai is fairly simple, although a copy of Nancy Chandler's *Map of Chiang Mai,* sold in bookshops, is a very worthwhile 150B investment. It shows all the main points of interest, shopping venues and oddities that you'd be most unlikely to stumble upon by yourself. *Groovy Map Chiang Mai Map'n'Guide* adds Thai script and more nightspots.

Information

Tourist Offices Chiang Mai has a friendly **TAT office** *(☎ 0 5324 8604; Th Chiang Mai-Lamphun; open 8am-4.30pm daily)*, opposite the Saphan Lek (Iron Bridge) just south of Saphan Nawarat.

Consulates Chiang Mai has a number of foreign-consular posts where you may be able to arrange visas. The Indian consulate is a familiar stopping-off point for travellers on their way to India; it takes about four days to process a visa.

Australia (☎ 0 5322 1083, fax 0 5321 9726) 165 Th Sirimankhalajan
Canada (☎ 0 5322 4851, 0 5322 4861, ☎/fax 0 5385 0147) 151 Th Chiang Mai-Lampang (Hwy 11)
China (☎ 0 5327 6125, 0 5320 0424, fax 0 5327 4614) 111 Th Chang Lor
France (☎ 0 5328 1466, 0 5327 5277, fax 0 5382 1039) 138 Th Charoen Prathet
Germany (☎/fax 0 5383 8735, e dekonsul@loxinfo.co.th) 199/163 Mu 3, Baan Nai Fan 2, Th Kan Khlong Chonlaprathan
India (☎ 0 5324 3066, 0 5324 2491, fax 0 5324 7879) 344 Th Faham (Charoen Rat)
UK & Northern Ireland (☎ 0 5326 3015, fax 0 5326 3016) 198 Th Bamrungrat
USA (☎ 0 5325 2629–31, fax 0 5325 2633) 387 Th Wichayanon

Immigration The Thai **immigration office** *(☎ 0 5320 1755-6)* is off Rte 1141 (Th Mahidon) near the airport.

Money All major Thai banks have several branches throughout Chiang Mai, many of them along Th Tha Phae; most are open 8.30am to 3.30pm.

In the well-touristed areas – for example, the Chiang Mai Night Bazaar, Th Tha Phae and Th Moon Muang – you'll find automatic teller machines (ATMs) and bank-operated foreign-exchange booths, open as late as 8pm.

SK Moneychanger *(☎ 0 5327 1864; 73/8 Th Charoen Prathet; open 8am-6pm Mon-Sat)*, near the Diamond Riverside Hotel, specialises in cash exchanges in several currencies (travellers cheques are also accepted) – sometimes at better rates than the banks.

If you need to send or receive money by wire, **Western Union** *(☎ 0 5322 4979, Central*

CENTRAL CHIANG MAI

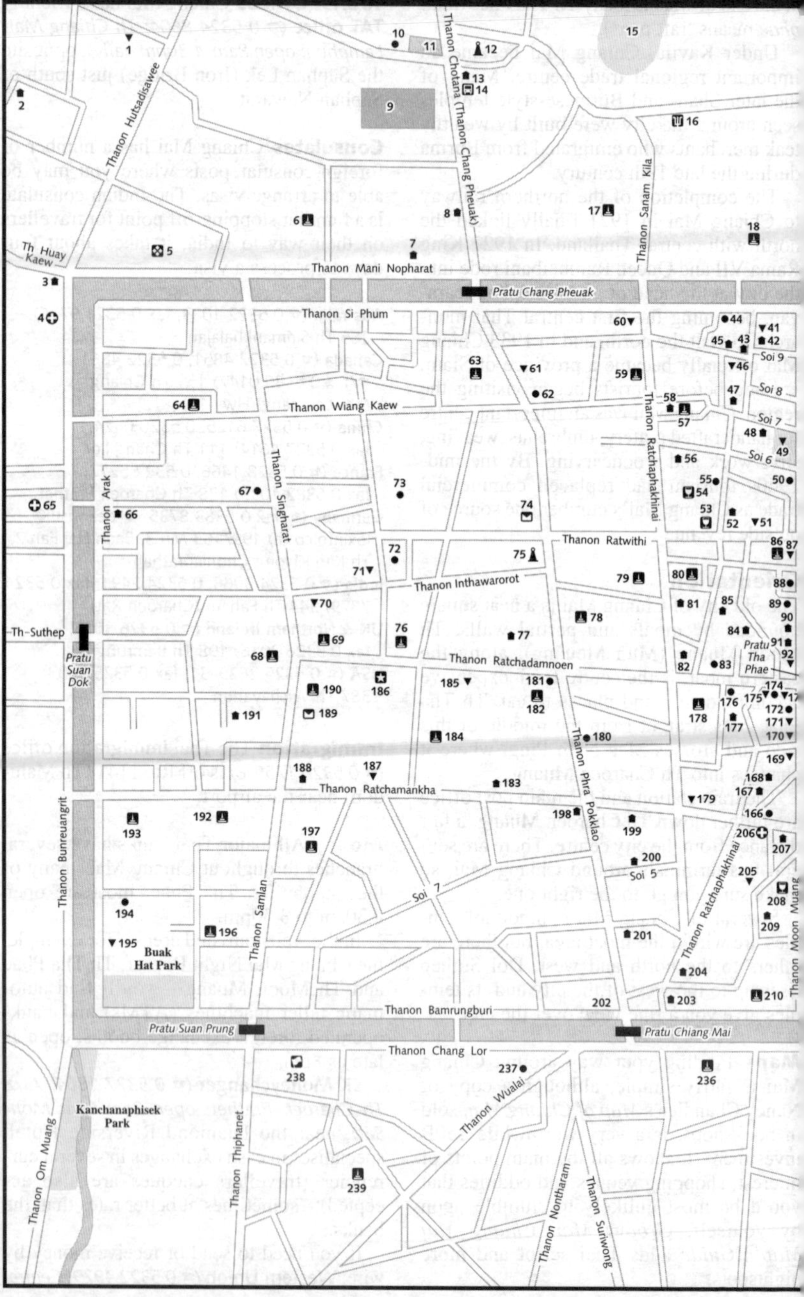

CENTRAL CHIANG MAI

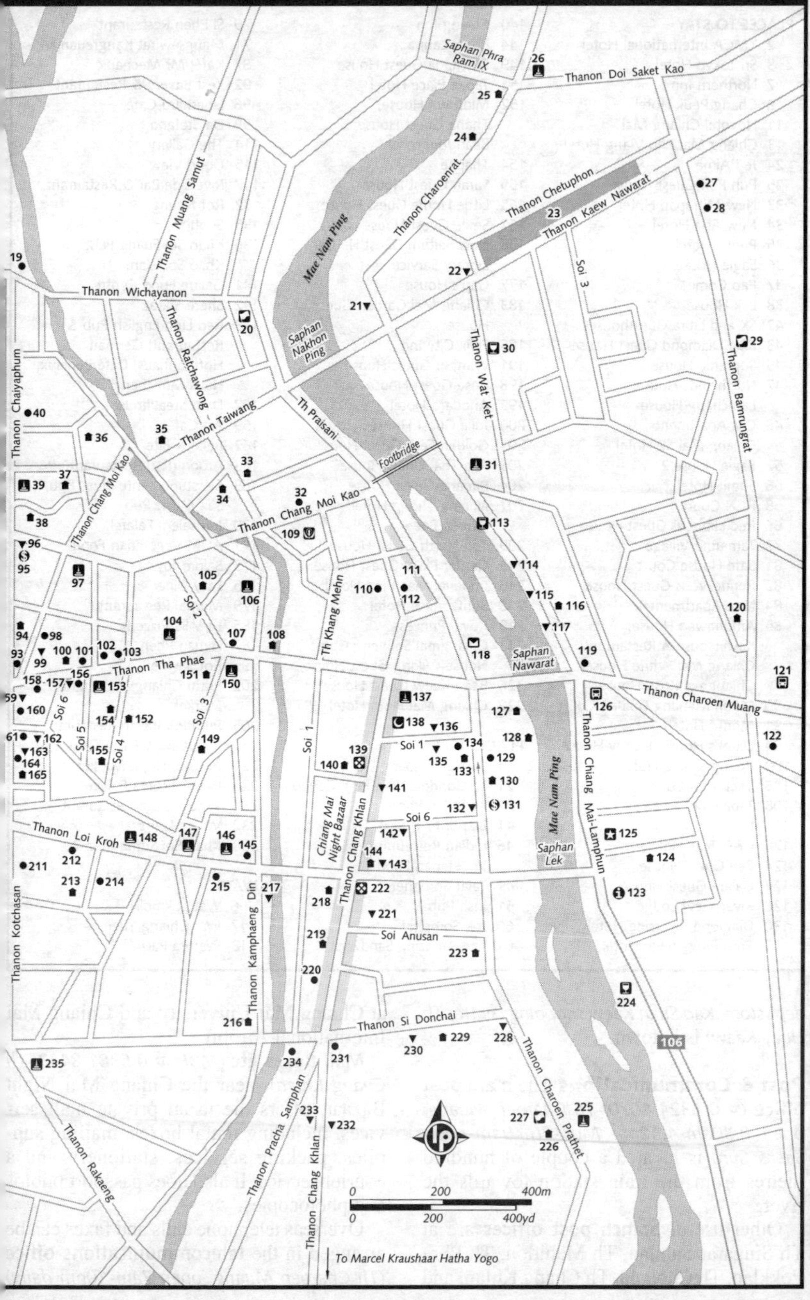

CHIANG MAI PROVINCE

CENTRAL CHIANG MAI

PLACES TO STAY
2 YMCA International Hotel
3 Sri Tokyo Hotel
7 Northern Inn
8 Chang Peuk Hotel
11 Novotel Chiang Mai
13 Chiang Mai Phu Viang Hotel
24 Je t'Aime
25 Pun Pun Guest House
33 New Mitrapap Hotel
34 New Asia Hotel
35 Prince Hotel
36 Eagle House 1
37 Pao Come
38 Lek House
42 SK and Libra Guesthouses
43 Blue Diamond Guest House
45 Supreme House
47 Northlands House; Lamchang House
48 CM Apartments; Chiang Mai SP Hotel
52 Eagle House 2
56 Sumit Hotel
58 RCN Court
66 Red Hibiscus Guest House
77 Tamarind Village
81 Safe House Court
82 Rendezvous Guest House
84 Nice Apartment
85 Amphawan House; Kavil House & Restaurant; Chiang Mai White House; Chiangmai Kristi House
90 Moon Meuang Golden Court
91 Montri Hotel
94 Daret's House; Happy House
100 Roong Ruang Hotel
105 Veerachai Court
108 Tapae Inn
116 Le Pont
120 C&C Teak House
124 Ben Guest House
127 Galare Guest House
128 River View Lodge
130 Diamond Riverside Hotel
133 Porn Ping Tower Hotel
140 Chiang Inn
144 Royal Lanna
149 Ratchada Guest House
151 Tapae Place Hotel
152 Midtown House; Thana Guest House; Baan Jongcome
154 Thapae
155 Sarah Guest House
165 Little Home Guest House
167 Smile Guest House
168 New Saitum Guest House; Library Service
177 Gap's House
183 Chiang Mai Garden Guest House
188 Felix City Inn
191 Wanasit Guest House
198 Rose Guest House
199 Anodard Hotel
200 Julie Guest House
201 Golden Fern Guest House
203 Pha Thai Guest House
204 Banana Guest House
207 Muang Thong Hotel; Queen Bee
209 Top North Guest House
213 Center Place Guest House
216 Imperial Mae Ping Hotel
218 Suriwongse Hotel
219 Royal Princess
223 Chiangmai Souvenir Guest House (Viking Guest House)
226 Baan Kaew Guest House
229 Chiang Mai Plaza Hotel

PLACES TO EAT
1 Sa-Nga Choeng Doi
21 La Gondola; Rim Ping Condo
22 Khao Soi Prince
41 Biaporn
46 Indian Restaurant Vegetarian Food
49 Talat Somphet
51 Irish Pub
60 Jok Somphet
61 The Amazing Sandwich
70 Si Phen Restaurant
71 Mangsawirat Kangreuanjan
87 Kafé; Mr Mechanic
92 Zest Bakery & Restaurant
96 Libernard Café
99 Da Stefano
114 The Gallery
115 Good View
117 Riverside Bar & Restaurant
132 Rot Neung
135 Sophia
136 Khao Soi Fuang Fah; Khao Soi Islam
141 Galare Food Centre
142 Shere Shiraz
143 Red Lion English Pub & Restaurant; German Hofbräuhaus; Café Benelux; Haus München
157 Dara Steakhouse
159 Art Café
162 Bake & Bite
163 Aroon (Rai) Restaurant
169 Bierstube; Pinte Blues Pub; Sax Music Pub
170 Jerusalem Falafel
171 AUM Vegetarian Food
173 Salom Joy
175 Easy Diner
179 Mitmai Restaurant
185 La Villa Pizzeria
187 Heuan Phen
195 Rot Sawoei
202 Pratu Chiang Mai Night Market
205 Pum Pui Italian Restaurant
217 Kuaytiaw Kai Tun Coke
221 Anusan Night Market
228 Piccola Roma Palace
230 Whole Earth Restaurant
232 Vihara Liangsan
233 Khao Soi Suthasinee 2

WATS
6 Wat Lokmoli
17 Wat Chiang Yuen
18 Wat Pa Pao

dept store, Kad Suan Kaew shopping centre, Th Huay Kaew) is in town.

Post & Communications The **main post office** *(☎ 0 5324 1070; Th Charoen Muang; open 8.30am-4.30pm Mon-Fri, 9am-noon Sat & Sun)* is located a couple of hundred metres from the train station towards the river.

Other useful **branch post offices** are at Th Singarat/Samlan, Th Mahidon, Th Phra Pokklao, Th Chotana, Th Chang Khlan, and at Chiang Mai University and Chiang Mai International Airport.

Mail Boxes Etc *(MBE; ☎ 0 5381 8433; Th Chang Khlan)*, near the Chiang Mai Night Bazaar, offers the usual private mail services, including rental boxes, mailing supplies, packing services, stationery and a courier service. It also does passport photos and photocopies.

Overseas telephone calls and faxes can be arranged in the **telecommunications office** *(Th Charoen Muang; open 7am-10pm daily)*

CENTRAL CHIANG MAI

26 Wat Chetuphon
31 Wat Ketkaram
39 Wat Chomphu
57 Wat Lam Chang
59 Wat Chiang Man
63 Wat Hua Khwang
64 Wat Pa Phrao Nai
68 Wat Phra Singh
69 Wat Thung Yu
76 Wat Chai Phra Kiat
78 Wat Duang Dii
79 Wat U Mong Klang Wiang
80 Wat Pan Ping
86 Wat Dok Euang
97 Wat U Sai Kham
104 Wat Chetawan
106 Wat Saen Fang
137 Wat Upakhut
146 Wat Chang Khong
147 Wat Loi Khraw
148 Wat Phan Tawng
150 Wat Bupparam
153 Wat Mahawan
178 Wat Phan An
182 Wat Phan Tao
184 Wat Chedi Luang
190 Wat Si Koet
192 Wat Meun Ngoen Kong
193 Wat Meh Thang
196 Wat Pheuak Hong
197 Wat Phra Jao Mengrai
210 Wat Sai Mun Myanmar
225 Wat Chaimongkhon
235 Wat Phuak Chang
236 Wat Muang Mang
239 Wat Sisuphan

OTHER

4 Chiang Mai Ram Hospital
5 Computer Plaza
9 Talat Thanin
10 Velocity
12 White Elephant Monument
14 Chang Pheuak (White Elephant) Bus Terminal (Provincial Buses)
15 Chiang Mai Stadium
16 Devi Mandir Chiang Mai
19 Big Bikes
20 US Consulate
23 Prince Royal's College
27 Thai Tribal Crafts
28 British Council
29 UK & Northern Ireland Consulate
30 Warm-Up
32 Chip Aun Thong Dispensary
40 Ban Nit Massage
44 Bike & Bite
50 Mr Kom
53 Yoy Pocket
54 Rasta Café
55 Baan Thai
62 Thai Airways International (THAI) Office
65 Malaria Centre
67 School
72 District Offices
73 Chiang Mai Central Prison
74 Post Office
75 Anusawari Sam Kasat
83 American University Alumni (AUA) Library
88 North Wheels
89 SP Bike Rental
93 Elephant Lightfoot
95 Money Exchange
98 Gecko Books; Backstreet Bookshop
101 City Silk
102 Ratana's Kitchen
103 Book Zone
107 Lost Heavans
109 Namdhari Sikh Temple
110 Talat Warorot
111 Flower Market
112 Talat Lamyai
113 Le Brasserie
118 Mae Ping Post Office
119 Raintree Resource Centre
121 Buses to Bo Sang & San Kamphaeng
122 San Pa Khoi Market
123 TAT
125 Tourist Police
126 Buses to Lamphun, Pasang, Chiang Rai & Lampang
129 Wild Planet-Contact Travel
131 SK Moneychanger
134 Roti Vendor Stall
138 Matsayit Chiang Mai
139 Chiang Inn Plaza
145 Hangdong Rattan
156 Broadway Photo
158 Journey Car Rent
160 Suriwongse Plaza; Dang Bike Hire
161 Shaman Books
164 Pop Rent-A-Car
166 Lost Book Shop
172 Chiang Mai Cookery School
174 Lek Chaiya Massage
176 American University Alumni (AUA)
180 Lanna Music
181 Chiang Mai Thai Language Center
186 Police (Inside the quadrangle on Th Ratchadamnoen)
189 Post Office
194 Mengrai Kilns
206 Mungkala
208 H3 Pub
211 DK Book House
212 Woven Dreams
214 Siam Thai Cookery School
215 Success Silk Shop
220 Mail Boxes etc
222 Chiangmai Pavilion
224 Gi Gi's
227 Alliance Française; French Consulate
231 Lanna Nakorn 1296
234 Suriwong Book Centre
237 Chiang Mai Flying Club
238 Chinese Consulate

around the side and upstairs from the main post office. International calls can also be made from **MBE** *(Th Chang Khlan)*. A few Internet cafés are able to arrange inexpensive Internet phone hook-ups.

Home Country Direct phones, with easy one-button connection to foreign operators in a number of countries around the world, are available at: Chiang Inn Plaza, 100/1 Th Chang Khlan, near the Chiang Mai Night Bazaar; Chiang Mai International Airport; the main post office on Th Charoen Muang; the Thai Airways International (THAI) office on 240 Th Phra Pokklao; and the TAT office on Th Chaing Mai-Lamphun.

The list of places to log on in Chiang Mai is rapidly growing and you'll find plenty of Internet centres along the following streets: Tha Phae, Moon Muang, Ratchadamnoen, Ratchadamri, Huay Kaew, Chang Khlan and Suthep.

Digital Resources The Chiang Mai Online website (W www.chiangmai-online.com) has an overall uneven information flow, although the accommodation listings are quite comprehensive and include room rates for guesthouses and hotels. Chiang Mai City Life (W www.chiangmainews.com) shows great potential, and posts articles on culture and art.

Bookshops If you're mainly travelling around northern Thailand, check out Lonely Planet's *Chiang Mai & Northern Thailand* guide. Local English expat Oliver Hargreave has written a colourful and authoritative guidebook to Chiang Mai entitled *Exploring Chiang Mai*, available around town for 350B.

Caravans of Northern Thailand

Dating from at least the 15th century, Chinese-Muslim caravans from Yunnan Province (China) used Chiang Mai as a 'back-door' entry and exit for commodities transported between China and the Indian Ocean port of Mawlamyaing (Moulmein) in Myanmar (Burma) for international seagoing trade.

British merchant Ralph Fitch, the first person to leave an English-language chronicle of Southeast Asian travel, wrote of his 1583 to 1591 journey through Thailand: 'To the town of Jamahey (Chiang Mai) come many merchants out of China, and bring a great store of Muske, Gold, Silver, and many other things of China worke.'

The main means of transport for the Yunnanese caravaneers were mules and ponies, beasts of burden that contrasted with the Southeast Asian preference for oxen, water buffalo and elephants. The Chinese Muslims who dominated the caravan traffic owed their preferred mode of conveyance, as well as their religious orientation, to mass conversions effected during the Mongol invasions of Yunnan in the 13th century. The equestrian nature of the caravans led the Thais to call the Yunnanese *jiin haw*, 'galloping Chinese'.

Three main routes emanated from the predominantly Thai Xishuangbanna (Sipsongpanna) region in southern Yunnan into northern Thailand, and onward to the Gulf of Martaban via Mawlamyaing. The western route proceeded southwest from Simao to Chiang Rung (now known as Jinghong), then went on through Chiang Tung (Kengtung) to Fang or Chiang Rai.

The middle route went south to Mengla near the border of China and Laos, crossed Laos via Luang Nam Tha, and entered Thailand at Chiang Khong (which was an independent principality at the time) on the Mekong River. At this point the middle route merged with the western route at Chiang Rai Province, and formed a single route through Chiang Mai to Mae Sariang, a line that continued along the Salawin River to Mawlamyaing in present-day Myanmar.

The third route went from Simao to Phongsali in northern Laos then via Luang Prabang (Laos), crossing the Mekong River to Nan and Phrae before curving northwestward via Lampang and Lamphun to Chiang Mai.

Principal southward exports along these routes included silk, opium, tea, dried fruit, lacquerware, musk, ponies and mules, while northward the caravans brought gold, copper, cotton, edible birds' nests, betel nut, tobacco and ivory. By the end of the 19th century many artisans from China, northern Burma and Laos had settled in the area to produce crafts for the steady flow of regional trade. The city's original transhipment point for such trade movements was a market district known as Ban Haw, a stone's throw from today's Night Bazaar in Chiang Mai.

Chiang Mai has several bookshops, the biggest being **Suriwong Book Centre** *(☎ 0 5328 1052; 54 Th Si Donchai)* and **DK Book House** *(Th Kotchasan)*. **Bookazine** *(☎ 0 5328 1370)*, in the basement of Chiang Inn Plaza, carries European and American newspapers and magazines, travel guides, maps and other English-language publications. A smaller place with a decent selection of books is The **Book Zone** *(☎ 0 5325 2418; Th Tha Phae)*, directly opposite Wat Mahawan.

The **American University Alumni (AUA) library** *(24 Th Ratchadamnoen; open 10am-6pm Mon-Fri, 9am-1pm Sat)* has one of the most comprehensive collections of English-language books and periodicals in Chiang Mai. Entry requires an annual 400B membership fee (100B for AUA students, 200B for other students) or a one-month temporary 150B membership fee for visitors. The **British Council** *(☎ 0 5324 2103, fax 0 5324 4781; 198 Th Bamrungrat)* also has a small English-language library.

Lost Book Shop *(34/3 Th Ratchamankha)*, on the northern side of this road (between Th Moon Muang and Th Ratchaphakhinai), and **Backstreet Bookshop** *(7/8 Th Chang Moi Kao)* have good used-book selections, going far beyond the usual airport pulp to include many books on arts and culture, as well as hardcovers. Most books for sale are in English, but books in French and German are also available. **Gecko Books** *(Th Chiang Moi Kao)*, directly behind Daret's House, is also very good. This section of Th Chang Moi Kao is quickly becoming a used-books district with **Hobo Books** and at least one other shop in the same area.

Shaman Books *(☎ 0 5327 5272; 2 Th Kotchasan)*, near the moat and Pratu Tha Phae, specialises in travel, fiction and spirituality.

Newpapers & Magazines The tourism-oriented *Guidelines Chiang Mai* and *Welcome to Chiangmai & Chiangrai* (both free) contain the usual assortment of brief cultural essays and maps embedded among stacks of advertisements for bars, pubs, restaurants and antique shops. Both have bus, train and airline timetables, which are updated about once a year. *Chang Puak/L'Elephant Blanc* appears occasionally and is printed almost entirely in French.

Oriented more towards residents than tourists, the monthly *Chiang Mai City Life* runs articles on local culture and politics, as well as a listing of local events and regular columns. The *Chiangmai Mail*, a new weekly newspaper affiliated with the *Pattaya Mail*, is also a good source of local news.

Film & Processing Outside of Bangkok, Chiang Mai has the best supply of quality photographic film in the country. **Broadway Photo** *(☎ 0 5325 1253; Th Tha Phae)*, about 100m east of Pratu Tha Phae, has a good selection of slide film, including hard-to-find (in Chiang Mai) Fujichrome slide film. Souvenir print processing is fine, but professional photographers will do better to wait until they're in Bangkok or back home for processing, as Chiang Mai's photo labs are notoriously unreliable.

Cultural Centres Several foreign cultural centres in Chiang Mai host film, music, dance, theatre and other cultural events.

Alliance Française (☎ 0 5327 5277) 138 Th Charoen Prathet. French films (subtitled in English) are screened at 4.30pm every Tuesday and at 8pm on Friday; admission is free to members, 30B to general public.

American University Alumni (AUA; ☎ 0 5327 8407, 0 5321 1377) 73 Th Ratchadamnoen. AUA offers English and Thai language courses (for details see Language & Culture under Courses later in this chapter).

British Council (☎ 0 5324 2103) 198 Th Bamrungrat. Features a small English-language library and offers the services of an honorary consul.

Medical Services The **McCormick Hospital** *(☎ 0 5324 1311, 0 5324 0832; Th Kaew Nawarat)*, an old missionary hospital, is good for minor treatment and is not expensive. As at most hospitals in Chiang Mai, many of the doctors speak English. **Chiang Mai Ram Hospital** *(☎ 0 5322 4861; Th Bunreuangrit)*, near the Sri Tokyo Hotel, is the most modern hospital in town. It's full of gleaming new equipment and costs a bit more than the other Chiang Mai hospitals.

Also recommended is the **Lanna Hospital** *(☎ 0 5335 7234; Th Superhighway)*, and **The Malaria Centre** *(☎ 0 5322 1529; 18 Th Bunreuangrit)*, which can do blood checks for malaria.

Chip Aun Thong Dispensary *(☎ 0 5323 4187; 48-52 Th Chang Moi)* offers traditional Chinese medicine and has a Chinese doctor on staff. **Mungkala** *(☎ 0 5327 8494, 0 5320 8431, fax 0 5320 8432; e mungkala@cm.ksc.co.th; 21-25 Th Ratchamankha)* is another good traditional Chinese clinic that offers acupuncture, massage and herbal therapy.

Emergency Chiang Mai's **tourist police** *(☎ 0 5324 8130, 0 5324 8974, emergency ☎ 1155; Th Chiang Mai-Lamphun; open 6am-midnight daily)* has an office about 100m north of the Tourism Authority of Thailand (TAT) office. Call ☎ 1155 in case of emergency (24 hours).

THINGS TO SEE

Wat Chiang Man

วัดเชียงมั่น

The oldest *wát* (temple) in the city, Wat Chiang Man was founded in 1296 and features typical northern Thai temple architecture, with massive teak columns inside the *bòt* (central sanctuary, called *sǐm* in northern Thai).

Two important Buddha images are kept in a glass cabinet in the smaller sanctuary to the right of the *sǐm*. The Phra Sila, a marble bas-relief Buddha standing 20cm to 30cm high, is supposed to have come from Sri Lanka or India 2500 years ago, but since no Buddha images were produced anywhere before around 2000 years ago, it must have arrived later. The well-known Phra Satang Man, a crystal seated Buddha image, was shuttled back and forth between Thailand and Laos like the Emerald Buddha. It's thought to have come from Lavo (Lopburi) 1800 years ago and stands just 10cm high.

The *sǐm* containing the venerated images is open 9am to 5pm daily. Wat Chiang Man is off Th Ratchaphakhinai in the northeastern corner of the old city.

Wat Phra Singh

วัดพระสิงห์

Started by King Pa Yo in 1345, the *wíhǎan* (large hall in a Thai temple) that houses the Phra Singh image was completed between 1385 and 1400. Architecturally it's a perfect example of the classic northern Thai or Lanna style followed during this period from Chiang Mai to Luang Prabang. The Phra Singh Buddha supposedly comes from Sri Lanka, but it is not particularly Singhalese in style. As it is identical to two images in Nakhon Si Thammarat and Bangkok, and has quite a travel history (Sukhothai, Ayuthaya, Chiang Rai, Luang Prabang – the usual itinerary for a travelling Buddha image, involving much royal trickery), no-one really knows which image is the real one, nor can anyone document its place of origin. The *sǐm* was finished in about 1600.

Wat Phra Singh *(☎ 0 5381 4164)* is at the end of Th Ratchadamnoen near Pratu Suan Dok.

Wat Chedi Luang

วัดเจดีย์หลวง

This temple complex *(☎ 0 5327 8595)* occupies a large piece of land off Th Phra Pokklao, surrounding a very large and venerable Lanna-style *chedi* (stupa) dating from 1441. It is now in partial ruins, damaged by either a 16th-century earthquake or the cannon fire of King Taksin in 1775 during the recapture of Chiang Mai from the Burmese. The Phra Kaew ('Emerald' Buddha), now in Bangkok's Wat Phra Kaew, sat in the eastern niche here in 1475.

A restoration of the great *chedi*, financed by Unesco and the Japanese government, has so far thankfully stopped short of creating a new spire, since no-one knows for sure how the original superstructure looked. New Buddha images have been placed in three of the four directional niches.

New porticoes and *naga* (serpent being) guardians for the chedi lack the finesse of the originals. On the southern side of the monument, six elephant sculptures in the pediment can be seen. Five are cement restorations; only the one on the far right – without ears and trunk – is original brick and stucco.

The *làk meuang* (guardian deity post) for the city is within the wát compound in the small building left of the main entrance.

Wat Phan Tao

วัดพันเตา

Diagonally adjacent to Wat Chedi Luang, this wát *(☎ 0 5381 4689)* contains a large, old teak *wíhǎan* that is one of the unsung treasures of Chiang Mai. Constructed of moulded wooden teak panels fitted together and supported by 28 gargantuan teak pillars, the *wíhǎan* features *naga* bargeboards inset with coloured mirror mosaic. On display inside are old temple bells, some ceramics, a few old northern-style gilded wooden Buddhas and antique cabinets stacked with old palm-leaf manuscripts. Also in the compound are some old monastic quarters.

There's a wall dividing Wat Phan Tao from Wat Chedi Luang, but you can walk through small gates from one to the other.

Wat Jet Yot

วัดเจ็ดยอด

Out of town on the northern highway loop near the Chiang Mai National Museum, this wát (☎ *0 5321 9483)* was built in the mid-15th century to host the eighth World Buddhist Council in 1477. Based on the design of the Mahabodhi Temple in Bodhgaya, India, the proportions for the Chiang Mai version are quite different from the Indian original, so it was probably modelled from a small votive tablet depicting the Mahabodhi in distorted perspective. The seven spires *(jèt yâwt)* represent the seven weeks Buddha was supposed to have spent in Bodhgaya after his enlightenment.

On the outer walls of the old *wíhăan* is some of the original stucco relief. There's an adjacent stupa of undetermined age and a very glossy *wíhăan*. The entire area is surrounded by well-kept lawns. It's a pleasant, relaxing temple to visit, although curiously it's not very active in terms of worship.

Wat Jet Yot is a bit too far from the city centre to reach on foot; by bicycle it's easy or you can take a red *săwngthăew* (pickup truck; also written *songthaew*).

Wat Suan Dok

วัดสวนดอก

Phaya Keu Na, the sixth Lanna king, built this temple (☎ *0 5327 8304)* in a forest grove in 1373 as a place where the visiting Phra Sumana Thera, a teaching monk from Sukhothai, could spend the rains retreat. The large, open *wíhăan* was rebuilt in 1932. The *bòt* contains a 500-year-old bronze Buddha image and vivid *jataka* (Buddha's past-life stories) murals. Amulets and Buddhist literature printed in English and Thai can be purchased at quite low prices in the *wíhăan*.

In the grounds is a group of whitewashed Lanna stupas, framed by Doi Suthep. The large central stupa contains a Buddha relic that supposedly self-multiplied. One relic was mounted on the back of a white elephant (commemorated by Chiang Mai's Pratu Chang Pheuak), which was allowed to wander until it 'chose' a site on which a wát could be built to enshrine it. The elephant stopped and died at a spot on Doi Suthep, where Chiang Mai residents built Wat Phra That Doi Suthep (see Doi Suthep under Around Chiang Mai later in this chapter).

Wat Ku Tao

วัดกู่เต้า

North of the moat, near Chiang Mai Stadium, Wat Ku Tao (☎ *0 5321 1842)* dates from 1613 and has a unique *chedi* that looks like a pile of diminishing spheres, claimed to be of possible Yunnanese design. The *chedi* is said to contain the ashes of Tharawadi Min, a son of the Burmese king Bayinnaung, ruler of Lanna from 1578 to 1607. Note the amusing sculptures on the outer wall of the wát.

Wat U Mong

วัดอุโมงค์

This forest wát (☎ *0 5327 3990)* was first used during Phaya Mangrai's rule in the 14th century. Brick-lined tunnels in an unusual large, flat-topped hill were supposedly fashioned around 1380 for the clairvoyant monk Thera Jan. The monastery was abandoned at a later date and wasn't reinstated until a local Thai prince sponsored a restoration in the late 1940s. The since-deceased Ajahn Buddhadasa, a well-known monk and teacher at southern Thailand's Wat Suanmok, sent a number of monks to re-establish a monastic community at U Mong in the 1960s. One building contains modern artwork by various monks who have resided at U Mong, including several foreigners. A marvellously grisly image of the fasting Buddha – ribs, veins and all – can be seen in the grounds on top of the tunnel hill, along with a very large *chedi*. Also on the grounds is a small lake.

A small library/museum with English-language books on Buddhism can be found on the premises. Resident foreign monks give talks in English on Sunday afternoon at 3pm by the lake.

To get to Wat U Mong, travel west on Th Suthep for about 2km and take the signed left; then follow the signs for another kilometre to Wat U Mong. Săwngthăew to Doi Suthep also pass the turn-off.

Wiang Kum Kam
เวียงกุมกาม

These excavated ruins are tucked away near the banks of the Mae Nam Ping, 5km south of the city via Hwy 106 (Th Chiang Mai-Lamphun). Apparently this was the earliest historical settlement in the Chiang Mai area, established by the Mon in the 11th or 12th century as a satellite town for the Hariphunchai kingdom. The city was abandoned in the early 18th century due to massive flooding, and visible architectural remains are few – only the four-sided Mon-style *chedi* of Wat Chedi Si Liam and the layered brick pediments of Wat Kan Thom (the Mon name; in Thai the temple was known as Wat Chang Kham) are left. Chedi Si Liam is said to have been inspired by the similar *chedi* at Wat Kukut in Lamphun.

Over 1300 inscribed stone slabs, bricks, bells and stupas have been excavated at the site – all are currently being translated at Chiang Mai University. So far, the most important archaeological discovery has been a four-piece inscribed stone slab, now on display in the Chiang Mai National Museum. These early-11th-century inscriptions indicate that the Thai script predates King Ramkhamhaeng's famous Sukhothai inscription (introduced in 1293) by 100 or more years.

An ideal way to reach Wiang Kum Kam is to hire a bicycle; follow Th Chiang Mai-Lamphun southeast for about 3km and look for a sign to the ruins on the right. From this junction it's another 2km to the ruins. You could also hire a *túk-túk* (motorised *săamláw*; a three-wheeled vehicle) or red săwngthăew to take you there for 50B or 60B (one way). Once you've finished looking around you can walk back to Th Chiang Mai-Lamphun and catch a săwngthăew or a blue Chiang Mai-Lamphun bus back into the city.

Other Temples, Shrines & Mosques

Temple freaks looking for more wát energy can check out **Wat Pheuak Hong** *(Th Samlan)*, behind Buak Hat Park off Th Samlan. The locally revered **Chedi Si Pheuak** is over 100 years old and features the 'stacked-spheres' style seen only here and at Wat Ku Tao. Another unique local temple is the 16th-century **Wat Chiang Yeun** *(Th Mani Nopharat)* on the northern side of the moat, between Pratu Chang Pheuak and the northeastern corner of the old city. Besides the large northern-style *chedi* here, the main attraction is an old Burmese colonial-style gate and pavilion on the eastern side of the school grounds attached to the wát. It looks like it dropped out of the sky from Yangon or Mandalay.

Three wát along Th Tha Phae, **Chetawan**, **Mahawan** and **Bupparam**, feature highly ornate *wíhăan* and *chedi* designed by Shan or Burmese artisans; most likely they were originally financed by Burmese teak merchants who immigrated to Chiang Mai 100 years ago or more. Burmese influence can easily be seen in the ever-present peacock symbol (a solar symbol common in Burmese and Shan temple architecture) and the Mandalay-style standing Buddhas found in wall niches. At Wat Mahawan no two guardian deity sculptures are alike; the whimsical forms include monkeys or dogs playing with lions and various mythical creatures. Wat Bupparam contains a precious little *bòt* constructed of teak and decorated in the Chiang Mai style.

A block-and-a-half east of Wat Phra Singh, **Wat Chai Phra Kiat** *(Th Ratchadamnoen)* contains a huge bronze Buddha cast by order of a Burmese military commander in 1565. **Wat Sisuphan** *(Th Wualai)*, south of the moat, was founded in 1502, but little remains of the original structures except for some teak pillars and roof beams in the *wíhăan*. The murals inside show an interesting mix of Taoist, Zen and Theravada Buddhist elements. Wat Sisuphan is one of the few wát in Chiang Mai where you can see the Poy Luang (Poy Sang Long) Festival, a Shan-style group ordination of young boys as Buddhist novices, in late March.

Muslim, Hindu & Sikh Of the 12 mosques in Chiang Mai, the oldest and most interesting is **Matsayit Chiang Mai** *(Chiang Mai Mosque; Soi 1, Th Charoen Prathet)*, sometimes called Ban Haw Mosque, between Th Chang Khlan and Th Charoen Prathet, not far from the Chiang Mai Night Bazaar.

Founded by *jiin haw* (Yunnanese Muslims) over 100 years ago, it still primarily caters to this unique ethnic group; you'll hear Yunnanese spoken as often as Thai within the compound. Along this *soi* (lane) are several Yunnanese Muslim restaurants that serve *khâo sàwy kài* (curried chicken and noodles) as a speciality.

The most colourful of Chiang Mai's two Hindu temples is the brightly painted, traditional shrine room *(mandir)* and tower *(sikhara)*, **Devi Mandir Chiang Mai** *(Th Ratanakosin)*, opposite Chiang Mai Stadium. **Namdhari Sikh Temple** *(Th Ratchawong)*, between Th Chang Moi and Th Tha Phae, is the place of worship for the Namdhari sect of Sikhism.

Chiang Mai National Museum

พิพิธภัณฑสถานแห่งชาติเชียงใหม่

This museum *(☎ 0 5322 1308; admission 30B; open 9am-4pm Wed-Sun)* has a good selection of Buddha images in all styles, including a very large bronze Buddha downstairs. Pottery is also displayed downstairs (note the 'failed' jar on the stairs), while upstairs there are household and work items. Look for the amusing wooden 'dog' used for spinning thread.

The museum is close to Wat Jet Yot on Hwy 11 (also known as Th Superhighway), which curves around the city. At present the museum is undergoing a major and much-needed renovation, so many of the display rooms should have an entirely new look within the near future.

Tribal Museum

พิพิธภัณฑ์ชาวเขา

Originally established in 1965 on the ground floor of the Tribal Research Institute on Chiang Mai University campus, this teaching museum *(☎ 0 5321 0872; admission free; open 9am-4pm Mon-Fri, closed public holidays; slide & video shows 10am-2pm)*, moved to its new location overlooking a lake in Ratchamangkhala Park on the northern outskirts of the city in 1997. The octagonal facility houses a large collection of handicrafts, costumes, jewellery, ornaments, household utensils, agricultural tools, musical instruments and ceremonial paraphernalia, along with various informative displays concerning the cultural features and backgrounds of each of the major hill tribes in Thailand. There is also an exhibition on activities carried out by the Thai royal family on behalf of the hill tribes, as well as various bits of research and development sponsored by governmental and nongovernmental agencies.

Chiang Mai Night Bazaar

The Chiang Mai Night Bazaar, arguably Chiang Mai's biggest tourist attraction, is in fact the legacy of the original Yunnanese trading caravans that stopped here along the ancient trade route between Simao (in China) and Mawlamyaing (on Myanmar's Gulf of Martaban coast). See also the Markets entry under Shopping later in this chapter.

Other Attractions

At the **Old Chiang Mai Cultural Centre** *(OCMCC; ☎ 0 5320 2993-5, 0 5327 4093, 0 5327 5097, fax 0 5327 4094; 185/3 Th Wualai; admission & dinner 270B; performances 7pm-10pm)*, 500km south of the city centre, northern-Thai and hill-tribe dances are performed nightly and include a *khan tòk* dinner (northern-style food eaten from low round tables). It's a touristy affair, but done well. Several big hotels around town offer similar events, but the OCMCC was the first and is still the best.

For a grander show that includes live elephants, try the newer **Lanna Nakorn 1296** *(☎ 0 5381 8249; 84 Th Chang Khlan; admission 250B; performances 8pm & 10pm nightly)*, in a former cinema house near the Chiang Mai Night Bazaar.

Anusawari Sam Kasat *(Three Kings Monument; Th Phra Pokklao)*, towards the Thai Airways International (THAI) office, is a set of three bronze sculptures depicting Phaya Ngam Meuang, Phaya Mangrai and Phaya Khun Ramkhamhaeng, the three northern Thai-Lao kings most associated with early Chiang Mai history. Behind the monument stands the graceful old **Sala Klang** (Provincial Hall), which is supposed to be converted into either a museum or a cultural centre. It's one of Chiang Mai's best examples of post-colonial Southeast Asian architecture.

The well-maintained **Buak Hat Park** *(Suan Buak Hat; open 8am-5pm daily)*, in the southwestern corner of the moat, is Chiang Mai's miniature counterpart to Bangkok's Lumphini Park, with pleasant expanses of grass, fountains and palms; many people jog in this area.

The **Chiang Mai University** campus on Th Huay Kaew is another quiet place to wander around. It's also interesting in the evenings, with a busy night bazaar of its own.

Out towards Doi Suthep, 6km northwest of the city centre, are the shady, nicely landscaped and hilly **Chiang Mai Zoo & Arboretum** (*☎ 0 5335 8116, 0 5322 2479; adult/child 30/5B, car/truck 30B, motorcycle & bicycle 10B; open 8am-5pm daily*). Except for the name of each species, most signs are in Thai only. Apparently over 5000 birds (150 species) fly about the zoo's Nakhon Ping Birdwatching Park. A few snack vendors scattered around the park offer simple rice and noodle dishes. The quiet, lush arboretum is a favourite local jogging spot. In 2002 there was much talk about moving the zoo south of town to Tambon Mae Hia, but if this happens it will probably be several years from now.

Along the same road nearby are the **Huay Kaew Fitness Park** and **Nam Tok Huay Kaew** (Huay Kaew Falls).

The slightly spooky **Foreign Cemetery** off Th Chiang Mai-Lamphun near the Gymkhana Club, contains some 100-year-old headstones bearing American, English and European names marking the remains of traders, missionaries and numerous other expats who have died in Chiang Mai. A bronze statue of Queen Victoria, imported from Calcutta, India, during the Raj era, stands sentinel.

ACTIVITIES

Aeronautics

The **Chiang Mai Flying Club** (*☎/fax 0 5320 0515, 0 1952 0144; e alpharom@samart.co.th; 185/12 Th Wualai*), based at an airstrip in Lamphun but with a Chiang Mai office, can offer pilot training as well as sightseeing flights. The latter run for a half-hour to 1½ hours, depending on the route (most are in the Lampang and Lamphun areas). They cost 1500B to 5500B per person, depending on the length of the flight and number of people. The cost includes transfers from Chiang Mai to Lamphun, the services of the pilot (also the guide) and membership to the club.

Ultralight-aircraft operation, **Chiang Mai Sky Adventure Club** (*☎ 0 5386 8460, 0 1993 6861, fax 0 5386 7646; e flying@cmnet.co.th; 143 Mu 6, Tambon Choeng Doi, Amphoe Doi Saket*), offers 15-minute flights over the Doi Saket area for 1200B per person, including transport from your hotel to the airfield.

Oriental Balloon Flights (*☎ 0 5339 8609*) arranges one-hour, early morning hot-air balloon cruises over the Chiang Mai countryside for US$190 per person, including transport to/from your hotel or guesthouse, plus a champagne breakfast.

Cycling

The **Chiang Mai Bicycle Club** (*☎ 0 5394 3018*) organises a trip almost every Sunday, between 7am and 7.30am from the square in front of Pratu Tha Phae. These trips typically take routes outside of town.

Horse Riding

The **Pack Squadron Riding Club** (*☎ 0 5329 7478*), with a stable of over 35 horses (many of them thoroughbreds), offers two-hour rides from 8am every Sunday. The cost is 300B per hour for nonmembers (200B if accompanied by a member) and 100B for members. The membership fee is 1500B per year. Riding lessons are held from 5pm to 6pm daily.

Jogging

Top spots for joggers are **Buak Hat Park**, at the southeastern corner of the city moat, the **arboretum** behind the Chiang Mai Zoo, the **Maharaj Hospital fitness park** off Th Suthep and the **700th Anniversary Stadium** north of town on the Chiang Mai to Mae Rim Highway. There are also tracks at the **Chiang Mai Stadium** and **Chiang Mai University**.

Thai Boxing

Lanna Muay Thai (*☎/fax 0 5389 2102; w www.lannamuaythai.com; 64/1 Soi Chiang Khian*), off Th Huay Kaew, (also known by its Thai name, Kiatbusaba) is a boxing camp that offers authentic *muay thai* (Thai boxing) instruction to foreigners as well as Thais. Several Lanna students have won stadium bouts, including the famous *kàthoey* (male transvestite) boxer Parinya Kiatbusaba (it's a tradition in Thailand for fighters to take the camp name as their ring surname), who wore lipstick and pink nail polish to his national weigh-in, then triumphed at Lumphini stadium in Bangkok. Rates are 250B a day or 7000B a month; simple camp accommodation is available for 3000B per month. Thai food is available at low cost, and Western food more expensively. The camp's management claims: 'Foreign boxers are much sought after and we offer match-ups with local boxers for all levels of competition'.

Rock Climbing

The largest rock-climbing wall in Southeast Asia stands in Chiang Mai at **The Peak Rock-Climbing Plaza** (*☎ 0 5382 0777; 28/2 Th Chang Khlan*). Rates are one trial 150B, one hour 200B and two hours 250B. Built to international competition climbing standards, this new attraction stands 15m high and 16m wide, and is designed to accommodate beginners as well as seasoned veterans. Nonclimbers can watch the action from several adjacent bars and restaurants. All rates include equipment rental.

Chiang Mai Rock Climbing Adventures (*☎ 0 6911 1470; W www.thailandclimbing.com; 8 Soi 1, Th Suriwong*) leads rock-climbing instruction trips (1500B per person, with a minimum of two people) to a set of limestone cliffs, called Crazy Horse Buttress by local *faràng* (Western) climbers, behind Tham Meuang On about 20km east of Chiang Mai. The price includes two guides, transport, food, fruit, drinking water, equipment rental, insurance – and T-shirt.

Swimming

Landlocked Chiang Mai can get very hot, particularly from March to July. Fortunately, local opportunities for a refreshing swim are many, providing an alternative to the usual tourist solution (vegetating in refrigerated rooms most of the day).

City Pools Chiang Mai has several swimming pools for public use; you can pay on a per-day basis, or buy an annual membership. Typical per-day fees cost 30B to 90B (public pools are cheaper than hotel or private pools), while annual memberships start at around 200B and go up to 300B.

Amari Rincome Hotel (☎ 0 5389 4884) Th Huay Kaew at Th Nimanhaemin
Chiang Mai University (☎ 0 5322 1699) Faculty of Education, Th Huay Kaew
Maharaj Hospital (☎ 0 5322 1310) Faculty of Medicine, Th Suthep
Physical Education College (☎ 0 5321 0825) 700th Anniversary Stadium
Pongpat Swimming Pool (☎ 0 5321 2812) 73/2 Th Chotana
Top North Guest House (☎ 0 5327 8900) 15 Soi 2, Th Moon Muang

Huay Teung Tao Reservoir This sizable lake about 12km northwest of the city is a great place for an all-day swim and picnic, especially during the hotter months. Windsurfing equipment can be rented for around 150B an hour. By car or motorcycle you can get to Huay Teung Tao by driving 10km north on Rte 107 (follow signs towards Mae Rim), then west 2km past an army camp to the reservoir.

Cyclists would do best to pedal to the reservoir via Th Chonlaprathan. Head west on Th Huay Kaew, then turn right just before the canal. Follow Th Chonlaprathan north until it ends at a smaller road between the reservoir and the highway; turn left here and you'll reach the lake after another 1km or so of pedalling. From the northwestern corner of the moat, the 12km bike ride takes about an hour.

If you don't bring your own, food is available from vendors at the lake, who spread mats out for people to sit on. Fishing is permitted if you'd like to try your luck at hooking lunch.

Tennis

Anantasiri Tennis Courts (*☎ 0 5322 2210*), off Hwy 11 and opposite the Chiang Mai National Museum, is the best public tennis facility in Chiang Mai. The eight courts are lit at night, and you can hire a 'knocker' (tennis opponent) for a reasonable hourly fee in addition to the regular court fee.

Other places with public tennis courts include:

Amari Rincome Hotel (☎ 0 5322 1130, 0 5322 1044; Th Huay Kaew)
Chiang Mai Land Village (☎ 0 5327 2821) Th Chiang Mai Land
Gymkhana Club (☎ 0 5324 1035) Th Ratuthit
Lanna Sports Club (☎ 0 5322 1911) Th Chotana

Massage

All of the places that teach massage (see Courses next) offer massage services as well, usually for 150B to 200B per hour. There are also dozens of *nûat phăen boraan* (traditional massage) centres all around the city, often doing massage for as little as 100B per hour, but most people find that the massage schools give the best service.

Let's Relax *(☎ 0 5381 8498; 145/27 Th Chang Khlan)*, on the 2nd floor of the small Chiangmai Pavilion shopping centre in the Chiang Mai Night Bazaar strip, offers massages that are generally of superior quality, and are performed in a very clean and professional atmosphere. In addition to full-body massage, it offers half-hour back and shoulder massage, arm massage and foot massage.

Traders Retreat Spa *(☎ 0 5340 9705; ⓔ info@siamesetraders.com; 85 Soi 2, Th Suksasem)*, near Lanna Hospital, is a new day spa specialising in Thai massage, Thai herbal sauna and teakwood tub mineral soaks in a tropical garden ambience. Prices are very reasonable.

Some of the top hotels have good massage staff. **Lanna Spa** *(☎ 0 5329 8181; Th Mae Rim-Samoeng Kao)*, at The Regent Chiang Mai Resort & Spa, about 20 minutes' drive north of Chiang Mai in Mae Rim, offers perhaps the best massage you can find associated with any hotel property in the Chiang Mai area. In addition to traditional Thai massage, it offers a skin-scrub massage using Thai herbs and spices, as well as aromatherapy oil massage. Facials and other kinds of spa treatments are also available. Expect premium prices and premium service.

COURSES

Language & Culture

The basic Thai course at **American University Alumni** *(AUA; ☎ 0 5327 8407, 0 5321 1377, fax 0 5321 1973; ⓔ aualanna@loxinfo.co.th; 73 Th Ratchadamnoen)* consists of three levels with 60 hours of instruction; there are also 30-hour courses in 'small talk', reading and writing, and northern Thai. Costs range from 2700B for the reading and writing and northern-Thai courses to 3500B per level for the 60-hour courses. More-expensive private tutoring is also available.

The **Australia Centre** *(☎ 0 5381 0552, fax 0 5381 0554; Soi 5, Th Suthep)*, at the back of Chiang Mai University in an old traditional Thai house, offers a 30-hour course in 'survival Thai' over a two-week period.

Payap University *(☎ 0 5330 4805 ext 250–1, fax 0 5324 5353; Th Kaew Nawarat)* offers intensive 60- and 120-hour Thai language courses at beginning, intermediate and advanced levels; these focus on conversational skills, as well as elementary reading and writing, and Thai culture. Costs for each course are 6000B (60 hours) and 12,000B (120 hours). It also offers a Thai Studies Certificate Program, which involves two semesters of classroom lectures and field trips. Costs include a US$40 application fee, plus US$1500 for tuition. Single courses can be taken for 3500B each.

The **Chiang Mai Thai Language Center** *(☎/fax 0 5327 7810; ⓔ cmat@loxinfo.co.th; 131 Th Ratchadamnoen)*, not far from AUA, is run by a Thai couple and offers Thai language courses for beginners to advanced learners. Its 30-hour course consists of reading/writing or speaking/conversation in group classes of no more than six students, while private lessons are also available. Tuition for private lessons starts at 200B, while the 30-hour group courses cost 2000B to 2200B.

Thai Cooking

Courses in Thai cuisine have become a real staple of Chiang Mai's vacation learning scene. Nowadays at least a dozen independent schools, as well as virtually every guesthouse in Chiang Mai, offer cooking classes from 700B to 900B a day.

Classes typically include an introduction to Thai herbs and spices, a local market tour, cooking instructions and a recipe booklet. Of course, you get to eat the delicious Thai food as well – everything from Chiang Mai-style chicken curry to steamed banana cake.

We've received good reports about the following courses.

Baan Thai (☎ 0 5335 7339, ⓔ info@cookinthai.com) 11 Soi 5, Th Ratchadamnoen
Chiang Mai Thai Cookery School (☎ 0 5320 6388, fax 0 5339 9036, ⓦ www.thaicookeryschool.com) 1-3 Th Moon Muang
Gap's Thai Culinary Art School (☎/fax 0 5327 8140, ⓔ gap_house@hotmail.com) Gap's House, 3 Soi 4, Th Ratchadamnoen
Siam Thai Cookery School (☎ 0 5327 1169, fax 0 5320 8950, ⓔ siam-kitchen@bangkok.com) 5/2 Soi 1, Th Loi Kroh

Traditional Massage

Over the years Chiang Mai has become a centre for Thai massage studies. The oldes

JERRY ALEXANDER

Young Lisu women, Chiang Dao, Chiang Mai Province

IZZET KERIBAR

Bo Sang Umbrella Festival, Chiang Mai Province

JERRY ALEXANDER

Lisu children, Chiang Dao, Chiang Mai Province

KRAIG LIEB
Artisan, Bo Sang, Chiang Mai Province

DENNIS JOHNSON
Teak handicrafts, Chiang Mai Province

JULIET COOMBE
Silverwork, Chiang Mai Province

JULIET COOMBE
Parasol production, Chiang Mai Province

and most popular place to study is the **Old Medicine Hospital** *(OMH; ☎ 0 5327 5085; 78/1 Th Chiang Mai-Hot)* on Soi Siwaka Komarat off Th Wualai, opposite the Old Chiang Mai Cultural Centre. The 11-day course runs daily from 9am to 4pm and costs 3500B, including all teaching materials. There are two courses a month year-round, except for the first two weeks of April. The OMH curriculum is very traditional, with a northern-Thai slant (the Thai name for the institute actually means Northern Traditional Healing Hospital). Classes tend to be large during the months of December to February, small the rest of the year.

New on the scene, **Thai Massage School of Chiang Mai** *(TMS; ☎ 0 5390 7193; w www.1thaimassage.com; Art Museum, Chiang Mai University)* offers certified courses from 18 hours for 2900B all the way up to a full year's intensive curriculum for 80,000B. The English-language standard appears to be particularly high here.

Another very well-recommended source of instruction is **Lek Chaiya** *(☎ 0 5327 8325; w www.nervetouch.com; 25 Th Ratchadamnoen)*. Khun Lek, a Thai woman who has been massaging and teaching for 40 years, specialises in *jàp sên* (similar to acupressure) and the use of medicinal herbs. Courses take three to five days, depending on the student's zeal or availability, and cost 4000B (including books).

A unique, one-on-one course is available at **Ban Nit** *(Soi 2, Th Chaiyaphum)*. The teacher is Nit, an older woman who is a specialist in deep-tissue, nerve and herbal massages. Her methods were handed down from a long line of ancestral Chinese healers. Length of study and payment for Nit's tutelage is up to the individual – according to what you can afford. Most students live in and eat meals with Nit and her family.

International Training Massage *(☎ 0 5321 8632; e itm60@hotmail.com; 171/7 Th Morakot)*, in Santitham district, features another OMH-inspired curriculum with a five- day, 1800B course.

Buddhist Meditation

Not far from Wat U Mong, Wat Ram Poeng is a large monastery that supports the well-known **Northern Insight Meditation Centre** *(☎ 0 5327 8620, fax 0 5381 0197; e watrampoeng@hotmail.com)*, where many foreigners have studied *vipassana*. Ten- to 26-day individual courses are taught by a Thai monk, with Western students or bilingual Thais acting as interpreters. A large *Tripitaka* (Buddhist scriptures) library houses versions of the Theravada Buddhist canon in Pali, Thai, Chinese, English and other languages.

The formal name for this wát is Wat Tapotaram. To get there by public transport, take a săwngthăew west on Th Suthep to Phayom Market. From Phayom Market, take a săwngthăew south along Th Khlong Chonlaprathan about 1km and get off when you see the signed wát entrance on the right. Or charter a săwngthăew or túk-túk all the way.

Meditation can also be learned from the monks at Wat U Mong. The best way to arrange this is to attend one of the Sunday talks (see the Wat U Mong entry under Things to See earlier in this chapter).

Monk Chat A room at **Wat Suan Dok** *(☎ 0 5327 3149, 0 5327 3105, 0 5327 3120; Th Suthep; open 5pm-7pm Mon, Wed & Fri)* is set aside for foreigners to meet and chat with novice monks studying at the monastic university on the monastery grounds. It's free, and provides an opportunity for the monastic students to practise their English and for foreigners to learn about Buddhism and Thai life. To reach the room, enter the wát from the main entrance and walk straight past the large *wíhăan* to a smaller building 100m or so into the temple grounds. Turn right at this smaller temple, and watch for the 'Monk Chat' signs pointing the way. The monastery asks that visitors dress modestly – covered shoulders, no shorts or short skirts – and that women visitors take care not to make physical contact with the monks.

Yoga

Hatha yoga classes with **Marcel Kraushaar Hatha Yoga** *(☎/fax 0 5327 1555; e marcelandyoga@hotmail.com; 129/79 Chiang Mai Villa 1)*, at the Pa Daet intersection, meet each weekday from 5.30am to 7.30am and 5pm to 7pm.

Informal Northern Thai Group

The 18-year-old Informal Northern Thai Group *(INTG; 138 Th Charoen Prathet; admission 20B)* meets at 7.30pm every second Tuesday at the Alliance Française. The usual evening format involves a lecture from a resident or visiting academic on some aspect of Thailand or Southeast Asia, followed by questions and answers and an informal drink afterwards at a local bar or restaurant. Topics covered have included 'The Use of Science in Contemporary Western Buddhist Apologetics' and 'Is Thailand One of the Few Non-Homophobic Countries in the World?'.

ORGANISED TOURS

River Cruises

From a small pier on Mae Nam Ping behind Wat Chaimongkhon, **Mae Ping River Cruises** (*☎ 0 5327 4822; Th Charoen Prathet*) offers two-hour day cruises in roofed boats that stop at a small fruit farm, about 40 minutes away, where free samples and a beverage are provided. The cost is 300B per person and tours run anytime between 8.30am and 5pm daily. The Thai dinner cruise offers a set menu (400B; alcoholic drinks cost extra) and goes from 7.15pm to 9.30pm nightly.

The **Riverside Bar & Restaurant** also offers dinner cruises; see its entry under Places to Eat later in this chapter.

SPECIAL EVENTS

The week-long **Winter Fair** *(thêtsàkaan ngaan reuduu năo)* in late December and early January is a great occasion, as is the April **Songkran Water Festival**, which is celebrated here with an enthusiasm bordering on pure pandemonium. In late January the **Bo Sang Umbrella Festival** *(thêtsàkaan rôm)* features a colourful umbrella procession during the day and a night-time lantern procession. Although it sounds touristy, this festival is actually a very Thai affair; a highlight is the many northern-Thai music ensembles that perform in shopfronts along Bo Sang's main street.

Perhaps Chiang Mai's most colourful festival is the **Flower Festival** *(thêtsàkaan mái dàwk mái pràdàp),* also called the Flower Carnival, held annually in February (dates vary from year to year). Events occur over a three-day period and include displays of flower arrangements, a parade of floats decorated with hundreds of thousands of flowers, folk music, cultural performances and the Queen of the Flower Festival contest. Most activities are centred at Buak Hat Park near the southwestern corner of the city moats. People from all over the province and the country turn out for this occasion, so book early if you want a room in town.

In May the **Intakin Festival** *(ngaan tham bun săo inthákin),* held at Wat Chedi Luang and centred around the city *làk meuang*, propitiates the city's guardian deity to ensure that the annual monsoon will arrive on time. Also in May – when the mango crop is ripe – a **Mango Fair** *(thêtsàkaan mámûang)* is celebrated in Buak Hat Park, with lots of mango eating and the coronation of the Mango Queen.

During the festival of **Loi Krathong**, usually celebrated in late October or early November, Chiang Mai's river banks are alive with people floating the small lotus-shaped boats that mark this occasion. In Chiang Mai this festival is also known as Yi Peng, and some *khon meuang* (people of northern Thailand) celebrate by launching cylindrical-shaped hot-air balloons, lighting up the night skies with hundreds of pinpoints of light.

PLACES TO STAY

At any one time there are about 300 hotels and guesthouses operating in Chiang Mai. Room prices range from 60B for a single room at Rose Guest House to US$425 for a garden-view room at The Regent Chiang Mai Resort & Spa.

PLACES TO STAY – BUDGET

Guesthouses

These are clustered in several areas: along Th Moon Muang (the inside of the east moat) and on streets off Th Moon Muang; along several lanes running south off Th Tha Phae; along Th Charoen Prathet, parallel to and west of Mae Nam Ping; and along Th Charoenrat east of Mae Nam Ping.

There are basically two kinds of budget guesthouse accommodation – old family homes converted into guest rooms (these usually have the best atmosphere although the least privacy) and hotel- or apartment-style places with rows of cell-like rooms. In both, the furnishings are basic – a bed and a few sticks of furniture. You can assume that rooms under 100B won't have a private bathroom but will probably have a fan.

The cheaper guesthouses make most of their money from food service and hill-tribe trekking rather than from room charges, hence you may be pressured to eat and to

Rip-Offs

Upon arrival in Chiang Mai by bus or train you're quite likely to be crowded by touts trying to get you to a particular hotel or guesthouse. As elsewhere in Thailand, the touts get a commission for every prospective guest they bring to a guesthouse or hotel.

The better guesthouses refuse to pay any commissions. At any rate if you call a guesthouse from the bus or train station, staff will be delighted to arrange a ride to avoid paying such exorbitant commissions.

Another scam to be aware of is the bus or minivan services from Th Khao San in Bangkok, which often advertise a free night's accommodation in Chiang Mai if you buy a Bangkok–Chiang Mai ticket. What usually happens on arrival is that the 'free' guesthouse demands you sign up for one of the hill treks immediately; if you don't, the guesthouse is suddenly 'full'. Sometimes they levy a charge for electricity or hot water. The better guesthouses don't play this game.

sign up for a trek. Places that charge 200B or more usually don't hassle guests in this way.

Many of the guesthouses can arrange bicycle and motorcycle rental. If you phone a guesthouse, most will collect you from the train or bus terminal for free if they have a room (this saves them having to pay a commission to a driver).

The following list is not exhaustive but covers most of the more reliable, long-running places.

Inner Moat Area Near Pratu Chiang Mai, **Banana Guest House** (☎ *0 5320 6285, fax 0 5327 5077;* ⓔ *onanong32@hotmail.com; 4/9 Th Ratchaphakhinai; dorm beds 70B, singles/doubles with private hot shower 100/120B)* is a small but friendly place, but often full in the high season. Call for free transport. **Pha Thai Guest House** (☎ *0 5327 8013, fax 0 5327 4075; 48/1 Th Ratchaphakhinai; rooms with fan & solar-heated shower 200-250B)*, in the same quiet southeastern corner of the inner moat area, has clean rooms in a modest three-storey building.

Golden Fern Guest House (☎ *0 5327 8423, fax 0 5327 8665;* ⓔ *thegoldenfern_chiangmai@hotmail.com; 20 Soi 8, Th Phra Pokklao; fan rooms with hot-water shower & fridge 250B, air-con, fridge & TV 350B, deluxe rooms with better beds & bath 450B)* is down a fairly quiet lane. The *faràng*-managed Golden Fern has been converted from a small apartment complex into a clean 30-room guesthouse.

Rose Guest House (☎ *0 5327 3869, 0 5327 6574; 87 Th Ratchamankha; singles/doubles/triples with fan & shared shower/toilet 60/80/120B)* is a friendly place, with a large sitting area downstairs as well as room to sit or do laundry on the roof. Like the Banana Guest House, it's often full in the high season.

Julie Guest House (☎ *0 5327 4355;* ⓔ *julie_chiangmai@yahoo.com; 7/1 Soi 5, Th Phra Pokklao; dorms 50B, rooms with shared bath 80B, singles/doubles/triples with private hot-water shower 120/130/180B)* is in the same general area as Banana Guest House, but is nicer. Rooms are on the small side, although the public areas, including a rooftop sitting area, are cosy.

New Saitum Guest House (☎ *0 5327 8575; Soi 2, Th Ratchamankha; rooms with bath 90-150B)* is near the Library Service. In a quiet setting and for a bargain rate, it offers basic, well-worn but relatively liveable wooden bungalows and balconies.

Smile Guest House (☎ *0 5320 8661, fax 0 5320 8663;* ⓔ *smile208@loxinfo.co.th; 5 Soi 2, Th Ratchamankha; singles/doubles with fan 250B, with air-con & TV 400B)* is farther along this same lane, almost on the corner with Th Ratchamankha, and offers rooms in an old Thai house surrounded by a row of newer rooms. The charming outdoor eating area attached to the renovated house is a plus. The guesthouse rents motorcycles and bicycles, and also offers other travel services. Historical footnote: This house once served as the 'safe house' of infamous Shan-Chinese opium warlord Khun Sa whenever he came to Chiang Mai.

Chiang Mai Garden Guest House (☎*/fax 0 5327 8881; 82-86 Th Ratchamankha; rooms with bath & fan/air-con 120/350B, 1 triple/quad with fan 150/200B)* is friendly and central, with clean rooms in an ageing two-storey building close to Heuan Phen, Mit Mai and several other restaurants. Wat Chedi Luang is in the next block. The Thai woman owner speaks French, German and English. Chiang Mai Garden will not pay commissions to túk-túk or săwngthăew drivers; call the guesthouse for free transport.

Eagle House 2 (☎ *0 5321 0620, fax 0 5321 6368; 26 Soi 2, Th Ratwithi; dorm beds 70B, singles/doubles/triples with shower & fan 170/200/270B, doubles/triples with hot water 240/320B, with air-con 290/360B)* is right around the corner from Irish Pub and convenient to several Thai bars along Th Ratwithi. The three-storey, modern building has a pleasant garden sitting area and is fairly quiet.

Along the narrow, red-bricked lane off Th Moon Muang is a plethora of other cheap places in several tacky, newer buildings. Soi 9, off Moon Muang near the northeastern corner of the moat, is a particularly good area to look if you're having trouble finding a vacant room during festivals, such as Songkran and the Flower Festival. **SK House** (☎ *0 5321 0690; 30 Soi 9, Th Moon Muang; singles/doubles 150/250B)* is OK, but if you don't sign up for a trek first, good luck getting a room. **Libra Guest House** *(☎/fax 0 5321 0687; 26 Soi 9, Th Moon Muang; rooms with fan & cold-/hot-water shower 100/150B)* next door to SK, is clean and friendly and has decent rooms, although it's often full, even in the low season.

Supreme House (☎ *0 5322 2480, fax 0 5321 8545; 44/1 Soi 9, Th Moon Muang; rooms with bath 100-250B)* has rooms in a three-storey, hotel-like building. A well-stocked paperback library on the bottom floor is a plus. **Northlands House** *(☎/fax 0 5321 8860; Soi 7, Th Moon Muang; rooms 250-350B)* is another hotel-like place on parallel Soi 7, west of Chiang Mai SP Hotel and CM Apartments. **Lamchang House** (☎ *0 5321 0586, 0 5321 1435; Soi 7, Th Moon Muang; rooms 80-150B)*, a little farther west on Soi 7, is a wooden Thai-style house run by a Thai family and is more atmospheric than some others. Simple rooms have shared toilet, fan and hot-water shower. There is a small garden restaurant and an information service.

Blue Diamond *(☎/fax 0 5321 7120; ⓔ bluediamondcm@hotmail.com; 35/1 Soi 7, Th Moon Muang; rooms 100-150B)*, also on Soi 7, offers well-kept rooms and above-average food, plus a friendly ambience.

Wanasit Guest House (☎ *0 5381 4042; ⓔ wanasit@writeme.com; 6 Soi 8, Th Ratchamankha; singles/doubles with bath from 150B)* is down a quiet lane, near Wat Phra Singh. Rooms are in a two-storey, modern Thai house.

Bridging the gap between budget and mid-range places are a couple of comfortable guesthouses in the 180B to 400B range. **Gap's House** *(☎/fax 0 5327 8140; ⓔ gap_house@hotmail.com; 3 Soi 4, Th Ratchadamnoen; singles/doubles 250/390B)*, behind the AUA, has wooden or brick houses built around a quiet garden that's filled with antiques. All rooms have carpet, air-con and private hot-water showers; rates include a filling breakfast. Gap's offers a Thai cooking course, as well as a tasty 80B vegetarian buffet from 7pm to 9pm nightly.

Rendezvous Guest House (☎ *0 5321 3763, fax 0 5341 9009; 3/1 Soi 5, Th Ratchadamnoen; singles/doubles with fan 180/250B, with air-con 300B)* is a three-storey inn on the other side of Th Ratchadamnoen down Soi 5 a bit. All rooms have hot water, TV, phone and fridge. Farther north along the same lane is a short string of three- and four-storey apartment-style places: **Kavil House & Restaurant** *(☎/fax 0 5322 4740; ⓔ kavilgh@chmai.loxinfo.co.th; 10/1 Soi 5, Th Ratchadamnoen; rooms 180-360B)* and **Amphawan House** (☎ *0 5321 0584; Soi 5, Th Ratchadamnoen; rooms 200-250B)* are both multistorey buildings with clean rooms that cost less for long-term stays. **Chiang Mai White House** (☎ *0 5335 7130; 12 Soi 5, Th Ratchadamnoen; rooms with fan/air-con 250/350B)* offers clean, quiet rooms with attached hot shower and cable TV (in the air-con rooms only). **Chiangmai Kristi House** (☎ *0 5341 8165; 14/2 Soi 5, Th Ratchadamnoen; rooms 150-180B)* is similar.

Top North Guest House (☎ *0 5327 8900, 0 5327 8684, fax 0 5327 8485; 15 Soi 2, Th Moon Muang; rooms with fan/air-con 300/500B, with TV & bath 600B)* is a popular, efficiently run place. Its rooms all have private hot-water shower. Facilities include a pretty swimming pool and a travel agency.

Safe House Court (☎ *0 5341 8955; 178 Th Ratchaphakhinai; rooms 350-400B)*, opposite Wat U Mong Klang Wiang, features very clean air-con rooms with phone, fridge, toilet and hot-water shower, plus daily maid service. Monthly rates are available. Its semi-classical architecture is of a more pleasing design than most apartment courts in Chiang Mai.

RCN Court (☎ *0 5341 8280-2, 0 5322 4619, fax 0 5321 1969; ⓔ rcncourt@chm.cscoms.com; 35 Soi 7, Th Moon Muang; rooms with* *fan 300-350B, with air-con 400-480B, rooms with fan/air-con per month 4000/5500B)* can be found if you head north along Th Ratchaphakhinai past Sumit Hotel, then right on Soi 7. Although the building exterior isn't as pleasing as that of Safe House Court, it's very clean, friendly, and offers fax and laundering services.

Pratu Tha Phae to the River Across the moat, and quite close to Pratu Tha Phae, **Daret's House** *(☎ 0 5323 5440; 4/5 Th Chaiyaphum; singles/doubles with cold water 70/100B, with hot water 80/120B)* has stacks of basic, well-worn rooms with private bathrooms. The large sidewalk café at the front is popular. **Happy House** *(☎ 0 5325 2619, fax 0 5325 1871; 11/1 Th Chang Moi Kao; singles/doubles with fan 100/180B, with air-con 280B)* is around the corner from Daret's, on narrow Th Chang Moi Kao, and is similar-looking but quieter. Its large, well-tended rooms have bathrooms with hot water.

Eagle House 1 *(☎ 0 5323 5387, fax 0 5321 6368; Soi 3, Th Chang Moi Kao; singles 90B, doubles 120-150B)*, a bit farther north than Pao Come, has simple rooms, each with private bath. The staff boast French, German, English and Spanish language skills. The rooms could use some additional maintenance, but at these prices it's hard to complain. Trekking is big here.

Soi 4, farther east (towards the river) along Th Tha Phae, has several newer, two-storey brick guesthouses with downstairs sitting areas: **Midtown House** *(☎ 0 5327 3191; 7 Soi 4, Th Tha Phae; rooms 100-200B)*, **Thapae** *(☎ 0 5327 1591; 2/2 Soi 4, Th Tha Phae; rooms 100-200B)* and **Sarah Guest House** *(☎ 0 5320 8271, fax 0 5327 9423; ⓔ sarahguesthouse@hotmail.com; 20 Soi 4, Th Tha Phae; fan rooms with cold-/hot-water shower 150/200B, with air-con & hot-water shower 350B)*. All are fine – a step up from the Pratu Tha Phae places – but we'd choose Midtown House for its friendly service and sense of privacy. Sarah Guest House has a nice garden setting.

Thana Guest House *(☎ 0 5327 9794, fax 0 5327 2285; 27/8 Soi 4, Th Tha Phae; singles/doubles with fan 160/180B, with air-con 250/300B)* caters to Israeli travellers (the management boasts 80% Israeli occupancy), with all signs in Thai and Hebrew. Good rooms have hot water, and there is a small restaurant on the premises serving kosher food. **Baan Jongcome** *(☎ 0 5327 4823; 47 Soi 4, Th Tha Phae; rooms with fan/air-con 350/450B)* is a little more upmarket, with comfortable rooms in a three-storey building.

Ratchada Guest House *(☎ 0 5327 5556; 55 Soi 3, Th Tha Phae; singles/doubles 100/150B)*, in the same general area, has quiet rooms with fan and hot-water shower.

Little Home Guest House *(☎ 0 5320 6939, fax 0 5327 3662; ⓔ littleh@loxinfo.co.th; 1/1 Soi 3, Th Kotchasan; singles/doubles with air-con & hot-water shower 200/280B)*, not far from the moat and DK Book House, leans towards the mid-range and offers large, clean, comfortable rooms in a modern Thai-style building. The upstairs rooms have private balconies.

The **Center Place Guest House** *(☎ 0 5327 1169, fax 0 5320 8950; ⓔ centerplace99@hotmail.com; 17/2 Soi 1, Th Loi Kroh; singles/doubles with fan & bath 150B)*, a well-run guesthouse, can be found on a lane off Th Loi Kroh, a good street for textile shopping and within walking distance of both the inner moat area and the Chiang Mai Night Bazaar.

Chiangmai Souvenir Guest House *(Viking Guest House; ☎ 0 5381 8786; 116 Th Charoen Prathet; rooms with fan 130-180B, with air-con 330B)* is one block east of the Chiang Mai Night Bazaar and right around the corner from the Anusan Night Market. It's a pleasant and inexpensive urban haven, complete with an outdoor eating area.

East of the River South of Saphan Nawarat and down a very narrow lane near the TAT office, **Ben Guest House** *(☎ 0 5324 4103; 4/11 Soi 2, Th Chiang Mai-Lamphun; rooms 150B)* offers very clean rooms with fan and private hot-water shower in a quiet compound. Food service is available in an adjacent garden, and the staff can arrange bicycle rentals. Although on the eastern side of the river, it's within walking distance of the Chiang Mai Night Bazaar.

There is a string of guesthouses along Th Charoenrat, parallel to the river – a bit far from the centre of town but recommended for those who are seeking a more scenic river setting. **Je t'Aime** *(☎ 0 5324 1912; 247-249 Th Charoenrat; singles 80-120B, doubles 100-160B)* is a long-running place with a variety of rooms in separate several-storey buildings on secure, landscaped grounds. The owner, a Thai artist, has placed paintings or some kind of original artwork in every room.

Pun Pun Guest House *(☎ 0 5324 3362, fax 0 5324 6140; e armms@iname.com; 321 Th Charoenrat; bungalows 150-200B, rooms 200-275B)* is American-owned and has very tidy bungalows with shared hot-water shower. Rooms with private bath in a quaint two-storey wooden Thai-style house vary in price, depending on the number of people and the time of year. Assets include a fully stocked bar, snooker table and riverfront promenade.

Le Pont *(☎ 0 5324 1661, 0 5324 1712, fax 0 5324 3673; 14 Th Charoenrat; rooms 450-550B)*, opposite the Riverside Bar & Restaurant near Saphan Nawarat, looks impressive, with its office, sitting area and restaurant housed in a 120-year-old teak residence. Air-con guest rooms in an adjacent modern wing are reduced to 450B per day for stays of a week or more. The only drawback is that you can hear the live music from the Riverside until the bands shut down around 1am.

C&C Teak House *(☎ 0 5324 6966; 39 Th Bamrungrat; singles/doubles 80/150B)*, closer to the train station than Mae Nam Ping (rather far from the old city), has quiet, comfortable rooms in a 100-year-old teak house in a secure, gated compound for a bargain rate. Bathroom facilities are shared; the upstairs shower has hot water.

Th Chang Khlan You need a Hostelling International membership to stay at **Chiang Mai Youth Hostel** *(☎ 0 5327 6737, fax 0 5320 4025; e chiangmai@tyha.org; 21/8 Th Chang Khlan; rooms with bath & fan/air-con 150/350B)*. A temporary membership valid for one night costs 50B. Call for free pick-up.

Riverfront Guest House *(Tha Nam; ☎/fax 0 5327 5125; e thanam@chmail.loxinfo.co.th; 43/3 Th Chang Khlan; rooms 400B)*, along the west bank of Mae Nam Ping (attached to the Riverfront Restaurant), offers air-con rooms in a classic Thai-style teak house that's more than 100 years old.

Th Huay Kaew The hostel **Uniserv** *(☎ 0 5322 4672, fax 0 5321 6244; Chiang Mai University; multi-bed fan room with shared facilities per bed 100B, 2-bed room with air-con & private hot-water shower 400B, 'VIP' room with TV & fridge 500-750B)* is on CMU campus, close to the Th Huay Kaew side. It's a large hotel-like structure with clean rooms, good service and a Thai restaurant downstairs. You do not have to be a student to stay here.

Hotels

Roong Ruang Hotel *(Roong Raeng; ☎ 0 5323 6746, fax 0 5325 2409; 398 Th Tha Phae; rooms upstairs/downstairs with fan & bath 250/280B, with air-con, hot-water shower & cable TV 350/400B)* is situated in a prime location, near Pratu Tha Phae, on the eastern side of the city moat. All rooms face an inner courtyard, with pleasant sitting areas out the front. This is a good place to stay for the Flower Festival in February as the Saturday parade passes right by the entrance, but for the same reason it's probably not the best choice for the raucous Songkran and Loi Krathong festivals. There's another entrance on Th Chang Moi Kao.

Tapae Inn *(☎ 0 5323 4640; rooms with fan/air-con 150/220B)*, just west of the canal on the northern side of Th Tha Phae, is a good budget choice.

Sumit Hotel *(☎ 0 5321 1033, ☎/fax 0 5321 4014; 198 Th Ratchaphakhinai; rooms with fan/air-con 200/300B)*, on a relatively quiet section of Th Ratchaphakhinai inside the old city, offers very clean, large rooms in the classic Thai/Chinese style. You can choose a room with one big bed or two twin beds for the same rate. All have private toilet and shower; air-con rooms have hot water. This is very good value for anyone avoiding the guesthouse scene – it's probably the best hotel deal in the old city.

New Mitrapap Hotel *(☎ 0 5323 5436, fax 0 5325 1260; 94-98 Th Ratchawong; rooms with fan/air-con 320/400B)*, in Chiang Mai's small Chinatown, lies between the east moat and Mae Nam Ping, and features adequate rooms; those with air-con are a better deal. It's close to several inexpensive Chinese restaurants, as well as the Talat Warorot.

Prince Hotel *(☎ 0 5325 2025, fax 0 5325 1144; 3 Th Taiwang; rooms from 440B)*, a little farther north, is an all air-con hotel with good, if time-worn, rooms. There's a restaurant, coffee shop and swimming pool.

Chiang Mai Phu Viang Hotel *(☎ 0 5322 1632; 5-9 Soi 4, Th Chotana; rooms with fan*

& bath from 200B, with air-con, bath & TV 280B), near the Chang Pheuak bus terminal, has small but clean rooms, and more spacious rooms with better facilities. A restaurant and coffee shop are on the premises.

Muang Thong Hotel *(☎ 0 5324 8378, fax 0 5327 4349; 5 Th Ratchamankha; singles/doubles with fan & bath 120/180B)*, on the corner of Th Ratchamankha and Th Moon Muang, is a funky, old Thai-style hotel in a good location inside the city moat. Street noise from busy Th Moon Muang could be a problem.

Montri Hotel *(☎ 0 5321 1069/70, fax 0 5321 7416; ⓔ montri-hotel@hotmail.com; 2-6 Th Ratchadamnoen; singles with air-con & hot water 575B, singles/doubles with air-con, hot water & cable TV 695B)* is a five-storey hotel on the busy corner of Th Moon Muang and Th Ratchadamnoen. Rates include tax, service and breakfast. Street-facing rooms are bombarded with noise from Th Moon Muang, which reflects off Tha Phae wall.

YMCA International Hotel *(☎ 0 5322 1819, 0 5322 2366, fax 0 5321 5523; 11 Th Mengrairasmi; old-wing dorm beds/singles/doubles with fan & shared facilities 75/130/190B, old-wing singles & doubles with fan & bath 220B, old-wing singles/doubles with air-con & bath 250/350B, new wing singles/doubles with air-con, phone, private bath & TV 500/600B)* is above the northwestern corner of the moat. Facilities at the hotel include a travel agency, handicraft centre and cafeteria.

Nice Apartment *(☎ 0 5321 0552, 0 5321 8290, fax 0 5341 9150; 15 Soi 1, Th Ratchadamnoen; rooms with fan 200-250B, with air-con 300-350B)*, on a lane behind the Montri Hotel, is a well-run place with clean, simple rooms with private hot-water bathroom, cable TV and either fan or air-con. Prices vary depending on season and length of stay. Discounted monthly rates, also depending on length of stay, are also available. **VIP** *(☎ 0 5341 8970, fax 0 5341 9199; 1 Soi 1, Th Ratchadamnoen; rooms with fan 200-250B, air-con 300-350B)* is on the same lane almost directly behind Zest Bakery & Restaurant. All rooms have private hot-water shower and TV.

On Soi 7, off Th Moon Muang, are a couple of good apartment-style places. **CM Apartments** *(☎ 0 5322 2100; 7 Soi 7, Th Moon Muang; rooms with private hot-water shower 250-450B)* and **Chiang Mai SP Hotel** *(☎ 0 5321 4522, fax 0 5322 3042; 7/1 Soi 7, Th Moon Muang; monthly rates 2500-3000B)* are both basic but clean, with many Thai residents.

Veerachai Court *(☎ 0 5325 1047, fax 0 5325 2402; 19 Soi2, Th Tha Phae; rooms with air-con, hot-water shower & TV per night/month 400/3500B)* features a nine-storey building on the eastern side of the lane, and a four-storey one on the western side. Rooms are clean and quiet but smallish.

Moon Meuang Golden Court *(☎ 0 5321 2779; Th Moon Muang; doubles with hot-water shower & fan/air-con 200/300B)*, off Th Moon Muang north of Pratu Tha Phae, is an apartment-style place with clean rooms. A small coffee shop is attached.

Anodard Hotel *(☎ 0 5327 0755, fax 0 5327 0759; 57-59 Th Ratchamankha; rooms with air-con from 450B)* stands off by itself in the inner-city area. It has well-kept rooms in a building that would have been called 'modern' 30 years ago, and a restaurant and swimming pool on the premises.

Pratu Chang Pheuak Area There are very few hotels north of the city walls. **Chawala Hotel** *(☎ 0 5321 4939, 0 5321 4453; 129 Th Chotana (Th Chang Pheuak); rooms with bath & fan/air-con 150/250B)*, far from the Tha Phae action, but near the Chang Pheuak bus terminal (for Chiang Dao, Fang and Tha Ton), is one such option. Its rooms are basic.

Chang Peuk Hotel *(☎ 0 5321 7513, fax 0 5322 3668; 133 Th Chotana, also called Th Chang Pheuak; rooms with air-con & with/without TV 350/250B)*, close to the Chang Pheuak bus terminal, has clean rooms. There's a good coffee shop on the premises.

PLACES TO STAY – MID-RANGE

In this range you can expect daily room cleaning, the option of air-con (some places have rooms with fan also) and – in hotels – TV and telephone. If there is anything that marks a guesthouse, it's the absence of these latter appliances.

Some of the places in this price category (500B to 1500B for Chiang Mai) really blur the line between 'hotel' and 'guesthouse', the difference often being in name only. **Galare Guest House** *(☎ 0 5382 1011, fax 0 5327 9088; ⓔ galare_gh@hotmail.com; 7/1 Soi 2,*

Th Charoen Prathet; rooms with air-con, hot-water shower, TV & refrigerator 860B) for example, is a well-managed place that has spacious rooms. It's popular with repeat visitors for its Mae Nam Ping location and proximity to both the Chiang Mai Night Bazaar and Mae Ping post office.

River View Lodge *(☎ 0 5327 1110, fax 0 5327 9019; 25 Soi 2, Th Charoen Prathet; rooms 1450-2000B)*, almost next door to the Galare Guest House, offers 36 well-appointed rooms in a two-storey, L-shaped building on spacious, landscaped grounds with a swimming pool. Discounts may be available from May to August. The friendly owner has a small collection of classic cars on display in the parking lot.

Porn Ping Tower Hotel *(☎ 0 5327 0099, fax 0 5327 0119; Th Charoen Prathet; singles/doubles 800/900B)*, which is almost opposite the decaying Diamond Riverside Hotel, is much better and has rooms that list for 1766B but at the time of writing were going for rates shown here. From the ambience of the reception area, one might expect to pay much more. The Porn Ping is most famous for Bubbles, still the most popular disco in town.

Royal Lanna *(☎ 0 5381 8773, fax 0 5381 8776; 119 Th Loi Kroh; rooms with air-con, hot-water shower & bath, TV, phone & refrigerator 900B)*, is a relatively new place that towers over the Chiang Mai Night Bazaar and has clean rooms. Rates include a breakfast buffet, and there are discounts for monthly rentals. There's a medium-sized swimming pool on the 4th floor.

Baan Kaew Guest House *(☎ 0 5327 1606, fax 0 5327 3436; 142 Th Charoen Prathet; rooms with hot-water shower & fan/air-con 350/450B)*, opposite Wat Chaimongkhon and two doors south of the Alliance Française, is set far back off the road, so it's very quiet. Very well-maintained rooms boast cross-ventilation and outdoor sitting areas. Meals are available in a small outdoor dining area.

Tapae Place Hotel *(☎ 0 5327 0159, 0 5328 1842, fax 0 5327 1982; 2 Soi 3, Th Tha Phae; rooms with air-con 700-1600B)*, off Th Tha Phae in the centre of town, offers rooms in a large, modern, L-shaped building. Although it's a bit worn, the hotel's main drawcard is that it's only a few steps away from the banks, shops and restaurants of Th Tha Phae.

Felix City Inn *(☎ 0 5327 0710, fax 0 5327 0709; ⓔ felix@cm.ksc.co.th; 154 Th Ratchamankha; rooms Nov-Jun/July-Oct 1900/942B)*, inside the old city, is friendly, efficient and offers 134 comfortable rooms, including breakfast.

Red Hibiscus Guesthouse *(☎ 0 5341 6074-5, fax 0 5321 7631; ⓔ hibiscus@cm.ksc.co.th; 1 Soi 2, Th Arak; rooms with air-con, hot water, phone & TV 650B, minisuites 1300B)* looks like a cross between a hotel and a modern Thai home. The clean, three-storey guesthouse has helpful English-speaking staff who can arrange everything from car rentals to flight reservations

New Asia Hotel *(☎ 0 5325 2426, fax 0 5325 2427; 55 Th Ratchawong; rooms with air-con 266-406B)* is a very Chinese place, with decent rooms – worth a try if you'd like to stay in Chiang Mai's bustling Chinatown.

Sri Tokyo Hotel *(☎ 0 5321 3899, fax 0 5321 1102; 6 Th Bunreuangrit; rooms with air-con 250B, suites 450-600B)* is next door to Chiang Mai Ram Hospital. It has OK rooms, plus suites. Street noise can be a problem in the front rooms.

Strung out along Th Huay Kaew to the immediate northwest of the old city are perhaps a dozen mid-range and top-end hotels. **Chiang Mai Phucome Hotel** *(☎ 0 5321 1026, fax 0 5321 6412; 21 Th Huay Kaew; rooms in old/new building 700/ 900B)*, once the best hotel in the city, is now very middle-of-the-road but a fair deal for a room with all amenities. It has a restaurant, coffee shop and massage centre. This hotel remains a favourite with many visiting Thais. **Quality Chiang Mai Hills** *(☎ 0 5321 0030, fax 0 5321 0035; 18 Th Huay Kaew; rooms with air-con 1200-1500B)*, near Phucome Hotel, has 249 well-appointed rooms and rates include breakfast. **The Providence** *(☎ 0 5389 3123, fax 0 5322 1750; 99/9 Th Huay Kaew; singles/doubles with air-con from 380B)*, farther out on Huay Kaew, has a restaurant, coffee shop and lobby bar.

Northern Inn *(☎ 0 5321 0002, fax 0 5321 5828; 234/18 Th Mani Nopharat; rooms with air-con 450B)* has OK rooms and is close to Pratu Chang Pheuak and the Chang Pheuak bus terminal. Mid-budget package tourists use this hotel extensively. **Iyara Hotel** *(☎ 0 5322 2245, 0 5321 4227, fax 0 5321 4401; 126 Th Chotana; rooms with air-con 450-700B)*, which is several long blocks farther north of Pratu Chang Pheuak and opposite the teachers college, Rajabhat Institute, has good accommodation.

Joy's House (*☎ 0 5385 4213, fax 0 5324 8960; e joys_house@hotmail.com; 114 Mu 9, San Phi Seua; rooms with fan, private hot-water shower, toilet & fridge from 950B*) represents a new concept in upper mid-range lodgings, a cross between a homestay and a boutique hotel with personalised services. Rooms are spread out among several large houses in a quiet area not far from the new City Hall on the city's northern outskirts. The more expensive 'Professor's Studio' has air-con and TV. A separate wing contains telephone, fax, computer with Internet access, TV and a bar. Prices include a welcome massage, herbal sauna, Thai dance, and transport by private car to/from and around Chiang Mai as necessary. For separate rates, it offers a range of activities from handicraft village visits to temple tours, all customised for the guest.

PLACES TO STAY – TOP END

In general, hotel rates for luxury hotels are lower in Chiang Mai than in Bangkok. You can expect to pay 1500B to 5000B for large, well-maintained rooms with air-con, TV and International Direct Dial (IDD) telephone in hotels with a restaurant (usually more than one), fitness centre and swimming pool. Booking through a travel agency or via the Internet almost always means lower rates, or try asking for a hotel's 'corporate' discount.

Chiang Mai

Tamarind Village (*☎ 0 5341 8898, fax 0 5341 8900; w www.tamarindvillage.com; 50/1 Th Ratchadamnoen; standard rooms 4000B, superior 5000B, deluxe 6000B, discounts available*), near the corner of Th Ratchaphakhinai, is the only place in the old city that scores a top-end qualification. A fusion of Thai and Mediterranean architectural styles, this quiet 40-room spread on the grounds of an old tamarind orchard features a nice pool, bar, modest restaurant, and perfect walking access to old city sights.

Chiang Mai Plaza Hotel (*☎ 0 5327 0036, fax 0 5327 2230; 92 Th Si Donchai; standard singles/doubles 2500B, discounted rates 1600/1800B*), a friendly hotel not far from the Chiang Mai Night Bazaar, boasts a spacious lobby with live northern-Thai music in the evenings, a lobby bar, restaurant, wood-panelled sauna, fitness centre and a well-kept pool area with shade pavilions. Nonsmoking rooms are available, which is unusual for a place charging less than 3000B.

Imperial Mae Ping Hotel (*☎ 0 5327 0160, fax 0 5327 0181; e maeping@loxinfo.co.th; 153 Th Si Donchai; singles/doubles 3000/3500B, deluxe singles/doubles 3750/4250B*), also near the Chiang Mai Night Bazaar, has well-outfitted standard rooms. A coffee shop, three restaurants and pool are on the premises.

Chiang Inn (*☎ 0 5327 0070, fax 0 5327 4299; e chianginn@chiangmai.a-net.net.th; rooms 1200-1500B*), behind the centre of the Chiang Mai Night Bazaar, off Th Chang Khlan, features comfortable rooms, with breakfast included. It also has a restaurant, popular disco and swimming pool. The Chiang Inn Plaza, with several restaurants and shops, is just opposite the front of the hotel.

Royal Princess (*☎ 0 5328 1033, fax 0 5328 1044; e rpc@dusit.com; 112 Th Chang Khlan; rooms from 3000B*), in the middle of the Chiang Mai Night Bazaar, has rooms with all amenities. Facilities include three restaurants, a lobby bar and a swimming pool. This hotel is mainly used by package tourists.

Suriwongse Hotel (*☎ 0 5327 0051, fax 0 5327 0063; e suriwongse_htl_cnx@hotmail.com; in Bangkok ☎ 0 2541 5275, fax 0 2541 5278; Th Loi Kroh; singles/doubles 1292/1420B*), around the corner from the Royal Princess, has large rooms (rates include tax, service and breakfast). It has a coffee shop, restaurant, swimming pool and massage centre. The 120B lunch buffet is popular with non-hotel guests.

Empress Hotel (*☎ 0 5327 0240, fax 0 5327 2467; e reservations@empresshotels.com; 199 Th Chang Khlan; singles/doubles from 3146/3630B*) is farther south down Th Chang Khlan, near Chiang Mai Central Hospital, and offers plusher surroundings than Suriwongse. Rates include tax and service charges. The hotel facilities include a restaurant, coffee shop, swimming pool, fitness centre and disco.

Westin Riverside Plaza (*☎ 0 5327 5300, fax 0 5327 5299; 318/1 Th Chiang Mai-Lamphun; rooms from 6200B*), across Saphan Mangrai from the Empress Hotel area, on the east bank of Mae Nam Ping, is the city's top property at the moment. The capacious rooms are commensurate in quality with the international reputation enjoyed by this management group. Facilities include three restaurants, a coffee shop, fitness centre, swimming pool, sauna and beauty salon.

Amari Rincome Hotel *(☎ 0 5322 1130, 0 5322 1044, fax 0 5322 1915; ⓔ rincome@amari.com; 1 Th Nimanhaemin; singles/doubles from US$88/96)*, on the corner of Th Huay Kaew and Th Nimanhaemin, offers standard rooms and is the most expensive option along Th Huay Kaew. Amenities include a well-received Italian restaurant, coffee shop, lobby bar, conference facilities, tennis court and swimming pool.

Amity Green Hills *(☎ 0 5322 0100, fax 0 5322 1602; ⓔ amity@loxinfo.co.th; 24 Th Chiang Mai-Lampang; rooms 1000-1600B)* is actually a short distance northeast off Th Huay Kaew, on Hwy 11 (Th Superhighway). The well-appointed rooms are listed at a relatively low price, no doubt because the location is less than ideal for walking to restaurants or attractions. Facilities include a restaurant, coffee shop, lobby bar, business centre, conference room, fitness room and swimming pool.

Two other top-drawer spots on Th Huay Kaew stand near Kad Suan Kaew shopping centre, not far from the corner of the moat: the **Chiang Mai Orchid Hotel** *(☎ 0 5322 2091, fax 0 5322 1625; 100 Th Huay Kaew; rooms from 2825B)* and the **Lotus Pang Suan Kaew Hotel** *(PSK; ☎ 0 5322 4444, fax 0 5322 4493; 99/4 Th Huay Kaew; rooms 1000-2783B)* are behind Kad Suan Kaew shopping centre. PSK has the most extensive facilities, including a beer garden, restaurant, coffee shop, fitness centre, nightclub, tennis and squash courts, swimming pool and, of course, sheltered access to the shopping centre.

Novotel Chiang Mai *(☎ 0 5322 5500, fax 0 5322 5505; ⓦ www.accorhotels-asia.com; 183 Th Chang Pheuak; singles/doubles 2600/2800B, deluxe 3000-3200B)*, north of Pratu Chang Pheuak, is a reliable choice and offers spacious, well-decorated rooms. You may be able to negotiate lower rates, as this isn't the most popular part of town to stay.

Out of Town

North of the city in the Mae Rim/Mae Sa area are a few plush countryside resorts. Most offer free shuttle vans to/from the city.

The Regent Chiang Mai Resort & Spa *(☎ 0 5329 8181, fax 0 5329 8190; Th Mae Rim-Samoeng Kao; garden-view suites from US$365)* is the *crème de la crème* of Chiang Mai's resorts, and features 64 vaulted pavilion suites (each around 75 sq metres), plus two- and three-bedroom residences spread amid eight hectares of landscaped gardens and rice terraces worked by water buffalo. On the premises are two full-service restaurants, a bar-restaurant, a health club, two swimming pools and two illuminated tennis courts. Rates, quoted in dollars only, don't include tax and service. The resort's 900-sq-metre Lanna Spa has earned much acclaim since its 1999 opening.

Chiang Mai Sports Club *(☎ 0 5329 8330, fax 0 5329 7897; ⓔ shotel@loxinfo.co.th; singles/doubles 2400B, suites 6500B)*, 7km from town on Th Mae Rim, has 45 rooms and three two-storey luxury suites on more than 113 sq km. Living up to its name, the resort boasts air-con squash courts, a badminton hall, grass- and hard-surface tennis courts, fitness centre, sauna, gymnasium and swimming pool; you have to pay extra for the badminton, squash and tennis facilities but everything else is free for guests. Official room rates are listed here, (plus a 400B high-season surcharge on holidays), although you may find discounts of up to 50% are available.

PLACES TO EAT

Chiang Mai has the best variety of restaurants of any city in Thailand outside of Bangkok. Most travellers seem to have better luck here than in Bangkok, though, simply because it's so much easier to get around and experiment.

Chiang Mai's guesthouses serve a typical menu of Western food along with a few pseudo-Thai dishes. If you're interested in authentic Thai cuisine, you'll have to leave the guesthouse womb behind.

Regional Thai

Si Phen Restaurant *(☎ 0 5331 5328; 103 Th Inthawarorot; dishes 25-60B; open 9am-5pm daily)*, an inexpensive place near Wat Phra Singh, specialises in both northern- and northeastern-style dishes. The kitchen prepares some of the best *sôm-tam* (spicy papaya salad) in the city, including a variation made with pomelo fruit. The *kài yâang* *khâo nĭaw* combo (grilled chicken and sticky rice) – another Isan favourite – is also very good, as is the *khâo sàwy* (chicken in a curried broth with noodles) and *khànŏm jiin* (Chinese noodles) with either *náam yaa* (fish sauce) or *náam ngíaw* (sweet, spicy sauce) – always incredible.

Aroon (Rai) Restaurant *(☎ 0 5327 6947; 45 Th Kotchasan; dishes 40-80B; open 8am-10pm daily)*, one of Chiang Mai's oldest and best known restaurants, is a large, open-air spot facing the moat near Pratu Tha Phae. Aroon specialises in both northern and central Thai dishes and has a huge menu; prices are inexpensive to moderate. Look for Chiang Mai specialities like *kaeng hang-leh, kaeng awm* and *kaeng khae*. Despite the Thai word *kaeng* (curry) in these dish names, only the first is a curry by the usual definition – that is, made from a thick, spicy paste; the latter two dishes are more like stews and rely on local roots and herbs for their distinctive, bitter-hot flavours. Aroon's standard, Indian-inspired chicken curry – *kaeng kàrìi kài* – is the best in town. Downstairs you'll find more exotic dishes in trays near the cashier, including bamboo grubs and other forest goodies. The spacious open-air dining area upstairs is favoured by night-time clientele, and in hot weather it's cooler than downstairs. Aroon is a good choice for a Thai breakfast of curry and rice.

Heuan Phen *(no Roman-script sign; ☎ 0 5327 7103; 112 Th Ratchamankha; dishes 40-100B; open 8.30am-3pm & 5pm-10pm daily)* is classy and highly regarded for northern Thai food. Among the house specialities are Chiang Mai and *jiin haw* dishes, such as *khànŏm jiin náam ngíaw*, *khâo sàwy*, *lâap khûa* (northern-style minced-meat salad), *náam phrík nùm* (chilli sauce made with roasted eggplant), *kaeng hang-leh*, *kaeng awm*, *kaeng khae*, and other *aahăan phéun meuang* (local food). It's almost opposite a kindergarten, east of the Felix City Inn. Daytime meals are served in a large dining room out the front, while evening meals are served in an atmospheric antique-decorated house at the back.

Heuan Sunthari *(no Roman-script sign; ☎ 0 5325 2445; 46/2 Th Wan Singkham; dishes 40-90B; open 10am-11pm daily)* is an atmospheric open-air restaurant built on several levels on the west bank of the river, a little north of Saphan Phra Ram IX. The owner – the famous northern Thai singer Soontaree Vechanont – performs at the restaurant nightly. The menu is a pleasant blend of northern, northeastern and central Thai specialities.

Khrua Phuket Laikhram *(no Roman-script sign; ☎ 0 5327 8909; 1/10 Th Suthep; dishes 40-100B; open 8.30am-2pm & 4pm-8.30pm daily; closed 12th, 13th, 27th & 28th of every month)*, a small family-run restaurant near Chiang Mai University, is worth hunting down for its delicious, cheap, authentic home-style southern-Thai cooking. If there are no seats downstairs, try the upstairs dining room. Along with the pans of curries displayed out the front, house specialities include *yâwt máphrâo phàt phèt kûng* (spicy stir-fried shrimp with coconut shoots), *khâo phàt pò tàek* (fried rice with seafood and kaffir lime) and *khâo yam* (a delicious southern Thai-style rice salad). The restaurant has daily specials, too. There are no English menus, and all signs are in Thai.

Ratana's Kitchen *(☎ 0 5387 4173; 320-322 Th Tha Phae; dishes 40-80B; open 9am-11pm daily)*, an air-con spot owned by an English-Thai couple and situated in a prime Th Tha Phae location, serves good Thai dishes from several regions, as well as a few *faràng* items. Located next to the Book Zone on Th Tha Phae, parking can be tight. If you're driving, you can usually park in the compound of adjacent Wat Chetawan.

Noodles

Khâo sàwy – a Shan-Yunnanese concoction of chicken (or, less commonly, beef), spicy curried broth and flat, squiggly, wheat noodles – is one of the most characteristic northern Thai noodle dishes. It's served with small saucers of shallot wedges, sweet-spicy pickled cabbage and a thick red chilli sauce.

The oldest area for *khâo sàwy* is Ban Haw, the *jiin haw* area around the Matsayit Chiang Mai on Soi 1, Th Charoen Prathet, around the corner from the Diamond Riverside Hotel and Galare Guest House and not far from the Chiang Mai Night Bazaar (in fact, this is where the *jiin haw* caravans of yore used to tie up). Yunnanese-run **Khao Soi Fuang Fah** and **Khao Soi Islam** *(no Roman-script signs for either; Soi 1, Th Charoen Prathet; dishes 20-40B; both open 5am-5pm daily)*, near Matsayit Chiang Mai, serve *khâo* *sàwy* as well as Muslim curries, *khànǒm jiin* (choice of two sauces, *náam yaa* or *náam ngíaw*) and *khâo mòk kài* (the Thai-Muslim version of chicken biryani). Khao Soi Islam also serves *khâo mòk pháe* (goat biryani).

Khao Soi Lam Duan *(Th Faham)*, just north of Saphan Phra Ram IX, serves large bowls of beef, pork or chicken *khâo sàwy*. Also on the menu are *kao-lǎo* (soup without noodles), *mǔu sà-té* (grilled spiced pork on bamboo skewers), *khâo sàwy* with beef or pork instead of chicken, *khànǒm rang phêung* (literally, beehive pastry, a coconut-flavoured waffle), Mekong rice whisky and beer. Two more very good *khâo sàwy* places along this same stretch of Th Faham are **Khao Soi Samoe Jai** and **Khao Soi Ban Faham**.

Khao Soi Prince *(Th Kaew Nawarat, near Prince Royal's College; dishes 20-35B; open 9am-3pm daily)* is regarded by many locals as their favourite spot for authentic *khâo sàwy*.

Rot Sawoei *(Th Arak; dishes 25-35B; open 11am-2.30am daily)*, around the corner from Buak Hat Park, is an unassuming place famous for very delectable *kǔaytǐaw kài tǔn yaa jiin*, rice noodles with Chinese herb-steamed chicken that practically melts off the bone. A normal bowl costs 25B, while a *phísèht* (special) order with extra chicken costs 35B. Its hours make it the perfect late-night spot for a snack.

Kuaytiaw Kai Tun Coke *(Th Kamphaeng Din; dishes 40B)*, a small food stall directly opposite the main entrance to the Imperial Mae Ping Hotel, does a simpler take on the same idea but substitutes Coca-Cola for the Chinese herbs. Here the chicken is marinated in cola and spices overnight before being steamed then served with rice noodles. It's actually quite good and has become famous as far away as Bangkok.

Rot Neung *(no Roman-script sign; Th Charoen Prathet; dishes 30B; open 9am-9pm daily)*, opposite the Diamond Riverside Hotel, serves some of the best *kǔaytǐaw lûuk chín plaa* (rice noodle soup with fish balls) in Chiang Mai. If you thought you didn't like fish balls – ground fish rolled into balls – give them a second try here, as this place makes them fresh and sells them to many other stands in town. A bowl is filled with noodles, fish balls, plus strips of fishcake and even delicious fish wonton.

Chinese

Mitmai Restaurant *(☎ 0 5327 5033; 42/2 Th Ratchamankha; dishes 35-65B; open 9am-9pm daily)* is a clean, simple and spacious Yunnanese place specialising in delicious vegetable soups made with pumpkin, taro, mushrooms, snowpeas or other vegetables. Especially tasty is the *tôm sôm plaa yâwt máphráo* (hot and sour fish soup with coconut shoots). The bilingual menu also includes *yam* (tangy, Thai-style salad) made with Chinese vegetables, as well as Yunnanese steamed ham, Chinese medicine chicken and many vegetarian dishes. Prices are moderate; no MSG is used in the cooking.

Salom Joy *(no Roman-script sign; Th Ratchadamnoen; dishes 20-40B; open around 6am-6pm daily)*, opposite Zest Bakery & Restaurant, is good for a quick Chinese breakfast. It has held out against the development of Pratu Tha Phae for many years and still serves cheap *jók* (rice congee), *paa-thâwng-kǒh* (Chinese 'doughnuts') and *náam tâo hûu* (hot soy milk). Later in the day noodle and rice plates are available.

Jok Somphet *(cnr Th Ratchaphakhinai & Th Si Phum; dishes 20-30B; open 6am-11pm)*, facing the northern moat, is popular for its namesake *jók*. The friendly proprietors also make decent *khâo sàwy kài* and other noodles – *bà-mìi* (wheat noodles), *kǔaytǐaw* (rice noodles) – with chicken, beef or pork.

China Palace *(☎ 0 5327 5300; Westin Riverside Plaza, 318/1 Th Chiang Mai-Lamphun; dishes 80-180B; open 11am-10pm daily)* is probably the best place to totally splurge on Chinese food in this plush spot at the Westin. It specialises in excellent Cantonese cuisine.

Chiang Mai has a small Chinatown in an area centred around Th Ratchawong north of Th Chang Moi. Here you'll find a whole string of Chinese rice and noodle shops, most of them offering variations on Tae Jiu (Chao Zhou) and Yunnanese cooking.

Indian, Muslim & Israeli

Along Soi 1, Th Charoen Prathet, between Th Chang Khlan and Th Charoen Prathet and near Chiang Mai (Ban Haw) Mosque, are a number of simple restaurants and alley vendors selling inexpensive but tasty Muslim curries and *khâo sàwy*. **Sophia** *(dishes 20-30B; open 8am-7pm Sat-Thur)*, on the opposite side of the lane from Khao Soi Islam and Khao Soi Fuang Fah (see Noodles earlier in this section), serves good curries and *khâo mòk kài*. *Néua òp hăwm* ('fragrant' Yunnanese Muslim-style dried beef), a speciality of Chiang Mai, is also sold along the lane. A **food vendor**, also on this lane, does delicious *rotii* (Indian flat bread) as well as chicken martabak (*mátàbà kài; rotii* stuffed with chicken).

Indian Restaurant Vegetarian Food (*☎ 0 5322 3396; Soi 9, Th Moon Muang*) is a very friendly, family-owned place that serves cheap and adequate vegetarian thalis as well as individual Indian dishes.

Shere Shiraz (*☎ 0 5327 6132; Soi 6, Th Charoen Prathet; dishes 50-100B; open about 9.30am-11pm daily*) serves mostly north-Indian food, with a few south-Indian dishes. The extensive menu includes many vegetarian dishes.

Arabia (*☎ 0 5381 8850; Anusan Night Market; dishes 30-80B, open 10am-10pm daily*) does north-Indian–Pakistani–Arab-style cuisine very well, perhaps better than any of the foregoing in terms of the freshness of the flavours. Don't let the fact that it's often empty or nearly so throw you off the trail; it has a steady and discerning, if small, clientele.

Jerusalem Falafel (*☎ 0 5327 0208; 35/3 Th Moon Muang; dishes 40-80B; open 9am-11pm Sat-Thur*) is a restaurant and bakery serving a selection of falafels, shasliks, hummus, and other Israeli specialities, as well as Thai and vegetarian food, baguettes, pizza, soups, salads, gelato, and delicious home-made cakes and pies.

Sa-Nga Choeng Doi (*no Roman-script sign; Th Charoensuk; dishes 25-35B; open 8am-4pm daily*) has probably the best *khâo mòk kài* and *mátàbà* in town, and if you happen to be near the YMCA in the Santitham district, it's a five-minute walk away. The home-made, unsweetened yogurt here is also highly recommended. The restaurant has no Roman-script sign – just look for the appropriate dishes on the tables.

Italian

Several enterprising Italians own and operate restaurants around town, and all of them have their strong points. **La Villa Pizzeria** (*☎ 0 5327 7403; 145 Th Ratchadamnoen; dishes 40-120B; open 11am-11pm daily*), in a large, old Thai house, serves delicious pizza baked in a wood-fired oven, and the rest of the Italian food on the menu is tops.

Da Stefano (*☎ 0 5387 4189; 2/1-2 Th Chang Moi Kao; dishes 60-120B; open about 11.30am-11pm Mon-Sat & 5.30pm-11pm Sun*) is an intimate, well-decorated, air-con place that focuses on fresh Italian cuisine, with one of the better wine lists in town. Prices are moderate, and the food and service are very good.

La Gondola (*☎ 0 5330 6483; behind Rim Ping Condo on Mae Nam Ping; dishes 60-120B; open 11am-midnight Tues-Sun*), a branch of Da Stefano, offers a similar menu with atmospheric, under-the-stars seating on a grassy area by the river.

Giorgio Italian Restaurant (*☎ 0 5381 8236; 2/6 Th Prachasamphan; dishes 100-200B; open 11am-11pm daily*) is Chiang Mai's newest Italian eatery and features a full range of pasta, all of it home-made, including *bigoli* (thick spaghetti). The salads are particularly good, while the slightly upscale decor is classy and retro.

Pum Pui Italian Restaurant (*☎ 0 5327 8209; 24 Soi 2, Th Moon Muang; dishes 50-120B; open 11am-11pm daily*), a more casual place near Top North Guest House, features a low-key garden setting and moderate prices; the menu includes olive pate and other antipasto, along with salads, several vegetarian selections, ice cream, breakfast, Italian wines and espressos. The complimentary Italian breads served at the beginning of all meals are excellent.

Piccola Roma Palace (*☎ 0 5327 1256; 144 Th Charoen Prathet; dishes 100-200B; open 11am-2pm & 5pm-11pm*), a luxurious place, is more of a splurge setting, with subdued lighting, sharp service and great attention to culinary detail. It also has very high prices (for Chiang Mai), the best salads in town and an excellent wine list – overall a good spot to celebrate an anniversary or the firing of your evil boss back home. Piccola Roma Palace offers free transportation to and from the restaurant – just call.

International

Art Café (*☎/fax 0 5320 6365; cnr Th Tha Phae & Th Kotchasan; dishes 40-100B; open 10am-10pm daily*), facing Pratu Tha Phae, is an air-con place offering a combination of vegetarian and nonvegetarian Italian, as well as Thai, Mexican and American food, including pizza, sandwiches, pasta, enchiladas, tacos, salads, ice cream, pies, tiramisu, shakes, fruit juices and coffees. It's the perfect place to go if you have a small group who can't decide what kind of food they want to eat. It occasionally hosts 190B Mexican buffets on Saturday. This restaurant is 100% smoke-free.

Zest Bakery & Restaurant *(formerly JJ Bakery & Restaurant; ☎ 0 5321 3088; cnr Th Moon Muang & Th Ratchadamnoen; Thai dishes 60-80B, breakfast 100-145B; open 6.30am-11pm daily)* is an amazing place that offers a very diverse menu of Western, Thai and Chinese dishes, all consistently good. It has very good coffee, inexpensive cocktails and a great selection of pies, cakes, croissants and cookies. Vegetarians may drool over the well-made brown-rice salad in the macrobiotic section of the menu.

Libernard Café *(☎ 0 5323 4877; 295-299 Th Chang Moi; dishes 40-100B; open 7.30am-5pm daily)* serves possibly the best coffee in town, fresh arabica grown in Thailand and roasted on the premises. The banana pancakes also deserve acclaim. A Thai menu is available as well.

Irish Pub *(☎ 0 5321 4554; 24/1 Th Ratwithi; dishes 50-100B; open 9am-midnight daily)* offers baked goods, good coffee, yogurt, muesli, sandwiches, pasta, pizza, vegetarian dishes, baked potatoes, ice cream, some Thai food, beer on tap, and fruit and vegetable juices. The homey indoor section is decorated with Irish kitsch and there's pleasant garden seating out the back.

Easy Diner *(☎ 0 5320 8989; 27/29 Th Ratchadamnoen; open Mon-Sat)* is an air-con place west of Pratu Tha Phae that specialises in American diner fare, such as burgers (vegetarian and chicken burgers included), hot dogs, ribs, chicken, salads, milk shakes and apple pie. Breakfast (including British style) is served all day, and there's a takeaway and delivery service.

Bake & Bite *(☎ 0 5328 5185; 6 Soi 1, Th Kotchasan; dishes 30-100B; open 7am-6pm Sun-Fri, 7am-3pm Sat)*, a tiny place wedged behind Suriwongse Plaza, prepares delicious European- and American-style pastries, pies and sandwiches on your choice of several breads. Good coffee, too.

Upper Crust Café *(☎ 0 5381 8183; Chiang Inn Plaza, Th Chang Khlan; dishes 40-80B; open 10am-11pm daily)* offers good pastries, mango cheesecake, Mexican dishes and sandwiches.

Little Pig Market *(☎ 0 5335 8148; 24/3 Th Nimanhaemin; dishes 20-50B; open 8am-7.30pm daily)*, is a small shop selling imported and locally produced groceries on the ground floor, while upstairs there's a cosy sitting area with baked goodies and various coffees.

Dara Steakhouse *(Th Tha Phae; dishes 40-120B; open 8am-9pm Mon-Sat)*, across from Roong Ruang Hotel, is a very casual spot, with an extensive Thai and Western menu and low prices.

The Amazing Sandwich *(☎ 0 5321 8846; 252/3 Th Phra Pokklao; dishes 60-90B; open 9am-8.30pm Mon-Sat)*, three doors north of the THAI office, is a small, very clean air-con place specialising in fresh baguettes with your choice of a dozen fillings, as well as lasagne, vegetable pie and quiche, plus juices, beers, wine, spirits and cocktails.

Popular among German expatriates and visitors are the **Bierstube** *(☎ 0 5327 8869; 33/6 Th Moon Muang; dishes 40-100B; open 7.30am-11pm daily)*, near Pratu Tha Phae, and **Haus München** *(☎ 0 5327 4027; 115/3 Th Loi Kroh; dishes 40-100B; open noon-midnight daily)*, east of Chiangmai Pavilion. Next to Haus München are three more European eateries, all in a row along Th Loi Kroh: **Red Lion English Pub & Restaurant**, **German Hofbräuhaus** and **Café Benelux**, each serving the type of cuisine their names imply.

Chez John *(☎ 0 5320 1551; 18/1 Th Mahidon; dishes 80-160B; open noon-2pm & 6.30pm-10pm daily)*, near the airport and opposite the customs office, offers moderately priced French cuisine as well as a large selection of wines. **Le Coq d'Or** *(☎ 0 5328 2024; ⓔ lecoqd'or@d-d-web.com; 68/1 Th Ko Klang; dishes 100-200B; open 11am-2pm & 6pm-11pm daily)* is more expensive and formal, and is a long-standing place that serves French haute cuisine in a lavishly decorated mansion off Th Chiang Mai-Lamphun east of the river.

The main fast-food district in Chiang Mai runs along Th Chang Khlan, in the Chiang Mai Night Bazaar area. This strip features the usual Western fast-food outlets, most of which are clustered within the Chiang Inn Plaza. Similar franchise-style places can be found in the Kad Suan Kaew shopping centre on Th Huay Kaew and at Central Airport Plaza near the airport.

Vegetarian

Chiang Mai is blessed with over 25 vegetarian restaurants, most of them very inexpensive. **AUM Vegetarian Food** *(☎ 0 5327 8315; 65 Th Moon Muang; dishes 30-70B; open 8am-9pm daily)*, near Pratu Tha Phae, has long been popular with travellers because of its easy location. The all-vegie menu features a varied list of traditional Thai and Chinese dishes, including northern and northeastern Thai dishes, prepared without meat or eggs. There is an upstairs eating area with cushions on the floor and low tables.

Mangsawirat Kangreuanjam *(Soi 1, Th Inthawarorot; dishes 10-20B; open 8am until early afternoon when everything's sold)* has a difficult-to-see English sign that reads 'Vegetarian Food'; look for a cluster of stainless steel pots. The cooks put out 15 to 20 pots of fresh, 100%-Thai vegetarian dishes daily. The dishes feature lots of bean curd, squash, peas, pineapple, sprouts and potato, and the desserts are good. Very good and very cheap – three items over rice cost just 15B to 20B, or figure 40B to 50B for three large bowls of food, two plates of rice and two bottles of water, more than enough to engorge two hungry stomachs.

Biaporn *(Soi 1, Th Si Phum; dishes 20-30B; open 10am-3pm)* is also within the old city quadrangle, just north of SK Guest House. It's an OK, very inexpensive Thai vegetarian place with a more limited selection of dishes.

The Asoke Foundation–sponsored **Vegetarian Centre of Chiang Mai** *(☎ 0 5327 1262; 14 Th Mahidon; dishes 10-15B; open 6am-2pm Sun-Thur)* operates an extremely cheap Thai vegetarian restaurant, south of the southwestern corner of the city walls. The food is served cafeteria-style – you push a tray down a rack and point at what you want. Warning: brown rice only. A small health-food section to one side of the restaurant offers dried gluten, nuts, beans, herbs, vegetarian chilli sauces, natural beauty products, herbal medicines and Dharma books (mostly in Thai). From Thursday afternoon to Saturday it's closed so that the staff can visit a retreat centre belonging to the Santi Asoke Buddhist sect in the *amphoe* (district) of Mae Taeng.

Suandok Vegetarian *(Th Suthep; dishes 10-20B; open 7am-2pm daily)*, just west of the entrance to Wat Suan Dok, offers a similar array of inexpensive, wholesome Thai vegetarian dishes and brown rice.

Whole Earth Restaurant *(☎ 0 5328 2463; 88 Th Si Donchai; dishes 90-200B; open 11am-11pm daily)*, past the Th Chang Khlan intersection, is associated with a Transcendental Meditation centre. The food is Thai and Indian (vegetarian and nonvegetarian) and the atmosphere is suitably mellow, although the food may be a bit overpriced and underspiced.

Vihara Liangsan *(☎ 0 5381 8094; 199/23 Th Chang Khlan; lunch about 25B; open 9am-2pm daily)* is around the corner from Whole Earth and south down Th Chang Khlan. Take a left off Th Chang Khlan into a small lane past the all-white Season (Si Suan) Plaza shopping centre and it's on your right. You serve yourself from a long buffet table (the food is a mix of Chinese and Thai vegetarian, with lots of tofu and gluten), then place your plate – including rice – on a scale and pay by weight. It's best to get here between 11am and 1pm as the food sometimes runs out.

All of the Indian restaurants mentioned earlier in this section feature short vegetarian sections in their menus; the Indian Restaurant Vegetarian Food's cuisine is all vegie.

Food Centres

At **Kad Suan Kaew shopping centre** on Th Huay Kaew and **Central Airport Plaza** on Th Mahidon, food centres gather together vendors selling all kinds of Thai and Chinese dishes at reasonable prices.

Galare Food Centre, a big indoor/outdoor cluster of permanent vendors opposite the main Chiangmai Night Bazaar building on Th Chang Khlan, is also good; free Thai classical dancing is featured nightly.

Night Markets

Chiang Mai is full of interesting day and night markets stocked with very inexpensive and very tasty foods. The **Somphet Market** *(Th Moon Muang)*, north of the Th Ratwithi intersection, sells cheap takeaway curries, yam, *lâap* (spicy minced meat), *thâwt man* (fried fish cakes), sweets and seafood. On the opposite side of the moat, the small **Somphet night market** *(Th Chaiyaphum)* has everything from noodles and seafood to the specialities of Yunnan. A lot of travellers eat here, so prices are just a bit higher than average, but the food is usually good.

Another good hunting ground is the very large and popular **Chiang Mai night market** *(along Th Bamrungburi near Pratu Chiang Mai)*. People tend to take their time here, making an evening of eating and drinking – there's no hustle to vacate tables for more customers.

In the upstairs section of **Talat Warorot** *(cnr Th Chang Moi & Th Praisani; open 6am-5pm daily)* are a number of basic stalls for *khâo tôm* (rice soup), *khâo man kài* (chicken rice), *khâo mŭu daeng* ('red' pork with rice), *jók* and *khâo sàwy*, with tables overlooking the market floor. It's not the best cooking in Chiang Mai by a long shot, but it's cheap. A set of vendors on the ground floor specialise in inexpensive noodles – this area is particularly popular.

Anusan Night Market *(between Th Chang Khlan & Th Charoen Prathet near Chiang Mai Night Bazaar)* attracts both the tourists and Thais. If you wander over here, look for the stalls that are crowded – they're usually the best. All of the places have English menus. The large *khâo tôm* place near the market entrance, **Uan Heh-Hah**, still packs in the customers; the most popular dish is the *khâo tôm plaa* (fish and rice soup), but other specialities worth trying include curried fish balls and curry-fried crab.

San Pa Khoi Market, midway between the river and the train station on Charoen Muang, has a better selection and lower prices than Anusan. A **curry stand** in San Pa Khoi Market is probably the only place in Chiang Mai where you can find fresh Thai curries past 11pm. It stays open until around 5am and is very popular with late-night partiers.

On the River

Riverside Bar & Restaurant *(☎ 0 5324 3239; Th Charoenrat; dishes 60-120B; open 5pm-1am daily)*, 200m north of Saphan Nawarat, has been the most consistent riverside place over the years. The food is always good, and it's as popular with Thais as with *faràng*. The atmosphere is convivial and there's live music nightly. Another plus is that you can choose from indoor and outdoor dining areas. There's also an 8pm dinner cruise – you can board the boat any time after 7.30pm.

Good View *(☎ 0 5324 1866; 13 Th Charoenrat; dishes 60-120B; open 6pm-1am daily)*, near Riverside, is newer, with more open-air areas, and it is more popular with Thais than *faràng*. The 122-item menu covers everything Thai. There's live music here also.

The Gallery *(☎ 0 5324 8601; 25-29 Th Charoenrat; dishes 60-120B; open noon-1am daily)* is another elegant eatery a little farther north along the river. It's a converted 100-year-old teak Chinese temple that's half art gallery, half restaurant. The quality of the food goes up and down, however; sometimes it's great, other times so-so. Ditto for service.

The Riverfront Restaurant *(Tha Nam; ☎ 0 5327 5125; 43/3 Th Chang Khlan; dishes 50-100B; open 8am-11pm)*, along the west bank of Mae Nam Ping, is housed in an old, northern Thai-style building. The Riverfront is pretty reliable for northern, northeastern and central Thai cuisine. A northern-Thai folk ensemble performs in the evenings.

See Regional Thai earlier in this section for a description of Heuan Soontharee, on the west bank of the river.

ENTERTAINMENT

Bars & Pubs

A section of Th Ratwithi extending a couple of blocks west of Th Moon Muang has become a good area for pubs, and Thais and foreigners, women as well as men, meet here for drinks and conversation. Mixed in among the pubs are a large art supplies store, a couple of homespun print shops, and other vaguely 'media-industrial' endeavours, some of them rather old.

Walking from Th Moon Muang, first is the long-running **Irish Pub** *(24/1 Th Ratwithi)* on the right, which has nothing particularly Irish about it other than some kitsch on the walls. The beers are all Thai-brewed, but it's quiet and the comfortable upstairs area is even suitable for solo reading or writing. Next, on the corner of Th Ratwithi and the lane that leads around the corner to Eagle House 2, sits the diminutive **Yoy Pocket** *(Th Ratwithi)*, a funky spot reminiscent of some of the homier cafés-pubs on Th Phra Athit in Bangkok.

Behind the building that houses the Yoy Pocket, the outdoor **Rasta Café** plays recorded reggae, dub, African and Latin music, and is quite popular in the high season. Look for other abandoned shopfronts along this street to give birth to more Thai pubs with creative decor – if the sagging economy permits.

Kafé *(Th Moon Muang, between Soi 5 & Soi 6)*, near Somphet Market, has a happy hour that is popular among expats and Thais. Farther south along Th Moon Muang, between Th Ratchadamnoen and Soi 3, is a string of small bars, some of these are strongly male-oriented in their overabundance of female staff, others good all-round places for a drink.

Pinte Blues Pub *(33/6 Th Moon Muang)* is a long-running place that serves espresso and beer, and plays tapes and CDs from a huge blues collection. **Sax Music Pub** *(Th Moon Muang)* in this same area plays a wide variety of CDs. The Pinte Blues Pub is the only bar in the Pratu Tha Phae vicinity where you generally see couples or *faràng* women, although during the high season the crowd at the Sax Music Pub can be relatively mixed.

Drunken Flower *(Mai Dokmai; ☎ 0 5321 2081)*, at the end of Soi 1 and off Th Nimanhaemin, is a cosy indoor/outdoor bar and restaurant with a mixed Thai and expat crowd, especially local nongovernmental organisation (NGO) staffers.

Darling Swiss Wine Pub & Bottle Shop *(☎ 0 5321 5167; Nantawan Arcade, 95/10 Nimanhaemin; open 5pm-midnight Tues-Sun)* serves fine wines by the glass or bottle in a sophisticated but relaxed atmosphere.

Most bars and pubs in Chiang Mai shut their doors at 1am, the legal closing time.

Discos

All the flashy hotels have discos with hi-tech recorded music and cover charges of 100B to 200B. The most active hotel discos in town are still **Fantasy Discotheque** (Chiang Inn), **Stardust** (Westin Riverside Plaza), **Crystal Cave** (Empress Hotel) and the ever popular **Bubbles** (Porn Ping Tower Hotel). Bubbles (actually the name has been 'updated' to Space Bubble, but everyone in town still calls it by the old name, which in Thai is pronounced 'Bubben') has the most regular local clientele.

Gi Gi's *(☎ 0 5330 2340-1; Th Chiang Mai-Lamphun)*, east of Mae Nam Ping, is one of the most popular nonhotel discos, along with **Discovery** *(Ground floor, Kad Suan Kaew shopping centre)*. In Thai parlance, these are 'kitchen discos' *(disco khrua)*, which means customers stand next to small, round, waist-height tables on the dance floor so that they dance close to their drinks and purses. **Nice Illusion** *(Th Chaiyaphum)*, near the moat, gets so crowded some nights there's barely room to move. At all three places, the crowd tends to be very young.

All Chiang Mai discos are legally required to close at 2am.

Live Music

Riverside Bar & Restaurant *(☎ 0 5324 3239; 9-11 Th Charoenrat; open until 2am or 3am)*, on Mae Nam Ping, is one of the longest-running live music venues in Chiang Mai. Two cover bands play at either end of the rambling wooden building nightly. It's usually packed with both foreigners and Thais on weekends, so arrive early to get a table on the veranda overlooking the river. There are two indoor bars, both full of regulars, with separate bands. **Good View** *(☎ 0 5324 1866; 13 Th Charoenrat)*, next door, changes bands more frequently and is also quite popular.

Le Brasserie *(☎ 0 5324 1665; 37 Th Charoenrat)*, a block or so north of the Good View has become a favourite late-night spot (11.15pm to 2am) to listen to a talented Thai guitarist named Took play energetic versions of Hendrix, Cream, Dylan, Marley, the Allmans, and other 1960s and 1970s gems. A couple of other local bands warm up the house before Took comes on, often to a packed house. Food service is available inside the bar or out the back by the river.

Warm-Up *(☎ 0 9993 2963; 60 Th Wat Ket)*, tucked away in an old two-storey wooden house a couple of blocks back from the river in the same neighbourhood as Le Brasserie, occasionally hosts nationally known Thai bands such as Modern Dog or T-Bone. On other nights local bands play Thai pop and reggae. This place is packed with students from Ratchamangkala Institute of Technology.

Until the recent police crackdown all of the above were open until 2am, the national legal closing time for places with live music.

Recently, local police have been forcing them to close at 1am.

Cinemas

Major Cineplex (*☎ 0 5328 3939; Cental Airport Plaza, 2 Th Mahidon*) is new and the best cinema in town. Along with the latest Thai films, first-run foreign films with English soundtracks are frequently shown. It boasts a state-of-the-art sound system along with 'honeymoon seats', pairs of seats without a middle armrest for romantic couples.

Two other cinemas showing first-run foreign as well as Thai films are the **Vista cinemas** at two shopping centres opposite one another on Th Huay Kaew: Kad Suan Kaew shopping centre and Vista 12 Huay Kaew.

The best source of information on current movie programming at all three cinema houses in Chiang Mai is the Thai homepage of Ⓦ www.movieseer.com (in English).

Every Sunday at 3pm, **Chiang Mai University** presents a different foreign film – usually art films of the Bergman and Buñuel variety – at the main auditorium of the Art & Culture Center. Admission is free.

SHOPPING

Hundreds of shops all over Chiang Mai sell hill-tribe and northern-Thai craftwork, but a lot of it is commercial and touristy junk churned out for the undiscerning. So bargain hard and buy carefully! The nonprofit outlets often have the best quality and, although the prices are sometimes a bit higher than at the Chiang Mai Night Bazaar, a higher percentage of your money goes directly to the hill-tribe artisans.

Thai Tribal Crafts (*☎ 0 5324 1043; 208 Th Bamrungrat*), near the McCormick Hospital, is run by two church groups on a nonprofit basis and has a good selection of quality handicrafts. **Hill-Tribe Products Promotion Centre** (*☎ 0 5327 7743; 21/17 Th Suthep*), near Wat Suan Dok, is a royally sponsored project; all profits go to hill-tribe welfare programs. The YMCA International Hotel also operates a nonprofit **handicrafts centre**.

The two commercial markets with the widest selections of northern-Thai folk crafts are **Talat Warorot** (*Th Chang Moi Kao*), at the eastern end of the road, and the **Chiang Mai Night Bazaar** (*off Th Chang Khlan*). See the separate entry for each of these under Markets following.

As Chiang Mai is Thailand's main handicraft centre, it's ringed by small cottage factories and workshops where you can watch craftspeople at work. In general, though, merchandise you see at factories outside the city will cost more than it would in Chiang Mai unless you're buying in bulk.

Markets

Talat Warorot (locally called *kàat lŭang*, northern Thai for 'great market') is the oldest and most famous market in Chiang Mai. Although the huge enclosure is quite dilapidated (ignore the scary-looking escalators, which haven't functioned for years), it's an especially good market for fabrics and cooking implements, along with inexpensive cosmetics, clothing, handicrafts and prepared foods (especially northern Thai foods). Across the street from Talat Warorot stands the very similar **Talat Lamyai**. Both markets are open from around 5am to 6pm daily.

Chiang Mai Night Market (*Talat Pratu Chiang Mai; Th Bamrungburi*), near Pratu Chiang Mai, is a fresh market that's particularly busy with locals shopping for takeaway Thai and northern Thai food. The indoor area is open from 4am until around noon, while outside vendors continue to sell until nightfall. A night food market then sets up across the street next to the moat and stays open past midnight.

Talat San Pa Khoi (*off Th Charoen Muang*) and **Talat Thiphanet** (*Th Thipanet*) are large municipal markets that offer all manner of goods and see few tourists. San Pa Khoi opens around 4am and does a brisk trade until around 10am, then slows until an hour before nightfall.

The best market for prepared foods is the clean and well-run **Talat Thanin** (*off Th Chotana; open 5am until early evening*), north of Pratu Chang Pheuak.

Just south of Talat Thiphanet, the **Chiang Mai Plant Market** (*Talat Dok Mai Chiang Mai; open around 9am until sunset*) is the perfect place to pick up some greenery to feather your Chiang Mai nest if you're settling in long term. A quick stop for flowers only, and especially fresh *phuang má-lai* (jasmine garlands), is the nameless **Flower Market** (*tàlaat dàwk mái*) on Th Praisani near Talat Warorot.

Talat Ton Phayom (*Th Suthep*), across from Chiang Mai University, features all manner of fresh produce and cooked foods. Because CMU students make up a good portion of the clientele, prices tend to be low.

Chiang Mai Night Bazaar

Chiang Mai Night Bazaar, the mother of all Chiang Mai tourist shopping, refers to a multiblock area stretching along Th Chang Khlan from Th Tha Phae to Th Si Donchai. Made up of several different roofed areas, ordinary glass-fronted shops and dozens of street vendors, the market offers a huge variety of Thai and northern Thai goods, as well as designer goods (both fake and licensed, so look carefully) at very low prices – if you bargain well. Many importers buy here because the prices are so good, especially when buying in large quantities.

Good buys include Phrae-style *sêua mâw hâwm* (blue cotton farmer's shirt), northern- and northeastern-Thai hand-woven fabrics, *yâam* (shoulder bags), hill-tribe crafts (many tribespeople set up their own stalls here; the Akha wander around on foot), opium scales, hats, silver jewellery, lacquerware, woodcarvings, iron and bronze Buddhas, as well as many other items.

If you're in need of new travelling clothes, a light cotton dress, trousers or *yâam* can be bought for less than 150B, and *sêua mâw hâwm* cost between 80B and 100B, depending on size. Spices – everything from a *tôm yam* (soup made with lemongrass, chilli, lime and usually seafood) herbal mix to pure saffron – are available from several vendors. Cashew nuts, roasted or raw, are often less expensive here than in southern Thailand where they're grown.

Chiangmai Night Bazaar Building *(Th Chang Khlan)* holds a couple of dozen permanent shops selling antiques, handicrafts, rattan and hardwood furniture, textiles, jewellery, pottery, basketry, silverwork, woodcarving and other items of local manufacture. Prices can be very good if you bargain hard. **Chiang Mai** *(2nd floor, Chiang Mai Night Bazaar Bldg)*, one of our favourite shops along the entire strip, carries a selection of well-made cotton T-shirts silk-screened with more than 30 different old Chiang Mai designs, along with equally well-designed silver-and-bead jewellery and a changing selection of interesting accessories.

Except in the few shops with fixed prices (like the aforementioned Chiang Mai), you must bargain patiently but mercilessly. The fact that there are so many different stalls selling the same items means that competition effectively keeps prices low, if you haggle. Look over the whole bazaar before you begin buying. If you're not in the mood or don't have the money to buy, it's still worth a stroll, unless you don't like crowds – most nights it's elbow to elbow.

Several restaurants and many food trolleys feed the hungry masses. Down Soi Anusan at the southern end of Th Chang Khlan, the **Anusan Night Market** *(Soi Anusan, Th Chang Khlan)* has lots of good Thai and Chinese food at night, and in the early morning (from 5am to 9am) you'll find fresh produce and noodle vendors.

Shopping Centres & Department Stores

Chiang Mai has over 15 shopping centres with department stores. **Kad Suan Kaew shopping centre** *(Th Huay Kaew)*, centred around a branch of Bangkok's Central department store, is the best, with **Central Airport Plaza** a close second. There are several upmarket shops in both complexes. **Computer Plaza** *(Th Mani Nopharat)*, near the northwestern corner of the moat, is the place to go for computer supplies.

Antiques

You'll see lots of antiques in the city. Check prices in Bangkok first, as Chiang Mai's shops are not always cheap. Also remember that worldwide there are a lot more instant antiques than authentic ones.

The **Chiang Mai Night Bazaar** area is probably the best place to look for fake antiques. Inside the Chiangmai Night Bazaar building, towards the back on the 2nd floor, are a few small shops with real antiques. Among the best is **The Lost Heavens** *(☎ 0 5327 8185; Stall 2, 2nd floor, Chiangmai Night Bazaar Bldg • ☎ 0 5325 1557; 234 Th Tha Phae)*, which specialises in Mien tribal artefacts. It's in the 'antiques corner' towards the back left of the Night Bazaar building. Its second store is opposite Wat Bupparam.

Under the Bo *(☎ 0 5381 8831)* at Stall 22-23 carries many unique pieces, in the form of furniture, antique bronze and wood figures, old doors, woodcarvings and weaving from Africa, South Asia and Southeast Asia. It isn't cheap, but many items are one-of-a-kind. It has another shop out on the road to Hang Dong, about 5km southwest of Th Mahidon.

Many more antique shops can be found along Th Tha Phae and especially along Th Loi Kroh. Burmese antiques are becoming more common than Thai, as most of the Thai stuff has been bought by collectors, and you can get some great buys on antique Burmese furniture from the British colonial period.

Hang Dong, 25km south of Chiang Mai, is even better for antique furniture of all kinds, especially the string of shops just east of Hang Dong on Th Thakhilek (the road to Ban Thawai), an area usually called Ban Wan. A couple of shops in Ban Wan make reproductions of Thai and Burmese antique furniture using salvaged old teak, which can be very good buys. **Srithong Thoprasert** (☎ *0 5343 3112, Th Thakhilek)* is one of the better ones. It's about 500m from the main Hang Dong intersection.

Nakee's Asia Treasures (☎ *0 5344 1357)*, a few hundred metres towards Ban Thawai from Srithong Thoprasert, has contemporary Thai furniture and designer accessories based on older themes updated for form and function (including some fusion with Santa Fe styles). It also sells good antiques – all very tasteful and of high quality. Ban Thawai itself is a woodcarving village offering mostly new pieces, though very little of high quality.

Bamboo Saxophones

Perhaps because northern Thailand is one of Asia's major locales for both wild and cultivated bamboo, Chiang Mai has attracted interest in the crafting of 'saxophones' from bamboo (although the first such instruments seem to have taken shape some 40 years ago in Jamaica). Actually a hybrid between the saxophone and the recorder (sax shape and sax reed, recorder fingering), the instruments come in two keys, G and F. For each saxophone the bamboo must be carefully selected, cut into short rings, which are roasted over a fire to temper them, and then fitted and glued into the familiar curved shape. The sonic characteristics of the bamboo perfectly compliment the traditional cane sax reed to produce a very mellow, slightly raspy sound.

Two Chiang Mai residents make these delightful little instruments, which produce amazing volume considering their relatively small size. **Joy of Sax** (☎ *0 5322 2505)* sells bamboo saxes through **The Lost Heavens** (☎ *0 5325 1557; 234 Th Tha Phae)*, opposite Wat Bupparum. You can also contact the Joy of Sax workshop directly. A sax in the key of G costs 4500B, and the slightly larger F sax 4800B; an instruction sheet and colourful hemp bag are included. **Elephant Lightfoot** (☎ *0 5387 9191; 4/1 Th Chaiyaphum)* has a shopfront near Pratu Tha Phae and makes F, G, B-flat and E-flat models, for about the same price as Joy of Sax.

Ceramics

Thai Celadon (☎ *0 5321 3541, 0 5321 3245; 112 Th Chotana; open Mon-Sat)*, about 6km north of Chiang Mai, turns out ceramics modelled on the Sawankhalok pottery that used to be made hundreds of years ago at Sukhothai and exported all over the region. With their deep, crackle-glaze finish, some ceramic pieces are very beautiful and the prices are often lower than in Bangkok.

Mengrai Kilns (☎ *0 5327 2063; 79/2 Th Arak)*, in the southwestern corner of the inner moat area near Buak Hat Park, is reliable. Other ceramic stores can be found close to the Old Chiang Mai Cultural Centre.

There are also several celadon operations in the nearby town of Hang Dong.

Clothes

All sorts of shirts, blouses and dresses, plain and embroidered, are available at very low prices, but make sure that you check the quality carefully. The Chiang Mai Night Bazaar and shops along Th Tha Phae and Th Loi Kroh have good selections. Also see the Tailors and Textiles entries in this section for other clothing options.

One shop selling good ready-made clothing made from northern-Thai textiles is **Sri Sanpanmai** (☎ *0 5389 4372; G-59 Kad Suan Kaew, Th Huay Kaew)*.

Lacquerware

Decorated plates, containers, utensils and other items are made by building up layers of lacquer over a wooden or woven bamboo base. Burmese lacquerware, smuggled into the north, can often be seen, especially at Mae Sai, the northernmost point of Thailand There are several lacquerware factories in San Kamphaeng, southeast of Chiang Mai.

Musical Instruments

Lanna Music (☎ *0 5327 4144; 148/1 Th Phra Pokklao)* sells and repairs northern-Thai musical instruments.

Rattan

Two cheaper rattan shops can be found along the northern side of Th Chang Moi Kao, two blocks east of the moat. This is the place to buy chairs, small tables, chaise longues, planters, floor screens, settees, bookshelves and other everyday household items. Most of the cheaper pieces, eg, a bookshelf or low-quality chair, cost around 800B, while a rattan chair of better, longer-lasting workmanship will cost 2000B to 5000B.

For higher-quality furniture and accessories made from this jungle vine, check out **Hangdong Rattan** *(☎ 0 5320 8167; 54-55 Th Loi Kroh)*. In addition to the many items on display, Hangdong takes custom orders.

Silverwork

There are several silverwork shops on Th Wualai close to Pratu Chiang Mai. **Sipsong Panna** *(☎ 0 5321 6096; 6/19 Th Nimanhaemin)*, in the Nantawan Arcade opposite the Amari Rincome Hotel, is a more up-market place for jewellery collected in Thailand, Laos, Myanmar and Southwest China. Hill-tribe jewellery, which is heavy, chunky stuff, is very nice.

Tailors

There are several tailor shops off Th Kotchasan near Aroon (Rai) Restaurant, including Florida, Chao Khun, Chaiyo and Progress. Another strip of tailors, catering mostly to tourists, can be found along Th Chang Khlan in the Chiang Mai Night Bazaar area. Prices are reasonable, and often cheaper than in Bangkok. **City Silk** *(☎ 0 5323 4388; 336 Th Tha Phae)*, more or less opposite Wat Mahawan, specialises in silk tailoring for women. English is spoken here, and service is friendly and professional. Ask to see some finished work before choosing a shop.

Textiles

Very attractive lengths of material can be made into all sorts of things. Thai silk, with its lush colours and pleasantly rough texture, is a particularly good bargain and is usually cheaper here than in Bangkok. **Talat Warorot** is one of the best and least expensive places to look for fabrics, but take care, as many items said to be silk are actually polyester.

Several individual shops in town focus on high-quality traditional (sometimes antique) Thai and Lao fabrics, sold by the metre or made up into original-design clothes. A list of the best places in town would have to include **Sbun-Nga** and **Nandakwang**, both in the Nantawan Arcade.

Studio Naenna *(☎/fax 0 5322 6042; 138/8 Soi Chang Khian, Th Huay Kaew)* is operated by Patricia Cheeseman, an expert on Thai-Lao textiles who has written extensively on the subject.

The Loom *(☎/fax 0 5327 8892; Chiang Inn Plaza, 100/1 Th Chang Khlan)* carries very fine fabrics from northern and northeastern Thailand, Laos and Cambodia.

Another good source of textiles is **Duangjitt House** *(☎ 0 5324 2291, 0 5324 3546)*, on a lane off Th Thung Hotel opposite the Northern Crafts Centre building – call for an appointment.

You'll also find several shops selling antique Thai and Lao textiles along Th Loi Kroh, including **Woven Dreams** *(☎ 0 5327 2569; 30/1 Th Loi Kroh)* and **Success Silk Shop** *(☎ 0 5320 8853; 56 Th Loi Kroh)*, which both feature Thai silk ready-made and made-to-order clothes using fabrics from Thailand, Laos and Cambodia. Many are patched together from old hand-woven textiles and made into dresses, skirts, shirts and jackets. They also offer silk scarves, woven hats and *yâam* – all more or less sized for *faràng*.

If you want to see where and how the cloth is made, go to the nearby town of San Kamphaeng for Thai silk, or to Pasang, south of Lamphun, for cotton.

Umbrellas

At Bo Sang, the 'umbrella village', 9km ease of Chiang Mai, you will find hand-painted paper umbrellas of all kinds, from simple traditional brown ones to giant rainbow-hued parasols.

Woodcarving

Many types of carvings are available, including countless elephants. Teak salad bowls are good and very cheap. Many shops along Th Tha Phae and near the Chiang Mai Night

Bazaar stock wood crafts, or you can go to the source – Hang Dong and Ban Thawai.

GETTING THERE & AWAY

Air

Regularly scheduled international flights arrive at **Chiang Mai International Airport** *(☎ 0 5327 0222)* from the following countries, as well as domestic flights from several other cities in Thailand.

Kunming (THAI; ☎ 0 5321 1044–7)
Singapore (Silk Air; ☎ 0 5327 6459)
Taipei (Mandarin Airlines; ☎ 0 5320 1268)
Vientiane, Luang Prabang (Lao Aviation; ☎ 0 5322 3401)
Yangon, Mandalay (Air Mandalay; ☎ 0 5381 8049)

The **THAI office** *(☎ 0 5321 1044-7; 240 Th Phra Pokklao)* is within the city moat area, behind Wat Chiang Man. THAI operates 11 one-hour flights between Bangkok and Chiang Mai daily (plus additional flights on certain days of the week). The fare is 2170B one way in economy class. THAI also flies between Chiang Mai, Mae Hong Son (690B) and Phuket (4520B).

Relative newcomer **Air Andaman** *(☎ 0 5327 8437; Chiang Mai International Airport)* has taken over several routes previously flown by THAI, connecting Chiang Mai with Chiang Rai (1200B), Mae Sot (1450B), Nan (1400B) and Phitsanulok (1500B).

Bangkok Airways *(☎ 0 5321 0043–4, fax 0 5328 1520; Chiang Mai International Airport)* operates daily flights to/from Bangkok via Sukhothai for 2170B.

Although rather small, Chiang Mai International Airport is quite well equipped with facilities for the traveller. Upstairs on the departure level is a branch of Suriwong Book Centre, selling magazines, newspapers and books, and a large restaurant operated by THAI, which serves Thai, Chinese and international food. On the ground floor are several fast-food outlets, a phone office (open from 8.30am to 8pm), a car-rental booth, money changers and ATMs, a tourist information booth and taxi service.

Bus

From Bangkok's newer Northern and Northeastern bus terminal (also known as Moh Chit) there are five ordinary buses daily to Chiang Mai. The 12-hour trip costs 215B via Nakhon Sawan and 200B via Ayuthaya. There are thirteen 2nd-class air-con buses a day – on which the air-con doesn't always work – for 314B; these take 10 to 11 hours to reach Chiang Mai.

First-class air-con buses with toilets and 34 seats leave every 30 minutes from 7am to 8.45pm and cost 403B one way. The government VIP buses, with 24 seats that recline a bit more than the seats in 1st class air, cost 625B; there are only a couple of departures each day, from either Bangkok or Chiang Mai, between 7pm and 9pm. The 1st-class and VIP buses take from nine to 10 hours to reach Chiang Mai, depending on the traffic.

Ten or more private tour companies run air-con buses between Bangkok and Chiang Mai, departing from various points throughout both cities. Return tickets are always somewhat cheaper than one-way tickets. The fares cost 300B to 400B, depending on the bus. The government buses from the Northern and Northeastern bus terminal are generally more reliable and on schedule than the private ones booked in Banglamphu and other tourist-oriented places.

Travel agencies in Bangkok are notorious for promising services they can't deliver, such as reclining seats or air-con that works. Several Th Khao San agencies offer bus tickets to Chiang Mai for as little as 200B, including a night's free stay at a guesthouse in Chiang Mai. Sometimes this works out well, but the buses can be substandard and the 'free' guesthouse may charge you 40B for electricity or hot water, or apply heavy pressure for you to sign up for one of its treks before you can get a room. Besides, riding in a bus or minivan stuffed full of foreigners and their bulky backpacks is not the most cultural experience.

Several readers have complained that they purchased tickets for large air-con or even VIP buses from Th Khao San and at the last minute were shunted into cramped minivans. We recommend avoiding these buses altogether; use public buses from Bangkok's Northern and Northeastern bus terminal instead.

Government buses between Chiang Mai and other northern towns depart frequently throughout the day (at least hourly), except for the Mae Sai, Khon Kaen, Udon, Ubon and Khorat buses, which have morning and evening departures only. (See the Bus

Destinations from Chiang Mai table for fares and destinations for government buses.)

For buses to destinations within Chiang Mai Province use the **Chang Pheuak bus terminal** (*☎ 0 5321 1586; Th Chotana*), while for buses outside the province use the **Chiang Mai Arcade bus terminal** (*☎ 0 5324 2664*), also called New Terminal. From the town centre, a túk-túk or chartered săwngthăew to the Chiang Mai Arcade terminal should cost 30B to 40B; to the Chang Pheuak terminal you should be able to get a săwngthăew at the normal 10B per person rate.

Train

Chiang Mai-bound rapid trains leave Bangkok's **Hualamphong station** (*☎ 0 2220 4334, 0 2220 1690*) daily at 3pm (air-con 2nd class and 3rd class) and 10pm (non-air-con 2nd-class sleeper and 3rd class), arriving at 6.05am and 11.55am respectively. Express diesel railcars depart at 8.25am and 7.25pm (air-con 2nd-class only) and arrive at 8pm and 7.40am.

Special express trains depart daily at 6pm (air-con 1st- and 2nd-class sleeper and non-air-con 2nd-class sleeper) and 7.40pm (air-con 1st- and 2nd-class only), arriving in Chiang Mai at 7.20am and 9.30am.

The basic 2nd-class one-way fare is 281B, plus either the special express (80B), express (60B) or rapid (40B) surcharges. Add 100B for an upper berth and 150B for a lower berth in a non-air-con 2nd-class rapid train (130B

Bus Destinations from Chiang Mai

destination	fare (B)	duration (hrs)
Chiang Dao*	25	1½
Chiang Khong	121	6½
air-con	169	6
1st class air-con	218	6
Chiang Rai	77	4
air-con	98	3
1st class	139	3
Chiang Saen	95	4
1st class air-con	171	3½
Chom Thong*	23	2
Fang*	61	3
van	100	3
Hang Dong*	8	½
Khon Kaen (via Tak)	243	12
air-con	340	12
1st class air-con	437	12
Khon Kaen		
(via Utaradit)	219	11
air-con	307	11
1st class air-con	394	11
Khorat	243	12
1st class air-con	437	12
VIP	510	12
Lampang	25	2
air-con	52	2
1st class air-con	70	2
Lamphun	12	
Mae Hong Son		
(via Mae Sariang)	143	8
air-con	257	8
via Pai	100	7
air-con	130	7

destination	fare (B)	duration (hrs)
Mae Sai	95	5
air-con	108	5
1st class air-con	171	5
Mae Sariang	78	4-5
1st class air-con	140	4-5
Mae Sot	134	6½
1st class air-con	241	6
Nan	128	6
air-con	179	6
1st class air-con	230	6
Pai 55B	4	
air-con	80	4
Phayao	67	3
air-con	94	2½
Phrae	79	4
air-con	111	3½
1st class air-con	142	3½
Phitsanulok	132-140	5-6
air-con	184-196	5
Sukhothai	122	6
air-con	171	5
Tha Ton*	70	4
Udon Thani	228	12
air-con	319	12
1st class air-con	410	12

**Leaves from Chang Pheuak bus terminal. All other buses leave from the Chiang Mai Arcade bus terminal (also called New Terminal) off Th Kaew Nawarat.*

Northern Thailand to Yunnan, China

It's possible to travel from Thailand to China's Yunnan Province by road via Laos, a land route that ties together the Golden Triangle and Yunnan's Xishuangbanna district (called Sipsongpanna in Thailand) in Southwest China. The Thais, Shan and Lao all consider Xishuangbanna to be a cultural homeland.

One can now cross into Laos from Thailand via at least six legal border crossings. Once in Laos, head to Luang Nam Tha or Udomxai, then proceed north to the Lao village of Boten on the Chinese border, close to the Xishuangbanna town of Mengla (Mong La). From Mengla, an existing road leads to Jinghong. To reach Luang Nam Tha from northern Thailand you may cross by ferry from Chiang Khong on the Thai side to Huay Xai on the Lao side. This crossing is fully operational; foreigners may enter Laos here with the proper visa. The Boten crossing is legal for all nationalities.

Another way to reach Boten is via Pakbeng in Laos' Udomxai Province. Pakbeng is midway along the Mekong River route between Huay Xai and Luang Prabang; from Pakbeng a Chinese-built road system continues all the way to Boten. To facilitate trade and travel between China and Thailand, the Chinese have offered to build a new road directly south to the Thai border (Nan Province) from the river bank opposite Pakbeng. For now, Thai authorities are not too happy about this proposed road extension, which is seen as a push towards an 'invasion' of Thailand. During the years of Thai communist insurgency, Communist Party of Thailand cadres used the Pakbeng road to reach Kunming, China, for training in revolutionary tactics.

In the long term, the Mekong River route is also promising. Chinese barges weighing up to 100 tonnes now ply the Mekong eight months a year; from the Chinese border to Chiang Khong, Thailand, the trip takes about five days. During the drier months, however, river transport north of Luang Prabang is hampered by rocks and shallows. Blasting and dredging could make way for boats of up to 500 tonnes to travel year-round, but could have devastating effects on the watercourse and lands downstream.

and 200B respectively on the special express). For air-con 2nd-class rapid trains, add 220/270B for upper/lower sleepers (250/320B on special express trains). For example, if you take a non-air-con 2nd-class upper berth on a rapid train, your total fare will be 461B (321B plus 100B plus 40B). Tickets for the 'express diesel railcar' (Nos 9 and 11) cost the same as air-con 2nd-class seats on an express.

The basic 1st-class fare is 593B; berths are 520B per person and are available on the special express and rapid trains only.

Trains leave Lopburi for Chiang Mai at 10.35am (express diesel railcar), 5.51pm (rapid), 8.26pm (special express), 9.33pm (express diesel) and 12.40am (rapid) arriving at the times listed for the same trains from Bangkok. Fares are 257/277B for 2nd-class rapid/express seats and 133/153B for 3rd-class rapid/express, including rapid/express surcharges.

Berths on sleepers to Chiang Mai are increasingly hard to reserve without booking well in advance; tour groups sometimes book entire cars. The return trip from Chiang Mai to Bangkok doesn't seem to be as difficult, except during the Songkran (mid-April) and Chinese New Year (late February to early March) holiday periods.

Chiang Mai's neat and tidy **train station** (*☎ 0 5324 5363; Th Charoen Muang*) has an ATM and two advance booking offices, one at the regular ticket windows outdoors (open 5am to 9pm daily), the other in a more comfortable air-con office (open 6am to 8pm daily). The booking office has a computerised reservation system through which you can book train seats for anywhere in Thailand up to 60 days in advance. There is also a left-luggage facility that is open 4.50am to 8.45pm daily. The cost is 10B per piece for the first five days and 15B per piece thereafter, with a 20-day maximum.

GETTING AROUND

To/From the Airport

There is only one licensed airport taxi service, charging 100B for comfortable sedan cars that can take up to four or five people and their luggage. Pick up a ticket at the taxi kiosk just outside the baggage-claim area, then present your ticket to the taxi drivers outside by the main arrival area exit. The airport is only 2km to 3km from the city centre.

You can charter a túk-túk or red săwngthăew from the centre of Chiang Mai to the airport for 50B or 60B.

Bus

Chiang Mai cancelled all city bus services in 1997. Most Chiang Mai residents now take săwngthăew and many also have their own bicycles or motorcycles.

Car & Motorcycle

Cars, 4WDs and minivans are readily available at several locations throughout the city. Be sure that the vehicle you rent has insurance (liability) coverage – ask to see the documents and carry a photocopy with you while driving.

Two of the best agencies in town for service and price are **North Wheels** *(☎ 0 5321 6189, fax 0 5322 1709; ⓔ sales@northwheels.com; 127/2 Th Moon Muang)* near Somphet Market, and **Queen Bee** *(☎ 0 5320 8988; Th Moon Muang)*, next to Muang Thong Hotel. Both offer hotel pick-up and delivery as well as 24-hour emergency road service; North Wheel's rates include insurance, while Queen Bee charges extra for insurance. Sample rentals at North Wheels include Suzuki Caribians for 1000B per 24-hour day and Toyota 4WD pickups for 1500B a day. Discounted weekly and monthly rates are available.

It's important to choose a car-rental agency carefully, by reputation rather than what's on paper. Also realise that whatever happens, you're still responsible for personal injury and medical payments of anyone injured in connection with a traffic accident.

Other prominent rental agencies include:

Avis (☎ 0 5320 1574) 14/14 Th Huay Kaew; (☎ 0 5320 1798–9) Chiang Mai International Airport
Budget (☎ 0 5320 2871) Chiang Mai International Airport
Journey Car Rent (☎ 0 5320 8787, fax 0 5327 3428, ⓔ journeycnx@thaimail.com) 283 Th Tha Phae
National Car Rental (☎ 0 5321 0118) Amari Rincome Hotel

If you're looking to hire a motorcycle, Honda Dream 100cc step-throughs can be rented for 100B to 200B a day, depending on the season, the condition of the motorcycle and length of rental. Prices are very competitive in Chiang Mai because there's a real glut of motorcycles. For two people, it's cheaper to rent a small motorcycle for the day to visit Doi Suthep than to go up and back in a săwngthăew. Occasionally you'll see slightly larger 125cc to 150cc Hondas or Yamahas for rent for 200B to 250B a day.

The availability of bikes bigger than 150cc varies from year to year but you can usually find Honda XL600s or Yamaha XT600s (800B to 900B a day), Honda AX-1 250s (500B, 350B low season), Honda Baja 250s (500B, 350B low season) and Honda XR 250s (400B) at a few of the agencies.

Motorcycle-rental places come and go with the seasons. Many of them are lined up along the eastern side of the moat on Th Moon Muang, Th Chaiyaphum and Th Kotchasan. Among the more established and more reliable are:

Bike & Bite (☎ 0 5341 8534) 23/1 Th Si Phum
Dang Bike Hire (☎ 0 5327 1524) 23 Th Kotchasan. This outfit rents big bikes.
Mr Mechanic 4 Soi 5 Th Moon Muang. Small motorcycles, Suzuki 4WD vehicles (insurance included) are available for hire.
Pop Rent-A-Car (☎ 0 5327 6014) Near Soi 2, Th Kotchasan. Rent motorcycles and cars (insurance included) from here.
SP Bike Rental (☎ 0 5335 7559) 99/1 Th Moon Muang, near Pratu Tha Phae
Tui Big Bike (☎ 0 5387 6227) On the corner of Th Wichayanon and Th Chaiyaphum. Big bikes are available here.

These agencies offer motorcycle insurance for around 50B a day, not a bad investment considering you could face a 25,000B to 60,000B liability if your bike is stolen. Most policies have a high deductible (excess), so in cases of theft you're usually responsible for a third to half of the bike's value – even with insurance. More casual rental places that specialise in quick, easy and cheap rentals of 100cc bikes can be found along Th Moon Muang, including **Mr Kom** *(2 Th Moon Muang)*, near Somphet Market.

Several car-rental places also rent motorcycles. See the Getting Around chapter for information on motorcycle touring.

Bicycle

Cycling is a good way to get around Chiang Mai if you don't mind a little traffic and, at the denser intersections, vehicular fumes. The city is small enough so that everywhere is accessible by bike, including Chiang Mai University, Wat U Mong, Wat Suan Dok and the Chiang Mai National Museum on the outskirts of town.

Basic Chinese- or Thai-manufactured bicycles can be rented for around 30B to 50B a day from several of the guesthouses or from various places along the east moat.

Bike & Bite (☎ 0 5341 8534) 23/1 Th Si Phum. This is a combination Thai restaurant and mountain bike rental/tour company.

SP Bike Rental (☎ 0 5335 7559) 99/1 Th Moon Muang, near Pratu Tha Phae

Velocity (☎ 0 5341 0665) 177 Th Chang Pheuak. Velocity rents mountain and racing bikes, offers guided tours and carries all kinds of cycling accessories.

Wild Planet-Contact Travel (☎ 0 5327 7178, fax 5327 9505, ⓔ adventure@thailine.com) 73/7 Th Charoen Prathet between Th Loi Kroh and Th Tha Phae. This outfit rents rugged 21-speed mountain bikes for 200B a day. It also operates cycling tours around the province.

Săwngthăew, Túk-túk & Săamláw

Hordes of red săwngthăew ply the streets of Chiang Mai looking for passengers. Flag one down, state your destination and if it is going that way you can ride for 10B. It's best to board one that already has passengers if you're worried about getting overcharged. Some drivers try to charge lone passengers (both Thais and *faràng*) 20B instead of the usual 10B. If you're the only passenger and you're going to an out-of-the-way place, that may be reasonable, but if you're going, say, from Pratu Tha Phae to Talat Warorot – a relatively short and well-travelled distance – you shouldn't have to pay more than the normal 10B fare. You can charter *(mǎo)* a săwngthăew anywhere in the city for 60B or less.

Túk-túk work only on a charter or taxi basis, at 30B for short trips and 40B to 60B for longer ones. After midnight in entertainment areas such as along Th Charoenrat near the Riverside and the Brasserie, or down towards Gi Gi's, most túk-túk charge a flat 50B for any trip back across the river.

Chiang Mai still has loads of săamláw (pedicabs, also spelt samlor), especially in the old city around Talat Warorot. Săamláw cost around 20B to 30B for most trips.

Around Chiang Mai

DOI SUTHEP

ดอยสุเทพ

Sixteen kilometres northwest of Chiang Mai is Doi Suthep, a 1676m peak named after the hermit Sudeva, who lived on the mountain's slopes for many years. Near its summit is **Wat Phra That Doi Suthep**; first established in 1383 under King Keu Naone, it is one of the north's most sacred temples. A staircase of 300 steps leads to the wát at the end of the winding road up the mountain. You also have the option of riding a tram from the parking lot to the wát grounds for 20B.

At the top, weather permitting, there are some fine views of Chiang Mai. Inside the cloister is an exquisite, Lanna-style, copper-plated *chedi* topped by a five-tiered gold umbrella – one of the holiest chedi in Thailand.

About 4km beyond Wat Phra That Doi Suthep is **Phra Tamnak Phu**, a winter palace for the royal family with **palace gardens** *(admission free; open 8.30am-12.30pm & 1pm-4pm Sat, Sun & holidays)*. The road that passes the palace splits off to the left, stopping at the peak of Doi Pui. From there, a dirt road proceeds for a couple of kilometres to a nearby Hmong hill-tribe village. If you won't have an opportunity to visit remote villages, it's worth visiting this one, even though it is well touristed. You can buy Hmong handicrafts here and see traditional homes and costumes, although these are mostly posed situations.

If you're cycling or driving to the summit, you can stop off along the way at the waterfalls, **Nam Tok Monthathon** *(admission 200B)*, 2.5km off the paved road to Doi Suthep. The trail is well marked; if you're interested in checking the falls out, have the săwngthăew driver drop you off on the way up the mountain. Pools beneath the falls hold water year-round, although swimming is best during or just after the annual monsoon. The falls can be a little crowded on weekends. The 200B fee allows you to visit other waterfalls on the road to Suthep.

Doi Suthep & Doi Pui National Park

Most visitors do a quick tour of the temple, the Hmong village and perhaps the winter palace grounds, altogether missing the surrounding park. This 261-sq-km reserve *(adult/child under 14 yrs 200/100B)* is home to more than 300 bird species and nearly 2000 species of ferns and flowering plants. Because of its proximity to urban Chiang Mai, development of the park has become a very sensitive issue. The western side of the park has been severely disturbed by poachers and land encroachers, including around 500 hill-tribe families.

There are extensive hiking trails in the park, including one that climbs 1685m Doi Pui; the summit is a favourite picnic spot. Other trails pass Hmong villages that rarely get *faràng* visitors. Bungalow and dormitory accommodation is available near the park headquarters (past the temple car park on the right). Depending on who's on duty at the park headquarters, there are also maps available here. Mountain bikers will find lots of fat-tyre fun.

A 4km trail also leads to the scenic and more isolated Nam Tok Sai Yai waterfalls, and connects with a trail that leads to Nam Tok Monthathon.

Getting There & Away

Săwngthăew to Doi Suthep leave Chiang Mai throughout the day from the western end of Th Huay Kaew in front of Chiang Mai University. Doi Suthep săwngthăew

NORTHERN CHIANG MAI

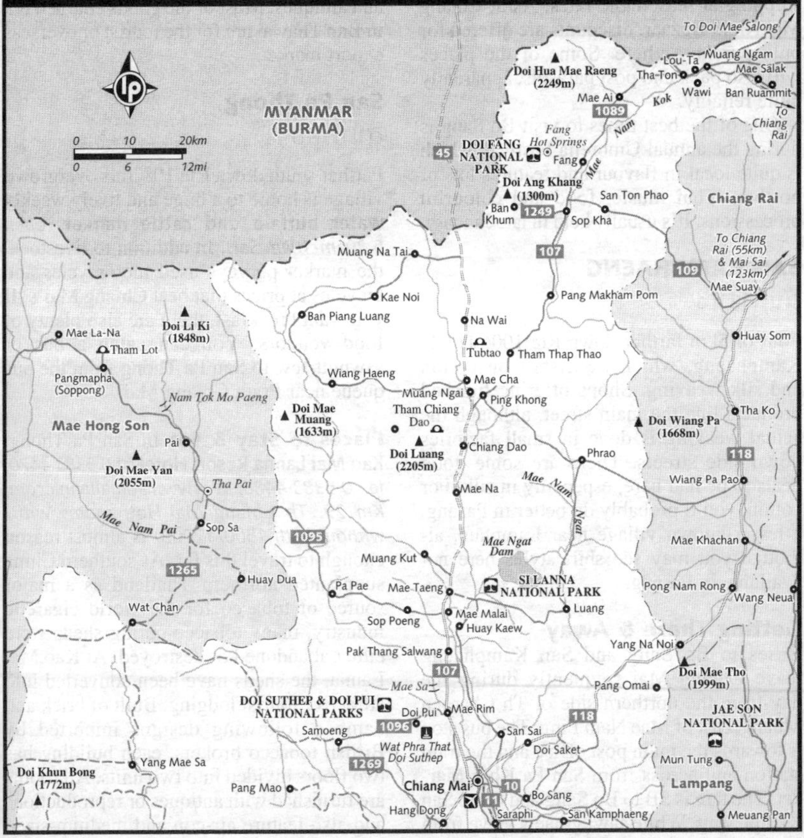

fares are 40B up and 30B back per person. Săwngthăew depart from Pratu Chang Pheuak and the Chiang Mai Zoo. To Phra Tamnak Phu Phing and Doi Pui add 20B in each direction.

BO SANG
บ่อสร้าง

Bo Sang (often spelt 'Baw Sang' or 'Bor Sang'), 9km east of Chiang Mai on Rte 1006, is usually called the Umbrella Village because of its many umbrella manufacturers. Almost the entire village consists of craft shops selling painted umbrellas, fans, silverware, straw handiwork, bamboo and teak, statuary, china, celadon and lacquerware, along with tacky Chiang Mai and northern-Thai souvenirs and some quality items.

The larger shops can arrange overseas shipping at reasonable rates. As at Chiang Mai Night Bazaar, discounts are offered for bulk purchases here. Some of the places will also pack and post parasols, apparently quite reliably.

One of the best times to visit Bo Sang is during the annual Umbrella Festival, which is quite local in flavour and features lots of northern-Thai music, food and colourful processions. It's usually held in late January.

SAN KAMPHAENG
สันกำแพง

Four or 5km farther down Rte 1006 is San Kamphaeng, which flourishes on cotton and silk weaving. Shops offering finished products line the main street, although the actual weaving is done in small factories down side streets. There are some good deals to be had here, especially in silk. For cotton, you'd probably do better in Pasang, a lesser-known village near Lamphun, although you may see shirt styles here not available in Pasang.

Getting There & Away

Buses to Bo Sang and San Kamphaeng leave Chiang Mai frequently during the day from the northern side of Th Charoen Muang, east of Mae Nam Ping. The bus stop is towards the main post office and the train station and across from San Pa Khoi Market. The fare is 5B to Bo Sang and 6B to San Kamphaeng. White săwngthăew leave from Chang Pheuak bus terminal and make the trip to either destination for 6B.

SOUTH OF CHIANG MAI

Hang Dong, Ban Wan & Ban Thawai
หางดง

Fifteen kilometres south of Chiang Mai on Rte 108 is Hang Dong, which is well known for ceramics, woodcarving and antiques. Many of the shops here deal in wholesale as well as retail, so prices are low. Catch a bus from Pratu Chiang Mai to Hang Dong (6B). The shops are actually strung out along Rte 108, starting about 2km before Hang Dong.

Immediately east of Hang Dong there are more antique and furniture shops in Ban Wan, and beyond that, in Ban Thawai. Ban Wan generally has the best-quality furniture and antiques. Most of the goods churned out in Ban Thawai are for the tourist or overseas export market.

San Pa Thong
สันป่าตอง

Farther south down Rte 108, this overgrown village is home to a huge and lively weekly **water buffalo and cattle market** *(open 5.30am-10am Sat)*. In addition to livestock, the market purveys used motorcycles and bicycles at prices that beat Chiang Mai's. If you want breakfast, there are also plenty of food vendors. You can catch a bus or săwngthăew to San Pa Thong from the bus queue near Pratu Chiang Mai.

Places to Stay & Eat In San Pa Thong, **Kao Mai Lanna Resort Hotel** *(☎ 0 5383 4470, fax 0 5383 4480; W www.kaomailanna.com; Km 29, Th Chiang Mai-Hot; rooms with/without bath 1500/1200B)* is almost reason enough to travel this far. As southern China supplanted northern Thailand as a major source of tobacco for the world cigarette industry, many tobacco-curing sheds were either abandoned or destroyed. At Kao Mai Lanna, the sheds have been converted into attractive tourist lodging. Built of brick and bamboo following designs imported by British tobacco brokers, each building has two floors divided into two units. All rooms are furnished with antiques or reproductions and also feature air-con and medium-sized refrigerators. Kao Mai Lanna offers free transport from the airport, train station or bus stations in Chiang Mai.

Even if you don't stay at Kao Mai Lanna, the outdoor restaurant serves superb Thai food at very reasonable prices.

MAE SA & SAMOENG

แม่สาและสะเมิง

This forested loop northwest of Chiang Mai via Mae Rim and/or Hang Dong makes a good day or overnight trip. Although dotted with tourist developments – resorts, orchid farms, butterfly parks, snake farms, elephant camps, botanic gardens, antique and handicraft shops – the Rte 1096/1269 loop through the Mae Sa Valley is very scenic in spots. **Nam Tok Mae Sa** is only 6km from the Mae Rim turn-off from Rte 107, which in turn is 12km north of Chiang Mai. Farther along the loop are several Hmong villages.

There are at least four places along the loop that call themselves elephant 'camp', 'farm' or 'village'. Best of the bunch is the **Maesa Elephant Camp** (*☎ 0 5329 7060; elephant show admission 80B*), near Nam Tok Mae Sa, which features one-hour elephant shows at 8am and 8.40am daily, plus 1.30pm during the high season. You can feed the elephants sugar cane and bananas, and visit the baby elephants in their nursery and training school. Call for more information.

Samoeng, at the westernmost extension of the loop (35km from Mae Rim), is the most peaceful area for an overnight stay, since

SOUTHERN CHIANG MAI

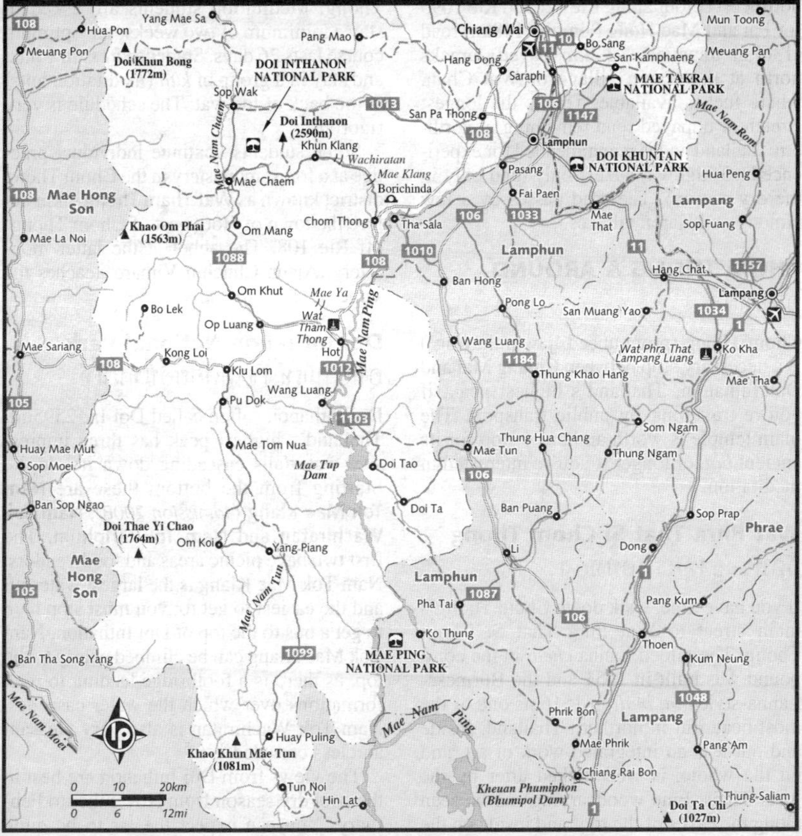

it's 5km north of the main loop junction between the highways to/from Mae Rim and Hang Dong via Rte 1269. **Samoeng Resort** (*☎ 0 5348 7072; bungalows with fan from 700B*), about 1.5km outside Samoeng village itself, has 15 quiet, well-designed bungalows with fan. It costs more for air-con.

Getting There & Away

You can get a săwngthăew to Samoeng from the Chang Pheuak bus terminal in Chiang Mai for 35B. There are two daily departures, one at 9am and another at 11am. It takes two hours and 40 minutes to reach Samoeng from Chiang Mai. In Samoeng the vehicles stop near the market, across from Samoeng Hospital.

Since it's paved all the way, the winding loop road makes a good ride by bicycle or motorcycle. From Samoeng you can take a northwest detour along Rte 1265 to Rte 1095 for Pai and Mae Hong Son; the 148km road (136km unpaved, 12.2km paved) breaks north at the Karen village of Wat Chan, where fuel is available. This is the longest stretch of unpaved road remaining in northern Thailand and is recommended for experienced off-highway bikers only (and only in the dry season). The road passes by a few Hmong and Karen villages.

CHOM THONG & AROUND

จอมทอง

Chom Thong (pronounced 'jawm thawng') is a necessary stop between Chiang Mai and Doi Inthanon, Thailand's highest peak, if you're travelling by public transport. The main temple is worth an hour's stop for its ancient *bòt*, or longer if you're interested in meditation.

Wat Phra That Si Chom Thong

วัดพระธาตุศรีจอมทอง

If you have time, walk down Chom Thong's main street to Wat Phra That Si Chom Thong. The gilded Lanna *chedi* in the compound was built in 1451 and the Burmese-Lanna-style *bòt*, *built* in 1516, is one of the most beautiful in northern Thailand. Inside and out it is an integrated work of art, and on the whole, is well looked after by the local Thais. Fine woodcarving can be seen along the eaves of the roof and inside on the ceiling, which is supported by massive teak columns. The impressive altar is designed like a small *prasat* (enclosed shrine), in typical Lanna style, and is said to contain a relic from the right side of the Buddha's skull.

Nearby is a glass case containing ancient Thai weaponry. Behind the *prasat* altar is a room containing religious antiques.

Vegetarian Restaurant (*Watjanee; dishes 25B; open 8am-4pm daily*), a few doors up from the wát compound, offers simple one-plate rice and noodle dishes that substitute meat with tofu and gluten. Look for the yellow pennants out the front.

Meditation Retreats Under the direction of Ajahn Thong, formerly of Wat Ram Poeng in Chiang Mai, meditation retreats in the style of the late Mahasi Sayadaw are held regularly at Wat Phra That Si Chom Thong. Meditation students are asked to stay a minimum of two weeks; the optimum course lasts 26 days. Students dress in white, and stay in a group of *kùtì* (meditation huts) at the back of the wát. The schedule is very rigorous.

Some students continue individual practice at a forest monastery in the Chom Thong district known as **Wat Tham Thong**, 5km before the town of Hot (west of Chom Thong) off Rte 108. The abbot at the latter monastery, Ajahn Chuchin Vimaro, teaches the same style of *vipassana*.

Doi Inthanon National Park

อุทยานแห่งชาติดอยอินทนนท์

Doi Inthanon (often called Doi In; 2595m), Thailand's highest peak has three impressive waterfalls cascading down its slopes. Starting from the bottom these are **Nam Tok Mae Klang** (*admission 200B*), **Nam Tok Wachiratan** and **Nam Tok Siriphum**. The first two have picnic areas and food vendors. Nam Tok Mae Klang is the largest waterfall and the easiest to get to; you must stop here to get a bus to the top of Doi Inthanon. Nam Tok Mae Klang can be climbed nearly to the top, as there is a footbridge leading to rock formations over which the water cascades. Nam Tok Wachiratan is also very pleasant and less crowded.

The views from Doi Inthanon are best in the cool dry season from November to February. You can expect the air to be quite chilly towards the top, so take a jacket or sweater. For most of the year a mist, formed by the condensation of warm humid air below, hangs around the highest peak. Along the 47km road to the top are many terraced rice fields, tremendous valleys and a few small hill-tribe villages. The mountain slopes are home to around 4000 Hmong and Karen tribespeople.

The entire mountain is a national park (482 sq km), despite agriculture and human habitation. One of the top destinations in Southeast Asia for naturalists and bird-watchers, the mist-shrouded upper slopes produce a bumper crop of orchids, lichens, mosses and epiphytes, while supporting nearly 400 bird varieties, more than any other habitat in Thailand. The mountain is also one of the last habitats of the Asiatic black bear, along with the Assamese macaque, Phayre's leaf-monkey and a selection of other rare and not-so-rare monkeys and gibbons, plus the more common Indian civet, barking deer and giant flying squirrel – around 75 mammalian species in all.

Most of the park's bird species are found between 1500m and 2000m; the best bird-watching season is from February to April, and the best spots are the *beung* (bogs) near the top.

Phra Mahathat Naphamethanidon, a *chedi* built by the Royal Thai Air Force to commemorate the king's 60th birthday in 1989, is off the highway between the 41km and 42km markers, about 4km before reaching the summit of Doi Inthanon. In the base of the octagonal *chedi* is a hall containing a stone Buddha image.

The 200B entry fee collected for Nam Tok Mae Klang near the foot of the mountain is good for all stops on the Doi Inthanon circuit; be sure to keep your receipt.

Places to Stay

Bungalows *(☎ 0 5331 1608; 8-person bungalows 800B, 10-person bungalows 900B & 1000B, tents 40B)*, 31km north of Chom Thong, can be booked at park headquarters in Chom Thong. Blankets hire is 10B.

In Chom Thong, inquire at Wat Phra That Si Chom Thong for a place to sleep.

Getting There & Away

Buses to Chom Thong leave regularly from just inside Pratu Chiang Mai at the south moat as well as from the Chang Pheuak bus terminal in Chiang Mai. Some buses go directly to Nam Tok Mae Klang and some go only as far as Hot, although the latter will let you off in Chom Thong. The fare to Chom Thong, 58km from Chiang Mai, is 23B.

From Chom Thong there are regular sǎwngthǎew to Mae Klang, about 8km north, for 15B. Sǎwngthǎew from Mae Klang to Doi Inthanon leave almost hourly until late afternoon and cost 30B per person. Most of the passengers are locals who get off at various points along the road, thus allowing a few stationary views of the valleys below.

For another 15B you can go south from Chom Thong to Hot, where you can get buses on to Mae Sariang or Mae Hong Son. However, if you've been to Doi Inthanon and the waterfalls, you probably won't have time to make it all the way to Mae Sariang or Mae Hong Son in one day, so you may want to stay overnight in the park or in Chom Thong.

North to Tha Ton

MAE TAENG & CHIANG DAO

แม่แตง/เชียงดาว

The mountainous area around Mae Taeng – especially southwest of the junction of Rtes 107 and 1095 – has become a major trekking area because of the variety of Lisu, Lahu, Karen and Hmong villages in the region. Rafting along Mae Taeng is so popular these days that there's a permanent rafting centre. **Maetaman Rafting & Elephant Camp** *(☎ 0 5329 7060, 0 5329 7283, fax 0 5329 7283; 535 Rim Tai, Mae Rim)* is west of Rte 107.

The **Elephant Training Centre Taeng-Dao** *(Km 56, Rte 107; adult/child 60/30B)*, off Rte 107 between Mae Taeng and Chiang Dao, is one of several training centres in the area that puts on elephant shows (at 9am and 10am daily) for tourists. If you haven't seen the one in Lampang Province (in Thung Kwian), this is a reasonable alternative.

From the main four-way junction at Chiang Dao, those with their own wheels – preferably a mountain bike, motorcycle or truck – can head east to visit Lahu, Lisu and Akha villages within a 15km ride. Roughly 13.5km from Rte 107 is the Lisu village of

Lisu Huay Ko, where rustic accommodation is available.

Tham Chiang Dao

The main attraction along the way to Fang and Tha Ton is this **cave complex** *(admission 5B)*, 5km west of Rte 107 and 72km north of Chiang Mai.

The complex is said to extend some 10km to 14km into 2285m Doi Chiang Dao; the interconnected caverns that are open to the public include Tham Mah (7365m long), Tham Kaew (477m), Tham Phra Non (360m), Tham Seua Dao (540m) and Tham Nam (660m).

Tham Phra Non and Tham Seua Dao contain religious statuary and are electrically illuminated (and thus easily explored on one's own), while Tham Mah, Tham Kaew and Tham Nam have no light fixtures. A guide with a pressurised gas lantern can be hired for 60B for up to eight people. The interior cave formations are quite spectacular in places – over 100 of them are named.

Local legend says this cave complex was the home of a *reusĭi* (hermit) for a thousand years. As the legend goes, the sage was on such intimate terms with the deity world that he convinced some *thewádaa* (the Buddhist equivalent of angels) to create seven magic wonders inside the caverns: a stream flowing from the pedestal of a solid-gold Buddha; a storehouse of divine textiles; a mystical lake; a city of *nagas*; a sacred immortal elephant; and the hermit's tomb. No, you won't find any of the seven wonders; the locals say these are much deeper inside the mountain, beyond the last of the illuminated caverns.

The locals also say that anyone who attempts to remove a piece of rock from the cave will forever lose their way in the cave's eerie passages.

There is a wát complex outside the cavern and a collection of vendors selling roots, herbs and snacks (mostly noodles).

The surrounding area is quite scenic and largely unspoiled. From the summit of Doi Chiang Dao there are spectacular views. Beyond Tham Chiang Dao along the same rural road is a smaller sacred cave retreat complex called **Samnak Song Tham Pha Plong** (Tham Pha Plong Monastic Centre), where Buddhist monks sometimes meditate. A long, steep stairway leads to a large stupa beautifully framed by forest and limestone cliffs.

Places to Stay

Malee's Nature Lovers Bungalows *(☎ 0 1961 8387; dorm beds 100B, doubles 300B)* is about 1.3km past the entrance to Tham Chiang Dao. Follow the left fork where the road splits 1km past the cave entrance, and you'll find Malee's on the right, about 100m off the road. Friendly and knowledgeable Thai owner Malee has dorm beds and six thatch-and-brick bungalows with private bath. Malee can arrange trekking, rafting and bird-watching trips in the area. If you'd rather hike on your own, maps are available showing hiking routes to the top of Doi Chiang Dao and through the nearby Chiang Dao Wildlife Sanctuary.

Pieng Dao Hotel *(☎ 0 5323 2434, 0 5334 4995; Ban Chiang Dao, Rte 107; singles/doubles with shared cold-water shower 100/150B, with private shower 200B)* is one of the old wooden hotels still operating in the north.

Chiang Dao Hill Resort *(☎ 0 5323 4995; bungalows 900-1800B)*, off the highway between Km 100 and Km 101, offers good tourist bungalows, and a **restaurant** *(open 7am-10pm)*. The **Royal Ping Garden Resort**, off the highway south of Chiang Dao, has more-expensive luxury rooms.

Getting There & Away

Buses to Chiang Dao from Chiang Mai's Chang Pheuak terminal depart every 30 minutes between 5.30am and 5.30pm (25B, 1½ hours).

DOI ANG KHANG

ดอยอ่างขาง

About 20km before Fang is the turn-off for Rte 1249 to Doi Ang Khang, Thailand's 'Little Switzerland'. Twenty-five kilometres from the highway, this 1300m peak has a cool climate year-round and supports the cultivation of flowers, fruits and vegetables that are usually found only in more temperate climates.

A few hill-tribe villages (Lahu, Lisu and Hmong) can be visited on the slopes. You can pick up a free map of the area at the main military checkpoint on Rte 1249. Some interesting do-it-yourself treks can be made in the area.

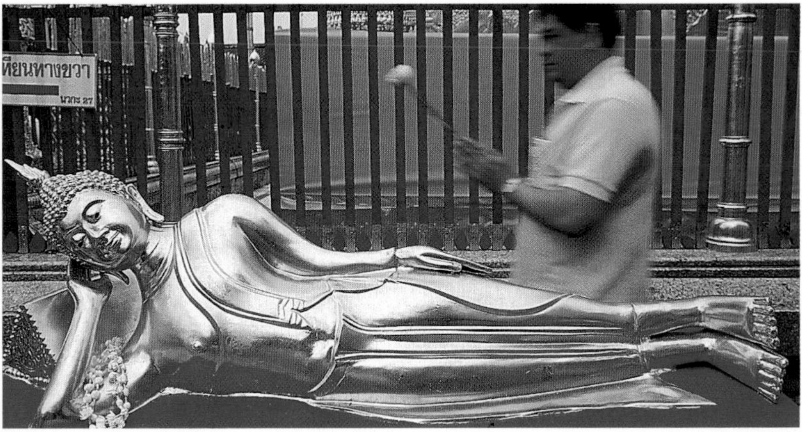

FRANK CARTER

Wat Phra That Doi Suthep, Doi Suthep, Chiang Mai Province

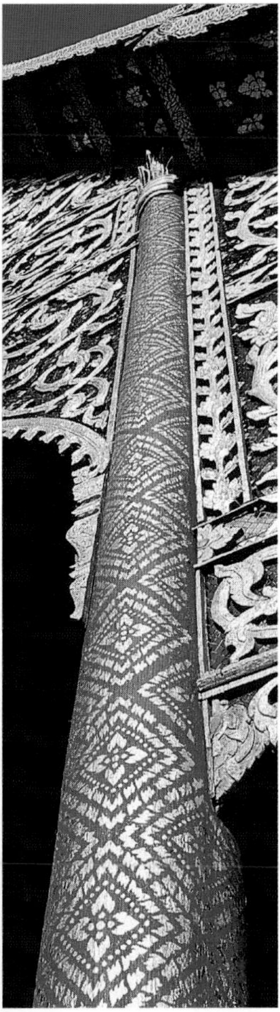

GLENN BEANLAND

Chiang Mai Province

RYAN FOX

Stupa, Doi Suthep, Chiang Mai Province

JERRY ALEXANDER

Young monks, Chiang Mai, Chiang Mai Province

Wat Phra That Doi Suthep, Chiang Mai, Chiang Mai Province

Traditional parasol, Chiang Mai Province

BOTH PHOTOGRAPHS BY FRANK CARTER

Nineteen kilometres before the turn-off to Doi Ang Khang you can make a 12km detour west on a dirt road to visit **Ban Mai Nong Bua**, another KMT village with an atmosphere like that of Doi Mae Salong.

Places to Stay & Eat

Near the summit of Doi Ang Khang, near the Yunnanese village of Ban Khum, there are several places to stay. Most are relatively modest A-frame bungalows positioned along a hillside, such as **Lung Kiat Chok Chai** and **Suwannaphum**, all charging from 100B for a very basic room with shared shower and toilet to 300B for a nicer one with private facilities. **Naha Guest House** *(☎ 0 5345 0008; Ban Khum, Tambon Mae Ngan, Fang; 6-person bungalows 1500B, 10-person bungalows 2000B or per person 100B)* has large bungalows with shared hot-water shower and toilet.

Angkhang Nature Resort *(☎ 0 5345 0110, fax 0 5345 0120; ⓔ angkhang@amari.com; 1/1 Mu 5, Ban Khum, Tambon Mae Ngan, Fang; rooms 3296-3659B, 20 Dec-10 Jan 4601-4238B)*, part of the Amari Hotel Group, and is an unexpectedly plush hotel that features large, tastefully designed bungalows spread out over a slope. There is a good, if pricey, restaurant on the premises.

At the base of the slope studded with cheaper bungalows are a couple of **open-air restaurants** serving a variety of dishes with an emphasis on Thai and Yunnanese Muslim cuisine.

FANG & THA TON

ฝาง/ท่าตอน

The present city of Fang was founded by Phaya Mangrai in the 13th century, although as a human settlement and trading centre for *jiin haw* caravans, the locale dates back at least 1000 years. North from Chiang Mai along Rte 107, Fang doesn't look particularly inviting, but the town's quiet backstreets are lined with interesting little shops in wooden buildings. The Shan/Burmese-style **Wat Jong Paen** (near the Wiang Kaew Hotel) has a very impressive stacked-roof *wíhǎan*.

There are Mien and Karen villages nearby that you can visit on your own, but for most people Fang is just a road marker on the way to Tha Ton, the starting point for Mae Nam Kok trips to Chiang Rai and for treks to the many hill-tribe settlements in the region. Most people prefer Tha Ton's more rural setting for spending the night. It's only half an hour or so by sǎwngthǎew to the river from Fang or vice versa.

Two **banks** along the main street in Fang offer currency exchange. Through the Wiang Kaew Hotel in Fang you can arrange tours to local villages inhabited by Palaung (a Karennic tribe that arrived from Myanmar around 14 years ago), Black Lahu, Akha and Yunnanese.

About 10km west of Fang at Ban Meuang Chom, near the agricultural station, is a system of **hot springs**, which are part of Doi Fang National Park. Just ask for the *bàw náam ráwn* (*baw nâam hâwn* in northern Thai). On weekends there are frequent sǎwngthǎew carrying Thai picnickers from Fang to the hot springs.

Tha Ton has a sǎwngthǎew stand and a collection of river boats, restaurants, souvenir shops and tourist accommodation along a pretty bend in Mae Nam Kok. Near the bridge is a **tourist police office** *(open 8.30am-4.30pm daily)*.

For something to do, climb the hill to **Wat Tha Ton** and the Chinese shrine for good views of the surrounding area. A large temple bell, which sounds every morning at 4am (wake-up call for monks) and again at 6am (alms-round call), can be heard throughout the valley surrounding Tha Ton.

Trekking & Rafting

There are some pleasant walks along Mae Nam Kok. Within 20km of Fang and Tha Thon you can visit Lahu and Palaung villages on foot, mountain bike or motorcycle.

Treks and raft trips can be arranged through Thip's Travellers House, Mae Kok River Village Resort or the Thaton River View Hotel, all in Tha Ton (see the following Places to Stay & Eat section). Thip's arranges economical bamboo house-rafts with pilot and cook for three days for 2000B per person (minimum four people), including all meals, lodging and rafting.

On the first day you'll visit several villages near the river and spend the night in a Lisu village; on the second day rafters visit hot springs and more villages, and spend the second night on the raft; and on the third day you dock in Chiang Rai.

You could get a small group of travellers together and arrange your own house-raft with a guide and cook for a two- or three-day journey down river, stopping off in villages of your choice along the way. A house-raft generally costs 500B to 600B per person per day, including simple meals, and takes up to six people – so figure on 1500B to 1800B for a three-day trip. Police regulations require that an experienced boat navigator accompany each raft – the river has lots of tricky spots and there have been some mishaps.

Near the pier (Tha Thon) you can rent inflatable kayaks to do your own paddling in the area. Upstream a few kilometres the river crosses into Myanmar.

Places to Stay & Eat

Fang Behind the Fang Hotel, off the main street, **Wiang Kaew Hotel** (*☎ 0 5245 1046; 22 Th Sai Rattabat; rooms with private bath 120-180B*) is a good choice. Rooms are basic but clean; the higher priced rooms have hot water.

Ueng Khum Hotel (*UK Hotel; ☎ 0 5345 1268; 227 Th Tha Phae; singles/doubles with fan 140/170B, with air-con 350B*), around the corner from Wiang Kaew, has bungalow-style accommodation around a courtyard; all rooms have hot-water showers.

Parichat Restaurant (*Th Rop Wiang; dishes 25-45B; open 8am-8pm daily*), near the highway market, serves *khâo sàwy* with chicken or beef, plus *kŭaytĭaw* (rice noodles), *khâo phàt* (fried rice) and other standards.

Farther down Th Rop Wiang is a row of cheap Isan restaurants and *lâo dawng* (herbal liquor) bars.

Tha Ton If you want to spend the night near the pier in Tha Ton, there are several options. **Thip's Travellers House** (*☎/fax 0 5349 5312; 1/7 Th Tha Phae; rooms with/without cold-water bath 100/80B*) is an old standby and just a short walk from the pier, quite near the bridge where the road from Fang meets the river. Rooms are thin-walled and facilities basic, but there's a nice little café out the front.

Chan Kasem (*☎ 0 5345 9313; rooms with shared bath 80B, with fan & cold-/hot-water bath 100B/150-250B, bungalows 300B*) down near the pier, has a restaurant on the river and rents a variety of none-too-clean rooms with shared bathroom in the older wooden section, singles/doubles with fan and bathroom and a brick bungalow. **Naam Waan Guest House** (*Th Tha Phae; rooms with fan & cold-water shower 150B*), near Chan Kasem, is a friendly place with 10 tidy rooms.

Apple Guest House (*rooms with hot-water shower & with/without TV 400/300B*) is opposite the boat landing in a new, two-storey building. It has an upmarket restaurant on the ground floor and spacious light-filled rooms above. Credit-card symbols on the front door seem to be merely decorative, as this place only accepts cash.

Maekok River Village Resort (*☎ 0 5345 9355, fax 0 5345 9329; W www.track-of-the-tiger.com; poolside suite 2250B, family villa 3250B*), farther along the river, is a newish place offering four-bed rooms as well as two-bed poolside rooms. On the grounds are a pool and restaurant. A variety of activities, including massage, cooking classes, trekking, rafting, mountain biking and caving can be arranged through the resort. It has several options for groups who want to use the facility; in fact the orientation is slanted towards school groups from around Thailand and abroad.

On the opposite side of the river there are three other places to choose from. **Garden Home** (*☎ 0 5337 3015; thatched-roof bungalows with hot-water shower 200-400B, stone bungalows with TV 800B*), is a tranquil place along the river about 150m from the bridge, and offers very clean thatched-roof bungalows spaced well apart among lots of litchi trees and bougainvillea. It also offers a few stone bungalows, and three larger, more luxurious bungalows on the river with small verandas, TV and fridge (1000B). From the bridge, turn left at the Thaton River View Hotel sign to find it.

Baan Suan Riverside Resort (*formerly Riverside House; ☎ 0 5337 3214, fax 0 5337 3215; bungalows with fan/air-con 300/500B, large bungalows 1000B*) is next along and is a newer place featuring small cement air-con bungalows with terraces back from the river, fan rooms in a cement building, also back off the river, and a couple of large air-con wooden bungalows with terraces right on the river. All rates include breakfast. The grounds are beautifully landscaped, and an attached restaurant overlooks the river.

Thaton River View Hotel (*☎ 0 5337 3173, fax 0 5345 9288; rooms 1320B*), farther along the river, is a well-designed hotel with 33 rooms facing the river and joined by wooden walkways. Rates include breakfast – better value at this price than Maekok River Village Resort. The hotel's restaurant is the best in the area, with Shell Chuan Chim honours (see the special section 'Thai Cuisine') for four different dishes on the menu.

Thaton Chalet *(☎ 0 5337 3155–7, fax 0 5337 3158; singles/doubles superior 1000/1200B, deluxe 2000B)*, right on the river next to the bridge, has a four-storey stone-facade. All rooms have carpet, air-con, TV and hot water. The hotel features a pleasant beer garden right on the river, as well as an indoor restaurant.

Several little noodle stands can be found in the vicinity of the bus queue, and there are a few rustic food stalls near the pier and near the bridge. **Racha Roti** in front of Thip's Travellers House features 16 flavours of *rotii*. A local culinary speciality is *lûu*, a northern-Thai salad made with pig's blood.

Asa's Guest Home *(bungalows per person 200B)* is about 15km northeast of Tha Ton, in Lou-Ta, the nearest Lisu village. Situated near the top of the village, with a bit of a view, Asa's offers four clean, basic bamboo-walled rooms in a bamboo-thatch house. Rates include two meals. The friendly family here can arrange various one- and two-day jungle trips in the area, including visits to Karen, Lahu, Lisu, Akha, Mien and Shan villages. To get to Asa's Guest Home take a yellow sǎwngthǎew from Tha Ton for 15B (or motorcycle taxi for 30B) and ask to get off in Lou-Ta.

Getting There & Away

Bus & Sǎwngthǎew Buses to Fang leave from the Chang Pheuak bus terminal in Chiang Mai every 30 minutes between 5.30am and 5.30pm (61B, 3½ hours). Air-con minivans make the trip to Fang every 30 minutes between 7.30am and 4.30pm (80B), leaving from behind the Chang Pheuak bus terminal on the corner of Soi Sanam Kila.

From Fang it's about 23km to Tha Ton. A sǎwngthǎew does the 40-minute trip for 12B; the larger orange buses from Fang leave less frequently and cost 12B. Buses leave from near the market, or you can wait in front of the Fang Hotel for a bus or sǎwngthǎew. Both operate from 5.30am to 5pm only.

Buses to Mae Sai cost 36B from Tha Ton, 45B from Fang.

The river isn't the only way to get to points north from Tha Ton. Yellow sǎwngthǎew leave from the northern side of the river in Tha Ton to Mae Salong in Chiang Rai Province every 30 minutes or so between 7am and 3pm (50B, 2½ hours). You can charter an entire sǎwngthǎew for 450B one way, 650B roundtrip. Hold on tight – the road is steep and winding.

If you're heading to/from Mae Hong Son Province, it's not necessary to dip all the way south to Chiang Mai before continuing westward or eastward. At Ban Mae Malai, the junction of Rte 107 and Rte 1095 (the Chiang Mai–Fang highway), you can pick up a bus to Pai for 45B; if you're coming from Pai, be sure to get off at this junction to catch a bus north to Fang.

Motorcycle Motorcycle trekkers can also travel between Tha Ton and Doi Mae Salong, 48km northeast along a fully paved but sometimes treacherous mountain road. There are a couple of Lisu and Akha villages on the way. The 27km or so between Doi Mae Salong and the village of Muang Ngam are very steep and winding – take care, especially in the rainy season. When conditions are good, the trip can be done in 1½ hours.

For an extra charge, you can take a motorcycle on most boats to Chiang Rai.

RIVER TRIP TO CHIANG RAI

From Tha Ton you can make a half-day long-tail boat trip to Chiang Rai down Mae Nam Kok. The regular passenger boat takes up to 12 passengers, leaves at 12.30pm and costs 250B per person. You can also charter a boat all the way for 1700B, which between six people works out to be about 33B more per person but gives you more room to move. A boat can be chartered any time between 7am and 3pm. The trip is a bit of a tourist trap these days as the passengers are all tourists (what local will pay 250B to take the boat when they can catch a bus to Chiang Rai for less than 40B?), and the villages along the way sell cola and souvenirs – but it's still fun. The best time to go is at the end of the rainy season in November when the river level is high.

The travel time down river depends on river conditions and the skill of the pilot, taking anywhere from three to five hours. You could actually make the boat trip in a day from Chiang Mai, catching a bus back from Chiang Rai as soon as you arrive, but it's better to stay in Fang or Tha Ton, take the boat trip, then stay in Chiang Rai or Chiang Saen before travelling on. You may sometimes have to get off and walk or push the boat if it gets stuck on sand bars.

Some travellers take the boat to Chiang Rai in two or three stages, stopping first in **Mae Salak**, a large Lahu village that is about a third of the distance, or **Ban Ruammit**, a Karen village about two-thirds of the way down. Both villages are well touristed these days (charter boat tours stop for photos and elephant rides), but from here you can trek to other Shan, Thai and hill-tribe villages, or do longer treks south of Mae Salak to **Wawi**, a large multiethnic community of *jiin haw*, Lahu, Lisu, Akha, Shan, Karen, Mien and Thai peoples. The Wawi area has dozens of hill-tribe villages of various ethnicities, including the largest Akha community in Thailand (Saen Charoen) and the oldest Lisu settlement (Doi Chang).

Another alternative is to trek south from Mae Salak all the way to the town of **Mae Suai**, where you can catch a bus on to Chiang Rai or back to Chiang Mai. You might also try getting off the boat at one of the smaller villages (see the boat fares table in this section). Another alternative is to make the trip (much more slowly) upriver from Chiang Rai – this is possible despite the rapids.

Near Ban Ruammit on the opposite river bank (50B, 1½ hours by boat from Chiang Rai,) are some very pretty **hot springs**. Don't even think about entering the water – it's scalding hot. From here you can hike about an hour to **Akha Hill House** (*☎ 0 5374 5140; W www.geocities.com/akhahouse; dorm beds 40B, singles/doubles without bath 70/120B, with bath 100/150B, bungalow 200B*), wholly owned and managed by Akha tribespeople. This rustic guesthouse is in a beautiful setting overlooking a mountain valley; a waterfall and several other villages (Akha, Mien, Lisu, Karen and Lahu) are within walking distance. It can organise overnight trips into the forest with guides who build banana-palm huts and cook meals using sections of bamboo. It can also be reached by road from Chiang Rai, 26km away. Call for free pick-up (once daily between 4pm and 4.30pm).

Several of the guesthouses in Tha Ton organise raft trips down the river – see Getting There & Away under Fang & Tha Ton earlier in this chapter.

A boat leaves once daily from the **Tha Ton public pier** (*☎ 0 5345 9427*) at 12.30pm. The following table shows boat fares from Tha Ton.

destination	fare (B)
Ban Mai	70
Mae Salak	80
Pha Tai	90
Jakheu	100
Kok Noi	110
Pha Khwang	120
Pha Khiaw	170
Hat Wua Dam	180
Pong Man Ron	200
Ban Ruammit	200
Chiang Rai	250

Northern Thailand

The first true Thai kingdoms arose in northern Thailand, hence this region is endowed with a wide range of traditional culture and architecture, including the country's most beautiful Thai temple ruins. It is also the home of Thailand's hill tribes, whose cultures are dissolving rapidly in the face of the country's modernisation and foreign tourism. Despite this, the scenic beauty of the north has been fairly well preserved – the region boasts more natural forest cover than any other – and a distinct northern Thai culture thrives.

Northern Thais *(khon meuang)* are known for their relaxed, easy-going manner, which shows up in their speech – the northern dialect *(kham meuang)* has a slower rhythm than Thailand's three other main dialects. Northern Thais are very proud of their local customs, considering northern ways to be part of Thailand's 'original' tradition and culture. Symbols frequently displayed by northern Thais to express cultural solidarity include clay water jars placed in front of homes, *kàlae* (carved wooden 'X' motifs) that decorate house gables, Shan or hill tribe–style shoulder bags and the ubiquitous *sêua mâw hâwm* (indigo-dyed rice-farmers' shirt) worn on Friday at many banks, universities and other institutions throughout the north.

Highlights

- Examine the finest collection of monuments to Thailand's 'golden age' Sukhothai and Si Satchanalai–Chaliang Historical Parks
- Explore unique northern-Thai temples plus this region's century-old teak homes and shophouses
- Visit the rural provinces with fertile river valleys and Thai Lü communities
- Take a cross-border trip to Myanmar's historic Thai Khün capital with crumbling Buddhas and colonial architecture
- Cave, trek and raft through the dense forests of Mae Hong Son Province
- Raft, hike and take an elephant ride to the spectacular waterfalls near Um Phang

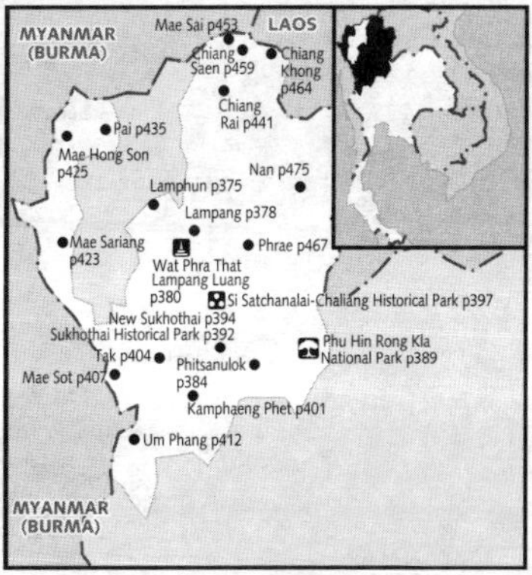

Lamphun Province

This tiny province southeast of Chiang Mai is very much one small city, Lamphun, surrounded by farms and villages.

LAMPHUN

อ.เมืองลำพูน

postcode 51000 • pop 15,200

Most often visited as a day trip from Chiang Mai, Lamphun was, along with Pasang, the centre of the small Hariphunchai principality (AD 750–1281) originally ruled by the semilegendary Mon queen, Chama Thewi. Long after its progenitor, Dvaravati, was vanquished by the Khmer, Hariphunchai succeeded in remaining independent of both the Khmer and the Chiang Mai Thais.

This oval-shaped provincial capital on the western bank of the Nam Mae Kuang is fairly quiet but there are a few places to stay if you want to get away from the hustle and bustle of Chiang Mai or want to study the temples here in depth. The number of historic temples in the capital is many times greater than the two described later.

During the second week of August, Lamphun hosts the annual **Lam Yai Festival**, which features floats made of fruit and, of course, a Miss Lam Yai contest.

NORTHERN THAILAND

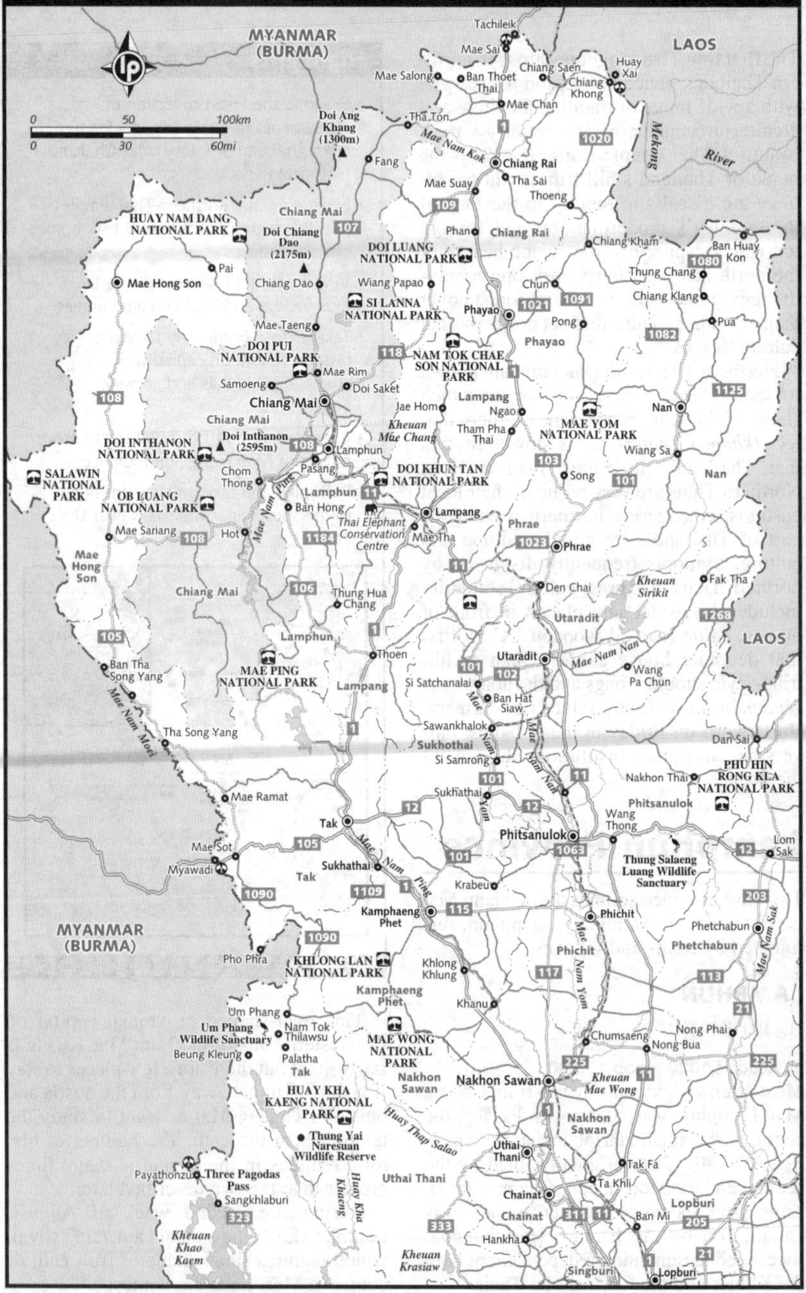

Wat Phra That Hariphunchai

วัดพระธาตุหริภุญชัย

This *wát* (temple), built on the site of Queen Chama Thewi's palace in 1044 (1108 or 1157 according to some datings), sits on the western side of the main road into Lamphun from Chiang Mai. The temple lay derelict for many years until Khruba Siwichai, one of northern Thailand's most famous monks, made renovations in the 1930s. It boasts some interesting post-Dvaravati architecture, a couple of fine Buddha images and two old *chedi* (stupa) of the original Hariphunchai style. The tallest *chedi*, Chedi Suwan, dates from 1418, measures 46m high and is surmounted by a nine-tiered gold umbrella weighing 6.5kg. Thais consider this to be one of the eight holiest *chedi* in Thailand.

Wat Chama Thewi

วัดจามเทวี

A more unusual Hariphunchai *chedi* can be seen at Wat Chama Thewi (popularly called Wat Kukut), which is said to have been erected in the 8th or 9th century as a Dvaravati monument, then rebuilt by the Hariphunchai Mon in 1218. As it has been restored many times since then it is now a mixture of several schools. The stepped profile bears a remarkable resemblance to the 12th-century Satmahal Prasada at Polonnaruwa in Sri Lanka.

Each side of the *chedi* – known as Chedi Suwan Chang Kot – has five rows of three Buddha figures, diminishing in size on each higher level. The standing Buddhas are in Dvaravati style, although made recently.

Lamphun National Museum

พิพิธภัณฑสถานแห่งชาติลำพูน

Across the street from Wat Phra That Hariphunchai, Lamphun's National Museum (*☎ 0 5353 0536; Th Inthayongyot; admission 30B; open 9am-4pm Wed-Sun*) has a small collection, which includes artefacts from the Dvaravati, Hariphunchai and Lanna kingdoms.

Places to Stay & Eat

Si Lamphun Hotel (*no Roman-script sign; ☎ 0 5351 1176; Soi 5, Th Inthayongyot; singles/doubles 100/200B*) is the easiest accommodation to find and is on the town's main street. It's a real dive – singles have grotty bathrooms. This place needs an overhaul and traffic noise is a problem.

Supamit Holiday Inn (*☎ 0 5353 4865, fax 0 5353 4355; Th Chama Thewi; singles/doubles with fan 250/300B, with air-con 350/400B*) bears no relation to the international hotel

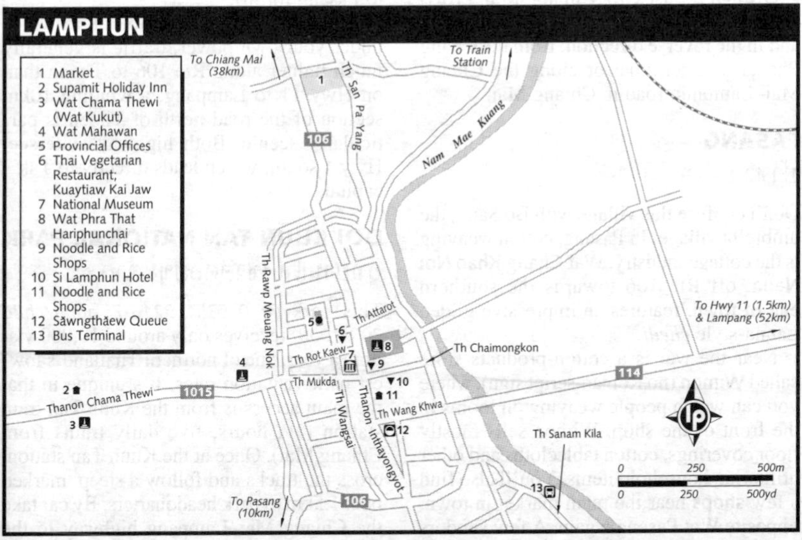

chain but is a clean and efficient 50-room establishment across from Wat Chama Thewi. Simple rooms have attached hot-water bathroom, fan or air-con, and balconies. An open-air restaurant on the 5th floor is quite good and offers a nice view of Lamphun.

Along Th Inthayongyot south of Wat Phra That is a string of OK **noodle and rice shops**.

A **Thai vegetarian restaurant** *(Th Wangsai; dishes 10-15B; open 7am-7pm Mon-Sat)* serves delicious meatless curries and stir-fried vegetables; dishes include rice. Look for the yellow pennant out front. Nearby **Kuaytiaw Kai Jaw** *(Th Wangsai)* specialises in the unusual combination of rice noodles with a sausage made from chicken, carrots and seaweed. It's more delicious than it sounds.

Getting There & Away

Blue *sǎwngthǎew* to Lamphun from Chiang Mai leave at 30-minute intervals throughout the day from the Chiang Mai–Lamphun road near the southern side of Saphan Nawarat. In the reverse direction, sǎwngthǎew leave Lamphun from the queue near the intersection of Th Inthayongyot and Th Wang Khwa. The 26km ride (10B) is along a beautiful country road, parts of which are bordered by tall dipterocarp trees.

Ordinary buses to Chiang Mai (10B) leave from the **bus terminal** *(Th Sanam Kila)*, and in the reverse direction, from the Chang Pheuak bus terminal or along the Chiang Mai–Lamphun road in Chiang Mai.

PASANG

ป่าซาง

Don't confuse this village with Bo Sang, the umbrella village. In Pasang, cotton weaving is the cottage industry. **Wat Chang Khao Noi Neua**, off Rte 106 towards the southern end of town, features an impressive gilded Lanna-style *chedi*.

Near the wát is a cotton-products store called **Wimon** (no Roman-script sign), where you can watch people weaving on looms in the front of the shop. Wimon sells mostly floor coverings, cotton tablecloths and other utilitarian household items. You'll also find a few **shops** near the main market in town, opposite Wat Pasang Ngam. A few vendors in the **market** also sell blankets, tablecloths, *phâakhamáa* (cotton wraparounds), shirts and other woven-cotton products.

Wat Phra Phutthabaht Tahk Phah

วัดพระพุทธบาทตากผ้า

This regionally famous wát belonging to the popular Mahanikai sect, about 9km south of Pasang or 20km south of Lamphun off Rte 106 in the subdistrict of Ma-Kok (follow Rte 1133 1km east), is a shrine to one of the north's most renowned monks, Luang Pu Phromma. It contains a lifelike resin figure of the deceased monk sitting in meditation.

One of his disciples, Ajahn Thirawattho, teaches meditation to a large contingent of monks who are housed in *kùtì* (a monk's hut or living quarters) of laterite brick. Behind the spacious grounds is a park and a steep hill mounted by a *chedi*. The wát is named after an unremarkable Buddha footprint *(phrá phútthábàat)* shrine in the middle of the lower temple grounds and another spot where Buddha supposedly dried his robes *(tàak phâa)*.

A sǎwngthǎew from Lamphun to the wát costs 20B.

Getting There & Away

A sǎwngthǎew will take you from Lamphun to Pasang for 8B.

If you're heading south to Tak Province under your own power, traffic is generally much lighter along Rte 106 to Thoen than on Hwy 11 to Lampang; a winding 10km section of the road north of Thoen is particularly scenic. Both highways intersect Hwy 1 south, which leads directly to Tak's capital.

DOI KHUN TAN NATIONAL PARK

อุทยานแห่งชาติดอยขุนตาล

This park *(☎ 0 5351 9216-7; adult/child 200/100B)* receives only around 10,000 visitors a year, one of northern Thailand's lowest park-visitation rates. It's unique in that the main access is from the Khun Tan train station (1½ hours, five daily trains from Chiang Mai). Once at the Khun Tan station, cross the tracks and follow a steep, marked path 1.5km to park headquarters. By car take the Chiang Mai–Lampang highway to the

Mae Tha turn-off, then follow signs along a steep unpaved road for 18km.

The 255-sq-km park ranges in elevation from 350m at the bamboo forest lowlands to 1363m at the pine-studded summit of Doi Khun Tan. Wildflowers, including orchids, ginger and lilies, are abundant. In addition to a well-marked **trail** covering the mountain's four peaks, there's also a trail to **Nam Tok Tat Moei** (7km round trip). Thailand's longest **train tunnel** (1352m), which opened in 1921 after six years of manual labour by a thousand Lao workers (several of whom are said to have been killed by tigers), intersects the mountain slope.

Bungalows, which can accommodate six to nine people, are available for around 600B to 1200B near the park headquarters and at Camp One on the first peak; at Camp Two on the second peak it's 250B per person, or you can pitch your own tent for 10B; food is available at a small **shop** near the park headquarters. The park is very popular on cool season weekends.

Lampang Province

LAMPANG

อ.เมืองลำปาง

postcode 52000 • pop 44,700

Lampang was inhabited as far back as the 7th century in the Dvaravati period and played an important part in the history of the Hariphunchai kingdom. Legend says the city was founded by the son of Hariphunchai's Queen Chama Thewi.

Like Chiang Mai, Phrae and other older northern cities, Lampang was built as a walled rectangle alongside a river (in this case Mae Wang). At the end of the 19th and beginning of the 20th centuries Lampang, along with nearby Phrae, became an important centre for the domestic and international teak trade. A large British-owned timber company brought in Burmese supervisors familiar with the teak industry in Burma to train Burmese and Thai loggers in the area. These well-paid supervisors, along with independent Burmese teak merchants who plied their trade in Lampang, sponsored the construction of more than a dozen impressive temples in the city. Burmese and Shan artisans designed and built the temples out of local materials, especially teak. Their legacy lives on in several of Lampang's best-maintained wát, now among the city's main visitor attractions.

Many Thais visit Lampang for a taste of urban northern Thailand without the crass commercialism of Chiang Mai.

Wat Phra Kaew Don Tao

วัดพระแก้วดอนเต้า

This wát, on the northern side of the Mae Wang, housed the Emerald Buddha (now in Bangkok's Wat Phra Kaew) from 1436 to 1468. The main *chedi* shows Hariphunchai influence, while the adjacent *mondòp* (a square, spire-topped shrine room) was built in 1909. The *mondòp*, decorated with glass mosaic in typical Burmese style, contains a Mandalay-style Buddha image. A display of Lanna artefacts (mostly religious paraphernalia and woodwork) can be viewed in the wát's **Lanna Museum**. A small admission fee is charged.

Other Temples

Two wát built in the late 19th century by Burmese artisans are **Wat Si Rong Meuang** and **Wat Si Chum**. Both have temple buildings constructed in the Burmese 'layered' style, with tin roofs gabled by intricate woodcarvings. The current abbots of these temples are Burmese.

Besides the *wíhăan* (any large hall in a Thai temple) at Wat Phra That Lampang Luang (for details see Around Lampang later in this section), the *mondòp* at **Wat Pongsanuk Tai** is one of the few remaining local examples of original Lanna-style temple architecture, which emphasised open-sided wooden buildings.

Wat Chedi Sao, about 6km north of town towards Jae Hom, is named for the 20 white-washed Lanna-style *chedi* on its grounds (*sao* is northern Thai for 20). It's a pretty, well-endowed wát, landscaped with bougainvillea and casuarina. At one edge of the wát stands a very colourful statue of Avalokiteshvara, while a pavilion in the centre features a gilded Buddha similar in style to the Phra Phutha Chinnarat in Phitsanulok. But the wát's real treasure is a solid-gold, 15th-century seated Buddha on display in a glassed-in **pavilion** *(open 8am-5pm daily)*, built over a square pond. The image weighs

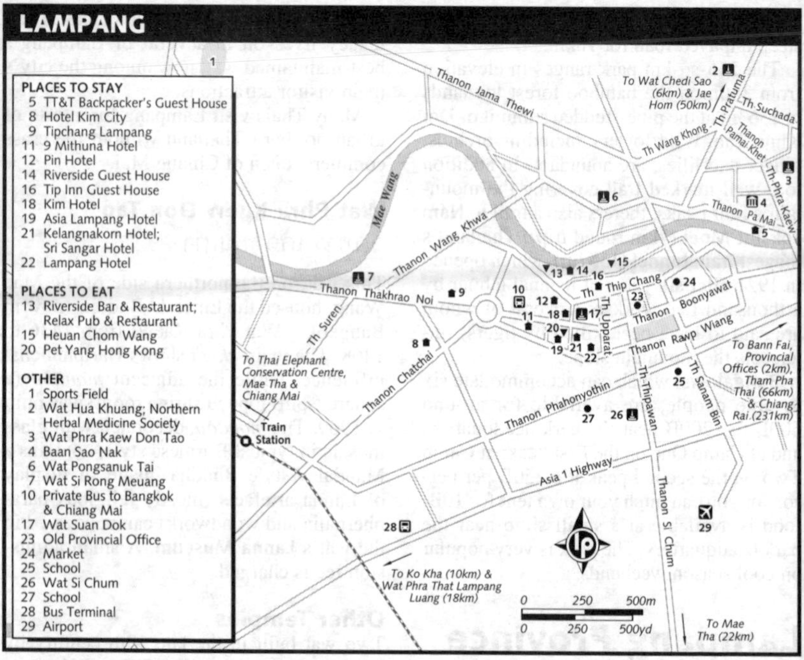

1507g, stands 38cm tall and is said to contain a piece of the Buddha's skull in its head and an ancient Pali-inscribed golden palm leaf in its chest; precious stones decorate the image's hairline and robe. A farmer reportedly found the figure next to the ruins of nearby Wat Khu Kao in 1983. Monks stationed at Wat Chedi Sao make and sell herbal medicines; the popular *yaa màwng* is similar to tiger balm.

Baan Sao Nak

บ้านเสานัก

Baan Sao Nak *(Many Pillars House; ☎ 0 5422 7653; admission 30B; open 10am-5pm daily)*, built in 1895 in the traditional Lanna style, is a huge teak house in the old Wiang Neua (north city) section of town, and is supported by 116 square teak pillars. Once owned by a local *khun yǐng* (a title equivalent to 'Lady' in England), it now serves as a local museum. The entire house is furnished with Burmese and Thai antiques; three rooms display antique silverwork, lacquerware, bronzeware, ceramics and other northern Thai crafts. The area beneath the house is sometimes used for ceremonial dinners.

Horse Carts

Lampang is known throughout Thailand as Meuang Rot Mah (Horse Cart City) because it's the only town in Thailand where horse carts are still used as public transport. These days, Lampang's horse carts are mainly for tourists. Trying to get a good price is difficult. A 20-minute horse cart tour around town costs 150B; for 200B you can get a half-hour tour that goes along the Mae Wang, and for 300B a one-hour tour that stops at Wat Phra Kaew Don Tao and Wat Si Rong Meuang. If there's little business you may be able to negotiate the price down to 120B per half-hour or 200B per hour. The main horse cart stands are in front of the old provincial office and the Tipchang Lampang.

Traditional Massage

The **Samakhom Samunphrai Phak Neua** *(Northern Herbal Medicine Society; 149 Th Pratuma; centre & sauna open 8am-8pm daily)*, next to Wat Hua Khuang in the Wiang Neua area, offers traditional northern-Thai massage (100B per half hour, 150B per hour) and herbal saunas (100B). Once you've paid, you can go in and out of the sauna as many times as you want during one visit.

Places to Stay – Budget & Mid-Range

There are several economical choices in Lampang along Th Boonyawat, which runs through the centre of town. **Sri Sangar Hotel** *(Si Sa-Nga; ☎ 0 5421 7070; 213-215 Th Boonyawat; singles/doubles 100/180B)* is centrally located and has clean rooms with fan and bathroom.

9 Mithuna Hotel *(☎ 0 5421 7438; 285 Th Boonyawat; fan/air-con rooms 204/286B)* off Th Boonyawat (with a second entrance off Th Rawp Riang), is a standard Thai-Chinese place – fine but not as good a deal as Sri Sangar. **Lampang Hotel** *(☎ 0 5422 7311; 696 Th Suan Dok; fan/air-con rooms 230/280B)* is similar to Mithuna Hotel. Rooms have bathroom and cost a bit more again with TV. A small parking lot can be found at the back.

Kim Hotel *(☎ 0 5421 7721, fax 0 5422 6929; 168 Th Boonyawat; rooms 220B)* is a three-storey hotel with clean, comfortable rooms with air-con, hot water and TV; parking is available. **Kelangnakorn Hotel** *(☎ 0 5421 6137; Th Boonyawat; rooms with fan/TV/air-con 210/250/340B)* diagonally across the street from Kim, is popular with travelling salesmen, and features air-con rooms with TV and phone. Off-street parking is provided.

Riverside Guest House *(☎ 0 5422 7005, fax 0 5432 2342; 286 Th Talat Kao; rooms with/without bath 250/150B, with balcony 350B, with air-con 600B)*, tucked away near the river, provides comfortable rooms in old teak buildings surrounded by beautiful landscaping. Rooms with fan have outside or private bathroom, and there are rooms with balconies overlooking the river. There is also one air-con room with a large living area. The guesthouse offers continental breakfast, fax service, international calls, motorcycle rental, laundering service and sightseeing tours.

Tip Inn Guest House *(☎ 0 5422 1821; 143 Th Talat Kao; singles with bath 100B, doubles with hot-water bath 160B)*, near Riverside Guest House, features nine adequate rooms off the street.

TT&T Backpacker's Guest House *(☎ 0 5422 5361, 0 1951 5154; 55 Th Pa Mai; beds 100B, singles/doubles 180/200B)*, on the northern side of the river off Th Pa Mai, has fairly clean, basic multibed rooms, singles or larger doubles, all with shared hot-water showers. A săwngthăew ride from the bus station to the guesthouse should cost about 20B per person.

Places to Stay – Top End

Asia Lampang Hotel *(☎ 0 5422 7844, fax 0 5422 4436; 229 Th Boonyawat; rooms 350B, suites 450-500B)* is a long-running place with good rooms facing the street and nicer, large, suite-style rooms on the 5th floor. All rooms have air-con, TV and fridge. The Asia's pleasant street-level café is its best feature.

Pin Hotel *(☎ 0 5422 1509, fax 0 5432 2286; 8 Th Suan Dok; air-con rooms 450B, deluxe rooms 650B, suites 900B)*, right behind the Kim Hotel in the town centre, has spacious, well-maintained, air-con rooms in an older section, or deluxe rooms and suites in a newer wing. All 59 rooms in this four-storey hotel come with air-con, satellite TV, fridge, phone and hot water; parking is available.

Tipchang Lampang Hotel *(☎ 0 5422 6501, fax 0 5422 5362; 54/22 Th Thakhrao Noi; rooms 600-800B)* is a big, modern place with a coffee shop, café, supper club, cocktail lounge, tennis courts and pool. Rates include breakfast.

Hotel Kim City *(☎ 0 5431 0238, fax 0 5422 6635; 274/1 Th Chatchai; rooms 500-900B)*, another big, modern place, sits a bit outside the city centre and is an OK choice only if you have your own wheels.

Places to Eat

Pet Yang Hong Kong *(Th Boonyawat; dishes 25-34B; open 8am-6pm)*, directly across from Kim Hotel, serves very tasty roast duck with rice or noodles. There are a few other **rice and noodle shops** in this area.

Riverside Bar & Restaurant *(328 Th Thip Chang; dishes 40-100B; open 11am-midnight daily)* is in a rambling old teak structure on the river. It serves vegetarian and northern Thai dishes as well as *faràng* (Western) pastries and ice cream and it has a full bar. It's a good choice for a drink or meal, with live folk music nightly and reasonable prices considering the high quality of the food and service. **Relax Pub & Restaurant**, a bit farther west, is more modern than Riverside and also has good food and live music.

Heuan Chom Wang *(Th Talat Kao; dishes 40-100B, open 11am-11pm daily)* is an atmospheric place that can be found by walking east about 100m from the Riverside Guest House on Th Talat Kao, then north down an alley on the left. This open-air restaurant, set in a beautiful, old, teak building overlooking the river, specialises in northern Thai food as well as more typical central Thai fare.

Getting There & Away

Air Daily flights between Lampang and Bangkok (1950B) are offered by **PB Air** *(☎ 0 5422 6238; Lampang Airport • in Bangkok ☎ 0 2261 0220)*.

Bus From Chiang Mai, buses to Lampang (25B, 50B to 65B air-con, two hours) leave from the Chiang Mai Arcade terminal about every half-hour during the day and also from next to Saphan Nawarat in the direction of Lamphun. Bus services also depart Lamphun (29B).

Air-con buses go to Lampang from Phitsanulok's main bus terminal (140B via the new route, four hours; 145B via the old route, five hours). Ordinary buses to/from Bangkok (7½ hours, four daily departures each way) cost 176B. There are also three 2nd-class air-con buses (246B), six 1st-class buses (317B) and one 24-seat VIP bus (490B) to/from Bangkok each day. The bus terminal in Lampang is some way out of town – 10B by shared săwngthăew.

To book an air-con bus from Lampang to Bangkok or Chiang Mai seek out the tour bus companies, which have offices in town along Th Boonyawat near the clock tower roundabout.

Train From Lampang to Chiang Mai (two hours) train fares will cost 37/15B for 2nd/3rd class.

AROUND LAMPANG

Wat Phra That Lampang Luang

วัดพระธาตุลำปางหลวง

Arguably the most beautiful wooden Lanna temple in northern Thailand, Wat Phra That Lampang is centred on the open-sided **Wihan Luang**. Thought to have been built in 1476, the impressive *wíhăan* features a triple-tiered wooden roof supported by teak pillars and is considered to be the oldest existing wooden building in Thailand. A huge gilded *mondòp* in the back of the *wíhăan* contains a Buddha image cast in 1563. The faithful leave small gold-coloured Buddha figures close to the *mondòp* and hang Thai Lü weavings behind it.

Early 19th-century **jataka murals** are painted on wooden panels around the inside upper perimeter of the *wíhăan*. The tall **Lanna-style chedi** behind the *wíhăan*, raised in 1449 and restored in 1496, measures 24m at its base and is 45m high. The small, simple **Wihan Ton Kaew**, to the north of the main *wíhăan,* was built in 1476 (standing with your back to the main gate). The oldest structure in the compound is the smaller 13th-century **Wihan Phra Phut** to the south of the main *chedi*; the *wíhăan* to the north of the *chedi* (Wihan Nam Taem) was built in the early 16th century and, amazingly, still contains traces of the original murals.

The **Haw Phra Phutthabaht**, a small white building behind the *chedi*, has been turned into a camera obscura. When you enter and shut the door an image of the *chedi* is projected, via a small hole in the door, onto a white sheet hanging on the wall.

WAT PHRA THAT LAMPANG LUANG

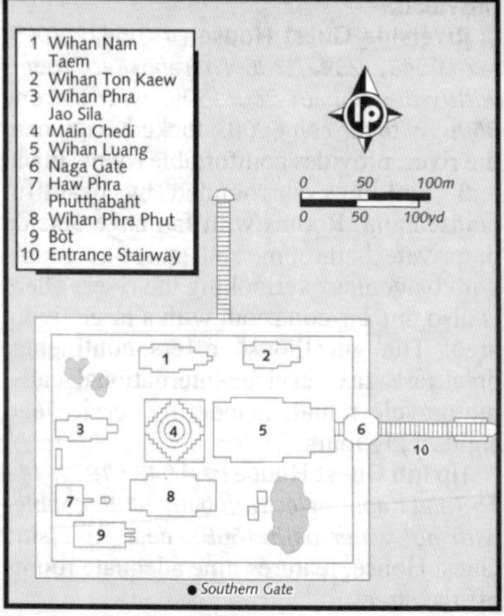

The lintel over the entrance to the compound features an impressive dragon relief – once common in northern Thai temples but rarely seen these days. This gate supposedly dates to the 15th century.

In the arboretum outside the southern gate, there are now three **museums** and they are all worthwhile. One displays mostly festival paraphernalia, plus some Buddha figures. Another, called 'House of the Emerald Buddha', contains a miscellany of coins, banknotes, Buddha figures, silver betel nut cases, lacquerware and other ethnographic artefacts, along with three small, heavily gold-leafed Buddhas placed on an altar behind an enormous repoussé silver bowl. The third, a fine small museum, features shelves of Buddha figures, lacquered boxes, manuscripts and ceramics, all well labelled in Thai and English.

Wat Phra That Lampang Luang is located 18km southwest of Lampang in Ko Kha. To get there by public transport from Lampang, catch a blue săwngthăew south on Th Praisani to the market in Ko Kha (10B), then a Hang Chat bound săwngthăew (5B) 3km north to the entrance of Wat Phra That Lampang Luang. A chartered motorcycle taxi from the Ko Kha săwngthăew station to the temple costs around 20B to 30B.

If you're driving or cycling from Lampang, head south on the Asia 1 Hwy and take the Ko Kha exit, then follow the road over a bridge and bear right. Follow the signs and continue for 2km over another bridge until you see the temple on the left. If you're coming from Chiang Mai via Hwy 11, turn south onto Rte 1034 18km northwest of Lampang at the Km 13 marker – this route is a 50km short cut to Ko Kha that avoids much of Lampang.

Thai Elephant Conservation Center

ศูนย์ฝึกลูกช้าง

In Hang Chat district northwest of Lampang, outside Thung Kwian at the Km 37 marker, this unique facility (*☎ 0 5422 8035, 0 5422 8108; admission 50B; public shows 10am & 11am daily, also 1.30pm Fri, Sat & holidays June-Feb*) promotes the role of the Asian elephant in ecotourism and provides free medical treatment and care for sick elephants from all over Thailand.

In addition to the standard tourist show, the 122-hectare centre offers exhibits on the history and culture of elephants as well as elephant rides (8am to 3.30pm, 300B for 15 minutes, 500B for 30 minutes) through the surrounding forest. At 9.45am (plus at 1.15pm on weekends) you can see the elephants bathing in the river. On weekends during the December to February high season, an ensemble of elephants play oversized musical instruments, including drums, to create a sort of chaotic trance music.

The camp staff are beginning to explore the use of elephant dung as a base for making decorative papers and to produce biogas for cooking and electricity. Admission to facilities used for dung paper and biogas production is free; follow the signs.

To reach the camp, you can take a bus or săwngthăew from Lampang's main bus terminal bound for Chiang Mai and get off at the Km 37 marker. Free vans shuttle visitors the 2km distance between the highway and the showgrounds.

Mahout Training The Thai Elephant Conservation Center now offers special programmes for those interested in learning the skills of the *khwaan cháang* or mahout (elephant caretaker). If you want a quick taste of the mahout's life, you can sign on for a one-day course for 1500B and learn a few simple commands for leading an elephant, experiment with dung paper, ride an elephant in the jungle and take a tour of the elephant hospital.

A more involved three-day, two-night homestay programme costs 5000B. This includes all meals, one night's lodging in a well-equipped, wood and bamboo bungalow and another at a jungle camp, plus a general introduction to elephant care and training. Those with a higher level of commitment can choose longer programmes of 10 days, a month, or longer, at a cost of 1500B per day including training, lodging and food.

Other Attractions

North and east of Lampang are the cotton-weaving villages of **Jae Hom** and **Mae Tha**. You can wander around and find looms in action; there are also plenty of shops along the main roads.

Tham Pha Thai is 66km north of Lampang, between Lampang and Chiang Rai about 500m off Hwy 1. Besides the usual formations (stalagmites and stalactites), the cave has a large Buddha image.

The province is well endowed with waterfalls. Three are found within Wang Neua district, roughly 120km north of the provincial capital via Rte 1053: **Wang Kaew**, **Wang Thong** and **Than Thong** (Jampa Thong). Wang Kaew is the largest, with 110 tiers. Near the summit is a Mien hill-tribe

Elephants in Thailand

The elephant is one of the most powerful symbols in Thai culture, and until 1917 a white elephant appeared on the Thai national flag. Historically Thais have worked side-by-side with elephants on farms and in the jungle, and elephants were the superweapons of Southeast Asian armies before the advent of tanks and big guns. Today elephants are still revered in Thai society and are a strong drawcard for Western tourists.

Current estimates put the number of wild elephants in Thailand at 2500 to 3200, more than India but fewer than Myanmar. The number of domesticated elephants hovers at around 2000. However, numbers of both wild and domestic animals are steadily dwindling. Around 1900 it was estimated that there were at least 100,000 elephants working in Thailand; by 1952 the number had dropped to 13,397. Today Tak Province has the highest number of elephants and is one of only three provinces (the other two are Mae Hong Son and Surin) where the elephant population has actually increased over the last 20 years.

Elephant mothers carry their calves for 22 months. Once they are born, working elephants enjoy a brief childhood before they begin training at around three to five years of age. The training, which is under the guidance of their mahouts, takes five years. Tasks they learn include pushing, carrying and piling logs, as well as bathing and walking in procession.

Working elephants have a career of about 50 years; hence when young they are trained by two mahouts, one older and one younger – sometimes a father-and-son team – who can see the animal through its lifetime. Thai law requires that elephants be retired and released into the wild at age 61. They often live for 80 years or more.

As a mode of jungle transport, the elephant beats any other animal or machine for moving through a forest with minimum damage – its large, soft feet distribute the animal's weight without crushing the ground. Interestingly, an adult can run at speeds of up to 23km/h but they put less weight on the ground per square centimetre than a deer!

In 1989 logging was banned in Thailand, resulting in much less demand for trained elephants. Some owners, however, continue to work their elephants in the illegal logging industry along the Thai-Myanmar border. Sadly, some animals are pumped full of amphetamines so they can work day and night.

The plight of these unemployed creatures is becoming an issue of national concern. Many domesticated elephants are increasingly neglected, mistreated or abandoned by owners who often cannot afford to care for them. Meanwhile, destruction of forests and ivory-trade poaching are placing the wild-elephant population in increasing jeopardy. The Asian elephant is now officially classified as an endangered species.

Rising numbers of unemployed elephants also means unemployed mahouts; many mahouts have begun migrating with their elephants to large Thai cities, even Bangkok. They earn money simply by walking the animal through the streets and selling bananas and sugarcane to people to feed the elephants. In these urban environments, the elephants often suffer; in 1998 an elephant died in Bangkok after getting one of its legs caught in a sewer culvert.

Elephant conservation experts are urging tourists *not* to feed elephants in the cities. A better way to make contact with these beautiful animals is at the Thai Elephant Conservation Center (TECC) in Lampang Province, or at other bona fide conservation facilities. 'The only viable alternative for Asian elephants today is tourism,' says Richard Lair, a long-time consultant to the TECC.

For more information about the state of elephants in Thailand check the TECC website (W www.changthai.com).

village. This area became part of the 1172-sq-km **Doi Luang National Park** in 1990; animals protected by the park include serow, barking deer, pangolin and the pig-tailed macaque.

In the Meuang Pan district, about halfway to Wang Neua from Lampang, is another waterfall, **Nam Tok Chae Son**, part of the 593-sq-km **Jae Son National Park**. Elevations in the park reach above 2000m. Jae Son has six drops, each with its own pool; close to the falls are nine hot springs. Small huts house circular baths, recessed into the floor and lined with clay tiles, that are continuously filled with water direct from the spring. For 20B you can take a 20-minute soak, preceded and followed by an invigorating cold-water shower.

Camping is permitted in both Jae Son and Doi Luang National Parks. Jae Son has a visitor centre, 12 **bungalows** for hire and a **restaurant**, but food must be ordered in advance of your visit. Several privately run **food/snack stalls** can provide sustenance as well. For further information, contact Jae Son National Park *(☎ 0 5422 9000; Tambon Jae Son, Amphoe Muang Ban, Lampang)* or the Natural Resources Conservation Office, **Royal Forest Department** *(☎ 0 2579 7223, 0 2579 5734; Th Phahonyothin, Chatuchak, Bangkok)*.

Phitsanulok Province

PHITSANULOK

อ.เมืองพิษณุโลก

postcode 65000 • pop 85,500

Under the reign of Ayuthaya King Borom Trailokanat (1448–88), Phitsanulok served as the capital of Thailand for 25 years. The town straddles Mae Nam Nan near a junction with Mae Nam Khwae Noi, hence it's sometimes referred to as Song Khwae (Two Tributaries), and it's the only city in Thailand where it's legal to reside on a houseboat within municipal boundaries. No new houseboats are permitted, however, so it's likely that they will gradually disappear.

This vibrant city makes an excellent base from which to explore the lower north. Besides the temples of Wat Phra Si Ratana Mahathat and Wat Chulamani, you can explore the attractions of historical Sukhothai, Kamphaeng Phet and Si Satchanalai, as well as the national parks and wildlife sanctuaries of Thung Salaeng Luang and Phu Hin Rong Kla, the former strategic headquarters of the Communist Party of Thailand (CPT). All of these places are within 150km of Phitsanulok.

The name Phitsanulok is often abbreviated as 'Philok'.

Information

Tourist Offices The **TAT office** *(☎/fax 0 5525 2742–3; e tatphs@loxinfo.co.th; 209/7-8 Th Borom Trailokanat; open 8.30am-4.30pm daily)*, in a lane off Th Borom Trailokanat, has knowledgeable and helpful staff (some of TAT's best) who give out free maps of the town and a sheet that describes a walking tour. The office also has information on Sukhothai and Phetchabun Provinces.

If you plan to do the trip from Phitsanulok to Lom Sak, ask for the sketch map of Hwy 12 that marks several waterfalls and resorts along the way.

Money Several banks in town offer foreign-exchange services and ATMs; only the **Bangkok Bank** *(35 Th Naresuan)* has an after-hours exchange window (usually open till 8pm). There's also an ATM inside the Wat Phra Si Ratana Mahathat compound.

Post & Communications If you need to deal with mail, go to the **main post office** *(Th Phuttha Bucha; open 8.30am-4.30pm Mon-Fri, 9am-noon Sat & Sun)*. The attached **Communications Authority of Thailand** *(CAT; open 7am-11pm daily)* office offers phone and Internet services.

Shops offering Internet access dot the central area of town near the railway station. The highest concentration of Internet cafés is on the western bank of the river near Saphan Ekathotsarot.

Wat Phra Si Ratana Mahathat

วัดพระศรีรัตนมหาธาตุ

The full name of this temple is Wat Phra Si Ratana Mahathat, but the locals call it Wat Phra Si or Wat Yai. The wát stands near the east end of the bridge over Mae Nam Nan (on the right as you're heading out of

Phitsanulok towards Sukhothai). The main *wíhăan* contains the **Chinnarat Buddha (Phra Phuttha Chinnarat)**, one of Thailand's most revered and copied images. This famous bronze image is probably second in importance only to the Emerald Buddha in Bangkok's Wat Phra Kaew. In terms of total annual donations collected (about 12 million baht a year), Wat Yai follows Wat Sothon in Chachoengsao.

The image was cast in the late Sukhothai style, but what makes it strikingly unique is the flame-like halo around the head and torso that turns up at the bottom to become dragon-serpent heads on either side of the image. The head of this Buddha is a little wider than standard Sukhothai, giving the statue a very solid feel.

The story goes that construction of this wát was commissioned under the reign of King Li Thai in 1357. When it was completed, King Li Thai wanted it to contain three high-quality bronze images, so he sent for well-known sculptors from Si Satchanalai, Chiang Saen and Hariphunchai (Lamphun), as well as five Brahman priests. The first two castings worked well, but the third required three attempts before it was decreed the best of all. Legend has it that a white-robed sage appeared from nowhere to assist in the final casting, then disappeared. This last image was named the Chinnarat (Victorious King) Buddha and it became the centrepiece in the *wíhăan*. The other two images, Phra Chinnasi and Phra Si Satsada, were later moved to the royal temple

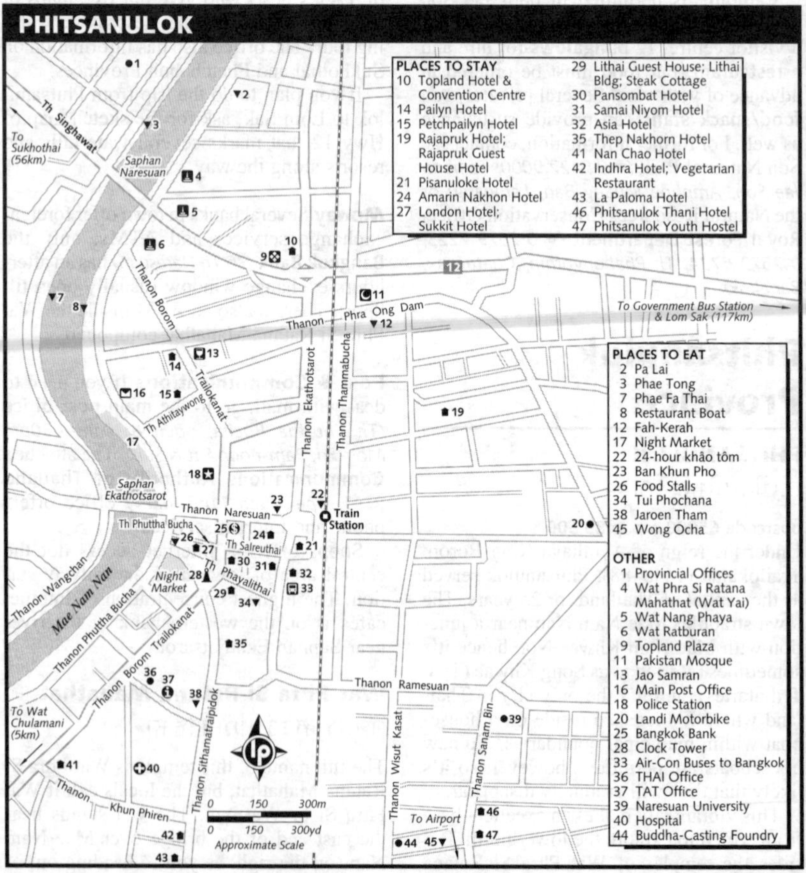

of Wat Bowonniwet in Bangkok. Only the Chinnarat image has the flame-dragon halo.

The walls of the *wíhăan* are low to accommodate the low-swept roof, typical of northern temple architecture, so the image takes on larger proportions than it might in a central or northeastern wát. The brilliant interior architecture is such that when you sit on the Italian marble floor in front of the Buddha, the lacquered columns draw your vision towards the image and evoke a strong sense of serenity. The doors of the building are inlaid with mother-of-pearl in a design copied from Bangkok's Wat Phra Kaew.

Another sanctuary to one side has been converted into a **museum** *(admission free; open 9am-5.30pm Wed-Sun)*, displaying antique Buddha images, ceramics and other historic artefacts. Dress appropriately when visiting this most sacred of temples – no shorts or sleeveless tops.

Near Wat Yai, on the same side of the river, are two other temples of the same period – **Wat Ratburan** and **Wat Nang Phaya**.

Wat Chulamani

วัดจุฬามณี

Five kilometres south of the city (a 4B trip on bus No 5 down Th Borom Trailokanat), Wat Chulamani harbours some ruins dating to the Sukhothai period. The original buildings must have been impressive, judging from what remains of the ornate Khmer-style tower. King Borom Trailokanat was ordained as a monk here and there is an old Thai inscription to that effect on the ruined *wíhăan*, dating from the reign of King Narai the Great.

The tower has little left of its original height, but Khmer-style door lintels remain, including one with a Sukhothai walking Buddha and a *dhammachakka* (Buddhist wheel of law) in the background.

Besides the tower and the *wíhăan*, the only original structures left are the remains of the monastery walls. Still, there is a peaceful, neglected atmosphere about the place.

Sergeant Major Thawi Buddha-Casting Foundry

โรงหล่อพระจ่าทวี

Not far from the Phitsanulok Youth Hostel, is a small factory *(Th Wisut Kasat; bus No 8; open 8.30am-4.30pm Wed-Sun)* where bronze Buddha images of all sizes are cast. Most are copies of the famous Phra Chinnarat Buddha at Wat Yai. Visitors are welcome to watch and there are even detailed photo exhibits demonstrating the lost-wax method of metal casting. Some of the larger images take a year or more to complete. The foundry is owned by Dr Thawi, an artisan and nationally renowned expert on northern Thai folklore. There is a small gift shop at the foundry where you can purchase bronze images of various sizes.

In addition to the foundry, there is a display of fighting cocks, which are bred and sold all over Thailand. The official English name for this part of the facility is 'The Centre of Conservative Folk Cock'!

Places to Stay – Budget

Phitsanulok has good coverage in the budget-accommodation category.

Guesthouses & Hostels Well above the usual standard of Thai Hostelling International Hostels is **Phitsanulok Youth Hostel** *(☎ 0 5524 2060; ⓔ phitsanulok@tyha.org; 38 Th Sanam Bin; rooms without bath 120B, row house singles/doubles/triples/quads 200/300/450/600B)*. Set amid a lush garden with aromatic jasmine vines and a spring, a 50-year-old house has been converted into a restaurant featuring Thai and European food. A lofty teak-wood *săalaa* (*sala;* open-sided pavilion) behind the house is built of salvaged timber from seven old Tak Province teak houses to create a pleasant, open-air sitting and dining area – a good place to sit back and relax over a glass of wine or freshly brewed, locally grown coffee while listening to the cadence of frogs and crickets.

The owner says he may soon be rebuilding all-new accommodation here, so look for rates to change. From the train station you can get to the hostel by *săamláw* (three-wheeled pedicab; 20B to 30B) or on a No 4 city bus. From the airport take a *túk-túk* (motorised săamláw; 30B) or a No 4 bus that passes by the hostel (on the right). From the bus terminal, take a săamláw (30B) or a No 1 city bus (get off at Th Ramesuan and walk the last 300m or so).

Lithai Guest House *(☎ 0 5521 9626, fax 0 5521 9627; Th Phayalithai; fan rooms without bath 200B, with bath & TV 220B, with air-con, TV, hot shower & á la carte Thai or European* *breakfast 300B, with fridge 360B)* is in the Lithai Building. Sixty clean, quiet rooms with plenty of light are strung out over three floors, giving more the feel of an apartment complex than a guesthouse. This might be a good choice for a long-term stay and, in fact, the Lithai offers one night free for every 15 you pay for. There's parking at the back.

Hotels Near the train station are several inexpensive hotels and places to eat. **Pisanuloke Hotel** *(☎ 0 5524 7555, 0 5524 7999; Th Ekathotsarot; 1/2-bed rooms with fan 180/280B, air-con rooms 350B)* is a classic in an old, two-storey building conveniently located right next to the station; all rooms have cold-water facilities. There's a *khâo kaeng* (rice-and-curry) vendor downstairs in the lobby, and plenty of places to eat nearby.

Asia Hotel *(☎ 0 5525 8378, fax 0 5523 0419; Th Ekathotsarot; singles/doubles with fan 250B, with air-con 300B)* is a four-storey hotel with quite decent rooms with private hot-water facilities. Street noise can be deafening, so ask for a room towards the back of the hotel. **Samai Niyom Hotel** *(☎ 0 5525 8575, 0 5524 7528; 175 Th Ekathotsarot; singles/doubles 280/380B)*, a three-storey place with rooms with air-con and hot water, stands across the street from Asia Hotel.

Pansombat Hotel *(☎ 0 5525 8179; Th Saireuthai; rooms with private shower & shared toilet 150B)* can be found by turning left out of the station and then taking the first right turn on to Th Saireuthai. It's noisy and has a bit of night traffic, however. **Sukkit Hotel** *(☎ 0 5525 8876; 20/1-2 Th Saireuthai; rooms 150B)* is a better deal for a clean room with fan and private bathroom. Although it's strictly basic and a little dark, it's centrally located a block from the river and is less noisy than hotels towards the station.

If you keep walking towards the river, Th Saireuthai changes name to Soi 1, Th Phuttha Bucha, where you'll find the London, the best cheapie in this area. **London Hotel** *(☎ 0 5522 5145; 21-22 Soi 1, Th Phuttha Bucha; fan rooms 100-150B)* is an old, wooden, Thai-Chinese hotel that has been spruced up and painted in cheery colours; clean rooms have shared cold-water facilities.

Petchpailyn Hotel *(☎ 0 5525 8844; 4/8 Th Athitayawong; fan/air-con room 300/400B)* is a friendly, old-fashioned, four-storey place half a block from the river and main post office. The large, clean rooms have private bathrooms and ceiling fans or air-con; those towards the back are considerably quieter. Some rooms have TVs.

Rajapruk Guest House Hotel *(☎ 0 5525 9203; 99/9 Th Phra Ong Dam; fan/air-con rooms 200/300B)* is behind the more upmarket Rajapruk Hotel. All rooms have hot-water showers and are good value. Guests may use the Rajapruk Hotel swimming pool.

Places to Stay – Mid-Range

Rajapruk Hotel *(☎ 0 5525 8477, fax 0 5525 1395; 99/9 Th Phra Ong Dam; rooms 500-800B)* offers good mid-range value. All rooms come with air-con, hot-water showers, carpeting, TV and telephone; there are also more expensive suites.

Indhra Hotel *(☎ 0 5521 7934; 103/8 Th Sithamatraipidok; air-con rooms 300B, with TV 360B)* is a good, clean, 45-room hotel next to La Paloma Hotel.

Places to Stay – Top End

Thep Nakhorn Hotel *(☎ 0 5524 4070, fax 0 5525 1897; 43/1 Th Sithamatraipidok; rooms 450B, suites 1000B)* is a six-storey hotel that offers quiet air-con rooms and suites. **Pailyn Hotel** *(☎ 0 5524 2424; 38 Th Borom Trailokanat; rooms from 900B)* is centrally located and rates include breakfast. Others in this category – places that were once Phitsanulok's flashiest digs but are now a little worn at the edges yet still quite comfortable – include **Nan Chao Hotel** *(☎ 0 5524 4702-5, fax 0 5524 4794; rooms from 600B)* and **Amarin Nakhon Hotel** *(☎ 0 5521 9069–75, fax 0 5521 9500; 3/1 Th Chao Phraya Phitsanulok; rooms from 800B)*.

Topland Hotel & Convention Centre *(☎ 0 5524 7800, fax 0 5524 7815; cnr Th Singhawat & Th Ekathotsarot; singles/doubles from 1030/1250B)* is connected to Topland Plaza shopping centre. It's a luxurious place with a beauty salon, café, snooker club, fitness centre, several restaurants and other facilities. The room rates are great value compared with Bangkok or Chiang Mai prices for similar quality. Free airport transfer is available.

La Paloma Hotel *(☎ 0 5521 7930, fax 0 5521 7937; 103/8 Th Sithamatraipidok; singles/doubles from 980B)*, a little way south of the Indhra Hotel, is a six-storey, 249-room luxury hotel with a bit of family orientation – the staff will arrange day care for children with advance notice. Rooms come with all the amenities.

Phitsanulok Thani Hotel *(☎ 0 5521 1065, fax 0 5521 1071 • in Bangkok ☎ 0 2314 3168; Th Sanam Bin; rooms regular/discounted rate 1600/980B, suites up to 4000B)* stands next door to the Phitsanulok Youth Hostel and is part of the Dusit chain. Suites include breakfast for two.

Places to Eat

Phitsanulok is a great town for eating – there must be more restaurants per capita here than in just about any other town in Thailand.

Tui Phochana *(Th Phayalithai; dishes 20-45B; open 8am-7pm daily)*, east of the Lithai Building, serves good, inexpensive Thai food. It makes fabulous *yam khànŭn* (curried jackfruit) at the beginning of the cool season, plus many other outstanding Thai curries year-round. There are plenty of other cheap Thai restaurants in this area, too.

Close to the Phitsanulok Youth Hostel are several small noodle and rice shops. South around the corner from the hostel, a permanent vendor stand called **Wong Ocha** *(no Roman-script sign; Th Sanam Bin; dishes 15-30B; open 10am-8pm daily)* sells delicious *kài yâang* (grilled, spiced chicken), *khâo nĭaw* (sticky rice) and *yam phàk kràchèt* (water mimosa salad).

There's a cluster of market-style **food stalls** *(dishes 20B)* just west of the London Hotel near the cinema.

Ban Khun Pho *(no Roman-script sign; Th Chao Phraya; dishes 25-30B; open 11am-11pm daily)* is a clean, new, air-con place decorated with antiques across from the Amarin Nakhon Hotel. The menu includes Thai, Japanese and Western selections.

Near the mosque on Th Phra Ong Dam are several Thai-Muslim cafés. **Fah-Kerah** *(dishes 7-20B; open 7am-7pm daily)* is one very famous one, where thick roti is served with *kaeng mátsàmàn* (Muslim curry). Ask for *rotii kaeng* to get the set plate. This small café also has fresh milk and yogurt.

A small **Thai vegetarian restaurant** *(Th Sithamatraipidok; open 8am-noon)* next to the Indhra Hotel offers very inexpensive vegetable dishes. **Jaroen Tham** *(Th Sithamatraipidok; open 8am-noon)*, around the corner from TAT, is similar.

Steak Cottage *(dishes 40-120B; open 7am-2pm & 5pm-9pm Mon-Sat)*, in the Lithai Building complex, is definitely not for vegetarians. Along with the namesake steak, other European dishes and Thai cuisine are served.

If you're out past midnight, your best bet is the very good **khâo tôm place** *(Th Ekathotsarot; dishes 15-40B; open 24hrs)* next to the train station or the **restaurant** *(dishes 30-80B; open 24hrs)* which is attached to the Amarin Nakhon Hotel, and serves Chinese and northeastern-Thai cuisine.

On the River Floating restaurants light up Mae Nam Nan at night. Some good choices include the **Phae Fa Thai** *(Th Wangchan; dishes 30-80B; open 11am-11pm daily)*, which has a talented chef, and **Phae Tong** *(Th Wangchan; dishes 40-80B; open 11am-11pm daily)*. South of the main string of floating restaurants is a pier where you can board a **restaurant boat** that cruises Mae Nam Nan every night. You pay a small fee – 20B to 40B – to board the boat and then order from a menu as you please – there is no minimum charge.

In the night market along the river, a couple of **street vendors** *(dishes 40-80B; open 5pm-midnight daily)* specialise in preparing *phàk bûng lawy fáa* (literally, floating-in-the-sky morning glory vine), which usually translates as 'flying vegetable'. This food fad originated in Chonburi but has somehow taken root in Phitsanulok. The dish is nothing glorious – basically water spinach stir-fried in soya bean sauce and garlic – but there is a performance thrown in: The cook fires up a batch of *phàk bûng* in the wok and then flings it through the air to a waiting server who catches it on a plate. The eating places on the river are now so performance-oriented that the server climbs to the top of a van to catch the flying vegetable! Tour companies bring tour groups here and invite tourists to try the catch – it's just as amusing watching the tourists drop *phàk bûng* all over the place as it is to watch the cook.

Pa Lai *(dishes 20-30B; Th Phuttha Bucha; open 10am-4pm daily)*, just back from the river and north of Wat Phra Si Ratana Mahathat, is old and established and famous for *kŭaytĭaw hâwy khăa* (literally, legs-hanging rice noodles). The name comes from the way customers sit on a bench facing the river, with their legs dangling below. At least two other copycat places in this area also offer this dish.

Entertainment

Along Th Borom Trailokanat near the Pailyn Hotel is a string of really popular Thai pubs. **Jao Samran** *(Th Borom Trailokanat)* features live Thai-folk and pop. The food service starts around 5pm or 6pm and the music comes on around 8pm.

The Phitsanulok Thani Hotel's semi-outdoor **Tree House** features live bands playing Thai and *faràng* covers.

Getting There & Away

Air The **THAI office** *(☎ 0 5525 8020; 209/26-28 Th Borom Trailokanat)* offers four 55-minute flights to Phitsanulok from Bangkok daily (1380B). **Air Andaman** *(☎ 0 5537 7941; Phitsanulok Airport)* fields flights to/from Chiang Mai for 1500B.

THAI provides a free shuttle van service a few times a day between Phitsanulok airport and Tak.

Bus Transport choices out of Phitsanulok are very good, as it's a junction for bus lines running both north and northeast. Bangkok is six hours away by bus and Chiang Mai 5½ hours. Buses leave Bangkok's Northern and Northeastern bus terminal for Phitsanulok several times daily (ordinary 125B, 2nd class air-con 185B, 1st class air-con 240B). Phitsanulok Yan Yon Tour and Win Tour both run VIP buses between Bangkok and Phitsanulok for 250B.

Buses to destinations in other northern and northeastern provinces leave several times a day from the Baw Khaw Saw (government bus station) just outside town on Hwy 12, except for the air-con buses that may depart only once or twice a day.

Bus Destinations from Phitsanulok

destination	fare (B)	duration (hrs)
Chiang Mai (via Den Chai)		
ordinary	132	5½
air-con	184	5
Chiang Mai (via Tak)		
ordinary	140	6
air-con	196	6
Chiang Rai		
ordinary	153	6
air-con	214, 290 (VIP)	5
Kamphaeng Phet*		
ordinary	43	3
air-con	58	2
Khon Kaen		
ordinary	130	6
air-con	173, 208 (1st)	6
Mae Sot		
air-con minivan	118	5
Nakhon Ratchasima (Khorat)		
ordinary	154	6
air-con	241, 290 (VIP)	6
Nan		
ordinary	112	9
air-con	148	8
Sukhothai**		
ordinary	24	1
air-con	33	1
Tak*		
ordinary	58	3
air-con	74	3
Udon Thani		
ordinary	125	7
air-con	205	7

**Buses to Kamphaeng Phet and Tak leave every hour.*

***Buses to Sukhothai leave every half-hour.*

Train Two ordinary trains (69B, 3rd class only, eight to nine hours) leave Bangkok for Phitsanulok at 7.05am (or Ayuthaya at 9.04am) and 8.35am (Ayuthaya 10.26am). For most people this is a more economical and convenient way to reach Phitsanulok from Bangkok than with the bus, since you don't have to go out to Bangkok's Northern and Northeastern bus station.

Rapid trains from Bangkok depart at 6.40am and 3.15pm, 6.10pm, 8pm and 10pm (about seven hours). The basic fare is 159B for 2nd class or 69B for 3rd class, plus a 40B surcharge for the rapid service. There are also three air-con, 2nd-class express diesel trains ('Sprinter' Nos 3, 5 and 7), at 9.30am and 4pm and 11.10pm daily that are about an hour quicker than the rapid service.

First class is available on the 3pm rapid train (2nd and 3rd class is also available) and 6pm special express train (2nd class is also available). The basic 1st-class and 2nd-class fares are 324B and 159B, not including the rapid and special express surcharges of 40B and 80B, plus any berth arrangements. Basic 3rd/2nd/1st-class train fares from Phitsanulok to Chiang Mai cost 52/122/269B (five hours); to Lopburi 41/95/201B (nine hours); and to Ayuthaya 54/124/258B (10 hours).

If you're going straight on to Sukhothai from Phitsanulok, a túk-túk ride from the train station to the bus station 4km away costs 30B to 40B. From there you can get a bus to Sukhothai, or you can catch a Sukhothai-bound bus in front of the Topland Hotel on Th Singhawat; a túk-túk to Th Singhawat costs 20B from the train station.

Getting Around

Săamláw rides within the town centre should cost 20B to 30B per person. Ordinary city buses cost 4B, and there are 13 routes so you should be able to get just about anywhere by bus. A couple of the lines also feature air-con coaches for 6B. The station for city buses is near the train station, off Th Ekathotsarot.

Motorcycles can be rented at **Landi Motorbike** (*☎ 0 5525 2765; 57/21-22 Th Phra Ong Dam*). Rates are 150B a day for a 100cc and 200B for a 125cc or 150cc.

Phitsanulok's airport is just out of town. Săwngthăew leave the airport for town every 20 minutes (10B); otherwise, you can catch the No 4 city bus (4B). The big hotels in town run free buses from the airport, and THAI has a door-to-door van service for 30B per person.

PHU HIN RONG KLA NATIONAL PARK

อุทยานแห่งชาติภูหินร่องกล้า

From 1967 to 1982, the mountain known as Phu Hin Rong Kla served as the strategic headquarters for the Communist Party of Thailand (CPT) and its tactical arm, the People's Liberation Army of Thailand (PLAT). The remote, easily defended summit was perfect for an insurgent army. Another benefit was that the headquarters was only 50km from the Lao border, so lines of retreat were well guarded after 1975 when Laos fell to the Pathet Lao. China's Yunnan Province is only 300km away and it was here that CPT cadres received their training in revolutionary tactics (this was until the 1979 split between the Chinese and Vietnamese communists, when the CPT sided with Vietnam).

For nearly 20 years the area around Phu Hin Rong Kla served as a battlefield for Thai troops and the communists. In 1972 the Thai government launched a major offensive against the PLAT in an unsuccessful attempt to rout them from the mountain. The CPT camp at Phu Hin Rong Kla became especially active after the Thai military killed hundreds of students in Bangkok during the October 1976 student-worker uprising. Many students subsequently fled here to join the CPT, setting up a hospital and a school of political and military tactics. By 1978 the PLAT ranks here had swelled to 4000. In 1980 and 1981 the Thai armed forces tried again and were able to recapture some parts of CPT territory. But the decisive blow to the CPT came in 1982, when the government declared an amnesty for all the students who had joined the communists after 1976. The departure of most of the students broke the spine of the movement, which had by this time become dependent on their membership. A final military push in late 1982 effected the surrender of the PLAT, and Phu Hin Rong Kla was declared a national park in 1984.

PHU HIN RONG KLA NATIONAL PARK

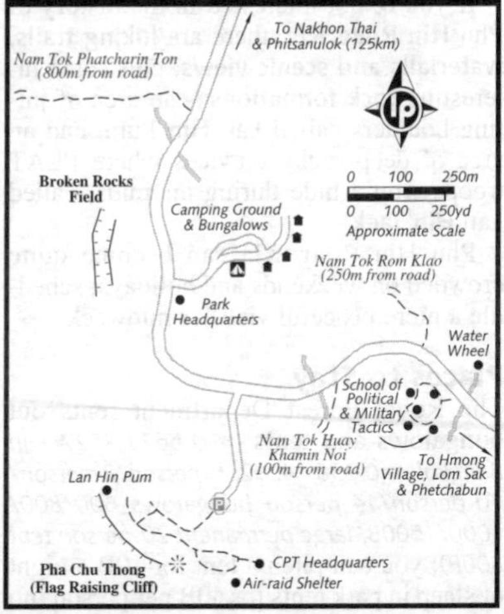

Orientation & Information

The park *(adult/child 200/100B)* covers about 307 sq km of rugged mountains and forest. The elevation at park headquarters is about 1000m, so the park is refreshingly cool even in the hot season. The main attractions on the main road through the park are the remains of the CPT stronghold, including a rustic meeting hall, the school of political and military tactics and the CPT administration building. Across the road from the school is a water wheel designed by exiled engineering students.

Things to See & Do

A trail leads to **Pha Chu Thong** (Flag Raising Cliff, sometimes called Red Flag Cliff), where the communists would raise the red flag to announce a military victory. Also in this area are an **air-raid shelter**, a **lookout** and the remains of the main **CPT headquarters** – the most inaccessible point in the territory before a road was constructed by the Thai government. The buildings in the park are made out of wood and bamboo and have no plumbing or electricity – a testament to how primitive the living conditions were.

At the park headquarters is a small **museum** that displays relics from CPT days, including medical instruments and weapons. At the end of the road into the park is a small White Hmong **village**. When the CPT was here, the Hmong were its ally. Now the Hmong are undergoing 'cultural assimilation' at the hands of the Thai government.

If you're not interested in the history of Phu Hin Rong Kla, there are **hiking trails, waterfalls and scenic views**, plus some interesting **rock formations** – an area of jutting boulders called **Lan Hin Pum**, and an area of deep rocky crevices where PLAT troops would hide during air raids, called **Lan Hin Taek**.

Phu Hin Rong Kla can become quite crowded on weekends and holidays; schedule a more peaceful visit for midweek.

Places to Stay

The Royal Forest Department rents out **bungalows and tents** *(☎ 0 5523 3527 • in Bangkok ☎ 0 2561 4292; 5-person/8-person/10-person/14-person bungalows 600/800/1000/1500B, large permanent 20-person tent 800B)*; you can pitch a tent for 10B a night or sleep in park tents for 40B per person (no bedding is provided, except blankets for 20B a night). If you want to build a fire, you can buy chopped wood for 150B a night. Book accommodation through the Royal Forest Department or **Golden House Tour Company** *(☎ 0 5525 9973, 0 5538 9002)* in Phitsanulok.

Places to Eat

Near the camping ground and bungalows are some vendors. The best are **Duang Jai Cafeteria** – try its famous carrot *sôm tam* – and **Rang Thong**.

Getting There & Away

The park headquarters is about 125km from Phitsanulok. To get here, first take an early bus to Nakhon Thai (30B, two hours, hourly from 6am to 6pm). From there you can catch a sǎwngthǎew to the park (25B, three times daily from 7.30am to 4.30pm).

A small group can charter a pick-up and driver in Nakhon Thai for about 600B to 800B for the day. Golden House Tour Co operates a van service from Phitsanulok once a day for 40B per person or 650B to charter the van one way. This is a delightful trip if you're on a motorbike as there's not much traffic along the way. A strong engine is necessary to make it up the hills to Phu Hin Rong Kla.

PHITSANULOK TO LOM SAK

Hwy 12 between Phitsanulok and Lom Sak (the scenic 'gateway' to northeastern Thailand) parallels the scenic and rapids-studded Lam Nam Khek. Along the way are several resorts and **waterfalls**. As in Phu Hin Rong Kla, the sites here tend to be more popular on weekends and holidays.

Any of the resorts along Hwy 12 can arrange **whitewater rafting trips** on the Lam Nam Khek along the section with the most rapids, which corresponds more or less with the length of Hwy 12 between Km 45 and 52.

The Phitsanulok **TAT office** distributes a sketch map of attractions along this 130km stretch of road that marks the resorts and three waterfalls. You may want to bypass the first two waterfalls, **Nam Tok Sakhunothayan** (at the Km 33 marker) and **Kaeng Song** (at the Km 45 marker), which are on the way to Phu Hin Rong Kla and hence get overwhelmed with visitors. The third, **Kaeng Sopha** at the Km 72 marker, is a larger area of small falls and rapids where you can walk from rock formation to rock formation – there are more or fewer rocks depending on the rains. **Food vendors** provide inexpensive *sôm-tam* and *kài yâang*.

Farther east along the road is the 1262-sq-km **Thung Salaeng Luang Wildlife Sanctuary** (entrance at the Km 80 marker), one of Thailand's largest and most important protected areas. Thung Salaeng Luang encompasses vast meadows and dipterocarp forests, and once was home to the PLAT. Among bird-watchers it's known as a habitat for the colourful Siamese fireback pheasant.

If you have your own wheels, you can turn south at the Km 100 marker onto Rte 2196 and head for **Khao Kho** (Khao Khaw), another mountain lair used by the CPT during the 1970s. About 1.5km from the summit of Khao Kho, you must turn onto the very steep Rte 2323. At the summit, 30km from the highway, stands a tall obelisk erected in memory of the Thai soldiers killed during the suppression of the communist insurgency. The **monument** is surrounded by an attractive garden. Gun emplacements and sandbagged lookout posts perched on the summit have been left intact as historical reminders. On a clear day, the 360-degree view from the summit is wonderful.

If you've made the side trip to Khao Kho you can choose either to return to the Phitsanulok–Lom Sak highway, or take Rte 2258, off Rte 2196, until it terminates at Rte 203. On Rte 203 you can continue north to Lom Sak or south to Phetchabun. On Rte 2258, about 4km from Rte 2196, you'll pass **Khao Kho Palace**. One of the smaller royal palaces in Thailand, it's a fairly uninteresting, modern set of structures but has quite a nice rose garden. If you've come all the way to Khao Kho you may as well take a look.

Places to Stay & Eat

There are several resorts just off Hwy 12 west of the Rte 2013 junction for Nakhon Thai. **Rainforest Resort** *(☎ 0 5529 3085, fax 0 5529 3086; Ⓔ rnforest@loxinfo.co.th; at the Km 44 marker; cottages 1000-1800B, cottage for 7 people 2400B)* is the best of the lot. Spacious, tastefully designed cottages spread over a hillside facing Mae Nam Khek accommodate up to four people, and there is also one cottage for up to seven people. All cottages come with air-con and hot water. An indoor-outdoor restaurant serves locally grown coffee and good Thai food. Other resorts in the area, **Wang Nam Yen** *(Hwy 12)* and **Thanthong** *(Hwy 12)*, are similarly priced. **SP Huts** *(☎ 0 5529 3402, fax 0 5529 3405; rooms from 500B)* is a bit cheaper.

Getting There & Away

Buses between Phitsanulok and Lom Sak cost 55B each way, so any stop along the way will cost less. During daylight hours it's easy to flag down another bus to continue your journey, but after 4pm it gets a little chancy.

Sukhothai Province

SUKHOTHAI

อ.เมืองสุโขทัย

postcode 64000 • pop 25,800

As Thailand's first capital, Sukhothai (Rising of Happiness) flourished from the mid-13th century to the late 14th century. The Sukhothai kingdom is viewed as the 'golden age' of Thai civilisation – the religious art and architecture of the era are considered to be the most classic of Thai styles.

The new town of Sukhothai is almost 450km from Bangkok and is undistinguished except for its good **municipal market** in the town centre. The *meuang kào* (old city) of Sukhothai features around 45 sq km of ruins (which have been made into a historical park) making an overnight stay in New Sukhothai worthwhile, although you can make a day trip to the old city ruins from Phitsanulok.

Information

The **tourist police** maintain an office in the Sukhothai Historical Park directly across from the Ramkhamhaeng National Museum.

A **TAT office** *(Th Prawet Nakhon; open 9am-5pm Mon-Fri)* can be found a bit north of the River View Hotel in New Sukhothai.

Siam Commercial Bank, on the southwestern corner of Th Singhawat and Th Tri Chat, has an ATM, as do several other banks in the vicinity.

The **post office** *(Th Nikhon Kasem; open 8.30am-noon Mon-Fri, 1pm-4.30pm Sat & Sun, 9am-noon holidays)* has an attached

CAT office *(open 7am-10pm daily)*, which offers international phone services.

There are several Internet centres in the vicinity of the Chinnawat Hotel.

Sukhothai Historical Park

อุทยานประวัติศาสตร์สุโขทัย

The original capital of the first Thai kingdom was surrounded by three concentric ramparts and two moats bridged by four gateways. Today the remains of 21 historical sites and four large ponds can be seen within the old walls, with an additional 70 sites within a 5km radius. The Sukhothai ruins are one of Thailand's World Heritage sites.

The ruins are divided into five zones – central, north, south, east and west – each of which has a 30B admission fee, except for the central section, which costs 40B. For a reasonable 150B you can buy a single ticket (from the kiosk at the entrance to the park) that allows entry to all the Sukhothai sites, plus Sawanwaranayok National Museum, Ramkhamhaeng National Museum and the Si Satchanalai and Chaliang ruins in nearby Sawankhalok. The ticket is good for repeated visits over 30 days. There are additional charges for bicycles/motorcycles (10/20B), săamláw/túk-túk (30B) and cars or vans (50B). Official hours are from 6am to 6pm.

Sukhothai temple architecture is most typified by the classic lotus-bud stupa, featuring a conical spire topping a square-sided structure on a three-tiered base. Some sites also exhibit other rich architectural forms introduced and modified during the period – bell-shaped Singhalese and double-tiered Srivijaya stupas.

See Getting Around in the Sukhothai section in this chapter for details on the best way to tour the park.

Ramkhamhaeng National Museum

The museum *(admission 30B; open 9am-4pm)* provides a good starting point for an exploration of the ruins. A replica of the famous Ramkhamhaeng inscription (see Wiang Kum Kam in the Chiang Mai Province chapter) is kept here among a good collection of Sukhothai artefacts.

Wat Mahathat Circa 13th-century and the largest wát in the city, Wat Mahathat is

SUKHOTHAI HISTORICAL PARK

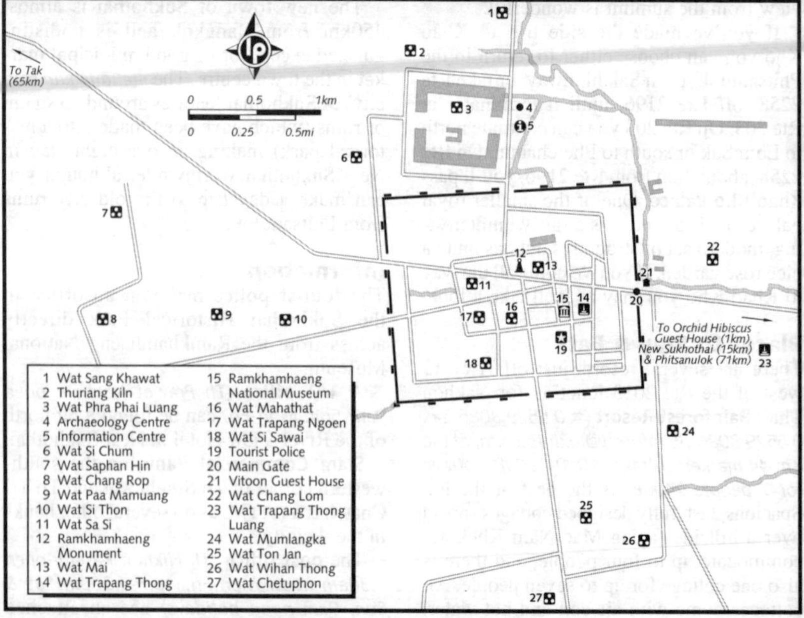

surrounded by brick walls (206m long and 200m wide) and a moat, said to represent the outer wall of the universe and the cosmic ocean. The stupa spires feature the famous lotus-bud motif, and some of the original stately Buddha figures still sit among the ruined columns of the old *wíhǎan*. There are 198 *chedi* within the monastery walls – a lot to explore in what many consider was the spiritual and administrative centre of the old capital.

Wat Si Sawai Just south of Wat Mahathat, this shrine (dating from the 12th and 13th centuries) features three Khmer-style towers and a picturesque moat. It was originally built by the Khmers as a Hindu temple.

Wat Sa Si Also known as 'Sacred Pond Monastery', Wat Sa Si sits on an island west of the bronze monument of King Ramkhamhaeng (the third Sukhothai king). It's a simple, classic Sukhothai-style wát with one large Buddha, one *chedi* and the columns of the ruined *wíhǎan*.

Wat Trapang Thong Next to the museum, this small, still-inhabited wát with its fine stucco reliefs is reached by a footbridge across the large lotus-filled pond that surrounds it. This reservoir, the original site of Thailand's **Loi Krathong Festival**, supplies the Sukhothai community with most of its water.

Wat Phra Phai Luang Outside the city walls in the northern zone, this somewhat isolated wát features three 12th-century Khmer-style towers, bigger than those at Wat Si Sawai. This may have been the centre of Sukhothai when it was ruled by the Khmers of Angkor prior to the 13th century.

Wat Si Chum This wát is northwest of the old city and contains an impressive, much-photographed *mondòp* with a 15m, brick-and-stucco seated Buddha. Archaeologists theorise that this image is the 'Phra Atchana' mentioned in the famous Ramkhamhaeng inscription. A passage in the *mondòp* wall that leads to the top has been blocked so that it's no longer possible to view the Jataka (stories of the Buddha's past lives) inscriptions that line the tunnel ceiling.

Wat Chang Lom Off Highway 12 in the east zone, Wat Chang Lom (Elephant Circled Monastery) is about a kilometre east of the main park entrance. A large bell-shaped *chedi* is supported by 36 elephants sculpted into its base.

Wat Saphan Hin A couple of kilometres to the west of the old city walls in the west zone, Wat Saphan Hin is on the crest of a hill that rises about 200m above the plain. The name of the wát, which means 'stone bridge', is a reference to the slate path and staircase leading to the temple, which are still in place. The site affords a good view of the Sukhothai ruins to the southeast and the mountains to the north and south.

All that remains of the original temple are a few *chedi* and the ruined *wíhǎan*, consisting of two rows of laterite columns flanking a 12.5m-high standing Buddha image on a brick terrace.

Wat Chang Rop On another hill west of the city, just south of Wat Saphan Hin, this wát features an elephant-base stupa, similar to that at Wat Chang Lom.

Swimming

Suan Nam Premsuk *(admission 40B; open 7am-9pm daily)*, at the Km 4 marker on Route 101, is a modest sports complex with a clean swimming pool, tennis courts and ping pong table. The admission allows you to use all facilities. Look for a couple of tall brick pillars supporting a blue-and-white sign.

Places to Stay

Guesthouses Most of the guesthouses in New Sukhothai offer reasonably priced accommodation in family homes (dorms and/or private rooms) and all rent out bicycles and motorcycles. Places continue to multiply and competition keeps the prices low. The local taxi mafia has its hooks in the guesthouse proprietors, so expect lots of opinions about where you want to go from the sǎamláw drivers.

Lotus Village *(☎ 0 5562 1484, fax 0 5562 1463; ⓔ lotusvil@yahoo.com; 170 Th Ratchathani; rooms without bath per person 120B, house without bath 400B, singles/doubles with hot-water shower 400B, deluxe rooms with fan/air-con 500/800B)*, on the east bank of Mae Nam Yom, is set in spacious grounds with a garden sitting area and is quite suitable for long-term stays. The attractive lobby/restaurant area with stacks of magazines and books is a pleasant place to hang out if you don't mind mosquitoes.

Somprasong Guest House (*☎ 0 5561 1709; 32 Th Prawet Nakhon; rooms with fan & shared bath 120B, with air-con & bath 300B*) is on the west bank of the river near the town centre. The rooms are arranged hotel-like on the 2nd floor of a large family house.

Ban Thai (*☎ 0 5561 0163; ⓔ guesthouse_banthai@yahoo.com; Th Prawet Nakhon; rooms without bath 120B, bungalows with bath 200B*) is newer than the next door Somprasong. It's run by yet another friendly family and has recently refurbished rooms; new bungalows were under construction when we stopped by. Ban Thai is a good place for reliable information on things to see and do in the Sukhothai area.

Garden House (*☎ 0 5561 1395; ⓔ toonosman@yahoo.com; 11/1 Th Prawet Nakhon; rooms 200B*) is a new guesthouse near Ban Thai featuring clean rooms in a two-storey house plus bungalows in the back. There's a **restaurant** downstairs.

TR Guest House (*☎ 0 5561 1663; ⓔ tr_guesthouse@thaimail.com; 27/5 Th Prawet Nakhon; fan rooms 150-200B, air-con 300B*) is another new place with good, clean rooms. The staff offer laundry service and motorcycle rental.

No 4 Guest House (*☎ 0 5561 0165; 140/4 Soi Khlong Mae Ramphan, Th Jarot Withithong; bungalows standard/larger 150/180B*),

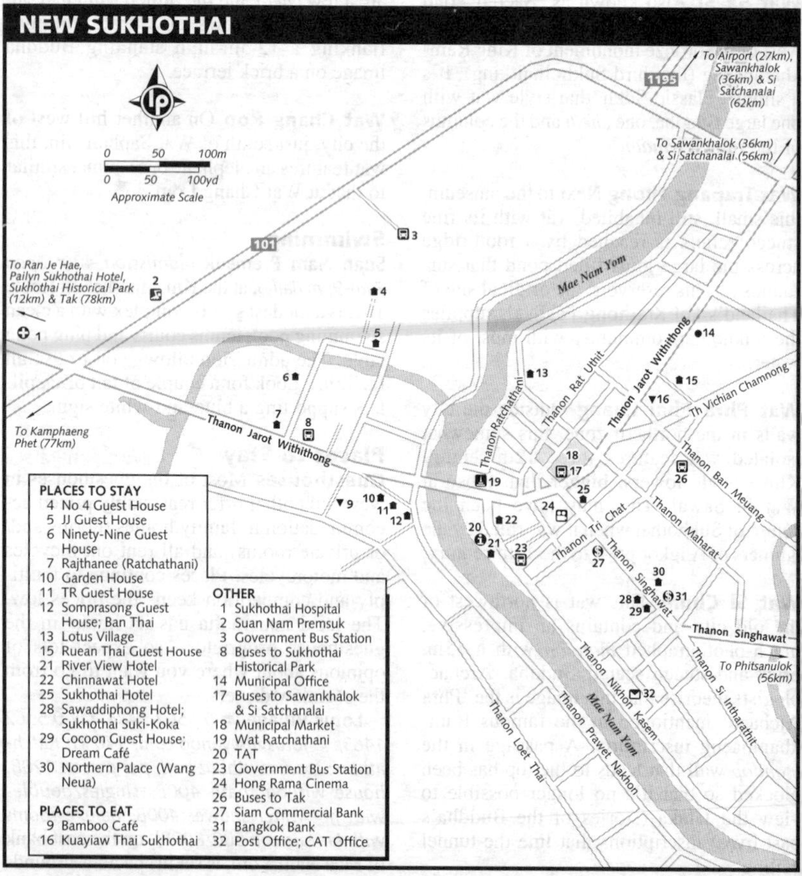

the first guesthouse in Sukhothai, has moved a couple of times and is now in its third location. Rustic, bamboo-thatch bungalows have private, open-air, cold-water bathrooms, fan and nicely furnished outdoor lounging areas; slightly larger ones cost a little more. There are several sitting areas on the property.

JJ Guest House *(Soi Khlong Mae Ramphan; rooms 150B)*, to the south and next door to No 4 Guest House, is a wood-and-cement house; it has basic rooms with shared hot-water bathroom.

Ninety-Nine Guest House *(☎ 0 5561 1315, 0 1972 9308; 234/6 Soi Panitsan; dorm beds 80B, singles/doubles 120/150B)* is a friendly place about 150m southwest on the opposite side of the canal. It offers rooms in a clean, two-storey teak house surrounded by gardens. Dorm beds are in a three-bed room, while singles and doubles have shared cold-water facilities upstairs, hot water downstairs.

Cocoon Guest House *(☎ 0 5561 2081, fax 0 5562 2157; 86/1 Th Singhawat; singles/doubles with cold water 250/350B, doubles with hot water 450B)* offers a few charming guest rooms in a wooden building behind Dream Cafe; all rooms have fan and attached shower. The owner has used recycled architectural features from old Thai houses throughout and the rooms are nicely decorated with local crafts and antiques.

Ruean Thai Guest House *(☎ 0 5561 2444; 181/20 Soi Pracha Ruammit, Th Jarot Withithong; rooms with fan 250B, with air-con up to 600B)* is a relatively new place on a lane between Th Jarot Withithong and Th Vichian Chamnong. It's in a nice residential neighbourhood and done in a traditional Thai style but with modern facilities. The house contains large and well-spaced guest rooms with lots of inviting sitting areas in between. All have modern, private hot-water facilities. The guesthouse rents out bicycles.

Vitoon Guest House *(rooms with fan/air-con 250/500B)*, in the old city close to the main entrance of the Sukhothai Historical Park, offers fan rooms with attached cold-water bathroom, and large, comfortable air-con rooms with TV and hot water. Vitoon also rents out bicycles.

Orchid Hibiscus Guest House *(☎/fax 0 5563 3284; ⓔ orchid_hibiscus_guest_house@hotmail.com; rooms 700B including breakfast)*, just 1km from the entrance to the Sukhothai Historical Park, has eight charming rooms with four-poster beds, air-con and private bath. Some of the rooms are furnished with antique reproductions. The guesthouse also features a garden and swimming pool. The guesthouse is on Route 1272 about 600m off Hwy 12 – the turnoff is between the Km 48 and Km 49 markers.

Hotels Once a travellers' favourite, **Sukhothai Hotel** *(☎ 0 5561 1133; 15/5 Th Singhawat; rooms with fan 170, with air-con 280B, add 100B for rooms with 2 big beds)* is now very much an also-ran. All rooms have cold-water bathroom. **Chinnawat Hotel** *(☎ 0 5561 1385; 1-3 Th Nikhon Kasem; rooms with fan 150-200B, with air-con 350B)* is also in need of renovation. Rooms with fan vary in price depending on whether they are in the old or new wing – the old wing is cheaper and a bit quieter. All rooms have bathrooms. Be sure to check that the air-con works before booking in.

River View Hotel *(☎ 0 5561 1656, fax 0 5561 3373; 38 Th Nikhon Kasem; rooms with 1/2 beds 350/420B, rooms with TV 500B, with TV & fridge 800B)*, which is near Mae Nam Yom, remains a favourite among small traders. River View's all air-con rooms are clean and there are slightly nicer rooms with TV. There is a large sing-song coffee shop downstairs.

Rajthanee *(Ratchathani; ☎ 0 5561 1031, fax 0 5561 2583; 229 Th Jarot Withithong; rooms with air-con & hot water 300B, with TV & fridge 600B)*, once the top hotel in town, has seen better days. **Northern Palace** *(Wang Neua; ☎ 0 5561 3522, fax 0 5561 2038; 43 Th Singhawat; rooms 450B)* has OK rooms with air-con, small TV and fridge. The hotel has a coffee shop.

Sawaddiphong Hotel *(☎ 0 5561 1567; 56/2-5 Th Singhawat)* was closed for renovations when we last visited, but should soon re-open with rooms in the 250B to 350B range.

Pailyn Sukhothai Hotel *(☎ 0 5563 3336, fax 0 5561 3317 • in Bangkok ☎ 0 2215 7110, fax 0 2215 5640; rooms from 1200B)* is about 8km from the city centre on the road between the old and new cities of Sukhothai. This huge hotel caters mostly to tour groups and has a disco, health centre and several restaurants.

Places to Eat

Dream Café *(☎ 0 5561 2081; Th Singhawat; dishes 40-100B; open 11am-10pm daily)*, opposite Bangkok Bank, is an air-con café decorated with 19th-century Thai antiques. Despite catering primarily to tourists, the café serves good food and the staff is attentive.

Sukhothai Suki-Koka *(Th Singhawat; dishes 30-90B; open 11am-11pm daily)*, in front of the Sawaddiphong Hotel, specialises in Thai-style sukiyaki.

Ran Je Hae *(Th Jarot Withithong; dishes 25-30B; open 10am-9pm daily)*, about 350m west of Rte 101, specialises in Sukhothai-style *kŭaytĭaw* – pork, coriander, green onions, pickled cabbage, pork skins, peanuts, chilli and green beans are added to the basic *kŭaytĭaw* recipe.

Kuaytiaw Thai Sukhothai *(Th Jarot Withithong; dishes 20-30B; open 9am-8pm daily)*, about 20m south of the turn-off for Ruean Thai Guest House, is another good spot to try Sukhothai-style *kŭaytĭaw*. The restaurant is in a nice wooden building with a fountain fashioned from ceramic pots out front.

Bamboo Cafe *(☎ 0 5561 2578; 62/15-16 Th Jarot Withithong; dishes 35-75B; open 9.30am-7pm Tues-Sun)* is located in a shophouse and mainly features Japanese food as well as a variety of tea and ice cream. It's a favourite hang out of Japanese backpackers and is a good source for travel information.

Getting There & Away

Air The so-called 'Sukhothai' airport is 27km outside of town off Route 1195 about 11km from Sawankhalok. It's privately owned by Bangkok Airways, and, like its Ko Samui counterpart, is a beautifully designed small airport that uses tropical architecture to best advantage. **Bangkok Airways** *(☎ 0 5563 3266–7, fax 0 5561 0908 • at the airport ☎ 0 5561 2448)* operates a daily flight from Bangkok (1820B, one hour and 10 minutes). In the reverse direction, the flight costs 1890B (because of an extra tax charged at this airport). Bangkok Airways charges 90B to transport passengers between the airport and Sukhothai.

Bangkok Airways flies daily from Chiang Mai to Sukhothai (750B), or from Sukhothai to Chiang Mai (830B); prices include tax. Fares for children are half the adult price. Bangkok Airways also flies daily to Luang Prabang.

Bus Sukhothai can be reached by road from Phitsanulok, Tak or Kamphaeng Phet. The bus to Sukhothai (24B ordinary, 33B air-con, one hour) leaves regularly throughout the day.

From Tak, get a Sukhothai bus at the Baw Khaw Saw station just outside town (31B ordinary, 43B air-con, 1½ hours); at last count there were 10 departures daily. Buses from Kamphaeng Phet cost 46B (one to 1½ hours).

Baw Khaw Saw buses to/from Chiang Mai via Tak (the shortest, fastest route) cost 122B ordinary, 171B air-con (4½ to five hours). Buses depart for Chiang Mai more or less hourly from 7pm to 2am. Buses to Chiang Rai cost 136B or 190B air-con (six hours); there are two departures a day of both air-con and ordinary buses.

All the private tour bus companies now use the new bus terminal located about 1km from Hwy 12. There are several departures to Phitsanulok, Tak, Khon Kaen and Chiang Mai throughout the day. Departures to Bangkok are roughly hourly from 7am to 2am. To Bangkok, an ordinary bus is 142B, 2nd class air-con 199B and 1st class air-con 256B (five to 5½ hours).

Buses to Sawankhalok (16B, 45 minutes) and Si Satchanalai (ordinary 27B, air-con 38B, one hour) leave hourly between about 6am and 6pm. Other destinations include Khon Kaen (ordinary 131B, air-con 183B, five hours), Phrae (air-con 92B, four times daily, three hours), Lamphang (ordinary 91B, air-con 127B, four hours), Nan (ordinary 104B, air-con 146B, six hours) and Si Satchanalai (ordinary 27B, air-con 38B, one hour). There's also a 12-seat van to Mae Sot for 100B (2½ hours).

Getting Around

Around New Sukhothai, a săamláw ride should not cost more than 20B to 30B. Săwngthăew run frequently from 6.30am to 6pm between New Sukhothai and Sukhothai Historical Park, leaving from Th Jarot Withithong near Mae Nam Yom; the fare is 10B (check with locals first to see if there's been a price increase) and it takes 20 to 30 minutes from the river to the park.

The best way to get around the historical park is by bicycle; these can be rented at shops outside the park entrance for 20B a day, or you can borrow or rent one at any guesthouse in New Sukhothai. Don't rent the first bikes you see at the bus stop in the old city as the better bikes tend to be found at shops around the corner, closer to the park entrance.

The park operates a tram service through the old city for 20B per person.

Transportation from the new private bus terminal into town in a chartered vehicle costs 30B, or 4B per person in a shared săwngthăew. Unfortunately, drivers often ask for 60B for a charter or even try to ask for 40B for a shared ride after you've arrived at your destination. In the latter case, just give them the 4B and walk away.

If you arrive in Phitsanulok by rail or air, take a city bus No 1 to the air-con bus station in the centre, or to the Baw Khaw Saw (government bus) station, for buses out of town.

AROUND SUKHOTHAI

Si Satchanalai–Chaliang Historical Park

อุทยานประวัติศาสตร์ศรีสัชชนาลัย/ชะเลียง

The 13th- to 15th-century ruins in the old cities of Si Satchanalai and Chaliang, about 50km north of Sukhothai, are in the same basic style as those in the Sukhothai Historical Park. The park *(open 8am to 6pm; admission 40B, plus 50B per car, 10B per bicycle, 30B per motorcycle, 40B per săamláw)* covers roughly 720 hectares and is surrounded by a 12m-wide moat. Chaliang, a kilometre to the southeast, is an older city site (dating to the 11th century), though its two temples date to the 14th century. This historical park has also been classified as a World Heritage site.

The ruins at Si Satchanalai are set among hills and are very attractive in the sense that they're not as heavily visited as the Sukhothai ruins. Some people actually prefer the more unrestored atmosphere at Si Satchanalai over Sukhothai. Those listed below represent only the more distinctive of the numerous Si Satchanalai ruins.

An **information centre** *(open 8.30am-5pm daily)* distributes free maps of the park and a small exhibit outlining the history and major attractions. There are bicycles for rent near the entrance to the park for 20B.

The nearby town of Sawankhalok is the main supply centre for the area.

Wat Chang Lom This fine temple, marking the centre of the old city of Si Satchanalai, has elephants surrounding a bell-shaped stupa but is somewhat better preserved than its counterpart in Sukhothai. An inscription says the temple was built by King Ramkhamhaeng between 1285 and 1291.

SI SATCHANALAI-CHALIANG HISTORICAL PARK

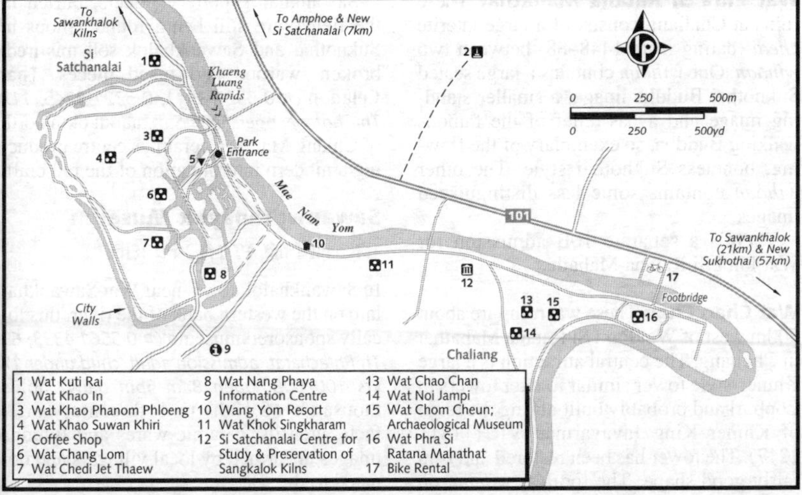

Wat Khao Phanom Phloeng On the hill overlooking Wat Chang Lom to the right are the remains of Wat Khao Phanom Phloeng, including a large seated Buddha, a *chedi* and stone columns that once supported the roof of the *wíhăan*. From this hill you can make out the general design of the once great city. The slightly higher hill west of Phanom Phloeng is capped by a large Sukhothai-style *chedi* – all that remains of Wat Khao Suwan Khiri.

Wat Chedi Jet Thaew Next to Wat Chang Lom, these ruins contain seven rows of *chedi*, the largest of which is a copy of one at Wat Mahathat in Sukhothai. An interesting brick-and-plaster *wíhăan* features barred windows designed to look like lathed wood (an ancient Indian technique used all over Southeast Asia). A *prasat* and *chedi* are stacked on the roof.

Wat Nang Phaya South of Wat Chang Lom and Wat Chedi Jet Thaew, this stupa is Singhalese in style and was built in the 15th or 16th century, a bit later than other monuments at Si Satchanalai. Stucco reliefs on the large laterite *wíhăan* in front of the stupa – now sheltered by a tin roof – date to the Ayuthaya period when Si Satchanalai was known as Sawankhalok. Goldsmiths in the district still craft a design known as *naang pháyaa*, modelled after these reliefs.

Wat Phra Si Ratana Mahathat These ruins at Chaliang consist of a large laterite *chedi* (dating from 1448–88) between two *wíhăan*. One *wíhăan* contains a large seated Sukhothai Buddha image, a smaller standing image and a bas-relief of the famous walking Buddha, so exemplary of the flowing, boneless Sukhothai style. The other *wihăan* contains some less distinguished images.

There's a separate 10B admission for Wat Phra Si Ratana Mahathat.

Wat Chao Chan These wát ruins are about 500m west of Wat Phra Si Ratana Mahathat in Chaliang. The central attraction is a large Khmer-style tower similar to later towers in Lopburi and probably built during the reign of Khmer King Jayavarman VII (1181–1217). The tower has been restored and is in fairly good shape. The roofless *wíhăan* on the right contains the laterite outlines of a large standing Buddha that has all but melted away from weathering.

Sawankhalok Kilns

เตาเผาสังคโลก

The Sukhothai–Si Satchanalai area was once famous for its beautiful pottery, much of which was exported to countries throughout Asia. In China – the biggest importer of Thai pottery during the Sukhothai and Ayuthaya periods – the pieces came to be called 'Sangkalok', a mispronunciation of Sawankhalok. Particularly fine specimens of this pottery can be seen in the national museums of Jakarta and Pontianak in Indonesia.

At one time, more than 200 huge pottery kilns lined the banks of Mae Nam Yom in the area around Si Satchanalai. Several have been carefully excavated and can be viewed at the **Si Satchanalai Centre for Study & Preservation of Sangkalok Kilns**, which opened in 1987. So far the centre has opened two phases of its construction to the public: a kiln centre in Chaliang with excavated pottery samples and one kiln; and a larger outdoor Sawankhalok Kilns site 2km northwest of the Si Satchanalai ruins. The exhibits are very well presented, although there are no English labels. More phases are planned, including one featuring a working kiln.

Sawankhalok pottery rejects, buried in the fields, are still being found. Shops in Sukhothai and Sawankhalok sell misfired, broken, warped and fused pieces. **Thai Celadon** *(☎ 0 5321 3541, 0 5321 3245; 112 Th Chotana; open Mon-Sat)*, about 6km north of Chiang Mai, is a ceramics centre producing a modern interpretation of the old craft.

Sawanworanayok Museum

พิพิธภัณฑ์สวรรค์วรนายก

In Sawankhalok town, near Wat Sawankhalam on the western bank of the river, this locally sponsored museum *(☎ 0 5561 4333; 69 Th Phracharat; admission adult/child under 17 yrs 100/50B; open 8am-5pm daily)* holds thousands of 12th- to 15th-century artefacts, utensils, ceramic wares and Buddha images unearthed by local villagers and donated to the wát.

Ban Hat Siaw
บ้านหาดเสี่ยว

This colourful village southeast of Si Satchanalai is home to the Thai Phuan (also known as Lao Phuan), a Tai tribal group that immigrated from Xieng Khuang Province in Laos about 100 years ago when the Annamese and Chinese were in northeastern Laos.

The local Thai Phuan are famous for **hand-woven textiles**, particularly *phâa sîn tiin jòk* (brocade-bordered skirts), which have patterns of horizontal stripes bordered by thickly patterned brocade. Men's *phâa khăo-mă̌a* (short sarong) from Hat Siaw, typically in dark plaids, are also highly regarded.

Practically every stilt house in the village has a loom beneath it; cloth can be purchased at the source or from shops in Sawankhalok. Vintage Hat Siaw textiles, 80 to 200 years old, can be seen at the Village Old Clothes Museum in central Si Satchanalai.

Another Thai Phuan custom is the use of **elephant-back** processions in local monastic ordinations; these usually take place in early April.

Places to Stay & Eat

Wang Yom Resort *(Sunanthana; ☎ 0 5563 1380; bungalows with fan/air-con 1200/1500B)*, just outside the Si Satchanalai Historical Park 400m before the southeastern corner of the old city, has bungalows and a 'handicraft village' set amid beautifully landscaped grounds along Mae Nam Yom. Spacious bungalows are overpriced and bargaining is in order. Wang Yom's large **restaurant** is reportedly very good. Food and drink are also available at a **coffee shop** in the historical park until 6pm.

Sawankhalok This charming town on Mae Nam Yom, about 11km south of the historical park, has a couple of options for visitors wishing to explore the area. **Saengsin Hotel** *(☎ 0 5564 1818, fax 0 5564 1828; 2 Th Thetsaban Damri 3; singles/doubles with fan 150/210B, with air-con 280/320B)* is centrally located on the main street that runs through Sawankhalok. It has clean and comfortable rooms and a **coffee shop**.

This isn't a big town for eating; most food places sell noodles and *khâo man kài* (Hainanese chicken rice) and not much else. There is a **night market** in Sawankhalok, which is held along the main streets.

Ko Heng *(☎ 0 5564 1616; 144/1 Th Na Meuang; dishes 40-90B; open 10am-3pm daily)* is an old riverside Chinese restaurant that's well past its prime and is now primarily a place for old Chinese cronies to sit and drink tea. The Hakka-style *kài òp* (baked chicken), however, is still excellent and sells out fast.

Kung Nam *(dishes 40-70B; 10am-11pm daily)*, a Thai and Chinese garden restaurant on the outskirts of Sawankhalok towards Sukhothai, is probably the best spot to eat.

Getting There & Away

Bus Si Satchanalai–Chaliang Historical Park is off Rte 101 between Sawankhalok and new Si Satchanalai. From New Sukhothai, take a Si Satchanalai bus (ordinary 27B, air-con 38B, one hour) and ask to get off at 'meuang kào' (old city).

There are two places along the left side of the highway where you can get off the bus and reach the ruins in the park; both involve crossing Mae Nam Yom. The first leads to a footbridge over Mae Nam Yom to Wat Phra Si Ratana Mahathat at Chaliang; the second crossing is about 2km farther northwest just past two hills and leads directly into the Si Satchanalai ruins.

Train King Rama VI had a 60km railway spur built from Ban Dara (a small town on the main northern trunk) to Sawankhalok just so that he could visit the ruins. The **original train station** in Sawankhalok is one of the main local sights. A vendor in the station sells real filtered coffee.

Amazingly, there is a daily special express from Bangkok to Sawankhalok, No 7, which leaves the capital at 11.10pm and arrives in Sawankhalok at 6.10am. Don't look for this train on your English train schedule as it's only listed on the Thai timetable. It's a 'Sprinter', which means 2nd class air-con, no sleepers, and the fare is 372B (this includes dinner and breakfast). You can also pick up this train in Phitsanulok at 5.30am; expect to pay about 33B for this shorter distance. In the reverse direction, No 4 leaves Sawankhalok at 7am.

There's also one local train daily, No 405, originating from Taphan Hin (which is 73km north of Nakhon Sawan). The train departs Phitsanulok at noon and arrives in

Sawankhalok at 2.45pm (21B 3rd class). The No 406 leaves Sawankhalok at 2.30pm and arrives at Sila at 4.45pm.

Getting Around

Bicycle is the best way to see the ruins. You can **rent bikes** from outside a barber shop at the gateway to Wat Phra Si Ratana Mahathat; rates are 20B a day.

Kamphaeng Phet Province

KAMPHAENG PHET

อ.เมืองกำแพงเพชร

postcode 62000 • pop 25,500

Formerly known as Chakangrao or Nakhon Chum, Kamphaeng Phet (Diamond Wall) was once an important front line of defence for the Sukhothai kingdom but is now mostly known for producing the tastiest *klûay khài* ('egg banana', a delicious kind of small banana) in Thailand. It's a nice place to spend a day or two wandering around the ruins and experiencing a small northern provincial capital that receives few tourists.

Information

A privately sponsored **tourist information centre** *(Th Thesa)*, the sign reads 'Chamber of Commerce', is a block south of the now defunct but still standing Chakungrao hotel and can answer general queries about accommodation and restaurants. It also has a good map of the town.

Kasikornbank and **Siam Commercial Bank** have branches with ATMs on Th Charoensuk, the road coming into town from Phitsanulok. Most of the major banks also have branches with ATMs along the main streets along the river.

The **main post office** *(Th Thesa)* is just south of the old city. There's an **MBE** (Mail Boxes Etc) opposite the Phet Hotel.

Old City

เมืองเก่า

The **Kamphaeng Phet Historical Park** *(admission 40B, plus 10B per bicycle, 20B per motorcycle, 30B per túk-túk, 50B per car; open 6am-6pm daily)* encloses the old city site and is cared for by the Fine Arts Department. The park was declared a Unesco World Heritage site in 1991. Here you'll find **Wat Phra Kaew**, which used to be adjacent to the royal palace (now in ruins). The weather-corroded Buddha statues have assumed slender, porous forms that remind many visitors of Alberto Giacometti (a Swiss sculptor and painter) sculptures. About 100m southeast of Wat Phra Kaew is **Wat Phra That**, distinguished by a large round-based *chedi* surrounded by columns. This park is a popular spot for joggers and walkers.

Kamphaeng Phet National Museum

พิพิธภัณฑสถานแห่งชาติกำแพงเพชร

Across the road and south 100m or so from these temples is a national museum *(☎ 0 5571 1570; admission 30B; open 9am-4pm Wed-Sun)*. Downstairs has the usual survey of Thai art periods while upstairs has a collection of artefacts from the Kamphaeng Phet area, including terracotta ornamentation from ruined temples and Buddha images in both the Sukhothai and Ayuthaya styles.

Kamphaeng Phet Chaloem Phrakiat Museum

พิพิธภัณฑ์กำแพงเพชรเฉลิมพระเกียรติ

Just south of the Kamphaeng Phet National Museum is the Kamphaeng Phet Chaloem Phrakiat Museum *(Kamphaeng Phet Museum; ☎ 0 5572 2341; admission free; open 9am-4pm daily)*, which consists of a series of central, Thai-style wooden structures on stilts set among nicely landscaped grounds. There are three main buildings: One focuses on history and prehistory, one features displays about geography and materials used in local architecture, and the third houses an ethnological museum featuring encased displays of miniature doll-like figures representing various tribes. Push-button recordings in English and Thai explain the displays.

San Phra Isuan

ศาลพระอิศวร

Near the Kamphaeng Phet Chaloem Phrakiat Museum, San Phra Isuan (Shiva Shrine) has

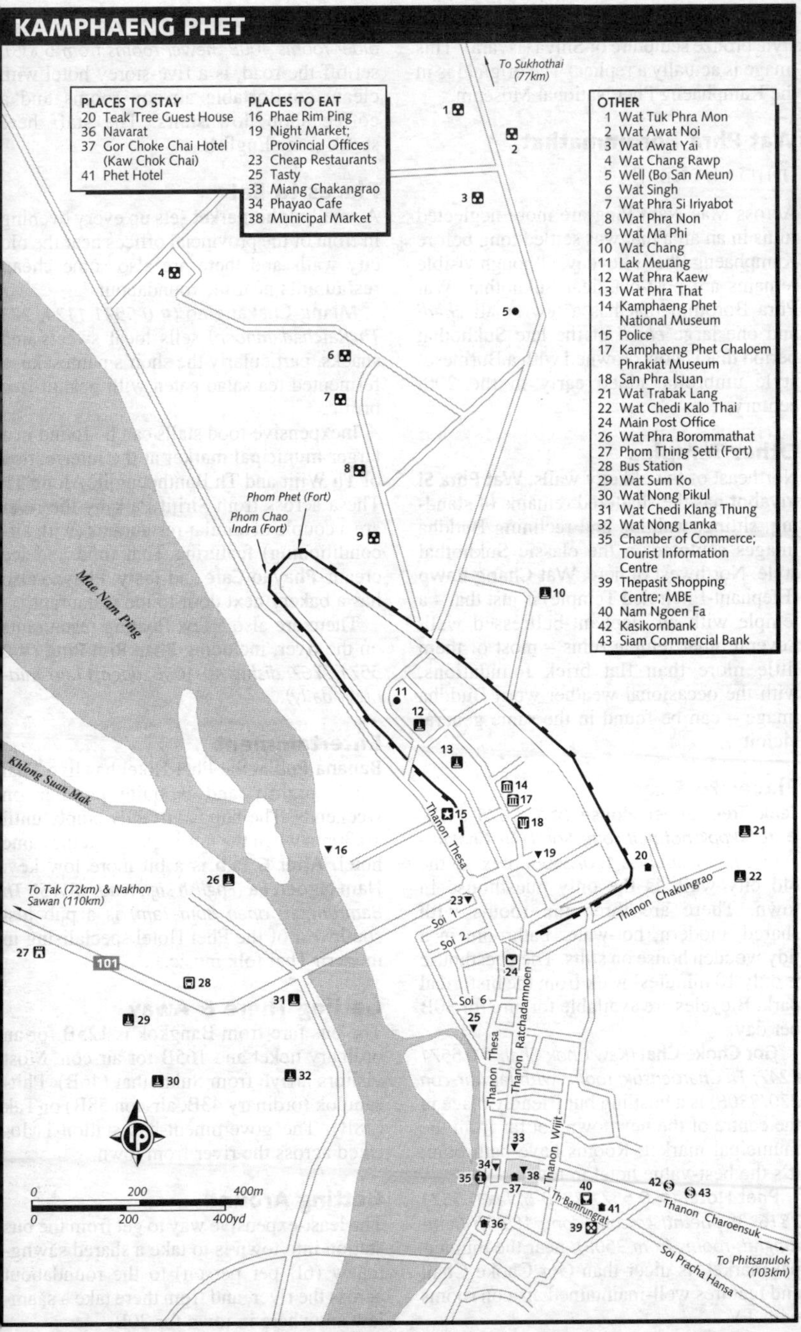
KAMPHAENG PHET
PLACES TO STAY
20 Teak Tree Guest House
36 Navarat
37 Gor Choke Chai Hotel (Kaw Chok Chai)
41 Phet Hotel
PLACES TO EAT
16 Phae Rim Ping
19 Night Market; Provincial Offices
23 Cheap Restaurants
25 Tasty
33 Miang Chakangrao
34 Phayao Cafe
38 Municipal Market
OTHER
1 Wat Tuk Phra Mon
2 Wat Awat Noi
3 Wat Awat Yai
4 Wat Chang Rawp
5 Well (Bo San Meun)
6 Wat Singh
7 Wat Phra Si Iriyabot
8 Wat Phra Non
9 Wat Ma Phi
10 Wat Chang
11 Lak Meuang
12 Wat Phra Kaew
13 Wat Phra That
14 Kamphaeng Phet National Museum
15 Police
17 Kamphaeng Phet Chaloem Phrakiat Museum
18 San Phra Isuan
21 Wat Trabak Lang
22 Wat Chedi Kalo Thai
24 Main Post Office
26 Wat Phra Borommathat
27 Phom Thing Setti (Fort)
28 Bus Station
29 Wat Sum Ko
30 Wat Nong Pikul
31 Wat Chedi Klang Thung
32 Wat Nong Lanka
35 Chamber of Commerce; Tourist Information Centre
39 Thepasit Shopping Centre; MBE
40 Nam Ngoen Fa
42 Kasikornbank
43 Siam Commercial Bank
To Sukhothai (77km)
Phom Phet (Fort)
Phom Chao Indra (Fort)
Mae Nam Ping
Khlong Suan Mak
Thanon Thesa
Thanon Chakungrao
To Tak (72km) & Nakhon Sawan (110km)
101
Soi 1
Soi 2
Soi 6
Thanon Ratchadamnoen
Thanon Wijit
Th Bamrungrat
Thanon Charoensuk
Soi Pracha Hansa
To Phitsanulok (103km)
0 200 400m
0 200 400yd

a sandstone base upon which is a Khmer-style bronze sculpture of Shiva (Isvara). This image is actually a replica: The original is in the Kamphaeng Phet National Museum.

Wat Phra Borommathat

วัดพระบรมธาตุ

Across Mae Nam Ping are more neglected ruins in an area that was settled long before Kamphaeng Phet's heyday, although visible remains are post-classical Sukhothai. Wat Phra Borommathat has a few small *chedi* and one large *chedi* of the late Sukhothai period that is now crowned with a Burmese-style umbrella added early in the 20th century.

Other Temples

Northeast of the old city walls, **Wat Phra Si Iriyabot** has the shattered remains of standing, sitting, walking and reclining Buddha images sculpted in the classic Sukhothai style. Northwest of here, **Wat Chang Rawp** (Elephant-Encircled Temple) is just that – a temple with an elephant-buttressed wall. Several other temple ruins – most of them little more than flat brick foundations, with the occasional weather-worn Buddha image – can be found in the same general vicinity.

Places to Stay

Teak Tree Guest House *(☎ 0 1675 6471; ⓔ teakkpp@hotmail.com; Soi 1 Th Chakungrao; singles/doubles 170/250B)*, next to the old city wall, is the only guesthouse in town. There are three fan rooms with shared, modern, hot-water bathroom in a tidy wooden house on stilts. The guesthouse is only 10 minutes' walk from the historical park. Bicycles are available for hire for 30B per day.

Gor Choke Chai *(Kaw Chok Chai; ☎ 0 5571 1247; Th Charoensuk; rooms with fan/air-con 270/330B)* is a bustling but friendly place in the centre of the new town not far from the municipal market. Rooms have bathroom; it's the best-value hotel in town.

Phet Hotel *(☎ 0 5571 2810-5, fax 0 5571 2816; ⓔ phethtl@cscoms.com; 189 Th Bamrungrat; rooms from 350B)*, near the municipal market, is nicer than Gor Choke Chai, and features well-maintained air-con rooms with TV.

Navarat *(Nawarat; ☎ 0 5571 1211; Th Thesa; older rooms 400B, newer rooms from 500B)*, set off the road, is a five-storey hotel with clean, comfortable air-con rooms and a coffee shop downstairs. The staff here speak some English.

Places to Eat

A small **night market** sets up every evening in front of the provincial offices near the old city walls and there are also some **cheap restaurants** near the roundabout.

Miang Chakangrao *(☎ 0 5571 1124; 273 Th Ratchadamnoen)* sells local sweets and snacks, particularly the shop's namesake, a fermented tea salad eaten with peanut-rice brittle.

Inexpensive food stalls can be found in a larger **municipal market** at the intersection of Th Wijit and Th Banthoengjit. Along Th Thesa across from Sirijit Park by the river are a couple of similar restaurants (with air-conditioning) featuring Thai food and ice cream, **Phayao Cafe** and **Tasty**. Phayao also has a bakery next door to the restaurant.

There are also a few floating restaurants on the river, including **Phae Rim Ping** *(☎ 0 5571 2767; dishes 40-100B; open 11am-midnight daily)*.

Entertainment

Banana Pub at the Phet Hotel has live Thai bands nightly and is quite popular on weekends. The pub is virtually empty until 10.30pm when the music starts. At the same hotel, **After 6 Pub** is a bit more low key. **Nam Ngoen Fa** *(English sign reads 'BWS'; Th Bamrungrat; open 8pm-1am)* is a pub just southwest of the Phet Hotel specialising in modern Thai folk music.

Getting There & Away

The bus fare from Bangkok is 125B for an ordinary ticket and 165B for air-con. Most visitors arrive from Sukhothai (46B), Phitsanulok (ordinary 43B, air-con 58B) or Tak (28B). The government-bus station is located across the river from town.

Getting Around

The least-expensive way to get from the bus station into town is to take a shared sǎwngthǎew (6B per person) to the roundabout across the river, and from there take a sǎamláw anywhere in town for 20B.

Tak Province

In the 1970s the mountains of western Tak were a hotbed of communist guerrilla activity. Since the 1980s the former leader of the local CPT movement has been involved in resort-hotel development and Tak is very much open to outsiders, but the area still has an untamed feeling about it. This province of only around 350,000 boasts Thailand's largest population of domesticated elephants, which are still commonly used by Karen villagers in western Tak for transport and agricultural tasks.

Western Tak has always presented a distinct contrast with other parts of Thailand because of strong Karen and Burmese cultural influences. The Thailand-Myanmar border districts of Mae Ramat, Tha Song Yang and Mae Sot are dotted with refugee camps, an outcome of the firefights between the Karen National Union (KNU) and the Myanmar government, which is driving Karen civilians across the border. As of mid-2002 there were an estimated 100,000 Burmese and Karen refugees along the border.

The main source of income for people living on both sides of the border is legal and illegal international trade. The main smuggling gateways on the Thailand side are Tha Song Yang, Mae Sarit, Mae Tan, Wangkha, Mae Sot and Waley. One important contraband product is teak, cut by the Karen or the Karenni (Kayah) and brought into Thailand from Myanmar on big tractor trailers at night. Up to 200,000B in bribes per truckload is distributed among local Thai authorities who conveniently look the other way. None of the trade is legal since the Thai government cut off all timber deals with the Burmese military in 1997.

Most of the province is forested and mountainous and is excellent for trekking. Organised trekking occurs, some farther north out of Chiang Mai, most of it locally organised. There are Hmong, Musoe (Lahu), Lisu and White and Red Karen settlements throughout the west and north.

In Ban Tak, 25km upstream along Mae Nam Tak from Tak, you can visit **Wat Phra Boromathat**, the original site of a Thai *chedi* that, according to legend, was constructed during the reign of King Ramkhamhaeng (1275–1317) to celebrate his elephant-back victory over King Sam Chon, ruler of an independent kingdom once based at or near Mae Sot. The wát's main feature is a large, slender, gilded *chedi* in the Shan style surrounded by numerous smaller but similar *chedi*. Many Thais flock to the temple each week in the belief that the *chedi* can somehow reveal to them the winning lottery numbers for the week.

Approximately 45km north of Meuang Tak via Rte 1 and then 17km west (between the Km 463 and Km 464 markers), via the road to Sam Ngao, is Kheuan Phumiphon (Bhumibol Dam), which impounds Mae Nam Ping at a height of 154m, making it the tallest dam in Southeast Asia and the eighth-tallest in the world. The shores and islands of the reservoir are a favourite picnic spot for local Thais.

TAK

อ.เมืองตาก

postcode 63000 • pop 49,200

Lying along the eastern bank of Mae Nam Ping, Tak is not particularly interesting except as a point from which to visit the Lan Sang and Taksin Maharat National Parks to the west or Kheuan Phumiphon to the north. Travellers heading to the Thailand-Myanmar border town of Mae Sot occasionally find themselves here for a few hours or overnight.

Although most of Tak exhibits nondescript, cement-block architecture, the southern section of the city harbours a few old teak homes. Residents are proud of the suspension bridge (for motorcycles, pedicabs, bicycles and pedestrians only) over Mae Nam Ping, which flows quite broadly here even in the dry season.

Information

TAT (*☎ 0 5551 4341; 193 Th Taksin; open 8.30am-4.30pm daily*) has an office in a beautiful contemporary Thai building off Th Mahat Thai Bamrung. You can ask questions or pick up tourist pamphlets and brochures here.

Several banks have branches along Th Mahat Thai Bamrung and Th Taksin, all with ATMs.

Places to Stay & Eat

Few people pause to spend the night in Tak, but if you do you'll find most of the town's

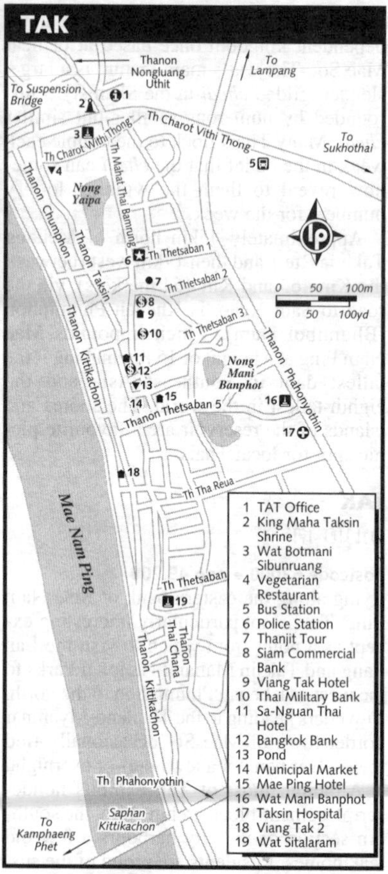

hotels are lined up on Th Taksin or Th Mahat Thai Bamrung in the town centre. **Mae Ping Hotel** *(☎ 0 5551 1807; 619 Th Taksin; rooms with fan/air-con 110/250B)* is slightly worn but has large clean rooms with bathroom in an old, wooden building. It's surprisingly quiet considering its location opposite the market.

Sa-Nguan Thai *(☎ 0 5551 1155; Th Mahat Thai Bamrung; singles/doubles with fan 170/200B, with air-con 300/350B)*, one street west of the Mae Ping Hotel, is an old, wooden, two-storey place. There is no sign, but this classic can be identified by the red Chinese lanterns on the 2nd-floor veranda. There's a decent Chinese-Thai **restaurant** downstairs.

Viang Tak 2 *(☎ 0 5551 1910; 236 Th Chumphon; rooms 650B, deluxe rooms 800-900B)*, by Mae Nam Ping, has comfortable standard and deluxe rooms for the discounted rate shown above – although listed rates are higher. Amenities at this eight-storey hotel include a coffee shop, karaoke bar and swimming pool. **Viang Tak** *(☎ 0 5551 1950, 25/3 Th Mahat Thai Bamrung; standard rooms 650B, deluxe rooms 800-900B)* is the older, bigger sibling of Viang Tak 2, and it features 100 rooms at roughly the same rates.

You can buy food at the **municipal market** *(Th Taksin; dishes 10-30B; open 6am-6pm daily)*. **Pond** *(Th Taksin; dishes 15-30B; open 8am-3pm daily)* is a simple place near the market specialising in Thai curries. On the southeastern corner of Th Taksin and Th Charot Withi Thong you'll find a **vegetarian restaurant** *(no Roman-script sign; dishes 10-30B; open 8am-4pm daily)*.

Getting There & Away

Tak airport, 15km out of town towards Sukhothai on Hwy 12, isn't operating at the moment; the nearest functioning airports are in Phitsanulok and Mae Sot. THAI provides a free shuttle van a few times a day between Phitsanulok airport and Tak. In Tak the vans stop at the Viang Tak 2 Hotel.

There are frequent buses to Tak from Sukhothai (31/43B ordinary/air-con, one to 1½ hours). Tak's **bus station** *(Th Charot Withi Thong)* is just outside town, but a túk-túk will take you to the town centre for around 20B.

Ordinary government buses depart for Bangkok three times daily (151B, 10 hours), while a 2nd-class air-con bus leaves once each day (184B, eight hours). There are four daily 1st-class air-con departures from Tak to Bangkok and one 10pm departure in the reverse direction (240B, six hours). **Thanjit Tour** and **Choet Chai Tour** offer 1st-class air-con buses with similar departures and fares.

Air-con buses to Mae Sot (50B) leave at 2pm, 4pm and 5pm. Minivans to Mae Sot leave much more frequently from the main station in Tak (35B, one to 1½ hours).

AROUND TAK

Taksin Maharat & Lan Sang National Parks

อุทยานแห่งชาติตากสินมหาราช

These small national parks *(adult/child 200/100B)* receive a steady trickle of visitors on weekends and holidays, but they are almost

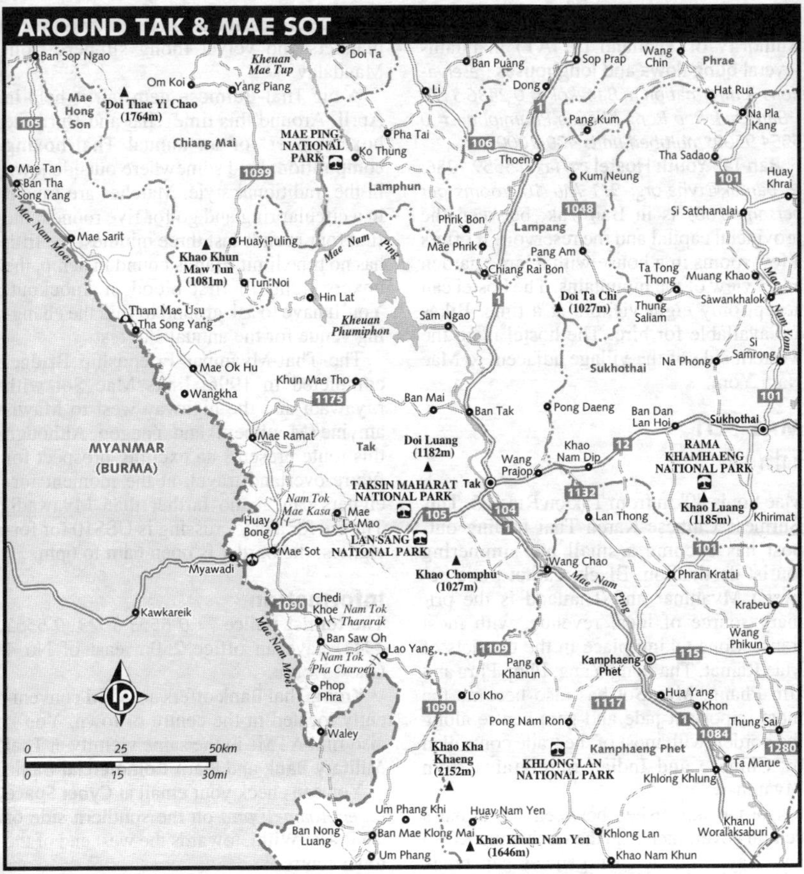

empty during the week. Taksin Maharat (established in 1981) covers 149 sq km; the entrance is 2km from the Km 26 marker on Rte 105/Asia Rte 1 (the so-called Pan-Asian Hwy, which would link Istanbul and Singapore if all the intervening countries allowed land crossings) to Mae Sot.

The park's most outstanding features are the 30m, nine-tiered **Nam Tok Mae Ya Pa** and a record-holding *tàbàak,* a dipterocarp that is 50m tall and 16m in circumference. Bird-watching is said to be particularly good here; known resident and migratory species include the tiger shrike, forest wagtail and Chinese pond heron.

Nineteen kilometres from Tak, Lan Sang National Park preserves 104 sq km surrounding an area of rugged, 1000m-high granite peaks, part of the Tenasserim Range. A network of trails leads to several **waterfalls**, including the park's 40m-high namesake. To reach the park entrance, take Rte 1103 3km south off Rte 105.

Places to Stay Lan Sang National Park rents out **bungalows** *(150-600B)* and also **tents** *(30B)*. Taksin Maharat National Park offers rustic **rooms** *(250B)*, and has a **camping ground** *(tent sites 10B)*. **Food service** can be arranged in both parks.

Kheuan Phumiphon

เขื่อนภูมิพล

This huge reservoir is a favourite canoeing, swimming, fishing and picnicking destination for Tak residents. The Electrical Generating Authority of Thailand (EGAT) maintains several **bungalows and longhouses** *(reservations & information in Bangkok ☎ 0 2436 3179 • Ban Phak Rap Rong Kheuan Phumiphon ☎ 0 5554 9509; multibed units 400-1000B)*.

Ban Tak Youth Hostel *(☎/fax 0 5559 1286; ⓔ bantak@tyha.org; 9/1 Mu 10; rooms per person 120B)* is in Ban Tak, between the provincial capital and the reservoir. It offers a few rooms in a house with a large garden and a view of the mountains. The hostel can accept only eight visitors at a time. Bikes are available for hire. The hostel is on the western side of the village adjacent to Mae Nam Yom.

MAE SOT
แม่สอด

Mae Sot is 80km from Tak on Rte 105. This Burmese-Chinese-Karen-Thai trading outpost has become a small but simmering tourist destination. Black-market trade between Myanmar and Thailand is the primary source of local revenue, with most transactions taking place in the districts of Mae Ramat, Tha Song Yang, Phop Phra and Um Phang. Mae Sot has also become the most important jade and gem centre along the border, with most of the trade controlled by Chinese and Indian immigrants from Myanmar.

Border skirmishes between Myanmar's central government and the weakening Karen and Kayah ethnic insurgencies can break out at any time, sending thousands of refugees – and the occasional mortar rocket – across the Thai-Myanmar border, elements that add to the area's perceived instability.

Walking down the streets of Mae Sot, you'll see an interesting mixture of ethnicities – Burmese men in their *longyi* (sarongs), Hmong and Karen women in traditional hill-tribe dress, bearded Indo-Burmese men and Thai army rangers. Shop signs along the streets are in Thai, Burmese and Chinese. Most of the temple architecture in Mae Sot is Burmese. The town's Burmese population is largely Muslim, while those living outside town are Buddhist, and the Karen are mostly Christian.

The large **municipal market** in Mae Sot, behind the Siam Hotel, sells some interesting stuff, including Burmese clothing, cheap cigarettes, roses, Indian food, sturdy Burmese blankets and velvet thong slippers from Mandalay.

A big **Thai-Burmese gem fair** is held in April. Around this time Thai and Burmese boxers meet for an annual **Thai-boxing competition**, held somewhere outside town in the traditional style. Matches are fought in a circular ring and go for five rounds; the first four rounds last three minutes, the fifth has no time limit. Hands bound in hemp, the boxers fight till first blood or knockout. You'll have to ask around to find the changing venue for the annual slugfest.

The Thai-Myanmar Friendship Bridge, completed in 1996, links Mae Sot with Myawadi and the highway west to Mawlamyine (Moulmein) and Yangon. Although this route presents an exciting prospect for future overland travel, at the moment foreigners can go no farther than Myawadi. The fee for a day-crossing is US$10 for foreigners; the border is open 6am to 6pm.

Information

The **tourist police** *(☎ 0 5553 3523, 0 5553 4341)* have an office 250m east of No 4 Guest House.

Krung Thai Bank offers an ATM conveniently located in the centre of town. You'll also find ATMs in the same vicinity at **Thai Military Bank** and **Siam Commercial Bank**.

You can check your email at **Cyber Space** *(open 10am-10pm)* on the southern side of Th Prasat Withi, towards the west end of the town centre.

DK Book House *(Th Intharakhiri)* is attached to the DK Mae Sot Square Hotel. The only English-language books it stocks so far are Penguin classics, but there are a few maps of the area for sale, including a detailed Thai military-surveyed topographic map (1:250,000) of the border area entitled *Moulmein*. This map covers as far north as Mae Ramat, to the south almost to Um Phang, west to Mawlamyine and only about 50km east of Mae Sot.

Herbal Sauna

At Wat Mani men can take a herbal sauna *(admission 20B; open 3pm-7pm)*. The sauna volunteers also sell herbal medicines made by the monks. The sauna is towards the back of the monastery grounds, past the monks' *kùti*.

MAE SOT

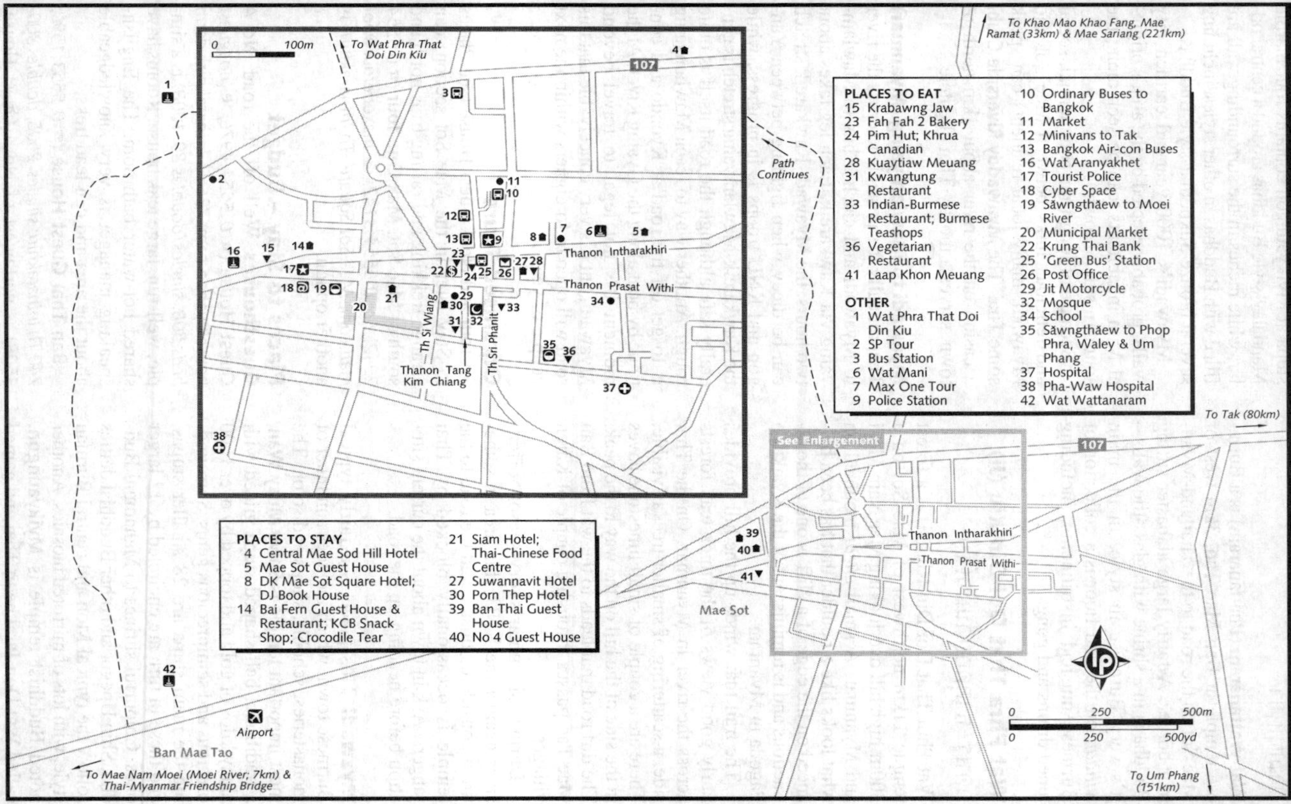
PLACES TO STAY
4 Central Mae Sod Hill Hotel
5 Mae Sot Guest House
8 DK Mae Sot Square Hotel; DJ Book House
14 Bai Fern Guest House & Restaurant; KCB Snack Shop; Crocodile Tear
21 Siam Hotel; Thai-Chinese Food Centre
27 Suwannavit Hotel
30 Porn Thep Hotel
39 Ban Thai Guest House
40 No 4 Guest House
PLACES TO EAT
15 Krabawng Jaw
23 Fah Fah 2 Bakery
24 Pim Hut; Khrua Canadian
28 Kuaytiaw Meuang
31 Kwangtung Restaurant
33 Indian-Burmese Restaurant; Burmese Teashops
36 Vegetarian Restaurant
41 Laap Khon Meuang
OTHER
1 Wat Phra That Doi Din Kiu
2 SP Tour
3 Bus Station
6 Wat Mani
7 Max One Tour
9 Police Station
10 Ordinary Buses to Bangkok
11 Market
12 Minivans to Tak
13 Bangkok Air-con Buses
16 Wat Aranyakhet
17 Tourist Police
18 Cyber Space
19 Săwngthăew to Moei River
20 Municipal Market
22 Krung Thai Bank
25 'Green Bus' Station
26 Post Office
29 Jit Motorcycle
32 Mosque
34 School
35 Săwngthăew to Phop Phra, Waley & Um Phang
37 Hospital
38 Pha-Waw Hospital
42 Wat Wattanaram
To Wat Phra That Doi Din Kiu
To Khao Mao Khao Fang, Mae Ramat (33km) & Mae Sariang (221km)
Path Continues
Thanon Intharakhiri
Thanon Prasat Withi
Th Si Wiang
Th Sri Phanit
Thanon Tang Kim Chiang
107
See Enlargement
Mae Sot
Airport
Ban Mae Tao
To Tak (80km)
To Um Phang (151km)
To Mae Nam Moei (Moei River; 7km) & Thai-Myanmar Friendship Bridge
0 100m
0 250 500m
0 250 500yd

Ban Mae Tao
บ้านแม่เฒ่า

Wat Wattanaram (Phattanaram) is a Burmese temple at Ban Mae Tao, 3km west of Mae Sot on the road to the Thailand-Myanmar border. A fairly large alabaster sitting Buddha is in a shrine with glass-tile walls – it's very Burmese in style. In the main *wíhăan* on the 2nd floor is a collection of Burmese musical instruments, including tuned drums and gongs.

Wat Phra That Doi Din Kiu (Ji)
วัดพระธาตุดอยดินกิว(จี)

Wat Phra That Doi Din Kiu (Ji) is a forest temple 11km northwest of Mae Sot on a 300m-high hill overlooking Mae Nam Moei and Myanmar. A small *chedi* mounted on what looks like a boulder that has been balanced on the edge of a cliff is one of the attractions and is reminiscent of the Kyaiktiyo Pagoda in Myanmar.

The trail that winds up the hill provides fairly good views of the thick teak forests across the river in Myanmar. On the Thai side, a scattering of smaller trees is visible. There are a couple of small limestone caves in the side of the hill on the way to the peak. The dirt road that leads to the wát from Ban Mae Tao passes through a couple of Karen villages.

During Myanmar's dry-season offensives against the KNU, this area is sometimes considered unsafe and the road to the temple is occasionally blocked by Thai rangers. Ask in town about the current situation before heading up the road.

Myawadi This place is a fairly typical Burmese town, which includes a number of monasteries, schools, shops and so on. The most important temple is **Shwe Muay Wan**, a traditional bell-shaped stupa gilded with many kilos of gold and topped by over 1600 precious and semiprecious gems. Surrounding the main stupa are 28 smaller stupas, and these in turn are encircled by 12 larger ones. Colourful shrines to Mahamuni Buddha, Shin Upagot and other Buddhist deities follow the typical Mon and central Burman style, with lots of mirrored mosaics. Another noted Buddhist temple is **Myikyaungon**, called Wat Don Jarakhe in Thai and named for its crocodile-shaped sanctuary. A hollow stupa at Myikyaungon contains four marble Mandalay-style Buddhas around a central pillar, while niches in the surrounding wall are filled with Buddhas in other styles, including several bronze Sukhothai-style Buddhas.

Myawadi's 1000-year-old earthen city walls, probably erected by the area's original Mon inhabitants, can be seen along the southern side of town.

Because of long-time commercial, social and religious links between Mae Sot and Myawadi, many local residents can speak some Thai. The **Myawaddy Riverside Club**, a casino on the river about 1km north of town, serves a mostly Thai clientele.

Myawadi to Mawlamyaing (Myanmar)
Theoretically it's possible to cross the river to Myawadi and catch a bus to Mawlamyaing via Kawkareik. Each leg takes about two hours; the Myawadi-Kawkareik stretch can be dicey when fighting between Yangon and KNU troops is in progress, while the Kawkareik-Mawlamyaing stretch is generally safe although the road itself is quite rough. Another way to reach Mawlamyaing is to get off the road at Kyondo and continue by boat along the Gyaing River. At the moment it's not legal to travel beyond Myawadi, but it's very conceivable that this road will open to foreigners within the next couple of years.

Organised Tours
SP Tour and No 4 Guest House (see Places to Stay later in the Mae Sot section) can arrange trekking and rafting trips north and south of Mae Sot. **Max One Tour** *(☎ 0 5554 2942, fax 0 5554 3142; ⓔ maxonetour@hotmail.com; Mae Sot Square, Th Intharakhiri)* is another option.

Places to Stay – Budget
Guesthouses Well off the road, **No 4 Guest House** *(☎ 0 5554 4976; ⓔ no4guesthouse@yahoo.com; 736 Th Intharakhiri; dorm beds 50B, singles/doubles 80/100B)* is a simple, well-run, large teak house. Rooms have shared hot-water bathroom. The English-speaking manager is very knowledgeable about the area and can lead treks.

Ban Thai Guest House *(☎ 0 5553 1590; 740 Th Intharakhiri; singles 250B, doubles 300-350B)* is northwest of No 4 Guest House, down an alley. This quiet, clean, two-storey guesthouse offers rooms with comfortable beds, Thai-style cushions and shared hot-water showers. Long-term discounts are available.

Bai Fern Guest House *(☎ 0 5553 3343; 660/2 Th Intharakhiri; singles/doubles 100/150B)*, near Crocodile Tear, is a fairly new place with basic rooms with shared hot-water showers in a rambling Thai house.

Mae Sot Guest House *(☎ 0 5553 2745; Th Intharakhiri; singles/doubles without bath 80/120B, with cold-water showers 280B)* offers not-so-great rooms with shared bathroom, and nicer air-con rooms with cold-water showers in a row house. The guesthouse's best feature is the pleasant open-air sitting area at the front. Local maps and information are available and the owner speaks English quite well.

Hotels All rooms have fan and bathroom at the **Suwannavit Hotel** *(☎ 0 5553 1162; Soi Wat Luang; rooms 150B)*, with an old wooden wing or a newer concrete one.

Siam Hotel *(☎ 0 5553 1376, fax 0 5553 1974; 185 Th Prasat Withi; rooms with fan 220B, with fan & TV 250B, with air-con 350B, with air-con & TV 500B)* has adequate rooms with a range of features. Although it's basically a truckers' and gem-traders' hotel, local rumour has it that Myanmar intelligence agents hang out at the Siam.

Places to Stay – Mid-Range

Porn Thep Hotel *(☎ 0 5553 2590; 25/4 Th Si Wiang; rooms with fan/air-con 250/400, deluxe rooms 700B)* is off Th Prasat Withi near the municipal market and is relatively clean and efficiently run. In the rear wing of the hotel, there are air-con singles and doubles with hot water, while rooms with fan and cold-water bathroom are cheaper. A few deluxe rooms with TV and hot water are available in the newer front wing. Porn Thep has security parking. Rates are sometimes discounted 50B during the rainy season.

DK Mae Sot Square Hotel *(☎ 0 5554 2648/9; 298/2 Th Intharakhiri; rooms with fan/air-con 250/450B)*, attached to DK Book House, is a three-storey hotel with small, apartment-style rooms with fan and private bathroom, or larger air-con rooms. The rooms tend to vary a lot in quality, so it might be best to look at a few before checking in.

Places to Stay – Top End

Central Mae Sod Hill Hotel *(☎ 0 5553 2601-8, fax 0 5553 2600 • in Bangkok ☎ 0 2541 1234; e cmhadm@cscoms.com; 100 Th Asia; standard rooms 900B, suites from 1200B)* is on the highway to Tak, just outside the town centre. It has a swimming pool, tennis courts, a good restaurant, a disco and a cocktail lounge. All rooms come with air-con, hot water, fridge, TV, video and telephone. Rates include breakfast.

Places to Eat

Mae Sot has an unusually good selection of places to eat. Near the Siam Hotel on Th Prasat Withi are several choices, including an adjacent **Thai-Chinese food centre** *(dishes 20-40B; open 8am-4pm daily)* with several different vendors serving noodles and curry. It's open morning to afternoon only. You can also try the rambling **market** behind the Siam Hotel for cheap Thai takeaway.

An **Indian-Burmese restaurant** *(dishes 10-30B; open 8am-8pm daily)* opposite the mosque (the sign reads 'Tea Shop') has good *rotii kaeng*, fresh milk, curries and *khâo sawy*. On the same side of the street about 50m south, a **Burmese Muslim tea-shop** *(10-30B; open 8am-7pm daily)* does cheap and tasty samosas, curries and naan.

A favourite local snack is *krabawng jaw* (Burmese for 'fried crispy'), a sort of vegetable tempura. The best place to eat it is at the small **vendor stand** west of Bai Fern Guest House on Th Intharakhiri. There's no sign – look for a bubbling wok in front of a two-storey house. They fire up the wok around 5pm and keep cooking until 7pm or until they've run out of ingredients.

Another local speciality to look out for is *kŭaytĭaw meuang,* a rich bowl of rice noodles covered with sliced pork, greens, peanuts, chilli and green beans very similar to *kŭaytĭaw sùkhŏthai*. Look for rice-noodle vendors along Th Prasat Withi; the best place is the **vendor** on the western side of Soi Sapphakan, running north off Th Prasat Withi.

Laap Khon Meuang *(Th Intharakhiril; open 10am-2pm)*, almost directly opposite No 4 Guest House, is known for both northern- and northeastern-style *lâap* (spicy minced meat salad), as well as *sôm-tam* made with various types of fruit.

Kwangtung Restaurant *(no Roman-script sign; dishes 30-90B; open 10am-10pm daily)*, is an air-con eatery that specialises in Cantonese cooking; it's the best Chinese restaurant in town. It's around the corner from the Porn Thep Hotel, south of Th Prasat Withi.

There are a few *faràng* restaurants along Th Tang Kim Chiang and Th Intharakhiri. On the former you'll find **Pim Hut** *(☎ 0 5553 2818; 415/11-12 Th Tang Kim Chiang; dishes 40-120B; open 7.30am-8pm daily)*, with decent pizza, steak, Thai and Chinese dishes, ice cream and international breakfasts at moderate prices, and brightly lit **Fah Fah 2 Bakery** *(☎ 0 5553 2569; 417/6-7 Th Tang Kim Chiang; open 7.30am-9pm daily)*, with a similar but slightly less-expensive menu. Both cater to tourists, foreign volunteer workers (from nearby refugee camps) and upper-middle-class Thais. **Khrua Canadian** *(☎ 0 5553 4659; Th Tang Kim Chiang; dishes 30-80B; open 7am-10.30pm daily)* serves breakfast, sandwiches and plenty of vegetarian food. It screens movies after 8.30pm.

KCB Snack Shop *(Th Intharakhiri; dishes 35-75B; open 8am-9pm daily)* is a friendly place a bit farther west past Soi Ruam Jai. **Bai Fern** *(☎ 0 5553 3343; Th Intharakhiri; dishes 35-75B; open 11am-midnight daily)* is next to the guesthouse of the same name. Both of these places have the usual mix of Thai and *faràng* dishes. The cosy, wood-furnished Bai Fern has the edge on atmosphere and the salads are especially good.

A small, no-name **vegetarian restaurant** *(dishes 10-20B; open 7am-7pm)*, next to the Um Phang sǎwngthǎew stop, offers good, inexpensive Thai vegetarian food until the food is sold out.

Khao Mao Khao Fang *(☎ 0 5553 3607; 382 Mu 5, Mae Pa; dishes 40-70B; open 10am- 10pm daily)* is a little north of town between the Km 1 and Km 2 markers on the road to Mae Ramat. It's the place to try if you're looking for an atmospheric evening out. A Thai botanist designed this open-air restaurant to make it feel as if you're dining in the forest, with lots of common and not-so-common live plants from around northern Thailand. The Thai cuisine is equally inventive, with such specialities as *yam hèt khon* (a spicy salad made with forest mushrooms available in September and October only) and *mǔu khâo mâo* (a salad of home-cured sausage, peanuts, rice shoots, lettuce, ginger, lime and chilli).

Getting There & Away

Air From Bangkok **Air Andaman** *(☎ 0 5554 4726; Mae Sot Airport)* flies to Mae Sot (2400B) every day except Saturday and to Chiang Mai (1500B) thrice weekly.

Bus & Sǎwngthǎew The locally famous 'green bus' is run by **Chai Wattana bus company** *(☎ 0 5553 2331; Th Intharakhiri)*. It goes to various points north, including Tak (ordinary/air-con 44/50B), Lampang (103/185B), Chiang Mai (134/241B), Chiang Rai (200/369B) and Mae Sai (219/394B). The buses leave from a dirt lot a block west of the post office, the ordinary bus at 6am daily and the air-con bus at 8am.

An orange bus to Mae Sot also leaves every day at 2pm, 4pm and 5pm from the Tak bus station and costs 50B. The more frequent orange-and-white minivans along the same route cost 35B per person and usually arrive a little quicker than the bus. The minivans depart from the roadside in front of the First Hotel in Mae Sot. The trip takes about 1½ hours and it takes you on a beautiful winding road through mountains.

Ordinary buses between Bangkok and Mae Sot (165B) depart three times each evening in both directions. First-class air-con buses run between Bangkok and Mae Sot five times daily (302B); 2nd-class air-con buses (232B) have similar departures.

VIP buses (24 seats) to/from Bangkok leave four times daily (460B, about eight hours). Thanjit Tour offers 32-seat VIP buses to Bangkok for only 345B, departing at 10pm. In Mae Sot, Bangkok-bound air-con and VIP buses leave from the northern side of Th Inthakhiri just west of the police station; ordinary buses to Bangkok leave from the bus station near the market north of the police station.

Sǎwngthǎew to destinations north of Mae Sot, such as Mae Sarit (66B, 2½ hours), Tha Song Yang (55B, 1½ hours) and Mae Sariang (165B, five to six hours) leave hourly between 6am and noon from the green bus station near the northern edge of town.

Sǎwngthǎew to Um Phang (120B, five hours) leave hourly between 7am and 3pm.

Getting Around

Most of Mae Sot can be seen on foot. **Jit Motorcycle** *(Th Prasat Withi)* rents out motorcycles for 160B a day. Make sure you test ride a bike before renting; some of the machines can be in rather poor condition. Cars and vans can be rented for around 1200B a day; ask at any hotel. Motorcycle taxis and sǎmláw charge 20B for trips around town.

AROUND MAE SOT

Karen & Burmese Refugee Camps

ค่ายผู้อพยพชาวกะเหรี่ยงและพม่า

A couple of refugee camps have been set up along the eastern bank of Mae Nam Moei in either direction from Mae Sot. Most of the refugees in these camps are Karen fleeing battles between Burmese and KNU troops across the border. The camps have been around for over a decade but the Thai government has generally kept their existence quiet, fearing the build-up of a huge refugee 'industry' such as the one that developed around the Indo-Chinese camps in eastern Thailand in the 1970s.

Although many Thai and foreign volunteers have come to the refugees' aid, the camps are very much in need of outside assistance. Tourists are no longer permitted to visit the camps, although if you meet a camp volunteer in Mae Sot you might be able to visit by invitation. Donations of clothes and medicines (to be administered by qualified doctors and nurses) may be offered to the camps via No 4 Guest House in Mae Sot.

Waley

บ้านวะเลย์

Thirty-six kilometres from Mae Sot, Rte 1206 splits southwest off Rte 1090 at Ban Saw Oh and terminates 25km south at the border town of Waley, an important smuggling point.

The Burmese side was once one of the two main gateways to Kawthoolei, the Karen nation, but in 1989 the Yangon government ousted the KNU. Until the Thai government cut off all timber trade with Myanmar's military government, teak was the main border trade. Nowadays there's a brisk trade in teak furniture instead.

One can visit hill-tribe villages near **Ban Chedi Kok**, or the **Highland Farm and Gibbon Sanctuary** *(ⓔ highland_ape@hotmail com; Km 42.8, Rte 1090)* near Phop Phra. The latter is a private facility that cares for gibbons and other animals who have been rescued from captivity.

There is a small **hotel** *(rooms 50B per person)* in Phop Phra.

Getting There & Away Sǎwngthǎew to Phop Phra (34B) and Waley (40B) depart frequently between 6am and 6pm from a stop southeast of the mosque in Mae Sot. If you go by motorcycle or car, follow Rte 1090 southeast towards Um Phang and after 36km take Rte 1206 southwest. From this junction it's 25km to Waley; the last 10km of the road are unpaved. Your passport may be checked at a police outpost before Waley.

Border Market & *Myawadi*

Sǎwngthǎew frequently go to the border, 6km west of Mae Sot: ask for Rim Moei (Edge of the Moei). The trip costs 10B and the last sǎwngthǎew back to Mae Sot leaves Rim Moei at 5pm.

A **market** about 100m from the river on the Thai side legally sells Burmese goods – dried fish and shrimp, dried bamboo shoots, mung beans, peanuts, woven-straw products, teak carvings, thick cotton blankets, lacquerware, tapestries, wooden furniture, jade and gems. You can also buy black-market kyat (Burmese currency) here at very favourable rates.

When the border is open, it's possible for foreigners to cross the international bridge to Myawadi for day visits. If your Thai visa is about to expire, you can cross the border here, turn around, and walk back into Thailand for an instant 30-day visa. Immigration procedures are taken care of at the Thai immigration booth at the bridge, although if you have any problems there's a larger immigration office in nearby Mae Moei Shopping Bazaar. It takes about 15 minutes to finish all the paperwork to leave Thailand officially, and then you're free to walk across the arched bridge. The bridge is open 6am to 6pm daily.

At the other end of the bridge is a rustic **Myanmar immigration booth**, where you'll fill out permits for a one-day stay, pay a US$10 fee and leave your passports as a deposit. Then you're free to wander around Myawadi as long as you're back at the bridge by 5pm to pick up your passport and check out with immigration.

UM PHANG & AROUND

อุ้มผาง

Rte 1090 goes south from Mae Sot to Um Phang, 150km away. This stretch of road used to be called the 'Death Highway' because of the guerrilla activity in the area that hindered highway development. Those days ended in the 1980s, but lives are still lost because of brake failure or treacherous turns on this steep, winding road through incredible mountain scenery.

Along the way – short hikes off the highway – are two waterfalls, **Nam Tok Thararak** (26km from Mae Sot) and **Nam Tok Pha Charoen** (41km). Nam Tok Thararak streams over limestone cliffs and calcified rocks with a rough texture that makes climbing the falls easy. It's been made into a park of sorts, with benches right in the stream at the base of the falls for cooling off and a couple of outhouse toilets nearby; on weekends **food vendors** set up here.

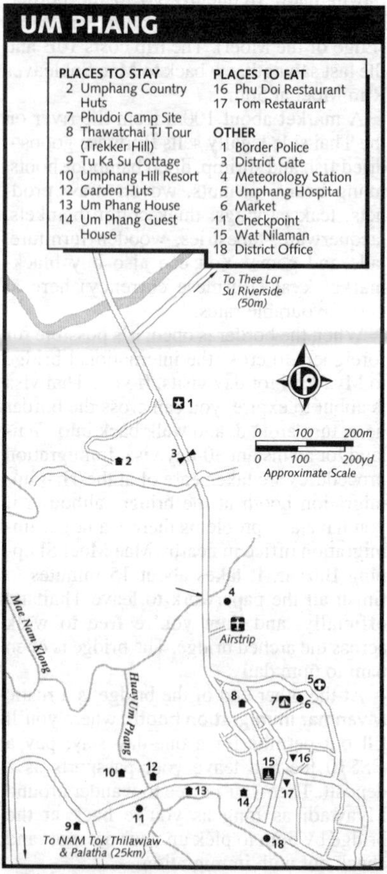

The eucalyptus-lined dirt road leaves the highway between the Km 24 and Km 25 markers. A side road at the Km 48 marker leads to a group of government-sponsored hill-tribe villages (Karen, Lisu, Hmong, Mien, Lahu). Just beyond Ban Rom Klao 4 – roughly midway between Mae Sot and Um Phang – is a very large Karen and Burmese refugee camp (called **Um Piam)** and several Hmong villages.

Sitting at the junction of Mae Nam Klong and Huay Um Phang, Um Phang is an overgrown village populated mostly by Karen. Many Karen villages in this area are very traditional, and elephants are used as much as oxen for farm work. *Yaeng* (elephant saddles) and other tack used for elephant wrangling are a common sight on the verandas of Karen houses outside of town. You'll also see plenty of **elephants** in other Karen villages throughout the district. The name for the district comes from the Karen word *umpha*, a type of bamboo container in which travelling Karen carried their documents to show to Thai border authorities.

An interesting **hike** can be done that follows the footpaths northeast of the village through rice fields and along Huay Um Phang to a few smaller Karen villages. At the border where Um Phang district meets Myanmar, near the Thai-Karen villages of Ban Nong Luang and Ban Huay, is a Karen **refugee village** inhabited by over 500 Karen who originally hailed from Htikabler village on the other side of border.

South of Um Phang, towards Sangkhlaburi in Kanchanaburi Province, Um Phang Wildlife Sanctuary links with the Thung Yai Naresuan and Huay Kha Kaeng Reserves as well as Khlong Lan and Mae Wong National Parks to form Thailand's **largest wildlife corridor** and one of the largest intact natural forests in Southeast Asia.

Nam Tok Thilawsu

น้ำตกทีลอซู

In Um Phang district you can arrange trips down Mae Nam Mae Klong to Nam Tok Thilawsu and Karen villages – inquire at any guesthouse. Typical three-day excursions include a raft journey along the river from Um Phang to the falls, then a two-day trek from the falls through the Karen villages of **Khotha** and **Palatha**, where a 4WD picks trekkers up and returns them to Um Phang (25km from Palatha by road). Some people prefer to spend two days on the river, the first night at a cave or hot springs along the river before Thilawsu and a second night at the falls. On the third day you can cross the river by elephant to one of the aforementioned villages to be met by a truck and returned to Um Phang. Or you can continue south along the road to Palatha 20km farther to the Hmong village of **Kangae Khi**. On the way back to Um Phang from Palatha you can stop off at **Nam Tok Thilawjaw**, which tumbles over a fern-covered cliff.

The scenery along the river is stunning, especially after the rainy season (November and December) when the 200m to 400m limestone cliffs are streaming with water and Nam Tok Thilawsu is at its best. This waterfall is Thailand's largest, measuring an estimated 400m high and up to 300m wide in the rainy season. There's a shallow cave behind the falls and several levels of pools suitable for swimming. The Thais consider Nam Tok Thilawsu to be the most beautiful waterfall in the country; it is now part of Um Phang Wildlife Sanctuary, declared a Unesco World Heritage site in 1999.

You can **camp** at the Um Phang Wildlife Sanctuary headquarters near the falls any time of year, and between December and May there are also **rooms** available for 100B per person. You must bring your own food. The 1.5km trail between the Um Phang Sanctuary headquarters and the falls has been transformed into a self-guided nature tour with the addition of well-conceived educational plaques. Surrounding the falls on both sides of the river are Thailand's thickest stands of natural forest, and the hiking in the vicinity of Nam Tok Thilawsu can be superb. The forest here is said to contain over 1300 varieties of palm; giant bamboo and strangler figs are commonplace, and the orchid tree *(Bauhinia variegata)* can even be seen along the road to Palatha.

Between 1 December and 1 June you can also drive to the falls via a rough 47km road from Um Phang suitable for 4WD or a skilled dirt-bike rider only. Or follow the main paved road south of Um Phang to Km 19; the walk to the falls is a stiff four hours from here via **Mo Phado** village. A săwngthăew goes to the km 19 marker from Um Phang once a day; ask for *kii-loh sìp kâo* and expect to pay 15B to 20B per person.

Um Phang Khi

This 'new' area for rafting, northeast of Um Phang, counts 47 sets of rapids rated at class III and class IV during the height of the rainy season. The rafting season for Um Phang Khi is short – August to October only – as other times of year the water level isn't high enough. Rafting trips arranged in Um Phang typically cost 2500B for a two-night, three-day programme, or 3000B if booked in Mae Sot.

Letongkhu to Sangkhlaburi

From Ban Mae Khlong Mai, a few kilometres north of Um Phang via the highway to Mae Sot, a graded dirt road (Rte 1167) heads southwest along the border to **Beung Kleung** (sometimes spelt Peung Kleung), a Karen, Burmese, Indo-Burmese, Talaku and Thai trading village where buffalo carts are more common than motorbikes. The picturesque setting among spiky peaks and cliffs is worth the trip even if you go no farther. Impressive **Nam Tok Ekaratcha** is an hour's walk away. Săwngthăew from Um Phang usually make a trip to Beung Kleung once a day, and it's possible to stay at the village clinic or in a private home for a donation of 100B per person. On the way you can stop off at the small, traditional Karen village of **Ban Thiphochi**.

Four hours' walk from here along a rough track (passable by 4WD in the dry season), near the Myanmar border on the banks of Mae Nam Suriya next to Sam Rom mountain, is the culturally singular, 109-house village of **Letongkhu** (Leh Tawng Khu). The villagers are for the most part Karen in language and dress, but they belong to a Hindu-like cult known as Talaku, with spiritual beliefs unique to this border region. They will eat only the meat of wild animals and hence do not raise chickens, ducks, pigs or beef cattle.

According to what little anthropological information is available, the villagers belong to the Lagu or Talaku sect, said to represent a form of Buddhism mixed with shamanism and animism. Letongkhu is one of only six such villages in Thailand; there are reportedly around 30 more in Myanmar. Each village has a spiritual and temporal leader called a *pu chaik* (whom the Thais call *reusǐi* – 'rishi' or 'sage') who wears his hair long – usually tied in a topknot – and dresses in white, yellow or brown robes, depending on the subsect.

The current 48-year-old *pu chaik* at Letongkhu is the 10th in a line of 'white-thread' priests dating back to their residence in Myanmar. The sage's many male disciples also wear their hair in topknots (often tied in cloth) and may wear similar robes. All *reusǐi* abstain from alcohol and are celibate. The priests live apart from the village in a temple and practise traditional medicine based on herbal healing and ritual magic. Antique elephant tusks are kept as talismans.

Evangelistic Christian missionaries have infiltrated the area and have tried to convert the Talaku, thus making the Talaku sensitive to outside visitation. If you visit Letongkhu, take care not to enter any village structures without permission or invitation. Likewise, do not take photographs without permission. If you treat the villagers with respect then you shouldn't have a problem.

Opposite Letongkhu on the Myanmar side of the border, the KNU has set up its latest tactical headquarters. Yangon government offensives against the KNU can break out in this area during the dry months of the year, but when this is happening or is likely to happen, Thai military checkpoints will turn all trekkers back. It wouldn't hurt to make a few inquiries in Um Phang first, just to make sure.

Sangkhlaburi (see Around Kanchanaburi Province in the Central Thailand chapter) is 90km or four to five days' walk from Beung Kleung. On the way (11km from Beung Kleung), about 250m off the road, is the extensive cave system of **Tham Takube**. From Ban Mae Chan, 35km on the same route, there's a dirt road branching across the border to a KNU-controlled village. The route to Sangkhlaburi has several branches; the main route crosses over the border into Myanmar for some distance before crossing back into Thailand. There has been discussion of cutting a newer, more direct road between Um Phang and Sangkhlaburi.

Because of the overall sensitive nature of this border area, and the very real potential for becoming lost, ill or injured, a guide is highly recommended for any sojourn south of Um Phang. You may be able to arrange a guide for this route in either Um Phang or Beung Kleung. Umphang Hill Resort in Um Phang can also arrange a trek but you need to give it a couple of weeks' notice. The best time of year to do the trek is October to January.

Organised Tours

Several of the guesthouses in Um Phang can arrange trekking and rafting trips in the area. The typical three-night, four-day trip costs about 4500B per person (four or more people). The price includes rafting, an elephant ride, food and guide service.

Longer treks of up to 12 days may also be available, and there are day trips to Nam Tok Thilawsu as well. It is worth checking to see what kind of rafts are used; most places have switched to rubber as bamboo rafts can break up in the rough rapids. Choose rubber, unless you are really looking for adventure – such as walking to your camp site rather than rafting there.

In Um Phang, **Tu Ka Su Cottage** and **Umphang Hill Resort** (see Places to Stay for details) have the best equipment and trip designs. Both offer basic three- to six-day rafting and hiking trips to Nam Tok Thilawsu and beyond, including one itinerary that takes rafters through 11 different sets of rapids on Mae Nam Mae Klong. Longer or shorter trips may also be arranged and elephant riding instead of walking is always an option.

Places to Stay

Accommodation in Um Phang is plentiful, but since the majority of visitors to the area are Thai, room rates tend to be a little higher than normal.

Thee Lor Su Riverside *(☎ 0 5556 1010; bungalows 600-1200B)* is the first place you come to as you enter Um Phang coming from Mae Sot. It's about 300m off the road, and features small wooden A-frame bungalows facing a stream. It's a bit overpriced even for this market, so best reserved for if everything else is full.

Umphang Country Huts *(rooms downstairs/upstairs 400/700B, larger rooms with private veranda 400-700B)*, off the highway 1.5km before Um Phang, is in a nice hilly setting. Rooms in a wood and thatch, two-storey building facing Huay Mae Klong share a common veranda, with benches. A downstairs room has a bathroom, while a larger upstairs room sleeps up to four. There are larger, more atmospheric rooms in another two-storey building that come with private verandas.

Thawatchai TJ Tour *(Trekker Hill; ☎ 0 5556 1090; beds 60B)* on a hillside near the village centre, offers beds in rustic thatched-roof shelters with shared facilities.

Phudoi Camp Site *(☎ 0 5556 1049, 0 1886 8783, fax 0 5556 1279; tent sites 50B, single/double bungalows 150/200B)*, around the corner from Trekker Hill towards the market, is a well-landscaped place on another hillside. You can pitch your own tent at the camping ground, or you can rent one of four clean, wooden bungalows. Additional bungalows were under construction when we visited. Discounts are available during the rainy season.

Um Phang Guest House *(☎ 0 5556 1021, fax 0 5556 1322; huts 100B, rooms in cottage/house 300/500B)* is farther south towards Huay Um Phang. Owned by BL Tour, it has rooms sleeping five to six in Thai-style houses, rooms in a cottage that sleep up to six and thatched huts for up to six people. The facilities, however, are in need of renovation.

Continuing towards Huay Um Phang, you'll find a few additional rustic guesthouses (referred to as 'resorts' in typical Thai fashion). **Um Phang House** *(☎ 0 5556 1073; rooms 150B, cottages 300B)* owned by the local *kamnan* (precinct officer), offers a few motel-like rooms with private bathroom that sleep up to three, and nicer wood-and-brick cottages with hot water and ceiling fans that sleep up to four (a solo traveller might be able to negotiate the price down a bit). There's a large outdoor **restaurant** in an open area near the cottages. Like Um Phang Guest House, the whole place could use spiffing up.

Garden Huts *(no Roman-script sign; Boonyaporn Guest House or Thaphae Resort; rooms without bath from 300B, bungalows with hot water up to 700B)* features five levels of accommodation ranging from bamboo huts with shared cold-water bathroom up to bungalows with attached hot-water bathroom; most of these rooms will sleep up to four people. You can get your fix of good, Thai-grown Arabica coffee here.

Umphang Hill Resort *(☎ 0 5556 1063, fax 0 5556 1065; ⓔ umphanghill@thaimail.com • in Mae Sot ☎ 0 5553 1409 • in Bangkok ☎ 0 2573 7942; large bungalows around 2000B, wooden bungalows 500B)*, on the opposite bank to Garden Huts, overlooks the stream. It's a friendly place where large wood-and-thatch bungalows have two or even three bathrooms, and price varies depending on the season; these are usually rented by Thai groups and can accommodate up to 20 people. When not full, the resort will rent out beds in these bungalows for 50B per person. There are also a few wooden bungalows with attached hot-water shower, small TV and refrigerator. This is one of the most popular places in Um Phang to book treks or raft trips.

Tu Ka Su Cottage *(Kin Ka Tu; ☎ 0 5556 1295, 0 1487 1643; rooms 1000-1500B)*, west of Huay Um Phang, is the cleanest and best-run of all the places offering accommodation in Um Phang. The attractive collection of brick-and-stone, multiroom cottages are surrounded by flower gardens. The largest sleeps 10, but it's possible to rent half of one of the smaller two-room cottages for between 600B and 750B. Tu Ka Su Cottage operates good local trekking-rafting trips as well.

Places to Eat

Um Phang has three or four simple noodle and rice shops plus a morning market and a small sundries shop. **Phu Doi Restaurant** *(dishes 20-40B; open 8am-10pm daily)*, on the main street into town, has very good food, especially the *phánaeng* (mild curry) dishes, but there are also rice dishes, noodles, *tôm yam* and cold beer. Phu Doi has a bilingual menu and seems to be virtually the only place open past 9pm.

There's a short string of noodle shops along the main road. **Tom Restaurant** *(dishes 20-40B; open 9am-8pm daily)* also does rice dishes.

Getting There & Away

There are several săwngthăew to Um Phang from Mae Sot (120B, 164km, five to six hours) that depart several times a day, starting around 7am and finishing around 3pm. Săwngthăew usually stop for lunch at windy **Ban Rom Klao 4** along the way. From Mae Sot to Um Phang, săwngthăew depart between 7am and 2.30pm.

If you decide to try to ride a motorcycle from Mae Sot, be sure it's one with a strong engine as the road has lots of fairly steep grades. Total drive time is around 3½ to four hours. The only petrol pump along the way is in Ban Rom Klao 4, 80km from Mae Sot, so you may want to carry 3L or 4L of extra fuel.

MAE SOT TO MAE SARIANG

Route 105 runs north from Mae Sot all the way to Mae Sariang in Mae Hong Son Province. The section of the road north of Tha Song Yang has finally been sealed and public transport is now available all the way to Mae Sariang (226km), passing through **Mae Ramat**, **Mae Sarit**, **Ban Tha Song Yang** and **Ban Sop Ngao** (Mae Ngao). In Mae Ramat a temple called **Wat Don Kaew**, which is behind the district office, houses a large Mandalay-style marble Buddha. Other attractions on the way to Mae Sariang include **Nam Tok Mae Kasa**, between the Km 13 and Km 14 markers, and extensive limestone caverns at **Tham Mae Usu**, at Km 94 near Ban Tha Song Yang. From the highway it's a 2km walk to Tham Mae Usu; note that in the rainy season, when the river running through the cave seals off the mouth, it's closed.

Instead of doing the Myanmar border run in one go, some people elect to spend the night in **Mae Sarit** (118km from Mae Sot), then start fresh in the morning to get to Ban Tha Song Yang in time for a morning săwngthăew from Ban Tha Song Yang to Mae Sariang.

Săwngthăew to Mae Sarit cost 66B and leave hourly between 6am and noon from the market north of the police station in Mae Sot (four hours). Mae Sarit to Ban Tha Song Yang costs 23B; from there to Mae Sariang costs 55B (three hours). If you miss the morning săwngthăew from Mae Sarit to Mae Sariang, you can usually arrange to charter a truck for 180B to 220B.

If you decide not to stay overnight in Mae Sarit you can take a direct Mae Sariang săwngthăew from Mae Sot for 165B. These large orange săwngthăew have the same departure times as the Mae Sot–Mae Sarit săwngthăew (about six hours).

Along the way you'll pass through thick forest, including a few stands of teak, and see Karen villages, the occasional work elephant and a large Thai ranger post.

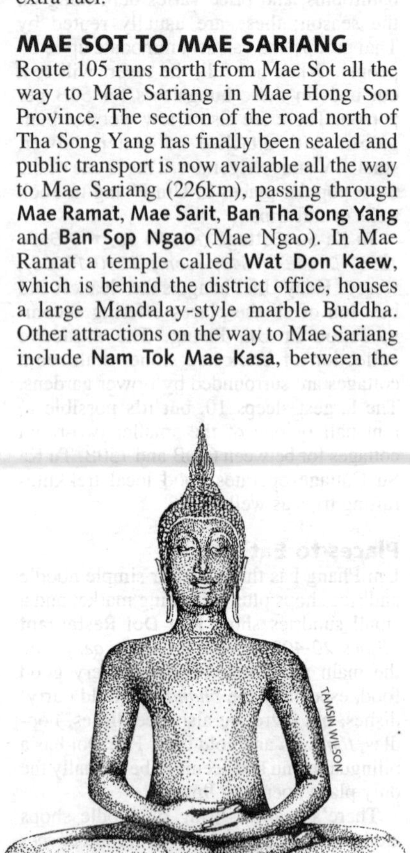

Buddha, in his myriad sculptural forms, is found throughout Thailand.

Places to Stay & Eat

Mae Salid Guest House *(singles/doubles 70/100B)* offers very basic rooms with private toilet and shared shower. This guesthouse is in Mae Sarit.

There are no guesthouses yet in Ban Tha Song Yang but it would probably be easy to arrange a place to stay by inquiring at the main market (where the săwngthăew stop) in this prosperous black-market town.

Krua Ban Tai *(☎ 0 1887 1102; Th Si Wattana; dishes 20-50B; open 8am-9pm daily)* is a two-storey wooden restaurant in the centre of Ban Tha Song Yang, around the corner from the main market. The creative menu includes very good *yam wún sên* (spicy noodle salad) made with freshwater shrimp, and *khâo phàt phánaeng* (phánaeng fried rice).

[Continued on page 422]

Hill Tribes

RYAN FOX

Young girl, Shan village

JOE CUMMINGS

Traditional Lisu headwear

BILL WASSMAN

Lahu girl, Chiang Mai Province

RYAN FOX

Young woman in traditional Hmong headwear

BILL WASSMAN

Mien woman

Ethnic minorities living in the mountainous regions of northern Thailand are often called 'hill tribes', or in the common Thai vernacular, *chao khăo* (mountain people). Each hill tribe has its own language, customs, mode of dress and spiritual beliefs.

Most are of semi-nomadic origin, having migrated to Thailand from Tibet, Myanmar, China and Laos during the past 200 years or so, although some groups may have been in Thailand much longer. They are 'fourth world' people in that they belong neither to the main aligned powers nor to the developing nations. Rather, they have crossed and continue to cross national borders, often fleeing oppression by other cultures, without regard for recent nationhood.

Language and culture constitute the borders of their world. Some groups are caught between the 6th and 21st centuries, while others are gradually being assimilated into modern life. Many tribespeople are also moving into lowland areas as montane lands become deforested by both traditional swidden (slash-and-burn) cultivation and illegal logging.

The Tribal Research Institute (**W** *www.chmai.com/tribal)* in Chiang Mai recognises 10 different hill tribes in Thailand, but there may be up to 20. The institute estimates the total hill-tribe population to be around 550,000.

The tribes most likely to be encountered in the region can be divided into three main linguistic groups: the Tibeto-Burman (Lisu, Lahu, Akha), the Karenic (Karen, Kayah) and the Austro-Thai (Hmong, Mien). Within each group there may also be several subgroups, eg, Blue Hmong, White Hmong; these names usually refer to predominant elements of clothing.

Hill tribes tend to have among the lowest standards of living in Thailand. Although it's tempting to correlate this with traditional lifestyles, their situation is compounded, in most cases, by a lack of Thai citizenship. Without the latter, they don't have the right to own land or even to receive the minimum wage, plus they may be denied access to health care and schooling. In the last couple of decades, efforts to integrate hill tribes into Thai society via free education and the issuing of Thai identity cards may have improved the lot of a minority of tribespeople. Of course the irony is that further Thai assimilation will threaten their cultural identities.

The Shan (Thai Yai, meaning large Thai) are not included in the descriptions below as they are not a hill-tribe group per se – they have permanent habitations and speak a language similar to Thai. The Shan are considered by Thai scholars to have been the original inhabitants of the area. Nevertheless, Shan villages are often common stops on hill-tribe treks.

The following comments on dress refer mostly to the female members of each group, as hill-tribe men tend to dress like rural Thais. The population figures indicated here are taken from the most recent estimates. For more detailed descriptions on Thailand's hill tribes, see some of the recommendations that are listed under Books in the Facts for the Visitor chapter.

Title page & inset: A woman from the Akha tribe wearing jewellery & headdress (Photograph by Bill Wassman)

Akha *(I-kaw)*

Pop 48,500
Origin: Tibet
Present locations: Thailand, Laos, Myanmar, Yunnan
Economy: rice, corn, opium
Belief system: animism, with an emphasis on ancestor worship
Cultural characteristics: headdress of beads, feathers and dangling silver ornaments. Villages are along mountain ridges or on steep slopes from 1000m to 1400m in altitude. The well-known Akha Swing Ceremony takes place from mid-August to mid-September, between planting and harvest. The Akha are among the poorest of Thailand's ethnic minorities and tend to resist assimilation into the Thai mainstream. Like the Lahu, they often cultivate opium for their own use.

Akha houses are constructed of wood and bamboo, usually atop short wooden stilts and roofed with thick grass. Guests are often received on a raised open verandah at the entrance of the house. At the entrance of every traditional Akha village stands a simple wooden gateway consisting of two vertical struts joined by a lintel. Akha shamans affix various charms made from bamboo strips to it to prevent malevolent spirits from entering the village. Standing next to the gateway are crude wooden figures of a man and a woman, each bearing exaggerated sexual organs, in the belief that human sexuality is abhorrent to the spirit world.

As their annual rice crop ripens in August or September, the Akha will erect a simple swing consisting of four tall saplings lashed into a pyramid configuration. Vines are hung from the top of the tree pyramid and tied to a wooden plank to form the swing. For four days, amid much feasting and merrymaking, the villagers – especially young teenage girls – will take turns riding the swing.

Opium & Trekking

Some guides are very strict now about forbidding the smoking of opium on treks. This seems to be a good idea, since one of the problems trekking companies have had in the past is dealing with opium-addicted guides! Volunteers who work in tribal areas also say opium smoking sets a bad example for young people in the villages.

Opium is traditionally a condoned vice of the elderly, yet an increasing number of young people in the villages are now taking opium, heroin and amphetamines. This is possibly due in part to the influence of young trekkers who may smoke once and a few weeks later be hundreds of kilometres away while the villagers continue to face the temptation every day. Addiction has negative effects for the village as well as the individual's health, including a reduced male labour force and corresponding increase in women's workloads (most addicts are men) and reduced overall agricultural production. Also, an increase in the number of villagers injecting heroin (needles are often shared) has led to sky-rocketing rates of HIV infection in hill-tribe villages. Given the already high incidence of HIV infection among northern-Thai prostitutes some welfare groups say that entire tribal communities will be wiped out unless the rate of infection can be stopped.

Lahu *(Musoe)*

Pop 73,200
Origin: Tibet
Present locations: south China, Thailand, Myanmar
Economy: rice, corn, opium
Belief system: theistic animism (supreme deity is Geusha); some groups are Christian
Cultural characteristics: black-and-red jackets with narrow skirts for women, bright green or blue-green baggy trousers for men. The Lahu tend to live at about 1000m altitude. They are known to be excellent hunters, and in fact the Thai term for this tribe, *musoe*, is derived from a Burmese word meaning 'hunter'.

Houses are built of wood, bamboo and grass, and usually stand on short wooden posts. Intricately woven Lahu shoulder bags *(yâam)* are prized by collectors. Lahu food is probably the spiciest of all the hill-tribe cuisines. There are five main groups – Red Lahu, Black Lahu, White Lahu, Yellow Lahu and Lahu Sheleh.

Lisu *(Lisaw)*

Pop 28,000
Origin: Tibet
Present locations: Thailand, Yunnan
Economy: rice, opium, corn, livestock
Belief system: animism with ancestor worship and spirit possession
Cultural characteristics: the women wear long multicoloured tunics over trousers and sometimes black turbans with tassels. Men wear baggy green or blue pants pegged in at the ankles. Premarital sex is said to be common (although some observers dispute this), along with freedom in choosing marital partners. Patrilineal clans have pan-tribal jurisdiction, which makes the Lisu unique among hill-tribe groups (most of which have power centred with either a shaman or a village headman). Lisu villages are usually in the mountains at about 1000m. Homes are built on the ground, rather than on stilts, and consist mostly of bamboo and grass. Older homes – today quite rare – may be made from mud brick or mud-and-bamboo thatch.

TOM COCKREM

Bottom: Detail of Lisu tribal costume in the hill village of Pan Baek

Mien *(Yao)*

Pop 40,300
Origin: central China
Present locations: Thailand, south China, Laos, Myanmar, Vietnam
Economy: rice, corn, opium
Belief system: animism with ancestor worship and Taoism
Cultural characteristics: women wear trousers and black jackets with intricately embroidered patches and red fur-like collars, along with large dark blue or black turbans. The Mien have been heavily influenced by Chinese traditions and they use Chinese characters to write their language. The Mien tend to settle near mountain springs at between 1000m and 1200m. Kinship is patrilineal and marriage is polygamous. The Mien are highly skilled at crafts such as embroidery and silversmithing.

Hmong *(Mong or Maew)*

Pop 124,000
Origin: south China
Present locations: south China, Thailand, Laos, Vietnam
Economy: rice, corn, opium
Belief system: animism
Cultural characteristics: tribespeople wear simple black jackets and indigo or black baggy trousers (White Hmong) with striped borders or indigo skirts (Blue Hmong) and silver jewellery. Sashes may be worn around the waist, and embroidered aprons draped front and back. Most women wear their hair in a large bun. They usually live on mountain peaks or plateaus above 1000m. Houses, made of wood or thatch, sit on the ground. Kinship is patrilineal and polygamy is permitted. The Hmong are Thailand's second-largest hill-tribe group and are especially numerous in Chiang Mai Province.

Karen *(Yang or Kariang)*

Pop 322,000
Origin: Myanmar
Present locations: Thailand, Myanmar
Economy: rice, vegetables, livestock
Belief system: animism, Buddhism, Christianity, depending on the group
Cultural characteristics: thickly woven V-neck tunics of various colours (unmarried women wear white). Kinship is matrilineal and marriage is monogamous. They tend to live in lowland valleys and practise crop rotation rather than swidden agriculture. Karen homes are built on low stilts or posts, with the roofs swooping quite low. There are four distinct Karen groups – the Skaw (or White) Karen, Pwo Karen, Pa-O (or Black) Karen and Kayah (or Red) Karen. These groups combined form the largest hill tribe in Thailand, numbering about half of all hill-tribe people.

CHRIS MELLOR

Visiting Villages

When visiting hill-tribe villages, try to find out what the local customs and taboos are, either by asking someone or by taking the time to observe local behaviour. Here are several other guidelines for minimising the impact you can have on local communities:

- Always ask for permission before taking photos of tribespeople and/or their dwellings. You can ask through your guide or by using sign language. Because of traditional belief systems, many individuals and even whole tribes may object strongly to being photographed.
- Show respect for religious symbols and rituals. Don't touch totems at village entrances or any other object of obvious symbolic value without asking permission. Unless you're asked to participate, keep your distance from ceremonies.
- Exercise restraint in giving things to tribespeople or bartering with them. If you want to give something to the people you encounter on a trek, the best thing is to make a donation to the village school or other community fund. Your guide can help arrange this. While it's an easy way to get a smile – giving sweets to children contributes to tooth decay – remember they probably don't have toothbrushes and toothpaste like you do.
- Set a good example to hill-tribe youngsters by not smoking opium or using other drugs.
- Don't litter while trekking or staying in villages.

You might also want to check the 'Guidelines for Visitors to Northern Thailand's Mountain Peoples' at W www.lanna.com/html/tourists.html.

Top: An Akha tribeswoman in traditional clothing, smoking a pipe

[Continued from page 416]

Mae Hong Son Province

Thailand's most northwestern province is a crossroads for ethnic minorities (mostly Karen, with some Hmong, Lisu and Lahu), Shan (known locally as Thai Yai) and Burmese immigrants. Reportedly 75% of the province consists of mountains and forest.

As the province is so far from the influence of sea winds and is thickly forested and mountainous, the temperature seldom rises above 40°C, while in January the temperature can drop to 2°C. The air is often misty with ground fog in the winter and smoke from slash-and-burn agriculture in the hot season.

The Mae Hong Son province has undergone a tourist miniboom over the last decade, with many resorts opening in the area around the capital. Few visitors seem to leave the beaten Mae Hong Son–Soppong–Pai track, however.

MAE HONG SON PROVINCE

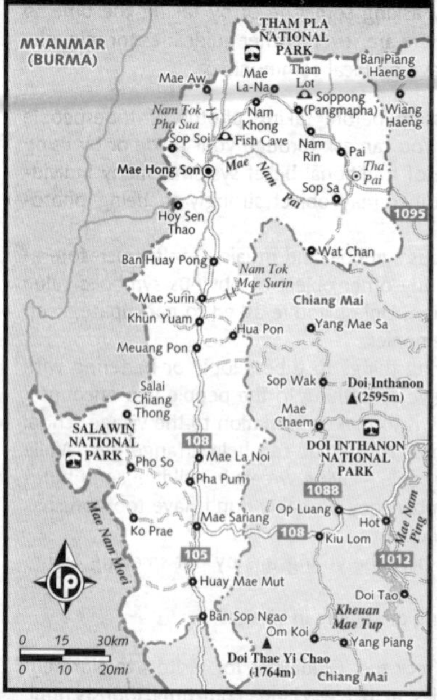

MAE SARIANG & KHUN YUAM

แม่สะเรียง/ขุนยวม

postcode 58110 • pop 7800

Many of the hill-tribe settlements in Mae Hong Son Province are concentrated in the districts and towns of Khun Yuam, Mae La Noi and Mae Sariang, which are good departure points for treks to Hmong, Karen and Shan villages. Of these three small towns, Mae Sariang is the largest and offers the most facilities for use as a base.

Although there is not much to see in Mae Sariang, it's a pleasant riverside town with a small travel scene. Two Burmese-Shan temples, **Wat Jong Sung** (Uthayarom) and **Wat Si Bunruang**, just off Mae Sariang's main street (not far from the Mae Sariang bus station), are worth a visit if you have time. Built in 1896, Wat Jong Sung is the more interesting of the two temples and has slender, Shan-style *chedi* and wooden monastic buildings.

About 5km outside Khun Yuan to the west, atmospheric **Wat To Phae** sits alongside a country stream and boasts a Mon-style stupa, antique wooden monks' residences and immaculate Burmese-style *wihǎan*. Inside the latter, take a look at the large, 150-year-old Burmese *kalaga* (embroidered and sequined tapestry) that's kept behind curtains to one side of the main altar. The tapestry depicts a scene from the Vessantara Jataka and local devotees believe one accrues merit simply by viewing it.

Guesthouses in Mae Sariang can arrange day and overnight **boat trips** on **Mae Nam Salawin** that include stops in Karen villages and **Mae Sam Laep**. You can take a boat upriver from Mae Sam Laep to **Salawin National Park**, a 722-sq-km protected area established in 1994. The boat trip takes about half an hour to reach the park headquarters. There are no lodgings, but in the dry season you can pitch a **tent** for free on a white-sand beach, called **Hat Thaen Kaew**, along the river in front of the park offices. There are good views of the river and Myanmar from the park headquarters. The park is heavily forested in teak, Asian redwood and cherrywood.

About 36km southeast of Mae Sariang at **Ban Mae Waen** is **Pan House** *(rooms per person 50B)*, where a guide named T Weerapan (Mr Pan) leads local treks. Ban Mae Waen itself is a mixed Thai/Karen village in

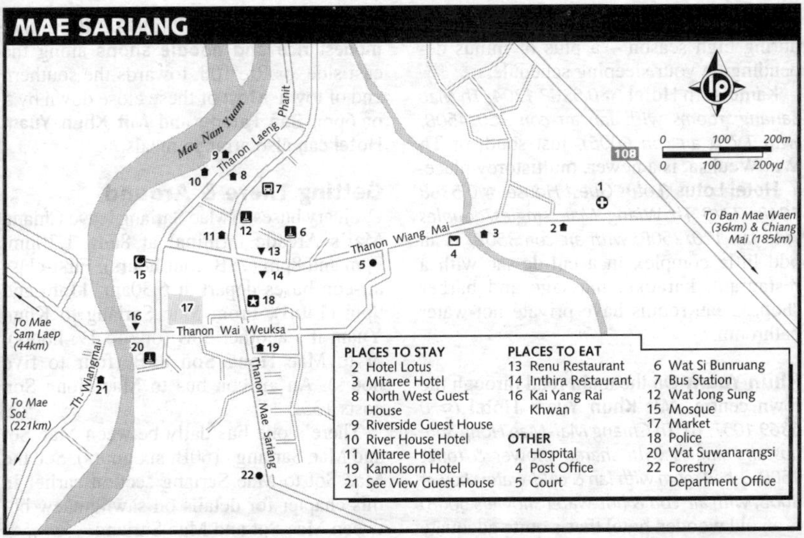

the middle of a Karen district. To get there, take a Chiang Mai-bound bus east on Rte 108 and get out at the Km 68 marker. Ban Mae Waen is a 5km walk south along a mountain ridge and (during the rainy season) across a couple of streams. If you're driving, 4WD will be necessary if the road is wet.

On the slopes of **Doi Mae U Khaw**, 25km from Khun Yuam via upgraded Rte 1263, is a Hmong village (Ban Mae U Khaw) and the 250m **Nam Tok Mae Surin** (50km northeast of Khun Yuam), reportedly Thailand's highest cataract. The area blooms with scenic *bua thawng* ('golden lotus', more like a sunflower than a lotus) in November; this is also the best time to view the waterfall.

Places to Stay

Mae Sariang Near the bus station, **Mitaree Hotel** *(☎ 0 5368 1110; Th Mae Sariang; old-wing singles/doubles 120/200B, new-wing rooms 250B, with air-con 400B)* is the oldest hotel in Mae Sariang. It has rooms in the old wooden wing (called the Mitaree Guest House) or rooms with hot-water shower in the new wing. The old wing is popular with Thai truckers.

Mitaree Hotel *(☎ 0 5368 1109; 24 Th Wiang Mai; singles/doubles with cold-water shower 120/150B, with hot-water shower 190/200-250B, with air-con 300/400B, cottages 600-1200B)*, near the post office, is another Mitaree Hotel run by the same family and sometimes referred to as 'New Mitaree'. The newer, wooden 'resort' cottages at the back have sitting areas in front, air-con and TV.

Riverside Guest House *(☎ 0 5368 1188; Th Laeng Phanit; singles/doubles 100/150B, with bath & river view 300/350B)*, by Mae Nam Yuam, is on a street that is incorrectly spelt on local street signs as 'Rang Phanich'. It's efficiently run and has basic rooms. There's a pleasant sitting and dining area overlooking the river.

North West Guest House *(☎ 0 5368 1956, fax 0 5368 1353; Th Laeng Phanit; singles/doubles 90/160B)*, on the opposite side of the street, offers rooms in a large wooden house. **River House Hotel** *(☎ 0 5362 1201, fax 0 5362 1202; ⓔ riverhouse@hotmail.com; 77 Th Laeng Phanit; fan rooms off the river 400B, air-con on the river 600B)* is a new, all-wooden place on the river under the same ownership as North West Guest House. Although the rooms here look nice at first glance, they're poorly ventilated.

See View Guest House *(☎ 0 5368 1556; rooms with fan/air-con 200/400B, bungalows 300B)* on the western side of Mae Nam Yuam, offers rooms with private hot-water shower in a row house far back from the river. Less attractive overpriced bungalows closer to the river are available. The open-air Old House **restaurant** on the premises sometimes features live Thai country music during high season – a plus or minus depending on your sleeping schedule.

Kamolsorn Hotel *(☎ 0 5368 1204; Th Mae Sariang; rooms with fan/air-con 350/450B, with TV & air-con 600B)*, just south of Th Wai Weuksa, is a newer, multistorey place.

Hotel Lotus *(Lotus Guest House; ☎ 0 5368 1048; 73/5 Th Wiang Mai; singles/doubles with fan 120/250B, with air-con 350B)* is an odd little complex in a cul-de-sac with a restaurant, karaoke, massage and barber shop. Clean rooms have private hot-water bathroom.

Khun Yuam On the main road through the town centre, **Mit Khun Yuam Hotel** *(☎ 0 5369 1057; 61 Th Chiang Mai-Mae Hong Son; upstairs singles with shared shower & toilet 150B, 3-bed room with fan & cold-water shower 300B, with air-con & hot-water showers 500B)* is an old wooden hotel that's quite adequate for a short stay.

Ban Farang *(☎ 0 5362 2086, 0 5369 1023; 499 Th Ratburana; dorm beds 50B, rooms 200B, bungalows 250-350B)* is a clean and friendly place off the main road towards the northern end of town (look for the signs). There are dorm beds, rooms in a row house with private facilities and newer bungalows.

Rustic accommodation is available at the Hmong village of **Mae U Khaw**, between Khun Yuam and Nam Tok Mae Surin.

Places to Eat

Riverside Guest House and **River House Hotel** in Mae Sariang (see Places to Stay earlier in this section) each serve relatively inexpensive Thai and *faràng* dishes in pleasant dining areas overlooking the river.

Inthira Restaurant *(Th Wiang Mai; dishes 30-75B; open 10am-10pm daily)* is the town's most popular restaurant. It features the standard Thai and Chinese dishes. **Renu Restaurant** *(Th Wiang Mai; dishes 30-75B; open 10am-11pm)*, across the street from Inthira and decorated with photos of King Bhumibol playing saxophone, offers such menu delights as 'nut-hatch curry'. Both restaurants have English menus.

At the foot of the bridge crossing towards See View Guest House, you'll find **Kai Yang Rai Khwan** *(dishes 10-50B; open 10am-5pm daily)* a great spot for Isan-style grilled chicken, sticky rice and *sôm tam*.

In Khun Yuam you'll find a collection of modest **rice and noodle shops** along the east side, or Rte 108, towards the southern end of town. Most of these close down by 5 or 6pm. **Ban Farang** and **Mit Khun Yuam Hotel** can also arrange meals.

Getting There & Around

Ordinary buses to Mae Sariang leave Chiang Mai's Arcade terminal at 8am, 1.30pm, 3pm and 8pm (78B, four hours). First-class air-con buses depart at 6.30am, 11am and 9pm (140B). From Mae Sariang to Khun Yuam it's another 50B (one to 1½ hours), or to Mae Hong Son 85B (four to five hours). An air-con bus to Mae Hong Son costs 135B.

There's one bus daily between Mae Sot and Mae Sariang (160B, six hours). See the Mae Sot to Mae Sariang section earlier in this chapter for details on sǎwngthǎew between Mae Sot and Mae Sariang.

Destinations anywhere in town are 10B by motorcycle taxi.

MAE HONG SON

อ.เมืองแม่ฮ่องสอน

postcode 58000 • pop 7400

Surrounded by mountains and punctuated by small but picturesque Nong Jong Kham (Jong Kham Lake), this provincial capital is still relatively peaceful despite the intrusion of daily flights from Chiang Mai. Much of the capital's prosperity is due to its supply of rice and consumer goods to the drug lords across the border. It has also become part of northern Thailand's standard tourist scene, with plenty of guesthouses, hotels and resorts in the area, most of them catering to Thais. The town's population is predominantly Shan. Several Karen and Shan villages in the vicinity can be visited as day trips, and farther afield are Lisu, Lahu and Musoe villages.

Mae Hong Son is best visited between November and March when the town is at its most beautiful. During the rainy season (June to October) travel in the province can be difficult because there are few paved roads. During the hot season, the Mae Pai valley fills with smoke from slash-and-burn agriculture. The only problem with going in the cool season is that the nights are downright cold – you'll need at least one thick sweater and a good pair of socks for mornings and evenings and a sleeping bag or several blankets.

Information

Tourist Offices Tourist brochures and maps can be picked up at the **TAT office** (*☎ 0 5362 3016; Th Khumlum Praphat; open 8.30am-4.30pm Mon-Fri*), in an old two-storey wooden building opposite the post office.

At the **tourist police office** (*☎ 0 5361 1812, emergency ☎ 1155; Th Singhanat Bamrung; open 8.30am-9.30pm daily*) you can report mishaps or lodge complaints against guesthouses and trek operators.

Money Foreign-exchange services are available at **Bangkok Bank, Kasikornbank** and **Bank of Ayudhya**, all located along Th Khunlum Praphat in the centre of town. Bangkok Bank and Kasikornbank have ATMs.

Post & Communications The Mae Hong Son **main post office** (*Th Khunlum Praphat; open 8.30am-4.30pm Mon-Fri, closed holidays*) is towards the southern end of Th Khunlum Praphat. International telephone service is available at the attached **CAT office** – hours are the same as the post office.

There's a Lenso International Phonecard telephone outside the entrance to the post office. A separate **CAT office** (*Th Udom Chow*), west of Pa Dim restaurant, also offers international phone service along with Internet access.

MAE HONG SON

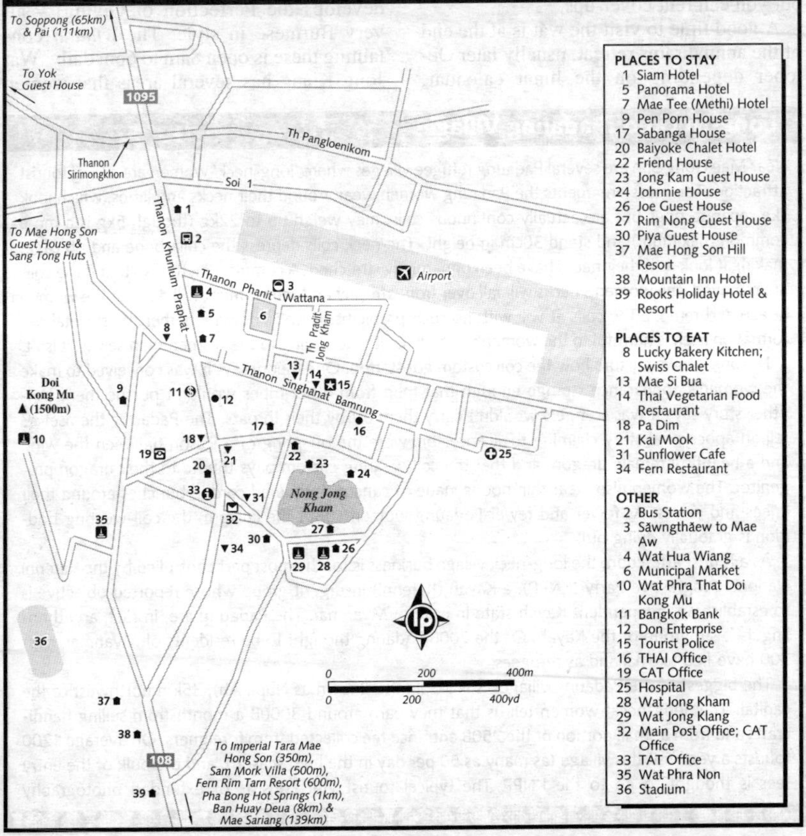

Several places around town, including **Sunflower Café** (see Places to Eat later in this Mae Hong Son section), provide Internet access by the minute.

Wat Phra That Doi Kong Mu

วัดพระธาตุดอยกองมู

Climb the hill west of town, Doi Kong Mu (1500m), to visit this Shan-built wát, also known as Wat Phai Doi. The view of the sea of fog that collects in the valley each morning is impressive; at other times of the day you get a view of the town. Two Shan stupas, erected in 1860 and 1874, enshrine the ashes of monks from Myanmar's Shan State. Around the back of the wát you can see a tall, slender, standing Buddha and catch views west of the ridge. No shorts or miniskirts are permitted in the wát grounds, but you can rent cover-ups.

A good time to visit the wát is at the end of the annual rains retreat, usually later October depending on the lunar calendar, when it fills with townspeople making merit by bringing food to feed a large number of monks.

Wat Jong Kham & Wat Jong Klang

วัดจองคำ/วัดจองกลาง

Next to Nong Jong Kham in the southern part of town are a couple of mildly interesting Burmese-style wát – Wat Jong Kham and Wat Jong Klang.

Wat Jong Kham was built nearly 200 years ago by Thai Yai (Shan) people, who make up about 50% of the population of Mae Hong Son Province. Wat Jong Klang houses 100-year-old glass Jataka paintings and has small rooms full of wooden reliefs and figures depicting the Vessantara Jataka (the popular Jataka in which the Bodhisattva develops the Perfection of Giving) – all very Burmese in style. The *wíhăan* containing these is open 8am to 6pm daily. Wat Jong Klang has several areas that women

'Long-Necked' Padaung Villages

Near Mae Hong Son are several Padaung refugee villages where 'long-neck' women are a local tourist attraction. The brass ornaments the Padaung women wear around their necks and limbs, which look like separate rings but are actually continuous coils, may weigh up to 22kg (though 5kg is a more common maximum) and stand 30cm in height. The neck coils depress the collarbone and rib cage, making it look as if their necks have been unnaturally stretched. A common myth says that if the coils are removed, the women's necks will fall over from atrophy and the woment will die, but the women attach and remove the coils at will with no such problems. It isn't known whether the skeletal deformation itself is harmful to the women's overall health; according to the women themselves, it isn't.

No-one knows for sure how the coil custom got started. One theory says it was conceived to make the women's appearance strange enough that men from other tribes wouldn't pursue them. Another story says it was so tigers wouldn't carry them off by their throats. The Padaung themselves tell an apocryphal story claiming their ancestors were the offspring of a liaison between the wind and a beautiful female dragon, and that the coil-wearing custom pays tribute to their dragon progenitor. The women also wear thin hoops made of cane or lacquered cord in bunches around their knees and calves. As fewer and fewer Padaung women adopt the custom, the coil-wearing tradition is gradually dying out.

As a tourist attraction, the long-neck village business is for the most part controlled by the Karenni National Progressive Party (KNPP), a Kayah (Karenni) insurgent group whose reported objective is to establish an independent Kayah state in eastern Myanmar. The Padaung are, in fact, an ethnolinguistic subgroup of the Kayah. Of the 7000 Padaung thought to be residents of Myanmar, over 300 have fled to Thailand as refugees.

The biggest of the Padaung villages is Nai Soi (also known as Nupa Ah), 35km northwest of the capital. The 'long-neck' women tell us that they earn around 3000B a month from selling handicrafts and from a small portion of the 250B entrance fee collected from foreigners. On average 1200 tourists a year visit this village (as many as 50 per day in the high season), and the bulk of the entry fees is thought to go to the KNPP. The typical tourist visit consists of extended photography are forbidden to enter – not unusual for Burmese-Shan Buddhist temples.

Wat Hua Wiang

วัดหัวเวียง

Although its wooden *bòt* (central sanctuary) is in an advanced state of decay, a famous bronze Buddha in the Mandalay style, called **Chao Phlalakhaeng**, can be seen in this wát *(Th Phanit Wattana)*, east of Th Khunlum Praphat.

Trekking

Trekking trips can be arranged at several guesthouses and travel agencies; **Mae Hong Son Guest House** has some of the most dependable and experienced guides. Guides at **Don Enterprise** *(☎ 0 5361 2236; 77/1 Th Khumlum Praphat)*, in the back of the night-market building, and **Sunflower Café** have also received good reviews. Typical rates for most treks are around 600B to 700B per day per person (if there are four or more people), with three to five days the normal duration. Popular routes include the Mae Pai valley, Khun Yuam district and north of Soppong. A straightforward six-day trek from east of Mae Hong Son to near Soppong costs 400B per day per person. As with trekking elsewhere in the north, be sure to clarify when a trek starts and stops or you may not get your money's worth. Nearby Karen villages can be visited without a guide by walking two hours outside of town – several guesthouses in town can provide a map.

Rafting

Raft trips on the nearby Mae Pai are gaining in popularity, and the same guesthouses and trekking agencies that organise treks from Mae Hong Son can arrange the river trips. The most common type of trip sets off from Tha Mae Pai (Pai River Pier) in **Ban Huay Deua**, 8km southwest of Mae Hong Son, for a day-long upriver journey of 5km. From the same pier, down-river trips to the 'long-neck' village of **Kariang Padawng**

'Long-Necked' Padaung Villages

sessions during which the coil-adorned Padaung women pose while weaving, or standing next to visitors. The women tell reporters they aren't bothered by the photography, which they consider to be part of their livelihood. As Nai Soi's Ma Nang was quoted in one of several stories the *Bangkok Post* has run on the Padaung, 'We had nothing in Myanmar. I had to work relentlessly in the rice fields. We miss our homes, but we don't want to go back.'

Opinions are sharply divided as to the ethics of 'consuming' the Padaung as a tourist attraction. Obviously there's the claim that the viewing of the long-necked Padaung in Thailand amounts to crass exploitation, but those who have taken the time to interview these people and learn about their lives have pointed out that this is the best opportunity they have available for making a living under current social conditions in Myanmar and Thailand. One thing seems certain: they are usually in Thailand by choice, having fled a potentially worse fate in Myanmar amid ethnic war. Thai authorities view Nai Soi as a self-sustaining refugee camp.

We see the long-neck phenomenon as sitting squarely on the same cline of ethnotourism as tribal trekking, one of the crasser forms to be sure, but only differing in degree from paying an Akha or a Guatemalan Indian to pose for a photo. Ethically it surely beats paying a trek operator for the privilege of photographing tribal people on a trek when the latter receive nothing.

If you want to see any of the Padaung settlements, you can choose among Hoy Sen Thao (11km west of Mae Hong Son, 20 minutes by boat from the nearby Ban Huay Deua landing), Nai Soi (35km northwest) and Huay Ma Khen Som (about 7km before Mae Aw). Travel agencies in Mae Hong Son arrange tours to these villages for 700B to 800B per person, which means they take in 450B to 550B over the village entry fees to pay for transport and expenses.

If you go to Nai Soi on your own, it's possible to arrange overnight accommodation in the village for 50B per person a night. At the entrance to the village your name, passport number and country of residence will be noted on a payment receipt issued by the 'Karenni Culture Department'. A couple of hundred metres beyond Nai Soi is a large Kayah refugee settlement, also controlled by the KNPP.

Kekongdu (Hoy Sen Thao) on the Thailand-Myanmar border are also possible. Another popular raft route runs between **Sop Soi** (10km northwest of town) and the village of **Soppong** to the west (not to be confused with the larger Shan trading village of the same name to the east). These day trips typically cost 500B per person if arranged in Ban Huay Deua, or 800B to 1200B if done through a Mae Hong Son agency.

The Mae Pai raft trips can be good fun if the raft holds up – it's not uncommon for rafts to fall apart or sink. The Myanmar trip, which attracts travellers who want to see the Padaung or 'long-necked' people, is a bit of a rip-off and, to some, exploitative – a four-hour trip through unspectacular scenery to see a few Padaung people who have fled to Mae Hong Son to escape an ethnic war in Myanmar. When there is fighting between Shan armies and Yangon troops in the area this trip may not be possible.

Special Events

Wat Jong Klang and Wat Jong Kham are the focal point of the **Poi Sang Long Festival** in March, when young Shan boys are ordained as novice monks during the school holidays in the ceremony known as *bùat lûuk kâew*. Like elsewhere in Thailand, the ordinands are carried on the shoulders of friends or relatives and paraded around the wát under festive parasols, but in the Shan custom the boys are dressed in ornate costumes (rather than simple white robes) and wear flower headdresses and facial make-up. Sometimes they ride on ponies.

Another important local event is the **Jong Para Festival**, held towards the end of the **Buddhist Rains Retreat** in October (three days before the full moon of the 11th lunar month – so it varies from year to year). The festival begins with local Shan bringing offerings to monks in the temples in a procession marked by the carrying of models of castles on poles. An important part of the festival is the folk theatre and dance, which is performed on the wát grounds, some of it unique to northwest Thailand.

During **Loi Krathong** – a national holiday usually celebrated by floating *kràthong* (small lotus floats) on the nearest pond, lake or river – Mae Hong Son residents launch balloons called *kràthong sàwăn* (heaven kràthong) from Doi Kong Mu.

Places to Stay – Budget

Guesthouses The town's first guest house, **Mae Hong Son Guest House** *(☎ 0 5361 2510; 295 Th Makasanti; rooms 100-150B, bungalows 250-500B)* has a secluded location on the northwestern outskirts of town (about 700m west of Th Khunlum Praphat). Rooms in a wooden longhouse have shared bathroom, bungalows have private bathroom. The guesthouse is a good source of information and inexpensive meals.

Sang Tong Huts *(☎ 0 5362 0680; e sangtonghuts@hotmail.com; huts with bath 500-1500B, without bath 350B)*, in the hills nearby, is equally secluded and has panoramic views. The setting is pretty and the huts have been renovated fairly recently. Smaller huts have shared facilities and there are nicely furnished huts with lots of windows, a balcony, fridge and spacious bathroom with hot-water shower. Set dinners are available in the dining area, with menus in English and German. Hill-tribe coffee and wine are also available.

Yok Guest House *(☎ 0 5361 1532; 14 Th Sirimongkhon; rooms with fan/air-con 250/400B)* is a small, very quiet, family-run place with nine super-clean rooms around a courtyard parking area. is on the right, if you continue northwest along this same road another 300m, past a wát. It has super-clean rooms around a courtyard parking area. All rooms have private hot-water shower. There are also a couple of rooms without carpet for 200B.

In the area of Nong Jong Kham are several very pleasant guesthouses. **Jong Kam Guest House** *(☎ 0 5361 1150; Th Pradit Jong Kham; singles/doubles 100/200B, double hut with hot-water bath 250B)* overlooks the lake from the north and has slightly worn but clean rooms in a row house plus some newer thatched huts, all with shared facilities.

Friend House *(☎ 0 5362 0119, fax 0 5362 0060; 20 Th Pradit Jong Kham; singles/doubles 100B, doubles with bath 250B, rooms for up to 4 300B)* has large clean rooms in a teak house. Singles and doubles have fan and shared hot-water shower, or there are doubles, which can accommodate up to four, with fan and attached bathroom. Upstairs rooms have a view of the lake. Friend House also rents out motorcycles. **Johnnie House** *(Th Pradit Jong Kham; singles/doubles without bath 80/100B, rooms with hot-water shower*

120B), northeast of Nong Jong Kam is a wooden row house with clean rooms.

Piya Guest House *(☎ 0 5361 1260; 1/1 Th Khunlum Praphat; rooms with air-con 600B)*, on the southwestern side of the lake, features good-sized rooms built around a garden and a bar/restaurant in front. All rooms have wood floors, private hot-water showers and air-con. **Sabanga House** *(☎ 0 5361 2280; 14 Th Udom Chaonithet; rooms 100B)*, farther north, is a basic bamboo row house; it has eight rooms with a mattress on the floor, fan and shared hot-water shower.

Rim Nong Guest House *(☎ 0 5361 1052; 4 Th Chamnan Sathit; dorm beds 120B, rooms with shared facilities 250B, one air-con room 500B)*, on the southern side of the lake, is a friendly place with a little **restaurant** on the water's edge. Somewhat cramped rooms have shared hot-water bathroom. **Joe Guest House** *(☎ 0 5361 2417; rooms without/with bath 100/250B)* occupies an old teak house across the street from the Rim Nong.

Pen Porn House *(☎/fax 0 5361 1577; 16/1 Th Wat Muay To; doubles/quads 250/400B)*, on the road to Wat Phra That Doi Kong Mu, sits in a residential neighbourhood on a slope on the western side of town. Clean, spacious row-house rooms have fan and private hot-water shower.

Other less-convenient places can be found around Mae Hong Son – the touts will find you at the bus station.

Hotels Most of the hotels in Mae Hong Son are along the main north-south road, Th Khunlum Praphat.

Siam Hotel *(☎ 0 5361 2148; 23 Th Khunlum Praphat; singles/doubles with fan 170/250B, rooms with air-con 350B)*, next to the bus station, has overpriced ordinary rooms.

Mae Tee Hotel *(Methi; ☎ 0 5361 2141, 0 5361 1141; 55 Th Khunlum Praphat; 1-bed/2-bed rooms with fan 150/160B, 1-bed/3-bed rooms with air-con 300/400B)*, farther south, is better value.

Places to Stay – Mid-Range & Top End

Panorama Hotel *(☎ 0 5361 1757, fax 0 5361 1790; 51 Th Khunlum Praphat; singles/doubles with fan 400/500B, rooms with air-con 800B)* has rooms with fan and hot-water shower or a simple, clean room with fridge, TV, air-con and hot-water shower.

Baiyoke Chalet Hotel *(☎ 0 5361 1486, fax 0 5361 1533; 90 Th Khunlum Praphat; rooms 1330B)*, towards the southern end of town near the post office, offers all the typical amenities. Low-season rates are 40% less, and breakfast is included. **Mountain Inn Hotel** *(☎ 0 5361 2284, fax 0 5361 1309; 112 Th Khunlum Praphat; rooms in low season 500-600B, in high season 800B)* is farther south and larger than Baiyoke Chalet. It has clean, medium-sized, air-con singles and doubles, with hot water, around a courtyard. The price also includes breakfast. The Mountain Inn has well-kept, nicely landscaped public areas.

Mae Hong Son Hill Resort *(☎/fax 0 5361 2475; 106/2 Th Khunlum Praphat; bungalows with fan/air-con 400/500B)*, near the stadium, is a quiet spot with 22 well-kept bungalows partially surrounded by gardens.

Rooks Holiday Hotel & Resort *(☎ 0 5361 2324, fax 0 5361 1524; ⓔ rooksgroup@hotmail.com; 114/5-7 Th Khunlum Praphat; rooms & bungalows 1800-2200B)* is a bit farther south, and definitely represents the top end in town, with rooms and bungalows. Facilities include a swimming pool, tennis courts, disco, snooker club, bakery, coffee shop and restaurant.

Out of Town Southwest of town a few kilometres towards Ban Huay Deua and Ban Tha Pong Daeng on the river are several 'resorts', which in the Thai sense of the term means any hotel near a rural or semirural area. **Imperial Tara Mae Hong Son Hotel** *(☎ 0 5361 1021–4, fax 0 5361 1252; ⓔ taramaehongson@imperialhotels.com; singles/doubles 3000/3500B)* is an upmarket, 104-room place with doubles (less than the listed rate if you request a discount) along with a pool, sauna and fitness centre.

Fern Rim Tarn Resort *(☎ 0 5361 1374, fax 0 5361 2363; ⓔ fernresort@maehongsontourism.net; 64 Mu Bo, Tambon Pha Bong; bungalows 950-1500B)* is about 5km southwest of town via Rte 108 and a turn-off for Ban Hua Nam Mae Sakut. This eco-friendly resort features Shan-style wooden bungalows adjacent to rice paddies; rates include breakfast. Low-season discounts are readily available, and there are good walks in the vicinity. A shuttle runs four times daily to the resort from the Fern Restaurant in town.

Farther off the highway, a couple more mid-range places worth considering are **Mae Hong Son Riverside Hotel** *(☎ 0 5361 1504, 0 5361 1406; Mu 3, Ban Huay Toe, Tambon Pha Bong; doubles from 1150B, discount rate 750B)* and **Sam Mork Villa** *(☎ 0 5361 1478; Tambon Pha Bong; doubles with fan/air-con from 500/800B)*.

Places to Eat

Mae Hong Son isn't known for its food, but there are a few decent places to eat besides the guesthouses. **Kai Mook** *(Khai Muk; ☎ 0 5361 2092; 23 Th Udom Chaonithet; dishes 25-60B; open 10am-2pm & 5pm-midnight daily)*, an outdoor restaurant just off Th Khunlum Praphat, is one of the better Thai-Chinese restaurants in town. The extensive menu includes house specialities such as *pèt yâang náam phêung* (roast duck with honey gravy), *plaa châwn sâi ùa* (serpent-headed fish with northern Thai sausage) and *yam bai kùt* (yam with fern leaves).

Fern Restaurant *(Th Khunlum Praphat; dishes 40-80B; open 10am-10pm daily)*, south of the post office, is another excellent, long-running spot. Specialities at Fern include *chùu-chìi kûng* (shrimp in a succulent curry sauce) and *hèt hǎwm òp sii-íu* (mushrooms baked in soy sauce and served with a roasted garlic sauce).

Pa Dim *(Th Khunlum Praphat; dishes 20-40B; open 8am-8pm daily)*, diagonally opposite Kai Mook, is a restaurant with dishes from every region in Thailand; it's popular because of its low prices and good-sized portions.

Thai Vegetarian Food Restaurant *(Th Singhanat Bamrung; dishes 10-30B; open 9am-3pm Mon-Sat)*, next to the tourist police office, serves inexpensive vegetarian Thai (as well as some nonvegetarian dishes). Nearby, on the same side of the street, **Mae Si Bua** *(Thai Yai Food; Th Singhanat Bamrung; dishes 15-35B; open 10am-6pm daily)* offers delicious Shan and northern Thai food.

Lucky Bakery Kitchen *(Th Singhanat Bamrung; dishes 40-100B; open 8am-9pm daily)*, west of Th Khunlum Praphat, does 'cowboy steak' and baked goods. **Swiss Chalet** *(☎ 0 5361 2050; dishes 40-80B; open 7am-1am daily)*, next door to Lucky Bakery, serves cheese fondue, roesti and pasta.

Sunflower Café *(Th Udom Chaonithet; dishes 20-100B; open 7.30-9pm daily)*, near the post office, offers fresh-baked, whole-wheat breads and cakes, pizzas and good coffee, plus information on local trekking.

Getting There & Away

Air THAI flies to Mae Hong Son from Chiang Mai three times daily (420B, 35 minutes). For many people, the time saved flying to Mae Hong Son versus bus travel is worth the extra money. Mae Hong Son has a **THAI office** *(☎ 0 5361 1297, 0 5361 1194; 71 Th Singhanat Bamrung; open 8am-5pm Mon-Fri)*.

Bus From Chiang Mai there are two bus routes to Mae Hong Son: the 270km northern route through Pai (100B ordinary, 147B air-con, seven to eight hours) and the 368km southern route through Mae Sariang (145B ordinary, 261B air-con, eight to nine hours). The fare is 78/140B as far as Mae Sariang.

Although it may be longer, the southern route through Mae Sariang is a much more comfortable ride because the bus stops every two hours for a 10- to 15-minute break and larger buses – with large seats – are used. Buses to Mae Hong Son via Mae Sariang leave Chiang Mai's Arcade bus station five times daily between 6.30am and 9pm. In the reverse direction, ordinary buses leave Mae Hong Son for Chiang Mai at 8am, 2pm, 8pm and 9pm; air-con buses depart at 6am, 10.30am and 9pm.

The Pai bus leaves the Chiang Mai Arcade station four times a day at 7am, 9am and 10.30am and 12.30pm. In the opposite direction, buses leave Mae Hong Son at 7am, 8.30am, 10.30am, 12.30pm and 4pm. The 4pm bus only goes as far as Pai. An air-con van (Pai 100B, Chiang Mai 200B) departs Mae Hong Son at 8am.

Buses to Soppong cost 35B (air-con 46B, one to 1½ hours), to Khun Yuam 35B (one to 1½ hours) and to Pai 53B (three hours).

The northern route through Pai, originally built by the Japanese in WWII, is very winding and offers spectacular views from time to time. Because the buses used on this road are smaller, they're usually more crowded and the younger passengers tend to get motion sickness.

Getting Around

It is pretty easy to walk around most of Mae Hong Son. Motorcycle taxis within town cost 20B; to Doi Kong Mu it's 30B one way or 50B return. Motorcycle drivers will also take passengers farther afield but fares out of town are expensive. There are now a few túk-túk in town, charging 20B to 30B per trip.

Several guesthouses rent out bicycles (20B to 30B) and motorcycles (150B for 24 hours). **Avis Rent-A-Car** *(☎ 0 5362 0457–8)* has an office at the Mae Hong Son airport.

AROUND MAE HONG SON

Pha Bong Hot Springs

บ่อน้ำร้อนผาบ่อง

Eleven kilometres south of the capital at the Km 256 marker on Rte 108, this public park with hot springs covers 12 sq km. Facilities include bathing rooms and a couple of simple **restaurants**.

Mae Aw & Around

แม่ออ

Another day trip you can do from the provincial capital is to Mae Aw, 22km north of Mae Hong Son on a mountain peak at the Myanmar border. Mae Aw is a Chinese Kuomintang (KMT) settlement, one of the last true KMT outposts in Thailand, although it's not as interesting as Doi Mae Salong or Ban Mai Nong Bua near Doi Ang Khang. There's no feeling of 'wow an exciting place filled with old renegade fighters', just a quiet place with people who basically ignore you, but it's an interesting trip.

The town lies along the edge of a large reservoir and the faces and signs are very Chinese. Occasionally there is fighting along the border between the KMT and the Mong Tai Army, formerly led by the infamous opium warlord Khun Sa but now operating as four splinter units under separate leaderships. When this happens, public transport to these areas is usually suspended and you are advised against going without a guide. The modern Thai name for Mae Aw is Ban Rak Thai (Thai-Loving Village).

Accommodation in thatched huts is available at **Roun Thai Guest House** *(rooms per person 50B, with 2 meals 150B)* in the Chinese/ Hmong village of **Na Pa Paek**, 7.3km southwest of Mae Aw. Two small tea shops set up for tourists serve tea, cola and snacks of dubious sterility. You can also purchase a cool souvenir here – a section of bamboo filled with tea labelled 'special blend tea, made by KMT' in English, Thai and Chinese. The better of the two is **Mr Huang Yuan Tea & Restaurant**.

From Na Pa Paek a rough dirt road leads southwest to the Hmong village of **Ma Khua Som** (3.5km) and the KMT village of **Pang Ung La** (6km) on the Myanmar border. Pang Ung La also has a guesthouse.

Since the sealing of the 22km road to Na Pa Paek, trips to Mae Aw are easier, although it's still a steep, winding route. The final unsealed 7km to Mae Aw can be very troublesome in the wet season.

There are rather irregular sǎwngthǎew going back and forth from Mae Hong Son for 50B to 60B per person, but it's so unpredictable these days that you're better off getting a group of people together and chartering a sǎwngthǎew. It will cost you 600B to 1300B (depending on whether the drivers have any paid cargo). This option lets you stop and see the sights along the way. Check Th Phanit Wattana near the municipal market at around 9am to see if there are any sǎwngthǎew going.

The trip takes two hours and passes Shan, Karen and Hmong villages, the **Pang Tong Summer Palace** and **waterfalls**. Mae Aw is also included on some day tours operated out of Mae Hong Son.

If you have your own transport, you can stop off at **Nam Tok Pha Sua** on the way to Mae Aw. About 17km north of Rte 1095, turn onto a marked dirt road. The multi-levelled cataract has water year-round; during the rainy season swimming can be dangerous due to thundering water flow. Facilities include picnic tables and toilets.

Tham Pla National Park A trip to Mae Aw could be combined with a visit to the recently established Tham Pla National Park centred on the animistic Tham Pla or **Fish Cave**, a water-filled cavern where hundreds of soro brook carp thrive. These fish grow up to 1m in length and are found only in the provinces of Mae Hong Son, Ranong, Chiang Mai, Rayong, Chanthaburi and Kanchanaburi. The fish eat vegetables and insects, although the locals believe them to be vegetarian and feed them only fruit and vegetables (which can be purchased at the park entrance).

You can see the fish through a 2-sq-metre rock hole at the base of an outer wall of the cave. A **statue** of a Hindu rishi called Nara, said to protect the holy fish from danger, stands nearby.

A path leads from the park entrance to a suspension bridge that crosses a stream and continues to the cave. The park is a shady, cool place to hang out; picnic tables are available. You can pitch a **tent** for free on the grounds. Last we checked admission to the park was still free, although the general increase in national park entry fees may mean the rangers will begin charging eventually. The park is 17km northeast of Mae Hong Son on the northern side of Hwy 1095.

Mae La-Na

แม่ละนา

Between Mae Hong Son and Pai, Rte 1095 winds through an area of forests, mountains, streams, Shan and hill-tribe villages and limestone caves. Some of Mae Hong Son's most beautiful scenery is within a day's walk of the Shan village of Mae La-Na (6km north of Rte 1095 via a half-sealed road), where overnight accommodation is available. From here you can **trek** to several nearby Red and Black Lahu villages and to a few caves within a 4km to 8km radius.

It's possible to walk a 20km half loop all the way from Mae La-Na to Tham Lot and Soppong, staying overnight in Red Lahu villages along the way. Ask for a sketch map at Top Hill (see Places to Stay & Eat later in this Around Mae Hong Son section). Experienced riders can accomplish this route on a sturdy dirt bike – but not alone or during the rainy season.

Local guides will lead visitors to nearby **caves** for set prices per cave. **Tham Mae La-Na**, 4km from the village, is largest and most famous – it's threaded by a 12km length of river – and a journey to the cave and through it costs 600B. Tham Pakarang (Coral Cave), Tham Phet (Diamond Cave), Tham Khao Taek (Broken Rice Cave) and Tham Khai Muk (Pearl Cave) all feature good wall formations and cost 200B each for guides. Rates are posted at a small *săalaa* near a noodle stand and petrol barrel pumps in the centre of the village; this is also where you may contact the guides during the day. If no-one's at the *săalaa* when you go there, just mention *thâm* (cave) to someone at the petrol pumps. Some of the caves may not be accessible during the rainy season.

Even if you don't go trekking or caving, Mae La-Na can be a peaceful and mildly interesting cul-de-sac to stay for a short while. Beyond the Shan-style **Wat Mae La-Na**, a school, some houses and the aforementioned 'downtown' area around the noodle shops and petrol pumps, there's little to see, but the surrounding montane scenery is quite pleasing.

The Mae La-Na junction is 55km from Mae Hong Son, 10km from Soppong (Pangmapha) and 56km from Pai. Twenty-seven kilometres west of the three-way junction is a short turn-off for **Wat Tham Wua Sunyata**, a peaceful forest monastery. The village is 6km north of the junction. Infrequent sǎwngthǎew from the highway to the village cost 20B per person – mornings are your best bet.

Tham Lot

ถ้ำลอด

About 8km north of Soppong is Tham Lot (pronounced *thâm lâwt* and also known as *thâm náam lâwt*), a large limestone cave with a wide stream running through it. Along with Tham Nam Lang farther west, it's one of the longest known caves in mainland Southeast Asia (although some as yet unexplored caves in southern Thailand may be even longer). It is possible to hike all the way through the cave (approximately 200m) by following the stream, although it requires some wading back and forth. Apart from the main chamber, there are three side chambers that can be reached by ladders – it takes two to three hours to see the whole thing. Where the stream exits the cave, thousands of bats and swifts leave the cave at dusk.

At the **park entrance** *(open 8am-5.30pm daily)* you must hire a gas lantern and guide for 100B (one guide can lead up to four people) to take you through the caverns; they no longer permit visitors to tour the caves alone. The guide fee includes visits to the first and third caverns; to visit the second cavern you must cross the stream. Raft men waiting inside the cave charge 10B per person per crossing; in the dry season you may be able to wade across. For 100B you can stay on the raft through the third cavern. If you decide to book a Tham Lot day tour from Mae Hong Son, ask if the tour cost includes guide, lamp and raft fees.

A row of **outdoor restaurants** *(dishes 15-35B; open 9am-6pm daily)* outside the park entrance offers basic Thai fare.

Soppong
สบป่อง

Soppong is a small but relatively prosperous market village a couple of hours northwest of Pai and about 70km from Mae Hong Son. Since the paving of Rte 1095, Soppong and Tham Lot have become popular destinations for minivan tours from Mae Hong Son and Chiang Mai.

Although for many years this town was known only as Soppong, lately the Thai government has been calling it 'Pangmapha', since the Pangmapha District Office is now located here. The two names seem to be used interchangeably.

Close to Soppong are several Shan, Lisu, Karen and Lahu **villages** that can easily be visited on foot. Inquire at the Jungle Guest House or Cave Lodge in Soppong for reliable information. It's important to ask about the current situation as the Myanmar border area is somewhat sensitive due to the opium trade and smuggling.

The rough back road between Soppong and Mae La-Na is popular with mountain bikers and off-highway motorcyclists.

Coffin Caves
ถ้ำผีแมน

A 900-sq-km area of Pangmapha and adjacent districts may contain more caves than any other region in the world. Over 30 of these limestone caverns are known to contain very old wooden coffins carved from solid tree logs. Up to 6m long, the coffins are typically suspended on wooden scaffolds inside the caves and bound with ceremonial tassels (very few of which have been found intact). The coffins – which number in the dozens – are of unknown age and origin, but Thai anthropologists have classified them into at least 14 different design schemes. Pottery remains associated with the sites have also been found.

The local Thais know these burial caves as *thâm phĭi* (spirit caves), or *thâm phĭi maen* (coffin caves). The eight coffin caves that scientists are investigating at the moment are off limits to the public, but you may be able to find guides in the Pangmapha district willing to tour others. **Tham Nam Lang**, 30km northwest of Soppong near Ban Nam Khong, is 9km long and said to be one of the largest caves in the world in terms of volume.

Places to Stay & Eat

Mae La-Na & Around On a hill overlooking the village, **Top Hill** *(bungalows per person 40B)* is run by Mae La-Na's village headman. It offers OK bungalow accommodation with shared facilities. **Mae Lana Guest House** *(dorm beds 40B, doubles 80B)* is closer to the valley floor; it rents out four large doubles with mosquito nets and a four-bed dorm. Mae Lana Guest House closes during the rainy season.

Wilderness Lodge *(huts per person 50B)* is at Ban Nam Khong. The Rte 108 turn-off for Wilderness Lodge is located 25km west of Soppong.

Thai Adventure Base Camp *(☎/fax 0 5369 9111; e rafting@activethailand.com; bungalows 100B)* is a new place in Ban Nam Khong near the rafting departure point used by Thai Adventure Rafting (see Trekking, Rafting & Elephant Riding in the Pai section, later). The basic bungalows have good beds; bathing facilities are shared. A river-view **restaurant** is attached.

About 12km north of Mae La-Na in the Black Lahu village of Ban Huay Hea (close to the Myanmar border) is the **Lahu Guest House** *(rooms 50B)*, run by a village teacher who speaks English. Lodging is simple and the money goes to a community fund.

Soppong Most accommodation in the area is concentrated around Soppong, which has developed into an important stop for both day and overnight package tours. **Lemon Hill Guest House** *(rooms 200-500B)*, just off the highway near the bus stop, features nice huts facing the Nam Lan and bougainvillea tumbling over the roofs. Rooms have private or shared hot-water shower. The more expensive huts have seating areas with a river view.

From the opposite side of the road to Lemon Hill, you'll find a narrow track leads a kilometre or so (the last half is accessible by foot or bicycle only) to a footbridge over a stream, where you'll come to **Charming Home** *(singles/doubles 120/150B)*. Two well-designed, well-spaced huts with private bathroom sit on a breezy hillside backed by primary forest. There are many birds in this area and you can easily hike to Lisu and Lahu villages nearby.

Soppong River Inn *(☎ 0 5361 7107; w www.soppong.com; rooms 450-600B)* features four spacious rooms combining American Southwestern, Thai and Balinese designs, all with innovative outdoor bathrooms, right on the river.

Jungle Guest House *(☎ 0 5361 7099; singles/doubles without bath 100/120B, with bath 250/300B)*, 1km west on the road to Mae Hong Son, is friendly and offers well-designed huts with shared hot-water shower or private facilities. The relatively new **restaurant** overlooking the river serves better fare than most of the other guesthouses in the area.

Little Eden Guest House *(formerly T Rex House; ☎ 0 5361 7054, fax 0 5361 7053; w www.littleeden-guesthouse.com; bungalows 250B, rooms 350B)*, well off the road in a nice river setting, features solar hot water and a swimming pool. Nine A-frame bungalows are available; all have private toilet and hot-water shower. There are also two VIP rooms in the main house. Discounts may be available during the rainy season.

A short distance out of town towards Mae Hong Son, at Km 143, open-air **Baan Kaafae** *(dishes 20-45B; open 8am-6pm daily)* serves good fresh coffee and snacks.

Tham Lot Near Tham Lot, several guesthouses have come and gone. At the moment there are only two, both within a few hundred metres of the cave.

Cave Lodge *(☎ 0 5361 7203; dorm beds 60B, bungalows without bath 120-250B, double/quad bungalows with bath 280/350B)* is a long-running place. Guided day hikes are available for a very reasonable 350B, inflatable kayak trips for 500B.

Lang River Guest House *(dorm beds 70B, bungalow singles/doubles 150/200B)* is on the banks of the stream that runs through the cave, west of the park entrance. It's relaxed and friendly, with a large shed-like dormitory back from the river with raised, partitioned sleeping platforms, each fairly wide with a mattress, mosquito net and built-in shelves. Bungalows are by the river, while two nicer bungalows are now reserved for tour groups. Trekking guides can also be arranged here.

Ban Nam Rin At this Lisu village 10km south of Soppong towards Pai, between the Km 132 and Km 133 markers, you can stay at **Lisu Lodge** *(Chiang Mai ☎ 0 5328 1789, fax 0 5328 1788; lodging/ecotour/trekking packages from 1960B per person)*. Be sure to book ahead, as the Lisu Lodge staff say it no longer accepts walk-ins.

Getting There & Around

Pai to Mae Hong Son buses stop in Soppong and there are two or three each day in either direction. From Mae Hong Son to Soppong, buses cost 35B, (46B air-con, 2½ hours). The trip between Pai and Soppong costs 30B (35B air-con, 1½ to two hours).

Motorcycle taxis stationed at the bus stop in Soppong will carry passengers to Tham Lot or the Cave Lodge for 50B per person; private pick-up trucks will take you and up to five other people for 200B.

PAI

ปาย

postcode 58130 • pop 3000

It first appears that there's not a lot to see in Pai (pronounced like the English word 'bye', *not* 'pie'), a peaceful crossroads town about halfway between Chiang Mai and Mae Hong Son on Rte 1095. But if you stick around a few days and talk to some of the locals, you may discover some beautiful spots in the surrounding hills.

Most of the town's population are Shan and Thai, but there's also a small but visible Muslim Chinese population. Attracted by easy living and a small live music scene, Pai nowadays also features a sizeable collection of long-term visitors – mostly *faràng* and Japanese – who use the town as a place to chill out between excursions elsewhere in Asia.

Northwest of town, a Shan village, a Lahu village and a Lisu village, a KMT village called **Ban Santichon** (San Ti Chuen in Yunnanese) and **Nam Tok Mo Paeng** can all be visited on foot. The Shan, Lisu and KMT villages lie within 4km of Pai, while the Lahu village is near Nam Tok Mo Paeng, which is another 4km farther from town (8km total).

You can cut the hike in half by taking a Mae Hong Son–bound bus north about 5km and getting off at a signpost for the falls; from the highway it's only 4km (about 2km beyond the Pai Mountain Lodge). A couple of pools at the base of the falls are suitable for swimming – best just after the rainy season, October to early December.

Across the Mae Pai and 8km southeast of town via a paved road is **Tha Pai Hot Springs** *(admission free; swimming or bathing 50B)*, a well-kept local park 1km from the road. A scenic stream runs through the park; the stream mixes with the hot springs in places to make pleasant bathing areas. There are also small public bathing houses to which hot spring water is piped.

Information

The **Krung Thai Bank** located on the eastern side of Th Rangsiyanon (the main road through town) has an ATM and foreign-exchange service.

Several places around town offer Internet services, including conveniently located **Avu Internet Café** *(☎ 0 5369 9824; Th Rangsiyanon; e peterjespersen1@yahoo.com; open 8am-10pm daily)*.

Siam Used Books *(Th Rangsiyanon)* carries a good selection of used fiction and nonfiction.

PAI

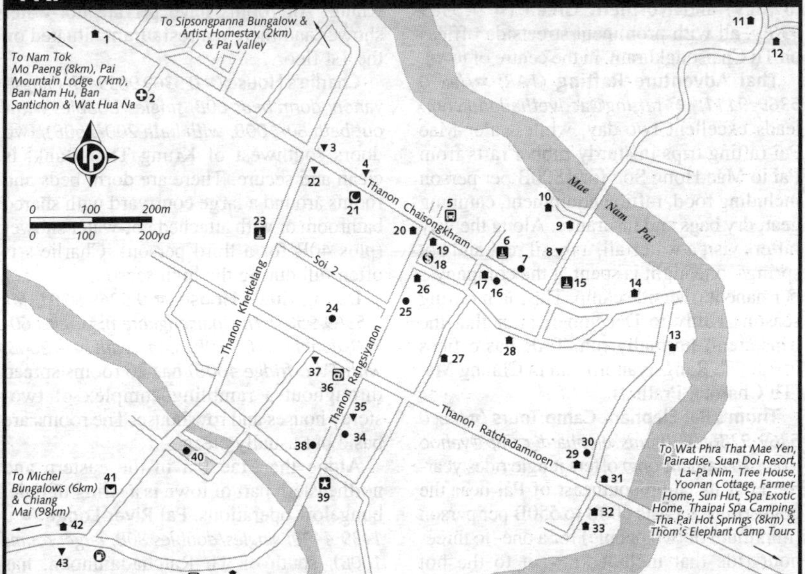

PLACES TO STAY
1 Mountain Blue Guest Cottages
9 Golden Hut
10 Riverside
11 Pai Watershed Guest House
12 View Point Bungalows
13 Baan Nam Pai
14 Rim Pai Cottage
17 Abodaya Guest House & Restaurant
19 Duang Guest House; Duang Trekking
20 Nunya's House
26 Charlie's House
27 Baan Pak Kunmun
28 Mr Jan's Bungalows & Massage
29 Pai Guest House
31 PP Orchid
32 Baan Tawan Guest House
33 Pai River Lodge
42 View Pai Hotel
45 Shan Guest House

PLACES TO EAT
3 Hut Ing Pai
4 All About Coffee
8 Edible Jazz
22 Nong Bia Restaurant
35 Chez Swan
37 Somtam Na Amphoe
40 Saengthongaram Market
43 Ban Benjarong

OTHER
2 Hospital
5 Bus Station
6 Wat Klang
7 Northern Green
15 Wat Pa Kham
16 Back Trax
18 Krung Thai Bank
21 Mosque
23 Wat Luang
24 District Office
25 Municipal Market
30 Pai Traditional Massage
34 Thai Adventure Rafting
36 Avu Internet Cafe
38 Siam Used Books
39 Police
41 Post Office
44 Bebop Cafe

Wat Phra That Mae Yen

วัดพระธาตุแม่เย็น

This temple sits atop a hill and has good views overlooking the valley. Walk 1km east from the main intersection in town, across a stream and through a village, to get to the stairs (a decent climb – 353 steps) that lead to the top. Or take the 400m sealed road that follows a different route to the top.

Trekking, Rafting & Elephant Riding

Any of the guesthouses in town can provide information on local trekking and a few do guided treks for as little as 500B per day if there are no rafts or elephants involved. Among the more established local agencies are **Back Trax** (☎ *0 5369 9739)*, **Duang Trekking** (see Duang Guest House in Places to Stay) and **Northern Green** *(☎ 0 5369 9385)*, all with prominent streetside offices on Th Chaisongkhram, in the centre of town.

Thai Adventure Rafting *(TAR; ☎/fax 0 5369 9111; ⓔ rafting@activethailand.com)* leads excellent two-day, white-water Mae Pai rafting trips in sturdy rubber rafts from Pai to Mae Hong Son for 1800B per person including food, rafting equipment, camping gear, dry bags and insurance. Along the way rafters visit a waterfall, a fossil reef and hot springs; one night is spent at the company's permanent riverside camp. The main rafting season is July to December; after that the trips aren't normally run. TAR has offices in Pai (Th Rangsiyanon) and in Chiang Mai (Th Charoen Prathet).

Thom's Pai Elephant Camp Tours *(☎/fax 0 5369 9286; ⓔ thoms_elephant_camp@yahoo.com; Th Ratdamrong)* offers jungle rides year-round at its camp southeast of Pai near the hot springs. It costs 300B to 550B per person (minimum of two people) for a one- to three-hour ride that includes a visit to the hot springs. It also arranges bamboo or rubber rafting trips down the Mae Pai. Combination elephant-trekking/river-rafting tours (1000B per person) include lunch and transport. Other combination tours/treks are available, including overnight stays in hill-tribe villages.

Traditional Massage & Herbal Sauna

Pai Traditional Massage *(☎ 0 5369 9121; Th Sukhapiban 1; open 4.30am-8.30pm Mon-Fri, 8.30am-8.30pm Sat & Sun)*, in a house near the river, has very good northern-Thai massage for 150B an hour, 230B for 1½ hours or 300B for two hours, as well as a sauna where you can steam yourself in *sàmŭn phrai* (medicinal herbs) for 60B per visit. The couple that do the massages are graduates of Chiang Mai's Old Medicine Hospital. A three-day massage course is available for around 2000B. Massage and sauna services are available on weekends.

For those into rougher stuff, another place in town called **Mr Jan's Massage** *(Soi Wanchalerm 18)* employs a harder Shan-Burmese massage technique.

Places to Stay

Abodaya Guest House & Restaurant *(☎ 0 5369 9041; Th Chaisongkhram; rooms 350B)* occupies a sturdy brick house opposite Wat Klang. All rooms have private hot-water shower and there's a **restaurant** situated on the 1st floor.

Charlie's House *(☎ 0 5369 9039; Th Rangsiyanon; dorm beds 60B, singles/doubles without bath 60/100B, with bath 200/250B)*, two doors southwest of Krung Thai Bank, is clean and secure. There are dorm beds and rooms around a large courtyard with shared bathroom or with attached hot-water shower (plus 40B for a third person). Charlie's is often full during the high season.

Duang Guest House *(☎ 0 5369 9101, fax 0 5369 9581; Th Chaisongkhram; singles 60-70B, doubles 120-130B, rooms with bath 200B, with TV & fridge 400B)* has 26 rooms spread throughout a rambling complex of two-storey houses and row house. The rooms are basic but usually clean.

Along the Mae Pai in the eastern and northeastern part of town is a string of quiet bungalow operations. **Pai River Lodge** *(☎ 0 1439 4490; singles/doubles 80B, larger rooms 100B)*, south of Th Ratchadamnoen, has simple huts arranged in a large circle with a dining and lounge area on stilts in the middle. There are older A-frame huts and a couple of slightly larger nicer ones. Because of its quiet, scenic location it's often full. Rates may be higher in peak season.

Baan Tawan Guest House *(☎ 0 5369 8116–7; ⓔ baantawan@yahoo.com; singles & doubles 200-300B)*, on the river near Pai River Lodge, is a collection of five bungalows and a two-storey house containing eight rooms. All are constructed of old, salvaged teak, with a modicum of charm and river views.

Baan Nam Pai *(☎ 0 1830 1161; e baannampai@hotmail.com; 88 Mu 3, Wiang Tai; huts 80-200B)* is a very friendly and well kept place that is usually quiet. All huts have shared shower and toilet facilities; price differences reflect the size of each hut. Eight new huts under construction at the time of writing will feature private facilities and cost more.

PP Orchid *(☎ 0 5369 9159; 80 Mu 3, Wiang Tai; singles/doubles 100/150B)*, close to the river, offers basic bungalows in a nicely landscaped area. **Pai Guest House** *(Wiang Neua; singles/doubles 70/90B, with bath 80/100B)*, near PP Orchid, has very basic rooms with thin mattresses on the floor.

Mr Jan's Bungalows *(☎ 0 5369 9554; Soi Wanchaloem 18; rooms without bath 70B, singles/doubles with bath 150/200B)*, part of Mr Jan's Massage, is tucked away and features 10 simple bamboo huts set among a large herb garden and fruit trees. All guests have access to facilities where you can bathe with heated, herb-infused water.

Baan Pak Kunmun *(Pohkamnam Guest House; ☎ 0 5369 9382; bungalows 80B, rooms 120B)*, down the lane that's opposite Wat Klang, offers either bungalows or row-house rooms; all have shared bathroom.

Rim Pai Cottage *(☎ 0 5369 9133, 0 5323 5931; Th Chaisongkhram; rooms and bungalows 500-800B)*, close to the river, has clean, quiet A-frames with bathroom, electricity and mosquito nets; there are also overpriced rooms in a row house. One large bungalow is available by the river. The rates here include breakfast.

Golden Hut *(☎ 0 5369 9949; dorm beds/doubles 50/100B, bungalows with shared hot-water bath 120B, singles/doubles/triples with bath 200/250/300B)* is a well-landscaped place north of Rim Pai Cottage offering simple thatched huts on stilts lined up along the river, plus dorm beds and double rooms in a large bamboo-thatch building. **Riverside** *(☎ 0 5369 9929; e the.riverside.guesthouses@gmx.net; 111/1 Mu 3, Wiang Tai; singles/doubles without bath 80/120B)* can be reached by a path that continues from Golden Hut along the river. Simple thatched bungalows are close to the river.

Shan Guest House *(☎ 0 5369 9162; bungalows 200B)*, on the southern edge of town off Th Rangsiyanon, is quiet and well-run. Well-worn bungalows have private hot-water showers. A rickety dining and lounging pavilion sits on stilts in the middle of a large pond. Long-term discounts are available.

View Pai Hotel *(☎ 0 5369 9174; rooms with fan/air-con 300/500B)*, farther south towards Chiang Mai past the petrol station, is a rather plain, three-storey place with overpriced rooms.

Mountain Blue Guest Cottages *(☎ 0 5369 9282; bungalows 50B, single cottages 80-100B, double cottages 100-150B)* is out towards the western end of Th Chaisongkhram near the hospital.

Out of Town Several guesthouses located across a bamboo slat bridge near Golden Hut closed due to flooding in 2002. At the time of writing they were rebuilding. If they re-open you'll have a choice of four or five simple hut operations offering accommodation for 80B to 250B.

Pai Watershed Guest House *(1 Mu 1, Ban Mae Yen; singles/doubles with shared shower & toilet 100/150B)* is about half a kilometre beyond the bamboo bridge, where the trail begins to climb up to a ridge. Here you'll find good views of the valley, plus quiet surroundings, which attract many long-term guests.

View Point Bungalows *(Wiang Tai; singles/doubles with shared shower & toilet 100/150B)* nearby offers a good view of the northeast part of town and terraced rice fields.

Pairadise *(☎ 0 9838 7521; e pairadise_gh@hotmail.com; 98 Mu 1, Ban Mae Yen; bungalows 350B)*, atop the ridge, offers a row of very nicely designed, spacious bungalows with private hot-water shower. Pairadise stands alongside a spring-fed pond suitable for swimming.

Suan Doi Resort *(Mu 1, Ban Mae Yen; huts 250-350B)*, just beyond Pairadise towards Wiang Neua, is a collection of wooden A-frame bungalows in a nice, wooded setting alongside a stream.

La-Pa Nim, **Tree House** and **Yoonaan Cottage** are all farther north of Suan Doi Resort with simple huts in the 100B to 300B range. None has a telephone. Yoonan Cottage can arrange Burmese meals.

Sipsongpanna Bungalow & Artist Homestay *(☎ 0 5321 6096, 0 1769 0142; e sipsongpanna33@hotmail.com; 60 Mu 5, Ban Juang,*

Wiang Neua; bungalows 150B), a couple of kilometres north of town in the village of Ban Wiang Neua, is a small but charming collection of wooden bungalows alongside the river with lots of deft little touches, such as private but separate toilet/ shower facilities for each. There are sitting areas sprinkled throughout the compound, along with a vegetarian **café** and art studio. Thai vegetarian cooking lessons are available.

Across the Mae Pai southeast of town are a number of places to stay along the road that leads to the hot springs, not far from Wat Phra That Mae Yen. Most offer simple thatched-roof huts for about 50B to 100B. **Farmer Home** *(☎ 0 5369 9378; 79 Mu 1, Ban Mae Yen; bungalows 50-200B)*, about 600m east of the river on a hillock, is a nice, friendly spot with a variety of huts.

Sun Hut *(☎ 0 5369 9730, 0 1960 6519; 28/1 Ban Mae Yen; singles/doubles without bath 100/120B, rooms with bath 120-200B)* is the best of the bunch; it has nicely spaced bamboo huts, plus one tree house, with shared bathroom. There are nicer units with private shower. The turn-off for Sun Hut comes right before a bridge over a stream, about 200m before the entrance to Wat Phra That Mae Yen.

Farther down this road are a couple of small resorts that take advantage of the local hot springs by piping the mineral-rich water into the facilities. **Spa Exotic Home** *(☎ 0 5369 9035, 0 5369 9145, fax 0 5369 9462; Ban Mae Hi; tent sites 100B, single/twin bungalows 500/700B)* features comfortable wooden bungalows with private hot-water shower and one or two large beds. You can get a 40% discount from May to August. You can also pitch a tent on the property. On the well-landscaped premises are a nicely designed set of outdoor hot tubs for the use of guests and a **restaurant** serving good Thai and Western food.

Thapai Spa Camping *(in Chiang Mai ☎ 0 5321 8583, fax 0 5321 9610; Ban Mae Hi; cottages 600-800B)*, near Spa Exotic Home, offers 15 wood and stone cottages with natural, hot, mineral-water showers. There's also an outdoor hot-water pool. Visitors may use the mineral baths here for 50B without staying overnight. Tent camping is available for 400B for two persons.

Pai Mountain Lodge *(☎ 0 5369 9068; Ban Mo Paeng; bungalows 500-600B, VIP bungalows 1000B)* is 7km northwest of Pai near Nam Tok Mo Paeng and several hill-tribe villages. Well-maintained spacious A-frames with hot-water showers and stone fireplaces sleep four and are good value. In town you can book a room or arrange transport at 89 Th Chaisongkhram, near Northern Green.

Michel Bungalows *(☎ 0 1951 4337; ⓔ michel@thailine.com; Ban Rong Yaeng; rowhouse rooms with hot water & fan 250B, bungalows 400B)* is about 6km outside Pai on the road to Chiang Mai and features a big pool with a stone filtration system. The bungalows are down a dirt lane about 200m off the main road. Rooms are discounted 50B if you stay more than one night.

Places to Eat

Nong Bia Restaurant *(☎ 0 5369 9103; Th Chaisongkhram; dishes 20-50B; open 8am-10pm daily)*, the most reliable and one of the oldest eateries in town, serves a good variety of inexpensive Thai and Chinese standards, as well as *khâo sawy*.

Hut Ing Pai *(Th Chaisongkhram; dishes 25-60B; open 7am-10pm daily)*, directly opposite Nong Bia, serves good *jók* (broken-rice congee) in the mornings and standard Thai fare the rest of the day.

Somtam Na Amphoe *(dishes 10-25B; open 8am-5pm daily)*, opposite the District Office, makes the best *sôm tam* in Pai, as well as other *tam* (pounded) salad-like dishes using green beans, cucumber and other vegies, along with fresh charcoal-grilled chicken.

Thai Yai *(☎ 0 5369 9093; Th Rangsiyanon; dishes 30-60B; open 7.30am-10pm Mon-Sat, 7.30am-noon Sun)* continues to provide the most dependable Thai-*faràng* menu in town, whether your tastes run from fresh-baked wholegrain bread to *kŭaytĭaw râat nâa* (rice noodles with vegetables and gravy). This place is also a popular meeting point for breakfast as only the municipal market opens earlier.

Edible Jazz *(dishes 25-75B; open 2pm-11pm daily)* is a relatively new spot on the lane leading to Golden Huts, near Wat Pa Kham. The menu's Thai and *faràng*, and the laid-back, cushions-on-the-floor atmosphere make it a good spot for a late lunch or leisurely dinner. Jazz CDs play in the background, and occasionally the Thai owner plays improvisational acoustic guitar.

All About Coffee *(Th Chaisongkhram; dishes 40-120B; open 8.30am-6pm Mon-Sat)* serves nice but pricey pastries, coffees, teas, fruit drinks and egg breakfasts.

Chez Swan *(☎ 0 5369 9111; Th Rangsiyanon; dishes 45-200B; open 8am-11pm daily)* serves French food – including several cheeses – in a nicely decorated old wooden house. The kitchen also makes excellent *khâo tôm* (rice soup).

Ban Benjarong *(Th Rangsiyanon; dishes 30-80B; open 11am-10pm daily)* serves a good range of Thai dishes in a pleasant partially open-air dining room with views of rice paddies out the back.

Every evening a row of local **food vendors** sets up in front of the day market. During the day, takeaway food can also be purchased at the larger **Saengthongaram Market** *(Th Khetkelang)*.

Entertainment

Pai boasts a small live-music scene. **Bebop Cafe** *(Th Rangsiyanon; open 6pm-1am daily)* is designed to look like a Shan-Yunnanese shophouse on the outside, and decorated with Asian hippie gear inside. The house band and occasional visiting bands play blues, R&B and rock nightly (starting at around 9.30pm).

Edible Jazz (see Places to Eat earlier) hosts occasional live acoustic music.

Getting There & Away

Buses (60B ordinary, 84B air-con) depart Chiang Mai's Arcade bus station at 8.30am and 11am and noon, 2pm and 4pm daily. The distance is only 134km but the trip takes about three hours due to the steep and winding road. From Mae Hong Son there are also five buses a day with the same departure times as the buses from Chiang Mai. This winding, 111km stretch takes three to four hours (53B, 74B). In the other direction, buses depart Pai for Chiang Mai and Mae Hong Son at 8.30am and 10.30am and noon, 2pm and 4pm. Buses from Pai to Soppong cost 30B ordinary, 35B air-con.

Getting Around

Most of Pai is accessible on foot. For local excursions you can **rent bicycles** or **motorcycles** at several locations around town. A place next door to Duang Guest House rents out bicycles for 50B per day (80B for newer bikes). Motorcycles can be rented at **MS Motorcycle Rent**, just south of Thom's Pai Elephant Camp Tours office – 100cc bikes cost 150B per 24 hours, larger bikes cost 200B. Motorcycle taxis can be hired from the taxi stand at the bus stop. Typical fares are 25B to Ban Nam Hu and Ban Wiang Neua, 35B to Nam Hu Lisaw and Nam Hu Jin, and 45B to Tha Pai.

AROUND PAI

Pai can be used as a base for excursions to hill-tribe villages, as described earlier in the Pai section. Farther afield, the area northeast of Pai has so far been little explored. A network of unpaved roads – some little more than footpaths – skirts a mountain ridge and the Mae Taeng valley all the way to the Myanmar border near **Wiang Haeng** and **Ban Piang Haeng**, passing several villages along the way. Near Ban Piang Luang is a Shan **temple** built by Khun Sa, the opium warlord.

This area can also be visited by road from Chiang Dao in Chiang Mai Province.

Chiang Rai Province

Chiang Rai, the northernmost province in Thailand, is one of the country's most rural areas. Half of its northern border, separating the province and nation from Laos, is formed by the Mekong River. Mountains form the other half, cleaving Myanmar from Thailand, with the junction of the Nam Ruak and Mekong River at Thailand's peak. The fertile Mekong flood plains to the east support most of the agriculture in the province; to the west the land is too mountainous for most crops. One crop that thrives on steep mountain slopes is opium, and until recently Chiang Rai was the centre for most of the opium in Thailand.

Crop substitution and other development projects sponsored by the late Princess Mother (the king's mother), along with accelerated law enforcement, have pushed much of the opium trade over the border into Myanmar and Laos. While there are undoubtedly still pockets of the trade here and there, even a few poppy patches, Chiang Rai's Golden Triangle fame is now mostly relegated to history books and museums.

CHIANG RAI

อ.เมืองเชียงราย

postcode 57000 • pop 40,000

Phaya Mangrai founded Chiang Rai in 1262 as part of the Lao-Thai Lanna kingdom and it didn't become a Siamese territory till 1786, then a province in 1910. Lots of wealthy Thais began moving to Chiang Rai in the 1980s, and in the early 1990s the area saw a development boom as local entrepreneurs speculated on the city's future. Things have calmed down a bit and a few guesthouses have closed down, although having an airport has increased its potential as a major tourist destination.

About 180km from Chiang Mai, the city northern Thais know as 'Siang Hai' has been marketed in tourist literature as 'the gateway to the Golden Triangle'. Thais often tout Chiang Rai as an alternative to Chiang Mai, although it's not nearly as colourful and there's less to do in town. On the other hand it's a little more laid-back, and anyone interested in trekking will find they can reach village areas quicker than from Chiang Mai.

Information

Tourist Offices The **TAT office** *(☎ 0 5374 4674, 0 5371 1433; Th Singkhlai; open 8.30am-4.30pm daily)* distributes maps of Chiang Rai as well as useful brochures on accommodation and transport.

Money Chiang Rai is well supplied with banks, especially along Th Thanalai and along Th Utarakit. **Bangkok Bank** *(Th Thanalai)* has an ATM, as do several other banks in town.

Post & Communications You can mail letters and parcels at the main **post office** *(Th Utarakit; open 8.30am-4.30pm Mon-Fri; 9am-noon Sat, Sun & holidays)*, south of Wat Phra Singh.

The **CAT office** *(cnr Th Ratchadat Damrong & Th Ngam Meuang; open 7am-11pm Mon-Fri)* offers international telephone and fax services. Both the CAT office and main post office feature Internet access as well.

Several Internet cafés can be found in the city centre, particularly in the vicinity of the Wang Come Hotel. The **Post Café** *(Th Phahonyothin; open 7.30am-9.30pm daily)* also offers mailing services.

Bookshops Although the stock is mostly Thai-language publications, **Ran Nai In** *(Th Phahonyothin)*, opposite Muang Thong Restaurant, does carry a few English-language books and newspapers.

Wat Phra Kaew

วัดพระแก้ว

Originally called Wat Pa Yia (Bamboo Forest Monastery) in local dialect, this is the city's most revered Buddhist temple. Legend says that in 1434 lightning struck the temple's octagonal *chedi*, which fell apart to reveal the Phra Kaew Morakot or Emerald Buddha (actually made of jade). After a long journey that included a long stopover in Vientiane, Laos, this national talisman is now ensconced in the temple of the same name in Bangkok.

In 1990 Chiang Rai commissioned a Chinese artist to sculpt a new image from Canadian jade. Named the Phra Yok Chiang Rai (Chiang Rai Jade Buddha), it was intentionally a very close but not exact replica of the Phra Kaew Morakot in Bangkok, with dimensions of 48.3cm across the base and 65.9cm in height, just 0.1cm shorter than the original. The image is housed in the impressive Haw Phra Kaew, which sits towards the back of the wát compound.

The main *wíhăan* is a medium-sized, nicely preserved wooden structure with unique carved doors. The *chedi* behind it dates to the late 14th century and is typical Lanna style.

Wat Jet Yot

วัดเจ็ดยอด

The namesake for this wát is a seven-spired *chedi* similar to the *chedi* in Chiang Mai's Wat Jet Yot but without stucco ornamentation. Of more aesthetic interest is the wooden ceiling of the front veranda of the main *wíhăan*, which features a unique Thai astrological fresco.

Wat Phra Singh

วัดพระสิงห์

Housing yet another copy of a famous Buddha image, this temple was built in the late 14th century during the reign of Chiang Rai's King Mahaphrom. A sister temple to Chiang

CHIANG RAI

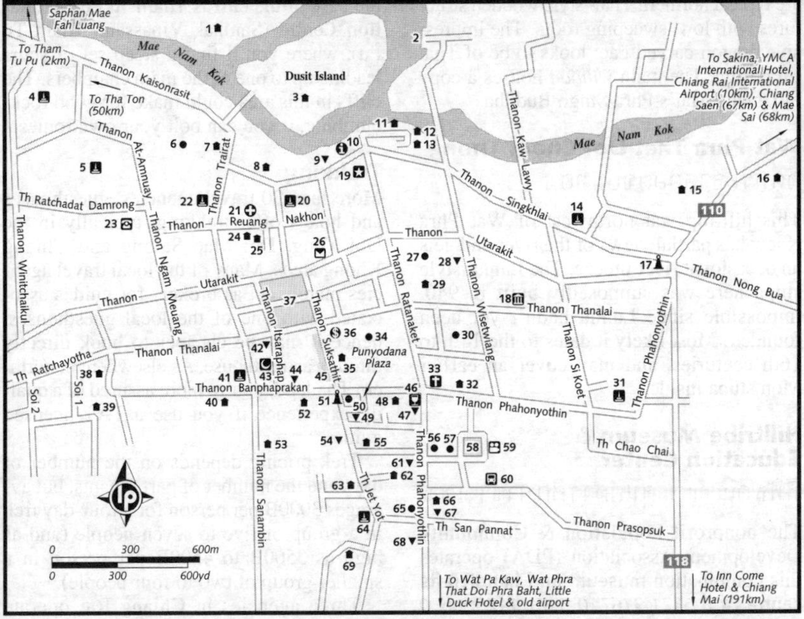

CHIANG RAI

PLACES TO STAY

1 Rimkok Resort
3 Dusit Island Resort; National Car Rental
7 Chat House
8 Mae Kok Villa
11 Bowling Guest House
12 Lotus Guest House
13 Mae Hong Son Guest House of Chiang Rai
15 White House Guest House
16 Wang Din Place
24 Ruang Nakhon Hotel
25 Kijnakorn Guest House
29 Pintamorn Guest House
32 Golden Triangle Inn; Budget Rent-A-Car
35 Chiengrai (Chiang Rai) Hotel
38 Lek House
39 Ben Guest House
40 Saenphu Hotel
48 Siam Hotel
52 Suknirand Hotel
53 Krung Thong Hotel
55 Wang Come Hotel; Mayura Bakery & Cafe
62 Baan Bua
63 Boonbundan Guest House
66 Wiang Inn
69 Tourist Inn

PLACES TO EAT

9 Cham Cha
28 Vegetarian Restaurant
42 Rot Prasoet
44 Phetburi; Ratburi
45 Rice & Noodle Restaurants
47 Nakhon Pathom
49 La Cantina; Chiang Rai Coffee Company
54 Pho Jai
58 Night Market
61 Post Cafe
67 Muang Thong Restaurant
68 Bierstube

OTHER

2 Tha Mae Nam Kok
4 Wat Phrat Tha Doi Chom Thong
5 Wat Ngam Meuang
6 Government Office; Town Hall
10 TAT Office
14 Wat Bunreuang
17 King Mengrai Monument
18 Hilltribe Museum & Education Center; Cabbages & Condoms
19 Police Station
20 Wat Phra Singh
21 Hospital
22 Wat Phra Kaew
23 CAT Office
26 Main Post Office
27 School
30 Old Jail
31 Wat Si Koet
33 Chiang Rai First Church
34 District Office
36 Bangkok Bank
37 Market
41 Wat Ming Meuang
43 Daru Aman Mosque
46 Teepee Bar
50 ST Motorcycle
51 Clock Tower
56 THAI Office
57 Centre Point Night Bazaar
59 Rama I Theatre
60 Bus Terminal
64 Wat Jet Yot
65 Ran Nai In

Mai's Wat Phra Singh, its original buildings are typical northern Thai–style wooden structures with low, sweeping roofs. The impressive dragon-carved gate looks to be of Thai Lü design. The main *wíhăan* houses a copy of Chiang Mai's Phra Singh Buddha.

Wat Phra That Doi Chom Thong

วัดพระธาตุดอยจอมทอง

This hill-top wát northwest of Wat Phra Kaew has partial views of the river and gets an occasional river breeze. The Lanna-style stupa here was supposedly built in 940, impossible since Lanna hadn't yet been founded! Most likely it dates to the 14th to 16th centuries, and may cover an earlier Mon stupa inside.

Hilltribe Museum & Education Center

พิพิธภัณฑ์และศูนย์การศึกษาชาวเขา

The nonprofit Population & Community Development Association (PDA) operates this combination **museum and handicrafts centre** *(☎ 0 5371 9167, 0 5371 1475, fax 0 5371 8869; ⓔ crpda@hotmail.com; 620/1 Th Thanalai; admission 50B; open 9am-7pm Mon-Fri, 10am-7pm Sat & Sun)*. Crafts for sale are displayed on the ground floor. The 3rd floor of the facility serves as a museum with typical clothing for six major tribes, folk implements and other anthropological exhibits. The centre also offers a 25-minute slide show on Thailand's hill tribes with narration in English, French, German, Japanese and Thai.

If you've already been to the Tribal Research Institute at Chiang Mai University, you'll have seen it all before; otherwise, it's a good place to visit before undertaking any hill-tribe treks. A branch of Bangkok's **Cabbages & Condoms** restaurant is on the premises (see Places to Eat later in this section for details; see also Trekking, following, for information on the PDA's trekking Agency).

Tham Tu Pu

If you follow the road across Saphan Mae Fah Luang to the northern side of Mae Nam Kok, you'll come to a turn-off for Tham Tu Pu, 800m from the bridge. Follow the dirt road 1.2km to arrive at this network of caves in the side of a limestone cliff. At the base of the cliff is **Tham Tu Pu Meditation Centre** (Samnak Vipassana Tham Tu Pu), where you'll find a steep set of stairs leading up to one of the main chambers. The cliffs in this area could make for good rock-climbing, if you can bolt your own routes.

Trekking

More than 20 travel agencies, guesthouses and hotels offer trekking, typically in the Doi Tung, Doi Mae Salong and Chiang Khong areas. Many of the local travel agencies merely act as brokers for guides associated with one of the local guesthouses; hence it may be cheaper to book directly through a guesthouse. As elsewhere in northern Thailand, you're more assured of a quality experience if you use a TAT-licensed guide.

Trek pricing depends on the number of days and the number of participants, but averages 3000B per person for a four-day trek in a group of five to seven people (and as high as 3500B to 4500B per person in a smaller group of two to four people).

Three agencies in Chiang Rai operate treks and cultural tours where profits from the treks go directly to community development projects.

Dapa Tours (☎ 0 5371 1354, 0 1764 5221, ⓦ www.dapatours.com) 115 Mu 2, Tambon Rim Kok. Run by Akha, specialises in tours to Akha areas.

Natural Focus (☎/fax 0 5371 5696, ⓔ natfocus@loxinfo.co.th) 129/1 Mu 4, Th Pa-Ngiw, Soi 4, Rop Wiang. Specialises in nature tours.

PDA Tours & Travel (☎ 0 5374 0088) Hilltribe Museum & Education Center.

From Tha Mae Nam Kok (Kok River Pier), boats can take you upriver as far as Tha Ton. (See Fang & Tha Ton in the Chiang Mai Province chapter.) An hour's boat ride from Chiang Rai is **Ban Ruammit**, which is a fair-sized Karen village. From here you can trek on your own to Lahu, Mien, Akha and Lisu villages – all of them within a day's walk. Inexpensive room and board (50B per person, meals 25B to 40B) are available in many villages in the river area. Another popular area for do-it-yourself trekkers is **Wawi**, south of the river town of Mae Salak near the end of the river route. (See River Trip to Chiang Rai at the end of the Chiang Mai Province chapter.)

Places to Stay – Budget & Mid-Range

Guesthouses Housed in a former school near Mae Nam Kok (for boats from Tha Ton), **Mae Kok Villa** *(☎ 0 5371 1786; 445 Th Singkhlai; dorm beds 80B, single/double bungalows with cold-water bath 120/150B, large singles/doubles/triples with hot-water shower 140/190/300B)* is housed in a former missionary school near the banks of the Mae Nam Kok. It's seen better days but is perfectly adequate and the TAT office is a short walk away. The owner speaks good English.

Chat House *(☎ 0 5371 1481; 3/2 Soi Saengkaew, Th Trairat; dorm beds 60B, singles/doubles without bath 80B, rooms with bath 100-150B)* is another nice place near Mae Nam Kok. It's an old Thai house; there are bicycles and motorcycles for rent, and 4WD and car rentals as well as guided treks can be arranged.

A bit east of here in a network of lanes off Th Singkhlai are a couple of small family run guesthouses. **Bowling Guest House** *(☎ 0 5371 2704; 399 Soi Nang Ing, Th Singkhlai; singles/doubles 80/100B)* is clean and friendly and has five rooms with attached cold-water shower; a hot-water shower is available. **Mae Hong Son Guest House of Chiang Rai** *(☎ 0 5371 5367; 126 Th Singkhlai; singles/doubles without bath from 100/120B, with bath 150/180B)* is so named because it was once run by the same family as the original guesthouse in Mae Hong Son. Now under Dutch-Thai management, it's a good place to gather info on what to see and do in the Chiang Rai area. The management also rents out motorcycles, teaches cooking courses and organises treks.

Lotus Guest House *(Soi Nang Ing, Th Singkhlai; singles/doubles without bath 80/100B, with cold shower 120/150B, single with hot shower 150B)*, near Mae Hong Son Guest House of Chiang Rai, is fairly new and has 16 well-kept rooms in row houses surrounding a grassy courtyard. One room with attached hot shower is available, while other rooms share hot-water facilities.

Pintamorn Guest House *(☎ 0 5371 4161, 0 5371 5427, fax 0 5371 3317; 509/1 Th Ratanaket; rooms without bath 100B, singles/doubles/triples with bath 200/250/300B, doubles with air-con 350B, room for 6 people 600B)* is located in the city centre near plenty of shops and restaurants. The rambling building contains a selection of fan and air-con rooms, including two adjoining air-con rooms that sleep six.

Boonbundan Guest House *(☎ 0 5371 7040, fax 0 5371 2914; 1005/13 Th Jet Yot; rooms with hot-water shower & fan 140B, larger singles/doubles with fan 200/250B, with air-con 300/350B)* is contained in a walled compound in the southern part of town. The choice of accommodation here includes small rooms off the garden, in huts or in the air-con building overlooking the garden – something to suit all budgets. Small dingy rooms with hot-water shower and fan are not such good value compared with other budget places in town.

Tourist Inn *(☎ 0 5371 4682; 1004/4-6 Th Jet Yot; rooms in old house 150B, in new building with fan/air-con 200/350B)* is also in this vicinity and offers fairly clean, large rooms with fan and private hot-water bathroom in the old house, or with fan/air-con in a new building. The proprietors speak English, Thai and Japanese and there is a good bakery on the premises. Car and motorcycle rentals can be arranged.

Lek House *(☎ 0 5371 3337; 95 Th Ratchayotha; singles & doubles without bath 70B, bungalows/row-house rooms with bath 120/130B)*, near the city centre, has rooms with shared bathroom in an old house, or small bungalows with private bathroom. A row house has rooms with private bathroom. Lek has motorcycles and a 4WD car for rent.

Ben Guest House *(☎ 0 5371 6775; 351/10 Soi 4 Th Sankhong Noi; singles/doubles without bath 80/100B, teak rooms with hot-water shower downstairs/upstairs 120/160B, brick rooms 200B)* is an ambitious place where there are clean rooms with fan and hot-water shower in a northern Thai–style building made of salvaged teak, and fan rooms with private bathroom in a newer brick building. A few rooms without facilities are available above the reception. Treks with licensed guides and motorcycle and 4WD rentals can be arranged.

Kijnakorn Guest House *(☎ 0 5374 4150–1; 24 Th Reuang Nakhon; rooms with fan 300B, with air-con 400-500B)* is in the town centre, a few steps away from Ruang Nakhon Hotel but set back from the road in a modern, four-storey building. All rooms come with TV, fridge and phone as well as hot-water

Trekking in Northern Thailand

Thousands of foreign travellers each year take part in treks into the hills of the north. Most come away with a sense of adventure, but there are a few who are disillusioned by the experience. The most important ingredient in a good trek is having a good leader/organiser, followed by a good group of trekkers. Some travellers finish a tour complaining more about the other trekkers than about the itinerary, food or trek leader.

Before Trekking

Hill-tribe trekking isn't for everyone. First, you must be physically fit to cope with the demands of sustained up and down walking, exposure to the elements and spotty food. Second, many people feel awkward walking through hill-tribe villages and playing the role of voyeur.

In cities and villages elsewhere in Thailand, Thais and other lowland groups are quite used to foreign faces and foreign ways (from TV if nothing else), but in the hills of northern Thailand the tribes lead largely insular lives. Hence, hill-tribe tourism has pronounced effects, both positive and negative. On the positive side, travellers have a chance to see how traditional, subsistence-oriented societies function. Also, since the Thai government is sensitive about the image of their minority groups, tourism may actually have forced it to review and sometimes improve its policies towards hill tribes. On the negative side, trekkers introduce many cultural items and ideas from the outside world that may erode tribal customs to varying degrees.

If you have any qualms about interrupting the traditional patterns of life in hill-tribe areas, you probably should not go trekking. If you do go, keep in mind that anyone who promises you an authentic experience is probably exaggerating at the very least, or at worst contributing to the decline of hill-tribe culture by leading travellers into untouristed areas.

Choosing a Company

Many trekking guides are freelance and go from one company to the next, so there's no way to predict which companies are going to give the best service at any time. Many guesthouses that advertise their own trekking companies actually act as brokers for off-site operations; they collect a commission for every guest they book into a trek. The Tourism Authority of Thailand (TAT) office in Chiang Mai maintains a list of licensed agencies and is making efforts to regulate trekking companies operating out of Chiang Mai. The TAT recommends that you trek only with members of the Professional Guide Association of Chiang Mai or the Jungle Tour Club of northern Thailand. Still, with more than 200 companies, it's very difficult to guarantee any kind of control. Ultimately the best way to shop for a trek is to talk to travellers who have just returned from one.

If you decide to do a trek keep these points in mind: choose your trek operator carefully, try to meet the others in the group (suggest a meeting), and find out exactly what the tour includes and does not include, as usually there are additional expenses beyond the basic rate. In the cool season, make sure sleeping bags are provided, as the thin wool blankets available in most villages are not sufficient for the average visitor. If everything works out, even an organised tour can be worthwhile. A useful check list of questions to ask are:

- How many people will there be in the group? (Six to 10 is a good maximum range.)
- Can the organiser guarantee that no other tourists will visit the same village on the same day, especially overnight?
- Can the guide speak the language of each village to be visited? (This is not always necessary, as many villagers can speak Thai nowadays.)
- Exactly when does the tour begin and end? (Some three-day treks turn out to be less than 48 hours in length.)
- Does the tour company provide transport before and after the trek or is it by public bus (which may mean long waits)?

In general, the trekking business has become more conscious of the need to tread carefully in hill-tribe villages than in previous decades. Most companies now tend to limit the number of visits to a

Trekking in Northern Thailand

particular area and are careful not to overlap areas used by other companies. Everyone benefits from this consciousness: The hill tribes are less impacted by trekkers, the trekkers have a better experience and the trekking industry runs at a sustainable rate.

You might find that places other than Chiang Mai or Chiang Rai offer better and less expensive tours from more remote and less trekked areas. Also, they are generally smaller, friendlier operations and the trekkers are usually a more determined bunch since they're not looking for an easy and quick in-and-out trek. You can easily arrange treks out of the Mae Hong Son, Pai, Mae Sai and Tha Ton. If you have a little time to seek out the right people, you can also go on organised treks from Mae Sariang, Khun Yuam, Soppong (near Pai), Mae Sot, Um Phang and various out-of-the-way guesthouses elsewhere in the north.

The down side, of course, is that companies outside of Chiang Mai are generally subject to even less regulation than those in Chiang Mai, and there are fewer guarantees with regard to trekking terms and conditions.

Costs

Organised treks out of Chiang Mai average from 1800B to 2100B for a three-day, two-night trek, to 7000B for a deluxe seven-day, six-night trek, including transport, guide, accommodation, three meals per day, sleeping bags, water bottles and rafting and/or elephant riding. Not included in the price are beverages other than drinking water or tea, lunch on the first and last days and personal porters. Rates vary, so it pays to shop around – although these days so many companies are competing for your business that rates have remained pretty stable for the last few years. Elephant rides actually become quite boring and even uncomfortable after an hour or two. Some companies now offer quickie day treks or one-night, two-day programmes. Don't choose a trek by price alone. It's better to talk to other travellers in town who have been on treks. Treks out of other towns in the north are usually less expensive.

Seasons

The best time to trek is November to February, when the weather is refreshing, there's little or no rain and wildflowers are in bloom. Between March and May the hills are dry and the weather is quite hot. The second-best time is early in the rainy season, between June and July, before the dirt roads become too saturated.

Independent Trekking

You might consider striking out on your own in a small group of two to five people. Gather as much information as you can about the area you'd like to trek in from the Tribal Museum in Chiang Mai. Browsing the displays will help you identify different tribes, and the inscriptions offer cultural information. Don't bother staff with questions about trekking as this is not their area of expertise.

Be prepared for language difficulties. Few people will know any English. Usually someone in a village will know some Thai, so a Thai phrasebook can be helpful. Lonely Planet publishes a *Hill Tribes phrasebook* with phrase sections for each of the six major hill-tribe languages.

As in Himalayan trekking in Nepal and India, many people now do short treks on their own, staying in villages along the way. It's not necessary to bring a lot of food or equipment, just money for food that can be bought en route at small Thai towns and occasionally in the hill-tribe settlements. (Obviously, be sure to take plenty of water and some high-energy snacks.) However, the TAT strongly discourages trekking on your own because of the safety risk. Check with the police when you arrive in a new district so they can tell you if an area is considered safe or not. A lone trekker is an easy target for robbers.

Safety

Thai police mount regular hill-country patrols and we haven't heard of any trekking groups being robbed for several years now. Still you shouldn't take anything along on a trek that you can't afford to lose. If you leave your valuables with a guesthouse, make sure you obtain a fully itemised receipt before departing on a trek.

showers. It's clean and relatively new, although not very atmospheric.

Baan Bua *(☎ 0 5371 8880, fax 0 5370 5357; ⓔ baanbua@yahoo.com; 879/2 Th Jet Yot; singles/doubles with fan 180/200B, rooms with fan & air-con 300B)*, in a quiet spot off Th Jet Yot, is a friendly place that offers 10 large, very clean rooms with hot showers, all in a cement row house with a garden out the front. The well-designed rooms feature screen doors on either side to allow for insect-free cross-ventilation.

White House Guest House *(☎ 0 5371 5081, fax 0 5371 3427; 789/7 Th Phahonyothin; singles/doubles with fan & bath 250/350B, with air-con & satellite TV 450/500B)* features 30 rooms, all with fans, hot showers and telephones, and plans for satellite TV in every room. The clean 14m swimming pool is a plus.

Hotels Chiang Rai has an abundance of inexpensive Thai-Chinese hotels. **Chiengrai Hotel** *(Chiang Rai; ☎ 0 5371 1266; 519 Th Suksathit; singles/doubles/triples 160/220/350B)*, near the clock tower and district government building, is an older, well-run place that is a favourite with Thai truck drivers and travelling salespeople. All rooms have fan and private bath while the 350B rooms also have air-con.

Suknirand Hotel *(☎ 0 5371 1055, fax 0 5371 3701; 424/1 Th Banphaprakan; rooms with fan/air-con from 300/500B)* is also centrally located between the clock tower and Wat Ming Meuang. The plain but clean rooms were renovated fairly recently.

Siam Hotel *(☎ 0 5371 1077; 531/6-8 Th Banphaprakan; singles/doubles 250/300B)* is yet another local bargain; all rooms have a fan and private hot-water shower. **Ruang Nakhon Hotel** *(☎ 0 5374 5000, fax 0 5374 5003; 25 Th Reuang Nakhon; quads with fan & bath 200B, doubles with air-con 300-400B)*, is near the hospital.

Krung Thong Hotel *(☎ 0 5371 1033, fax 0 5371 7848; 412 Th Sanambin; singles/doubles with fan 250/290B, rooms with air-con 340B)* has larger than average, clean rooms and is popular with both tourists and Thai business travellers.

Golden Triangle Inn *(☎ 0 5371 1339, 0 5371 6996, fax 0 5371 3963; 590/2 Th Phahonyothin; singles/doubles Nov-Feb 650/950B, Apr-Oct 500/600B)* has 39 tasteful rooms with tile floors, air-con and hot water (even bathtubs); rates include American breakfast. During the low season, April to October, the Golden Triangle knocks 100B off these rates. The landscaped grounds include a café, a Japanese-Thai garden, a Budget car-rental office and an efficient travel agency. It's a popular place, so book in advance to ensure you get in.

Saenphu Hotel *(☎ 0 5371 7300, fax 0 5371 7309; 389 Th Banphaprakan; singles & doubles from 500B)* is centrally located and good value. Rooms have all the amenities – air-con, TV, phone, fridge – and start at a bargain rate. The hotel's basement nightclub has live music and is a very popular local rendezvous spot.

Inn Come Hotel *(☎ 0 5371 7850, fax 0 5371 7855; 176/2 Th Ratbamrung; singles & doubles from 650B)*, south of the city centre, offers similar rooms to Saenphu Hotel and has a restaurant, coffee shop, karaoke and a popular disco.

YMCA International Hotel Chiangrai *(☎ 0 5371 3785, fax 0 5371 4336; 70 Th Phahonyothin; dorm beds 90B, singles/doubles with fan 300/400B, with air-con 400/500B)*, a very modern establishment with dorm beds and singles/doubles with private bathroom, is out of town on the highway to Mae Sai. All rooms come with hot water and a telephone. Facilities include a restaurant, convention room, daycare centre, a small swimming pool, Thai massage and herbal sauna.

Places to Stay – Top End

Wiang Inn *(☎ 0 5371 1533 • in Bangkok ☎ 0 2513 9804-5, fax 0 2513 2926; ⓔ wiang inn@samart.co.th; 893 Th Phahonyothin; singles/doubles 1400/1600B, deluxe singles/doubles 2100/2300B)* offers comfortable rooms, a swimming pool, massage parlour, bar, restaurant, coffee shop and karaoke.

Wang Come Hotel *(☎ 0 5371 1800, fax 0 5371 2973 • in Bangkok ☎ 0 2252 7750; 869/90 Th Premawiphat; rooms 1060-1600B, suites 2000-5500B)* has comfortable rooms with air-con, carpet, TV, fridge and phone. The hotel has a pool, banquet room, disco, coffee shop, two restaurants and a nightclub.

Dusit Island Resort *(☎ 0 5371 5777–9, fax 0 5371 5801 • in Bangkok ☎ 0 2636 3333; ⓔ chiangrai@dusit.com; rooms from 2800B)* is perched on its own island in Mae Nam

Kok (you can't miss seeing its stacked white facade if you arrive in Chiang Rai by boat). This is an island unto itself, insulating its guests from the rigours of laid-back Chiang Rai. Facilities include Chinese and European restaurants, a coffee shop, pub, swimming pool and fitness centre.

Rimkok Resort *(☎ 0 5371 6445, fax 0 5371 5859 • in Bangkok ☎ 0 2279 0102; 6 Mu 4, Th Chiang Rai/Tha Ton; rooms 1806-2477B)* sits opposite the Dusit Island Resort north of the river amid lush grounds. Designed with plenty of Thai-style flair, it's Chiang Rai's most impressive-looking hotel, although recent reports say it could be better-maintained.

Wang Din Place *(☎ 0 5371 3363, fax 0 5371 6790; 341 Th Khae Wai; bungalows 800B)*, in the northeastern corner of town near the river, is another good choice. Sturdy, Thai-style bungalows have fridge, TV, aircon and private hot-water shower.

Little Duck Hotel *(☎ 0 5371 5620, fax 0 5371 5639 • in Bangkok ☎ 0 2691 5941–6; ⓔ chitpong@loxinfo.co.th; 199 Th Phahonyothin; rooms 900-1200B)*, south of the city past the old airport, has picked up a regular clientele of Thai politicos and entrepreneurs in spite of its distance from the new airport and town. Amenities include a pool and a restaurant.

Places to Eat

Thai You'll find plenty of restaurants in the city centre, especially along Th Banphaprakan and Th Thanalai. **Phetburi** and **Ratburi** restaurants on Th Banphaprakan have stacks of platters heaped with cheap, decent central Thai and Chinese food. The Phetburi has a particularly good selection of Thai curries.

Nakhon Pathom *(no Roman-script sign; Th Phahonyothin; dishes 30-80B; open 8am-3pm daily)*, yet another local restaurant named after a central Thailand city, is very popular for inexpensive *khâo man kài* and *kŭaytĭaw pèt yâang* (roast duck with rice noodles).

Muang Thong Restaurant *(☎ 0 5371 1162; Th Phahonyothin; dishes 30-80B; open 11am-10pm daily)*, just south of the Wiang Inn, has an extensive Thai and Chinese menu and is packed nightly. One of the house specialities is *kaeng pàa pèt*, a delicious duck curry.

Cham Cha *(Th Singkhlai; dishes 35-90B; open 7am-4pm daily)*, beside the TAT office, is a very good place for breakfast or lunch if you arrive at TAT tired and hungry. It has all the usual Thai and Chinese standards along with a few Isan dishes not on the English menu, such as *lâap* and *sôm tam*, and ice cream, too.

Rot Prasoet *(English sign reads 'Muslim food'; Th Itsaraphap; dishes 20-30B; open 7am-8pm daily)* is a Thai-Muslim restaurant next to the mosque on Th Itsaraphap. It serves the usual Thai Muslim favourites, including *khâo mòk kài*, a Thai version of chicken biryani. **Sakina** *(Th Phahonyothin; dishes 15-25B; open 8am-5pm Sun-Thur, 8am-noon Fri)*, on the highway to Mae Sai north of town, has much more impressive Muslim fare. The *kaeng masala kài* (chicken masala curry) is especially good here, along with *mátàbà* (roti stuffed with a spicy mix of potatoes and chicken or beef) and *khâo sawy*.

Cabbages & Condoms *(☎ 0 5374 0784; 620/1 Th Thanalai; dishes 35-90B; open 8am-midnight daily)*, on the grounds of the Hilltribe Museum & Education Center, serves northern Thai food in a casual indoor/outdoor eating area. Profits from the restaurant are used by the PDA for HIV/AIDS education with the intention to make condoms as easy to find as cabbages.

There's a small, pleasant, family run **Thai vegetarian restaurant** *(100/2 Th Utarakit; dishes 10-30B; open 7am-2pm daily)* opposite the Chiang Rai Condotel, off Th Utarakit on Th Wisetwiang.

Pho Jai *(Th Jet Yot; dishes 20-30B; open 8am-3pm daily)* is a very good *khâo sawy* place directly behind the Wang Come Hotel.

Mayura Bakery & Cafe, attached to the Wang Come Hotel, sells baked goods and a selection of Thai and Western dishes. Near the bus terminal are the usual **food stalls**; the **night market** (next to the station and Rama I cinema) is also good. There's a string of inexpensive **rice and noodle restaurants** near the Chiengrai Hotel along Th Jet Yot (between Th Thanalai and the clock tower).

International South of the Wiang Inn, **Bierstube** *(☎ 0 5371 4195; Th Phahonyothin; dishes 40-80B; open 9am-11pm)* has been recommended for German food. There are several other Western-style pubs along here and on Th Suksathit/Jet Yot near the Wang Come Hotel.

La Cantina *(Th Wat Jet Yot; dishes 45-100B; open 8am-10pm)* has a long menu featuring a variety of Italian dishes. La Cantina is open for breakfast. Nearby you can order breakfast and coffee at the new **Chiang Rai Coffee Company**, a narrow café with wooden tables and chairs.

Entertainment

Chiang Rai is pretty quiet at night. A string of bars along Th Wat Jet Yot capture most of the expat business. **Teepee Bar** *(Th Phahonyothin)*, next to the Nakhon Pathom restaurant, is a hang-out for backpackers and Thai hippies and a good place to exchange information.

Punyodana (formerly Sapkaset Plaza), an L-shaped lane between Th Banphaprakan and Th Suksathit, has become a go-go bar centre.

Free northern Thai music and dance performances are given nightly on a stage at **Centre Point Night Bazaar**.

Shopping

Prices for antiques and silverwork are sometimes lower in Chiang Rai than in Chiang Mai. Several shops worth checking for handicrafts, silver and antiques can be found along Th Phahonyothin, including **Gong Ngoen** at No 873/5, **Silver Birch** at No 891 and **Chiangrai Handicrafts Center** at No 237. **Ego** *(869/81 Th Premawiphak)*, carries upmarket items like antique textiles.

It's cheaper to buy direct from the craft vendors who set up on the sidewalk in front of the northern entrance to the bus station nightly. Adjacent to the bus station is a tourist-oriented night market that resembles Chiang Mai's but on a much smaller scale.

Getting There & Away

Air The **Chiang Rai International Airport** is 10km north of the city. The terminal has several snack vendors, a THAI-owned restaurant, souvenir shops, a Chinese tea shop, a money exchange, a post office (open 7am to 7pm daily) and rental car booths.

Air Andaman *(☎ 0 5379 3726; Chiang Rai International Airport)* flies five times daily between Chiang Rai and Chiang Mai (1200B economy, 40 minutes). Daily flights are also available via **THAI** *(☎ 0 5371 1179; 870 Th Phahonyothin)* to/from Bangkok (2200B, 1¼ hours). There has been talk of flights from Hong Kong, Kunming, Vientiane and Mandalay, but as long as Chiang Mai's airport fields flights from these cities they're not likely to be added to the schedule.

Taxis into town from the airport cost 150B. Out to the airport you can get a túk-túk for 80B to 100B.

Bus There are two routes to Chiang Rai from Chiang Mai: an old and a new. The old route *(săi kào)* heads south from Chiang Mai to Lampang before heading north through Ngao, Phayao and Mae Chai to Chiang Rai. If you want to stop at these cities, this is the bus to catch, but the trip will take up to seven hours. In Chiang Mai the bus leaves from Th Chiang Mai–Lamphun, near Saphan Nawarat; the fare is 83B (ordinary only).

The new route *(săi mài)* heads northeast along Rte 118, stopping in Doi Saket and Wiang Papao, and takes about four hours. The fare is 77B ordinary, 98B 2nd-class air-con or 139B for 1st-class air-con. New-route 'green buses' *(rót meh khĭaw)* leave from Chiang Mai's Arcade bus terminal. Chiang Mai to Chiang Rai buses are sometimes stopped for drug searches by police.

The **bus terminal** *(Th Prasopsuk)* is several blocks south of Th Phahonyothin.

See the 'Bus Destinations from Chiang Rai' table, following, for fares and destinations for other bus services.

Boat Another way to reach Chiang Rai is via boat along Mae Nam Kok from Tha Ton (for details see River Trip to Chiang Rai at the end of the Chiang Mai Province chapter).

For boats heading upriver, go to the pier in the northwestern corner of town. The boats leave daily at 10.30am. Regular long boats from Chiang Rai stop at the following villages (times are approximate for ideal river conditions).

destination	fare (B)	duration (hrs)
Ban Ruammit	50	1
Hat Yao	100	2¼
Kok Noi	150	3
Mae Salak	170	4
Pha Khwang	130	2½
Pong Nam Rawn	60	1½
Tha Ton	250	5

You can charter a boat to Ban Ruammit for 650B or all the way to Tha Ton for 1600B.

RYAN FOX
Mae Hong Son Province

CHRIS MELLOR
Karen woman, Golden Triangle

JOE CUMMINGS
Young monk, Nan Province

ALAIN EVRARD
Young novice monks, Mae Hong Son Province

PAUL DYMOND
Sukhothai Historical Park, Sukhothai Province

CHRIS MELLOR
Parasol, Northern Thailand

PAUL DYMOND
Sukhothai Historical Park

BILL WASSMAN
Chiang Mai soldier, Bangkok

MICK ELMORE
Rafting, Chiang Rai Province

Bus Destinations from Chiang Rai

destination	fare (B)	duration (hrs)
Bangkok		
air-con	370	10
1st class	452	10
VIP	700	10
Ban Huay Khrai (for Doi Tung)		
ordinary	15	1
Basang		
ordinary	15	¾
Chiang Khong		
ordinary	42	2½
Chiang Saen		
ordinary	25	1½
Fang		
ordinary	45	2½
Khon Kaen		
ordinary	239	13
air-con	335	13
1st class	430	13
Khorat		
ordinary	262	14
air-con	472	13
VIP	550	13
Lampang		
ordinary	35	2½
air-con	55	2
1st class	80	2
Mae Sai		
ordinary	20	1½
air-con	37	1½
Mae Sot		
ordinary	200	7½
air-con	369	7½
Mae Suay		
ordinary	18	1¼
air-con	34	1
1st class	40	1¼
Nan		
ordinary	95	6
Phayao		
ordinary	25	1¾
air-con	45	1¾
1st class	55	1¾
Phitsanulok		
ordinary	153	6
air-con	214	5
VIP	290	5
Phrae		
ordinary	80	4
air-con	124	4
1st class	155	4
Tak		
ordinary	150	6½
air-con	200	6½

Call **Chiang Rai Boat Tour** *(☎ 0 5375 0009)* for further information.

Getting Around

A săamláw ride anywhere in central Chiang Rai should cost 20B to 30B. Túk-túk cost twice that. A city săwngthăew system (10B fare) circulates along the main city streets; there are also route túk-túk that charge 15B to 20B. Several small agencies near the Wang Come Hotel rent out cars (around 1200B a day), vans (1300B to 1500B) and Suzuki Caribian 4WDs (800B). The following charge a little more than the local offices.

Avis Rent-A-Car (☎ 0 5379 3827) Chiang Rai International Airport
Budget Rent-A-Car (☎ 0 5374 0442–3) 590 Th Phahonyothin, Golden Triangle Inn complex
National Car Rental (☎ 0 5379 3683) Chiang Rai International Airport; Dusit Island Resort

Bicycles and motorcycles can be hired at **ST Motorcycle** *(☎ 0 5371 3652; Th Banphaprakan • ☎ 0 5375 2526; Th Wat Jet Yot)*, which appears to take good care of its motorcycles. It's near the clock tower, but get there early as it often runs out in the morning. Daily bike rental costs 60B to 100B a day. Motorcycle rentals start at 150B per day for older Honda Dreams (200B for newer ones) up to 660B per day for a 250cc Yamaha TTR. Motorcycles can also be rented at many of the guesthouses.

MAE SALONG

แม่สลอง(สันติคีรี)

postcode 57240 • pop 10,000

Aside from Bangkok's Yaowarat district, there is no place in Thailand that more resembles China than Mae Salong. But here, rather than calling to mind brash Hong

Kong or Taipei, the atmosphere is more reminiscent of a small Chinese mountain village. The combination of pack horses, hill tribes (Akha, Lisu, Mien, Hmong) and southern Chinese-style houses conjures up images of a small town or village in China's Yunnan Province.

The village of Mae Salong was originally settled by the 93rd Regiment of the KMT, which fled to Myanmar from China after the 1949 Chinese revolution. After futile intermittent rearguard action against the Chinese communists, the renegades were forced to flee Myanmar in 1961 when the Yangon government decided they wouldn't allow the KMT to remain legally in northern Myanmar. Crossing into northern Thailand with their pony caravans, the ex-soldiers and their families settled into mountain villages and re-created a society much like the one they left behind in Yunnan.

After the Thai government granted the KMT refugee status in the 1960s, efforts were made to incorporate the Yunnanese KMT and their families into the Thai nation. Until the late 1980s they didn't have much success, as many ex-KMT persisted in involving themselves in the Golden Triangle opium trade in a three-way partnership with opium warlord Khun Sa and the Shan United Army (SUA). Because of the rough, mountainous terrain and lack of sealed roads, the outside world was rather cut off from the goings-on in Mae Salong. Hence the Yunnanese were able to ignore attempts by Thai authorities to suppress opium activity and tame the region.

Infamous Khun Sa made his home in nearby Ban Hin Taek (now Ban Thoet Thai) until the early 1980s when he was finally routed by the Thai military. Khun Sa's retreat to Myanmar seemed to signal a change in local attitudes and the Thai government finally began making progress in its pacification of Mae Salong and the surrounding area.

In a further effort to separate the area from its old image as an opium fiefdom, the Thai government officially changed the name of the village from Mae Salong to Santikhiri (Hill of Peace). Until the 1980s pack horses were used to move goods up the mountain to Mae Salong, but today the 36km road from Basang (near Mae Chan) to Santikhiri is paved and well travelled. The

GOLDEN TRIANGLE

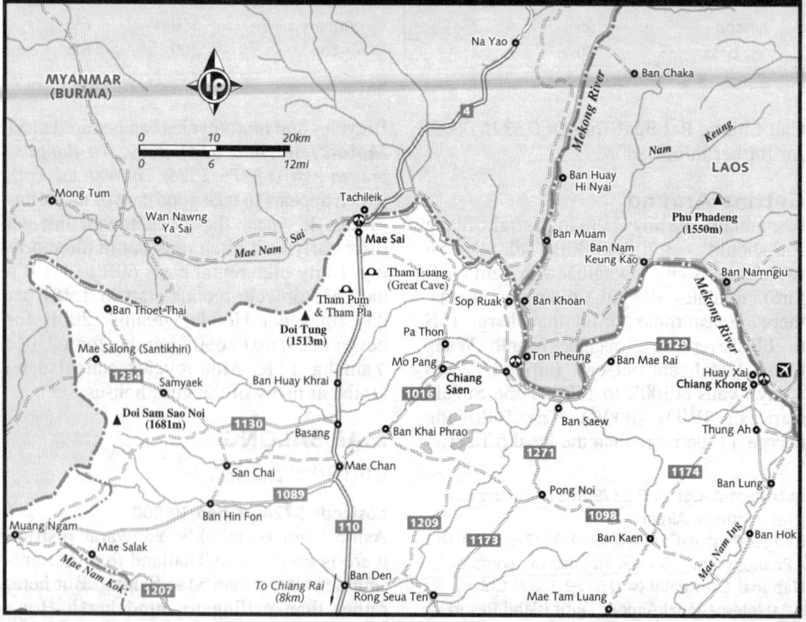

Yunnanese immigrants' equestrian history, alien to the Thais, has led the latter to refer to them as *jiin haw* ('galloping Chinese').

Despite the ongoing 'Thai-isation' of Mae Salong, the town is unlike any other in Thailand. It's not unusual for hotels and restaurants in Mae Salong to boast satellite reception of three TV channels from China and three from Hong Kong. Although the Yunnanese dialect of Chinese remains the lingua franca, the new generation of young people look more to Bangkok than Taipei for their social and cultural inspirations. Many have left for greater educational and career opportunities.

One of the most important government programmes is the crop-substitution plan to encourage hill tribes to cultivate tea, coffee, corn and fruit trees. This seems to be quite successful, as there are plenty of these products for sale in the town markets, and tea and corn are abundant in the surrounding fields. There is a **tea factory** in town where you can taste the fragrant Mae Salong teas (originally from Taiwan). The local illicit corn whisky is much in demand – perhaps an all-too-obvious substitution for the poppy. Another local speciality is Chinese herbs, particularly *yaa dawng,* a kind that are mixed with liquor. Thai and Chinese tourists who come to Mae Salong frequently take back a bag or two of assorted Chinese herbs.

The weather is always a bit cooler on **Doi Mae Salong** than on the plains below. During the cool and dry months, November to February, nights can actually get cold – be sure to bring sweaters and socks for visits at this time of year.

An interesting **morning market** convenes from around 5am to 7am (5am to 6am is the peak time) at the T-junction near Shin Sane Guest House. The market attracts town residents and many tribespeople from the surrounding districts.

Minivans full of Thai day-trippers begin arriving in Mae Salong around 10am and leave by 4pm. If you can stay overnight you'll pretty much have the place to yourself in the mornings and evenings.

Trekking

Shin Sane Guest House has a wall map showing approximate routes to Akha, Mien, Hmong, Lisu, Lahu and Shan villages in the area. Nearby Mien, Akha and Lisu villages are less than half a day's walk away.

The best hikes are north of Mae Salong between Ban Thoet Thai and the Myanmar border. Ask about political conditions before heading off in this direction (towards Myanmar), however. Shan and Wa armies competing for control over this section of the Thailand-Myanmar border occasionally clash in the area. A steady trade in amphetamines and, to a lesser extent, heroin, flows across the border via several conduit villages.

It's possible to walk south from Mae Salong to Chiang Rai in three or four days, following trails that pass through fairly remote hill-tribe villages. There are also several easily reached hill-tribe villages along the highway between Basang and Mae Salong, but these days they're full of day tourists from Chiang Rai.

Shin Sane Guest House arranges six-hour horseback treks to four nearby villages for about 600B per day. It's possible to hire ponies as pack animals or horses for riding. You could also trek the 12km to the Lahu village of **Ja-Ju** on your own. A basic **guesthouse** there offers rooms and two meals a day for 50B per person.

Places to Stay

Since the road from Mae Salong to Tha Ton opened, fewer visitors are opting to stay overnight in Mae Salong. The resulting surplus of accommodation often makes prices negotiable, except at holidays when they tend to increase.

Shin Sane Guest House *(Sin Sae; ☎ 0 5376 5026; 32/3 Th Mae Salong; rooms without bath per person 50B, singles/doubles with bath 200B)*, Mae Salong's original hotel, is a wooden affair with a bit of atmosphere. Information on trekking is available, including a good trekking map; there is also a nice little eating area and a place for doing laundry. Calls to prayer from a mosque behind Shin Sane will bring you closer to Allah bright and early in the morning.

Golden Dragon Inn *(☎ 0 5376 5009; 13/1 Th Mae Salong; bungalows 300B, rooms 500B)*, directly opposite the mosque, offers clean bungalows with balconies and private hot-water showers. Newer hotel-type rooms have two double beds and include private hot shower.

Mae Salong Villa *(☎ 0 5376 5114–9, fax 0 5376 5039; 5 Mu 1; rooms 600-1200B)*, just below the town centre, has clean rooms and bungalow-style accommodation in a garden setting – this is better value than the Mae Salong Resort. The **restaurant** offers a nice view of the mountains and the food is quite good. High-quality tea, grown on the proprietor's tea estate, can be purchased here.

Mae Salong Resort *(☎ 0 5376 5014, fax 0 5376 5135; Mu 1; rooms 500-2000B)* is a 59-room place with a variety of so-so rooms and bungalows (they look good from a distance but are none too clean). An exhibit hall on the grounds displays interesting old photographs, captioned in English, from the KMT era. The Yunnanese **restaurant** here is very good – especially tasty are the fresh-mushroom dishes.

Khumnaiphol Resort *(☎ 0 5376 5001–3, fax 0 5376 5004; 58 Mu 1; singles & doubles 500B)* on the road to Tha Ton on the opposite side of town near the afternoon market, is not as well kept as it once was. Modern hotel-style rooms are available.

Places to Eat

Paa-thâwng-kŏh (Chinese doughnut) and hot soybean milk at the **morning market** are a good way to start the day. Don't miss the many street **noodle vendors** who sell *khànŏm jiin náam ngíaw*, a delicious Yunnanese rice-noodle concoction topped with a spicy pork sauce – Mae Salong's most famous local dish and a gourmet bargain at 15B per bowl.

Around town you'll find a variety of places serving simple Chinese snacks like fluffy *mantou* (plain steamed Chinese buns) and *saalaabao* (pork-stuffed Chinese buns) with delicious pickled vegetables. Many of the Chinese in Mae Salong are Muslims so you'll find several **Muslim Chinese restaurants** serving *khâo sawy*.

Salema Restaurant *(Th Mae Salong)*, located halfway between the Shin Sane Guest House and the day market, serves tasty Yunnanese dishes using locally grown shitake mushrooms at moderate prices.

Of the hotel restaurants, the **Mae Salong Villa's** is best. Try the local speciality of black chicken steamed in Chinese medicinal herbs.

Several **tea houses** in town sell locally grown teas and offer complimentary tastings in very traditional, elaborate procedures involving the pouring of tea from a tall, narrow cup into a round cup, said to enhance the tea's fragrance.

Getting There & Away

Mae Salong is accessible via two routes. The original road, Rte 1130, winds west from Ban Basang, about 2km north of Mae Chan. Newer Rte 1234 approaches from the south, allowing easier access from Chiang Mai. The older route is definitely more spectacular.

To get to Mae Salong by public transport, take a bus from Mae Sai or Chiang Rai to Ban Basang. From Ban Basang, there are săwngthăew up the mountain to Mae Salong for 50B per person (down again costs 40B); the trip takes about an hour. This service stops at around 5pm; you can charter a săwngthăew in either direction for 300B.

The bus fare from Chiang Rai to Ban Basang is 15B. You can also reach Mae Salong by road from Tha Ton. See Fang & Tha Ton under the North to Tha Ton section in the Chiang Mai Province chapter for details.

BAN THOET THAI
บ้านเทิดไทย

Those with an interest in Khun Sa history can make a side trip to this Yunnanese-Shan village, 11km off the road between Ban Basang and Mae Salong.

Today many of Ban Thoet Thai's 3000 residents – a mix of Shan, Yunnanese, Akha, Lisu and Hmong – claim to have fond memories of the man once hunted, but never captured, by heroin-consuming countries. The warlord's former camp headquarters, a simple collection of wood and brick buildings on a hillside overlooking the village, has been turned into a rustic **museum**. There are not set opening hours, and admission is free, so you simply have to turn up at the place and ask one of the caretakers to open the exhibition room for you.

Inside the walls are hung with maps of the Shan States and Mong Tai (the name the Shan use for the independent nation they hope to establish in the future) homelands, a photograph of the former Kengtung (East Shan State) palace and a few political posters. It's not much considering Khun Sa's six years (1976–82) in the area, and of course there is no mention of opium.

A busy **morning market**, part of which was once used to store the Shan United

Army arsenal, trades in goods from Thailand, Myanmar and China. Khun Sa was also responsible for the construction of **Wat Phra That Ka Kham**, a Shan-style monastery near his former camp.

Gredpetch Rimtaan Guest House *(☎/fax 0 1961 6961; bungalows 300-500B)* has adequate accommodation in sturdy bungalows next to a stream in case you find your self stuck in Ban Thoet Thai overnight.

MAE SAI

แม่สาย

postcode 57130 • pop 60,000

The northernmost town in Thailand, Mae Sai can be used as a launching point from which to explore the Golden Triangle, Doi Tung and Mae Salong. It's also a good spot to observe border life, as Mae Sai is one of the few official land crossings open between Myanmar and Thailand. Don't come expecting bags of atmosphere; the town is little more than a modern trading post.

Foreigners are permitted to cross the border to Tachileik (the town opposite Mae Sai, spelt Thakhilek by the Thais) and continue as far as Kengtung, 163km from Thailand and 100km short of China. Within a few years, the road should be open all the way to the Chinese border – already the town seems to be gearing up for Thailand-China traffic. (See the Around Mae Sai section for current details on this trip.) In spite of the opening, Thai tourists are much more commonly seen in Mae Sai than *faràng*.

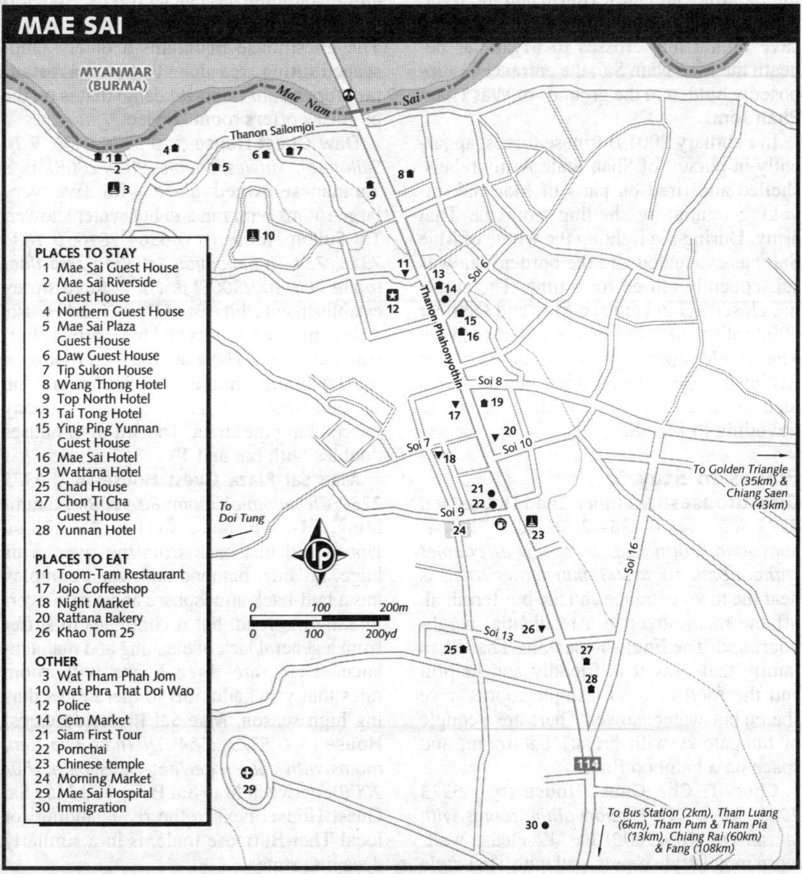

Burmese lacquerware, gems, jade and other goods from Laos and Myanmar are sold in **shops** along the main street. Many Burmese come over during the day from Tachileik to work or do business, hurrying back by sunset. Gem dealers from as far away as Chanthaburi frequent the **gem market** opposite the police station.

Take the steps up the hill near the border to **Wat Phra That Doi Wao**, west of the main street, for superb views over Myanmar and Mae Sai. This wát was reportedly constructed in memory of a couple of thousand Burmese soldiers who died fighting KMT here in 1965 (you'll hear differing stories around town, including a version wherein the KMT are the heroes). There are also some interesting **trails** in the cliffs and hills overlooking the Mae Sai Guest House and the river. A persistent rumour says there's a gated cave tunnel that crosses to Myanmar beneath the Mae Nam Sai; the entrance is supposedly hidden in the grounds of **Wat Tham Phah Jom**.

In February 2001 Burmese forces, apparently in pursuit of Shan State Army rebels, shelled and fired on parts of Mae Sai, invoking retaliatory shelling from the Thai army. During the fighting the whole of Mae Sai was evacuated and the border area was subsequently closed for a time. The crossing closed again between May and October 2002 following a political spat between the Thai and Myanmar governments. As of this writing it's open again, but it would be a good idea to check the current situation before travelling to Mae Sai.

Places to Stay

Guesthouses Old-timer **Chad House** *(☎ 0 5373 2054, fax 0 5364 2496; 32/1 Th Phahonyothin; dorm beds 50B, singles/doubles without bath 100/150B, bungalows 200B)* is near the town entrance and the bus terminal, off the main street in a residential neighbourhood. The English-speaking Thai-Shan family that runs it is friendly and helpful and the food is good. Simple rooms have shared hot-water shower. There are a couple of bungalows with private bathroom, and space on a bamboo floor.

Chon Ti Cha Guest House *(☎ 0 5373 2068; Soi 14, Th Phahonyothin; rooms with fan/air-con 180/300B)* has 12 clean, well-worn motel-style rooms – all with Thai-style toilet and cold-water shower, and TV. A Thai **restaurant** is attached, but very little English is spoken.

Ying Ping Yunnan Guest House *(☎ 0 5364 0507; Soi 6, Th Phahonyothin; rooms 200-250B)* is farther down the same lane as Mae Sai Hotel and offers 12 very clean rooms with fan, TV, phone and hot-water shower – good value. There's a Chinese **restaurant** on the premises. Not much English is spoken.

Northern Guest House *(☎ 0 5373 1537; 402 Th Tham Pha Jum; rooms without bath from 60B, doubles with bath 300B, doubles with air-con 350B)* is a friendly place on Nam Ruak west of the international bridge. A variety of rooms and huts are available including doubles with hot-water shower and river views, some with air-con; a new air-con building has fancier rooms. Add 50B to 100B to these rates in the high season. The guesthouse maintains a nicely landscaped sitting area along the river; a **restaurant** *(open 7am-midnight daily)* that is on the premises offers room service.

Daw Guest House *(☎ 0 5364 0476; 9 Th Sailomjoi; singles/doubles 160/200B)* is a Yunnanese-owned place with five very large rooms with fan and hot-water shower. **Tip Sukon House** *(☎ 0 5364 2816, 0 1883 7318; 734 Th Sailomjoi; 1st-/2nd-/3rd-floor rooms 200/400/300B)* is a new, three-storey establishment a bit east of Daw Guest House. All rooms are spotless and have private hot-water showers. There are one-bed rooms on the 1st floor, while air-con VIP rooms on the 2nd floor each have TV and a balcony overlooking the street. The 3rd floor houses doubles with fan and TV.

Mae Sai Plaza Guest House *(☎ 0 5373 2230; Th Sailomjoi; rooms 80-120B)* is a rambling, 71-room place west of Tip Sukon House and just back from the river. This huge, hillside, bamboo and wood complex has a laid-back atmosphere and a café overlooking the road, but it continues to suffer from a general lack of cleaning and maintenance. There are three levels with room rates that vary; add 50B to these rates during high season. **Mae Sai Riverside Guest House** *(☎ 0 5373 2554; Th Tham Pha Jum; rooms with cold-water/hot-water bath 150/200B)*, between Mae Sai Plaza and Mae Sai Guest House, next to the river landing for local Thai-Burmese trade, is in a similarly decaying state.

Mae Sai Guest House *(☎ 0 5373 2021; Th Sailomjoi; single/double bungalows without bath 100/150B, with bath 300-400B)*, 150m west of Mai Sai Riverside, has a nicely landscaped and scenic location on the river across from Myanmar. It's a walk of about a kilometre from the end of Mae Sai's main road and thus very quiet. Nicely designed bungalows have shared hot-water shower or private bathroom, and unlike at the previous two guest houses, standards have been maintained. The **restaurant** is decent, and staff can arrange treks.

Hotels Strictly a budget choice, **Mae Sai Hotel** *(☎ 0 5373 1462; Soi 6, Th Phahonyothin; rooms with fan 230B, with air-con 350B)* is a solid if worn hotel where you get a choice of rooms with fan and private cold-water shower, or with air-con and hot water. **Wattana Hotel** *(☎ 0 5373 1002; Th Phahonyothin; rooms with fan/air-con 200/300B)* is on the same side of Th Phahonyothin. The rooms are fairly well kept.

Top North Hotel *(☎ 0 5373 1955, fax 0 5373 2331; 306 Th Phahonyothin; fan singles/doubles with bath 300/400B, rooms with hot water 500B, with air-con 550B, with air-con, fridge & TV 600B)*, on the western side of Th Phahonyothin towards the bridge, has comfortable rooms with private bathroom and is only about five minutes' walk from the bridge crossing to Myanmar.

Yunnan Hotel *(☎ 0 5364 2169; 688 Th Phahonyothin; fan rooms with hot water & TV 350B, air-con VIP rooms 500B)*, about 100m south of the turn-off for Chad House, is a friendly but somewhat gaudy-looking place with a beer garden in front. Nice rooms sleeping up to three people have fan, hot water and TV; air-con VIP rooms have the same plus sofa and fridge.

At **Tai Tong Hotel** *(Thai Thong; ☎ 0 5373 1975, fax 0 5364 0988; 6 Th Phahonyothin; standard/larger rooms 300/500B, suites 900B)* the rates for the larger rooms and suites include breakfast for two; all rooms come with air-con and hot water.

Wang Thong Hotel *(☎ 0 5373 3388–95, fax 0 5373 3399; 299 Th Phahonyothin; singles & doubles 750B, suites up to 1500B)*, a nine-storey hotel off Th Phahonyothin in the northern part of town, entertains brisk traffic among business travellers. Spacious, international-class rooms come with all the amenities, while suites are available; rates do not include tax and service. Facilities include a swimming pool, pub, disco and restaurant. Off-street parking is available in a guarded lot behind the hotel.

Places to Eat

Many **food stalls** offering everything from *khâo sawy* to custard set up at night on the sidewalks along Th Phahonyothin. The **night market** is rather small but the Chinese vendors do good *kŭaytĭaw phàt sii-íu* (rice noodles stir-fried in soy sauce) and other noodle dishes. You can also get fresh *paa-thâwng-kŏh* and hot soy milk.

Jojo Coffeeshop *(☎ 0 5373 1662; 233/1 Th Phahonyothin; dishes 25-50B; open 6.30am-4.30pm)* serves very good Thai curries and Thai vegetarian dishes, plus ice cream and Western snacks. You'll eat well while contemplating the collection of Lanna-style wooden Buddhas along the walls. Across from the district office is a **vegetarian restaurant** – the sign simply reads 'vegetarian food'.

Khao Tom 25 *(Th Phahonyothin; dishes 20-45B; open noon-4am daily)*, near Chad House, is your best bet for late eats. **Toom-Tam Restaurant** *(Th Phahonyothin)* is a Muslim place with good curries and *khâo mòk*, and is north of the police station.

Rattana Bakery *(☎ 0 5373 1230; 18 Th Phahonyothin; dishes 10-35B; open 8am-5pm)*, north of Soi 10 on the main drag, offers Thai- and Western-style pastries and cakes.

Getting There & Away

Mae Sai's **government bus station** *(☎ 0 5364 6437)* is 2km south of the immigrations office, a 5B shared sǎwngthǎew ride from the city centre. Buses to Mae Sai leave frequently from Chiang Rai and cost 20B (37B air-con, 1½ hours). To/from Chiang Saen by bus costs 20B via Mae Chan. See Getting Around in the Chiang Saen section for details on different routes between Mae Sai and Chiang Saen.

To/from Chiang Mai it's 95B by ordinary bus (three departures daily) or 108/171B 2nd-class/1st-class air-con (seven daily); this trip takes about four to five hours.

To Mae Sot there's one 1st-class bus daily (394B, 11½ hours) and to Nakhon Ratchasima (Khorat) there are four 1st-class buses departing daily (505B, 15 hours).

There are also direct buses to Mae Sai from Fang (45B, two hours) and Tha Ton (36B, 1½ hours) via the Tha Ton–Mae Chan road. Other destinations include Doi Tung (40B, 1½ hours), Mae Chan (14B, 30 minutes), Mae Salong (60B, 2½ hours) and Sop Ruak (34B, one hour).

You'll find blue săwngthăew that leave Mae Sai for Chiang Saen daily for 40B.

Bangkok Second-class air-con government buses to Bangkok cost 374B and depart at 5.20pm and 5.45pm; the trip takes 13 hours. First-class air-con buses (481B, 12 hours) depart several times throughout the day and VIP buses (685B) are also available. These leave at 7am, 5.30pm and 5.45pm.

Siam First Tour operates a 1st-class air-con bus from Mae Sai to Bangkok for 561B. **Sombat Tour** and **Phitsanulok Yan Yon** both offer air-con buses to Bangkok for 481B.

VIP buses to Bangkok leave Mae Sai at 6.30pm, 7pm and 7.10pm.

Getting Around

Săwngthăew around town are 5B shared. Túk-túk cost 20B to 30B and motorcycle taxis 10B to 20B. Honda Dreams can be rented at **Pornchai** *(Th Phahonyothin)* between Siam First Tour and the petrol station for 150B per day. **Thong Motorbike**, across from Tip Sukon House, also rents motorcycles at similar rates.

AROUND MAE SAI

Tham Luang

ถ้ำหลวง

About 6km south of Mae Sai off Rte 110, this large cave extends into the hills for at least a couple of kilometres, possibly more. The first cavern is huge, and a narrow passage at the back leads to a series of other chambers and side tunnels of varying sizes. The first kilometre is fairly easy going but after that you have to do some climbing over piles of rocks to get farther in. At this point the roof formations become more fantastic and tiny crystals make them change colour according to the angle of the light. For 30B you can borrow a gas lantern from the caretakers in front of the cave or you can take someone along as a guide (for which there's no fixed fee; just give them whatever you want). Guides aren't always available during the week.

Tham Pum & Tham Pla

ถ้ำปุ้ม/ถ้ำปลา

Only 13km south of Mae Sai, just off Rte 110 at Ban Tham, are a couple of caves with freshwater lakes inside. Bring a torch to explore the caves as there are no lights. Another attraction here is the unique cake-like *chedi* in front of the cave entrance. It's a very large, multitiered structure stylistically different from any other in Thailand.

Doi Tung

ดอยตุง

About halfway between Mae Chan and Mae Sai on Rte 110 is the turn-off west for Doi Tung. The name means 'Flag Peak', from the northern Thai word for flag *(tung)*. King Achutarat of Chiang Saen ordered a giant flag to be flown from the peak to mark the spot where two *chedi* were constructed in AD 911; the *chedi* are still there, a pilgrimage site for Thai, Shan and Chinese Buddhists.

But the main attraction at Doi Tung is getting there. The 'easy' way is via Rte 1149, which is mostly paved to the peak of Doi Tung. But it's winding, steep and narrow, so if you're driving or riding a motorcycle, take it slowly.

Along the way are Shan, Akha and Musoe (Lahu) villages. Travelling after 4pm – when traffic thins out – is not advised except along the main routes. It is not safe to trek in this area without a Thai or hill-tribe guide simply because you could be mistaken for a United States Drug Enforcement Agency agent (by the drug traders) or drug dealer (by the Thai army rangers who patrol the area). You may hear gunfire from time to time, which might indicate that the rangers are in pursuit of the Mong Thai Army (MTA) or Karen rebels or others who have been caught between two hostile governments.

On the theory that local hill tribes would be so honoured by a royal presence that they will stop cultivating opium, the late Princess Mother (the king's mother) built the **Doi Tung Royal Villa**, a summer palace, on the slopes of Doi Tung near Pa Kluay Reservoir. The beautifully landscaped **Mae Fah Luang Garden** is open to the public, and the royal villa itself has been converted into a **museum** that preserves everything in the house almost exactly as it was before the Princess Mother's death in 1995.

Another royal project nearby, **Doi Tung Zoo**, covers an open space of over 32 hectares. The zoo was first established as a wildlife breeding and animal conservation station, to help reintroduce many species to a reforested Doi Tung. These include Siamese fireback pheasants, peacocks, bears, sambar deer, barking deer and hog deer.

At the peak, 1800m above sea level, **Wat Phra That Doi Tung** is built around the twin Lanna-style *chedi*. The *chedi* were renovated by famous Chiang Mai monk Khruba Siwichai early in the 20th century.

Pilgrims bang on the usual row of temple bells to gain merit. Although the wát isn't that impressive, the high, forested setting will make the trip worthwhile. From the walled edge of the temple you can get an aerial view of the snaky road you've just climbed.

A walking path next to the wát leads to a spring and there are other short walking trails in the vicinity. A bit below the peak is the smaller **Wat Noi Doi Tung**, where food and beverages are available from vendors.

Places to Stay & Eat If you want to spend the night, **Baan Ton Nam** *(☎ 0 5376 7003, fax 0 5376 7077; ⓔ tourism@doitung.org; Doi Tung Development Project, Mae Fah Luang District; singles/doubles Jan-Sept 1800/2300B; Oct-Dec 2000/2500B)* opened in 2000 and offers 45 deluxe twin rooms with attached hot-water shower, air-con, refrigerators and satellite TV. A semi-outdoor **restaurant** *(open 7am-9pm)* offers excellent meals made with local produce, including lots of fresh mushrooms.

Getting There & Away Buses to the turn-off for Doi Tung are 15B from either Mae Chan or Mae Sai. From Ban Huay Khrai, at the Doi Tung turn-off, a sǎwngthǎew to Ban Pakha is 30B (30 minutes), or 60B all the way to Doi Tung, 18km away (one hour).

Road conditions to Doi Tung vary from year to year depending on the state of repair; during bad spells, the section above Baa Pakha can be quite a challenge to climb, whether you're in a truck, 4WD or motorcycle.

You can also travel by motorcycle between Doi Tung and Mae Sai along an even more challenging, 16km, unevenly sealed road that starts in the Akha village of Ban Phame, 8km south of Mae Sai (4km south along Rte 110, then 4km west), and joins the main road about two-thirds of the way up Doi Tung – about 11km from the latter. You can also pick up this road by following the dirt road that starts in front of Mae Sai's Wat Phra That Doi Wao. West of Ban Phame the road has lots of tight curves, mud, rocks, precipitous drops, passing lorries and occasional road repair equipment – figure on at least an hour by motorcycle or 4WD from Mae Sai. Although now paved, this is a route for experienced bikers only. The road also runs high in the mountains along the Myanmar border and should not be travelled alone or after 4pm. Ask first in Mae Sai about border conditions. If you want to do a full loop from Mae Sai, ride/drive to Doi Tung via Rte 110 south of Mae Sai, then Rte 1149 up to Doi Tung. Once you've had a look around the summit, return to Mae Sai via the Bang Phame aforementioned roads; this means you'll be running downhill much of the way.

Cross-Border Trips to Tachileik & Beyond

Foreigners are ordinarily permitted to cross the bridge over the Nam Ruak into Tachileik. On occasion the border may close temporarily for security reasons, so be prepared for possible disappointment if the political situation between Bangkok and Yangon deteriorates again.

For now you can enter Myanmar at Tachileik and travel to **Kengtung** or **Mengla** for two weeks upon payment of a US$10 fee and the exchange of US$100 for 100 FEC (foreign exchange certificates), the phoney money Myanmar's government uses to dampen black-market currency exchange. You can use the FEC to pay for hotel rooms and plane tickets, but that's about all. Or change them for Myanmar kyat at the going black-market rate. Your two-week tourist visa can be extended for another two weeks at the immigration office in Kengtung.

If you only want to cross the border into Tachileik for the day, the cost is US$5 or 250B. There is no FEC exchange requirement for day trips. Besides shopping for Shan handicrafts (about the same price as on the Thai side, and everyone accepts baht) and eating Shan/Burmese food, there's little to do in Tachileik. About 4000 people cross the bridge to Tachileik daily, most of them Thais shopping for dried mushrooms, herbal medicines, cigarettes and other cheap imports from China. Be wary of cheap cartons of Marlboros and other Western-brand cigarettes, as many are filled with Burmese cigarettes instead of the real thing.

Three-night, four-day excursions to the town of Kengtung (called Chiang Tung by the Thais and usually spelt Kyinetong by the Burmese), 163km north, may be arranged on your own as described earlier.

Kengtung is a sleepy but historic capital for the Shan State's Khün culture – the Khün speak a northern Thai language related to Shan and Thai Lü and use a writing script similar to the ancient Lanna script. It's a bit more than halfway between the Thai and Chinese borders – eventually the road will be open all the way to China but for now Kengtung is the limit. Built around a small lake and dotted with ageing **Buddhist temples** and crumbling British **colonial architecture**, it's a much more scenic town than Tachileik, and one of the most interesting towns in Myanmar's entire Shan State. About 70% of all foreign visitors to Kengtung are Thais seeking a glimpse of ancient Lanna. Few westerners are seen around town save for contract employees working for the United Nations Drug Control Project (UNDCP).

Harry's Guest House & Trekking *(☎ 0 1012 1418; 132 Mai Yang Lan)* in Kengtung rents out basic rooms in a large house for US$5 per person. Harry is an English-speaking Kengtung native who spent many years as a trekking guide in Chiang Mai. **Noi Yee Hotel** *(rooms per person US$8-15)*, near the centre of town, has large multibed rooms.

For a complete description of Kengtung and the surrounding area, see Lonely Planet's *Myanmar* guidebook.

Beyond Kengtung Eighty-five kilometres north of Kengtung lies the Sino-Burmese border district of Mengla (or Mong La as it's sometimes spelt). Although Mengla is mainly a Thai Lü district, in a deal worked out with the Myanmar military it's currently controlled by ethnic Wa, who once fought against Yangon troops but who now enjoy peaceful relations with Yangon (in return for a sizable share in the Wa's thriving amphetamine and opium trade, it is suspected). A **Drug Free Museum** contains an exhibit on how to refine heroin from opium. The district receives lots of Chinese tourists, who come to peruse Mengla's well-known **wildlife market** and to gamble in the district's several casinos. The largest and plushest, the **Myanmar Royal Casino**, is an Australian-Chinese joint venture. There are also plenty of karaoke bars, discos and other staples of modern Chinese entertainment life. The main currency used in town is the Chinese yuan.

In order to proceed to Mengla from Kengtung, you must first register at the Kengtung immigration office. The staff at **Harry's Guest House** can help you accomplish this.

The obvious question is, can you cross the border from Mengla into Daluo, China? The simple answer is we haven't tried, and we don't know anyone who has.

Getting There & Away The cheapest form of transport to Kengtung is the săwngthăew that leave each morning from Tachileik, but reports say Myanmar authorities aren't allowing foreigners to board these. Give it a try anyway, as this sort of situation tends to change. You can rent 4WDs on either side of the border, but Thai vehicles with a capacity of five or fewer passengers are charged a flat US$50 entry fee, US$100 for vehicles with a capacity of over five. Burmese vehicle hire is more expensive and requires the use of a driver. Whatever the form of transport, count on at least six to 10 gruelling hours (depending on road conditions) to cover the 163km stretch between the border and Kengtung.

The road trip allows glimpses of Shan, Akha, Wa and Lahu villages along the way.

CHIANG SAEN

เชียงแสน

postcode 57150 • pop 55,000

Once the site of an important northern Thai kingdom, Chiang Saen today is a small crossroads town on the banks of the Mekong River. Scattered throughout the town are the ruins of the 14th-century Chiang Saen kingdom. Surviving architecture includes many *chedi*, Buddha images, *wihăan* pillars and earthen city ramparts. A few of the old monuments still standing predate Chiang Saen by a couple of hundred years; legend says this pre–Chiang Saen kingdom was called Yonok. Formerly loosely affiliated with various northern Thai kingdoms, as well as 18th-century Myanmar, Chiang Saen didn't really become a Siamese possession until the 1880s. A 19th-century American missionary wrote that the city was:

> …admirably situated for purposes of trade, at the intersection of routes leading from China, Burmah, Karenni, the Shan States, Siam, Tonquin and Annam. It forms, in fact, a centre of intercourse between all the Indo-Chinese races and the point of dispersion for caravans along the diverging trade routes.

Yunnanese trade routes extended from Simao, Yunnan, through Laos to Chiang Saen and then on to Mawlamyine in Burma, via Chiang Rai, Chiang Mai and Mae Sariang. A lesser-used route proceeded through Utaradit, Phayao and Phrae.

Today huge river barges from China moor at Chiang Saen, carrying fruit, engine parts and all manner of other imports, keeping the old China–Siam trade route open. Despite this trade and despite commercialisation of the nearby Golden Triangle, the sleepy town hasn't changed too much over the last decade. Practically everything in Chiang Saen closes down by 9pm.

Chiang Saen is an official border crossing for Thai and Lao citizens travelling by ferry to and from the Lao People's Democratic Republic town of Ton Pheung on the opposite side of the river.

Information

The **visitors centre** *(Th Phahonyothin; open 8.30am-4.30pm Mon-Sat)*, on the left-hand side as you come into town from the west, has a good relief display showing the major ruin sites as well as photos of various stupas before, during and after restoration.

Chiang Saen's **immigration office** has two branches, the main office on the southwestern corner of the town's main intersection, and a smaller one next to the Mekong River pier (for crossings to Ton Pheung).

Siam Commercial Bank *(Th Phahonyothin)* is on the main street leading from the highway to the Mekong River, has an ATM and currency exchange.

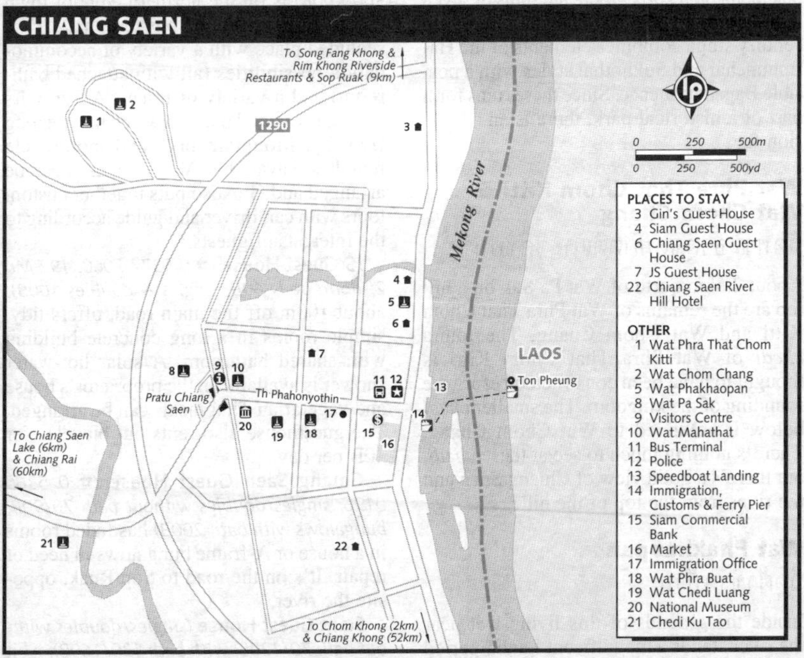

Chiang Saen National Museum
พิพิธภัณฑ์แห่งชาติเชียงแสน

Near the town entrance, a small museum *(☎ 0 5377 7102; 702 Th Phahonyothin; admission 30B; open 9am-4pm Wed-Sun)* displays artefacts from the Lanna period and prehistoric stone tools from the area, as well as hill-tribe crafts, dress and musical instruments.

Wat Chedi Luang
วัดเจดีย์หลวง

Behind the museum to the east are the ruins of Wat Chedi Luang, which features an 18m octagonal *chedi* in the classic Chiang Saen or Lanna style. Archaeologists argue about its exact construction date but agree it dates to some time between the 12th and 14th centuries.

Wat Pa Sak
วัดป่าสัก

About 200m from the Pratu Chiang Saen (the historic main gateway to the town's western flank) are the remains of Wat Pa Sak *(admission 20B)*, where the ruins of seven monuments are visible. The main mid-14th century stupa combines elements of the Hariphunchai and Sukhothai styles with a possible Bagan influence. Since these ruins form part of a historical park, there is an admission fee.

Wat Phra That Chom Kitti & Wat Chom Chang
วัดพระธาตุจอมกิตติและวัดจอมช้าง

About 2.5km north of Wat Pa Sak on a hill top are the remains of Wat Phra That Chom Kitti and Wat Chom Chang. The round *chedi* of Wat Phra That Chom Kitti is thought to have been constructed before the founding of the kingdom. The smaller *chedi* below it belonged to Wat Chom Chang. There's nothing much to see at these *chedi*, but there's a good view of Chiang Saen and the river from the top of the hill.

Wat Phakhaopan
วัดผ้าขาวป้าน

Inside the grounds of this living wát near the river stands a magnificent Lanna-period *chedi*. The large, square base contains walking Lanna-style Buddhas in niches on all four sides. The Buddha facing east is sculpted in the so-called 'calling for rain' *mudra*, with both hands held straight at the image's sides – a pose common in Laos and not so common in Thailand.

Mekong River Trips
A relatively new boat landing and customs station stand alongside the Chiang Saen waterfront. Boats from China, Laos and Myanmar can be seen unloading their cargoes in the mornings.

Six-passenger speedboats will go to Sop Ruak (half an hour) for 400B per boat one way or 700B return, or all the way to Chiang Khong (1½ to two hours) for 1300B one way or 1700B return, depending on your bargaining skills.

See Mekong River Cruises in the Sop Ruak section later in this chapter for information on services from that town.

Places to Stay
Gin's Guest House *(☎ 0 5365 0847, 0 5365 1023; 71 Mu 8; singles 150-250B, doubles 300-400B)* is on the northern edge of town (about 1.5km from the bus terminal). It's a secluded place with a variety of accommodation possibilities (all with attached bathroom) and a variety of prices. An upstairs veranda is a good place to watch the Mekong flow by. Mountain bike and motorcycle rentals are available. Visas for Laos can be arranged and Gin also puts together custom tours with car, driver and guide according to the interests of guests.

JS Guest House *(☎ 0 5377 7060; 192 Mu 2; dorm beds 60B, singles & doubles 100B)*, about 100m off the main road, offers tidy, simple rooms in a long concrete building with shared bathroom. A solar hot-water shower is available in the proprietor's house and vegetarian Thai meals can be arranged. The guesthouse also rents out bicycles for 40B per day.

Chiang Saen Guest House *(☎ 0 5365 0196; singles/doubles without bath 70/90B, bungalows with bath 200B)* has faded rooms in a house or A-frame bungalows in need of repair. It's on the road to Sop Ruak, opposite the river.

Siam Guest House *(singles/doubles without bath 70/120B, with bath 130/160B)*, a bit farther along this road on the same side as Chiang Saen Guest House, offers rooms in huts with mosquito nets. Oddly enough, none of the rooms have fans. This guesthouse also has a pleasant-looking café.

Chiang Saen River Hill Hotel (*☎ 0 5365 0826, fax 0 5365 0830 • in Bangkok ☎ 0 2748 9046–8, fax 0 2748 9048; 714 Mu 3 Tambon Wiang; high-season singles/doubles 1000B, low-season rooms 850B*) is a clean, four-storey hotel that features good service and some nice northern Thai touches to the furnishings. All the rooms contain a fridge, TV and phone, along with a floor sitting area furnished with Thai axe pillows, a Thai umbrella and a small rattan table.

Places to Eat

Cheap noodle and rice dishes are available at **food stalls** in and near the market on the river road and along the main road through town from the highway, near the bus stop. A small **night market** sets up each evening at the latter location and stays open till around midnight.

During the dry months, **riverside vendors** sell sticky rice, green papaya salad, grilled chicken, dried squid and other fun foods for people to eat while sitting on grass mats along the river bank in front of Chiang Saen Guest House – a very pleasant way to spend an evening. Local specialities include fish or chicken barbecued inside thick joints of bamboo, eaten with sticky rice and *sôm-tam*.

Song Fang Khong (*dishes 35-100B; open 11am-11pm daily*) and **Rim Khong** (*dishes 35-100B; open 11am-11pm daily*) are two *sŭan aahăan* (food garden–style) riverside restaurants off the river road out of Chiang Saen towards Sop Ruak, and both offer extensive menus of Thai, Chinese and Isan food. Bring your Thai-language skills.

Two kilometres south of town via Rte 1129, **Chom Khong** (*dishes 35-100B; open 11am-11pm daily*), back from the river, is a very nice spot amid fruit gardens.

Getting There & Away

There are frequent buses from Chiang Rai to Chiang Saen for 25B (40 minutes to 1½ hours, depending on traffic and passenger numbers etc).

From Chiang Mai, ordinary/air-con buses cost 95/171B (up to five hours). In either direction, be sure to ask for the new route (*săi mài*) via Chiang Rai. The old route (*săi kào*) passes through Lamphun, Lampang, Ngao, Phayao and Phan, a trip that takes from seven to nine hours. You can also take a bus first to Chiang Rai then change to a Chiang Saen bus (about 4½ hours).

Laos A 30B ferry service between Ton Pheung, Laos, and Chiang Saen is open only to Thai and Lao citizens for the time being. The crossing is open 8am to 6pm.

Getting Around

A good way to see the Chiang Saen–Mae Sai area is on two wheels. Mountain bikes (50B a day) and motorcycles (15B to 200B) can be rented at Gin's Guest House, while JS Guest House rents out regular bicycles for 40B.

From Mae Sai to Chiang Saen there's a choice of two scenic paved roads (one from the centre of Mae Sai and one near the town entrance), or a wider, busier paved road via Rte 110 to Mae Chan and then Rte 1016 to Chiang Saen.

The roads out of Mae Sai are considerably more direct but there are several forks where you have to make educated guesses on which way to go (there are occasional signs). The two roads join near the village of Mae Ma, where you have a choice of going east through Sop Ruak or south through Pa Thon. The eastern route is more scenic.

If you're heading south to Chiang Khong, Rte 1129 along the river is the road to take.

AROUND CHIANG SAEN

Sop Ruak

สบรวก

Nine kilometres north of Chiang Saen is Sop Ruak, the official 'centre' of the Golden Triangle where the borders of Myanmar, Thailand and Laos meet, at the confluence of Nam Ruak and the Mekong River. In historical terms, 'Golden Triangle' actually refers to a much larger geographic area, stretching thousands of square kilometres into Myanmar, Laos and Thailand, within which the opium trade is prevalent. Nevertheless hoteliers and tour operators have been quick to cash in on the name by referring to the tiny village of Sop Ruak as 'the Golden Triangle', conjuring up images of illicit adventure even though the adventure quotient here is close to zero. In northern Thai this village is pronounced 'Sop Huak'; many out-of-town Thais don't know either Thai name and simply call it 'Sam Liam Thong Kham' (*sǎam lìam thawng kham*; Thai for 'Golden Triangle').

Tourists have replaced opium as the local source of gold. Sop Ruak has in fact become something of a tourist trap, with souvenir stalls, restaurants, a massage place and bus loads of package-tour visitors during the day. In the evenings things are quieter.

One place worth a visit is the **House of Opium** *(admission 20B; open 7am-6pm daily)*, a small museum with historical displays pertaining to opium culture. Exhibits include all the various implements used in the planting, harvest, use and trade of *Papaver somniferum* resin, including pipes, weights, scales and so on, plus photos and maps. Most labels are in Thai only. The museum is at Km 30, at the southeastern end of Sop Ruak.

On the southern edge of town a huge pier and attached Thai-Lao-Chinese-Myanmar Department Store shopping centre complex has been under construction for several years. The pier is meant to serve passenger-boat traffic between Sop Ruak and China – once the red tape has cleared and such a service becomes established. On our last visit we were told everything was 'almost' ready for a regular boat circuit to China and that a company called **Star Cruisers** would soon begin offering three-day cruises to China for 15,000B.

On the Burmese side of the river junction stands the Paradise Resort's Golden Triangle, a huge hotel and casino financed by Thai and Japanese business partners who have leased nearly 480 hectares from the Myanmar government. Only two currencies – baht and dollars – are accepted at the hotel and casino.

Ten kilometres north of Chiang Saen on a plot of about 40 hectares opposite Baan Boran Resort & Spa, the Mah Fah Luang Foundation has established a 5600-sq-metre **Opium Exhibition Hall**. After it's expected opening at the end of 2003, this impressive facility will become the world's leading exhibit and research facility for the study of the history of opiate use around the world.

Mekong River Cruises Local long-tail boat or speedboat trips can be arranged through several local agents. The typical trip involves a 40-minute circuit around a large island and upriver for a view of the Burmese casino hotel for 300B per person, or 500B per boat, with a maximum of five persons. Longer trips head downriver as far as Chiang Khong for 1800B per person return. There's a fee of 250B to go onto the casino island for the day (they'll stamp you in and out at the same time), 500B if you stay overnight.

On longer trips you can stop off at a Lao village on the large river island of Don Sao, roughly halfway between Sop Ruak and Chiang Saen. The Lao immigration booth here is happy to allow day visitors onto the island without a Lao visa. A 20B arrival tax is collected from each visitor. There's not a lot to see, but there's an official post office where you can mail letters or postcards with a Laos PDR postmark, a few shops selling T-shirts and Lao handicrafts, and the **Sala Beer Lao**, where you can drink Lao beer and munch on Lao snacks.

Places to Stay & Eat Most budget travellers stay in Chiang Saen these days. Virtually all the former budget places in Sop Ruak have given way to souvenir stalls and larger tourist hotels. **Akha Guest House** *(Th Chiang Saen, Sop Ruak; singles & doubles 200B)*, a kilometre south of Sop Ruak on the road to Chiang Saen, offers simple thatched huts. **Bamboo Hut** *(☎ 0 5365 0077, 0 5376 9084; Th Chiang Saen, Sop Ruak; singles & doubles 190B)*, just south of Akha Guest House near the Mekong River, is a cluster of bamboo huts with shared bathroom and a central bar area.

Imperial Golden Triangle Resort *(☎ 0 5378 4001–5, fax 0 5378 4006 • in Bangkok ☎ 0 2653 2201; 222 Ban Sop Ruak; rooms from 2500B)*, on a hillside overlooking the river, offers 1st-class accommodation including buffet breakfast.

Baan Boran Resort & Spa *(☎ 0 5378 4084, fax 0 5378 4090; ⓔ info@baanboran.com; rooms US$120-160)* sits on a secluded hillside off the road between Sop Ruak and Mae Sai, directly opposite the new Opium Exhibition Hall. Designed by Thai architect ML Tridhosyuth Devakul, the Baan Boran melds classic northern Thai design motifs with modern resort hotel tricks, which include cathedral ceilings and skylights. To fit the naughty Golden Triangle image, poppy motifs festoon the **Suan Fin** (Opium Field) restaurant. Windows off the dining area serve up a view of Myanmar and Laos in the distance. A swimming pool, jacuzzi, tennis and squash courts, gym, sauna, medical clinic and new spa round out the amenities. Baan Boran Resort, recently purchased by Thailand's Royal Garden hotel group, may soon change its name to Anantara Spa & Resort.

Of the several tourist-oriented restaurants overlooking the Mekong River in Sop Ruak, the best is **Sriwan**, opposite the Imperial Golden Triangle Resort.

Getting There & Away From Chiang Saen to Sop Ruak, a sǎwngthǎew/share taxi costs 10B; these leave every 20 minutes or so throughout the day. It's an easy bike ride from Chiang Saen to Sop Ruak.

CHIANG KHONG

เชียงของ

postcode 57140 • pop 9000

At one time Chiang Khong was part of a small river-bank *meuang* (city-state) called Juon, founded in AD 701 by King Mahathai. Over the centuries Juon paid tribute to Chiang Rai, then Chiang Saen and finally Nan before being occupied by the Siamese in the 1880s. The territory of Chiang Khong extended all the way to Yunnan Province in China until the French turned much of the Mekong River's northern bank into French Indochina in 1893.

More remote yet more lively than Chiang Saen, Chiang Khong is an important market town for local hill tribes and for trade with northern Laos. Nearby are several villages inhabited by Mien and White Hmong. Among the latter are contingents who fled

Plaa Bèuk

The Mekong River stretch that passes Chiang Khong is an important fishing ground for the *plaa bèuk* (giant Mekong catfish, *Pangasianodon gigas* to ichthyologists), probably the largest freshwater fish in the world. A *plaa bèuk* takes at least six and possibly 12 years (no-one's really sure) to reach full size, when it will measure 2m to 3m in length and weigh up to 300kg. Locals say these fish swim all the way from Qinghai Province (where the Mekong originates) in northern China. In Thailand and Laos its meaty but mild-tasting flesh is revered as a delicacy.

These fish are taken only between mid-April and May when the river depth is just 3m to 4m and the fish are swimming upriver to spawn in Erhai Lake, Yunnan Province, China. Before netting them, Thai and Lao fishermen hold a special annual ceremony to propitiate Chao Mae Pla Beuk, a female deity thought to preside over the giant catfish. Among the rituals comprising the ceremony are chicken sacrifices performed aboard the fishing boats. After the ceremony is completed, fishing teams draw lots to see who casts the first net, and then take turns casting.

Only a few catfish are captured in a typical season, and the catfish hunters guild is limited to natives of Ban Hat Khrai. Fishermen sell the meat on the spot for up to 500B or more per kilo (a single fish can bring 100,000B in Bangkok); most of it ends up in Bangkok, since local restaurants in Huay Xai and Chiang Khong can't afford such prices. During harvest season, dishes made with giant catfish may be sold in a makeshift restaurant near the fishermen's landing in Ban Hat Khrai.

Although the *plaa bèuk* is on the Convention on International Trade in Endangered Species (Cites) list of endangered species, there is some debate as to just how endangered it is. Because of the danger of extinction, Thailand's Inland Fisheries Department has been taking protective measures since 1983, including a breed-and-release programme. Every time a female is caught, it's kept alive until a male is netted, then the eggs are removed (by massaging the female's ovaries) and put into a pan; the male is then milked for sperm and the eggs are fertilised in the pan. As a result, well over a million *plaa bèuk* have been released into the Mekong since 1983. Of course, not all of the released fish survive to adulthood. Reservoirs elsewhere in Thailand have had moderate success breeding this fish, however.

At the moment the greatest threat to the catfish's survival is the blasting of Mekong River rapids in China, which is robbing the fish of important breeding grounds.

Laos during the 1975 communist takeover and who are rumoured to be involved in an organised resistance movement against the current Lao government.

The **Si Ayuthaya**, **Kasikornbank** and **Siam Commercial Bank** have branches in town with ATMs and foreign-exchange services.

The current town of Chiang Khong has several northern Thai-style wát of minor interest. **Wat Luang**, on the main road, was once one of the most important temples in Chiang Rai Province and features a *chedi* dating to the 13th century (restored in 1881).

On a hill overlooking the town of Chiang Khong and the river is a **Nationalist Chinese Soldiers Cemetery**, where over 200 KMT soldiers have been buried. The grave mounds are angled on the hill so that they face China. A shrine containing old photos of KMT soldiers-in-arms stands at the top of the hill.

The village of **Ban Hat Khrai**, about 1km south of Chiang Khong, is famous as being one of the few places where *plaa bèuk* (giant Mekong catfish) are still occasionally caught (for more information see the 'Plaa Bèuk' boxed text earlier). During the *plaa bèuk* season, April and May, you can watch the small fishing boats coming and going from **Tha Pla Beuk**, about 2km south of Chiang Khong on the Mekong; the turn-off is near the Km 137km.

Huay Xai, opposite Chiang Khong on the Lao side of the river, is a legal point of entry for Laos. Anyone with a valid Laos visa may cross by ferry. From Huay Xai it's 250km

CHIANG KHONG

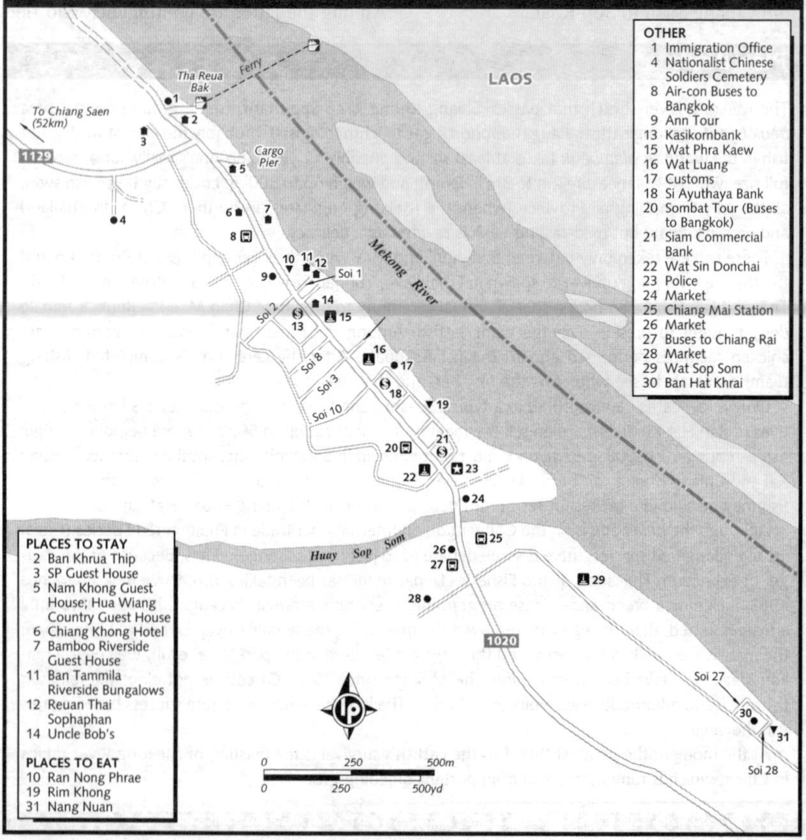

OTHER
1 Immigration Office
4 Nationalist Chinese Soldiers Cemetery
8 Air-con Buses to Bangkok
9 Ann Tour
13 Kasikornbank
15 Wat Phra Kaew
16 Wat Luang
17 Customs
18 Si Ayuthaya Bank
20 Sombat Tour (Buses to Bangkok)
21 Siam Commercial Bank
22 Wat Sin Donchai
23 Police
24 Market
25 Chiang Mai Station
26 Market
27 Buses to Chiang Rai
28 Market
29 Wat Sop Som
30 Ban Hat Khrai

PLACES TO STAY
2 Ban Khrua Thip
3 SP Guest House
5 Nam Khong Guest House; Hua Wiang Country Guest House
6 Chiang Khong Hotel
7 Bamboo Riverside Guest House
11 Ban Tammila Riverside Bungalows
12 Reuan Thai Sophaphan
14 Uncle Bob's

PLACES TO EAT
10 Ran Nong Phrae
19 Rim Khong
31 Nang Nuan

to Luang Nam Tha, a short distance from Boten, a legal border crossing to and from China – see Border Crossing (Laos) under Getting There & Away later in the Chiang Khong section for more information.

Trade between Thailand and China via Chiang Khong is steady. Thai goods going north include dried and processed food and beverages, cosmetics, machinery, spare parts and agro-industrial supplies.

Places to Stay

Overlooking the river, **Bamboo Riverside Guest House** *(☎ 0 5379 1621, 0 5379 1629; ⓔ sweepatts@hotmail.com; 71 Mu 1 Hua Wiang; dorm beds 70B, units 150-250B)* offers bamboo-thatched dorm rooms as well as private rooms, all with fan and attached hot shower. A restaurant perched on a deck with views of Laos serves good Mexican food.

Ban Tammila Riverside Bungalows *(☎ 0 5379 1234; ⓔ baantammila@hotmail.com; 113 Mu 8; huts with/without bath 300/200B)* is an old standby offering simpler huts overlooking the river; there's also a very pleasant sitting/dining area by the river. Ban Tammila receives a lot of repeat business.

Reuan Thai Sophaphan *(☎ 0 5379 1023; Th Sai Klang; rooms 350-600B)*, next door to Ban Tammila Riverside Bungalows, is more upmarket, with rooms in nicely designed multi floor wooden buildings.

Chiang Khong Hotel *(☎ 0 5379 1182; 68/1 Th Sai Klang; singles/doubles 150/200B)*, farther north and towards the river road from Chiang Saen, has plain but nicely kept rooms with hot-water shower and fan.

There are several guesthouses at the northern end of town in a neighbourhood called Ban Wiang Kaew. **Ban Khrua Thip** *(☎ 0 5363 5859; doubles 250B)* is a guesthouse/restaurant near the main pier. The guesthouse features clean sturdy wooden huts with good beds. The rooms are a bit sparse, but each hut has an attached hot-water shower, and towels, toilet paper and soap are supplied.

Near the cargo-ferry pier, **Nam Khong Guest House** *(☎ 0 5365 5102; ⓔ phayao98@hotmail.com; Th Rim Khong)* and **Hua Wiang Country Guest House** *(Th Rim Khong)* have a variety of simple hut accommodation overlooking the Mekong (40B to 150B); huts have separate hot showers.

SP Guest House *(☎ 0 5379 1767, fax 0 5379 1802; ⓔ spguesthouse@hotmail.com; row-house rooms 60-150B, thatched huts 120B)* is a quiet place well off the road on a wooded hillside. Rates for rooms in the row house vary depending on the number of beds and whether or not there's a bathroom. The guesthouse provides van service to Chiang Mai leaving at noon (220B; five hours).

Uncle Bob's *(☎ 0 5379 1929; Th Sai Klang; dorm beds 50B, singles/doubles 80/120B)*, a little northwest of Wat Phra Kaew, has rooms in an old wooden building with shared facilities (including a hot-water shower).

Places to Eat

There are a number of rice and noodle shops along the main street, none of them particularly good. **Ran Nong Phrae** *(dishes 30-80B; open 11am-9pm daily)*, just northwest of the entrance to Ban Tammila Riverside Bungalows, serves good *khâo sawy*, Western breakfasts, *kŭaytĭaw* and food made to order.

Rim Khong *(dishes 30-80B; open 11am-9pm daily)*, on a narrow road down by the river, is a simple indoor-outdoor restaurant overlooking the river. The bilingual menu is much shorter than the Thai menu; yam are the house speciality, but the kitchen can make just about anything.

Nang Nuan *(dishes 40-120B; open 9am-midnight daily)*, next to Tha Pla Beuk, is a pleasant, open-air place overlooking the Mekong River. Nang Nuan specialises in fresh river fish, including *plaa bèuk*.

Bamboo Riverside Guest House (see Places to Stay earlier for details) has good Thai and *faràng* food, as well as a few Mexican dishes. It is probably the only guesthouse worth seeking out for a meal even if you're staying there.

Chiang Doi Fishing Park *(☎ 0 5370 1701; Km 5, Rte 1020, Tambon Tha Sai; dishes 40-90B; open 10am-11pm daily)* is a good place to stop if you're travelling by road along Rte 1020 from Chiang Rai. The fare at this unassuming roadside place is excellent. You don't have to fish your own meal from the adjacent lake, though some people try.

Getting There & Away

From Chiang Saen, graded and paved 52km-long Rte 1129 is the quickest way to come from the west. A second 65km road curving along the river has also been paved and provides a slower but less trafficked alternative. With mountains in the distance and the Mekong to one side, this road passes through picturesque villages and tobacco and rice fields before joining Rte 1129 just outside Chiang Khong.

Buses leave hourly between Chiang Rai and Chiang Khong from around 4am to 5pm; ditto to/from Chiang Saen. Buses from Chiang Rai and beyond use roads from the south (primarily Rte 1020) to reach Chiang Khong. The Chiang Rai bus costs 42B (2½ hours). These stop more or less opposite the Bamboo Riverside Guest House, although the main terminal is near the market at the southeast end of town.

Buses to/from Bangkok use the same patch of turf opposite the Bamboo Riverside. First-class air-con buses between Bangkok and Chiang Khong cost 573B, while the more comfortable 24-seat VIP buses cost 760B. The trip takes 12½ hours in either direction and there's usually one departure from either end at around 7pm.

Boats taking up to 10 passengers can be chartered up the Mekong River from Chiang Khong to Chiang Saen for 1800B. Boat crews can be contacted near the customs pier behind Wat Luang, or farther north at the pier for ferries to Laos.

Border Crossing (Laos) Ferries to Huay Xai, Laos (20B one way), leave frequently between 8am and 5.30pm from Tha Reua Bak, a pier at the northern end of Chiang Khong, for 20B each way. A new pier was recently built about 100m southeast of the Tha Reua Bak, but is used for cargo only.

As long as you hold a visa valid for Laos, there should be no problem crossing. If you don't already have a visa, **Ann Tour** *(☎ 0 5365 5198, fax 0 5379 1218)*, on the main road in town near Ban Tammila Riverside Bungalows, can arrange a 15-day visa for 1200B. If you submit your passport to the office at 8am, it will have it back to you, complete with visa, by 3pm – in time to get across the river and start your Laos journey. A 30-day visa takes three to five days to process; the fee ranges from 1800B to 2000B, depending on your nationality. Ann Tour can also arrange vehicle permits to take cars or motorcycles into Laos.

Plans to build a bridge across the Mekong River here were aborted in 1997 following the baht crash. If the bridge ever gets built, it will, of course, replace the ferry service. Completion of a bridge might also affect the visa situation. Either way there continues to be talk of allowing visas on arrival in Huay Xai. Ask at the local guesthouses for the latest information.

Once on the Lao side you can continue on by road to Luang Nam Tha and Udomxai or by boat down the Mekong River to Luang Prabang and Vientiane. **Lao Aviation** *(☎ 312022)* flies from Huay Xai to Vientiane a couple of times a week.

Phrae Province

Phrae Province is probably most famous for the distinctive *sêua mâw hâwm*, the indigo-dyed, cotton, farmer's shirt seen all over Thailand. 'Made in Phrae' has always been a sign of distinction for these staples of rural Thai life, and since the student-worker-farmer political solidarity of the 1970s, even Thai university professors like to wear them. The cloth is made in Ban Thung Hong outside the town of Phrae.

The annual **Rocket Festival** kicks off the rice-growing season in May. In Phrae the biggest celebrations take place in Long and Sung Men districts. Look for launching towers in the middle of rice fields for the exact location.

Sung Men district is also known for **Talat Hua Dong**, a market specialising in carved teak wood. Phrae has long been an important teak centre. Along Rte 101 between Phrae and Nan you'll see a steady blur of teak forests (they are the thickest around the Km 25 marker). Since the 1989 national ban on logging, these forests are all protected by law. Most of the provincial teak business now involves recycled timber from old houses. Specially licensed cuts taken from fallen teak wood may also be used for decorative carvings or furniture (but not in house construction).

The province of Phrae and its neighbouring province of Nan have been neglected by tourists and travellers alike because of their remoteness from Chiang Mai, but from Den Chai – on the northern train route – they're easily reached by bus along Rte 101.

PHRAE

อ.เมืองแพร่

postcode 54000 • pop 21,200

Like Chiang Mai and Lampang, Phrae has an old city partially surrounded by a moat alongside a river (here, Mae Nam Yom). Unlike Chiang Mai, Phrae's old city still has lots of quiet lanes and old teak houses – if you're a fan of traditional Thai teak architecture, you'll find more of it here than in any other city of similar size anywhere in Thailand. The local temple architecture has successfully resisted central Thai influence over the centuries as well. It's a bit unusual since you'll find a mix of Burmese, northern Thai (Nan and Lanna) and Lao styles.

Southeast of the old city, the newer, more modern Phrae looks like any other medium-sized town in Thailand.

Information

Phrae's **main post office** *(Th Charoen Meuang; open 8.30am-4.30pm Mon-Fri, 9am-noon Sat)* stands near the centre of the old city near the traffic circle. Long-distance calls can be made at the **CAT office** *(open 8am-8pm daily)*, attached to the main post office.

Bangkok Bank and **Krung Thai Bank**, both on Th Charoen Meuang, offer foreign-exchange services during normal banking hours (8.30am to 3.30pm weekdays); both also have ATMs.

You can catch up on your email at **KSC Internet Service Centre** *(open 8am-8pm daily)*, near the north end of Th Ratsadamnoen.

Wat Luang

วัดหลวง

This is the oldest wát in the city, probably dating to the founding of the city in the 12th or 13th century. **Phra That Luang Chang Kham**, the large octagonal Lanna-style *chedi*, sits on a square base with elephants supporting it on all four sides, surrounded by *kùtì* and coconut palms. As is sometimes seen in Phrae and Nan, the *chedi* is usually swathed in Thai Lü fabric.

The veranda of the main *wíhăan* is in the classic Luang Prabang–Lan Xang style but has unfortunately been bricked in with laterite. Opposite the front of the *wíhăan* is

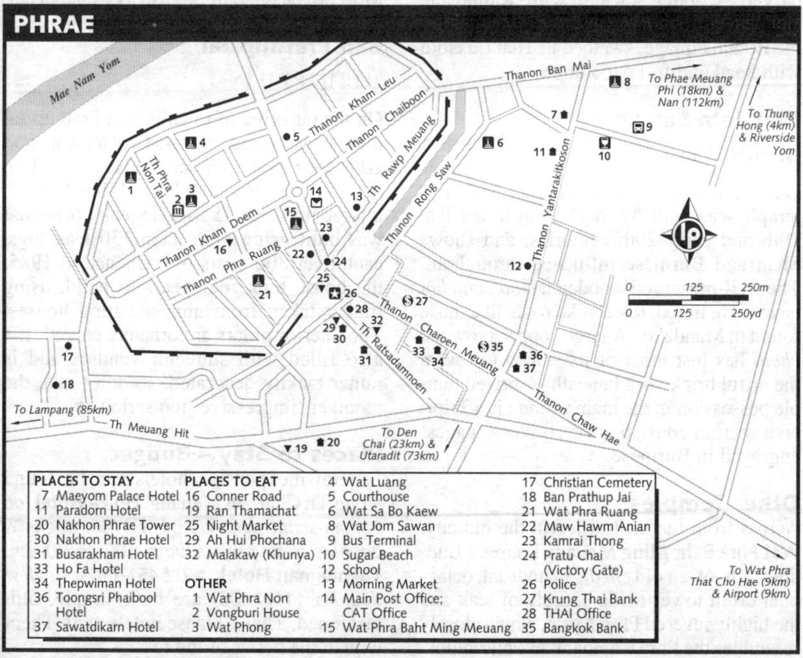

Pratu Khong, part of the city's original entrance gate. No longer used as a gate, it now contains a statue of Chao Pu, an early Lanna ruler. The image is sacred to local residents, who leave offerings of fruit, flowers, candles and incense.

Also on the temple grounds is a **museum** displaying temple antiques, ceramics and religious art dating from the Lanna, Nan, Bago and Mon periods. A 16th-century, Phrae-made sitting Buddha on the 2nd floor is particularly exquisite. There are also some 19th-century photos with English labels on display, including some gruesome shots of a beheading. The museum is usually open weekends only, but the monks will sometimes open it on weekdays on request.

Wat Phra Non

วัดพระนอน

Southwest a few hundred metres from Wat Luang is a 300-year-old wát named after its highly revered reclining Buddha image *(phrá nawn)*. The *bòt* was built around 200 years ago and has an impressive roof with a separate, two-tiered portico and gilded, carved, wooden facade with Ramayana scenes. The *wíhăan* behind the *bòt* contains the Buddha image, swathed in Thai Lü cloth with bead and foil decoration.

Wat Jom Sawan

วัดจอมสวรรค์

Outside the old city on Th Ban Mai, this temple was built by local Shan in the late 19th and early 20th centuries, and shows Shan and Burmese influence throughout. The well-preserved wooden *wíhăan* and *bòt* have high, tiered, tower-like roofs like those found in Mandalay. A large copper-crowned *chedi* has lost most of its stucco to reveal the artful brickwork beneath. A prized temple possession in the main *wíhăan* is a Tripitaka section consisting of 16 ivory 'pages' engraved in Burmese.

Other Temples

Across from the post office in the old city, **Wat Phra Baht Ming Meuang** houses a Buddhist school, an old *chedi*, an unusual, octagonal drum tower made entirely of teak and the highly revered Phra Kosai, which closely resembles the Phra Chinnarat in Phitsanulok. Just outside the northeastern corner of the moat, **Wat Sa Bo Kaew** is a Shan-Burmese-style temple similar to Wat Jom Sawan. **Wat Phra Ruang**, inside the old city, is typical of Phrae's many old city wát, with a Nan-style, cruciform-plan *bòt*, a Lao-style *wíhăan* and a Lanna *chedi*. Or is this unique mix a coherent design of local (Nan-Phrae) provenance that has yet to be identified?

Vongburi House

บ้านวงศ์บุรี

Opened as a private **museum** *(☎ 0 5462 0153; Th Phra Non Tai; admission 30B; open 8am-5pm daily)* in 1997, this two-storey teak house was constructed between 1897 and 1907 for Luang Phongphibun (the last prince of Phrae) and his wife Chao Sunantha, who once held a profitable teak concession in the city. Elaborate carvings on gables, eaves, balconies and above doors and windows are in very good condition. Inside, many of the house's 20 rooms display late 19th-century teak antiques, documents (including early 20th-century slave concessions), photos and other artefacts from the bygone teak-dynasty era. Most are labelled in English as well as Thai.

Ban Prathup Jai

บ้านประทับใจ

On the outskirts of town is Ban Prathup Jai *(Impressive House; ☎ 0 5451 1008; admission 20B; open 8am-5pm daily)*, also called Ban Sao Roi Ton (Hundred Pillar-Filled House), a large northern Thai–style teak house that was built using more than 130 teak logs, each over 300 years old. Opened in 1985, the house took four years to build, using timber taken from nine old rural houses. The interior pillars are ornately carved. It's also filled with souvenir vendors and is rather tackily decorated, so don't take the moniker 'impressive' too seriously.

Places to Stay – Budget

Several inexpensive hotels can be found along Th Charoen Meuang. **Ho Fa Hotel** *(no Roman-script sign; ☎ 0 5451 1140; singles & doubles with private bath 100-150B)* and **Thepwiman Hotel** *(☎ 0 5451 1103; singles/doubles 110/160B)* are both simple, old-fashioned, Thai-Chinese hotels, with Thepwiman the better of the two.

Toongsri Phaibool Hotel *(Thung Si Phaibun; ☎ 0 5451 1011; 84 Th Yantarakitkoson; rooms with fan 130-180B, with air-con 300B)*, a friendly place, has clean rooms with bathroom. **Sawatdikarn Hotel** *(☎ 0 5451 1032; 76-78 Th Yantarakitkoson; singles & doubles from 100B)* is similar to the Toongsri Phaibool but not as well kept.

Busarakham Hotel *(☎ 0 5451 1437; Th Ratsadamnoen; rooms with fan/air-con per person 180/300B)* is southeast of the Nakhon Phrae Hotel on the same side of Th Ratsadamnoen. It has decent rooms with fan or air-con.

Places to Stay – Mid-Range & Top End

Nakhon Phrae Hotel *(☎ 0 5451 1122, fax 0 5452 1937; 29 Th Ratsadamnoen; old-wing rooms with/without TV 250/200B, new-wing rooms with TV & fan 350B, with TV & air-con 500B, with TV & fridge 560B)* is a mere two-minute walk from the old city. The hotel's two wings are on opposite sides of the street; rooms are large. Local tourist information is available in the lobbies of both wings.

Paradorn Hotel *(Pharadon; ☎ 0 5451 1177; 177 Th Yantarakitkoson; singles/doubles with fan 200/250B, rooms with air-con 350B)* has OK-priced rooms with bathroom and fan or air-con. Information on local attractions is available in the lobby, but the hotel is looking a bit run-down these days.

Maeyom Palace Hotel *(☎ 0 5452 1028–38, fax 0 5452 2904; 181/6 Th Yantarakitkoson; singles/doubles 1000/2000B, discounted to 650/800B)* stands about 100m northeast of the Paradorn. Rooms have air-con, carpet, TV, phone and fridge; low occupancy rates mean you can easily get a discounted rate. Hotel facilities include a pool and two restaurants; the hotel also provides free transport to and from the Phrae bus terminal and airport.

Nakhon Phrae Tower *(☎ 0 5452 1321, fax 0 5452 1937; 3 Th Meuang Hit; standard rooms 1200B)*, a luxury hotel, offers quality similar to that found at the Maeyom Palace. Official rates for a standard room with all the amenities are readily discounted to 660B.

Places to Eat

A very good **night market** convenes just outside the Pratu Chai intersection every evening. Several **food vendors** also set up nightly in the lane opposite the Sawatdikarn hotel. There's another **night market** a block or two behind the Paradorn Hotel on weekday evenings only.

Malakaw *(Khunya; Th Ratsadamnoen; dishes 40-80B; open 3.30pm-midnight daily)*, diagonally opposite the Busarakham Hotel, offers good-quality Thai food and drink in a rustic ambience of rough-cut wooden tables and chairs beneath lots of hanging plants.

Also on Th Ratsadamnoen, near the Nakhon Phrae Hotel and Busarakham Hotel, are several other eating spots. **Ah Hui Phochana** *(Th Ratsadamnoen; dishes 20-60B; open 5pm-midnight daily)*, a Chinese coffee shop next to the Nakhon Phrae Hotel, offers strong coffee and various noodle and rice dishes in the evening.

Conner Road *(Th Kham Doem; dishes 40-90B; open 10am-11pm)*, an indoor/outdoor place two blocks southwest of the traffic circle in the old city, is decorated with lots of wood and old movie photos and serves good rice and noodle dishes as well as Thai food. The indoor section is air-con. An English menu is available and there's live music in the evenings.

Ran Thamachat *(no Roman-script sign; Th Saisibut; dishes 15-40B; open 7am-7pm)* is a Thai vegetarian place.

Entertainment

Sugar Beach, one of the more salubrious local nightspots, is a large, open-air pavilion near the bus terminal. It's basically just a bar-restaurant but on some nights there's live music.

Riverside Yom, a cluster of pavilions fashioned from grass thatch and pine, sits alongside the river and features live bluegrass and *phleng phêua chii-wít* music nightly. It's about 2km northeast of the city centre amid a maze of roads, and thus quite difficult to find; it's best to take a sǎamláw or sǎwngthǎew.

Shopping

A good place to buy *mâw hâwm* in Phrae is **Maw Hawm Anian**, a shop about 60m from the southeastern gate (Pratu Chai) into the old city.

If you're in the market for baskets or woven mats, a shop called **Kamrai Thong** *(no Roman-script sign)* in the same area carries a fine selection of hand-woven basketry.

Getting There & Away

Air THAI flies to Phrae daily from Bangkok (2300B, 1½ hours). There's a free shuttle service between the airport **THAI office** (☎ *0 5451 1123; 42-44 Th Ratsadamnoen*), near the Nakhon Phrae Hotel.

Bus Ordinary buses from Bangkok's Northern and Northeastern bus terminal depart twice daily (9am and 10pm) and cost 172B. Air-con buses cost 319B to 372B depending on the bus and leave twice nightly; VIP (sleeper) buses cost 495B and leave twice nightly.

From Chiang Mai's Arcade bus terminal, ordinary buses leave daily at 6.30am and 9am (79B, four hours). Air-con buses leave from the same terminal several times daily between 8am and 10pm (111B, 142B 1st class).

From Chiang Rai bus services take around four hours to reach Phrae (ordinary 80B, 2nd-class air-con 124B, 1st-class air-con 155B).

Train Tickets to Den Chai station from Bangkok cost 90B for 3rd class, 207B for 2nd class and 431B for 1st class, plus supplementary charges. Trains that arrive at a decent hour are the No 101 rapid (2nd and 3rd class only, departs Bangkok at 6.40am and arrives in Den Chai at 4.03pm), the No 205 ordinary (3rd class only, leaves at 7.05am and arrives at 6.15pm), the No 9 express diesel (2nd class only, leaves at 8.25am and arrives at 3.32pm) and the No 109 rapid (2nd and 3rd class, departs at 10pm and arrives at 8.07am). On the latter you can get a 2nd-class sleeper.

Blue sǎwngthǎew and red buses leave the Den Chai station frequently for the 23km jaunt to Phrae (20B). You can catch them anywhere along the southern end of Th Yantarakitkoson.

Mabri Hill Tribe

Along the border of Phrae and Nan Provinces live the remaining members of the Mabri (sometimes spelt Mrabri or Mlabri) hill tribe, whom the Thais call *phīi tawng lěuang* ('spirits of the yellow leaves'). The most nomadic of all the tribes in Thailand, the Mabri customarily move on when the leaves of their temporary huts turn yellow, hence their Thai name. Now, however, their numbers have been greatly reduced (possibly to as few as 150) and experts suspect that few of the Mabri still migrate in the traditional way.

Traditionally the Mabri are strict hunter-gatherers, but many now work as field labourers for Thais or other hill-tribe groups, such as the Hmong, in exchange for pigs and cloth. Little is known about the tribe's belief system, but it is said that the Mabri believe they are not entitled to cultivate the land for themselves. A Mabri woman typically changes partners every five or six years, taking any children from the previous union with her. The Mabris' knowledge of medicinal plants is said to be enormous, encompassing the effective use of herbs for fertility and contraception, and for the treatment of snake or centipede poisoning. When a member of the tribe dies, the body is put in a tree top to be eaten by birds.

In Phrae Province there is a small settlement of around 40 Mabri living in Rong Kwang district (northeast of the provincial capital, near Phae Meuang Phi) under the protection (control?) of American missionary Eugene Long. Long calls himself 'Boonyuen Suksaneh' and the Mabris' village 'Ban Boonyuen' – a classic scenario right out of Peter Mathiessen's *At Play in the Fields of the Lord*. **Ban Boonyuen** can only be reached on foot or by elephant; the nearest village, which is linked by road, is about 12km away.

Several Mabri families have reportedly abandoned Ban Boonyuen and are now living in Hmong villages in Phrae and Nan. The remaining 100 or so Mabri live across the provincial border in Nan.

The Thai government operates a 'Pre-Agricultural Development of Mabri Society Project' in both provinces to ease the Mabri into modern rural society without an accompanying loss of culture.

According to project leaders, the effort is necessary to protect the Mabri from becoming a slave society within northern Thailand's increasingly capitalist rural economy. Because of their anti-materialist beliefs, the Mabri perform menial labour for the Hmong and other hill tribes for little or no compensation.

Getting Around

A sǎamláw anywhere in the old town costs 20B to 30B; farther afield to somewhere like Ban Prathup Jai it can cost up to 40B. Motorcycle taxis are available at the bus terminal; a trip from here to, say, Pratu Chai should cost around 20B.

Shared sǎwngthǎew ply a few of the roads (mainly Th Yantarakitkoson) and cost 5B to 10B depending on the distance.

AROUND PHRAE

Wat Phra That Cho Hae

วัดพระธาตุช่อแฮ

On a hill about 9km southeast of town off Rte 1022, this wát is famous for its 33m-high gilded *chedi*. Cho Hae is the name of the cloth that worshippers wrap around the *chedi* – it's a type of satin thought to have originated in Xishuangbanna (Sipsongpanna, literally 12,000 Rice Fields, in northern Thai). Like Chiang Mai's Wat Doi Suthep, this is an important pilgrimage site for Thais living in the north. The **Phra Jao Than Jai** Buddha image here, which is similar in appearance to Phra Chinnarat in Phitsanulok, is reputed to impart fertility to women who make offerings to it.

The *bòt* has a gilded wooden ceiling, rococo pillars and walls with lotus-bud mosaics. Tiered *naga* stairs lead to the temple compound; the hill top is surrounded by a protected forest of mature teak trees.

Sǎwngthǎew between the city and Phra That Cho Hae are frequent and cost 12B.

Phae Meuang Phi

แพะเมืองผี

The name means 'Ghost-Land', a reference to this strange geological phenomenon about 18km northeast of Phrae off Rte 101. Erosion has created bizarre pillars of soil and rock that look like giant fungi. The area has been made a provincial park; a few trails and viewpoints are recent additions. There are picnic pavilions and food vendors selling *kài yâang*, *sôm tam* and sticky rice near the entrance – you may need a drink after wandering around the baked surfaces between the eroded pillars.

Getting there by public transport entails a bus ride 9km towards Nan, getting off at the signposted turn-off for Phae Meuang Phi, and then catching a sǎwngthǎew another 6km to a second right-hand turn-off to the park. From this point you must walk or hitch about 2.5km to reach the entrance.

Nan Province

Formerly a government-designated 'remote province', Nan before the early 1980s was so choked with bandits and PLAT insurgents that travellers were discouraged from visiting.

With the successes of the Thai army and a more stable political machine in Bangkok during the last two decades, Nan has opened up considerably. The roads that link the provincial capital with the nearby provinces of Chiang Rai, Phrae and Utaradit pass through exquisite scenery of rich river valleys and rice fields. Like Loei in the northeast, this is a province to be explored for its natural beauty and its likeable people.

Nan remains a largely rural province with not a factory or condo in sight. Most of the inhabitants are agriculturally employed, growing sticky rice, beans, corn, tobacco and vegetables in the fertile river plains. Nan is also famous for two fruits: *fai jiin* (a Chinese version of Thailand's indigenous *máfai* fruit) and *sôm sǐi thawng* (golden-skinned oranges). The latter are Nan's most famous export, commanding high prices in Bangkok and Malaysia. Apparently the cooler winter weather in Nan turns the skin orange (lowland Thai oranges are mostly green) and imparts a unique, sweet-tart flavour. Thung Chang district supposedly grows the best *sôm sǐi thawng* in the province. Nan is also famous for its *phrík yài hâeng* (long hot chillies) similar to those grown in China's Sichuan Province. During the hot season, you'll see lots of these chillies drying by the roadside.

Geography

Nan shares a 227km border with Laos. Only 25% of the land is arable (and only half of that actively cultivated), as most of the province is covered by heavily forested mountains; **Doi Phu Kha**, at 2000m, is the highest peak. Half the forests in the province are virgin upland monsoon forest. Most of the province's population of 364,000 live in the Mae Nam Nan valley, which is a

NAN PROVINCE

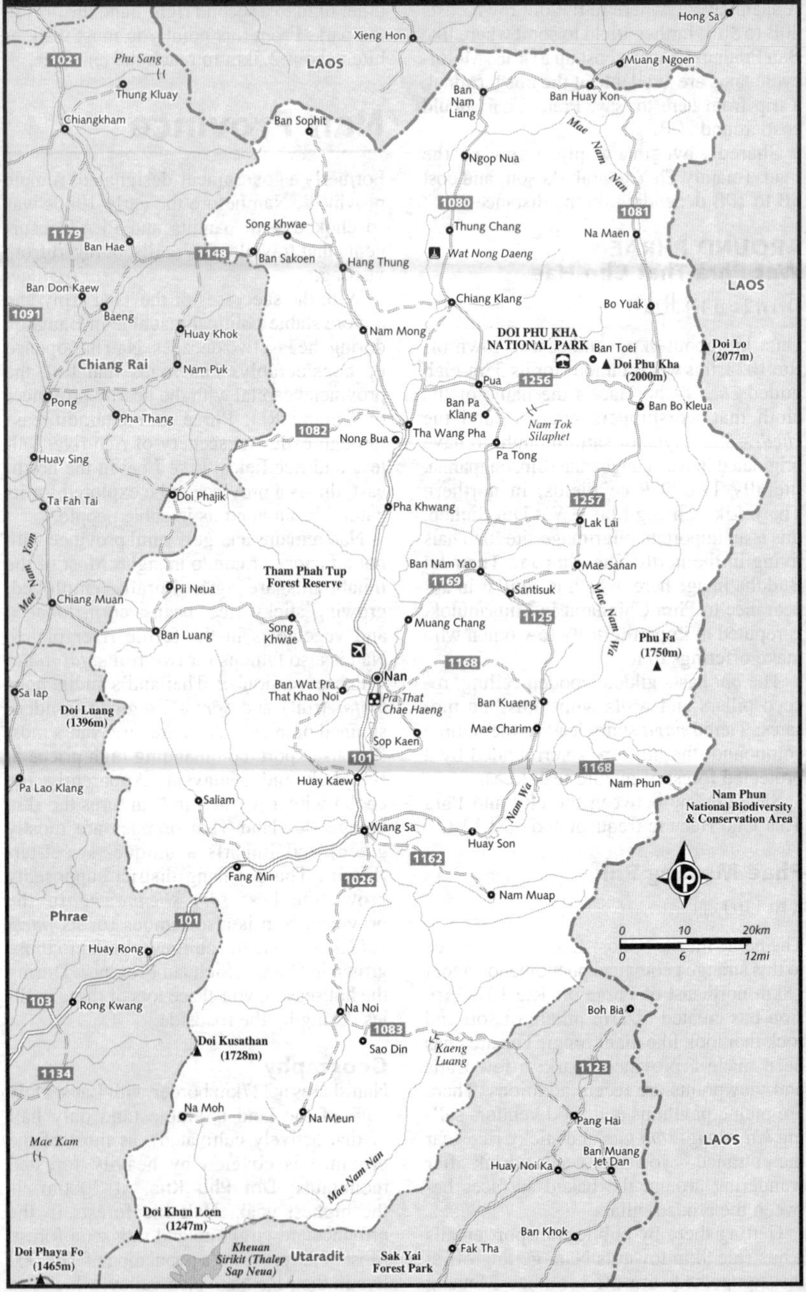

bowl-shaped depression ringed by mountains on all sides.

The major river systems in the province include the Nan, Wa, Samun, Haeng, Lae and Pua. At 627km, Mae Nam Nan is Thailand's third-longest river after the Mekong and the Mun.

Population & People

Nan is a sparsely populated province and the ethnic groups found here differ significantly from those in other northern provinces. Outside the Mae Nam Nan valley, the predominant hill tribes are Mien (around 8000), with smaller numbers of Hmong. During the Vietnam War, many Hmong and Mien from Nan (as well as Chiang Rai and Phetchabun) were recruited to fight with the Communist Pathet Lao, who promised to create a Hmong-Mien king following a Pathet Lao victory in Laos. Some of these so-called 'Red Meos' even trained in North Vietnam.

Along the southwestern provincial border with Phrae are a few small Mabri settlements. What makes Nan unique, however, is the presence of three lesser-known groups seldom seen outside this province: the Thai Lü, Htin and Khamu.

Thai Lü Originally from Xishuangbanna (Sipsongpanna) in China's Yunnan Province, the Thai Lü migrated to Nan in 1836 in the wake of a conflict with a local lord. Phra Jao Atityawong, ruler of the Nan kingdom at the time, allowed the Thai Lü to stay and grow vegetables in what is now Tha Wang Pha district. Their influence on Nan (and to a lesser extent, Phrae) culture has been very important. Like most Siamese Thai, the Thai Lü are Theravada Buddhists, and the temple architecture at Wat Phra That Chae Haeng, Wat Phumin and Wat Nong Bua – typified by thick walls with small windows, two- or three-tiered roofs, curved pediments and *naga* lintels – is a Thai Lü inheritance. Thai Lü fabrics are among the most prized in northern Thailand and the weaving motifs show up in many Nan handicrafts.

The Thai Lü build traditional wooden or bamboo-thatched houses on thick wooden stilts, beneath which they place their kitchens and weaving looms. Many still make all their own clothes, typically sewn from indigo-dyed, cotton fabrics. Many Thai Lü villages support themselves by growing rice and vegetables. In Nan they maintain a strong sense of tradition; most Thai Lü communities still recognise a *jâo meuang* (lord) and *măw meuang* (state astrologer), two older men in the community who serve as political and spiritual consultants.

Htin Pronounced 'Tin', this Mon-Khmer group of about 3000 live in villages of 50 or so families spread across remote mountain valleys of Chiang Klang, Pua and Thung Chang districts. A substantial number also live across the border in Sayaburi Province, Laos. They typically subsist by hunting for wild game, breeding domestic animals, farming small plots of land and, in Ban Bo Kleua, by extracting salt from salt wells.

Htin houses are usually made of thatched bamboo and raised on bamboo or wooden stilts. No metal – including nails – is used in the construction of houses because of a Htin taboo.

The Htin are particularly skilled at manipulating bamboo to make everything needed around the house; for floor mats and baskets the Htin interweave pared bamboo with a black-coloured grass to create bold geometric patterns.

They also use bamboo to fashion a musical instrument of stepped pipes (similar to the *angklung* of central Thailand and Indonesia) which is shaken to produce musical tones. The Htin don't weave their own fabrics, often buying clothes from neighbouring Miens.

Khamu Like the Thai Lü, the Khamu migrated to Nan around 150 years ago from Xishuangbanna and Laos. There are now over 5000 in Nan (more than anywhere else in Thailand), mostly in the Wiang Sa, Thung Chang, Chiang Klang and Pua districts. Their villages are established near streams; their houses have dirt floors like those of the Hmong but their roofs sport crossed beams similar to the northern Thai *kàlae* (locally called *kapkri-aak*).

The Khamu are skilled at metalwork and perform regular rituals to placate Salok, the spirit of the forge. Khamu villages are usually very self-sufficient; villagers hold fast to tradition and are known to value thrift and hard work. Ban Huay Sataeng in Thung Chang district is one of the largest and easiest Khamu villages to visit.

NAN

อ.เมืองน่าน

postcode 55000 • pop 23,000

Just over 668km from Bangkok, little-known Nan is steeped in history. For centuries it was an isolated, independent kingdom with few ties to the outside world. Ample evidence of prehistoric habitation exists, but it wasn't until several small *meuang* (city-states) consolidated to form Nanthaburi on Mae Nam Nan in the mid-14th century – concurrent with the founding of Luang Prabang and the Lan Xang (Million Elephants) kingdom in Laos – that the city became a power to contend with. Associated with the powerful Sukhothai kingdom, the *meuang* took the title Waranakhon and played a significant role in the development of early Thai nationalism.

Towards the end of the 14th century Nan became one of the nine northern Thai–Lao principalities that comprised Lan Na Thai (now known simply as Lanna) and the city-state flourished throughout the 15th century under the name Chiang Klang (Middle City), a reference to its position roughly midway between Chiang Mai (New City) and Chiang Thong (Golden City, which is today's Luang Prabang).

The Burmese took control of the kingdom in 1558 and transferred many inhabitants to Myanmar as slaves; the city was all but abandoned until western Thailand was wrested from the Burmese in 1786. The local dynasty then regained local sovereignty and remained semi-autonomous until 1931 when Nan finally accepted full Bangkok sponsorship.

Parts of the old city wall and several early wát dating from the Lanna period can be seen in present-day Nan. Meuang Nan's wát are distinctive: Some temple structures show Lanna influence, while others belong to the Thai Lü legacy brought from Xishuangbanna, the Thai Lü's historical homeland.

Orientation & Information

The **provincial office** *(Th Suriyaphong; open 9am-4.30pm Mon-Fri, 9am-noon Sat)* has a friendly tourist centre, although not much English is spoken. Maps are sometimes available. A new **tourist information centre** *(open 8am-5pm daily)*, complete with coffeeshop, stands opposite Wat Phumin.

Bangkok Bank and **Kasikornbank**, on Th Sumonthewarat near the Nan Fah and Dhevaraj hotels, operate foreign-exchange services and ATMs.

The **main post office** *(Th Mahawong; open 8.30am-4.30pm Mon-Fri, 9am-noon Sat, Sun & holidays)* is in the centre of the city. The attached **CAT office** *(open 7am-10pm daily)* offers a Home Country Direct Phone.

Internet services are available at **Vichart Telecom** *(Th Anantaworarittidet)* and at **R&T Computer**, on the corner almost opposite Fhu Travel Service.

Nan National Museum

พิพิธภัณฑสถานแห่งชาติน่าน

Housed in the 1903-vintage palace of Nan's last two feudal lords (Phra Jao Suriyapongpalidet and Jao Mahaphrom Surathada), this museum *(☎ 0 5477 2777, 0 5471 0561; Th Pha Kong; admission 30B; open 9am-noon & 1pm-4pm Mon-Sat)* first opened its doors in 1973. Relatively recent renovations have made it one of the most up-to-date provincial museums in Thailand. Unlike most provincial museums in the country, this one also has English labels for many items on display.

The ground floor is divided into six exhibition rooms with ethnological exhibits covering the various ethnic groups found in the province, including the northern Thais, Thai Lü, Htin, Khamu, Mabri, Hmong and Mien. Among the items on display are silverwork, textiles, folk utensils and tribal costumes. On the 2nd floor of the museum are exhibits on Nan history, archaeology, local architecture, royal regalia, weapons, ceramics and religious art.

The museum's collection of Buddha images includes some rare Lanna styles as well as the floppy-eared local styles. Usually made from wood, these standing images are in the 'calling for rain' posture (with hands at the sides, pointing down) and they show a marked Luang Prabang influence. The astute museum curators posit a Nan style of art in Buddhist sculpture; some examples on display seem very imitative of other Thai styles, while others are quite distinctive, with the ears curving outwards. Also on display on the 2nd floor is a rare 'black' (actually reddish-brown) elephant tusk said to have been presented to a Nan lord over 300 years ago by the Khün ruler of Chiang

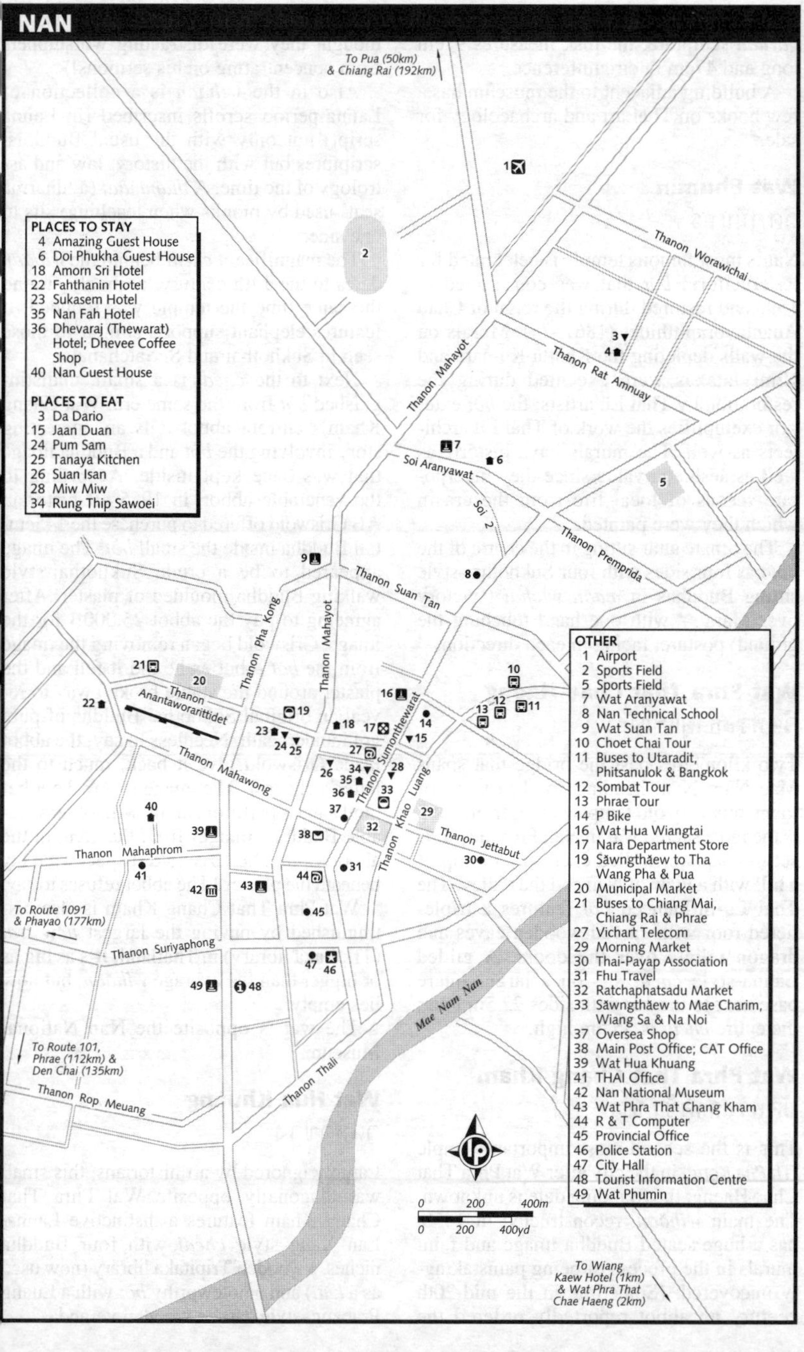
NAN
PLACES TO STAY
4 Amazing Guest House
6 Doi Phukha Guest House
18 Amorn Sri Hotel
22 Fahthanin Hotel
23 Sukasem Hotel
35 Nan Fah Hotel
36 Dhevaraj (Thewarat) Hotel; Dhevee Coffee Shop
40 Nan Guest House
PLACES TO EAT
3 Da Dario
15 Jaan Duan
24 Pum Sam
25 Tanaya Kitchen
26 Suan Isan
28 Miw Miw
34 Rung Thip Sawoei
OTHER
1 Airport
2 Sports Field
5 Sports Field
7 Wat Aranyawat
8 Nan Technical School
9 Wat Suan Tan
10 Choet Chai Tour
11 Buses to Utaradit, Phitsanulok & Bangkok
12 Sombat Tour
13 Phrae Tour
14 P Bike
16 Wat Hua Wiangtai
17 Nara Department Store
19 Săwngthăew to Tha Wang Pha & Pua
20 Municipal Market
21 Buses to Chiang Mai, Chiang Rai & Phrae
27 Vichart Telecom
29 Morning Market
30 Thai-Payap Association
31 Fhu Travel
32 Ratchaphatsadu Market
33 Săwngthăew to Mae Charim, Wiang Sa & Na Noi
37 Oversea Shop
38 Main Post Office; CAT Office
39 Wat Hua Khuang
41 THAI Office
42 Nan National Museum
43 Wat Phra That Chang Kham
44 R & T Computer
45 Provincial Office
46 Police Station
47 City Hall
48 Tourist Information Centre
49 Wat Phumin
To Pua (50km) & Chiang Rai (192km)
Thanon Worawichai
Thanon Mahayot
Thanon Rat Amnuay
Soi Aranyawat
Soi 2
Thanon Prempridа
Thanon Suan Tan
Thanon Pha Kong
Thanon Anantaworarittidet
Thanon Mahawong
Thanon Sumonthewarat
Thanon Khao Luang
Thanon Jettabut
Thanon Mahaphrom
Thanon Suriyaphong
Thanon Rop Meuang
Thanon Thali
Mae Nam Nan
To Route 1091 & Phayao (177km)
To Route 101, Phrae (112km) & Den Chai (135km)
To Wiang Kaew Hotel (1km) & Wat Phra That Chae Haeng (2km)
0 200 400m
0 200 400yd

Tung (Kengtung). Held aloft by a wooden *garuda* sculpture, the tusk measures 97cm long and 47cm in circumference.

A building adjacent to the museum has a few books on Thai art and archaeology for sale.

Wat Phumin
วัดภูมินทร์

Nan's most famous temple is celebrated for its cruciform *bòt* that was constructed in 1596 and restored during the reign of Chao Anantavorapitthidet (1867–74). Murals on the walls depicting the Khatta Kumara and Nimi Jatakas were executed during the restoration by Thai Lü artists; the *bòt* exterior exemplifies the work of Thai Lü architects as well. The murals have historic as well as aesthetic value since they incorporate scenes of local life from the era in which they were painted.

The ornate altar sitting in the centre of the *bòt* has four sides with four Sukhothai-style sitting Buddhas in *maan wíchai* ('victory over Mara' – with one hand touching the ground) posture, facing in each direction.

Wat Phra That Chae Haeng
วัดพระธาตุแช่แห้ง

Two kilometres past the bridge that spans Mae Nam Nan, heading southeast out of town, this very old temple dating from 1355 is the most sacred wát in Nan Province. It is set in a square, walled enclosure on top of a hill with a view of Nan and the valley. The Thai Lü-influenced *bòt* features a triple-tiered roof with carved wooden eaves and dragon reliefs over the doors. A gilded Lanna-style *chedi* sits on a large square base next to the *bòt* with sides 22.5m long; the entire *chedi* is 55.5m high.

Wat Phra That Chang Kham
วัดพระธาตุช้างค้ำ

This is the second-most important temple *(Th Pha Kong)* in the city after Wat Phra That Chae Haeng; the founding date is unknown. The main *wíhǎan*, reconstructed in 1458, has a huge seated Buddha image and faint murals in the process of being painstakingly uncovered. (Sometime in the mid-20th century an abbot reportedly ordered the murals to be whitewashed because he thought they were distracting worshippers from concentrating on his sermons!)

Also in the *wíhǎan* is a collection of Lanna-period scrolls inscribed (in Lanna script) not only with the usual Buddhist scriptures but with the history, law and astrology of the time. A *thammâat* (a 'dharma seat' used by monks when teaching) sits to one side.

The magnificent *chedi* behind the *wíhǎan* dates to the 14th century, probably around the same time the temple was founded. It features elephant supports similar to those seen in Sukhothai and Si Satchanalai.

Next to the *chedi* is a small, undistinguished *bòt* from the same era. Wat Chang Kham's current abbot tells an interesting story involving the *bòt* and a Buddha image that was once kept inside. According to the venerable abbot, in 1955 art historian AB Griswold offered to purchase the 145cm-tall Buddha inside the small *bòt*. The image appeared to be a crude Sukhothai-style walking Buddha moulded of plaster. After agreeing to pay the abbot 25,000B for the image, Griswold began removing the image from the *bòt* – but as he did it fell and the plaster around the statue broke away to reveal an original Sukhothai Buddha of pure gold underneath. Needless to say, the abbot made Griswold give it back, much to the latter's chagrin. The image is now kept behind a glass partition, along with other valuable Buddhist images from the area, in the abbot's *kùtì*. Did Griswold suspect what lay beneath the plaster? The abbot refuses to say.

Wat Phra That Chang Kham is also distinguished by having the largest *hǎw trai* (Tripitaka library) in Thailand. It's as big as or bigger than the average *wíhǎan*, but now lies empty.

The wát is opposite the Nan National Museum.

Wat Hua Khuang
วัดหัวข่วง

Largely ignored by art historians, this small wát diagonally opposite Wat Phra That Chang Kham features a distinctive Lanna/Lan Xang–style *chedi* with four Buddha niches, a wooden Tripitaka library (now used as a *kùtì*) and a noteworthy *bòt* with a Luang Prabang–style carved wooden veranda.

Inside are a carved wooden ceiling and a huge *naga* altar. The temple's founding date is unknown, but stylistic cues suggest this may be one of the city's oldest wát.

Wat Suan Tan
วัดสวนตาล

Reportedly established in 1456, Wat Suan Tan *(Palm Grove Monastery; Th Suan Tan)* features an interesting 15th-century *chedi* (40m high) that combines prang and lotus-bud motifs of obvious Sukhothai influence. The heavily restored *wíhǎan* contains an early Sukhothai-style bronze sitting Buddha.

Wat Suan Tan is near the northeastern end of Th Pha Kong.

Trekking & Rafting

Nan has nothing like the organised trekking industry found in Chiang Rai and Chiang Mai, but there is one company that leads two- or three-day excursions into the mountains. **Fhu Travel Service** *(☎ 0 5471 0636, 0 5471 0940, 0 1472 8951, fax 0 5477 5345; e fhutravel@hotmail.com; 453/4 Th Sumonthewarat)* offers treks to Mabri, Hmong, Mien, Thai Lü and Htin villages.

A one-day 'soft' trek costs 700B to 1200B per person depending on the number of participants (two-person minimum); a two-day, one-night journey costs 1200B to 2000B per person; and three days and two nights costs 1500B to 2700B per person. The trekking fees include transport, meals, accommodation, sleeping bag and guide services.

Fhu also runs boat trips on Mae Nam Nan in December and January when the water level is high enough. White-water rubber rafting trips on the Nam Wa in Mae Charim are offered all year. The prices run from 1300B per person (for trips of seven to eight people) to 2500B per person (for trips of two people). This price includes transport, guide, lunch and safety equipment. Three-day rubber-rafting trips are 3000B to 6000B per person, depending on the number of people. Elephant tours are also available. Tours of the city and surrounding area cost 500B for up to five people.

Outside High Attitude Company *(☎ 0 2942 0578; e totorockz@hotmail.com; 1 Mu 11, Lat Phrao, Bangkok 10230)* offers three-day, white-water rafting trips with lodging in bamboo huts on the river. The 5800B (per person) package includes eight meals, transportation, dry pack, raft, rafting captain and crew, safety gear, an English-speaking guide, accommodation and insurance.

Nan Pang Chang *(☎ 0 5478 1316, 0 1724 0579, 0 1952 4709, fax 0 5478 1212)* is a tour operator in Wiang Sa with adventure programmes for travellers. One-day trips include elephant treks along the Nam Wa for 700B per person or 950B if you add rafting. Longer trips include a two-day, one-night trekking/camping package to Doi Phu Kha for 2300B per person (six-person minimum required). Call for more details.

Places to Stay

Guesthouses An old favourite, **Doi Phukha Guest House** *(☎ 0 5475 1517; 94/5 Soi 1 Th Sumonthewarat; singles/doubles from 70/100B)* has reopened after having been closed for renovation. It's basically just a rambling old house, but as it's in a residential neighbourhood it's fairly quiet and the management is very helpful with local info.

Nan Guest House *(☎ 0 5477 1849; 57/16 Th Mahaphrom; singles/doubles/triples without bath 70/100/130B, rooms with bath 200B)* is in a large house at the end of a lane off Th Mahaphrom, near the THAI office. Clean rooms come with shared bathroom. Nan Guest House also does tours and rents out mountain bikes for 30B.

Amazing Guest House *(☎ 0 5471 0893; 23/7 Th Rat Amnuay; singles/doubles/triples/quads 100/160/210/260B)* is in a tidy, two-storey house on a quiet lane off Th Rat Amnuay. It's a friendly place that offers five fan rooms upstairs, all with wooden floors, clean beds and hot shared showers. Discounts are available for long-term stays.

Hotels With basic fan rooms, **Amorn Sri** *(no Roman-script sign; ☎ 0 5471 0510; 62/1 Th Anantaworarittidet; singles/doubles 170/250B)* is a bit overpriced. The hotel is at a very busy intersection so it may not be the quietest choice. **Sukasem Hotel** *(☎ 0 5471 0141, fax 0 5477 1581; 29/31 Th Anantaworarittidet; singles & doubles with fan 180B, with fan & TV 210B, with air-con 350B)* has much better rooms than Amorn Sri, with bathroom and fan or air-con.

Dhevaraj Hotel *(Thewarat; ☎ 0 5471 0094, fax 0 5477 1365; 466 Th Sumonthewarat; singles/doubles with fan 320/400B, with air-con*

500/600B, VIP rooms 700B) is a four-storey place built around a tiled courtyard with a fountain. It's not really fancy but it's a pleasant place and is one of the best hotels Nan has to offer. Parts of the hotel were undergoing renovation when we last visited, so prices may change. Large, clean rooms on the 2nd floor have fan and private bathroom. Prices for these are a bit steep due to the lack of competition, but the rooms are a cut above the usual room with fan. Rooms towards the back of the hotel are quieter than those towards the front. Rooms on the 3rd floor are all air-con. On the top floor are newly renovated 'VIP' rooms with double-glazed windows, carpet, cable TV and minifridge.

Nan Fah Hotel *(☎ 0 5471 0284; 438-440 Th Sumonthewarat; singles & doubles from 380B)*, an all-wood place next to the Dhevaraj Hotel, is well known for a supporting teak pillar that extends for three storeys. All rooms come with air-con, TV, fridge and hot-water showers. Khrua Rak Nan Fa **restaurant** is attached to the hotel.

Wiang Kaew Hotel *(☎ 0 5475 0573, fax 0 5477 4573; Km 1, Rte 1168; rooms with fan/air-con 240/380B)* is a friendly place at the Km 1 marker on Rte 1168, 1km from the bridge on the road that leads to Wat Phra That Chae Haeng. Although the rooms are in row houses, they have the appearance of separate bungalows. There's no lounge or karaoke so it's quiet at night. All rooms come with hot water, TV, refrigerator and phone.

Fahthanin Hotel *(☎ 0 5475 7321–4; 303 Th Anantaworarittidet; rooms 700B, with bathtub 800B)* is a fairly new, seven-storey hotel that offers rooms with TV, air-con, hot shower and minifridge, or slightly larger versions with bathtubs. Rates include breakfast. The **restaurant/coffee shop** has very good Thai food.

Places to Eat

Rung Thip Sawoei *(Th Sumonthewarat; dishes 25-60B; open 6am-4.30pm daily)* is an old, brick and wood eatery with the most dependable Thai-Chinese food in the vicinity of the Nan Fah and Dhevaraj hotels. The restaurant also serves homemade coconut ice cream.

Miw Miw *(no Roman-script sign; Th Sumonthewarat; dishes 20-50B; open 8am-10pm daily)*, opposite the **Kasikornbank**, is a bit cleaner than Rung Thip Sawoei and has good *jók*, noodles and real coffee.

Suan Isan *(Th Sumonthewarat; dishes 25-60B; open 11am-11pm)* is the best choice in town for Isan food. If you turn left at the lane next to Rung Thip Sawoei and follow it about 200m, you'll come to this semi-outdoor place.

Tanaya Kitchen *(☎ 0 5471 0930; 75/23-24 Th Anantaworarittidet; dishes 15-35B; open 7am-9pm)*, near the Sukasem Hotel, is a clean place that serves a range of reasonably priced vegetarian dishes (plus nonveg), and a mostly tourist clientele. Two doors east of Sukasem Hotel, **Pum Sam** has a large selection of Thai and Chinese standards. Opposite the Nara department store, **Jaan Duan** *(no Roman-script sign)* features ice cream, coffee, and curries over rice. It's open morning and evening.

Dhevee Coffee Shop *(☎ 0 5471 0094, fax 0 5477 1365; Dhevaraj Hotel, 466 Th Sumonthewarat; dishes 40-100B; open 6am-2am)*, inside the Dhevaraj Hotel, is a modest, clean and reliable restaurant; it's open when many other places are closed.

Da Dario *(☎ 0 5475 0258; 37/4 Th Rat Amnuay; dishes 50-100B; open 10am-2pm & 5pm-10pm Mon-Sat, 5pm-10pm Sun)*, next to Amazing Guest House, is a Swiss-run Italian-Thai restaurant; prices are reasonable and the food and service are very good.

Shopping

Good buys include local textiles, especially the Thai Lü weaving styles from Xishuangbanna. Typical Thai Lü fabrics feature red and black designs on white cotton in floral, geometric and animal designs; indigo and red on white is also common. A favourite is the *lai náam lăi* ('flowing-water design') showing stepped patterns representing streams, rivers and waterfalls.

Local Mien embroidery and Hmong applique are of excellent quality. Htin grass-and-bamboo baskets and mats are worth a look, too.

Thai-Payap Association *(☎ 0 5471 0230; 24 Th Jettabut)* is one of Thailand's most successful, nonprofit, village self-help projects and has a shop near the morning market. Supported by Britain's Ockenden Venture from 1979 to 1990, the association now involves over 20 villages and has become totally self-sufficient. The handiwork offered through Thai-Payap is among the highest quality available, often including intricate, time-consuming designs. All proceeds go directly to the participating villages – even the administrative staff are trained village representatives.

There are several small, artisan-operated shops along Th Sumonthewarat and along Th Mahawong and Th Anantaworarittidet.

Getting There & Away

Air You can fly to Nan on **Air Andaman** *(☎ 0 5471 1222; Nan Airport)* from Chiang Mai (1400B, four flights, weekly) or Bangkok (2600B, daily). Air Andaman offers free transport between Fahthanin Hotel and the airport.

Bus Baw Khaw Saw (government) buses run from Chiang Mai, Chiang Rai and Phrae to Nan. The fare from Chiang Mai's Arcade bus terminal is 128B ordinary (air-con 179B, 1st class air-con 230B, six to seven hours). From Chiang Rai there's one daily bus at 9.30am (No 611, 110B) that takes six to seven gruelling hours via treacherous mountain roads – get a window seat as there's usually lots of motion sickness. Buses from Phrae to Nan leave frequently, cost 44B (air-con 62B, two to 2½ hours).

From Nan, buses to Chiang Mai, Chiang Rai and Phrae leave from a terminal west of the large market along Th Anantaworarittidet.

Regular government-run air-con buses to Bangkok cost 300B (daily at 8am, 8.30am and 7pm), 1st-class air-con is 420B (daily at 8am and 7pm) and 24-seat VIP buses are 620B (daily at 7pm). The journey takes 10 to 13 hours.

Private 1st-class and VIP Bangkok buses leave from offices located along the eastern end of Th Anantaworarittidet, not far from the Baw Khaw Saw terminal. **Sombat Tour** and **Phrae Tour** both run VIP buses to Bangkok for as low as 450B – check the number of seats before booking, although. **Choet Chai Tour** offers 1st-class air-con buses to Bangkok. Most of these private buses depart between 6.15pm and 6.45pm.

Train The northern railway makes a stop in Den Chai, which is a 46B, three-hour bus ride from Nan.

A Bangkok-bound Sprinter leaves Den Chai at 12.25pm and arrives in Bangkok at 8.10pm. There are also a couple of evening Rapid train departures each day; to be sure of meeting any of these trains, take an early afternoon (1pm or 2pm) Den Chai–bound bus from Nan's Baw Khaw Saw bus terminal.

Trains bound for Chiang Mai depart Den Chai at 8.07am (rapid), 10.55am (ordinary) and 3.32pm (express), arriving at Chiang Mai at 12.55pm, 4.10pm and 8pm respectively. The 2nd- and 3rd-class fares to/from Chiang Mai are 74/31B, plus the rapid/express surcharges.

See Getting There & Away in the Phrae section for more Den Chai train information.

Săwngthăew Pick-ups to districts in the northern part of the province (Tha Wang Pha, Pua, Phah Tup) leave from the petrol station opposite Sukasem Hotel on Th Anantaworarittidet. Southbound săwngthăew (for Mae Charim, Wiang Sa, Na Noi) depart from the car park opposite Talat Ratchaphatsadu on Th Jettabut.

Getting Around

P Bike *(no Roman-script sign; ☎ 0 5477 2680; 331-3 Th Sumonthewarat)*, opposite Wat Hua Wiangtai, rents out Honda Dreams for 150B a day including helmet and third-party insurance. Bicycles are also available, and P Bike does repair work.

Oversea Shop *(☎ 0 5471 0258; 488 Th Sumonthewarat)*, a few doors down from the Dhevaraj Hotel, rents out bicycles and motorbikes and can also handle repairs.

Săamláw around town cost 20B to 30B. Green săwngthăew circulating around the city centre charge 5B to 10B per person depending on distance.

AROUND NAN

Doi Phu Kha National Park

อุทยานแห่งชาติดอยภูคา

This national park *(adult/child 200/100B)* is centred on 2000m-high Doi Phu Kha in the Pua and Bo Kleua districts of northeastern Nan (about 75km from Nan). There are several Htin, Mien, Hmong and Thai Lü **villages** in the park and vicinity, as well as a couple of **caves** and **waterfalls** and endless opportunities for forest **walks**.

The park offers 14 **bungalows** that rent for 250B per double room. You must bring food and drinking water in from town, as the park office no longer offers food service.

Bamboo Hut *(103 Mu 10, Tambon Phu Kha, Amphoe Pua, Nan 55120; singles & doubles 100B)* in Ban Toei, a Lawa-Thai village near the summit at the edge of the park, is a much better choice than the park bungalows. Bamboo Hut offers five clean, well-spaced bamboo-thatch huts with shared bathroom and stupendous mountain and valley views. It leads guests on one- to three-day treks for 500B per day, including all meals. Treks visit local waterfalls, limestone caves (Tham Lawng is the biggest cave – about a one-day walk from the guesthouse) and hill-tribe villages. This area gets quite cool in the winter months – evening temperatures of 5°C to 10°C are not uncommon – so dress accordingly.

To reach the park by public transport you must first take a bus or sǎwngthǎew north of Nan to Pua (25B), and then pick up one of the infrequent sǎwngthǎew to the park headquarters or Bamboo Hut (30B). The one from Nan to Pua leaves about 6am, the one from Pua to Ban Toei at about 7am.

Ban Bo Kleua is a Htin village southeast of the park where the main occupation is the extraction of salt from local salt wells. It's easy to find the main community salt well, more or less in the centre of the village. Many small shops and vendor stands sell the local salt in 2kg bags for 20B; it's delicious stuff. Rte 1256 meets Rte 1081 near Ban Bo Kleua; Rte 1081 can be followed south back to Nan (107km) via a network of unpaved roads.

Nong Bua
หนองบัว

This neat and tidy Thai Lü village near the town of Tha Wang Pha, approximately 30km north of Nan, is famous for Lü-style **Wat Nong Bua**. Featuring a typical two-tiered roof and carved wooden portico, the *bòt* design is simple yet striking – note the carved *naga* heads at the roof corners. Inside the *bòt* are some noteworthy but faded Jataka murals; the building is often locked when religious services aren't in progress, but there's usually someone around to unlock the door. Be sure to leave at the altar a donation for temple upkeep and for its restoration.

You can also see Thai Lü weavers in action in the village. The home of **Khun Janthasom Phrompanya**, a few blocks behind the wát, serves as a local weaving centre – check there for the locations of looms or to look at fabrics for purchase. Large *yâam* (hill-tribe–style shoulder bags) are available for just 50B, while nicely woven neck scarves cost more. There are also several weaving houses just behind the wát.

Getting There & Away Sǎwngthǎew to Tha Wang Pha (15B) leave from opposite Nan's Sukasem Hotel. Get off at Samyaek Longbom, a three-way intersection before Tha Wang Pha, and walk west to a bridge over Mae Nam Nan, then left at the dead end on the other side of the bridge to Wat Nong Bua. It's 3.1km from the highway to the wát.

If you're coming from Nan via your own transport on Rte 1080, you'll cross a stream called Lam Nam Yang just past the village of Ban Fai Mun but before Tha Wang Pha. Take the first left off Rte 1080 and follow it to a dead end; turn right and then left over a bridge across Mae Nam Nan and walk until you reach another dead end, then left 2km until you can see Wat Nong Bua on the right.

Tham Phah Tup Forest Reserve
ถ้ำผาตูบ

This limestone cave complex is about 10km north of Nan and is part of a relatively new wildlife reserve. Some 17 **caves** have been counted, of which nine are easily located by means of established (but unmarked) trails.

From Nan, you can catch a sǎwngthǎew bound for Pua or Thung Chang; it will stop at the turn-off to the caves for 10B. The vehicles leave from the petrol station opposite the Sukasem hotel.

Sao Din
เสาดิน

Literally 'Earth Pillars', Sao Din is an erosional phenomenon similar to that found at Phae Meuang Phi in Phrae Province – tall columns of earth protruding from a barren depression. The area covers nearly 3.2 hectares off Rte 1026 in Na Noi district about 60km south of Nan.

Sao Din is best visited by bicycle or motorcycle since it's time consuming to reach by public transport. If you don't have your own wheels, take a sǎwngthǎew to Na Noi from the southbound sǎwngthǎew station opposite the Ratchaphatsadu Market in Nan. From Na Noi you must get yet another sǎwngthǎew bound for Fak Tha or Ban Khok, getting off at the entrance to Sao Din after 5km or so. From here you'll have to walk or hitch 4km to Sao Din itself. There are also occasional direct sǎwngthǎew from Na Noi.

Northwest of Sao Din, off Rte 1216, is a set of earth pillars called **Hom Chom**.

Other Attractions

There are a couple of interesting destinations in and around the Thai Lü village of **Pua**, roughly 50km north of Nan. In Pua itself you can check out another famous Thai Lü temple, **Wat Ton Laeng**, which is admired for its classic three-tiered roof. **Nam Tok Silaphet** is southeast of Pua just off the road between Pua and Ban Nam Yao. The water falls in a wide swath over a cliff and is best seen at the end of the monsoon season in November. On the way to the falls and west of the road is the Mien village of **Ban Pa Klang**, worth a visit to see silversmiths at work. This village supplies many silver shops in Chiang Mai and Bangkok. Other silverwork Mien villages can be found on Rte 101 between Nan and Phrae.

Off Rte 1148, north of the village of Ban Sakoen, is a huge, 200m-wide cave called **Tham Luang**. The path to the cave is not signposted, but if you ask at the police checkpoint in Ban Sakoen you should be able to get directions or you might even find a guide.

Thaleh Sap Neua (Northern Lake) formed by Kheuan Sirikit is an important freshwater fishery for Nan, as well as a recreational attraction for Nan residents. **Ban Pak Nai** on its northwestern shore is the main fishing village. Just before Mae Nam Nan feeds into the lake at its extreme northern end, there is a set of river rapids called **Kaeng Luang**.

Border Crossing (Laos)

Ban Huay Kon (140km north of Nan) in Thung Chang District is a legal border crossing for Lao and Thais, and it may be promoted to an international crossing in the foreseeable future. From this crossing it's just 152km to Luang Prabang or about 300km to the Chinese border at Boten, Laos. From the Lao side of the border crossing, a dirt road leads north-northeast about 45km to the banks of the Mekong River in Laos' Udomxai Province. From here you can either take a boat downriver to Luang Prabang or cross the river and pick up Rte 2 to Muang Xai, the provincial capital. From Muang Xai it's only a couple of hours to the international border with China's Yunnan Province.

Nan residents are excited by the prospect of linking again the five *chiang* (cities) of the Lanna–Lan Xang–Xishuangbanna diaspora: Chiang Mai, Chiang Rai, Chiang Thong (the original name for Luang Prabang), Chiang Rung (Yunnan's Jinghong) and Chiang Klang (Nan).

There is an **immigration office** in the district capital of Thung Chang, 100km north of Nan; if you find out that the border crossing is open to foreigners, you should stop in to get a Thai exit stamp in your passport.

Every Saturday morning from around 5am to 11am there's a lively Lao-Thai **market** in Thung Chang.

Northeastern Thailand

While the northeast gets relatively few first-time visitors to Thailand, it's a favourite with Western travellers and expatriates who know Thailand well. Compared to the rest of Thailand the pace is slower, the people friendlier and prices are cheaper in the Isan provinces; and, although fewer people speak or understand English, travel in the northeast is relatively easy.

Sites of historical and archaeological significance abound in the northeast and many of them have been restored or excavated. Scattered around the region are 202 known *prasat, prang* and *ku,* 182 of which are of Khmer origin. Most of these sites are found in four provinces: Buriram (61 sites), Khorat (26), Surin (33) and Si Saket (12).

Generally speaking, *prasat* (from the Sanskrit architectural term *prasada*) refers to large temple sanctuaries with a cruciform floor plan, while *prang* refers to a Khmer-style tower that may constitute an entire *chedi* (or stupa) or part of a *chedi,* and *ku* is a smaller *chedi* that is partially hollow and open. However, many Thais use these terms interchangeably. *Prasat* is sometimes translated in Thai tourist literature as 'castle' or 'palace', but these Khmer monuments were never used as royal residences. Observant visitors will find these monuments quite different in style from the Thai-built Buddhist monuments at Ayuthaya and Sukhothai, most noticeably in the use of sandstone blocks (some of which are exquisitely carved) instead of brick.

The Khorat Plateau extends across most of northeastern Thailand and is divided by the Phu Phan mountain range into two wide drainage basins, the Sakon Nakhon Basin in the upper northeast (fed by the Mekong River and its tributaries) and the Khorat Basin in the lower northeast (fed by the Mae Nam Chi and Mae Nam Mun rivers).

Isan (or *ìsǎan,* the collective term for the northeastern region) officially consists of an amalgamation of 19 provinces: Amnat Charoen, Buriram, Chaiyaphum, Kalasin, Khon Kaen, Loei, Mahasarakham, Mukdahan, Nakhon Phanom, Nakhon Ratchasima, Nong Bualamphu, Nong Khai, Roi Et, Sakon Nakhon, Si Saket, Surin, Ubon Ratchathani, Udon Thani and Yasothon.

Highlights

- Admire the lovingly restored Angkor-period temples at Phanom Rung and Prasat Hin Phimai
- Enjoy a meal and a spectacular Mekong view from one of Nakhon Phanom's rustic riverside restaurants
- Do a crash course in Hindu-Buddhist cosmology at the curious and folksy Sala Kaew Ku sculpture gardens in Nong Khai
- Hike through Khao Yai National Park – home to some of the lush tropical scenery in the film *The Beach*
- Visit traditional weaving villages where the looms have been clacking rhythmically for thousands of years

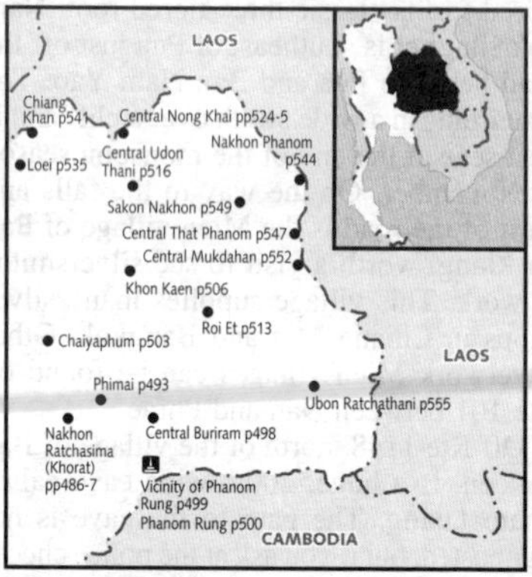

History

The region has a long history, beginning with the 4000-year-old bronze culture of Ban Chiang, which predates both Mesopotamia and China as a metallurgical and agricultural site.

Thais use the term *ìsǎan* to classify the region *(phâak ìsǎan)*, the people *(khon ìsǎan)* and the food *(aahǎan ìsǎan)* of northeastern Thailand. The name comes from Isana, the Sanskrit name for the Mon-Khmer kingdom that flourished in what is now northeastern Thailand and pre-Angkor Cambodia; Isana was a precursor to the Funan empire (1st to 6th centuries AD). Funan was in turn absorbed by the Chenla empire during the late 6th to 8th centuries and divided into Upper (Water) and Lower (Land) Chenla, which corresponded with parts of modern-day Isan, southern Laos and northwestern Cambodia. After the 9th century, Chenla was superseded by the Angkor empire, which extended into Isan and beyond.

Isan remained more-or-less autonomous from early Thai kingdoms until the arrival of the French in the 18th century created the Indochinese state of Laos, thus forcing Thailand to define its northeastern boundaries. Rama V divided the region into four *monthon* (Thai pronunciation of the Pali-Sanskrit *mandala*), or semi-autonomous satellite states, including Lao Phuan (northeastern Isan), Roi Et (central Isan), Lao Klang (southwestern Isan) and Ubon (southeastern Isan). The *monthon* system was changed to the *jangwàt* (province) system in 1933.

Traditionally Thailand's poorest region, due to the infertility of the soil and lack of rain in comparison with the rest of the country, the northeast was fertile ground for the communist movement. Ho Chi Minh spent 1928 to 1929 proselytizing in Udon Thani, Sakon Nakhon and Khorat (Nakhon Ratchasima's more common name); in the 1940s a number of Indochinese Communist Party leaders fled to Isan from Laos and helped strengthen the Communist Party of Thailand. From the 1960s until 1982 or so, Isan was a hotbed of guerrilla activity, especially in the provinces of Buriram, Loei,

NORTHEASTERN THAILAND

Ubon Ratchathani, Nakhon Phanom and Sakon Nakhon. Almost immediately following the amnesty of 1982, the northeastern strongholds of the Communist Party dissolved rapidly (the fact that tens of thousands of refugees from recently communist Laos and Cambodia had been pouring into camps in Isan to escape their oppressive governments did little to promote communism among the Thai). The process was hastened by a decade of economic growth that drew large numbers of Isan peasants from the forests and rice fields to various provincial capitals and to Bangkok.

During the boom years only the larger cities of the northeast were able to ride the coat-tails of Thailand's rising income. The rural areas have the lowest per-capita income of the country's four major regions.

Culture

Isan culture and language are marked by a mixture of Lao and Khmer influences. The Khmers left behind Angkor Wat-like monuments near Surin, Khorat, Buriram and other northeastern towns. Along the Mekong River–Lao border are several Lao-style temples, including Wat Phra That Phanom. Many of the people living in this area speak Lao – or Thai dialects that are very close to Lao dialects spoken in Laos – and in fact there are more people of Lao heritage in northeastern Thailand than in all of Laos. In certain areas of the lower northeast, Khmer is the most common language.

Isan food is famous for its pungency and choice of ingredients. Well-known dishes include *kài yâang* (grilled spiced chicken) and *sôm-tam* (spicy salad made with grated papaya, lime juice, garlic, fish sauce and fresh chillies). Northeasterners eat glutinous rice with their meals, squeezing the almost translucent grains into wads with their hands, and then dipping the rice into the main dish before popping it into their mouths. Meals are communal affairs that traditionally take place on the floor.

The music of northeastern Thailand is highly distinctive in its folk tradition, using instruments such as the *khaen,* a reed instrument with two long rows of bamboo pipes strung together; the *ponglaang,* which is like a xylophone and made of short wooden logs; and the *phin,* a type of small three-stringed lute played with a large plectrum. The most popular song forms are *lûuk thûng* (literally, children of the fields) types – a very rhythmic style in comparison to the classical music of central Thailand.

The best silk in Thailand is said to come from the northeast, particularly Khorat, Khon Kaen and Roi Et. A visit to northeastern silk-weaving towns can uncover bargains, as well as provide an education in Thai weaving techniques. Cotton fabrics from Loei, Nong Khai and Nakhon Phanom are highly regarded, especially those woven using *mát-mìi* methods (in which cotton threads are tie-dyed before weaving, similar to Indonesian *ikat*).

For real antiquity, Udon Thani Province offers prehistoric cave drawings at Ban Pheu, south of Nong Khai, and a look at the ancient ceramic and bronze culture at Ban Chiang to the east of Udon. The latter harbours remains of what appears to be the world's oldest agricultural society and first bronze metallurgy.

Travellers who want to know more about northeastern Thailand should read the works of Pira Sudham, a Thai author born in Buriram. His autobiographical *People of Esarn* is especially recommended.

Getting There & Away

The main train and bus lines in the northeast are between Bangkok and Nong Khai, and between Bangkok and Ubon Ratchathani. The northeast can also be reached from northern Thailand by bus or from Phitsanulok, with Khon Kaen as the gateway.

Nakhon Ratchasima Province

Thailand's largest province (20,500 sq km) is most well known for silk weaving. Some of the country's best silk is made in the village of Pak Thong Chai, 30km southwest of Nakhon Ratchasima (more commonly known as Khorat) on Rte 304. Many of the Bangkok silk houses have their cloth made there, so don't expect to get any special bargains just because you went all that way. There are also a couple of silk shops in Khorat that are just as good – sometimes better – for their selection and price. Still, Pak Thong Chai is worth a trip if you're interested in observing Thailand's silk-weaving methods.

Khorat's other big attraction is the Angkor-period Khmer ruins scattered around the province. Most are little more than a stack of stones and a plaque, but the completed restoration at Prasat Hin Phimai and ongoing work at Prasat Phanomwan are very impressive. In addition to Khmer religious shrines, there are some 192 ancient city sites – Mon, Lao and Khmer – in the province. Most are visible only to archaeologists trained to look for the odd earthen rampart, boundary stone or laterite (red clay) foundation.

Not much is known about the early history of the province except that, as indicated by an AD 937 inscription, it was part of a kingdom known as Sri Janas (Si Janat), which apparently extended over the entire Khorat Plateau. The inhabitants of Sri Janas – or at least its elite royal inhabitants – practised a mixture of Mahayana Buddhism and Brahmanist Shiva worship, hence it was quite possibly an Angkor satellite.

NAKHON RATCHASIMA (KHORAT)

นครราชสีมา(โคราช)

postcode 30000 • pop 210,600

Exactly 250km from Bangkok, *amphoe meuang* (provincial capital) Khorat was once the capital of Lao Klang, a Thai *monthon* that covered present-day Khorat, Chaiyaphum and Buriram Provinces. Up until the mid-Ayuthaya era it was actually two towns, Sema and Khorakpura, which merged under the reign of King Narai. To this day, Khorat has a split personality of sorts, with the older, less commercial half to the west, and the newer central half inside the city moats to the east. Sema and Khorakpura were originally built in present-day Sung Noen (35km southeast).

No longer the quaint Isan town it once was, busy Khorat has become an important transportation hub and burgeoning industrial centre, and is Thailand's second-largest city. Often cited only as a train or bus stop away from the nearby Phimai ruins, Khorat is a fairly interesting place if you don't mind putting up with the heat and grubby air, which can be almost as bad as Bangkok's. Those who prefer a quieter setting might want to spend the night in Phimai instead, making day trips to Khorat; those who like city life might consider the opposite tactic.

One of seven air bases in Thailand used by the US armed forces to launch air strikes on Laos and Vietnam in the 1960s and '70s was just outside Khorat. A few retired GIs still live in the area with their Thai families, and the Veterans of Foreign Wars Cafeteria is still open on Th Phoklang (Phoklang Rd). But the heavy US influence that was obvious in the late 1970s after the base was closed has all but faded away.

Khorat's most popular annual event is the **Thao Suranari Festival**, a celebration of Thao Suranari's victory over the Lao (see the Thao Suranari Memorial entry later in this section). It's held from late March to early April and features parades, *lí-keh* (Thai folk dance-drama), *phleng khorâat* (Khorat folk song) and a beauty contest. (See also the special section 'Music, Theatre & Dance'.) Thousands of participants from around Khorat Province and beyond attend the festivities.

Orientation

Central Khorat is contained within a road loop formed on the west and north by the Friendship Hwy (Hwy 2), also known as Th Mittaphap; and connecting routes to the east and south. A historic moat further subdivides the city in two, with the more densely developed half to the east of the Thao Suranari Memorial and a slightly more low-key section to the west, around the Khorat train station and Bus Terminal 1. Khorat has expanded in all directions well beyond these main areas, but the parts of the city most visitors deal with are found in these central sections.

Information

Tourist Offices The **Tourism Authority of Thailand office** *(TAT; ☎ 0 4421 3666, fax 0 4421 3667; 2102-2104 Th Mittaphap; open 8.30am-4.30pm daily)*, at the western edge of town, is worth a visit. The friendly staff have plenty of information about Khorat as well as Buriram, Surin and Chaiyaphum, so if you're headed to one of those provinces you can stop here and get maps and advice. The TAT office is quite far from the city centre, a *túk-túk* (motorised *săamláw,* a three-wheeled vehicle) ride should cost 40B.

A **tourist police office** *(☎ 0 4434 1777–9, emergency ☎ 1155)* is located opposite bus terminal 2, off the highway to Nong Khai north of the city centre. There is also a small tourist police booth adjacent to the Thao Suranari Memorial.

Money The best area for banks is Th Chumphon, where you'll find **Bangkok Bank**, **Kasikornbank** and **Siam Commercial Bank**, all of which offer foreign-exchange services from 8.30am to 3.30pm, Monday to Friday. **Bangkok Bank of Commerce** *(Th Phoklang)*, opposite the Fah Thai Hotel, has an **exchange window** *(open 8.30am-8pm daily)*.

Post & Communications The main **post office** *(Th Mittaphap; open 8.30am-4.30pm Mon-Fri, 9am-1pm Sat)* is conveniently located. There is a **branch post office** *(Th Jomsurangyat)* between Klang Plaza 2 shopping centre and the Chao Phraya Inn, and another **post office** *(Th Atsadang)* further east. International telephone calls are best made from the **Communications Authority of Thailand office** *(CAT; open 7am-11pm daily)* attached to the Atsadang post office.

Mahawirawong National Museum

พิพิธภัณฑสถานแห่งชาติมหาวีรวงศ์

In the grounds of Wat Sutchinda, directly across from the government buildings off Th Ratchadamnoen and just outside the city moat, this museum *(admission 10B; open*

NAKHON RATCHASIMA (KHORAT)

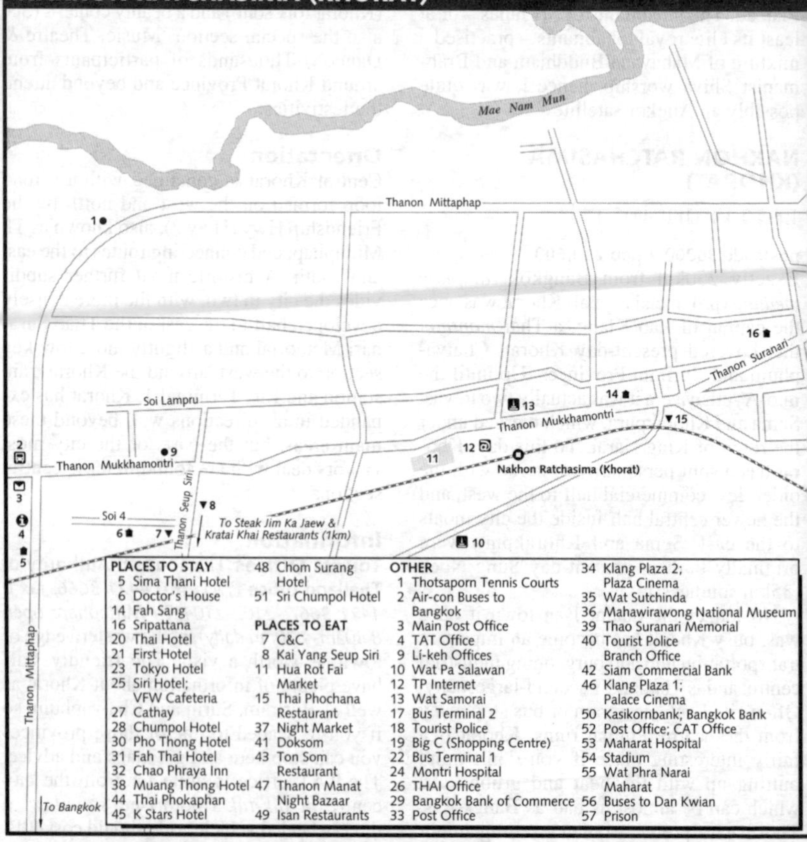

9am-4pm daily) has a good collection of Khmer art objects, especially door lintels, as well as objects from other periods.

Thao Suranari Memorial
อนุสาวรีย์ท้าวสุรนารี

At the Chumphon Gate to central Khorat, on the western side, is this much-worshipped memorial shrine to Thao Suranari (also known as Khun Ying Mo), a courageous Thai woman who led the local citizens in a battle against Lao invaders from Vientiane during the rule of Rama III (1824–51). At least that's the official version of events. Some scholars have suggested that the legend was in fact invented by the Thai to instill a sense of Thai-ness in the ethnic-Lao people of the province.

Hundreds of unique offerings, such as a miniature model of a bus donated by local bus drivers, find their way to the shrine in the hope that Thao Suranari's spirit will protect the supplicants from danger or any ill will.

Khorat Song In the evenings you can see performances of *phleng khorâat,* the traditional Khorat folk song, on a stage near the shrine and next to the tourist-police booth. It's usually performed by groups of four singers hired by people whose supplications to Thao Suranari have been honoured. To show gratitude to the spirit, they pay for the performance. Over 100 groups are available for hire, usually for 400B to 500B per half-hour performance.

NAKHON RATCHASIMA (KHORAT)

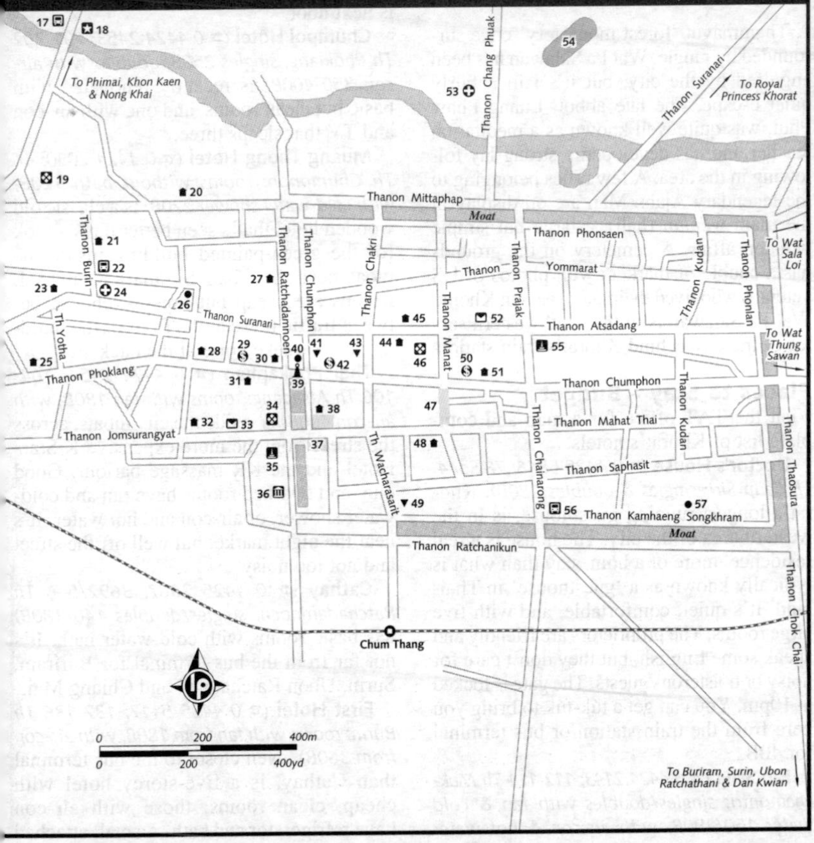

Wat Phra Narai Maharat
วัดพระนารายณ์มหาราช

This monastery *(Th Prajak)* is of interest for two main reasons: it has a Khmer sandstone sculpture of Phra Narai (Narayana or Vishnu), and it also houses Khorat's *làk meuang* (city pillar). The *wát* (temple) is between Th Atsadang and Th Chumphon.

Wat Sala Loi
วัดศาลาลอย

This modern 'Temple of the Floating Pavilion' is 400m east of the northeastern corner of the moat and has a *bòt* (central chapel) shaped like a Chinese junk.

Wat Pa Salawan
วัดป่าสาละวัน

A Thammayut 'forest monastery' once surrounded by jungle, Wat Pa Salawan has been engulfed by the city, but it's still a fairly quiet escape. The late abbot, Luang Phaw Phut, was quite well known as a meditation teacher and has developed a strong lay following in the area. A few relics belonging to the legendary Ajahn Man are on display in the main *wíhǎan* (hall), a large but simple wooden affair. A cemetery on the grounds has a couple of markers with photos of US veterans who lived their later years in Khorat. Wat Pa Salawan is in the southwestern sector of the city behind Khorat's train station.

Places to Stay – Budget
Visit the TAT office for a map and complete list of Khorat's hotels.

Doctor's House *(☎ 0 4425 5846; 78 Soi 4, Th Seup Siri; singles & doubles 180B)*, Khorat's longest-running guesthouse, is in the western area of the city. The house is a real residence, more of a homestay than what is typically known as a 'guesthouse' in Thailand. It's quiet, comfortable, and with five large rooms. The proprietors are friendly and speak some English, but they don't care for noisy or boisterous guests. The gate is locked at 10pm. You can get a túk-túk to bring you here from the train station or bus terminal for 40B.

Fah Sang *(☎ 0 4424 2143; 112-114 Th Mukkhamontri; singles/doubles with fan & cold water 150/190B, with air-con & hot water 330/360B)*, not far from Khorat train station, has OK rooms and friendly staff, although the location is noisy. Rooms with fan are in the old wooden section, while those with air-con are in a newer building.

Pho Thong Hotel *(☎ 0 4424 2084; 658 Th Phoklang; rooms with fan 180-220B, with air-con 300B)* has rooms with bath; air-con rooms have TV. It's on the corner of Th Ratchadamnoen at the west city gate, right in the centre of things, and is overall better value than the Fah Sang.

Siri Hotel *(☎ 0 4424 2831; 167-168 Th Phoklang; rooms with fan 120-180B, with air-con 300-400B)*, in the same vicinity as Pho Thong, is even better value. It's quiet, friendly and well located, a couple of blocks west of the city moats. Rooms are large and have a strange feature – they can be divided in half with a curtain! The VFW Cafeteria is next door.

Chumpol Hotel *(☎ 0 4424 2453; 701-702 Th Phoklang; singles 250B, doubles with air-con 350-400B)* is recently renovated with basic but clean rooms, and one with air-con and TV that sleeps three.

Muang Thong Hotel *(☎ 0 4424 2090; 46 Th Chumphon; rooms without bath 120B, with cold-water shower 220B)* is a classic old wooden hotel that's seen better days – look for the green-painted building inside the moat near the Thao Suranari Memorial. Rooms are cheap but noisy – choose between traffic noise at the front of the building and karaoke noise at the back.

Thai Phokaphan *(☎ 0 4424 2454; 104-106 Th Atsadang; rooms with fan 180B, with air-con 400B)* is inside the city moats, across the street from the more expensive K Stars Hotel and the KR massage parlour. Good one- and two-bed rooms have fan and cold-water shower, or air-con and hot water. It's near the night market but well off the street and not too noisy.

Cathay *(☎ 0 4425 2067; 3692/5–6 Th Ratchadamnoen; singles/doubles 140/180B)* has basic rooms with cold-water bath. It's not far from the bus terminal for Buriram, Surin, Ubon Ratchathani and Chiang Mai.

First Hotel *(☎ 0 4425 5117; 132-136 Th Burin; rooms with fan from 180B, with air-con from 360B)*, even closer to the bus terminal than Cathay, is a five-storey hotel with cheap, clean rooms; those with air-con have refrigerator and bath. A small attached restaurant serves basic Thai food at reasonable prices.

Sri Chumpol Hotel *(☎ 0 4424 2460; 133 Th Chumphon; singles/twins with fan 180/220B, singles & twins with air-con 280B)* is a bit quieter than the other Thai-Chinese places on Th Phoklang and Th Ratchadamnoen, and it's cleaner than most. Rooms with fan have cold-water bath, while those with air-con have hot water.

Tokyo Hotel *(☎ 0 4424 2873, fax 0 4424 2788; 329-333 Th Suranari; rooms with fan/air-con 160/400B)* has OK rooms – quieter than most on Th Phoklang – with fan and cold-water bath, or with air-con and hot water.

Places to Stay – Mid-Range

Fah Thai Hotel *(☎ 0 4426 7390, fax 0 4425 2797; 35-39 Th Phoklang; singles/doubles with fan 200/250B, with air-con 350B)* has rooms with private bath. It's good for a Th Phoklang Thai-Chinese place. There is a small attached **restaurant** *(open 7am-8pm daily)*.

Chao Phraya Inn *(☎ 0 4424 3825; 62/1 Th Jomsurangyat; rooms 420B)*, well located near the Klang Plaza 2 shopping centre, has simple but comfortable air-con rooms with cold-water bath. There's a 24-hour coffee shop on the premises.

Thai Hotel *(☎ 0 4427 1613; 644-650 Th Mittaphap; rooms with fan 250-300B, with air-con 320-380B)*, not far from the bus terminal, has similar digs to Chao Phraya, plus less-expensive rooms with fan.

Places to Stay – Top End

Sripattana *(☎ 0 4425 1652, fax 0 4425 1655; 346 Th Suranari; rooms 500B, suites 900-1200B)*, at the bottom of the top end, has clean and comfortable rooms with air-con, hot-water bath and TV. The suites are often discounted. This circa-1965 hotel has a pub, 24-hour coffee shop and a swimming pool, and offers Thai massage. Breakfast is included with the room rates. It's excellent value overall.

Chom Surang Hotel *(☎ 0 4425 7088, fax 0 4425 2897; 2701/2 Th Mahat Thai; rooms from 880B)* offers air-con throughout, and also has a pool.

K Stars Hotel *(☎/fax 0 4425 7057; 191 Th Atsadang; rooms from 450B, deluxe suites 1500B)* is a multistorey hotel that has clean, comfortable air-con rooms and deluxe suites. It offers a 24-hour coffee shop, minimart, massage, and nightclub.

Sima Thani Hotel *(☎ 0 4421 3100, fax 0 4421 3121; superior rooms from 1000B, deluxe rooms 1300-1500B)* originally opened in 1992 as a Sheraton but is now owned by a Thai hotel group. All rooms have air-con, IDD phone, satellite TV, fridge and safe. The hotel has a lobby bar, restaurant, pub and pool.

Royal Princess Khorat *(☎ 0 4425 6629–35, fax 0 4425 6601; 1137 Th Suranari; rooms from 1000B)*, on the northeastern outskirts of the city, was opened by Thailand's Dusit Group, perhaps in an effort not to be outdone by Sima Thani. Starting rates are for standard rooms, and include an excellent breakfast buffet featuring Chinese, Thai and Western food. All rooms have a fridge, bath, satellite TV and air-con. Amenities include a lobby bar, restaurant, large pool and business centre.

Places to Eat

Khorat has many excellent Thai and Chinese restaurants, especially along Th Ratchadamnoen near the Thao Suranari Memorial and western gate to central Khorat. **Hua Rot Fai Market** *(Th Mukkhamontr)* near the Khorat train station is a great place to eat in the evening, as is the **Th Manat night bazaar**; both are at their best from 6pm to 10pm.

Thai Phochana Restaurant *(142 Th Jomsurangyat; dishes 40-60B)* is air-conditioned and well known for its mix of standard Thai and local specialities, including *mìi khorâat* (Khorat-style noodles) and *yam kòp yâang* (roast frog salad). Also good is *kaeng phèt pèt* (duck curry).

C & C *(Cabbages & Condoms; dishes 60-120B; open 10.30am-10pm daily)*, just around the corner from Doctor's House, is a branch of the same restaurant in Bangkok. Like the original, it's a nonprofit operation sponsored by the Population & Community Development Association; the food is good but a bit pricey for Khorat.

Doksom *(☎ 0 4425 2020; Th Chumphon; drinks & desserts 20-40B)*, near the Thanon Suranari Memorial, is air-conditioned and a good place to cool off with some delicious ice cream or cold drinks.

Ton Som Restaurant *(☎ 0 4425 2275; Th Wacharasarit; dishes 60-100B; open until*

NORTHEASTERN THAILAND

midnight daily), near Doksom, is an upmarket Thai restaurant.

Isan Two very unassuming Isan places along the eastern side of Th Wacharasarit between Th Saphasit and Th Kamhaeng Songkhram, **Suan Sin** and **Samran Lap** serve locally popular Isan fare, such as *plaa chonnábòt* (freshwater fish steamed with vegetables and served with a tart, spicy sauce), *súp hăang wua* (oxtail soup) and *lín yâang* (barbecued tongue). They also serve *lâap* (spicy minced-meat salad) and other Isan standards.

A line of excellent Isan sidewalk restaurants can be found along Th Seup Siri in the evenings. **Steak Jim Ka Jaew** *(Steak Lao; dishes 30-60B)* is located at the mouth of Soi 39. Nearby and also popular is **Kratai Khao**. It's quite easy to tell which restaurants are the better ones: they're so full of customers that you may have to share a table with strangers. Restaurants along this street set up around 7pm and stay open until midnight.

Kai Yang Seup Siri *(Th Seup Siri; dishes 20-40B; open 10.30am-3pm or 4pm daily)*, near Doctor's House, has the best *kài yâang* (grilled spiced chicken) and *sôm-tam* (grated papaya salad) in town. There are two Isan places next door to each other here – look for the one with chickens on the grill out the front. Food is usually sold out by 3pm or 4pm.

International Next to the Siri Hotel, **VFW Cafeteria** *(Th Phoklang; dishes 40-80B)* has cheap American-style breakfasts, as well as steaks, ice cream, pizza and salads. It gets mixed reviews, however, so let's just say it's a good imitation of an American 'greasy spoon', for all that term implies. The central tables are often taken by a tight-knit group of US Vietnam War veterans chatting about the old days.

Cleaner and more reliable – if more expensive – are the American-style restaurants in Klang Plaza 2 shopping centre, including **KFC**, **Dunkin' Donuts**, **Black Canyon Coffeeshop** and **Royal Home Bakery**. Klang Plaza also has a large **supermarket**, should you want to shop for groceries.

Entertainment

Phlap-Phla Dawan Restaurant, in the Sima Thani Hotel, hosts a well-executed cultural performance of Thai, Lao and Khmer dancing nightly from 7pm to 8pm. It's actually a dinner show with a set menu and a choice of Thai, Chinese or *faràng* (foreigner) food that costs 250B to 300B per person.

The city boasts several Thai-style **nightclubs** and a couple of hotel **discos**. You can get a complete list of nightlife venues from the TAT office.

Shopping

The **Thanon Manat night bazaar** *(Th Manat)* features cheap clothes, flowers, sunglasses, watches, fruit and food vendors – nothing spectacular, but it's a fine place to spend time.

Klang Plaza 2 *(Th Jomsurangyat)* offers five floors of shops purveying everything from videos to homewares. There's also **Klang Plaza** *(Th Atsadang)* near the Thai Phokaphan Hotel.

Big C shopping centre *(Th Mittaphap)*, near the Thai Hotel, has two floors of small shops, a good pharmacy and restaurants, including a KFC.

Khorat has many shops that specialise in silk. Several can be found along Th Ratchadamnoen near the Thao Suranari Memorial.

Getting There & Away

Air From Bangkok **Air Andaman** *(in Bangkok ☎ 0 2229 9555; 0 4424 6261)* flies to Khorat daily, except Sunday (1500B).

Thai Airways International (THAI) to/from Buriram (775B). There is a **THAI office** *(☎ 0 4425 2114; 40-44 Th Suranari)* in the centre of town.

Bus Ordinary buses leave the Northern bus terminal in Bangkok every hour from 5am to 7pm. The fare is 96B and the trip takes four hours. Air-con buses cost 154B.

For buses from Khorat to other places in Thailand, there are two main bus terminals. **Bus terminal 1**, off Th Burin in the city centre near the intersection of the Th Mittaphap loop and the highway north to Nong Khai, is for destinations within the province. Many of these buses also stop at bus terminal 2 on their way out of town.

Buses to points outside Khorat Province leave from **bus terminal 2**, off the highway to Nong Khai north of the city centre. The following table lists buses and fares to/from Khorat.

Bus Destinations to/from Nakhon Ratchasima (Khorat)

destination	fare (B)	duration (hrs)
Chiang Mai		
air-con	385	12
VIP	444	10
Loei		
air-con	221	3
Nakhon Phanom		
air-con	264	4½
Nong Khai		
ordinary	110	4
air-con	214	3½
Pattaya		
air-con	223	5½
Phitsanulok		
air-con	218	4
VIP	288	4
Rayong		
air-con	216	4
Roi Et		
air-con	140	2½
Sakon Nakhon		
ordinary	111	4½
air-con	200	4
Ubon		
ordinary	149	6
air-con	260	5
Udon		
ordinary	98	4
air-con	206	3
Yasothon		
ordinary	79	5
air-con	143	3

Train An express train bound for Ubon Ratchathani departs from Bangkok's Hualamphong station at 9pm, arriving in Khorat at 2.40am.

Rapid-train services on the Ubon Ratchathani line depart from Bangkok daily at 6.40am, 6.45pm and 10.45pm, arriving in Khorat at 12.14pm, 12.09am and 4.11am respectively.

There are also four ordinary trains (3rd class only) that depart from Bangkok at 9.10am, 11.45am and 11.10pm, arriving in Khorat about 5½ to six hours after departure. Express diesel railcars (aka 'Sprinters'; 2nd class air-con only) depart from Bangkok's Hualamphong station at 11.05am and 9.50pm and arrive in Khorat at 3.23pm and 3.24am respectively.

A special express train (1st and 2nd class) leaves at 5.45am and arrives in Khorat at 10am.

The 1st-class fare (express train only) is 230B, 2nd class is 115B and 3rd class 50B. Add 40B for the rapid trains, 60B for the express and 80B for the special express. The train passes through some great scenery on the Khorat Plateau, including a view of the enormous white Buddha figure at Wat Theppitak on a thickly forested hillside.

Getting Around

Túk-túk cost 40B to most places around town (30B for a short hop), 50B to 60B for longer trips. Motorbike taxis cost about the same.

The city once had a fairly extensive bus system, but it's been slowly falling out of use due to the fact that most locals use motorbikes to get around. Unless you want to spend an hour waiting for the bus, we suggest you take a túk-túk or motorbike taxi.

AROUND NAKHON RATCHASIMA

Pak Thong Chai

ปักธงชัย

Thirty-two kilometres south of Khorat on Rte 304 is Pak Thong Chai, one of Thailand's most famous **silk-weaving** villages. Several varieties and prices of silk are available, and most weavers sell directly to the public. However, prices are not necessarily lower than in Khorat or Bangkok. There are around 70 silk factories in the district.

Achan Pan and **Pak Thong Chai** hotels are both on the main road through town and have rooms from 80B.

Buses to Pak Thong Chai leave bus terminal 1 in Khorat every 30 minutes, the last trip leaving at 6pm (the last bus from Pak Thong Chai to Khorat leaves at 5pm). The 12B trip takes about 40 minutes, depending on the number of stops.

Dan Kwian

ด่านเกวียน

Travellers interested in Thai **ceramics** might pay a visit to Dan Kwian, 15km southeast of Khorat. This village has been producing

AROUND NAKHON RATCHASIMA

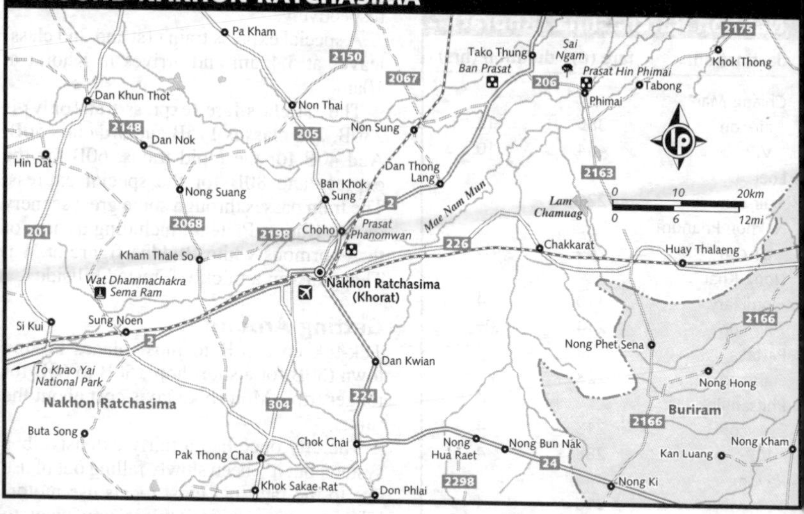

pottery for hundreds of years; originally it was a bullock-cart stop for traders on their way to markets in old Khorat (*dàan kwian* means 'bullock-cart checkpoint'). Dan Kwian pottery is famous for its rough texture and rust-like hue – only kaolin from this district produces such results.

Several more-or-less permanent **shops** line the highway. Prices are very good – many exporters shop for Thai pottery here. It's not all pottery, though – clay is shaped and fired into all kinds of art objects, from jewellery to wind chimes. There are also a couple of workshops that produce interesting reproductions of the ancient Khmer sandstone sculpture found at Prasat Hin Phimai and other local sites. There's also a display of old bullock carts from around the country.

To get here from Khorat, hop on a *sǎwng-thǎew* (pick-up truck) from the south or east city gates; the fare to Dan Kwian is 10B.

Phimai
พิมาย

The small town of Phimai is nothing much, but staying a night or two is pleasant enough if you're here to visit the ruins (Prasat Hin Phimai). If you want to visit the ruins as a day trip from Khorat, the 8am bus will give you plenty of wandering time at the ruins with time to spare for the return bus trip in the late afternoon. If Khorat's not your cup of tea, do it the other way around; stay in Phimai and take a day trip to Khorat.

Outside the town entrance, a couple of kilometres up Rte 206, is Thailand's largest and oldest banyan tree, a mega-florum spread over an island in a large pond (actually a state irrigation reservoir). The locals call it **Sai Ngam** (Beautiful Banyan); you can walk through the banyan branches via walkways built over the pond. Due to the banyan's extensive system of roots cascading from all but the smallest branches, the huge tree really looks more like a small forest. **Food vendors** and astrologers offer their services to picnickers in the vicinity.

Since 1991 the town has hosted a **festival** during the second weekend of November to celebrate Prasat Hin Phimai history. Events include a sound-and-light show at the ruins, historical and cultural exhibits, classical dance-drama performances and a lamp-lit procession between temples. Tickets cost 200B to 500B and can be bought ahead of time at the TAT office in Khorat.

Information There's a **Kasikornbank** next door to Baiteiy Restaurant, and a branch of the **Thai Military Bank** near the Prasat Hin Phimai Historical Park entrance. Banking hours are from 8.30am to 3.30pm Monday to Friday. There is also a **post office** *(open 8.30am-4.30pm Mon-Fri, 9am-noon Sat)*.

Prasat Hin Phimai National Historical Park The Angkor-period Khmer shrine monument here *(admission 40B; open 6am-6pm daily)*, 60km northeast of Khorat, makes Phimai worth a visit. Originally started by Khmer King Jayavarman V in the late 10th century and finished by King Suriyavarman I (r. AD 1002–49) in the early 11th century, this Hindu-Mahayana Buddhist temple projects a majesty that transcends its size.

The 28m-tall main shrine, of cruciform design, is made of white sandstone, while the adjunct shrines are of pink sandstone and laterite. The sculptures over the doorways to the main shrine are particularly impressive.

The Phimai temple, like many other Khmer monuments in this part of Thailand, predates the famous Angkor Wat complex in Cambodia. When the Angkor empire was at its peak, and encompassed parts of Thailand, Phimai was directly connected to the Angkor capital by road.

Reconstruction work by the Fine Arts Department has been completed and, although the pieces do not quite fit together as they must have originally, this only seems to add to the monument's somewhat eerie quality.

Phimai National Museum The exhibits at this nicely designed new museum *(admission 30B; open 9am-4pm daily)* are mostly dedicated to Khmer sculpture, with many of the best lintels and statues from Phimai,

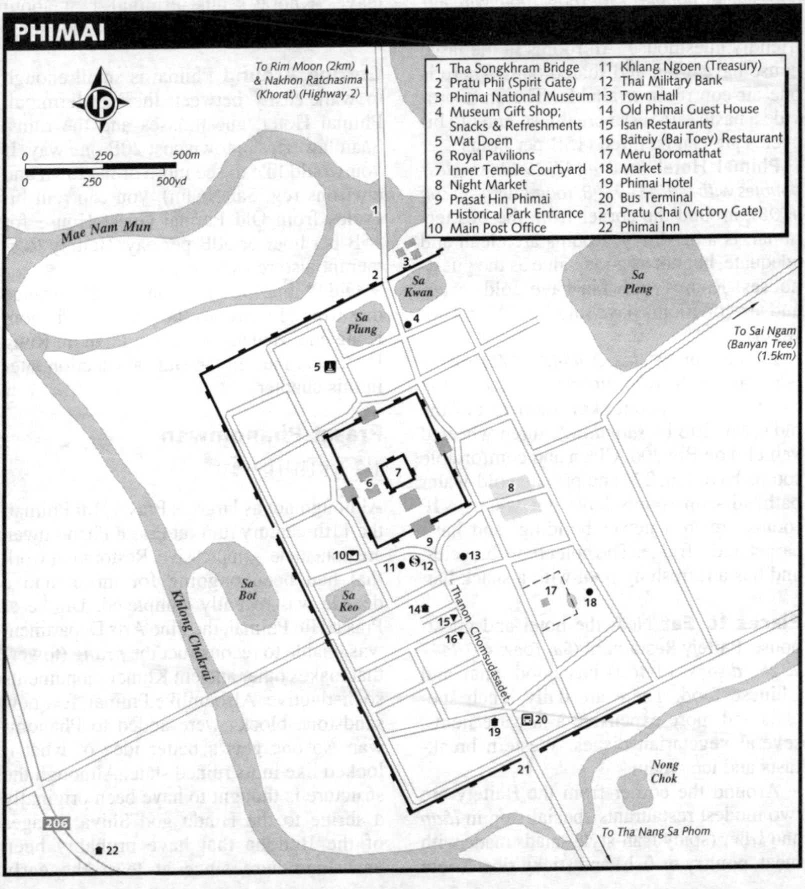

Phanom Rung, Phanomwan and other Khmer sites in Thailand, as well as ceramics from nearby Ban Prasat.

The museum's most prized possession, a stone sculpture of Angkor King Jayavarman VII, comes from Prasat Hin Phimai National Historical Park – it looks very much like a sitting Buddha.

An open-air sculpture garden, next to the main hall, displays ornate boundary stones and other Khmer figures from Phimai. A small bookshop is attached to the museum.

There's also a gift shop and a restaurant that serves simple Thai dishes and ice cream.

Places to Stay On an alley off the main street leading to the ruins, **Old Phimai Guest House** *(☎ 0 4447 1918; dorm beds 80B, singles/doubles 130/160B, room with air-con 350B)* is a spartan but comfortable and friendly guesthouse. All rooms in the large house have a fan and shared bath. There is one air-con room available. The staff provide a basic self-serve breakfast, and old bicycles are can be hired (15B per hour).

Phimai Hotel *(☎ 0 4447 1940; singles/doubles with fan 200/240B, rooms with air-con 400B)*, around the corner from the bus terminal, is a bit dingy. Rooms are clean and adequate, but not as good value as the guesthouses. Rooms with fan have cold water, and air-con rooms have satellite TV and hot water.

Phimai Inn *(☎/fax 0 4447 1175; rooms with fan 250B, with air-con 350-380B, VIP rooms 500B)* is about 2km southwest of the old town (20B by *săamláw,* a three-wheeled vehicle) on Rte 206. Clean and comfortable rooms have fan, TV and private cold-water bath; air-con rooms have hot water. VIP rooms are in a newer building, and have carpet and a fridge. The hotel rents bicycles, and has a refreshing pool with a snack bar.

Places to Eat Near the hotel and guesthouse, **Baiteiy Restaurant** *(Bai Toey; ☎ 0 4447 1725; dishes 30-40B)* has good Thai and Chinese food. There are daily lunch specials and more-expensive à la carte items, several vegetarian dishes, Western breakfasts and ice cream.

Around the corner from the Baiteiy are two modest restaurants specialising in *lâap* and *kâwy* (spicy Isan-style salads made with meat, poultry or fish) and sticky rice. There is also a decent collection of food vendors at a **night market** *(open 6pm to midnight)* just north of the regular day market.

Rim Moon *(dishes 60-120B; open daily)*, on a tributary of the Mae Nam Mun about 2km northwest of town, is a typical rural garden restaurant. It features a live band nightly.

Getting There & Away Buses for Phimai leave every half-hour during the day from Khorat's bus terminal 1. The trip to Phimai (35B) takes from one to 1½ hours, depending on the number of passengers that are picked up along the way. The bus terminal in Phimai is around the corner from the Phimai Hotel and down the street from Prasat Hin Phimai. The last Phimai bus leaves Khorat's bus terminal 1 at about 10pm; from Phimai the last bus is at 6pm.

Getting Around Phimai is small enough to walk easily between the bus terminal, Phimai Hotel, guesthouses and the ruins. Săamláw trips in town cost 20B one way. If you would like to see more of the town and environs (eg, Sai Ngam), you can rent bicycles from Old Phimai Guest House for 15B per hour or 50B per day. Baiteiy Restaurant also rents bikes.

Old Phimai Guest House can also arrange day trips (1500B) to the ruins of Phanom Rung and Meuang Tam (see Phanom Rung Historical Park in the Buriram section later in this chapter).

Prasat Phanomwan

ปราสาทพนมวัน

Although not as large as Prasat Hin Phimai, the 11th-century ruins at Prasat Phanomwan are nonetheless impressive. Restoration work that had been ongoing for more than a decade was recently completed. Unlike at Prasat Hin Phimai, the Fine Arts Department was unable to reconstruct the *prang* (tower) that makes other ancient Khmer monuments so distinctive. Also unlike Phimai, few new sandstone blocks were added to Phanomwan, so one gets a better idea of what it looked like in its ruined state. Although the structure is thought to have been originally a shrine to the Hindu god Shiva, images of the Buddha that have probably been enshrined here since at least the early

Ayuthaya period are still in place and still the objects of veneration. Until the restoration began the ruins were actually part of a Buddhist monastery and monks were in charge of maintaining the site. On our last visit the Fine Arts Department was not yet charging admission, but it is likely you'll be charged 30B in the near future.

Getting There & Away There are direct buses from Khorat's bus terminal 1 between 7am and 5.30pm. The fare is 21B.

Sandstone Reclining Buddha Image

พระพุทธไสยาสน์หินทราย

Located within Wat Dhammachakra Sema Ram in Khorat's Sung Noen district, this is Thailand's oldest reclining Buddha. Thought to date back to the 8th century, the Dvaravati-style image is unique in that it hasn't been covered with a layer of stucco and a coat of whitewash – it actually looks as old as it is purported to be. The crude but appealing image is protected from the elements by a huge roof, and an altar has been built before it. On display at the wát is a stone rendition of the Buddhist Wheel of Law, also found on the site, which is thought to pre-date the reclining Buddha image.

Getting There & Away Located 36km southwest of Khorat, this is best done as a day trip from there. Sung Noen is on the railway line to Bangkok (although only local trains stop here). It can also be reached by taking any Bangkok-bound non-air con bus from Khorat, though the trip may take as long as an hour. From the Sung Noen train station you'll have to hire a túk-túk or motorbike taxi for the final 5km to the wát. Expect to pay about 200B for the return trip, as well as a wait of around an hour or so.

Ban Prasat

บ้านปราสาท

Forty-five kilometres northeast of Khorat near the banks of Lam Than Prasat (Than Prasat River; off Hwy 2 between Non Sung and Phimai), Ban Prasat is the oldest archaeological site in the Khorat Basin. Excavations completed in 1991 show that the site, which is also known as the Ku Tan Prasat Mound, was inhabited by an agricultural-ceramic culture at least 3000 years ago. This culture lasted around 500 years and may even have predated Udon Thani Province's Ban Chiang by 1000 years.

Archaeological evidence suggests the Ban Prasat culture spun thread for weaving cloth, made sophisticated coloured pottery, planted rice, raised domestic animals and – towards the end of the culture's 500 years of prosperity – developed bronze metallurgy. Other layers uncovered indicate the site was later taken over by a pre-Dvaravati Mon city, followed by a 10th-century settlement whose main legacy is a small brick sanctuary known locally as **Ku Than Prasat**. This structure shows both Dvaravati and Khmer characteristics, and may have been a cultural transition point between Mon kingdoms to the west and the Khmer principalities to the east.

Several excavation pits are on display; the new **museum** *(open 8.30am-4pm Wed-Sun)* houses pottery and skeletons found in the pits.

Places to Stay & Eat The village of Ban Prasat along with the TAT has started a **cultural homestay programme** *(reservations village headman, ☎ 0 4436 7075)* that allows villagers to offer their homes as accommodation to visitors. Although mostly geared towards groups of urban Thai students who want to learn about Isan culture, it is possible for foreign visitors to take part in the programme. The cost is 400B per person per night and includes two meals. Reservations should be made at least one week in advance through the TAT office in Khorat or by calling the village headman, Mr Tiam La-Ongkan.

Getting There & Away Ordinary buses between Phimai and Khorat will stop in Ban Prasat for 16B. In Ban Prasat a motorbike taxi can take you 1.5km to all three excavation sites, including waiting time of about 15 minutes at each site for about 80B, but you'll have to haggle to get this price.

KHAO YAI NATIONAL PARK

อุทยานแห่งชาติเขาใหญ่

Established in 1961, this is Thailand's oldest national park *(adult/child 200/100B)*; it covers 2172 sq km and includes one of the largest intact monsoon forests in mainland Asia. Considered by many experts to be among the world's best national parks, Khao Yai was designated an Association for South East Asian Nations (Asean) National Heritage Site and has been nominated for international status by the UN. More recently, millions of movie-goers unknowingly gazed upon one of Khao Yai's landmarks while watching the 2000 film *The Beach:* the waterfall that appears repeatedly in the film is Nam Tok Hew Suwat (Hew Suwat Falls). The park's terrain covers five vegetation zones: evergreen rainforest (100m to 400m); semi-evergreen rainforest (400m to 900m); mixed deciduous forest (northern slopes at 400m to 600m); hill evergreen forest (over 1000m); and savannah and secondary-growth forest in areas where agriculture and logging occurred before it was protected.

Some 200 to 300 wild elephants reside within the park boundaries; other mammals recorded include sambar deer, barking deer, gaur, wild pig, Malayan sun bear, Asiatic black bear, tiger, leopard, serow, and various gibbons and macaques. In general these animals are most easily spotted during the rainy season from June to October. Khao Yai also has Thailand's largest population of hornbills, including the great hornbill (*nók kòk* or *nók kaahang* in Thai), king of the bird kingdom; as well as the wreathed hornbill (*nók ngaa cháang;* literally, elephant-tusk bird), Indian pied hornbill *(nók khàek)* and rhinoceros hornbill *(nók râet)*. Hornbills breed from January to May, the best time to see them. They also feed on figs, so ficus trees are good places to find them. Caves in the park are home to rare wrinkle-lipped bats and Himalayan ribbed bats.

The park has over 50km of hiking trails, many of them formed by the movement of wildlife. Elevations range from 100m to 1400m where the western edge of Cambodia's Dangrek mountain range meets the southern edge of the Khorat Plateau. You can get a rather inaccurate trail map from the park headquarters. It's easy to get lost on the longer trails so it's advisable to hire a guide. Rangers may be able to act as guides for 200B per day. If you do plan to go walking, it is a good idea to take boots as leeches can be a problem – although mosquito repellent does help to keep them away. There are also three wildlife-watching towers in the park.

Colour topographical maps of the park are usually on sale at the visitors centre at the park headquarters.

In nearby Pak Chong, you can arrange tours from two or three different agencies. Currently the most reputable seem to be those organised by **Wildlife Safari** *(☎ 0 4431 2922; 39 Th Pak Chong)*, and **Green Leaf Tours** *(☎ 0 4436 5024)* at Green Leaf Guest House (see Places to Stay & Eat). We've received a number of reports that the latter company is quite friendly and professional. Package tours lasting 1½ days cost from 950B per person, including guides, entrance fee, transport and lunch. Lodging is at the guesthouse.

Places to Stay & Eat

All commercial visitor accommodation was removed at the end of 1992. Forestry department **bungalows** *(Bangkok ☎ 0 2561 4292)* that sleep 12 are available for 1500B. There is also a very basic **dorm shelter** for 30B per person at Yaowachon (Youth) Camp, but you need to supply your own bedding; a sleeping bag is a must during the cooler months. You can pitch your own **tent** for 20B per person per night here. A small **restaurant** *(open 6am-6pm daily)* serves reasonably priced Thai food.

Phubade Hotel *(Phubet; ☎ 0 4431 4964; 781/1 Soi 15, Th Thetsaban; rooms with fan 200B, with air-con 300B)* is in the nearby market town of Pak Chong, just off Th Mittaphap – walk past the night market towards the road to Khao Yai and take a left at Th Thetsaban 15, then a left at the sign that reads 'Hotel'. Clean, well-maintained rooms catering to businesspeople and Thai government officials have private bath.

Green Leaf Guest House *(☎ 0 4436 5024; rooms with bath 200B)* is 7.5km out of town (just past the International School) on the way to Khao Yai. Friendly, clean and comfortable, it serves good food, and is getting rave reviews for its informative tours, including bird-watching and night-time 'spotlight' tours to look for nocturnal animals.

Khao Yai Garden Lodge *(☎ 0 4436 5167; rooms with fan 500B, with air-con 900-1000B)* is about 7km out of town on the way to Khao Yai. Reports from travellers indicate that the service and tours offered here are not as good as they once were, but the place seems to be popular with German package tourists.

Also along this road, from 17km to 25km out of Pak Chong, there are at least a dozen 'resorts', including the **Wan-Ree Resort**, **Golden Valley Resort** and **Juldis Khao Yai Resort**, which offer upmarket bungalows in the 1000B to 5000B range on weekends. During the week you should be able to haggle the rates down by half.

Near the main highway intersection in Pak Chong is an excellent **night market** *(open 5pm-11pm)* purveying a wide range of Thai and Chinese food. There are also a few decent **Thai restaurants** on the highway through town. **Krua Sonont**, on the lane leading to the train station off the main highway through town, is clean, air-conditioned and has a good Thai-Chinese menu. The owner speaks excellent English and is helpful with local information.

Getting There & Away

From Bangkok take a bus (ordinary 89B, air-con 146B; every 15 minutes; 5am to 10pm) from the Northern bus terminal to Pak Chong. From Pak Chong you can catch a sǎwngthǎew to the park gates for 10B from in front of the 7-Eleven store. You may also be able to take a direct bus from Bangkok at certain times of year – inquire at the Northern bus terminal. Ordinary buses do the trip in about three hours, air-con buses are an hour faster. Minivans to Bangkok are available from next to Pak Chong's air-con bus terminal for 120B.

From Khorat take a Bangkok-bound bus and get off in Pak Chong (ordinary 26B).

You can also easily get to Pak Chong from Ayuthaya by ordinary train (3rd/2nd class 25/56B) in around three hours. From Bangkok the train costs 36B in 3rd class and 82B in 2nd class, excluding the surcharge (40B) for rapid trains. The ordinary train takes around four hours from Bangkok; the rapid is 30 minutes shorter.

Buriram Province

Buriram is a large province (the 18th-largest of 76) with a small capital and a long history. During the Angkor period this area was an important part of the Khmer empire. The restored ruins at Phanom Rung (formally known as Prasat Hin Khao Phanom Rung) are the most impressive of all Angkor monuments in Thailand; other lesser-known ruins in the province include Prasat Meuang Tam, Ku Rasi, Prasat Ban Khok Ngiu, Prasat Nong Hong, Prasat Ban Thai Charoen, Prasat Nong Kong, Prang Ku Samathom, Prang Ku Khao Plaibat, Prang Ku Suwan Taeng, Prang Ku Khao Kadong and many others. If one includes all ancient city sites (including Dvaravati and pre-Dvaravati), the province contains 143 ruins, second in number only to Nakhon Ratchasima Province.

Until recently, most of the ruins in Buriram were little more than piles of laterite blocks by the side of a road or out in a field. The Fine Arts Department's restoration programme has transformed many of these into stacks of laterite blocks with a plaque, and surrounded by manicured lawns. Many of these sites are of interest only if you're really into Khmer history, though the locals are justifiably proud of them, and they are sometimes the focus of annual Buddhist festivals.

Contemporary Buriram Province is famous among Thais for the 320-hectare **Dong Yai Forest**, once protected by monk Prajak Kuttajitto, who 'ordained' trees with monastic robes and sacred thread so people wouldn't cut them down. In 1991 he and his followers were finally run out of the forest by the Thai military, but not without the sustained protests of thousands of sympathetic Thai citizens.

BURIRAM

บุรีรัมย์

postcode 31000 • pop 30,000

Buriram is a small provincial capital where there is not much to do, and the accommodation is a bit on the sleazy side. The town is an adequate base for visiting the fine Khmer temple ruins around the province (such as Phanom Rung), but then again so are Nang Rong and the provincial capital of Surin, where accommodation options are superior.

Information

The **post office** *(open 8.30am-4.30pm Mon-Fri)* has an **international telephone** *(open 7am-10pm daily)*. There is an **international phonecard telephone** in front of the post office.

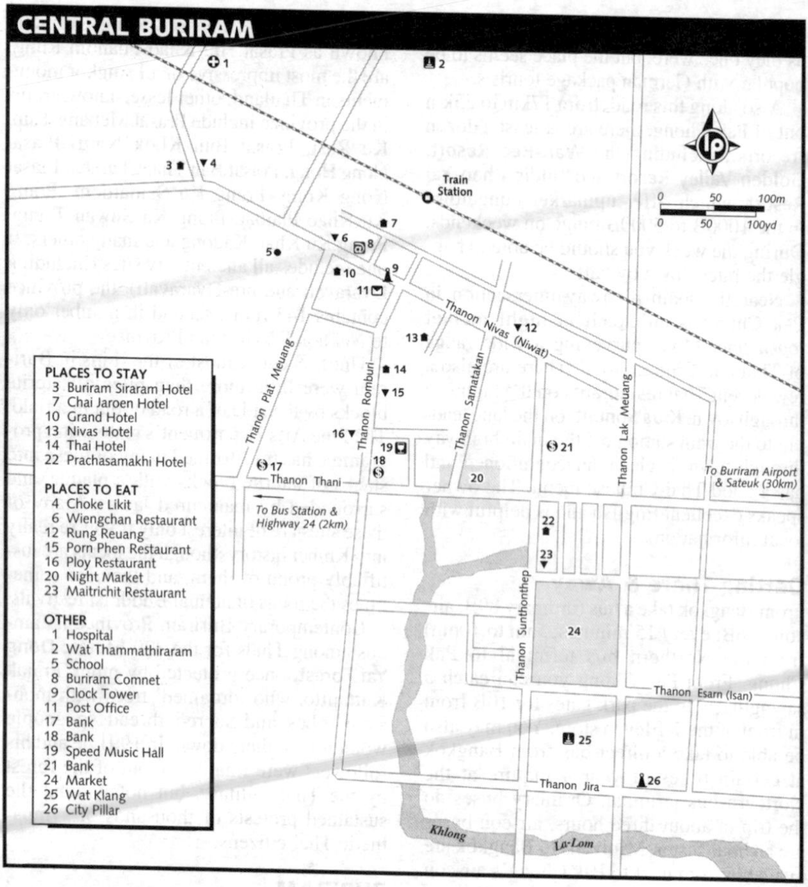

Phanom Rung Historical Park

อุทยานประวัติศาสตร์เขาพนมรุ้ง

Phanom Rung *(admission 40B between 8am-5.30pm)* is on an extinct volcanic cone (383m above sea level) that dominates the flat countryside for some distance in all directions. To the southeast you can clearly see Cambodia's Dongrek mountains and it's in this direction that the capital of the Angkor empire once lay. The Phanom Rung temple complex is the largest and best restored of all the Khmer monuments in Thailand (it took 17 years to complete the restoration) and, although it's not the easiest place to reach, it's well worth the effort.

During the week of the nationwide Songkran Festival in April, the local people have their own special celebration, **Phanom Rung Festival**, which commemorates the restoration of Phanom Rung. During the day there is a procession up Phanom Rung Hill, and at night sound-and-light shows and dance-dramas are performed in the temple complex.

Phanom Rung is Khmer for 'Big Hill', but the Thais have added their own word for hill *(khăo)* to the name as well as the word for stone *(hĭn)* to describe the *prasat*. Its full name is Prasat Hin Khao Phanom Rung.

The Phanom Rung temple was built between the 10th and 13th centuries, the bulk of it during the reign of King Suriyavarman II (r. AD 1113–50), which by all accounts was the apex of Angkor architecture. The complex faces east, towards the original Angkor capital. Of the three other great Khmer monuments of Southeast Asia, Cambodia's Angkor Wat faces west, its Prasat Khao Wihan faces north and Thailand's Prasat Hin Phimai faces southeast. Nobody knows for sure whether these orientations have any special significance, especially as most smaller Khmer monuments in Thailand face east (towards the dawn – typical of Hindu temple orientation).

The Sanctuary Phanomrung, by Dr Sorajet Woragamvijya, is an informative booklet published by the Lower North-East Study Association (LNESA). Sometimes it is available for sale near the entrance to the complex. Several English-speaking guides also offer their services at the complex – fees are negotiable. Downhill a bit from the main sanctuary is a visitor's centre that houses a scale model of the area as well as some artefacts found at the site.

The best time to visit Phanom Rung is before 10 am – this beats most bus tours, it's cooler and the light is better for photography.

Design One of the most remarkable design aspects of Phanom Rung is the promenade leading to the main gate. This is the best surviving example in Thailand. It begins on a slope 400m east of the main tower, with three earthen terraces. Next comes a cruciform base for what may have been a wooden pavilion. To the right of this is a stone hall known locally as the White Elephant Hall (Rohng Cháng Phèuak). On the northern side of this hall are two pools that were probably once used for ritual ablutions before entering the temple complex. Flower garlands to be used as offerings in the temple may also have been handed out here. After you step down from the pavilion area, you'll come to a 160m avenue paved with laterite and sandstone blocks, and flanked by sandstone pillars with lotus-bud tops, said to be early Angkor style (AD 1100–80). The avenue ends at the first and largest of three *naga* (serpent) bridges.

These *naga* bridges are the only three that have survived in Thailand. The first is flanked by 16 five-headed *naga* in the classic Angkor style – in fact, these figures are identical to those found at Angkor Wat. After passing this bridge and climbing the stairway you come to the magnificent east gallery leading into the main sanctuary. The central *prasat* has a gallery on each of its four sides and the entrance to each gallery is itself a smaller version of the main tower. The galleries have curvilinear roofs and false-balustrade windows. Once inside the temple walls, have a look at each of the galleries and the *gopura* (entrance pavilion), paying particular attention to the lintels over the porticoes. The craftsmanship at Phanom

VICINITY OF PHANOM RUNG

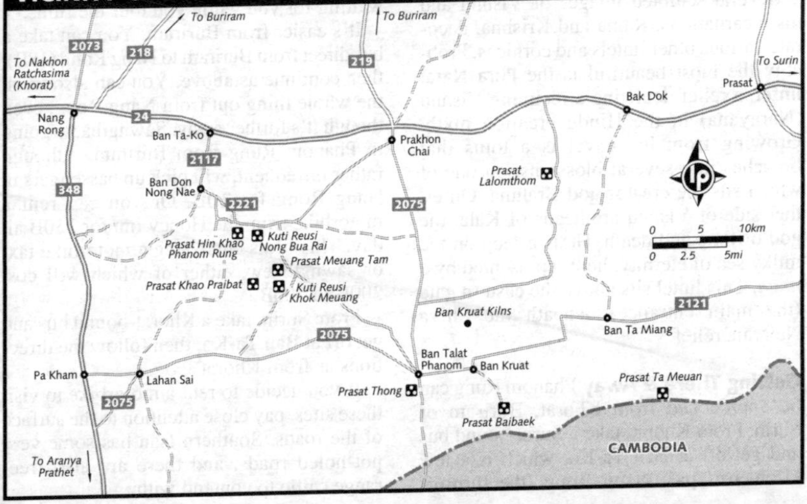

PHANOM RUNG

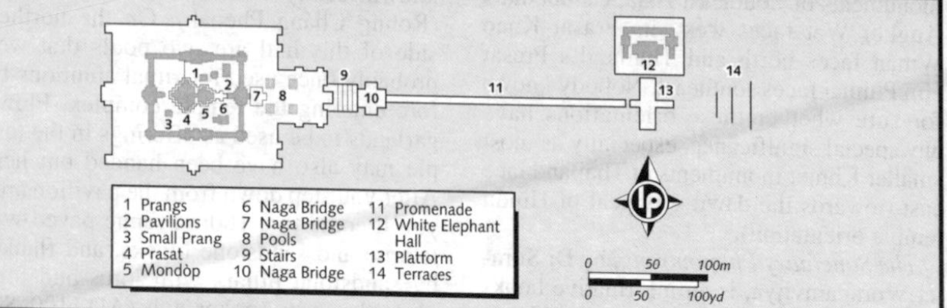

Rung represents the pinnacle of Khmer artistic achievement, on a par with the reliefs at Angkor Wat in Cambodia.

Sculpture The Phanom Rung complex was originally built as a Hindu monument and exhibits iconography related to the worship of Vishnu and Shiva. Excellent sculptures of both Vaishnava and Shaiva deities can be seen in the lintels or pediments over the doorways to the central monuments and in various other key points on the sanctuary exterior.

On the east portico of the *mondòp* is a Nataraja (Dancing Shiva), which is in the late Baphuan or early Angkor style, while on the south entrance are the remains of Shiva and Uma riding their bull mount, Nandi. The central cell of the *prasat* contains a Shivalingam (phallus image).

Several sculpted images of Vishnu and his incarnations, Rama and Krishna, decorate various other lintels and cornices. Probably the most beautiful is the **Phra Narai lintel**, a relief depicting a reclining Vishnu (Narayana) in the Hindu creation myth. Growing from his navel is a lotus that branches into several blossoms, on one of which sits the creator god Brahma. On either side of Vishnu are heads of Kala, the god of time and death. He is asleep on the milky sea of eternity, here represented by a *naga*. This lintel sits above the eastern gate (the main entrance) beneath the Shiva Nataraja relief.

Getting There & Away Phanom Rung can be approached from Khorat, Buriram or Surin. From Khorat, take a Surin-bound bus and get off at Ban Ta-Ko, which is a few kilometres past Nang Rong (the turn-off north to Buriram). The fare should be about 35B; Ban Ta-Ko is well marked as the turn-off for Phanom Rung. Once in Ta-Ko you have several options. At the Ta-Ko intersection you can wait for a săwngthăew that's going as far as the foot of Phanom Rung (20B, 12km) or one that's on the way south to Lahan Sai. If you take a Lahan Sai truck, get off at the Ban Don Nong Nae intersection (you'll see signs pointing the way to Phanom Rung to the east). From Ta-Ko to Don Nong Nae will cost 6B. From Don Nong Nae, get another săwngthăew to the foot of the hill (10B) or charter a pick-up (50B) one way.

If you don't have the patience to wait for a săwngthăew, take a motorbike taxi from Ta-Ko to Don Nong Nae (40B) or all the way to Phanom Rung (100B). A return trip will cost 150B; for an extra 50B the drivers will add Meuang Tam. These rates include waiting for you while you tour the ruins.

It's easier from Buriram. You can take a bus direct from Buriram to Nang Rong (18B), then continue as above. You can also work the whole thing out from Nang Rong, even though it's further away. Săwngthăew going to Phanom Rung from Buriram, although rather infrequent, will pick up passengers in Nang Rong for 10B. Or you can rent a motorbike from the Honey Inn for 250B all day. This beats chartering a motorbike taxi or săwngthăew, either of which will cost 300B to 500B.

From Surin, take a Khorat-bound bus and get off at Ban Ta-Ko, then follow the directions as from Khorat.

If you decide to rent a motorbike to visit these sites, pay close attention to the surface of the roads. Southern Isan has some very pot-holed roads, and there are also free-range cattle to contend with.

Prasat Meuang Tam & Other Ruins

About 8km southeast of Phanom Rung, this Khmer site *(admission 30B, open 8am-5.30pm)* dates to the late 10th century and was sponsored by King Jayavarman V. This temple complex is probably Isan's third most interesting – after Phanom Rung and Khorat's Phimai – in terms of size, atmosphere and the quality of restoration work. The whole complex is surrounded by laterite walls, within which are four lotus-filled reservoirs, each guarded by whimsical five-headed *naga*. Sandstone galleries and *gopura*, the latter exquisitely carved, surround five brick *prang* (Khmer-style towers). The towers themselves, being brick, are not nearly as tall or as imposing as the sandstone *prang* at Phanom Rung, but the plan is based on the same design as that of Angkor Wat: the five peaks of Mt Meru, the mythical abode of the Hindu gods. A lintel on one of the towers, depicting Shiva and his consort Uma riding the sacred bull Nandi, suggests that the temple was once a shrine to Shiva. A Shivalingam was also found in the central tower.

North of Meuang Tam and east of Phanom Rung are the much smaller Khmer ruins of **Kuti Reusi Nong Bua Rai** and **Prasat Khao Praibat**. East of these are **Prasat Lalomthom**, **Prasat Thong** and **Prasat Baibaek**. South of Prasat Meuang Tam is **Kuti Reusi Khok Meuang**. All of these have been restored or stabilised to some degree by the Fine Arts Department and are marked by signs along the highways, though unless you have your own vehicle, they're not the easiest places to reach. They're spotted on the Vicinity of Phanom Rung map in case you want to rent a motorbike and look for them yourself. Or you can contact the guide Khun Pirom in Surin (see Places to Stay in the Surin section later in this chapter), work out your own itinerary and he will drive you there in his Land Rover.

From Prasat Meuang Tam you can continue southeast via Ban Kruat and Ban Ta Miang (along Rtes 2075 and 2121) to **Prasat Ta Meuan**, off a secluded Khmer ruins complex on the Thai-Cambodian border (see the Surin section later in this chapter for details). From Ta Miang you can then proceed north to Surin town or continue east along the border to Si Saket and Ubon Ratchathani Provinces.

Places to Stay

Buriram's choice of accommodation is a bit on the sleazy side. Nearly all of the establishments in the provincial capital double as short-time hotels. If you are put off by this, consider staying in nearby Nang Rong (see later in this section).

Several cheap hotels are within walking distance of the Buriram train station. **Chai Jaroen Hotel** *(☎ 0 4460 1559; 114-116 Th Nivas; singles & doubles from 120B)*, in front of the station, has dreary rooms with fan and bath.

Nivas Hotel *(Niwat; ☎ 0 4461 1640; singles/doubles 60/80B)*, on a desolate lane just off Th Nivas, is cheaper than Chai Jaroen, but definitely a step or three down in quality, with barely adequate rooms. **Grand Hotel** *(☎ 0 4461 1179; Th Nivas; singles/doubles with fan 150/200B, doubles with air-con 350B)*, in the other direction to Nivas, has fair rooms with cold-water bath. A small restaurant is attached.

Prachasamakhi Hotel *(☎ 0 4461 1198; Th Sunthonthep; rooms with/without bath 120/100B)*, further south of the train station, is a four-storey Chinese hotel with a restaurant downstairs. Rooms are simple but adequate.

Thai Hotel *(☎ 0 4461 1112, fax 0 6441 2461; 38/1 Th Romburi; singles/doubles with fan 160/200B, with air-con & TV 350/390B, deluxe room 500B)* is fairly nice and has clean rooms with bath. There is also a larger 'deluxe' room with bath.

Buriram Sirarom Hotel *(☎ 0 4461 1740; rooms with air-con, TV & fridge 400-600B)* near the town entrance from Rte 218, is the best accommodation in town – and about the only place whose rooms don't reek of urinal cakes. It's rarely full though and discounts are sometimes given.

Nang Rong You can also stay closer to Phanom Rung by spending the night at this tiny town off the highway.

Honey Inn *(☎ 0 4462 2825; 8/1 Soi Si Kun; rooms with fan 150-250B)* is run by a local schoolteacher who speaks English. It's really more of a homestay than a 'guesthouse' in the Thai sense of the word. Rooms are clean and comfortable. To find it, walk 100m from the bus stop to the main road, turn east and go 100m past a petrol station on the left, then turn left just before the hospital and it's about 150m further on the right (past a reservoir). Or take a sǎamláw for 30B. Good food is available here also. A couple of motorbikes can be rented for 250B per day – very handy for visiting the Phanom Rung and Meuang Tam ruins.

Nang Rong Hotel *(☎ 0 4463 1014; singles & doubles with fan 120B, with air-con 400B)* is run-down and peephole-ridden, but has an attached restaurant.

Places to Eat

In front of the train station there are a few restaurants that are open during the day for breakfast and lunch. The **restaurant** on the corner of the clock tower opens early in the morning, and sells coffee, tea and *paa-thâwng-kǒh* (Chinese doughnuts).

At the Th Samatakan and Th Thani intersection there is a large **night market** that has mostly Chinese as well as a few Isan vendors. The curiously named **Choke Likit** *(Th Nivas; dishes 60-80B)*, near the Buriram Sirarom Hotel, also has Isan food in a slightly more upmarket atmosphere.

Maitrichit Restaurant *(Th Sunthonthep; dishes 30-40B)* near the Prachasamakhi Hotel, has a large selection of Thai and Chinese standards that are served from morning until night. It offers bakery items as well.

Ploy Restaurant *(☎ 0 4461 3747; Th Romburi; dishes 60-80B)*, opposite and about 100m south of the Thai Hotel, serves very good Thai food and Western breakfasts with real coffee, and even has a selection of wines.

Porn Phen Restaurant *(Phawn Phen; ☎ 0 4461 1553; Th Romburi; dishes 30-50B)*, near the Thai Hotel, is also good for basic Thai food and Isan dishes.

Rung Rueng *(Rung Reuang; ☎ 0 4461 1778; Th Nivas; dishes 25-40B)*, near the train station, offers decent Thai-Chinese fare and is open until late.

Entertainment

Speed Music Hall is a modern dance club with state-of-the-art sound equipment and an impressive light show. Fellow patrons are very friendly, especially if you are willing to pick up the tab.

Getting There & Away

Air From Bangkok **Air Andaman** *(in Bangkok ☎ 0 2229 9555)* flies to Buriram daily (1800B, 1¼ hours); tickets are available through **Phusiam Tours** *(☎ 0 4462 5066; 24/23 Th Romburi)*. The airport is about 30km northeast of Buriram, on Rte 219, near the town called Sateu. There's also a flight to/from Khorat (775B).

Bus Ordinary buses heading from Khorat to Buriram leave every 20 minutes between 4.30am and 8pm (55B, about 2½ hours). From Surin ordinary buses head for Buriram at a similar frequency (30B, about an hour).

From Bangkok's Northern bus terminal there are seven air-con departures (215B), and ordinary buses (139B) also.

Train Buriram is on the Bangkok–Ubon Ratchathani line. Fares are 67B in 3rd class, 155B in 2nd class and 316B in 1st class, excluding supplementary charges for rapid (40B) or express (60B) service. Express diesel railcars or 'Sprinters' (2nd class air-con only) to Buriram from Bangkok depart at 11.05am and 9.50pm. Ordinary 3rd-class trains depart at 11.45am and 11.10pm. These take around seven hours to reach Buriram; rapid and express trains are about 50 minutes faster – see Getting There & Away in the Nakhon Ratchasima (Khorat) section earlier for information on the departure times from Bangkok.

From Khorat there are 14 trains to Buriram (3rd/2nd class 17/40B; 1¾ hours; departures at 12.23am, 2.50am, 3.34am, 4.21am, 5.19am, 5.34am, 7.50am, 10.10am, 10.55am, 12.24pm, 2.30pm, 3.33pm, 5.25pm and 9.35pm). Trains from Surin take only 50 minutes and cost just 6B in 3rd class.

Getting Around

Sǎamláw and túk-túk going from the Buriram train station to the town centre charge 20B.

Chaiyaphum Province

Bounded by Phetchabun, Lopburi, Nakhon Ratchasima and Khon Kaen Provinces, right in the centre of Thailand, Chaiyaphum might as well be in the middle of nowhere considering its low tourist profile. The least visited of any province in the country, it's so remote from national attention that even many Thai citizens can't tell you exactly where it is – or even whether it's in the northern or the northeastern region.

The several Khmer shrine ruins in the province – none of which are major sites – indicate that the territory was an Angkor, and later Lopburi, satellite during the 10th and 11th centuries.

CHAIYAPHUM
ชัยภูมิ

postcode 36000 • pop 55,500

During the late 18th century a Lao court official brought 200 Lao from Vientiane to settle this area, which had been abandoned by the Khmers 500 years earlier. The community paid tribute to Vientiane but also cultivated relations with Bangkok and Champasak. When Prince Anou (from Vientiane) declared war on Siam in the early 19th century, the Lao ruler of Chaiyaphum, Jao Phraya Lae, wisely switched allegiance to Bangkok, knowing that Anou's armies didn't stand a chance against the more powerful Siamese. Although Jao Phraya Lae lost his life in battle in 1806, the Siamese sacked Vientiane in 1828 and ruled most of western Laos until the coming of the French near the end of the 19th century. Today a statue of Jao Phraya Lae (renamed Phraya Phakdi Chumphon by the Thais) stands in a prominent spot in central Chaiyaphum.

Chaiyaphum residents celebrate a week-long **festival** in Jao Phraya Lae's honour each year in mid-January. Activities focus on his statue and on a **shrine** erected on the spot where he was killed by Vientiane troops in 1806 – at the base of a tamarind tree about 3km west of town off the road to Ban Khwao (Rte 225).

The main reason people visit Chaiyaphum today is to tour **Ban Khwao** (15km west) and other nearby silk villages. Silk can also be purchased at Chaiyaphum shops or in the municipal market in the centre of town. Buses to Ban Khwao leave from the bus terminal every 20 minutes between 6am and 6pm (6B). If you've never observed the silk process – from the cultivation of mulberry trees and propagation of silkworms to the dyeing and weaving of silk thread – you're in for an interesting day.

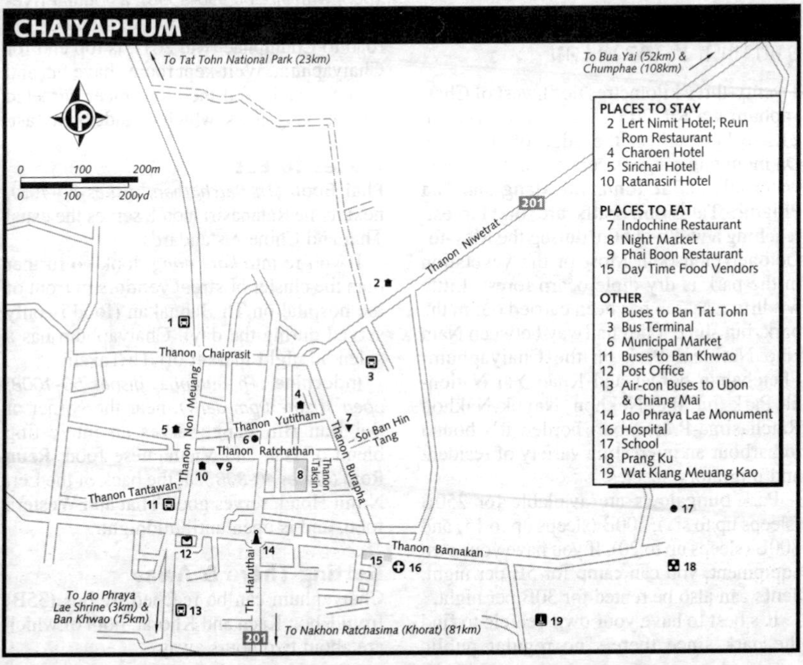

Information

The **post office** *(Th Bannakan; open 8.30am-4.30pm Mon-Fri)* is near the corner of Th Non Meuang.

Prang Ku

ปรางค์กู่

This hollow Khmer *prang* was constructed during the reign of the final Angkor king, Jayavarman VII (AD 1181–1219) as a place of worship at a 'healing station' on the Angkor temple route between the Angkor capital in Cambodia and Prasat Singh in Kanchanaburi Province. It's really not much to look at, just a pile of laterite blocks a few metres high, however Chaiyaphum residents consider this a very holy spot and many make daily offerings of flowers, candles and incense. The Buddha figure inside the *ku* (hollow, cave-like stupa) purportedly hails from the Dvaravati period (6th to 10th centuries). Also on the small grounds are a Shivalingam pedestal and a venerable tamarind tree.

Prang Ku is about 1km east of the Jao Phraya Lae monument.

Tat Tohn National Park

อุทยานแห่งชาติตาดโตน

Twenty-three kilometres northwest of Chaiyaphum via Rte 2051, this seldom-visited, 218-sq-km park at the edge of the Laen Da mountain range is centred on the scenic waterfalls of **Tat Tohn**, **Tat Klang** and **Pha Phiang**. Tat Tohn Falls are the largest, reaching a width of 50m during the May-to-October monsoon. Most of the vegetation in the park is dry dipterocarp forest. Little wildlife research has been carried out in the park, but since it lies halfway between Nam Nao National Park on the Chaiyaphum-Phetchabun border and Khao Yai National Park on the Nakhon Nayok-Nakhon Ratchasima-Prachinburi border, it's bound to harbour an interesting variety of resident and migratory species.

Park **bungalows** are available for 250B (sleeps up to six), 500B (sleeps up to 15) and 800B (sleeps up to 20). If you have your own equipment, you can **camp** for 5B per night. **Tents** can also be rented for 30B per night.

It's best to have your own vehicle to find the park since there's no regular public transport from Chaiyaphum. Alternatively, you can get a săwngthăew from Chaiyaphum as far as Ban Tat Tohn (around 6B), then hire a pick-up truck on to the park for about 100B one way.

Places to Stay

Ratanasiri Hotel *(☎ 0 4482 1258; cnr Th Non Meuang & Th Ratchathan; rooms with fan 160-220B, with air-con 350B)* is an efficiently run place with one floor of rooms with fan, and two floors with air-con and hot water. All rooms come with TV.

Sirichai Hotel *(☎ 0 4481 1461; singles & doubles with fan 200-300B, doubles with air-con 400B)*, on the opposite side of Th Non Meuang further north, is a friendly place with slightly more upmarket rooms than Ratanasiri, all with TV. The restaurant serves American breakfasts and good Thai food.

Charoen Hotel *(☎ 0 4481 1194; 196/7 Soi 1, Th Yutitham; rooms with fan 150-200B, with air-con 250-350B)*, further east than Sirichai, is run-down and has rooms with fan and cold water, or air-con.

Lert Nimit Hotel *(☎ 0 4481 1522, fax 822335; Th Niwetrat; rooms with fan 200-250B, with air-con 550-850B)*, a popular five-storey hotel, east of the bus terminal on the road to Chumphae (Rte 201), is top end for Chaiyaphum. Well-kept rooms have fan and attached bath, and there are nicer carpeted air-con bungalows, which include breakfast.

Places to Eat

Phai Boon *(Th Ratchathan; dishes 20-40B)*, next to the Ratanasiri Hotel, serves the usual Thai and Chinese standards.

If you're into *kài yâang,* look no further than the cluster of **street vendors** in front of the hospital on Th Bannakan (food is only served during the day). Chaiyaphum has a splendid **night market** off Th Taksin.

Indochine *(Th Burapha; dishes 50-100B; open 10am-10pm daily)*, near the corner of Soi Ban Hin Tang, serves an interesting blend of Isan and Vietnamese food. **Reun Rom** *(dishes 40-80B)*, at the back of the Lert Nimit Hotel, serves good Thai and Western food, and is open until midnight.

Getting There & Away

Chaiyaphum can be reached by bus (35B) from Khon Kaen and Khorat, both of which are about two hours away.

Buses from Bangkok's Northern bus terminal cost 186B to 212B for air-con (five hours, 19 daily); and 99B for ordinary (six hours, every half-hour from 6am to 9pm).

Getting Around

A túk-túk should cost no more than 20B for any destination in town.

Khon Kaen & Roi Et Provinces

Khon Kaen and Roi Et are mostly rural provinces where farming and textiles are the main occupations. At the heart of the Isan region, these provinces are good to explore Isan culture – its language, food and music.

KHON KAEN

ขอนแก่น

postcode 40000 • pop 145,300

Khon Kaen is about a 2½-hour bus trip from either Khorat or Udon Thani, and 450km from Bangkok. It is also the gateway to the northeast if you are coming from Phitsanulok in northern Thailand.

The fourth-largest city in Thailand, Khon Kaen is an important commercial, financial, educational and communications centre for Isan. **Khon Kaen University**, the largest university in the northeast, covers 8.1 sq km in the northwestern part of Khon Kaen.

The city has grown fantastically over the last decade, with lots of added neon and the heaviest automotive traffic in the northeast after Khorat. Unlike in Khorat, the air is fairly clean.

With its international cuisine restaurants, air-con hotels and modern banking facilities, Khon Kaen makes a good spot to take a rest from small-town and village travel in the northeast. It can also be used as a base for day trips to Chonabot (57km southwest), which is a centre for good quality *mát-mìi* silk, and the Khmer ruins of Prasat Peuay Noi (66km southeast). See Chonabot and Prasat Peuay Noi in the following Around Khon Kaen section for information.

History

The city is named after Phra That Kham Kaen, a revered *chedi* at Wat Chetiyaphum in the village of Ban Kham in Nam Phong district, 32km to the northeast. Legend says that early in the last millennium a *thâat* (reliquary stupa) was built over a tamarind tree stump that miraculously came to life after a contingent of monks carrying Buddha relics to Phra That Phanom (in today's Nakhon Phanom Province) camped here overnight. There was no room at That Phanom for more relics, so the monks returned to this spot and enshrined the relics in the new That Kham Kaen (Tamarind Heartwood Reliquary). A town developed nearby, but was abandoned several times until 1789 when a Suwannaphum ruler founded a city at the current site, which he named Kham Kaen after the *chedi*. Over the years the name has changed to Khon Kaen (Heartwood Log).

Information

Tourist Offices The TAT *(☎ 0 4324 4498, fax 0 4324 4497; 15/5 Th Prachasamoson; open 8.30am-4.30pm daily)* has a branch office in Khon Kaen. The English-speaking staff distribute good maps of the city, and can answer general queries on Khon Kaen and the surrounding provinces.

Khon Kaen's **tourist police** *(☎ 0 4323 6937, emergency ☎ 1155)* have an office next door to TAT.

Consulates The Lao People's Democratic Republic operates a **consulate** *(☎ 0 4322 3698, 0 4322 1961; 123 Th Photisan)*, which issues 30-day visas for Laos. The bad news is that visas can take up to three days to issue (as opposed to four hours in Bangkok). The consulate's location on the outskirts of town also makes it a hassle to find twice (most locals have never heard of it – try saying *sathăan kongsŭn lao* to the túk-túk drivers). Unless you were already planning to spend some time in Khon Kaen, it's easier to get a Lao visa before leaving Bangkok.

The **Vietnamese consulate** *(☎ 0 4324 2190; 65/6 Th Chatapadung)* issues visas for Vietnam in three days.

Money Every major Thai bank has a branch in Khon Kaen, most of which are clustered along the southern side of Th Si Chan west of Th Na Meuang, and along Th Na Meuang between Th Si Chan and Th Reun Rom.

Bangkok Bank *(Th Si Chan)* has an ATM and foreign-exchange facilities.

Post & Communications The **main post office** *(cnr Th Si Chan & Th Klang Meuang; open 8.30am-4.30pm Mon-Fri, 9am-noon Sat)* has a **CAT international-telephone office** attached. You can also make international phone calls at the **CAT office** *(Th Lang Sunratchakan)* in the northern part of town.

Things to See

About the only tourist attraction is the very well-curated **Khon Kaen National Museum** *(Th Lang Sunratchakan; admission 30B; open 9am-noon & 1pm-5pm Wed-Sun)*, which features Dvaravati objects, *sĕmaa* (ordination-precinct marker stones) from Kalasin and Meuang Fa Daet, and bronze and ceramic artefacts from Ban Chiang.

On the banks of Khon Kaen's 100-hectare **Beung Kaen Nakhon** (Kaen Nakhon Pond) is **Wat That**, with the extra-elongated spires typical of this area. At the southern end of Beung Kaen Nakhon, **Wat Nong Wang Muang** features a relatively new nine-tier *chedi*. This lake and **Beung Thung Sang** in the northeastern section of town are favourite venues for evening strolls.

Language Courses

The **American University Alumni** *(AUA; ☎ 0 4324 1072)* has a branch at Khon Kaen University, where Thai-language instruction may be available.

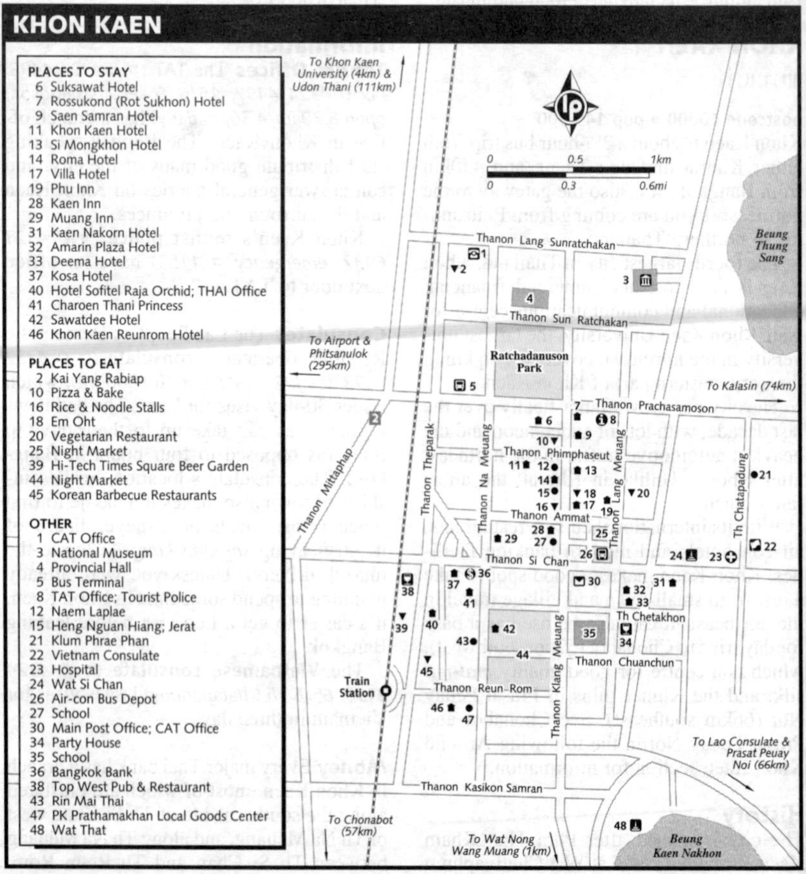

Special Events

Khon Kaen's biggest annual event is the **Silk and Phuk Siaw Festival**, held for 10 days and nights from late November to early December. Centred on Ratchadanuson Park and in the field in front of the Provincial Hall (Sala Klang), the festival celebrates the planting of the mulberry tree, a necessary step in the production of silk. Another aspect of the festival is *phùuk sìaw* ('friend-bonding'), a reference to the *bai sĭi* ceremony in which sacred threads are tied around one's wrists for spiritual protection. The ritual also implies a renewal of the bonds of friendship and reaffirmation of local tradition. Other activities include parades, Isan music, folk dancing, and the preparation and sharing of Isan food.

The **Flowers** and **Khaen Music Festival** takes place during Songkran, the Thai lunar New Year in mid-April. Along with the customary ritual bathing of important Buddha images at local temples, activities in Khon Kaen include parades of floats bedecked with flowers and plenty of Isan music.

Places to Stay – Budget

As Khon Kaen is a large city and an important transit point, there is a huge choice of hotels. **Si Mongkhon** *(61-67 Th Klang Meuang; rooms with/without bath 150/100B, with air-con 350B)*, is an all-wooden place and the best budget choice. Rooms with air-con have TV and hot water.

Saen Samran Hotel *(☎ 0 4323 9611; 55-59 Th Klang Meuang; singles/doubles with fan 150/250B)* is reputedly Khon Kaen's oldest hotel, and the sturdy wooden building does have some character. Rooms are basic but clean.

Suksawat Hotel *(☎ 0 4323 6472; rooms without bath 100B, with bath & fan 120-160B)*, off Th Klang Meuang, is quieter as it's a bit off the main streets. It has clean rooms.

Roma Hotel *(☎ 0 4323 7177, fax 0 4324 2450; 50/2 Th Klang Meuang; rooms with fan/air-con 200/350B)* is a friendly, long-running place with large rooms with fan, plus refurbished rooms with air-con. The coffee shop serves basic Thai dishes at reasonable prices.

Sawatdee Hotel *(☎ 0 4322 1600, fax 0 4332 0345; 177-179 Th Na Meuang; singles/doubles with fan from 200/250B, rooms with air-con 550B)* is clean and modern. All rooms have hot water; rooms with air-con have a bath, fridge, large TV, private balcony and carpet.

Villa Hotel *(☎ 0 4324 1545; cnr Th Klang Meuang & Th Ammat; rooms 350B)* is mainly a short-time place attached to a massage parlour 'entertainment complex', but it has rooms with air-con and hot water. The sign on the hotel's façade has a wonderfully retro 1960s-era Thai font, for those who appreciate such things.

Places to Stay – Mid-Range

Khon Kaen excels in this category, with a fine selection of accommodation in the 400B to 600B range.

Deema Hotel *(☎ 0 4332 1562, fax 0 4332 1561; 133 Th Chetakhon; rooms with fan 250B, with air-con 450B)*, near the bus depot and night market, is a good deal. It has clean rooms with private hot-water bath; rooms with air-con come with satellite TV.

Muang Inn *(☎ 0 4324 5870, fax 0 4333 4411; Th Na Meuang; standard/VIP rooms 450/550B)* is at a convenient location and offers tidy air-con singles and doubles with air-con, telephone and TV; VIP rooms have refrigerator. There's an excellent bakery and restaurant on the ground floor.

Amarin Plaza Hotel *(☎ 0 4332 1660; rooms 350-550B)*, off Th Lang Meuang, is a modern, six-storey hotel and offers nice rooms with air-con and hot water.

Phu Inn *(☎ 0 4324 3174, fax 0 4324 3176; rooms 300-500B)* a similar mid-range spot near the night market, has 97 rooms with air-con. The slightly more expensive rooms on the upper floors are in better condition than those on the ground floor. There's a coffee shop that's open until late.

Khon Kaen Reunrom Hotel *(☎ 0 4322 3522, fax 0 4322 0567; 335 Th Reun Rom; rooms 300B)*, near the train station, has 72 rooms with air-con; all come with TV, minibar, carpet and hot water – good value in this range – but it's starting to show wear.

Kaen Nakorn Hotel *(☎ 0 4322 4268, fax 0 4322 4272; Th Si Chan; rooms 300-600B)* has fairly clean and comfortable rooms with air-con.

Places to Stay – Top End

Khon Kaen Hotel *(☎ 0 4324 4881, fax 0 4324 2458; Th Phimphaseut; singles/doubles 460/560B, suites from 960B)* is a seven-storey hotel with 134 clean, comfortable rooms that include air-con, refrigerator and private balcony.

Rossukond Hotel *(Rot Sukhon; ☎ 0 4323 8576, fax 0 4323 8579; Th Klang Meuang; singles/doubles 550/700B, suites 2000B)* is similar to the nearby Khon Kaen Hotel and has rooms with air-con. Discounts are readily given in the low season.

Kosa Hotel *(☎ 0 4322 5014, fax 0 4322 5013; Th Si Chan; rooms from 900B)* is popular and has rooms with all the amenities, as well as suites. The attached karaoke club attracts a steady flow of Thai businessmen. There's also a swimming pool.

Hotel Sofitel Raja Orchid *(☎ 0 4332 2155, fax 0 4332 2150; Th Theparak; rooms from 2400B)* near Kosa, has well-decorated rooms and suites. There are nonsmoking floors, facilities for the disabled and several restaurants. The Underground entertainment complex beneath the hotel even has a German *brauhaus* where it brews its own 'Kronen beer'.

Kaen Inn *(☎ 0 4324 5420, fax 0 4323 9457; 56 Th Klang Meuang; rooms 800B)* is friendly and used to be the top hotel in the city. Rooms have air-con, TV, telephone and fridge. On the premises are Chinese and Japanese restaurants, a karaoke lounge, coffee shop, barber shop and snooker club.

Charoen Thani Princess *(☎ 0 4322 0400, fax 0 4322 0438; 260 Th Si Chan; rooms from 990B)* towers over the city. Well-appointed rooms have all the mod-cons (add tax and service charge).

Places to Eat

Khon Kaen has a lively **night market** *(Th Reun Rom)*, between Th Klang Meuang and Th Na Meuang next to the air-con bus terminal, with plenty of good food stalls. It convenes each evening from around sunset to 11pm. Look for the busy **Khun Aem** *jók* stall, which serves exemplary broken-rice congee. More late-night food stalls can be found along Th Ruen Rom near the train station. Another area to look for food stalls both day and night is along the west side of Th Klang Meuang between Th Phimphaseut and Th Ammat.

Also in the evenings, a row of outdoor, cook-it-yourself **Korean Barbecue Restaurants** can be found on Th Theparak, just north of the train station, though these places are good only if you're with a group. Don't show up alone!

Kai Yang Rabiap *(Th Theparak; dishes 20-30B)*, near the corner of Th Lang Sunratchakan, is a good spot for local Isan food.

Em Oht *(Th Klang Meuang; dishes 30-40B)*, across from the Roma Hotel, is a good place for breakfast. It serves real coffee and specialises in *kài kàthá* (eggs served in a cooking pan with local sausages).

A family-oriented restaurant, **Pizza & Bake** *(dishes 30-70B; open 6.30am-11.30pm)* has two locations; one on Th Maliwan west of the railway line and another on the corner of Th Phimphaseut and Th Klang Meuang. Pizza is the main focus, but the restaurant also prepares a variety of other European and Thai dishes, as well as a full line of espresso drinks.

You could try **Vegetarian Restaurant** *(Th Lang Muang; dishes 15-25B; open 8am-9pm daily)*, which serves Thai vegetarian dishes.

Shopping

Khon Kaen is a good place to buy handcrafted Isan goods such as silk and cotton fabrics (you can get *mát-mìi* cotton and silk), silver and basketry. A speciality of the northeast is the *mǎwn khwǎan* ('axe pillow'), a stiff triangle-shaped pillow used as an elbow support while sitting on the floor. These come in many sizes, from small enough to carry in a handbag to large enough to fill your entire backpack. Perhaps the most practical way to acquire axe pillows while on the road is to buy them unstuffed (*mâi sài nûn,* 'no kapok inserted') – the covers are easily carried and you can stuff them when you get home.

If textiles are your main interest, try **PK Prathamakhan Local Goods Center** *(☎ 0 4322 4080; 79/2-3 Th Reun Rom)* just west of Th Na Meuang – a local handicraft centre with a small museum.

Also good are **Rin Mai Thai** *(☎ 0 4322 1042; 412 Th Na Meuang)*, and **Klum Phrae Phan** *(☎ 0 4333 7216; 131/193 Th Chatapadung)*. Klum Phrae Phan is run by the Handicraft Centre for Northeastern Women's Development.

Several shops selling local preserved foods and other Isan products can be found along Th Klang Meuang between Th Prachasamoson and Th Si Chan, including **Jerat**, **Naem Laplae** and **Heng Nguan Hiang**.

The emphasis in these shops is *năem* (a kind of sausage made of raw pickled pork) and other types of sausage or processed meats, such as *sâi kràwk, mŭu yaw, kun siang mŭu* and *kun siang kài*. Still, behind the stacks of sausage you can often ferret out some good handicraft purchases.

Getting There & Away

Air THAI flies six times daily between Bangkok and Khon Kaen (1500B one way, 55 minutes).

Khon Kaen has a **THAI office** *(☎ 0 4322 7701–5)* located in the Hotel Sofitel Raja Orchid. The **airport** *(☎ 0 4323 6523, 0 4323 8835)* is a few kilometres west of the city centre off Hwy 12; minivan shuttles between the airport and the city are available through THAI.

Bus Ordinary buses arrive at and depart from a **bus terminal** *(☎ 0 4323 7300; Th Prachasamoson)*, while air-con buses use a **depot** *(☎ 0 4323 9910)* near the night market off Th Klang Meuang.

An air-con bus from Bangkok's Northern bus terminal costs 246B to 315B. Departures are approximately every half-hour between 7.30am and 11.30pm. Ordinary buses (142B) leave several times between 8am and 10pm. This is a seven- to eight-hour bus trip.

The Phitsanulok-to-Khon Kaen road runs through spectacular scenery, including two national parks. Ordinary buses to Khon Kaen from Phitsanulok leave several times throughout the day (108B, six hours). Air-con buses leave Phitsanulok less frequently (around 160B to 200B, depending on the company).

Air-con night buses from Khon Kaen to Chiang Mai depart from the bus terminal on Th Prachasamoson via Phitsanulok (348B to 407B).

Other air-con bus destinations from Khon Kaen include: Nakhon Phanom (141B, five to six hours), Ubon Ratchathani (198B, five hours), Nong Khai (104B, three hours), Loei (111B, four hours), Udon Thani (51B to 70B, two hours), Roi Et (54B, two hours)

NORTHEASTERN THAILAND

Bai Sĭi Ceremony

Northeastern Thais commonly participate in *bai sĭi* (sacred thread) ceremonies on auspicious occasions such as birthdays, farewells and times of serious illness, and during certain festivals such as Khon Kaen's annual *phùuk sìaw* ('tying friends') festival. In the *bai sĭi* ceremony, the 32 guardian spirits known as *khwăn* are bound to the guest of honour by white strings tied around the wrists. Each of the 32 *khwăn* are thought to be guardians over different organs or functions in a person's body.

Khwăn occasionally wander away from their owner, which isn't considered much of a problem except when that person is about to embark on a new project or on a journey away from home, or when they're very ill. At these times it's best to perform the *bai sĭi* to ensure that all the *khwăn* are present and attached to the person's body. A *măw phawn* ('wish doctor') – usually an elder who has spent some time as a monk – presides over the ritual. Those participating sit on mats around a tiered vase-like centrepiece *(phakhuan)*, which is decorated with flowers, folded banana leaves and branches with white cotton strings hanging down; pastries, eggs, bananas, liquor and money are placed around the base as offerings to the spirits in attendance.

After a few words of greeting, the *măw phawn* chants in a mixture of Isan and Pali to convey blessings on the honoured guest, while all in attendance place their hands in a prayer-like, palms-together pose. For part of the chanting segment, everyone leans forward to touch the base of the *phakhuan*; if there are too many participants for everyone to reach the base, it's permissible to touch the elbow of someone who can reach it, thus forming a human chain.

Once the *măw phawn* has finished chanting, each person attending takes two of the white strings from the *phakhuan* and ties one around each wrist of the honoured guest, while whispering a short, well-wishing recitation. When all have performed this action, the guest is left with a stack of strings looped around each wrist. Small cups of rice liquor are passed around, sometimes followed by an impromptu *ram wong* (circle dance). For the intended effect, the strings must be kept around the wrists for a minimum of three full days. Some Isan people believe the strings should be allowed to fall off naturally rather than cut off – this can take weeks.

and Sakon Nakhon (104B, three to four hours).

There are ordinary buses from Khon Kaen to Khorat (64B, 2½ to three hours). Other destinations include Udon Thani (49B, two hours), Chaiyaphum (34B, two hours) and Surin (71B, 5½ hours).

Train Rapid train Nos 137 and 133 (2nd and 3rd class) depart from Bangkok's Hualamphong station at 6am and 6.30pm, arriving in Khon Kaen at 2.32pm and 3.56am respectively. The only overnight sleeper train that arrives at a semi-decent hour is express No 69 (1st/2nd/3rd class 368/179/77B, express and rapid surcharges excluded), which leaves Bangkok at 8.45pm and arrives in Khon Kaen at 5.19am.

Getting Around

A regular săwngthăew system plies the central city for 8B per person, and colour-coded city bus routes cost 5B. If you want to charter a vehicle you usually have to pay a săwngthăew or túk-túk driver 30B to 60B.

AROUND KHON KAEN

Chonabot

ชนบท

This small town located southeast of the provincial capital of Khon Kaen is famous for *mát-mìi* cotton and silk. *Mát-mìi* is a method of tie-dyeing the fabric threads before weaving and is similar to Indonesian *ikat*. The easiest place to see the fabrics is at **Sala Mai Thai** (Thai Silk Exhibition Hall), on the campus of Khon Kaen Industrial & Community Education College (Withayalai Kan Achip Khon Kaen). This resource centre for the local silk industry contains a well-organised exhibit of silk products. There are a couple of traditional northeastern wooden houses next to the exhibition hall. The campus is 1km west of Chonabot on Rte 229, near the Km 12 marker.

Textiles can be purchased directly from silk-weaving houses along Chonabot's off-highway streets – look for the tell-tale looms beneath the wooden homes. Even if you're not interested in buying, it's worth wandering around to take a look at the amazing variety of simple wooden contraptions devised to spin, tie, weave and dry silk.

Some of the more reputable weaving households include those belonging to Khun Songkhram, Khun Suwan, Khun Thongsuk and Khun Chin. Very little English is spoken in Chonabot so it helps considerably if you bring someone along who can speak Thai.

Getting There & Away Săwngthăew to Chonabot depart from the bus terminal in Khon Kaen hourly between 5.30am and 5.30pm (19B, 45 minutes to an hour); the last one back from Chonabot leaves the market around 3.30pm or 4pm.

Chonabot can also be reached from the south (eg, Khorat) by taking either a bus or train to Ban Phai, which is 167km northeast of Khorat.

Prasat Peuay Noi

ปราสาทเปือยน้อย

Also known as Ku Peuay Noi, and locally known as That Ku Thong, this 12th-century Khmer temple was recently restored at Khon Kaen-government expense. About the size of Buriram's Prasat Meuang Tam, the east-facing monument consists of a large central sandstone sanctuary surmounted by a partially collapsed *prang* and surrounded by laterite walls with two major gates. The site is rich in sculpted lintels; the restored pediments of sandstone are also intricately carved.

Getting There & Away Although Prasat Peuay Noi can be time-consuming to approach if you don't have your own transport, it's a rewarding visit because of the quiet scenery along the way, even if you're not a Khmer temple buff. On your own from Khon Kaen, proceed 44km south on Hwy 2 to Ban Phai, then east on Hwy 23 (signposted to Borabeu) and 11km to Rte 2297. Follow Rte 2297 for 24km southeast through a scenic tableau of rice fields and grazing cattle to the town of Peuay Noi. The ruins are at the western end of town on the southern side of the road; you can't miss their grey eminence on your right as you enter the town.

By public transport from Khon Kaen, take a bus or train to Ban Phai, then a săwngthăew to Peuay Noi. Start early in the morning if you plan to do this in one day;

AROUND KHON KAEN

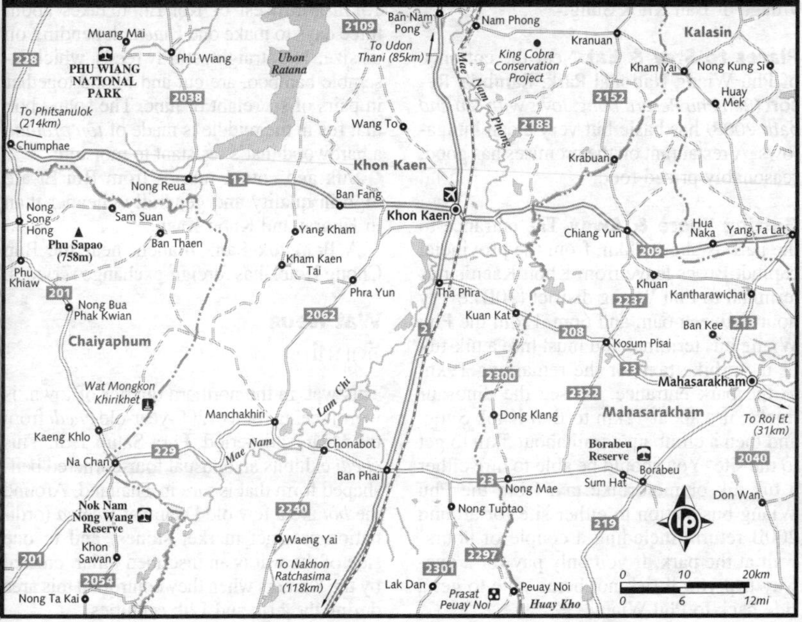

the last săwngthăew back to Ban Phai from Peuay Noi leaves around 3pm. Hitching may be possible. See Getting There & Away in the previous Chonabot section for details on transport to Ban Phai.

King Cobra Conservation Project
โครงการอนุรักษ์งูจงอาง

Northeast of Khon Kaen via Hwy 2 and Rte 2039, this labour of love in the village of Ban Khok Sa-Nga seeks to protect and breed Thailand's endangered king cobra (*nguu jong aang* in Thai). Dozens of king cobras can be seen in their cages here – virtually every household in the village raises a cobra or two. Other snakes, including the python (*nguu lăam*) are also on display. For a donation, the staff will put on a show that includes 'snake parades' and 'snake boxing'. If you arrive at the right time of day you may be able to watch the snakes being fed small rodents.

By bus, leave from Khon Kaen's bus terminal to the turn-off to Khok Sa-Nga (21B, one hour) and then walk or take a motorbike taxi (20B) for the remaining 1.5km to the village. If you're driving from Khon Kaen, just after passing through Nam Phong take the turn-off marked 'Kranuan', near the Km 33 marker. Along the way to Kranuan you should begin seeing English signs for the 'King Cobra Club'.

Phu Wiang National Park
อุทยานแห่งชาติภูเวียง

The discovery of dinosaur fossils while a French team was exploring for uranium lead to some 32,000 hectares of forested land being set aside as a national park *(admission 200B; open 8am-5pm Thur-Tues)* in 1991. Since then, Khon Kaen has celebrated its prehistoric mascots, though only until recently has it been easy to get a look at the digs. The park includes a small but free museum, with life-size models of the species of dinosaurs found in the area labelled in Thai and English. A 'Dinosaur Trail' within the park can be taken to the digs, which are now enclosed and protected from the elements within 'exhibition centres'. There also small dinosaur tracks in solid stone (a total of 68 are said to have been found) in the park, but they are about 17km from the digs, near the village of Ban Khok Sung.

Places to Stay & Eat Near the entrance of Phu Wiang National Park, **Rambo's Resort** *(Ban Phu Resort; bungalows with fan and bath 200B)* has basic but very clean bungalows. A restaurant on the premises has good, reasonably priced food.

Getting There & Away The entrance to the park is about 78km from the provincial capital. Buses leave from Khon Kaen's bus terminal to Phu Wiang district (30B) every hour between 6am and 6pm. From the Phu Wiang bus terminal you must hire a túk-túk or motorbike taxi for the remaining 19km to the park entrance. To see the dinosaur tracks, it's about 12km to Ban Khok Sung, and then a climb up a trail about 5km to get to the site. You should be able to hire either a túk-túk or motorbike taxi from the Phu Wiang bus station to either site for around 200B return, including a couple of hours' wait at the park. If you only pay for a one-way trip you'll risk not being able to get a ride back to Phu Wiang.

NORTHEASTERN THAILAND

ROI ET
อ.เมืองร้อยเอ็ด

postcode 45000 • pop 36,000

Roi Et is the fairly small but growing capital of a province which, three centuries ago, probably served as a buffer between Thai and Lao political conflict. Old Roi Et had 11 city gates and was surrounded by its 11 vassal colonies. The name Roi Et means 'one hundred and one'; this could be an exaggeration of the number 11.

The capital is now on an entirely new site, with the large **Beung Phlan Chai** artificial lake in the centre. An island in the middle, reached by north, west and south causeways, features a fitness park surrounding a tall walking Buddha – demonstrating perhaps that even the Buddha walked for health? A new and imposing city gate has also been erected, of note because it sports the old name of Roi Et (Saket Nakhon) spelled out in Lao script.

Roi Et Province is known for the crafting of the quintessential Isan musical instrument, the *khaen,* a kind of panpipe made of the *mâi kuu* reed and wood. The best *khaen* are reputedly made in the village of **Si Kaew**, 15km northwest of Roi Et. It takes about three days to make one *khaen*, depending on its size. The straight, sturdy reeds, which resemble bamboo, are cut and bound together in pairs of six, eight or nine. The sound box that fits in the middle is made of *tôn pràduu,* a hardwood that's resistant to moisture.

Silk and cotton fabrics from Roi Et are high in quality and generally cheaper than in Khorat and Khon Kaen.

A **Bangkok Bank** branch, near the Ban Chong Hotel, has foreign-exchange services.

Wat Neua
วัดเหนือ

This wát, in the northern quarter of town, is worth seeing for its 1200-year-old *chedi* from the Dvaravati period, Phra Satup Jedi. This *chedi* exhibits an unusual four-cornered bell-shaped form that is rare in Thailand. Around the *bòt* are a few old Dvaravati *sěmaa* (ordination-precinct marker stones) and to one side of the wát is an inscribed pillar, erected by the Khmers when they controlled this area during the 11th and 12th centuries.

Wat Burapha
วัดบูรพา

The tall, standing Buddha that towers above Roi Et's minimal skyline is the Phra Phuttha-ratana-mongkon-mahamuni (Phra Sung Yai for short) at Wat Burapha. Despite being of little artistic significance, it's hard to ignore. From the ground to the tip of the *ùtsànít* (flame-shaped head ornament) it's 67.8m high, including the base. You can climb a staircase through a building that supports the figure to about as high as the Buddha's knees and get a view of the town.

Places to Stay
Ban Chong Hotel *(Banjong; ☎ 0 4351 1235; 99-101 Th Suriyadet Bamrung; rooms 100-200B)* is friendly and has clean rooms with fan and cold-water bath. **Saithip Hotel** *(☎ 0 4351 1985; 133 Th Suriyadet Bamrung; rooms with fan 260-280B, with air-con 340-360B)*, on the same street as Ban Chong, has semi-clean rooms with fan, while air-con rooms have hot water; this one's often full.

Khaen Kham Hotel *(☎ 0 4351 1508; 52-62 Th Rattakit Khlaikhla; rooms with fan 180-220B,*

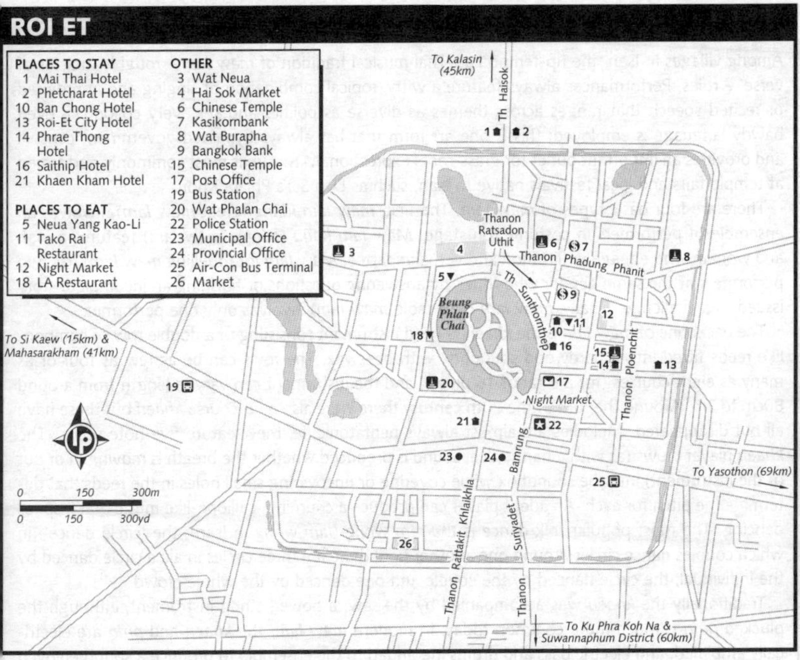

with air-con 320B) has clean but very worn rooms with bath. A coffee shop is attached.

Phrae Thong Hotel *(☎ 0 4351 1127; 45-47 Th Ploenchit; rooms 120-220B)*, next to a Chinese temple, is noisy but has comfortable rooms with fan.

Mai Thai Hotel *(☎ 0 4351 1036–8; 99 Th Haisok; doubles 380B, VIP rooms 580B)* has well-worn rooms with air-con, TV and hot-water bath. 'VIP' rooms have a bath tub. **Phetcharat Hotel** *(☎ 0 4351 1235; rooms 350-450B)*, opposite the Mai Thai, has clean mid-range rooms with air-con and hot water. Ask for a room off the road – they're quieter.

Roi-Et City Hotel *(☎ 0 4352 0387, fax 0 4352 0401; Th Ploenchit; rooms 880-990B, VIP rooms 1200B)*, formerly the Roi-Et Thani and near the Phrae Thong Hotel, has rooms with air-con, bath, IDD phone (with data-ports), TV, fridge and carpet, plus some nicer VIP rooms. Breakfast is included, and there are two **restaurants** on the premises.

Places to Eat

Around the edge of Beung Phlan Chai are several medium-priced garden restaurants. **Neua Yang Kao-Li** *(dishes 40-120B)*, on the northwestern side, has a pleasant atmosphere, a menu in English and good food; the name-sake house speciality is cook-it-yourself Korean beef.

LA Restaurant *(dishes 40-100B)* is another good lakeside place offering an English menu, including soups, sandwiches and English breakfast, as well as Thai dishes.

You'll find a string of cheaper **restaurants** along Th Ratsadon Uthit, which runs east off the lake from the northeastern corner.

Tako Rai Restaurant *(Th Sukkasem; dishes 20-40B)*, around the corner from the Ban Chong Hotel, serves some of the best Isan food in town. The **night market** area is a couple of streets east of the Ban Chong and Saithip Hotels. A decent **night market** also assembles each evening along a street a block south of the post office.

Shopping

If you want to buy local handicrafts, the best place to go is the shopping area along Th Phadung Phanit, where you'll find shops selling *mǎwn khwǎan, phâa mát-mìi* (thick cotton or silk fabric woven from tie-dyed

Măw Lam & the Khaen

Among villages in Isan, the up-tempo Lao-Thai musical tradition of *măw lam* – roughly 'master of verse' – rules. Performances always feature a witty, topical combination of singing and improvised or recited speech that ranges across themes as diverse as politics and sex. Very colloquial, even bawdy language is employed; this is one art form that has always bypassed government censors and provides an important outlet for grass-roots expression. *Măw lam* is most commonly performed at temple fairs and local festivals native to Isan, such as Dan Sai's Phi Ta Khon.

There are four basic types of *măw lam*. The first, *măw lam lŭang* (great *măw lam*), involves an ensemble of performers in costume, on stage. *Măw lam khûu* (couple *măw lam*) features a man and woman who engage in flirtation and verbal repartee. *Măw lam jòt* (duelling *măw lam*) has two performers of the same gender who 'duel' by answering questions or finishing an incomplete story issued as a challenge. Finally, *măw lam dìaw* (solo *măw lam*) involves only one performer.

The backbone of *măw lam* is the *khaen*, a wind instrument consisting of a double row of bamboo-like reeds fitted into a hardwood soundbox with beeswax. The rows can be as few as four or as many as eight courses (for a total of 16 pipes), and the instrument can vary in length from around 80cm to 2m. Around the turn of the 20th century there were also nine-course *khaen* but these have all but disappeared. Melodies are almost always pentatonic; ie, they feature five-note scales. The *khaen* player blows (as with a harmonica, sound is produced whether the breath is moving in or out of the instrument) into the soundbox while covering or uncovering small holes in the reeds that determine the pitch for each. An adept player can produce a churning, calliope-like music that inspires dancing. The most popular folk dance is the *ram wong* (*lam wong* in Isan), the 'circle dance', in which couples dance circles around one another until there are three circles in all: a circle danced by the individual, the circle danced by the couple and one danced by the whole crowd.

Traditionally the *khaen* was accompanied by the *saw*, a bowed string instrument, although the plucked *phin* is much more common today. In modern *măw lam*, the *khaen* and *phin* are electrically amplified, and electric bass and drums are added to the ensemble to produce a sound enjoyed by Isan people young and old.

threads), sticky-rice baskets, traditional musical instruments and Buddhist paraphernalia. **Phaw Kan Kha** *(377-379 Th Phadung Phanit)* has a particularly good selection of fabrics but, as always, you must bargain skilfully to get good prices. **Charin** *(Jarin; 383-385 Th Phadung Phanit)*, a few doors to the east, is also good; the owner speaks some English and he also sells gourmet Thai groceries.

Roi Et's street **fabric vendors** have better prices but less of a selection (and lower quality) than the shops – don't be surprised if your 'silk' purchase turns out to be synthetic.

Weavers themselves buy from **Mae Bang Long** *(371 Th Phadung Phanit)*; here you may see local betel-munchers squatting on the floor checking out dyes, pattern books and pre-knotted skeins.

Getting There & Away

PB Air *(☎ 0 4351 8572, in Bangkok ☎ 0 2261 0222–5)* flies to Roi Et from Bangkok once daily (one way 1720B).

Buses to Roi Et cost 43B from Udon Thani (air-con 101B), 38B from Khon Kaen (air-con 54B) and 61B from Ubon Ratchathani (99B air-con). If you're coming straight from Bangkok's Northern bus terminal, you can catch an air-con bus for 275B to 400B (seven hours, five times in the morning and eight times in the evening between 6pm and 10.45pm).

Ordinary-bus destinations include Surin (40B) and Yasothon (25B).

Getting Around

It costs 20B to take a săamláw around Roi Et. To take a túk-túk, you'll be paying 20B to 30B.

AROUND ROI ET

Ku Phra Koh Na

กู่พระคูนา

Around 60km southeast of Roi Et town, in Suwannaphum district, are the ruins of an 11th-century Khmer shrine. The monument comprises three brick *prang* facing east from a sandstone pediment, surrounded by a sandstone-slab wall with four gates. The middle *prang* was replastered in 1928 and Buddha niches were added. A Buddha footprint shrine, added to the front of this *prang*, is adorned with the Khmer monument's original Baphuon-style *naga* sculptures.

The two other *prang* have been restored but retain their original forms. The northern *prang* has a Narai (Vishnu) lintel over one door and a *Ramayana* relief on the inside gable. Watch out for monkeys looking for something to eat – it's best not to carry any food.

Getting There & Away Suwannaphum can be reached by frequent buses (20B) and săwngthăew (12B) from the provincial capital via Rte 215. From Suwannaphum it's another 6km south via Rte 214 to Ku Phra Koh Na; any Surin-bound bus can stop at Ban Ku, which is at the T-intersection with Rte 2086 east to Phon Sai. The ruins are in a wát compound known locally as Wat Ku.

The ruins can also be approached from Surin, 78km south. From Surin to Ban Ku costs 25B on an ordinary bus and takes about two hours. These buses run more-or-less hourly from about 8am to 5.30pm, and there is plenty of time to go there and back in one day.

Udon Thani Province

UDON THANI

อุดรธานี

postcode 41000 • pop 227,200

Just over 560km from Bangkok, Udon (often spelt Udorn) is one of several northeastern cities that boomed virtually overnight when US air bases were established nearby during the Vietnam War. There are still annual reunions of war veterans who served here, both Thai and American.

Udon is an important transport hub and an agricultural market centre for surrounding provinces. Except as a base for touring nearby Ban Chiang, Ban Pheu or *khít*-weaving villages, the city has little to offer for visitors. For Western expats living in more rural parts of northern Isan (and Vientiane, Laos), Udon is a place to come to shop for things that can't be found anywhere else in the region.

Information

The **TAT office** (*☎ 0 4232 5406, fax 0 4232 5408; 16/5 Th Mukkhamontri; open 8.30am-4.30pm daily*) is near Nong Prajak (there's another entrance off Th Thesa). This office has printed material on Udon, Loei and Nong Khai Provinces. Next to the TAT is the **tourist-police office** (*☎ 0 4224 0616, emergency ☎ 1155*).

Several banks along the main avenues provide foreign-exchange services and ATMs. Only the **Bangkok Bank** (*Th Prajak Silpakorn*) has an after-hours exchange window, usually open until 8pm.

The **main post office** (*Th Wattananuwong; open 8.30am-4.30pm Mon-Fri, 9am-noon Sat, Sun & holidays*) has an upstairs **telephone office** (*open 7am-10pm daily*). Phone calls can also be made at the **telephone office** (*Th Wattanuwong) located east along the same street (also called Wattana)*. There is a Lenso **international card-phone** right outside the TAT office.

The **Aek Udon International Hospital** (*☎ 0 4234 2555; 555/5 Th Pho Si*) is the best medical facility in the upper northeastern region. Most employees are fluent in English, and there are translation services for all major languages. **Wattana Hospital** (*☎ 0 4232 5500; Th Suphakit Janya*), near Nong Prajak, is also a good choice.

Things to See & Do

In the northeastern corner of the Thung Si Meuang (City Field) is the **Lak Meuang** (city Phallus-Pillar), where the city's guardian deity is thought to reside. Encrusted with gold leaf and surrounded by offerings of flowers, candles and incense, the pillar shrine sits next to a smaller shrine containing Phra Phuttha Pho Thong, a Buddha stele of undetermined age. Nearby is the huge and garish Pu Ya Shrine, a recently built Chinese shrine that attests to the wealth of the local Thai-Chinese merchant class. Take photos of it now before the vivid colours start to fade.

To get away from the busy central area, walk around **Nong Prajak**, a reservoir and park in the northwestern part of town. This

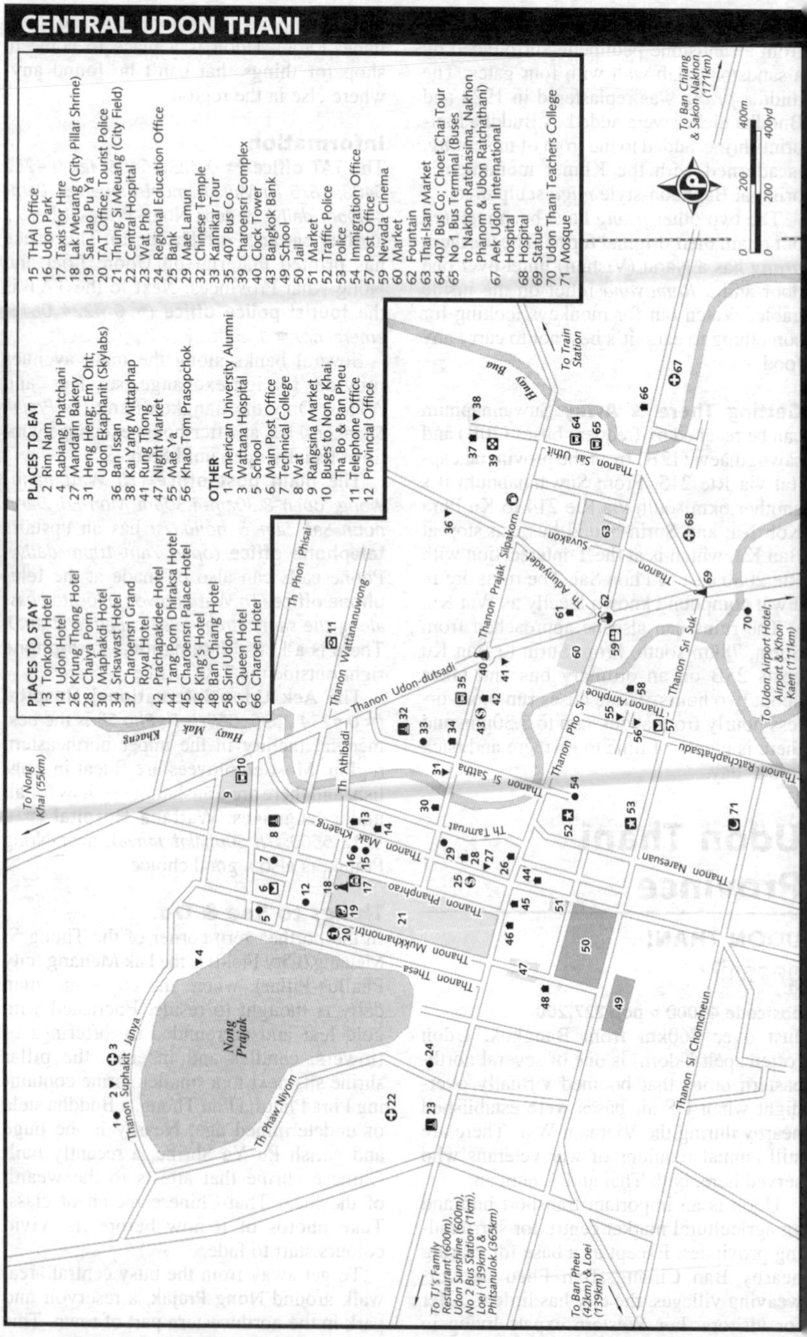
CENTRAL UDON THANI
PLACES TO STAY
13 Tonkoon Hotel
14 Udon Hotel
26 Krung Thong Hotel
28 Chaiya Porn
30 Maphakdi Hotel
34 Srisawast Hotel
37 Charoensri Grand Royal Hotel
42 Prachapakdee Hotel
44 Tang Porn Dhiraksa Hotel
45 Charoensri Palace Hotel
46 King's Hotel
48 Ban Chiang Hotel
58 Siri Udon
61 Queen Hotel
66 Charoen Hotel
PLACES TO EAT
2 Rim Nam
4 Rabiang Phatchani
27 Mandarin Bakery
31 Heng Heng; Em Oht; Udon Ekaphanit (Skylabs)
36 Ban Issan
38 Kai Yang Mittaphap
41 Rung Thong
47 Night Market
55 Mae Ya
56 Khao Tom Prasopchok
OTHER
1 American University Alumni
3 Wattana Hospital
5 School
6 Main Post Office
7 Technical College
8 Wat
9 Rangsina Market
10 Buses to Nong Khai, Tha Bo & Ban Pheu
11 Telephone Office
12 Provincial Office
15 THAI Office
16 Udon Park
17 Taxis for Hire
18 Lak Meuang (City Pillar Shrine)
19 San Jao Pu Ya
20 TAT Office; Tourist Police
21 Thung Si Meuang (City Field)
22 Central Hospital
23 Wat Pho
24 Regional Education Office
25 Bank
29 Mae Lamun
32 Chinese Temple
33 Kannikar Tour
35 407 Bus Co
39 Charoensri Complex
40 Clock Tower
43 Bangkok Bank
49 School
50 Jail
51 Market
52 Traffic Police
53 Police
54 Immigration Office
57 Post Office
59 Nevada Cinema
60 Market
62 Fountain
63 Thai-Isan Market
64 407 Bus Co; Choet Chai Tour
65 No 1 Bus Terminal (Buses to Nakhon Ratchasima, Nakhon Phanom & Ubon Ratchathani)
67 Aek Udon International Hospital
68 Hospital
69 Statue
70 Udon Thani Teachers College
71 Mosque
To Ban Chiang & Sakon Nakhon (171km)
To Train Station
To Udon Airport Hotel, Airport & Khon Kaen (111km)
To Nong Khai (55km)
To TJ's Family Restaurant (600m), Udon Sunshine (600m), No 2 Bus Station (1km), Loei (139km) & Phitsanulok (365km)
To Ban Pheu (42km) & Loei (139km)
Nong Prajak
Huay Mak Khaeng
Huay Bua
Thanon Udon-dutsadi
Thanon Wattananuwong
Th Phon Phisai
Th Athibadi
Thanon Mak Khaeng
Thanon Phanphrao
Thanon Mukkhamontri
Thanon Thesa
Thanon Suphakit Janya
Th Phaw Niyom
Th Tamrui
Thanon Si Sattha
Thanon Prajak Silpakorn
Th Adunyadet
Thanon Suvakon
Thanon Sai Uthit
Thanon Pho Si
Thanon Amphoe
Thanon Sri Suk
Thanon Ratchaphatsadu
Thanon Naresuan
Thanon Si Chomcheun
0 200 400m
0 200 400yd

is a favourite area for locals to go jogging, to picnic, and to meet and socialise.

Udon Sunshine This nursery just northwest of the city in Ban Nong Samrong is famous for producing 100% natural orchid perfumes. Recently it has become even more famous for cultivating a 'dancing plant' bred from several generations of Thai gyrants selected for their inexplicable propensity to sway and jitter when exposed to certain sounds. The mature gyrant (despite the way it has been described in the Thai press, it is not an orchid) has long oval leaves, plus smaller ones of similar shape. If you sing or talk to the plant in a high, gentle voice (saxophone or violin works even better), the smaller leaves will begin making subtle back-and-forth motions, sometimes quick, sometimes slow. This is no hype; we've seen it for ourselves. The experience of talking or singing to the plants is said to produce a calming influence on troubled spirits, and several local psychotherapists bring patients here for sessions.

The nursery (*☎ 0 4224 2475; open daily year-round*) is open to the public. The plants are most active from November to February, the cool season. If you come in the hot or rainy seasons it's best to try to arrive between 7am and 10am or 4.30pm and 7pm; noon is OK if it's cloudy. The owner speaks very good English and is happy to show people around the nursery for a donation of 30B. All proceeds earned from viewing the plant go to an HIV/AIDS project at Udon Hospital. The plants are not for sale, and the owner is careful to remove all flowers from plants on public display so that no-one can pilfer them and grow their own. You can, however, buy 'Miss Udon Sunshine', a rare orchid bred for fragrance (and the first ever to be made into a perfume). Call for further information.

To get here, follow signs to Ban Nong Samrong off Hwy 2024, then after 200m, follow the sign reading 'Udon Sunshine'. A túk-túk from Udon's city centre would cost about 50B each way.

Places to Stay – Budget

Queen Hotel (*☎ 0 4222 1451; 6-8 Th Udondutsadi; rooms with fan 120-160B, with air-con 240B*) located in a busy market area, has 22 simple rooms, all with bath.

Maphakdi Hotel (*☎ 0 4222 1212; Th Prajak Silpakorn; singles/doubles without bath 100/120B*), conveniently located near several cafés and bakeries, is an ancient-looking Thai-Chinese place, built partially of wood, with a basic restaurant downstairs. It's noisy and grubby, but if you speak some Thai or Lao there's always a friendly card game going on in the back of the restaurant.

Tang Porn Dhiraksa Hotel (*☎ 0 4222 1032; Th Mak Khaeng; rooms with/without bath 200/140B*) is nicer than both hotels already mentioned, yet not much more expensive, with large, fairly quiet rooms with fan.

Chaiya Porn (*☎ 0 4222 1913; 209-211 Th Mak Khaeng; rooms with fan 150-200B, with air-con 350B*) is a friendly place, and all rooms have private bath.

Siri Udon (*☎ 0 4222 2330; rooms with fan/air-con 180/380B*), on a lane between Th Pho Si and Th Sri Suk, has 50 clean rooms.

King's Hotel (*☎ 0 4222 1634; Th Pho Si; rooms with fan 100B, with air-con 200B*) is a Vietnam War–era place formerly called the Victory Hotel, and offers cheap but decent rooms off the street, all with hot-water shower. It's at the south end of the City Field.

Travellers preferring something quieter and calmer might consider staying in nearby Ban Chiang (for details see Around Udon Thani Province later in this section).

Places to Stay – Mid-Range

Udon Hotel (*☎ 0 4224 8160, fax 0 4224 2782; 81-89 Th Mak Khaeng; rooms 420-500B*), a move up in quality and price, is enlarged and upgraded, and has comfortable air-con rooms, including breakfast. The cheaper rooms are in a 1960s era building. A favourite with travelling businesspeople because it has a parking lot, this hotel is often full.

Tonkoon Hotel (*☎ 0 4232 6336, fax 0 4232 6349; 50/1 Th Mak Khaeng; singles/doubles 500/600B*), next door to Udon Hotel, is a six-storey place that offers air-con rooms with satellite TV, fridge and phone.

Charoensri Palace Hotel (*☎ 0 4224 2611, fax 0 4224 2612; 60 Th Pho Si; rooms with air-con 400-800B*) has decent air-con rooms with hot water, and rooms with carpet and a fridge.

Charoen Hotel (*☎ 0 4224 8155, fax 0 4224 1093; 549 Th Pho Si; rooms old wing 600B, new wing up to 800B*) has air-con rooms in either the old or new wing. Facilities include a pool, cocktail lounge, restaurant and disco.

Udon Airport Hotel *(☎/fax 0 4234 6223; 14 Mu 1, Th Udon-Nongbualamphu; rooms from 450B)*, formerly the Sleep Inn, is a relatively new, modern, three-storey hotel with 121 rooms and suites, 3km outside of town, near the airport on Rte 210. All rooms feature air-con, fridge, cable TV and IDD phone. Breakfast is included. Other amenities include a restaurant, beer garden, parking and free transport to/from the Udon airport.

Places to Stay – Top End

Charoensri Grand Royal Hotel *(☎ 0 4234 3555, fax 0 4334 3550; singles/doubles 1400/1600B, suites from 2000B)* is at the Charoensri Complex, off the southeastern end of Th Prajak Silpakorn. Luxury rooms and suites are offered over 14 floors. Secure covered parking is available.

Ban Chiang Hotel *(☎ 0 4232 7911, fax 0 4322 3200; Th Mukkhamontri; rooms 900B)* is a 10-storey hotel with deluxe rooms; rates include breakfast. There's a convention centre attached to the hotel.

Places to Eat

There is plenty of good food in Udon, especially Isan fare. **Ban Issan** *(☎ 0 4224 8128; 177-179 Th Adunyadet; dishes 30-40B)* serves tasty *kài yâang* and *sôm-tam,* along with other northeastern specialities. **Kai Yang Mittaphap**, an outdoor place across from the Charoensri Complex, is another good choice for grilled chicken.

Rung Thong *(dishes 30-40B; open until about 5pm)*, on the western side of the clock tower roundabout, sells excellent Thai curries and is also cheap; this is one of the longest-running curry shops in northeastern Thailand.

Mandarin Bakery *(Th Mak Khaeng; dishes 30-40B; open until 11pm)*, adjacent to the Chaiya Porn Hotel, is air-conditioned and roomy, and serves Thai, Chinese and *faràng* food at reasonable prices, in addition to takeaway pastries. Several other small restaurants are scattered along nearly the entire length of Th Mak Khaeng.

Heng Heng *(Th Prajak Silpakorn; dishes 30-40B)*, between Th Mak Khaeng and Th Si Sattha, is a very popular *khâo tôm* (boiled rice soup) place that stays open quite late. **Em Oht**, nearby, is a long-running breakfast coffee shop serving real coffee.

Khao Tom Prasopchok *(Th Ratchaphatsadu; dishes 30-40B)*, near the post office, is an open-air place specialising in *khâo tôm* and Thai curries; it's open until late. **Mae Ya** *(☎ 0 4222 3889; Th Ratchaphatsadu; dishes 30-40B)*, near Khao Tom, is a clean, two-storey air-con restaurant serving a variety of Thai dishes.

Rim Nam and **Rabiang Phatchani** are two decent open-air Thai restaurants on the banks of the Nong Prajak reservoir off Th Suphakit Janya.

There's also a good **night market** *(Th Mukkhamontri) for snacks.*

Almost opposite the turn-off for Udon Sunshine, **TJ's Family Restaurant** *(dishes 60-120B; open 9am-10pm daily)* is the best place in town for *faràng* food. Reminiscent of Khorat's VFW Cafeteria (but a lot cleaner), the small eatery offers hamburgers, sandwiches, American-style chilli, steaks, Southern fried chicken and huge breakfasts with grits and homefries. TJ's annually plays host to groups of visiting American veterans who were stationed at Udon during the Vietnam War.

The **Charoensri Complex** at the southeastern end of Th Prajak Silpakorn contains the usual international fast-food chains and a huge **supermarket**.

Entertainment

Udon Park *(☎ 0 4232 4755; 36 Th Mak Khaeng)*, just across from the Tonkoon Hotel, has a restaurant, lush beer garden and stage where traditional Isan song and dance are performed nightly. Prices for meals are moderate (80B to 160B).

Shopping

Udon's main shopping district is centred on Th Pho Si, between the fountain circle and Th Mak Khaeng.

Mae Lamun *(Th Prajak Silpakorn)* is a good local craft shop just east of Th Mak Khaeng; it's on the 2nd floor of a shop selling Buddhist paraphernalia. Mae Lamun has a selection of quality silks and cottons, silver, jewellery, Buddha images and ready-made clothes tailored from local fabrics. Prices start high but are negotiable. Another good craft shop – especially for pillows – is **Thi Non Michai** *(208 Th Pho Si)*.

The relatively new **Charoensri Complex**, off Th Prajak Silpakorn, is the largest shopping centre in Isan, with 22,000 sq metre of retail space filled with standard Thai department stores, a huge supermarket, a flock of designer clothing boutiques, several restaurants and coffee shops (see Places to Eat earlier), and the attached Charoensri Grand Royal Hotel (see Places to Stay).

If you're in the market for a large túk-túk – a motorised three-wheel taxi known across the river in Vientiane as a 'jumbo', and called *rót sàkailáep* ('Skylab', named for the space capsule of many years ago) throughout Isan – Udon Thani is its manufacturing capital in Thailand. You can buy a new Skylab at **Udon Ekaphanit** *(117/2-4 Th Prajak Silpakorn)*, next door to Em Oht coffee shop. They come in several models depending on the engine, from one powered by a Honda 90cc to a 125cc job. Ekaphanit's motto is 'In Lampang, ride a horse cart – in Udon, ride a Skylab'.

Getting There & Away

Air THAI flies to Udon from Bangkok four times daily (1785B, one hour). There is a **THAI office** *(☎ 0 4224 6697, 0 4224 3222; 60 Th Mak Khaeng)*.

Bus There are buses leaving Bangkok's Northern bus terminal for Udon throughout the day (air-con 269B, 24-seat VIP 450B; 10 to 11 hours; 5am to 11pm).

Buses leave the main bus terminal in Khorat every half-hour during the day and arrive in Udon five hours later. The cost is 98B (air-con 206B).

The No 2 bus terminal is on the northwestern outskirts of the city next to the highway, and has buses to Loei (ordinary/air-con 59/101B), Nakhon Phanom (ordinary/air-con 128/211B), Si Chiangmai (ordinary 28B), Nong Khai (ordinary 26B) and Bangkok (air-con 269B to 339B).

The No 1 bus terminal is off Th Sai Uthit near the Charoen Hotel in the southeastern end of town. Buses from here go mostly to points south and east of Udon, including Khorat, Sakon Nakhon, Nakhon Phanom, Ubon Ratchathani, Khon Kaen, Roi Et and Bangkok, and also to Beung Kan.

There are also private air-con buses to Bangkok. The company with the best local reputation is **407 Bus Co** *(☎ 0 4222 1121; 125/3 Th Prajak Silpakorn)*. It has many daily departures to Bangkok (32-seat VIP 308B) and Khon Kaen (air-con 79B). Nearby **Choet Chai Tour** *(no Roman-script sign; ☎ 0 4224 3243; Th Prajak Silpakorn)* has VIP buses to Bangkok departing around 8pm.

Train The 8.45pm *Nong Khai Express* (No 69) from Bangkok arrives in Udon at 7.24am the next day. Rapid trains leave Bangkok on the Nong Khai line at 6am and 6.30pm, arriving in Udon at 4.35pm and 6.02am. Two special diesel railcars (Nos 75 and 77) depart from Bangkok at 8.20am and 8pm, reaching Udon at 5.20pm and 4.56am. The 1st-class fare is 457B, 2nd class is 219B and 3rd class is 95B, plus applicable charges for sleeper and express service.

In the reverse direction, the No 70 express leaves Udon at 8.02pm, while rapid trains (Nos 134 and 138) depart at 7.04pm and 9.15am, and special diesel railcars (Nos 76 and 78) leave at 7.26am and 6.35pm.

To reach Khorat from Udon, the only available trains are the No 78 special diesel rail car that leaves at 6.35pm and arrives in Khorat at 10.53pm, and the local trains (Nos 416 and 418) that leave Udon at 5.54am and 1.34pm, and arrive at Khorat six hours later.

Getting Around

You can get anywhere around town by túk-túk for between 20B and 40B. Săamláw rates should be about the same.

Three car-rental places opposite the Udon Hotel offer sedans, jeeps and vans for hire from around 1200B. Should you want to hire a car with driver, a cheaper alternative is to negotiate for one of the old four-door Nissan and Toyota taxis waiting at the bus stop on Th Phanphrao at the northeastern corner of Thung Si Meuang. Figure on no more than 1000B per day for one of these, including the services of a driver, who will be happy to go anywhere in the province, and as far out of the province as Nong Khai or Khon Kaen.

AROUND UDON THANI PROVINCE

Ban Chiang

บ้านเชียง

Ban Chiang is 50km east of Udon Thani. As well as the original excavation pit of an ancient Ban Chiang burial ground at **Wat Pho Si Nai** *(admission 30B)* at the village edge, there is a relatively new **national museum** *(admission 30B; open 9am-4.30pm daily)* with extensive Ban Chiang exhibits. The excavation pit displays 52 human skeletons, in whole or in part, along with lots of pottery. This is worth a trip if you're at all interested in the historic Ban Chiang culture, which goes back at least 4000 years. The well-conceived museum exhibits pottery from all Ban Chiang periods, plus myriad bronze objects recovered from the Pho Sin Nai excavation, including spearheads, sickles, axeheads, fish hooks, chisels, arrowheads, bells, rings and bangles.

The Ban Chiang culture, an agricultural society that once thrived in northeastern Thailand, is known for its early bronze metallurgy and clay pottery, especially pots and vases with distinctive burnt-ochre swirl designs, most of which were associated with burial sites. Seven layers of civilisation have been excavated; the famous swirl-design pottery comes from the third and fourth layers. The area was declared a Unesco World Heritage site in 1992.

The locals attempt to sell Ban Chiang artefacts, real and fake, but neither type is allowed out of the country, so don't buy them. Some of the local handicrafts, such as thick hand-woven cotton fabric, are good buys; over 50 local families are involved in the spinning and weaving of such textiles, along with ceramics and basket-weaving. The other main local livelihoods are rice cultivation, fishing and hunting.

Places to Stay & Eat A five-minute walk from the museum, **Lakeside Sunrise Guest House** *(☎ 0 4220 8167; singles/doubles 120/160B)* is nicely landscaped with upstairs rooms and one larger room. Clean, shared facilities are downstairs, while the upper floor boasts a spacious wooden veranda overlooking the lake.

Across from the national museum entrance are a couple of restaurants. One such eatery, **Nakhon Sawan**, specialises in rice noodles that have been made with Thai pumpkin to produce bright-yellow noodles *(mìi lěuang)*; they're delicious when prepared *râat-nâa* style (with sauce poured over the top).

AROUND NONG KHAI & UDON THANI

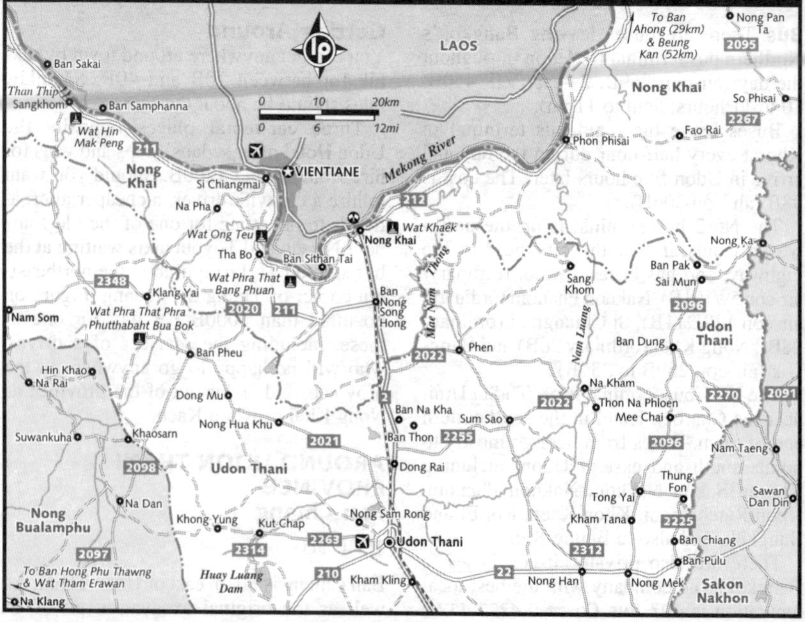

Getting There & Away Săwngthăew run regularly from Udon Thani to Ban Chiang from late morning until around 3.45pm (25B). In the reverse direction they're frequent from around 6.30am until 10.30am. Catch them from in front of the museum.

Alternatively, take a bus bound for Sakon Nakhon or Nakhon Pathom and get off at the Ban Pulu turn-off, a 10-minute săamláw ride from Ban Chiang. Buses leave in either direction several times a day, but the last leaves Ban Chiang in the late afternoon.

Ban Pheu
บ้านผือ

Ban Pheu district, 42km northwest of Udon Thani, has a peculiar mix of prehistoric cave paintings, bizarre geological formations and Buddhist shrines, the bulk of which are at **Phra Phutthabaht Bua Bok Park** *(admission 30B)*, 12km outside Ban Pheu on Khao Phra Baht hill.

The formations are a collection of balanced rocks, spires and whale-sized boulders, with several shrines and three wát built in and around them. A well-marked trail meandering through the park takes around two hours to negotiate at a normal walking pace. Some of the trees are labelled with their Latin names, and a climb beyond the rock formations, to the edge of the escarpment, affords a fine view of the mountains of Laos to the north.

At the entrance to the area is the largest temple in the historical park, **Wat Phra That Phra Phutthabaht Bua Bok**, with its namesake Lao-style *chedi*. Prehistoric paintings in several grottos feature wild animals, humans and cryptic symbols. To the southeast of the main wát are the caves of **Tham Lai Meu** and **Tham Non Sao Eh**, and to the west are **Tham Khon** and **Tham Wua Daeng**. These are really more like grottos or rocky overhangs than caves. There are also some small but sophisticated rock carvings of Buddha images dating back to when the Mon and later Khmer ruled this area. For Isan residents, this is an important place of pilgrimage. For visitors, the side-by-side progression from rock art to Buddhist stupa represents a localised evolution of thought and aesthetics.

Most of the bizarre rock formations to be found here are featured in an enchanting local legend about a king, his stunningly beautiful daughter, a hermit, and a lovestruck prince from another kingdom. The most striking rock formation, a mushroom shaped outcropping with a shrine built into it, is said to be the tower where the beautiful princess was forced to live by her overprotective father. Many of these rock formations are signposted with names in Thai and English alluding to the legend, but, unless you're familiar with it, they'll make little sense to you. If you're staying at the Mutmee Guest House in Nong Khai, you might try getting Julian, the owner, to tell you the story before you go.

Getting There & Away The park has three new **bungalows** *(☎ 0 4291 0107; 300B per person)* if you want to spend some time here, but they're really more geared for visiting groups of Thai students. Otherwise, Phra Phutthabaht can be visited as a long day trip from either Udon or Nong Khai. From Udon it's an 18B săwngthăew ride to Ban Pheu; it's 26B from Nong Khai. From Ban Pheu, take a săwngthăew for 12B to Phra Phutthabaht. You could also charter a motorbike in the Ban Pheu market to take you all the way to Phra Phutthabaht. If you're using public transport you should plan on leaving the park by 2.30pm.

Easiest of all is to visit the park by rented motorbike from Nong Khai.

Weaving Villages

Two villages renowned for *khít*-pattern fabrics are **Ban Na Kha** and **Ban Thon**, around 16km north of Udon via Hwy 2 on the way to Nong Khai. *Khít* is a geometric, diamond-grid minimal weft brocade commonly used for the centre square of *măwn khwăan* fabrics or other decorative items. Ban Na Kha is just east of Hwy 2, while Ban Thon is 2km further east along a laterite road. Shops in Ban Na Kha that are used to dealing with foreigners include **Songsi Isan Handicraft** *(184/1 Mu 1)* and **Chanruan Nakha** *(92 Mu 1)*.

Ban Nong Aw Tai, in the district of Nong Wua Saw, about 40km southwest of Udon via Rte 210, produces high-quality silk. In this same district is **Wat Tham Kok Du**, a famous meditation wát presided over by abbot Phra Ajahn Kham Fong, whose simple, direct style of teaching has attracted a large number of lay students. Nong Wua Saw is actually part of Nong Bualamphu Province.

Tham Erawan

ถ้ำเอราวัณ

If you happen to be travelling along Rte 210 between Loei Province and Udon, you can stop off and visit Tham Erawan, a large cave shrine high up on the side of a limestone mountain. A huge seated Buddha in the cave can be seen gazing out over the plains from several kilometres away.

The cave is at the back of **Wat Tham Erawan**, which is 2km north of a turn-off between the Km 31 and Km 32 markers on Rte 210. It's near the village of Ban Hong Phu Thawng, west of the town of Na Klang. There is a smaller cave wát near this turn-off – keep going north until you can see the larger, higher cave in the distance.

Nong Khai Province

Nong Khai Province is a narrow 300km strip along the Mekong River. At its widest point the province measures only 50km across. Even if you don't cross into Laos, Nong Khai is a fascinating province to explore, with long, open views of the Mekong River and Laos on the other side. The capital boasts one of Asia's most intriguing sculpture gardens, located on the outskirts of the city.

NONG KHAI

หนองคาย

postcode 43000 • pop 61,500

More than 620km from Bangkok and 55km from Udon Thani, Nong Khai is where Hwy 2 (also known as Mittaphap Hwy, Friendship Hwy and Asia 12) ends, at the Thai-Lao Friendship Bridge over the Mekong River. Across the river is the Lao People's Democratic Republic.

Nong Khai was once part of the Vientiane (Wiang Chan) kingdom, which for much of its history vacillated between independence and tribute to either Lan Xang (AD 1353–1694) or Siam (late 18th century until 1893). In 1827 Rama III gave a Thai lord, Thao Suwothamma, the rights to establish Meuang Nong Khai at the present city site. In 1891, under Rama V, Nong Khai became the capital of *monthon* Lao Phuan, an early Isan satellite state that included what are now Udon, Loei, Khon Kaen, Sakon Nakhon, Nakhon Phanom and Nong Khai Provinces, as well as Vientiane.

The area came under several attacks by Jiin Haw (Yunnanese) marauders in the late 19th century. The 1886-vintage **Prap Haw Monument** (*pràap haw* means 'defeat of the Haw') in front of the former Provincial Office (now used as a community college) commemorates Thai-Lao victories over Haw invasions in 1874, 1885 and 1886.

When western Laos was partitioned off from Thailand by the French in 1893, the *monthon* capital was moved to Udon, leaving Nong Khai to fade into a provincial backwater.

The opening of the Thai-Lao Friendship Bridge on 8 April 1994 marked the beginning of a new era of development for Nong Khai as a regional trade and transport centre. New multistorey hotels and office buildings were built along the outskirts of town near the relatively new Hwy 2 (Mittaphap Hwy) bypass that leads to the Thai-Lao Friendship Bridge.

Today's Nong Khai has a handful of old buildings of French-Chinese architecture along Th Meechai, east of Th Haw and parallel to the river. There are also a few remaining examples of the old, wooden Thai-Chinese shophouses in the city centre. The Governor's Mansion, near the Mutmee Guest House, is a fine example of early-20th-century Thai architecture constructed at a time when the country was under pressure to appear 'modern' to colonising European powers. Unfortunately, local developers have razed some of the historic buildings in Nong Khai and replaced them with the uninteresting tinted-glass architecture common all over urban Asia. Few visitors linger in Nong Khai these days – most are on their way to or from Vientiane via the Thai-Lao Friendship Bridge – but Nong Khai is still a pleasant leafy town and certainly worth a couple of days if you have time to spare.

Like many other cities in the northeast, Nong Khai has a large **Rocket Festival** *(ngaan bun bâng fai)* during the full moon of May, and a **Candle Festival** *(ngaan hàe* *thian)* at the beginning of *phansăa,* or the Buddhist Rains Retreat, in late July. The city also holds a **Nong Khai Festival** in March. During the full moon of October the chance to catch a glimpse of **naga fireballs** *(bâng fai phayaa nâak)*, mysterious floating lights sometimes seen over this stretch of the Mekong, draws thousands of curious from as far away as Bangkok (see the boxed text 'Great Balls of Fire' later in this section).

Information

Tourist Offices A small **TAT office** *(☎ 0 4246 7844)* is tucked away in a row of shophouses next to the Thai-Lao Friendship Bridge checkpoint. The staff distribute information on Nong Khai and surrounding provinces, as well as some information on Vientiane.

Visas for Laos Nong Khai is one of five crossings open to foreigners along the Thai-Lao border (the other four are Chiang Khong, Nakhon Phanom, Mukdahan and Chong Mek) and citizens of the two countries are allowed to cross at will for day trips.

The Lao government issues 15-day Tourist Visas on arrival at the Friendship Bridge, which spans the Mekong River near Nong Khai. To receive this visa on arrival you must present the following: US$30 cash or the baht equivalent (travellers cheques and *kip* are not accepted, and it's a good idea to bring the exact amount of cash – change is not always available); a passport photo; and the name of a hotel you will be staying at in Vientiane.

If you want to save money or you'd like to stay in Laos longer than 15 days, you can obtain your visa ahead of time at the Lao embassy in Bangkok, which can usually issue a 30-day visa on the same day of application. See the Khon Kaen section earlier for information on obtaining visas at the Lao consulate there.

Lonely Planet's *Laos* guidebook contains extensive visa and travel information.

Immigration Offices Should you need to extend your visa, the **Nong Khai immigration office** is on the highway bypass that leads to the Friendship Bridge, south of the bridge shuttle-bus stop.

Money Several banks along Th Meechai offer ATMs and foreign-exchange services.

Post & Communications There is a **main post office** *(Th Meechai; open 8.30am-4.30pm Mon-Fri, 9am-noon Sat, Sun & holidays)*. Long-distance phone calls can no longer be placed there, but a new **CAT office** has opened 5km from the intersection of Rte 212 and Hwy 2, on the eastern side of the road to Udon Thani (Hwy 2); signs at the post office give directions.

Thai-Lao Friendship Bridge
สะพานมิตรภาพไทยลาว

The US$30 million, Australian-financed Saphan Mittaphap Thai-Lao (Thai-Lao Friendship Bridge) spans the Mekong River from Ban Jommani (3km west of Nong Khai) to Tha Na Laeng (19km southeast of Vientiane) on the Lao side. An 8.2km highway bypass was added to link the bridge with Hwy 2/Asia 12 just south of Nong Khai.

The 1174m-long bridge opened in April 1994 amid much hoopla about how it would improve transport and communications between Thailand and Laos. It was the second bridge to be erected anywhere along the Mekong's entire length (the first was in the People's Republic of China).

In spite of its two 3.5m-wide traffic lanes, two 1.5m-wide footpaths and space for a railway down the centre, the bridge has done little to fulfil its design potential. City planners have been saying for years that eventually a train link will extend from the Nong Khai railhead across the 12.7m-wide bridge and on to Vientiane. So far the rails go from the new Nong Khai train station all the way to the centre of the bridge where they abruptly stop. Apparently the Lao are waiting for some donor country with deep pockets to come and finish the job.

For bridge transport information, see Laos under Getting There & Away later in this section.

Wat Pho Chai
วัดโพธิชัย

Wat Pho Chai *(Phra Sai; main hall open 7am-5pm daily)*, off Th Prajak in the southeastern part of town, is renowned for its large Lan Xang–era sitting Buddha. The head of the image is pure gold, the body is bronze and the *ùtsànít* (flame-shaped head ornament) is set with rubies. The altar on which

NORTHEASTERN THAILAND

the image sits features elaborately executed gilded wooden carvings and mosaics, while the ceiling bears wooden rosettes in the late Ayuthaya style.

Murals in the *bòt* depict the image's travels from the interior of Laos to the banks of the Mekong, where it was put on a raft. A storm capsized the raft and the image sat at the bottom of the river from 1550 to 1575, when it was salvaged and placed in a temple now called Wat Pradit Thammakhun on the Thai side of the river. The highly revered image was moved to Wat Pho Chai during the reign of King Mongkut (1852–68).

During the annual Songkran Festival (April), the Phra Sai image is taken out in procession around town.

Phra That Nong Khai

พระธาตุหนองคาย

Also known as **Phra That Klang Nam** (Holy Reliquary in the Middle of the River), this Lao *chedi* is submerged in the Mekong River and can only be seen in the dry season when the Mekong lowers about 30m. The *chedi* slipped into the river in 1847 and continues to slide – it's near the middle now. For the best view of the *chedi*, walk east along Th Meechai past the marine police post, then past three wát on the right, then turn left on Soi Paphraw (Paa Phrao) 3. Follow this lane until it ends at the new riverside promenade and look for the *chedi* in the river. Once the top of the *chedi* has cleared the water during the dry season, coloured flags are fastened to the top to make it easier to spot.

You can get a closer look at the *chedi* by taking the nightly sunset cruise from Tha Wat Hai Sok – see the Sunset Cruise entry later in this section for details.

Wat Noen Phra Nao

วัดเนินพระเนาว์

This forest wát at the southeastern edge of town boasts a *vipassana* (insight meditation) centre on nice, tree-shaded grounds. Many Westerners meditated here in the 1960s and 1970s. Some extremely ornate temple architecture, including perhaps the most rococo bell tower we've ever seen, stands in contrast with the usual ascetic tone

CENTRAL NONG KHAI

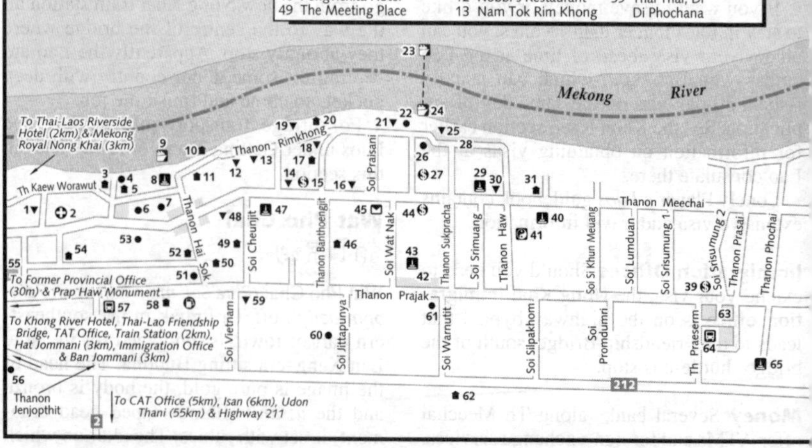

of such forest monasteries. There's a Chinese cemetery on the grounds.

Sala Kaew Ku

ศาลาแก้วกู่

Also called Wat Khaek *(Indian Temple; admission 20B; grounds open 7.30am-5.30pm daily)* by locals, this strange Hindu-Buddhist shrine, established in 1976, is a tribute to the wild imagination of Luang Pu Bunleua Surirat. Luang Pu (Venerable Grandfather) was a Brahmanic yogi-priest-shaman who made a concoction of Hindu and Buddhist philosophy, mythology and iconography into a cryptic whole. He developed a large following in northeastern Thailand and Laos, where he lived for many years before fleeing to Nong Khai after the communists took over Laos in 1975. In fact, there is a cruder version of this sculpture garden just across the river in Laos. If you have the chance to visit both places, it's interesting to compare the work. Luang Pu died in 1996.

The temple has many bizarre cement statues of Shiva, Vishnu, Buddha, and every other Hindu and Buddhist deity imaginable, as well as numerous secular figures, all supposedly cast by unskilled artists under Luang Pu's direction. Some of the sculptures are quite amusing – if you're travelling with kids they'll enjoy the serene and stately elephant wading though a pack of anthropomorphic dogs. The tallest sculpture, a Buddha seated on a coiled *naga* with a spectacular multiheaded hood, is 25m high. Also of interest is a circular-shaped compound filled with sculptures designed to teach laypersons of the Hindu-Buddhist cycles of birth, life and death. Note that the sculptures have become miniature shrines – bits of sacred thread have been tied around the wrists of many images.

The main shrine building is full of framed pictures of Hindu and Buddhist deities, temple donors, and Luang Pu at various ages, plus smaller bronze and wooden figures of every description and provenance, guaranteed to throw an art historian into a state of disorientation. Luang Pu's corpse lies in state under a glass dome in the upper room. Although the room is not open to the public and Luang's Pu's corpse is not on display, we were told that his hair is miraculously still growing.

CENTRAL NONG KHAI

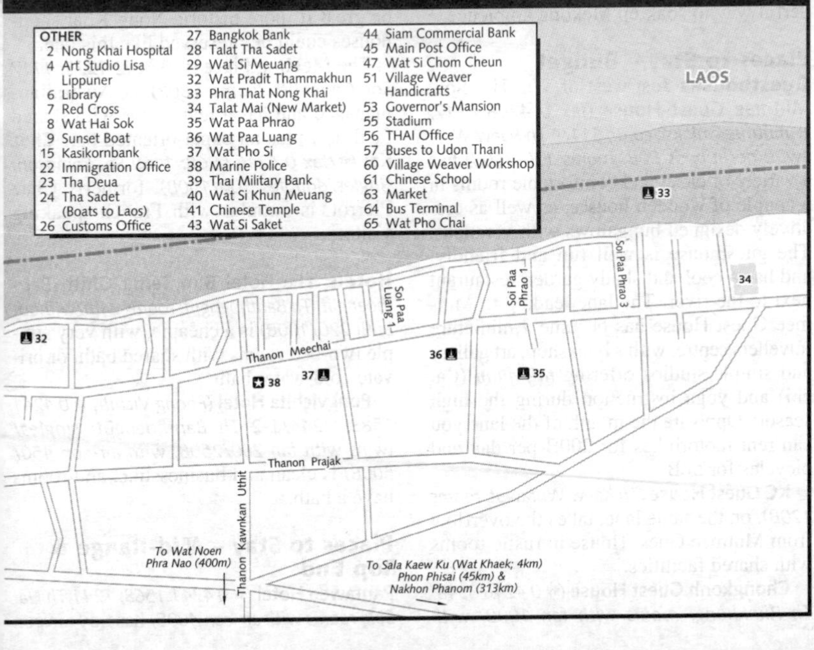

Getting There & Away To get to Sala Kaew Ku, board a sǎwngthǎew heading southeast towards Beung Kan and ask to get off at Wat Khaek, which is 4km to 5km outside the town, near St Paul Nong Khai School. The fare should be about 15B. A chartered túk-túk costs 50B.

Sala Kaew Ku is an easy 3km bike ride from town.

Hat Jommani
หาดจอมมณี

This sand 'beach' along the Mekong River only appears during the dry season. Next to the Thai-Lao Friendship Bridge in Ban Jommani, 3km west of Nong Khai, Hat Jommani is a favourite picnic destination for local Thais.

During the dry season a rustic thatched shelter with straw mats becomes a restaurant serving delicious *kài yâang, plaa pîng* (grilled fish), *sôm-tam* and cold beer.

Sunset Cruise

Sunset boat rides are available daily at around 5pm aboard a floating restaurant behind Wat Hai Sok. It's only 30B (plus the cost of whatever you order) and it's a wonderful way to soak up Mekong ambience.

Places to Stay – Budget

Guesthouses Just west of Wat Hai Sok, **Mutmee Guest House** *(fax 0 4246 0717; e mutmee@nk.ksc.co.th; 111/4 Th Kaew Worawut; dorm beds 80B, rooms 110-360B)* has a variety of clean and comfortable rooms in a couple of wooden houses, as well as creatively designed bungalows with verandas. The guesthouse is well run and friendly, and has a cool and shady garden restaurant next to the river. The lane leading to Mutmee Guest House has become a miniature travellers centre, with a bookshop, art gallery and simple studios offering *taijiquan* (t'ai chi) and yoga instruction during the high season. Opposite the mouth of the lane you can rent motorbikes for 200B per day and bicycles for 50B.

KC Guest House *(Th Kaew Worawut; rooms 120B)*, on the same lane, takes the overflow from Mutmee Guest House in rustic rooms with shared facilities.

Chongkonh Guest House *(☎ 0 4246 0548; Th Rimkhong; rooms with fan 100B, with air-con 300B)* is housed in an older two-storey wooden building on the river. Rooms have shared bath.

Maekhong Guest House *(☎ 0 4246 0689; Th Rimkhong; rooms per person 120B, larger singles/doubles 150/250B, rooms with air-con 500B)*, further east along Th Rimkhong, has basic but clean rooms overlooking the river, plus a couple of larger rooms. Hot showers are available. In a Thai-style wooden bungalow on an upstairs deck overlooking the river are large rooms with air-con and private hot-water shower. There's an Internet café next door.

Rimkhong Guest House *(☎ 0 4246 0625, fax 0 4242 0967; Th Rimkhong; singles/doubles 100/150B)*, between the Maekong and Mutmee guesthouses, on a quiet spot near the river, has 12 decent rooms in three wooden houses with shared bath.

Sawasdee Guest House *(☎ 0 4241 2502, fax 4242 0259; 402 Th Meechai; rooms with fan 100/140B, with air-con 300B, with TV & fridge 380B)* is in one of Nong Khai's old shophouses, restored and refurbished to provide small but very clean rooms with fan and shared bath, or air-con and hot-water shower. A large room at the front of the building is pleasant for sitting – it would be great if more historic Nong Khai shophouses could be preserved like this one.

The Meeting Place *(☎ 0 4242 1223; 1117 Soi Chuenjit; rooms 180B)* is Australian-managed and has a few rooms with shared facilities, plus an expat-oriented bar. **Chez Kai** *(☎/fax 0 4246 0968; 1160 Soi Samoson; singles/doubles 100/150B)*, formerly Chez Pierrot, is popular with French-speaking visitors.

Hotels The **Hotel Bun Terng Ghitt** *(Banthoengjit; Th Banthoengjit; rooms with/without bath 220/100B)* is a cheapie, with very simple two-bed rooms with shared bath, or private cold-water bath.

Pongvichita Hotel *(Phong Vichitr; ☎ 0 4241 1583; 1244/1-2 Th Banthoengjit; singles/twins with fan 200/250B, with air-con 450/500B)* is clean and businesslike, and rooms have a bath.

Places to Stay – Mid-Range & Top End

Pantawee Hotel *(☎ 0 4241 1568; 1241 Th Hai Sok; rooms with air-con 400B)* has tidy air-con rooms with hot water. There's a decent coffee shop downstairs. **Pantawee Bungalows**, across the street and under the same management, charges the same rates. It's a bit on the noisy side.

Nong Khai Grand Hotel *(☎ 0 4242 0033, fax 0 4241 2026; singles/doubles 1000/1300B, suites 2500B)* is a nine-storey hotel on Rte 212, a bit south of the town centre. Modern rooms come with all the amenities, and discounts are readily available. On the premises are a restaurant, coffee shop, swimming pool, conference room and disco.

Mekong Royal Nong Khai *(☎ 0 4242 0024, fax 0 4242 1280; rooms from 900B)*, a nine-storey, 208-room hotel, was built in hopes of reaping a profit from the bridge opening and sits on the highway bypass near Ban Jommani, east of the town centre. Plush rooms include breakfast. Hotel facilities include a restaurant, coffee shop, cocktail lounge, pool, miniature golf, a jogging track and conference rooms. It also provides access (and one room) for the mobility impaired.

Thai-Laos Riverside Hotel *(☎ 0 4246 0263, fax 0 4246 0317; 051 Th Kaew Worawut; rooms 500B, with breakfast 700B)*, in the same general vicinity as Mekong Royal, is a new seven-storey hotel, with 72 rooms featuring air-con, IDD phone, satellite TV and fridge. Some upper-storey rooms have a river view. Facilities include a restaurant, karaoke, Thai massage and parking.

Places to Eat

Out of all the guesthouses in town, the **Mutmee** *(Th Kaew Worawut; dishes 40-80B)* has the best food, including many vegetarian dishes. Its riverside location also has the best atmosphere.

This Puerto Rican–managed place, **José Ramon's Restaurant & Cantina** *(1128/11 Th Takai; dishes 40-60B)* is near the Mutmee Guest House, just west of the Nong Khai Hospital. It specialises in Latin American and Mexican food, as well as steaks, burgers and fries.

Dukada Bakery *(Th Meechai; dishes 30-40B)* has Western breakfasts and Thai food, although the once-plentiful pastry selection has become a bit thin. **Danish Baker** *(Th Meechai)*, next to the **Kasikornbank**, serves good coffee. It's open for breakfast, lunch and dinner.

Darika *(no Roman-script sign; Th Meechai; breakfasts 20-30B)* serves cheap egg-and-toast breakfasts, real Thai coffee, banana pancakes and Lao-style baguette sandwiches, plus *khànǒm jìip* (Chinese dumplings), *jók* and *kǔaytǐaw* (rice soup).

Daeng Naem Neuang *(no Roman-script sign; Th Banthoengjit; dishes 30-40B)* has very good Vietnamese food; the house speciality is the namesake *nǎem neuang* – spicy pork sausage served with lettuce leaves, sliced starfruit and various condiments.

Udom Rot Restaurant, *(no Roman-script sign; Th Rimkhong; dishes 30-40B)*, overlooking the Mekong and Tha Sadet (the ferry pier for boats to/from Laos), has good food and atmosphere. **Tha Dan Restaurant** *(Customs Pier)* is a more expensive restaurant on the other side of the pier to Udom Rot, which also has a souvenir shop at the front. **Nong Naen Pla Phao** is on your left if you wander east along Th Rimkhong into the covered part of Talat Tha Sadet. This rustic but clean Lao-style restaurant offers delicious salt-baked *plaa châwn* stuffed with herbs, plus *kài yâang, kaeng lao* (Lao-style bamboo-shoot soup), grilled sausage and grilled prawns (shrimp). The eating area overlooks the river.

Rabieng Mekhong *(Th Rimkhong; dishes 40-100B)*, next to the Maekhong Guest House, is another riverside choice. **Nam Tok Rim Khong** *(Th Rimkhong; dishes 30-40B)*, on the opposite side of the street, is a restaurant specialising in Isan dishes, including *néua náam tòk* (literally, waterfall beef) – a spicy, tart salad of barbecued beef served with sticky rice.

Nobbi's Restaurant *(Th Rimkhong; dishes 50-120B)* caters to the older expat crowd in the city with European favourites, such as home-made German sausage, goulash, bratwurst, steaks, sandwiches, salads, pizza and spaghetti.

Night vendors set up each evening on Th Prajak, along the south side of Wat Si Saket.

Further east, there's a **vegetarian restaurant** (a Roman-script sign reads 'Vegetarian Food') right next to Wat Si Meuang on Th Meechai.

Shopping

A shop called **Village Weaver Handicrafts** *(☎ 0 4242 2651; W www.thaivillageweaver.com; 1020 Th Prajak)* sells high-quality, moderately priced hand-woven fabrics and ready-made clothes. The shop was established by the Good Shepherd Sisters as part of a project to encourage local girls to stay in the villages and earn money by weaving, rather than leaving home to seek work in urban centres. The hand-dyed *mát-mìi* cotton is particularly good here. The **workshop** (☎ *0 4241 1236; 1151 Soi Jittapanya)* and looms where some of the fabric is produced are located off Th Prajak, and visitors are welcome to observe the methods of weaving. The Thai name for the project is Hatthakam Sing Thaw.

The Good Shepherd Sisters have also recently established the **Isan Weaving** and **Isan Pottery** training centres to further provide alternative vocational skills and employment to local people. A new shop called **Isan**, 6km outside Nong Khai on the road to Udon Thani, carries the items produced at these centres.

Art Studio Lisa Lippuner (☎ *0 4246 1110;* e *mira@nk.ksc.co.th)*, on the same lane as Mutmee Guest House, houses a gallery exhibiting the naturalistic paintings of a longtime Swiss resident.

Getting There & Away

Air The nearest airport is approximately 55km south at Udon Thani. THAI flies to Udon; see Getting There & Away in the Udon Thani section earlier for flight details. THAI operates an express van between Udon airport and Nong Khai's **THAI office** (on the southern side of Rte 212, about 300m west of Hwy 2) for 120B per person (35 minutes). You can get a túk-túk to the office for about 20B.

Bus Nong Khai's main bus terminal, off Th Prajak, has buses to Si Chiangmai, Beung Kan, Loei, Udon Thani, Ubon Ratchathani, Tha Bo, Bangkok and Rayong.

Buses to Nong Khai leave Udon Thani approximately every half-hour throughout the day from Udon's No 2 bus terminal (26B, 1¼ hours).

Buses to Loei (No 507) leave Nong Khai throughout the day between 6am and 4pm (81B); Nakhon Phanom buses (No 224) depart 16 times each day between 6.30am and 4.30pm (ordinary/air-con 79/143B).

If you're coming from Loei Province, you can get buses from Chiang Khan or Pak Chom without having to double back to Udon Thani. From Nakhon Phanom you can travel via Beung Kan along the Mekong River or you can cut through Sakon Nakhon and Udon Thani.

Bangkok First-class air-con and VIP buses leave nightly between 7.30pm and 8.30pm; 1st class costs 409B, while 24-seat VIP is 525B. Most people prefer to take the Bangkok–Nong Khai train – you can wander around a bit rather than sit on a narrow bus seat for 10 or more hours.

Laos Shuttle buses ferry passengers back and forth across the bridge for 10B per person; there are departures every 20 minutes from 6am to 7.30pm. You must arrange your own transport to the bridge from Nong Khai; figure on around 40B by túk-túk. The shuttle bus leaves from the Thai immigration office at the bridge, where you pay 10B for the ticket. After the three-minute drive across the bridge, the bus drops you off at Lao immigration and customs. Coming from Laos, you'll have to walk about 100m beyond the bridge to find a túk-túk, as they're not allowed to park and wait for passengers in the vicinity of the immigration office. There are usually taxi drivers loitering around the office, but they're more interested in big spenders who want to hire the car for a sprint to the airport at Udon (500B).

The bridge is open from 6am to 8pm. If you're driving, a toll of 20B is collected for cars; 30B for trucks under one tonne; 50B for mini or medium buses; 100B for bus coaches; and 100B to 300B for larger trucks, depending on the number of wheels.

Train From Bangkok, the Nong Khai express (No 69) leaves Hualamphong station daily at 8.45pm, arriving in Nong Khai at 8.10am – it's about the same speed as the bus but considerably more comfortable. Two rapid trains leave daily at 6am and 6.30pm, arriving at 5.25pm and 7am. One-way fares are 497B in 1st class, 238B in 2nd class and 103B in 3rd class, excluding surcharges for express or rapid service (60B and 40B) or sleeping berths.

A more inexpensive way to go by train most of the way is to take a 3rd-class diesel railcar as far as Udon Thani (95B) and hop on a bus from there for another 17B – see

Getting There & Away in the Udon Thani section earlier for schedule information.

In the reverse direction, the Nong Khai express (No 70) departs from Nong Khai at 7.05pm and arrives in Bangkok at 6.15am. There are also two Bangkok-bound rapid trains leaving Nong Khai at 6.05pm and 8.20am – both offer 2nd- and 3rd-class services only, but make only one more stop than the express.

A new train station was recently opened in Nong Khai. If you're stuck here waiting for a train, you can leave your bag at the left-luggage room and have a poke around the food and refreshment stalls across the road.

Getting Around

Sǎamláw around the town centre cost 20B; túk-túk are 20B, or 40B to the Friendship Bridge shuttle-bus terminal and the train station.

AROUND NONG KHAI PROVINCE

Wat Phra That Bang Phuan

วัดพระธาตุบังเผือน

Twelve kilometres south of Nong Khai on Hwy 2 and then 11km west on Rte 211, Wat Phra That Bang Phuan *(admission free, donations appreciated)* is one of the most sacred sites in the northeast because of the old Indian-style stupa here. It's similar to the original *chedi* beneath the Phra Pathom Chedi in Nakhon Pathom, but no-one knows when either *chedi* was built. It's speculated that it must have been in the early centuries AD – the *chedi* supposedly

Great Balls of Fire

Mass hysteria? Methane gas? Drunken Lao soldiers? Or perhaps the fiery breath of the sacred *naga*, a dragon-like being that populates folkloric waterways throughout Theravada Buddhist Southeast Asia. For the people who live along a certain stretch of the Mekong River in Thailand's Nong Khai Province, it's not a matter of whether or not to believe. For as long as anyone can remember, the sighting of the *bâng fai phayaa nâak* (loosely translated '*naga* fireballs') has been an annual event. Locals who have witnessed the phenomena often describe them as reddish or pinkish balls of fire that emerge from the Mekong River just after dusk and float into the air, sometimes as high as 300m, before disappearing without a trace. Most claim that the *naga* fireballs are soundless, but others say that a hissing can be heard if one is close enough to where they emerge from the surface of the river. On both sides of the Mekong the event has long been explained as a sign that the resident *naga* were celebrating the end of the Buddhist Rains Retreat (*Awk Phansǎa* in Thai), which coincides with the 15th waxing moon of the 11th lunar month.

Naga fireballs have only recently come to the attention of the rest of Thailand. TV news has been reporting the annual sightings for years, but it wasn't until the 2002 release of a film based on the phenomena that Thais really began to take notice. Entitled *Sìp Hâa Khâm Deuan Sìp-èt* or *Fifteenth Waxing Moon of the Eleventh Lunar Month* in Thai (the film was released with English subtitles under the curious title *Mekhong Full Moon Party*), the debut of the film not long before the scheduled event had an expected effect. Thousands of Thais from Bangkok and the rest of the country converged on the banks of the Mekong in Nong Khai Province and waited for the show to begin. Sadly, it rained that year. But that didn't dampen enthusiasm and *naga* fireballs were witnessed right on schedule.

So what, you might ask, is the real cause behind *naga* fireballs? Various theories have been put forth. One, which was aired on a Thai TV expose-style programme, claimed that Lao soldiers taking part in festivities on the other side of the Mekong were firing their rifles into the air. Interestingly, the reaction to the TV programme was anger and a storm of protest from both sides of the river. A more sensible theory perhaps, is that methane gas, trapped below the mud on the river bottom, reaches a certain temperature at that time of year and is released. Whatever the real cause, we may never find out. There are plans to blast a series of rapids along the Nong Khai stretch of the Mekong as part of a four-nation agreement (between Thailand, China, Myanmar and Laos) to make the river more navigable. Whatever subtle balance of nature has produced this mysterious event year after year may be lost forever.

enshrines some chest bones of the Buddha himself.

In 1559 King Jayachettha of Chanthaburi (not the present Chanthaburi in Thailand, but Wiang Chan – now known as Vientiane – in Laos) extended his capital across the Mekong and built a newer, taller, Lao-style *chedi* over the original as a demonstration of faith (just as King Mongkut did in Nakhon Pathom). Rain caused the *chedi* to lean precariously and in 1970 it fell over. The Fine Arts Department restored it in 1976 and 1977. The current *chedi* stands 34.25m high on a 17.2-sq-metre base.

But it is the remaining 16th-century Lao *chedi* in the compound (two contain semi-intact Buddha images in their niches) that give the wát its charm. There is also a roofless *wíhăan* with a large Buddha image, and a massive round brick base that must have supported another large *chedi*. A small museum displays site relics and a collection of old wooden spirit houses.

Getting There & Away To get to Wat Phra That Bang Phuan, get a săwngthăew or bus in Nong Khai bound for Si Chiangmai or Sangkhom and ask for Ban Bang Phuan (15B). Most Sangkhom-bound buses automatically stop at Phra That Bang Phuan. Otherwise, get any bus south on Hwy 2 and get off in Ban Nong Song Hong, the junction for Rte 211. From there take the next bus (from either Udon or Nong Khai) that's going to Si Chiangmai and get off near the wát. The fare should be about 15B to the road leading off Rte 211; it's an easy walk to the wát from that point.

Tha Bo
ท่าบ่อ

postcode 43110 • pop 16,000

Along the Mekong River and Rte 211, between the town of Nong Khai and the Loei Province border, are several smaller towns and villages where life revolves around farming and (minimal) trade between Laos and Thailand.

Surrounded by banana plantations and vegetable fields flourishing in the fertile Mekong floodplains, Tha Bo is the most important market centre between Nong Khai and Loei. An open-air market along the main street probably offers more wild plants and herbs than any market along the Mekong, along with Tha Bo's most famous local product – tomatoes. Annual tomato exports from Tha Bo often exceed 80,000 tonnes. Tobacco is also grown in fairly impressive quantities.

The **Kheuan Huay Mong** (Huay Mong Dam), which crosses the Mekong at the western edge of town, irrigates 108 sq km of land around Tha Bo. This relatively small-scale pumping project is one of the most successful hydrology efforts in Thailand, running at higher efficiency than any of the country's larger dam facilities and with less-extreme environmental impact. There is a pleasant public park next to the dam.

Aside from the market and dam, the town's only other claim to fame is **Wat Ong Teu** (also known as Wat Nam Mong), an old Lao-style temple sheltering a 'crying Buddha'. According to local legend, the left hand of the 300-year-old bronze image was once cut off by art thieves; tears streamed from the Buddha's eyes until the hand was returned. The wát is 3km west of town off Rte 211.

Places to Stay & Eat On the main street through town, **Suksan Hotel** *(☎ 0 4243 1665; Th Santisuk; rooms 80-100B)* has basic rooms. **Tha Bo Bungalow** *(☎ 0 4243 1196; Th Charoen Sawan; rooms 140-200B)*, on a back street not far from the town centre, has passable rooms with fan and bath.

Getting There & Away All săwngthăew and buses from Nong Khai (25km to the east) bound for Si Chiangmai will drop passengers in Tha Bo for 10B to 12B. If you're cycling from Nong Khai, you have a choice of the scenic river road or the slightly less scenic Rte 211, which makes up for it with whimsical topiary spaced along the highway every 500m or so.

Si Chiangmai
ศรีเชียงใหม่

Just across the river from Vientiane, Si Chiangmai has a large number of Lao and Vietnamese who make their living from the manufacture of rice-paper spring-roll wrappers. You can see the translucent disks drying in the sun on bamboo racks all over town. Si Chiangmai is one of the world's leading exporters of spring-roll wrappers! Many of the Vietnamese and Lao residents are Roman Catholic and there is a small cathedral in town. A local bakery prepares fresh French rolls every morning in an outdoor brick oven.

Wat Hin Mak Peng, Ban Pheu and various local villages can be visited from Si Chiangmai – inquire at Tim Guest House for the latest information.

Ferries now cross regularly to Vientiane – there are immigration and customs offices in town – but foreigners are not allowed to cross here.

Places to Stay & Eat The only guesthouse in town, **Tim Guest House** *(☎/fax 0 4245 1072; Th Rim Khong; singles from 90B, doubles up to 130B)* is run by a friendly Swiss-French man who speaks English, French, German and Thai. Rooms range from a small single to a large double with a river view. Simple Thai and *faràng* food is served in a dining area downstairs. Maps of the vicinity, massage and herbal sauna, laundry service, and bicycle and motorbike rental are available. Boat trips along the Mekong to Nong Khai, Wat Hin Mak Peng and Sangkhom can also be arranged. The guesthouse is near the river in the centre of town – walk west from the bus terminal and turn right at Soi 17, then turn left at the end of the road and you'll find it on the left.

Hotel Suthisuwan *(☎/fax 0 4245 1127; rooms with fan 200B, with air-con 350B)*, a bit southeast of Tim, is located in a historic building (check out the impressive upper floor), but is rather basic itself.

Maneerat Resort *(☎ 0 4245 1311; rooms 390B, VIP rooms 800B)*, about 700m southeast of Hotel Suthisuwan, is a new three-storey hotel. It has rooms with air-con and a few special larger VIP rooms. The hotel has a restaurant with a few tables across the road on the river, as well as a karaoke lounge.

Getting There & Away First-class air-con buses to Bangkok cost 402B and leave in the evening between 7pm and 9pm. To/from Loei the three-hour trip costs 64B. To/from Udon Thani costs 26B. To/from Nong Khai sǎwngthǎew (20B) take about an hour.

Wat Hin Mak Peng
วัดหินหมากเป้ง

Sixty-four kilometres northwest of Nong Khai between Si Chiangmai and Sangkhom, Wat Hin Mak Peng is worth a trip just for the scenery along Rte 211 from Nong Khai. This monastery is locally known for its *thúdong* (Pali: *dhutanga*) monks – monks who have taken ascetic vows in addition to the standard 227 precepts. These vows include, for example, eating only once a day and wearing only forest robes made from discarded cloth, plus a strong emphasis on meditation. There are also several *mâe chii* (Thai Buddhist nuns) living here. The place is very quiet and peaceful, set in a cool forest with lots of bamboo groves overlooking the Mekong. The *kùtì* (monastic huts) are built among giant boulders that form a cliff high above the river; casual visitors aren't allowed into this area, though. Below the cliff is a sandy beach and more rock formations. A Lao forest temple can be seen directly across the river. Fisherfolk occasionally drift by on house rafts.

The abbot at Wat Hin Mak Peng requests that visitors to the wát dress politely – no shorts or sleeveless tops. Those who don't observe the code will be denied entrance.

Getting There & Away To get here, take a sǎwngthǎew from Nong Khai to Si Chiangmai (20B) and ask for a sǎwngthǎew directly to Wat Hin (there are a few) or to Sangkhom, which is just past the entrance to the wát – the other passengers will let you know when the truck passes it (the sǎwngthǎew usually makes a stop here anyway). The second sǎwngthǎew is 18B. On the way to Wat Hin Mak Peng you'll see many examples of **topiary** along both sides of Rte 211.

Sangkhom
สังคม

The tiny town of Sangkhom could be used as a rest stop on a slow journey along the Mekong River from Loei to Nong Khai. Wat Hin Mak Peng is nearby, and there are some good hikes to caves and waterfalls in the area. The guesthouses hand out maps.

Opposite the River Huts guesthouse (see Places to Stay & Eat later), in the middle of the Mekong River, the Lao island of **Don**

Klang Khong appears during the dry season. From around the beginning of December a couple of rustic outdoor eating areas with thatched-roof shelters and tables and chairs are set up in the river shallows.

One of the largest local waterfalls is **Nam Tok Than Thip**, 3km from Rte 211 between the Km 97 and Km 98 markers, and a few kilometres west of Sangkhom. The waterfall has two major levels; the upper level is cleaner and has a deep pool (during or just after the rainy season) that is good for a dip. The falls are a long walk from the road – this is a trip best accomplished by motorbike.

Nam Tok Than Thong, 11.5km east of Sangkhom at the Km 73 marker off the northern (river) side of Rte 211, is more accessible but can be rather crowded on weekends and holidays.

Wat Aranyabanphot is a forest wát on a nearby hilltop with a very good sunset-over-the-Mekong view. A recent addition to the wát is a Lanna-style gilded *chedi*.

Places to Stay & Eat The town's guesthouses are off the main road through town and near the river.

River Huts *(singles & doubles 100B)* has a secluded location well off the main road. It's friendly and efficient, and has thatched huts overlooking the river. The food is good and bicycles are available for rent.

Bouy's Guest House *(☎/fax 0 4244 1065; singles/doubles 80/100B)* out on the main road is the original; a very pleasant place with huts on the river. Its better-than-average restaurant is worth a stop for lunch even if you're not staying overnight. Sandwiches, as well as Thai food, are available.

Two or three other guesthouses seem to come and go with the seasons, including **Riverside Guest House** and **Garden Home**. Outside town a little bit, on the way to Si Chiangmai, are the similar **Dee Dee Guest House** (just west of the Km 83 marker, opposite a PTT petrol station) and **Pak Som Guest House** (a bit further east), neither of which is anything special.

There are a couple of riverside **restaurants**. Ask around and you may be able to find a taste of *náam yân*, the sweetest moonshine from Laos.

Getting There & Away Buses from Nong Khai are 35B, and the trip takes about two hours. From Loei it costs 55B (three or four hours). From nearby Si Chiangmai the fare is 15B.

West of Pak Chom, săwngthăew are less frequent because the road worsens; the fare to Chiang Khan is 20B.

BEUNG KAN
บึงกาฬ

This is a small dusty town on the Mekong River, 185km east of Nong Khai by Rte 212. You may want to break your journey here if you are working your way around the northeastern border from Nong Khai to Nakhon Phanom (as opposed to the easier but less interesting Udon Thani–Sakon Nakhon–Nakhon Phanom route).

Between Nong Khai and Nakhon Phanom you'll pass many towns with 'Beung' or 'Nong' in their names: both terms refer to shallow bodies of fresh water fed by seasonal streams (a *beung* is usually larger than a *năwng*).

The closer you get to Nakhon Phanom Province, the more Vietnamese people you will see working in the rice fields or herding cows along the road. Nearly all the farmers in this area, whether ethnic Vietnamese or Thai, wear a simple conical Vietnamese-style straw hat to fend off the sun and rain.

The district of Beung Kan itself isn't much but there are some mildly interesting spots, including a nicely landscaped promenade along the waterfront. During the dry season the Mekong River recedes from Beung Kan and reaches its narrowest point along the Thai-Lao border.

East of town is **Nam Song Si** (Two Colour River), where the broad, muddy Huay Songkhram replenishes the Mekong.

Near the clock tower is a **Kasikornbank** with an ATM.

Wat Phu Thok
วัดภูทอก(วัดเจดีย์คีรีวิหาร)

Travellers interested in northeastern forest wát can visit Wat Phu Thok (Wat Chedi Khiri Wihan), a massive sandstone outcropping in the middle of a rather arid plain and a real hermit's delight. The entire outcropping, with its amazing network of caves and breathtaking views, belongs to the wát. The wát mountain is climbed by a series of stairs (seven levels) representing the seven factors of enlightenment in Buddhist psychology. Monastic *kùtì* (monks' dwellings) are scattered around the mountain, in caves and on cliffs. As you make the strenuous climb, each level is cooler than the one before. It is the cool and quiet isolation of this wát that entices monks and *mâe chii* from all over the northeast to come and meditate here.

This wát used to be the domain of the famous meditation master Ajahn Juan, a disciple of the fierce Ajahn Man who passed away in 1949. Ajahn Juan died in a plane crash about 20 years ago, along with several other highly revered forest monks who were flying to Bangkok for Queen Sirikit's birthday celebration.

To get to Wat Phu Thok you'll have to take an early morning sǎwngthǎew south on Rte 222 to Ban Siwilai (10B, 25km), then another sǎwngthǎew east (left) on a dirt road, 20km to the wát (15B). Hitching might be possible if you miss the truck. Occasionally you can find a local túk-túk going to the wát in the afternoon from Siwilai for 15B. If solitude is your main objective, it's best to tour Phu Thok early in the morning before the crowds of Thai pilgrims arrive.

If you're driving or pedalling yourself, a more direct route to the monastery is to continue southeast along Rte 212 from Beung Kan (in the direction of Nakhon Phanom) until you reach the Km 61 marker, then turn right (southeast) at a road signed for Jet Si, Tham Phra and Chut Na waterfalls. After 17km make a right on another road heading southwest, signed (in Thai only) for Phu Thok. You'll come to a monastery gate on the right after another 3.5km.

Ban Ahong

บ้านอาฮง

This village at the Km 115 marker on Rte 212 between Beung Kan and Nong Khai (23km west of Beung Kan) makes an interesting alternative to staying overnight in Beung Kan. The friendly Hideaway Guest House (see Places to Stay & Eat) next to the Mekong River is just a 200m walk from one of Isan's smallest and most intriguing wát. Set among giant boulders along the river, **Wat Pa Ahong Silawat** is a pretty riverside wát.

The narrow stretch of Mekong River opposite the wát has some refreshing **pools** for swimming during the dry season when the river is fairly clear. This area is also considered a highly auspicious spot to spend the evening of *wan àwk phansǎa*, the end of the Buddhist Rains Retreat. According to local legend, supernatural lights, *bâng fai pháyaa nâak* (*naga* fireballs), emerge from beneath this stretch of the Mekong River each year and arc across the sky (see the boxed text 'Great Balls of Fire' earlier in this section).

Hideaway Guest House can arrange boat trips to nearby river islands.

Places to Stay & Eat

Beung Kan The modest **Samanmit** *(rooms 60-80B)* and **Santisuk** *(☎ 0 4249 1114; rooms 150-350B)* are both on Th Prasatchai not far from the town clock tower; the Samanmit has the best overall appearance, while the Santisuk has a nice eating area downstairs.

Mekong Guest House *(☎/fax 0 4249 1341; rooms with fan/air-con 250/350B)*, a new two-storey place, sits across from the riverbank and offers clean rooms with private hot shower. The attached **Joy's Restaurant** *(dishes 30-40B)* downstairs serves reasonably priced tasty Thai dishes.

Ban Ahong Behind the village school next to the river (turn off at the Km 115 marker), **Hideaway Guest House** *(singles/doubles without bath 100/120B, rooms with bath 150B)* has a circle of simple, quiet huts on stilts with shared or private bath. Meals are available, there is a pleasant riverside sitting area nearby and you can go for walks in the village.

Getting There & Away

The bus from Nong Khai to Beung Kan (49B) departs every half-hour from 6am to 6.30pm. Buses from Nakhon Phanom to Beung Kan cost 94B and buses between Beung Kan and Ban Ahong cost 18B.

Loei Province

Loei is one of Thailand's most beautiful and unspoiled provinces. The terrain is mountainous and the temperature goes from one extreme to the other – hotter than elsewhere in Thailand during the hot season and colder than anywhere else during the cold season. This is the only province in Thailand where temperatures can drop to as low as 0°C, a fact the tourist brochures love to trumpet – though they're less keen on promoting the extreme heat!

The culture is an unusual mixture of northern and northeastern influences – a mixture that has produced more than one local dialect. Rural life outside the provincial capital has retained more of a traditional village flavour than many other places in Thailand, with the possible exceptions of Nan and Phetchabun, which were also once classified as remote or closed provinces.

Within the province, Phu Kradung and Phu Reua National Parks, in addition to the district of Chiang Khan, are worth a look and are good places to explore natural attractions. For hiking, the best time to visit Loei is during the cool months of mid-October through February.

LOEI

อ.เมืองเลย

postcode 42000 • pop 32,500

Nearly 520km from Bangkok, 140km from Udon Thani, 269km from Phitsanulok via Lom Sak and 200km via Nakhon Thai, the remote provincial capital of Loei has little to hold the interest of the ordinary traveller. Cotton is one of the province's major crops, so the town is a good place to buy cotton goods, especially the heavy cotton quilts

LOEI PROVINCE

(quite necessary during the chilly nights of Loei's cool months) made in Chiang Khan district – they're priced by the kilogram.

During the first week of February, Loei holds a **Cotton Blossom Festival** that culminates in a parade of cotton-decorated floats and, naturally, a Cotton Blossom Queen beauty contest. Loei also celebrates with fervour its own annual **Rocket Festival**, held in May. The city has even imported the colourful Phi Ta Khon procession from nearby Dan Sai district (see 'The Arrival of the Spirits' boxed text later in this section).

Information

Directly opposite the Thai Udom Hotel is a branch of **Bangkok Bank** *(Th Charoenrat)*, with an ATM.

Loei's **main post office** *(Th Charoenrat)* is not far from the Muang Fai Hotel. The **telephone office** is on the southern side of Th Chumsai, just east of Th Ruamjit.

Places to Stay – Budget

Friendship Guest House *(☎ 0 4283 2408; Th Charoenrat; rooms 150-200B)* has only three rooms (often rented out to long-termers). Toilet and shower facilities are shared. The owner, Khun Dum, speaks good English.

Sarai Thong Hotel *(☎ 0 4281 1582; rooms 120B)*, off Th Ruamjit, has 56 none-too-clean rooms in three buildings, all with fan and bath. The service isn't great, but it's off the street so it's usually quiet.

Places to Stay – Mid-Range & Top End

Phu Luang Hotel *(☎ 0 4281 1570; 55 Th Charoenrat; singles & doubles with air-con 400-600B)*, is near the night market, there's a late-night coffee shop and nightclub on the premises.

Thai Udom Hotel *(☎ 0 4281 1763; 122/1 Th Charoenrat; singles/doubles with fan 250/300B, rooms with air-con 500B, VIP rooms 600B)*, across from the Bangkok Bank, is a friendly hotel; its VIP rooms are largest. Overall it's a better choice than the Phu Luang, especially if you get a room away from the street.

Kings Hotel *(☎ 0 4281 1701, fax 0 4281 1235; Th Chumsai; singles with fan 240B, singles/doubles with air-con 380/399B)* is a well-run three-storey hotel. Rooms with fan

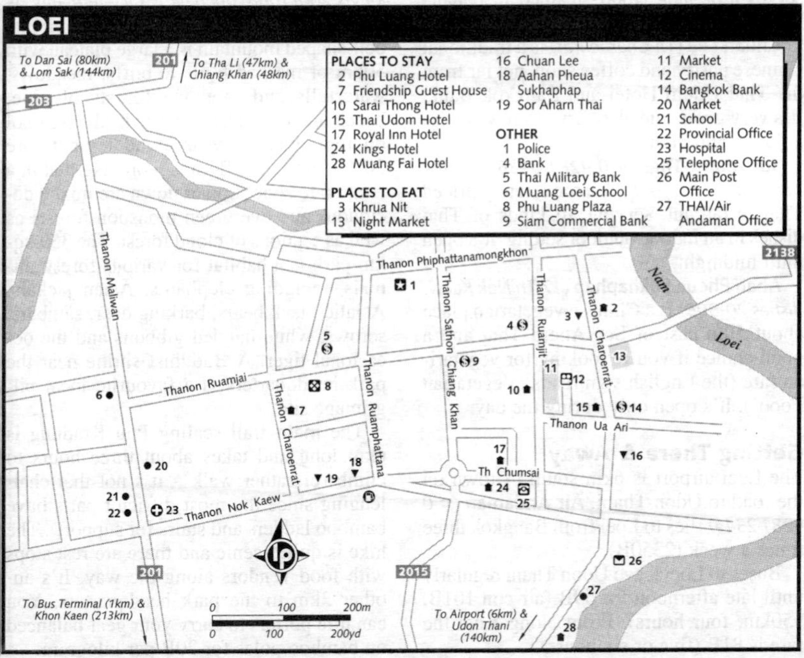

have bath, and those with air-con have hot water. An attached restaurant serves Thai, Vietnamese, Chinese and European dishes.

Royal Inn Hotel *(☎ 0 4281 2563, fax 0 4283 0878; singles/doubles 350/400B)*, just off Th Chumsai, is also in the King Hotel vicinity, and offers nice modest apartments with TV and air-con.

Muang Fai Hotel *(☎ 0 4281 1302; Th Charoenrat; rooms with fan/air-con 150/300B, deluxe with air-con 350B)* is a four-storey hotel near the THAI/Air Andaman office and main post office. Although the official rack rates are much higher, it offers very pleasant rooms for the rates shown here. It's a well-run place with a decent coffee shop.

Places to Eat

The **night market**, near the intersection of Th Ruamjai and Th Charoenrat, has cheap eats and other items of local provenance. Look for the local speciality, *khài pîng* (eggs-in-the-shell toasted on skewers).

Khrua Nit *(☎ 0 4281 3013; Th Charoenrat; dishes 20-40B; open 6am-8.30pm daily)*, opposite Phu Luang Hotel, is inexpensive and serves *hàw mòk* (food steamed in banana leaves) and other central-Thai dishes

Chuan Lee *(Th Charoenrat)* is a traditional Chinese pastry and coffee shop, not far from the Thai Udom Hotel and Bangkok Bank. It's very good, and also serves a few curries at lunch and dinner.

Sor Aharn Thai *(☎ 0 4281 3436; Th Nok Kaew; dishes 30-40B)* is a moderately priced Thai restaurant, serving all kinds of Thai dishes in an indoor-outdoor setting. It's open until midnight.

Ahan Pheua Sukhaphap *(17 Th Nok Kaew; dishes 20-30B)* is a Chinese vegetarian place about 50m east of Sor Aharn Thai and a good choice if you're looking for vegetarian fare (the English sign reads 'Vegetarian Food'). It's open only during the day.

Getting There & Away

The Loei airport is 6km south of town on the road to Udon Thani. **Air Andaman** *(☎ 0 4281 2344)* flies to Loei from Bangkok three times a week (2350B).

Buses to Loei leave Udon Thani regularly until late afternoon for 59B (air-con 101B, 150km, four hours). From Nong Khai the fare is 81B (five or six hours).

A direct bus between Phitsanulok and Loei costs 79B (air-con 145B) and takes four to five hours. Buses between Loei and Dan Sai cost 42B, and depart from Loei nine times between 5am and 5pm.

Air-con buses to Loei from Bangkok's Northern bus terminal leave several times daily (1st class 250B to 320B, 10 hours). A VIP bus leaves nightly at 8.40pm and costs 491B. Ordinary buses cost 178B and leave several times daily. In Loei you can get air-con buses to Bangkok from the bus terminal at the southwestern edge of town or from an agency in the lobby of the Kings Hotel.

Getting Around

You'll find plenty of túk-túk waiting at the bus station to take you into town. The fare is 5B per passenger, or about 30B for a chartered ride.

AROUND LOEI PROVINCE

Phu Kradung National Park

อุทยานแห่งชาติภูกระดึง

At 1360m, Phu Kradung *(adult/ child under 14 yrs 200/100B; open early Oct–mid-July)* is the highest point in Loei. On top of this bell-shaped mountain is a large plateau with 50km of marked trails to cliffs, meadows, waterfalls and montane forests of pine, beech and oak. The weather is always cool on top (average year-round temperature 20°C), hence the flora is more like that in a temperate zone. Lower down are mixed deciduous and evergreen monsoon forests as well as sections of cloud forest. The 359-sq-km park is a habitat for various forest animals, including elephants, Asian jackals, Asiatic black bears, barking deer, sambars, serows, white-handed gibbons and the occasional tiger. A Buddhist **shrine** near the park headquarters is a favourite local pilgrimage site.

The **main trail** scaling Phu Kradung is 6km long and takes about three hours to climb (or rather walk – it's not that challenging since the most difficult parts have bamboo ladders and stairs for support). The hike is quite scenic and there are rest stops with food vendors along the way. It's another 3km to the park headquarters. You can hire porters to carry your gear balanced on bamboo poles for 20B per kilogram.

During the hottest months, from March to June, it's best to start the climb about dawn. Temperatures in December and January can drop as low as 3°C to 4°C; blankets can be hired. Bring sweaters and thick socks.

Phu Kradung is closed to visitors during the rainy season because it is considered too hazardous, being slippery and subject to mud slides. The park can get crowded during school holidays (especially March to May, when Thai schools are closed).

A **visitors centre** at the base of the mountain distributes detailed maps and collects your admission fee. This entrance is open only from 7am to 3pm.

Places to Stay & Eat Lots of young Thai people, mainly college students, **camp** in the park. The park offers tents and tiny A-frame cabins for 100B and 200B respectively, or you can pitch your own tent for 50B. Mats, blankets and pillows are also available for rent. Other **park accommodation** includes several different units that sleep up to 10 people and cost 100B per person. Keep in mind, however, that these are really set aside for Thai students who come by the busload on weekends and during summer vacation. Foreign visitors who want to use this accommodation will have to rent the whole unit (800B for an eight-bed unit, 1000B for a 10-bed unit etc). There are a bunch of small **open-air eateries** here that do the usual stir-fry dishes for 30B to 40B.

Getting There & Away Buses on the Khon Kaen line go to the town (actually an *amphoe,* or district) of Phu Kradung. Departures from the Loei bus terminal are scheduled every half-hour from 4am until 6.30pm (but don't forget the park entrance closes at 3pm) for the 34B, 77km trip. From Phu Kradung, hop on a sǎwngthǎew (10B) to the park visitors centre at the base of the mountain, 7km away.

The last bus back to Loei from Phu Kradung leaves around 6pm.

Phu Reua National Park

อุทยานแห่งชาติภูเรือ

This relatively small park of 121 sq km surrounds Phu Reua (Boat Mountain), so-named because a cliff jutting from the peak is shaped like a Chinese junk. The easy 2½-hour hike to the summit (1375m) passes from tropical forest to broad-leaf evergreen forest to pine forest. In December, temperatures near the summit approach freezing at night.

The park entrance is about 50km west of the provincial capital on Rte 203. The usual admission fees apply. Although there is public transport from Loei to the town of Phu Reua, it is difficult to find sǎwngthǎew all the way to the park except on weekends and holidays. A well-marked 16km trail from the park **visitors centre** (3km off the highway) covers a good sample of what the park has to offer, including fine views of a mountain range in Sainyabuli Province, Laos.

Places to Stay & Eat The forestry department **bungalows** cost from 250B a night for up to five people, or you can rent a two-person tent for 50B.

On weekends and holidays, food is sometimes available from **vendors** in the park; at other times you may be able to arrange food through the park rangers.

In the nearby town of Phu Reua, there are several rustic but rather pricey 'resorts', including the **Phu Reua Chalet** *(☎ 0 4289 9012; rooms 500-1000B)* and **Rai Waranya** *(☎ 0 4289 9020; bungalows 600-2000B)*, which offers large bungalows on the road to the park entrance.

Getting There & Away Nine buses a day run between Loei and Dan Sai between 5am and 5pm, passing through Phu Reua town on the way. The fare should be around 25B.

Dan Sai

ด่านซ้าย

About 80km west of Loei is the small town of Dan Sai, which is famous for its unique form of the **Bun Phra Wet Festival**. The three-day festival occurs during the fourth lunar month (usually in June) and actually combines the Phra Wet Festival – during which recitations of the Mahavessantara Jataka are supposed to enhance the listener's chance of being reborn in the lifetime of the next Buddha – with the Bun Bang Fai (Rocket Festival). The latter usually takes place a month or so earlier throughout the northeast in May.

Nobody seems to know how or when Dan Sai's distinctive festival first began,

NORTHEASTERN THAILAND

The Arrival of the Spirits

Without a doubt, Dan Sai's three-day **Bun Phra Wet Festival** – also known as the Phi Ta Khon *(phǐi taa khǒn)* Festival – is one of the most colourful and unique annual events in Thailand. On the first day of the festival, the current village shaman – Jao Phaw Kuan – dons white clothing and a white headband, and, along with his shaman wife, Jao Mae Nang Tiam (also dressed in white with a white cloth wrapped around her hair), leads the propitiation of the all-important *tiam*. The latter are a class of spirits similar to the Lao-Thai *khwǎn* but perceived to be at a higher level.

Assisting in the rites are a group of male and female lesser mediums. Ceremonies begin around 3.30am in a procession from Dan Sai's Wat Phon Chai to the Mae Nam Man. Rites are performed at the riverside to coax Phra Upakhut – a water spirit supposedly embodied in an invisible piece of white marble – to join the proceedings. Phra Upakhut is believed to have once been a monk with supernatural powers, who transformed himself into white marble 'to live a solitary and peaceful existence below the water', according to local descriptions. It's possible he is somehow related to the *bodhisattva* (Buddhist saint) Upagupta, who in Mahayana Buddhist mythology is thought to reside in the ocean. The procession – accompanied by the invisible spirit – then returns to the wát, where resident monks receive ceremonial food at around 7am.

Shortly thereafter the summoning of additional spirits takes place at Jao Phaw Kuan's home, which doubles as the most important spirit shrine in Dan Sai. Villagers are invited to attend the ceremony, and all present participate in a *bai sǐi* (sacred thread-tying) ceremony. After some incantations and lighting of candles, villagers crawl up to the Jao Phaw and Jao Mae, seated cross-legged on the floor in a semi-trance, and tie lots of sacred thread on their arms, which are propped up by pillows. The attendants also tie single loops of sacred thread around one wrist of everyone present. While all this is taking place, free food is served on round trays and everyone downs shots of *lâo khǎo* ('white spirit') to get in the mood for what comes next.

As the tying of threads finishes up, the shaman's attendants take down bundles of special costuming kept on a high altar near the ceiling of the house, put the clothing on and gather in front of the house. Most of the costumes look like something from Shakespearian theatre meant for beggar or jester roles – ragged and tattered but very colourful. To complete the transformation into *phǐi taa khǒn* (an untranslatable term basically meaning 'Phra Wet spirits'), each attendant dons a huge mask made from a *hûat* (crescent-shaped basket used for steaming sticky rice), cut and re-shaped to fit atop the head, and a thick sheath from the base of a coconut palm frond. On the typical mask, small eye-openings have been cut into the palm sheath and a large, curving wooden nose added, and the whole affair is custom-painted to suit the wearer with all manner of designs. Brightly coloured cloth hangs from the basket top to cover the back of the head.

Two of the attendants, however, wear tall bamboo frames assembled in vaguely human shapes, covered with white cloth, and topped with giant heads standing perhaps 2m above their own heads.

but another aspect to the festival has to do with tribal Thai – possibly Thai Dam – spirit cults. In fact the dates for the festival are divined by Jao Phaw Kuan, a local spirit medium who channels the information from Jao Saen Meuang, the town's guardian deity.

The festival has grown in popularity among outsiders and now has a steady following among Thais from nearby provinces and as far away as Bangkok. A few Westerners are beginning to find their way here as well. See the boxed text 'The Arrival of the Spirits'.

About 1km outside town off Rte 2113 stands **Phra That Si Songrak**, a large Lao-style *chedi* with a very wide base, giving a much stronger-looking profile than the average Lao *chedi*. The most highly revered stupa in Loei Province, the whitewashed *chedi* stands 30m high and was built in AD 1560 as a gesture of national friendship between the Lao kingdom of Wiang Chan (Vientiane) and the Thai kingdom of Ayuthaya. A smaller stupa in front is semi-hollow and attached to a pavilion. The open repository contains a very old chest that supposedly contains an even older carved stone Buddha about 76cm long. Shoes can't be worn anywhere in the compound. The *chedi* caretaker is none other than Jao Phaw Kuan, Dan Sai's main spirit medium.

The Arrival of the Spirits

One figure is male, the other female, as is obvious from the huge, exaggerated sexual organs attached to the front of the figures – a giant penis (controlled from inside by a string that makes it flop up and down) for one, a large hairy vaginal triangle and conical breasts for the other. These are the *phĭi taa khŏhn yài* (big Phra Wet spirits), and exactly what they represent is anyone's guess nowadays. These figures, surrounded by regular *phĭi taa khŏhn* as well as 'civilians', then lead a boisterous procession from the Jao Phaw's house back to the monastery, with musical accompaniment supplied by *khaen, pin* and other Isan instruments.

More *lâo khăo* is passed around and soon the knees and elbows get moving and everyone starts dancing down the road. Once the procession reaches the wát grounds, the participants begin circumambulating the main *wíhăan* (hall) and continue for a couple hours, becoming increasingly rowdy with each turn. There's lots of sexual innuendo and older village women take turns grabbing the lengthy penis of the male *phĭi taa khŏhn yài* and giving it a few good shakes, laughing all the while. The whole thing ends around noon and people stagger back home to sleep it off.

On the second day all the locals get into costume and accompany Jao Phaw Kuan, Jao Mae Nang Tiam and the four female assistant mediums in a procession from Chum Chon Dan Sai School to the temple. In earlier years the Jao Phaw/Jao Mae and their shaman court rode on wood or bamboo palanquins, but these days they sit on colourful dais in the back of pick-up trucks. Bamboo rockets ride along with them. As on the first day, there's plenty of music and dancing, but this time there are hundreds more participants, and spectators marvel at the many different costume designs cooked up for this year's event. Some show real creative genius. Many of the costumed *phĭi taa khŏhn*, both men and women, carry carved wooden phalli (or a knife or sword with a phallic handle) in one or both hands, waving them about as talismans or using them to tease the crowd while they dance and strut down the street. Tin cans and wooden cowbells may be hung from the costumes to create more of a racket.

Once again, when they reach the wát, the participants circumambulate the *wíhăan* many times, dancing along the way. Fuelled by the consumption of much *lâo khăo*, the rounds continue for hours and become more raucous and spontaneous as the day wears on. At the same time in the main courtyard in front of the wát there's live *măw lam* music, and lots more dancing and wooden penis antics. If it has rained recently, participants will revel in the mud. As one Western observer remarked, 'It's like Woodstock and Halloween rolled into one'.

In the late afternoon of the second day the bamboo rockets are fired. Be prepared to run for cover if one of the rockets loses its course and comes spiralling back into the crowd.

The third day is much more solemn as the villagers assemble at the temple to listen to Mahavessantara Jataka recitations and Dhamma sermons by local and visiting monks. By custom, 13 sermons are delivered in a row.

Wat Neramit Wiphatsana, on a wooded hill just southwest of town, is a meditation wát where most of the buildings are made of unplastered laterite blocks. Famous Thai temple muralist Pramote Sriphrom has been painting images of *jataka* (past-life stories of the Buddha) tales on the interior walls of the *bòt* for the last seven years and estimates it will take him another five to finish the job. The wát is dedicated to the memory of the late Ajahn Mahaphan (also known as Khruba Phawana), a much-revered local monk.

Further from the town on Rte 203 near the Km 61 marker is the entrance for **Chateau de Loei Vineyards**, Thailand's most serious and respected vineyard. Visitors are welcome to tour the vineyards, after obtaining a pass at the Chateau de Loei store-restaurant about 30m from the vineyard entrance.

Na Haew district, about 30km northwest of Dan Sai, is separated from Laos by the Mae Nam Heuang (also known locally as the Nam Man, although cartographers say the Man is a tributary of the Heuang and starts further south). There is an official border crossing at the village of Meuang Phrae in Na Haew. A toll is collected from Lao and Thais who cross here. They cross either by wading across the river when the water level is low, or by raft when the water is high. For the moment foreigners cannot cross here legally.

Places to Stay & Eat Very close to Wat Phon Chai, **Yensuk Guest House** *(rooms 200B)* offers six featureless rooms in a row house, each with private bath, but no ventilation. During the festival, the owners ask as much as 400B for these rooms. Further away but still in town, **Wiang Kaew Guest House** *(rooms 200B)* has three larger rooms than Yensuk's, with ceiling fans and attached bath. It's off the road, so it's fairly quiet. Rates are the same as Yensuk – rising to 400B during the festival. You may want to ask the staff to clean your room before checking in.

Phak Thanapho *(T Guest House; ☎ 0 4289 1702; Soi Thetsaban 4; rooms without bath 150B)* is nicer than either mentioned so far and is in a wooden house at the edge of town. Simple but clean, quiet rooms have shared bath (and possibly cost more during the festival).

Out on Rte 203 towards Loei, near the Km 61 marker, there's a good choice if you can spend a little more and have your own transport. **Rangyen Resort** *(☎ 0 4289 1089, fax 0 4289 1423; rooms with fan 850B, with air-con 1100-1450B, two-room bungalows 3500B)* is spread out over several hectares of land that also hold a large pond, a swimming pool, badminton court and tennis courts. Large rooms have two beds, minibar and satellite TV, and even during the festival discounts are readily available. There's a large restaurant and a karaoke bar on the premises – the place seems to be geared towards Thai business or civil service conventions. It's at least a 20-minute drive off the highway, so you can forget about using public transport to get here or to get from here to Dan Sai.

There are a few **noodle and rice stands** near Wat Phon Chai. **Restaurant Je-Boy** *(dishes 30-40B)* is a small open-air place on Rte 2114 just north of Dan Sai and is one of the best places to eat.

Getting There & Away Phitsanulok–Udon Thani express buses going in both directions make stops in Dan Sai in the afternoon. The fare in either direction from Dan Sai is about 50B. There are also several departures to/from Loei from 6am to 5pm.

CHIANG KHAN
เชียงคาน

Chiang Khan is about 50km north of Loei, on the Mekong River in a large valley surrounded by mountains. The shophouses along the backstreets are wooden and give the place a bit of a frontier atmosphere, and there are some nice views of the river.

Boat trips upriver as far as the Mae Nam Heuang junction or downriver to Kaeng Khut Khu can be arranged at Tonkhong Guest House (see Places to Stay later) for as little as 200B per person, depending on the size of the group.

Chiang Khan comes alive during *wan àwk phansăa,* the end of the **Buddhist Rains Retreat** in late October and early November. There's a week-long festival that features displays of large carved wax *prasat* (shrines) at each of the temples in town, as well as boat races on the river. At night there are performances of *măw lam* (Isan-style folk music) in the field facing the main post office.

Temples

The town's wát feature a style of architecture rarely seen in Thailand – *wíhăan* with colonnaded fronts and painted shutters that seem to indicate a French (via Laos) influence. A good example in the centre of town is **Wat Pa Klang**, which is about 100 years old and features a new glittery superstructure; in the grounds of this wát is a small Chinese garden with a pond, waterfall, and Chinese-style sculptures of Buddha and Kuan Yin.

Wat Mahathat in the centre of town is Chiang Khan's oldest temple; the *bòt,* constructed in 1654, has a new roof over old walls, with faded murals on the front. **Wat Si Khun Meuang** *(Th Chiang Khan)*, between Soi 6 and Soi 7, contains a Lao-style *chedi* and *bòt* (*sĭm* in Lao), plus a topiary garden.

Temple structures at **Wat Santi** and **Wat Thakhok** are similar to those at Wat Pa Klang (minus the Chinese garden). The walls of the temple buildings are stained red from all the dust and mud that builds up in the dry and rainy seasons.

Wat Tha Khaek is a 600- to 700-year-old temple, 2km outside town, on the way to Ban Noi. The seated Buddha image in the *bòt* is sacred and it is said that holy water

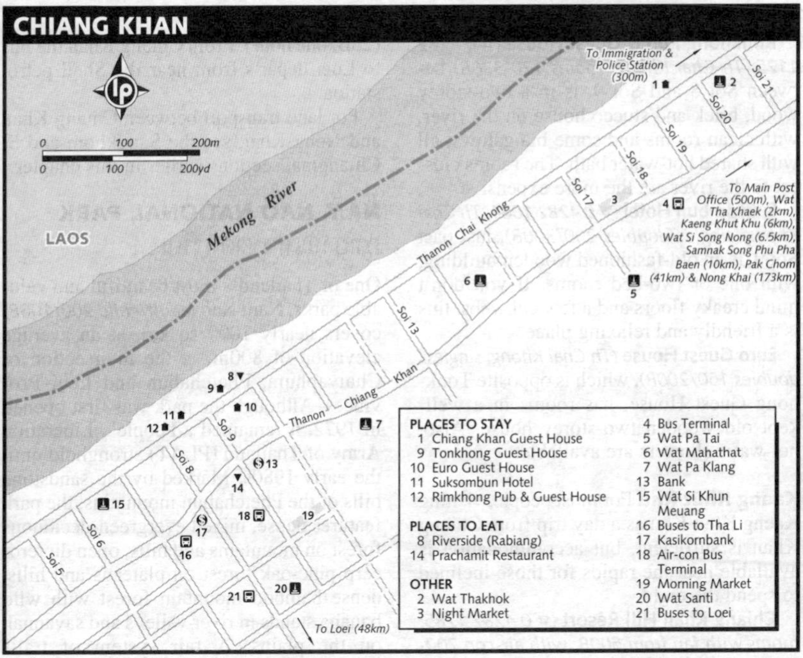

prepared in front of the image has the power to cure any ailing person who drinks it or bathes in it.

Other well-known monastic centres in the area include **Samnak Song Phu Pha Baen**, 10km east of Chiang Khan, where monks meditate in caves and on tree platforms; and **Wat Si Song Nong**, west of Kaeng Khut Khu (within easy walking distance) on the river. The latter is a small forest wát where the highly respected Ajahn Maha Bun Nak resides.

Kaeng Khut Khu

แก่งคุดคู้

About 6km downstream from Chiang Khan is Kaeng Khut Khu, a stretch of rapids (best in the dry, hot season) with a park on the Thai side and a village on the Lao side. You can hire a boat to reach the rapids. The park has thatched-roof picnic areas with reed mats on raised wooden platforms. **Vendors** sell delicious Isan food such as *kài yâang, sôm-tam* and *khâo nĭaw* (sticky rice), as well as *kûng tên* (literally, dancing shrimp; fresh river prawns served live in a light sauce of lime juice and chillies), *kûng thâwt* (the same fried whole in batter) and drinks. One large restaurant called **Khrua Nucha** serves sit-down meals. This is a great place to spend a few hours.

Nearby **Wat Noi** houses three very old stone Buddha images; they're placed on a ledge high above a larger, modern Buddha in the wát's new *bòt*.

Places to Stay

Chiang Khan The **Chiang Khan Guest House** (*☎ 0 4282 1691; Th Chai Khong; single/double/triple rooms 150/200/300B*) has fair rooms, and rooms with shared bath. The dining area overlooks the river and food is served for groups with advanced notice. It's between Soi 19 and Soi 20, on a street that runs along the Mekong.

Tonkhong Guest House (*☎ 0 4282 1547; Th Chai Khong; rooms with/without bath 200/150B*), in an older building between Soi 9 and Soi 10, is a friendly riverside place with rooms with shared facilities. There's a nice view from the 2nd-storey vegetarian restaurant. Two-hour trips to the rapids can be arranged with comfortable boats that carry up to 18 people. (See Getting There & Away later for other options.)

Rimkhong Pub & Guest House *(☎ 0 4282 1125; Th Chai Khong; rooms 120-320B)* between Soi 8 and Soi 9, is in a two-storey wood, brick and stucco house on the river, with clean rooms and some bungalows, all with shared hot-water bath. The rooms closest to the river are the more expensive.

Suksombun Hotel *(☎ 0 4282 1064; Th Chai Khong; singles/doubles 200/300B)*, just past Soi 9, is an old-fashioned wooden building, with one or two-bed rooms. If you don't mind creaky floors and a few cobwebs, this is a friendly and relaxing place.

Euro Guest House *(Th Chai Khong; singles/doubles 150/200B)*, which is opposite Tonkhong Guest House, has rooms in a well-kept old wooden two-storey house. Also, hot-water showers are available.

Kaeng Khut Khu For most people, visiting Kaeng Khut Khu as a day trip from Chiang Khan is sufficient, but accommodation is available near the rapids for those inclined to spend the night.

Chiang Khan Hill Resort *(☎ 0 4282 1285; rooms with fan from 500B, with air-con 700-900B, air-con bungalows up to 1800B)* offers rooms with fan and air-con as well as solid, brick bungalows, near the rapids. However, air-con is hardly necessary at night and it only drowns out the sound of the river. The attached restaurant serves good breakfasts.

Places to Eat

Riverside *(Rabiang; dishes 30-40B)* and **Rimkhong Pub & Guest House** *(dishes 30-40B)* are modest Thai restaurants in old shophouses on the river.

A few more eating places are clustered on Soi 9 and around the intersection of Soi 9 and Th Chiang Khan. **Prachamit Restaurant**, on the southwestern corner of the intersection, serves inexpensive Thai and Chinese dishes. For cheap breakfasts, head for the morning market off Soi 9 near Wat Santi. Between 5am and 7.30am there are two **stalls** selling *kaafae thŭng* (Thai coffee), curries and *paa-thâwng-kŏh* (Chinese doughnuts). The **riverside restaurant** at the Suksombun Hotel serves good Thai and Chinese standards.

Getting There & Away

Săwngthăew to Chiang Khan leave almost every hour from the Loei bus terminal (26B, one hour). From Chiang Khan the bus to Loei departs from near the Shell petrol station.

For land transport between Chiang Khan and Nong Khai, see the Sangkhom and Si Chiangmai sections earlier in this chapter.

NAM NAO NATIONAL PARK
อุทยานแห่งชาติน้ำหนาว

One of Thailand's most beautiful and valuable parks, Nam Nao *(adult/child 200/100B)* covers nearly 1000 sq km, at an average elevation of 800m, at the intersection of Chaiyaphum, Phetchabun and Loei Provinces. Although the park was first opened in 1972, it remained a People's Liberation Army of Thailand (PLAT) stronghold until the early 1980s. Marked by the sandstone hills of the Phetchabun mountains, the park features dense, mixed evergreen-deciduous forest on mountains and hills, open dipterocarp pine-oak forest on plateaus and hills, dense bamboo mountain forest with wild banana stands in river valleys and savannah on the plains. A fair system of trails branches out from the park headquarters; the scenic and fairly level **Phu Khu Khao** trail cuts through pine forest and grass meadow for 24km. The park also features several waterfalls and caves. The park's highest peak, **Phu Pha Jit**, reaches a height of 1271m.

Although it's adjacent to 1560-sq-km **Phu Khiaw Wildlife Sanctuary**, a highway bisecting the park has unfortunately made wildlife somewhat more accessible to poachers, so many native species are in decline. There are no villages within the park boundaries, however, so incidences of poaching and illegal logging remain fairly minor. Elephants and banteng (wild cattle) are occasionally spotted, as well as Malayan sun bears, tigers, leopards, Asian jackals, barking deer, gibbons, langurs and flying squirrels. Rumours of rhinoceros (last seen in 1971, but tracks were observed in 1979) persist, and the bizarre fur-coated Sumatran rhino may survive here. Phu Khiaw itself is a sandstone mountain in Khon San district covered with thick forest that harbours crocodiles, banteng, gaurs, tigers, elephants, serows, leopards and barking deer. Three rivers are sourced at Nam Nao: the Chi, Saphung and Phrom.

NORTHEASTERN THAILAND

Temperatures are fairly cool year-round, especially nights and mornings; the best time to go is from November to February, when morning frost occasionally occurs.

A small **museum** in the visitors centre contains a collection of confiscated guns and traps used by poachers, an ecological map and a bird list.

The Royal Forest Department operates **accommodation**, including 500B units that sleep up to eight people, as well as 1000B units sleeping up to 24. Two-person tents are available for rent (50B). **Vendors** next to the visitors centre offer noodles, Thai and Isan food.

Daily buses run through the park from Chumphae or Khon Kaen (103km). Look for the park office sign on Hwy 12 at the Km 50 marker; the office is 2km from there.

Nakhon Phanom Province

Nakhon Phanom Province has a strong Lao and Vietnamese presence, although its capital is largely ethnic Chinese. If you plan to visit That Phanom, you'll probably have to stop here first to change buses, unless you go directly to That Phanom from Sakon Nakhon via Rte 223. The province is dotted with temples with Lao-style *thâat* (four-sided, curvilinear *chedi*).

NAKHON PHANOM

อ.เมืองนครพนม

postcode 48000 • pop 31,700

Nakhon Phanom is 242km from Udon Thani and 296km from Nong Khai. It's a rather ordinary town that just happens to have a panoramic view of the Mekong River and the craggy mountains of Laos beyond – in fact, the Sanskrit-Khmer name Nakhon Phanom means 'city of hills'.

A landscaped promenade was added along the river at either end of town to take advantage of the views. If you were choosing a northeastern-Thai capital to live in, Nakhon Phanom might make a good candidate since the streets are well laid out, there are many green areas, the riverside is scenic and there's not much traffic – the only drawback is there's almost nothing to do!

Just south of the Mae Nam Khong Grand View Hotel is a river 'beach', where locals and visitors gather to watch the sun set and buy snacks from the vendors. On hot, still days an upside-down mirror image of the river island **Don Don** appears to hang in the air above the real thing.

The interior murals of the *bòt* at **Wat Si Thep**, in town on the street of the same name, show *jataka* (past-life stories of the Buddha) along the upper part, and kings of the Chakri dynasty along the lower part. On the back of the *bòt* is a colourful triptych done in modern style.

The Lao town on the other side of the river is **Tha Khaek**. Foreigners with Lao visas are now permitted to cross by ferry. Thai and Lao government officials are currently mulling over the possibility of adding a bridge over the Mekong here. This would link Nakhon Phanom with the Vietnamese seaport of Vinh on the Gulf of Tonkin via the 240km Rte 12 across Laos and Vietnam.

Information

The **TAT** *(☎ 0 4251 3490, fax 0 4251 3492; e tat.ne@npu.msu.ac.th; cnr Th Sala Klang & Th Sunthon Wijit; open 8.30am-4.30pm daily)* has an office in a beautiful colonial-style building. The staff distribute information on Nakhon Phanom, Mukdahan and Sakon Nakhon Provinces.

There is a **main post office** *(cnr Th Ratchathan & Th Sunthon Wijit; open 8.30am-4.30pm Mon-Fri, 9am-noon Sat, Sun & holidays)* and a separate **CAT telephone office** *(Th Sala Klang; open 8.30am-4.30pm Mon-Fri)*.

Places to Stay – Budget

Charoensuk Hotel *(no Roman-script sign; ☎ 0 4251 1130; Th Bamrung Meuang; singles/doubles 150/200B)*, directly opposite the Bangkok Bank, is the cheapest place in town, with simple but clean and surprisingly large rooms with fan and bath. The hotel is set back from the street with off-street parking at the front. **Grand Hotel** *(☎ 0 4251 1526, fax 0 4251 1283; cnr Th Si Thep & Th Ruamjit; rooms 230B, with air-con from 320B)* is similar to Charoensuk, with simple but well-kept rooms, all of which have bath and TV. **First Hotel** *(☎ 0 4251 1253; 370 Th Si Thep; rooms with fan 160-210B, with air-con 280-300B)* has well-worn rooms with bath, some with TV.

Places to Stay – Mid-Range & Top End

Windsor Hotel (☎ *0 4251 1946; 692/19 Th Bamrung Meuang; rooms with fan 250B, with air-con 350-400B)* is a former budget place that was upgraded a bit and now has rooms with attached bath and TV. It's friendly and probably the best-value place to stay in town.

Nakhon Phanom Hotel *(☎ 0 4251 1455; 403 Th Aphiban Bancha; rooms with air-con 300-450B)* has rooms with air-con, carpet, TV and hot water. The more expensive rooms have been recently renovated and are fairly comfortable. The cheap rooms are rather depressing.

Mae Nam Khong Grand View Hotel *(☎ 0 4251 3564, fax 0 4251 1037; rooms 495-595B)*, an all air-con hotel overlooking the river at the southern end of town, offers spacious rooms with all the amenities. Rooms with a river view and balcony are more expensive. **Nakhon Phanom River View** *(☎ 0 4252 2333, fax 0 4252 2777; rooms 900B)*, about 350m further south along the same road, is newer than Grand View and is now the town's most luxurious hotel, with well appointed rooms, all with air-con, TV, hot-water bath and fridge. Breakfast is included in the price of the room.

Places to Eat

Most of the better restaurants are along the river on Th Sunthon Wijit; they include **Plaa Beuk Thong** *(Golden Giant Catfish; dishes 60-120B)*, **New Rapmit**, **Rim Nam** and **New Suan Mai**. New Suan Mai, Plaa

NAKHON PHANOM

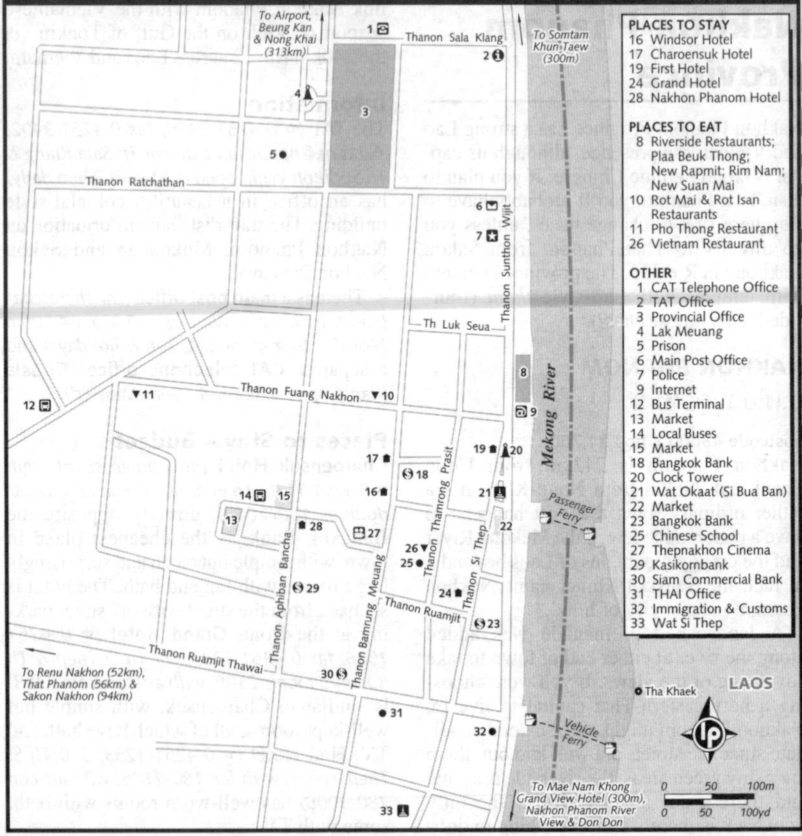

JOE CUMMINGS

Sculpture garden, Sala Kaew Ku, Nong Khai Province

JOE CUMMINGS

Chiang Khan, Loei Province

BILL WASSMAN

Temple ruins, Prasat Hin Phimai, Nakhon Ratchasima Province

JOE CUMMINGS

Phanom Rung Historical Park

CASEY & ASTRID WITTE MAHANEY

Khao Yai National Park, Nakhon Ratchasima Province

JOHN HAY

Dyed silk, northeastern Thailand

JOHN ELK III

Wat Phra That Phanom, That Phanom

JOHN ELK III

Internet café, Nakhon Ratchasima (Khorat), Nakhon Ratchasima Province

Beuk Thong (also open for breakfast) and Rim Nam are the best of the bunch; Rim Nam has an open-air, floating platform at the back that gets a breeze. At these restaurants giant Mekong catfish is occasionally available, though if you ask for it and none is at hand, you'll likely be served some other kind of fish and charged an exorbitant amount for it. A sunset dining boat leaves from the back of Rim Nam at 5pm for 40B per person plus the cost of whatever you order. Diners may hire a *mǎw lam* ensemble to entertain on special occasions.

There are several good, inexpensive restaurants serving dishes like noodles and curry-and-rice along Th Bamrung Meuang north of the Windsor and Charoensuk Hotels. **Rot Mai** and **Rot Isan**, two small rice shops near the Charoensuk Hotel, serve local specialities, including *jàew hâwn*, a sukiyaki-style soup with noodles, beef and vegetables. Other popular dishes at these restaurants are *lâap pèt* (spicy duck salad) and *yâang sěua ráwng hâi* ('grill that would make a tiger cry' – beef grilled with chillies).

Pho Thong Restaurant *(Th Fuang Nakhon; dishes 30-40B)* is a larger place serving Isan food. **Somtam Khun Taew** *(Th Suthon Wijit)*, two blocks north of the TAT office, is one of the most famous *sôm-tam* shops in Isan. Here Khun Taew will pound an order of the spicy green papaya salad made to your specifications. She also makes good *súp nàw mái* (spicy bamboo-shoot salad), *plaa châwn phǎo* (grilled serpentfish) and *hǎwy khǒm* (freshwater snails).

Vietnam Restaurant *(Th Thamrong Prasit; dishes 30-40B)* serves Vietnamese specialities, including *nǎem neuang* (barbecued pork meatballs) and *yáw* (spring rolls), usually sold in 'sets' *(sùt)* with cold rice noodles, fresh lettuce leaves, mint, basil, various dipping sauces, sliced starfruit and sliced green plantain.

Opposite and south of the Si Thep Hotel are **restaurants** *(dishes 15-30B)* selling *jók* and *khài kàthá*.

Getting There & Away

Air THAI fields daily flights to/from Bangkok (2195B, 1¼ hours). THAI runs a shuttle van between the airport, 16km away, and the city centre. The **THAI office** *(☎ 0 4251 2940; 13 Th Ruamjit Thawai)* is at Bovon Travel. In the near future this route is scheduled to be taken over by **PB Air** *(☎ 0 4258 7207, in Bangkok ☎ 0 2261 0222–5)*.

Bus Regular buses run from Nong Khai to Nakhon Phanom via Sakon Nakhon for 79B. There are air-con buses hourly from 6am to 11am for 143B. If you want to go through Beung Kan, you can get a bus to Beung Kan (about 40B) first, then change to a Nakhon Phanom bus. The journey all the way from Udon Thani costs 128/211B by ordinary/air-con bus.

Between Nakhon Phanom and Mukdahan there are hourly departures between 5am and 5pm for 42B (air-con 70B); ordinary buses between Nakhon Phanom and Sakon Nakhon run on a similar schedule for 39B (air-con 61B).

Air-con buses run between Khorat and Nakhon Phanom thrice daily for 264B.

From Bangkok's Northern and Northeastern bus terminal there are different classes of air-con buses to Nakhon Phanom each day between 6am and 8pm (360B to 579B).

Boat A ferry boat across the Mekong River to Tha Khaek, in Laos, costs 40B per person; the fare is the same in the reverse direction. Anyone with a valid visa for Laos is permitted to cross here.

Nakhon Phanom Festival

On the full moon of the 11th lunar month (usually late October) at the end of the Buddhist Rains Retreat, Nakhon Phanom residents celebrate Wan Phra Jao Prot Lok – a holiday in honour of Buddha's descent from the Devaloka (Deity World), where legend says he had spent a Rains Retreat offering teachings. Besides the usual wát offerings, festival activities include the launching of *reua fai* (fire boats), on the Mekong. Originally these 8m to 10m boats were made of banana logs or bamboo, but modern versions can be fashioned of wood or synthetic materials. The boats carry offerings of cakes, rice and flowers; at night the boats are launched on the river and illuminated in a spectacular display.

During this same festival in the daytime, the city hosts longboat races similar to those seen in many towns along the Mekong River.

AROUND NAKHON PHANOM

Renu Nakhon

เรณูนคร

The village of Renu Nakhon is known for cotton and silk weaving, especially *mát-mìi* designs. The local Phu Thai, a Thai tribe separate from mainstream Siamese and Lao, also market their designs here. Each Saturday there's a big **market** near Wat Phra That Renu Nakhon where you can find many stalls selling local hand-woven fabrics and some handicrafts. On other days you can buy from a string of shops and vendors near the temple or directly from weavers in the village.

The *thâat* at **Wat Phra That Renu Nakhon** exhibits the same basic characteristics as That Phanom but in less elongated proportions. Renu Nakhon is worth a visit if you're in the vicinity, even during the week.

During local festivals the Phu Thai sometimes hold folk-dance performances called *fáwn lákhon thai,* which celebrate their unique heritage. They also practise the *bai sĭi* custom common in other parts of the northeast as well as in Laos, in which a shaman ties loops of sacred string around a person's wrists (see the 'Bai Sĭi Ceremony' boxed text earlier in this chapter).

Getting There & Away The turn-off to Renu Nakhon is south of Nakhon Phanom at the Km 44 marker on Rte 212. Since it's only 10km further to That Phanom, you could visit Renu on the way, or if you are staying in That Phanom, visit Renu as a day trip. From Rte 212, it's 7km west on Rte 2031 (7B by săwngthăew from the junction).

Tha Khaek

ท่าแขก

This Lao town across the river from Nakhon Phanom traces its roots to French colonial construction between 1911 and 1912. Before the war (and during the war until the North Vietnamese Army and Pathet Lao cut the road north to Vientiane), Tha Khaek was a thriving provincial capital and a gambling centre for day-tripping Thais. Today it's a quiet transport and trade outpost with some French colonial architecture, though not nearly as much as in Savannakhet to the south.

If you hold a valid Lao visa, you can catch a 40B ferry ride across the river; the border is open 8.30am to 5pm weekdays and until 12.20pm Saturday. Buses from Tha Khaek to Vientiane take 10 hours. For more information see Lonely Planet's *Laos* guidebook.

THAT PHANOM

ธาตุพนม

That Phanom is 56km south of Nakhon Phanom and 70km southeast of Sakon Nakhon. The centre of activity in this small town is Wat Phra That Phanom.

The short road between Wat Phra That Phanom and the old town on the Mekong River passes under a large Lao arch of victory, which is a miniature version of the arch on Th Lan Xang in Vientiane (which leads to Vientiane's Wat That Luang). This section of That Phanom is interesting, with a smattering of French-Chinese architecture reminiscent of old Vientiane or Saigon.

Hundreds of Lao merchants cross the river for the **market** from around 8.30am to noon on Monday and Thursday. There are two market locations in town, one on the highway near the wát and one on the river north of the pier. The latter is where the Lao congregate on their twice-weekly visits. Exotic offerings include Lao herbal medicines, forest roots, Vietnamese pigs and animal skins; the maddest haggling occurs just before the market closes, when Thai buyers try to take advantage of the Lao's reluctance to carry unsold merchandise back to Laos.

About 20km south of town (turn-off for Wan Yai, between the Km 187 and Km 188 markers) is a wooded park next to **Kaeng Kabao**, a set of rapids in the Mekong River. Nearby hills afford views over the river and to Laos on the other side. The usual food vendors make this a good spot for an impromptu picnic – it's an easy and interesting bicycle ride from That Phanom.

During the **That Phanom Festival** in mid-February, hordes of visitors descend from all over Isan. Lao cross over to visit the wát, Thais cross over to Laos and the town hardly sleeps for seven days.

Information

The **Thai Military** and **Siam Commercial Banks**, both on Th Chayangkun, offer foreign-exchange services and ATMs.

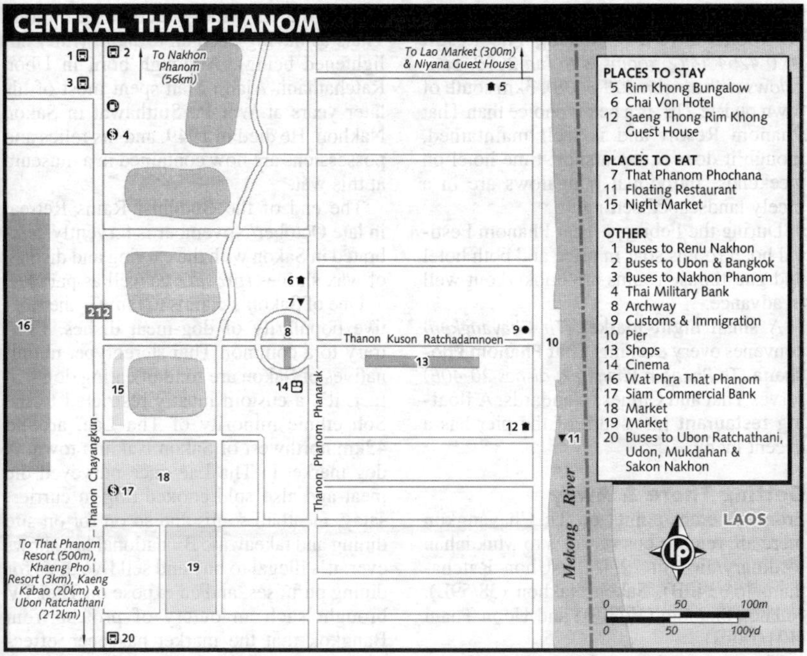

Wat Phra That Phanom

วัดพระธาตุพนม

The centrepiece of this wát is a huge *thâat*, or Lao-style *chedi*, more impressive than any *chedi* in present-day Laos. The monument, which caved in during heavy rains in 1975 and was restored in 1978, is a talismanic symbol of Isan and is highly revered by Buddhists all over Thailand. The age of the wát is disputed, but some archaeologists set it at about 1500 years. The *chedi* is 57m high (or 52m, depending on whom you believe) and the spire is decorated with 110kg of gold. Surrounding the famous *chedi* is a cloister filled with Buddha images and behind the wát is a shady park.

Places to Stay & Eat

Niyana Guest House *(☎ 0 4254 0088; singles/doubles 70/120B)*, opposite Wat Hua Wiang at the northern end of town, offers rooms with shared bath in an old house and a few dorm beds. There's a good information board and a nice upstairs sitting area. Food can be prepared with advanced notice.

Rim Khong Bungalow *(☎ 0 4254 1634; rooms with fan 250B, with air-con 400-500B)* is one block south of Niyana and has basic rooms with fan and slightly better ones with air-con. It seems to act as a second choice when the Niyana is full.

Saeng Thong Rim Khong Guest House *(☎ 0 4252 5614; singles/doubles with fan 250/300B, doubles with air-con 400B)* is near the boat landing and features nine clean rooms in a modern L-shaped building, each with ceiling fan. More expensive rooms have hot-water shower.

Chai Von Hotel *(☎ 0 4254 1391; Th Phanom Phanarak; rooms with/without bath 150/120B, with air-con 350B)*, to the north of the arch (turn left as you pass under it), is an historic little Franco-Chinese–style place with lots of character and friendly, but pretty basic rooms. Rooms have shared or private Thai-style bath. There is one room with air-con and the rate varies, depending on length of stay.

That Phanom Resort *(☎ 0 4254 1047; singles/doubles with fan 250/350B, with air-con 500B)* is on the southern edge of town off Rte 212 on the river, and has rooms in two clean but rather uninspiring buildings. All rooms have TV. **Khaeng Pho Resort** *(☎ 0 4254 1412; rooms with fan 200B, bungalows with air-con 400-800B)*, 3km south of town on Rte 212, is a better choice than That Phanom Resort and is well maintained, though it does act as a short-time hotel on weekends. Individual bungalows are in a nicely landscaped setting.

During the February That Phanom Festival hotel rooms soar in price and both hotel and guesthouse rooms are booked out well in advance.

A small **night market** *(Th Chayangkun)* convenes every evening. **That Phanom Phochana** *(Th Phanom Phanarak; dishes 20-40B)* serves Thai and Chinese standards. A **floating restaurant** just south of the pier has a decent menu.

Getting There & Away

From different points on Th Chayangkun there are regular bus services to Mukdahan (ordinary/air-con 22/46B), Ubon Ratchathani (65/140B), Sakon Nakhon (38/59B), Nakhon Phanom (17/30B) and Udon Thani (121/189B).

The air-con Khorat–Nakhon Phanom bus makes a stop at That Phanom. The fare (264B) is the same as all the way to Nakhon Phanom.

Săwngthăew to That Phanom leave regularly from the intersection near the Nakhon Phanom Hotel in Nakhon Phanom and cost 17B. Stay on the bus until you see the *chedi* on the right. The trip takes about 1½ hours. The last săwngthăew to That Phanom leaves around 6pm; the last vehicle leaves That Phanom for Nakhon Phanom at 8pm.

At the moment only Thai and Lao citizens are permitted to cross the river to/from Laos here.

Sakon Nakhon Province

Sakon Nakhon Province is known among Thais as the one-time home of two of the most famous Buddhist monks in Thai history, Ajahn Man Bhuridatto and Ajahn Fan Ajaro. Both were ascetic *thúdong* monks who were thought to have attained high levels of proficiency in *vipassana* meditation. Ajahn Man is widely recognised among Thais as having been an *arahant* (fully enlightened being). Although born in Ubon Ratchathani, Ajahn Man spent most of his later years at Wat Pa Sutthawat in Sakon Nakhon. He died in 1949, and his relics and possessions are now contained in a museum at this wát.

The end of the Buddhist Rains Retreat in late October/November is fervently celebrated in Sakon with the carving and display of wax shrines *(prasat)*, as well as parades.

One of Sakon's claims to fame is the relative popularity of dog-meat dishes. Contrary to a common Thai stereotype, not all natives of Sakon are fond of eating dog – in fact, it's a custom mostly restricted to the Soh ethnic minority of Tha Lae, around 42km northwest of Sakon Nakhon town. A dog market in Tha Lae once purveyed the meat and also sold cooked dog in curries, satay, meatball soups and so on for on-site dining and takeaway. By national law, however, it's illegal to buy and sell live dogs for dining purposes, and an expose on Thai TV brought such an outcry of protest from Bangkok that the market has been effectively driven underground. Of course, the dog-eating continues, albeit discreetly. If you're able to read Thai, you'll notice the cryptic signs around Tha Lae proclaiming *neúa mii* (literally, 'meat have') or *neúa mòt* ('meat finished') posted in front of places where dog meat is sold.

SAKON NAKHON

สกลนคร

postcode 47000 • pop 67,700

As the secondary agricultural market centre (after Udon Thani) for upper Isan, the provincial capital is mostly a collection of shops selling farm equipment. For most visitors, the only reason to stay in the city is to visit Wat Phra That Choeng Chum and Wat Phra That Narai Jaeng Waeng.

A **city monument** in a field in the northwestern corner of the city centre was obviously inspired by Vientiane's Patuxai or That Phanom's gate. In this case the arch-like structure consists of four big, ornate, cement pillars standing over a bowl filled with *naga* (serpent) beings.

Along the eastern edge of town is **Nong Han**, Thailand's largest natural lake. *Don't* swim in the lake – it's infested with liver flukes, which can cause a nasty liver infection known as opisthorchiasis. The villagers around the lake have among the highest incidences of opisthorchiasis in the world, since many of them eat snails gathered from the lake. These snails play host to the flukes, which bore through human or animal skin and breed in the internal organs. (See Infectious Diseases under Health in the Facts for the Visitor chapter.)

Ajahn Man Museum
พิพิธภัณฑ์พระอาจารย์มั่น

In the grounds of Wat Pa Sutthawat, on the southwestern outskirts of town (off the road to Kalasin), this museum *(open 8am-6pm daily)* contains an exhibition of the personal effects of Thailand's most famous forest monk. The building looks a bit like a modern Christian church, with arches and stained-glass windows. A bronze image of Ajahn Man surrounded by flowers sits on a pedestal at one end. Articles and photos associated with the monk's history are on display behind glass.

Wat Phra That Choeng Chum
วัดพระธาตุเชิงชุม

Next to the Nong Han Lake, this wát features a 25m-high Lao-style *chedi*, which was erected during the Ayuthaya period over a smaller 11th-century Khmer *prang*. To view the *prang* you must enter through the adjacent *wíhăan*. If the door to the *chedi* is locked, ask one of the monks to open it – they're used to having visitors. Around the base of the *prang* is a collection of Lao and Khmer Buddha images.

Also on the grounds is a small Lan Xang-era *bòt* and a *wíhăan* built in the cruciform shape reminiscent of Lanna styles found in northern Thailand. *Lûuk nímít*, spherical ordination-precinct markers that look like cannonballs, are arranged on the grass near the *wíhăan*; next to the monastery's east gate is the base for an original Khmer Shiva-lingam (phallic object).

A drum tower donated by the local Vietnamese population bears upon it the inscription 'Viêt Kieu Luu Liem' – so this wát features Thai, Lao, Vietnamese and Khmer elements.

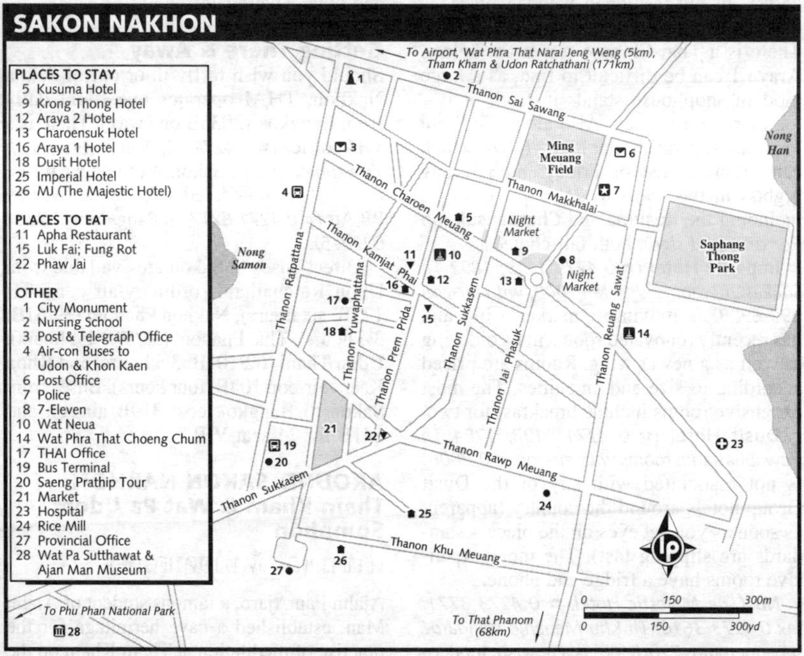

Wat Phra That Narai Jaeng Waeng

วัดพระธาตุนารายณ์แจงแวง

About 5km west of town at Ban That (3km past the airport), this wát has a 10th- to 11th-century Khmer *prang* in the early Bapuan style. Originally part of a Khmer Hindu complex, the five-level sandstone *prang* features a reclining Vishnu lintel over its eastern portico and a dancing Shiva over its northern one.

To get to the temple by public transport, catch a sǎwngthǎew west towards the airport on Th Sai Sawang and get off at Talat Ban That Nawaeng (5B). From there it's a pleasant 1km walk to the wát through a village.

The wát is called Phra That Nawaeng (contraction of Narai Jaeng Waeng) for short.

Places to Stay

Araya 1 *(☎ 0 4271 1097; cnr Th Prem Prida & Th Kamjat Phai; singles/twins with fan 150/250B, with air-con 250/330B)* has rooms that are passable, though it's a bit of a short-time place on weekends. **Araya 2** *(☎ 0 4271 1054; Th Prem Prida; rooms with/without bath 200/150B)*, an old-fashioned wooden place, is diagonally opposite and has rooms with fan. There is a Thai-Chinese restaurant below. Araya 1 can be difficult to find, as a large modern shophouse stands in front of it – look around the back. Also along Th Prem Prida are several similar hotels (all of which can get quite busy on Friday and Saturday nights) in the 150B to 250B price range, including the **Kusuma** and **Charoensuk** *(no Roman-script sign)*, both fair choices.

Imperial Hotel *(☎ 0 4271 1119; 1892 Th Sukkasem; rooms with fan 290B, with air-con 390-690B)* is moving upmarket a bit, and has recently renovated rooms in its old wing as well as a newer wing. Rooms are priced according to size and amenities. The most expensive rooms include breakfast for two.

Dusit Hotel *(☎ 0 4271 1198; 1784 Th Yuwaphattana; rooms with air-con 300-500B)* is not associated with any of the Dusit Group hotels around the country (apparent as soon as you set eyes on the place – standards are slipping fast). The more expensive rooms have a fridge and phone.

MJ *(The Majestic Hotel; ☎ 0 4273 3771, fax 0 4273 3616; Th Khu Meuang; standard/superior rooms 720/840B)* is a newish, modern all air-con hotel offering standard or superior rooms. The more expensive rooms have a small sitting area. If you can afford it, the extra 200B makes quite a difference in standards of cleanliness and service. Additional facilities include a restaurant, cocktail lounge, pub, café, massage, snooker club and karaoke.

Places to Eat

Night markets are open each evening near the roundabout at Th Charoen Meuang and Th Jai Phasuk, and also at the intersection of Th Charoen Meuang and Th Sukkasem. Both markets are very popular nightspots, and are open until late.

Along Th Prem Prida are several inexpensive Thai-Chinese restaurants with passable food at cheap prices. **Phaw Jai** *(dishes 20-30B)*, at the three-way intersection of Th Sukkasem, Th Prem Prida and Th Rawp Meuang, serves a good variety of Thai and Chinese dishes; as do **Luk Fai** *(no Roman-script sign)* and **Fung Rot**, both on Th Kamjat Phai.

Apha Restaurant *(dishes 20-30B)*, about a block west on the opposite side of Th Kamjat Phai, is clean and specialises in curries and other Thai dishes.

Getting There & Away

Should you wish to fly in or out of Sakon Nakhon, THAI operates one flight daily from Bangkok (2035B one way). There is a **THAI office** *(☎ 0 4271 2259–60; 1446/73 Th Yuwaphattana)* in Sakon. In the near future this route is scheduled to be taken over by **PB Air** *(☎ 0 4271 6217, in Bangkok ☎ 0 2261 0222–5)*.

Direct buses to Sakon are available from Ubon Ratchathani (ordinary/air-con 101/173B, six hours), Nakhon Phanom (39/61B, 3½ hours), That Phanom (38/59B 1½ hours), Udon Thani (62/101B, 3½ hours) and Khon Kaen (air-con 104B, four hours). Buses from Sakon to Bangkok cost 319B air-con and 541B for 24-seat VIP.

AROUND SAKON NAKHON

Tham Kham & Wat Pa Udom Somphon

ถ้ำขามและวัดป่าอุดมสมพร

Ajahn Fan Ajaro, a famous student of Ajahn Man, established a cave hermitage for the practise of meditation at Tham Kham on the mountain of Khao Phu Phan, 17km off Hwy 22 (the turn-off comes between the Km 125 and Km 126 markers on Hwy 22 on the way from Udon Thani). He was also affiliated with Wat Pa Udom Somphon in his home district of Phanna Nikhom, 37km from Sakon Nakhon towards Udon Thani off Hwy 22. A **museum** well outside the wát compound at Ban Phanna commemorates the life of Ajahn Fan, who died in 1963. Unlike Wat Pa Sutthawat, which has become a *wát thîaw* (tourist wát), Wat Pa Udom Somphon is still a strict forest meditation monastery. Visitors are welcome to tour the museum, but only those with a serious interest in Buddhism or meditation should enter the compound of the adjacent monastery.

Phu Phan National Park

อุทยานแห่งชาติภูพาน

This 645-sq-km nature reserve *(admission 200B)* is in the Phu Phan mountains near the Sakon Nakhon-Kalasin border. Deer, monkeys and other smaller, forest animals are common to the park, and wild elephants and tigers are occasionally seen as well.

The mountain forests are thick and the area is fairly undeveloped. It has been used as a hiding spot by two guerrilla forces – the Thai resistance against the Japanese in WWII and the PLAT guerrillas in the 1970s.

The park has only a few **hiking trails**, but there are good views along Rte 213 between Sakon Nakhon and Kalasin. Three waterfalls – **Tat Ton**, **Hew Sin Chai** and **Kham Hom** – can be visited fairly easily.

The **Tham Seri Thai** cave was used by the Thai Seri (see WWII & Postwar Periods in the Facts about Thailand chapter) during WWII as an arsenal and mess hall.

Yasothon & Mukdahan Provinces

YASOTHON

อ.เมืองยโสธร

postcode 35000 • pop 22,900

Yasothon is a bit out of the way, but if you happen to be in the area (say, in Ubon Ratchathani, which is about 100km away) during May, it might be worth the two-hour bus trip (from Ubon) to catch the annual **Rocket Festival** that takes place from 8 to 10 May. The festival (Bun Bang Fai in Thai) is prevalent throughout the northeast as a rain and fertility rite, and is celebrated most fervently in Yasothon, where it involves parades and rocket-launching contests. The name of the town, which has the largest Muslim population in the northeast, comes from the Sanskrit 'Yasodhara' (meaning 'preserver or maintainer of glory') and is also the name of one of Krishna's sons by Rukmini in the *Mahabharata*.

In town, **Phra That Phra Anon** (also known as Phra That Yasothon) at Wat Mahathat is a highly venerated Lao-style *chedi*. It's said to be over 1200 years old and to enshrine holy relics of Phra Anon (Ananda), the Buddha's personal attendant monk and one of his chief disciples.

The village of **Ban Si Than** in Pha Tiu district, about 20km east of Yasothon off Rte 202, is renowned for the crafting of firm, triangle-shaped *mǎwn khwǎan,* which are said to rival those of Roi Et.

Phra That Kong Khao Noi

Located in Ban Tat Thong off Hwy 23 (between the Km 194 and Km 195 markers) heading towards Ubon Ratchathani, this a brick-and-stucco *chedi* dating from the late Ayuthaya period. It's name *kawng khâo náwy* actually means 'small sticky-rice basket', a reference to the *chedi's* unusual shape and a local legend. According to an old story, a young farmer who had toiled all morning in the hot sun murdered his mother in a fit of rage when she brought his lunch to the fields late – and in the smallest of sticky-rice baskets. The farmer, eating his lunch over his mother's body, realised that the small basket actually contained much more sticky rice than he could eat. To atone for his deed he then built the *chedi*.

Places to Stay

Yot Nakhon *(☎ 0 4571 1122; 141-143/1-3 Th Uthairamrit; rooms with/without air-con from 300/220B)* is the cleanest and friendliest of Yasothon's cheapies. There are others in this vicinity, and around the market, but all are rather dank and sleazy.

JP Emerald Hotel *(☎ 0 4572 4851, fax 0 4572 4855; Th Jaeng Sanit; rooms 880-1650B)* is Yasothon's newest and most expensive accommodation, offering rooms with air-con and all the amenities. There is a coffee shop and restaurant on the premises.

Getting There & Away

An ordinary bus to Yasothon from Ubon Ratchathani costs 43B (76B air-con); from Khorat it costs 79B (143B air-con).

MUKDAHAN

อ.เมืองมุกดาหาร

postcode 49000 • pop 34,300

Fifty-five kilometres south of That Phanom, 170km north of Ubon Ratchathani and directly opposite the city of Savannakhet in Laos, Mukdahan is known for its beautiful Mekong scenery and as a Thai-Lao trade centre. Among Thais it's most known for the **Talat Indojin** (Indochina Market), a Thai-Lao-Vietnamese affair that gathers around Wat Si Mongkhon Tai near Tha Mukdahan. On weekends the market spills over onto nearby streets; you'll see *khaen* (Isan panpipes) and bolts of cloth from around Isan in addition to the usual Lao, Vietnamese and Chinese imports. The more formal **Danang Market**, in the town centre, contains shopfronts selling many of the same goods.

According to agreements between the Thai, Lao and Vietnamese governments, a bridge between Mukdahan and Savannakhet on the opposite bank of the Mekong should be completed by 2005. Vietnam, Laos and Thailand have likewise agreed to finish development of Laos' Rte 9 to link Mukdahan, Savannakhet and Danang by 2004. Such discussions have prompted lots of construction around town as speculators position themselves for an anticipated economic boom. South of Hotel Muk, the ambitious **Haw Kaew Mukdahan** (Mukdahan Jewel Hall) is a tall needle-shaped shopping and business centre.

For town views, climb the 500m **Phu Narom** hill, 3km south of town. **Phu Mu**, a local picnic spot with scenic views, is 34km south of town off Rte 212 – just south of Ban Taw Khet and the Mukdahan Province line between the Km 29 and Km 30 markers.

Information

The **Bangkok Bank of Commerce** *(Th Samut Sakdarak)* has a currency-exchange service.

CENTRAL MUKDAHAN

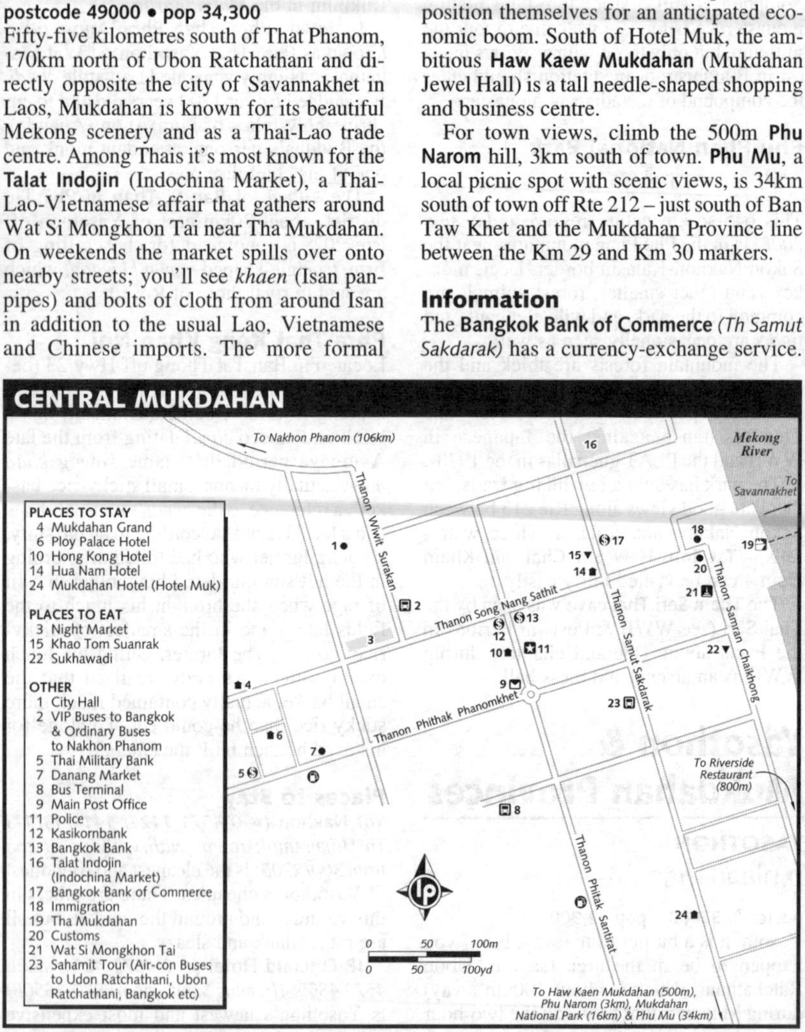

Mukdahan National Park
อุทยานแห่งชาติมุกดาหาร

Formerly known as Phu Pha Thoep National Park, this hilly area of caves and unusual mushroom-shaped rock formations is located 16km south of Mukdahan, off Rte 2034. Two groups of rock formations (Phu Pha Thoep and Hin Thoep) are situated about 200m from the park headquarters. Besides the rock formations, the park *(admission 200B)* is a habitat for barking deer, wild boar, monkeys and civets. About 2km west into the park (and up a hill) is a collection of dozens of small **Buddha images** within a grotto, known as Phu Tham Phra. Nearby is a scenic waterfall, Nam Tok Phu Tham Phra. It takes a couple of hours to walk the well-marked trail from the park headquarters to the grotto and back.

Getting There & Away Unless you have your own wheels, it's kind of difficult to get to the park. Săwngthăew to Amphoe Don Tan (which leave from the bus terminal in Mukdahan every hour between 6am and 2pm) pass the turn-off to the park entrance, but you'll have to walk or hitch the remaining 2km to the park headquarters.

Places to Stay
If you've come to Mukdahan with the intention of crossing over to Savannakhet in Laos, you might as well press ahead, as there are more atmospheric hotels to be found there. If you get stuck in Mukdahan, there are a handful of decent choices.

Hua Nam Hotel *(☎ 0 4261 1197; 20 Th Samut Sakdarak; singles/doubles with fan 200/220B, with air-con 250/300B)* has passable rooms that see lots of action on Friday and Saturday nights. Unless you're really pinching your baht, spend a bit more and sleep on clean sheets at another hotel.

Hong Kong Hotel *(☎ 0 4261 1143; 161/1-2 Phitak Santirat; rooms with fan 160B)* is similar in function to the Hua Nam but a bit nicer. All rooms come with TV.

Mukdahan Hotel *(Hotel Muk; ☎ 0 4261 1619; Th Samut Sakdarak; rooms with fan 180B, with air-con 300-450B)* is still the best deal in town, although it's a little away from the centre of town. Rooms are clean and the staff friendly. Rooms with air-con all have TV and hot-water shower. Larger rooms with fridge are the most expensive.

A couple of upmarket hotels seem to be begging for business. **Ploy Palace Hotel** *(☎ 0 4261 1329; Th Phithak Phanomkhet; rooms from 1500B, discount rate 900B)* features impressive marble-and-wood public areas, and 150 rooms outfitted with stereo TV, fridge, air-con and hot water, (discounted by 50% when business is slow). The nearby **Mukdahan Grand** *(☎ 0 4261 2020, fax 0 4261 6021; Th Song Nang Sathit; rooms 750-2700B)* is similar to Ploy Palace, but has larger rooms.

Places to Eat
The **night market** along Th Song Nang Sathit has *kài yâang, sôm-tam, khâo jìi* (Lao baguette sandwiches) and *pàw-pía* (Vietnamese spring rolls), either fresh *(sòt)* or fried *(thâwt)*. **Khao Tom Suanrak**, next to Hua Nam Hotel, is a Chinese rice-soup place that's open all night.

South of the pier along the river is a string of moderately priced indoor-outdoor restaurants, including the well-patronised **Sukhawadi** *(☎ 0 4261 1882; Th Samran Chaikhong; dishes 40-90B)*, which closes at 9.30pm. **Riverside** *(☎ 0 4261 2845)*, also on the river and about 1km south of the pier, has a shady outdoor area with a view of Savannakhet. The menu covers mostly Thai and Chinese dishes, but *lâap* (spicy minced meat salad) is also served. Prices are moderate and the beer is cold. It stays open until 11pm.

Getting There & Away
There are frequent buses from either direction – 42B ordinary (70B air-con) from Nakhon Phanom, half that price from That Phanom and 55B (105B air-con) from Ubon Ratchathani.

VIP (sleeper) buses to Bangkok (565B) and ordinary buses to Nakhon Phanom leave from the intersection of Th Wiwit Surakan and Th Song Nang Sathit, near the government-bus office. **Sahamit Tour** *(Th Samut Sakdarak)* has air-con buses to Bangkok, Nakhon Phanom, Udon Thani, Ubon Ratchathani and Sakon Nakhon.

SAVANNAKHET (LAOS)
Just across the Mekong from Mukdahan, this Lao city of 45,000 is the capital of Savannakhet Province in southern Laos, and a major relay point for trade between Thailand and Vietnam.

The 570km Rte 9 extends east all the way to the Vietnamese border at Lao Bao, where it continues eastward to the port of Dong Ha on the lower Gulf of Tonkin. If you have the proper visas, this is the easiest route to go overland between Thailand and Vietnam. Visas for Laos and Vietnam are available in Bangkok and Khon Kaen, but you cannot get a Lao visa in Mukdahan.

Like Luang Prabang, Savannakhet has a fair number of French colonial and Franco-Chinese buildings, but with less of a Western presence and fewer tourists.

Places to Stay

Sayamungkhun Guest House *(Th Latsawongseuk; rooms US$5-6)*, where the sign out the front reads simply 'Guest House', is near the centre of town and is good value. All rooms in this well-kept villa come with bath and air-con, and cost the Lao kip equivalent of the listed US-dollar rate.

Getting There & Away

Ferries cross the Mekong between Savannakhet and Mukdahan frequently between 9am and 3.30pm Monday to Saturday, and 10.30am to 3pm on Sunday (50B). From Savannakhet it is possible to catch a bus north to Vientiane, south to Pakse or east to Vietnam. For more information on Savannakhet, see Lonely Planet's *Laos* guidebook.

Ubon Ratchathani Province

Ubon Ratchathani is the northeast's largest province and its provincial capital is one of the larger towns in Thailand. About 300km of the province shares a border with Laos and around 60km borders Cambodia. The local TAT office is trying to promote the area where the three countries meet as the 'Emerald Triangle' in counterpart to northern Thailand's Golden Triangle. The 'emerald' ostensibly refers to the hundreds of square kilometres of intact monsoon forest in this part of the province – an area that has been sparsely populated because of war tensions. Now that the Khmer Rouge has disappeared from the scene, travel in the tri-border zone is safe.

Mekong

The Thai name for the river is Mae Nam Khong. Mae Nam means river (literally, Water Mother) and Khong is its name (from the Sanskrit *ganga*). The Thais themselves sometimes shorten the name to 'Maekhong' (on the Laos side they prefer 'Nam Khong'), hence the Western term 'Mekong River' is, in some ways, redundant. By agreement between the Thai and Lao governments, all islands in the Mekong – including sandbars that appear only in the dry season – belong to Laos.

Ubon's Mae Nam Mun and Mae Nam Chi river basins were centres for Dvaravati and Khmer cultures many centuries ago. Following the decline of the Khmer empires, the area was settled by groups of Lao in 1773 and 1792. By the early Ratanakosin era it had become part of *monthon* Ubon, a southeastern Isan satellite state extending across what are now Surin, Si Saket and Ubon Provinces – as well as parts of southern Laos – with Champasak, Laos, as *monthon* capital. Today the Lao influence in the province predominates over the Khmer.

UBON RATCHATHANI

อ.เมืองอุบลราชธานี

postcode 34000 • pop 109,800

Ubon (sometimes spelt Ubol – the 'l' is pronounced like an 'n') is 557km from Bangkok, 271km from Nakhon Phanom and 311km from Khorat. Situated on the banks of the Mae Nam Mun – Thailand's second-longest waterway after the Mekong – Ubon is a financial, educational, communications and agricultural market centre for eastern Isan. Like Udon Thani and Khorat, it served as a US air base in the Vietnam War days. The main attractions are a few wát and a national museum. Now that the Thai-Lao border crossing at nearby Chong Mek is open to foreigners, Ubon is receiving more and more travellers who are finding it a good place to decompress after the comparatively rustic food and accommodation of southern Laos.

Ubon's **Candle Festival** is actually a parade of gigantic, elaborately carved wax sculptures that is held during Khao Phansa, a Buddhist holiday marking the commencement of *phansăa*, the Rains Retreat (Buddhist Lent), in July. The festival is very popular with Thai tourists and the city's hotel rooms are often all booked for the event.

Information

The **TAT** (*☎ 0 4524 3770; 264/1 Th Kheuan Thani; open 8.30am-4.30pm daily*) has a very helpful branch office here, opposite the Sri Kamol Hotel. The office distributes free maps of Ubon, and information handouts about Si Saket and Yasothon Provinces also. The local **tourist-police office** (*☎ 0 4524 5505, emergency ☎ 1155; Th Suriyat*) is directly behind the police station.

Ubon's main **post office** (*open 8.30am-4.30pm Mon-Fri, 9am-noon Sat & Sun*) is near the intersection of Th Luang and Th Si Narong. The **telephone office** (*open 7am-11pm daily*) is next door.

A handful of places with Internet access are located on Th Saphasit.

The **Rom Kao Hospital** (*Th Uparat*) near the bridge is the best medical facility in the lower northeast.

Ubon National Museum

พิพิธภัณฑสถานแห่งชาติอุบลราชธานี

Housed in a former palace of the Rama VI era, west of the TAT office, Ubon National Museum (*Th Kheuan Thani; admission 30B; open 9am-4pm Wed-Sun*) is a good place to learn about Ubon's history and culture before exploring the city or province. Most of

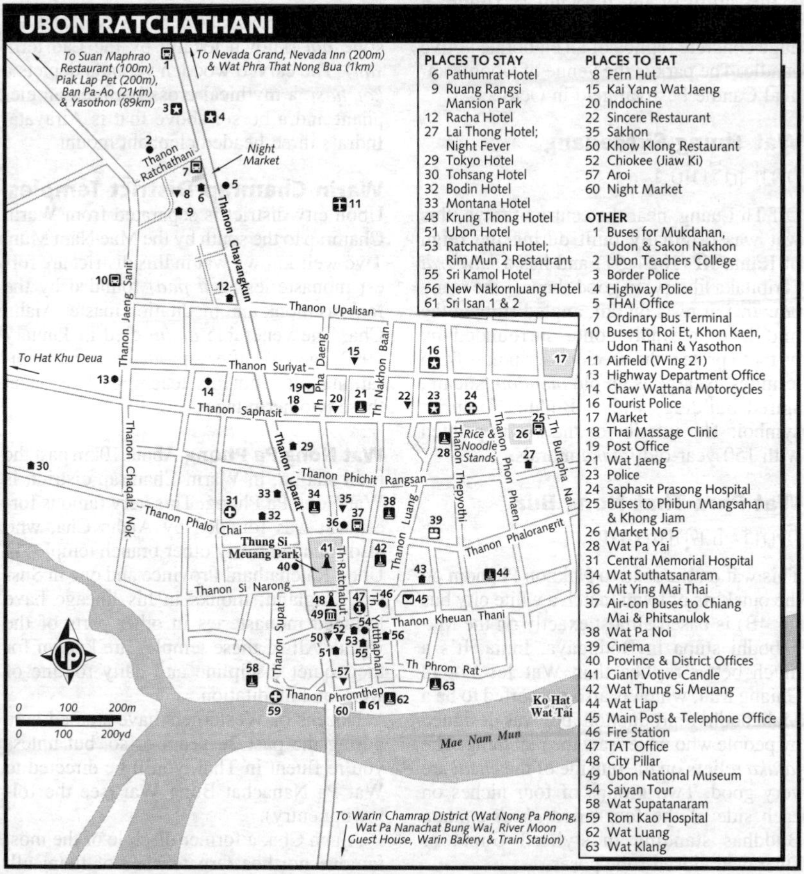

the exhibits have bilingual labels. Flanking the main entrance are a large Buddhist ordination-precinct stone from the Dvaravati period and some Pallava-inscribed pillars from the Khmer era. A prehistory room displays stone and bronze implements, burial urns and 1500- to 3000-year-old pottery from the northeast. Another gallery contains many of the real treasures of mainland Southeast Asian art, including Hindu-Khmer sculpture from the Chenla and Angkor eras, Lao Buddhas, Ubon textiles, local musical instruments and folk utensils (eg, rice containers, fish traps and betel nut holders).

Among the museum's most prized possessions are a rare standing Dvaravati Buddha image and a Dong Son bronze drum.

Just north of the museum is **Thung Si Meuang Park**, the centrepiece of which is a huge concrete replica of an elaborate votive candle. The park is the venue of Ubon's annual Candle Festival held in October.

Wat Thung Si Meuang
วัดทุ่งศรีเมือง

Off Th Luang, near the centre of town, this wát was originally built during the reign of Rama III (1824–51) and has a *hăw trai* (Tripitaka library) in good shape. Like many *hăw trai,* it rests on tall, angled stilts in the middle of a small pond, surrounded by water to protect the precious scriptures from termites. Nearby is an old *mondòp* (square, spired building) with a Buddha footprint symbol. The interior of the *bòt* is painted with 150-year-old *jataka* murals.

Wat Phra That Nong Bua
วัดพระธาตุหนองบัว

This wát on the road to Nakhon Phanom on the outskirts of town (catch a white city bus for 4B) is based almost exactly on the Mahabodhi stupa in Bodhgaya, India. It's a much better replica than Wat Jet Yot in Chiang Mai, which is also purported to be a Mahabodhi reproduction, but was designed by people who never saw the real thing. The *jataka* reliefs on the outside of the *chedi* are very good. Two groups of four niches on each side of the four-sided *chedi* contain Buddhas standing in stylised Gupta or Dvaravati closed-robe poses.

Wat Supatanaram
วัดสุปัฎนาราม

Called Wat Supat for short, the unique 19th-century *bòt* at this temple features a mix of Khmer, European and Thai styles. In contrast to the usual Thai- or Lao-style temple structures of the region, the *bòt* is made entirely of stone, like the early Khmer stone *prasat*, and the roof corners display dragons.

On display in the *bòt* is one of Thailand's oldest surviving Khmer stone carvings, a lushly carved stone lintel dating to the 7th century. In front of the *bòt* stands the largest wooden bell in Thailand.

Wat Jaeng
วัดแจ้ง

This wát *(Th Saphasit)* has a typical Lao-style *bòt* (known locally by the Lao term *sĭm*). The carved wooden veranda depicts a *kotchasi,* a mythical cross between an elephant and a horse; above that is Airavata, Indra's three-headed elephant mount.

Warin Chamrap District Temples

Ubon city district is separated from Warin Chamrap to the south by the Mae Nam Mun. Two well-known wát in this district are forest monasteries *(wát pàa)* founded by the famous monk and meditation master Ajahn Cha. The venerable *ajahn* died in January 1992, aged 75, after a productive and inspirational life, but his teachings live on at these two hermitages.

Wat Nong Pa Phong About 10km past the train station, in Warin Chamrap district, is Wat Nong Pa Phong. This very famous forest wát was founded by Ajahn Cha, who also founded many other branch temples in Ubon Ratchathani Province and one in Sussex, England; monks in his lineage have founded monasteries in other parts of the world. All of these temples are known for their quiet discipline and daily routine of work and meditation.

Dozens of Westerners have studied here during the past 20 years or so, but unless you're fluent in Thai, you'll be directed to Wat Pa Nanachat Bung Wai (see the following entry).

Ajahn Cha, a former disciple of the most famous northeastern teacher of them all,

Ajahn Man, was known for his simple and direct teaching method that seemed to cross all international barriers. His funeral, which was held here, drew thousands of followers from around the world.

The wát features a small **museum** and a *chedi* where Ajahn Cha's ashes are interred. To get to the wát from Ubon, take a pink city bus No 3 to the ordinary-bus terminal, then catch a sǎwngthǎew going to the wát.

Wat Pa Nanachat Bung Wai The abbot here is Australian and most of the monks are European, American or Japanese. As English is the main language spoken here, Wat Pa Nanachat is a better place to visit than Wat Nong Pa Phong if you don't speak Thai and are interested in more than sightseeing. The wát is very clean, cool and quiet.

Generally only those with a serious interest in Buddhism – preferably with previous practical experience – are permitted to stay overnight. Both men and women are welcome. Write in advance to avoid disappointment (Wat Pa Nanachat, Ban Bung Wai, Amphoe Warin, Ubon Ratchathani 34310); during the March-to-May hot season monks go into retreat and overnight guests aren't usually accepted.

From Ubon, take a white city bus No 1 south down Th Uparat, cross the bridge over the Mae Nam Mun and get off as the bus turns right in Warin Chamrap for the train station. From there, catch any sǎwngthǎew heading south (though heading west eventually, on Rte 2193 towards Si Saket) and ask to be let off at Wat Pa Nanachat – everybody knows it. You can also get there by catching a Si Saket bus from Ubon for 8B to Bung Wai, the village across the road from Wat Pa Nanachat.

There is a sign in English at the edge of the road – the wát is in the forest behind the rice fields. You can also hire a túk-túk direct to the wát from town for about 100B.

Ko Hat Wat Tai

เกาะหาดวัดใต้

This is a small island in the Mae Nam Mun on the southern edge of town. During the hot and dry months, from March to May, it is a favourite **picnic spot** and there are 'beaches' where you can **swim**. You can get here by boat from the northern shore of the river.

Hat Khu Deua

หาดคูเดื่อ

Hat Khu Deua is a 'beach' area on the northern bank of the river west of town, off Th Liang Meuang. Several thatched *sǎalaa* (pavilions) offer shade for picnicking or napping by the river; you can even stay overnight in simple raft houses at no charge.

Traditional Massage The **Thai Massage Clinic** *(☎ 0 4525 4746; 369-371 Th Saphasit; open 9am-9pm daily)* offers traditional-style massage. Rates are 100B per hour.

Ubon also has several *àap òp nûat* (bathe-steam-massage) places that probably got their start when a US air base was located outside town. The most notorious is the Pathumrat Hotel's **Long Beach** *(Th Chayangkun)*, which Ta Mok and other Khmer Rouge commanders visited regularly until Pol Pot finally kicked the bucket.

Places to Stay – Budget

River Moon Guest House *(☎ 0 4428 6093; 43 Th Sisaket; rooms 100-200B)* is located across the Mae Nam Mun, near the train station in Warin Chamrap. It's in a rustic wooden house and gets lots of travellers on their way to/from Laos. All rooms come with fan, and bathrooms are shared.

Sri Isan 1 & 2 *(☎ 0 4525 4204, 0 4524 2444; 60-66 Th Ratchabut; singles/doubles with fan 100/150B, with air-con 260B)* is a good budget choice and rooms have private bath; the rooms with air-con are in a separate building. The mosaic railing on the staircase in the old wing is worth a look.

New Nakornluang Hotel *(☎ 0 4525 4768; 84-88 Th Yutthaphan; rooms with fan/air-con 190/270B)* has decent rooms with private bath. The more expensive rooms with fan have TV.

Tokyo Hotel *(☎ 0 4524 1739; 178 Th Uparat; old-building rooms with fan/air-con 250/300B, new-building rooms with fan 350B, with air-con 450-800B)* is well kept, near the town centre and preferable to all the foregoing hotels if you can afford it. There are comfortable rooms in the old building with fan and bath, or with air-con and TV. In the new building there are rooms with fan, or rooms with air-con, TV and fridge.

Places to Stay – Mid-Range

Racha Hotel *(☎ 0 4525 4155; 149/21 Th Chayangkun; singles/doubles with fan 280/350B, with air-con 400/500B)* is a friendly place north of the town centre, and has clean rooms with bath.

Krung Thong Hotel *(☎ 0 4525 4200; Th Si Narong; rooms with fan 280B, doubles with air-con 450B)*, near Wat Thung Si Meuang, is a clean and comfortable place offering rooms with TV.

Nevada Inn *(☎ 0 4531 3351; Th Chayangkun; air-con rooms 650B)*, opposite (and owned by) the more expensive Nevada Grand, is a good mid-range choice with comfortable, newish rooms and helpful staff.

Ubon Hotel *(Kao Chan; ☎ 0 4524 1045; 333 Th Kheuan Thani; singles with fan 280-400B, with air-con 350-450B)* used to be the city's number-one lodgings but has gone steadily downhill over the years. Singles – some quite OK, others rather dank – have a bath and a choice of fan or air-con.

Ratchathani Hotel *(☎ 0 4524 4388; 297 Th Kheuan Thani; singles/doubles with fan 330/450B, with air-con 500/650B)* is similar in price to the Ubon Hotel but in better condition, having recently undergone renovations. The Rim Mun restaurant next door is a plus.

Ruang Rangsi Mansion Park *(☎ 0 4524 4745–7; apartments per night 400-450B, per month 3800-4300B)*, in the Ruang Rangsi Complex off Th Ratchathani, offers apartments with air-con for rent by the day or month. The landscaped grounds are conveniently adjacent to the Fern Hut restaurant, various shops and a branch post office.

Sri Kamol Hotel *(Si Kamon; ☎ 0 4524 1136; 22/2 Th Ubonsak; rooms 450-550B)*, near the Ratchathani Hotel, has decent rooms with all the amenities; discounts are available for stays of longer than three days.

Phathumrat Hotel *(☎ 0 4524 1501; 337 Th Chayangkun; singles/doubles 800/1000B)*, once the top-end hotel in Ubon, has slid into the mid-range. The staff are friendly; however, the rooms are not great for these prices, though breakfast is included in the price.

Places to Stay – Top End

Tohsang Hotel *(☎ 0 4524 1925, fax 0 4524 4814; 251 Th Phalo Chai; rooms 950-1700B)* offers large, pleasant rooms with air-con, TV and fridge, including breakfast. Facilities include a coffee shop and Chinese restaurant.

Lai Thong Hotel *(☎ 0 4526 4271, fax 0 4526 4270; 50 Th Phichit Rangsan; singles/doubles 1200/1300B)* has comfortable rooms with all the amenities, including breakfast. There's a swimming pool on the premises.

Nevada Grand *(☎ 0 4528 0999, fax 283424; 434 Th Chayangkun; rooms 900-1600B)* is a relatively new luxury hotel. Formerly part of the Felix chain, the hotel's standards don't seem to have slipped with the new management. Decked-out rooms include breakfast.

Places to Eat

Regional Ubon is famous for its Isan food – many Thai gourmets claim it has the best in all of Isan. *Lâap pèt* (spicy duck salad) is the local speciality, often eaten with *tôm fák* (squash soup) and Chinese mushrooms. Good places for *lâap pèt* include **Jak Kan Lap Pet** *(Th Suriyat)*, **Piak Lap Pet** *(Th Jaeng Sanit)*, next to a radio relay station, and **Suan Maphrao**, near the Km 288 marker on the road to Yasothon.

Kai Yang Wat Jaeng *(Th Suriyat)*, a block north of Wat Jaeng, is considered by everyone in town to be the best purveyor of *kài yâang* (grilled Lao-style chicken), another dish that Ubon is also big on. The chicken is sold from 9am to 2pm only, after which the vendor switches to curries. Other specialities include *hàw mòk* (soufflé-like curry steamed in banana leaves) – choice of fish *(plaa)*, or chicken *(kài)*.

Sakhon *(☎ 0 4524 1101; Th Pha Daeng; dishes 40-60B)*, near the provincial courthouse, is a simple and long-running Ubon institution, with a full array of Isan dishes available. A favourite with local Thai families, there's also an English menu.

Indochine *(no Roman-script sign; ☎ 0 4525 4126; Th Saphasit; open 10am-6pm daily)*, near Wat Jaeng, specialises in tasty Vietnamese food, including good-value set meals.

Sincere Restaurant *(Th Saphasit; open 9am-11pm Mon-Sat)* is an air-con place a little further east along the same side of the road as Indochine, and serves interesting Thai-French cuisine.

Noodles & Rice Next to the Ratchathani Hotel, **Rim Mun 2** *(Th Kheuan Thani; dishes 20-30B)* is a late-night *khâo tôm* restaurant that can prepare just about any Thai or Chinese dish that you can name.

Aroi *(no Roman-script sign; Th Ratchabut; buffet 30-50B)*, located towards the southern end of the road, has a good Thai-Chinese buffet.

The cheapest string of **rice and noodle** places in town runs along Th Saphasit just opposite Saphasit Prasong Hospital.

Vegetarian Located in front of the Ubon Hotel, **Khow Klong Restaurant** *(dishes 15-25B)* offers pre-cooked vegetarian food that you can point out and have served with rice. It's only open during the day.

Breakfasts & Bakeries The French-Lao influence in Ubon means people are somewhat more accustomed to pastries and Western breakfasts than in many parts of Thailand. **Chiokee** *(Jiaw Ki; Th Kheuan Thani; dishes 20-30B)* is very popular among local office workers for both Chinese and Western breakfasts: it serves everything from *khâo tôm* to ham and eggs. *Jók* is a speciality.

Fern Hut *(☎ 0 4524 4305)*, down a lane opposite the teachers' college *(wíthayaalai khruu)*, sells good cakes and other baked items, plus Thai dishes. It closes at 10pm.

Warin Bakery *(Th Pathumthepphakdi)*, in Warin, near a Bangkok Bank branch, offers decent baked goods, coffee and breakfasts.

Night Markets Ubon has two night markets that are open from dusk to dawn, one by the river near the bridge (*tàlàat yài* or big market), and the other near the bus terminal on Th Chayangkun – convenient to hotels on Th Chayangkun and Th Suriyat.

Shopping

One of the major local specialities is silver betel-nut containers moulded using the lost-wax process. The **Ubon National Museum** *(Th Kheuan Thani)* has a good exhibit of locally produced betel boxes; to see them being made visit Ban Pa-Ao, a ilversmithing village between Yasothon and Ubon off Hwy 23.

Phanchat *(☎ 0 4524 3433; 158 Th Ratchabut)* carries a range of Ubon handicrafts, although it specialises in hand-woven fabrics, as does **Mit Ying Mai Thai** *(cnr Th Phalorangrit & Th Pha Daeng)*.

Getting There & Away

Air THAI has three daily flights from Bangkok to Ubon. The fare is 1895B and the flight takes an hour and five minutes. The **THAI office** *(☎ 0 4531 3340–4; 364 Th Chayangkun)* operates a shuttle van between its city office and the airport.

Bus Ordinary buses to Ubon from Bangkok cost 180B to 226B (depending on the route) and leave the Northern bus terminal in Bangkok hourly from around 4.30am to nearly midnight. First-class air-con buses cost 401B, and leave twice in the morning (8.30am and 9.30am) and eight times in the evening between 7.45pm and 11pm. There is one 520B VIP departure nightly at 8pm. From Ubon's **ordinary bus terminal** *(Th Chayangkun)*, there are morning and evening departures of air-con buses for Bangkok.

Other fares to/from Ubon are in the table on the following page. Some fares differ according to alternative routes taken between the same terminals – longer routes are usually cheaper – or class of air-con service.

Train The Ubon Ratchathani express leaves Bangkok nightly at 9pm, arriving in Ubon at 7.40am the next morning.

The basic 1st-class fare is 460B and 2nd class is 221B, excluding surcharges for express service or a sleeping berth.

Rapid trains leave at 6.40am, 6.45pm and 10.45pm, arriving in Ubon about 11 hours later. There is no 1st class on the rapid trains. Ordinary trains take only about an hour longer to reach Ubon. There are two departures daily in either direction; the fare is 95B.

Rapid train services from Khorat leave at 12.23am, 4.21am and 12.24pm, arriving in Ubon Ratchathani at 5.40am, 10am and 5.45pm respectively. The basic fares for rapid trains are 45/106B in 2nd/3rd class.

Ordinary trains to Bangkok leave Ubon at 6.55am and 1.05pm, arriving in Bangkok about 12 hours later. Rapid trains leave at 5pm and 7.15pm. One express train departs from Ubon for Bangkok nightly at 6.10pm. The basic fare is 95/221B for 3rd/2nd class.

Ubon's train station is in Warin Chamrap; take a white No 2 city bus (5B) to reach Th Chayangkun in Ubon's city centre.

Getting Around

A city bus system runs large buses along the main avenues (5B) – very convenient for getting from one end of town to the other cheaply. Săamláw around town cost around 30B per kilometre.

Motorbikes, vans and cars can be rented at **Chaw Wattana** (*☎ 0 4524 1906; 39/8 Th Suriyat*).

Bus Fares to/from Ubon

destination	fare (B)
Buriram	
ordinary	66
air-con	148
Kantharalak (for Khao Phra Wihan)	
ordinary	20
Khong Jiam	
ordinary	40
Khon Kaen	
ordinary	96
air-con	198
Khorat	
ordinary	149
air-con	260
Mukdahan	
ordinary	55
air-con	105
Phibun Mangsahan	
ordinary	22
Prakhon Chai (for Phanom Rung)	
ordinary	84
Roi Et	
ordinary	61
air-con	99
Sakon Nakhon	
ordinary	101
air-con	173
Si Saket	
ordinary	29
air-con	40 to 60
Surin	
ordinary	72
air-con	129
That Phanom	
ordinary	65
air-con	140
Udon Thani	
ordinary	122
air-con	219
Yasothon	
ordinary	43
air-con	76

NORTHEASTERN THAILAND

AROUND UBON PROVINCE

Phibun Mangsahan to Khong Jiam

The small riverside district of Khong Jiam is 75km east of Ubon via Rte 217 – to Phibun Mangsahan and then over the Mae Nam Mun by bridge at the western end of Rte 2222. Visitors often stop in Phibun to see a set of rapids called **Kaeng Sapheu** next to the river crossing. Phibun Mangsahan is also the location of the Ubon immigration office; visa extensions as well as exit visas (for crossings into Laos) are available here. The office is about 1km from town on the way south to Chong Mek – look for a large communications antenna nearby.

Ban Khawn Sai, 500m west of Phibun on Rte 217 between the Km 23 and Km 24 markers, is a small village whose main livelihood is the forging of bronze gongs for temples and classical Thai music ensembles. You can watch the gong-makers hammering the flat metal discs into beautiful instruments and tempering them in rustic fires – often in temporary shelters just off the road. Should you care to make a purchase or two, small gongs cost 400B to 500B each, larger ones 4000B to 5000B; the huge 2m gongs run as high as 50,000B.

Ban Pa-Ao Northwest of Ubon on Hwy 23, is another village that produces household utensils of brass using the lost-wax casting method. The turn-off for the village is near the Km 19 marker on Hwy 23 – from there it is another 3km to the village. Nearly all buses to Yasothon pass this way.

Further east along Rte 2222 you can stop at **Nam Tok Sae Hua Maew** and **Wat Tham Hew Sin Chai**. The latter is a cave temple with a waterfall cascading over the front of the cave; it's just a 2km walk southwest of Khong Jiam. Other waterfalls in Ubon Province are **Nam Tok Pak Taew** in Nam Yeun district – a tall vertical drop – and the low but wide **Nam Tok Tat Ton**.

Khong Jiam At the confluence of the Mae Nam Mun and the Mekong, Khong Jiam sits on a picturesque peninsula formed by these rivers. Huge conical fish traps are made here for local use – they look very much like the fish traps that appear in the 3000-year-old murals at Pha Taem (see the Pha Taem National Park entry later in this

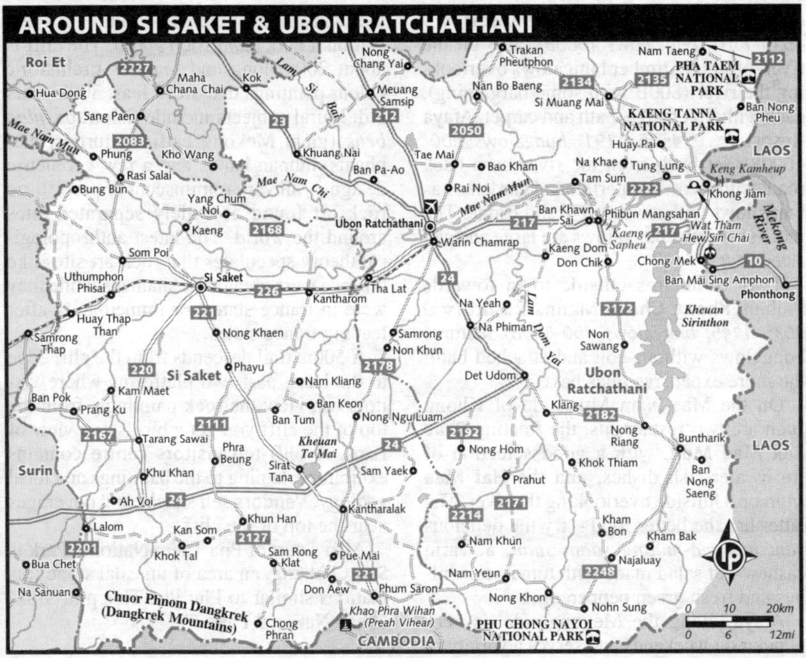

section). Thais visit Khong Jiam to see the so-called **Mae Nam Song Si** (Two Colour River), the contrasting coloured currents formed at the junction of the Mae Nam Mun and the Mekong. Along the Mekong side is a simple but pleasant park with benches and **food vendors**.

For 200B to 300B per hour you can charter 15-person capacity long-tail boats from a landing next to the Pak Mun Restaurant to see Two Colour River and various small river islands; Thais can cross the Mekong to Laos. While this is not an official crossing for foreigners, it is sometimes possible to persuade boatmen to take you to the Lao village across the river for an hour or two, especially during Buddhist festival days, when regulations get lax. (Foreigners are, however, officially permitted to cross into Laos 32km further south at Chong Mek.)

Places to Stay & Eat In Phibun Mangsahan, near the bus stop in the centre of town, **Phiboonkit Hotel** (☎ *0 4544 1201; rooms with fan 200B, singles/doubles with air-con 300/350B)* has rooms with fan and bath, as well as air-con rooms. It's a bit of a short-time place, and can be noisy on Friday and Saturday nights.

Sanamchai Guest House (☎ *0 4544 1289; rooms with fan 200B, with air-con 300B)*, 3km north of Phibun, has rather worn bungalows and gets a fair bit of short-time traffic on weekends, but it's friendly and cheap. There's a pub and a garden restaurant opposite the guesthouse.

Near the bridge to Rte 2222 is a simple **restaurant** famous for *saalaapao* (Chinese buns) and *năng kòp* (frog skin, usually fried). Thais visiting Pha Taem like to stop here on the way to stock up on these items.

Apple Guest House (☎ *0 4535 1160; Th Kaewpradit; rooms with fan/air-con 150/300B)*, in Khong Jiam, has a total of 16 basic but comfortable rooms, all with attached bath, in a couple of buildings off the main road. Rates are reasonable; windows are screened, and soap and towels provided. Motorbikes are available for rent and there is a restaurant nearby.

Khong Jiam Guest House (☎ *0 4535 1074; rooms with fan 150B, with air-con 350B)* is a friendly, motel-like place near the river, where rooms have a bath, and air-con rooms come with TV. **Ban Rim Khong Resort** *(☎ 0 4535 1101; bungalows 1000B)*, also on the river, offers six timber bungalows overlooking the river (800B with some bargaining), each with TV, fridge, bath and carpet. **Araya Resort** *(☎ 0 4535 1191; bungalows 500-1000B)*, set back from the river on a back road, with its own waterfall and gardens, has bungalows with air-con, TV and fridge. The more expensive bungalows are large and can sleep four.

Two kilometres outside town towards Phibun, **Khong Chiam Marina Resort** *(☎ 0 4535 1145; bungalows 450-500B)* features bungalows with air-con and attached bath; the more expensive ones have TV.

On the Mae Nam Mun side of Khong Jiam are two restaurants, the floating **Phae Rak Mae Mun**, with a good selection of freshwater fish dishes, and the **Hat Mae Mun** on a hillside overlooking the river. The latter has the better food – try the delicious *yam mét má-mûang sǎam sǔan*, a warm cashew-nut salad made with tomatoes, chillies and fresh green peppercorns.

Araya, along the Mekong side, is very popular on weekends and serves a variety of freshwater fish, Thai-Lao standards, river turtle *(tà-phâap náam)* and wild pig. Depending on how you feel about eating wildlife versus penned protein, you may want to avoid this one. **Pak Mun** and **Mae Nam Song Si** are two other restaurants in this vicinity.

Getting There & Away From Ubon, direct buses to Khong Jiam (74km) cost 40B and leave from the Warin Market or the bus queue behind the Lai Thong Hotel.

When direct buses aren't running to Khong Jiam, catch a Phibun bus (22B) from Ubon's train station in Warin between 5am and 3.30pm, and change to a Khong Jiam bus (20B) in Phibun.

If you're driving or cycling to Khong Jiam from the Sirinthon Reservoir area via Rtes 217 and 2396, you'll have to cross the Mae Nam Mun by vehicle ferry (look for the sign that says 'ferpy boat'). The ferry is 40B per vehicle.

Pha Taem National Park

อุทยานแห่งชาติผาแต้ม

In Khong Jiam district, 94km northeast of Ubon, is a tall stone cliff called Pha Taem – the centrepiece of the 340-sq-km Pha Taem National Park *(admission 200B)*. The cliff is about 200m long and features **prehistoric** colour paintings that are at least 3000 years old. Mural subjects include fish traps, *plaa bèuk* (giant Mekong catfish), turtles, elephants, human hands and a few geometric designs – all very reminiscent of prehistoric rock art found at widely separated sites around the world. The latest anthropological theory speculates that rock-art sites like this one were created by shamans while they were in trance states, or immediately after leaving trance states.

A 500m trail descends from the cliff edge to the base, past two platforms where visitors can view the rock paintings; from the top of the cliff you get a bird's eye view of Laos. A cliff-top **visitors centre** contains exhibits pertaining to the paintings and local geology. **Vendors** sell snacks and beverages near the top of the cliff.

Also a part of Pha Taem National Park is **Sao Chaliang**, an area of unusual stone formations similar to Phu Pha Thoep in Mukdahan National Park.

Places to Stay If you have your own equipment, **camping** is permitted in a designated area near the park headquarters between the turn-off from Rte 2112 and the visitors centre.

Getting There & Away Pha Taem is 20km beyond Khong Jiam via Rte 2112, but there's no direct public transport there. The bus from Ubon to Khong Jiam will pass the final turn-off to Pha Taem on request; then you can walk or hitch 5km to the cliff.

By car, bike or motorbike from Ubon, go east on Rte 217 to Phibun Mangsahan, then turn left and head north across the Mae Nam Mun on Rte 2222 and follow this road to Khong Jiam.

From Khong Jiam, take Rte 2134 northwest to Ban Huay Phai and then go northeast at the first turn-off to Pha Taem.

Chong Mek & the Emerald Triangle

ช่องเม็กและสามเหลี่ยมมรกต

South of Khong Jiam, via Rte 217, is the small trading town of Chong Mek on the Thai-Lao border. If you possess a valid Lao visa, Chong Mek is the only place in Thailand where you can cross into Laos by land (that is, you don't have to cross the Mekong). The southern Lao capital of Pakse is about an hour by road and ferry from Ban Mai Sing Amphon, the village on the Lao side of the border.

Thai visitors come to Chong Mek to browse through cheap goods from China, Vietnam and Laos. Foreign visitors won't find much of interest to purchase here, unless they're in the market for toiletries (from China), camouflage clothing (from Vietnam) or buckets of live frogs (from Laos).

In July of 2000 an armed band of Lao nationals and ethnic Lao from Ubon staged an attack on the Lao border outpost here in which at least five were killed. The attackers, who had been using Ubon Province as a base, were in possession of a flag of the defunct Kingdom of Laos when routed by the Lao army and forced to flee back into Thailand.

About 5km west of Chong Mek is the northeastern shore of the huge **Kheuan Sirinthon** (Sirinthon Reservoir), an impoundment of a Mae Nam Mun tributary. On forested hills near the dam at the northern end of the reservoir is a recreation area frequented by local picnickers.

Further south, near the intersection of the Lao, Thai and Cambodian borders (in the area sometimes called the 'Emerald Triangle' for its relatively healthy forest cover) is the little-known **Phu Chong Nayoi National Park**. Established in 1987, the 687-sq-km park's predominant attractions include the **Bak Taew Yai Waterfall** (3.5km from the park headquarters), which plunges 40m over a cliff in two separate but parallel streams; a number of interesting rock formations; a couple of fresh springs; and some nice views of the surrounding countryside from a cliff called **Pha Pheung**. The park's highest point reaches 555m. Fauna includes the endangered white-winged wood duck. There is no accommodation at the park but camping is permitted in a designated area if you bring your own equipment. To get there from Ubon, take a bus from Warin Market to the town of Najaluay. Buses leave hourly between 10am and 1pm, cost 40B and the trip takes about an hour. From Najaluay, săwngthăew can be hired for 400B to 500B for the journey, including return. If you have your own wheels, take Hwy 24 south and turn onto Rte 2182 at the town of Det Udom. From there it's 45km to the town of Buntharik, where you turn south onto Rte 2248. The turn-off to Phu Chong Nayoi National Park is a few kilometres beyond Najaluay. The park headquarters is 7km from the turn-off. Admission is 200B.

Getting There & Away Săwngthăew run between Phibun and Chong Mek for 25B. There are two daily air-con buses that run directly from Chong Mek to Bangkok and vice versa. They both leave Chong Mek at 5pm and arrive at the Northern and Northeastern bus terminal in Bangkok at about 6am the next day.

Surin & Si Saket Provinces

These adjacent provinces between Buriram and Ubon Ratchathani border Cambodia and are dotted with the ruins of ancient Khmer structures built during the Angkor empire. The only other major attraction in the area is the Surin Annual Elephant Roundup. Few elephants are still used as work animals in Surin; they are brought out for ceremonial occasions such as parades and monastic ordinations.

SURIN
สุรินทร์

postcode 32000 • pop 41,200

Surin, 452km from Bangkok, is a quiet provincial capital, except during the **Elephant Roundup** in late November. At that time a carnival atmosphere reigns, with elephants providing the entertainment. If you have ever wanted to see a lot of elephants in one place, this is your opportunity. Events include parades of elephants that have been given psychedelic paint jobs, elephant soccer, and re-enactments of famous events from Thai history in which combatants do battle while riding fearsome tuskers.

Culturally, Surin represents an intersection of Lao, central Thai, Khmer and Suay peoples, resulting in an interesting mix of dialects and customs.

To see Surin's elephants during the low season, visit **Ban Tha Klang** in Tha Tum district, about 60km north of Surin. Many of the performers at the annual festival are trained here, but their presence is seasonal – inquire in Surin before making a trip.

Silk weaving can be observed at several local villages, including **Khwaosinarin** and **Ban Janrom**.

Prasat Ta Meuan
ปราสาทตาเมือน

The most atmospheric – and most difficult to reach – of Surin's temple ruins is a series of three sites known collectively as Prasat Ta Meuan in Ban Ta Miang district on the Cambodian border. Ban Ta Miang is 25km east of Ban Kruat and 49km west of Kap Choeng via Rte 2121. The sites are 10.5km from Ban Ta Miang via a mediocre dirt road. This trip is best done by hired motorbike or car – Pirom's House (see the Places to Stay entry later) can also arrange day trips by Land Rover if you can get a small group together.

The first site, **Prasat Ta Meuan** proper, was built in the Jayavarman VII period (AD 1121–1220) as a rest stop for pilgrims. It's a fairly small monument with a two-door, eight-window sanctuary constructed of laterite blocks; only one sculpted sandstone lintel over the rear door remains.

To the south, about 500m along a winding road, is the more impressive **Prasat Ta Meuan Toht**, which is said to have been the chapel for a 'healing station' or 'hospital' like Prang Ku outside Chaiyaphum. The ruins consist of a *gopura* (entrance pavilion), *mondòp* and main sanctuary, which is surrounded by a laterite wall. This site has fairly recently been restored and the strangler figs cut away.

Further south, right next to the Cambodian border, is the largest site, **Prasat Ta Meuan Thom**. Built mostly of sandstone blocks on a laterite base, on a slope that drops off at the southern end to face the Cambodian border, the walled complex has been rather badly reassembled into a jumble of sculpted blocks. Unfortunately, some of the sculpted blocks from the highly ornate southern gate have ended up haphazardly inserted into other structures in the compound. This temple was occupied by the Khmer Rouge in the 1980s and many of the best carvings were pried or blasted from the temple and sold to unscrupulous Thai dealers. Just beyond the southern gate the forest is cordoned off by barbed wire and red skull-and-crossbone signs (Khmer and English) warning of undetonated mines.

Mines and undetonated hand grenades around the Prasat Ta Meuan sites are a real danger; *don't* veer from the cleared paths around and between the monuments. In the not-so-distant past, firefights between the Khmer Rouge and Phnom Penh government troops could be heard almost daily during the dry season. The demise of the Khmer Rouge has brought peace to the border but banditry is still a possibility. A Thai military checkpoint along Rte 2121 screens all visitors and they may turn back nonresidents if the situation at the border is volatile.

Other Khmer-Temple Ruins

The southern reach of Surin Province along the Cambodian border harbours several minor Angkor-period ruins, including **Prasat Hin Ban Phluang** *(admission 30B, open 8am-4pm daily)*, 30km south of Surin. The solitary sandstone sanctuary, mounted on a laterite platform, exhibits well-sculpted stone lintels.

A larger Khmer site is seen 30km northeast of town at **Prasat Sikhoraphum** *(admission 30B, open 8am-4pm daily)*, 500m north of Rte 226 at the Km 34 marker. Sikhoraphum (or Si Khonphum) features five Khmer *prang*, the tallest of which reaches 32m. The doorways to the central *prang* are decorated with stone carvings of Hindu deities in the Angkor Wat style. Sikhoraphum can be reached by bus or train from Surin town.

The ruined **Prasat Phumpon** in Sangkha district (59km southeast of Surin via Rte 2077) is the oldest Khmer *prasat* in Thailand, dating from the 7th or 8th century AD. Unless you're adamant about ticking off every Khmer site in Thailand, you'll most likely be disappointed by this jumble of bricks.

Surin can also be used as a base to visit the Khmer ruins at Phanom Rung and Meuang Tam, about 75km southwest of Surin in Buriram Province (see the Buriram Province section and the entry for Phanom Rung Historical Park in that section, earlier in this chapter).

Places to Stay

Pirom's House *(☎ 0 4451 5140; 242 Th Krung Si Nai; singles/doubles 100/150B)* has rooms in a traditional wooden house. Pirom knows the area well and can suggest ideas for day trips around Surin, including excursions to lesser-known Khmer temple sites. He also owns a Land Rover and can lead reasonably priced all-day tours of several Khmer temple sites along the Cambodian border (about 600B per person if you go in a group of four, including a Thai lunch prepared by his wife). Besides trips to Khmer temples, Pirom can also do tours of little-known weaving villages populated by ethnic Lao, Khmer and Suay people. If you're at all interested in getting an in-depth look at Isan culture, take advantage of Pirom's informative and flexible tours. Pirom's wife speaks some French.

Hotel rates may increase during the Elephant Roundup and hotels may fill up, but otherwise **Krung Si Nai** *(☎ 0 4451 1037; 185 Th Krung Si Nai; rooms 200-300B)* offers some options. **New Hotel** *(☎ 0 4451 1341; 22 Th Thanasan; rooms with fan from 180B, with air-con from 350B)*, next to the train station, has rooms with fan and some with air-con. **Thanachai Hotel** *(Th Thetsaban 1; rooms 100B)*, just off the roundabout near the post office, has somewhat dark and dingy rooms.

Nid Diew Hotel *(☎ 0 4451 2099; 279-283 Th Thanasan; rooms with fan 200B, with air-con 400B)*, formerly the Saeng Thong, is moving upmarket just a bit, and is very clean and well run; air-con rooms have TV and hot water. **Memorial Hotel** *(☎ 0 4451 1637; Th Lak Meuang; doubles with fan 300-350B, doubles with air-con 500-600B)*, just west of Th Thanasan, has good rooms with fan but no TV, or fan and air-con rooms with TV and fridge.

Phetkasem Hotel *(☎ 0 4451 1274; 104 Th Jit Bamrung; singles & doubles 450-550B)* is businesslike and all of its rooms have air-con. **Thong Tarin Hotel** *(☎ 0 4451 4281; 60 Th Sirirat; rooms 720-810B)* is Surin's top-end place to stay, with 205 air-con rooms with all the amenities, including breakfast. The more expensive rooms were recently renovated.

Places to Eat

Along the northern end of Th Thanasan between the Nid Diew Hotel and the Surin train station are a handful of good, inexpensive Thai and Chinese restaurants. **Surin Phochana** is a long-running place along this stretch that serves dependable curries and noodles.

A small **night market** assembles in front of the Surin train station each evening. There is also a larger **night market** next to the main municipal market along Th Krung Si Nai, close to Pirom's House and the Krung Si Nai Hotel.

Ying Di *(no Roman-script sign; dishes 20-30B)*, next to the train station, serves reliable stir-fries with rice during the day. At the roundabout nearby is **Thapparot**, which is similar.

Getting There & Away

Air From Bangkok **Air Andaman** *(in Bangkok ☎ 0 2229 9555)* flies to/from Surin thrice weekly (1850B).

Bus Ordinary buses to Surin leave from Bangkok's Northern bus terminal (145B) at 7.30pm and 9pm. There are many air-con bus departures throughout the day and into the evening (285B to 313B).

During the Elephant Roundup celebration there are many special air-con bus services to Surin organised by major hotels and tour companies.

Surin lies about halfway between Ubon Ratchathani and Khorat; buses from either direction take around four hours (ordinary/air-con 72/129B).

Train Most people travel to Surin by rapid train No 135, which leaves Bangkok at 6.40am, arriving in Surin at 3.04pm. The 2nd-class fare for this service is 209B, including the rapid surcharge. You should probably book your seats at least two weeks in advance for travel during November. If you prefer night train travel, the rapid No 141 leaves Bangkok at 10.45pm and arrives in Surin at 7.05am.

Ordinary 3rd-class trains take around nine hours from Bangkok, cost 73B and leave daily at 11.45am and 11.10pm. Surin can also be reached by train from any other station along the Ubon Ratchathani line, including Buriram, Si Saket and Ubon Ratchathani.

Getting Around

Săamláw around central Surin cost about 20B per kilometre.

SI SAKET
ศรีสะเกษ

postcode 33000 • pop 42,800

Si Saket's provincial capital has gained in size and wealth on Surin's; however, with no major drawcards like Surin's Elephant Roundup, the town has less of a tourist infrastructure – a boon for visitors in search of laid-back, authentic Isan ways. Also, Si Saket Province has more Khmer ruins of significance within its borders than Surin Province.

When Khao Phra Wihan (a major Angkor site just over the provincial border in Cambodia) first reopened in the 1990s, many thought the town's fortunes would change as it became the gateway for visitors to the ruins. Unfortunately, the border crossing to the ruins has closed again since then, and the droves of visitors have yet to materialise.

Khao Phra Wihan
เขาพระวิหาร

For many years both Thailand and Cambodia claimed the territory on which this great temple complex is found *(admission 200B; open until 4pm daily)*. In 1963 the World Court finally awarded it to Cambodia. Privately many Thais still seethe at the concession, pointing out that Khao Phra Wihan (Preah Vihear) sits in an upland valley attached to Thailand's Khorat Plateau and has little geographic connection with the Cambodian interior. Apparently the World Court was influenced by the argument that the Angkor-period complex represented Cambodian patrimony, in spite of the fact that there are over 2000 Khmer archaeological sites within Thailand's borders. Perhaps the court thought Thailand had enough Khmer ruins.

Lying just across the Cambodian border opposite Si Saket Province's Kantharalak district, the impressive Khao Phra Wihan (Preah Vihear) ruins are virtually inaccessible from the Cambodian side, and until a Khmer Rouge cease-fire was reached in Cambodia they were also off-limits from the Thai side. After a year of negotiations between the Cambodian and Thai governments, the ruins finally opened to the public in 1991, then closed down again during the 1993–97 Phnom Penh offensive against the Khmer Rouge. In August 1998, following the death of Pol Pot and the banishment of the Khmer Rouge from its nearby Anglong Veng base, the ruins once again opened to the public. Sadly, the border and access to the temple closed again due to political bickering, and at the time of writing it was unclear when it would reopen – though there were rumours that it could open again very soon. Before setting out to visit Khao Phra Wihan, we suggest you call Ubon's TAT office *(☎ 0 4524 3772–7)* and ask what the current situation is.

Khao Phra Wihan was built over two centuries under a succession of Khmer kings, beginning with Rajendravarman II in the mid-10th century and ending with Suryavarman II in the early 12th century – it was the latter who also commanded the construction of Angkor Wat. The hill itself was sacred to Khmer Hindus for at least 500 years before the completion of the temple complex, however, and there were smaller brick monuments on the site prior to the reign of Rajendravarman II.

One of the most impressive of all Angkor-period archaeological sites, Phra Wihan sits atop a 600m cliff at the edge of the Dangrek (Dong Rek) escarpment, commanding a dramatic view of the Cambodian plains to the east. Built originally as a Hindu temple in the classic Baphuon and early Angkor Wat styles, the complex extends a linear 850m, encompassing four *gopura,* and a large *prasat* surrounded by a courtyard and galleries. A stepped *naga* approach ascends approximately 120m from the foot of the hill to the sanctuary.

The temple complex is semi-restored – the general condition is somewhere between that of Prasat Phanomwan in Khorat and Phanom Rung in Buriram. During Khmer Rouge occupation it suffered a heavy loss of artefacts – lintels and other carvings in particular – although some of this smuggled art has been intercepted and will eventually be returned to the site. One *naga* balustrade of around 30m is still intact; the first two gopura have all but fallen down and many of the buildings are roofless, but abundant examples of stone carving are intact and visible. The doorways to the third gopura have been nicely preserved and one (the inner door facing south) is surmounted by a well-executed carved stone lintel depicting Shiva and his consort Uma sitting on Nandi

(Shiva's bull), under the shade of a symmetrised tree. A Vishnu creation lintel is also visible on the second gopura; in contrast to the famous Phanom Rung lintel depicting the same subject, this one shows Vishnu climbing the churning stick rather than reclining on the ocean below.

The main *prasat* tower in the final court at the summit is in need of major restoration before the viewer can get a true idea of its former magnificence. Many of the stone carvings from the *prasat* are either missing or lie buried in nearby rubble. The galleries leading to the *prasat* have fared better and have even kept their arched roofs.

From the Thai border, visitors must walk down and then up a rocky and sometimes steep slope. You may tour only the immediate surroundings of the complex. There are still plenty of land mines and live ordnance in the fields and forests nearby; stick to the designated safety lanes leading to the ruins.

Getting There & Away Rte 221 leads 95km south from Si Saket to Saron – 11km short of the temple – via Kantharalak. Catch a săwngthăew from near the bus terminal adjacent to the main day market in Si Saket for 25B. If you miss the infrequent direct săwngthăew service, you may have to take a bus first to Kantharalak (24B) and pick up another săwngthăew to Phum Saron (8B). Buses to Kantharalak leave every half-hour from around 6am to 5pm. From either Kantharalak or Phum Saron, you'll have to hire a motorbike taxi to the border entrance to Khao Phra Wihan – figure on 200B return from Kantharalak or Phum Saron, with a couple of hours waiting time (100B one way). Motorbike taxi drivers in Kantharalak seem to be much more reasonable than their grasping counterparts in Phum Saron, who are aware that visitors will be unwilling to backtrack to Kantharalak in search of a better deal. On weekends, when the temple complex is open, there are sometimes direct săwngthăew from Si Saket all the way to the border entrance for 25B.

Pha Maw I Daeng

ผามออีแดง

If border entry to Khao Phra Wihan is closed, you can still walk to the edge of this cliff, around 400m from the temple site on the Thai side. In addition to good views of the plains below and the Dangrek mountain range in the distance, you can also make out the Khao Phra Wihan ruins over a chasm on a hill opposite the cliff – binoculars will certainly enhance the view. In early 1994, we watched from the relative safety of this cliff as Phnom Penh troops bombarded a Khmer Rouge position on the plains below. A railed stairway cut into the edge of the cliff leads down to a well-sculpted relief executed directly onto the upper cliff face. The relief depicts three figures whose identities are an enigma to archaeologists and art historians. Although they give the general impression of representing deities, angels or kings, the iconography corresponds to no known figures in Thai, Mon or Khmer mythology. Stylistically the relief appears to date back to the Koh Ker (AD 921–45) period of Khmer art, when King Jayavarman IV ruled from his capital at Koh Ker.

For information on how to get here see Getting There & Away under Khao Phra Wihan earlier.

Other Khmer Ruins

Forty kilometres west of Si Saket in Uthumphon Phisai district, **Prasat Hin Wat Sa Kamphaeng Yai** features a striking 10th-century sandstone *prang* with carved doorways. The ruined sanctuary can be found on the grounds of Wat Sa Kamphaeng Yai's modern successor.

About 8km west of town via Rte 226 is **Prasat Sa Kamphaeng Noi**, consisting of a pile of laterite and not much else.

Places to Stay & Eat

Si Saket Most accommodation in Si Saket costs between 120B and 220B (for simple rooms with fan). None of them are all that great (they're all short-time hotels to some degree). If you're squeamish or travelling with kids, you'd probably be better off in Ubon Ratchathani or Surin. Accommodation options include: **Santisuk** *(☎ 0 4561 1496; 573 Soi Wat Phra To)*; **Si Saket** *(☎ 0 4561 1846; 384-385 Th Si Saket)*; and **Thai Soem Thai** *(☎ 0 4561 1458; Th Si Saket)*.

Phrom Phiman *(☎ 0 4561 2677; 849/1 Th Lak Meuang; singles/doubles with fan 230/270B, with air-con 300/490B)* has rooms. Security is lax here, though – keep an eye on your belongings.

Ketsiri Hotel *(☎ 0 4561 4006, fax 0 4561 4008; 1102-1105 Th Khukhan; air-con rooms 750-850B)* is the best of the lot, and is 100m south of the telephone office. It has comfortable rooms, and discounts are sometimes available on the listed rack rates.

There are many **small restaurants** on the street in front of the train station. A **night market** convenes 200m east of the train station, with good Isan and Thai food. **Chu Sin Than** *(no Roman-script sign; dishes 15-20B)* is a friendly vegetarian restaurant around the corner from the Thai Soem Thai Hotel, with good Thai vegie dishes.

Kantharalak This is the place to stay if you want to see Khao Phra Wihan early in the morning. **Kantharalak Palace Hotel** *(☎ 0 4566 1084; 131 Th Sinpadit; rooms with fan 280B, with air-con 350-550B)* is a comfortable place on the main street, with air-con rooms. The only eating options in this town are the usual **rice and noodle shops**.

Getting There & Away

From Bangkok's Northern bus terminal there are several departures to Surin in the morning, as well as in the evening. Any bus going to Ubon Ratchathani will also get you there. Air-con buses take about eight hours and cost 337B to 370B. Ordinary buses leave four times daily and cost 169B to 185B, depending on the route taken.

Ordinary buses from Ubon Ratchathani cost 29B (40B to 60B air-con) and take about an hour to reach Si Saket, depending on how many stops the bus makes along the way.

A 3rd-class train from Ubon to Si Saket costs 8B and takes 1½ hours.

Upper Southern Gulf

Heading south from Bangkok, Thailand's upper southern gulf follows the Burmese border along three provinces (Phetchaburi, Prachuap Khiri Khan and Chumphon), ending at the Isthmus of Kra, the region's narrowest point and official beginning of the Thai-Malay peninsula.

This coastal area has yet to be discovered by the majority of foreign tourists, who head further south to well-known island destinations such as Ko Samui or Phuket. But it has plenty to offer the adventure-seeker: Kaeng Krachan National Park, Thailand's largest and covering nearly half of Phetchaburi Province; the laid-back seaside resorts of Cha-am and Hua Hin (among many others); and provincial cities such as Phetchaburi and Prachuap Khiri Khan, which give a good sense of what regular Thai towns are like (as well as yielding a few surprises).

The rural areas are agricultural, with fishing and pineapple-growing the economic mainstays. The upper southern gulf is one of coastal Thailand's least-expensive areas to visit. Some parts of it require more initiative to see – the most interesting shoreline isn't necessarily signposted, and few guided tours or easy-to-book, public-transport options reach many of the off-the-beaten-track spots.

UPPER SOUTHERN GULF

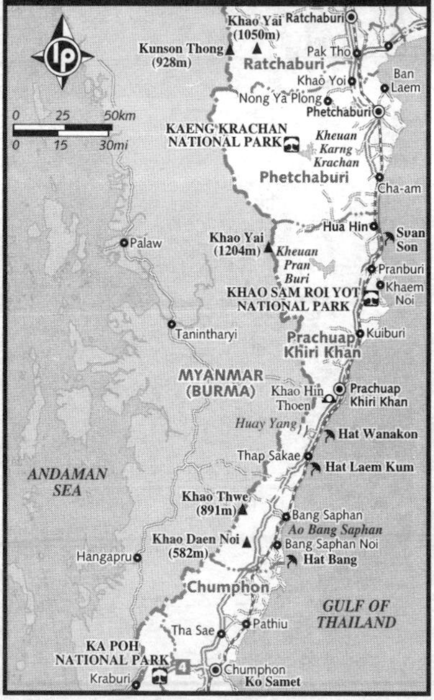

Highlights

- Feast your eyes on Phetchaburi's rich culture at its collection of temples
- Relax on Cha-am's long, casuarina-lined beach – deserted on weekdays and lively on weekends
- Mingle with tourists at Hua Hin's beaches, restaurants and markets
- Spot the wildlife and diverse scenery at Kaeng Krachen and Khao Sam Roi Yot National Parks
- Chill out at the peaceful and uncrowded Hat Ban Krut, Bang Saphan Yai and other nearby beaches

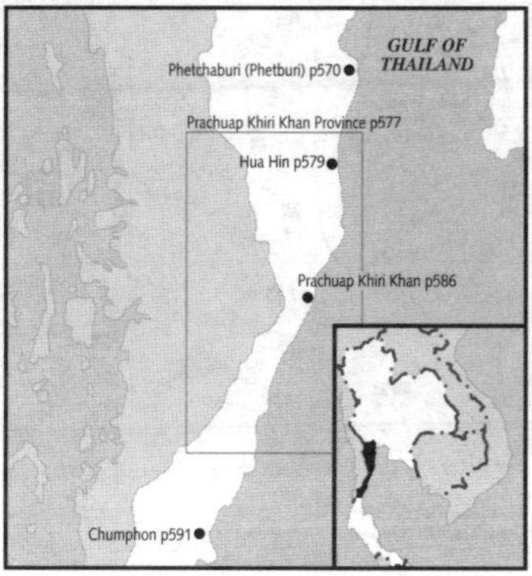

Phetchaburi Province

PHETCHABURI (PHETBURI)

อ.เมืองเพชรบุรี

postcode 76000 • pop 43,400

Situated 160km south of Bangkok, Phetchaburi (commonly known as Phetburi, and

PHETCHABURI (PHETBURI)

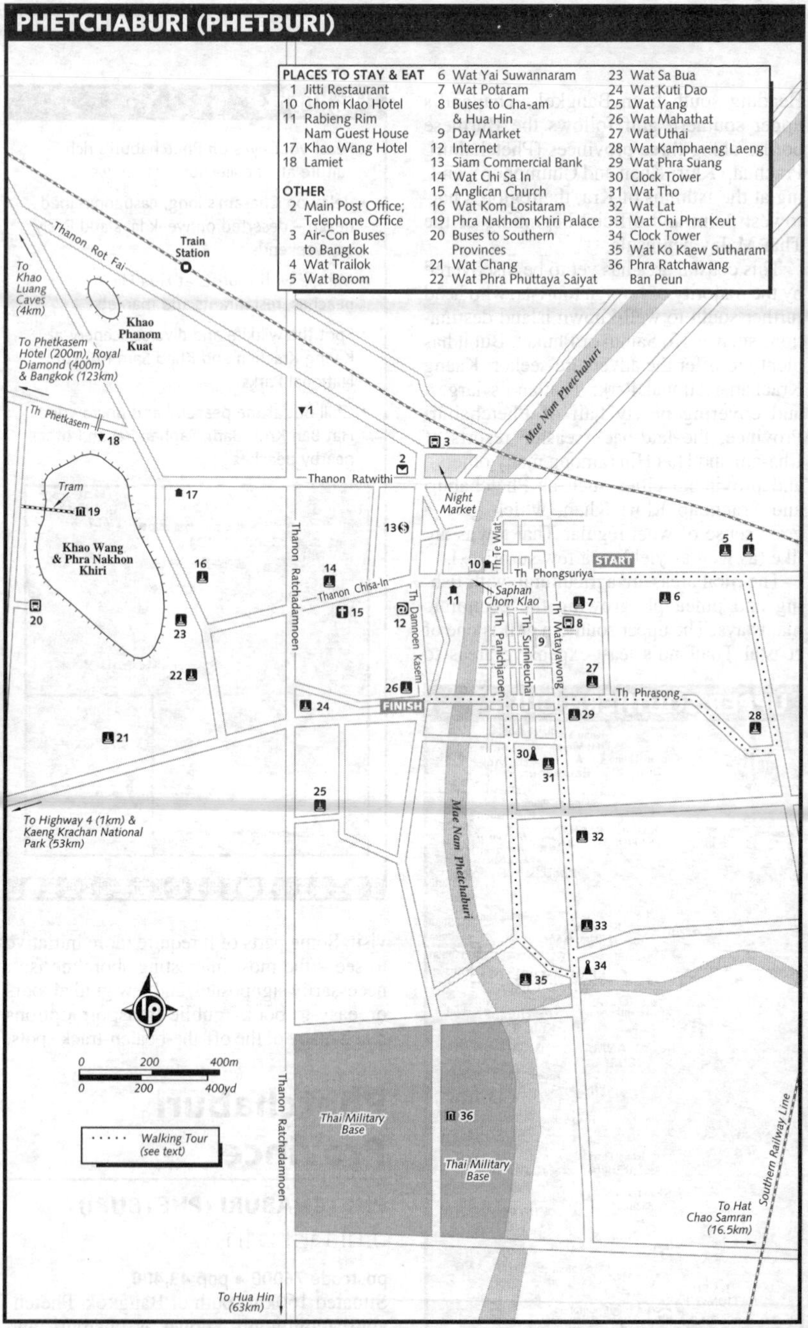

UPPER SOUTHERN GULF

Walking Tour – Phetchaburi Temples

Wat Yai Suwannaram

After you've crossed Mae Nam Phetchaburi, by Saphan Chomrut, and passed the Nam Chai Hotel on the left, walk about 300m farther along Th Phongsuriya until you see a big temple on the right. This is Wat Yai Suwannaram, originally built in the 17th century and renovated during the reign of King Rama V (r. 1868–1910). The main *bòt* (central sanctuary) is surrounded by a cloister filled with sombre Buddha images. The murals inside the *bòt* date to the 1730s and are in good condition. Next to the *bòt*, in a murky pond, is a beautifully designed old *hăw trai*, or Tripitaka library.

Wat Borom & Wat Trailok

These two wát are next to one another on the opposite side of Th Phongsuriya from Wat Yai Suwannaram, a little to the east. They aren't especially attractive, but do have distinctive monastic halls and long, graceful, wooden 'dormitories' on stilts.

Wat Kamphaeng Laeng

This is a pleasant, 13th-century Khmer site with five *prang* (Khmer-style tower) and part of the original laterite wall *(kamphaeng laeng)* still standing. The front *prang* contains a Buddha footprint. Of the other four, two contain images dedicated to famous *lŭang phâw* (venerated monks), and two have been restored from ruins. The structures were built as Hindu monuments, so the Buddhist symbols are later additions.

Wat Ko Kaew Sutharam

Follow Th Phrasong back towards the centre of town, turning left onto Th Matayawong. After about 800m turn right at the clock tower and look for signs leading to the Ayuthaya-period Wat Ko Kaew Sutharam (Wat Ko). Two different *soi* on the left lead to the wát, which is behind the shops along the curving street. The *bòt* features early 18th-century murals that are among the best conceived in Thailand. One panel depicts what appears to be a Jesuit priest wearing the robes of a Buddhist monk, while another shows other foreigners undergoing Buddhist conversions. There is also a large wooden monastic hall on stilts, similar to the ones at Wat Borom and Wat Trailok, but in much better condition.

Wat Mahathat

Follow the street running in front of Wat Ko back towards central Petchaburi and turn left onto Th Phrasong; soon you'll reach Wat Mahathat. The large white *prang* of this wát can be seen from a distance – it is a typical late Ayuthaya–early Ratanakosin adaptation of the *prang* of Lopburi and Phimai.

also Meuang Phet) is a medium-sized, unpretentious city dotted with an unusually large number of old *wát* (temples) that span several centuries. These temples have made very few concessions to the 20th and 21st centuries and thus provide a glimpse of the traditional Siamese urban wát. The more interesting ones can be seen on a long walk around the city.

Also noteworthy is the forested Khao Wang hill, just west of the city centre, which has the remains of a King Rama IV palace and several wát, along with a good aerial view of the area. Phra Ratchawang Ban Peun, a European-style palace built for King Rama V, and the underground Buddhist shrine at the Khao Luang Caves, north of the city, are also worth a few hours of your time.

Information

You can exchange money at the **Siam Commercial Bank** *(2 Th Damnoen Kasem)*. Other nearby banks also offer foreign exchange and ATMs. The **main post office** *(cnr Th Ratwithi & Th Damnoen Kasem; open 8.30am-4.30pm Mon-Fri, 9am-12pm Sat & Sun)* has an upstairs international **telephone office** *(open 7am-10pm daily)*. There's an Internet café *(open 9.30am-9pm daily)* on Th Damnoen Kasem, near Th Chisa-In.

Khao Wang & Phra Nakhon Khiri
เขาวัง/อุทยานประวัติศาสตร์พระนครคีรี

Just west of the city is the prominent hill of Khao Wang, the site of King Rama IV's palace, Phra Nakhon Khiri *(admission 40B; open 9am-4pm daily)*, which is now a museum. Leafy brick paths undulate throughout the pleasant, woods, where wát and various other historical sites provide a base for awe-inspiring views. Though the walk up looks easy, it's actually fairly strenuous – and you'll want to keep an eye out for aggressive monkeys lining the paths. Save yourself strained muscles and primate encounters by catching the **tram** *(tickets 30B; 9am-5.30pm daily)*.

Phra Ratchawang Ban Peun
พระราชวังบ้านปืน

Just over 1km south of the city centre, and located inside a block-long Thai military base, is Phra Ratchawang Ban Peun *(Ban Peun Palace; ☎ 0 3242 8083; admission 50B; open 8am-4pm Mon-Fri)*. Construction began in 1910 at the behest of King Rama V (who passed away not long after the project was started) and was completed in 1916. German architects hired to do the job used the opportunity to showcase contemporary German innovations in construction and interior design. The structure is typical of the early 20th century, a period that saw a Thai craze for erecting European-style buildings – seemingly in an effort to keep up with the 'modern' architecture of its colonised neighbours. While the exterior of this two-storey palace promises little excitement, the exquisite glazed tiles in the interior, particularly on the columns in the domed foyer, are worth a peep.

UPPER SOUTHERN GULF

Khao Luang Caves
ถ้ำเขาหลวง

Five kilometres north of Phetchaburi is the cave sanctuary of Khao Luang *(admission by donation)*. Steps lead down into a main cavern lined with impressive stalactites and old Buddha statues (including a large reclining Buddha). Many of these were put in place by King Rama IV. Sunlight from a hole in the chamber ceiling illuminates the images and makes for a good photo opportunity. To the rear of the main cavern is an entrance to a third, smaller chamber, also lit by a hole. On the right of the entrance is Wat Bunthawi, with a *sǎalaa* (meeting hall) designed by the abbot of the wát himself and a *bòt* with impressively carved wooden door panels. Around the cave you may meet brazen monkeys waiting for handouts.

Sǎamláw (three-wheeled pedicabs, 50B) and motorcycle taxis (30B) provide transport from Phetchaburi.

Places to Stay

Accommodation is not one of Phetchaburi's highlights.

Chom Klao Hotel *(☎ 0 3242 5398; rooms with/without bath 160/120B)* is right on the river, though it doesn't really take advantage of this fact. It's a somewhat bleak and basic, but friendly, Chinese hotel.

Rabieng Rim Nam Guest House *(☎/fax 0 3242 5707; 1 Th Chisa-In; singles/doubles with fan 120/240B)* caters to backpackers, with a laundry service, bicycle and motorcycle rental, tours to nearby Kaeng Krachan National Park and a pleasant old-style **restaurant** overlooking the river. The six rooms are very cramped and noisy, however.

Khao Wang Hotel *(☎ 0 3242 5167; rooms with fan/air-con 230/330B)*, on Th Ratwithi and near Khao Wang hill, is a 50-room favourite among travelling salesmen and not as sleazy as the town's other Chinese hotels. Its basic rooms are fairly clean and some have TV.

Phetkasem Hotel *(☎ 0 3242 5581; 86/1 Th Phetkasem; singles/doubles with fan from 170/250B, with air-con from 300/450B)* is on the western edge of town and is good value. Clean, airy and large rooms sport outdated furniture and line industrial halls, and the management is friendly. It's a long walk to the centre of town, however.

Royal Diamond *(☎ 0 3241 1062, fax 0 3242 4310; 555 Mu 1, Th Phetkasem; rooms 800B)* is a 60-room, upmarket hotel and *the* place to stay if you need the comforts of mid-range surroundings (these being air-con, fridge, cable TV and carpeting). Unfortunately it's also quite a walk from the town centre.

Places to Eat

Local dishes for which Phetchaburi is famous include *khànǒm jiin thâwt man* (thin noodles with fried, spicy fish cake), *khâo châe phétbùrii* (moist chilled rice served with sweetmeats, a hot-season speciality) and *khànŏm mâw kaeng* (egg custard). You'll find these, along with a range of standard Thai and Chinese dishes, at several good restaurants in the Khao Wang area. A variety of cheap eats is available at the **night market**, near the northern end of town.

Other good eating places can be found in the town centre along the main street to the clock tower. North of Khao Wang, **Lamiet** (no Roman-script sign) sells good *khànŏm mâw kaeng* and *făwy thawng* (sweet shredded egg yolk). It's a bit hard to find among all the other shops hawking similar fare.

Attractive and casual **Rabieng Rim Nam** *(dishes 30-70B; open 8.30am-1am daily)*, at the guesthouse of the same name, features a Thai and English menu with over 150 items, including seafood and 30 kinds of *yam* (spicy salads). **Jitti Restaurant** *(dishes 30-80B; open 9am-11pm daily)* is set back from busy Th Ratchadamnoen and offers a leafy and peaceful ambience, along with basic Thai food.

Getting There & Away

There are frequent services to/from Bangkok's Southern bus station (1st class, 90B to 101B; 2nd class, 70B; 2½ hours). The bus terminal is across from the night market. Other bus destinations to/from Phetchaburi include: Cha-am (25B, 40 minutes), Hua Hin (30B to 36B, 1½ hours) and Prachuap Khiri Khan (80B, three hours). Ordinary buses to the southern provinces leave from the bus station near Khao Wang; those to nearby Hua Hin and Cha-am leave from the town centre.

Frequent services run to/from Bangkok's Hualamphong train station. Fares (3rd class, 74B to 94B; 2nd class, 118B to 258B; 1st class, up to 753B; three hours) vary widely depending on the train and class. Taking the bus is faster, unless you include getting out to Bangkok's Southern bus station.

Fair Enough

The Phra Nakhon Khiri Fair takes place in early February and lasts for about eight days. Centred on Khao Wang and Phetchaburi's historic temples, the festivities include a sound-and-light show at the Phra Nakhon Khiri Palace, temples festooned with lights and performances of Thai classical dance-drama, *lákhon chatrii*, *lí-keh* (see the special section 'Music, Theatre & Dance') and modern-style historical dramas.

A twist on the usual beauty contest provides a showcase for Phetchaburi widows.

Getting Around

Săamláw and motorcycle taxis go anywhere in the town centre for 20B; you can also charter them for the whole day (from 200B to 300B). *Săwngthăew* (pick-up trucks) cost 10B around town. It's a 20-minute walk from the train station to the town centre.

Rabieng Rim Nam Guest House rents out bicycles (120B per day) and motorcycles (250B per day).

KAENG KRACHAN NATIONAL PARK

อุทยานแห่งชาติแก่งกระจาน

This 3000-sq-km park *(☎ 0 3245 9293; admission 200B)* is Thailand's largest, covering nearly half of Phetchaburi Province along the Myanmar border. In spite of its size and proximity to Bangkok, however, Kaeng Krachan doesn't get many visitors – and it's hard to visit without your own wheels. Abundant rainfall nourishes rich forest areas, though there are also savanna-like grasslands, mountains, steep cliffs, caves, waterfalls, long-distance hiking trails and two rivers, Mae Nam Phetchaburi and Mae Nam Pranburi, which are suitable for rafting.

Animals living in Kaeng Krachan include wild elephants, deer, tigers, bears, gibbons, boars, hornbills, bantengs, dusky langurs, gaurs and wild cattle. Small Karen settlements have taken their toll on the park via illegal farming and poaching. According to Gray, Piprell & Graham's *National Parks of Thailand*, 'Kaeng Krachan…could become one of the world's premier reserves if properly managed in the future'.

Eighteen-tiered **Nam Tok Tho Thip** is a three-hour, 4km hike from the 36km marker on the road into the park; longer hikes can reach the headwaters of Mae Nam Phetchaburi or the summit of **Phanoen Thung**, the park's highest point. To the south, near

La-U Reservoir, are the twin waterfalls of **Pa La-U Yai** and **Pa La-U Noi**; these are reachable with 4WD from the south (closer to Hua Hin) via Hwy 3219.

Hiking and camping are possible with your own supplies and camping gear. The best months for this activity are between November and April.

Near the visitors centre is a large, scenic reservoir stocked with fish. You can rent boats here for 400B per hour.

Places to Stay & Eat

Bungalows *(up to four people 800B)* near park headquarters were being rebuilt at the time of writing. To reserve, call the **Royal Forest Department** *(Bangkok ☎ 0 2579 5734)*. There are also a few **campsites** *(per person 30B)* in the park, including a pleasant one near the reservoir at the visitors centre (where there's also a modest **restaurant**). **Tents** *(150-300B)* can be rented.

Accommodation is also available a few kilometres before entering the park. Some blue-roofed riverside **bungalows** *(no Roman-script sign; ☎ 0 1807 7264; bungalows 1500-2000B)* offer air-con and TV and are located after crossing the bridge, about 850m past the police station as you near the park. Look for the small Pepsi sign on the right. Three hundred metres past the bungalows, on the left side of the road and 3.5km before hitting the visitor's centre, **A&B Bungalows** *(☎ 0 1763 3824; rooms & bungalows 600-1200B)* is less scenic but still pleasant. The grounds are grassy and there's a **restaurant**.

Getting There & Away

Kaeng Krachan is 60km southeast of Phetchaburi, with the southern edge of the park lying about 35km from Hua Hin. From Phetchaburi, drive 20km south on Hwy 4 to the city of Tha Yang. Turn right (west) and after 40km you'll reach the visitors centre (follow the 'Special Forces Training Camp' signs). You'll need a 4WD vehicle if you want to explore the dirt roads within the park.

There is no direct public transport all the way to the park, but you can get a săwngthăew from Phetchaburi (near the clock tower) to the village of Ban Kaeng Krachan, 4km before the park. Go early as the last săwngthăew leaves at 2pm. The trip costs 30B and takes about 1½ hours. Motorcycle taxis from Ban Kaeng Krachan to the visitors centre also cost 30B.

CHA-AM

อำเภอชะอำ

postcode 76120 • pop 43,900

Sandwiched 40km south of Phetchaburi and 25km north of Hua Hin, the sprawling beach town of Cha-am is a popular weekend destination for provincial Thai families, though more Westerners are visiting this casuarina-lined resort as well. Hotels, restaurants, small beach shops and various tourist services stretch out along the busiest 3km of decent seashore and murky green waters, and you'll never be too far from food vendors or umbrella and sling-chair rentals. There are occasional public bath and toilet facilities, and plenty of bicycles to rent – including three- and four-seaters. The mayor of Cha-am keeps bars off the beach strip, but if you need to let it out a bit, you can find them on Th Narathip and various streets off the beach strip.

Cha-am has a way to go before becoming a cutting-edge international beach resort, and in the meantime visitors can enjoy the casual, 'untucked around the edges' feel of this unglamorous beach town.

Orientation

Phetkasem Hwy runs right through Cha-am's busy centre. This area is where you'll find the main bus 'terminal' (more like a bus stop), most banks, the main post office, an outdoor market, the train station and various government offices. About 1km east, via the main connecting road, Th Narathip, is the long beach strip where you'll be headed. The road that runs along this strip (and where most beach accommodation and services are located) is Th Ruamjit.

Information

A very helpful, English-speaking office of the **Tourism of Thailand** *(TAT; ☎ 0 3247 1005, 0 1486 4936; ⓔ tatphet@tat.or.th; open 8.30am-4.30pm daily)* is inconveniently way out on Phetkasem Hwy, about 500m south of the town. A less helpful **tourist information office** is conveniently located on the corner of Th Ruamjit and Th Narathip, but staff do not speak English.

The beach strip has a few practical tourist services, including a bank (across from the tourist information office), a small post office with an international telephone service, and the occasional Internet café, including the **Coffee Wave** *(246/10 Th Ruamjit; open 8.30am-7.30pm daily)*.

Places to Stay – Budget & Mid-Range

Cha-am is a big weekend destination, so from Friday to Sunday expect a 20% to 50% increase on most prices listed here.

Jitravee Resort *(☎ 0 3247 1382, fax 0 3243 3925; 241/20 Th Ruamjit; rooms with air-con from 250B)* offers cheap plain rooms where concrete and tile predominate. It's good value though, and you can dish out more baht for a TV, a fridge or hot water.

Prathonchok House *(☎ 0 3247 1215; 240/3 Th Ruamjit; rooms with fan/air-con 250/300B)* is a basic cheapie with white-tiled halls; ask to see several rooms or you may end up with a 'wall' view. Rooms with shared bath cost less; those with TV and/or fridge cost more.

Anantachai Guest House *(☎ 0 3243 3396; 235/8-9 Th Ruamjit; singles/doubles with air-con 300/500B)* is a decent corner place run by a friendly Chinese family. The daughter speaks good English and provides information on the area. Rooms have sea views and TV, and there's an inexpensive Thai **restaurant** downstairs. Call for a pick-up from the highway.

Rua Makam Villa *(☎ 0 3247 1073; singles/doubles with fan 300/600B)* has spacious but spartan wood-and-concrete cottages on bleak grounds. Baths are Thai-style, and TV and air-con cost more.

Cha-am Villa *(☎ 0 3247 1597; 241/2 Th Ruamjit; rooms with air-con from 400B; bungalows with air-con from 1500B)* has accordion-shaped buildings, lots of concrete and a pool. Good rooms and bungalows come with TV, fridge and hot water, and some have wooden floors.

Sea Pearl Hotel *(☎ 0 3247 1118; 263/32 Th Ruamjit; rooms with fan/air-con 400/500B)* aspires to mediocrity, with yawn-inducing, stuffy, carpeted rooms. There is, however, hot water, and some of the pricier rooms are larger and come with tub, TV and partial sea views.

Savitree Resort *(☎ 0 3243 4088; 263/1 Th Ruamjit; rooms with air-con 500B)* is a small place with several attractive, semidetached brick bungalows. Rooms come with fridge and TV.

Jolly & Jumper *(☎ 0 3243 3887; W www.jolly-jumper.info; 274/3 Th Ruamjit; rooms with fan 150-250B, with air-con 500B)* is a clean place that's run by an eccentric Dutch couple. Rooms are large and colourful, all with shared baths. There's a good **restaurant** below and free use of bicycles for guests.

Thiptari Place *(☎ 0 3247 1879; 247/33-35 Th Ruamjit; rooms with air-con 500-600B)* sports sizable rooms with wooden floors and simple decor. All have fridge and TV, and some have balconies with sea views (more like casuarina-tree views).

Places to Stay – Top End

Remember to ask for better rates if you show up on a weekday; significant discounts should apply.

Santisuk Bungalows & Beach Resort *(☎ 0 3247 1212; 263/3 Th Ruamjit; bungalows 2000-3500B)* has large grounds dotted with early Cha-am–style wooden bungalows of various sizes (most two to three bedroom), some up on stilts and all with outdoor decks. It's simple, good value especially for unfussy couples travelling together.

Cha-am Methavalai Hotel *(☎ 0 3247 1028, fax 0 3247 1590; 220 Th Ruamjit; rooms from 2800B)* is the best hotel in town, with a luxurious lobby, well-kept modern rooms and an inviting pool lined with *faràng* (Westerners). The pool can be used by nonguests (50B) when the hotel's not full. There's also a good restaurant on the premises.

Gems Cha-am *(☎ 0 3243 4060, fax 0 3243 4002; W www.gemscha-amhotel.com; rooms from 1500B)* is a towering white goliath of a hotel, sporting good rooms facing the sea, with the usual top-end amenities. Stunning views and a small pool await on the 17th floor, and there's also a fitness centre and sauna. The rates include breakfast and the sign at its long driveway proclaims it a 'healthy & nice hotel'.

Long Beach Cha-am Hotel *(☎ 0 3247 2442, fax 0 3247 2287; 225/75 Th Ruamjit; rooms from 2600B)* offers typical upmarket amenities but isn't an especially good deal, with slightly scruffy rooms and only partial sea views (which sometimes include ugly neighbouring buildings). Negotiate a price; you're sure to get a better deal than the posted rack rate.

Several huge, luxurious and modern resort hotels have sprung up on the beaches south of town, on the road to Hua Hin. These include **Springfield Beach Resort** *(☎ 0 3245 1181, fax 0 3245 1194; W www.springfieldresort.com; rooms in low/high season from 3500/5000B)* and **Dusit Resort & Polo Club** *(☎ 0 3252 0009, fax 0 3252 096; W www.dusit.com; rooms from US$125)*.

Places to Eat

Opposite the beach are a few good **seafood restaurants**, which are reasonably priced – unlike the bungalow restaurants. Cheap **food vendors** on the beach sell all manner of barbecued and fried seafood.

Poom Restaurant *(☎ 0 3247 1036; 274/1 Th Ruamjit; dishes 80-150B; open 9am-midnight daily)* is across from the beach and has a large, pleasant outdoor patio shaded with trees; it's very popular among visiting Thais.

Anantachai Guest House *(☎ 0 3243 3396; 235/8-9 Th Ruamjit; dishes 40-60B)* cooks up affordable, no-frills Thai and seafood dishes in an open, casual atmosphere. Service is friendly.

Jolly & Jumper *(☎ 0 3243 3887; 274/3 Th Ruamjit; dishes 40-300B; open 9.30am-10pm)* presents a huge menu of Western and Thai food, which is good, there are lots of alcoholic drinks, a variety of rehabilitated birds cheep from their cages, and the decor is interesting; no wonder it's often full of *faràng*.

Coffee Wave *(☎ 0 9742 0925; 246/10 Th Ruamjit; dishes 35-80B; open 8.30am-7.30pm)* is good for breakfast, serving fancy coffees, such as cappuccino, latte and Irish coffee; just what you need to kick-start your day. The digs are clean, airy and spartan, and there's Internet access.

Scandy Restaurant *(☎ 0 3247 1926; 274/32-33 Th Ruamjit; dishes 50-200B; open 9am-11pm)* grills up Western and Thai grub in amiable and cosy surroundings. It's next to **Thiptari Place**, which is similar.

The luxury hotels have generally fine seafood and Thai and Western cuisine at standard hotel prices. The seafood and Thai cuisine are especially good at the Cha-am Methavalai Hotel's **Sorndaeng Restaurant**, the fanciest restaurant in town.

Getting There & Away

Most ordinary and air-con buses stop in the town centre, on Phetkasem hwy. Some

Culture of the South

Although under Thai political domination for several centuries, the south has always remained culturally apart from the other regions of Thailand. Historically, the peninsula has been linked to cultures in ancient Indonesia, particularly the Srivijaya empire, which ruled a string of principalities in what is today southern Thailand, Malaysia and Indonesia. The influence of Malay-Indonesian culture is still apparent in the ethnicity, religion, art and language of the *thai pàk tâi* (southern Thais).

The *thai pàk tâi* dress differently, build their houses differently and eat differently from Thais in the north. Many are followers of Islam, so there are quite a few mosques in southern cities; men often cover their heads and the long sarong is favoured over the shorter *phâa khăo măa* worn in the northern, central and northeastern regions. There are also a good many Chinese living in the south – their influence can be seen in the old architecture and in the baggy Chinese pants worn by rural non-Muslims.

Southern Thais speak a dialect that confounds even visitors from other Thai regions. Diction is short and fast and the clipped tones fly into the outer regions of intelligibility. In the provinces nearest Malaysia, many Thai Muslims speak Yawi, an old Malay dialect.

Southern architecture follows three basic threads. In rural areas, simple bungalows constructed from thatched palm leaves and bamboo strips affixed to wooden or bamboo frames are common. A Malay style of construction emphasises sturdy houses of wood with square tile roofs. In the older cities you'll come across splendid examples of Sino-Portuguese architecture, featuring arched windows and porticoes and curved tiled roofs.

Southern-Thai cuisine combines Chinese, Malay and Thai elements to create brightly coloured, heavily spiced dishes. Look for *khànŏm jiin náam yaa*, thin noodles doused in a fish curry sauce, and *rotii kaeng*, Malay-style flat bread served with a curry dip. Seafood is an everyday staple.

Washing day, Prachuap Khiri Khan Province

BILL WASSMAN

Soft-drink signs, Surat Thani

DENNIS JOHNSON

Ko Nang Yuan, Surat Thani Province

PAUL BEINSSEN

Ko Pha-Ngan

PAUL DYMOND

Ko Samui, Surat Thani Province

JERRY ALEXANDER

JOHN HAY
Fisherman, Hua Hin, Prachuap Khiri Khan Province

RICHARD NEBESKY
Drying fish, Na Thon, Ko Samui

CHRIS MELLOR
Shoe polisher, Chumphon Province

private air-con buses to/from Bangkok conveniently go all the way to the beach, stopping at a small terminal a few hundred metres south of the Th Narathip intersection.

Frequent bus services opertaing to/from Cha-am include Bangkok (air-con/ordinary 113/95B, three hours), Phetchaburi (25B, 40 minutes) and Hua Hin (20B, 30 minutes).

The train station is inland on Th Narathip, west of Phetkasem Hwy and a 20B motorcycle ride to/from the beach. From Bangkok three train stations have daily services to Cha-am from Hualamphong (3.50pm), Sam Sen (9.27am) and Thonburi (7.15am, 1.30pm, 7.05pm). Tickets cost from 80B to 193B. Cha-am isn't listed on the English-language train schedule.

Getting Around

From the city centre to the beach it's a quick motorcycle (20B) or share-taxi (5B) ride. Motorcycle taxis around town cost 20B. Sometimes a driver will pretend he doesn't know where your hotel is, and take you somewhere else where he can get a commission. Just say 'But my friend is waiting for me!' to help jog his memory.

You can rent motorcycles for 200B to 300B a day. Bicycle rentals are available everywhere for 30B per hour, or 150B per day, and are a great way to get about town.

AROUND CHA-AM

Just before the border between Phetchaburi and Prachuap Khiri Khan Provinces is reached – 9km south of Cha-am – stands **Phra Ratchaniwet Marukhathayawan** (*☎ 0 3247 2482; admission 50B; open 8.30am-4.30pm daily*) a summer palace built during the reign of King Rama VI. The collection of one- and two-storey buildings are constructed of prime golden teak and interlinked by covered boardwalks, all raised high above the ground on stilts. Along with the high, tiled roofs and tall, shuttered windows, this design allows for maximum air circulation – a tropical building technique sorely missing in most modern Thai architecture. Unlike the current summer palace situated farther south at Hua Hin, this one is open daily to the public. It's surrounded by the grounds of Camp Rama VI, a military post, but with proper check-in at the gate you should have no trouble receiving permission to tour the palace.

Prachuap Khiri Khan Province

HUA HIN

อำเภอหัวหิน

postcode 77110 • pop 41,800

The beaches of Hua Hin first came to the country's attention in 1926, when King Rama VI's royal architect constructed **Phra Ratchawang Klai Kangwon** (Far-From-Worries Palace), a seaside summer palace of golden teak, just north of what was then a small fishing village. Once endorsed by the royal family, Hua Hin became a traditional favourite among Thais, especially after the beaches of Pattaya and Phuket had been taken over

PRACHUAP KHIRI KHAN PROVINCE

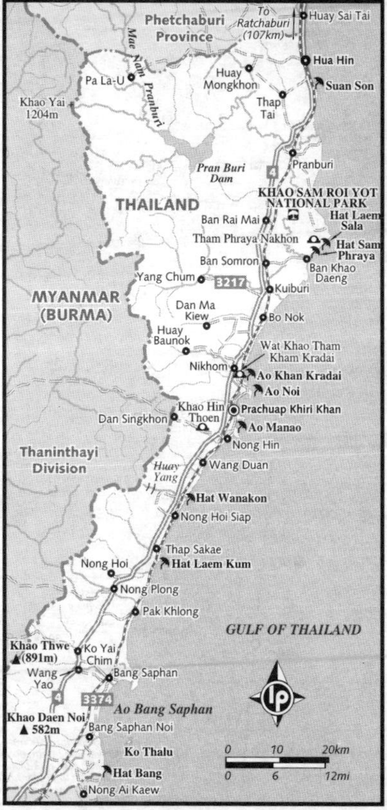

by foreign tourists. The palace is still used by the royal family.

In the late 1980s the colonial-style Hua Hin Railway Beach Hotel (now the Sofitel Central Hua Hin Resort), built in 1923, was renovated by a major French hotel group, attracting international attention. Major American hotel chains such as the Hilton, Hyatt and Marriott have recently dropped anchor in town, setting the scene for an invasion of sorts. Certainly Europeans have already discovered Hua Hin: a large a number of cafés and bistros offering Spanish, French, Italian and German cuisine have claimed their share of prime real estate. And there's no shortage of expats now living and working in the city.

But evolution brings its own problems. Hua Hin is not completely clear of that seedy factor plaguing the likes of Pattaya, which is the other main beach destination near Bangkok. Girlie bars have taken over a small lane in the centre of town, creating a small sex industry. Hua Hin has almost entirely lost its fishing-village atmosphere – the fishing fleet has been moved out and the town's infamous squid-drying piers have been replaced by hotels. Even the charming wooden pier houses along the shore on Th Naretdamri are slated to go – though this has been the plan for quite a few years now, and so far nothing has happened.

On the bright side, a sewage treatment plant and municipal sewer system have been constructed and the shore is cleaner than ever. The main swimming beach still has thatched umbrellas and long chairs; vendors

UPPER SOUTHERN GULF

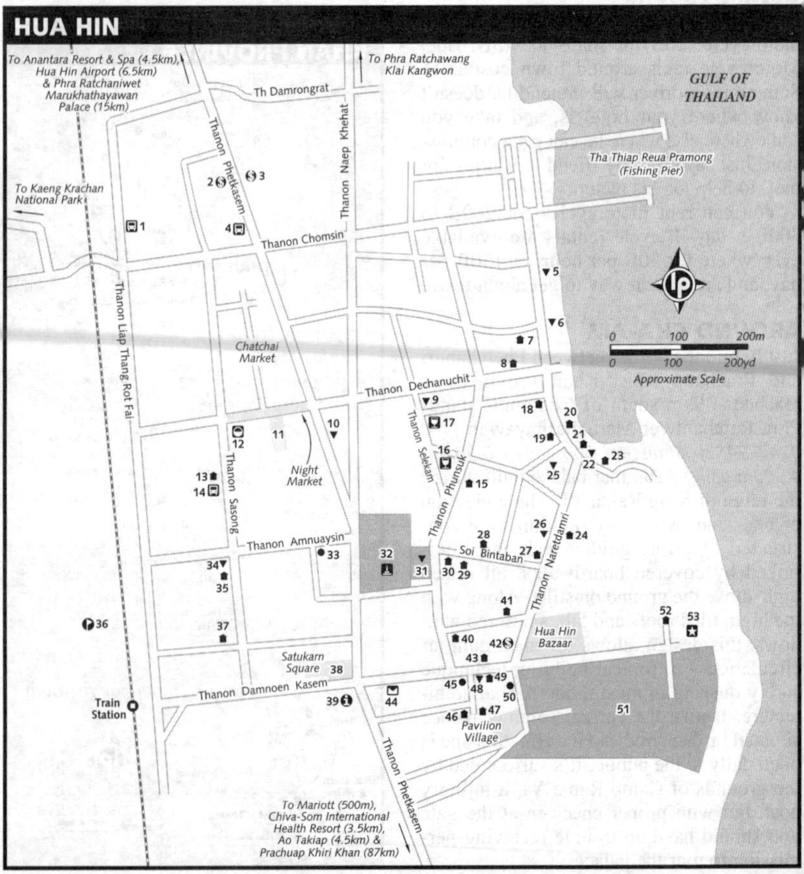

from the nearby food stalls will bring you steamed crab, mussels and beer (look for them near the public entrance to the beach, or to the south of the Sofitel).

The city's 5km of beaches are studded with large, smooth boulders, enough to give the beach a scenic appeal but not enough to hinder **swimming**. The surf is safe for bathers year-round, although jellyfish are an occasional problem during the rainy season (May to October) and water sports that are available include sailing and jet-skiing. In the city itself, a plethora of souvenir stands and tourist markets appeal to those seeking that modern, bustling beach-town atmosphere. Hua Hin remains a safe place for foreign visitors and their families, with its popularity growing by the year.

Information

Tourist Information *(☎ 0 3251 1047; cnr Th Phetkasem & Th Damnoen Kasem; open 8.30am-4.30pm daily)* provides advice about Hua Hin and its surrounding area and sells bus tickets to southern destinations.

The **tourist police** *(☎ 0 3251 5995)* sit at the eastern end of Th Damnoen Kasem, ready to serve.

The *Welcome to Hua Hin* brochure contains useful information on hotels, restaurants and transport. *Hua Hin Observer*, an expat-published newsletter with short features in English (and a few in German), on eating out, culture and entertainment.

There are several banks with ATMs around town. Conveniently located is the exchange booth at **Bank of Ayudhya** *(open 10am-8pm)*, across from the Hua Hin bazaar.

The **main post office** *(open 8.30am-4.30pm Mon-Fri, 9am-12pm Sat & Sun)* is next to the **CAT office**, which offers international phone service. Internet access is available all over Hua Hin.

Bookazine *(☎ 0 3253 2071; 166 Th Naretdamri; open 9am-10pm daily)* has a branch here, offering many maps, books in English and travel books – including Lonely Planet guides.

Western Tours *(☎ 0 3253 3303; 11 Th Damnoen Kasem; open 8.30am-7pm)* does tours to surrounding attractions, books hotel and bus tickets, and helps with local transportation. There's another branch on Th Amnuaysin.

Mai Thai Cruise & Travel *(☎ 0 3251 5919; 47/2 Th Dechanuchit)* is an agency that operates a beautifully restored and modified Thai fishing boat for cruises into the gulf and to Monkey island. The cruises, which include lunch and hotel shuttle, cost 1950B per person. It also organises and runs fishing trips for 2000B per person.

HUA HIN

PLACES TO STAY
- 7 Pattana
- 8 All Nations
- 13 Siripetchkasem Hotel
- 15 Sand Inn
- 18 Memory
- 19 Fulay Hotel; Orchids
- 20 Fulay Guest House
- 21 Sirima; Mod
- 23 Bird Guest House
- 24 Hilton Hua Hin Resort & Spa
- 27 Fresh Inn; Lo Stivale
- 28 Phuen Guest House & Happy Bar
- 29 Ban Pak Hua Hin
- 30 Sukwilai
- 35 Kung
- 37 Euro Hua Hin Hotel
- 40 Ban Boosarin
- 41 Lucky
- 43 Sirin
- 46 Ban Somboon
- 47 Patchara House
- 49 Puangpen Villa Hotel; PP Villa Guest House; Western Tours
- 51 Sofitel Central Hua Hin Resort
- 52 Central Hua Hin Village

PLACES TO EAT
- 5 Seafood Restaurants
- 6 Brasserie de Paris
- 9 Corner Bar; Mai Thai Cruise & Travel
- 10 Khuang Seng; Thara Jan; Clocktower
- 11 Night Plaza
- 22 Taj Mahal
- 25 Luciano's Pizza House
- 26 Sunshine Restaurant & Bakery
- 31 Food Stalls
- 34 Ruammit Restaurant & German Bakery
- 38 Tourist Market
- 48 Buffalo Bill's

OTHER
- 1 Bus Station
- 2 Kasikornbank (ATM)
- 3 Bangkok Bank (ATM)
- 4 Non-Air-Con Buses to Phetchaburi & Cha-am
- 12 Săwngthăew to Ao Takiap
- 14 Air-Con Buses to Bangkok
- 16 Coconuts Bar
- 17 Octopussy Bar
- 32 Wat Hua Hin
- 33 Western Tours
- 36 Royal Hua Hin Golf Course
- 39 Tourist Information
- 42 Bank of Ayudhya
- 44 Main Post Office; CAT Office
- 45 Money Exchange
- 50 Bookazine
- 53 Tourist Police

Beaches & Temples

The main beach runs about 2km along the southern half of town, with the nicest stretch of sand edging the Sofitel. Smooth granite boulders pierce the surf and are the source of the town's name, which means 'Stone Head'.

Along Ao Takiap, 8km to 13km south of Hua Hin, are the beaches of **Hat Takiap**, **Suan Son** and **Khao Tao**, all served by relatively new resort hotels. Two hill-top temples can be visited here. **Wat Khao Thairalat** is well off the beach on a rocky hill and nothing special, but at the end of the bay is the more interesting **Wat Khao Takiap**. Climb the steps for a good view of the bay.

Places to Stay – Budget

There's heaps of cheap accommodation in Hua Hin. Most of it basic, no-frills guesthouses. A cluster lies along or just off Th Naretdamri.

Lucky *(☎ 0 3253 2062; rooms with shared bath 150-200B)* offers decent and clean rock-bottom rooms that aren't too small. One room has air-con and costs 350B.

Phuen Guest House & Happy Bar *(☎ 0 3251 2344; rooms with fan 150-200B, with air-con 350B)* is home to some depressingly small and rather ramshackle rooms. There's a surprisingly nice common area, however, and it's within easy staggering distance of the nearby sleazy bars.

Sukwilai *(☎ 0 3251 3523; rooms with fan 150-250B, with air-con 400-800B)* is a large, decent and impersonal place. The wide variety of OK rooms range from shared bath to those with TV, hot water and fridge.

Ban Pak Hua Hin *(☎ 0 3251 1653, fax 0 3253 3649; rooms with fan/air-con 250/ 350B)* is an acceptable budget choice. It's neat and clean, though a bit rough around the edges and sports outdated architectural details.

Farther up Th Naretdamri is a string of wooden guesthouses built on piers and overlooking the sea.

Memory *(☎ 0 3251 1816; rooms with fan/ air-con from 200/500B)* has good clean rooms and pleasant halls on two levels; the more amenities you want, the more you pay.

Fulay Guest House *(☎ 0 3251 3145; rooms with fan 250-350B, with air-con 750-850B)* has decent fan rooms, though for air-con try the nearby **Fulay Hotel**, which is a much better deal for the same price.

Mod *(☎ 0 3251 2296; rooms with fan 250-450B, with air-con 550B)* takes up two storeys and exudes wooden charm. The upstairs rooms cost more but are airy and have better views.

Sirima *(☎ 0 3251 1060; rooms with fan 350-450B, with air-con 650B)* comes in pastel colours, with a long hallway leading to the highlight: a common deck overlooking the water. Rooms are small and nondescript.

Bird *(☎ 0 3251 1630; rooms with fan/air-con 350/600B)* is nearby and also popular for its deck and small rooms.

Going inland a bit you'll find a few more budget options.

All Nations *(☎ 0 3251 2747; 10-10/1 Th Dechanuchit; singles 150B, doubles 250-300B, rooms with air-con 450B)* has small, plain, warren-like rooms with shared bath. There's a small **restaurant** and bar downstairs.

Pattana *(☎ 0 3251 3393, fax 0 3253 0081; e huahinpattana@hotmail.com; rooms with fan 250-450B)* has simple, good rooms in old and beautiful teakwood buildings. Security is good and there's an outdoor **restaurant**.

Siripetchkasem Hotel *(☎ 0 3251 1394, fax 0 3251 1464; 7/5-8 Th Sasong; rooms with fan/ air-con 250/400B)* is a roomy, clean, fairly comfortable place served by indifferent staff. It's right next to where the air-con buses to Bangkok leave.

Euro Hua Hin Hotel *(☎ 0 3251 3130, fax 0 3251 4181; rooms with fan/air-con 300/ 500B)* may still have the old sign up, which says 'Srichan'. The rooms are fairly adequate, clean and simply furnished. The entrance is around the corner and then down an alley.

Kung *(☎ 0 1683 2844; cnr Th Sasong & Th Amnuaysin; rooms with fan/air-con 350/ 450B)* only has four rooms, but they're relatively good deals. Very large, clean, modern spaces come with new furniture, TV and fridge. Baths are shared between two rooms, however, and it's located well inland.

Ban Somboon *(☎/fax 0 3251 1538; 13/4 Soi Damnoen Kasem; rooms with fan/air-con 450/700B)* charms you with nicely furnished, cosy rooms in an older wooden house with garden. A TV, hot water and breakfast are included, and some rooms have fridges.

Sand Inn *(☎ 0 3253 3667; 38 Th Phunsuk; e sand-inn@prachuab.a-net.net.th; rooms with air-con 500B)* presents you with a dark and dreary stone lobby, but it's friendly. The good-sized rooms come with TV and hot water.

Places to Stay – Mid-Range

Hua Hin's mid-range places are typically small, sedate, modern hotels with air-con rooms and luxuries such as phones and fridges.

Patchara House *(☎ 0 3251 1787; 13/5 Soi Damnoen Kasem; rooms with air-con in low/high season 700/900B)* is down a quiet alley and offers good-value rooms with TV and fridge. There's hot water when the sun shines, as showers are solar powered.

Fulay Hotel *(☎ 0 3251 3670, fax 0 3253 0320; 110/1 Th Naretdamri; rooms with air-con 750B)* offers good, comfortable, immaculate rooms and well-decorated stairways. Also on the list are cable TV, fridge and, if you're lucky, sea-view balconies. There's a good French **restaurant** downstairs.

PP Villa Guest House *(☎ 0 3253 3785, fax 0 3251 1216; e ppvillahotel@hotmail.com; 11 Th Damnoen Kasem; rooms with air-con 750-850B)* has decent mid-range rooms and a garden with pool. The beach is about 200m away. Sharing the grounds and contact information is the more expensive **Puangpen Villa Hotel**. Rates rise during the high season and on weekends.

Ban Boosarin *(☎ 0 3251 2076; 8/8 Th Phunsuk; rooms with air-con in low/high season 850/1000B)* has very large, carpeted rooms with balcony and all the basic amenities.

Fresh Inn *(☎ 0 3251 1389; 132 Th Naretdamri; rooms with air-con 850-950B)* is very clean and nice, with rooms that have pleasant furniture, TV and fridge. There's a popular **restaurant** and small, attractive lobby.

Sirin *(☎ 0 3251 1150, fax 0 3251 3571; 6/3 Th Damnoen Kasem; rooms with air-con from 990B)* is a fine hotel for the price. The rooms are great and include fridge, bath, balcony and simple decor. There's a small pool and parking.

Just beyond the Marriott Hotel, 1km south of Hua Hin, is a small low-key neighbourhood of almost identical, mid-range guesthouses (ex-townhouses), a large number of which are run by *faràng*-Thai couples. None are right on the beach, but it's only a short walk away. Prices (rooms from 600B to 750B July to September, from 800B to 1000B October to June) and facilities (clean, comfortable, modern) are approximately the same at almost every one. We recommend **Royal Beach** *(☎/fax 0 3253 2210; e royalbeach@hotmail.com)*, **Thipurai** *(☎ 0 3251 2210; e thipurai@hotmail.com)*, **Leng** *(☎ 0 3251 3546; w www.go.to/leng)*, **Sunny Clown** *(☎ 0 3251 2936; w www.sunnyclown.com)* and **Jinning Beach** *(☎/fax 0 3251 3950; w www.jinningbeachguesthouse.com)*.

Places to Stay – Top End

There are some wonderful upmaket hotels in Hua Hin, but you'll find a few more options either north or south of town as well.

Remember that these hotels will add almost 18% to your bill for service charges and tax. Also, during peak-holiday periods supplemental charges are often tacked on to the usual prices.

Sofitel Central Hua Hin Resort *(☎ 0 3251 2021, fax 0 3251 1014, in Bangkok ☎ 0 2233 0980; w www.sofitel.com; rack rates from 6150B)* is a magnificent, two-storey colonial-style place with three pools, expansive grounds along the beach, spa facilities and excellent service. Rooms are beautiful and luxurious, with charming old-time touches. Discounts may be possible with advance booking through Bangkok.

Central Hua Hin Village *(☎ 0 3251 2036, fax 0 3251 1014; w www.hotels-huahin.com; bungalows from 3900B)*, right across from the Sofitel, is a collection of gorgeous one- and two-bedroom wooden beach bungalows. The tropical grounds are beautiful (and extend to the beach), the Thai **restaurant** is good, and there's a stunning pool. Discounts may be possible with advance booking through Bangkok.

Hilton Hua Hin Resort & Spa *(☎ 0 3251 2888, fax 0 3251 1135, in Bangkok ☎ 0 2253 0123, fax 0 2250 0999; w www.huahin.hilton.com; rooms US$140-190)* offers rooms with balconies and sea views, and an elephant theme throughout. There's a 17th-floor rooftop **restaurant**, a beachside pool and all the amenities a Hilton can offer, including complete spa services.

Hua Hin Marriott *(☎ 0 3251 1881, fax 0 3251 2422; w www.marriotthotels.com/hhqmc; rooms 16 Apr-31 Sept 3950B, 1 Oct-15 Apr 5800B)* claims its own beachfront territory, which includes over 200 rooms, two tennis courts, a large pool and four **restaurants**. Relaxing, open lounges and gorgeously landscaped grounds make this hotel one of the most comfortable stays in the Hua Hin area. The Marriott is just south of the town on Th Phetkasem.

Chiva-Som International Health Resort (*☎ 0 3253 6536, fax 0 3251 1154; W www.chivasom.com; Th Phetkasem; singles US$420, doubles per person US$315*), south of town about 2.5km, is one of the world's top health resorts, and your wellness is paramount here. Forty ocean-view rooms and 17 Thai-style pavilions decorate the three beachside hectares. Rates include all meals, fitness consultations and massage – nonguests can also use the spa services. One-week packages to 30-year memberships are also available. It's a good idea to book ahead for this place.

Places to Stay – Out of Town

Ao Takiap, 4.5km south of Hua Hin, boasts plenty of upper mid-range accommodation options.

Nern Chalet (*☎ 0 3251 1288, fax 0 3251 1288; W www.nernchalet.com; rooms Mon-Thur 1200-1700B, Fri-Sun 1700-2500B*) lies at the northern end of Ao Takiap. It has very pleasant, tiled-floor rooms on three floors in a nice, relatively intimate building. All rooms have sea views (the beach is right there) and most have balconies. Rates include breakfast.

Hua Hin Bluewave Beach Resort (*☎ 0 3251 1036, fax 0 3253 6245; rooms Mon-Thur from 1250B, Fri-Sun 1450B*) sits 6km south of town. It's a beachside high-rise and home to almost 150 good rooms, all with balcony (though only the junior suites have frontal sea views). Amenities include pool, sauna, fitness centre and billiards room. Rates include breakfast.

Ta-kiab Beach Resort (*☎ 0 3251 2639, fax 0 3251 5899; W www.takiabbeach.com; rooms Mon-Thur 900B, Fri-Sun 1500B*) stands right behind the Bluewave, 150m away from the beach – a less expensive option, if you don't need sea views. At least there's a pool.

About 4.5km north of Hua Hin **Anantara Resort & Spa** (*☎ 0 2477 0800, fax 0 2476 6165; W www.anantara.com; rooms US$100-165*) is a beautiful, Thai-style place on large, tropical grounds that adjoin the beach. Rooms are tastefully done and comfortably restful after your spa regime, for which Anantara is well known.

UPPER SOUTHERN GULF

Places to Eat

One of Hua Hin's major attractions has always been the colourful and inexpensive Chatchai Market in the centre of town, where vendors gather nightly to cook fresh seafood for hordes of hungry Thais. It's also excellent for Thai breakfasts – there's very good *jók* and *khâo tôm* (rice soups). Fresh-fried *paa-thâwng-kŏh* (Chinese doughnuts) in the Hua Hin–style – small and crispy, not oily – cost 2B for three. A few vendors also serve hot soy milk in bowls (5B) – break a few *paa-thâwng-kŏh* into the soy milk.

A **night market** sets up on Th Dechanuchit, in front of the touristy Night Plaza. **Satukarn Square** also caters to tourists with a few food carts (among the souvenir stalls).

The best seafood to eat in Hua Hin is *plaa sămlii* (cotton fish or kingfish), *plaa kràphong* (perch), *plaa mèuk* (squid), *hăwy málaeng phûu* (mussels) and *puu* (crab). Enjoy it at the Night Plaza off Th Dechanuchit, or near the fishing pier at the northern end of town. Two Chinese-Thai seafood places along Th Phetkasem are **Khuang Seng** and **Thara Jan**, neither of which have Roman-script signs; both are fairly good value.

Taj Mahal (*☎ 0 3251 2613; 31/1 Th Naretdamri; dishes 40-90B; open 9.30am-11pm daily*), next to Bird guesthouse, serves cheap and decent Indian food, such as tandoori bread and meat. There's also mutton and vegetable offerings, and the ambience is intimate and modern.

Lo Stivale (*☎ 0 3251 3800; 132 Th Naretdamri; dishes 140-280B; open 1pm-11.30pm daily*) is a popular place serving the usual Italian dishes, pizza and a few Thai choices. For dessert, there's banana split (120B).

Luciano's Pizza House (*☎ 0 3253 0709; 7 Soi Selakam; dishes 70-200B; open 2pm-midnight daily*) is another place that does Italian food, with checkered tablecloths and a bistro-like atmosphere.

Sunshine Restaurant & Bakery (*☎ 0 3253 2475; 130/2 Th Naretdamri; dishes 65-220B; open 9am-10.30pm daily*), opposite the Hilton, serves German, European and Thai food in a pleasant atmosphere with lattice and rattan touches. Drinks include coffee, wine and beer. A few baked goods are sold, and there's even Internet access.

Buffalo Bill's (*☎ 0 3253 2727; 13 Th Damnoen Kasem; dishes 150-320B; open 'morning* *to night')* grills up great Australian steaks, burgers and fish 'n' chips in a large, clean and well-lit environment. It's British-run and boasts a huge and extensive menu you could beat someone over the head with.

Bamboo Hut *(☎ 0 3253 2692; Hua Hin Bazaar; dishes 80-150B; open 10am-3pm & 5.30pm-10pm daily)* doesn't offer sushi, but does have a Japanese picture menu, making ordering easy. It's a tiny place and apparently the only Japanese restaurant in Hua Hin, other than the fancy one at the Hilton. Look for it next to Berny's.

Ruammit Restaurant & German Bakery *(☎ 0 3251 1228; cnr Th Amnuaysin & Th Sasong; dishes 100-310B; open 8am-8pm daily)* claims the best breakfast in town. It serves German food and is (unsurprisingly) a magnet for German tourists. There's a large, pleasant patio out front.

Orchids *(☎ 0 3251 3670; 110/1 Th Naretdamri; open 7am-midnight daily)* cooks up semi-authentic French food along with more authentic Thai food. It's an intimate, airy place with pleasant timber decor and satisfied *faràng*.

Brasserie de Paris *(☎ 0 3253 0637; 3 Th Naretdamri; dishes 120-395B; open 11am-11pm daily)* offers just a few upmarket French dishes, cooked by a French chef. There's a good view of the sea from upstairs, and the ambience is modern and comfortable.

Corner Bar *(☎ 0 3251 3327; 47/1 Th Dechanuchit; dishes 60-150B; open 3pm-1am daily)* has basic Thai food on the menu, with some sandwiches for variety. Busy sidewalk tables are popular with travellers, who also come here to drink. It's a casual place – nothing fancy.

Coconuts *(☎ 0 3253 2507; 85 Th Selekham; dishes 50-80B; open 9am-2am daily)* has soup, rice dishes, noodles, breakfast and pub fare. The owner also conducts unique five-hour cave tours (600B).

The Hua Hin Bazaar has a handful of British-style pubs offering 'home cooking', along with a few Thai dishes (and we don't mean the staff).

Billy's Bar & Restaurant *(Hua Hin Bazaar; dishes 65-160B; open 9.30am-2am daily)* offers Thai food, sandwiches and breakfasts. All types of spirits are served, and tables spill out onto the shopping lane.

Berny's *(Hua Hin Bazaar; dishes 80-250B; open 24hr)* is another British-run place with similar pub fare. Food is served during meal hours. This is also the place for golf information.

Entertainment

Several *faràng* bars under European management can be found in the Hua Hin Bazaar. Some of these offer the familiar Thai-hostess atmosphere but a few bill themselves as 'sports bars' and have wide-screen TVs. **Berny's** *(open 24hrs)* is a sports bar, but concentrates especially on golf. It's British-run, and pub food is served during meal hours. **Billy's Bar & Restaurant** *(open 9.30am-2am daily)* attracts older male *faràng* in the evenings, and sports a typical pub atmosphere. There's a pool table for entertainment and plenty of drinks to make it fun.

There are some interesting bars on Th Selekam as well.

Octopussy *(☎ 0 3251 1087; 27/1-2 Th Selekam; open noon-midnight daily)* is a hard-grit drinking bar, attracting strange types with darts, a nice back area and plenty of cocktails. There is also sport on the TV and two pool tables.

Coconuts *(Hard Cock Cafe; ☎ 0 3253 2507; 85 Th Selekam; open 9am-2am daily)* is a casual, expat-run place festively decorated with dozens of neon coconuts. Reasonably priced drinks are poured, and there's a pool table. Get your picture taken with the python.

Anyone looking for sleazy nightlife need not go far. Soi Bintaban, just a short walk further down from Octopussy and Coconuts, is lined with girly bars doing their best to attract clientele. It's not a dangerous place per se, just a peek into the seedier side of tourism.

Getting There & Away

Bangkok Airways *(airport ☎ 0 3252 2305)* flies to Bangkok and Ko Samui four times weekly; to Phuket it goes daily.

There are frequent air-con buses to/from Bangkok's Southern bus station (1st class/2nd class 128/99B, 3½ hours). These leave from next to the Siripetchkasem Hotel.

The main bus station has air-con buses to/from Phetchaburi (60B, 1½ hours), Cha-am (40B, 30 minutes), Prachuap Khiri Khan (50B, 1½ hours), Chumphon (125B, four hours), Surat Thani (210B, seven hours), Phuket (305B, 10 hours) and Krabi (280B, nine hours). Frequent non-air-con buses to

Phetchaburi (30B, 1½ hours) and Cha-am (20B, 30 minutes) leave from near the intersection of Th Chomsin and Th Phetkasem.

There are frequent trains to/from Bangkok's Hualamphong train station (2nd class, 142B to 192B; 3rd-class 80B; four hours) and other stations on the southern railway line.

Getting Around

The airport is about 6km north of town, only a 150B taxi ride away.

Local buses (7B) and săwngthăew (10B) to Ao Takiap leave from the corner of Th Sasong and Th Dechanuchit.

Săamláw will tempt you with fares from the train or bus stations to the middle of Th Naretdamri (approximately 40B), though your bags may cost you more.

Motorcycles (200B per day) and bicycles (150B per day) can be rented from a couple of places on Th Damnoen Kasem. For car rental, **Avis** has offices at the **Sofitel** *(☎ 0 3251 2021)* and the **Hilton** *(☎ 0 3251 2888)*. Local agencies will charge less, however.

KHAO SAM ROI YOT NATIONAL PARK

อุทยานแห่งชาติเขาสามร้อยยอด

Called Three Hundred Mountain Peaks *(☎ 0 3261 9078; admission 200B)* this 98-sq-km park is mostly filled with lagoons and coastal marshlands that are excellent for bird-watching. There are magnificent views of the ocean and surrounding areas from the top of Khao Daeng, a short hike from park headquarters, but if you have more time and energy you can climb the 605m **Khao Krachom** for even better views. With luck you may even come across a serow (Asian goat-antelope). Along the coast you may see the occasional pod of Irrawaddy dolphins *(plaa lohmaa hŭa bàat)*.

Be sure to bring insect repellent along. King Rama IV and a large entourage of Thai and European guests convened here on 18 August 1868 to see a total solar eclipse – predicted, so the story goes, by the monarch himself – and enjoy a feast prepared by a French chef. Two months later the king died from malaria, contracted from mosquito bites inflicted here. The risk of malaria in the park is relatively low, but the mosquitoes can be pesky.

Fauna

Notable wildlife includes barking deer, crab-eating macaque, slow loris, Malayan pangolin, fishing cat, palm civet, otter, serow, Javan mongoose and monitor lizard. Khao Sam Roi Yot is considered an exceptional place to view dusky langur.

Because the park lies at the intersection of the East Asian and Australian fly ways, as many as 300 migratory and resident bird species have been recorded, including yellow bittern, cinnamon bittern, purple swamp hen, water rail, ruddy-breasted crake, bronze-winged jacana, grey heron, painted stork, whistling duck, spotted eagle and black-headed ibis. The park protects Thailand's largest freshwater marsh (along with mangroves and mudflats), and is one of only three places in the country where the purple heron breeds.

Waterfowl are most commonly seen in the cool season. Encroachment by shrimp farmers in the vicinity has sadly destroyed substantial portions of mangroves and other wetlands, thus depriving the birds of an important habitat.

September to March are the best bird-watching months for waterfowl.

Beaches & Mangroves

A sandy beach, flanked on three sides by dry limestone hills and casuarinas, **Hat Laem Sala** is the location for a small visitor centre, restaurant, bungalows and camping area. Boats can be hired from Bang Pu to the beach (a 15-minute ride) for 200B return. You can also reach the beach via a steep trail, about a 20-minute hike.

Hat Sam Phraya, 5km south of Hat Laem Sala, is a 1km-long beach with a restaurant and washrooms. The **park headquarters** and another visitors centre are located about 6km south of here.

A 4km canal trip in a 10-person boat along **Khlong Khao Daeng** can be arranged in Ban Khao Daeng (300B, 1½ hours). The boat passes by mangrove remnants and waterfowl habitats; the birds are most active in early morning or late afternoon. You might also spot monitor lizards and monkeys.

Caves

Other attractions at Khao Sam Roi Yot are caves. **Tham Phraya Nakhon** is the most visited and can be reached by boat or on foot.

The boat trip only takes about half an hour return, while it's half an hour each way on foot along a steep, rocky trail. There are two large caverns, with sinkholes that allow light in. In one cave is a royal *săalaa* built for King Rama V, who would stop off when travelling between Bangkok and Nakhon Si Thammarat.

Tham Kaew, 2km from the Bang Pu turn-off, features a series of chambers connected by narrow passageways; you enter the first cavern by means of a permanent ladder. Stalactites and other limestone formations, some of which glitter with calcite crystals as if diamond encrusted (hence the cave's name, 'Jewel Cave'), are plentiful. Lamps can be rented, but Tham Kaew is best visited in the company of a park guide because of the dangerous footing.

Tham Sai is ensconced in a hill near Ban Khung Tanot, about 2.5km from the main road between Laem Sala and Sam Phraya beaches. Villagers rent out lamps at a shelter near the cave mouth. A 280m trail leads up the hillside to the cave, which features a large single cavern. Be careful of steep drop-offs in the cave.

Places to Stay

The **Forestry Department** *(Bangkok ☎ 0 2561 2920)* rents large **bungalows** near park headquarters and at Hat Laem Sala. The bungalows sleep four to 20 people and cost 1200B per night for one to five people. Two-person tents are available for 120B a night. You can also pitch your own tent at **camp sites** *(20B per person)* near park headquarters, Hat Laem Sala or Hat Sam Phraya. There are restaurants at Hat Laem Sala and Hat Sam Phraya.

One private accommodation option is **Bayview Laguna Resort** *(☎/fax 0 3262 2165; bungalows with fan/air-con 750/1400B)*, next to a lagoon and within walking distance of Bang Pu.

Getting There & Away

The park is about 60km south of Hua Hin (40km south of Pranburi) and it's best seen by car. If you don't have your own wheels, catch a bus or train to Pranburi and then a săwngthăew (40B) to Bang Pu, the small village inside the park. From Bang Pu you can walk to Hat Laem Sala.

You can can also hire a săwngthăew for 400B, or a motorcycle taxi for 250B, from Pranburi all the way to the park. Be sure to mention you want to go to the national park *(ùtháyaan hàeng châat)* rather than Ban Khao Sam Roi Yot.

PRACHUAP KHIRI KHAN

อ.เมืองประจวบคีรีขันธ์

postcode 77000 • pop 27,700

Roughly 80km south of Hua Hin and capital of its province, Prachuap Khiri Khan lies in the large, 8km-long muddy bay of Ao Prachuap, which is surrounded by faraway limestone cliffs and dotted with colourful fishing boats. There are no real swimming beaches in town, although these can be found to the north and south of it. The seafood is tasty and affordable, and fishing is still the mainstay of the local economy.

Prachuap Khiri Khan (specifically Ao Manao) was one of seven points on the Gulf of Thailand coast where Japanese troops landed on 8 December 1941 during their invasion of Thailand. Several street names around town commemorate the ensuing skirmish: Phitak Chat (Defend Country); Salachip (Sacrifice Life); Suseuk (Fight Battle).

Information

At the northern end of town there's a **tourist office** *(☎ 0 3261 1491; open 8.30am-4.30pm daily)* and if you're lucky you'll get the good English speaker who dispenses excellent information on the area. If you need a visa extension, ask about the possiblity of obtaining one near the Myanmar border in Dan Singkhon.

There's an **Internet café** *(open 8.30am-9.30pm daily)* on Th Sarachip near Th Maitri Ngam. Another **Internet café** *(open noon-8pm daily)*, near the train station on Th Kong Kiat, sells steamed buns (3B each).

Local resident **Pinit Ounope** *(☎ 0 3255 0059; 144 Th Chai Thaleh)* arranges tours to nearby national parks, beaches and waterfalls, among other sites. His house is rather difficult to find, so take a motorcycle taxi. Tours cost about 500B per person.

Things to See & Do

North of the city is **Khao Chong Krajok** (Mirror Tunnel Mountain – named after the hole in the mountain that appears to reflect the sky). At the top is **Wat Thammikaram**,

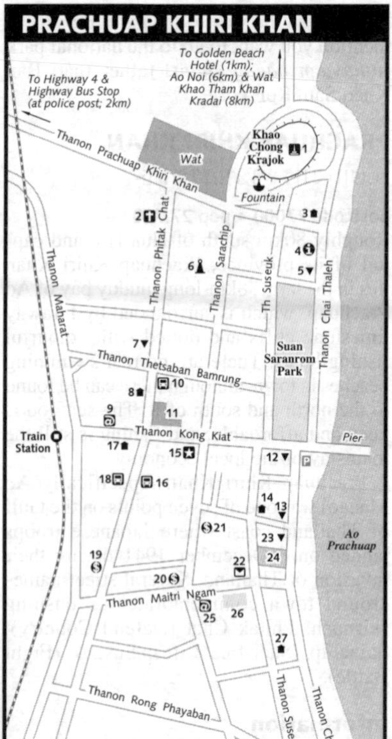

PLACES TO STAY
3 Thaed Saban Bungalows
8 Inthira Hotel; Ordinary Buses to Chumphon
14 Suksan
17 Yuttichai Hotel
24 Hadthong Hotel
27 Prachuapsuk Hotel

PLACES TO EAT
5 Sai Thong Restaurant
7 Chiow Ocha
11 Food Stalls
12 Pramong
13 Pan Phochana Restaurant
23 Phloen Samut Restaurant

OTHER
1 Wat Thammi Karam
2 Ave Maria Church
4 Tourist Office
6 City Pillar
9 Internet Café
10 Ordinary Buses to Hua Hin
15 Police
16 Air-Con Buses to Cha-am, Hua Hin, Phetchaburi, Bangkok
18 Air-Con Buses to Bangkok
19 Kasikornbank
20 Bangkok Bank
21 Siam Commercial Bank
22 Main Post Office
25 Internet Café
26 Municipal Market

established by King Rama VI. You can climb the hill for a view of the town and bay; a ladder leads from the grounds of the wát into the tunnel.

Near the base of this mountain is a small **fountain** that hordes of monkeys sometimes dive into (from 15ft up) while chasing each other. It's hugely entertaining. If they're not here you'll no doubt see the monkeys somewhere else on the mountain – stay alert, though, as they can be aggressive. The 'stooping-to-pick-up-a-rock' motion works wonders.

If you continue north along the beach road you'll come to a small boat-building village on **Ao Bang Nang Lom**, where wooden fishing vessels are still made using traditional Thai methods. It takes about two months to finish a 12m boat, which will sell for around 400,000B. The industrious folks here also catch a fish called *plaa ching chang,* which they dry and store for Sri Lankan traders. A few kilometres north of Ao Bang Nang Lom is another bay, **Ao Noi**, the site of a small fishing village.

Six kilometres south of the city is the scenic, island-dotted **Ao Manao**, a bay ringed by a clean white-sand beach. A Thai air-force base guards access to the bay (a possible legacy of the 1941 Japanese invasion). The beach itself is 2km to 3km past the base entrance, where you'll probably have to show your passport.

There are several *sǎalaa* here, along with a hotel and restaurant. You can rent chairs, umbrellas and inner tubes, and buy food and drink. In early December there's a public ceremony at the base commemorating Thai WWII heroes.

Nine kilometres south of Ao Manao, and just past **Hat Khlong Wan**, is the pleasant, casuarina-lined **Hat Wa Kaw**, which is even quieter and cleaner than Ao Manao. The **King Mongkut Memorial Park of Science and Technology** *(☎ 0 3266 1098; admission free; open 8.30am-4.30pm daily)* commemorates the 1868 solar eclipse that the king and his 15-year-old son Prince Chulalongkorn came south to witness. Also on display is a US-built steam locomotive (Baldwin Locomotive Works, 1925).

Places to Stay

Central Prachuap has plenty of budget accommodation, but anything above that is limited. There are better mid-range choices to the north or south of the city, though getting to them isn't always easy.

Yuttichai Hotel (*☎ 0 3261 1055, fax 0 3260 1755; 115 Th Kong Kiat; rooms with shared bath 120-180B, with private bath 180-240B*) offers large, dim, old, clean and decent fan rooms. It's close to the bus stops, and the friendly staff even speak a little English.

Inthira Hotel (*☎ 0 3261 1418; 120 Th Phitak Chat; rooms with fan/air-con 200/300B*), around the corner from Yuttichai, is also friendly and has basic rooms. TV is extra.

Prachuapsuk Hotel (*☎ 0 3261 1019, fax 0 3260 1711; 69-71 Th Suseuk; rooms 180B, with air-con 300B*) has all the charm of a two-car garage. It's a friendly, family run place with rock-bottom rooms. It has a small Roman-script sign.

Suksan (*☎ 0 3261 1145; 11 Th Suseuk; rooms with fan/air-con from 250/370B*) is about two notches above 'rock-bottom'. All acceptably worn rooms have a balcony, but there's no elevator so you'll get plenty of exercise.

Thaed Saban Bungalows (*☎ 0 3261 1204; rooms with fan/air-con 300/400B, bungalows with fan from 600B*) sit forlornly in a run-down, treeless lot and are very rustic in that almost completely charmless way. They're made of concrete and wood, and are large and outdated, though some do face the sea; groups of up to eight can fit themselves inside.

Hadthong Hotel (*☎ 0 3260 1050, fax 0 3260 1057; w www.hadthong.com; 21 Th Suseuk; rooms from 675B*) is definitely the place to go if you're at all queasy about staying at grungy places. The shower in room 204 was especially nice. Rooms are modern but not spiffy, and come with fridge, cable TV and chipped furniture. Sea view rooms are worth the extra baht. There's also a murky pool outside.

North of town there's coastline to explore, along with a few places to stay.

Golden Beach Hotel (*☎ 0 3260 1626, fax 0 3255 1199; 113 Th Suanson; rooms with air-con 400-600B*), about 1km north of the city, is across from the beach and offers a couple of different kinds of nondescript, modern rooms – the better ones cost more, naturally. There are mangroves behind the hotel.

Ao Noi Beach Resort (*☎ 0 3260 1350; 206 Tambon Ao Noi; rooms with fan/air-con 400/600B*), about 6km north of the city, is set on pleasant, leafy grounds next to the beach, though the buildings could've used some planning. Fan rooms at least have windows facing the sea; air-con ones just have a wall. It's a casual, friendly place far away from anything touristy, though there's a wát nearby.

Eight kilometres south of town, past Ao Manao and the small town of Khlong Wan, are a few islolated and low-key places to stay on the beach (Hat Khlong Wan). Săwngthăew from Prachuap will cost 20B; motorcycle taxis or *săaleng* (a kind of túk-túk) charge 70B.

Ban Rim Thalee (*no Roman-script sign; ☎ 0 3266 1734, Th Prachuap-Khlong Wan; rooms with air-con 800-1200B*) is a modern, tidy and new place with comfortable rooms. There isn't much to do here except hang out on the beach; Khlong Wan is 2km north and has a bank and 7-Eleven. Look for the wagon wheels at the entrance.

Ban Forty (*☎/fax 0 3266 1437; w www.hellohuahin.com/baanforty; 555 Th Prachuap-Khlong Wan; rooms & bungalows 800B, house 2500B*), 200m past Ban Rim Thalee, offers four simple but clean concrete bungalows surrounded by grass and gravel, and some palm trees; there's also a seven-bed house. It's owned by a friendly policeman of Thai-English descent. Simple meals can be served.

Places to Eat

Because of its well-deserved reputation for fine seafood, Prachuap Khiri Khan has many restaurants for its size. One of the seafood specialities that you shouldn't miss is *plaa sămlii dàet diaw* – whole cottonfish that's sliced lengthways and left to dry in the sun for half a day, then fried quickly in a wok. It's often served with mango salad on the side. It may sound awful, but the taste is sublime.

There are some good cheap places in town, with large, open and very casual dining rooms. These include **Sai Thong Restaurant** (*no Roman-script sign; ☎ 0 3255 0868; Th Chai Thaleh; dishes 50-160B; open 10am-10pm daily*), **Chiow Ocha** (*no Roman-script sign; ☎ 0 3261 1118; 100 Th Phitak Chat; dishes 50-80B; open 8am-7pm daily*) and **Pramong** *(no Roman-script sign; ☎ 0 3261 1168; 36 Th Chai Thaleh; dishes 50-80B; open 7am-10pm daily)*.

If you're looking for more upmarket, great-tasting seafood, at reasonable prices and with added sea views, you're not asking too much. Try **Pan Phochana Restaurant** *(☎ 0 3261 1195; 40 Chai Thaleh; dishes 50-120B; open 8am-10pm daily)*, which is famous for its *hàw mòk hǎwy* (ground fish curry steamed in mussels on the half-shell), or **Phloen Samut Restaurant** *(☎ 0 3261 1115; 44 Th Chai Thaleh; dishes 50-120B; open 8.30am-10pm daily)*, with its extensive menu.

The best place for your baht and adventurous taste buds are the **food stalls** that convene near the district office in the middle of town.

Getting There & Away

Inquire at the efficient tourist-information office for current bus and train schedules and prices.

There are frequent services to/from Bangkok (1st/2nd class 176/140B, four to five hours), Hua Hin (50B, 1½ hours), Cha-am (60B, 2½ hours) and Phetchaburi (80B, three hours). These air-con buses leave from Th Phitak Chat near the centre of town. For southern destinations such as Phuket, Krabi or Hat Yai, hike out to the police station on the highway to catch passing buses (motorcycle taxis will take you for 30B). One exception is the local bus No 426 to Chumphon (75B), which leaves from in front of the Inthira Hotel.

There are frequent train services to/from Bangkok (2nd class 175B to 225B; 3rd class 98B). Other destinations include Hua Hin (19B to 59B) and Chumphon (34B to 258B).

Getting Around

Prachuap is small enough to get around on foot, but you can hop on a motorcycle or *sǎaleng* around town for 20B. Other destinations include Ao Noi (30B to 40B) and Ao Manao (20B to 25B), whose beach is accessible via a Thai air-force base. Motorcycles aren't permitted past the gate unless both driver and passenger are wearing helmets.

Hiring the services of a motorcycle taxi for three hours costs 300B.

AROUND PRACHUAP KHIRI KHAN

Wat Khao Tham Khan Kradai

วัดเขาถ้ำคานกระได

About 8km north of town, following the road beyond Ao Noi, is this small cave wát at one end of **Ao Khan Kradai** (also known as Ao Khan Bandai) – a long, beautiful bay.

A trail at the base of the limestone hill leads up and around the side to a small cavern and then to a larger one that contains a reclining Buddha. If you have a torch you can proceed to a larger second chamber also containing Buddha images.

From this trail you get a good view of Ao Khan Kradai. The beach here is suitable for swimming and is virtually deserted. A motorcycle ride here is 30B.

Dan Singkhon

ด่านสิงขร

Just south of Prachuap Khiri Khan is a road leading west to Dan Singkhon, on the Myanmar border. This is the narrowest point in Thailand between the Gulf of Thailand and Myanmar – only 12km across. The Myanmar side changed from Karen to Yangon control following skirmishes in 1988–9. The border is open to Thai-Burmese citizens only. On the Thai side there is a small frontier village and a Thai police camp with wooden semi-underground bunkers built in a circle.

Off the road on the way to Dan Singkhon are a couple of small cave hermitages. The more famous one at **Khao Hin Thoen** is surrounded by a park of the same name. It contains some interesting rock formations and sculptures.

The road to Khao Hin Thoen starts where the paved road to Dan Singkhon breaks left. **Khao Khan Hok** (also known as Phutthakan Bang Kao) is a less well-known cave nearby where an elderly monk, Luang Phaw Buaphan Chatimetho, lives.

HAT BAN KRUT & BANG SAPHAN YAI

หาดบ้านกรูดและบางสะพานใหญ่

These two low-key destinations lie about 40km and 60km south of Prachuap Khiri Khan, where a string of fairly good surrounding beaches attracts a handful of Thai tourists but very few *faràng*. It's popular on weekends and school holidays, and during January and February – when waves bring more sand onto the beach. Islands off the coast to the south, including **Ko Thalu** and **Ko Sing** offer good **snorkelling** and **diving** from the end of January to mid-May. Coral Resort and Suan Luang Resort in Bang Saphan Yai can arrange half-day diving excursions to these islands.

Hat Ban Krut is edged by a road, which makes the 10km beach handy to cars and services but detracts from a completely peaceful beach experience. The sand is nice and soft, however, and the beach is long enough for crowds not to be a problem.

Bang Saphan Yai is nothing special as a town, but its long coastline has begun to attract some speculative development. Don't confuse this place with Bang Saphan Noi, which is further south about 15km.

Relatively frequent buses and trains connect Hat Ban Krut and Bang Saphan Yai to Bangkok (227B), Prachuap Khiri Khan and Chumphon. The train station is located around 4km from the beach, with motorcycle taxis the only form of public transport available. Public transport is limited within this area, so getting around can be a problem. Having your own wheels makes things a lot easier, as distances between the beaches are fairly long. Motorcycles can be hired from some of the guesthouses.

Places to Stay

Hat Ban Krut Just north of the Hat Ban Krut headland (topped by Wat Ton Sai) is **Ban Krut Youth Hostel** *(☎ 0 3261 9103; e hostthai@ksc.th.com; dorm beds 200-250B, bungalows with fan 500B, with air-con 700-1000B)*. It's brand-spanking new and very plush for a hostel, with four- or five-bed dorms in a large, spiffy building complete with conference room. Basic wooden bungalows come with fan and 'outdoor' baths, while fancier air-con bungalows sit nearer the beach and are furnished with large TV, fridge and hot water. On the grounds are a small beachside pool with jacuzzi and nearby bar. There are plans to add a sport courts, an aviary and garden, and rent bicycles and motorcycles. Breakfast is included but sheet rental is not; hostel cards glean a small discount. Call the staff for a nearby pick-up (40B).

The following are all on the beach road south of the wát-topped headland.

Reun Chun Seaview *(☎ 0 3269 5061, fax 0 3269 5322; 300 Mu 3; bungalows with 1/2 bedrooms 600/1500B)* is towards the northern end of the beach and features modern, crowded bungalows with a somewhat impersonal feel, though the management is friendly. There are large verandas and solid furniture, and the restaurant is huge.

Ban Klang Aow Beach Resort *(no Roman-script sign; ☎ 0 3269 5086, fax 0 3269 5430; w www.baan-klang-aow.co.th; bungalows Mon-Thur 1400-2600B, Fri-Sun 1600-2800B)* has nicely appointed, spacious one- and two-bedroom bungalows with dark log walls and large verandas. They're set around wonderfully leafy tropical paths and two pools. A romantic **restaurant** at the resort offers nourishment, while bicycles and kayaks provide exercise. Look for the upmarket thatched roofs.

Siam Garden Beach Resort *(☎/fax 0 1458 7877; e siamgarden@hotmail.com; rooms with fan/air-con 550/750B)* is located way at the southern end of the beach. The rooms are large, modern and adequate, and furnished with TV and fridge. Four-person bungalows are available, and rates include breakfast. There are also bicycles (150B) and motorcycles (250B) available for rent.

Bang Saphan Yai The following are just north of the town and on the coast.

Hat Somboon Sea View *(☎ 0 3254 8344, fax 0 3254 8343; 32/1 Mu 5; singles/doubles with air-con 400/500B)* has seen grander days, but still maintains decently furnished rooms (some large) with carpet, TV, fridge and some personality. It's across from the beach on a corner.

Nipa Beach Bungalows *(☎ 0 3269 1583; bungalows with air-con 550B)* is a friendly place across the street from the Hat Somboon Sea View. It has large, cute, modern bungalows on a sparse garden lot.

Van Veena Hotel *(☎ 0 3269 1251, fax 0 3269 1548; 163 Th Mae Rampheung; rooms with fan/air-con 250/450B)*, 300m further up the beach, offers cold industrial halls and unexciting rooms with fridge and TV. There's a pleasant **restaurant** across the street on the beach, however.

The following are about 5km south of town, and on or near the coast.

Suan Luang Resort *(☎ 0 3269 1663, fax 0 3269 1664; ⓔ suanluang@prachuab.net; 13 Mu 1; bungalows with fan/air-con 400/600B)* lies 500m down a side road; the beach is 700m further on. It's run by a friendly Thai woman who speaks English and French. Spacious bungalows have mosquito proofing; wooden ones come with fans and concrete ones have hot water, TV and air-con. Motorcycles can be rented (250B) and tours to surrounding areas can be organised. Call for a pick-up from the train station.

Coral Hotel *(☎ 0 3269 1667; ⓦ www.coral-hotel.com; 171 Mu 9; rooms with air-con 995-1620B)* is a French-managed hotel at the beach (700m past Suan Luang Resort). It's an upmarket place with a pleasant pool and grounds. All rooms have TV, fridge and hot water, with the best ones actually being the cheapest ones. Four-person cottages are also available. Water-sports equipment can be hired, and tours are also offered. Rates do not include tax and service.

Chumphon Province

CHUMPHON

อ.เมืองชุมพร

postcode 86000 • pop 50,000

About 500km south of Bangkok and 184km from Prachuap Khiri Khan, Chumphon is a junction town (its name derives from the Thai *chumnumphon,* which means 'meeting place'), where you turn west for Ranong and Phuket or continue south on the newer road to Surat Thani, Nakhon Si Thammarat and Songkhla. The provincial capital is a busy place, but of no particular interest except that this is where southern Thailand really begins in terms of ethnic markers such as dialect and religion.

Pak Nam, Chumphon's port, is 10km from Chumphon, and in this area there are a few beaches and a handful of islands with good reefs for diving. The best local beach is 4km-long Hat Thung Wua Laen (12km north of town), also known locally as 'Hat Cabana' because of the long-running Chumphon Cabana Resort & Diving Center here.

In March or April the city hosts the **Chumphon Marine Festival**, which features cultural and folk-art exhibits, a windsurfing competition at Hat Thung Wua Laen and a marathon. In October, the five-day **Lang Suan Buddha Image Parade & Boat Race Festival** includes a procession of temple boats and a boat race on Mae Nam Lang Suan (Lang Suan River), about 60km south of the capital.

Pak Nam is a departure point for boats to Ko Tao, which is a popular island north of Ko Samui and Ko Pha-Ngan. Many travellers bound for Ko Tao stop for a night in Chumphon.

Information

Basic tourist information is available from inside the municipal office *(☎ 0 7751 1024; open 8.30am-4.30pm Mon-Fri).*

Depending on whether it's open you may or may not get help from **Chumphon Tourist Services Center**, located in the provincial office building; but little English is spoken here.

Several banks in town offer foreign exchange and ATMs; most are located along Th Sala Daeng and are open from 8.30am to 3.30pm Monday to Friday.

The **main post office** *(open 8.30am-4.30pm Mon-Fri, 9am-noon Sat & Sun)* is found at the southeastern end of town. The **CAT office** *(open 8.30am-9pm daily)* is about 1km east of the post office and has international calls. **Fame Tour & Service** *(188/87-88 Soi Saladang; open 11am-7am daily)* offers Internet access.

DK Book Store *(open 8am-9pm daily)* has a spinning rack full of plastic-wrapped English-language books, including Lonely Planet guides. Maps are also sold.

Chumphon is full of travel agencies. A couple of good ones are **Infinity Travel** *(☎ 0 7750 1937; 68/2 Tha Taphao)*, a dependable agency that does tours and ticketing as well as motorcycle rental, and **Fame Tour & Service** *(☎ 0 1676 6900; 188/87-88 Soi Saladang)*, located in a restaurant and offering similar services; it also runs a small branch outside the train station.

Places to Stay

The hotels here aren't world class, and budget guesthouses (which cater to quick overnight stays) constitute the bulk of options. Remember that 'single' means one bed, 'double' means two beds. Chumphon is a major gateway to Ko Tao; all the following places can sell you a ferry ticket there.

Infinity Guest House (☎ *0 7750 1937; 224/37 Soi 1, Th Krom Luang; rooms with fan 100-150B)* has six decent rooms in a two-storey wooden house, though the baths are grungy.

Chumphon Guest House *(Miao; ☎ 0 7750 2900; rooms with fan 120-150B)*, just around the corner from Infinity, features big, airy rooms in an old teak house along with a row of simple cubicles out front. There's a nice outdoor common area where breakfast and snacks are served, and there's motorcycle rental.

Sooksamer Guest House (☎ *0 7750 2430, fax 0 7757 1584; e sooksamerguesthouse@hotmail.com; 118/4 Th Suksamoe; singles/doubles with fan 100/150B)* has tiny, airless rooms barely big enough for the bed. There's a shared bath downstairs; at least the common area is nice and cosy.

Farang Bar (☎ *0 1597 7381; Th Tha Taphao; singles/doubles/triples with fan 120/160/210B)* is a centrally located cheapie, with a bar for the lobby. The best room is on the 2nd floor; all are spartan with shared hot-water bath.

Mayazes Resthouse (☎ *0 7750 4452, fax 0 7750 2217; 111/35 Soi Bangkok Bank; w www.thaisouth.com/mayazes; singles/doubles with fan 200/250B, with air-con 280/350B)* offers very nice budget rooms with some personality (and shared bath). The best rooms are at the top, and there's a good traveller vibe.

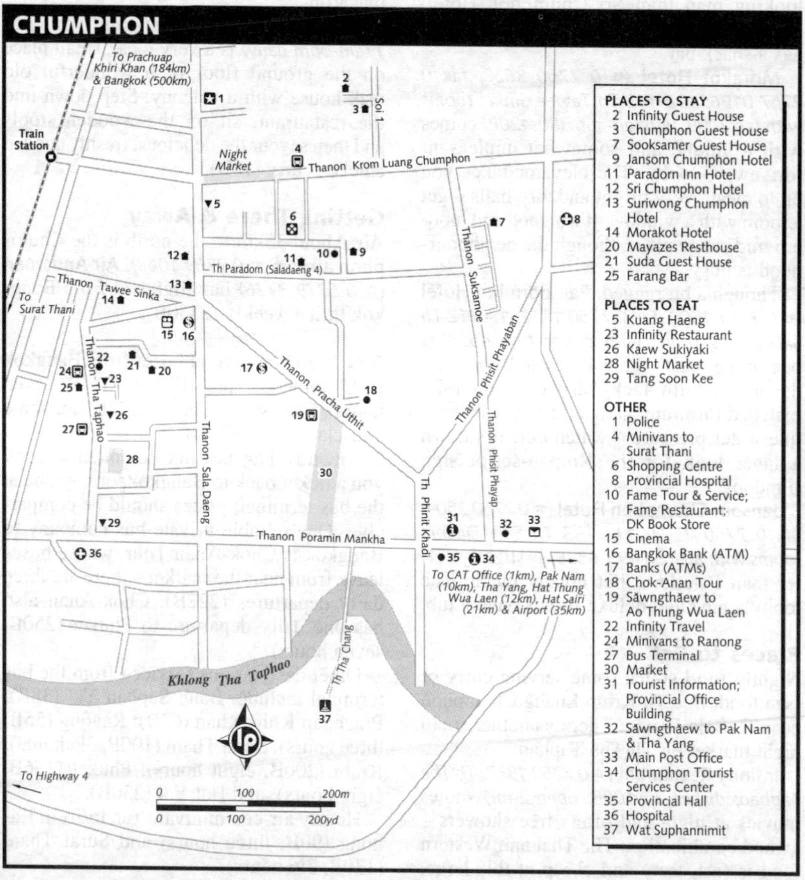

Suda Guest House *(☎ 0 7750 4366; 8 Soi Bangkok Bank; rooms with air-con 200-400B)* has only two rooms, including a large one that can sleep two couples. If the owner isn't here, look for her at Infinity Travel around the corner.

If hotels were men, **Sri Chumphon Hotel** *(☎ 0 7751 1280, fax 0 7750 4616; 127/22-24 Th Sala Daeng; rooms with fan 250-350B, with air-con 500-600B)* would be large and plain-looking – with a dud personality. The lobby is dark and the halls big and impersonal; most rooms are tiled, and those with two beds are bigger.

Suriwong Chumphon Hotel *(☎ 0 7751 1203, fax 0 7750 2699; 125/27-29 Th Sala Daeng; rooms with fan 260-300B, with air-con 360-400B)* would be a friendlier, better-looking man than Sri Chumphon Hotel. Rooms are clean and good, and the lobby has a snack bar.

Morakot Hotel *(☎ 0 7750 3628, fax 0 7757 0196; 102-112 Th Tawee Sinka; rooms with fan 300B, with air-con 380-420B)* comes with a unique and somewhat unpleasant 'driveway' lobby. The elevator takes you up to clean, very bright and airy halls – get a room with a window. It's a good and modern mid-range place, though the neighbourhood is busy.

Though a bit ragged, **Paradorn Inn Hotel** *(☎ 0 7751 1500, fax 0 7750 1112; 180/12 Th Sala Daeng; rooms with air-con from 450B)* is one of the 'best' hotels in town. Rooms are decorated with tacky artwork and mismatched furniture, and baths have elephantine water pressure – watch out! It's down a lane; look for the Roman-script sign 'Pradon'.

Jansom Chumphon Hotel *(☎ 0 7750 2504, fax 0 7750 2503; 118/138 Th Sala Daeng; rooms with air-con 495-638B)* is slightly better than Paradorn, but not by much. The lobby's nice and deluxe rooms have a tub.

UPPER SOUTHERN GULF

Places to Eat

Nightly **food stalls**, some serving curry or Isan food, line Th Krom Luang Chumphon near Th Sala Daeng. There's another small night market on Th Tha Taphao.

Infinity Restaurant *(☎ 0 7750 1937; Th Tha Taphao; dishes 35-100B; open 24hr)* shows movies at night and offers free showers – a good combination. The Thai and Western food is fast, tasty and cheap at this large, open cafeteria. It's off the main street, a little down a driveway.

Fame Restaurant *(☎ 0 7757 1077; dishes 50-120B; open 11am-3am daily)* prepares popular Thai and Western meals within a traveller-oriented atmosphere. There's also a travel agency and Internet access here.

Tang Soon Kee *(no Roman-script sign; ☎ 0 7751 1120; dishes 60-150B; open 8.30am-9.30pm daily)* is a very popular Chinese place that has only four large tables. Look for it across from the motorcycle shop.

Kaew Sukiyaki *(dishes 50-100B; open 11am-midnight daily)* lies across from the bus station; look for the Roman-script sign on the wall inside. It has a nice, clean, open ambience with wooden furniture and serves basic Thai dishes, and, scarily, sashimi *and* macaroni.

Kuang Haeng *(no Roman-script sign; open 11am-5pm daily)* is a very local, small place on the ground floor of a wonderful old teak house with a balcony. Step down into the restaurant, sit on the wooden stools and then savour the delicious, freshly cooked chicken curry (18B).

Getting There & Away

Air About 35km to the north is the **Chumphon airport** *(☎ 0 7759 1068)*. **Air Andaman** *(☎ 0 5379 3726)* has flights to/from Bangkok thrice weekly (2350B).

Bus There are several buses from Bangkok to Chumphon: one VIP bus (317B, seven hours), five 1st-class buses (272B) and three 2nd-class buses (211B).

Any travel agency in Chumphon will sell you a ticket back to Bangkok, or buy one at the bus terminal; prices should be comparable. One reliable private-bus company to Bangkok is Chok-Anan Tour, whose buses leave from near the market – there are three daily departures (222B). Chok-Anan also has one daily departure to Phuket (250B, seven hours).

Other destinations serviced from the bus terminal include: Bang Saphan Yai (38B); Prachuap Khiri Khan (63B); Ranong (55B; three hours); Surat Thani (100B, 3½ hours); Krabi (200B, eight hours); Phuket (196B, eight hours); and Hat Yai (230B).

Hourly air-con minivans run to/from Ranong (90B, three hours) and Surat Thani (130B, 3½ hours)

Train There are frequent services to/from Bangkok (2nd class, from 230B to 280B; 3rd class, 122B, 7½ hours)

Other destinations from Chumphon (all in 3rd-class berths) include Prachuap Khiri Khan (34B); Surat Thani (34B); and Hat Yai (79B). Southbound rapid and express trains – the only trains with 1st and 2nd class – are much less frequent and can be difficult to book out of Chumphon in high season (November to February).

Boat Ko Tao can be reached by boat from two piers near Pak Nam, an area 10km southeast of Chumphon. There are several boat services to the small island; except for the midnight boat, all include transport from Chumphon to the piers. Remember that the speedboats are faster but the ride is rougher, and some may not have air-con or bathrooms. Also be aware that the following schedule of services is very changeable.

Săwngthăew from Chumphon run frequently to both piers between 6am and 6pm (10B). Your best option for the midnight boat, however, is the 10pm van that travel agencies and guesthouses send to the pier – this costs 50B per person. Motorcycles charge at least 100B, although this isn't a good option unless you travel light and like to haggle.

If you somehow manage to get stuck in the pier area and don't want to return to Chumphon, try the **Thayang Seaport Hotel** *(☎ 0 7755 3052; rooms with fan 200B, with air-con 250-300B)*, which has surprisingly good-value rooms.

Getting Around

Săwngthăew and motorcycle taxis around town cost a flat 10B per trip. Săwngthăew to Hat Sairi and Hat Thung Wua Laen cost 20B.

Motorcycles can be rented at many travel agencies (such as Infinity) and guesthouses or hotels (such as Chumphon, Morakot, Suda) for 200B to 250B per day. Car rental costs between 1000B and 1500B per day; *(188/87-88 Soi Saladang; open 11am-7am daily)* is one place that rents them.

Boat Services

Boat	price (B)	departure time	duration (hrs)	frequency
Lomprayah Catamaran	550	1pm	1½	daily
Lomlahk Catamaran	500	1pm	1½	Sat & Sun
Lomlahk Speedboat	400	7.30am	1¾	daily
Koh Tao Cruiser	400	7am	3	daily
High Speed Ferry	400	7am	2½	daily
Songserm Express	400	7.30am	3	daily
Midnight Boat	200	12pm	6	daily

Lower Southern Gulf

While the scenery of the Southern Gulf may not be as dramatic as that of the Andaman coast, its vistas of coconut groves alongside azure seas evoke images of a tropical paradise in the classic sense. Composed of the provinces of Surat Thani, Nakhon Si Thammarat, Songkhla, Yala, Pattani and Narathiwat, it forms the eastern coast of Thailand's portion of the Malay peninsula. As with the provinces of the Andaman coast, there are large populations of Thai Muslims in the countryside, while ethnic Chinese dominate the cities. The former are, for the most part, fisherfolk and tillers of the soil, the latter merchants and professionals.

Except for landlocked Yala, the provinces of the Southern Gulf have an abundance of inviting beaches. Of course, the Southern Gulf isn't just about beaches. Inland you'll find protected areas that are home to endangered species inhabiting pockets of the primeval jungle that once covered much of Southeast Asia. But if you're coming for the beach or for water sports such as diving, it's important to get your timing right.

Mid-September through to the end of November is the rainiest time along the Southern Gulf. The seas are choppy and hence visibility is poorest at this time of year. If somehow you find yourself on a rain-soaked beach, don't despair: The weather on the Andaman coast might be bright and sunny – and it's a relatively short trip across the peninsula to find out.

Highlights

- Explore Khao Sok National Park's rainforests, waterfalls, limestone cliffs and lakes – home to a plethora of flora and fauna, including tigers and the world's largest flower
- Discover why Ko Samui's fine-sand beaches, easy accessibility and wide range of accommodation make it one of Thailand's most popular island resorts
- Dive at Ko Pha-Ngan, laze on its isolated beaches, take a day trip to Ang Thong National Marine Park, or get lost at one of its infamous full-moon raves
- Head straight for Ko Tao, Thailand's diving mecca, with great visibility and amazing underwater pinnacles; and there's great beaches to boot
- Soak up the traditional southern way of life in bustling Hat Yai, historical Pattani and serene Narathiwat – where Buddhism and Islam meet
- Get to know Songkhla, with its interesting museum, twin hills and popular coastline; then, explore the peaceful villages and roads of nearby Ko Yo

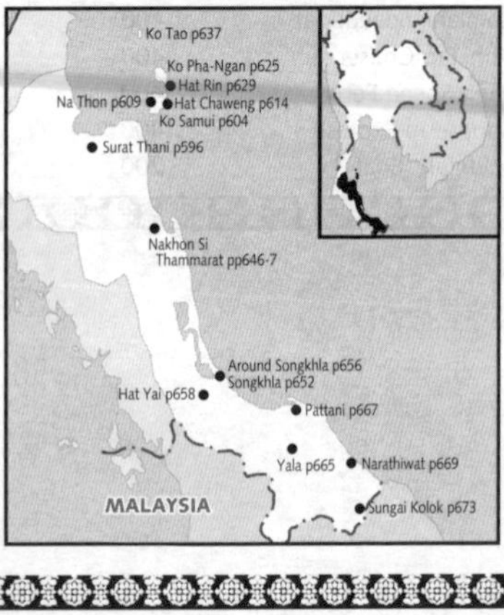

Surat Thani Province

SURAT THANI

สุราษฎร์ธานี

postcode 84000 • pop 117,700

There is little of historical interest in Surat Thani, a busy commercial centre and port dealing in rubber and coconut, but the town's waterfront lends some character nonetheless. It's 651km from Bangkok and the first point in a southbound journey towards Malaysia that really feels and looks like southern Thailand. For most people Surat Thani (often known simply as 'Surat') is only a stop on the way to Ko Samui or Ko Pha-Ngan, scenic islands 32km off the coast.

If you find yourself with some time to kill in Surat, you can do a one- or two-hour

LOWER SOUTHERN GULF

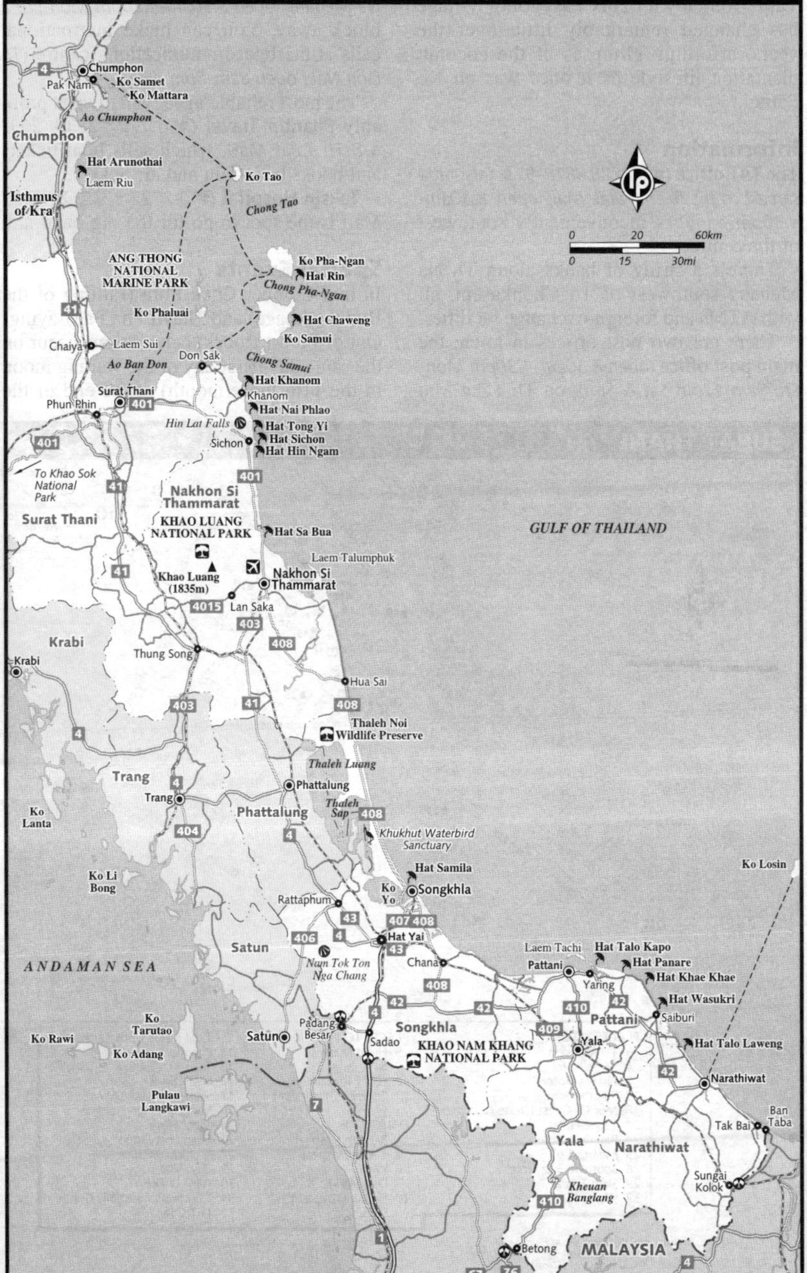

tour of **Bang Ban Mai**, across Mae Nam Tapi from town. This easygoing village has changed remarkably little over the years, affording glimpses of the coconut plantation lifestyle as it once was on Ko Samui.

Information

The **TAT office** (☎ *0 7728 8818–9;* ⓔ *tatsurat@samart.co.th; 5 Th Talat Mai; open 8.30am-4.30pm daily)* is inconveniently southwest of the centre.

There's a string of banks along Th Na Meuang southwest of Th Chonkasem, all with ATMs and foreign-exchange facilities.

There are two post offices in town; the **main post office** *(open 8.30am-4.30pm Mon-Fri, 9am-12pm Sat & Sun)*, on Th Talat Mai and a smaller **branch** *(cnr Th Chonkasem & Th Na Meuang; open 8.30am-4.30pm Mon-Fri)* a block away. You can make international calls at the **telecommunications centre** *(Th Don Nok; open 8am-8pm daily)*.

The most reliable agency in town is probably **Phantip Travel** (☎ *0 7727 2230; 293/6-8 Th Talat Mai)*, which sells boat tickets and books bus, train and air tickets.

Taksin Hospital (☎ *0 7727 3239; Th Talat Mai)* is the spot to go for the big band-aid.

Special Events

In mid-October **Chak Phra** (Pulling of the Buddha Image) and **Thawt Pha Pa** (Laying-Out of Forest Robes) celebrations occur on the same day (first day of the waning moon in the 11th lunar month) at the end of the

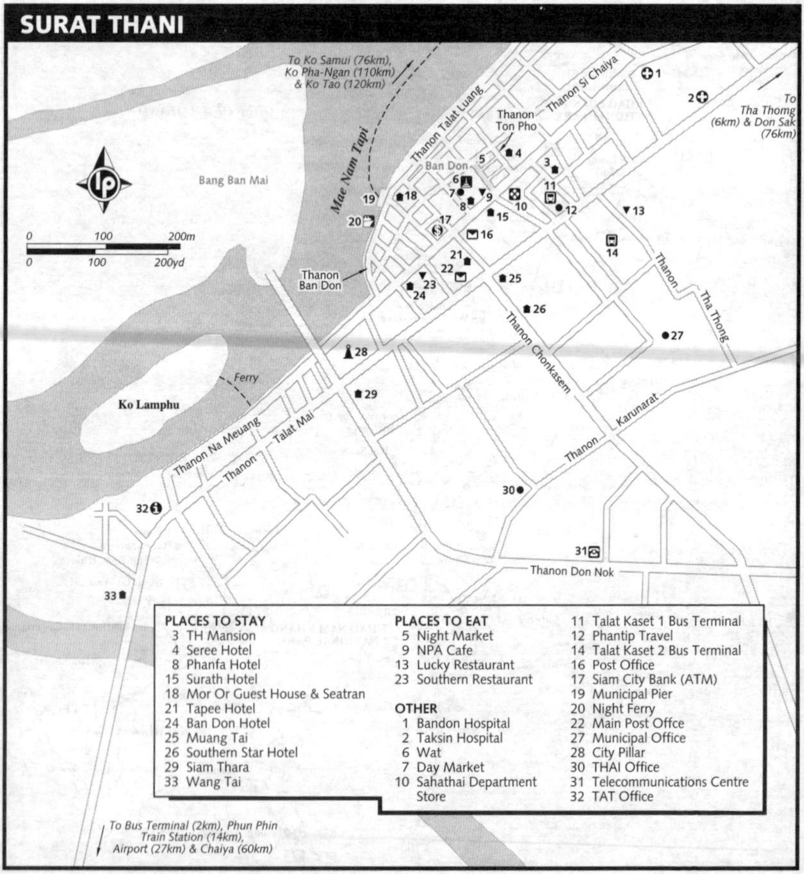

Buddhist Rains Retreat and are major events for Surat Thani Province.

Thawt Pha Pa begins at dawn with the offering of new monastic robes to the monks, while Chak Phra takes place during the day and evening. During Chak Phra, local lay devotees place sacred Buddha images on boats for a colourful procession along Mae Nam Tapi. A similar landborne procession uses trucks and hand-pulled carts. Lots of food stalls and musical performances, including *lí-keh* (folk plays featuring dancing, comedy, melodrama and music) are set up for the occasion.

Places to Stay

For many of Surat Thani's cheaper hotels, business is largely 'short-time' trade. This doesn't necessarily make them less suitable as regular hotels, though there's likely to be more noise, as guests arrive and depart frequently. It can be worth dishing out a few more baht for nicer amenities, though.

Mor Or Guest House *(☎ 0 7721 0268; 136 Th Na Meuang; rooms 150B)*, opposite the night ferry pier, is the cheapest digs in Surat Thani – but you get what you pay for. Rooms are tiny, nondescript and decorated only with beds. There's a travel agency, Seatran, and Internet connection downstairs.

Surath Hotel *(☎ 0 7727 2243; 496 Th Na Meuang; rooms with fan 180-350B, with air-con 380-480B)* offers good, large, bright budget rooms – those on the 2nd floor are more appealing. At the rear are some quiet, renovated rooms.

Phanfa Hotel *(☎ 0 7727 2287; 247/2-5 Th Na Meuang; rooms with fan 180-280B)*, opposite and similar to the Surath Hotel, has rooms with Thai bath and solid old furniture.

Seree Hotel *(☎ 0 7727 2279; 2/2-5 Th Ton Pho; rooms with fan/air-con 200/270B)* has mostly airless, musty, boring rooms, but it's the cheapest air-conditioned hotel in town.

Ban Don Hotel *(☎ 0 7727 2167; 268/2 Th Na Meuang; rooms with fan/air-con 250/400B)* is a cleaner, newer, less worn place than most, with tidy but uninspired rooms (the cheapest with squat toilets). A decent Chinese restaurant sits downstairs.

Muang Tai *(☎ 0 7727 2559; 390-392 Th Talat Mai; rooms with fan 240-460B, with air-con 340-420B)* has good-sized rooms with outdated furniture, and they're either too noisy (facing a busy intersection) or have views of a wall. Otherwise this mid-range place is OK.

Tapee Hotel *(☎ 0 7727 2575, fax 0 7728 2433; 100 Th Chonkasem; rooms with fan 300B, with air-con 430-460B)* has old, spacious rooms worn similarly to the Muang Tai, but it's a more quiet and bright place. It's set off the busy street a bit.

TH Mansion *(☎ 0 7721 2701; 70/1-4 Th Mit Kasem; rooms with fan/air-con 300/350B)* presents average, well-sized rooms that are furnished decently enough. It's another OK choice.

Siam Thara *(☎ 0 7727 3740; 1/144 Th Don Nok; rooms with air-con 395-960B)* is a more upscale place a bit southwest of the town centre. While it's not luxurious, rooms are carpeted, comfortable and nice – a good deal overall.

Wang Tai *(☎ 0 7728 3020, fax 0 7728 1007; 1 Th Talat Mai; rooms with air-con 950-1100B)* starts with a posh lobby and leads up to 300 modern, fine and quiet rooms (some with pool views). It's southwest of town, though local buses are frequent.

Southern Star Hotel *(☎ 0 7721 6414, fax 0 7721 6427; 253 Th Chonkasem; rooms with air-con from 1100B)* is the tallest building in town, and rooms are perfectly fine for the price. The restaurant on the 16th storey has great views; other facilities include a coffee shop and karaoke pub. The rates include breakfast.

Phun Phin So you've somehow become stranded in Phun Phin (the nearby town where the Surat Thani train leaves from) or want to get an early morning train before the bus service starts from Surat. Luckily there's one acceptable accommodation option in this small town, along with a couple banks with ATMs and plenty of cheap eats.

Queen *(☎ 0 7731 1003; 916/10-13 Th Mahasawat; rooms with fan 200-300B, with air-con 400B)* is around the corner from the train station, on the road to Surat Thani. Some of the fair budget rooms are brighter, larger and less dingy than others, so see a couple before deciding.

Places to Eat

The **night market** *(Th Ton Pho)* is *the* place for fried, steamed, grilled or sauteed delicacies – look for the crunchy insect tidbits. You may also see large trays of greens on diners' tables – this is southern-style *khànŏm jiin* (curry noodles served with vegetables and herbs).

During the day, many **food stalls** near the bus terminal specialise in *khâo kài òp* (marinated baked chicken on rice), which is very tasty. During mango season, street vendors in Surat sell incredible *khâo nĭaw mámûang* (coconut-sweetened sticky rice with sliced ripe mango).

The **NPA Cafe** (*☎ 0 7727 2623; 259/4 Th Na Meuang; dishes 40-130B; open 8.30am-9.30pm daily*) has soothing air-conditioning, and serves Western breakfasts, burgers, salads, macaroni, spaghetti, sandwiches, pizza, and Thai and Chinese food – plus beer to wash it all down.

Lucky Restaurant (*☎ 0 7727 3267; 452/84-85 Th Tha Thong; dishes 50-300B; open 10am-10pm daily*) cooks curries, meats and seafood, among other Thai dishes. It has a comfortable, dim environment – like the inside of a log cabin, but in Thailand.

Southern Restaurant (*☎ 0 7727 2894; dishes 30-100B; open 9am-11.30pm daily*) offers a cosy pub-like atmosphere along with breakfasts, Thai food and pizza.

Getting There & Away

Air There is a twice daily service to Bangkok on **Thai Airways International** (*THAI; ☎ 0 7727 2610; 3/27-28 Th Karunarat*) for 2445B (70 minutes).

Bus & Minivan Most long-distance public buses run from the Talat Kaset bus terminals 1 and 2. Air-con minivans leave from Talat Kaset 2; they tend to have more frequent departures than buses, though they're not always cheaper.

There's a bus terminal 2km west of town (on the way to Phun Phin train station), but it's used less frequently than the two terminals in town. To get into town from there take an orange local bus (9B), which comes by every 10 minutes. Just make sure it's going back into town rather than out to Phun Phin (it does a loop). *Săwngthăew* (pickup truck) are another option into town; they cost 10B.

Shop around if buying bus or minivan tickets from travel agencies, as some may quote you inflated prices and/or give you false information on trip durations. See the boxed text 'Traveller beware in Surat Thani' in this section.

Some destinations to/from Surat are included in the table on the following page.

Train There are several trains from Bangkok to Phun Phin (the closest station to Surat Thani; it's 14km west of town). Fares are 147B in 3rd class, 288B to 358B in 2nd class and 1199B in 1st class. The trip takes around 11 to 12 hours, so if you take an early evening train from Bangkok you'll arrive in Surat Thani in the morning. Not all trains have sleeping berths, however.

Traveller Beware in Surat Thani

It's a lucrative business, this shuttling of travellers back and forth between Surat Thani and Bangkok, the islands or southern destinations. And a lucrative transport business will always attract its share of shady travel agencies…

One agency that should be avoided at all costs is Chaw Wang Tours. We've received numerous complaints from readers, year after year, about rip-offs involving this company. Travellers who have used this service report that they have:

- ended up on inferior buses;
- been told they 'must change money' before heading south (at very bad exchange rates);
- been told they must pay a (bogus) 'visa fee'; and/or
- been lied to and treated very rudely.

These rip-offs are not restricted to Chaw Wang Tours alone, though it is a high-profile offender. Check out any agency you are thinking of using before purchasing tickets.

Also, take care when booking private air-con and VIP buses out of Surat. Some companies have been known to sell tickets for VIP buses to Bangkok, then pile hapless travellers onto an ordinary air-con bus and refuse to refund the fare difference. If possible get a recommendation from another traveller or inquire at the TAT office. And watch those touts!

Bus Destinations to/from Surat Thani

destination	fare (B)	duration (hrs)
Bangkok		
VIP	590	10
1st class	380	10
2nd class	295	11
ordinary	211	11
Hat Yai		
1st class	380	4
2nd class	295	5
minivan	180	3½
Krabi		
1st class	120-180	3
2nd class	80	4
minivan	120	2
Nakhon Si Thammarat		
1st class	90	2
2nd class	45	2
minivan	120	2
Phang-Nga		
1st class	130	3
2nd class	110	4
Phuket		
1st class	160	5
2nd class	105-120	6
minivan	180	4
Ranong		
1st class	180	4
2nd class	80	5
minivan	130	3½
Trang		
2nd class	120	3

The train station has a 24-hour left-luggage room that charges 10B a day for the first five days, 15B a day thereafter. The advance ticket office is open from 6am to 6pm (with a 11am to noon lunch break) daily.

At certain busy times it's difficult to book long-distance trains out of Phun Phin; taking the bus can be easier, especially if heading south. Trains are very often full and it's a drag to bus it out to the train station just to be turned away – though you could buy a 'standing room only' 3rd-class ticket and wait hopefully for a seat to become available. Many travel agencies in town (including Phantip Travel) book advance train reservation, so if you have a fixed return schedule you can make an onward reservation *before* getting on the boat to Ko Samui. If you don't know when you're coming back to the mainland, you could always try booking a train ticket from a travel agency on Samui itself.

Boat There are nightly ferries to Ko Tao (400B, eight hours), Ko Pha-Ngan (200B, seven hours) and Ko Samui (150B, six hours). All leave from the night ferry pier at 11pm. These are freighters, not luxury boats; bring food and water, and watch your bags.

Seatran (☎ *0 7727 5060; 136 Th Na Meuang*), whose office is below Mo Or Guest House and near the night ferry pier, operates a bus/boat combination to Ko Samui for 150B (3½ hours, six a day).

Raja Ferry (☎ *0 7737 4523)* also operates bus/boat combinations to Ko Tao (500B, four hours, two a day), Ko Pha-Ngan (250B, 3½ hours, three a day) and Ko Samui (140B, 2½ hours, seven a day). Buy tickets at **Phantip Travel** (☎ *0 7727 2230; 293/6-8 Th Talat Mai)*.

In the high season there may also be bus/boat services to Ko Samui and Ko Pha-Ngan directly from the train station.

Getting Around

Air-con vans to/from the airport cost 70B to 80B per person. They'll drop you off at your hotel; buy tickets at travel agencies or the **THAI office** (☎ *0 7727 2610; 3/27-28 Th Karunarat)*.

Orange buses run from Phun Phin train station to Surat Thani every 10 minutes from 6am to 8pm (9B, 25 minutes). For this ride taxis charge 100B. Other taxi rates are posted just north of the train station (at the metal pedestrian bridge).

Taxis from Surat Thani to Don Sak pier cost 500B; Phantip Travel runs frequent vans and charges 50B per person.

Around town, săwngthăew cost 10B, while *săamláw* (three-wheeled vehicles) charge 20B to 30B.

AROUND SURAT THANI

Chaiya

ไชยา

Chaiya is a small, calm and friendly town about 60km north of Surat Thani, basically consisting of a few streets (with some old

LOWER SOUTHERN GULF

Arriving in Surat Thani by Train

Most travellers arriving by train here don't plan on staying long, which is fine because there really isn't much to do in Surat. They want to go to Phuket, Phang-Nga or the Krabi area (all on the Andaman coast), which is also fine since there's lots to do in these places. But first, they must negotiate busy little Phun Phin…

The first thing you must realise is that you'll actually be arriving in Phun Phin, the town where Surat Thani's train station is located. It's approximately 14km west of Surat. The second thing to realise is that you don't necessarily have to leave Phun Phin to reach your Andaman coast beach destination. There are buses directly from the train station to Phuket, Phang-Nga and Krabi – some via Takua Pa, a junction city farther west. They may not exactly be air-con, though, and their departures may not fit your arrival schedule – but if you catch the right bus at the right time you could save yourself a few hours' worth of back-and-forth-to-Surat travel time. Look for the big white wall just south of the train station – there's a Pepsi symbol and sign proclaiming 'Coffee shop and fast food'. This is where those buses stop.

Of course, if you've missed the last bus (or Ko Samui is your actual destination – it's on the *other* coast) you'll have to hike it into Surat after all, as there are more transport options there. This isn't hard to do, as local orange buses chug between Phun Phin and Surat (a 25-minute ride) every 10 minutes, and it only costs 9B. And, you'll get to see Surat Thani!

teak buildings) and a nice **day market** in front of the train station. There are some **wát** (temples) and a couple of **museums** to see in the vicinity; these are all best visited as a day trip from Surat.

Chaiya is one of the oldest cities in Thailand, dating back to the Srivijaya empire. The name may in fact be a contraction of Siwichaiya, the Thai pronunciation of the city that was a regional capital between the 8th and 10th centuries. Previous to this time the area was a stop on the Indian trade route in Southeast Asia. Many Srivijaya artefacts in the National Museum in Bangkok were found in Chaiya, including a famous Avalokiteshvara Bodhisattva bronze that's considered a masterpiece of Buddhist art.

Wat Suan Mokkhaphalaram
วัดสวนโมกข์พลาราม

The very calm and non-showy Wat Suanmok (short for Wat Suan Mokkhaphalaram – or literally, Garden of Liberation) is a modern forest wát founded by Ajahn Buddhadasa Bhikkhu, arguably Thailand's most famous monk. Born in Chaiya in 1906, Buddhadasa was ordained as a monk when he was 21 years old. He spent many years studying the Pali scriptures and then retired to the forest for six years of solitary meditation. Returning to ecclesiastical society, he was made abbot of Wat Phra Boromathat, a high distinction, but conceived of Suanmok as an alternative to orthodox Thai temples. During Thailand's turbulent 1970s he was branded a communist because of his critiques of capitalism, which he saw as a catalyst for greed. Buddhadasa died in July 1993 after a long illness.

Buddhadasa's philosophy was ecumenical in nature, comprising Zen, Taoist and Christian elements, as well as the traditional Theravada schemata. Today, the hermitage is spread over 120 hectares of wooded hillside and features huts for up to 70 monks, a 'spiritual theatre' and a museum-library. This latter building has bas-reliefs on the outer walls that are facsimiles of sculptures at Sanchi, Bharhut and Amaravati in India. The interior walls feature modern Buddhist painting – eclectic to say the least – executed by the resident monks. The wát is 7km from Chaiya and not visible from the highway.

At the affiliated **International Dhamma Hermitage** (IDH), across the highway 1.5km from Wat Suanmok, resident monks hold meditation retreats during the first 10 days of every month. Anyone is welcome to participate; the cost is 1200B (120B per day for 10 days), which includes meals. Advance registration is not possible; simply arrive in time to register on the final day of the month preceding the retreat. You can get information about this retreat at **Wat Suanmok** (*w www.suanmokkh.org*).

Other Attractions

The restored **Borom That Chaiya** at Wat Phra Boromathat, just 800m outside Chaiya, is a *chedi* (stupa) that is a fine example of Srivijaya architecture and strongly resembles the *candi* (stupas) of central Java – a stack of ornate boxes bearing images of Kala, a peacock (a symbol for the sun), Airavata, Indra and the Buddha (facing east as usual).

In the courtyard surrounding the *chedi* are several pieces of sculpture from the region, including an unusual two-sided *yoni* (the uterus-shaped pedestal that holds the Shivalingam, or phallic shrine), *reusǐi* (masters) performing yoga and a number of Buddha images.

The small but well-done **National Museum** *(admission 30B; open 9am-4pm Wed-Sun)*, right next to Wat Phra Boromathat, displays historic and prehistoric artefacts of local origin, as well as local handicrafts and a shadow puppet exhibit.

About 500m farther along the highway towards Chaiya, and down a side road a few hundred metres, is the ruined stupa at **Wat Kaew** (also known as Wat Long). It's also from the Srivijaya period, which shows a central Javanese influence (or perhaps vice versa) as well as Cham (9th-century southern Vietnam) characteristics.

At the intersection of the aforementioned side road and the highway, about 300m from Chaiya, is Wat Wiang, which contains Chaiya's **Folklore Museum** *(admission by donation; open 8am-9pm daily)*. You may need to get a friendly monk to open it up and show you the mishmash of items: old instruments, china, pottery, shadow puppets, work implements, buffalo-hide sandals and a ceramic opium pillow.

Places to Stay

Chaiya is easily done as a day trip from Surat; if you want to stay longer, you can request permission from the monks to stay in the guest quarters at Wat Suanmok. Or, you can stay at Chaiya's only hotel.

Udomlap Hotel *(☎ 0 7743 1123; rooms with fan 150-250B, with air-con 400-450B)* is friendly and modern, and generally a good hotel. The cheapest rooms share baths in an old wing, while the pricier rooms are in a more modern wing. Many *faràng* (foreigners) stay here for the meditation retreat at Wat Suanmok.

Getting There & Away

If you're going to Surat Thani by train from Bangkok, you can get off at the small Chaiya train station, then later catch another train to Phun Phin, which is Surat's nearest train station. If you're already in Surat you can take the train north to Chaiya, although this does involve getting out to the train station in Phun Phin and taking much longer than just hopping on a sǎwngthǎew from the centre of Surat.

Sǎwngthǎew leave from Talat Kaset 2 bus terminal (30B, one hour) in Surat. A convenient way to see the region is to take this sǎwngthǎew first to Wat Suanmok (30B), then another one to Wat Phra Boromathat (10B), then walk on to Wat Kaew and Wat Wiang (10 to 15 minutes), and next walk to Chaiya (five minutes). Wat Suanmok is 7km before Chaiya, so you're working your way there. All attractions are on or just off the same wide highway, and it's hard to get lost. You can also do this tour in the other direction. Motorcycle taxis between Surat and Chaiya cost 50B.

Sǎwngthǎew going back to Surat may end their route at Phun Phin, Surat's train station; from there Surat is only a 9B bus ride (or 10B sǎwngthǎew ride) away.

KHAO SOK NATIONAL PARK

อุทยานแห่งชาติเขาสก

Established in 1980, this 646-sq-km park *(☎ 0 7739 5025; admission 200B)* lies in the western part of Surat Thani Province, off Rte 401 about a third of the way from Takua Pa to Surat Thani. The park has thick native rainforest with waterfalls *(náam tòk)*, limestone cliffs, numerous streams, an island-studded lake and many trails, mostly along rivers. According to Thom Henley, author of the highly informative *Waterfalls and Gibbon Calls*, the Khao Sok rainforest is in fact a remnant of a 160-million-year-old forest ecosystem that is much older and richer than the forests of the Amazon and central African regions.

Khao Sok is connected to two other national parks, Kaeng Krung and Phang-Nga, as well as the Khlong Saen and Khlong Nakha wildlife sanctuaries. Together, these form the largest contiguous nature preserve – around 4000 sq km – on the Thai peninsula. Khao Sok shelters a plethora of wildlife, including wild elephants, leopards, serow, banteng, gaur, dusky langurs, tigers and Malayan sun bears, as well as over 180 bird species.

A major watershed for the south, the park is filled with lianas, bamboo, ferns and rattan, including the giant rattan *(wǎi tào phráw)* with a stem over 10cm in diameter. A floral rarity in the park is *Rafflesia kerri meyer*, known to the Thais as *bua phút* (wild lotus), the largest flower in the world. Found only in Khao Sok and an adjacent wildlife sanctuary (different varieties of the same species are found in Malaysia and Indonesia), mature specimens can reach 80cm in diameter. The flower has no roots or leaves of its own; instead it lives parasitically inside the roots of the liana, a jungle vine. From October to December, buds burst forth from the liana root and swell to football size. When the bud blooms in January and February it emits a potent stench resembling rotten meat, which attracts pollinating insects.

Orientation & Information

The best time of year to visit Khao Sok is December to May, when trails are less slippery, river crossings are easier and riverbank camping is safer due to the lower risk of flash flooding. There are also fewer leeches to worry about. During the June to November wet season, on the other hand, you're more likely to see Malayan and Asiatic black bears, civets, slow loris, wild boar, gaur, deer and wild elephants – and tigers if you're very, very lucky – along the trail network. During dry months the larger mammals tend to stay near the reservoir in areas without trails.

The **park headquarters** and the **visitors centre** are 1.8km off Rte 401, close to the 109km marker. Besides the **camping area** and **bungalows** here, there are several private guesthouse operations nearby – some have so-called 'tree house' bungalows (most are actually bungalows on stilts near trees).

At the visitors centre, as well as at various bookshops in southern Thailand, you can purchase a copy of Henley's inspirational wildlife guide, *Waterfalls and Gibbon Calls*. The author pulls no punches when it comes to his critiques of park management and national policy.

Leeches are quite common in certain areas of the park, so make sure to take the usual precautions – wear closed shoes when hiking and apply plenty of repellent.

Things to See & Do

Various trails from the visitors centre lead to the waterfalls of **Sip-Et Chan** (4km), **Than Sawan** (9km) and **Than Kloy** (9km), among other destinations. A rough map showing trails and sights can be obtained here. Any guesthouse will happily arrange guided tours and hikes that include waterfalls, caves and river-running.

An hour's drive east of the visitors centre is the vast **Chiaw Lan Lake**, 165km at the longest point. It was created in 1982 by the 95m-high, 700m-long, shaled-clay dam of Ratchaprapha (Kheuan Ratchaprapha or Kheuan Chiaw Lan). Limestone outcrops protruding from the lake reach a height of 960m, over three times higher than the formations in the Phang-Nga area. A cave known as **Tham Nam Thalu** contains striking limestone formations and subterranean streams, while **Tham Si Ru** features four converging passageways used as a hideout by communist insurgents between 1975 and 1982. **Tham Khang Dao**, high on a limestone cliff face, is home to many bat species. All three caves can be reached on foot from the southwestern shore of the lake. You can **rent boats** from local fishermen to explore the coves, canals, caves and cul-de-sacs along the lakeshore, while three floating raft houses belonging to the national park provide overnight accommodation.

Places to Stay & Eat

Near the visitors centre you can pitch your own **tent** *(2 people 30B)* or rent **bungalows** *(1-4 people 800B, 5-8 people 1000B)*. For reservations, call ☎ 0 7739 5025; a few restaurants nearby provide nourishment. At Chiaw Lan Lake, two substations have **floating raft houses** *(☎ 0 7729 9318; houses per person 500B)*. Call to reserve these raft houses; rates include meals.

On the 1.8km road from Hwy 401 to the visitors centre, and on a dirt side road off this main road, are several private, simple guesthouse operators and their restaurants. All have rooms with fan; there are no rooms with air-con in these parts. Prices rise in the high season from about November to February. The following accommodation options are on the highway.

Pantoorat Mountain Lodge, which is near Rte 401, looks to be one of the more 'up-market' choices in the area. It was closed at the time of writing, but perhaps you'll have more luck.

Lotus *(☎ 0 7739 5012; bungalows 100-200B)* is down a little way and is a fair deal for its small bungalows with mosquito nets.

Freedom Resort *(☎ 0 7739 5019; e free domresort@yahoo.com; bungalows 150-200B)* has 11 basic wooden bungalows in a woodsy setting.

Bamboo House II *(☎ 0 7739 5013; rooms 300-500B)* maintains bright, well-built concrete and brick bungalows with tiled floors and verandahs; it's located near a river.

Khao Sok Rainforest Resort *(☎ 0 7739 5006; w www.krabidir.com/khaosokrainforest; rooms 400-600B)*, on the other side of the river from Bamboo House II, has simple riverside bungalows and a pleasant garden; fancier mountain bungalows are a short hike up.

Treetop River Huts *(☎ 0 7742 1155; w www.treetops-riverhuts.com; bungalows 250-700B)*, right at the visitors centre, has a wide variety of bungalows in a jungle-like area. Nearby **Riverside Bungalow** *(☎ 0 7739 5015; bungalows 200-300B)* is across a rickety footbridge and on a large lot; it's more basic.

The following are on the dirt side road leading off the highway.

Bamboo House *(☎ 0 1787 7484; rooms 100-600B)* has a wide variety of rustic bungalows; two very basic ones precariously overlook the river.

Nung House *(☎ 0 7739 5024; w www.nunghouse.com; bungalows 150-300B)* sits a little beyond Bamboo House. There's a range of basic bungalows on a large grassy lot, including a true treehouse by the river. Some are newer than others, so see a couple before deciding.

Art's Riverview Jungle Lodge *(☎/fax 0 7739 5009; rooms & bungalows 350-550B)*, beyond Bamboo House 400m, has a pleasant range of simple, solid and airy rooms with mosquito nets. The more expensive ones have verandas/hammocks, and all are in a beautiful, tranquil and lush setting. You can view wild macaques from the riverside restaurant.

Our Jungle House *(☎ 0 9909 6814; e ihtravel@inet.co.th; bungalows 400-600B)*, 800m past Bamboo House, is Australian-run. Basic wooden bungalows are set on very jungle-like paths along a river, which sits across from a limestone cliff.

Getting There & Around

Khao Sok is 40km from Takua Pa (on the west coast) and almost 100km from Surat Thani (on the east coast).

From the Surat Thani area, catch a bus going towards Takua Pa – you'll be getting off well before hitting this destination (tell the bus driver 'Khao Sok'). You can also come from the west coast by bus, but you'll have to go to Takua Pa first. Buses from Takua Pa to the park cost 25B (one hour, nine a day). All buses will drop you off on the highway, 1.8km from the visitors centre; if you're not met by guesthouse touts, you'll have to walk to your chosen guesthouse (from 50m to 2km).

To arrive at Chiaw Lan Lake, go east on Rte 401 from the visitors centre and take the turn-off between the Km52 and Km53 markers, at Ban Takum. It's another 14km to the lake. If you don't have your own wheels you'll have to bus it to Ban Takum, then hope to hitch a ride to the lake. The best option without private transport would be to join a tour, which any guesthouse can arrange for 1000B (2000B to 2500B with an overnight stay).

KO SAMUI

เกาะสมุย

postcode 84140 • pop 50,000

Ko Samui is one of Thailand's most popular islands and its third-largest. It's also part of an archipelago that includes 80 smaller islands, of which only six – Pha-Ngan, Ta Loy, Tao, Taen, Ma Ko and Ta Pao – are also inhabited.

Samui's first settlers were islanders from Hainan Island (now part of the People's Republic of China) who took up coconut farming here around 150 years ago. You can still see a map of Hainan on the *sǎan jâo* (Chinese spirit shrine) near Siam City Bank in Na Thon, the oldest town on the island.

The island has had a legendary status among travellers to Asia for the past quarter century or so, but it wasn't until the late 1980s that it escalated to the touristy proportions of other similar getaways, such as

Goa and Bali. Since the advent of the Don Sak ferry and the opening of the airport in 1989, things have been changing fast. During the high seasons (late December to February and July to August) it can be hard to find a place to stay, even though most beaches are crowded with bungalows and resorts. There are nearly a dozen daily flights to Samui from Bangkok, and the island has rushed into top-end development.

Nevertheless, Samui is an enjoyable place to spend some time, and plenty of old-time travellers are still coming here despite all the changes. It still has some of the best-value accommodation in Thailand and a casual, do-as-you-please atmosphere that makes it quite attractive. Even with an airport, it has the advantage of being off the mainland and far away from Bangkok. Coconuts are still an important part of the local economy – millions are shipped to Bangkok each month.

But there's no going back to 1971, when the first two tourists arrived on a coconut boat from Bangkok. The main difference is that there are now many more places to stay, most of them in the mid- to high range by Thai standards. And of course, with this 'something for everyone' climate there's more people, more traffic, more noise and more rubbish, but so far not in intolerable proportions. Samui residents are beginning to formulate policies to deal with these social and environmental challenges and the prognosis is, tentatively, optimistic – only time will tell.

Perhaps due to the Hainanese influence, Samui culture differs from that of other islands in southern Thailand; and its inhabitants refer to themselves as *chao samŭi* (Samui folk) rather than Thais. They can be even friendlier than the average upcountry Thai, in our opinion, and have a great sense of humour, although those who are in constant contact with tourists can be a bit jaded. Nowadays many of the resorts, restaurants, bars and other tourist enterprises are owned or operated by Bangkok Thais or Europeans, so you have to get into the villages to meet true *chao samŭi*.

The island has a distinctive cuisine, influenced by the omnipresent coconut, which is still the main source of income for *chao samŭi*, who have disproportionately less ownership in beach property than outsiders. Coconut palms blanket the island, from the hillocks right up to the beaches. The durian, rambutan and *langsat* (a small round fruit similar to rambutans) are also cultivated.

Ecology & Environment

Samui's visitors and inhabitants produce an incredible amount garbage each day, much of it plastic. Not all of it is properly disposed of, and quite a few plastic bottles end up in the sea, where they wreak havoc on marine life. You could try to fill your own water bottle from the guesthouse or hotel restaurant's large, reusable canisters. On Ko Tao the TAT arranges monthly volunteer rubbish collections with half a dozen dive agencies that offer discounts to participating customers; ask your Samui dive shop if a beach cleanup is planned.

Orientation

Samui has plenty of beaches to choose from, with bungalows popping up around more small bays all the time. The most crowded beaches for accommodation are **Chaweng** and **Lamai**, both are on the eastern side of the island. Chaweng has more bungalow options, plus several snazzy and some very upmarket hotels. It also boasts the longest beach (more than twice the length of Lamai) with **Ko Mat Lang** just offshore. Both Lamai and Chaweng have clear blue-green water, coral reefs and enough nightlife.

Chaweng is the target of current upmarket development because of its long beach. Another factor is that only Chaweng (and the northern part of Lamai) has water deep enough for swimming from October to April; at most other beaches on the island the water becomes very shallow during these months.

At the wát in Ban Lamai is the **Ban Lamai Cultural Hall**, a sort of folk museum displaying local ceramics, household utensils, hunting weapons and musical instruments.

The drawback to Lamai is the rather sleazy atmosphere of the strip of beer bars on the main road though town, though they're not necessarily offensive; Chaweng's bar-and-disco strip is more sophisticated and international.

For more peace and quiet, try the beaches along the north, south and west coasts. **Mae Nam**, **Bo Phut** and **Bang Rak** (Big Buddha) are along the northern end. The water here is not quite as clear as at Chaweng or Lamai, but the feeling of seclusion is greater, and accommodation is cheaper.

Ao Thong Yang is on the western side of the island and is even more secluded. There are only a few sets of bungalows, but the beach here isn't great by Samui standards. The southern end of the island now has many bungalows, set in little out-of-the-way coves – it's worth seeking them out. And then there's everywhere in between – every bay, cove or cape with a strip of sand gets a bungalow nowadays.

When to Go The best time of year to visit Ko Samui is during the hot and dry season, from February to late June. From July to October it can be raining on and off, and from October to January there are sometimes heavy winds. On the other hand, many travellers have reported fine weather (and fewer crowds) in September and October. November tends to get some of the rain that also affects the east coast of Malaysia at this time. Prices tend to soar from December to July, whatever the weather.

Maps In Surat Thani or on Ko Samui, you can pick up the TAT's helpful *Surat Thani* map, which has maps of Surat Thani, the province, Ang Thong National Marine Park and Ko Samui, along with travel information. A couple of private companies now do maps of Ko Samui, Ko Pha-Ngan and Ko Tao, which are available for 50B to 70B in the tourist areas of Surat and on the islands.

Visid Hongsombud's *Guide Map of Koh Samui, Koh Pha-Ngan & Koh Tao* is also good.

Information

Tourist Offices The helpful **TAT office** *(☎ 0 7742 0504; open 8.30am-4.30pm daily)* is at the northern end of Na Thon. South of town is the **tourist police** *(open 24hr; ☎ 0 7742 1281, emergency ☎ 1155)*.

Immigration Offices Travellers can extend tourist visas by 30 days (or visa on arrival by 10 days) for a fee of 500B at the Ko Samui **immigration office** *(☎ 0 7742 1069; open 8.30am-noon & 1pm-4.30pm Mon-Fri, closed public holidays)*. It's about 2km south of Na Thon.

Money Changing money isn't a problem in Na Thon, Chaweng or Lamai, where several banks (with ATMs) or exchange booths offer daily exchange services.

Post & Communications The island's **main post office** *(open 8.30am-4.30pm Mon-Fri, 9am-noon Sat)* is located in Na Thon, but other parts of the island have privately run branches.

International telephone service is available at the **CAT office** *(open 7am-10pm daily)* at the main post office. Many private phone offices on the island will make a connection for a surcharge above the Telephone Organization of Thailand (TOT) or CAT rates.

There's no shortage of Internet facilities in any of the bigger towns, and even the smaller ones have access to the World Wide Web. For information on Ko Samui, check Ⓦ www.sawadee.com, which contains lists of information on dive centres, tours and accommodation, plus timetables for Bangkok Airways, ferries, trains and VIP buses.

Travel Agencies Efficient and reliable **Travel Solutions** *(☎ 0 7723 0203;* Ⓦ *www.travelsolutions.co.th)*, on Chaweng beach near the Samui Mandalay Resotel, can help with the usual international travel plans, transport bookings, accommodation and visa arrangements. Languages spoken include English, Spanish, French and Thai.

Newspapers & Magazines A locally produced, tourist-oriented newspaper with articles in German, English and Thai, *Samui Welcome*, comes out monthly (free). *What's on Samui*, *Samui Guide* and the pocket-sized *Accommodation Samui* are also free and have listings of hotels, restaurants and suggestions of things to do, buried beneath scads of ads.

Medical Services Clinics catering to foreigners are common on Chaweng and Lamai; for more serious stuff head to **Samui International Hospital** *(Chaweng Hospital; ☎ 0 7723 0781, 0 7742 2272;* Ⓦ *www.sih.co.th)*. This is your best bet for just about any medical or dental problem. Emergency ambulance service is available 24 hours and credit cards are accepted for treatment fees. It's opposite the Muang Kulaypan Hotel.

Dangers & Annoyances Several travellers have written to warn others to take care when making train and bus bookings. Bookings sometimes aren't made at all, the bus turns out to be far inferior to the one expected or other hassles develop. Sometimes travel agents say that economy class is fully booked and only business class is available; the agent then sells the customer an air ticket – at business-class prices – that turns out to be economy class.

As on Phuket, the rate of fatalities on Samui from road accidents is quite high. This is due mainly to the large number of tourists who rent motorcycles only to find out that Samui's winding roads, stray dogs and coconut trucks can be lethal to those who have never dealt with them. If you feel you must rent a motorcycle, protect yourself by wearing a helmet, shoes and appropriate clothing when driving.

Theft isn't unknown on the island. If you're staying in a beach bungalow, consider depositing your valuables with the management while off on excursions around the island or swimming at the beach. Most of the theft reports continue to come from Lamai and Mae Nam beaches.

Waterfalls

Besides the beaches, Samui has a couple of waterfalls. **Nam Tok Hin Lat** (Hin Lat Falls) is only worth a visit if you're bored from waiting in Na Thon for a boat out. You can get here by sǎwngthǎew (30B), go 2km and get off after the 7-Eleven, then walk

2km, or walk the whole way – walk 2km or so south of town on the main road and turn left at the first major intersection. Head straight along another 2km to the waterfall (you'll see the vendors). From here, it's almost an hour's hike along a slippery trail to the top of the opaque trickle of water.

Nam Tok Na Muang, in the centre of the island (the turn-off is 10km southeast of Na Thon), is more scenic and less frequented. There are several levels. The lower falls are smaller, but have a large pool suitable for swimming, and are directly accessible from the road. To reach the upper falls requires a 1.5km hike – from the uppermost level the view extends to the sea.

Temples

For temple enthusiasts **Wat Laem Saw**, at the southern end of the island near the village of Ban Bang Kao, features an interesting and highly venerated old Srivijaya-style *chedi*. This *chedi* is very similar to the one in Chaiya (see its section under Around Surat Thani earlier in this chapter).

At the northern end, on a small rocky island that's joined to Samui by a causeway, is **Wat Phra Yai** (Temple of the Big Buddha). Erected in 1972, the modern image is about 12m high, and makes a pretty silhouette against the tropical sky and sea behind it. The image is surrounded by *kùtì* (meditation huts). A sign in English requests that proper attire (no shorts or sleeveless shirts) be worn on the premises.

There is also an old semi-abandoned temple, **Wat Pang Bua**, near the northern end of Hat Chaweng, where 10-day *vipassana* (insight meditation) courses are occasionally held for *faràng*; the courses are led by monks from Wat Suanmok in Chaiya.

Near the car park at the entrance to Nam Tok Hin Lat is another trail left to **Suan Dharmapala**, a meditation temple. Another attraction is the ghostly **mummified monk** at Wat Khunaram, south of Rte 4169 between Ban Thurian and Ban Hua Thanon. The monk, Luang Phaw Daeng, has been dead over two decades but his corpse is preserved sitting in a meditative pose and sporting a pair of sun glasses.

At **Wat Samret** near Ban Hua Thanon you can see a typical Mandalay sitting Buddha carved from solid marble – common in northern Thailand, but rarer in the south. A collection of antique Buddha images is housed in a hall on the monastery grounds; to view them, ask one of the monks to unlock the hall, and leave a small donation.

Ang Thong National Marine Park
อุทยานแห่งชาติหมู่เกาะอ่างทอง

This archipelago of around 40 small islands combines sheer limestone cliffs, white-sand beaches, hidden lagoons, and dense vegetation to provide a nearly postcard-perfect opportunity to enjoy gulf islands. The park lies 31km northwest of Ko Samui and encompasses 18 sq km of islands, plus 84 sq km of marine environments.

Tour operators run popular day trips to the park, leaving from Na Thon or Mae Nam. Lunch is included, along with a climb to the top of a 240m hill to view the whole island group; some tours visit **Tham Bua Bok**, a cavern containing lotus-shaped cave formations. There's officially a 200B admission fee for foreigners, though it should be included in any tour you take. Bring shoes with good traction, snorkelling gear, a hat, and plenty of sunscreen and drinking water. You can also join a more active but more expensive Ang Thong kayak trip; see Paddling later in this section. Overnight tours are also available.

At the **park headquarters** *(☎ 0 7728 6025)* on Ko Wat Ta Lap, there are bungalows available, but you may not be able to reserve them unless you go with a tour.

Buffalo Fighting

Local villagers love to bet on duelling water buffaloes and events are arranged on a rotating basis at seven rustic fighting rings around the island in Na Thon, Ban Saket, Na Muang, Hua Thanon, Ban Chaweng, Mae Nam and Ban Bo Phut. In these events two buffaloes face off and, at their owners' urging, lock horns and/or butt one another until one of the animals backs down. The typical encounter lasts only a few seconds, and rarely are the animals injured. As such events go, it's fairly tame – certainly far more humane than dog-fighting, cockfighting or Spanish bullfighting. Tourists are charged 150B to 200B entry.

Diving

The best diving is really in the Ko Tao area, and many dive trips starting from Samui end up there – plenty of dive operations around the island will eagerly take you. Bigger and more well-known shops are often good, but smaller shops may try harder – and some go out with smaller groups as well. The only hyperbaric chamber on the island is in Hat Bang Rak (Big Buddha Beach).

Beach dives cost around 1000B per day. Dives from boats start from 3000B, and two- to four-day certification courses cost 6000B to 9500B. An overnight dive trip to Ko Tao, including food and accommodation, can be done for about 3500B.

The highest concentration of dive shops is at Hat Chaweng.

Calypso Diving (☎ 0 7742 2437, w www.calypso-diving.com) Hat Chaweng
Dive Indeep (☎ 0 7723 0155, e indeep@samart.co.th) Hat Chaweng
Samui International Diving School (SIDS; ☎ 0 7724 2386, w www.planet-scuba.net) Hat Lamai, Bo Phut & Hat Chaweng
Silent Divers (☎ 0 7742 2730, w www.silentdivers.com) Hat Chaweng
The Dive Shop (☎/fax 0 7723 0232, e diveshop@samart.co.th) Hat Chaweng

Paddling

Blue Stars *(☎ 0 7741 3231; w www.gallerylafayette.com/bluestars)*, in Hat Chaweng, offers guided kayak trips in Ang Thong National Marine Park (1990B) and two-day overnight tours to the beautiful bay filmed in the movie *The Beach* (4750B).

Sea Canoe *(☎/fax 0 7723 0484; w www.seacanoe.net)*, in Hat Lamai, is another good company with trips to the marine park and more.

Any travel agency worth its salt should be able to book a kayak tour.

Cooking Courses

Samui Institute of Thai Culinary Arts *(Sitca; ☎/fax 0 7741 3172; w www.sitca.net; 46/6 Soi Colibri)* offers daily Thai cooking classes, as well as courses in the aristocratic Thai art of carving fruits and vegetables into intricate floral designs. Quick lunchtime classes cost 995B (three courses), while dinner classes are 1400B (four courses). Of course you get to eat your work, and even invite a friend along for the meal. Sitca is also planning to open a restaurant on the 2nd floor. To find it, look for a blue 'Save Way Travel' sign; it's down that lane.

Na Thon

หน้าทอน

Na Thon, on the northwestern side of the island, is the small town where ferries from the Surat Thani area arrive; some from Ko Pha-Ngan also dock here. Most hotels, restaurants, banks with ATMs, souvenir shops, markets and travel agencies are found on the two main streets. Though it's basically a tourist town now, Na Thon still sports a few old teak Chinese shophouses and cafés along Th Ang Thong, and there's a colourful day market in town, too.

The staff at **Asia Travel** *(☎ 0 7723 6120; open 8.30am-6pm Mon-Sat)* speak English and can help with visas (both Thai and nearby countries), as well as travel arrangements. If you need beach reading, head for **Na Thon Bookshop** *(open 10am-6pm daily)*, which has a wide selection of used books for sale or trade.

Places to Stay The **Palace Hotel** *(☎ 0 7742 1079; rooms with fan/air-con 350/500B)*, near the old pier, is a bit dark and old and has saggy mattresses, but it's OK.

Win Hotel *(☎ 0 7742 1500, fax 0 7742 1454; rooms with air-con & TV 450-550B)* is a good, friendly place with only a few sea-view rooms.

Nathon Residence *(☎ 0 7723 6058; rooms with air-con & TV 500B)* is a beautiful new place – the best of the lot in town. It's modern, clean and central, and there's a pleasant guesthouse feel.

Sea View Guest House *(☎ 0 7723 6236; rooms with fan 200-300B, with air-con 400-450B)* is an eclectically run old digs, with basic, large, well-furnished rooms. Some have paint chips missing but most are decent and bright.

Dum Rong Town Hotel *(☎ 0 7742 0359; rooms with air-con 450-550B)* has quiet, large rooms, with bathrooms; they're not new but remain perfectly acceptable.

Places to Eat The open-air **food stalls**, near the ferry pier area, are cheap and fun. The **day market** is good for fruit.

Roung Thong Bakery *(dishes 50-190B; open 6.30am-7pm daily)* attracts waiting travellers with its good hangout atmosphere. There's lots of choice on the menu, as well as bakery items for the boat ride out.

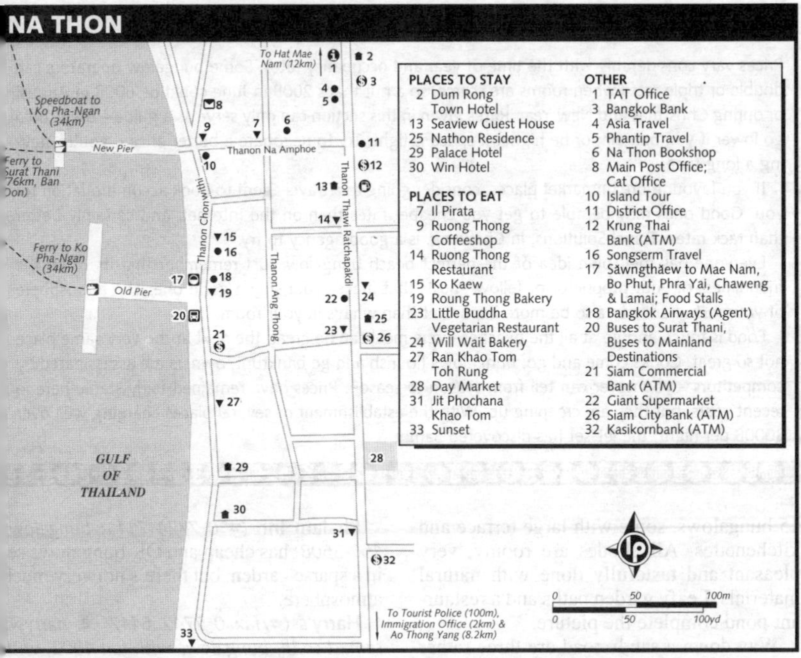

Ko Kaew *(dishes 25-150B; open 7am-9pm daily)*, near Roung Thong Bakery, serves cheap Thai food in a friendly, casual setting.

Roung Thong Restaurant *(dishes 50-190B; open 6.30am-7pm daily)* has good offerings (including lots of coffees), with airy bench seats outside to catch the breeze along the side street.

Roung Thong Coffee shop *(dishes 60-180B; open 6am-9pm daily)* is the fanciest of the three, offering similar fare for the trendy.

Jit Phochana Khao Tom *(dishes 35-80B; open 24hr)* is cheap and friendly.

Il Pirata *(dishes 50-150B; open 8am-9pm daily)* serves Thai and Western food in some friendly but tacky surroundings (too many mirrors). It has a busy corner location.

Will Wait Bakery *(dishes 50-200B; open 7.30am-5.30pm daily)* is a friendly, casual place with just a few bakery offerings, but also serves Thai and Western foods, and breakfast.

Little Buddha Vegetarian Restaurant *(dishes 60-125B; open 8am-6pm daily)* is a tiny place with a few tables; half the space is artwork. Vegie items, including pastries and tofu, are served, along with fancy coffees.

Sunset *(dishes 50-250B; open 10am-10pm daily)* sits at the southern end of the coast street, and offers great seaside atmosphere. On tap are Thai, Western and seafood dishes.

Ban Tai (Ao Bang Po)
บ้านใต้(อ่าวบางปอ)

This is the first beach area north of Na Thon with accommodation; there are just a handful of places to stay here. The beach has fair snorkelling and swimming.

Healing Child Resort *(☎ 0 7742 0124, fax 0 7742 0125; W www.healthoasisresort.com; rooms with fan 675B, with air-con 1350-1800B)* is a New Age spot on pleasant sunny grounds; modern rooms are comfortable and well balanced. The restaurant serves vegetarian food, and communal meals are 120B. Services offered include massage, colonic cleansing, 'vortex astrology', lymphasising and all sorts of other uplifting things. The ethereal Internet is available as well.

Axolotl Village *(☎/fax 0 7742 0017; W www.axolotlvillage.com; rooms & bungalows 500-1000B)* is Italian-run and boasts

Places to Stay & Eat

Prices vary considerably with the time of year and occupancy rates. Some bungalow operators can double or triple rates when rooms are scarce, so a hut that's 200B in June could be 600B in August or during Christmas and New Year. Rates given in this section can only serve as a guide – they could go lower if you bargain, or be higher if space is tight. Try to negotiate a better price if you're staying a long time.

If you favour more upmarket places, consider going to a travel agent to book accommodation for you. Good ones may be able to get you cheaper rates than on the Internet, and certainly better than rack rates. Travel Solutions, in Chaweng, is a good agency to try.

Everyone has their own idea of the perfect beach bungalow. Just remember that its often the friendliness of your proprietor or fellow guests that makes your stay a good one. The atmosphere of your restaurant can also be more important than what's in your room.

Food is touch and go at all the beaches – one meal can be great, the next at the very same place not so great. Cooks come and go, bungalows flourish and go bankrupt, owners are assassinated by competitors – you never can tell from season to season. Prices have remained fairly stable here in recent years, but they are creeping up. With the establishment of several places charging well over 3000B per night, the jet-set has discovered Samui.

15 bungalows, some with large terrace and kitchenettes. All abodes are roomy, very pleasant and tastefully done with natural materials. Leafy garden paths and a restaurant pond complete the picture.

Way down a sandy road are three rather isolated places.

Moon (*☎ 0 7724 7371; bungalows 150-350B*) has nice and comfortable inland bungalows, along with sea view ones. There's a great casual restaurant area by the beach, and traveller services are available.

Ban Tai (*☎ 0 9874 7357; 1-person huts 100B, bungalows 200-250B*) has 12 pretty, airy and comfortable bungalows that are good deals.

Sunbeam (*☎ 0 7742 0600; bungalows 200-400B*) is the most upmarket of the lot, with a variety of big, comfortable and rustic bungalows by the sea. There's a great garden with brick paths and a relaxing restaurant.

Hat Mae Nam
หาดแม่น้ำ

Hat Mae Nam, 14km from Na Thon, is expanding rapidly in terms of bungalow development – there are still a few cheapies left but prices are going steadily up. Bungalow operations are a bit spread out along inland sand tracks. The beach in front of Wat Na Phalan is undeveloped and the locals hope it will stay that way; please avoid going topless here.

Phalarn Inn (*☎ 0 7724 7111; bungalows 150-350B*) has cheap and OK bungalows set in a sparse garden, but there's not very much atmosphere.

Harry's (*☎/fax 0 7742 5447; e harrys@samart.co.th; bungalows with fan 400B, with air-con 500-800B*) starts with a tiled walkway, which leads you to a sandy garden with a few trees. Concrete and floor-tiled bungalows are good, though inland from the beach. Its best feature is the pool.

Sea Fan (*☎ 0 7742 5204, fax 0 7742 5350; w www.seafansamuihotel.com; rooms with air-con 3000-3300B*) has well-built wood and thatch luxury bungalows connected by wooden walkways along spacious gardens. There's a pool, and on Christmas day there's a 2500B compulsory 'Gala' dinner.

Anong Villa (*☎ 0 7724 7256; bungalows with fan 300-500B, with air-con 800-1000B*) has a wide range of nice-looking bungalows, from cheapies on the beach to some more upmarket ones at the back (but facing a sandy driveway).

New Sunrise Village (*☎ 0 7724 7219; bungalows 200-500B*) is scruffy but not unpleasant. There's a wide assortment of bungalows; rates vary depending on size and proximity to the beach.

Palm Point Village (*☎/fax 0 7742 5095; bungalows with fan 350-400B, with air-con 800B*) has a small, well-maintained garden and bright, good bungalows with creative wooden rails; those with fan are close to the beach, while larger air-conditioned ones are farther inland.

Maenam Resort *(☎/fax 0 7742 5116; ⓔ maenamrs@samart.co.th; bungalows 700-1200B)* is a good deal; nicely maintained and upmarket bungalows have a rich, dark ambience and are relatively private. The beautiful, lush garden paths lead to the shady beachside restaurant.

Santiburi Dusit Resort *(☎ 0 7742 5031, 0 7742 5040; ⓦ www.dusit.com; rooms with air-con US$374-990)* is for the type of people who probably wouldn't be caught dead using a Lonely Planet guidebook.

Lolita *(☎ 0 7742 5134; bungalows with fan 400-600B, with air-con 1500B)* offers attractive, large wooden bungalows at or near the beach. It's a good place, with a slightly upmarket atmosphere that's good for families. The circular restaurant has classic styling and is tastefully done.

Mae Nam Beach Bungalows *(☎ 0 7742 5060; bungalows 150-350B)* is a backpacker's special; friendly, basic shacks or more modern bungalows sit on a shady lot, and there's a good beach atmosphere.

New La Paz Villa *(☎ 0 7742 5296, fax 0 7742 5402; rooms with fan 300-500B, with air-con 700-1000B)* is a quite pleasant and popular place, with a nice garden, pool and decent beachside restaurant.

New Star *(☎ 0 7742 7623; huts 150-250B)* must be among the cheapest places to stay on the entire island. Small huts and bigger bungalows are a bit grungy but OK. There's a colourful restaurant with a pool table and a good atmosphere.

Maenam Villa *(☎ 0 7742 5501; bungalows with fan 200-400B, with air-con 1200B)* features large, modern, orange-coloured bungalows and a rather bleak-looking restaurant.

SR Bungalow *(☎ 0 7742 7530, fax 0 7742 7531; ⓔ sr_bungalow@hotmail.com; bungalows 300-400B)* sports well-maintained bungalows with a decent beach area; they look nicer than Maenam Villa's bungalows.

Hat Bo Phut

หาดบ่อผุด

This beach has a reputation for peace and quiet, and those who regularly come here hope it will stay that way; don't show up looking for a party. The beach tends to be a little on the muddy side and the water can be too shallow for swimming during the dry season – a curse that can be a blessing because it keeps development rather low key and has preserved the village atmosphere.

The following are off the main road and west of the central village area.

Sunny *(☎ 0 7742 7031; bungalows 250-400B)* offers 12 small, basic bungalows on a sandy lot with coconut palms – there's not much action, but it's a decent choice for backpackers who don't need much.

Zazen *(☎ 0 7742 5085, fax 0 7742 5177; ⓦ www.samuizazen.com; rooms & bungalows with air-con in low season 800-1500B, in high season 1000-3000B)* is a lusciously unique place; 28 artistically decorated, multilevel abodes are trimmed in wood and nicely painted. There's a billiard-table pavilion, great swimming pool, tasty beachside restaurant and small spa, all surrounded by attractive grounds.

Sandy Resort *(☎ 0 7742 3534, fax 0 7742 5325; bungalows with fan 500B, with air-con 800-1000B)*, next door, has well-appointed bungalows of wood and concrete – some have log walls and saggy mattresses.

Free House *(bungalows 400-700B)* is a casual little place with a leafy, pretty garden and large, simple bungalows (some with sea view).

World Resort *(☎ 0 7742 5355; bungalows with air-con 1050-2150B)* has stylish, large rooms with nice terraces, a pool with a bar, and appealing grounds. Breakfast is included.

Peace Bungalow *(☎ 0 7742 5357, fax 0 7742 5343; ⓦ www.peaceresort.com; rooms with air-con 1850-3300B)* has shiny, upmarket, wooden bungalows in a shady tropical garden. It's a very comfortable place, with a beachside swimming pool and restaurant.

Samui Euphoria *(☎ 0 7742 5100, fax 0 7742 5107; ⓦ www.samuieuphoria.com; rooms with air-con 2500-3000B)* has lush gardens surrounded by unobtrusive, hotel-like room blocks; it's not spic-and-span though, and with another coat of paint would probably gain a half-star.

The heart of Bo Phut runs along a calm inland road near the beach, where you'll find a concentrated number of restaurants and other services. Good eateries include Thai restaurants along with *faràng*-oriented ones. Locals recommend **Angela's Harbourside Cafe**, **Pudding House** and **Frog & Gecko Pub**.

All the following, except The Lodge, are on the inland side of the road/village, just a few steps from the beach.

Hello Diving & Guesthouse (☎ *0 9872 7056, fax 0 7742 7542;* Ⓦ *www.hello-diving.com; dorm beds with fan/air-con 100/150B)* is a unique traveller's crash pad run by a knowledgable expat. There are good, intimate dorms and a nice ground-floor communal room. The only drawback so far is its lack of a restaurant and the limited bathroom facilities.

Eden (☎ *0 7742 7645, fax 0 7742 7644;* Ⓦ *www.sawadee.com/samui/eden; bungalows with air-con 800-1600B)* is an exceptional find. It has 12 spacious and creative rooms, and a gorgeous garden with pool. It's a pleasant stay, but you may want to reconfirm your reservations (if you make them) before you arrive.

Summer Night (☎ *0 7724 5288; bungalows with fan 300-450B, with air-con 700-800B)* has large, basic, good no-frills bungalows in a sparse inland garden.

The Lodge (☎ *0 7742 5337, fax 0 7742 5336; rooms with air-con 1350-1550B)* is a small, personal and upmarket place right on the beach. The 10 luxurious rooms are beautiful, cosy and super-comfortable.

Smile House (☎ *0 7742 5361, fax 0 7742 5239;* Ⓔ *smilehousesamui@hotmail.com; rooms 500-1600B, bungalows 1400-6500B)* features little white bungalows all lined up in a row, along an attractive but sparse garden and pool area. The property has a rather impersonal feel; the best bungalows are at the back.

Ziggy Stardust (☎ *0 7742 5173; bungalows with fan/air-con 400/1000B)* has good-sized thatched-roof bungalows along nice, calm garden pathways. It's a good deal, but poorly signed; look for its thatched-roof restaurant on the beach, west of Smile House.

Hat Bang Rak (Big Buddha Beach)

หาดบางรักษ์

This place is more like an 'area' and not really a conventional town. Bungalow operations are spread out along the main road. Nearby is an island, Ko Fan, connected to the mainland by a causeway; Wat Phra Yai's big Buddha statue attracts tourists and view-seekers. For an exceptional meal, be sure to check out **The Mangrove** (☎ *0 7742 7584; open 11.30am-late daily)* on an inland road nearby. The kitchen is run by an ex-Poppies chef who cooks up an ever-changing menu of French cuisine. Reservations are highly recommended, as seating is limited.

Nara Garden Beach Resort (☎ *0 7742 5364, fax 0 7742 5292;* Ⓔ *naragarden@hotmail.com; rooms with air-con from 1470B)* is a pleasant, intimate and well-laid out place with a small beachside pool surrounded by green shrubs. Rooms are situated either around this pool or a leafy garden. Ask for discounts off the rack rate.

Pongpetch Servotel (☎ *0 7724 5100, fax 0 7742 5148;* Ⓦ *www.pongpetchhotel.com; rooms & bungalows with fan 600-1200B, with air-con 700-1350B)* has small but good and homey abodes around a cute garden with fountain and sitting areas; it's a nice little place that isn't fancy but is comfortable enough.

Secret Garden Bungalows (☎ *0 7742 5419, fax 0 7724 5253;* Ⓦ *www.secretgarden.co.th; bungalows with fan/air-con 500/ 1500B)* has grounds that aren't wholly unattractive, but not especially pretty either – and management can be dour, depending on who helps you. The bungalows themselves are good enough, though.

Shambala (☎*/fax 0 7742 5330;* Ⓦ *www.shamui-shambala.com; bungalows 400-700B)* is a great traveller's pad. This English-run place has spacious grounds and bright, roomy bungalows that are pleasant and well run. There are traveller services in the cool restaurant and a floating lounger in the sea.

Chez Ban-Ban & Le Mar de Provence (☎ *0 7724 5135, fax 0 7742 5515;* Ⓔ *ban-ban@samui-info.com; cottages with fan/air-con 450/1000B)* holds dear 10 very tiny and cute, Heidi-like cottages with rattan floors. They surround a nice little garden along with a French restaurant.

Como Resort (☎ *0 7742 5210;* Ⓦ *www.yucom.be/home.html; rooms & bungalows with air-con 1000B)* is a cosy little place with just a handful of sweet rooms and bungalows. There's a wading pool too.

Ao Thong Sai & Hat Choeng Mon

อ่าวท้องทรายและหาดเชิงมน

The largest cove following Ao Thong Sai has several names, but the beach is generally known as Hat Choeng Mon. It's clean, quiet and recommended for families or for those who don't need nightlife and a variety of restaurants (easily found at nearby Hat Chaweng anyway). Opposite the beach is **Ko Fan Yai**, an island that can be reached on foot in low tide.

Imperial Boat House Hotel *(☎ 0 7742 5041, fax 0 7742 5460; W www.imperialhotels.com; rooms & bungalows with air-con US$120-225)* has a definite boat theme, and if you're a rich seafarer you'll want to stay here. The fanciest bungalows are converted teak rice barges, one of two pools is boat-shaped, and oars decorate the entrance. It's a stunning, sophisticated and unique place, with an almost postmodern feel.

Island View *(☎ 0 7742 5031, fax 0 7742 5081; bungalows with fan/air-con 400/800B)* is a friendly place on the beach in an attractive, though not isolated, area. It has nice, large, modern bungalows and is a good budget choice.

Choeng Mon Bungalow *(☎ 0 7742 5372, fax 0 7742 5219; bungalows with fan 300-450B, with air-con 650-1200B)* offers clean, spacious and OK bungalows facing a sandy parking lot with a few palms; it's not totally unpleasant, though paths could use a bit of maintenance.

The White House *(☎ 0 7724 5315, fax 0 7742 5318; e info@samuidreamholiday.com; rooms with air-con 4400-6000B)* is perfect for those seeking a cosy, romantic getaway. Beautifully appointed rooms are artfully decorated, have creative wooden details and come with peaked roofs. Duvets top every bed, and on arrival you'll receive fresh fruit and flowers. Water-filled urns dot the lush garden paths and there's an elegant pool, a restaurant and private spa areas – it's simply a gorgeous place.

PS Villa *(☎ 0 7742 5160, fax 0 7742 5403; bungalows with fan 400-600B, with air-con 500-1200B)* features a good range of bungalows and amenities in a spacious, well-maintained garden area.

Tongsai Bay *(☎ 0 7742 5015, fax 0 7742 5462; W www.tongsaibay.co.th; suites 10,000-50,000B)* is not for the masses, needless to say. Expansive, nicely maintained and hilly grounds make buildings here look like a small village, and golf carts are employed to zoom guests around. All super luxury suites have day-bed rest areas, a gorgeous romantic decor, stunning views, large terraces and creatively placed tubs (you'll see). Facilities include salt- and fresh-water pools, a tennis court, spa and three restaurants.

Hat Chaweng
หาดเฉวง

Hat Chaweng, Samui's longest beach, has the island's highest concentration of bungalows and tourist hotels – it's a pretty upmarket place, though if you look hard enough you may find a budget gem here and there.

The main road parallel to the beach is a commercial strip that is jam-packed with restaurants, Internet outlets, travel agencies, currency-exchange booths, motorcycle rentals, souvenir shops, massage parlours, bars and discos (there are so many business, in fact, that you may get lost finding a path back down to the beach).

If you need a book to complement your hammock or deck chair, try **Bookazine** (near McDonald's), which sells new books and magazines, or **Saai Bookshop** (a bit north near Siam Bank), which sells and exchanges used books.

Water sports are really big here, so if you enjoy parasailing, sailboarding, scuba diving, water-skiing, banana boating or whatever, you won't be disappointed. If you're a swimmer, be careful from November to January, when riptides are a possibility. Ask around to be safe.

The following places were researched in the mid- to high month of August. Be aware that prices zoom spaceward during the holiday period from late December to mid-January, and that exact high or peak seasons are defined differently from place to place. Also, since so many bungalow operations are being upgraded or expanded, prices are sure to waver a bit. Use the following tariffs as a guide only.

Places to Stay The accommodation options in this section are divided between three areas: North Chaweng, Central Chaweng and Chaweng Noi.

You may find that, as a whole, North Chaweng has more inexpensive places than farther south – though there are pricey digs up here too. This makes sense since it's not as central and away from certain convenient services. But if you're looking for a more

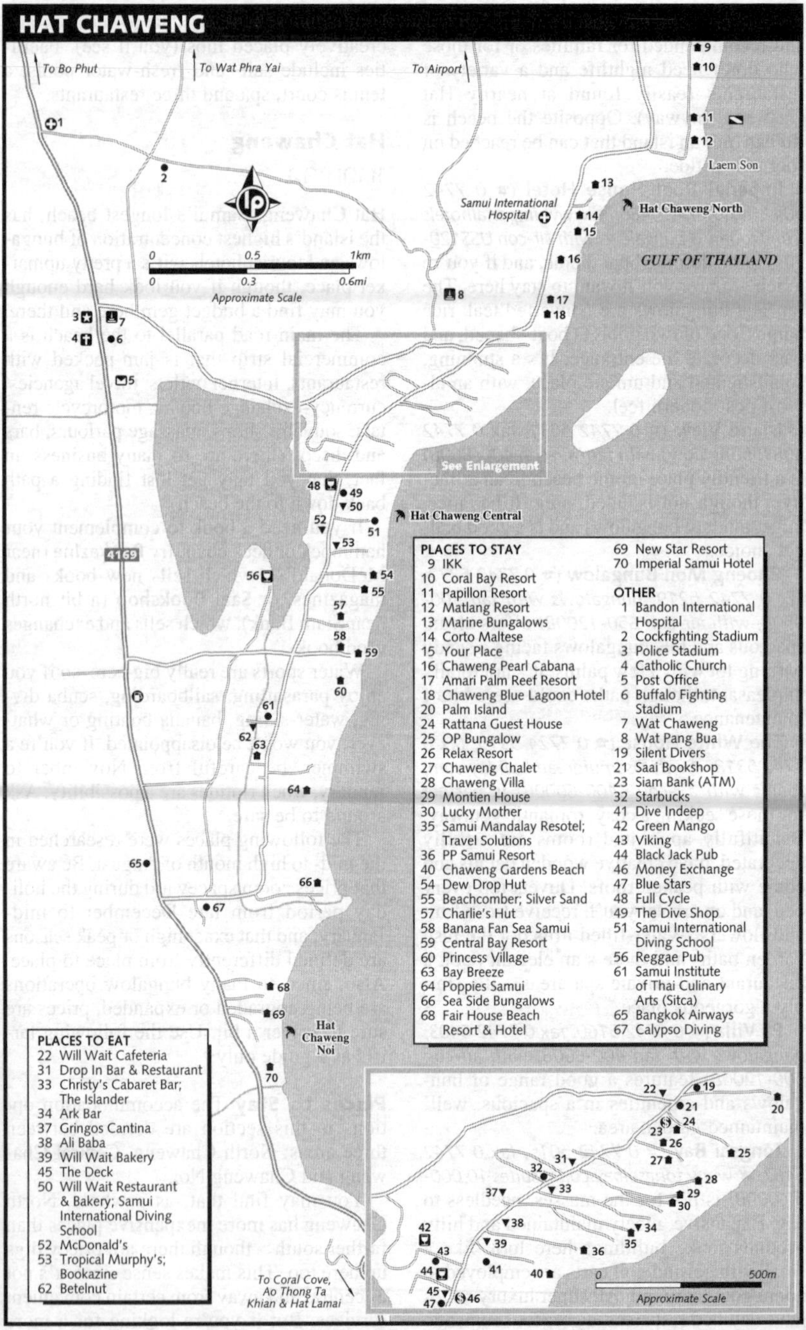
HAT CHAWENG
To Bo Phut
To Wat Phra Yai
To Airport
Samui International Hospital
Laem Son
Hat Chaweng North
GULF OF THAILAND
0 0.5 1km
0 0.3 0.6mi
Approximate Scale
See Enlargement
Hat Chaweng Central
4169
Hat Chaweng Noi
To Coral Cove, Ao Thong Ta Khian & Hat Lamai
0 500m
Approximate Scale
PLACES TO STAY
9 IKK
10 Coral Bay Resort
11 Papillon Resort
12 Matlang Resort
13 Marine Bungalows
14 Corto Maltese
15 Your Place
16 Chaweng Pearl Cabana
17 Amari Palm Reef Resort
18 Chaweng Blue Lagoon Hotel
20 Palm Island
24 Rattana Guest House
25 OP Bungalow
26 Relax Resort
27 Chaweng Chalet
28 Chaweng Villa
29 Montien House
30 Lucky Mother
35 Samui Mandalay Resotel; Travel Solutions
36 PP Samui Resort
40 Chaweng Gardens Beach
54 Dew Drop Hut
55 Beachcomber; Silver Sand
57 Charlie's Hut
58 Banana Fan Sea Samui
59 Central Bay Resort
60 Princess Village
63 Bay Breeze
64 Poppies Samui
66 Sea Side Bungalows
68 Fair House Beach Resort & Hotel
69 New Star Resort
70 Imperial Samui Hotel
OTHER
1 Bandon International Hospital
2 Cockfighting Stadium
3 Police Stadium
4 Catholic Church
5 Post Office
6 Buffalo Fighting Stadium
7 Wat Chaweng
8 Wat Pang Bua
19 Silent Divers
21 Saai Bookshop
23 Siam Bank (ATM)
32 Starbucks
41 Dive Indeep
42 Green Mango
43 Viking
44 Black Jack Pub
46 Money Exchange
47 Blue Stars
48 Full Cycle
49 The Dive Shop
51 Samui International Diving School
56 Reggae Pub
61 Samui Institute of Thai Culinary Arts (Sitca)
65 Bangkok Airways
67 Calypso Diving
PLACES TO EAT
22 Will Wait Cafeteria
31 Drop In Bar & Restaurant
33 Christy's Cabaret Bar; The Islander
34 Ark Bar
37 Gringos Cantina
38 Ali Baba
39 Will Wait Bakery
45 The Deck
50 Will Wait Restaurant & Bakery; Samui International Diving School
52 McDonald's
53 Tropical Murphy's; Bookazine
62 Betelnut

quiet area away from throbbing discos, consider staying here.

IKK *(☎ 0 7741 3281; bungalows 500-700B)* sports 15 identical bungalows whose price is determined by beach proximity. It's a small but somewhat isolated and pleasantly calm place. On board are nice garden paths and an atmospheric restaurant area.

Coral Bay Resort *(☎ 0 7742 2223, fax 0 7742 2392; W www.coralbay.net; rooms & bungalows 2500-9000B)* has thatched roofs all over. The accommodation is great, sporting natural materials and unique wooden details in spacious surroundings. Gardens are lush, hilly and meandering, and there's a tastefully designed pool area with overlooking restaurant. It's an ecological resort of sorts.

Papillon Resort *(☎/fax 0 7723 1169; W www.papillonsamui.com; rooms & bungalows with air-con from 1500B)* offers some imaginative, two-level rooms with elegant decor and lofts, along with a lush garden, beautiful restaurant and tiny pool. It's a creative place.

Matlang Resort *(☎ 0 7742 2172; bungalows with fan 400-700, with air-con 800B)* has solid thatch-roof, wooden bungalows that vary in price and are surrounded by garden paths. It's friendly and has good rooms.

Marine Bungalows *(☎ 0 7742 2416, fax 0 7742 2263; bungalows with fan 300-600B, with air-con 800B)* maintains decently built bungalows, most inland on shady, spacious and hilly grounds.

Corto Maltese *(☎ 0 7723 0041, fax 0 7742 2535; W www.corto.kohsamui.net; rooms with air-con from 2490B)*, well designed and decorated, has creative baths and comfortable rooms. It's popular, and there's a pool. The rates include breakfast.

Your Place *(☎ 0 7723 0039; bungalows with fan 300-500B, with air-con 600B)* features 27 cute bungalows, most around a garden square, that are a good deal (especially air-con ones). It's a friendly place too.

Chaweng Pearl Cabana *(☎ 0 7742 2116; bungalows with fan 300-400B, with air-con 500-600B)* offers brusque service, which is tolerable for some of the cheapest rooms around. You'll also have to deal with dim rooms and saggy mattresses, though for a budget sleeps it's still OK.

Amari Palm Reef Resort *(☎ 0 7742 2015, fax 0 7742 2394; W www.amari.com; rooms & bungalows with air-con from 5500B)* is a luxurious, ultra-tastefully done resort with a gorgeous pool area and spacious, comfortable rooms. Thai-style cottages have lofts, and there are two swimming pools.

Chaweng Blue Lagoon Hotel *(☎ 0 7742 2041, fax 0 7742 2388; W www.bluelagoonhotel.com; bungalows with air-con from 4500B)* is a lovely upmarket resort with nice tropical touches and Thai-style decor.

Hat Chaweng's central area has the most bungalows, hotels, restaurants (many with videos), bars (including the girlie kind), discos, video parlours, minimarts, tailors, souvenir shops and currency-exchange booths. Expect accommodation prices to be the most expensive on the island; after all, it *is* the prettiest beach, and where most folks want to stay.

OP Bungalow *(☎ 0 7742 2424, fax 0 7742 2425; bungalows with fan/air-con 550/900B)* offers decent, good-looking bungalows on tropical grounds – just ignore the ugly driveway. The restaurant has a good view of the beach.

Rattana Guest House *(☎ 0 7742 2441; rooms 400-500B)* is a hotel-like building that's well inland but cheap. Some rooms are good, large and come with balconies; others are not quite as nice but are located along more attractive hallways. The atmosphere is local and hardly festive, though it's good value.

Palm Island *(☎ 0 7723 0654, fax 0 7741 3140; W www.palmislandsamui.com; rooms & bungalows 1800-5500B)* offers good, sizable rooms in a hotel block, and nice-looking wooden bungalows. There's also a pleasant pool with a wide patio area. It's an affordable mid-range choice and not too far from the town centre.

Relax Resort *(☎ 0 7742 2280, fax 0 7742 2113; bungalows with fan/air-con 600/1200B)* has nice rooms with fans in an appalling location off the driveway; on the other hand, the rooms with air-con are gorgeously charming, with attractive architecture (some have wonderful lofts) and creative details. They are in the back of the complex, along nice garden paths.

Chaweng Chalet *(☎ 0 7741 3732, fax 0 7741 3731; e chaletsamui@hotmail.com; bungalows with air-con from 1200B)* offers 15 good, clean, solid bungalows with rustic wooden decor and good amenities. They live on pleasing grounds in a good location. The restaurant is pretty cool, too.

Chaweng Villa *(☎ 0 7723 1123, fax 0 7723 1124; w www.chawengvilla.com; rooms & bungalows with air-con 1700-2600B)* has nicely kept, vine-covered rooms and bungalows on grassy grounds. The pool and restaurant are near the beach.

Montien House *(☎ 0 7742 2169, fax 0 7742 2145; e montien@samart.co.th; rooms & bungalows with air-con 1600/1800B)* is a special place, offering well-designed bungalows amid peaceful, gorgeous gardens. There's also a large, beautiful pool by the beach, and tranquil music at the restaurant.

Lucky Mother *(☎ 0 7723 0931; bungalows 250-700B)* is a true cheapie among the diamonds. Backpackers will appreciate the shared baths and rickety wooden bungalows reminiscent of old Samui. The rest of your picky family can stay at Montien House next door.

Samui Mandalay Resotel *(☎ 0 7723 1157; bungalows with fan 500-800B, with air-con 1000B)* has dark but sweet and well-designed bungalows on pleasant garden paths. There's a small pool and ubiquitous beachside restaurant. It's a good mid-range choice.

PP Samui Resort *(☎ 0 7742 2540, fax 0 7742 2324; rooms with air-con 900-1000B)* comes very modern and clean. The white, stylish one- or two-storey buildings have tiled roofs and good rooms. Brick garden pathways lead all the way to the beach.

Chaweng Gardens Beach *(☎/fax 0 7742 2265; rooms & bungalows with air-con 750-1000B)* features beautiful, well-spaced, two-storey abodes among lush tropical gardens. The grounds are spacious and the restaurant has a wonderful ambience.

Dew Drop Hut *(☎ 0 7723 0551; bungalows 400B)* offers basic wooden bungalows on stilts or on concrete blocks among a sparse jungle garden. It's a good bare-bones budget choice on the beach.

Beachcomber *(☎ 0 7742 2037, fax 0 7742 2041; w www.kohsamui.net/beachcomber; rooms with air-con from 3000B)* offers pretty decent housing in a hotel-like block among well-maintained gardens. The pool's set a little inland, but the restaurant is right over the beach.

Silver Sand *(☎ 0 7723 1202, fax 0 7742 2089; rooms & bungalows 400-500B)* has bungalows with shaky wooden floors, but they're cute and OK. Rooms are dark but decent, and prices are good all around.

Charlie's Hut *(☎ 0 7742 2343; bungalows 250-500B)* is popular for its cheap bungalows on well-kept, lush grounds – though it's not the friendliest of places. There's a lot of in-and-out, so take care of your valuables.

Banana Fan Sea Samui *(☎ 0 7741 3483, fax 0 7741 3487; w www.bananafansea.com; rooms & bungalows with air-con 3500-7000B)* starts with an impressive lobby and leads to wonderfully appointed rooms with sparkling clean baths. There's a small beachside pool with Jacuzzi.

Central Bay Resort *(☎/fax 0 7742 2119; bungalows with fan 500-700B, with air-con 1200-1500B)* has bungalows that look a bit worn, and the grounds could be lusher. It's a decent choice, though more for travellers who don't need extra frills and expect just modern, clean and pleasant rooms at a good price.

Princess Village *(☎ 0 7742 2216, fax 0 7742 2386; w www.samuidreamholiday.com; bungalows with air-con from 3300B)* has to be the most atmospheric stay on the island; you'll feel like royalty. Ayuthaya-period houses, high on stilts, are beautifully constructed and tastefully decorated. They're spaced out in a lush garden with ponds. It's a very special place that would be perfect for honeymooners.

Bay Breeze *(☎ 0 7742 2198; bungalows with fan/air-con 300/500B)* seems like such a good deal, but…it's not on the beach. Look for it on the inland side of the road. It's also a bit old, but is friendly and has decent large rooms with cheap air-con.

Poppies Samui *(☎ 0 7742 2419, fax 0 7742 2420; w www.kohsamui.net/poppies; rooms with air-con US$192)* emulates a cosy elfland; the gorgeous garden comes with bubbling stream, while the beautifully built cottages are luxuriously comfortable. Boulders edge the small swimming pool and, of course, the restaurant is top-notch. The rates include breakfast.

Sea Side Bungalows *(☎ 0 7742 2364, fax 0 7742 2364; e benjaporn2022@hotmail.com; bungalows with fan 850B, with air-con 1250-1500B)* is a friendly, good-feel spot harbouring neat, personable bungalows with good furniture and some artwork on the walls. The large, grassy garden is pleasing, and the rates include breakfast.

The Chaweng Noi area is off by itself around a southern headland. The following places are upmarket and not great value.

Fair House Beach Resort & Hotel (☎ *0 7742 2256, fax 0 7742 2373;* 🅦 *fairhousesamui.com; rooms with air-con 3500-5400B)* is a decent, though not stunning resort, with tropical grounds, two pools and comfortable, tasteful rooms with good amenities.

New Star Resort (☎ *0 7742 2407, fax 0 7742 2325;* 🅦 *www.samuinewstar.com; bungalows 1700-3000B)* is very pleasant, with good, clean, spacious bungalows rolling down a hill to the beach. A remodel may change prices, however.

Imperial Samui Hotel (☎ *0 7742 5041, fax 0 7742 5460;* 🅦 *www.imperialhotels.com; bungalows with air-con 5885-7190B)* has a great pool and cute pueblo-style architecture with rustic elegance…but it has seen better days. Give it a good coat of paint and it may be worth the asking price.

Places to Eat You won't have a difficult time finding a place to eat in Chaweng; all tastes are accounted for, from Thai to European to American fast-food to Indian to lots of seafood. For the best ambience, though, get off the strip and head to the beach, where many bungalow operators set up tables on the sand and have glittery fairy lights at night. With the waves sounding in the background, you can't get much more relaxed than this.

Ali Baba (☎ *0 7723 0253; dishes 70-200B; open 10am-11pm daily)* has mostly Indian and Thai food, though it will serve burgers and pizza also. It's good for vegies too, and has friendly service in a homey space.

Will Wait Restaurant & Bakery (☎ *0 7742 2613; dishes 80-250B; open 7am-midnight daily)* is a good restaurant and excellent bakery that's especially popular for breakfast. It's pleasantly modern, and has lots of drinks along with Western grub and Thai dishes. **Will Wait Cafeteria** *(open 10.30am-10.30pm daily)* is another branch farther north a few blocks, which has good, cheap Thai food.

Drop In Bar & Restaurant (☎ *0 7741 3221; dishes 80-260B; open 12pm-midnight daily)* is in a beautiful lofty thatched hut, with a stream and waterfalls adding an elegant ambience. Western and Thai food pleases the tourists, and there's also a calm bar nearby.

The Deck (☎ *0 7723 0897; dishes 80-200B; open 8am-midnight daily)* is an open-air restaurant cooking up Thai food, burgers, souvlaki, pasta and salad, among other dishes. There's a loud bar, too.

Gringos Cantina (☎ *0 7741 3267; dishes 145-230B; open 2pm-midnight daily)* is a Mexican *cocina* with quesadillas, tacos, tostadas and burritos. There are burgers and pizza too, along with margaritas, piña coladas and tequila shooters.

Poppies (☎ *0 7742 2419; dishes 220-640B; open 7am-11pm daily)* is where high elegance goes for fine cuisine. It's a classy place where reservations are recommended and worn threads are not – dress up a bit. There is occasional live music, and Saturday is Thai night (expect dance, music and culture).

The Islander (☎ *0 7723 0836; dishes 90-210B; open 8am-2am daily)* is a popular, pub-style place with Western and Thai food, a kids' menu, outdoor tables, a pool table and sports on TV – something for almost everyone.

Tropical Murphy's (☎ *0 7741 3614; dishes 75-295B; open 8am-2pm daily)*, across from McDonald's, is fairly similar to The Islander and just as popular with *faràng*. On the menu are steak and kidney pie, fish and chips, lamb chops, Irish stew and desserts.

Betelnet (☎ *0 7741 3370; 46/27 Chaweng; open 6pm-midnight daily)* is a small, modest upmarket place just a bit south of the town centre. Gourmets trek here for California-Thai fusion specials, like sesame-crusted salmon, jumbo prawns with *tôm yam* (soup made with lemon grass, chilli, lime and usually seafood) and roast duck in pineapple curry. Wines include Chilean, South African, Italian and Australian. Reservations are highly recommended.

Entertainment There's plenty of nightlife in Chaweng to keep you entertained, livened up and out late.

Reggae Pub *(open 7.30pm-2am daily)* looms like a gorgeous monster at the end of a girlie bar line-up. It's a two-storey, tastefully done, open building sporting long bars, pool tables, good seating, a live-music stage and lake views. It's also a virtual shrine to Bob Marley. Across the street is an open-air cinema and more bars. Needless to say, it's popular with both foreigners and Thais – despite being far from the town centre.

Green Mango *(☎ 0 7742 2148; beers from 80B, cocktails 170-190B)* is another popular, cavernous and very loud *faràng* bar with blazing lights, soccer on TV and expensive drinks.

Full Circle *(☎ 0 7741 3061; open 3pm-2am daily)*, a restaurant that turns into a nightclub after everyone has eaten, has live nightly music from 5pm. It's a popular, central spot.

The Deck *(☎ 0 7723 0897; open 5pm-2am daily)*, next door, is a multiterraced, open-air bar with comfortable lounging platforms and good views of the street scene below.

Drop In Bar & Restaurant *(open 11am-1am daily)* is a mellow, more sophisticated yet casual place, with bar stools, a projector TV (think soccer), wooden details, a few outdoor tables and great ambience in general.

Black Jack Pub *(☎ 0 1748 3740; open 5pm-2am daily)* comes casual, friendly and popular, with two pool tables and lots of soccer on TV. It's a small and cosy place run by an expat, and doesn't have girls to draw in the foreign men.

Christy's Cabaret Bar *(admission free; open 7pm-2am daily)* attracts a mixed clientele of both sexes, but there are also transvestites to drag customers in, so to speak. Inside, the music's outdated and the show's not great, but maybe you'll luck out somehow.

Viking *(☎ 0 9909 6779; open 8pm-2am daily)* is Swede-run and thus draws in Scandinavians; it plays them homesick music in a cosy space. Its claim to fame is a Swede who downed 11 vodka shots in 9.86 seconds. Newcomers are cautiously invited to break this record (though you'll probably have to pay for your booze).

Coral Cove & Ao Thong Ta Khian

อ่าวท้องยางและอ่าวท้องตะเคียน

There's another series of beautiful capes, coves and beaches beyond Hat Chaweng.

Coral Cove Resort *(☎ 0 7742 2126, fax 0 7741 3097; e coral@samart.co.th; bungalows with fan 650-900B, with air-con 900-1950B)* is a small place with a nice brick patio, but the wood and concrete bungalows are placed a bit too close together. The boulder-framed cove here is pretty.

Coral Cove Chalet *(☎ 0 7742 2242, 0 7742 2496; e coralcc@samart.co.th; bungalows with air-con 2600-4500B)* is a small, upmarket place with tiny thatched bungalows by the beach. The pool, Jacuzzi and restaurant overlook a pleasant, grassy hillside with palms.

Blue Horizon Bungalows *(☎ 0 7742 2426, fax 0 7723 0293; e bluehorizon@samuitourism.com; rooms & bungalows with fan 400B, with air-con 700-900B)*, above an intimate beach, has sweet little things for bungalows. They come with fridge, deck and views; the only drawback is the restaurant – it's perched near the busy road.

Hi Coral Cove *(☎ 0 7742 2495, fax 0 7741 3220; e hicoral@samuinet.com; bungalows with fan 300B, with air-con 700-1000B)* offers no-frills bungalows with air-con. Although worn around the edges, they're cheap and a pretty good deal overall. Breakfast is included, but the eating area is inland and uninspired.

Beverly Hills Hotel Resort *(☎/fax 0 7742 2232; bungalows with fan 350-600B, with air-con 800B)* has nothing to do with LA's Beverly Hills. The bungalows with fan are basic but come with great views. Those with air-con are large and OK, but nothing fancy. The restaurant has great views of the hillside and ocean beyond, but there's no beach below.

Crystal Bay *(☎ 0 7742 2677, fax 0 7742 2678; rooms with fan/air-con 400/800B)* features new, modern rooms, some much better located than others. There's a great terrace for guests, and a fine-sand beach. It's a good, friendly place and not too fancy.

Thong Ta Kian Villa *(☎/fax 0 7723 0978; rooms with fan 400B, with air-con 600-1000B)* offers pleasant rooms, though most have no sea views and are situated on a boring lot. The priciest rooms are huge, beautiful and new; they're almost in a different class.

Samui Yacht Club *(☎ 0 7742 2225, fax 0 7742 2400; w www.samuiyachtclub.com; bungalows with air-con 1800-3300B)* lives with its misnomer; this definitely ain't no yacht club. Rather, it offers huge, romantic Thai-style abodes with four-poster beds, mosquito nets, great furniture, TV and fridge. The garden and paths are lush and well designed, and there's a pool near the beach. A good deal for those seeking something special.

Hat Lamai

หาดละไม

After Chaweng, this is Samui's most popular beach for travellers. It's a calmer, smaller strip of sand backed by a wall of green hills. Fewer beach hawkers come by, and there's less noise in general. There's also less choice of eateries and little of Chaweng's glitz, but this is what attracts folks to Hat Lamai.

South of town are the interesting **Grandfather** and **Grandmother** rock formations. These explicit natural formations attract plenty of giggling Thai tourists. There are also plenty of souvenir vendors and parking attendants in the area. It's worth a peek; there's no charge (financial, that is).

Places to Stay Accommodation at the northeastern tip of the beach is quieter and moderately priced than the central and southern areas, although the beach isn't very wide. Businesses and services are farther south, so you'll have to walk a bit to take advantage of them – or not.

Star Bay Beach & Garden *(☎ 0 7742 4546, fax 0 7742 4547; W www.starbay-beach.com; 1- or 2-bedroom houses 2200-2500B)* caters to longer-term guests (two weeks or so) with large, beautiful houses near the beach. They're good for families, with a pool and beachside restaurant. The gardens are nice and leafy. If business is slow, shorter stays may be possible.

Jungle Park Hotel *(☎/fax 0 7742 4110; W www.jungle-park.com; rooms with fan 900-1800B, with air-con 1200-3800B)* is affordable luxury. Rooms are tastefully decorated, have lots of light and great baths. There's a wonderful amoeba-shaped pool near the beach, along with a restaurant and bar; breakfast is included.

Long Island Resort *(☎ 0 7742 4202, fax 0 7742 4023; bungalows with fan 750B, with air-con 1800-2100B)* features some well-laid out thatched bungalows along brick paths. There's a nice blue pool and neat, grassy grounds with banana trees. It's a popular mid-range choice.

Rose Garden *(☎ 0 7742 4115, fax 0 7742 4410; bungalows with fan 400B, with air-con 600-700B)* has good but basic average-sized bungalows with fan and nicer ones with air-con (the cheapest are near the road); all are in a large, lush garden.

Tamarind Retreat *(☎ 0 7742 4221, fax 0 7742 4311; W www.tamarindretreat.com; villas US$98-188)*, located well inland and on a hillside, offers eight gorgeously built and decorated villas – each with a different cultural theme. Some have boulders built into walls and floors, private ponds or creative outdoor baths. There's a five-night minimum stay, free pickup at the airport and breakfast included. There's no restaurant, but food delivery is possible. Tamarind is also a fine spa, with a full range of services and massage. It's often fully booked, so reserve well in advance.

Spa Resort *(☎ 0 7723 0855, fax 0 7742 4126; W www.spasamui.com; bungalows 250-600B, suites 1800B)* is a New Age place that offers herbal sauna, massage, clay facials, meditation and colon cleansing. Activities include *taijiquan* (t'ai chi) and yoga. The restaurant serves healthy dishes, and simple bungalows are available – but since this place is often booked out, reserve ahead of time (by email is best). Nonguests are welcome to participate in the programmes. It has another location 4km inland as well.

Sukasem *(☎ 0 7742 4119, fax 0 7723 1084; e sukasem@altavista.com; bungalows with fan/air-con 300/800B)* has beautiful, clean, tiled, white bungalows facing a sandy and palmy lot. It's not a bad deal, but hardly atmospheric and close to the main road.

New Hut *(☎ 0 1477 7237; e newhut@hotmail.com; huts 100-200B)* offers pennypinchers a rare cheapie, with tiny A-frame huts (just a mattress inside) on the beach. More solid wooden bungalows are cramped and airless, though. There's a great restaurant to hang-out and a shady deck.

Beers House *(☎ 0 7723 0467; bungalows 150-350B)* is a friendly place with 16 small, tidy bungalows near the beach. The cheapest have shared bath.

The central part of the beach is closest to Ban Lamai village and the beginning of the Lamai 'scene'. Many services are available here, including currency-exchange offices, medical clinics, small groceries, souvenir shops, motorcycle rentals, travel agencies, restaurants (many with videos), discos and bars.

Pavilion Resort *(☎ 0 7742 4420, fax 0 7742 4029; W www.pavilionsamui.com; rooms & bungalows with air-con 2500-4000B)* offers octagonal bungalows a little too crowded together, although very comfortable, beautiful and spacious inside. Rooms are cheaper, but unexciting. The pool is gorgeous, however, with turtle statues spouting water – and the restaurant pavilion makes you feel like royalty. It's a somewhat stark but sophisticated place. The rates include breakfast.

Utopia *(☎ 0 7723 3113, fax 0 7723 3115; w www.utopia-samui.com; bungalows with fan 400B, with air-con 700-800B)* features comfortable, roomy and solid bungalows with good mattresses and amenities. There's a pleasant restaurant area and a jungle-like garden.

Sand Sea Resort *(☎ 0 7742 4026, fax 0 7742 4415; bungalows with air-con 1000-1200B)* presents 30 amenable green-shack bungalows with tiled baths, sitting under coconut palms. There's a unique clover-shaped pool, too.

Magic *(☎ 0 7742 4229; e magicresortlamai@hotmail.com; bungalows with fan 250-350B, with air-con 750B)* could use a spell of good maintenance, but it will do in a pinch for budget-watchers. The smallest bungalows are simply tiny.

Lamai Inn 99 *(☎ 0 7742 4427, fax 0 7742 4211; e lamaiinn@samart.co.th; bungalows with fan 500B, with air-con 1000-1200B)* is a somewhat impersonal place with heaps of inland bungalows; those with fan are small and OK, while the air-con bungalows are neat and acceptable. Grounds are pleasing enough, and there's a beachside eatery.

Marina Villa *(☎ 0 7742 4426, fax 0 7723 2342; rooms & bungalows with air-con 700-1200B)* neatly presents attractive, good-value accommodation. Rooms are inland, while pricier bungalows sit near the beach.

Galaxy Resort *(☎ 0 7742 4441, fax 0 7742 4137; w www.galaxysamui.com; rooms & bungalows with air-con 1200-2200B)* is a decent mid-range resort. Its good, comfy rooms have a few scratches. The pricier bungalows are beautifully presented, with Thai-style architecture and decor, and huge bathtubs. There's also a nice pool. The rates include breakfast.

Mira Mare *(☎ 0 7742 4262; bungalows with fan 300-500B, with air-con 800B)* is a fine, casual place popular with Italians; must be the name.

Golden Sand *(☎ 0 7742 4031, fax 0 7742 4430; rooms & bungalows 1300-2500B)* is a very pleasant place with beautiful expansive grounds and very good facilities. Rooms and bungalows are nicely decorated with tropical furniture. The restaurant overlooks the inland garden, while the bar sits on the beach.

Sea Breeze *(☎ 0 7742 5607, fax 0 7742 5592; e seabreeze@sawadee.com; bungalows with fan 200-500B, with air-con 600-1200B)* has an affordable variety of bungalows and is an excellent choice for budget travellers. It's an attractive place, though the restaurant is inland.

Aloha *(☎ 0 7742 4418, 0 7742 4419; w www.alohasamui.com; rooms & bungalows with air-con 2500-5500B)* offers fairly pleasant bungalows with solid, nondescript furniture. The rooms are more modern. Both the bungalows and rooms have good amenities, and it has a cosy feel for a larger resort. The wonderfully tropical, blue-tiled pool overlooks the beach.

Amadeus *(☎ 0 7742 4568, fax 0 7742 4582; e amadeusbungalow@hotmail.com; bungalows 250-300B)* is a friendly and popular place a couple of minutes' walk from the beach. Basic bungalows are sprinkled on a shrubby green hillside. It's a good budget choice.

Amity *(☎ 0 7742 4084; bungalows 120-500B)* offers ramshackle bungalows with shared bath, as well as nice modern ones – there's no theme, just cheap bungalows that change style depending on the price range.

Bill Resort *(☎ 0 7742 4403, fax 0 7742 4286; w www.samui.sawadee.com/billresort; rooms & bungalows 1200-1800B)* has uniquely wonderful rooms and bungalows set in an overflowing lush garden with a few fountains. There's great use of colourful materials and textures here.

Green Canyon *(☎/fax 0 7741 8687; e greencanyon@samuinet.com; bungalows with fan 250-500B, house with air-con 2500B)* is not on the beach (it's a three-minute-walk away). A handful of bungalows are set on a cool green hillside near a canyon, and are basic but nice. The restaurant has a good traveller atmosphere.

Nice Resort *(☎ 0 7742 4027, fax 0 7742 4028; e nice1@sawadee.com; rooms & bungalows with fan 500B, with air-con 1000-1800B)*; like the name says, it's *nice* enough, though the driveway is unappealing. Leafy foliage surrounds the good rooms and bungalows, and there's a sparkling pool near the beach.

Sun Rise *(☎ 0 7742 4433; bungalows with fan 350-650B, with air-con 1000B)* isn't an especially great deal, but it's near the grandparent rocks. Bungalows with fan are small and simple, while those with air-con are more modern (no surprise here). There's a small jungle-like garden patch.

South of Hat Lamai Ao Bang Nam Cheut is a bay just south of Hat Lamai. The swimming here is best during the rainy season, when water levels rise in the shallow beach. Look for the well-known phallus-like Grandfather and yoni-like Grandmother rock formations – just follow the crowd.

Swiss Chalet *(☎ 0 7742 4321, fax 0 7723 2205; rooms/bungalows 200/400B)* is a friendly place with park-like grounds and very widely placed bungalows. It feels a bit isolated; the beach is a short walk down, while the restaurant is up near the entrance.

Rocky *(☎ 0 7741 8367, fax 0 7741 8366; W www.rockyresort.net; bungalows with fan 715-975B, with air-con 1485-3390B)*, is a friendly resort and is a great place for families. Bungalows are very clean and pleasant, and are surrounded by a safe, peaceful and relaxing environment. There's a beachside pool and restaurant.

Places to Eat Lamai doesn't have as wide a variety of places to eat as Chaweng, but there's still plenty of choice. The following are all located on the main road through town.

Lamai Food Centre is a cluster of several open, casual seafood restaurants, at least one of which is open all night. Look for the yellow sign 70m south of McDonald's, on the inland side.

Bauhaus Bistro *(☎ 0 9972 2241; dishes 50-220B; open 8.30am-11pm daily)* is a huge wooden structure serving specials like beef in Guinness (120B), but the regular stuff includes burgers, salads, sandwiches, snacks and Thai food. Also on tap is a great lounging area with large TV.

Churchill's *(☎ 0 7741-8687; dishes 130-230B; open 9am-2am daily)* has indoor and outdoor seating, and plates of steak and other pub fare. There is sport on TV and a pool table.

Rising Sun *(☎ 0 7741 8015; dishes 60-295B; open 9.30am-2am daily)* serves decent burgers, steaks, vegie stuff, coffees and drinks. It's popular with *faràng* for its outdoor, casual seating.

The Terrace *(☎ 0 7723 2361; dishes 80-200B; open 10.30am-midnight daily)* is the choice for fancier Thai meals in elegant surroundings. Choose your seafood at the front.

Il Tempio *(☎ 0 7723 2307; dishes 130-230B; open 9am-2am daily)* cooks up all the Italian specialities, along with a few Thai ones. There's appealing, open but covered seating around a small pond, and a gelataria also.

Will Wait *(☎ 0 7742 4263; dishes 50-200B; open 8am-11pm daily)* does Western and Thai dishes, along with breakfast, pastries, and lots of drinks and dessert. There's pleasant seating at a breezy location.

Entertainment What would a Thai tourist beach town be without its Pattaya-style girlie bars? Lamai's no exception, but there *are* clean places to taste alcohol. A few pub/restaurants cater to *faràng*, such as **Churchills** and **Mawney Arms**, but for a beach atmosphere you need to head to **Chillout Bar** *(open 10am-2am daily)*, toward the northern end of the beach. It has a sand floor; what more is there to say?

On the main drag is **Bauhaus Pub** *(open 6pm-2am daily)*, with huge wooden beams and high rattan ceiling under a thatched roof. It turns into a disco if enough people are willing, and you may occasionally luck out with short drag shows and *muay thai* (Thai boxing) demos.

South Coast

The south end of Ko Samui is spotted with rocky headlands and smaller beach coves, and around the Laem Set promontory is a long reef with good snorkelling – though the swimming isn't all that great. There are a few mid-range to top-end places to stay.

Samui Marina Cottage *(☎ 0 7723 3395, fax 0 7742 4024; e smaria@loxinfo.co.th; bungalows with air-con 1600-1800B)* sports lots of good, concrete bungalows all lined up obediently along a shady garden; near the beach is the restaurant and a huge rectangular swimming pool.

Wanna Samui Resort *(☎ 0 7723 2130; W www.sawadee.com/samui/wanna; bungalows with fan 400B, with air-con 900-1200B)* has two-level bungalows and is similar to Marina Cottage in layout, but the grounds are sunnier, grassier and palmier. The pool is also smaller.

Central Samui Village *(☎ 0 7742 4020, fax 0 7742 4022; W www.centralhotelsresorts.com;*

bungalows from 4200B) features stylish, modern wooden cottages with garden or sea views, linked by wooden walkways over well-maintained landscaped areas. A deliciously welcoming pool and a beautiful restaurant lies above the beach.

Laem Set Inn *(☎ 0 7742 4393, fax 0 7742 4394; w www.laemset.com; bungalows with fan US$75, rooms with air-con US$120-185, suites US$200-450)* is a beautiful place trickling down a hillside, along with waterways, a lush tropical garden and lots of stairs. The rooms and bungalows are surrounded by rich, dark natural materials, and the restaurant has a stunning view. There's a full-service spa, also.

A few kilometres farther west, Ao Thong Krut provides mooring for local fishing boats. If you need a place to stay, **TK Tour & Restaurant** *(☎ 0 7742 3258; bungalows with fan 300-500B, with air-con 800B)* has a relaxing restaurant overlooking the jetties. From here you can arrange tours to some offshore islands – including **Ko Mat Sum**, which is great for snorkelling. Day tours from Ao Thong Krut cost 500B to 650B and include snorkelling equipment and snacks.

Another nearby island is **Ko Taen**, which sports three nature trails and some accommodation. On the east shore are **Tan Village** *(☎ 0 1968 4130; bungalows 350-650B)*, with pretty bungalows in a garden, and the **Coral Beach Bungalows** *(☎ 0 7741 5465; bungalows 350-650B)*. In a sharply curving bay on the western side are the similar **Dam Bungalows** *(huts 100-150B)* and **BS Cove** *(huts 100-150B)*. **Annie Tour** *(☎ 0 1894 1822)*, at Tonsai Restaurant on Ao Thong Krut, can book you accommodation on Ko Taen for no commission, and helps with transport there, which can cost as much as 200B unless you book with a bungalow operator.

West Coast

Several bays along Samui's western side have accommodation options, including Ao Thong Yang, where the Don Sak and Khanom vehicle ferries dock. The beaches here turn to mud flats at low tide, however.

Around the hook-shaped Laem Hin Khom is little **Ao Phangkha**. Here you'll find **Emerald Cove** *(☎ 0 7742 3082; bungalows 200-400B)*, which doesn't offer much more than cheap seaside bungalows with saggy beds. **Pearl Bay** *(☎ 0 7742 3110; bungalows 200B)* is better, with bungalows up the hill. Next door is **Seagull** *(☎ 0 7742 3091; bungalows 150-300B)*, with a few semi-modern bungalows facing the breezy, picturesque cove.

In **Ao Taling Ngam**, up north a couple of kilometres, you'll find **Wiesenthal** *(☎/fax 0 7723 5165; e wisnthal@samart.co.th; bungalows with fan 400B, with air-con 800-1200B)*, with 13 good, well-spaced bungalows amid a pleasant garden with coconut palms. All have partial or full sea views.

Just beyond and above Wiesenthal perches the resplendent **Le Royal Meridian Baan Taling Ngam** *(☎ 0 7634 0480, fax 0 7634 0479, in Bangkok ☎ 0 2653 2201; w www.lemeridien.com; rooms with air-con US$400-720, villas US$570-2170)*. It's Samui's most exclusive resort, boasting a sauna, beauty salon, babysitting service, two bars, three restaurants, two tennis courts, seven swimming pools, a dive school, water sports of all kinds, conference rooms, shuttles to the beach – and, of course, Samui's best rooms. Don't forget the 20% tax and service.

In serene Ao Thong Yang is **Ar An Resort** *(☎ 0 7742 3189; bungalows with fan/air-con 300/600B)*, which is nothing special but does have cheap, modern bungalows with air-con on a shady, sandy and palmy lot with views of the old ferry dock. Not too far away is **In Foo Palace** *(☎ 0 7742 3066; rooms with fan 500B, with air-con 800-1000B)*, a bit more upmarket than Ar-An, with nice, modern rooms with partial sea views.

On the way north to Na Thon is sweeping Ao Chon Khram. Here is the hefty **International Bungalows & Big John Seafood Restaurant** *(☎ 0 7742 3025; e international@sawadee.com; bungalows with fan 600B, with air-con 1200-1700B, house with air-con 1700-2500B)*, which offers solid thatch-roof bungalows around sandy, grassy lots. It's family friendly (there's a playground), and it has a large restaurant.

Rajapruek Samui Resort *(☎ 0 7742 3115, fax 0 7742 3115; rooms & bungalows with fan 500-600B, with air-con 800-1000B)* is a friendly place with a variety of mostly good amenities and bungalow styles, with strange building layouts. There's a nice garden. Farther down is **Lipa Lodge** *(☎ 0 7742 3028; e lipalodge@hotmail.com; bungalows with fan 350-650B, with air-con 1200B)*, with ramshackle rattan bungalows along with more solid versions – there's no theme here, and the grounds aren't well tended. It's not a good deal, but has a *Gilligan's Island* feel.

Next along the coast is the **Siam Residence Resort** *(☎ 0 7742 0008, fax 0 7742 0009; Ⓦ www.siamresidence.com; bungalows with air-con US$160-200)*, which is for rich, quiet and fastidious guests. The sunny garden is meticulously maintained; check out the topiary hedges. Bungalows are huge and classically beautiful, but they're all clones of each other and seem impersonal. There's a pool and tennis court.

Sawai Home *(☎ 0 7723 4031; bungalows 400-600B)* is close by, with spacious wood and bamboo bungalows in a very attractive jungle-like garden.

Getting There & Away

Air Bangkok Airways flies about 16 times daily between Ko Samui and Bangkok. There is a **Bankgok Airways office** *(in Chaweng ☎ 0 7742 2512 • airport ☎ 0 7742 5209)*. The flight takes about one hour and 20 minutes.

Other destinations from Samui include Phuket, Pattaya, Hua Hin and Chiang Mai. At the time of writing there were no flights to Krabi from here. During the high season flights may be completely booked out as many as six weeks in advance, so be sure to plan accordingly. If Samui flights are full, you might try flying to Surat Thani first, then taking a boat.

The Samui airport departure tax is 400B for domestic and international flights. The attractive Samui airport is open-air, and has a nice bar, restaurant, money-exchange outlet and hotel reservations counter.

Bus It can be cheaper and less stressful to get bus/ferry combination tickets that take you all the way to (and from) Ko Samui.

The government-bus fares from Bangkok's Southern bus terminal don't include the cost of the ferry. These are 660B for VIP, 430B for 1st class and 337B for 2nd class. Most private buses from Bangkok charge around 400B for the same journey and include the ferry fare. From Th Khao San in Bangkok it's possible to get bus/ferry combination tickets for as little as 250B, but service is substandard and theft is more frequent than on the more expensive buses. If an agency on Th Khao San claims to be able to get you to Samui for less, it is almost certainly a scam as no profit can be made at such low prices. Surat Thani bus companies **Phantip Travel** *(☎ 0 7742 1221)* and **Songserm Travel** *(☎ 0 7742 0157)* have offices in Na Thon.

From Na Thon, air-con buses head to Surat (150B), Krabi (250B), Phuket (280B), Hat Yai (290B) and Bangkok (450B). Most departures are at 7.30am, and fares include the ferry ride.

Train You can buy train/bus/ferry tickets straight through to Samui from Bangkok. Buying these combination tickets are worth saving you the hassle (though you really don't save much money – especially if you count getting to the train station etc). See Getting There & Away in the Surat Thani section earlier for details on train travel.

Boat The ferry situation is complicated: there are four ferry piers on the Surat Thani

Buying Tickets in Samui: A Local Travel Agent's view

So many people's holidays are marred by poor communication – they feel like they've been ripped-off because tickets in one office are a different price from another office. People here are just trying to get by, and would like to be able to live the lives the tourists seem to live, travelling to distant countries for two months at a time. We're talking differences of 50B at times – that's barely over a dollar for a traveller. The only reason prices differ is that companies try to undercut each other – competition is fierce. While many travellers are on tight budgets, visitors to Thailand fail to consider that profit margins are ridiculously slim here and rents vary immensely from place to place. People often ask why it is 400B by VIP bus from Bangkok to Samui and yet 450B to go back. Land in Chaweng/Lamai costs substantially more to lease than in Bangkok, the cost of living is also higher. It's like asking, why does a cup of coffee cost more in London than Manchester? People on Samui seem to be so cheerful all of the time, but really they live such desperate lives in comparison to people here on holiday.

Philippa

coast (Ao Ban Don, Tha Thong, Don Sak, Khanom) and three on Ko Samui (Na Thon, Mae Nam and Big Buddha). When going to Ko Samui, the boat (and pier) you use will probably depend on what's available next when you arrive in Surat Thani (after all, you don't really want to hang around in Surat).

Schedules and prices are always in flux. Expect more departures during the busy season and fewer during the rainy times. Prices may fall during slow seasons. Nothing stays the same, so use the following as general guidelines only. And remember that tickets from a travel agency cost more but include a transfer to the pier.

There are frequent daily boat departures between Samui and Surat Thani. These cost from 150B to 350B and take 2½ to six hours, depending on the boat. A couple of these departures can connect directly with the train station in Phun Phin. The slow night boat to Samui leaves from central Surat Thani each night at 11pm, reaching Na Thon around 5am (150B). This boat is recommended if you arrive in town too late for the fast boats and don't want to stay in Surat Thani overnight. Going back to Surat, the slow night boat leaves Na Thon at 9pm, arriving at around 3am or 4am. Watch your bags on this boat.

There are almost 10 daily departures between Samui and Ko Pha-Ngan. These take from 30 minutes to an hour and cost 115B to 250B. On Ko Pha-Ngan there are two piers (Hat Rin and Thong Sala), so decide where you want to go before you buy your ticket. There are also around a half-dozen daily departures between Samui and Ko Tao. These take 1½ to three hours and cost 280B to 550B.

During the low season (any time except December to February or August), young Thai touts often throng Samui-bound travellers, trying to convince them to stay at their bungalow. This isn't necessarily a bad thing, and you may actually find a good, out-of-the-way place to stay.

Getting Around

To/From the Airport Private taxi fares from the airport are as follows: Chaweng 200B to 250B, Lamai 250B to 300B, Na Thon 400B. Minivans also do the run; the more passengers in the van, the cheaper it is for you. Destinations and rough prices are: Bang Rak 30B; Bo Phut 70B; Chaweng and Mae Nam 100B; and Na Thon and Lamai 120B. Cheapest are the săwngthăew: Chaweng 50B; Lamai and Mae Nam 80B; and Na Thon 100B.

Săwngthăew Fares from Na Thon include Mae Nam 30B, Bo Phut 40B, Hat Bang Rak 50B, Lamai 50B, Chaweng 50B and Choeng Mon 50B. Săwngthăew drivers love to try and overcharge you, so it's always best to ask a third party for current rates (in case these have changed). These vehicles run regularly during daylight hours only.

A rough rate for motorcycle taxis is around 20B for a five-minute ride.

Car & Motorcycle You can rent motorcycles (and bicycles) from several places in Na Thon, Chaweng and Lamai, as well as various bungalows around the island. The going rate is 150B per day for a small motorcycle, but for longer periods try and negotiate a better rate. Take it easy on the bikes; every year several *faràng* die or are seriously injured in motorcycle accidents on Samui, and besides, the locals really don't like to see their roads used as race tracks. A helmet law is enforced with some vigour from time to time.

Also, don't put valuables in the basket on the front of the bike. Snatch thieves can easily scoot by on their own motorcycles and grab your bag. And even if you attach your bag with its straps you could be thrown off-balance. Using bungee cords across the top may be a good visible barrier.

Suzuki Caribian jeeps can be hired for around 1000B per day from a number of Na Thon agencies as well as at Chaweng and Lamai.

KO PHA-NGAN

เกาะพงัน

postcode 84280 • pop 10,300

Ko Pha-Ngan, about a half-hour boat ride north of Ko Samui, has become a good alternative for those who find Samui too crowded, too expensive or just...too big. There's a beach for everyone on this casual island; if you're looking for a party, wait for a full moon and head to Hat Rin, which then hosts the biggest beach party in the world. But if this isn't your scene, there are plenty of more isolated beaches with simple huts, and snorkellers will also find some good coral formations around the island.

Ko Pha-Ngan's lack of an airport and relative absence of good roads have so far spared the island from tourist-hotel and package-tour development, though a new pier built in Thong Sala looks big enough to accept cruise ships. And these days more roads are turning from rutty dirt paths to smooth, concrete thoroughways leading to previously secluded beaches. Perhaps it's now time to see Ko Pha-Ngan, before things change even more.

Dangers & Annoyances

While many travellers like to sample the local herb, it's wise to think twice. There are constant reports of travellers being sold marijuana or other drugs by restaurant or bungalow owners, and then being promptly busted by police who were in the know.

Police roadblocks that are set up near Ban Khai are a major hassle during the days leading up to the infamous full moon party on Hat Rin (officers are shipped in specifically for this party). These aren't casual checks, either; if you're on a motorcycle the police look in the fuel tank, check the tyres and search all your gear, looking for any sort of illegal drug. If they find it, the result is often a steep fine (about 50,000B) and in some cases deportation – not exactly the makings of a laid-back vacation. Take a taxi – they run all night and aren't checked as much.

KO PHA-NGAN

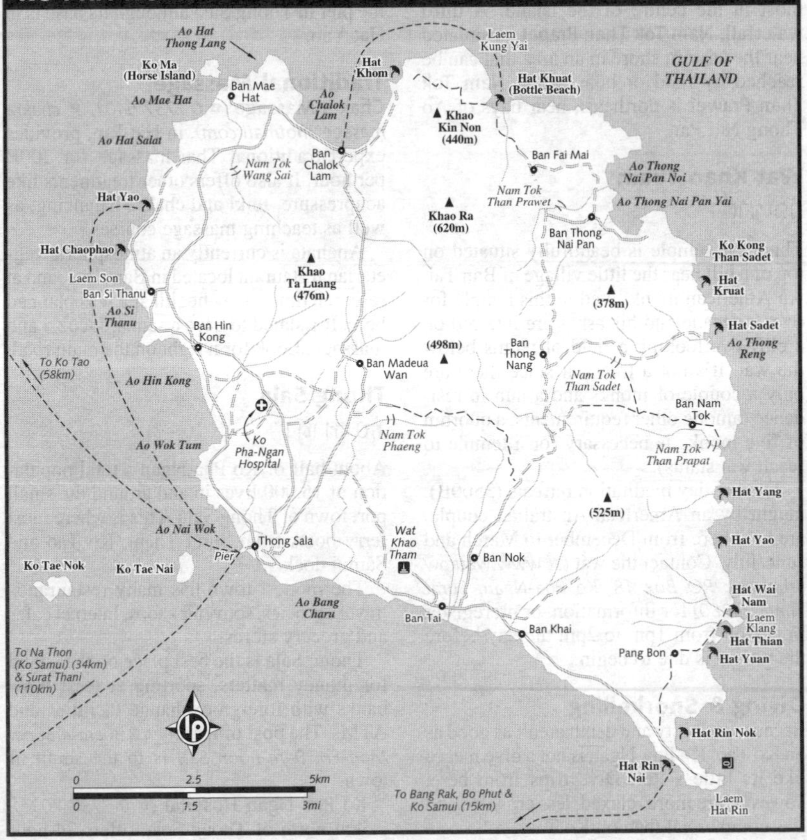

Waterfalls

In the interior of the island are four year-round waterfalls and a number of more seasonal ones. Boulders carved with the royal insignia of Rama V, Rama VII and Rama IX, all of whom have visited the falls, can be found at **Nam Tok Than Sadet**, which cascades along Khlong Than Sadet in the eastern part of the island. Rama V so liked this island that he made 18 trips here between 1888 and 1909. A pleasant way to get to the falls is with one of the Cactus bar's boat trips (see Entertainment under Hat Rin later in this section), which leaves from Hat Rin Nok at 11am and returns at sunset. Included are stops at Hat Khuat and Hat Khom. The cruise costs 300B per person, including food, refreshments and snorkel gear.

Nam Tok Phaeng is off the main road between Thong Sala and Ban Chalok Lam, almost in the centre of the island. A third waterfall, **Nam Tok Than Prapat**, is situated near the eastern shore in an area that can be reached by road or boat, while **Nam Tok Than Prawet** is northeast, near bays of Ao Thong Nai Pan.

Wat Khao Tham

วัดเขาถ้ำ

This cave temple is beautifully situated on top of a hill near the little village of Ban Tai. An American monk lived in this temple for over a decade and his ashes are interred on a cliff overlooking a field of palms below the wát. It's not a true wát since there are only a couple of monks and a nun in residence (among other requirements, a quorum of five monks is necessary for a temple to reach wát status).

The ten-day meditation retreats (3500B), taught by an American-Australian couple, are held here from December to March and June/July. Contact the wát *(W www.watkowtahm.org; PO Box 18, Ko Pha-Ngan, Surat Thani 84280)* for information, or preregister in person from 1pm to 2pm the day before the retreat is due to begin.

Diving & Snorkelling

Because visibility and depth aren't as good as on Ko Tao, Ko Pha-Ngan is not a dive mecca like its little sister. Dive trips from here, however, are more relaxed, less crowded and less commercial than on Ko Tao.

There are intermittent coral reefs around the island – the deepest and healthiest can be found off the west coast (best from January to April). On the northwest coast are more dive sites (best from September to October), and farther away are the major attractions of Sail Rock (to the north) and Ang Thong National Marine Park (to the west).

There are only about a half-dozen dive operators on Ko Pha-Ngan, and all charge similar prices: 700B for beach dive trips; 2000B for a dive trip to Sail Rock or Ang Thong National Marine Park; and 8000B for full certification, including lunch and two dives. A snorkelling set can be rented for 100B to 150B.

Phangan Divers *(☎ 0 7737 5117; W www.phangandivers.com)* is in Hat Rin and Hat Yao, while **Haad Yao Divers** *(☎ 0 1229 4744; W www.haadyaodivers.com)* has an office at the pier in Thong Sala although its base is in Hat Yao.

Traditional Massage

Chakra Massage *(☎ 0 7737 5401; e chakramasage@hotmail.com)*, in Hat Rin, provides expert traditional Thai massage for 200B per hour. It also offers other treatments like acupressure, reiki and chakra balancing, as well as teaching massage courses.

Anahata is currently an atmospheric vegetarian restaurant located in Ban Khai, and at research time a new **health spa** was planned here. It's slated to have a sauna, Jacuzzi and massage. Look for it right on the main road.

Thong Sala

ท้องศาลา

About half of Ko Pha-Ngan's total population of 15,000 lives in and around the small port town of Thong Sala. This is where most ferry boats from Surat Thani, Ko Tao and Samui dock.

The modest town has many restaurants, travel agencies, souvenir shops, Internet cafés and grocery stores.

Thong Sala is the best place on the island for money matters, sporting at least three banks with foreign-exchange facilities and ATMs. The **post office** *(open 8.30am-4.30pm Mon-Fri, 9am-noon Sat)* is to the south of town.

Ko Pha-Ngan Hospital *(☎ 0 7737 7034)*, 2.5km north of Thong Sala, offers 24-hour emergency services, but if it's serious wait until you reach Bangkok, or go to Ko Samui's International Hospital.

Rent motorcycles at **Ko Pha-Ngan car and motorcycle rentals** *(☎ 0 7737 7150; 53/4 Mu 1)*, where an American expat has well-maintained motorcycles for around 200B per day; bicycles are 75B per day.

Places to Stay & Eat Thong Sala wouldn't be the first choice of places to stay; it's a small city, after all, and you're on an island ringed with beaches. But consider bunking here to wait for an early boat out, since transport times from other parts of the island can be unpredictable. Or try nearby Ao Nai Wok (see later in this section), which has a few places on the beach.

Pha-Ngan Chai Hotel *(☎/fax 0 7737 7068; rooms with air-con 900-1000B)*, on the bay, is a big hotel with dim, carpeted, modern rooms. Rooms facing the sea have a great view of the ugly new pier. The rates include breakfast.

Sea Mew *(☎ 0 1477 7076; rooms 200B)* is next door to Pha-Ngan Chai and has impersonal but modern and fluorescent lit, good-sized rooms in the back building. The restaurant at the front is interesting.

Bua Kao Inn *(☎ 0 7737 7226; ⓔ buakao@samart.co.th; rooms with fan 450-480B, with air-con 550B)*, in the middle of town, is fastidiously maintained by an expat and is worth a stay for the showers alone. The five rooms (one with air-con) come very clean and nicely decorated; there's one single for 350B. Downstairs is a very popular and good restaurant.

Asia Hotel *(☎ 0 7723 8607; rooms with air-con 400-700B)*, near Bua Kao Inn, offers some tiny rooms – pay more for the space as you'll need to breathe. Things are fairly modern and decent here.

Ao Nai Wok is just a few minutes' walk north of Thong Sala. Its beach isn't spectacular, but if you want to be near Thong Sala it's a fairly nice area to while away a few days. Swimming is best from December to April. To get here, go north past the Asia Hotel about 250m to the T-intersection, where you go left again for 100m.

Phangan *(☎ 0 7737 7191; bungalows 150-400B)* has two lines of peaceful bungalows on grassy grounds with coconut palms. There's one large bungalow with two rooms.

Sun Town *(☎ 0 7737 7411; bungalows 150-200B)* is near Phangan and has small, basic bungalows on a more intimate lot.

Siriphun *(☎ 0 7737 7140, fax 0 7737 7242; bungalows 300-700B)* is friendly and offers a pretty garden area and solid bungalows with mosquito screens. There's also large, modern bungalows with air-con.

For food, consider **Swiss Bakery** *(dishes 30-170B; open 6am-5pm Mon-Sat, closed Sun)*, a little paradise serving great homemade stuff like breads, yogurt and pancakes. It's inside the block behind Bua Kao Inn, which itself has a tasty restaurant called **A's Coffee shop**, and is surrounded by other *faràng*-oriented eateries. On the main road up from the pier is **Pizza Chiara**, an Italian place serving great thin-crust pizza, pasta and tiramisu.

Beaches

Most travellers to Ko Pha-Ngan stay in the Hat Rin area, which is no surprise considering it's the most happening place on the island. If you're looking for more peace and quiet, however, there are heaps of more sedate beaches to explore. The northern destinations of Hat Khuat (Bottle Beach) and Ao Thong Nai Pan/Yai are good choices if you're looking for beaches in between 'too busy' and 'too isolated'.

During the peak months (December to February and July and August), there can be a shortage of rooms at the most popular beaches and even the boats coming to the island can be dangerously overcrowded. In the low seasons, however, you should be able to negotiate bungalow rates down quite a bit. Rates quoted here are for August; note that prices zoom higher during holiday periods.

Be aware that since some of the cheapest bungalows make most of their profits from their restaurants, bungalow owners have been known to eject guests after a few days if they don't take meals where they're staying.

Ao Bang Charu South of Thong Sala, the shallow beach here is not one of the island's best, but it's close to town. All of the following are located on the beach down 50m dirt driveways off the main road.

Pha-Ngan Villa *(☎ 0 7737 7083; ⓔ phanganvilla@hotmail.com; bungalows 130-250B)* is sitting pretty with well-maintained, pleasant bungalows on tended grounds. There are hammocks and the place feels good. Also pleasant and right next door is **Moonlight** *(☎/fax 0 7723 8398; bungalows 150-400B)*.

CoCo Garden *(☎ 0 7737 7721; rooms with fan/air-con 300/600B)* comes with small rooms with fan and large rooms with air-con; there are great rails made from natural branches. The restaurant is nice but the garden sparse. Look for the blue roofs.

Or-Rawarn *(☎ 0 7737 7713; ⓔ or_rawarn@hotmail.com; bungalows with fan 200-300B, with air-con 500-600B)*, next to CoCo Garden, is well-run and a good choice, with green roofs.

Charm Beach *(☎ 0 7737 7165; bungalows 150-300B)* comes with quite charming high-pitched roofs, though the cheap rooms aren't as snazzy as the larger, more expensive ones. There are hammocks for snoozing.

Chokana *(☎ 0 7723 8085; bungalows with fan 150-500B, with air-con 800B)* is a popular, friendly place with good deals; the rooms with air-con have a bath, fridge and gorgeous wooden details.

Ban Tai & Ban Khai Between the villages of Ban Tai and Ban Khai is a series of sandy beaches with quite a few well-spaced bungalow operations. From the main road, the signs to these places can be small and hard to see. A săwngthăew from Thong Sala is 30B per person to this area.

Dewshore *(☎ 0 7723 8128; rooms with fan 350-500B, with air-con 800-1300B)* has small, concrete, pastel blue bungalows that are passable.

Emerald Ocean *(bungalows 150-200B)* has nice, clean, and basic bungalows. Next door and not as good a deal is **Liberty** *(☎ 0 7723 8171; huts 150-200B)*, a ramshackle cheapie with colourful huts.

Hansa *(☎ 0 7737 7494; bungalows with fan 500-650B, with air-con 1000B)* isn't bad for an upmarket place, with pretty thatched-roof bungalows of stucco and wood. It's new, so the garden is just starting out.

Mac Bay *(☎ 0 7723 8443; bungalows with fan 300-400B, with air-con 600-800B)* is a good deal where even the cheaper bungalows are decent and modern. Pricier ones come with stone details and gnarly branches for rails.

Rainbow Bungalows *(☎ 0 7723 8236; ⓦ www.rainbowbungalows.com; bungalows 100-250B)*, at the southern end of Ban Khai, has decent bungalows with hammocks and mosquito nets.

If you're hungry in Ban Khai, check out **Anahata** *(dishes 125-145B; open 6pm-11pm Mon-Sat, 7am-11am Sun in high season, closed Mon-Tues in low season)*, near Rainbow Bungalows. It serves good Thai, European and vegetarian food. There's a legendary Sunday buffet brunch, and some cool decks to hang-out.

Hat Rin This area has become the most popular place on Ko Pha-Ngan, with two beaches sandwiching a busy peninsula that ends in a cape. Businesses crowded together in this self-contained village and travel agencies, moneychangers, minimarts, restaurants, bars, tattoo shops and outdoor discos all compete for your tourist dollar. It's a pretty exciting little scene.

Hat Rin Nok (Sunrise Beach), on the east side, is along a sandy bay lined with bungalows and coconut palms, and is busy with boat traffic. The snorkelling here is pretty good, but between October and March the surf can be a little hairy. This beach is famous for monthly 'full moon parties', featuring all-night beach dancing and the ingestion of various illicit substances – forget about sleeping on these nights unless you get a place off the beach. Even when the moon isn't full, several establishments blast dance music all night long – head for the western side if you prefer a quieter atmosphere for you holiday.

Hat Rin Nai (Sunset Beach), on the west side, has another nice beach, but it's often too shallow for swimming – though at least there aren't too many long-tail boats to bash your head against. The pier is located here, which serves boats from the northwest coast of Ko Samui, a half-hour away. It's a straighter beach than Hat Rin Nok and pleasantly relaxed, with much less activity and a more isolated feeling, but it can get trashy when the wind blows.

There are plenty of telephone offices and Internet cafés on Hat Rin. To fix your 'Ko Pha-Ngan tattoo' (motorcycle accident scrape), head to **Sang's Clinic** *(☎ 0 1896 2195; open 5pm-10pm Mon-Fri, 10am-10pm Sat & Sun)*, next to Phangan divers near the pier.

Places to Stay Remember that these are the island's most popular beaches, and one reason for that popularity is the Full Moon Party. Prices not only rise in the days before this phenomenal event, but bungalow operations expect you to stay for a minimum number of days. And if you arrive the day before or the day of the party, you may not find anywhere to sack out (but party all night and you won't need to). Also be aware that during this time some bungalows might get broken into; secure your room and stash valuables somewhere safe. Prices quoted below are mid-season, non-full-moon-party rates.

The following places are right on Hat Rin Nok and listed from the south up.

Paradise Bungalows *(☎ 0 7737 5244; W www.paradisebungalow.com; bungalows 250-500B)* lives on its name; this is were the Full Moon parties started. Past the fancy entrance sign are unattractive grounds, though the various bungalows are better-located on a hillside. Movies are shown in the restaurant.

Haadrin Resort *(☎ 0 7737 5259; bungalows 300-450B)* offers crowded but good bamboo-concrete bungalows in a shady garden. There's a pleasant restaurant offering movies and sea views.

Phangan Orchid Resort *(☎ 0 7737 5156; rooms with fan 400-700B, with air-con 800-1200B)* has a tidy, sunny garden and modern bungalows. Prices depend on size, and the air-con ones are closest to the beach.

Sunrise Resort *(☎ 0 7737 5145; e or999@hotmail.com; bungalows 250-300B)* lies in a leafy, shady garden with solid wood and concrete bungalows; there are also bungalows with log-style walls.

Pha-Ngan Bayshore Resort *(☎ 0 7737 5227; bungalows with fan 400-500B, with air-con 800-1800B)* has decent bamboo bungalows, pleasant grounds, though the staff could be more helpful. It's at the end of the road.

Tommy Resort *(☎ 0 7737 5253; bungalows with 200-800B, without bath 150B)* has fair but worn bungalows on not especially attractive grounds. The bungalows closer to the beach cost more.

Palita *(☎ 0 7737 5170; e palitas9@hotmail.com; bungalows with fan 150-800B, with air-con 1200B)* is a friendly place with a good range of well-maintained bungalows. The garden is sparse rather than lush, and the restaurant serves up tasty food and screens movies.

HAT RIN

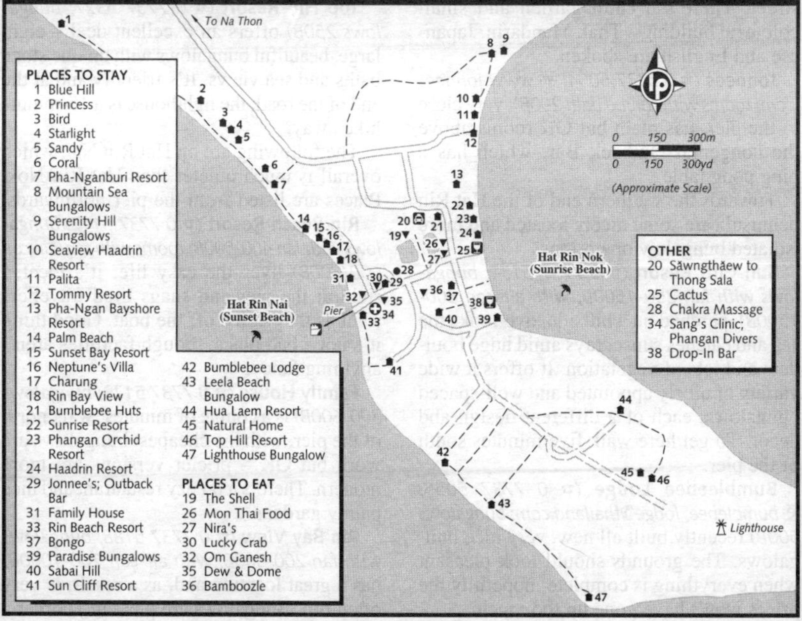

Sea view Haadrin Resort (☎ *0 7737 5160; bungalows with fan 250-700B, with air-con 1000-1200B)* features some plain but nice, roomy bungalows; the fancier ones (with beautiful archways) cost more.

Mountain Sea Bungalows (☎ *0 7737 5347; bungalows 300-600B)*, on the rocky headland north of Hat Rin, has a selection of decently maintained, blue and white, bungalows on a grassy hillside; most have views.

Serenity Hill Bungalows (☎ *0 9937 1066; bungalows 200-350B)* has some really ratty bungalows on a crumbling hillside – but the views are nice.

The following places are about a block inland from the beaches.

Bongo (☎ *0 7737 5268;* e *bongomoo@yahoo.com; bungalows with fan/air-con 400/800B)* has modern, sturdy bungalows of all different sizes; larger ones are beautiful, clean and spacious. There's a peaceful and shady garden; this place is a good deal.

Bumblebee Huts (☎ *0 7737 5157; bungalows 200B)* is cheap and inland, with OK bamboo and wooden huts.

Sabai Hill (☎ *0 7737 5199;* e *sabai_hill_bun@hotmail.com; dorm beds 150B, rooms with fan 300-350B, with air-con 800B)* is a peaceful and hippie-like place down a side street. There's a calm garden and small colourful buildings. Thai, Mandarin, Japanese and English are spoken.

Jonnees (☎ *0 7737 5054;* w *www.jonnees.com; rooms with shared bath 200B)*, very close to the pier, has plain but OK rooms above the congenial Outback Bar, which has a ping pong table.

Towards the southern end of the Hat Rin peninsula are some nicely located and more isolated bungalow operations.

Sun Cliff Resort (☎ *0 7737 5134; bungalows with fan 250-1500B, with air-con 800-1500B)*, perched on a hillside, overlooks the sea and catches sunset rays amid huge boulders and lots of vegetation. It offers a wide variety of nicely appointed and well-spaced bungalows, each of a different design and decor. To get here walk five minutes south of the pier.

Bumbleebee Lodge (☎ *0 7737 5055;* e *bumblebee_lodge@thailand.com; bungalows 500B)* recently built all new, very nice bungalows. The grounds should look pleasant when everything is complete; hopefully the prices won't have gone up too much.

Leela Beach Bungalows (☎ *0 7737 5094;* w *www.leelabeach.com; huts 100-300B)*, a 15-minute walk from the pier, isn't an especially good deal, with mostly very basic, rickety shacks in a scraggly garden and on a hillside. There's a nice laid-back beachside restaurant, however.

Lighthouse Bungalow (☎ *0 7737 5075; bungalows with/without bath 350/200B)* goes from cheap, nondescript shacks with outside bath to nicer, more modern bungalows with great views. The restaurant is beautiful and homey with lots of breezes. A renovation may happen soon. To get here go past Leela and walk along the shore on the scary wooden walkway (20 minutes' walk from the pier, or hire a boat).

Hua Laem Resort *(Sunsmile;* ☎ *0 7737 5222; bungalows 200-350B)* is about a 15-minute walk from the pier, and welcomes you with inspirationally located bungalows. All have great views and decks, hammocks and mosquito nets, and are simple yet comfortable. It's a great deal.

Natural Home (☎ *0 7737 5134; bungalows 250-350B)* offers good, large bungalows along a sparse but shady hillside; sea views, if any, are only partial. More bungalows may be on the way.

Top Hill Resort (☎ *0 7737 5327; bungalows 250B)* offers an excellent deal – eight large, beautiful bungalows with unique stone baths and sea views. It's friendly and at the end of the road; the lighthouse is a 15-minute hike away.

The following are on Hat Rin Nai, which overall is much quieter than Hat Rin Nok. Places are listed from the pier northwards.

Rin Beach Resort (☎ *0 7737 5112; bungalows with fan 400-500B; rooms with fan/air-con 600/800B)* lives the easy life; it's located right at the pier and snags tired travellers right as they come off the boat. Good thing it's not a bad place, though facilities aren't anything fancy.

Family House (☎ *0 7737 5173; bungalows 300-600B)* is a couple of minutes' walk north of the pier, with the cheapest bungalows are worn but OK – pricier versions are more modern. There's a breezy restaurant and nice palmy gardens

Rin Bay View (☎ *0 7737 5188; bungalows with fan 200-500B, with air-con 700-1000B)* has a great location and, as a result, is very often full. Bungalows are pleasant, border a leafy garden strip and come in many price ranges.

Charung *(☎ 0 1968 0173; bungalows with fan 150-400B, with air-con 500-700B)* is also popular, well located and offers a wide variety of rooms.

Neptune's Villa *(☎ 0 7737 5251; ⓔ neptune1@thaimail.com; bungalows with fan 150-500, with air-con 750B)* is an attractive place, with small, neat, clean bungalows around a cute, well-kept garden. The most basic bungalows are wood-thatched or clapboard, and nothing special.

Sunset Bay Resort *(bungalows 150-250B)* features decent bungalows on scruffy land by the beach. The same family owns the newer **Haadrin Thai Resort** *(bungalows 300-350B)*, inland and upwards on a hillside.

Palm Beach *(bungalows 100-1000B)* has a range of accommodation from cheap shacks with shared bathroom to more solid-looking wooden things to nice, modern and new air-con bungalows with log walls.

Pha-Nganburi Resort *(☎ 0 7737 5330; bungalows 300B)* offers attractive bungalows on the outside with worn and musty baths on the inside. The spacious grounds could use some maintenance and the staff a dose of hospitality, but it's not a bad deal.

Coral *(☎ 0 7737 5241; bungalows 100-200B)* has good bungalows with tiled floors, colourful curtains and pebbly walls – too bad they're in a dusty lot inland from the beach. The cheaper ramshackle wooden bungalows are closer to shore but so basic it hurts. The restaurant is wonderfully relaxing, though, with cushioned lounging areas and a wide vista of the sea.

Sandy *(☎ 0 7737 5138; bungalows 200-300B)* offers nothing other than nice bungalows (not terribly worn) on pleasant garden grounds.

Starlight *(☎ 0 7737 5018; ⓔ starlight_haadrin@hotmail.com; bungalows 200-300B)* has OK green pastel bungalows either with or without shared bath. Grounds are grassy and the family friendly.

Bird *(☎ 0 7737 5191; bungalows 150-500B)* contains bungalows ranging from small, plain ones with shared bath to large, nice wooden ones with sea views.

Princess *(☎ 0 7739 5025; rooms 300-400B)* is something different in this area; a hotel building. It's new, it's nice and it has good modern rooms with balconies. Hopefully prices won't skyrocket after the garden gets planted.

Blue Hill *(☎ 0 1922 4963; bungalows 150-200B)* is at the end of the line, about a 25-minute walk from the pier. On call are good-sized but very basic, shanty-like bungalows on a hillside with lots of stairs. It's a great place for shoestringers who want no-frills isolation. The seaside restaurant is also a bit shaky but intimate and laid-back.

Places to Eat There's no shortage of Thai, Western or seafood in the Hat Rin area.

Om Ganesh *(☎ 0 7737 5123; dishes 60-130B; open 9am-11pm daily)*, right near the pier, has good Indian food in a colourful ambience. Hindu gods will be watching from the wall mural as you consume curries, biryani rice, roti and lassies. Try a combination of *chicken malai tikka* and garlic naan.

Lucky Crab *(☎ 0 1891 3150; dishes 60-250B; open 8am-11pm daily)*, not far from the pier, has a huge menu of Thai, Indian, Mexican and Italian food – the question is, are they any good? Stick to the seafood.

Dew & Dome *(☎ 0 7737 5262; dishes 70-200B; open 8am-11.30pm daily)*, near Lucky Crab, serves pizza, sandwiches and seafood in a cosy setting.

Outback Bar *(☎ 0 7737 5126; dishes 120-220B; open 9am-2am daily)* is expat-run, which in this case means that the Western food is pretty authentic. Order caesar salad, lambchops, Swedish meatballs and shepherd's pie, followed by a good selection of beers…yum. It's a large space divided into smaller areas, which include a pool room. There's sport on the TV and artwork on the walls.

The Shell *(☎ 0 7737 5149; dishes 90-130B; pizzas 140-220B; open 11am-11.30pm daily)* serves good Italian food like gnocchi, ravioli and pizza, along with gelato, tiramisu and Italian coffees. It's in an open, peaceful area beyond the lily ponds.

Bamboozle *(dishes 70-180B; open 2pm-midnight daily)* serves up Mexican food such as chilis rellenos, burritos and nachos on a lofty, beautiful platform.

Nira's *(☎ 0 7737 5109; dishes 60-150B; open 24hr)* is a very popular breakfast spot, brewing up fancy coffees like iced mochas (70B) and double espressos (60B). The food is also good and includes sandwiches, pizza, baked potatoes, salads and Thai dishes. The

Full Mooning

Ravers from all around the globe have been gathering for over 10 years to celebrate Hat Rin's infamous full moon parties. Some 3000 to 5000 ravers – sometimes over 12,000 during the December-to-February peak season – turn up to dance, drink and smoke the night away. A half-dozen music stages belt out house, trance, hip-hop, techno, ambient and R&B (whatever's trendiest), while groovers spill out of open-air dance halls and onto the beach. Fire swinging and fireworks light up the night. The number of partygoers peaks at around 2am to 3am, and the last of the DJs don't shut down till around 11am. As you can guess, it's a pretty wild and hazy time for everyone.

And what would the world's biggest beach party be without drugs? Yes, they're still available these days, though the more hardcore partakers have moved on to other beaches due to a pumped-up police presence (both uniformed and undercover). It's wise to take care when using illicit substances; more than a few deaths have been attributed to drug use at this party. And, if you stay in control of yourself, you'll remember what a good time you had.

The whole event is well organised by Thai residents who run the bungalows and bars along Hat Rin. And these same proprietors, along some of the more conscientious foreign travellers, come together to clean the beach of substantial morning-after litter when the party is finally over.

Check your lunar calendar for upcoming full-moon party dates.

Full Moon Party Tips

Religious protests have recently forced Hat Rin's full moon parties to actually take place either before or after the actual full moon date; these are related to Buddhist holidays that occur around the full moon about four times yearly. Double-check if any changes are in store when you plan to attend the party.

Safety Be watchful of your personal belongings and personal safety. Try not to bring extra money; travel light. Don't keep valuables in your bungalow – it's a big night for break-ins, especially at the cheaper huts. Be careful with fireworks and even stray live wires. Wear protective shoes! Don't go swimming under the influence of drugs or alcohol – drownings account for many full moon party deaths. Don't accept consumables from strangers. If you're staying alone on the western side of the peninsula, think about having friends escort you home after dark. And, remember to eat all your vegetables.

Accommodation If you arrive on the day of the full moon or even the day before, you can forget about finding a vacant room or bungalow anywhere near Hat Rin – many ravers nail down a room four days in advance. Head over the rocky hills to the southern end of the cape, or try some of the nearby beaches – though even these are likely to be full. Loads of partygoers, especially Thais, boat over from Samui during the afternoon, party all night, then boat back the next morning, thereby side-stepping the accommodation dilemma.

Food Beachfront barbecues offer fresh grilled seafood until around 11pm, after which the pickings are slim. Several beach bungalows shut down their restaurants the morning after so that staff can get some sleep. If you wake before noon you may have to wander into the village between inner and outer Hat Rin to find something to feed your abused stomach.

Transport If you're coming over from Ko Samui for the party, take one of the thrice-daily ferries from Big Buddha pier at Hat Bang Rak on Samui (100B), or hop on one of the frequent speedboats in operation the day and night of the full moon (one way 200B to 250B, return 350B to 400B). The speedboats continue to depart from Big Buddha pier and Bo Phut pier until around 1am, reaching a peak number of trips between 8pm and midnight. After the party, return tickets are at a premium; if you don't get a return ticket, you may be overcharged on the way back.

Drugs Thai police often set up inspection points on the road between Thong Sala and Hat Rin on days leading up to full moon parties. All vehicles, including bicycles and motorcycles, are stopped and the passengers searched thoroughly. People go to jail, or pay through the nose. The going rate – or 'fine' if you wish – for escaping a small pot bust is 50,000B.

service could use some help, though. There's a luscious bakery next door.

Mon Thai Food *(☎ 0 7735 7095; dishes 35-80B; open 24hr)* is a great place for budget travellers, with cheap but good Thai food, pizza and spaghetti; it also shows loud videos.

Entertainment There are plenty of bars in which to meet the floor intimately.

Drop-In Bar *(open 4pm-late daily)* is the kind of place that uses any excuse for a party. The walls are colourful and the staff strangely eclectic, and the throat lubricants include piña coladas, kamikazes and Long Island iced teas. Tunes run from rock to hip hop, pop, house and trance – 'every night is different,' says the Rasta dude.

Cactus *(☎ 0 7737 5308; open 9pm-late daily)* is a more mainstream bar, central and good-sized, with four types of beer and cocktails for 80B to 130B. It also offers 'Cactus Boat Trips' to beaches and waterfalls for 300B, including snorkelling gear and snacks.

Getting There & Away Săwngthăew hop between Hat Rin and Thong Sala for 50B. This road is a smooth, narrow, concrete, hair-raising roller-coaster of a ride from just outside Hat Rin to Ban Khai. Unless you're very good on a motorcycle, you shouldn't attempt this road.

There are three daily boats between Hat Rin and Ko Samui (Big Buddha pier; 100B, 50 minutes). For more departure options head to Thong Sala. During the monthly full moon party the number of departures increases (as does the boat ticket price), and by midnight speedboats are leaving these piers every 15 or 30 minutes until around 3am or 4am. You may wish to take a day boat as they're safer and less crowded.

East Coast Beaches Along the east coast of Ko Pha-Ngan are a few little coves and beaches where enterprising bungalow operations have been built. You can hike from the Hat Rin Nok area to Hat Wai Nam, but after that you'd be better off going by boat.

There are a some cool places to stay on **Hat Yuan**, which is very rapidly becoming crowded. Try **Big Blue** *(☎ 0 1270 1537; bungalows 250-350B)*, the largest place here, with a range of nice bungalows on the beach and hillside; **Good Hope** *(bungalows 250B)*, the kind of place that advertises hash brownies; **Bamboo Hut** *(bungalows 150-220B)*, with well-built, good-vibe bungalows and a lush garden; and **Haad Yuan Bungalows** *(rooms 100B)*, the most basic of all, with claustrophobic bamboo rooms.

Next up and close by is **Hat Thian**, wherein lies **The Sanctuary & Wellness Centre** *(from 9am-1pm ☎ 0 1271 3614; w www.thesanctuary-kpg.com; dorm beds 60B, bungalows 300-1000B, houses 3000B)*. There's a great community feeling here, and health and nature are stressed. The creatively built restaurant serves wonderful vegetarian dishes and seafood. On offer are daily yoga and full spa treatments, and electricity is available from 6pm to midnight. Boats from Hat Rin cost 50B; by rough trail it's a 1½-hour hike.

Nearby, **Haad Tien Resort** *(☎ 0 1229 3919; bungalows 120-200B)* has beautiful peaked wood-and-bamboo bungalows, while **Horizon** *(e eck_horizon@hotmail.com; bungalows 150B)* is up the hill with basic bamboo huts in a sparse garden area. Hidden farther inland is **Silver Star** *(bungalows 250B)*, with 10 comfortable bungalows.

A five-minute hike over the next headland is **Wai Nam Hut** *(huts 150-200B)*, with seven simple huts situated on a pleasantly small beach.

Farther north just a few kilometres (take a boat) is the pretty coast **Ao Thong Reng**. On this pleasantly intimate beach is **Thong Reng Resort** *(bungalows 100-150B)* and **Than Sadet Resort** *(huts 150-250B)*, with nice-looking accommodation. Past the rocky headland is **Hat Sadet**, a larger but still relaxed beach cove. Here lies a string of modestly simple places, including **Silver Cliff** *(bungalows 150-250B)*, with large, airy bungalows on the northern hill; **JS Hut** *(bungalows 150-500B)*, another operation that's just below Silver Cliff; and **Mai Pen Rai** *(☎ 0 7737 7414; bungalows 120-500B)*, with all kinds of beach shacks right near the sands.

Ao Thong Nai Pan This bay is really made up of two bays, **Ao Thong Nai Pan Yai** and **Ao Thong Nai Pan Noi**. The latter has the best all-round swimming beach, but the sand on both is equally nice and soft. The two bays are separated by a steep 20-minute hike over a headland, though you can always take a long-tail boat. A couple of dive shops are found here, along some Internet connections.

Săwngthăew from Thong Sala to Thong Nai Pan cost 80B. Getting here shouldn't be attempted by motorcycles, unless the road's been paved by now; otherwise, drivers should be experienced on steep, rutty dirt roads.

The following places to stay are on Ao Thong Nai Pan Yai.

White Sand *(bungalows 400B)*, at the east end, has large, concrete and sunny bungalows with wooden floors. They're lined up perpendicular to the water.

Dolphin *(bungalows 300B)* hides behind a richly ambient bar and lush tropical vegetation. Relaxing lounging areas and great bungalows give this place a gold star. It's run by a Kiwi/Thai family.

AD View *(bungalows 100-300B)* features 12 bungalows, from small and rustic to larger and cute. All sit on pleasant grounds.

Nice Beach *(☎ 0 7723 8547; bungalows 200-500B)* has either small bungalows with Thai-style baths or attractive, large bungalows with Western baths. The restaurant is good and plays decent music.

Central *(☎ 0 7729 9059; e central_cottage@hotmail.com; bungalows with fan 200-500B, with air-con 600-800B)* offers solid, concrete bungalows, some with stone walls. The cheapest are thatch, bamboo and wood, but remain very decent; all sit on leafy grounds.

Pen's *(bungalows 150-600B)* isn't any different; cheap bungalows are very small but airy, while more expensive ones are more solid. The grounds are nice, and there's a restaurant with shady tables on the sand.

Pingjun Resort *(☎ 0 7729 9004; bungalows 150-300B)* is a popular oldie, with cute wooden shacks in a grassy area.

Dreamland *(☎ 0 7723 8539; e dreamland_resort@yahoo.com; bungalows 150-600B)* watches over an empire, with almost 40 different types of bungalows crowded together rather impersonally.

Candle *(☎ 0 7737 7070; bungalows with fan 400-500B, with air-con 700B)* is for the more upmarket traveller, with small, bright and airy bungalows. It's a new place, so the garden needs to fill out.

The following options are on Ao Thong Nai Pan Noi.

Panviman Resort *(☎ 0 2587 8491 in Bangkok; w www.panviman.com; rooms with fan/air-con 1500/2000B; bungalows with air-con 3000B)* sits on top of the headland separating the two bays. It's definitely upmarket, with fine accommodation on hilly, lush grounds interlaced with brick paths. Rooms have balconies and nice furniture. There's a taxi service from Thong Sala.

Star Hut *(☎ 0 7729 9005; bungalows 200-350B)* goes from simple thatched huts with shared bath to more expensive, better versions. There's a reasonably priced, popular restaurant that offers some traveller services.

Baan Panburi *(☎ 0 7723 8593; w www.baanpanburi.bigstep.com; bungalows with fan 200-940, with air-con 2600B)* is an upscale place but still offers basic bungalows with shared bath. Mid-range bungalows are pleasant and airy, while the fanciest are pretty comfortable. The restaurant is great.

Thong Ta Pan Resort *(☎ 0 7723 8538; e tontapan@yahoo.com; bungalows 300-500B)* offers good-sized, nice bungalows of wood or concrete; they're well spaced and sprinkled along a lovely hillside.

Thong Ta Pong *(bungalows 150-350B)*, at the northern end and across a rickety footbridge, has small, neat bungalows going up a rocky hillside with some trees. The restaurant's sound system is pretty loud, though.

Hat Khuat (Bottle Beach) & Hat Khom

These two pretty bays (especially Hat Khuat) are becoming big destinations because of their fine, comfortable-sized beaches, calm waters and low-key atmosphere. There's snorkelling around the points, and electricity only at night. Get here early to secure a room, and remember that your bungalow owners may become miffed if you don't always eat at their restaurant (negotiate in advance).

Săwngthăew run from Thong Sala to Ban Chalok Lam (50B), where there are boats to Hat Khom and Hat Khuat (40B to 50B). You can walk to Hat Khom in about 20 minutes, or take a taxi; motorcycles should be able to negotiate the hard, sandy road. You can also hike the 2.5km from Hat Khom to Hat Khuat (one hour), but the trail is challenging and you can easily get lost; take a guide if possible.

On Hat Khuat, the one family runs **Bottle Beach I** *(bungalows 100-400B)*, with solid bungalows and a fancier restaurant; **Bottle Beach II** *(bungalows 120-350B)*, with basic huts and a good hang-out restaurant; and **Bottle Beach III** *(bungalows 100-250B)*, with even more basic huts and a not quite as happenin' restaurant.

Smile Bungalow *(bungalows 250-350B)* is slightly better than the Bottle Beach conglomerates, with well-spaced, quieter bungalows trickling down a hillside and located in a pretty, jungle-like garden with views.

OD Bungalows *(bungalows with shared bath 100B)* is the most bare-bones and ramshackle of all, with bungalows tucked away up on the rocks on the western hill; the family is sweet and welcoming, though.

Hat Khom is smaller and more peaceful than Hat Khuat, with only three places to stay. **Had Khom** *(bungalows 150-400B)* is an OK place, but not especially memorable.

Ocean View *(in Thong Sala ☎ 0 7737 7231; rooms & bungalows 150-380B)* is a good deal, with attractive, modern and well-decorated bungalows sporting hammocks and huge decks. Rooms are shady and pleasant.

Ocean Bay *(☎ 0 7737 4245; bungalows 150-450B)*, up on the headland, is a friendly place with 30 pleasant abodes with some great views. They range from basic huts with shared bath to large, fancy and creatively done bungalows with balconies. The restaurant has a super deck and serves vegetarian food. Call for free transport.

Ban Chalok Lam This fishing village has a few restaurants, groceries, laundry and Internet services, money exchange, motorcycle rental and a dive school. It's a pleasant enough town in which to stay – with beaches just a short boat ride away – and only becoming a little bit touristed. Săwngthăew to/from Thong Sala cost 50B.

During the high season boats run regularly from here to Hat Khuat, though private charters are always available. On rough days boats won't run, so you can get stuck; plan accordingly.

Rose Villa *(☎ 0 7737 4013; ⓔ rosevilla 2000@hotmail.com; bungalows with fan 300-500B, with air-con 1000B)* is a good place for some shut-eye, with neat brick and concrete bungalows in a sparse beachside garden.

Nanthawan *(bungalows 150-250B)*, nearby, has cheap shacks in a bleak lot for budget backpackers; it's not located very well, but the family is friendly.

Fanta *(☎ 0 7737 4132; ⓔ fantaphangan@ yahoo.com; bungalows 150-500B)*, a bit farther on, has 40 decent bungalows of varying comfort. The beach is nice and there's a good traveller vibe.

Try Tong Resort *(☎ 0 7737 4115; bungalows with fan 150-300B, with air-con 800-1500B)* lies across the river from Fanta. There are old, large bungalows with some views, or newer rooms with air-con. The restaurant is inland and just OK.

Some restaurants to try include **Seaside** *(dishes 30-100B; open 7am-10.30pm daily)*, at the west end of town, and **Cafe del Mar** *(dishes 35-120B; open 8am-2am daily)*, near the entrance to town, serving international food.

Ao Mae Hat Just past Ban Mae Hat (another small fishing village) is the bay of Ao Mae Hat, harbouring some decent bungalow resorts. The beach isn't fantastic, but there is a bit of coral offshore, and you can walk to Ko Ma (Horse Island) via a sandbar. A bit south are the cascades of **Nam Tok Wang Sai**. Săwngthăew to/from Ban Chalok Lam cost 20B.

Mae Haad Bay Resort *(☎/fax 0 1968 2740; ⓔ maehaad-bay-resort@hotmail.com; bungalows 200-250B)* has nice wooden bungalows with hammocks; the best are away from the road.

Island View Cabana *(huts 70-250B)*, nearby, isn't particularly friendly, but the cheapest shacks have shared bath. Other bungalows are blue pastel clapboards.

Royal Orchid Resort *(☎ 0 7737 4182; bungalows 150-200B)* is a good deal for its small wooden bungalows, all nice and lined up on spacious grounds.

Wang Sai Resort *(☎ 0 7737 4238; bungalows 100-500B)*, next door but down its own driveway, has decent bamboo huts along with more solid bungalows. There are boulders and a garden, and the beach is over the footbridge.

Ko Ma Dive Resort *(bungalows 200-300B)* is on Ko Ma, opposite the beach, and has a few bungalows.

Hat Yao This long, pretty beach has a reasonable drop-off that makes it one of the island's best swimming beaches, and there is good snorkelling too.

Bayview *(☎ 0 1476 3226; bungalows 100-300B)*, on a hill to the north, offers small, OK bungalows with decks and good lofty views.

Long Bay Resort *(☎ 0 7737 7289; bungalows with fan 500B, with air-con 1500-2500B)* is the fanciest offering on the beach, with comfortable bungalows with fan and large, beautiful bungalows with air-con. There's a pool.

Long Beach (*☎ 0 7737 7015, fax 0 7723 8242; bungalows 300-1000B*) has good-sized bungalows lined up away from the beach.

Silver Beach (*bungalows with fan 150-500B, with air-con 1000B*) is a friendly place with a variety of wood and rattan bungalows on pleasant-enough grounds.

Ibiza (*☎ 0 1968 4727; bungalows 150-200B*) has cramped, basic bungalows, but they're in a nice garden. It's a budget traveller's special.

Tantawin Bungalows (*☎ 0 7734 9108; e yup_pat@hotmail.com; bungalows 250B*), on a hillside, is a pleasant retreat with pool. It has a good French-Thai restaurant and beautiful views over the bay.

Hat Chaophao & Ao Si Thanu Farther south of Hat Yao are these two areas, where you'll see the occasional mangrove along the coast; inland there's a pretty lagoon at the southern end of Hat Chaophao. The following accommodation options are in Hat Chaophao.

Great Bay (*bungalows 100-200B*) is not for the timid, with dark, basic, small shacks, though the 200B ones are bigger. The bar has an OK atmosphere.

Hut Sun (*bungalows 150-300B*) is a good, friendly cheapie, where the bungalows line a leafy garden.

Jungle Huts (*e jungle_huts@hotmail.com; bungalows 100-250B*), amid a lush jungle, has old, ratty and cheap huts close to the beach; pricier bungalows are a good deal.

Pha-Ngan Cabana (*☎ 0 1958 0182; bungalows with fan/air-con from 300/600B*) has a resort feel, with upmarket but crowded bungalows lined up inland from the beach. A large, snazzy restaurant sits by the sea, and there's also a pool. Bungalows with air-con zoom to 2000B during holidays.

Sri Thanu (*no Roman-script sign; bungalows with fan 150-400B, with air-con 700B*) has a rather nice garden. The best (and priciest) rooms are the spacious, seaside bungalows with big windows. Look for the 'Bovy' driveway and go right.

The following are in Ao Si Thanu.

Laem Son I & II (*☎ 0 1856 6027; bungalows 150-200B*) both have small but nice bungalows, some with hammocks. Most are on the beach and there's a definite backpacker feel. The seaside restaurant has decent music.

Seaview Rainbow (*☎ 0 7727 4105; bungalows 200-400B*) has decent, spacious concrete bungalows in an open garden.

Loy Fa (*☎ 0 7737 7319; bungalows 150-200B, large cottages 500B*) is a good place with various kinds of sea-view bungalows fanned out over an attractive hillside. The restaurant shows movies.

Chai (*☎ 0 1271 6967; bungalows 150-200B*) isn't as nice as its neighbour Loy Fa, with small trails and a closed-in feel. Some of the 11 small bungalows have great views, though.

Ao Hin Kong & Ao Wok Tum This long bay – sometimes divided in two by a stream that feeds into the sea – is just a few kilometres north of Thong Sala, but so far has relatively subdued tourist development.

Lipstick Cabana (*☎ 0 7737 7294; rooms 100-500B*), about 300m north of the cement road junction in Ban Hin Kong, is a friendly place near some local village houses. Seven abodes are available here, the pricier ones are bigger and nicer. Bring a book and chill out.

A couple of kilometres closer to Thong Sala, lining the cape that separates Ao Wok Tum from Ao Nai Wok, is a cluster of bungalow operations.

Woktum Bay (*☎ 0 7737 7430; bungalows 100-200B*) is a friendly family place with smaller, older concrete bungalows and some newer, larger wooden ones – these are more expensive, naturally.

Sea Scene (*bungalows with fan/air-con 400/800B*) has beautiful, upmarket and modern bungalows in a well-tended garden. There's a good, clean feel to the whole place; it's a great deal.

Bounty (*bungalows 150B*) offers basic bungalows with hammocks, and they're all in a pleasant garden and open grounds – a good deal at this price.

Porn Sawan (*☎ 0 7737 7599; bungalows 100-250B*) offers just OK bungalows; the big restaurant has a sandy floor and a football table. Internet facilities are available.

Beach 99 (*☎ 0 7737 7518; bungalows 250-700B*) is a hike down from the driveway. Pricier bungalows are large, wooden and solid, with nice sitting areas. Cheap bungalows are unmemorable.

Getting There & Away

Note that exact numbers of boat departures are determined by weather and season. Also, slower boats tend to be cheaper and no-frills, while faster ones are more expensive and more comfortable.

There are almost 10 daily departures between Ko Pha-Ngan and Ko Samui. These boats leave throughout the day from 7.30am to 4.30pm, take from 30 minutes to an hour and cost 115B to 250B. All leave from either Thong Sala or Hat Rin on Ko Pha-Ngan and arrive either in Na Thon, Mae Nam or the Big Buddha pier on Ko Samui. If the final location matters, state your preferences while buying your ticket.

There are over six daily departures between Ko Pha-Ngan and Surat Thani. These boats leave throughout the day from 7am to 10pm, take from 2½ to seven hours and cost 200B to 370B. All leave from Thong Sala.

There are about six daily departures between Ko Pha-Ngan and Ko Tao. These boats leave throughout the day from 8.30am to 1pm, take from one to three hours and cost 180B to 350B. These also leave from Thong Sala.

Getting Around

Roads on the island are becoming paved at a rapid rate, which will no doubt mean fewer low-speed accidents and more high-speed ones. The worst place for motorcycle riding is between Ban Khai and Hat Rin, which is a paved, but very hilly road. Also bad is the mid-section to Ao Thong Nai Pan, which is a rutty, dirt road (though this could be paved by the time you read this book). Be careful and slow down.

Some places can only be reached by boat, such as Hat Khuat and some sections of the east coast. If you find trails, they can be overgrown and not recommended for walking if you're wearing a heavy pack. Always carry water and a torch, just in case.

From Thong Sala, sǎwngthǎew cost 50B per person to anywhere on the island except for Ban Khai (30B) and Ao Thong Nai Pan (80B). Rates jump at sunset.

Long-tail boats from Ao Chalok Lam to Hat Khuat cost 50B per person with at least three persons. Boats between Thong Sala and Hat Yao also cost 50B per person from January to September (in calm weather only). You can charter a boat ride from beach to beach for about 150B per 15 minutes of travel.

Motorcycles are available for rent in Thong Sala and at bungalows here and there for about 200B per day, depending on the season. Cars go for about 1000B.

KO TAO

เกาะเต่า

pop 5000

Ko Tao translates as 'turtle island', so-named because of its shape (it does not, however, look like a turtle). It's only about 21 sq km, and if the local folk aren't involved in tourism, they mostly fish and grow coconuts. The beaches are pleasant and scenic enough, but most are too shallow for swimming (with the exception of Ao Leuk). Diving has become a major industry on this island because of the surrounding water's particularly good visibility and abundance of fishy wildlife and coral.

Ko Tao is a popular island and getting more popular all the time. Large numbers of resorts have gone up in the last few years, and during the high season many of them

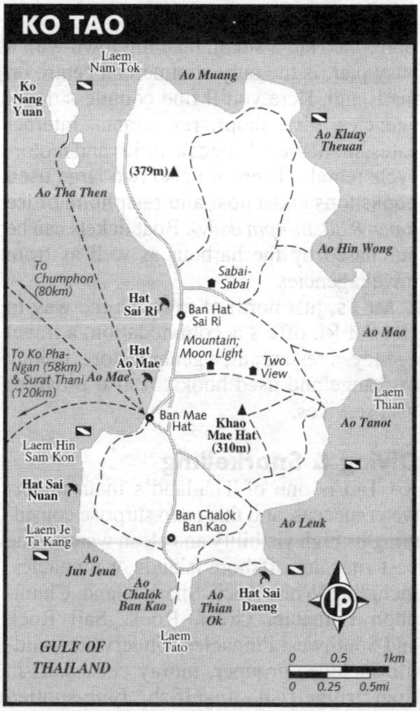

are full. Electricity is still sporadic, with few resorts providing 24-hour service, but this situation will no doubt improve (bring a torch for the dark trails). Unfortunately, growth always brings about its own problems, and Ko Tao's not an exception. A lack of seasonal rain brought water shortages in 2002, while rubbish collection has also become a serious issue.

Ban Mae Hat, on the western side of the island, is where boats dock. The only other villages on the island are **Ban Hat Sai Ri**, about midway up the western coast, and **Ban Chalok Ban Kao** to the south. Just 1km off the northwestern shore of the island is **Ko Nang Yuan**, which is really three islands joined by a sand bar.

The granite promontory of **Laem Tato** at the southern tip of Ko Tao makes a nice hike from Ban Chalok Ban Kao. About the only thing of historic interest on the island is a large **boulder** where King Rama V had his initials carved to commemorate a royal visit in 1900. The boulder, located at the southern end of Hat Sai Ri, has become something of a local shrine and is the focus of a small ceremony every October.

Information

Ban Mae Hat, a small, bustling town with a busy pier, is the only commercial centre on the island. Here you'll find countless travel agencies, dive shops, restaurants, Internet cafés, money-exchange facilities and motorcycle rentals. There are also two large **used bookshops** and a **post and telephone office** *(open 8.30am-4pm daily)*. Boat tickets can be purchased by the harbour as well as from travel agencies.

Mr J's, just north of town on the way to Hat Sai Ri, offers accommodation, a travel agency, a restaurant, a general store, money exchange and used books. It also provides visa services.

Diving & Snorkelling

Ko Tao is one of Thailand's main underwater meccas, and this is no surprise considering its high visibility and clean waters. The best sites are offshore islands or pinnacles, including White Rock, Shark Island, Chumphon Pinnacle, Green Rock, Sail Rock and Southwest Pinnacles. Underwater wildlife includes grouper, moray eels, batfish, titan triggerfish, angelfish, blue-spotted stingrays, sea snakes and the occasional whale shark.

About 40 dive operators eagerly offer their services to travellers. Some of these are small dive shops and just offer dive services, while others are 'dive resorts' that also have accommodation (sometimes only to clients – in the high season, it can be difficult finding a place to stay that will accept you as a non-diver). Many are run by Western staff, who seem to be travellers extending their vacations by finding jobs as 'dive masters' (an entry-level position obtained after some instruction).

The larger, more well-known dive operators aren't necessarily better than the smaller ones, and will often take out bigger groups of divers. These operators usually have more than one branch office around the island (like at Ban Mae Hat and at Hat Sai Ri). The quality of your dive experience, however, will ultimately depend on the experience and abilities of your dive shop's staff. It's a good idea to ask around for a recommendation.

Rates are similar everywhere, and typically cost 800B per dive to 5400B for a 10-dive package. An all-inclusive introductory dive lesson costs 1600B, while a four-day, open-water PADI certificate course costs around 8000B – these rates include gear, boat, instructor, food and beverages. Ko Tao's nearest decompression chamber is on Ko Samui, a two-hour boat ride away.

Any bungalow can arrange snorkelling trips for 250B per person.

Martial Arts & Traditional Massage

Here & Now *(☎ 0 9970 1525; Ⓦ www.hereandnow.be)*, at CFT (see Places to Stay following), offers classes in the Chinese martial arts of *taijiquan* and *qi gong*, taught by a German expat. Nine-session early-morning or evening courses cost 2800B. His wife and daughter also offer traditional Thai yoga massage for 550B for 2½ hours.

Places to Stay

Ko Tao's reputation as a dive destination is not unfounded; many places here are dive resorts and cater to those taking dive trips. In the high season, some places won't let you stay unless you plan a trip with their dive centre; in the low season, they may be more amenable to non-divers. A few won't take non-divers no matter what the season. Ko Tao isn't exclusively for divers, however, so please don't feel you'll be unwelcome everywhere if you don't dive.

Many of the smaller, more isolated and least expensive bungalow operations rely on guests eating at their restaurant for extra income. Some may become miffed if you go elsewhere, and a few may even try to give you the boot.

Unless stated, rates here are approximately for April to November; expect them to skyrocket from December to March. During this time it's wise to call ahead to confirm prices and secure a room. Many simple places have electricity only at night, and not even all the fancy places have electricity 24 hours a day – yet.

Hat Ao Mae This shallow bay, just north of Ban Mae Hat, has plenty of coral, but the southern end can get some rubbish from the pier area at Ban Mae Hat.

To get to Hat Ao Mae, get off the pier and turn left at Cafe del Sol. For the most part, all places to stay following are listed clockwise around the island.

Crystal (*☎ 0 7745 6107, fax 0 7745 6105; W www.crystaldive.com; bungalows with fan/air-con 500/1200B)* is for divers only and offers neat rows of standard, modern bungalows. If you dive with Crystal the price drops to 200/750B; if you take a beginners' course, the room is free. This place has electricity almost 20 hours a day, which is longer than most.

Beach Club (*☎ 0 7745 6222; rooms & bungalows with fan/air-con in low season 800/1500B, in high season 1000-1800B)* has small, bamboo bungalows that face seaward, and larger, more modern rooms with fridge and comfy furniture.

Queen Resort (*☎ 0 7745 6002; bungalows with/without bath 500/200B)*, on a headland overlooking the bay, has rustic wooden bungalows in a scraggly jungle. The best ones are closest to the water. There's a decent restaurant on the premises, too.

Tommy's Resort (*☎ 0 7745 6039; e tommy_resorts@hotmail.com; rooms & bungalows in low season with fan 350-800B, with air-con 800-1500B, in high season 1500-2500B)* offers a good deal, with clean, bright, modern rooms and bungalows terraced down to the water. Most have hammocks and balconies. There's a good-feeling restaurant and deck.

View Cliff Bungalows (*☎ 0 7745 6353; e viewcliff@ksc.th.com; bungalows with fan 600-800B, with air-con 1100B)*, just beyond Tommy's, has good, plain bungalows. Rates stay the same year-round, but head north during Thai holidays.

Just south of Hat Ao Mae and the pier is a cluster of nicer places.

Blue Diamond (*☎ 0 7745 6255; W www.kohtaotravel.com/bluediamond; bungalows 400-800B)* maintains its prices all year. It's a friendly family place with two grades of bungalows; unsurprisingly, the cheaper ones are smaller and less spiffy.

Ko Tao Royal Resort (*☎ 0 7745 6156, fax 0 7745 6157; bungalows with fan 800B, with air-con 2800-3500B)*, beyond Blue Diamond, is another smart place with beautiful, modern bungalows.

Sensi Paradise Resort (*☎ 0 7745 6244, fax 0 7745 6245; W www.kohtaoparadise.com; rooms with fan 450-2500B, with air-con 3900-8000B)* is a mostly upmarket place with some gorgeous Thai-style rooms in rich dark wood. Artsy indoor/outdoor baths are great, and the beautiful decor makes everything comfortable. It's pretty romantic overall, with covered decks (great for lounging) overlooking the sea. The bigger villas are perfect for families, and there are also some more basic bungalows.

Hat Sai Ri Around the headland to the north is the longest, busiest beach, with a string of dive operations, bungalows, travel agencies, minimarkets and Internet cafés. The pathway here is now paved the whole way, so watch out for motorcycles that will mow you down.

In Touch (*☎ 0 7722 2723; bungalows 250-350B)*, a 15-minute walk from the pier, has darkish bamboo and wooden bungalows with tin roofs. They're located in a jungle-like area and come with mosquito nets. The highlight here is its restaurant, set at the beach, and sporting driftwood decor and nice decks.

AC Resort I (*☎ 0 7745 6197; bungalows with fan 300-600B, with air-con 1000B)* features small bungalows with fan and mosquito nets, while those with air-con can come with huge beds. They're all located on pleasantly grassy, hilly and palmy grounds.

AC Resort II *(☎ 0 7745 6195)* is next door, and similar.

Ban's Diving Resort *(☎ 0 7745 6061; W www.amazingkohtao.com; rooms & bungalows with fan 400B, with air-con 800-1200B)* maintains its prices year-round. Modern rooms with balconies are set in a hotel block and overlook the pool out the back, while at the front decent but no-frills bungalows lie in a nicely tended, hilly garden. It has 24-hour electricity.

SB Cabana *(☎ 0 7745 6005; bungalows 250-300B)* has small, bare-bones and well-kept wooden bungalows in an unexciting locale.

Sai Ree Cottages *(☎/fax 0 7745 6374; bungalows 250-500B)* is a bit more pleasant than SB Cabana, with thatched-roof bungalows ringing a grassy lot with palm trees. There's a popular, relaxing restaurant.

Sea Shell Resort *(☎ 0 7745 6299; W www.kohtaoseashell.com; bungalows with fan 400-850B, with air-con 1500B)* offers wood and bamboo bungalows, the more modern versions with bathtubs (very rare). The grounds are beautiful, and you can stay here without diving.

Lotus Resort *(☎ 0 7745 6271; rooms with fan 400-850B, bungalows with fan/air-con 1200/1600B)* is run by the same quality management as Sea Shell Resort, but the bamboo bungalows here are bigger and nicer. The garden isn't as lush or shaded, though, but the place is clean and well run.

Silver Sand Beach Resort *(☎ 0 7745 6303; e silversand_kohtao@hotmail.com; bungalows with fan in low season 250B, in high season 500-600B)* is next in line, with plain wooden bungalows that are basic, cheap and popular.

Big Blue Resort *(☎ 0 7745 6050; W www.bigbluediving.com; rooms & bungalows with fan 200-300B, with air-con 500-1700B)* keeps its rates year-round. On the premises is a variety of accommodation with 24-hour electricity. It takes non-divers in the low season.

Sunset Buri Resort *(☎ 0 7745 6266, fax 0 7745 6101; bungalows with fan 700-900B, with air-con 1300-2500B)* is 30 minutes' walk from the pier. There's a pool and reasonably shaded modern bungalows lined up in two rows going inland. A leafy garden area completes the picture.

Blue Wind *(☎ 0 7745 6116; bungalows 250-400B)* claims its spot on the beach with small, cute, rustic and shady bungalows. The restaurant is small but popular enough.

Pranee's *(☎ 0 7745 6080; bungalows 300-450B)* is another popular and similar place, with good bungalows of wood and rattan-woven walls; all are partly shaded by palms.

Koh Tao Coral Grand Resort *(☎ 0 7745 6431, fax 0 7745 6430; W www.kohtaocoral.com; bungalows with fan/air-con from 1900/3800B)* lies a bit beyond Hat Sai Ri. It's a spanking-new and fancy resort with pastel-coloured, double-peaked bungalows in geometric shapes. They're very comfortable inside, boasting wooden floors, bright linen and wooden tubs. The grounds will be a bit sparse until the foliage takes hold, but there's a pool!

Ko Tao Palace *(☎/fax 0 7745 6250; e kohtaopalace@ppdw-card.com; bungalows with fan in low season 1300B, in high season 1500-1800B)* offers a good luxury deal, but you'll have to live without air-con. This new place has large, Fred Flintstone-like bungalows with tropical decor and creative indoor/outdoor baths. All are smooth and circular and overlook the sea from under shady palms.

North of the beach, in a hilly area called Ao Ta Then, are several operations with very inexpensive and very basic bungalows – most high above the water – including **Silver Cliff** (up a rough driveway), **Sun Sea** (high on top of the rocks) and **Sun Lord** (down below Sun Sea). All charge about 200B and some have awesome views – an excellent deal if you love the ultra-rustic and isolated, and aren't afraid of dust or a few bugs in your bed.

Thipwimarn *(☎ 0 7745 6409, fax 0 7745 6024; e thipwimarn@excite.com; bungalows with fan/air-con in low season 1750/2450B, in high season 2500/3500B)* lies 200m beyond the cheapies and at the other end of the comfort spectrum. A beautifully located and circular restaurant greets you, sporting a handful of intimate floor-level tables and an outstanding view. The attractive bungalows themselves spill down the hillside among boulders and greenery, while the myriad stairs keep you fit.

CFT *(☎ 0 9970 1525; W www.hereandnow.be; bungalows 100-350B)* sits at the end of the road about 300m past Thipwimarn. It's German-run and offers traditional Thai yoga massage (550B for 2½ hours). This is a spiritual place, but not at all fancy; it's best for those who can let go of modern creature comforts. All bungalows are basic, and the cheapest have shared baths. The jungle-like grounds are strewn with magnificent boulders. Săwngthăew from Ban Mae Hat cost 50B.

Ko Nang Yuan The **Ko Nangyuan Dive Resort** (*☎/fax 0 7745 6093; www.nangyuan.com; bungalows with fan 750-1700B, with air-con 2000B*) monopolises a trio of islands, northwest about 1km offshore, connected by an idyllic sandbar. Bungalows are quite comfortable and well spaced. The emphasis here is on diving; stay three nights with a four-day dive course for around 10,000B (rates depend on the season). Daily boats from Ban Mae Hat leave at 10.30am, 3pm and 5.30pm (60B return). Due to rubbish concerns, plastic bottles aren't allowed on the island. For more information, see its booking office in Ban Mae Hat.

Ao Hin Wong to Ao Tanot On the east side of Ko Tao is tranquil Ao Hin Wong, with a few accommodation options; there isn't really a beach, but the snorkelling is decent. The road here is paved in parts, but still hairy on a motorcycle. From Ban Mae Hat, săwngthăew cost 50B per person; longtail boats from Ban Mae Hat cost 200B.

Hin Wong Bungalows (*☎ 0 1229 4810; bungalows with fan in low season 250B, in high season 300-500B*) has some beautiful new wooden bungalows with great big modern baths; older bungalows are OK too, but obviously not as fancy.

Green Tree (*bungalows with fan & shared/private bath 100/200B*) is a friendly place 150m farther along the road. It has white bungalows (which are a bit more basic than Hin Wong's) set in a jungle-like area. The restaurant is nice enough.

View Rock (*☎ 0 1229 4307; bungalows with shared/private bath 100/300B*) is 600m up the dirt road from Green Tree; you climb the hill to get to the entrance, but climb back down (it's around a headland) to access the seaside bungalows and restaurant. It's worth it, though; brand-new bungalows are a great deal at these prices, and the best have large spaces and super sea views.

South of Ao Hin Wong, past Ao Mao, is the scenic cape of Laem Thian.

Laem Thian (*☎ 0 7745 6477; huts 100-150B, with bath 600-800B, rooms 300-350B*), sitting by itself, has some very cheap and rustic bungalows, while pricier ones are nice and comfy. Rooms in the hotel block are beautifully modern and come with balconies – the best have sea views. All over the hilly grounds are huge boulders, just great to bound around and even jump into the water from. The road here is very rough; catch a săwngthăew from Ban Mae Hat (50B), which depart at around 10.30am and 2.30pm.

Farther south from Laem Thian is Ao Tanot – one of the island's best spots for snorkelling, though the swimming is not so good. Two dive operators compete in this small, boulder-strewn cove, while several bungalow operators line the beachfront. There are a couple of simple shops in the area. Get here by săwngthăew (50B), which leave Ban Mae Hat five times daily.

Tanote Bay Resort (*☎ 0 1970 4703; bungalows with fan 500-1000B, with air-con 2500B*) keeps its rates the same all year. It's another place with good, modern and clean bungalows on a hillside.

Bamboo Hut (*☎ 0 1968 6000, fax 0 7745 6186; bungalows 150-500B*) has 20 decked bungalows, the older they are the smaller they are. The kitchen here specialises in spicy southern Thai-style food.

Black Tip Dive Resort (*☎ 0 7745 6488; www.blacktip-kohtao.com; bungalows with fan 400-700B; rooms with air-con 1250B*), part of a dive shop, has a handful of very nice bungalows and keeps its rates year-round.

Diamond Beach (*☎ 0 1958 3983; bungalows 400-500B*) is nice and plays upbeat music. Bungalows are relatively new, modern and comfortable. At the time of writing it was building a new restaurant.

Poseidon (*☎ 0 1958 8917; bungalows 350-500B*) offers very simple and very unmemorable bungalows; the onsite restaurant is nice, though.

Mountain Reef Resort (*☎ 0 1956 2916; bungalows 350-400B*), at the south end of the bay, has peaceful bungalows and a raised restaurant with a good view.

Ao Leuk to Ao Thian Ok The dirt road to Ao Leuk gets steep, rough and rutty, especially towards the end; don't attempt it on a motorcycle unless you're an expert. At the end of the road are **Ao Leuk Resort** and **Nice Moon**, both with bungalows from 300B to 400B. They are neighbours and share the same small beach. Nice Moon is up the hill, with simple bungalows and good views; the restaurant is a bit shaky, though (literally).

At Hat Sai Daeng, **Coral View Resort** *(☎ 0 1970 22807; bungalows 450-600B)* features well-built bungalows run by a friendly Aussie/Thai couple. It's best getting here by long-tail boat from Ban Mae Hat, as the road is rough and may require you to hike a little.

Even farther west is pretty Ao Thian Ok, where **Rocky** *(☎ 0 7745 6035; rooms low/high season 200-350/350-500B)* monopolises one end of the beach with haphazardly built, unattractive bungalows. It's the only place here, so at least it's pretty tranquil. Across the bay from Rocky and up the hill is **New Heaven Restaurant**, with a simply grand view over the bay (see Places to Eat following this section).

Ao Chalok Ban Kao This nicely situated coral beach has heaps of bungalows to choose from. Just past Laem Khlong Resort, and accessible via a raised walkway, is the stilted, stunningly located **Taraporn Restaurant**; it's right over the water and a super casual place to hang out (see Places to Eat following this section).

Ko Tao Cottage Dive Resort *(☎ 0 7745 6198; Ⓦ www.kotaocottage.com; rooms & bungalows 740-940B)*, towards the eastern end of the bay and about 500m past Tropicana, isn't too friendly but has good sea-view bungalows, a leafy garden and a large terraced restaurant.

Tropicana *(☎ 0 7745 6167; bungalows low/high season 300-400/400-500B)* is simple and sweet, with large, modern and clean abodes.

Buddha View Dive Resort *(☎ 0 7745 6074; Ⓦ www.buddhaview-diving.com; rooms 300-400B)* has OK bungalows for divers only – the swimming pool is also used for dive courses. Look for it on the right as you enter Ao Chalok Ban Kao.

Sunshine *(☎ 0 7745 6219; bungalows 250-400B)*, next door to Buddha View, has decent, modern rooms that don't stand out. Electricity runs for 22 hours here.

Sunshine II *(rooms & bungalows from 350-400B)* offers good abodes in two rows facing each other across a nice garden. It's popular restaurant has a good vibe.

Laem Khlong Resort *(☎ 0 7745 6083; rooms & bungalows with fan 150-500B)* lies on a hill overlooking the bay. Modern rooms and bungalows are large, have blue-tiled floors and boast sea views.

Viewpoint Bungalows *(☎ 0 7756 6444; bungalows with fan 200-1000B)* is a friendly, family-run place just past Taraporn Restaurant. Cheap bungalows are airy and well maintained, and some have partial sea views. Expensive bungalows, however, are large and beautiful, and claim wide vistas along with beautiful decks.

Ao Jun Jeua to Hat Sai Nuan A trail follows past Viewpoint Bungalows, going both along the beach and inland, eventually turning into a full-on thin, steep hiking trail that's difficult to navigate while wearing a large pack. It eventually circles back to Ban Mae Hat, but you may get lost along the way. Long-tail boats are a good form of transport to this coastal area; with a decent number of people they cost 50B per person for these destinations. Or you can take a taxi to the Hat Sai Nuan area, then find your way on the trail from there.

Sunset *(Ⓦ www.earth2marsh.com/sunset; bungalows low/high season 100-150/150-180B)* is a 15-minute walk from the centre of Ao Chalok Ban Kao. It has a great seaside location, but appeals to minimalists seeking the simple life – bungalows are very basic (mattress on floor). There's a vegetarian restaurant, good swimming and snorkelling offshore, and yoga classes are occasionally offered.

Moondance *(☎ 0 1958 2971; bungalows 250B)*, on Ao Jun Jeua along with Sunset, has just 10 old bungalows terraced up a hillside with many stairs; all have sea views. It's a clean and decent budget choice.

Tao Thong Villa *(bungalows with shared bath 100-350B)* features very rustic, no-frills bungalows with great views. Laem Je Ta Kang, the headland on which this place is located, forms a small double bay with two beaches on either side; it's a great spot, if you can make it here. There's a pleasant, lofty restaurant also.

Sai Thong Resort *(☎ 0 7745 6476; Ⓔ saithongresort@hotmail.com; bungalows with fan 100-800B, with air-con 1500-2000B)* offers a good range of bungalows, from basic hillside huts to nicer beachside abodes. It has a great relaxing restaurant complete with hammocks and sun deck and a small, private beach.

Siam Cookie *(bungalows with fan & shared bath 200B)*, on Hat Sai Nuan, is basic, cheap and comes with peaceful sea views. There are similar places nearby.

Khao Mae Hat In the middle of the island, a rutty dirt road leads up the slopes of 310m-high Khao Mae Hat. Even 4WD vehicles in the dry season hesitate to climb this road, but strong (unladen) hikers can reach the top in about 30 minutes.

Moon Light *(☎ 0 9599 9558; bungalows in low season 200-250B, in high season 300-350B)* is about 250m up a very steep, paved driveway. It's a casual place with basic bungalows, though some have spectacular views of land and sea – as does the restaurant. Climbing many stairs makes this possible, so come fit. **Mountain** *(bungalows with fan 100B)* sits under Moon Light and the views aren't as good.

Two View *(e twoview@hotmail.com; w www.geocities.com/twoview2000; huts with shared bath 100B)* is at the apex of this boulder-strewn mountaintop, about a 20-minute hike from Moon Light and about a 40-minute hike from Ao Tanot Bay (on the east side). You can see both sunrise and sunset from this aerie. Life is simple up here; there's no telephone, no electricity and just some simple, bare-bones bamboo huts. Colon-cleansings, Chakra-balancing, rebirthing sessions and yoga/meditation retreats are offered, and there's Thai cooking and Swedish massage classes. Email to reserve a room in the high season.

Places to Eat

Practically all bungalows on the island have their own restaurant, since food is a good moneymaker. Most of the following restaurants are in Ban Mae Hat, which is full of *faràng*-oriented places.

Baan Yaay *(☎ 0 7745 6262; dishes 50-200B; open 11am-11pm daily)* has an airy, casual deck over the water, and serves salads, soups and fried rice/noodle dishes. You can also order cocktails to make things interesting.

Liab Thale *(set menus 49B; open 8.30am-6pm daily)*, near Baan Yaay, is near the water and has a back area that overlooks the busy pier area and its surrounds. It's popular for its location (folks waiting for the boat...) and its good, cheap Thai food.

La Matta *(☎ 0 1229 4718; dishes 90-235B; open 11am-10.30pm daily)*, on the uphill road, is an Italian-run place serving dishes like pasta, sandwiches, salads and omelettes. Some locals prefer it to Farango next door, another Italian eatery.

Swiss Bakery *(open 6.30am-6.30pm daily)* is a very popular morning spot serving juices, breakfast, sandwiches, baked goods and hit-or-miss pastries. It has large tables and wooden benches, and is across from La Matta.

Yang *(dishes 30-50B; open 8am-11pm daily)*, near Swiss Bakery, is great for cheap but good Thai food; slam it down with a cool fruit shake (20B). Portions are generous, which attracts backpackers like bees to honey.

Tattoo and **Whitening** (see Entertainment following) are bars in Ban Mae Hat that also serve good Thai and Western food

New Heaven Restaurant *(☎ 0 7745 6462; dishes 50-200B; open 8am-9.30pm daily)*, on the rocky headland of Laem Tato, has a simply grand view over the bay. The menu isn't extensive and the portions aren't large, but you're here for the scenery.

Taraporn Restaurant *(☎ 0 7745 6457; dishes 40-80B; open 8.30am-10.30pm daily)*, in Ao Chalok Ban Kao, serves good Thai and Western food (and hard drinks) at another unbeatable location. It's a more casual place built right over the water at the edge of the shallow bay, and reached via a long walkway. The intimate tables are at floor level, while cushions encourage quick naps.

Entertainment

Ko Tao has a few bars to get you nicely lubricated. If you're looking for parties, though, check out the ubiquitous fliers posted on trees and walls; venues are always changing.

The following are in Ban Mae Hat.

Whitening *(☎ 0 7745 6199; open 11am-midnight daily)* is a trendy bar/restaurant right at the beach; the 'floors' are sandy, the music is moody and the lighting glitters romantically at night (think tiki torches). Many different drinks are served, including margaritas. It has a definite upmarket feel, but it's comfortable; there's a great deck over the water. Staff throw an open party every Friday night at 10pm.

Tattoo *(open 7am-2am daily)* is 30m south of Whitening (at the edge of town). It's a more casual and intimate bar, with some tables and a TV lounge area. Breezes blow through the friendly and laid-back spaces, and there are plans to build a barbecue patio alongside. If you're hungry, try the big Aussie burger (120B).

The **Dragon Bar** *(☎ 0 7745 6423)* caters to those seeking snazzy, cutting-edge surroundings in which to be seen. It's an exception to other places in Ban Mae Hat, and may start an upscaling trend. There's a large, modernistic conversation-pit area and everything's dimly lit, moody and relaxing (not a party atmosphere). There's a large variety of cocktails, and plans to add tapas to the food menu.

Sea Monkey *(open 5pm-1am daily)* sits on the 2nd floor across from Cafe del Sol. It's a colourful place, with a pool table, upbeat atmosphere and glowing bubble tubes. Groovy tunes change themes nightly, and only drinks are served (no food) – a short and sweet list.

Safety Stop Bar has a great location by the pier and is the best place to watch soccer on TV while downing Mexican food snacks.

Getting There & Away

Chumphon & Surat Thani See the Chumphon section in the Upper Southern Gulf chapter for details on getting to Ko Tao. If you're heading *to* Chumphon, you can choose from about a half-dozen daily boats, from the slow ferry to catamarans (200B to 550B, 1½ to six hours).

Every night, depending on the weather, two slow ferries chug between Surat Thani and Ko Tao (400B, eight hours). Boats depart from Surat Thani at 11pm and Ko Tao at 9pm. There are also several morning ferries travelling to Surat Thani (400B to 500B, four to seven hours).

Ko Pha-Ngan & Ko Samui Depending on weather conditions, about six boats – from slow ferries to speedboats – run daily from 9.30am to 3pm from Ko Tao to either Ko Pha-Ngan or Ko Samui.

From Ko Tao there are boats to Ko Pha-Ngan (180B to 350B, one to three hours) and to Ko Samui (280B to 550B, 1½ to 2½ hours).

Exact times can vary from year to year, so check the schedules during your visit.

Islands for Cheap

You're on Th Khao San in Bangkok, shopping around for combination tickets to Ko Tao (or Ko Phan-gan or Ko Samui) and the prices seem unbelievable: 250B from Bangkok to Ko Tao? Straight through to Ko Samui for 300B? Sounds like a good deal, right?

Well, sometimes it is...and sometimes it's not. Some unscrupulous bus companies make their profits by, well, stealing from travellers. Ruses have included bus personnel sneaking below and rifling through bags (while the bus is enroute), sneaking along the aisle while everyone is asleep (and the lights are off) and just a lot of sneaky business in general. Some travellers show up and don't get the bus they were expecting. Others have extra transport charges added to their fare. A very few have even reported being gassed to unconsciousness and robbed right in their seats!

It's important to note we're not saying that this always (or even often) happens with cheap bus/boat tickets, but remember that no-one's in business to lose money. It's always best to have a chat with other travellers who've recently come back from where you're going.

Getting Around

Săwngthăew cost 50B per person to anywhere on the island. Many have scheduled departure times to the east coast of Ko Tao (four to five daily). Private charters are, of course, significantly more, especially at night. Long-tail boats can be chartered for up to 2000B a day, depending on the number of passengers carried.

Walking is an easy way to get around the island, but some remote trails aren't clearly marked and can be difficult to follow. You can walk around the whole island in a day, although the hilly paths make it a challenge.

Many tourists rent motorcycles on Ko Tao (150B per day). If you're confident on two wheels then this is a good way to get around, though there aren't a whole lot of roads on the island. The main ones are paved, but the more remote ones are rutted dirt paths that can be steep at times. These should *not* be attempted by novices. If you plan to rent a motorcycle, see the boxed text 'Renting Motorcycles' in this section for advice.

Nakhon Si Thammarat Province

Much of this large southern province is covered with rugged mountains and forests, which were, until recently, the last refuge of Thailand's communist insurgents. The province's eastern border is formed by the Gulf of Thailand, and much of the provincial economy is dependent on fishing and prawn farming. Along the north coast are several nice beaches: **Hat Khanom**, **Hat Nai Phlao**, **Hat Tong Yi**, **Hat Sichon** and **Hat Hin Ngam**.

In the interior are several caves and waterfalls, including **Nam Tok Phrom Lok**, **Tham Thong Phannara** and **Nam Tok Yong**. Besides fishing, Nakhon residents earn a living by growing coffee, rice, rubber and fruit (especially *mangkhút*, or mangosteen).

NAKHON SI THAMMARAT

อ.เมืองนครศรีธรรมราช

postcode 80000 • pop 122,400

Centuries before the 8th-century Srivijaya empire subjugated the peninsula, there was a city-state here called Ligor (or Lagor), the well-known capital of the Tambralinga (or Tampaling) kingdom. Later, when Sri Lankan-ordained Buddhist monks established a monastery at the city, the name was changed to the Pali-Sanskrit Nagara Sri Dhammaraja (City of the Sacred Dharma-King), which is rendered in Thai phonetics as Nakhon Si Thammarat.

An overland route between the western port of Trang and eastern port of Nakhon Si Thammarat functioned as a major trade link between Thailand and the rest of the world, as well as between the western and eastern hemispheres. Clergy from Hindu, Muslim, Christian and Buddhist denominations established missions here over the centuries, and even in contemporary Nakhon Si Thammarat you'll find active temples, shrines, mosques and churches representing each of these faiths.

During the early development of the various Thai kingdoms, Nakhon Si Thammarat also became a very important centre for religion and culture. Thai shadow theatre *(nǎng tàlung)* and classical dance-drama (*lákhon* – the Thai pronunciation of Lagor) were both developed here, and buffalo-hide

Renting Motorcycles

It sure is tempting: rent your own wheels for cheap, feel the wind blowing through your hair, go anywhere you like and keep cool while you're at it. Who wouldn't want the convenience of renting a motorcycle, especially on a tropical island with lots of secluded beaches?

If there weren't any downsides, it would be great. But there's always a chance of taking a spill, and this can be especially dangerous where traffic rules are often bent until they break. Heeding the few tips below may help, but just remember there are no guarantees.

1. Use a helmet. Ninety per cent of foreigners don't, but you can be one of the smart ones. Conking your delicate head on cement is not fun. It's also one less excuse for policemen to stop you.
2. Think about what your right hand is doing. Many accidents involving inexperienced riders occur when they try to brake but accelerate instead. The braking hand motion on bicycles and the accelerating hand motion on motorcycles is somewhat similar, and if you're panicked you could easily get them confused.
3. If you're relatively inexperienced, avoid going on steep, dirt hills. It's very easy to slip in a rut or slide on loose gravel, sand or dirt. And to keep control, use lower gears on hilly paved roads.
4. Avoid a superficial 'island tattoo' (exhaust-pipe burn mark on your calf, or skinned shoulder from an accident) by wearing protective clothing. Decent protective shoes are also a good idea.

Some motorcycle-rental places note any damage on their motorcycles and charge steep fees accordingly; check the bike beforehand to note previous damage. Any leftover fuel from the previous renter is usually drained when you receive the motorcycle; you can return it empty as well. And remember to watch your valuables if you place them in the motorcycle's basket; some thieves in tourist places zoom by on their own bikes and snatch unprotected packs!

shadow puppets along with dance masks are still being made. Other crafts for which Nakhon is famous include *thŏm* (nielloware) silver and basketry.

Today, Nakhon Si Thammarat is a very long, thin city divided into two sections: the historic half is south of the clock tower, and the new city centre north of the clock tower. The new city centre has all the hotels and most of the restaurants.

Information

The helpful, friendly **TAT office** (*☎ 0 7534 6515; e tatnakon@nrt.cscoms.com; open 8.30am-4.30pm daily*) is housed in a 1926-vintage building near the police station. Staff are helpful with transport information. There's another **tourist information office** (*open 8.30am-4.30pm daily*) in the city hall building farther north, but it's less helpful (though still friendly).

The **main post office** (*open 8.30am-4.30pm Mon-Fri*) has an upstairs **telephone office** (*open 8am-11pm daily*) with international service.

Nakhon Si Thammarat National Museum

พิพิธภัณฑสถานแห่งชาตินครศรีธรรมราช

Since the Tambralinga kingdom traded with Indian, Arabic, Dvaravati and Champa states, much art from these places found its way to the Nakhon Si Thammarat area, and some is now on display in this museum (*admission 30B; open 9am-4pm Wed-Sun*). Notable are the Dong-Son bronze drums, Dvaravati Buddha images and Pallava (south Indian) Hindu sculpture. Upstairs are folk crafts, such as elaborate walking sticks, fishing cages and pottery, along with an amusing coconut-grating device.

If you've already had your fill of the usual Thai art-history surveys from Ban Chiang to Ayuthaya (hasn't everybody?), go straight to the Art of southern Thailand exhibit. Here you'll find many fine images of Nakhon Si Thammarat provenance, including the Phutthasihing, U Thong and late Ayuthaya styles. The Nakhon Si Thammarat-produced Ayuthaya style seems to be the most common, with distinctive, almost comical, crowned faces. The so-called Phutthasihing-style Buddha looks a little

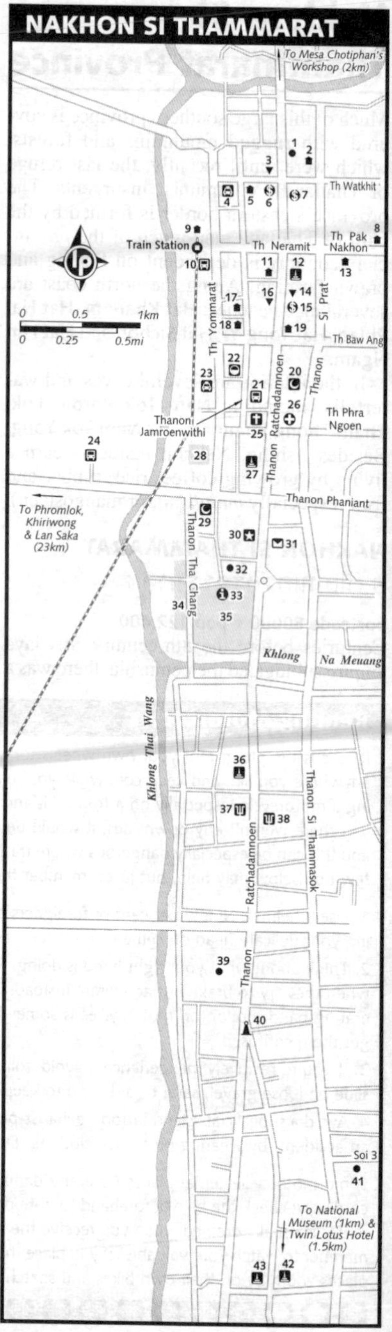

NAKHON SI THAMMARAT

PLACES TO STAY

2 Taksin Hotel
5 Thai Fa Hotel
8 Nakorn Garden Inn
9 Phetpailin Hotel
11 Thai Hotel
13 Grand Park Hotel
17 Muang Thong Hotel
18 Bue Loung (Bua Luang) Hotel
19 Thai Lee Hotel

PLACES TO EAT

3 Dam Kan Aeng
14 Bovorn Bazaar
16 Kuang Meng

OTHER

1 THAI Office
4 Minivans to Surat Thani
6 Bangkok Bank
7 Kasikornbank
10 Minivans to Hat Yai
12 Wat Buranaram
15 Siam Commercial Bank
20 Matsayit Yamia (Friday Mosque); City Hall (Tourist Information)
21 Minivans to Phuket & Krabi
22 Săwngthăews to Khiriwong
23 Share-Taxi Terminal
24 Bus Terminal
25 Bethlehem Church
26 Christian Hospital
27 Wat Maheyong
28 Market
29 Mosque
30 Police Station
31 Main Post Office & Telephone Office
32 Lak Meuang (City Pillar)
33 TAT Office
34 Handicraft Shops
35 Sanam Na Meuang (City Park)
36 Wat Sema Meuang
37 Shiva Shrine
38 Vishnu Shrine
39 Provincial Offices; Phra Phuttha Sihing Chapel
40 Clock Tower
41 Suchart Subsin's Workshop
42 Wat Na Phra Boromathat
43 Wat Phra Mahathat

like the Palla-influenced Chiang Saen Buddha, but is shorter and more 'pneumatic'.

The museum is on Th Ratchadamnoen, 1km south of Wat Mahathat. Any săwngthăew scooting south will take you there for a mere 6B.

Wat Phra Mahathat

วัดพระมหาธาตุ

This is the city's most historic site, reputed to have been founded by Queen Hem Chala over a thousand years ago. Bronze statues representing the queen and her brother stand in front of the east wall facing Th Ratchadamnoen, and her spirit is said to be associated with the large standing Buddha in the southeastern cloister. Locals make daily offerings of flower garlands to both this Buddha image and the statue of the queen, believing her spirit watches over the city and its residents.

This is the biggest wát in southern Thailand, comparable to Wat Pho and other large Bangkok wát. If you like wát, this one is well worth a trip. Reconstructed in the mid-13th century, the huge complex features a 78m *chedi*, crowned by a solid gold spire weighing several hundred kilograms. Numerous smaller grey-black chedi surround the main one.

Besides the distinctive *bòt* (central sanctuary) and *chedi* there are many intricately designed *wíhăan* (halls) surrounding the *chedi*, several of which contain crowned Nakhon Si Thammarat/Ayuthaya-style Buddhas in glass cabinets. One of the *wíhăan* houses a funky museum with some carved wooden *khrút* (Garuda, Vishnu's mythical bird-mount); old votive tablets; Buddha figures of every description, including a standing Dvaravati figure; a Buddha styled after the Siwichai *naga*; pearl-inlaid alms bowls; and other oddities. A *mondòp*, the fortress-looking structure towards the northern end of the temple grounds, holds a Buddha footprint – one of the better designs in Thailand.

Across the street from this wát stands **Wat Na Phra Boromathat**, the residence for monks serving at Mahathat. There is a nice Gandhara-style fasting Buddha in front of the *bòt* here.

Both wát are on Th Ratchadamnoen, 2km south of town. Any săwngthăew chugging south will take you there for a bargain 6B.

Phra Phuttha Sihing Chapel (Haw Phra Phuttha Sihing)

หอพระพุทธสิหิงค์

This chapel is located next to the provincial offices and contains one of Thailand's three identical Phra Singh Buddhas. One of these was supposed to have been cast in Sri Lanka before being brought to Sukhothai (through Nakhon Si Thammarat), Chiang Mai and, later, Ayuthaya. The other images are at Wat

Nakhon Si Thammarat Festivals

Every year in mid-October there is a southern Thai festival called Chak Phra Pak Tai held in Nakhon Si Thammarat (as well as Songkhla and Surat Thani). In Nakhon Si Thammarat the festival is centred on Wat Mahathat and includes performances of *năng tàlung* (shadow-puppet theatre) and *lákhon* as well as the parading of Buddha images around the city to collect donations for local temples.

In the third lunar month (February to March) the city holds the colourful Hae Phaa Khun That, in which a lengthy cloth *jataka* painting is wrapped around the main *chedi* at Wat Phra Mahathat.

Phra Singh in Chiang Mai and the National Museum in Bangkok – each is claimed to be the original.

Other Places of Worship

In addition to the original Sri Lankan monks who arrived in 13th-century Nakhon to teach Theravada Buddhism, many other missionaries – Catholics from Portugal, Hindus from India, Muslims from the Middle East and Mahayana Buddhists from Japan – also stationed themselves in the city. A legacy of these visitors is the variety and number of non-Theravadin places of worship surviving today.

Two **Hindu shrines**, one to Shiva and one to Vishnu, can be found along Th Ratchadamnoen inside the city walls. Brahman priests from these temples take part each year in the Royal Ploughing Ceremony in Bangkok. One temple houses a locally famous Shivalingam (phallic object) that is worshipped by women hoping to bear children.

Farther north is the green-hued **Matsayit Yamia** (Friday Mosque), and there are at least two other mosques in the area. On the opposite side of the road, a bit farther south, is the quaint **Bethlehem Church**.

Nakhon's most important non-Buddhist shrine is the **Lak Meuang** (City Pillar). Five *chedi*-like structures of stucco and marble are arranged like the dots on a die, while the porticoes bear a depiction of Rahu swallowing the sun. The tip of the pillar is decorated with eight faces and resembles an elaborate *mukhalinga* (a phallus with a face – this is a symbol of Shiva in his function as divine creator).

Shadow-Puppet Workshops

Traditionally, there are two styles of the shadow puppets: *năng tàlung* and *năng yài*. The former are similar in size to the Malay- and Indonesian-style puppets, while the latter are nearly life-size and are unique to Thailand. Both are intricately carved from buffalo hide. Performances of Thai shadow theatre are rare nowadays (usually only during festivals), but there are two places in town where you can see the puppets being made.

The acknowledged master of shadow-puppet manufacture and performance is **Suchart Subsin** (*☎ 0 7534 6394; Soi 3, 110/18 Th Si Thammasok*). Khun Suchart has received several awards for his mastery and preservation of the craft, and has performed for the king. You can visit his workshop and watch a performance (50B, two people minimum). Puppets can also be purchased at reasonable prices. On some puppets the fur is left on the hide for additional effect – these cost a bit more as special care must be taken in tanning them.

Another craftsperson, **Mesa Chotiphan** (*☎ 0 7534 3979; 558/4 Soi Rong Jeh, Th Ratchadamnoen*) has a workshop in the northern part of town. To get there, go north from the city centre on Th Ratchadamnoen and, 500m north of the sports field, take the soi opposite the Chinese cemetery.

Places to Stay

Thai Lee Hotel (*☎ 0 7535 6948; 1130 Th Ratchadamnoen; rooms 120-140B*) is friendly and has spacious rooms that are either bright and noisy or dark and quiet. It's secure and a good budget choice.

Thai Fa Hotel (*☎ 0 7535 6727; Th Wat Kit; rooms 120-180B*) is a basic, depressing old place with Thai-style baths. Rooms are worn and not very clean. Staff are friendly, though.

Muang Thong Hotel (*☎ 0 7534 3026, fax 0 7535 6177; 1459/7-9 Th Jamroenwithi; rooms 160-220B*) has dark, industrial halls and rooms, which are bleak and screened at the top (read: noisy).

Thai Hotel *(☎ 0 7534 1509, fax 0 7534 4858; 1375 Th Ratchadamnoen; rooms with fan 200-290B, with air-con 420-490B)* offers good mid-range rooms with TV and just a few scratches. The more expensive rooms with air-con are larger, better furnished and have a fridge. There's a small lobby café, and the whole place is pretty central.

Taksin Hotel *(no Roman-script sign; ☎ 0 7534 2790; 1584/23 Th Si Prat; rooms with air-con, TV & fridge 360-450B)* could use a new coat of paint. Rooms are worn but OK. Look for the big six-storey white building.

Bue Loung Hotel *(Bua Luang; ☎ 0 7534 1518, fax 0 7534 2977; Soi Luang Meuang; rooms with fan/air-con from 170/270B)* features small, unexciting rooms, though they're decent and bright (some even have partial mountain views). It's not a bad deal.

Phetpailin Hotel *(☎ 0 7534 1896, fax 0 7534 3943; 1835/38-39 Th Yommarat; rooms with fan/air-con 180/380B)*, next to the train station, has quiet rooms with mountain views at the back, and noisy rooms at the front. The rooms with fan are basic and musty but OK; those with air-con are plain and adequate. Halls are long and bleak.

Nakorn Garden Inn *(☎ 0 7531 3333, fax 0 7534 2926; 1/4 Th Pak Nakhon; rooms with air-con 445B)* is where you would want to stay if you can possibly afford it (make an exception if you can't). Tidy, homey, brick-walled rooms have good wooden furniture, TV and refrigerator. They're set around a quiet, sparse garden, and there's plenty of parking.

Grand Park Hotel *(☎ 0 7531 7666, fax 0 7531 7674; 1204/79 Th Pak Nakhon; rooms with air-con from 600B)* offers fine, modern rooms with TV and fridge – nothing too fancy or luxurious. They're on seven floors, some with grand views of the city. Downstairs is a nice lobby and a restaurant.

Twin Lotus Hotel *(☎ 0 7532 3777, fax 0 7532 3821; 97/8 Th Phattanakan Khukhwang; rooms with air-con from 1100B)* is a few kilometres southeast of town. It's a 16-storey, 413-room hotel that offers all the top amenities in this class. It shouldn't hurt to ask for a discount.

Places to Eat

Th Jamroenwithi is the city's main culinary centre. At night the entire block running south from Th Neramit is lined with cheap **food stalls** serving rice and noodle dishes, as well as delicious Muslim food like *rotii klûay* (banana pancakes), *khâo mòk kài* (chicken biryani) and *mátàbà* (murtabak; pancakes stuffed with chicken or vegetables).

The **Ligor Home Bakery** *(Bovorn Bazaar; dishes 30-60B; open 7.30am-5.30pm daily)* bakes European-style pastries in a modern atmosphere. It also serves breakfast, Thai food and good coffee. It has the same menu as Hao Coffee following.

Hao Coffee *(☎ 0 7534 6563; Bovorn Bazaar; dishes 30-60B; open 7am-7pm daily)* is a good place to try some of Nakhon's excellent coffee. Originally a Hokkien-style coffee shop, it now serves international coffees as well as southern-Thai Hokkien-style coffee ('Hao coffee' on the menu) in a renovated, antique-like atmosphere.

Khrua Nakhon *(☎ 0 7531 7197; Bovorn Bazaar; open 6am-3pm daily)*, near Hao Coffee, is a large cafeteria-style place serving Nakhon cuisine. Order *khâo yam* (southern-style rice salad), *kaeng tai plaa* (spicy fish curry) and *khànŏm jiin* (curry noodles served with a huge tray of vegies). Get there early as it's only open until mid-afternoon.

Ban Lakhon *(Bovorn Bazaar; open 11am-10pm daily)* is behind Khrua Nakhon in an old house built around a large tree. Step up to the 2nd floor for good Thai food.

Dam Kan Aeng *(☎ 0 7534 4343; Th Watkhit; open 8.30am-9.30pm daily)* is a popular, cheap and simple Thai-Chinese eatery, packed with hungry customers nightly.

Kuang Meng *(1343/12 Th Ratchadamnoen; open 6am-7pm daily)* is friendly, very small Hokkien coffee shop with marble-top tables and delicious pastries.

Rock 99 Bar & Grill *(☎ 0 7534 7846; Bovorn Bazaar; dishes 65-180B; open 11am-11pm daily)* has a pet store-like feel with its wall-lined fish tanks. As well as a few cocktails, the kitchen serves steak, pizza, spaghetti and sandwiches – but don't expect authenticity.

Getting There & Away

Air Flights to/from Bangkok are available twice daily (once on Saturday) with **THAI** *(☎ 0 7534 2491; 1612 Th Ratchadamnoen)* for 2520B.

Bus & Minivan There are several daily buses to/from Bangkok (1st class/2nd class

454/353B, non-air-con 252B to 325B, 12 to 13 hours). One VIP departure leaves nightly (705B). Ordinary buses to Bangkok leave from the bus terminal, but a couple of private bus companies on Th Jamroenwithi sell air-con bus tickets to Bangkok and buses leave from here rather than from the bus terminal. Look for Saphan Tour or Moung Tai Tours, which are both easy to find.

Other destinations from the bus terminal include Hat Yai (73B to 102B, three hours), Krabi (67B to 94B, three hours), Ko Samui (bus-boat 135B), Phuket (125B to 200B, seven hours), Songkhla (70B to 98B, three hours), Surat Thani (45B to 90B) and Trang (69B, 1½ hours)

When looking for minivan stops, look for small desks set near the footpath (minivans and waiting passengers may or may not be present nearby). Frequent minivans to Krabi (120B, 2½ hours) and Phuket (200B, five hours) leave from Th Jamroenwithi. Minivans to Surat Thani (95B) leave from Th Watkhit. Minivans to Hat Yai (90B) leave from Th Yommarat.

Train Most southbound trains from Bangkok stop at Thung Song, about 40km west of Nakhon (from where you must take a bus or taxi to the coast), though the 173 and 85 make it all the way to Nakhon. Second-class fares cost 468B to 688B.

Share Taxi The large share-taxi terminal on Th Yommarat has taxis to Yala (150B), Hat Yai (90B), Surat Thani (90B) and Songkhla (90B), among other destinations.

Getting Around

Săwngthăew run north–south along Th Ratchadamnoen and Th Si Thammasok for 6B (a bit more at night). Motorcycle taxi rides start at 20B and cost up to 50B for the longer distances.

AROUND NAKHON SI THAMMARAT

Khao Luang National Park

อุทยานแห่งชาติเขาหลวง

Known for its beautiful mountain and forest walks, cool streams, waterfalls and the fruit orchards, this 570-sq-km park (☎ *0 1228 2051; admission 200B)* surrounds **Khao Luang** (1835m), the highest peak in peninsular Thailand. Along with other forested igneous peaks to the west, Khao Luang provides a watershed that feeds Mae Nam Rapi. Local Thais practise a unique form of agriculture called *sŭan rôm* (shade garden, or shade farm). Instead of clear-cutting the forest, they leave many indigenous trees intact, randomly interspersing them with betel, mangosteen, rambutan, langsat, papaya, durian and banana trees. Cleverly placed bamboo and PVC pipes irrigate the mixed orchards without the use of pumps.

Wildlife includes clouded leopard, tiger, elephant, banteng, gaur, tapir, serow, musk deer, macaque, civet, binturon and Javan mongoose, plus over 200 bird species. More than 300 orchid varieties (including several indigenous species) find roots in the humid environments here, along with begonias and a wide variety of ferns.

Activities include hiking and rafting (both are possible June to December, the rainy season).

Park bungalows *(☎ 0 7530 9664 for reservations; 4-12 people 250-1200B)* are available, and **camping** is permitted on the trail to the summit of Khao Luang (see Hiking Trails following). There are a few private **bungalows** and **restaurants** on the road to the park offices that offer accommodation and food.

The best months to visit are January to April, when it's cooler and drier. If you're coming from Nakhon Si Thammarat, visit the **TAT office** there and pick up a small, informative English booklet to the park.

Hiking Trails

You can hike 2.5km through dense tropical forest to the top of **Nam Tok Karom** from the national park headquarters near Lan Saka (25km from Nakhon Si Thammarat), off Rte 4015. Every 500m or so there are shelters and seats. To reach seven-tiered **Nam Tok Krung Ching**, a half-day walk, you'll have to take the Krung Ching nature trail from Nopphitam at the northeastern border of the park, off Rte 4140.

Along the way you'll pass the world's largest tree ferns, an old communist insurgent camp, **Tham Pratuchai** (a cave also used by the communists) and a mangosteen forest. This trail, too, is lined with seats and shelters. The falls are most impressive right after the rainy season has ended in November and December.

A more challenging trail leads from a car park near Khiriwong to the **summit** of Khao Luang, a 14-hour walk best divided into two or more days. Night-time temperatures at the summit can drop to 5°C, so come prepared with plenty of warm clothing. At 600m, Kratom Suan Sainai offers a simple-roofed **shelter** and also marks the upper limit of the fruit plantations. In the dry season you can **camp** next to a riverbed at Lan Sai, about a six-hour walk from the car park. A five-hour walk farther on, along a section of very steep trail, you'll enter a cloud forest full of rattan, orchids, rhododendrons, ferns and stunted oaks. From here it's another three hours to the summit, where, if the weather is clear, you'll be rewarded with stunning views of layer after layer of mountains rolling into the distance.

The best and safest way to appreciate the Khao Luang trek is to go with a guide from the **Kiriwong Village Ecotourism Club** *(☎ 0 7530 9010, 0 9501 2706)* in Khiriwong. For 1500B per person the villagers can arrange three-day, two-night treks, along with all meals and guide services. The guides can point out local flora and fauna that you might otherwise miss. The only time to do this hike is January to around June, when the trails are drier and leeches not as bad. During heavy rains the trail can be impassable for days.

Getting There & Away

To reach the park, take a săwngthăew (20B) from Nakhon Si Thammarat (on Th Jamroenwithi) to the village of Khiriwong at the base of Khao Luang. The entrance to the park and the offices of the Royal Forest Department are 33km from the centre of Nakhon on Rte 4015, an asphalt road that climbs almost 400m.

Songkhla Province

SONGKHLA

สงขลา

postcode 90000 • pop 86,700

Songkhla, 950km from Bangkok, is another former Srivijaya satellite on the east coast. Not much is known about the pre-8th-century history of Songkhla, a name derived from the Yawi *singora* – a mutilated Sanskrit reference to a lion-shaped mountain (today called Khao Daeng) opposite the harbour. Though the original settlement lay at the foot of Khao Daeng, the city later moved across the harbour to its present site on a peninsula between Thaleh Sap Songkhla (an inland sea) and the South China Sea (or Gulf of Thailand, depending on how you look at it).

Today it's a pleasant place with a colourful market, charming older section (west of Th Ramwithi) and plenty of coastline. Seafood served along the peaceful, white-sand beaches is excellent, although the water is not that great for swimming (especially if you've just come from the Ko Samui archipelago). The town has plenty of other curiosities to offer, however.

The population is a mixture of Thais, Chinese and Malays, and the local architecture and cuisine reflect this combination. Over the last decade Songkhla has become increasingly Westernised due to the influx of multinational oil company employees – particularly British and American. This, along with a strong Thai navy presence, has created a wealthier-than-average Thai city.

Information

The Songkhla **post office** *(Th Wichianchom; open 8.30am-3.30pm Mon-Fri, 9am-noon Sat & Sun)* is opposite the market; **international calls** can be made upstairs. **Dotcom Internet** *(open 8am-10pm daily)*, next to Mrs Brown's guesthouse, provides links to the web.

Consulates in town include those for Malaysia *(☎ 0 7431 1062; 4 Th Sukhum)*, China *(☎ 0 7431 1494; Th Sadao)* and Indonesia *(☎ 0 7431 1544; Th Sadao)*. File for visa extensions at the **immigration office** *(☎ 0 7431 3480; open 8.30am-4.30pm Mon-Fri)*.

Corner Bookshop *(☎ 0 7431 2577; cnr Th Saiburi & Th Phetchakhiri; open 7am-7.30pm daily)* sells novels, maps, newspapers, magazines and Lonely Planet guidebooks (all in English).

Songkhla is well supplied with banks.

National Museum

พิพิธภัณฑสถานแห่งชาติสงขลา

Housed in a 100-year-old building of southern Sino-Portuguese architecture is this picturesque national museum *(☎ 0 7431 1728; Th Wichianchom; admission 30B; open 9am-4pm*

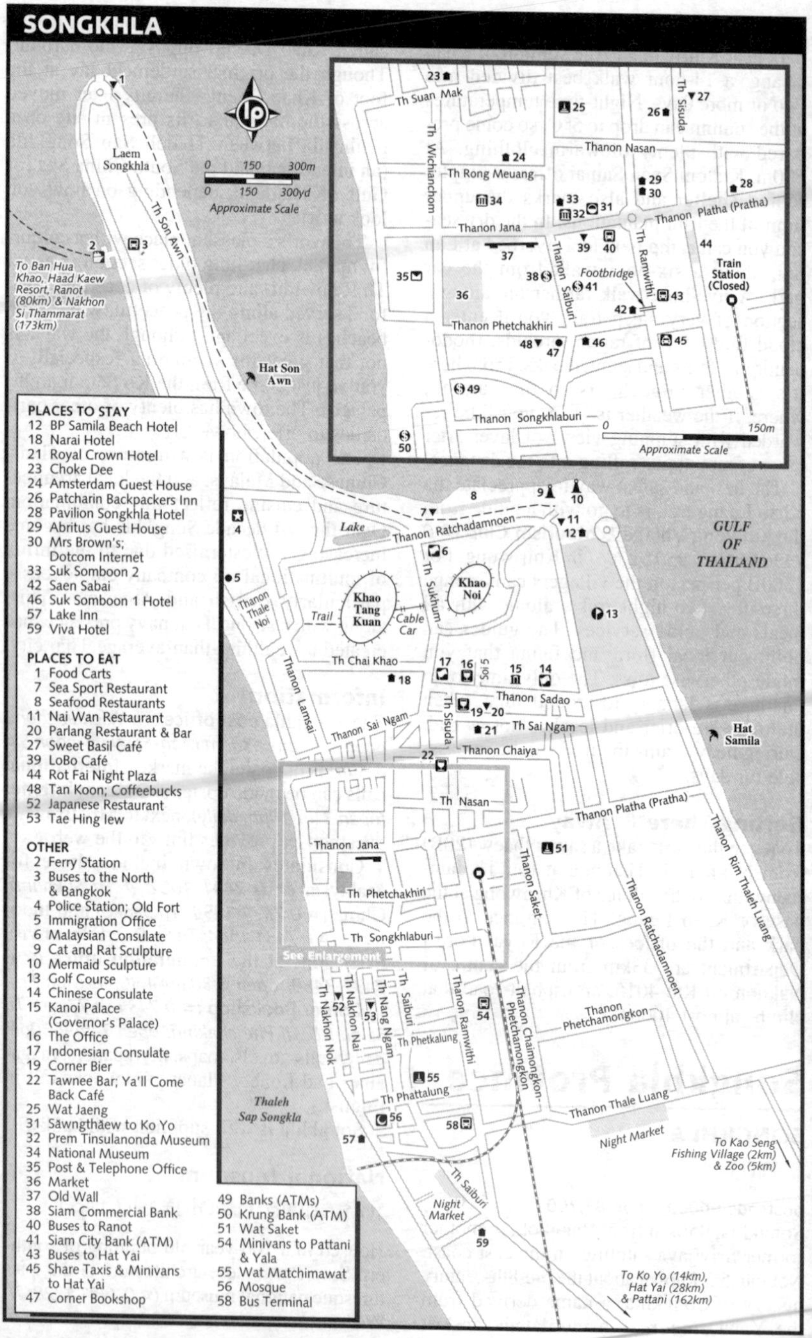
SONGKHLA
PLACES TO STAY
12 BP Samila Beach Hotel
18 Narai Hotel
21 Royal Crown Hotel
23 Choke Dee
24 Amsterdam Guest House
26 Patcharin Backpackers Inn
28 Pavilion Songkhla Hotel
29 Abritus Guest House
30 Mrs Brown's; Dotcom Internet
33 Suk Somboon 2
42 Saen Sabai
46 Suk Somboon 1 Hotel
57 Lake Inn
59 Viva Hotel
PLACES TO EAT
1 Food Carts
7 Sea Sport Restaurant
8 Seafood Restaurants
11 Nai Wan Restaurant
20 Parlang Restaurant & Bar
27 Sweet Basil Café
39 LoBo Café
44 Rot Fai Night Plaza
48 Tan Koon; Coffeebucks
52 Japanese Restaurant
53 Tae Hing Iew
OTHER
2 Ferry Station
3 Buses to the North & Bangkok
4 Police Station; Old Fort
5 Immigration Office
6 Malaysian Consulate
9 Cat and Rat Sculpture
10 Mermaid Sculpture
13 Golf Course
14 Chinese Consulate
15 Kanoi Palace (Governor's Palace)
16 The Office
17 Indonesian Consulate
19 Corner Bier
22 Tawnee Bar; Ya'll Come Back Café
25 Wat Jaeng
31 Săwngthăew to Ko Yo
32 Prem Tinsulanonda Museum
34 National Museum
35 Post & Telephone Office
36 Market
37 Old Wall
38 Siam Commercial Bank
40 Buses to Ranot
41 Siam City Bank (ATM)
43 Buses to Hat Yai
45 Share Taxis & Minivans to Hat Yai
47 Corner Bookshop
49 Banks (ATMs)
50 Krung Bank (ATM)
51 Wat Saket
54 Minivans to Pattani & Yala
55 Wat Matchimawat
56 Mosque
58 Bus Terminal
Laem Songkhla
Th Son Awn
Hat Son Awn
0 150 300m
0 150 300yd
Approximate Scale
To Ban Hua Khao, Haad Kaew Resort, Ranot (80km) & Nakhon Si Thammarat (173km)
Th Suan Mak
Th Wichianchom
Th Rong Meuang
Thanon Nasan
Th Sisuda
Thanon Platha (Pratha)
Thanon Jana
Th Ramwithi
Thanon Saiburi
Footbridge
Train Station (Closed)
Thanon Phetchakhiri
Thanon Songkhlaburi
0 150m
Approximate Scale
Lake
Thanon Ratchadamnoen
GULF OF THAILAND
Khao Noi
Khao Tang Kuan
Th Sukhum
Cable Car
Trail
Thanon Thale Noi
Thanon Lamsai
Th Chai Khao
Soi 5
Thanon Sadao
Th Sisuda
Thanon Sai Ngam
Th Sai Ngam
Thanon Chaiya
Hat Samila
Th Nasan
Thanon Platha (Pratha)
Thanon Rim Thaleh Luang
Thanon Jana
Th Phetchakhiri
Th Songkhlaburi
See Enlargement
Thanon Saket
Thanon Ratchadamnoen
Thanon Ramwithi
Thanon Chaimongkon-Phetchamongkon
Thanon Phetchamongkon
Th Nakhon Nok
Th Nakhon Nai
Th Nang Ngam
Th Saiburi
Th Phetkalung
Th Phattalung
Thaleh Sap Songkla
Thanon Thale Luang
Night Market
To Kao Seng Fishing Village (2km) & Zoo (5km)
Th Saiburi
Night Market
To Ko Yo (14km), Hat Yai (28km) & Pattani (162km)

Wed-Sun, closed national holidays). Along with the innate architectural charms of its curved rooflines and thick walls, it's a quiet, breezy building with a tranquil garden at the front. The museum contains exhibits from all national art-style periods, particularly the Srivijaya, including a 7th- to 9th-century Shivalingam found in Pattani. Also on display are Thai and Chinese ceramics, and sumptuous Chinese furniture and a lacquer bookcase owned by the area's local Chinese aristocracy.

Prem Tinsulanonda Museum

พิพิธพัณฑ์เปรมติณสูลานนท์

The Prem Tinsulanonda Museum *(cnr Th Jana & Th Saiburi; admission free; open 8.30am-4pm Tues-Sun)* is touted as the birthplace of Thailand's 16th prime minister, who served from 1980 to 1988. The 'museum' is a wooden house that was actually built recently upon the site of Prem's birthplace, and contains some of the furniture and personal effects that graced the original home. While something of a shrine to Prem, the museum is worth a visit even if you have little interest in Thai politics – it's a charming example of the combination of breezy verandas and cosy interiors that constitutes the traditional Thai house.

Temples & Chedi

Wat Matchimawat *(Wat Klang; Th Saiburi)* typifies the Sino-Thai temple architecture of 17th-century Songkhla. One of the *wíhăan* contains an old marble Buddha image and a small museum. Another temple with similar characteristics, **Wat Jaeng** *(Th Ramwithi)*, was recently renovated.

There is a Singhalese-style *chedi* and royal pavilion on top of **Khao Tang Kuan**, a hill rising up at the northern end of the peninsula; to reach the top you'll have to climb 305 steps.

Songkhla Architecture

All that remains of the old King Narai-era city is a lengthy section of wall along Th Jana near the national museum and main market in the centre of town. A few patches of 19th- and early-20th-century architecture can be seen near the inland sea waterfront. Walk along the back streets parallel to the waterfront – Th Nang Ngam, Th Nakhon Nai and Th Nakhon Nok – to find older Songkhla buildings showing Chinese, Portuguese and Malay influence. Many of them disappeared during Thailand's economic boom, but a few have been restored and hopefully the city will support some sort of historical architectural legacy.

Beaches

Hat Samila is a casuarina-lined beach and pleasant for strolling. At the north end, sitting atop some rocks, a **bronze mermaid sculpture** is depicted squeezing water from her long hair in a tribute to Mae Thorani (the Hindu-Buddhist earth goddess). Locals treat the figure like a shrine, tying the waist with coloured cloth and rubbing the breasts for good luck. Near the mermaid statue is a **cat and rat statue**, which represents the islands offshore (who are supposed to look like their namesake animals).

The less-frequented **Hat Son Awn** extends north of Hat Samila. There are a few seafood restaurants at the south end of this stretch, with less pleasant ones farther north on the other side of the road. Jogging or bicycle riding are good activities here; rent bicycles at Amsterdam or Abritus guesthouses.

Other Attractions

To the north of centre are the two forested hills of **Khao Tang Kuan** and **Khao Noi** (also known as Monkey mountain, since hordes of monkeys live here). They're safe to explore during the day, but be careful at night, when druggies find refuge there. A cable car is being built on the east side of Khao Tang Kuan and may be operational when you visit.

Just north of Khao Tang Kuan is a manmade **lake** full of catfish. If there's anyone selling fish food, you buy some, toss the stuff in and watch the waters boil to a feeding frenzy. A legendary 2m catfish is supposed to inhabit this lake.

A few kilometres south of Hat Samila is **Kao Seng**, a quaint Muslim fishing village – this is where the tourist photos of gaily painted fishing vessels are taken. Săwngthăew run regularly between Songkhla and Kao Seng for 8B per person.

Places to Stay – Budget

If you're a budget traveller, you're in luck here; Songkhla has an exceptional number of good and inexpensive guesthouses that cater to travellers.

Amsterdam Guest House *(☎ 0 7431 4890; 15/3 Th Rong Meuang; rooms with shared bath 180-200B)* is a popular homey place set up to serve travellers. Bicycles/motorcycles are available to rent for 100/200B per day. Rooms are basic, and there's a lounge and restaurant nearby.

Abritus Guest House *(☎ 0 7432 6047; e abritus_th@yahoo.com; 28/16 Th Ramwithi; rooms with shared bath 200B)* offers four spacious, clean rooms. Downstairs is a good restaurant and one Internet connection. English, German, Russian and Bulgarian are spoken, and bikes and motorcycles are available for rent.

ABC Guest House *(☎ 0 7431 2558; 28/14 Th Ramwithi; w www.abcguesthouse.info; dorm beds 130B, rooms 220-300B)* is a brand-new place a couple of doors down from Abritus, and has a Thailand rarity: dorm beds.

Mrs Brown's *(☎ 0 7432 7475; 28/19 Th Ramwithi; rooms 150-180B)* is right near Abritus and run by a friendly Englishman. It's a popular place with well-furnished rooms; in the future there may also be small dorm rooms.

Patcharin Backpackers Inn *(☎ 0 7431 1821; 65 Th Sisuda; rooms with shared bath 230-250B)* offers six beautiful, large rooms. It's new, clean, friendly and central to Songkhla's bar scene. There's a tiny garden at the front.

Narai Hotel *(☎ 0 7431 1078; 14 Th Chai Khao; rooms with shared bath 150-200B)* hardly looks like a hotel; it's a faded yellow wooden house with overgrown yard. It's friendly but not central, and rooms are clean and fairly quiet. There is one huge double room with bathroom for 250B.

Choke Dee *(☎ 0 7431 2275; 14/19 Th Wichianchom; rooms with fan 280, with air-con 380-400B)* offers a good deal, with large, clean, modern and bright tiled rooms along spacious halls and sitting areas. Pastel blues and a modern ambience emanate from this place, which is a bit less homey than those mentioned previously.

Suk Somboon 1 Hotel *(☎ 0 7431 1049; 40 Th Phetchakhiri; rooms with fan 180-250B, with air-con 300B)* has reasonable budget rooms with some personality. Rooms facing east are brighter than those on the other side, which sport wall views.

Saen Sabai *(☎ 0 7444 1027; 1 Th Phetchakhiri; rooms with shared bath 150B, with fan/air-con 220/270B)*, right behind the Caltex petrol station, is a small place with dark, musty rooms – but it's friendly!

Places to Stay – Mid-Range & Top End

Suk Somboon 2 *(☎ 0 7431 3809; 14 Th Saiburi; rooms with fan 200B, with air-con 400-500B)* is actually two buildings, an old and a new, right next to each other. The new half has pleasant smallish mid-range rooms with good showers, TV and fridge, while the old half is much more basic.

Royal Crown Hotel *(☎ 0 7431 2174, fax 0 7432 1027; 38 Th Sai Ngam; rooms with air-con 400-450B)* comes with good, carpeted mid-range rooms, and is located right near the bar area.

Viva Hotel *(☎ 0 7432 1033; 547/2 Th Nakhon Nok; singles/doubles with air-con 500/600B)* has decent, modern (though not luxurious) rooms. There's a coffee shop with karaoke, and the lobby is nice, but the place isn't central.

Lake Inn *(☎ 0 7432 1044; e lakeinn@hotmail.com; 301 Th Nakhon Nok; rooms with air-con 390-590B)* isn't really worth it except for the 590B rooms with balconies and the views. The halls are worn and rooms modest.

BP Samila Beach Hotel *(☎ 0 7444 0222, fax 0 7444 0442; 8 Th Ratchadamnoen; rooms with air-con from 1150B)* lies like a swanky monster next to the beach, Songkhla's best accommodation. All the amenities are on tap; pay the extra 100B for sea views, as they're worth it. Balconies are large, the amoeba-like pool is inviting and the Internet is available near the grand lobby. It's not a bad deal at all, if you can afford it, and rates include breakfast.

Pavilion Songkhla Hotel *(☎ 0 7444 1850, fax 0 7432 3716; w www.pavilionhotel.co.th; 17 Th Platha; rooms with air-con from 750B)* is a great deal. The lobby is fancy, the location is good, and the large, luxurious rooms have some wood panelling, satellite TV and carpeting.

Haad Kaew Resort *(☎ 0 7433 1059, fax 0 7433 1220; bungalows 527B, rooms with air-con 771-899B)* is actually a long drive outside Songkhla, on the peninsula north of the channel. This large, pleasant resort has its own lagoon, beach front and pool on its landscaped grounds. Comfortable rooms and bungalows come with all the amenities.

Places to Eat

For cheap food, try the string of good, inexpensive **seafood** places along Th Ratchadamoen near Hat Samila. Right at the tip of Songkhla's northern finger are **food carts** that set out mats in the grassy park-like waterfront area. And, at the south end of Th Sisuda is a night market called **Rot Fai Night Plaza** – on Sunday, a morning market pops up here.

Sea Sport Restaurant (*☎ 0 7432 7244; Th Ratchadamnoen; dishes 50-200B; open 4pm-midnight daily*) is highly recommended by locals for its seafood. The ambience is unbeatable, at least when it's not raining: outside wooden benches (some shaped like boats) are set on a grassy, bricked terrace while a cloth tarp blows overhead. At night everything's lit up romantically, and the breezy sea is right there.

Nai Wan Restaurant (*☎ 0 7431 1295; Th Ratchadamnoen; dishes 35-200B; open 10am-9.30pm daily*) is popular for its crab dishes (bring moist wipes!). Also on the menu are Thai salads, soups and other seafood offerings, as well as a few vegie entries. The large, casual space is near the little mermaid sculpture.

Tan Koon (*☎ 0 7431 3297; cnr Th Phetchakhiri & Th Saiburi; dishes 35-100B; open 8.30am-7.30pm daily*), set back from the street and inside a leafy garden area, is a small Thai place with some breakfast items. From Th Phetchakhiri you go through a shop to reach the restaurant. **Coffeebucks** is next door and brews passable java for 20B to 50B per shot.

LoBo Cafe (*☎ 0 7431 1788; T10/1-3 Th Platha; dishes 40-120B; open 7am-10pm daily*) cooks up Western breakfasts and Thai food in a modern, homey and friendly atmosphere. It rents motorcycles, too.

Ya'll Come Back Café (*Tawnee Bar; Th Sisuda; dishes 150B; open 8am-6pm daily*) is energetically run by two southern boys from the USA. Generous portions of home-cooked Creole and southern dishes, such as Jambalaya, chicken dumplings and Spanish omelettes (as well as other breakfast items), are served in a tiny, dim bar atmosphere.

Sweet Basil Cafe (*50/2-3 Th Sisuda; dishes 50-120B; open 10am-midnight daily*) serves good Vietnamese and Thai food in a pretty, peaceful setting – at least compared to the bar scene outside. The service is good, and a large picture menu makes ordering easy.

Tae Hieng Iew (*85 Th Nang Ngam*), south of the town centre, serves locally recommended seafood in a decent atmosphere with nice wooden furniture. Look for it just south of the elaborate Chinese cinema.

Abritus Guest House and **Mrs Brown's** both have their own popular restaurants, with a half-dozen tables and CNN on TV. Food reflects their clientele's tastes: there are Western breakfasts, burgers and basic Thai dishes. Abritus adds Bulgarian meatballs and kebabs.

The seafood of Ko Yo (see Around Songkhla) has a reputation for being some of the best in the area. Restaurants are located near the main island road, next to the water.

Entertainment

A string of bars just east of the Indonesian consulate is jokingly referred to among local expats as 'The Dark Side'. Not as ominous as it sounds, this strip caters mainly to oil company employees and other Westerners living in Songkhla. **The Office**, the bar nearest Soi 5, is run by an Englishman.

On nearby happenin' Th Sisuda, interspersed with some restaurants, are a few other casual bars worth checking out. **Corner Bier** is a small corner place where Songkhla's Canadian community hangs out. **Parlang**, where the Hash House Harriers meet every Saturday at 3pm, is another popular expat place – the cashew chicken here has been especially recommended.

Getting There & Away

Air THAI operates several daily flights between Bangkok and nearby Hat Yai; see the Hat Yai section later in this chapter for details.

Bus, Minivan & Share Taxi Songkhla is something of a Hat Yai transport satellite; from Songkhla, you'll have to go to Hat Yai to reach most long-distance destinations in the south. There are a few destinations originating in Songkhla, though.

Across from the ferry station is a small, strangely located government bus terminal. Four 2nd-class buses go daily to Bangkok

(437B); these stop in Chumphon (245B), Nakhon Si Thammarat (100B) and Surat Thani (150B), among other places. One VIP bus to Bangkok leaves at 4.45pm (870B), while three 1st-class buses (562B) leave late afternoon and evening. There's one ordinary bus (312B) at 11.30am.

To Hat Yai, buses (16B), minivans (20B) share taxis (25B) take around 40 minutes and leave from Th Ramwithi. Minivans to Pattani and Yala (70B) leave from the southern part of Th Sisuda, while ordinary buses to Nakhon Si Thammarat (70B) leave from the not-very-useful bus terminal south of town.

Boat Towards the head of Laem Songkhla (Songkhla's finger-like peninsula), there is a government-run ferry that plies the short distance across the channel where the Thaleh Sap Songkhla inland sea meets the Gulf of Thailand. The barge-like ferry carries about 15 cars, plus assorted motorcycles and pedestrians. The fare for the seven-minute ride is 18B per car, 5B per motorcycle and 1B per person; it runs 5am to 9pm daily.

Getting Around

Share taxis to the Hat Yai airport cost 150B to 180B; private taxis charge 400B.

Săwngthăew circulate around town for 10B. Motorcycle taxis around town cost 10B to 20B; rates double at night.

Amsterdam and Abritus guesthouses rent bicycles and motorcycles; LoBo Cafe just rents motorcycles. Prices are 100B per day for bicycles, 200B for motorcycles.

AROUND SONGKHLA

Songkhla Zoo

This is a new (and not quite finished), surprisingly humane and unusual zoo *(☎ 0 7433 6038; admission per person/car/motorcycle 30/30/10B; open 9am-6pm daily)*. The hilly enclosures are large and in a natural setting, with lots of greenery between exhibits. So much greenery, in fact, that the whole place really needs to be explored in a vehicle – distances are almost too long to walk. Roads lace the mountainside where the zoo is located, connecting the exhibits to each other (this lofty setting affords occasional good views of the surrounding countryside). Unfortunately the zoo's roads are pretty close to the animals, who are no doubt exposed to the motor noises.

Animals on display include rhinos, elephants, ostriches, camels, orang-utans, chimpanzees, and birds such as flamingos, parrots and hornbills. If you're lucky you can watch the tigers being fed: plucked chickens are suspended from ropes, and the beasts take running leaps out to grab them.

The zoo is south of Songkhla about 5km, on the Songkhla–Chana road. Follow the signs; the turn-off is at the Esso petrol station, then it's another 500m to the gate. It's best to rent a motorcycle (or bicycle if you like pedalling up hills) to get here, since then you'll have transport within the zoo.

Ko Yo

เกาะยอ

An island set in the inland sea, Ko Yo (pronounced kaw yaw) is a peaceful, country-road-filled place surrounded by fish farms and supporting a small **cotton-weaving** industry. The good-quality, distinctive *phâa kàw yaw* is hand woven on rustic looms and available on the spot at 'wholesale' prices – meaning you still have to bargain but have a chance of undercutting the usual city price.

There are many different households around the island engaged in cotton weaving and they sell their wares at a small market off the highway.

You can hire a motorcycle in Songkhla (make sure you know how to operate one first, however) and tour the quiet backroads of Ko Yo: tiny villages, scenic coastline, forested hills, spiritual wát – it's a very local treat, and off the beaten track. And don't leave Ko Yo without trying its famous seafood: look for shorefront restaurants along the island's main road.

Folklore Museum At the northern end of the island, about 2km past the market, is this large and excellent museum *(☎ 0 7433 1184; admission 50B; open 8.30am-5pm daily)* run by the Institute of Southern Thai Studies. Opened in 1991, the complex of Thai-style pavilions overlooking the Thaleh Sap Songkhla contains well-curated collections of folk art, as well as a library and souvenir shop. Be ready to hike, however; the museum ripples down a hillside, each display room connected by stairs, stairs and more stairs. Displays include pottery, beads, shadow puppets, basketry, textiles, musical instruments, jewellery, boats, religious art, weapons, and various household, agricultural and fishing implements. Among these is a superb collection of coconut-grater seats carved into various animal and human shapes, as well as a glassware display that Martha Stewart would salivate over.

On the institute grounds is a series of small gardens, including one occasionally used for traditional shadow-theatre performances; a medicinal herb garden; and a bamboo culture garden.

Getting There & Away Frequent săwngthăew to Ko Yo leave from Th Platha in Songkhla (10B, 30 minutes). To stop at the small market ask for *nâa tàlàat,* 'in front of the market'. To get off at the museum, about 2km past the market, ask for *phíphítháphan*. Buses to Ranot pass through Ko Yo for the same fare.

You could also hire a motorcycle in Songkhla and scoot your way here, even making a loop north, coming back into town via the short ferry ride across the channel. This is a long distance, though – about 20km – and it includes hairy highways and windy bridges. Make sure you've completely mastered the art of motorcycle driving in Thailand.

Of course you could also rent a bicycle to do this ride, but unless you're a Greg LeMonde wannabe you probably shouldn't risk the next-day leg-muscle cramps.

Khukhut Waterbird Sanctuary
อุทยานนกน้ำคูขุด

On the eastern shore of the Songkhla inland sea, about 30km north of Songkhla near the village of Sathing Phra, is a 520-sq-km sanctuary for waterbirds. Together with the similar Thaleh Noi Wildlife Preserve in Phattalung, the wetlands are habitat for over 200 resident and migrant bird species from the entire Thaleh Sap, including bitterns, egrets and herons (these three are called *nók yaang* in Thai), rare Javanese pond herons, fishing eagles *(nók yìaw plaa)*, cormorants *(nók kaa náam)*, storks, kites, hawks, falcons, plovers, sandpipers, terns *(nók naang nuan)* and kingfishers.

A book that's available from the **park office** *(☎ 0 7439 7042)* has detailed information on the waterbirds and maps showing their habitat. The best months to go birdwatching are November and December, and the worst are from May to August.

The park office also arranges boat trips – it's about 250B for a one-hour bird-watching excursion, and 500B for two hours to see birds and stop at two islands. Each boat can hold up to seven people.

Buses to Sathing Phra are 20B – take a red Ranot-bound bus. From the bus stop in front of the Sathing Phra district office you can walk the 3km to the park, or get a motorcycle taxi for 20B.

HAT YAI
หาดใหญ่

postcode 90110 • pop 191,200

Hat Yai, 933km from Bangkok, is southern Thailand's commercial centre and one of the kingdom's largest cities, although it's only a district in Songkhla Province. A steady stream of customers from Malaysia once kept Hat Yai's central business district booming, but Southeast Asia's economic doldrums, along with the Malaysian government's ban on the exchange of Malaysian currency anywhere outside Malaysia, has slowed things down a bit. You wouldn't know it by walking along its streets, though – it's still very much a bustling international market town, and everything from dried fruit to stereos is sold in shops along the parallel streets of Th Niphat Uthit Nos 1, 2 and 3.

Visually, Hat Yai is a big city with big buildings, including some large department stores. Busy streets are filled with traffic, while walkways are lined with hawkers and their shoppers. Culturally, Hat Yai is very much a Chinese town at its centre, with loads of gold shops, Chinese restaurants and Mandarin-specked conversations. A substantial Muslim minority is concentrated in certain sections of the city, especially near the mosque off Th Niphat Songkhrao.

Hat Yai is a major transport hub for travel around southern Thailand and between Thailand and Malaysia. Many travellers stop over in the city on their way to/from Malaysia.

Information

The **TAT office** (☎ *0 7424 3747;* ⓔ *tathatyai@hatyai.inet.co.th; 1/1 Soi 2, Th Niphat Uthit 3; open 8.30am-4.30pm daily)* is towards the south end of town. Nearby is the **tourist police** *(☎ 0 7424 6733; open 24hr)*.

The Hat Yai **immigration office** *(☎ 0 7424 3019; Th Phetkasem)* is near the railway bridge, in the same complex as a police station. The nearest Malaysian consulate is in Songkhla.

Hat Yai is loaded with **banks**, especially along Th Niphat Uthit 2 and 3 near the Th

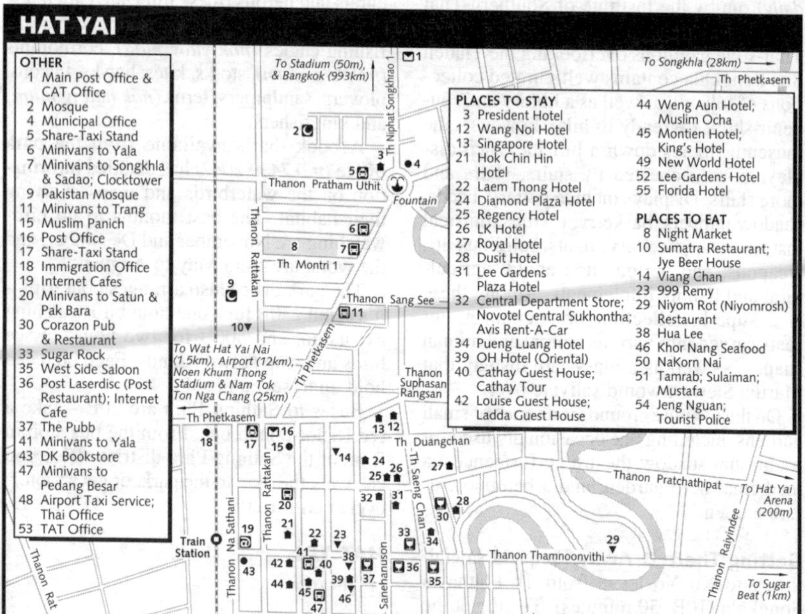

Thamnoonvithi intersection. If you have Malaysian ringgit, the banks won't take them but many mid-range and top-end hotels will.

Hat Yai's **main post office** *(1 Th Niphat Songkhrao; open 8.30am-4.30pm Mon-Fri, 9am-noon Sat & Sun)* is at the very north of town; it has an adjacent **telephone office** *(open 7am-11pm daily)*. A more convenient **post office** *(Th Na Sathani)* lies two blocks northeast of the train station.

IO Net *(open 9am-midnight daily)*, right in front of the train station, is one of two Internet cafés next to each other.

Hat Yai is full of travel agencies. If you can't get a recommendation, try **Cathay Tour** *(☎ 0 7423 5044; 93/1 Th Niphat Uthit 2)*. Staff are used to dealing with *faràng* and offer a full range of services, including visa advice.

Wat Hat Yai Nai

วัดหาดใหญ่ใน

About 1.5km west of town, on Th Phetkasem, this wát features a 35m reclining Buddha (Phra Phut Mahatamongkon). Inside the image's gigantic base is a curious little museum and mausoleum with a souvenir shop. To get here, hop on a săwngthăew near the intersection of Th Niphat Uthit 1 and Th Phetkasem and get off after crossing Saphan U Taphao (U Taphao Bridge) – it costs about 10B.

Bullfighting

Bullfighting, involving two bulls in opposition rather than a person and a bull, takes place on the first Saturday of each month, or on the second Saturday if the first Saturday is a *wan phrá* (Buddhist worship day; full, half or new moon). Fights are held at Noen Khum Thong Stadium on the way to the airport (15B by săwngthăew).

On the first Sunday of each month another round is held in Klonggit district (between Hat Yai and Sadao). Matches take place continuously from 9am to 4pm and entry is 20B to 70B or more per round, depending on the bulls' reputation – although many hundred times that amount changes hands during the nonstop betting by Thai spectators. Check with the TAT office for details.

Places to Stay – Budget

Hat Yai has dozens of hotels within walking distance of the train station. During Chinese New Year (late February to early March), the prices double for most budget rooms. Malaysian holidays also cause a steep hike in room prices.

Cathay Guest House *(☎ 0 7424 3815, fax 0 7435 4104; 93/1 Th Niphat Uthit 2; dorm beds 100B, rooms with fan 160-250B)*, three blocks east of the train station, is a backpacker magnet. Very handy are its four-bed dorms and basic rooms, laundry service, accessible travel information and its good location. There's a communal area upstairs at reception, and a reliable travel agency sits downstairs at the entrance.

Weng Aun Hotel *(☎ 0 7426 1045; Th Niphat Uthit 1; rooms from 120B)* is a friendly place four doors down from the Muslim Ocha restaurant. It's one of Hat Yai's last remaining examples of Sino-Portuguese architecture. It's a charmingly decrepit building with very basic singles.

Hok Chin Hin Hotel *(☎ 0 7424 3258, fax 0 7435 0131; Th Niphat Uthit 1; singles/doubles 150/240B)* is another good deal a couple of blocks from the train station. Bright, clean rooms have fans and good furniture, and there's a restaurant downstairs

Ladda Guest House *(☎ 0 7422 0233; 13-15 Th Thamnoonvithi; rooms with fan 200-240B, rooms with air-con 290-320B)* has some comfortable, very good budget rooms that are well furnished and clean. Stairs and halls are narrow enough to make you worry about the lack of fire exits, though.

Louise Guest House *(☎ 0 7422 0966; 21-23 Th Thamnoonvithi; rooms with fan/air-con 300/400B)* comes with cosy halls and small, decent rooms – though some have no views. This place is set back from the road a bit.

Laem Thong Hotel *(☎ 0 7435 2301, fax 0 7423 7574; ⓔ laemthong99@hotmail.com; 46 Th Thamnoonvithi; rooms with fan 260B, with air-con 300-450B)* is not far from the train station. There are large, basic and noisy rooms – especially those that are facing the street. It's a popular place, though, and is a decent deal.

Singapore Hotel *(☎ 0 7423 7478; 62-66 Th Suphasan Rangsan; rooms with fan 270B, with air-con 380-450B)* is friendly, with good, clean, carpeted rooms that aren't too fancy or bright. The better ones have satellite TV and hot water.

Pueng Luang Hotel *(☎ 0 7424 4548; 241-245 Th Saeng Chan; rooms with fan/air-con*

270/400B) has some huge, dark rooms with high porthole windows. It could use more furniture to fill the bleak spaces and cover the peeling walls.

Wang Noi Hotel (☎/fax 0 7423 1024; 114/1 Th Saeng Chan; rooms with fan 270-340B, with air-con 370-390B) gives you good-sized, tiled abodes. The rooms with air-con are functional and unexciting, while avoid the windowless rooms with fans. Halls are bleak and worn.

Dusit Hotel (☎ 0 7423 2141, fax 0 7423 6479; 25/3 Th Pracharom; rooms with fan/air-con 300/400B) is Chinese-run, with good, clean and well-presented rooms. It's not anything special, but is on a quieter side street near some bar and music venues.

King's Hotel (☎ 0 7426 1700, fax 0 7423 6103; 126 Th Niphat Uthit 1; rooms with air-con 390-490B) offers nice, clean, dark rooms with fridge, satellite TV and wall views. The outdoor halls are set back a bit, and there's a little café on the ground floor.

Places to Stay – Mid-Range

For some reason hotels in Hat Yai take a disproportionate leap upwards in quality once you pay another 100B to 200B a night.

New World (☎ 0 7423 0100, fax 0 7423 0105; 152-156 Th Niphat Uthit 2; rooms with air-con 500B) offers acceptable, nice rooms with fridge and TV, though a few have wall views. It's not a bad deal.

OH Hotel (☎ 0 7423 0142, fax 0 7435 4824; 135 Th Niphat Uthit 3; rooms with air-con 550-600B) was, at the time of writing, offering free massage and breakfast (not necessarily together) – no guarantee that this deal still holds, however. Good, comfortable rooms come with fridge, satellite TV and bright, large windows.

Royal Hotel (☎ 0 7435 1451, fax 0 7424 3246; 106 Th Prachathipat; rooms with air-con from 580B) is a large, white hotel with 136 good-sized, comfortable rooms with TV and fridge. The Sharky Pub on the premises presents itself as 'extremely fizzy night after night…hosted by hottest sexy teenager singers'. This has to be good.

Montien Hotel (☎ 0 7423 4386, fax 0 7423 0043; 120-124 Th Niphat Uthit 1; rooms with air-con 550B) offers some very nice central rooms with TV and fridge. There's Internet access in the lobby, and as a whole this place is a good deal.

Places to Stay – Top End

Top-end accommodation in Hat Yai is mainly geared to Malaysian Chinese week-end visitors, so rates are considerably lower than in Bangkok or Chiang Mai. All rooms are air-conditioned.

Lee Gardens Hotel (☎ 0 7423 4422, fax 0 7423 1888; 1 Th Lee Pattana; rooms 600-700B) should not be confused with its rather more extravagant sister uptown. Very nice rooms live in this fairly quiet locale, though the hall carpets beg to be replaced. The hotel is half-way elegant and a good deal overall.

President Hotel (☎ 0 7434 9500, fax 0 7423 0609; 420 Th Phetkasem; rooms 600-1200B) is a good choice in a quiet, though not central, location. Rooms are clean, neat and comfortable.

Florida Hotel (☎ 0 7423 4555, fax 0 7423 4553; 8 Th Siphunawat; rooms 895B) looms at the southern edge of the city centre. Rooms aren't posh enough for the price, though you could try to bargain a bit. The location is quiet, and there's also a restaurant and pub downstairs.

Diamond Plaza Hotel (☎ 0 7423 0130, fax 0 7423 9824; W www.diamondplaza.co.th; 62 Th Niphat Uthit 3; rooms 990-2800B) claims to be 'the most generous and gentle hotel' – at least the rooms are worth the price range. The location is central and there's a pool.

Regency Hotel (☎ 0 7435 3333, fax 0 7423 4102; W www.regencyhatyai.com; 23 Th Prachathipat; rooms from 1398B) features 436 rooms on 26 floors. It's OK, not ultra-luxurious. There's a restaurant, coffee shop and pool on the 5th floor, and the entrance is on the corner.

Lee Gardens Plaza Hotel (☎ 0 7426 1111, fax 0 7435 3555; W www.leeplaza.com; 29 Th Pratchathipat; rooms from 1549B) shouldn't be confused with the Lee Gardens Hotel farther south. This one is much more upmarket, with a dramatic 10th-floor lobby (though getting there via elevators from the shopping mall downstairs forces you to mix with the rabble). The acceptable rooms have great views, and there's a 12th-floor pool and park-like spaces. The rates include breakfast.

Novotel Central Sukhontha (☎ 0 7435 2222, fax 0 7435 2223; W www.centralhotelsresorts.com; 3 Th Sanehanuson; rooms from 2200B) has a nice 6th-floor lobby and comfortable, fully outfitted rooms. The facilities include a pool, sauna, restaurants and fitness centre, as well as a business centre. It's right above a shopping mall and the rates include breakfast.

Places to Eat

You won't go hungry in this city: Hat Yai is southern Thailand's gourmet mecca, offering fresh seafood from both the Gulf of Thailand and the Andaman Sea, Muslim *rotii* and curries, Chinese noodles and dim sum. There are also plenty of birds' nest and sharks' fin soup places, but harvesting methods for the animals involved is exceptionally cruel – think twice before partaking in these Chinese delicacies.

Lots of good, cheap restaurants can be found along the three Niphat Uthit roads, in the markets off side streets between them, and also near the train station. For fancier Chinese food try upmarket hotels. Many Hat Yai restaurants, particularly the Chinese ones, close in the afternoon between 2pm and 6pm – unusual for Thailand.

For cheap eats or self-catering, go to the basement of **Central department store**, which has a cafeteria and large supermarket. The extensive **night market** along Th Montri 1 offers fresh, inexpensive seafood dishes.

Hua Lee *(cnr Th Niphat Uthit 3 & Th Thamnoonvithi; dishes 30-50B; open 4.30pm-2am daily)* displays a great photograph from the flood that visited Hat Yai in 2000; the water level mark can be seen on the wall. It's an open, casual and very busy corner place, with good Chinese food that arrives quickly at your table. Its staff are used to travellers.

Jeng Nguan *(no Roman-script sign; cnr Th Niphat Utit 1 & Th Siphunawat; open 11am-2pm & 5pm-9pm)* offers dishes like *tâo hûu thâwt kràwp* (fried bean curd), *bàmìi plaa phàt* (fried noodles with fish) and *kíaw plaa* (fish wonton). It's a cop hangout, since the police station is around the corner.

Viang Chan *(☎ 0 7424 3668; 12 Th Niphat Uthit 2; dishes 50-100B; open 10.30am-9pm daily)* is a good, clean and non-pretentious Chinese restaurant.

Niyom Rot *(Niyomrosh; 219-221 Th Thamnoonvithi; open 10.30am-2pm & 5pm-9.30pm daily)* is an old, established Thai restaurant across from the lime green Spa Hotel. The *plaa kràbàwk thâwt* (whole sea mullet fried with eggs intact) is particularly prized here. It's set up for big groups, so the atmosphere is not intimate.

Khor Nang Seafood *(☎ 0 7423 8071; 162-1164 Th Niphat Uthit 3; dishes 35-80B; open 6pm-11pm daily)* serves up locally recommended seafood; the stuff's displayed right out the front. Dim sum is also available in the industrial setting, as is regular Thai food.

999 Remy *(Th Niphat Uthit 2; open 6am-9.30pm daily)* is a small no-frills place serving lots of cheap curries and fried food in a casual environment.

NaKorn Nai *(☎ 0 7423 2550; 16-7 Th Niphat Uthit 2; dishes 30-60B; open 7.30am-8pm Fri-Wed)* ensconces you in a new, modern and trendy atmosphere. Thai and Western foods are both served, as is breakfast.

Muslim Ocha *(Th Niphat Uthit 1; dishes 25-40B; open 6am-7pm daily)* is a small, clean place that's still going strong, with *rotii kaeng* (*roti chanai* in Malay) in the mornings and curries all day. This is one of the few Muslim cafés in the town where women – even non-Muslim or foreign women – seem welcome.

Sumatra Restaurant *(☎ 0 7424 6459; 55/1 Th Rattakan; dishes 30-100B; open 6am-9pm daily)* is located in a light green building. It's large, clean and modern, and serves a bit of everything: curries, seafood, vegetables, beef, chicken and salad dishes.

Jye Beer House *(☎ 0 7423 6521; 49/3 Th Rattakan; dishes 45-110B; open 9am-10pm daily)*, near Sumatra, caters to Western tastes with steak, Italian food and Heineken beer; the decidedly Western decor is smart and comfortable. There's also Thai food and Singha beer on the menu, however.

On Th Niyomrat, between Niphat Uthit 1 and 2, are **Sulaiman**, **Tamrab** and **Mustafa**, all casual and inexpensive Muslim restaurants open from approximately 7am to 9pm daily.

Entertainment

Most of the many clubs and coffee shops in town cater to Malaysian clientele. Try the bigger hotels for discos, which charge about 150B for cover. Other entertainment options include:

Post Laserdisc *(☎ 0 7423 2027; Th Thamnoonvithi; open 9am-2am daily)* seems more of a restaurant than a bar, and serves Thai, Western and Chinese foods, which include breakfast. Plenty of alcoholic drinks can be ordered as well (especially during happy hour from 4pm to 9pm) and there's live music nightly at 8.45pm. A large projector screen shows movies, music videos and sports shows.

The Pubb *(☎ 0 7423 1029; open 3pm-2am Mon-Fri, 11.30am-2am Sat & Sun)*, near Post Laserdisc, offers similar fare for similar clientele: live music, sports on a big screen, and decent food selections. It's a good place.

Sugar Rock *(open 8am-midnight daily)* is also nearby and exudes a split personality: one side has nostalgic decor, while the other is modern and trendy. Food and drinks are easily available.

West Side Saloon *(☎ 0 7435 4833; 135/5 Th Thamnoonvithi; open 6am-2am daily)* attracts Thais, Malays and *faràng* to its dim, rustic and pub-like space. Tables are set in front of a stage, where live music rocks nightly from 8.30pm.

Corazon *(☎ 0 7435 0360; 41 Pracharom; open 6pm-2am daily)* is a cosy Latin disco-pub, eclectically but well decorated. There's live and DJ music (of all kinds, including Latin), and Thai and Western-style foods are served.

Sugar Beat *(☎ 0 7423 3333; 444 Th Thamnoonvithi; open 6pm-2am daily)*, not to be confused with Sugar Rock, is 2km east of town. It's a popular place that doesn't get going until after 10pm. Live bands play in the dark and moody atmosphere, which has a personal feel despite being a fairly large place. Reasonably priced Thai food is available. A motorcycle ride here costs 20B.

Shopping

Shopping is Hat Yai's number-one drawcard, with most of the market action taking place along Th Niphat Uthit 2 and 3. Here you'll find Thai and Malaysian batik, cheap electronics and inexpensive clothing. There are also plenty of large department stores in town, such as **Central department store**.

Muslim Panich *(☎ 0 7423 3555; 17 Th Niphat Uthit 1; open 8am-6pm)* has an excellent selection of textiles, including Thai, Malay and Indonesian batik. Although you'll find cheaper at the markets, they can't compare with Muslim Panich in terms of quality and selection.

DK Bookstore *(no Roman-script sign; ☎ 0 7423 0759; 2/4-7 Th Thamnoonvithi; open 9am-6pm daily)* has some books in English, such as novels, picture books and Lonely Planet guides. Maps are sold too. Look for the big yellow building.

Getting There & Away

Air Flights to Bangkok with **THAI** *(☎ 0 7423 3433; 182 Th Niphat Uthit 1)* are available five times daily (3095B, 1½ hours). There are also daily flights that go to Phuket and Singapore.

Hat Yai international airport has a post office, a restaurant, a coffee shop, money-exchange services and car-rental counters.

Bus, Minivan & Share Taxi The bus terminal is 2km southeast of the town centre, though many buses make stops in town. See the Bus Destinations from Hat Yai table on the following page.

Minivans leave from various spots around town. See the Hat Yai map for locations. Destinations and fares include Padang Besar (40B), Pak Bara (70B), Sadao (45B), Satun (60B), Songkhla (20B), Trang (90B) and Yala (70B).

Crossing into Malaysia from Hat Yai

The Malaysian border is about 50km south of Hat Yai, and many travellers come through town just to extend their Thai visas.

To get an in-and-out stamp, head to Padang Besar, the nearest Malaysian border town. Private taxis cost 500B return (one hour), share taxis are 100B (one hour, leave when full), minivans 40B (1½ hours, hourly) and buses 26B (1½ hours, every 25 minutes). It's also possible to take the train, but this option is not very fast or frequent.

If you need a longer Thai visa, you'll have to see the Thai consulate in Georgetown, on Penang Island (accessible through the mainland town of Butterworth). Buses from Hat Yai to Butterworth cost 230B (four hours) and share taxis are 250B. Again, trains from Hat Yai to Butterworth are slower and less frequent.

Cathay Tour (☎ *0 7423 5044; 93/1 Th Niphat Uthit)* runs express minivans to Krabi (160B), Ko Samui (280B to 300B), Phuket (280B), Surat Thani (150B), Sungai Kolok (150B) and Trang (120B).

Share taxis are a good, quick way of getting from one southern province to another. There are several share-taxi stands in Hat Yai, each stand specialises in transport to certain destinations.

Bus Destinations from Hat Yai

destination	fare (B)	duration (hrs)
Bangkok		
ordinary	315	17
air-con	416-567	14
VIP	830	14
Butterworth (for Penang)		
air-con	230	4
Ko Samui		
air-con	270	7
Krabi		
air-con	173	5
Kuala Lumpur		
air-con	350-450	9
Pak Bara		
ordinary	46	2½
Padang Besar		
ordinary	26	1½
Pattani		
ordinary	41	2
Phuket		
ordinary	150	8
air-con	210-420	8
Satun		
ordinary	36	2
air-con	65	1½
Singapore		
air-con	450-600	16
Songkhla		
ordinary	14	½
Sungai Kolok		
air-con	148	4
Surat Thani		
ordinary	115	6½
air-con	165-170	5½
Trang		
ordinary	60	3
Yala		
ordinary	53	2½

In general, share taxis cost about the same as air-con buses, but are quite a bit faster. Share taxis also offer door-to-door drop-offs. The downside is that the drivers wait around for enough passengers (usually five) before they depart. If you get lucky the taxi may leave immediately; otherwise you may have to wait for half an hour or more. The drivers also drive at hair-raising speeds – not a pleasant experience for highly strung passengers.

There is one other small drawback associated with share taxis. The locations of share-taxi stands tend to change frequently. Share taxis are only semi-legal and therefore the locations of the taxi stands are somewhat fluid. When police inevitably crack down on one location, the share taxis move to another one, usually just around the corner. Look for them near the President Hotel, or across from the post office on Th Rattakan – they may be there during your tenure in Hat Yai, unless, of course, they've moved.

Train There are five daily trains to/from Bangkok. Fares range from 189B to 745B depending on the class. There are also daily trains to Sungai Kolok (42B to 122B, seven a day), Butterworth (two a day) and Padang Besar (57B or 322B, two a day).

There is an **advance booking office** and **left-luggage office** at the train station; both are open 6am to 6pm daily.

Getting Around

An **Airport Taxi Service** *(☎ 0 7423 8452)* makes the run to/from the airport seven times daily (60B per person). The service leaves for the airport from the THAI office on Th Niphat Uthit 1; coming into to Hat Yai, the service offers hotel drop-off. A private taxi for this run costs about 200B.

Avis Rent-A-Car *(☎ 0 7435 2222)* has an office at the Novotel Central Sukhontha. You can arrange car rental (for approximately 1000B per day) through some other travel agencies in town, such as **Cathay Tour** *(☎ 0 7423 5044; 93/1 Th Niphat Uthit)*. The airport also has some car-rental counters for those flying in.

Săwngthăew run along Th Phetkasem and charge 5B per person. Túk-túk around town cost 10B per person, though they like to charge foreigners 20B instead.

AROUND HAT YAI

Nam Tok Ton Nga Chang

น้ำตกต้นงาช้าง

Nam Tok Ton Nga Chang (Elephant Tusk Falls), 25km west of Hat Yai via Hwy 4 in Rattaphum district, is a beautiful, 1200m seven-tier cascade that falls in two streams (thus resembling two tusks). It can take three hours to walk to the seventh tier. If you're staying in Hat Yai, the falls make a nice break from the hustle and bustle of the city. The waterfall looks its best at the end of the rainy season, from October to December.

To get here take a sǎwngthǎew bound for Rattaphum (25B) from anywhere along Th Phetkasem and ask to get off at the *náam tòk* (waterfall). Many travel agencies in Hat Yai have tours to these falls, which cost about 150B.

Khao Nam Khang Tunnels

อุโมงค์ประวัติศาสตร์เขาน้ำค้าง

Located in the Khao Nam Khang National Park, this tunnel complex *(admission 200B; open 9am-4pm daily)* was once used by Communist Party of Malaysia (CPM) guerrillas as a base camp until they finally gave up the struggle in 1989. At least 1km of tunnels on three levels has been preserved and a portion of these have been widened to accommodate visitors. The underground base boasted conference rooms, a radio room, an operating room and, oddly, three long, straight passageways where the tunnel-bound communists could practice riding their motorcycles! The whole complex is said to have taken two years to build.

There are no buses here, so you'll have to drive your own vehicle. From Hat Yai take Hwy 4 south toward Sadao, turning left at the Sadao district office and driving for another 26km. The tunnels are located about 4km beyond the park headquarters.

Yala Province

Yala is the most prosperous of the four predominantly Muslim provinces in southern Thailand, mainly due to the income derived from rubber production. It is also the prime business and education centre for the region.

YALA

อ.เมืองยะลา

postcode 95000 • pop 76,300

Despite its reputation as a clean city, the capital city of Yala is not an exciting place to be. The streets are large and lined with homely buildings that aren't terribly nice to look at, and there aren't any museums or other such attractions near the town centre. The population is a mix of Thai, Chinese and Muslims, and this latter group most prominently stands out. You'll notice this especially in Yala's market area, and north of town where one of Yala's tallest buildings and the largest mosque in Thailand is located.

About the most exciting time to be here is during the **Asean Barred Ground Dove Competition**, usually held in March. Over 1,000 feathered competitors are literally 'pitched' against each other, judged on stamina, melody, volume, and of course pitch. This is the World Cup for songbirds, and attracts dove-lovers from all over Thailand, as well as Malaysia, Indonesia and Singapore. Another large festival in Yala is held during May or June and pays respect to the city's guardian spirit, **Jao Phaw Lak Meuang**. Also celebrated here with some zest is **Chinese New Year**.

Information

Send letters to your loved ones at the **post office** *(Th Siriros; open 8.30am-4.30pm Mon-Fri, 9am-noon Sat)*, though you can also call them at international telephone office next door.

Things to See & Do

Phrupakoi Park, south of town and west of the roundabout, has a big artificial lake where you can fish, boat and eat in floating restaurants. Yala residents seem to be obsessed with water recreation, possibly as a consequence of living in the only land-locked province in the south.

Places to Stay

Yala has lots of cheap old Chinese hotels, though most are at the bottom of the barrel, so to speak. Stick to the higher-end if you want a few comforts.

On the same block of Th Ratakit are three cheapie options: **Shanghai Hotel** (☎ *0 7321*

2037; rooms with fan 80-140B), **Saen Suk Hotel** *(rooms with fan 80B)* and **Muang Thong Hotel** *(☎ 0 7321 2671; rooms with fan 100B)*. All of these are dreary and slightly sleazy Chinese hotels with restaurants on the ground floor. These are best for those penny-pinching travellers who consider old, worn, and once-possibly charming, buildings quaint.

Metro Hotel *(☎ 0 7321 2175; Th Ratakit; rooms with shared bath 100-140B, with private bath 130-170B)* is across from the aforementioned 'Three Stooges' and has a more familial atmosphere. Rooms are still very basic, though larger ones are tidier and less depressing.

Aun Aun Hotel *(☎ 0 7321 2216; Th Pipitpakdee; rooms with/without bath 140/100B)* is another bleak and dreary place, but has some weirdly fascinating architectural details, like urinals in hall alcoves and saloon-style doors over the regular ones. English is semi-spoken here.

Thepvimarn Hotel *(☎ 0 7321 2400; Th Sribumrung; rooms with fan 150-200B, with air-con 330-390B)* is a large, friendly place with no-frills, but acceptable, upper-budget rooms that are fine for a couple of nights. It's about 90% clean.

Sri Yala Hotel *(☎ 0 7321 2299; 18-22 Th Chaijarus; rooms with fan 180-240B, with air-con 300-350B)* has some dark, airless and very unexciting rooms on the ground floor, so avoid these. Otherwise rooms are OK, and you get an elevator, restaurant and coffee shop to boot, so it's good value.

Yala Rama *(☎ 0 7321 2563, fax 0 7321 4532; 21 Th Sribumrung; rooms with air-con 420B)* features nine floors of large, bright, carpeted and clean mid-range rooms; a great deal for the price, unless the karaoke lounge really gets going. A sign on the counter demands 'Please identify yourself'.

Chang Lee Hotel *(☎ 0 7324 4597, fax 0 7324 4599; 318 Th Siriros; rooms with air-con 680B, suites from 1100B)* offers Yala's best beds, and can offer promotions as low as 400B – which would make this place a bargain. All plush rooms have carpet, hot water and TV, and facilities include a pool, business centre, karaoke, nightclub and coffee shop. It's on a big street and not central, though (a 15-minute walk from the train station).

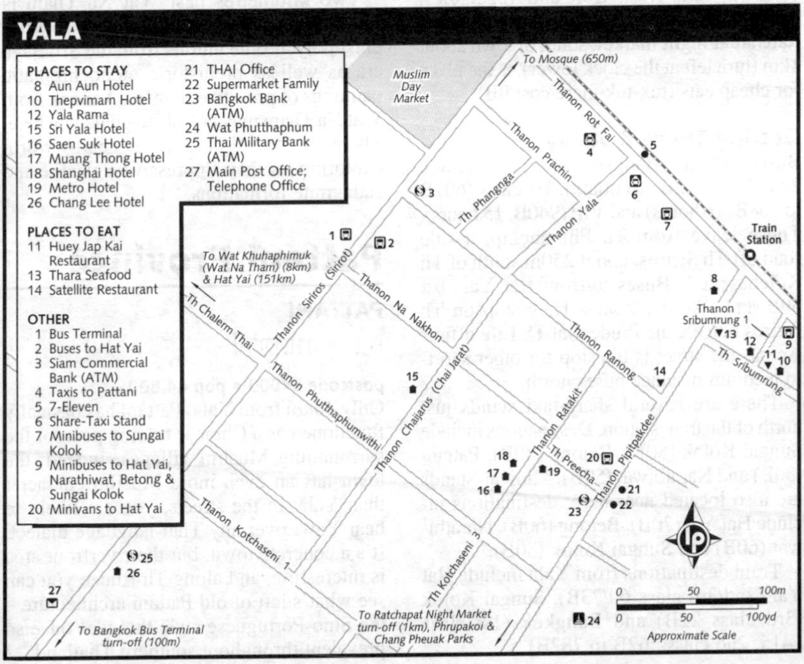

Places to Eat

Yala is hardly a culinary destination, though there are a couple of decent eateries in town. Chinese restaurants proliferate along Th Ratakit and Th Ranong.

Thara Seafood *(no Roman-script sign; cnr Th Pipitpakdee & Th Sribumrung; dishes 65-300B; open 3pm-10pm daily)* is popular for its excellent, moderately priced seafood. House specialities include *kûng phăo* (grilled prawns) and *plaa òp bai toei* (fish baked in pandanus leaves), and they're temptingly cooked on the sidewalk.

Satellite *(cnr Th Pipitpakdee & Th Ranong; open 6.30am-10pm daily)* is another popular corner restaurant with worn tables and chairs and a few food carts out the front – you just have to point at the steamed and fried dishes. It also does good *jók* (rice congee) and Chinese dumplings.

Huey Jap Kai Restaurant *(no Roman-script sign; Th Sribumrung; open 6am-midnight daily)*, right next to the Thipvimarm Hotel, is great for a cheap breakfast noodle soup (25B). It's a large, popular, clean cafeteria-style place located on a breezy corner.

The Muslim **day market**, in the north part of town, sells fresh fruit and vegetables; try to wear modest clothing around here. **Ratchapat night market**, south of town about 1km (turn left at the clock tower), is the place for cheap eats (túk-túk there cost 9B).

Getting There & Away

Buses between Bangkok and Yala include 2nd class (472B, 16 hours), 1st class (607B to 708B, 16 hours) and VIP (940B, 15 hours). These leave from Th Phumachip, a side road off Th Siriros, about 250m south of Th Kotchaseni 1. Buses to/from Hat Yai cost 59B and take 2½ hours. They stop on Th Siriros outside the Prudential TS Life office. Across the street is the stop for other short- to medium-distance buses north.

There are several share-taxi stands just north of the train station. Destinations include Sungai Kolok (80B), Betong (80B), Pattani (30B) and Narathiwat (50B). Minivan stands are also located near here; destinations include Hat Yai (70B), Betong (60B), Narathiwat (60B) and Sungai Kolok (80B).

Train destinations from Yala include Hat Yai (2nd/3rd class 60/23B), Sungai Kolok (3rd class 22B) and Bangkok (1st class 1415, 2nd class 462B to 782B).

Getting Around

THAI has a shuttle service to Hat Yai international airport (220B). Túk-túk should only charge 9B for rides around town, but you could pay as much as 20B.

AROUND YALA

Wat Khuhaphimuk

Outside town, about 8km west off the Yala–Hat Yai road, is Wat Khuhaphimuk (also called Wat Na Tham, Cave-Front Temple), a Srivijaya-period cave temple established around AD 750. Inside the cave is Phra Phutthasaiyat, a long, reclining Buddha image sculpted in the Srivijaya style. For Thais, this is one of the three most-venerated Buddhist pilgrimage points in southern Thailand (the other two are Wat Boromathat in Nakhon Si Thammarat and Wat Phra Boromathat Chaiya in Surat Thani). There is a small **museum** in front of the cave, with artefacts of local provenance.

To get here, take a săwngthăew (7B) going west towards the town of Yaha via Rte 4065 and ask to get off at the road to Wat Na Tham. It's about a 1km walk to the wát from the highway.

Two kilometres past Wat Na Tham is **Tham Silpa**, a well-known cave with Buddhist polychrome murals from the Srivijaya era as well as prehistoric monochromatic paintings of primitive hunters. A monk from Wat Na Tham may be able to guide you here. There are several other caves nearby worth exploring for their impressive stalactite and stalagmite formations.

Pattani Province

PATTANI

อ.เมืองปัตตานี

postcode 94000 • pop 44,800

Only 40km from Yala, Pattani has basically functioned as a Chinese trading post for the surrounding Muslim villages. Indeed, the town has an even more Muslim character than Yala; in the streets, you are likely to hear Yawi over any Thai-language dialect. It's a concrete town, but the riverfront area is interesting, and along Th Rudee you can see what's left of old Pattani architecture – the Sino-Portuguese style that was once so prevalent throughout southern Thailand.

Pattani was until quite recently the centre of an independent principality that included Yala and Narathiwat. It was also one of the earliest kingdoms in Thailand to host international trade; the Portuguese established a trading post here in 1516, the Japanese in 1605, the Dutch in 1609 and the British in 1612. A cosmopolitan collection of antique cannons unearthed at Pattani and now on display at the national museum in Songkhla attests to the competitive nature of trade during early Pattani times. During WWII, Japanese troops landed in Pattani to launch attacks on Malaysia (then called Malaya) and Singapore.

Information

If you're in need of some cash, check out the banks along the southeastern end of Th Pipit.

The front of Pattani's **main post office** *(Th Pipit; open 8.30am-4.30pm Mon-Fri, 9am-noon Sat & Sun)* sheltered this author during a heavy rainstorm. The attached **CAT office** *(open 8.30am-4.30pm daily)* provides overseas telephone service.

There's an **Internet café** *(Th Prida)* that's often full of kids playing loud video games.

Mosques

Thailand's second-largest mosque is the **Matsayit Klang**, a traditional structure of green hue, probably still the most important mosque in southern Thailand. It was built in the early 1960s.

The oldest mosque in Pattani is the **Matsayit Kreu-Se**, built in 1578 by an immigrant Chinese named Lim To Khieng, who had married a Pattani woman and converted to Islam. The brick, Arab-style building was never finished, and has been left in its original semi-completed, semi-ruined form – but the faithful keep up the surrounding grounds. It's in the village of Ban Kreu-Se, about 7km east of Pattani next to Hwy 42 at the Km10 marker; a gaudy Chinese temple has been built next to it. For the full legend, see the boxed text 'The Unfinished Mosque' in this section.

The tree from which Lim Ko Niaw hanged herself has been enshrined at the **San Jao Leng Ju Kieng** (or San Jao Lim Ko Niaw), the site of an important Chinese-Muslim festival in late February or early March. During the festival a wooden image of Lim Ko Niaw is carried through the streets;

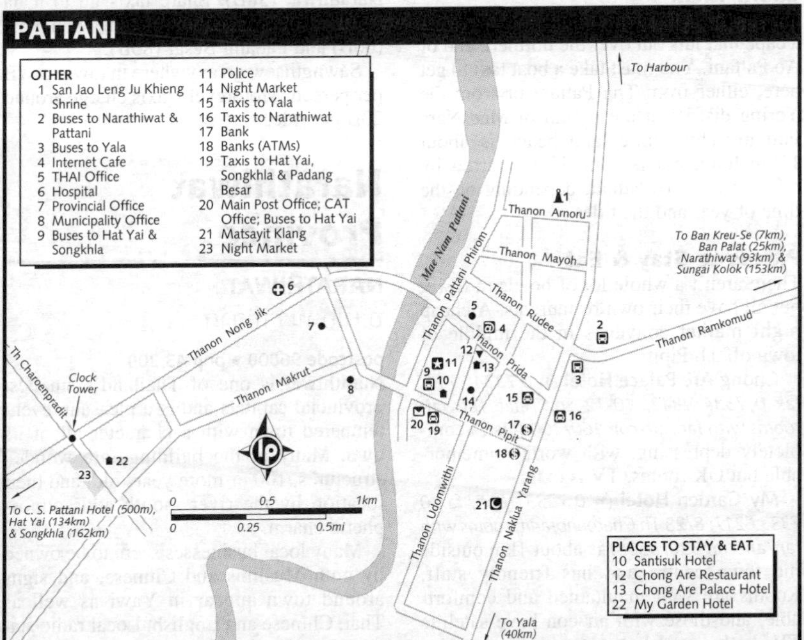

The Unfinished Mosque

According to legend, Lim To Khieng's sister, Lim Ko Niaw, sailed from China on a sampan to try to persuade her brother to abandon Islam and return to his homeland. To demonstrate the strength of his faith, To Khieng began building the Matsayit Kreu-Se. His sister then put a curse on the mosque, saying it would never be completed. Then, in a final attempt to dissuade To Khieng, she hanged herself from a nearby cashew tree. In his grief, Khieng was unable to complete the mosque, and to this day it remains unfinished; supposedly every time someone tries to work on it, lightning strikes.

additional rites include fire-walking and seven days of vegetarianism. The shrine is in the northern end of town towards the harbour.

Another festival fervently celebrated in Pattani is **Hari Rayo**, the Muslim month of fasting during the 10th lunar month.

Laem Tachi

The only beach near town is at Laem Tachi, a cape that juts out over the northern end of Ao Pattani. You must take a boat taxi to get here, either from Tha Pattani or from the Yaring district at the mouth of Mae Nam Pattani. This white-sand beach is about 11km long, but is sometimes marred by refuse from Ao Pattani, depending on the time of year and the tides.

Places to Stay & Eat

There aren't a whole lot of hotels in town, but all have their own restaurants. A cheap **night market** convenes in the middle of town off Th Pipit.

Chong Are Palace Hotel (*☎ 0 7334 9711, fax 0 7334 9842; 10-12 Soi Talat Tetiwat; rooms with fan/air-con 160/300B*) isn't completely depressing, with worn, unmemorable but OK rooms. TV is extra.

My Garden Hotel (*☎ 0 7333 1055, fax 0 7333 6217; 8/28 Th Charoenpradit; rooms with fan/air-con 330/550B*) is about 1km outside the town centre and has friendly staff. Rooms are well maintained and comfortable, and those with air-con have satellite TV, bath, good hot-water showers and a fridge. The restaurant is proud to have 'musicians to full you and entertain you while beautiful waitresses wait on you'.

CS Pattani (*☎ 0 7333 5093, fax 0 7333 1620; ⓔ cspatani@cscoms.com; rooms with air-con from 1500B*), about 3km west of the town centre, is the best place to stay in town. Large, luxurious rooms come with all the amenities, and facilities include a fitness room, pool and beautiful restaurant. Promotional rates are often available; all include breakfast.

Shopping

Thai Muslims in southern Thailand use traditional batik methods similar to the batik of northeastern Malaysia. The **Palat Market** (Talat Nat Palat) sells this style of batik. The market is off Hwy 42 between Pattani and Saiburi in Ban Palat, and is held on Wednesday and Sunday. There are also some shops along Th Rudee that sell local and Malaysian batik.

Getting There & Around

Buses destinations to/from Pattani include Yala (16B, one hour), Hat Yai (50B) and Narathiwat (38B). Share taxis go to Yala (30B, 30 minutes), Hat Yai (70B), Songkhla (60B) and Padang Besar (80B).

Săwngthăew go anywhere in town for 7B per person. Motorcycle taxis charge around 20B per ride.

Narathiwat Province

NARATHIWAT

อ.เมืองนราธิวาส

postcode 96000 • pop 43,300

Narathiwat is one of Thailand's smallest provincial capitals and is a pleasant, even-tempered town with a character all of its own. Many of the buildings are wooden structures, 100 or more years old, and their location by the river mouth adds atmospheric charm.

Many local businesses seem to be owned by both Muslims and Chinese, and signs around town appear in Yawi as well as Thai, Chinese and English. Local radio stations broadcast in a mix of Yawi, Thai and

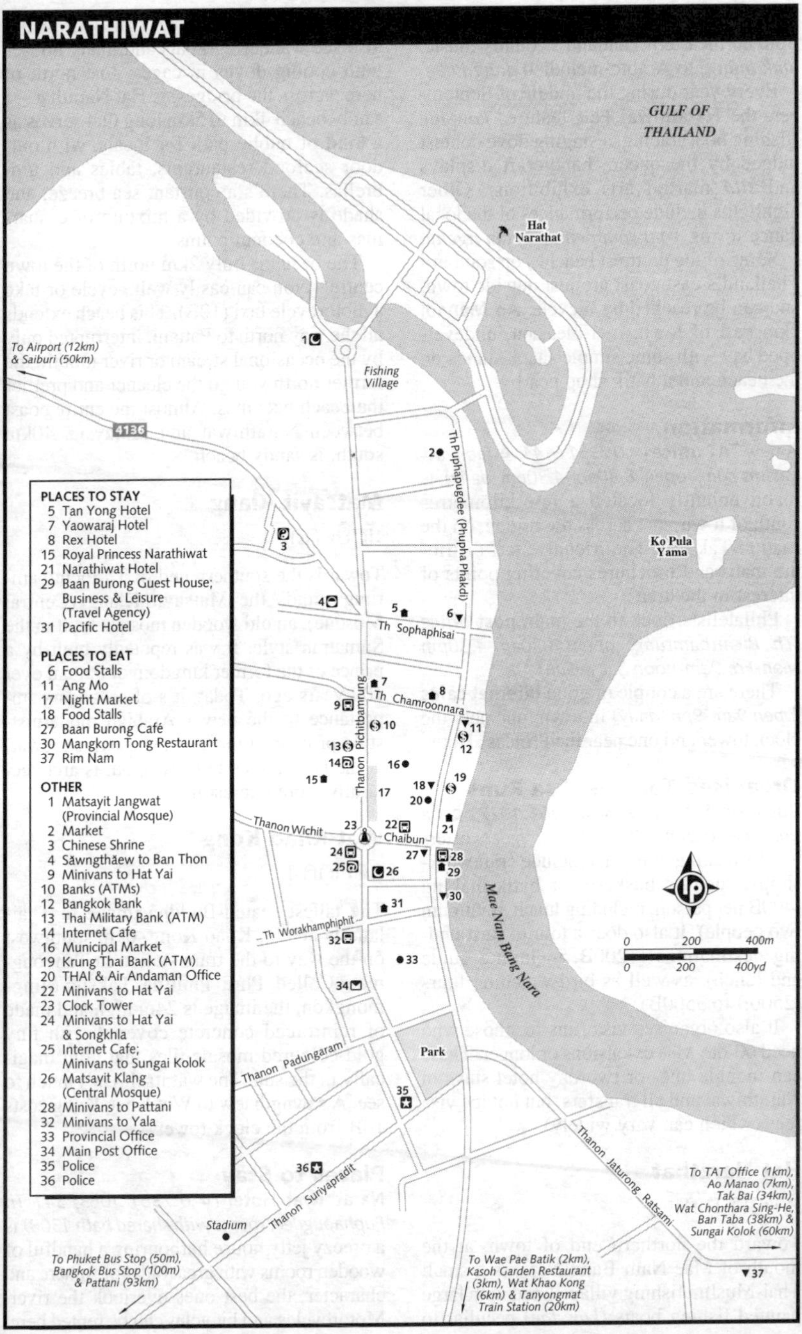
NARATHIWAT
GULF OF THAILAND
Hat Narathat
Ko Pula Yama
Fishing Village
To Airport (12km) & Saiburi (50km)
4136
Th Puphapugdee (Phupha Phakdi)
Th Sophaphisai
Th Chamroonnara
Thanon Pichitbamrung
Thanon Wichit
Chaibun
Th Worakhamphiphit
Thanon Padungaram
Thanon Suriyapradit
Thanon Jaturong Ratsami
Mae Nam Bang Nara
Park
Stadium
0 200 400m
0 200 400yd
To TAT Office (1km), Ao Manao (7km), Tak Bai (34km), Wat Chonthara Sing-He, Ban Taba (38km) & Sungai Kolok (60km)
To Wae Pae Batik (2km), Kasoh Garden Restaurant (3km), Wat Khao Kong (6km) & Tanyongmat Train Station (20km)
To Phuket Bus Stop (50m), Bangkok Bus Stop (100m) & Pattani (93km)
PLACES TO STAY
5 Tan Yong Hotel
7 Yaowaraj Hotel
8 Rex Hotel
15 Royal Princess Narathiwat
21 Narathiwat Hotel
29 Baan Burong Guest House; Business & Leisure (Travel Agency)
31 Pacific Hotel
PLACES TO EAT
6 Food Stalls
11 Ang Mo
17 Night Market
18 Food Stalls
27 Baan Burong Café
30 Mangkorn Tong Restaurant
37 Rim Nam
OTHER
1 Matsayit Jangwat (Provincial Mosque)
2 Market
3 Chinese Shrine
4 Săwngthăew to Ban Thon
9 Minivans to Hat Yai
10 Banks (ATMs)
12 Bangkok Bank
13 Thai Military Bank (ATM)
14 Internet Cafe
16 Municipal Market
19 Krung Thai Bank (ATM)
20 THAI & Air Andaman Office
22 Minivans to Hat Yai
23 Clock Tower
24 Minivans to Hat Yai & Songkhla
25 Internet Cafe; Minivans to Sungai Kolok
26 Matsayit Klang (Central Mosque)
28 Minivans to Pattani
32 Minivans to Yala
33 Provincial Office
34 Main Post Office
35 Police
36 Police

Malay, with musical selections to match – from northeastern Thailand's country music, *lûuk thûng*, to Arabic-melodied *dangdut*.

Every year during the middle of September, the **Narathiwat Fair** features *kaw-lae* (fishing boat) racing, a singing dove contest judged by the queen, handicraft displays and *sìlá* martial arts exhibitions. Other highlights include performances of the local dance forms, *ram sam pen* and *ram ngeng*.

Some of the prettiest beaches on southern Thailand's east coast are just outside town, and can be reached by bicycle. **Ao Manao**, 7km east of town, is a pleasant, undeveloped bay with some simple snack stands on the beach and a batik shop nearby.

Information

A new **TAT office** *(☎ 0 7351 6144; e tatnara@cscoms.com; open 8.30am-4.30pm daily)* is inconveniently located a few kilometres south of town, just across the bridge, on the road to Tak Bai. The friendly staff distribute maps and brochures covering points of interest in the area.

Philatelists flock to the **main post office** *(Th Pichitbamrung; open 8.30am-4.30pm Mon-Fri, 9am-noon Sat & Sun)*.

There are a couple of good **Internet cafés** *(open 9am-9pm daily)* in town; one near the clock tower and one near the Princess Hotel.

Organised Tours & Visa Runs

Business & Leisure *(☎ 0 7351 1027; e natini@chaiyo.com; 399 Th Puphapugdee)* offers local kayaking tours that include craft workshops, such as basketry or batik-making (400B per person, including lunch, minimum two people). It also does a tour to surrounding destinations (1200B, including guide and lunch), as well as bird-watching tours (2500B to 3500B).

It also organises visa runs for those who need 60-day visa extensions or longer. These can include one- or two-day hotel stays in Narathiwat and all transfers, but not the visa fees (which can vary widely).

Hat Narathat

หาดนราทัศน์

Toward the northern end of town, at the mouth of Mae Nam Bang Nara, is a small Thai-Muslim fishing village lined with large painted fishing boats *(kaw-lae)* peculiar to Narathiwat and Pattani. You'll probably also see wandering goats and many houses with cooing doves in cages. Just north of here, across the bridges, is Hat Narathat – a sandy beach 4km to 5km long that serves as a kind of public park for locals, with outdoor seafood restaurants, tables and umbrellas. There's a constant sea breeze, and shade is provided by a mixture of casuarinas and coconut palms.

The beach is only 2km north of the town centre – you can easily walk, cycle or take a motorcycle taxi (10B). This beach extends all the way north to Pattani, interrupted only by the occasional stream or river mouth; the farther north you go the cleaner and prettier the beach becomes. Almost the entire coast between Narathiwat and Malaysia, 40km south, is sandy beach.

Matsayit Klang

มัสยิดกลาง

Towards the southern end of Th Pichitbamrung stands the Matsayit Klang (Central Mosque), an old wooden mosque built in the Sumatran style. It was reputedly built by a prince of the former kingdom of Pattani over 100 years ago. Today it's of secondary importance to the newer Arabian modernist-style provincial mosque (Matsayit Jangwat) at the northern end of town, but is architecturally more interesting.

Wat Khao Kong

วัดเขากง

The tallest seated-Buddha image in Thailand is at Wat Khao Kong, 6km southwest on the way to the train station in Tanyongmat. Called Phra Phuttha Taksin Mingmongkon, the image is 24m high and made of reinforced concrete covered with tiny gold-coloured mosaic tiles that glint magically in the sun. The *wát* itself isn't much to see. A *sǎwngthǎew* to Wat Khao Kong costs 10B from the clock tower.

Places to Stay

Narathiwat Hotel *(☎ 0 7351 1063; 341 Th Puphapugdee; rooms with shared bath 130B)* is a breezy jetty house harbouring a handful of wooden rooms with great old atmosphere and character; the best ones overlook the river. Motorcycles and bicycles can be rented here.

Rex Hotel (*☎ 0 7351 1134, fax 0 7351 1190; 6-6/1 Th Chamroonnara; rooms with fan 200-320B, with air-con 350-430B*) starts with a bleak lobby, but has large, bright, basic rooms upstairs, and is a fair deal. TV costs more.

Yaowaraj Hotel (*☎ 0 7351 1148; 131 Th Pichitbamrung; rooms 160-360B*) gives you good, decent, no-frills rooms at a range of prices. The incessant hotel problem pops up here: Outside rooms are noisy with street traffic, while those inside are dark.

Tan Yong Hotel (*☎ 0 7351 1477, fax 0 7351 1834; 16/1 Th Sophaphisai; rooms with fan 400B, with air-con 698-745B*) features musty, dark rooms with fans and impressive wall views. Rooms with air-con are better, but upgrade to a 'deluxe' room, with partial river views and small balconies. A restaurant, café and karaoke sit downstairs.

Pacific Hotel (*☎ 0 7351 1076; 42/1-2 Th Worakhamphiphit; rooms with air-con 400-430B*) offers large, clean and good modern rooms with TV; breakfast is included.

Baan Burong Guest House (*☎ 0 7351 1027, fax 0 7351 2001; e natini@chaiyo.com; 399 Th Puphapugdee; rooms with air-con & shared bath 400-500B*) offers just three nice, homey and clean rooms in an old shophouse, with an intimate common TV area next to the river. A breakfast of toast and coffee or tea is included, and there's free use of bikes and kayaks. Friendly Natini runs the place, speaks excellent English and plans to add seven more rooms above her tiny café across the street.

Royal Princess Narathiwat (*☎ 0 7351 5041, fax 0 7351 5040; e pnn@dusit.com; 228 Th Pitchitbamrung; rooms with air-con 1200-1600B*) is the best hotel in town, a relatively new place offering eight storeys of clean rooms. There's a small pool and modest lobby, and free airport transfers are provided for guests.

Places to Eat

For inexpensive food treats, try the **night market** on Th Pichitbamrung. Also serving cheap eats is a cluster of **food stalls** on Th Sophaphisai at Th Puphapugdee.

Baan Burong Café (*dishes 25-80B; open 9am-11pm daily*) serves breakfast, snacks and light meals – do try the refreshing fruit frappes or the very good selection of coffee and teas. It's a tiny place, with just four small tables; the few baked items available are wonderful.

Mangkorn Tong Restaurant (*☎ 0 7351 1835; 433 Th Puphapugdee; dishes 60-180B*) offers a seafood menu, but the great riverside setting is why you're here; there's a floating dining section out the back. The food's pretty good and the prices are quite reasonable.

Rim Nam (*☎ 0 7351 1559; Th Jaturong Ratsami; dishes 50-200B; open 9am-10pm daily*) is about 2km south of town (across from the petrol station; look for colourful flags). It cooks up fresh seafood in a modern, airy atmosphere, and also has a floating platform. Recommended dishes include the fried shrimp salad (100B) and the lemon chicken (80B).

Kasoh Garden Restaurant (*☎ 0 7352 1700; 1/3 Tambon Lamphu; dishes 40-150B; open 11am-10pm daily*) is an airy, spacious and upmarket place that serves tasty seafood, vegetable dishes, Thai soups and salads. The ambience is great, with a nearby garden and fish-filled pond. This place is south of town a bit; Natini at Baan Burong Guest House can arrange free transport here.

On the corner of Th Puphapugdee and Th Chamroonnara is the excellent **Ang Mo**, with outdoor tables. You can tell it's good because it's packed every night. Very cheap and tasty food is served, and you can point to the displayed dishes; try the duck.

Shopping

Several batik factories near town will sell batik direct to visitors at decent prices. **Wae Pa Batik** (*☎ 0 7351 2452; 96/3 Mu 8 Tambon Lamphu; closed Friday*) is on the way to Wat Khao Kong and has good prices. A motorcycle taxi ride is 30B. **Ao Manao Batik**, in Ao Manao, is another place where you can stock up on the stuff.

Getting There & Away

Air THAI has one flight daily between Narathiwat and Phuket, connecting with flights to Bangkok. To book flights, go to the **THAI office** (*☎ 0 7351 3090; 322-324 Th Puphapugdee*), which also doubles as the Air Andaman office. The airport is 12km north of town.

Bus, Minivan & Share Taxis Narathiwat is connected by bus to Sungai Kolok (30B),

Hat Yai (80B) and Pattani (38B); buses run along Th Pichibamrung.

Buses to Bangkok and Phuket leave from two separate small shop terminals on Th Suriyapradit, south of town a few hundred metres past the police stations. The buses to Phuket (396B) go three times daily via Pattani, Hat Yai, Songkhla, Trang, Krabi and Phang-Nga. Buses to Bangkok (VIP/1st/2nd class 1035/666/518B) operate four times daily. You can buy tickets from Business & Leisure (see Organised Tours & Visa Runs earlier).

Minivans head to Hat Yai (120B), Pattani (60B), Songkhla (120B), Sungai Kolok (50B) and Yala (60B) from different spots around the centre of town.

Share taxis leave from in front of the Royal Princess Narathiwat hotel; prices are approximate to minivans.

Săwngthăew to the border at Ban Taba cost 20B.

Train Narathiwat's train station is located in Tanyongmat, 20km west of town (30B by săwngthăew).

Getting Around

Narathiwat is easy to navigate on foot. If you don't feel like walking, motorcycle taxis will take you around for 10B to 20B, depending on the distance.

The **THAI office** (☎ *0 7351 3090; 322-324 Th Puphapugdee)* operates airport shuttles for 50B per person; these include hotel pick-up.

Baan Burong Guest House (☎ *0 7351 1027, fax 0 7351 2001)* rents bicycles (50B per day) and motorcycles (250B per day), and can also arrange taxi hire (500B to 700B per day) or car rental.

AROUND NARATHIWAT

Matsayit Wadi Al Husen (Talo Mano)

มัสยิดวาดินฮูเซ็น

Matsayit Wadi Al Husen (Wadi Al Husen Mosque) is also known locally as 'Matsayit Song Roi Pi' (200-Year-Old Mosque), and is one of the most interesting mosques in Thailand. Constructed in 1769 of Malabar ironwood, it mixes Thai, Chinese and Malay architectural styles to good effect. It's in the village of Lubosawo in Bajo (Ba-Jaw) district, about 15km northwest of Narathiwat off Hwy 42 (costs about 10B by săwngthăew).

Wat Chonthara Sing-He

วัดชลธาราสิงเห

During the British colonisation of Malaysia (then called Malaya), the Brits tried to claim Narathiwat as part of their Malayan empire. The Thais constructed the riverside Wat Chonthara Sing-He near the Malayan border to prove that Narathiwat was indeed part of Siam, and as a result the British relinquished their claim.

Today it's most notable because of the genuine southern-Thai architecture, rarely seen in a Buddhist temple – this is the Thai-Buddhist equivalent of the Wadi Al Husen Mosque. A wooden *wíhăan* here very much resembles a Sumatran-style mosque. An 1873 *wíhăan* on the grounds contains a reclining Buddha decorated with Chinese ceramics from the Song dynasty. Another *wíhăan* on the spacious grounds contains murals painted by a famous Songkhla monk during King Mongkut's time (r. 1910–1925). The murals are religious in message but also

Crossing into Malaysia from Narathiwat

You've got two options if you're heading south from Narathiwat to the Malaysian town of Kota Bharu. You can go through the northern border crossing at Ban Taba (săwngthăew/minibus 20/30B, 1½ hours), a grungy little town with a few passable hotels and a bank. The border is open year-round from 6am to 4pm daily. From here you'd take a ferry (10B) across to Pengkalan Kubor and then frequent buses or taxis from there to Kota Bharu.

Or, you can take the much more popular route via Sungai Kolok (bus/minivan 30/50B, 1½ hours), a much larger city, but not any more charming than Ban Taba. Crossing the border should be a straightforward proposition, and on the other side is Rantau Panjang, which has frequent connections to Kota Bharu. The border here is open year-round from 5am to 9pm daily.

depict traditional southern-Thai life. There is also a larger, typical Thai *wíhăan*.

There's also a small new **museum** *(admission free; open 10am-6pm daily)* on the grounds, with surprisingly well-displayed exhibits on the wát's history, southern Thai-style houses, batik-making, ecclesiastical fans and china. A carved-wood pulpit here is also impressive. Look for the pastel painted building just to the right as you enter the grounds; you may have to ask a monk to open it up for you.

To get here from Narathiwat, take a minivan (30B) or săwngthăew (20B) bound for Ban Taba and get off in Tak Bai; the trip takes 30 minutes. There are also săwngthăew from Sungai Kolok (20B, one hour). The wát is about 500m from the main Tak Bai intersection (follow the sign).

SUNGAI KOLOK
สุไหงโกลก

pop 38,800

Sungai Kolok's biggest money-maker is the Thai-Malaysian shipping industry, and there is an entire district in the northeastern part of town dedicated to warehouses that store goods moving between countries. The city's second biggest source of income is prostitution, and you may notice this if you spend the night at a cheap hotel. As a border town, however, Sungai Kolok isn't so terribly sleazy – it could be a lot worse – and it lights up pleasantly at night, providing you don't look too closely. But since most of the city is unexciting concrete, so there's no reason to really hang around.

The Thai government once planned to move the border crossing from Sungai Kolok to Ban Taba in Tak Bai district, which is on the coast 32km northeast. The Taba crossing is a shorter and quicker route to Kota Bharu, the first Malaysian town of any size, but Sungai Kolok is more convenient and will probably remain open as well for a long time.

The Thailand–Malaysia border is open from 5am to 9pm daily, all year.

Information
The **TAT office** *(☎ 0 7361 2126; open 8.30am-4.30pm daily)*, tourist police and immigration facilities are all located at the border. There's another **Thai immigration office**

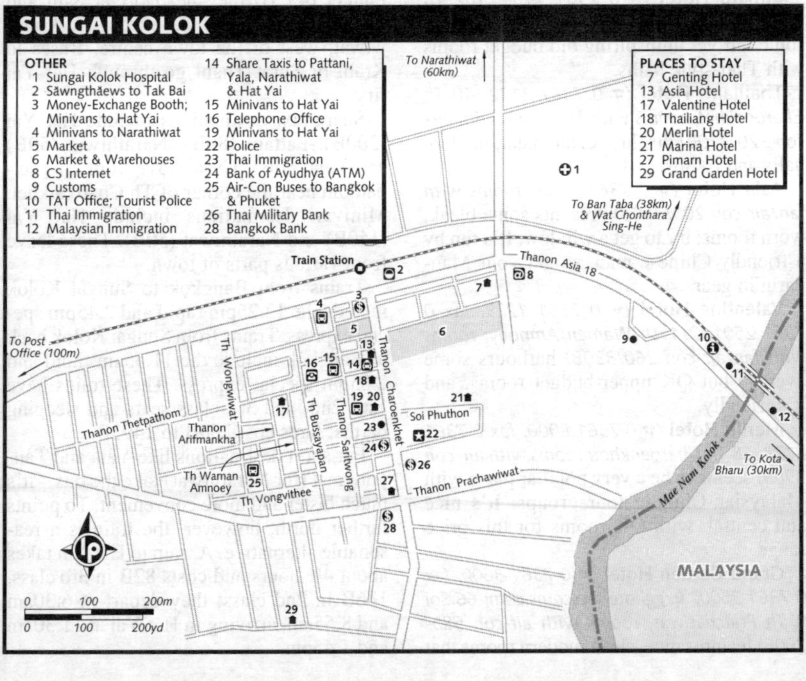

(open 9am- 4pm Mon-Fri) in town, near the Merlin Hotel.

Take a hike to the **post office** *(Th Asia 18; open 8.30-4.30 Mon-Fri, 9am-noon Sat & Sun)*, because it's on the western edge of town. The **telephone office** *(Th Thetpathom; open 8.30am-4.30pm Mon-Fri)* is more central, however.

There are plenty of banks with ATMs in town (open 8.30am to 3.30pm Monday to Friday), though they're closed on Saturday and Sunday. During this time you'll have to rely on money-changing booths, which are open 6am to 5pm daily; there's one across from the train station.

For surfing the Internet, check out **CS Internet** *(Th Asia 18; open 10am-10pm daily)*, across from the Genting Hotel.

Places to Stay & Eat

As a border town Sungai Kolok sees its share of short-time trade, so if you're trying to avoid this it's wise to shell out a few more baht. Most places in Sungai Kolok will take Malaysian ringgit as well as Thai baht for food or accommodation. Upmarket hotels will also change money for you, at a price.

Pimarn Hotel *(☎ 0 7361 1464; 102 Th Charoenkhet; rooms with fan 200B)* sponsors some fair yet uninspiring old budget rooms with Thai-style baths.

Thailiang Hotel *(☎ 0 7361 1132; 40 Th Charoenkhet; rooms with fan 200B, with air-con 320-370B)* displays clean, neat, modern halls and rooms.

Asia Hotel *(☎ 0 7361 1101; rooms with fan/air-con 200/350B)* presents some bleak, worn rooms; try to get a window. It's run by a friendly Chinese man, so get your Mandarin in gear.

Valentine Hotel *(☎ 0 7361 1229, fax 0 7361 2501; 2/1 Th Waman Amnoey; rooms with fan/air-con 260/330B)* harbours some average but OK upper-budget rooms, and it's friendly.

Merlin Hotel *(☎ 0 7361 8000, fax 0 7361 8123; 68 Th Charoenkhet; rooms with air-con 390B)* seems to be a very popular place with Malaysian-Chinese tour groups. It's nice and central, with OK rooms for this price range.

Grand Garden Hotel *(☎ 0 7361 3600, fax 0 7361 3500; ⓔ gghotel@cscoms.com; 66 Soi 3 Th Pratchatiwat, rooms with air-con 585-700B)* features nice, clean modern rooms that are well maintained and quite comfortable. There's also a small pool outside and karaoke inside.

Genting Hotel *(☎ 0 7361 3231, fax 0 7361 1259; 250 Th Asia 18; rooms with air-con 645-710B)* comes with only a few scuff marks on the walls and carpets, otherwise it's mostly up to snuff, with good mid-range rooms away from the seedier areas. There's a pool, restaurant and karaoke, of course. It's a tall, white behemoth of a building.

Marina *(☎ 0 7361 3881, fax 0 7361 3385; Soi Phuthon; rooms with air-con 990-1750B)* may be worth it for the views; this hotel has 15 storeys with a sky lounge on the top floor. Modern rooms are decent, and there's a 3rd-floor pool.

The town has plenty of food stalls selling Thai, Chinese and Malay food, while a cluster of reliable **Malay food vendors** can be found at the market and in front of the train station.

Getting There & Away

Air-con buses to Bangkok (VIP/1st/2nd class 1090/702/546B, 17 to 18 hours) depart at 8am, 11.30am and 12.30pm; to Phuket (432B) they head off at 8am and 5.30pm. These buses leave from Th Wongwiwat, west of the town centre. Buses to Krabi or Surat Thani go through Hat Yai first.

Share-taxi destinations include Hat Yai (200B), Pattani (80B), Narathiwat (50B) and Yala (80B). These leave from Th Thetpathom near the corner of Th Charoenkhet. Minivan destinations include Hat Yai (150B) and Narathiwat (50B). These leave from various parts of town.

Trains from Bangkok to Sungai Kolok include the 12.25pm rapid and 2.45pm special express. Trains from Sungai Kolok back to Bangkok include the 11.55am rapid and 2.05pm special express. These trains have 1st-, 2nd- and 3rd-class seats and sleeping berths; fares cost 260B to 1493B.

For short destinations like Yala and Tanyongmat (for Narathiwat) take the bus – it's much faster and more convenient. To points farther north, however, the train is a reasonable alternative. A train to Hat Yai takes about 4½ hours and costs 82B in 3rd class, 136B in 2nd class; they depart at 6.30am and 8.55am, arriving in Hat Yai at 11.30am and 1.45pm.

Getting Around

The border is about 1km from the centre of Sungai Kolok or the train station. Transport around town is by motorcycle taxi – it's 20B for a ride to the border. Coming from Malaysia, just follow the old train tracks to your right or, for the town, turn left at the first intersection and head for the high-rises. From Rantau Panjang (Malaysian side), a share taxi to Kota Bharu will cost about RM5 per person (or RM20 to charter the whole car) and takes around an hour. To Kota Bharu it costs RM3.50 on the regular yellow and orange bus.

Andaman Coast

A heady mix of sandy beaches framed by soaring mountains of jagged limestone, Thailand's Andaman coast offers some of Southeast Asia's most striking scenery. Comprised of Ranong, Phang-Nga, Phuket, Krabi, Trang and Satun Provinces, the Andaman coast is bordered to the north by Myanmar and to the south by Malaysia. Culturally, it shares virtually all of the same characteristics as the neighbouring provinces of the southern gulf: An ethnic Chinese merchant class dominates the cities while Muslim Thais (many of whom are ethnic Malay) inhabit the rural areas.

For the visitor to Thailand's southern provinces and its famed beaches, the main concern is weather. The Andaman coast gets more rain than the southern gulf provinces – with May to October being the months of heaviest rainfall. During this time passenger boats to some islands, such as the Surin and Similan Archipelagos, are suspended. On the other hand, the southern gulf provinces are comparatively dry until October, with rainfall heaviest in November. Of course the abundance of microclimates makes it difficult to generalise but, fortunately, the peninsula on which southern Thailand sits is somewhat narrow. If you find the weather on the Andaman coast unpleasant, you can easily travel to the other side and hope to find the sun shining.

Highlights

- Dive at world-class destinations such as Phuket, Ko Phi-Phi, and the Surin and Similan Archipelagos
- Explore some of the most scenic landscape in the world: incredible limestone formations, karst caves, gushing waterfalls, secluded islands and fine white-sand beaches
- Live it up at the luxurious resorts, lively entertainment, shopping and – of course – wonderful beaches on Phuket
- Experience the remote and virtually uninhabited Ko Tarutao National Marine Park, one of the most pristine coastal areas in Thailand
- Chill out at the densely forested interior, long sandy beaches and mangrove swamps filled with tropical birds and butterflies on Ko Lanta

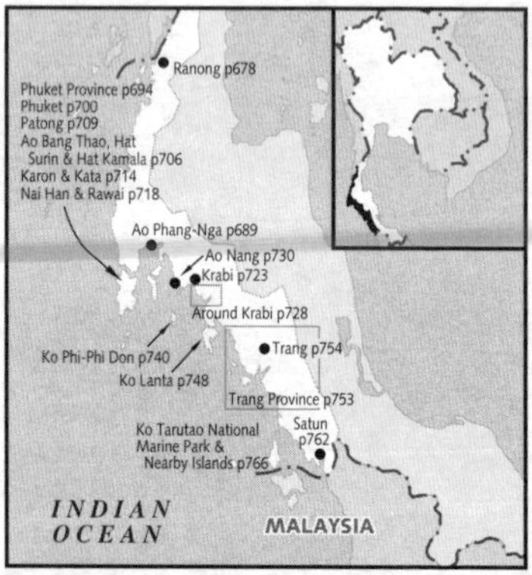

Ranong Province

Thailand's least populated province is approximately 80% forest and 70% mountains, and is supported mainly by mineral extraction and fishing, along with rubber, coconut and cashew production. Like much of southern Thailand it experiences two monsoons, but the mountains here tend to hold the rains over the area longer, so it gets the highest average annual rainfall in the country. Consequently, it's incredibly green overall and there are lots of waterfalls. However, it's swampy near the coastline and mainland beaches are almost nonexistent. For some time on the sand, you could head out to Ko Chang and Ko Phayam, pleasant laid-back islands just off the coast from the town of Ranong.

RANONG

อ.เมืองระนอง

postcode 85000 • pop 24,500

This small and friendly provincial capital has a bustling fishing port and is separated from Myanmar only by Pak Chan, the estuary of Mae Nam Chan (Chan River). Burmese residents from nearby Kawthoung (Ko Song) hop across to trade in Thailand or work on fishing boats. Many Burmese people now

ANDAMAN COAST

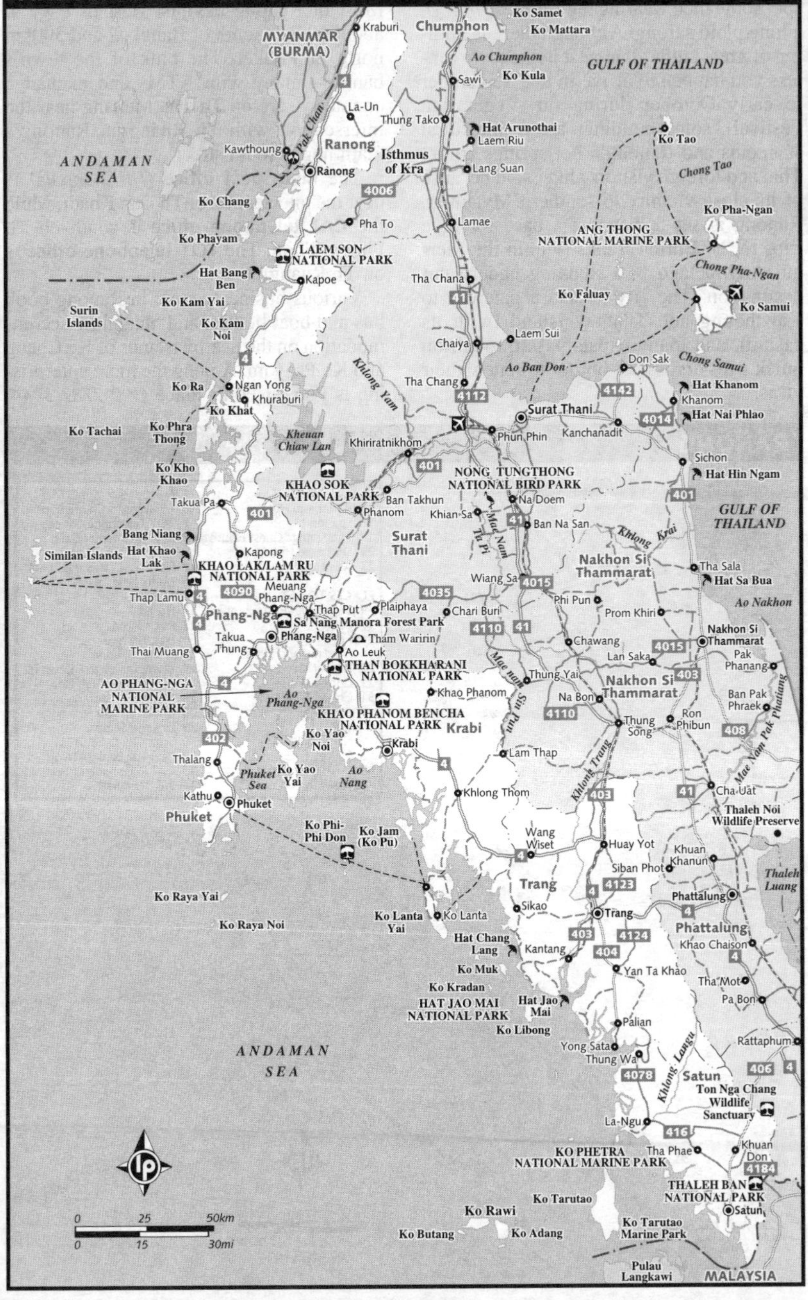

reside in Ranong as well, and you might spot some men wearing the Burmese *longyi*, a long plaid sarong. Although there is nothing of great cultural interest in the town (unless you happen to arrive in late September to early October during the Vegetarian Festival), some buildings are architectural standouts and Ranong's hot springs attract Thai and foreign visitors alike. And because of its close vicinity to southern Myanmar, Ranong is set to become a base for dive trips to the Burma Banks (within the Mergui Archipelago) – a stunning underwater destination. The city is also a gateway to Kawthoung and Thahtay Island (with its casino), and many expats pass through on quick trips across the border to renew their visas.

Orientation & Information

Most of Ranong lies just west of Hwy 4, about 600km south of Bangkok and 300km north of Phuket. The bulk of the town's banks – many with ATMs and exchange counters – are on Th Tha Meuang near the intersection with Th Ruangrat, Ranong's main north–south street.

The **main post office** *(Th Chonraua)* is near the intersection of Th Dap Khadi, while the **CAT telephone office** is south on Th Phoem Phon. The **TOT telephone office** is on Th Ruangrat.

Various businesspeople in Ranong book bus and boat tickets, and bungalow accommodation on the nearby islands of Ko Chang and Ko Phayam. Among the more enterprising is Pon, at **Pon's Place** *(☎ 0 7782 3344;*

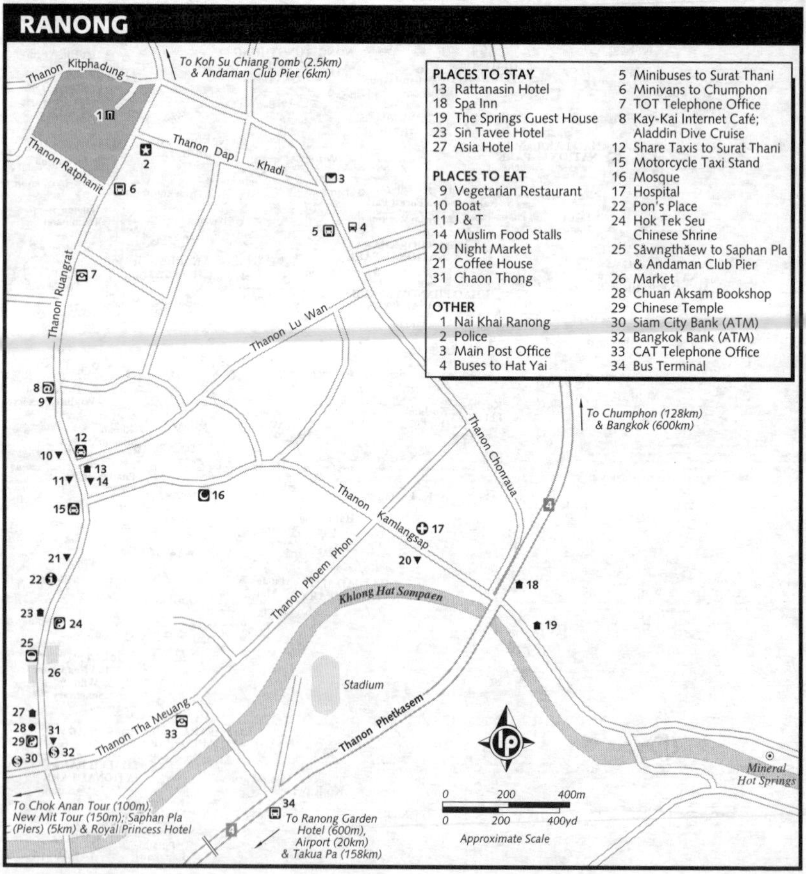

Th Ruangrat; open 7.30am-midnight daily), who also rents motorcycles and cars. He is also a good source of information on the area's ins and outs.

Kay-Kai Internet Café *(open 8.30am-11pm daily)*, on Th Ruangrat north of the cinema, has several computers with speedy and cheap (15B per hour) Internet connections, and serves snacks as well. And if you want reading material in English, try **Chuan Aksam bookshop** *(☎ 0 7781 1154; Th Ruangrat; open 8am-9.30pm daily)*, near the corner of Th Tha Meuang.

Hot Springs

About 1km east of Spa Inn, at Wat Tapotaram, is the Ranong Mineral Hot Springs. Water temperatures hover around 65°C – hot enough to boil eggs. The spring water is thought to be sacred as well as having miraculous healing powers.

You can bathe in rustic rooms where you mix water from separate hot- and cold-water tanks, sluicing the mixed water over your body. Note: Don't get inside the tanks, as you'll spoil the water. Some hotels along Th Phetkasem pipe this water into baths for their clients.

Nai Khai Ranong
ในค่ายระนอง

During the reign of King Rama V, a Hokkien named Koh Su Chiang became governor of Ranong (thus gaining the new name Phraya Damrong Na Ranong) and his former residence, Nai Khai Ranong, has become a clan house and shrine. It's on the northern edge of town and is worth a visit.

Of the three original buildings, one still stands and is filled with mementoes of the Koh family. A much larger building lies in ruins to the southwest, beneath a shelter. Parts of the original wall surrounding the entire compound also remain.

Koh Su Chiang's tomb is set into the side of a hill nearly 3km farther northwest, on the road to the Andaman Club pier. Along the way you'll pass a few other Chinese tombs; Koh's is signed and is the most elaborate, with a great deal of statuary.

Diving

Dives in the Ranong area include trips out to the impressive Burma Banks (a part of the Mergui Archipelago) as well as the world-class Surin and Similan Islands. Because of the distances involved, dive trips are mostly live-aboards and not cheap. Expect to pay more than US$200 for a two-day/two-night deal.

A couple of dive shops in Ranong can get you started: **Aladdin Dive Cruise** *(☎ 0 7781 2967; Ⓦ www.aladdindivecruise.de)*, at Kay-Kai Internet Café, and **A-One-Diving** *(☎/fax 0 7783 2984; Ⓦ www.a-one-diving.com; 77 Saphan Pla)*.

Places to Stay

As elsewhere in Thailand, at the cheaper hotels 'single' means a room with one large bed (big enough for two) while 'double' means a room with two beds.

Asia Hotel *(☎ 0 7781 1113; 39/9 Th Ruangrat; rooms with fan 290-350B, with air-con 600B)*, near the market, has spacious and clean rooms. Information on local islands is posted in a corridor beyond the lobby.

Sin Tavee Hotel *(Thawi; ☎ 0 7781 1213; 81/1 Th Ruangrat; singles/doubles with fan 160/240B, doubles with air-con 280B)* is north of the market. Reception is relaxed and doubles come with tile floors, good beds, hot water, soap and towels. It's good value; where's the catch, you ask? Some of the sinks empty straight out of the bottom, splashing water on your feet.

Rattanasin Hotel *(cnr Th Ruangrat & Th Lu Wan; singles/doubles 100/170B)* has a very small sign in Roman script. It's a typical Thai-Chinese hotel that looks a bit worse for wear, though rooms have good beds and fans. Some of the bathrooms have squat toilets, and showers consisting merely of a pipe jutting out of the wall, but at least it's cheap.

The following three places to stay are on or near Th Phetkasem (Hwy 4) and can be reached from town by *săwngthăew* No 2 (7B). From the bus station, the farthest is 1km away.

The Springs Guest House *(☎ 0 7783 4369; cnr Th Kamlangsap & Th Phetkasem; dorm beds 80-100B, rooms with fan 150-200B, with air-con 230-250B)* is a block east of Th Phetkasem. Savour the tinted windows; this used to be a karaoke joint. It's geared toward the foreign traveller, with a pool table and satellite TV in the bar/restaurant area downstairs, left luggage, and lots of local information. Rates vary depending on the number of people. It's a fairly small place, with a three-bed dorm – but when it fills up, bathroom access may be a problem.

Spa Inn *(no Roman-script sign; ☎ 0 7781 1715; Th Phetkasem 1/15; rooms with air-con 380-480B)* is on Hwy 4 just north of the river. It's getting rather tatty but has no pretensions and is friendly enough. The rooms are large and have bathtubs you can fill with hot mineral water piped in from the springs upstream. The back rooms look out on lush green mountainside.

Ranong Garden Hotel *(☎ 0 7783 2174, fax 0 7783 2183; 6/54 Th Phetchkasem; rooms with air-con 975-1075B)* is about 800m south of the bus station and is a decent hotel, with modern carpeted rooms and a few mid-range amenities. Prices are often discounted during slow times. Keeping drinks cold in your room will cost more, though.

Royal Princess *(☎ 0 7783 5240, fax 0 7783 5238; w www.royalprincess.com; rooms with air-con in low/high season 990/1800B)* is the fanciest pad in town, with mineral-water bathrooms, Jacuzzi, gym and pool. The rooms are fine enough but are looking slightly piqued. Breakfast is usually included in the price.

Places to Eat

Not far from Hwy 4 and the Spa Inn is a night market with several **food stalls** *(Th Kamlangsap)*. Towards Th Ruangrat's southern end, and occupying space on both sides of the street, the town **market** offers inexpensive Thai and Burmese meals, as well as fresh produce, fish and meats.

The following restaurants are located on Th Ruangrat, and are listed here from north to south.

Kay-Kai *(open 8.30am-11pm daily)*, just north of the cinema, is a friendly eatery with a good variety of dishes and inexpensive ice-cream concoctions, plus a row of computers providing cheap and fast Internet access. A **vegetarian restaurant** *(open 7am-6pm Mon-Sat)*, next door to Kay-Kai, cooks you very inexpensive Thai vegie dishes.

Boat *(☎ 0 7782 3996)* is a large and modern air-con restaurant (and rather bleak guesthouse) that does a lot of ice-cream business. It also serves Thai and Western food.

J&T *(dishes 20-45B)* is a similar air-con place that fills up with Thai families on Sunday afternoon. The food is closer to cafeteria than haute cuisine, but it's filling and dirt-cheap. Try the Indonesian stir-fried rice (35B), which comes topped with a fried egg and accompanied by shrimp crisps, chopped cucumber and slices of chicken.

Muslim food stalls *(open Sun-Fri)* are three modest eateries strung to the south along the opposite side of the street from J&T. You can get Malaysian-style curry, rice, roti, pickled cucumbers and tea for 35B.

Coffee House, across the street and about a block farther south, is tiny and friendly, and serves Western-style breakfasts and light meals. Look for the small paper sign in Roman script.

Pon's Place *(☎ 0 7782 3344; open 7.30am-midnight daily)* serves good cheap food and dishes out lots of local information as well; there's a helpful travel desk in front.

Chaon Thong *(open 6am-9.30pm daily)* is a clean, inexpensive indoor/outdoor (air-con indoors) café with plenty of fresh-cooked Thai dishes and Western breakfasts.

Getting There & Away

Air Contact **Phuket Airlines** *(☎ 0 7782 4590; w www.phuketairlines.com)* for daily flights between Ranong and Bangkok. Flights between Ranong and Phuket leave Friday, Saturday and Sunday at 11.30pm. At the time of writing, the airline had plans for services between Ranong and points in Myanmar.

Bus The bus terminal is on Hwy 4 toward the south end of town, though some buses stop in town before proceeding on to the terminal. Săwngthăew No 2 (blue) passes the terminal. See the 'Bus Destinations from Ranong' table on the following page.

Two private bus companies offer routes to Bangkok: **Chok Anan Tour** *(☎ 0 7781 1337)* operates 1st-class air-con buses at 8am and 8pm daily (333B), as well as a VIP bus (389B) and a super VIP bus (515B), both which leave at 8pm. **New MIT Tour** *(☎ 0 7781 1150)* has VIP buses (389B) at 8.30am and 8.10pm. Both companies are located on Th Meuang a few hundred metres west of Th Ruangrat.

Minivans head to Surat Thani (130B, three hours) and Chumphon (80B, three hours); see the map for departure locations. Share taxis also go to Surat Thani (130B) from just south of the post office.

Bus Destinations from Ranong

destination	fare (B)	duration (hrs)
Bangkok		
VIP	389-515	10
1st class	333	10
2nd class	259	10
ordinary	185	10
Chumphon		
2nd class	70	3
ordinary	50	3
Hat Yai		
2nd class	300	5
Khuraburi		
air-con	60	1½
ordinary	40	1½
Phang-Nga		
ordinary	90	5
Phuket		
air-con	185	5
ordinary	103	6
Surat Thani		
1st class	180	4
2nd class	80	5

Getting Around

Ranong airport is 20km south of town, off Hwy 4. Săwngthăew to Saphan Pla are 7B. Motorcycle taxis will take you most anywhere in town for 15B, to the hotels along Hwy 4 for 20B and to the pier for boats to Koh Chang, Ko Panyam and Myanmar for 40B. Pon's Place (see Orientation & Information earlier for details) can assist with motorcycle and car rentals.

AROUND RANONG

Kawthoung

เกาะสอง

The small port of Kawthoung (Ko Song) at the southernmost tip of mainland Myanmar is separated from Thailand by Pak San, the broad estuary of Mae Nam Chan. To the British it was Victoria Point and to the Thais it's Ko Song, which means Second Island. Kawthoung, the Burmese name, is probably a corruption of the latter.

The main business here is trade with Thailand, followed by fishing. Among the Burmese, Kawthoung is perhaps best known for producing some of the country's best kick boxers. Most residents are bilingual, speaking Thai and Burmese. Many people born and raised around Kawthoung, especially Muslims, also speak Pashu, a dialect that mixes Thai, Malay and Burmese. Nearby islands are inhabited by bands of nomadic Moken, or sea gypsies.

At the moment Kawthoung is only accessible to foreigners by boat from Ranong, Thailand. It's probably not worth making a special trip to Ranong just to visit Kawthoung, but if you're in the area and decide to cross over, you'll find it's similar to southern Thailand except that many more men wear the *longyi* (the Burmese sarong). It is now legal to travel from Kawthoung into the interior of Myanmar – eg, Dawei (Tavoy) or Yangon – by plane or by ship. Road travel north of Kawthoung, however, is forbidden by the Myanmar government due to security concerns.

Places to Stay So far there are only two places in Kawthoung approved to accept foreigners. Thai baht are readily accepted here.

Honey Bear Hotel *(in Yangon ☎ 0 1229 6190; rooms with air-con 700B)*, a five-minute walk from the pier, is modern and friendly, sporting clean rooms with satellite TV and cold-water shower; it's not a great deal by Thai standards but a comfortable enough hotel.

Kawthoung Motel *(rooms 1000B)* is the other option – a mouldy joint about 300m beyond the main immigration office and about 500m from the pier. For simple double rooms with private cold-water shower, foreigners pay dearly, and the money goes into the military regime's pocket. Breakfast is included.

On nearby Thahtay Island is **Andaman Club Hotel** *(in Ranong ☎ 0 7783 1227, in Bangkok ☎ 0 2679 8238; W www.andamanclub.com; rooms with air-con in low/high season from 1560/1920B)* is on nearby Thahtay Island and is where well-heeled Thai and Singaporean gamblers shack up. It's a huge five-star hotel complex sporting a casino and over 200 modern rooms with sea views. Also on the premises are a wonderful pool, fitness centre, sauna, and all those other things that make rich people happy.

Getting There & Away When the Thai/Myanmar border is open, boats to Kawthoung leave the pier at Saphan Pla (Pla

Bridge), about 4.5km from the centre of Ranong. Departures are frequent from around 8.30am until 6pm, and cost 60B to 100B per person. Take sǎwngthǎew No 2 from Ranong (7B; some have destinations in English on the side) and get off at the **immigration office** *(☎ 0 7782 2016; Th Ruangrat; open 8.30am-6pm daily)*, 700m north of the pier, to get your passport stamped. Walk or catch another sǎwngthǎew the rest of the way. There's a small tollbooth at the entrance to the pier area; turn to the right here and walk down the lane that leads past the north side of the PTT petrol station (ie, you'll pass the station on your left). At the end of the lane are boats to Kawthoung. Chartering a boat holding six to seven people costs around 500B return.

Bear in mind when you are returning to Thailand that Myanmar time is a half hour behind Thailand's. This has caused problems in the past for returning visitors who got through Burmese immigration before its 6pm closing time only to find the Thai office closed. Though Thai immigration seems to have changed their hours in order to avoid this unpleasantness, you should double-check with them when leaving the country.

Upon arrival at the Kawthoung jetty there's a stop at Myanmar immigration. At this point you must inform the authorities whether you're a day visitor – in which case you must pay a fee of US$5 or 300B for a day permit. If you're staying the night and inform them you'll be staying at the Kawthoung Motel (see Places to Stay earlier), the permit *might* be issued more readily, since this motel is government-run. If you have a valid Myanmar visa in your passport, you'll be permitted to stay up to 28 days, but are required to buy US$200 worth of foreign exchange certificates (FECs).

A more expensive alternative to the process outlined earlier, and one favoured by many expats on 'visa runs', is to take a fast air-con boat for a visit to the Andaman Club Hotel (see Places to Stay earlier) from its private pier about 7km northwest of Ranong centre. The pier has a large covered car park and a deluxe **ticket office** *(☎ 0 7783 0461)* with its own customs and immigration counters. Boats leave 15 times a day between 7am and 11.50pm Monday to Thursday, and hourly from 7am to midnight Friday to Sunday and holidays. You pay 250B return (or 500B if you want the staff to process your Myanmar visa). For an extra 100B the Andaman Club van will pick you up in Ranong and bring you to the pier. Or you can catch a 20B sǎwngthǎew bound for Sam Laem (ask for the Andaman Club pier) from the market on Th Ruanrat in Ranong.

Perhaps because it is such a money-maker, the Andaman Club route tends to be open even when the border is officially closed. Immigration officers at the Saphan Pla office hand out maps to the club's pier, complete with phone number.

Yangon Airways *(1/1 Bogyoke Lan, Kawthoung)* sometimes flies an ATR-72 to Yangon for US$145. To Yangon by ship it's two nights (one night each is spent in Dawei and Myeik) – 36 hours in total.

Ko Chang
เกาะช้าง

The waters around this rustic and laid-back island (not to be confused with the larger Ko Chang in Trat Province) are clouded by effluent from the muddy estuary, but that doesn't stop adventurous travellers from enjoying the mangroves on the east coast and a hilly, forested interior. There's a small main village where boats land (in high season), dirt trails meandering around the island, and so far no electricity – the resorts either do without or generate their own. Beaches are found along the western shore and if you're lucky, you may catch sight of sea eagles, Andaman kites and even hornbills.

Bungalow operations on the island can arrange boat trips to Ko Phayam and other nearby islands for around 200B per person (including lunch) in a group of six or more. Dive trips are also possible; check with **Aladdin Dive Cruise** *(in Ranong ☎ 0 7781 2967; Ⓦ www.aladdindivecruise.de; Kay-Kai Internet Café, Th Ruangrat • on Ko Chang ☎ 0 1229 6667)*.

Places to Stay & Eat Several beach places have opened up over the last few years, although for the most part they're only open from November to April. Some have limited electricity.

Ko Chang Contex *(☎ 0 7781 2730, in Ranong ☎ 0 7783 3137; bungalows 100-200B)*, which is north of the village, is run by a Thai family and offers basic bungalows on a rocky headland above the beach, along with an à la carte restaurant menu.

Eden Bistro Cafe *(☎ 0 7782 0172; bungalows 250-300B)*, southwest of Ko Chang Contex, is a friendly café that offers a handful of small bungalows with shared bathroom and one large bungalow with attached shower.

Sunset Bungalow *(☎ 0 7782 0171; bungalows 100-250B)*, just down the beach from Eden, offers nicely built bungalows in a shady, breezy spot.

Cashew Resort *(☎ 0 7782 4741; bungalows 200-600B)*, the oldest and largest resort on the island, has a range of abodes, from wooden A-frame huts to larger, more solid bungalows. Cashew, Eden and Sunset will pick prospective guests up at J&T restaurant in Ranong.

Chang Thong Bungalows *(☎ 0 7783 3820; bungalows with/without bath 150/100B)* and **Pheung Thong**, a few hundred metres past the pier, are friendly side-by-side operations. They have solid wooden bungalows set on a sandy lot with some trees. Chang Thong often picks up visitors at Chaon Thong in Ranong.

Lae Tawan *(☎ 0 1788 5683; bungalows 150-200B)* is located in a nearby small bay, offering a handful of wood-and-concrete bungalows on a tree-spotted hillside. **Ta Daeng Bay** *(huts 100-200B)* is nearby, with thatched huts.

N & X Bungalows *(huts 100B)*, by itself at the southern end of the island at **Ao Lek** (Small Bay), offers very basic thatched huts.

Getting There & Away From Ranong take a săwngthăew (7B; will likely have destination signs in English) to Saphan Pla, getting off by the PTT petrol station and toll booth. Look for a lane on the left just before the toll booth (there may be a sign referring to Ko Chang) and follow it down a few hundred metres, zigzagging along the way; turn left at the T-intersection and walk about five minutes to reach the pier.

Two or three boats leave every morning from November to April; turn up around 9am to see when they're going, as they don't usually leave before this hour. During the high season – December to March – there's a consistent noon departure daily. Boats return to Ranong at 8am the next day. The fare is 100B per person, though if you book your accommodation ahead of time the boat ride can be included.

Ko Phayam

This friendly and demure little island is populated by only a few hundred inhabitants – mostly Thais and Burmese – with a smattering of expats and a few dozen *chao leh* (sea gypsies) thrown into the mix. While spotlighted by two main bays and their beaches, Ko Phayam also has a couple of sizeable, forested hills and plenty of scenic agricultural land to boot. Locals support themselves mostly on prawn fishing and cashew-nut farming. Interesting fauna in the area include wild pigs, hornbills, monkeys and snakes.

There's one sizeable 'village' on the island, where lies the main pier, a couple of simple eateries, some small grocery stalls and one surprisingly modern bar. (The only other bar on the island is Banana Bar, which has an isolated and natural setting and is located towards Ao Yai, near Bamboo Bungalows.) From the pier area, motorcycle taxis scoot you to the 15 or so bungalow operations around the island, almost all of which are pretty basic and located on the two bays. A new motorcycle 'highway', running down the middle of Ko Phayam, augments smaller concrete roadways and dirt driveways.

Places to Stay & Eat Practically all the bungalows on Ko Phayam only have fans, and electricity is usually available from sunset to 10pm or 11pm only. All have their own restaurant and many, unlike on nearby Ko Chang, stay open all year.

The following places are on Ao Yai, whose 3km-long beach is sandy and pleasant and gets more waves than Ao Khao Fai. Prices may vary a bit depending on the season or demand.

Bamboo Bungalows *(☎ 0 7782 0012; bungalows 100-500B)* is run by a friendly Israeli/Thai couple. There are a wide variety of bungalows here, from the most basic A-frames to solid concrete-and-tile-floor structures with creative baths. Garden areas are pleasant and the restaurant is good. It's near the middle of the beach, and boogie boards can be rented.

Coconuts *(☎ 0 7782 0011; bungalows 200-400B)*, near Bamboo, is another friendly business that features some nice, well-spaced wooden bungalows, the larger of which cost more. Next door is **Ao Yai Bungalows** *(☎ 0 7782 1753; ✉ gilles_patchara@hotmail.com; bungalows 200B)*, with more decent wooden bungalows.

The next few places are at **Ao Khao Fai**, a little bit north of Ao Yai. This shallow beach is more sheltered, but not quite as good for swimming. It's also more affected by the tides than Ao Yai. It's still quite a scenic bay to hang your towel, however.

Vijit *(☎ 0 7783 4082; 🌐 www.geocities.com/vijitbungalows; bungalows 100-200B)*, toward the southern end of the bay, has about a dozen basic bungalows around a sandy lot planted with young trees. Each bungalow has been built in a slightly different style. At high tide, the beach here thins out. Contact the staff for free transport from Ranong.

JPR *(bungalows 150-200B)* is farther north and has nine no-frills bungalows spread out between trees, on a dusty hillside above the beach. It's friendly, pretty isolated and down a long driveway.

Mountain Resort *(☎ 0 7782 0098; bungalows 350B)*, north of JPR at the top of the bay, has five large, solid and attractive bungalows. They lie on grassy, palm-shaded grounds off the beach, and are some of the most modern ones on the island.

Located about a 10- to 15-minute walk north of the village (turn right after the pier) is **Anan Bungalows** *(☎ 0 1892 4795; ✉ arnon87@hotmail.com; bungalows 200-300B)*, with four attractive wooden abodes. Unlike the rest of the businesses mentioned here, Anan is inland and not near the bays or beaches.

Getting There & Away See the Ko Chang Getting There & Away section for details on getting to Ranong's Saphan Pla, from where boats head to Ko Phayam.

There are daily boats from Saphan Pla to Ko Phayam's pier at around 8am and 3pm (100B, 1½ to two hours). From Ko Phayam back to Ranong the boats run at 9am and 2pm. During the high season there may be three runs daily. Long-tail boat charters to the island cost 1500B to 2000B.

There was talk of a new boat service running from Ranong directly to the two main bays on Ko Phayam, saving you a hefty motorcycle ride. This service would run November to May only and cost 100B per person. It may be worth asking around Ranong and seeing if this boat run got off the ground, so to speak.

Getting Around Transport around the island is provided by motorcycle taxis; there are no cars or trucks (yet), and roads are pleasantly motorcycle-sized. A ride to your bungalow will cost 50B to 100B. Walking is possible but distances are long – it's about 45 minutes from the pier to Ao Khao Fai, the nearest bay.

Motorcycle rentals are available at **Oscar's** *(☎ 0 7782 4236)*, the only bar in the village – you can't miss it. Rates are about 250B per day. Some of the bigger guesthouses might be able to arrange rentals also.

Phang-Nga Province

Covering the coastline between Ranong and Phuket Provinces, Phang-Nga Province has plenty of natural beauty to offer the intrepid traveller. The Surin and Similan Island Archipelagos are national marine parks – harbouring some of the world's top diving destinations. Along the shoreline are the up-and-coming beach destinations of Bang Niang and Hat Khao Lak. Ao Phang-Nga has stunning limestone mountains and rock formations. And let's not forget the small but uniquely fascinating national parks scattered here and there throughout Phang-Nga Province, which is also a gateway to Phuket Island, the Krabi region and Khao Sok National Park.

SURIN ISLANDS NATIONAL MARINE PARK

อุทยานแห่งชาติหมู่เกาะสุรินทร์

A national park since 1981, the Surin Islands *(admission 200B; open mid-Nov–mid-May)* number five in all and are famous for their excellent diving and snorkelling. The two main and largest islands, Ko Surin Neua (north) and Ko Surin Tai (south), lie about 55km from Thailand's coast and 5km from Thailand's marine border with Myanmar. Some of the best diving can be found in the channel between these two islands. The park office, visitors centre and best hiking trails are at Ao Mae Yai (the south bay) on Ko Surin Neua. On Ko Surin Tai is a village of *chao náam* who hold a major ancestral worship ceremony (Loi Reua) in April. Long-tail boats ferry passengers between the two islands.

Surrounding the Surin Archipelago are some of the best-developed coral colonies in Thailand. There are seven major dive sites in the immediate vicinity of the Surin Islands; the best are at **HQ Bay**, **Ko Chi** and **Richelieu Rock** (a seamount 14km south-east of Ko Surin Tai). Whale sharks – the largest fish in the world – are often spotted near Richelieu, especially during the months of March and April. Snorkelling is excellent in many areas due to relatively shallow reef depths of 5m to 6m – all you need to do is bring your equipment.

The **Burma Banks** are a gorgeous system of submerged seamounts about 60km north-west of the Surin Islands. The only way to visit – unless you have your own boat – is by way of seven- to 10-day live-aboard dive trips out of Phuket, Khao Lak or Ranong. The three major banks, **Silvertip**, **Roe** and **Rainbow**, provide four- to five-star diving experiences, with fields of psychedelic coral laid over flat, underwater plateaus. There are heaps of large oceanic as well as smaller reef marine species, including reef, silver-tip, nurse and leopard sharks.

Places to Stay & Eat

Accommodation is available in the **park longhouses** *(in Bangkok ☎ 0 2561 2919–21; 1-6 person longhouses 1200B)* or at the **camp-site** *(mainland office ☎ 0 7649 1378; camping per person 40B, onsite tent for 2 people 300B)*. The park also offers a daily package of three good **meals** (mostly seafood) for 400B per person. Electricity is generated from 6pm to 11pm.

Should you need to stay nearby on the mainland, Khuraburi offers the friendly, very basic and somewhat charming **Tararain River Hut Resort** *(☎ 0 7649 1789; bungalows with fan/air-con 300/500B)*, north of town just over the bridge. Fan bungalows are tiny and no-frills; air-con bungalows are tiny and a bit more modern. At the other end of the scale is the **Kuraburi Greenview Resort** *(☎ 0 7642 1360; rooms & bungalows 1900-2200B)*, where rooms have luxurious amenities. Breakfast is included in the rates. It's actually south of Khuraburi about 12km, right off Hwy 4.

Getting There & Away

Boat travel is only considered safe between mid-November and mid-May. The park is officially closed from mid-May to mid-November.

Ko Surin National Park's **mainland office** *(☎ 0 7649 1378)* is in Ngan Yong, the little fishing village where boats to the islands depart. The short (2km) road to Ngan Yong turns off Hwy 4 at the Km 110 marker, about 6km north of Khuraburi and 109km south of Ranong.

Ordinary/air-con buses between Khuraburi and Ranong cost 40/60B and take about an hour and 20 minutes; ask to be let off at Ngan Yong (say 'Ko Surin'). To/from Phuket, buses cost 60B and take about three hours. Motorcycle taxis between Khuraburi to Ngan Yong are 50B.

Ko Surin is not a bargain destination. Ask about in-season daily boat departures at the mainland office (boats leave at 9am); park staff can help book you seats (1000B per person return; four hours). You can also charter a private boat for about 6000B return.

Dive operators in Phuket, Khao Lak and even Ranong have live-aboard diving excursions to the Surin Islands. Because of the distances involved, Ko Surin is the most expensive dive destination in Thailand; costs about 10,000B to 12,000B for a two-day or three-day trip.

TAKUA PA

This sizeable town should not be on your 'to-see' list; it's not necessarily unpleasant, but it just isn't a tourist destination. You may find yourself travelling through here, however, as Takua Pa is 3.5km from the junction of Hwy 4 (which leads north towards Ranong and south towards Phuket) and Hwy 401 (which leads east to Khao Sok National Park).

Places to Stay

If you need some shut-eye, consider the decent **Extra Hotel** *(☎ 0 7642 1026, fax 0 7642 1412; rooms with fan/air-con 300/450B)*, located right behind the Esso petrol station in the middle of town.

Getting There & Away

The bus station is 200m north of town, across the bridge. Destinations from this cheap-restaurant-filled transit point include Bangkok (air-con 427B to 498B), Surat Thani (ordinary/air-con 65/90B), Phuket (ordinary/air-con 55/75B), Ranong (ordinary/air-con 65/90B), Krabi (ordinary 65B) and Khao Sok National Park (ordinary 25B, nine a day).

BANG NIANG & HAT KHAO LAK
บ้านเนียงและหาดเขาหลัก

About 30km south of Takua Pa and separated by 3km are the pleasant, laid-back resorts of Bang Niang and Hat Khao Lak. The beach along this pretty stretch is very long and occasionally studded with granite boulders; swimming and beach strolling are great time-burners here. An offshore coral reef suitable for snorkelling is 45 minutes away by boat, and many dive shops offer excursions to this reef or to the Similan and Surin Islands.

Bang Niang is quite a bit smaller than Hat Khao Lak, but still offers Internet service, small food stores and a few shops. The waterfalls of **Chong-Fa** *(admission 200B)* are about 6km up a side road from the highway.

Hat Khao Lak has a few more restaurants and services (such as dive shops and car-rental agencies) than Bang Niang, as well as the swankiest resorts in the area. As with Bang Niang, the basic services are all spread out along the highway, while most resorts are hidden away by the coast on side streets off the highway. Both towns are growing rapidly, so expect more services to be at your disposal.

Diving

Khao Lak is a dive haven – there are around 15 dive shops here now, with more on the way. Ready access to the Ko Surin and Ko Similan National Park Archipelagos explains this phenomenal growth, as these islands offer some of the best diving in Thailand.

Since both Ko Surin and Ko Similan are relatively far from the mainland – around 60km away – most dive trips do 'live-aboard' trips, meaning you spend the night on the boat. These cost around 3700/9000/12,000B for one-day/two-day/three-day packages. Trips to local coral reefs start around 1300B. The best diving months are December to May.

Some of the more established dive shops in town are **Sea Dragon** *(☎ 0 7642 0420; w www.seadragondivecenter.com)*, **Phuket Divers** *(☎ 0 7642 0628; w www.phuketdivers.com)*, **Sea Bees** *(☎ 0 7642 0581; w www.sea-bees.com)* and **Kon Tiki** *(☎ 0 7642 0208; w www.kontiki-khaolak.com)*. All of these have staff who speak several languages.

Places to Stay – Budget & Mid-Range

Bang Niang The following businesses are located at or near the beach, approximately 1km from the highway down a side road from the main intersection in town. Most have their own restaurant.

Baan Soraya *(☎ 0 7642 0192; w www.geocities.com/baansoraya; rooms with fan in low/high season 700/1000B, with air-con 800/1200B)* is a small, intimate place with only six modern and tastefully decorated rooms. It has a seaside restaurant/bar area.

Pascha Resort *(☎ 0 7642 0280; e pascha43@hotmail.com; rooms with air-con in low season 1000-1200B, in high season 1800-2500B)* is an upscale resort about 20m from the beach. Wood and brick bungalows surround a pool area, and there's a large restaurant near reception.

Baan Thai Resort *(☎ 0 7642 0531, fax 0 7642 0506; e baanthairesort@hotmail.com; bungalows with fan 500-800B)* offers basic, thatched bungalows (along with fancier tiled ones) surrounding a nice leafy path. Prices drop 50% in low season; it's just inland from Mai's Quiet Zone Bungalows.

Mai's Quiet Zone Bungalows *(☎ 0 7642 0196, fax 0 7642 0197; e maisquietzone@yahoo.com; bungalows with fan 600-850B, family units 1000B)* is a great traveller's find: charmingly rustic bungalows, beach swings, cool spots to lounge, a great seaside restaurant deck – all surrounded by lush garden. Canoes are also available to rent. Prices drop 30% in low season.

Wunder Bungalow *(☎ 0 7642 0595, fax 0 7642 0596; e wunder@pop.co.th; bungalows in low/high season 400/800B)* wasn't quite open at the time of writing, but these new wood bungalows – set away from the beach a little – look very pleasant. It's located almost at the northern tip of the beach road.

Hat Khao Lak All of the businesses listed here are located on the beach, 500m from the highway down a side road from the main intersection in town.

Nang Thong Bay Resort *(☎ 0 7642 0088, fax 0 7642 0090; ⓔ nangthong1@hotmail.com; bungalows with fan in low/high season 700/1200B)* is the first resort you hit on the beach. Very comfortable bungalows are *mostly* well spaced on pleasant grounds with a stream running through.

Nang Thong Bay Resort II *(☎ 0 7642 0078, fax 0 7642 0080; ⓔ nangthong2@hotmail.com; bungalows with fan in low/high season 600/900B, with air-con 800/1200B)* is 300m south of its sister resort. Beautiful palmy grounds, shrub-lined paths and (an eroding) beachside restaurant terrace compliment good bungalows.

Green Beach *(☎ 0 7642 0046; bungalows with fan in low/high season 400/900B, with air-con 600/1300B)* is 200m north of Nang Thong Bay Resort and has interesting bamboo, wood and stone bungalows lined up along a garden path that leads to the beach. The bungalows are not fancy inside, just basic but adequate.

Garden Beach Resort *(☎ 0 7642 0121, fax 0 7642 0129; ⓔ gardenbeachresort@hotmail.com; bungalows with fan 300-600B)* is 200m north of Green Beach, and only open in high season. Over 60 small and plain bungalows rest on large, scruffy, tree-specked grounds. Prices vary depending on proximity to the beach.

Happy Lagoon *(☎ 0 1719 9387; bungalows with fan in low season 180-200B, in high season 250B)* offers 10 very basic thatched bungalows; they're the cheapest digs on this beach and for hard-core budget backpackers only. Happy Lagoon is at the northern end of town, 800m from the highway down its own dirt driveway (look across from the shopping strip).

Places to Stay – Top End

Hat Khao Lak The following are located south on Hwy 4, within 2km of town. Expect luxurious amenities like air-con and fancy drapes. All prices include breakfast but not service charges or taxes.

Khao Lak Laguna Resort *(☎ 0 7642 0200, fax 0 7642 0206; ⓦ www.khaolaklaguna.net; rooms & bungalows in low season 1650-2100B, in high season 3300-4200B)* lies 900m from town and is charming and in a beautiful setting. Expansive grassy grounds intertwine with lagoons, while wood or brick walkways keep you above it all. The bungalows and rooms are very comfortable and there's a beachside pool, billiards room and nice Thai restaurant.

Khao Lak Palm Beach Resort *(☎ 0 7642 0096, fax 0 7642 0095; ⓦ www.khaolakpalmbeach.com; rooms in low season 1800-4250B, in high season 3600-8500B)* is 1.9km from town and offers gorgeous rooms with nice details – the buildings have traditional peaked roofs. There are four types of rooms; the best have large baths and sunken tubs. The grounds are a lush jungle with streams. A spa, gym and two pools complete the picture.

Khao Lak Sunset Resort *(☎ 0 7642 0075, fax 0 7642 0075; ⓦ www.khaolaksunset.com; rooms from 1200-3290B)* is 2km from town. It's a modern resort boasting comfortable, well-appointed rooms with a balcony and sea views, as well as a Thai restaurant and a large pool near the beach.

Getting There & Away

Any bus travelling between Thai Muang and Takua Pa will stop at Bang Niang or Hat Khao Lak. From Bangkok (ordinary/2nd class 120/168B, six hours) there are several buses.

KHAO LAK/LAM RU NATIONAL PARK

อุทยานแห่งชาติเขาหลัก/แหลมรู

The area to the immediate south of Hat Khao Lak is encompassed by this 125-sq-km park *(☎ 0 7642 0243; admission 200B)*. Situated within its borders are a collection of beautiful sea cliffs, 1000m-high hills, beaches, waterfalls, estuaries and mangroves. Wildlife seen in the area include hornbills, drongos, tapirs, gibbons, monkeys and Asiatic black bears. The **visitors centre**, just off Hwy 4 between the Km 56 and Km 57 markers, has little in the way of maps or printed information, but there's a very nice open-air **restaurant** *(open 9am-9pm daily)* perched on a shady slope overlooking the sea.

There are coastal trails to explore, and you may be able to take long-tail boat trips up the scenic Khlong Thap Liang estuary – if you're lucky you'll spot mangrove communities of crab-eating macaques. Ask at the visitors centre for more information.

Khao Lak/Lam Ru National Park is less than 3km south of Khao Lak and can easily be visited on day trips. If you'd like to stay within the park, however, two- to four-person **bungalows** can be rented for 250B to 500B. Tents are also available for 100B to 200B. For reservations, call the park.

SIMILAN ISLANDS NATIONAL MARINE PARK

อุทยานแห่งชาติหมู่เกาะสิมิลัน

The Similan Islands *(admission 200B; open Nov-May)* are world-renowned among diving enthusiasts for incredible underwater sightseeing at depths ranging from 2m to 30m. Huge and smooth granite rock formations plunge into the sea and form seamounts, rock reefs and dive-throughs. As elsewhere in the Andaman Sea, the best diving months are December to May when the weather is good and the sea at its clearest.

The Thais sometimes refer to the Similan Islands as Ko Kao, or Nine Islands, because there are nine of them – each has a number as well as a name. In fact, the name 'Similan' comes from the Malay word *sembilan* meaning nine. Counting in order from the north, they are Ko Bon, Ko Ba-Ngu, Ko Similan, Ko Payu, Ko Miang (which is actually two islands close together), Ko Payan, Ko Payang and Ko Hu Yong. They're relatively small islands and uninhabited except for park officials and the occasional tourist group.

Ko Miang, the second largest island after Ko Similan, is where you'll find a visitors centre, the park headquarters and accommodation. Venturing inland from the beach, you should catch glimpses of the Nicobar pigeon or the hairy-legged mountain land crab. If you're not into aqualungs, the beaches on this island are good for snorkelling, as is the channel between Ko Miang and Ko Payu.

Ko Similan is also good for hiking and snorkelling. In a small bay on the Similan's western side you may be able to see spiny lobsters resting in rock crevices, along with sea fans and plume worms. The largest granite outcrop in the Similan Islands is also found on Ko Similan; scramble to the top to enjoy a sweeping view of the sea.

On the nine islands there are 32 species of birds, including the Brahminy kite and white-breasted waterhen. Migratory species of note include the pintail snipe, grey wagtail, cattle egret, watercock and the roseate tern. Fairly common mammal residents such as the bush-tailed porcupine, common palm civet, flying lemur and bottlenose dolphin call these islands home, along with reptiles and amphibians like the banded krait, reticulated python, white-lipped pit viper, common pit viper, hawksbill turtle, leather turtle, Bengal monitor lizard, common water monitor lizard and the ornate froglet.

Diving

The best place for dive trips to the Similan Islands is Hat Khao Lak. Many dive shops there offer multi-day dive excursions; see Bang Niang & Hat Khao Lak earlier in this chapter for more details.

Phuket also has many dive shops offering Similan Islands excursions, however, Phuket is far from the Similans – some 90km by boat, as opposed to 60km from Hat Khao Lak. This longer distance makes the excursions more expensive; expect to pay about US$440 for a three-day/four-night dive trip with equipment included.

Places to Stay & Eat

Accommodation, including camping, is only allowed on Ko Miang. The park *(mainland office ☎ 0 7659 5045; camping per person 80B, 2-person onsite tents for 400B, bungalows for 4/6/8 people 600/1200/1600B, for 2 people with bath 1000B)* rents **bungalows** and tents.

The only source of food is a privately run **restaurant** on Ko Miang. Prices are high, so it's a good idea to bring some of your own.

Getting There & Away

The Similan Island's **mainland park office** *(☎ 0 7659 5045)* is in Thap Lamu, 39km south of Takua Pa and 4km off Hwy 4. Just 500m past this office is the pier where boats leave to the islands, 60km away.

From November to May boats depart daily at 8.30am for about 2300B return; you can buy boat tickets at **Met Sine Tours** *(☎/fax 0 7644 3276)*, near the pier. The trip takes about three hours. Boats return from the Similans in the afternoon; schedules can be fluid, so call Metsine or the mainland park office for more information.

AO PHANG-NGA & PHANG-NGA

อ่าวพังงา/อ.เมืองพังงา

postcode 82000 • pop 9500

Over 95km northeast of Phuket, this sheltered pocket of the Andaman Sea is blessed with plenty of verdant limestone cliffs, odd rock formations, submerged karst caves and quaint fishing villages. All around the coast are the turquoise waters and scenic islands for which the Phang-Nga region is known. On the high cliffs of more isolated islands, swiftlets build their delicate saliva nests, which are collected for use in birds'-nest soup (a Chinese delicacy). Much of this area is part of **Ao Phang-Nga National Marine Park** and can be explored by boat or kayak.

If you're arriving in the Ao Phang-Nga area from Krabi on Hwy 4, you can either turn right or left just after Thap Put. Turning left will keep you on the shorter, straighter main highway, while turning right will take you onto a narrow, very curvy and pretty stretch of highway that's 5km longer than the main highway. It's your choice.

Phang-Nga is a somewhat spread out, modestly sized town with one main street (Hwy 4), and is nicely located near some limestone cliffs. There isn't a whole lot to see or do unless you happen to be there during the annual Vegetarian Festival in late September or early October (see the boxed text 'Vegetarian Festival' later in this chapter). It does have **Somdet Phra Sinakharin**, a public park at the south end of town, which contains dramatic karst formations like water-filled caves and tunnels; there's even a hole in a cliff you can drive through. One of the larger caves, **Tham Reusi Sawan**, is marked by a gilded statue of a *reusǐi* (Hindu sage).

Information

Phang-Nga town doesn't have a tourist office, but the one in Phuket town (see that entry later in this chapter) provides maps and good information on the region.

The bus terminal is in the centre of town, as are several banks with ATMs. The post and telephone offices are about 2km south of the centre. There's a good Internet café across from the 7-Eleven.

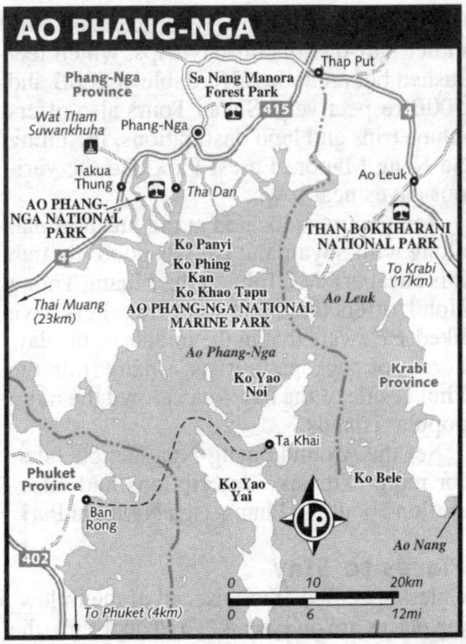

Phang-Nga's **immigration office** *(☎ 0 7641 2011; open 8.30am-4.30pm Mon-Fri)* is a few kilometres south of town; you'll probably never find it on your own, so take a motorcycle taxi.

Boat Tours

About 8.5km south of the town centre is Tha Dan, the pier area from where you can charter boats to see half-submerged caves, oddly shaped islands and a Ko Panyi, a Muslim village on stilts. There are also tours to 'James Bond Island' (the island rock in *The Man with the Golden Gun*) and Ao Phang-Nga National Park (400B to 500B per person for a two- to three-hour tour). Takua Thung, another pier area about 10km farther south of Tha Dan, also has private boats for hire, for similar prices; ask at the restaurants. Unless you enjoy haggling with boatmen, it's much easier (and not that expensive) to go with an arranged tour through an agency in town.

Sayan Tours *(☎ 0 7643 0348; W www.sayantourphangnga.com)* has been doing tours of Ao Phang-Nga for many years now, and these continue to receive good reviews from travellers. Overnight tours costs 750B per person and include **Tham Lawt** (a large water cave), **Ko Phing Kan** ('James Bond Island') and **Ko Panyi**, among other destinations. Meals and very rustic accommodation on Ko Panyi are part of the package.

This overnight trip is recommended over either half-day or full-day trips, which feel rushed but are more affordable at 200B and 500B respectively. Sayan Tours also offers canoe trips and land destinations, including Sa Nang Manora Forest Park and the various caves near town.

Kean Tours is located at the bus terminal along with Sayan, but isn't as good (though it is cheaper). **MT Tour**, at the Muang Thong Hotel, offers tours that some travellers have liked. Be aware that in the middle of the day, hordes of package tourists – many from the Phuket side of the bay – can crowd the more popular islands.

See the Around Phang-Nga section, later, for more extensive descriptions and information about Ao Phang-Nga National Park.

Places to Stay

Unless specified otherwise, all of the following places are on Hwy 4 (Th Phetkasem), the main street.

Thawisuk *(☎ 0 7641 2100; 77-79 Th Phetkasem; rooms with fan 150-200B)* is a rambling, pastel blue building in the middle of town. It's friendly and offers bright, simple rooms. There's a rooftop with good views. Similarly decked out are the nearby **Ratanapong** *(rooms with fan 150-200B; with air-con 350-450B)* and **Muang Thong** *(rooms with fan 150-200B)*, with a tour agency downstairs.

Phang-Nga Guest House *(☎ 0 7641 1358; rooms with fan 220-250B, with air-con 350-400B, room for 4-6 people 800-1000B)* is the best-value budget digs in town, with 12 clean, neat and pleasant rooms.

New Lukmuang Hotel *(☎ 0 7641 2218; rooms 450-670B)* is an ageing, noisy hotel next to the PTT petrol station just north of town. Its best-value rooms are actually the cheapest ones, but even those aren't anything special. Frosted windows obstruct views of anything.

Phang-Nga Inn *(☎ 7641 1963; ⓔ phang-ngainn@png.co.th; 2/2 Soi Lohakit; rooms with air-con 500-1400B)* is the most pleasant hotel in town. A converted family mansion holds 12 homy, quiet rooms. All are comfortably modern and well furnished; there's an eating area in front. It's on a side street off the main road near the centre of town.

Phang-Nga Valley Resort *(☎ 0 7641 2201; bungalows with air-con 560B, house with 3 bedrooms 2500B)* is on the southern outskirts of town, 350m south of the highway to Krabi. It's down a 400m driveway, best reached with private transport. The hilly grounds are green and expansive, but the buildings have definitely seen better days. The 10 OK bungalows still in use are hardly spiffed up inside – just hope the air-con works. At least it's nicely secluded.

Phang-Nga Bay Resort Hotel *(☎ 0 7641 2067, fax 0 7641 2070; rooms with air-con 1050B)*, south of town 8.5km at Tha Dan, increases the rates considerably during holidays. Rooms (which can be huge or small) come with TV, fridge, balcony and faded carpets. Facilities include a pool and restaurant. It has great views of the bay.

Places to Eat

Bismilla *(☎ 0 1125 6440; dishes 60-120B; open 8.30am-11pm daily)*, opposite the 7-Eleven, is a tidy restaurant up a few stairs that serves Thai Muslim dishes with interesting names such as 'Yum fish's spawn'.

Chai Thai *(no Roman-script sign)* is across from Soi Langkai and offers a few dim sum items in an open, casual and absolutely no-frills space.

Phang-Nga Satay *(184 Th Phetkasem; open 1pm-7pm daily)* is a tiny shack that specialises in Malay-style satay; the shrimp satay is good. It's two doors down from Chai Thai (past the wedding-dress store).

Cha-Leang *(☎ 0 7641 3831; dishes 40-90B; open 10am-10.30pm daily)* is one of the best and most popular restaurants in town, cooking up well-priced seafood dishes – try the 'clams with basil leaf and chilli', or 'edible inflorescence of banana plant salad'. There's a simple but pleasant back patio.

Several **food stalls** on the main street of Phang-Nga sell delicious *khànŏm jiin* (thin wheat noodles) with chicken curry, *náam yaa* (spicy ground-fish curry) or *náam phrík* (sweet and spicy peanut sauce). One vendor in front of the market (opposite Bangkok Bank) serves *khànŏm jiin* with about 10 free vegetable accompaniments.

Rotii kaeng is available in the **morning market** from around 5am to 10am. There's a small **night market** just south of Soi Lohakit open Tuesday and Thursday nights only.

Getting There & Away

Phang-Nga's bus terminal is located just off the main street on Soi Bamrung Rat. Buses to/from Bangkok to Phang-Nga include VIP (685B, 12 hours, one daily), 1st class (441B to 459B, 12 to 13 hours, two daily) and 2nd class (357B, 12 hours, three to four daily). Other destinations include the following.

destination	price (B)	duration (hrs)	frequency
Ko Pha-Ngan	400	6	2 daily
Ko Samui	240	5	2 daily
Krabi	35-59	1½	frequent
Hat Yai	175-220	6	2 daily
Ranong	90	5	4 daily
Satun	221	6	2 daily
Surat Thani	60-130	3	9 daily
Trang	139	3½	frequent
Phuket	35-65	1½	frequent

Getting Around

Most of the town is easily accessible on foot. Motorcycle taxis around town cost 20B.

Sayan Tours, located at the bus terminal, can assist with motorcycle rental (200B per day). Săwngthăew/motorcycle taxis to Tha Dan cost 20/40B.

AROUND PHANG-NGA

Sa Nang Manora Forest Park
สวนป่าสระนางมโนราห์

This beautiful and little-visited park *(admission free)* features an impressive fairy-land setting, with plenty of dense rainforest, rattan vines, moss-encrusted roots and rocks and multilevel waterfalls with several pools suitable for swimming. Primitive trails follow along (and at times through) the falls level after level and beyond – you could easily get a full day's hiking in without walking along the same path twice. Bring plenty of drinking water – although the shade and the falls moderate the temperature, the humidity in the park is quite high.

The park's name comes from a local folk belief that the mythical Princess Manora bathes in the pools of the park when no-one else is around. Facilities include some picnic tables here and there, plus a small restaurant. To get here, head north out of town on Hwy 4. Go past the Shell petrol station 3.2km, then turn left and go down a curvy road another 4km. Motorcycle taxis from Phang-Nga cost 50B.

Wat Tham Suwankhuha
วัดถ้ำสุวรรณคูหา

South of Phang-Nga about 10km is Wat Tham Suwankhuha *(Heaven Grotto Temple; admission 10B)*, a cave wát full of Buddha images. The shrine consists of two main caverns, a larger one containing a 15m reclining Buddha and tiled with *laikhraam* and *benjarong* (two coloured patterns more common in pottery), and a smaller cavern displaying spirit flags and a rishi *(reusĭi)* statue. Royal seals of several kings, including Rama V, Rama VII and Rama IX – as well as those of lesser royalty – have been inscribed on one wall of the latter cave. Monkeys hang around the area, so lock your car doors or they'll break in to get at your snacks.

To get here without your own transport, hop on any săwngthăew running between Phang-Nga and Takua Thung (20B). The wát is a down a side road.

On this same side road, about 6km beyond the cave wát, is **Raman Forest Park** (admission free) a pretty little park with a beautiful waterfall running through a small valley. You can follow alongside this cascade about 3km; it's a gorgeous trail, and swimming is possible at a couple of pools.

The park is relatively isolated, so it's difficult to get here without your own transport. Try hitching from the cave wát or you could rent a motorcycle in Phang-Nga – but, because you'd be riding along the busy highway, ensure you have decent riding skills.

Ao Phang-Nga National Park
อุทยานแห่งชาติอ่าวพังงา

Established in 1981, covering an area of 400 sq km, Ao Phang-Nga National Park *(admission 200B)* is noted for its classic karst scenery, created by fault movements on the mainland that pushed massive limestone blocks into geometric patterns. As these blocks extend southward into Ao Phang-Nga, they form over 40 islands with huge vertical cliffs. The bay itself is composed of large and small tidal channels that originally connected with the mainland fluvial system. The main tidal channels – Khlong Ko Phanyi, Khlong Phang-Nga, Khlong Bang Toi and Khlong Bo Saen – run through vast mangroves in a north–south direction and today are used by fisherfolk and island inhabitants as aquatic highways. These mangroves are the largest remaining primary mangrove forest in Thailand. Over 80% of the area within the park boundaries is covered by the Andaman Sea.

The biggest tourist spot in the park is so-called 'James Bond Island', known to Thais as **Ko Phing Kan** (Leaning on Itself Island). Once used as a location setting for *The Man with the Golden Gun,* the island is now full of vendors hawking coral and shells that should have stayed in the sea, along with butterflies, scorpions and spiders encased in plastic.

The Thai name for the island refers to a flat limestone cliff that appears to have tumbled sideways to lean on a similar rock face, which is in the centre of the island. Off one side of the island in a shallow bay stands a tall slender limestone formation that looks like a big rock spike that has fallen from the sky.

There are a couple of caves you can walk through and a couple of small sand beaches, often littered with rubbish from tourist boats. About the only positive development has been the addition of a concrete pier so that tourist boats don't have to moor directly on the island's beaches, but this still happens when the water level is high and the pier is crowded with other boats.

For information on Ko Yao, which is part of Ao Phang-Nga National Marine Park, see Around Phuket Province later in this chapter.

Flora & Fauna Two types of forest predominate in the park; limestone scrub forest and true evergreen forest. The marine limestone environment favours a long list of reptiles, including the Bengal monitor, flying lizard, banded sea snake, dogface water snake, shore pit viper and Malayan pit viper. Keep an eye out for the two-banded (or water) monitor *(Varanus salvator)* which looks like a crocodile when seen swimming in the mangrove swamp and can measure up to 2.2m in length (only slightly smaller than the Komodo dragon, the largest lizard in the Varanidae family). Like its Komodo cousin, the water monitor (called *hîa* by the Thais, who generally fear or hate the lizard) is a carnivore that prefers to feed on carrion but occasionally preys on live animals.

Amphibians in the Ao Phang-Nga area include the marsh frog, common bush frog and crab-eating frog. Avian residents of note are the helmeted hornbill (the largest of Thailand's 12 hornbill species, with a body length of up to 127cm), the edible-nest swiftlet *(Aerodramus fuciphagus),* white-bellied sea eagle, osprey and Pacific reef egret.

Over 200 species of mammals reside in the mangrove forests and on some of the larger islands, including the white-handed gibbon, serow, dusky langur and crab-eating macaque.

Rock Art Many of the limestone islands in Ao Phang-Nga feature prehistoric rock art painted or carved onto the walls and ceilings of caves, rock shelters, cliffs and rock massifs. In particular you can see rock art on Khao Khian, Ko Panyi, Ko Raya, Tham Nak, and Ko Phra At Thao. Khao Khian (Inscription Mountain) is probably the most visited of the sites. The images contain scenes of human figures, fish, crabs, shrimp, bats, birds and elephants, as well as boats and fishing equipment – it's obvious this was some sort of communal effort tied to the all-important harvesting of sustenance from the sea. Some drawings also contain rows of lines thought to be some sort of cabbalistic writing. The rock paintings don't fall on any one plane of reference; they may be placed right-side up, upside-down or sideways. Most of the paintings are monochrome, while some have been repeatedly traced several times over in orange-yellow, blue, grey and black.

Places to Stay & Eat There are **national park bungalows** *(☎ 0 7641 2188; bungalows with fan 500B, with air-con 700-900B)* near the park headquarters. Small bungalows sleep two to four people, while larger ones sleep up to 15. **Camping** is permitted in certain areas within park boundaries but you should ask permission at the visitors centre first.

There's a small, clean **restaurant** in front of the visitors centre.

Getting There & Around From the centre of town drive south on Hwy 4 about 6km, then turn left onto Rte 4144 and travel 2.6km to the park headquarters. Beyond here 400m is the visitors centre. Without your own transport you'll need to take a sǎwngthǎew to Tha Dan (20B).

Plenty of private boats, ready to zoom off on Ao Phang-Nga tours, await your bargaining skills (400B to 500B per person for a two- to three-hour tour).

Ko Panyi & Muslim Stilt Villages
เกาะปันหยีและหมู่บ้านมุสลิม

This small island is famous for the Muslim fishing village built almost entirely on stilts and nestled against its towering limestone cliffs. The village appears very commercialised during the day, when hordes of tourists invade to eat lunch at the village's many overpriced seafood restaurants while buying tacky souvenirs at the many stalls. Once the tourist boats depart, however, the village returns to its usual, normal self.

The 200 households here – home to perhaps a total of 2000 people – are said to descend from two seafaring Muslim families that arrived here from Java around 200 years ago. Ko Panyi's primary livelihood is still fishing, since only during the dry season do a significant number of tourists visit the island. In addition to a big green mosque, a health clinic and a school, you'll find a market filled with small shops selling clothes, toiletries, medicines and all the other staples seen in markets all over Thailand – except for any type of alcoholic beverage. Besides alcohol, two other things forbidden on the island are dogs and pigs. Houses mixed in with the shops vary from grubby little shacks to homes with fancy tile fronts and curtained windows. The people are generally quite friendly, especially if you can speak a little Thai. Village men often gather to gossip and watch the sunset over the western side of the village near the mosque.

If you fancy a look at similar but less well-known Muslim stilt villages in Ao Phang-Nga, take a boat to one of the villages in the huge mangrove forests at the northern end of the bay. These include **Ban Ling** (Monkey Village), **Ban Mai Phai** (Bamboo Village) and **Ban Sam Chong** (Three Channels Village).

Places to Stay & Eat Very basic **accommodation** *(rooms 100B)* with shared toilet and scoop shower is available at a tattered set of thin-walled rooms near Ko Panyi's northern pier. Although the rooms aren't much, they do have windows that catch sea breezes. Overnight tours from Phang-Nga use these rooms; if they're full you should be able to find a room in a village home for about the same or less. Ask at one of the restaurants.

Along with the more expensive seafood restaurants built out over the sea in front of the village (which are generally open for lunch only), there are some smaller cafés and restaurants along the interior alleys where locals eat. *Khâo yam* (southern-Thai rice salad) and roti are available in the morning. The villagers raise grouper in floating cages, selling them to the island and mainland restaurants. A local culinary speciality is *khànŏm bâo lâng*, a savoury dish made with black sticky rice, shrimp, coconut, black pepper and chilli steamed in a banana leaf – a breakfast favourite.

Getting There & Away Most visitors to the island arrive on tour boats, whether for brief day visits or overnight stays. You can also take a long-tail boat from Tha Dan (30B, 25 minutes). These leave when full, from dawn to dusk, arriving and departing from the village's northern pier (the southern pier is mostly reserved for tourist boats). Chartering your own long-tail boat costs 150B.

Phuket Province

Dubbed 'Pearl of the South' by the tourist industry, Phuket (poo-**get**) is Thailand's largest, wealthiest, most populous and most visited island, and a province in itself. The jagged coastal terrain of this 810-sq-km island encompasses broad, sandy bays, rocky peninsulas, limestone cliffs and tropical vegetation. Phuket's interior supports rice paddies, rubber, cashew-nut, cacao, pineapple and coconut plantations, along with the island's last bit of rainforest. Although Phuket is connected to Phang-Nga Province by a causeway, most visitors arrive via the island's international airport, located near its northern tip.

Formerly called Ko Thalang and before that Junk Ceylon (an English corruption of the Malay 'Tanjung Salang' or Cape Salang), Phuket has a culture all of its own. It combines Chinese and Portuguese influences (like neighbouring western Malaysia) with

PHUKET PROVINCE

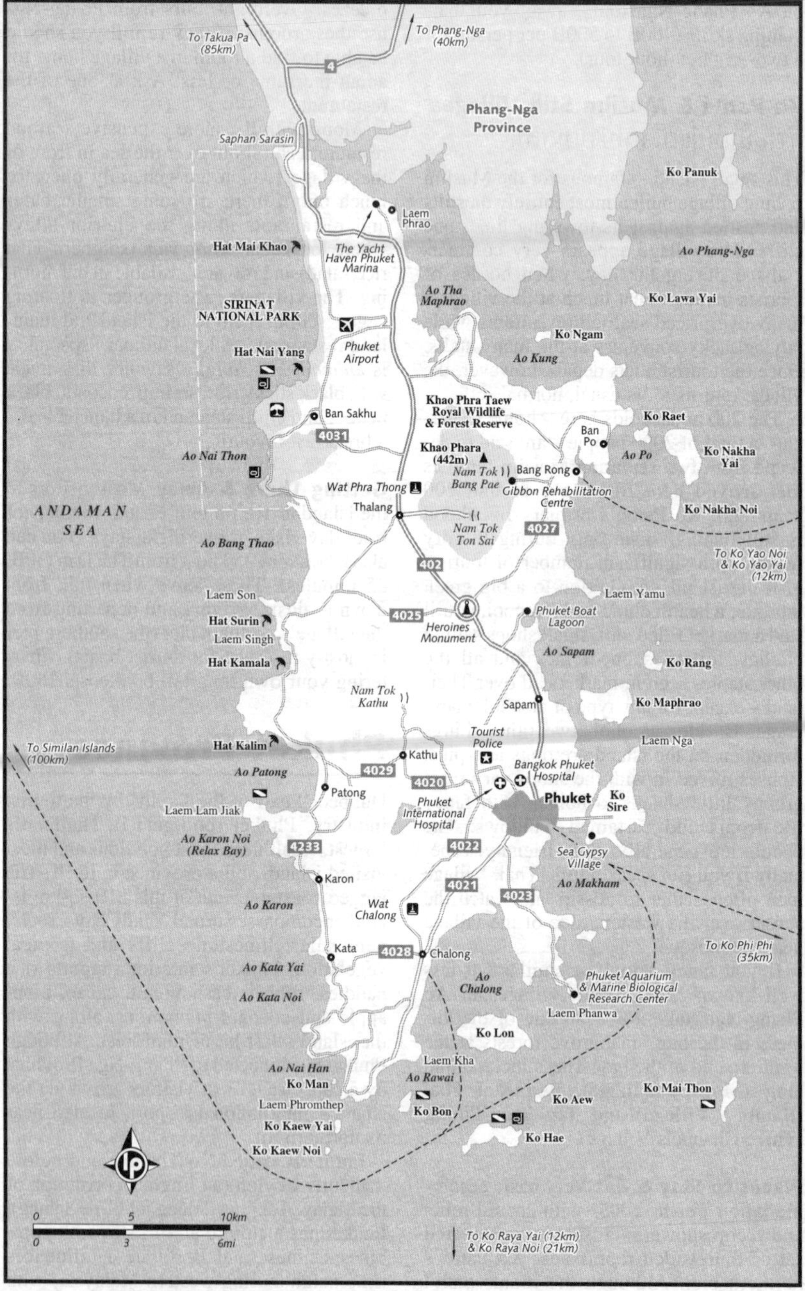

Phuket Warning

Every year about 20 people drown in accidents off Phuket's beaches, especially on the west coast (Surin, Laem Singh and Kamala). Red flags are posted on beaches to warn bathers of riptides and other dangerous conditions. If a red flag is flying at a beach, don't go into the water.

Renting a motorcycle can be a high-risk proposition. Thousands of people are killed or injured every year on Phuket's highways. Some are travellers who weren't familiar enough with riding motorcycles and navigating the island's roads, highways and traffic patterns. If you must rent a motorcycle, make sure you at least know the basics – and wear a helmet!

that of southern Thais and the *chao náam*, an indigenous ocean-going people. About 35% of the island's population are Thai Muslims, and there are about as many mosques as Buddhist wát here.

Visitors will find a lot to do (and spend money on) in Phuket, such as sampling the delicious seafood and taking scuba diving or snorkelling trips. And while most tourists seeking entertainment flock to the flashy beach towns of Patong, Karon and Kata, there are calmer spots, such as Nai Han and Kamala – and even the relatively untouched northern coasts of Nai Yang, Nai Thon and Mai Khao.

Capitalism rules on Phuket, and you shouldn't assume that an activity won't be harmful to the environment. At least some beach resorts seem to have realised the advantage of long-term, sustainable practices. However, the general growth of commercialism along the island's main roads sometimes detracts from Phuket's appeal. The island's beaches and relatively unspoiled northern interior remain its natural attractions, and the responsible traveller can only hope that this is what provincial authorities as well as the business sector will recognise and support.

INFORMATION
Digital Resources

Phuket Island Access (W www.phuket.com) offers a sophisticated compendium of many kinds of information, including accommodation on the island. Other sites offering good information on Phuket include W www.phuket.net, W www.phukettourism.org and W www.phuketmagazine.com.

Newspapers & Magazines

The fortnightly English-language *Phuket Gazette* (20B) publishes lots of information on activities, events, dining and entertainment in Phuket town, as well as around the island. It can be accessed online at W www.phuketgazette.net. The same publisher issues *Gazette Guide*, a 385-page listing of businesses and services on the island.

There are also the usual tourist freebies around, such as *South*. *Phuket* magazine is like an in-flight magazine that relies heavily on advertising but still manages to publish an interesting article about Phuket once in a while.

The small-format *Phuket Holiday Guide* (120B) contains lots of solid information and insiders' tips on accommodation, transport and other travel practicalities on the island. It also contains the most unbiased sightseeing information, since it has less advertising.

Medical Services

International doctors rate the **Phuket International Hospital** (*☎ 0 7624 9400, emergency ☎ 0 7621 0935; Airport Bypass Rd*) as the best on the island. **Bangkok Phuket Hospital** (*☎ 0 7625 4421; Th Yongyok Uthit*) is reputedly the favourite with locals. Both hospitals are equipped with modern facilities, emergency rooms and outpatient-care clinics.

ACTIVITIES
Diving & Snorkelling

Although there are many, many places to dive around Thailand, Phuket is indisputably the primary centre for the Thai scuba-diving industry and one of the world's top 10 dive destinations. The island is ringed by good to excellent dive sites, including several small islands to the south – Ko Hae, Ko Raya (Noi and Yai), Hin Daeng and Hin Muang, and to the east – Ko Yao (Noi and Yai). Live-aboard excursions to the fantastic Surin and Similan islands, or to the Burma Banks/Mergui Archipelago off the southern coast of Myanmar, are also possible from Phuket (though these destinations are far away).

Phuket has heaps of 'dive' shops – at last count there were over 100, though most of

Which Dive Shop to Pick?

Choosing the right dive shop can be intimidating business. After all, there are so many flashy storefronts advertising the wonders of the diving world – over 100 in Phuket alone – how on earth can you make sure you're making the right choice?

When choosing a dive company on Phuket (or anywhere in Thailand, for that matter) there are a few key questions you should ask. For example, how long has the dive shop existed? How many divers will be on the boat? What is the dive instructor-to-client ratio? What kind of insurance do they have and what does it cover? Is it a licensed Tourism Authority of Thailand (TAT) operator? If it's a live-aboard trip, is there oxygen on board? Talk to the staff (if they're not out diving); how experienced are they, and how much of this experience is local? Do they make you feel comfortable and confident? If you're taking a class, what kind of certification do the instructors have? And do they speak your language well enough so you understand each other? One last thing: Look at the equipment – is it in good shape and well-maintained?

Perhaps the best way to choose an excellent dive operation, however, is to get a glowing recommendation from other divers who've already done the underwater deed. Word-of-mouth is often the best indicator of the quality of a company – and in the competitive diving world, a good reputation can really make or break a business.

them are the equivalent of a booking agency. The more serious ones often operate their own boat(s), so ask if you're concerned. And it doesn't hurt if an operator is a five-star PADI dive centre, though this isn't always the best criteria for dive shops. Many of these operations are centred at Hat Patong or Ao Chalong, though the smaller beach towns certainly have their share. Some of the bigger (but not necessarily better) places have multiple branch offices all over Phuket.

Typical one-day dive trips to nearby sites cost 1600B to 2500B, including two dives and equipment. Nondivers (and snorkellers) are permitted to join such dive trips for a significant discount. PADI open-water certification courses cost around 8000B to 11,000B for four days of instruction and all equipment. Most places also rent all the basic equipment.

It's very wise to obtain your own private diving insurance before travelling. PADI or DAN is best – regular insurance doesn't often cover diving accidents or recompression costs, but you could check with your insurance representative. Your dive shop will also have some insurance, but some shops have better insurance than others; ask around.

There are three **hyperbaric chambers** on Phuket. **Wachira Hospital** (*☎ 0 7621 1114*) and **Phuket International Hospital** (*☎ 0 7624 9400, emergency ☎ 0 7621 0935*) are both just outside Phuket town; a private chamber (*☎ 0 7634 2518; W www.hst-sss-network.com*) is in Patong. The chamber at Phuket International Hospital is considered the best of the three. Dive shop affiliation with the private hyperbaric chamber in Patong mostly means that clients who need to use that chamber will be charged US$200 rather than US$800 per hour of treatment (five-hour minimum), though if a dive shop has the right kind of insurance it will cover much of this cost. Again, ask for specifics if you're concerned.

Snorkelling is best along Phuket's west coast, particularly at the rocky headlands between beaches. Mask, snorkel and fins can be rented for around 250B a day. As with scuba diving, you'll find better snorkelling, with greater visibility and variety of marine life, along the shores of small outlying islands like Ko Hae, Ko Yao and Ko Raya.

As elsewhere in the Andaman Sea, the best diving months are December to May, when the weather is good and the sea is at its clearest (and boat trips are much safer).

There are numerous dive shops with supplies. **Andaman Sea Sport** (*☎ 0 7621 1752; 69 Th Phuket, Phuket town*) stocks some diving and snorkelling supplies.

Phuket Wetsuits (*☎ 0 7638 1818; W www.phuketwetsuit.com; Th Chao Fa west, Ao Chalong*) offers both custom and ready-made wet suits. This place is located 2km north of Ao Chalong.

Dive Supply (*☎ 0 7634 2513; W www.divesupply.com; 189 Th Rat Uthit, Patong*) has a great variety of diving equipment, and offers a good service in several languages.

Yachting

Phuket is one of Southeast Asia's main yacht destinations, and you'll find all manner of craft anchored along its shores – from 80-year-old wooden sloops that look like they can barely stay afloat, to the latest in hi-tech motor cruisers. Marina-style facilities with year-round anchorage are presently available at two locations on the protected eastern side of the island: **Phuket Boat Lagoon** (*☎ 0 7623 9055, fax 0 7623 9056*) at Ao Sapam, about 20km north of Phuket town on the eastern shore, and **The Yacht Haven Phuket Marina** (*☎ 0 7620 6705, fax 0 7620 6706; W www.yacht-haven-phuket.com*) at Laem Phrao on the northeastern tip. However, the new US$25 million **Royal Phuket Marina** is due to be finished sometime in 2003 and will be located just south of Phuket Boat Lagoon. Luxury villas, townhouses and a hotel are planned to join 190 berths and a spa here.

Until then, Phuket Boat Lagoon offers an enclosed marina with tidal channel access, serviced pontoon berths, 60- and 120-tonne travel lifts, hard-stand area, plus a resort hotel, laundry, coffee shop, fuel, water, repairs and maintenance services. The Yacht Haven boasts 130 berths, a scenic restaurant and also does yacht maintenance. If you need sails, **Rolly Tasker Sailmakers** (*☎ 0 7628 0347, fax 7628 0348; W www.rollytasker.com; Ao Chalong*) can outfit you with these; riggings, spars and hardware are also available.

Port clearance is rather complicated; both Phuket Boat Lagoon and The Yacht Haven will take care of the paperwork (for a fee of course) if notified of your arrival in advance. For information on yacht charters – both bareboat and crewed – yacht sales and yacht deliveries, contact the following.

Faraway Sail & Dive Expeditions (☎/fax 0 7628 0701, W www.far-away.net) Hat Karon
Siam Sailing (☎/fax 0 7620 0507, W www.sailing-charter-thailand.com)
SEAL (☎ 0 7634 0406, fax 0 7634 0586, W www.seal-asia.com) Hat Patong
Sunsail Yacht Charters (☎ 0 7623 9057, fax 0 7623 8940, e sunthai@phuket.loxinfo.co.th) Phuket Boat Lagoon
Thai Marine Leisure (☎ 0 7623 9111, e tml@thaimarine.com) Hat Patong
Yachtpro International (☎ 0 7634 8117–8, fax 0 7634 8119, W www.sailing-thailand.com) Yacht Haven Marina, Phuket

The TAT office in Phuket town also has an extensive list of yacht charters and brokers. Charters aboard 32ft to 44ft yachts start at 1000B per day, while larger ones (to 85ft) start at 18,000B. Significant discounts are available June to October. Day trips usually include boat, crew, lunch and soft drinks, plus snorkelling and fishing gear. For insurance purposes, it's a good idea to see if the boat you want to charter is registered in Thailand.

Paddling

Several companies based in Phuket offer canoe tours of scenic Ao Phang-Nga.

Sea Canoe Thailand (*☎ 0 7621 2252, fax 0 7621 2172; W www.seacanoe.net; 367/4 Th Yaowarat*), based in Phuket town, was the first and is still the most famous. The kayaks are able to enter semi submerged caves (which Thai fishermen have called *hâwng* or 'room' for centuries) inaccessible by the long-tail boats. A day paddle costs 2970B per person and includes meals, equipment and transfer; also available are all-inclusive, three- or six-day camping trips. The day trips can be booked from Ao Nang in Krabi for 1700B, but a different area without semi submerged caves is explored.

Another canoe company with an excellent reputation is **Paddle Asia** (*☎/fax 0 7624 0893; W www.paddleasia.com; 19/3 Th Rasdanusorn*), also based in Phuket town. It caters to beginners and those who don't enjoy being surrounded by noisy tour groups. Groups are small (two to six people) and multi day tours are offered. Other canoeing companies include **Sea Cave Canoe** (*☎ 0 7621 0434; W www.seacavecanoe.com; 2/2 Th Chumphon, Phuket town*) and **Andaman Sea Kayak** (*☎ 0 7623 5353; W www.andamanseakayak.com*), which can be booked through many travel agencies on the island.

ORGANISED TOURS

Siam Safari (*☎ 0 7628 0116*) and **Adventure Safaris** (*☎ 0 7634 1988*) combine 4WD tours of the island's interior with short elephant rides and short hikes for around 2200B a day. Half-day trips are also available, although the difference in price is not that great.

COOKING COURSES

Pat Thienthong (*☎ 0 7626 3366; e thaicookingclass@hotmail.com*), who worked as a chef

Vegetarian Festival

Phuket's most important festival is the Vegetarian Festival, which takes place during the first nine days of the ninth lunar month of the Chinese calendar. This is usually in late September or early October.

Basically, the festival celebrates the beginning of the month of 'Taoist Lent', when devout Chinese abstain from eating all meat and meat products. In Phuket, the festival activities are centred around five Chinese temples, with the Jui Tui temple on Th Ranong the most important, followed by Bang Niaw and Sui Boon Tong temples. Events are also celebrated at temples in the nearby towns of Kathu (where the festival originated) and Ban Tha Reua.

The TAT office in Phuket prints a helpful schedule of events for the Vegetarian Festival each year. If you plan to attend the street processions, consider bringing earplugs for the firecrackers. The festival is also big in Trang, Krabi and other southern towns.

Besides abstention from meat, the Vegetarian Festival involves various processions, temple offerings and cultural performances and culminates with incredible acts of self-mortification – walking on hot coals, climbing knife-blade ladders, piercing the skin with sharp objects and so on. Shopkeepers along Phuket's central streets set up altars in front of their shopfronts offering nine tiny cups of tea, incense, fruit, candles and flowers to the nine emperor gods invoked by the festival.

Those participating as mediums bring the nine deities to earth for the festival by entering into a trance state and piercing their cheeks with all manner of objects – sharpened tree branches (with leaves still attached!), spears, slide trombones, daggers; some even hack their tongues continuously with saw or axe blades. During the street processions these mediums stop at the shopfront altars, where they pick up the offered fruit and either add it to the objects piercing their cheeks or pass it on to bystanders as a blessing. They also drink one of the nine cups of tea and grab some flowers to stick in their waistbands. The shopkeepers and their families stand by with their hands together in a *wâi* gesture, out of respect for the mediums and the deities by whom they are temporarily possessed.

The entire atmosphere is one of religious frenzy, with deafening firecrackers, ritual dancing, bloody shirt fronts and so on. Oddly enough, there is no record of this kind of activity associated with Taoist Lent in China. Some historians assume that the Chinese here were somehow influenced by the Hindu festival of Thaipusam in nearby Malaysia, which features similar acts of self-mortification. The local Chinese claim, however, that the festival was started by a theatre troupe from China that stopped off in nearby Kathu around 150 years ago. The story goes that the troupe was struck seriously ill because the members had failed to propitiate the nine emperor gods of Taoism. The nine-day penance they performed included self-piercing, meditation and a strict vegetarian diet.

at a Thai restaurant in California for six years, is offering Thai cooking courses at her home, located just outside Phuket town. Half-day courses for either lunch or dinner cost 1200B. She can be contacted by telephone during the day, or by stopping in at **Phuket Reminder** (*☎ 0 7621 3765, 0 1538 8276; 85 Th Rasada*), a souvenir shop in Phuket town.

PHUKET TOWN

อ.เมืองภูเก็ต

postcode 83000 • pop 68,700

Centuries before Phuket began attracting sand-and-sea hedonists, it was an important trade centre for Arab, Indian, Malay, Chinese and Portuguese traders who came here to exchange goods with the rest of the world for tin and rubber. Francis Light, the British colonialist who made Penang the first of the British Straits Settlements, married a native of Phuket and tried unsuccessfully to pull this island into the colonial fold. Although this polyglot, multicultural heritage has all but disappeared from most of the island, a few vestiges can be seen and experienced in the province's *amphoe meuang* (provincial capital), Phuket.

In the older town centre you'll see some Sino-Portuguese architecture, characterised by ornate two-storey Chinese shophouses fronted by Romanesque arched porticoes that were a 19th-century tradition in Malaysia, Singapore, Macau and Hainan Island. For a time it seemed this wonderful old architecture was all being torn down and replaced with modern structures but, over the course of the last 10 years, a preservation ethic has taken hold.

Information

Tourist Offices The **TAT office** *(☎ 0 7621 2213, 0 7621 1036; ⓔ tathkt@phuket.ksc.co.th; 73-75 Th Phuket; open 8.30am-4.30pm daily)* has maps, brochures, a list of the standard săwngthăew fares to the various beaches and a wealth of other information.

The **tourist police** *(☎ 0 7635 5015, 0 7625 4693, emergency ☎ 1155)* can be reached via telephone. Phuket town's **immigration office** *(☎ 0 7621 2108)* is south of town almost at the end of Th Phuket.

Maps Although it doesn't look like it, the advertisement-plastered *A-O-A Phuket Map* is probably the best one if you're planning to drive around. It's more accurate than the other freebies, and it has all the route numbers marked. The free Thaiways map isn't very good for island navigation, although the inset maps for Patong and Karon-Kata are better than those in *A-O-A Phuket Map*. You can pick up both maps at the TAT office and other places around the island.

Groovy Map's informative new *Phuket Day & Night Map 'n' Guide* (100B) features five maps (Phuket Town, Phuket Island, Patong, Kata and Karon, and a boat route map) as well as a selection of short reviews of restaurants, pubs, nightclubs and beaches in Phuket and Krabi. Bus routes and fares are also included.

Money The highest concentration of banks with ATMs is on Th Rasada.

Post & Communications Stamps can be purchased at the **main post office** *(Th Montri; open 8.30am-4.30pm Mon-Fri, 9am-noon Sat, Sun & holidays)* and at a smaller **post office** *(open 8.30am-4.30pm Mon-Fri)* on Th Krung Thep.

Mail Boxes Etc *(MBE; ☎ 0 7625 6409; 168/2 Th Phuket; open 8.30am-6pm Mon-Fri, 9am-4pm Sat)* has a branch almost opposite The Books (see Bookshops). MBE rents private mail boxes, sells packaging and mailing materials and offers photocopying, laminating, binding, passport photo and business card services.

Two courier services at your service include **DHL** *(☎ 0 7665 8500; 61/4 Th Thepkasatri)*, which is in town, and **UPS** *(☎ 0 7626 3989; 64/53 Th Chao Fa)*, which is about 4km south of town on the way to Ao Chalong.

The **Phuket Telecommunications Centre** *(Th Phang-Nga; open 8am-midnight daily)* offers Home Country Direct service and a kick-ass Internet connection with air-con and no kids playing games.

There are many **Internet cafés** in Phuket town; just have a walk around and you'll find them.

Bookshops If you're starved for good reading material, head to **Southwind Books** *(Th Phang-Nga; open 9am-7.30pm Mon-Sat)*, which sells and trades lots of used books. For newer versions there's **The Books** *(☎ 0 7622 4362; open 10am-9.30pm daily)*, with a great selection of English-language books and maps.

Things to See & Do

For historic **Sino-Portuguese architecture**, have a meander down Thalang, Dibuk, Yaowarat, Ranong, Phang-Nga, Rasada and Krabi streets. The most magnificent examples in town are the Standard Chartered Bank – Thailand's oldest foreign bank – on Th Phang-Nga and the THAI office on Th Ranong, but there are lots of other interesting buildings along these streets. The best residences are found along Th Dibuk and Th Thalang.

Phuket's main **day market** on Th Ranong is fun to wander through, and a few old **Chinese temples** can be found in this area. Most are standard issue, but one that's a little bit different is the **Shrine of the Serene Light** *(San Jao Sang Tham; open 8.30am-noon & 1.30pm-5.30pm daily)*, tucked away at the end of a 50m alley off Th Phang-Nga. Said to be 100 to 200 years old, the shrine was only restored five years ago.

Walk up **Khao Rang**, sometimes called Phuket Hill, northwest of town, for a nice view of the city, jungle and sea. If, as many people say, Phuket is a corruption of the Malay word *bukit* (hill), then this is probably the hill it was named after.

Places to Stay – Budget

On On Hotel *(☎ 0 7621 1154; 19 Th Phang-Nga; rooms with fan 120B, with fan & bath 180-250B, with air-con 360B)* remains popular despite old and musty rooms. The 49-room

PHUKET

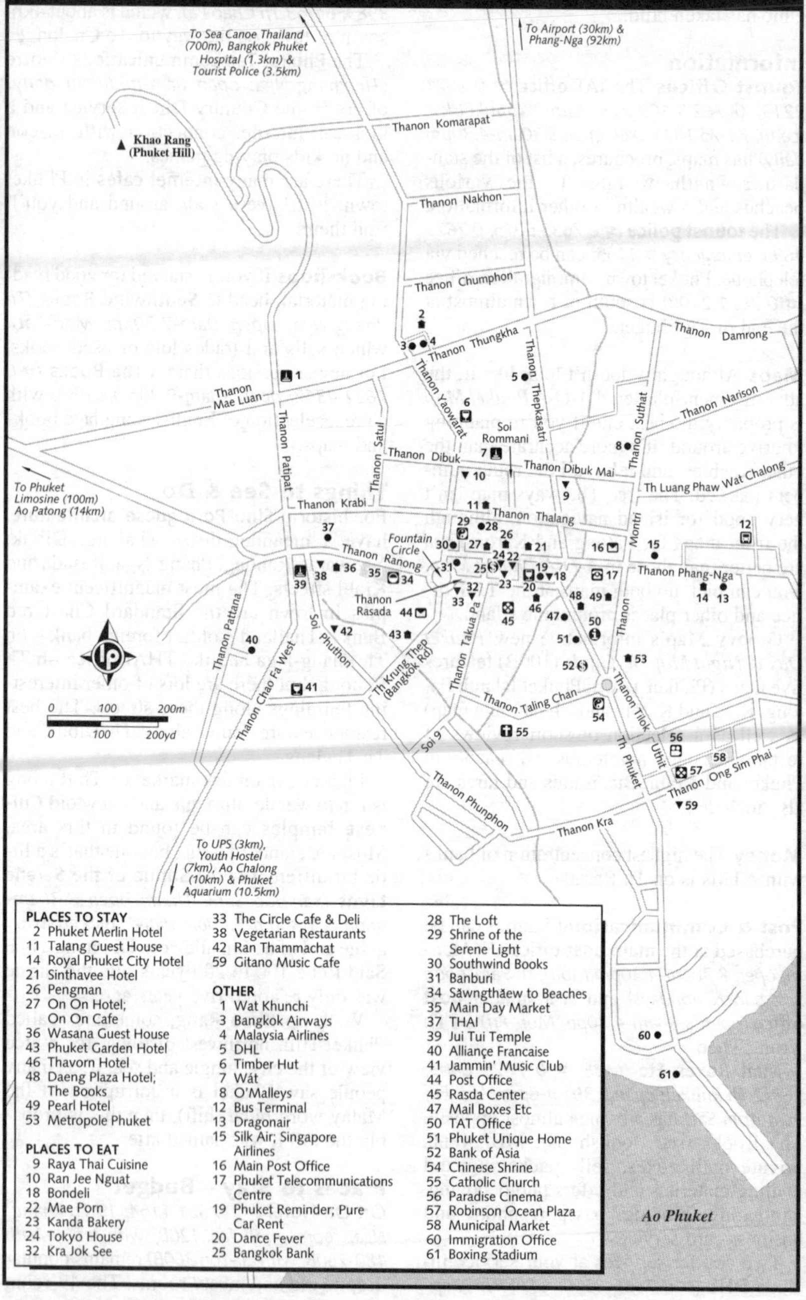
To Sea Canoe Thailand (700m), Bangkok Phuket Hospital (1.3km) & Tourist Police (3.5km)
To Airport (30km) & Phang-Nga (92km)
Khao Rang (Phuket Hill)
Thanon Komarapat
Thanon Nakhon
Thanon Chumphon
Thanon Damrong
Thanon Thungkha
Thanon Yaowarat
Thanon Thepkasatri
Thanon Suthat
Thanon Narisorn
Thanon Mae Luan
Thanon Patipat
Thanon Satul
Soi Rommani
Thanon Dibuk
Thanon Dibuk Mai
Th Luang Phaw Wat Chalong
To Phuket Limosine (100m) Ao Patong (14km)
Thanon Krabi
Thanon Thalang
Fountain Circle
Thanon Ranong
Thanon Montri
Thanon Phang-Nga
Thanon Rasada
Thanon Pattana
Soi Phuthon
Thanon Chao Fa West
Th Krung Thep (Bangkok Rd)
Thanon Takua Pa
Thanon Taling Chan
Thanon Tilok Uthit
Th Phuket
Thanon Ong Sim Phai
Soi 9
Thanon Phunphon
Thanon Kra
0 100 200m
0 100 200yd
To UPS (3km), Youth Hostel (7km), Ao Chalong (10km) & Phuket Aquarium (10.5km)
Ao Phuket

PLACES TO STAY
2 Phuket Merlin Hotel
11 Talang Guest House
14 Royal Phuket City Hotel
21 Sinthavee Hotel
26 Pengman
27 On On Hotel; On On Cafe
36 Wasana Guest House
43 Phuket Garden Hotel
46 Thavorn Hotel
48 Daeng Plaza Hotel; The Books
49 Pearl Hotel
53 Metropole Phuket

PLACES TO EAT
9 Raya Thai Cuisine
10 Ran Jee Nguat
18 Bondeli
22 Mae Porn
23 Kanda Bakery
24 Tokyo House
32 Kra Jok See
33 The Circle Cafe & Deli
38 Vegetarian Restaurants
42 Ran Thammachat
59 Gitano Music Cafe

OTHER
1 Wat Khunchi
3 Bangkok Airways
4 Malaysia Airlines
5 DHL
6 Timber Hut
7 Wát
8 O'Malleys
12 Bus Terminal
13 Dragonair
15 Silk Air; Singapore Airlines
16 Main Post Office
17 Phuket Telecommunications Centre
19 Phuket Reminder; Pure Car Rent
20 Dance Fever
25 Bangkok Bank
28 The Loft
29 Shrine of the Serene Light
30 Southwind Books
31 Banburi
34 Săwngthăew to Beaches
35 Main Day Market
37 THAI
39 Jui Tui Temple
40 Alliançe Francaise
41 Jammin' Music Club
44 Post Office
45 Rasda Center
47 Mail Boxes Etc
50 TAT Office
51 Phuket Unique Home
52 Bank of Asia
54 Chinese Shrine
55 Catholic Church
56 Paradise Cinema
57 Robinson Ocean Plaza
58 Municipal Market
60 Immigration Office
61 Boxing Stadium

hotel exudes decrepit charm from its old Sino-Portuguese architecture. It's near the centre of town and services include an Internet café, travel agency, motorcycle rentals and nearby restaurant.

Pengman *(☎ 0 7621 1486; 69 Th Phang-Nga; rooms with fan 130B)* is bare-bones, budget and bleak, but basically bearable.

Talang Guest House *(☎ 0 7621 4225; 37 Th Thalang; rooms with fan 240-280B, with air-con 370-410B)* is central, in a classic and tidy three-storey shophouse. It offers decent, large rooms with one bed and fan as well as air-con rooms with three or four beds. Rates include toast and coffee or tea in the morning.

Wasana Guest House *(☎ 0 7621 1754; 159 Th Ranong; rooms with fan/air-con 250/350B)*, next to Th Ranong Market, has a very bleak lobby and impersonal halls, but the clean rooms are fair-sized and bright.

Places to Stay – Mid-Range

Thavorn Hotel *(☎ 0 7621 1333, fax 0 7621 5559; ⓔ budgethotel@email.com; 74 Th Rasada; rooms with fan/air-con 230/550B)* features an impressive, museum-like lobby with much less impressive, gruff-like reception. It's not a bad deal, though; carpeted rooms with firm beds and bathtubs offset the bad air-con. Fan rooms in the older wing are smaller and simpler, while in the newer wing they're larger and flashier.

Phuket Garden Hotel *(☎ 0 7621 6900, fax 0 7621 6909; ⓔ pghhkt@hotmail.com; rooms with air-con in low/high season 780/1330B)* is a better deal in the low season; all rates include breakfast. Glass elevators take you to pleasant, clean and tidy rooms. There's a grassy garden outside, and it's close to the centre of town.

Sinthavee Hotel *(☎ 0 7621 1186, fax 0 7621 1400; 85-91 Th Phang-Nga; rooms with air-con in low season 650-950B, in high season 960-1200B)* has seen better days; the small, lacklustre rooms need a facelift, and the whole hotel could use some welcoming, 'feel-good' decor. A plus is that it's very central. Facilities include a coffee shop and business centre.

Daeng Plaza Hotel *(☎ 0 7621 6428, fax 0 7621 3884; ⓦ www.phukettoday.com/daengplaza; rooms with air-con in low season 590B, in high season 800-1000B)* is a lone, white high-rise, and the large, carpeted rooms come with fridge and TV. Beds are old and springy, but it's still a good deal.

Places to Stay – Top End

Pearl Hotel *(☎ 0 7621 1044, fax 0 7621 2911; 42 Th Montri; rooms in low/high season 942/1271B)* welcomes you with cold air-con in the lobby. Rooms are small, carpeted and very nice. Amenities include a 12th-floor restaurant, cocktail lounge and pool.

Phuket Merlin Hotel *(☎ 0 7621 2866, fax 0 7621 6429; 158/1 Th Yaowarat; rooms with air-con in low/high season 1044/1531B)* spruces up 180 pleasant rooms for your pleasure. The lobby is functional, the 2nd-floor pool fine, the plant-filled halls relaxing. It's not so central, but is fair value overall.

Metropole Phuket *(☎ 0 7621 5050, fax 0 7621 5990; ⓔ metropole@phuketinternet.co.th; rooms with air-con in low season 2000-2500B, in high season 3000-3500B)*, located in a busy area, offers 248 plush rooms, some with far-away sea views. There are 18 floors, with the pool on the 4th. There's an escalator to the first two floors, which overlook a beautiful lobby. Facilities include eating (and drinking) facilities, a business centre and an airport shuttle bus. Rates include breakfast.

Royal Phuket City Hotel *(☎ 0 7623 3333, fax 0 7623 3335; ⓦ www.royalphuketcity.nu; 154 Th Phang-Nga; rooms with air-con in low season 2933-3101B, in high season 4190-5028B)* is the best hotel in town to plunk your spare change. Start at the grand marble lobby and work your way towards the 251 perfect rooms (some with sea views) or 19th-floor Thai restaurant. The service is great, and facilities include pool, gym and spa. Discounts may be possible, and rates include breakfast.

Places to Eat

There's good food in Phuket town, and meals here cost a lot less than at the beach. Southeast of the centre is the town's **municipal market**, where you can buy fresh fruit and vegetables. Around three sides of this market you'll find a **night market** that features Thai and Chinese food. Nearby is the Robinson Ocean Plaza, which has a **food court** for those who need modern surroundings. A couple of **vegetarian restaurants** on Th Ranong (east of the garish Jui Tui Chinese temple) serve good Chinese vegetarian food during daylight hours.

Ran Jee Nguat *(no Roman-script sign; Th Yaowarat; open 7am-2pm daily)*, four doors down from the corner, is a long-running local institution serving Phuket's most famous dish – delicious *khànŏm jiin náam yaa phuukèt* – Chinese noodles in a puréed fish and curry sauce, with fresh vegetables on the side – for about 20B.

On On Cafe *(dishes 60-100B; open 7am-8pm daily)*, beside the On On Hotel, serves rice dishes, curries and breakfast at reasonable prices. It's a very casual place run by teenage girls.

Mae Porn *(☎ 0 7621 1389; cnr Th Phang-Nga & Soi Pradit; open 9am-9.30pm daily)* attracts both *faràng* and Thais to its casual, open corner location. It's friendly with indoor and outdoor tables, and cooks up some mean curries, seafood and Thai specialties – all at very reasonable prices.

Kanda Bakery *(☎ 0 7622 3410; Th Rasada; dishes 50-120B; open 7.30am-7.30pm daily)* is a small, modern and popular eatery with Thai and Western foods, breakfast and bakery items. Kanda Bakery also serves brewed coffee and *khâo tôm* (boiled rice) specialities.

The Circle Café & Deli *(☎ 0 7635 5233; 8 Th Rasada; dishes 60-150B; open 9am-6pm Mon-Sat, 10am-6pm Sun)* serves up breakfast and snacks, along with a wide selection of coffees. Goran and Natasha, who run this café, are good sources of information on Phuket.

Kra Jok See *(☎ 0 7621 7903; 26 Th Takua Pa; dishes 180-480B; open 6.30pm-10pm Tues-Sun)*, hidden away behind some greenery, offers great old-time decor and an intimate ambience. There aren't a whole lot of dishes, but the selection is enough if you like meat and fish; try the delicious *hàw mòk thálèh* (steamed seafood curry). Look for it next to Ban Boran Antiques.

Raya Thai Cuisine *(☎ 0 7621 8155; 48 Th Dibuk Mai; dishes 60-150B; open 10am-11pm daily)* is a bit tourist-oriented but nicely housed in a two-storey Sino-Portuguese mansion with tall ceilings. The food is good, but a bit overpriced.

Bondeli *(cnr Th Rasada & Th Thepkasatri; dishes 65-170B; open 7.30am-5.30pm daily)* offers a calm, air-con haven despite its busy corner locale. Quick eats such as burgers, sandwiches and pizzas line the menu, and breakfast is also possible.

Gitano *(☎ 0 7622 5797; dishes 100-135B; open 4pm-midnight daily)* grills up a few Latin main dishes, but since it's a bar scene you're more likely to order appetisers like nachos, quesadillas and fajitas. Toss them down with margaritas (135B) or sangria (150B). The decor is very tasteful and hip.

Tokyo House *(☎ 0 7625 6735; 34-38 Th Phang-Nga; open 11am-11pm daily)* slices up sushi, sashimi, *nigiri* and *moriawase*. Be warned, though; prices are geared toward homesick Japanese, and can be very expensive. Better value are the set meals and noodle dishes – mostly authentic though you could still end up with spaghetti noodles in your udon soup. Wine and sake are poured.

Ran Thammachat *(Natural Restaurant; no Roman-script sign; ☎ 0 7622 4287; 62/5 Soi Phuthon; dishes 60-100B; open 9am-midnight Tues-Sun)* is deservedly popular for its well-priced Thai food. Best of all, though, is the atmosphere: The thatched, two-storey structure is engulfed by plants. It's a great spot and worth the walk there.

Entertainment

Bars, Clubs & Pubs A bit far from the city centre, **Jammin' Music Club** *(☎ 0 7622 0189; 78/28-29 Th Krung Thep; open 8pm-2am daily)* is popular for its live music (nightly at 10pm). International tunes in the rock, pop and jazz genres are played to two floors of intimate atmosphere.

Dance Fever *(Th Rasada; open 8pm-2am daily)* caters to the deaf, with very loud, heart-stopping bass beats. It's more like a large bar with a stage on which live Thai bands perform; there isn't much room to dance.

Gitano Music Cafe *(☎ 0 7622 5797; Th Kra; open 4pm-midnight daily)* is the only venue for Latin music and treats such as nachos and fajitas. Toss-me-down drinks include margaritas, sangrias and *caipirinhas* (130B to 150B).

Timber Hut *(Th Yaowarat; open 6pm-2am daily)* is a popular pub with attractive rustic decor, and also serves up Thai food and live music after 10pm.

Cinemas For those addicted to celluloid, there's **Paradise Cinemas**, next to Robinson Ocean Plaza on Th Tilok Uthit.

Alliance Française *(☎ 0 7622 2988; 3 Soi 1, Th Phattana; open 2.30pm-6pm Mon,*

9.30am-12.30pm & 2.30am-6pm Tue-Fri, 9am-noon Sat) offers weekly showings of French films (subtitled in English). It also has a library and a TV with up-to-date news broadcasts.

Spectator Sports

Thai boxing can be witnessed Tuesday and Friday nights at 8pm. Seats cost 500B, 700B or 1000B, with one-way transport included. The stadium is at the southern edge of town near the pier; túk-túk cost 70B. Get your tickets at the On On Hotel.

Shopping

There's some decent shopping in the provincial capital. The Th Ranong **day market**, near the town centre, traces its history back to the days when pirates, Indians, Chinese, Malays and Europeans traded in Phuket. You might still find some fabrics from Southeast Asia, though it's mostly food now. At the **Municipal market**, southeast of the centre, the focus is on fresh produce and other things to eat; the **Robinson Ocean Plaza** is nearby.

Along Th Yaowarat, just north of the circle, are a few Indian-run tailor and fabric shops such as **Banburi** *(☎ 0 7622 3966; open 9am-7pm daily)*, which has bolts of silk. Chinese gold shops are lined up opposite the Th Ranong market.

The Loft *(☎ 0 7625 8160; 36 Th Thalang)* and **Ban Boran Antiques** *(☎ 0 1893 6735; Th Takua Pa)* sell Asian antiques; there are more shops on Th Rasada near the circle. **Phuket Unique Home** *(☎ 0 7621 2093; 186 Th Phuket; open 9am-6pm Mon-Sat)* carries original designs in dishware, home decor accessories and furniture, much of it a blend of old and new influences.

Getting There & Away

Air Thirty kilometres to the north of the city centre, **Phuket international airport** *(☎ 0 7632 7230)* has a post office, bookshop, restaurants and cafés, left luggage (40B per piece per day; open 6am to 10pm daily) and very expensive Internet connection (100B per 15 minutes) in the domestic departure area, plenty of foreign exchange in both sections and, in the arrivals area, ATMs and a tourist office.

THAI operates about a dozen daily flights from Bangkok; it also has regular flights to/from Hat Yai and Narathiwat. THAI's international destinations from Phuket include Penang, Langkawi, Kuala Lumpur, Singapore, Hong Kong, Taipei and Tokyo.

Phuket Air and Air Andaman have flights between Phuket and Bangkok as well, while Air Andaman also goes from Phuket to Ranong, Chumphon and Hua Hin. Bangkok Airways flies between Phuket and Bangkok four times daily; it also flies between Phuket and Ko Samui two to three times daily.

International airlines that have offices in Phuket include the following.

Bangkok Airways (☎ 0 7622 5033) 58/2-3 Th Yaowarat
Dragonair (☎ 0 7621 5734) Th Phang-Nga
Malaysia Airlines (☎ 0 7621 6675) 1/8-9 Th Thungkha
Silk Air (☎ 0 7621 3891) 183/103 Th Phang-Nga
Singapore Airlines (☎ 0 7621 3891) 183/103 Th Phang-Nga
THAI (☎ 0 7625 8236) 78/1 Th Ranong

Bus Phuket town's bus terminal is just east of centre, within walking distance of many hotels. See also the 'Bus Destinations from Phuket' table on the following page.

Minivan Some Bangkok travel agencies sell tickets for air-con minivans down to Ko Samui; the fare includes ferry transport. Air-con minivan services to Surat, Krabi and Ranong are also available. Departure locations vary, but the TAT office knows where they are. Expect to pay more than an ordinary bus and less than an air-con bus for the same destination.

Ferry During the high season several boats ply the waters between Ton Sai Bay (Ko Phi-Phi) and a few different ports on Phuket. Fares range from 300B to 500B and take about 1½ hours. It's also possible to reach Phuket from Ko Lanta, but you'll have to stop in Ko Phi-Phi along the way.

Getting Around

To/From the Airport Minivans from the airport to Phuket town cost 80B per person; to Patong, Karon and Kata they're 120B per person. If you're heading to the airport, **Phuket Limosine** *(☎ 0 7624 8596)* runs hourly shuttles from 6.30am to 7.30pm for 100B. Unfortunately they're located west of the town centre about a kilometre.

Bus Destinations from Phuket

destination	fare (B)	duration (hrs)
Bangkok		
ordinary	278	15
air-con	389-500	13-14
VIP	755	13
Chumphon		
air-con	195-250	6½
Hat Yai		
ordinary	150	8
air-con	210-270	6-7
Ko Samui (bus/boat)		
air-con	260	8
Krabi		
ordinary	65	4
air-con	91-117	3½
Nakhon Si Thammarat		
ordinary	125	8
air-con	175-200	7
Phang-Nga		
ordinary	36	2½
Ranong		
ordinary	103	6
air-con	185	5
Surat Thani		
ordinary	104	6
air-con	160-170	5
Takua Pa		
ordinary	54	3
Trang		
ordinary	105	6
air-con	147-189	5

Taxis between the airport and Phuket town cost 400B; between the airport and beaches 500B to 600B. The fledgling metered taxi service that was starting up at the time of writing may undercut these rates and perhaps even bring them down (see the boxed text 'Phuket's metered taxis').

Car & Motorcycle There are cheap car rental agencies on Th Rasada near Pure Car Rent. Suzuki jeeps go for about 1000B per day (including insurance), though in the low season the rates can go down to 700B. And if you rent for a week or more, you should get a discount.

The rates are always better at local places than at the better-known internationals, though you may be able to get deals with the familiar companies if you reserve in advance.

Avis Rent-A-Car (airport ☎ 0 7635 1243, in Patong ☎ 0 7634 5540, w www.avisthailand.com) Charges a premium (around 1500B a day) but has outlets at some bigger resort hotels.

Pure Car Rent (☎ 0 7621 1002) 75 Th Rasada. This is a good choice in the centre of town.

Via Rent-A-Car (☎ 0 7638 5718, w www.via-phuket.com) 189/6 Th Rat Uthit, Patong. This offers similar rates to Pure, and can deliver to anywhere on the island.

Motorcycle taxis around town are 20B. You can rent motorcycles on Th Rasada near Pure Car Rent, or from various places at the beaches. Costs are anywhere from 150B to 300B per day, and can vary depending on the season. Bigger bikes (over 125cc) can be rented at a couple of shops at Patong and Karon.

You should think seriously about whether or not it's worth the convenience to rent a motorcycle on Phuket. In the last few years, thousands of people were injured and hundreds have been killed in motorcycle accidents here. A significant number of the victims were foreign visitors. If you have an accident you're unlikely to find that medical attention is up to international standards. And remember that a minor spill while wearing reasonable clothes will leave you bruised and shaken, but for somebody clad in shorts it could result in enough skin loss to end your travels right there.

Săwngthăew & Túk-Túk Săwngthăew run regularly from Th Ranong (at the day market) to the various Phuket beaches for 20B to 25B per person – see the Getting There & Away sections for the respective beaches for details. These run from around 7am to 5pm; outside these times you have to charter a túk-túk to the beaches. These will set you back 200B to Patong, 230B to Karon and Kata, and 300B for Nai Han and Kamala. You'll probably have to bargain for a good price.

Beware of tales about the tourist office being 5km away, or that the only way to reach the beaches is by taxi, or even that you'll need a taxi to get from the bus terminal to the town centre (the bus terminal is more or less *in* the town centre).

For a ride around town, túk-túk should charge 20B.

GLENN BEANLAND

Long-tail boat, Ao Nang, Krabi Province

PAUL BEINSSEN

Movie posters, Krabi, Krabi Province

DALLAS STRIBLEY

Local woman, near Krabi, southern Andaman Coast

ANDERS BLOMQVIST

Hat Tham Phra Nang, Krabi Province

MARK STRICKLAND

Reef fish, Similan Islands National Marine Park, Phang-Nga Province

Phuket's Metered Taxis

Tired of haggling with those infernal túk-túk drivers who seem to want to squeeze every last baht from your wallet? Try one of Phuket's new metered taxis. All you need to do is call ☎ 0 7623 2157 or ☎ 0 7623 2158 and a yellow and blue steed will be dispatched to your door, 24 hours a day. Expect to pay the metered fare plus a 20B surcharge (or approximately 30B for the first 2km and 4B for each additional kilometre), which might end up being significantly less than what you might pay a túk-túk right off the street – and without the bouts of stressful 'negotiation'. Don't expect to see many metered taxis roaming the streets, however; there are only about six in the fleet so far.

AROUND PHUKET PROVINCE

This section goes anti-clockwise around the island, beginning in the northeast, well north of the city of Phuket, then skipping to the west coast and following the shoreline.

Khao Phra Thaew Royal Wildlife & Forest Reserve

อุทยานสัตว์ป่าเขาพระแทว

This mountain range, in the northern interior of the island, protects 23 sq km of rainforest (evergreen monsoon forest). There are nice jungle hikes in this reserve, and a couple of waterfalls, **Ton Sai** and **Bang Pae**. The falls are best seen in the rainy season between June and November; in the dry months they slow to a trickle. Because of its royal status, the reserve is better protected than the average Thai national park.

A German botanist, Dr Darr, discovered a rare and unique species of palm in Khao Phra Thaew about 50 years ago. Called the white-backed palm or langkow palm, the fan-shaped plant stands 3m to 5m tall and is found only here and in Khao Sok National Park. The highest point in Khao Phra Thaew Royal Wildlife & Forest Reserve is 442m **Khao Phara**.

Tigers, Malayan sun bears, rhinos and elephants once roamed the forest here, but nowadays resident mammals are limited to humans, gibbons, monkeys, slow loris, langur, civets, flying foxes, squirrels, mousedeer and other smaller animals. Watch out for cobras and wild pigs.

Near Nam Tok Bang Pae (Bang Pae Falls) is the **Phuket Gibbon Rehabilitation Centre** *(☎ 0 7626 0492; W warthai.org; admission by donation; open 9am-4pm daily)*. Financed by donations and run by volunteers, the centre cares for gibbons that have been kept in captivity and reintroduces them to the wild. Visitors who wish to help may 'adopt' a gibbon for 1500B, which will pay for one animal's care for a year. The programme includes keeping you updated on your adopted gibbon's progress throughout the year of adoption. Check the website for more information about this programme.

Ao Bang Thao

อ่าวบางเทา

Ao Bang Thao laps against a lovely 8km-long crescent of white-sand beach on Phuket's west coast. A steady breeze makes the bay ideal for **sailboarding**; since 1992 the annual Siam World Cup windsurfing championships have been held here. A system of lagoons inland from the beach has been incorporated into Laguna Phuket, a complex of five upscale resorts dominating the central portion of the beach.

Traditional Massage About 800m west of Hwy 4030, **Hideaway Day Spa** *(☎ 0 7627 1549; open 11am-9pm daily)* offers traditional Thai massage, sauna, mud body wraps and other treatments beginning at 1500B for a 90-minute massage. The facility is very nicely laid out in a tranquil wooded setting next to one of Bang Thao's lagoons. Reservations are recommended.

Places to Stay Most beachside accommodation on Bang Thao is quite swanky, and priced accordingly. The two exceptions are listed first; both are near the southern end of the bay. Some of the more expensive places hike rates during the holidays, and you're often obligated to pay for 'gala dinners' at Christmas and New Year's Eve.

Bangtao Lagoon Bungalows *(☎ 0 7632 4260, fax 0 7632 4168; W www.phuket-bangtaolagoon.com; bungalows in low season 400-1000B, in high season 630-1680B, suites in low/high season 1300/2100B)* has a swimming pool, great beach frontage and a restaurant

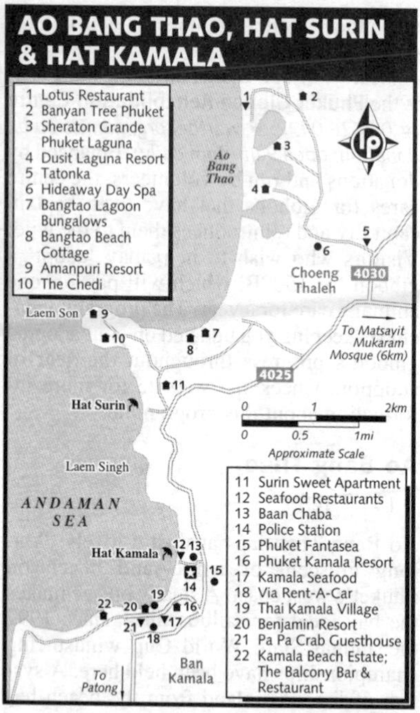

serving Thai and European dishes. A mere four of the 70 clean, tile-floored units are available at the cheapest fan-only rate. The rest have air-con and come in a variety of grades. However, most are on the small side.

Bangtao Beach Cottage *(☎ 0 7632 5418, fax 0 7632 5419; W www.bangtaobeachcottage.com; cottages in low season 2200-4300B, in high season 3900-6000B)* is a small operation with a delightful aesthetic and a beachfront restaurant. The seven 'cottages' are set in lush landscaped grounds and have unique flourishes, making much use of rich-hued tropical woods – in both construction and furnishing – that contrast wonderfully with the flagstone flooring. Each cottage has air-con and a ceiling fan, minibar and a hair dryer in a large bathroom.

The five resorts in the **Laguna Phuket complex** *(W www.lagunaphuket.com)* have a total of more than 1100 rooms and 30 restaurants (the gargantuan Sheraton Grande alone has 325 rooms and eight restaurants). The complex boasts an 18-hole golf course, and guests at any one of the resorts can use the dining and recreation facilities at all of them. Frequent shuttle buses make the rounds of all the hotels, as do pontoon boats (via the linked lagoons). Two of the five are described further here.

Dusit Laguna Resort *(☎ 0 7632 4324, fax 0 7632 4174, in Bangkok ☎ 0 2636 3333; W www.phuket.dusit.com; rooms in low season from US$150, suites up to US$250, rooms & suites Nov-Apr US$280-400)* offers 226 guest rooms and suites; a spa, fitness centre and tennis courts; and free use of windsurfers and sailboats.

Banyan Tree Phuket *(☎ 0 7632 4374, fax 0 7632 4375; W www.banyantree.com; villas in low season US$570-1300, in high season US$685-1425)* has 120 villas, all with private landscaped gardens, open-air sunken bathtubs and various combinations of Jacuzzi and/or private swimming pool, sauna, steam room etc). You'll also find a golf course, full-service spa, three tennis courts, a lap pool and a free-form swimming pool. The Banyan Tree specialises in spiritual and physical spa treatments, including massage, seaweed packs, yoga and meditation, but in addition to the food for the soul, there are seven restaurants. In 1998 it was voted the world's best spa resort by readers of *Condé Nast Traveler*.

Places to Eat Despite what local hoteliers would have you believe, there is some good food to be had outside the confines of Bang Thao's luxury hotels.

Lotus Restaurant *(dishes 50-100B)* is an open-walled eatery 500m west of the entrance to Banyan Tree Phuket, and the first in a row of beachside Thai and seafood restaurants that stretches to the south. It's clean, breezy and friendly, and has an amazing assortment of live crab, lobster, shrimp, fish and other visual and culinary delights in very well-tended tanks. Check out the crazy mantis shrimp!

Tatonka *(☎ 0 7632 4349; dishes 250-300B; open from 6pm-late Thur-Tues)*, 100m west of Hwy 4030 on the road to the Laguna Phuket resort complex, features 'globetrotter cuisine', which owner-chef Harold Schwarz developed by taking fresh local products and combining them with cooking and presentation techniques learned in Europe, Colorado and Hawaii. The eclectic, tapas-style selection includes creative vegetarian and seafood dishes and such delights as

Peking duck pizza (220B), as well as a tasting menu (750B per person, minimum two people) that lets you try a little of everything. Call ahead in high season. Tatonka arranges free transportation for guests of the resort complex.

Getting There & Away A sǎwngthǎew between Phuket's Th Ranong and Bang Thao costs 25B per person. In Bang Thao sǎwngthǎew can be caught along Rtes 4030 and 4025. Túk-túk charters are 200B.

Hat Surin

หาดสุรินทร์

Hat Surin is a pleasant beach, with occasionally heavy surf, south of Ao Bang Thao and separated from it by a cape. When the water is calm, there's fair snorkelling here; lounge chairs and beach umbrellas can be rented for 50B. Surin is popular with local Thais, who come for nibbles at the dozen or so seafood stands above the beach. Just to the east, in Bang Thao Village No 2, is one of southern Thailand's most beautiful mosques, **Matsayit Mukaram**, a large, whitewashed, immaculate structure with lacquered wooden doors.

Places to Stay To sleep close to the water, you need to hit the cape at Surin's northern end and shell out big bucks at one of the exclusive resorts – the Amanpuri and the Chedi – that sit on Pansea Beach, a secluded offshoot of Hat Surin.

Surin Sweet Apartment *(☎ 0 7627 0863, fax 0 7627 0865; rooms in low/high season 600/800B)* is set well back from the central section of the beach. It looks awful from the outside, but management is friendly and the rooms are large and clean, with tile floors, air-con, balconies and rare shower curtains.

The Chedi *(☎ 0 7632 4017, fax 0 7632 4252; ⓔ hotel@chedi-phuket.com; rooms in low season US$190-495, in high season US$350-675)* has tennis courts, a beachside pool and many water sports on offer. Lodging is in cottages, many with teak floors and private verandas. Rates skyrocket during the December to January holidays.

Amanpuri Resort *(☎ 0 7632 4333, fax 0 7632 4100; ⓦ www.amanresorts.com/puri_m.html; rates US$700-8200)* plays host to Thailand's celebrity traffic, with each guest getting a 133-sq-metre pavilion or private two- to six-bedroom villa home (with live-in maid and cook); the staff-to-guest ratio is 3½ to one. It was designed by the architect who did the former Shah of Iran's Winter Palace. Rates come down in the low season, but are still up there. The resort offers six tennis courts, a spa, Thai and Italian restaurants, and about 20 watercraft for sailing, diving and overnight charters.

Getting There & Away A regular sǎwngthǎew between Phuket's Th Ranong and Hat Surin costs 25B per person and túk-túk charter is 250B to 300B.

Hat Kamala

หาดกมลา

Hat Kamala is a lovely stretch of sand and sea about 4km south of Surin and 25km from Phuket. The northern end (the nicest area) is shaded by casuarina trees and features a small thatched-roof snack bar. Please note: Most of the locals here are Muslim and would find topless bathing extremely offensive.

Phuket Fantasea *(☎ 0 7638 5000; ⓦ www.phuket-fantasea.com; admission with/without dinner 1500/1000B; open 5.30pm-11.30pm Wed-Mon)*, a US$60 million 'cultural theme park', is located just north of Hat Kamala. Despite the billing, there aren't any rides but there is a truly magical show that manages to capture the colour and pageantry of traditional Thai dance and costumes and combine them with state-of-the-art light and sound techniques that rival anything found in Las Vegas (think 30 elephants). All of this takes place on a stage dominated by a full-scale replica of a Khmer temple reminiscent of Angkor Wat. Kids especially would be captivated by the spectacle. There is also quite a good and varied collection of souvenir shops in the park offering Thai-made handicrafts. The Thai buffet dinner is surprisingly good. Tickets can be booked through most hotels and tour agencies.

Places to Stay Kamala is seeing a fair bit of development as small places expand and go upscale, but budget options can be found.

Baan Chaba *(☎/fax 0 7627 9158; ⓦ www.baan-chaba.com; rooms with air-con in low season 800B, in high season 1200B)* is just a few minutes' walk from the beach. There are eight beautiful, comfortable, clean and well-furnished rooms at this small and intimate hotel. All come with hot water, TV, fridge and good decor.

Benjamin Resort *(☎/fax 0 7638 5739; W www.phuketdir.com/benjaminresort; rooms with air-con in low season 350-500B, in high season 700-800B)* is very good value. All rooms have TV, minibar and a terrace with table and chairs. The more expensive rooms have sea views, some of which are glorious. The hotel, built in 2001, is on the beach.

Pa Pa Crab Guesthouse *(☎/fax 0 7638 5315; rooms with fan/air-con in low season 450/700B, in high season 600/850B)* has 10 well-decorated, comfortable rooms and a lovely colour scheme, but will close in low season if business is slow.

Thai Kamala Village *(☎ 0 7627 9795, fax 0 7627 9797; e thaiexin@e-mail.in.th; rooms in low/high season 1200/1800B)* is another almost-new hotel directly on the beach. All of the 17 air-con rooms face the bay, offering excellent views from their balconies. They are simply but tastefully decorated, and aligned perfectly to catch the sea breeze. There's a restaurant as well, which is open in the high season only.

Phuket Kamala Resort *(☎ 0 7621 2775, fax 0 7621 1841; bungalows with air-con in low/high season 1250/1650B)* is a moderately upmarket resort across the street from the beach. It features tennis courts, a pool and a fitness centre. The 40 bungalows have private balconies, minibar and TV.

Kamala Beach Estate *(☎ 0 7627 9756, fax 0 7632 4115; W www.kamalabeachestate.com; apartments in low season US$95-190, in high season US$120-235, villas low/high season US$255/350)* is at the southern end of the bay, overlooking the beach. It boasts fully equipped, high-security modern apartments, suites and villas – some with a kitchen and fantastic sea views. The manicured grounds feature an outdoor Jacuzzi, a lovely pool and an on-site restaurant. Each unit is individually owned and thus uniquely different; 20% are solely owner-occupied. The villas are especially beautifully laid out, with huge flagstone terraces and loads of comfortable and bright space.

Places to Eat The best value for eating is the friendly no-name **thatched-roof restaurant** at the northern end of the beach. There are others like it a little to the south. **Kamala Seafood** *(closed in low season)*, near the centre of the beach, is a decent family-run Thai seafood restaurant catering to *faràng*.

The Balcony Bar & Restaurant *(☎ 0 7627 9756 ext 132; dishes 80-250B)*, at Kamala Beach Estate on the southern end of the bay, is the most upmarket place to eat; it offers good views of the bay, reliable Thai and Western food and a decent wine list.

Getting There & Around A regular săwngthăew between Kamala and Patong costs 20B per person, while a charter costs 250B. You can rent vehicles at **Via Rent-A-Car** *(☎ 0 7638 5718; W www.via-phuket.com)*.

Patong
ป่าตอง

Patong is the most popular destination on Phuket – a seething concentration of souvenir shops, sleazy girlie bars, pricey seafood restaurants, dive shops, travel agencies, hotels and guesthouses and everything else in between that makes for the perfect tourist trap. It isn't necessarily unpleasant, however, as there is a decent beach here, good trinket shopping and plenty of bare skin (both *faràng* and Thai) to go along with the exciting day and nightlife that this town holds in spades. The sort of people drawn to this teeming, neon-lit atmosphere will adore Patong, while the more peace-loving souls (you know who you are) might want to stay far, far away. You might want to think twice about bringing your young kids into this town.

Although this began as Phuket's most expensive beach, prices are stabilising as the local accommodation market has become saturated with tons of places to stay. There are some decent and affordable guesthouses in town, but they won't be near the beach – that's were the luxury resorts are.

Information There are two **post offices** in Patong; one is toward the north end of Th Rat Uthit while the other is near the centre of Th Thawiwong. **Money exchange booths** and **Internet cafés** are commonplace. For English-language maps, guidebooks, magazines and newspapers head to **Bookazine** *(☎ 7634 5833; open 11am-midnight daily)*.

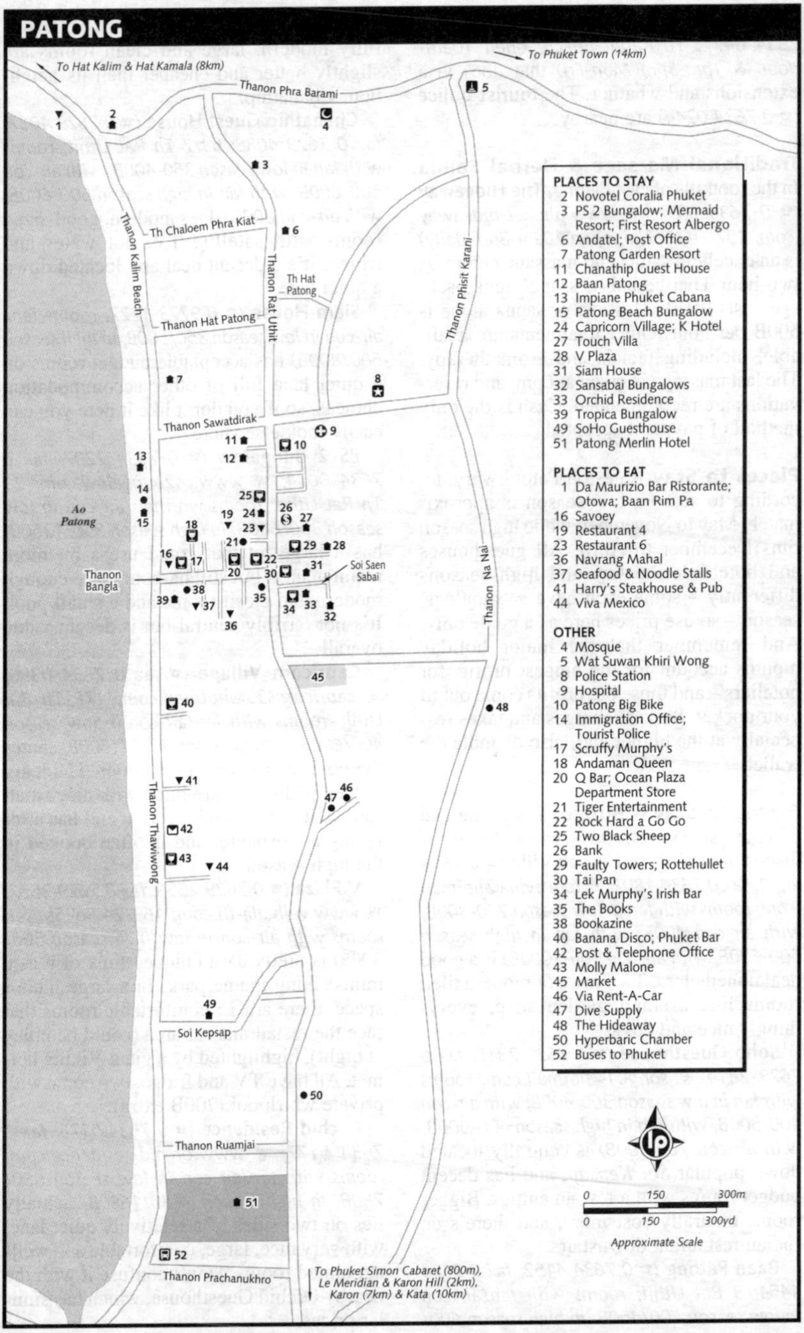
PATONG
To Phuket Town (14km)
To Hat Kalim & Hat Kamala (8km)
Thanon Phra Barami
Th Chaloem Phra Kiat
Thanon Kalim Beach
Thanon Rat Uthit
Th Hat Patong
Thanon Phisit Karani
Thanon Hat Patong
Thanon Sawatdirak
Ao Patong
Thanon Bangla
Soi Saen Sabai
Thanon Na Nai
Thanon Thawiwong
Soi Kepsap
Thanon Ruamjai
Thanon Prachanukhro
To Phuket Simon Cabaret (800m), Le Meridian & Karon Hill (2km), Karon (7km) & Kata (10km)
PLACES TO STAY
2 Novotel Coralia Phuket
3 PS 2 Bungalow; Mermaid Resort; First Resort Albergo
6 Andatel; Post Office
7 Patong Garden Resort
11 Chanathip Guest House
12 Baan Patong
13 Impiane Phuket Cabana
15 Patong Beach Bungalow
24 Capricorn Village; K Hotel
27 Touch Villa
28 V Plaza
31 Siam House
32 Sansabai Bungalows
33 Orchid Residence
39 Tropica Bungalow
49 SoHo Guesthouse
51 Patong Merlin Hotel
PLACES TO EAT
1 Da Maurizio Bar Ristorante; Otowa; Baan Rim Pa
16 Savoey
19 Restaurant 4
23 Restaurant 6
36 Navrang Mahal
37 Seafood & Noodle Stalls
41 Harry's Steakhouse & Pub
44 Viva Mexico
OTHER
4 Mosque
5 Wat Suwan Khiri Wong
8 Police Station
9 Hospital
10 Patong Big Bike
14 Immigration Office; Tourist Police
17 Scruffy Murphy's
18 Andaman Queen
20 Q Bar; Ocean Plaza Department Store
21 Tiger Entertainment
22 Rock Hard a Go Go
25 Two Black Sheep
26 Bank
29 Faulty Towers; Rottehullet
30 Tai Pan
34 Lek Murphy's Irish Bar
35 The Books
38 Bookazine
40 Banana Disco; Phuket Bar
42 Post & Telephone Office
43 Molly Malone
45 Market
46 Via Rent-A-Car
47 Dive Supply
48 The Hideaway
50 Hyperbaric Chamber
52 Buses to Phuket
0 150 300m
0 150 300yd
Approximate Scale

Patong has an **immigration office** *(☎ 0 7634 0477; Th Kalim Beach; open 10am-noon & 1pm-3pm Mon-Fri)* that does visa extensions and whatnot. The **tourist police** *(☎ 0 7634 0244)* are nearby.

Traditional Massage & Herbal Sauna In the foothills of east Patong, **The Hideaway** *(☎ 0 7634 0591; W www.phuket-hideaway.com; 157 Th Na Nai; open 10am-8pm daily)* is an excellent sauna and massage centre. A two-hour Thai herbal massage/sauna package costs 950B. Massage or sauna alone is 500B per hour. Other treatments are available, including facials and aromatherapy. The last massage is given at 6pm, and reservations are recommended. Cash is the only method of payment accepted.

Places to Stay Rates on Patong vary according to season; low season is approximately May to November, while high season runs December to April. All guesthouses and hotels define low and high seasons differently – some even have a 'shoulder' season – so use prices here as a guide only. And remember that the major holiday months account for the biggest profits for hoteliers – and those big profits come out of your pocket. Service charges and taxes (especially at the higher end) also dwindle the wallet.

Places to Stay – Budget It's at the end of a busy side street, so you can still hear the discos thumping, but **Touch Villa** *(☎ 0 7634 4011, fax 0 7634 1802; e touchvilla@hotmail.com; rooms with fan in low season 250-300B, with air-con 400B, with fan in high season 500-600B, with air-con 900-1000B)* is a good deal nonetheless. Two rows of modern tiled rooms line a small garden strip; everything's nice and cosy.

Soho Guesthouse *(☎ 0 7629 2815, fax 0 7629 2814; e soho01@hotmail.com; rooms with fan in low season 300-400B, with air-con 400-500B, with fan in high season 400-500B, with air-con 700-800B)* is centrally located down popular *Soi Kepsap*, and has decent budget rooms with a few amenities. Bigger rooms naturally cost more, and there's an Indian restaurant downstairs.

Baan Patong *(☎ 0 7634 4152, fax 0 7634 4454; 3 Rat Uthit; rooms with fan/air-con in low season 300/450B, in high season 600/800B)* is a great deal at this price. Beautifully modern, large and clean rooms are slightly better and cheaper than its neighbour Chanathip.

Chanathip Guest House *(☎ 0 7629 4087, fax 0 7629 4088; 53/7 Th Rat Uthit; rooms with fan in low season 350-400B, with air-con 500-600B, with fan in high season 500-600B, with air-con 800B)* does modern, good-sized rooms with satellite TV, hot water and fridge. It's a decent deal and located down a quiet lane.

Siam House *(☎ 0 9723 1727; rooms fan/air-con in low season 350/500B, in high season 500/800B)* has acceptable budget rooms on a quiet lane full of other accommodation choices, so if you don't like it here you can easily look elsewhere.

PS 2 Bungalow *(☎ 0 7634 2207, fax 0 7634 0034; W www.ps2bungalow.com; 21 Th Rat Uthit; rooms with fan/air-con in low season 350/600B, in high season 850/1350B)* has a large lot that could use a bit more maintenance, but still harbours nice enough modern and clean rooms and a small pool. It's not terribly central but is decent value overall.

Capricorn Village *(☎/fax 0 7634 0390; e capricorns39@hotmail.com; 178 Th Rat Uthit; rooms with fan/air-con in low season 400/600B, in high season 1000/1500B)* shares the pool with K Hotel next door. The leafy garden paths here are lined with nice small rooms. It's in a good location and has a relaxing atmosphere, and is often booked in the high season.

V Plaza *(☎ 0 7629 2556, fax 0 7629 2557; W www.valhalla-th.com; 163/24 Soi Sunset; rooms with air-con in low/high season 500/800B)* is pretty darn unique; think of it as a mini-Viking theme park. In a large indoor space, there are 13 comfortable rooms that face the restaurant/bar area (could be noisy at night), highlighted by a giant Viking helmet. All have TV and fridge; two come with private whirlpool (700B extra).

Orchid Residence *(☎ 0 7634 5176, fax 0 7634 5177; W www.orchid-residence.com; rooms with fan/air-con in low season 580/780B, in high season 1480/1680B)* actually lies on two sides of a relatively quiet lane, with very nice, large, comfortable and well-appointed rooms. Don't confuse it with the nearby Orchid Guesthouse, which has similar prices.

Places to Stay – Mid-Range The rooms at **First Resort Albergo** (*☎/fax 0 7634 0980; w www.phuket.com/firstresort; rooms with air-con in low/high season 800/1600B*) are very nice, modern and clean, and have a somewhat boring view of a plain, grassy garden. Still, they do come with satellite TV, hot water, fridge, balcony and breakfast.

K Hotel (*☎ 0 7634 0832, fax 0 7634 0124; w www.k-hotel.com; 180 Th Rat Uthit; rooms with air-con in low/high season 800/2000B*) consists of a long, two-storey building along pleasant paths; rooms face the pool and garden and are pretty comfortable.

Patong Garden Resort (*☎ 0 7634 1197, fax 0 7634 0123; 188 Th Thawiwong; rooms with air-con in low season 900-1400B, in high season 1800-3000B*) has interesting slant-faced buildings and leafy paths. Some rooms are located better than others, so get one you like – most are large and comfortable, and there's a nice shady pool with a bar. Easy parking completes this picture.

Sansabai Bungalows (*☎ 0 7634 2948, fax 0 7634 4888; w www.phuket-sansabai.com; 171/21 Soi Saen Sabai; rooms with fan in low season 450B, with air-con 600-800B, with fan/air-con in high season 950/1200B*), at the quiet end of a lane, has a great secluded location next to a large pond. However, it doesn't play this advantage, harbouring musty rooms and a large scruffy garden. Larger rooms cost more; cheaper ones are small but OK. There's plenty of parking.

Andatel (*☎ 0 7629 0489; w www.andatelhotel.com; rooms with air-con in low/high season 1000/1800B*) offers great rooms, all with patio or balcony and some creative touches, in traditional peaked Thai buildings. There's a pool to splash around in, plus an attractive restaurant out front. And it's right next to the post office, in case you desperately need to mail that postcard.

Patong Beach Bungalow (*☎ 0 7634 0117, fax 0 7634 0213; w www.patongbeachbungalows.com; rooms & bungalows with air-con in low season 1200-2000B, in high season 3000-3900B*) offers good, large rooms with the usual amenities in this class (TV, fridge, decent furniture), plus a small pool and beachside locale.

Mermaid Resort (*☎ 0 7634 5670, fax 0 7634 5251; w www.mermaid-resort.com; rooms with air-con in low/high season 1200/2200B*) is a great new resort with 24 spiffy rooms (all with balcony or patio), a nice little garden and a small but pleasant pool. Breakfast is included.

Tropica Bungalow (*☎ 0 7634 0204, fax 0 7634 0206; e tropica@phuket.loxinfo.co.th; rooms with air-con in low/high season 1000/2500B*) is a much better deal in low season – rates simply skyrocket in the high season (though they include breakfast). Small but beautiful and artistically decorated rooms are clean, neat and modern. They're set in a lush garden, and there's a pool to savour.

Places to Stay – Top End A monster resort engulfing almost a whole block, **Patong Merlin Hotel** (*☎ 0 7634 0037, fax 0 7634 0394; w www.merlinphuket.com; rooms with air-con in low/high season from 2800/5650B*) covers much of what you'd expect in a high-class resort: Beautiful grounds, beautiful pools, beautiful rooms. Beachside restaurants and a wide range of sport facilities are naturally included.

Impiana Phuket Cabana (*☎ 0 7634 0138, fax 0 7634 0178; w www.impiana.com; rooms with air-con in low season 2900-3900B, in high season 6500-7500B*) is close to the top of the heap, presenting gorgeously perfect rooms, grounds and lobby – all decked out in traditional Thai decor. Thatch-roof restaurants and lush gardens await your pleasure. Rates include breakfast.

Novotel Coralia Phuket (*☎ 0 7634 2777, fax 0 7634 2168; w www.phuket.com/novotel; rooms with air-con in low season 2900-6500B, in high season 4900-11000B*), at the northern edge of town, has nice rooms with views – although some are strangely located in the back with unattractive open halls. Novotel has a unique pool with scenic views and three levels are separated by tiled waterfalls.

Le Meridien Phuket (*☎ 0 7634 0480, fax 0 7634 0479; w www.lemeridien.com; rooms with air-con in low/high season from US$230/250*) is south of town about 1.5km and has a great set-up: Restaurants sit amid expansive swimming pools close to the beach. The 470 rooms feature things like safes, satellite TV and coffeepots. There are four tennis courts, two squash courts, beach volleyball, mini golf, a climbing wall, water sports equipment and, of course, the beautiful pools. It's a great place if you like to swim.

Places to Eat Patong has stacks of restaurants, some of them quite good, and many of them quite expensive. This is no surprise, considering Patong is one of the most popular beaches on Thailand's most upscale island. There are, however, a few bargain **seafood and noodle stalls** down a tiny lane opposite Soi Eric on Th Bangla.

Restaurant 6 (*☎ 0 7634 2219; 186 Th Rat Uthit; dishes 40-120B; open 8.30am-midnight daily*) found the secrets of restaurant success, which are (1) serve good food; (2) serve large portions; (3) serve it quickly; and (4) don't charge a whole lot. Both Thai and *faràng* flock to this small casual eatery, making you feel sorry for its neighbour restaurants.

Restaurant 4 (*☎ 0 1787 3167; seafood sold by weight; open 5pm-11pm daily*) lives in a no-nonsense, fluorescent-lit shed off Th Bangla. The most reasonably priced seafood can be found here; add your name to the graffiti on the walls when you've finished dining.

Savoey (*☎ 0 7634 1171; 136 Th Thawiwong; dishes 120-350B; open 10am-midnight daily*) slays 'em and weighs 'em – seafood, that is. And you can see it all from the sidewalk, where you'd be choosing your dinner critter from atop its mound of ice. It's a hugely popular, open-style café.

Harry's Steakhouse & Pub (*☎ 0 1787 3167; 110/2 Soi Big One; dishes 100-495B; open 8am-midnight daily*) is a tourist magnet, with a comfortable Western atmosphere and food to match – there are burgers, steak and pizza on the menu. It's also part pub, so you can order plenty of heady drinks to throw down.

Navrang Mahal (*☎ 0 7629 2280; dishes 90-210B; open 11.30am-11.30pm daily*) serves good Indian food. Another international eatery is **Viva Mexico**, down a lane off Th Thawiwong, which also has Arabic and Scandinavian restaurants.

Just north of town, on the coast, are a trio of expensive restaurants with romantic atmospheres. They are a good choice for a special night out.

Baan Rim Pa (*☎ 0 7634 4079; dishes 215-475B; open noon-11pm daily*), set above a thicket of mangrove trees, offers stunning ocean-view tables – but you'll have to make reservations to get them. Actually, you'll have to make reservations anyway. And, this being a high-class restaurant, come dressed accordingly. The Thai food served is only slightly toned down for foreign palates.

Otowa (*☎ 0 7634 4254; dishes 295B to sky-high group dishes; open noon-10.30pm daily*), next door to Baan Rim Pa, serves Japanese food (including sushi) just above the crashing waves. The ambience doesn't seem appropriately upscale considering the prices, type of food and its two fancy sister-restaurants nearby.

Da Maurizio Bar Ristorante (*☎ 0 7634 4079; dishes 450-950B; open noon-11pm daily*), next door to Otowa, is an Italian restaurant in the same classy genre as the others. Call for both reservations and a complimentary ride to the restaurant. It's set down on the rocks.

Entertainment There is no shortage of entertainment options in Patong.

There are dozens of simple bars around town, many of them little more than a few stools around an open-air bar with a handful of scantily-dressed Thai women whose main objective is to hook passers-by and keep them drinking long enough to pay the rent. Th Bangla has the main cluster, though they are everywhere. They are definitely loud and sleazy, but for certain visitors this adds to Patong's, uh, appeal. There are also plenty of other, much more upscale bars catering to the yuppie crowd.

Molly Malone's (*☎ 0 7629 2771; Th Thawiwong; open 10am-2am daily*) rocks with Irish gigs every night at 9.45pm. There's a good atmosphere, lots of pricey pub food, and some great tables out front from which to admire the ocean and legions of tourist passers-by. Guinness is available for a mere 349B per pint.

Scruffy Murphy's (*☎ 0 7629 2590; 5 Th Bangla; open 11am-2am daily*) competes with Molly Malone's by offering its own live Irish music at 9.45pm. It's also clean and air-conditioned. It cooks up pub and Thai food and offers big screens for watching sports. It's located amid the strips of cheap bars, though it doesn't play the girlie game.

Q-Bar (*☎ 0 7629 2114; open noon-2am daily*) is a small, delicate and hip bar next to the big department store on Th Bangla. It specialises in DJ music amid modern and simple decor.

Two Black Sheep (*open 9am-2am daily*) serves breakfast, surprisingly. It's mostly an intimate bar atmosphere, however, with good live rock music nightly in a trendy, dark space.

V Plaza *(☎ 0 7629 2556; 163/24 Soi Sunset; open 8am-2am daily)* contains 'Odin's Cave', something of an enclosed Nordic theme park for beer drinkers, complete with Viking ship and giant helmet. You have to see this V Plaza to believe it. Food and rooms are also available.

Phuket Bar *(☎ 0 1271 2469; open 5pm-2am daily)* is a great place for older, more conservative drinkers. It's right under Banana Disco, and is a nice and comfortable drinking hole. Live music plays outside on the patio area.

Off Th Rat Uthit, near Th Bangla, are some lanes full of bars. Most of them are the girlie kind, but a few are small and personal places good for meeting people. They're often run by expats and cater to older male foreigners. These include **Faulty Towers**, **Rottehullet** and **Lek Murphy's Irish Bar**.

The cover charge at the nightclub **Tiger Entertainment** *(☎ 0 7634 5112; admission 100B; open 9pm-2am daily)* includes one drink. It's in a huge primeval structure with a tiger head theme: Walk upstairs into the tiger's mouth. There are girlie bars downstairs and a Thai boxing ring next door.

Banana Disco *(☎ 0 1271 2469; 96 Th Thawiwong; admission 200B; open 9.30pm-2am daily)* is decorated in an Aztec-like theme. It's on the main beach strip and the cover charge includes two drinks.

Tai Pan *(☎ 0 1271 2469; Th Rat Uthit; open 8.30pm-2am daily)* is large and is patrolled by a staff of T-shirted young women who glow under the blue lights. The Western music is loud and sometimes comes to you good and live.

Rock Hard a Go Go *(☎ 0 7634 0409; cnr Th Bangla & Th Rat Uthit; open 5pm-2am daily)* is one of the cleaner go-go bars, where decently-clad girls swing on the poles both upstairs and down. Despite the entertainment it exudes a comfortable air, and welcomes couples and women. It serves a good range of Western food.

Andaman Queen *(Th Bangla; admission free; open 9pm-2am daily)*, at the end of Soi Kathoey, presents a go-go and cabaret show that's sleazier than Phuket Simon Cabaret but more of a hoot. There are three shows nightly. This is a great venue for transvestites.

Phuket Simon Cabaret *(☎ 0 7634 2011; admission 550B)*, south of town about 300m, offers entertaining transvestite shows. The 600-seat theatre is grand, the costumes are gorgeous, and the 'ladyboys' are convincing. The house is often full. Performances are given at 7.30pm and 9.30pm nightly.

Getting There & Around Săwngthăew from Phuket town leave from the day market and cost 20B. The after-hours charter fare is 150B. Buses to Phuket town leave from the south end of Th Thawiwong and cost 15B.

Túk-túk service Patong for 10B per ride. **Patong Big Bike** *(☎ 0 7634 0380; Th Rat Uthit)* rents a few kinds of motorcycles. **Via Rent-A-Car** *(☎ 0 7638 5718; W www.via-phuket.com)*, based in Kamala, has an unmanned office in town (you call from the telephone there) and delivers rental cars to Patong.

Travel agencies on Patong will eagerly arrange for you day cruises to nearby islands.

Karon

กะรน

Karon is a long, gently curving beach with small sand dunes and a few palms and casuarina trees. The main stretch of beach features a paved promenade with streetlights, and the area has blended with Hat Kata to the south to produce a self-contained village inhabited by a mixture of tourists, seasonal residents and year-rounders. It is still a fairly peaceful beach, though going more upmarket as the number of high-rise hotels increases. Unlike Kata, Karon still has large empty tracts of land facing the beach. They have a look of impending development about them, but with some luck room supply will soon outstrip demand and construction will not reach the proportions of Kata's Club Med.

In the off season, Karon is largely shut down by about 11.30pm, and those looking for nightlife must seek it in neighbouring Kata, to the south.

Dino Park *(☎ 0 7633 0625; adult/child 120/90B, with use of golf course 240/180B; open 10am-midnight daily)*, next to Marina Cottage, features an 18-hole minigolf course and a fake waterfall, among other things. The theme is Flintstones; staff wear caveman outfits with a loose necktie, the restaurant

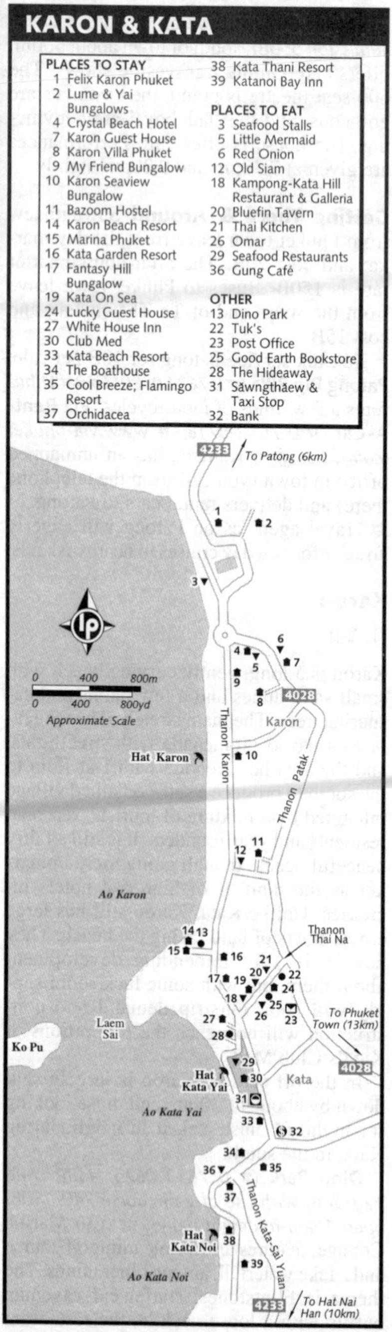

serves Bronto Burgers and you can drink at the Dino Bar.

Places to Stay – Budget & Mid-Range

Karon is lined with inns and deluxe bungalows, along with some cheaper places. Ask for discounts in the low season and if you stay more than just a few days. Less expensive places will naturally be found well off the beach, often on small hillocks to the east of the main road.

Bazoom Hostel (*☎/fax 0 7639 6914; ⓔ bazoom@loxinfo.co.th; dorm beds in low/high season 80/120B, rooms in low season 200-400B, in high season 290-490B*) is eclectically painted. The dorm is a bit large at 14 beds, and the rooms are pretty small. There's a cool Internet café downstairs. Bring your padlock for the lockers.

Fantasy Hill Bungalow (*☎ 0 7633 0106; bungalows with fan/air-con in low season 200/500B, in high season 300/700B*) sits in a lush garden on a hill; it's up a steep, short driveway off the main road. Fan bungalows are small and OK, while air-con ones are new, large and good. It's not fancy, but it is somewhat peaceful.

Crystal Beach Hotel (*☎ 0 7639 6580, fax 0 7639 6584; ⓔ crystalbeach@phuketinternet.co.th; rooms in low season 400-500B, in high season 700-900B*) is just east of the roundabout, near the beach. All rooms have air-con, tile floors and minibars. It has a bit of a split personality with upscale aspirations but low-rent smells, however, it is basically good value.

Karon Guest House (*☎ 0 7639 6860; rooms with fan/air-con in low season 400/600B, in high season 600/800B*), 300m east of the roundabout, has decent rooms (particularly the air-con ones) and offers free left-luggage service and safe deposit, plus satellite TV in the lobby. Guests have pool privileges at the nearby Golden Sands Hotel.

Karon Seaview Bungalow (*☎ 0 7639 6798, fax 0 7639 6799; rooms with fan/air-con in low season 400/800B, in high season 450/1000B*) is nothing special, but it's quiet, across from the beach and has a restaurant. Rooms have tile floors; some of the fan rooms are nicer than the air-con units.

My Friend Bungalow (*☎ 0 7639 6344, fax 0 7639 6345; ⓦ www.myfriendbungalow.com; rooms in low/high season 500/1500B*) is popular, friendly and opposite the beach. All of the very clean, modern rooms have air-con, tile floors and fridge; and there's a café out front. Unless you get a room with a sea view, the high-season prices are a bit too high. The owner has plans to build a hotel out back, so stay tuned.

Lume & Yai Bungalows (*☎ 0 7639 6382, fax 0 7696 6096; rooms with fan 600-800B*), at the north end of town, is up some stairs on a hillside with partial views of the bay. It was being renovated at the time of writing, so things might be nice and spiffy when you arrive. A dalmatian who doesn't seem to like certain men, however, patrols the grounds. Rates should drop in low season.

Places to Stay – Top End Many of the remaining places in Karon are newer resort-type hotels with rooms starting at 1500B or above, with air-con, swimming pools, multiple restaurants etc. Overbuilding has made it easier to bargain even at these larger places, and especially from May to October. During the holidays, however, rates zoom skyward.

Felix Karon Phuket (*☎ 0 7639 6666, fax 0 7639 6853; W www.felixphuket.com; rooms with air-con 3800-4500B*), at the northern end of town, is an older but well-maintained property with two pools and three bars. The rooms have some very nice touches, and all come with safe, phone, fridge and colour TV. The bathrooms are delightful. The official room rates only change in the high season (20 December to 15 January), when an 800B surcharge is added. In the low season it will sometimes offer rooms (including the deluxe poolside units) as low as 1600B.

Marina Phuket (*☎ 0 7633 0625, fax 0 7633 0516; W www.marinaphuket.com; rooms with air-con in high season US$100-160*) is one of the more exemplary options at the top end. Formerly called Marina Cottage, it's a long-running, medium-scale, low-rise, low-density resort on shady, palm-studded grounds near the southern end of the beach. Some rooms have ocean views while others are set back in a wooded area. There is a 50% discount in the low season if you book online.

Karon Beach Resort (*☎ 0 7633 0006, fax 0 7633 0529; W www.katagroup.com; rooms with air-con 5200B*), near the Marina Phuket, occupies a scenic spot right on the southern end of the beach, and has a pool and 80 smallish rooms with all the modern conveniences.

Karon Villa Phuket (*☎ 0 7639 6139, fax 0 7639 6122; W www.karonvilla.com; rooms with air-con in low/high season 6500/6800B, bungalows 3400/6300B*) is an enormous complex: Its lobby is off Th Patak, but the bungalows extend nearly to the beach road (golfcarts are on call to transport guests). It boasts three pools, a fitness centre, tennis courts, a spa and four restaurants, and offers classes in Thai cooking, batik painting, garland making etc. The bungalows are spacious and well constructed.

Places to Eat As usual, almost every place to stay provides some food. There are a few cheap Thai and seafood places off the roundabout (including beachside **seafood stalls** 100m north of it), but overall you'll find more selection farther south at Hat Kata Yai and Hat Kata Noi.

Little Mermaid (*☎ 0 7639 6638; dishes 70-300B; open 24hrs*), about 80m east of the roundabout, serves a good breakfast all day and has a long menu (available in 12 languages!) that includes burgers and steaks, Danish sandwiches, cheeses and Thai food.

Red Onion (*☎ 0 7639 6827; 486 Th Patak; dishes 60-150B; open 4pm-11pm daily*) attracts *faràng* like nobody's business. It's about 300m east of the roundabout – look for the coloured lights. There is Thai food on the menu, along with Western tidbits like schnitzel and spaghetti. Cocktails and wine selections complement the meals, so try to forget the bad music.

Old Siam (*☎ 0 7639 6090; dishes 195-300B, buffet 750B; open 6pm-10.30pm daily*), part of the Thavorn Palm Beach, is a large open-air restaurant constructed in a traditional central Thai style. It produces regional dishes for the tourist palate. Every Wednesday and Sunday in the high season it offers a Thai buffet with a traditional dance show from 8pm to 9pm.

Getting There & Away See the Kata Getting There & Away section for details on transport to Karon.

Kata

กะตะ

Just around a headland south from Karon, Kata is a more interesting beach and divided into two – Hat Kata Yai and Hat Kata

Noi. The main commercial street of Th Thai Na is perpendicular to shore and has most of the restaurants and shops, along with some cheaper places to stay. For reading material head to the **Good Earth Bookstore** *(open 10am-9pm daily)*, across from Bluefin Tavern, which sells and exchanges second-hand books.

The small island of Ko Pu is within swimming distance of the shore (if you're a strong swimmer); on the way are some OK coral reefs. Careful of riptides, however; heed the red flags and don't go past the breakers (ask about swimming conditions). Both Hat Kata Yai and Noi offer decent surfing waves from April to November.

If you feel like firing up the stove, The Boathouse offers a two-day **Thai cooking class** each weekend for 2800B per person; one-day courses are 1800B (for contact details see Places to Stay – Mid-Range & Top End). Or perhaps you'd like a spa treatment? **The Hideaway** *(☎ 0 7633 0914; 116/9 Th Patak)* has a branch here, offering traditional Thai massage, sauna, mud body wraps and other treatments.

Places to Stay – Budget Low season runs from May to September, while high season rakes your wallet from October to April. Definitions of 'high season' dates (and rates) may vary slightly from place to place, however. You can certainly expect price hikes during holiday periods.

Kata On Sea *(☎ 0 7633 0594; bungalows with fan in low/high season 200/300B)* is up a short, steep driveway. Twenty-nine basic and modest but large bungalows dot a quiet green hilltop.

Lucky Guest House *(☎ 0 7633 0572, fax 0 7633 0334; rooms & bungalows with fan in low season 250-300B, with air-con 450-500B, with fan in high season 500-600B, with air-con 750-850B)* won't win any special prizes, but does offer basic and decent accommodation on large, unpretentious grounds with plenty of room for your car. It's inland, just off the main street in a central location.

Katanoi Bay Inn *(☎ 0 7633 3308, fax 0 7633 0570; e katanoi_bayinn@hotmail.com; rooms with fan/air-con in low season 300/600B, with fan in high season 700B, with air-con 1200-1500B)*, across from the beach near the end of the road, has some modern new rooms with air-con, fridge, TV and large sliding glass doors; these are much nicer than the worn fan rooms. There's a restaurant downstairs.

White House Inn *(☎ 0 7633 0405, fax 0 7633 0689; rooms with air-con in low season 400-800B, in high season 1000-1500B)* offers 17 good rooms of different sizes. Some aren't energy efficient, however; open screens at the top of some rooms don't go well with air-conditioning. At least it's a central location, near a busy intersection but set back in a leafy garden. The beach is a 10-minute walk away.

Flamingo Resort *(☎ 0 7633 0776, fax 0 7633 0814; w www.flamingo-resort.com; bungalows with fan in low/high season 600/1000B)*, across from The Boathouse, sports just 10 large and decent bungalows on a hillside. Most have fridges, sizeable verandas and good views. It has a restaurant downstairs.

Cool Breeze *(☎ 0 7633 0484, fax 0 7633 0173; e coolbreeze.bungalows@yahoo.com; bungalows with fan/air-con in low season 350/550B, with fan in high season 700-900B, with air-con 1200-1500B)* features fair but basic and unexciting bungalows tumbling down a steep hillside; those at the top offer the most exercise and best views.

Places to Stay – Mid-Range & Top End The **Orchidacea Resort** *(☎ 0 7633 0181, fax 0 7633 0794; w www.orchidacearesort.com; rooms with air-con in low/high season from 1200/2200B)* features very nice beach-view rooms with balcony, fridge and TV. It's on a hillside terrace with nice gardens; be prepared to climb stairs. A pleasant pool lies towards the bottom.

Kata Beach Resort *(☎ 0 7633 0530, fax 0 7633 0128; w www.katagroup.com; rooms with air-con in low season 3000-3500B, in high season 6000-7000B)* is your basic luxury resort, with 262 nice rooms in hotel-like buildings and a large, amoeba-shaped pool under swaying palms. Rates include breakfast; check the website for discounts.

The Boathouse *(☎ 0 7633 0015, fax 0 7633 0561; w www.theboathousephuket.com; rooms with air-con in low season 3500-4000B, in high season 6500-7000B)* is a gorgeous boutique resort that boasts art-filled halls and 36 intimate rooms filled with tasteful wood and bamboo furniture. All of the rooms come with balcony and there are two pools. The restaurant is good here and so is the location.

Kata Thani Resort *(☎ 0 7633 0124–6, fax 0 7633 0426; w www.katathani.com; rooms with air-con in low season US$140-170, in high season US$190-220)* is an enormous, three-storey 530-room resort that commands most of the beach at Kata Noi. It's also one of the choice spots anywhere along Karon or Kata. It has upmarket, well-appointed rooms on nicely landscaped grounds, tennis courts, four swimming pools, a fitness centre and six restaurants round out the amenities.

Club Med *(☎ 0 7633 0456, fax 0 7633 0461; w www.clubmed.com; rooms with air-con in low/high season per person 3900/7000B)* caters to active travellers by not putting TVs in any rooms. It's a monster resort, though, with 306 rooms, expansive grounds and large pools. The beach is across the street, while the entrance is on the inland side of the block. Rates include all meals and activities; check the website for discounts.

Places to Eat There's some surprisingly classy food in Kata, though you'll be paying dearly for it. Easier on the bank account are the many **eateries** on Th Thai Na, which has more than its share of Italian and Scandinavian restaurants. A cluster of affordable, casual **seafood restaurants** can be found on Th Patak near the shore, though unfortunately they're not within view of the sea.

The Boathouse *(☎ 0 7633 0015; dishes 180-600B; open 11am-10.30pm daily)* is the best restaurant in the entire area, including Karon and Patong to the north. It boasts an excellent wine collection and the nightly seafood buffet is excellent. It's pricey but the atmosphere is casual and the service is first-rate; it's a great place to bring a fussy date.

Gung Cafe *(☎ 0 7633 0015; dishes 160-550B; open 11am-10.30pm daily)* is next to The Boathouse and under the same ownership. It's a bit more casual though, but still upscale and with romantic seaside tables. The seafood, meats and Thai food on the menu help to thin your wallet.

Kampong-Kata Hill *(☎ 0 7633 0103; dishes 80-260B; open 4pm-11.30pm daily)*, up many stairs on a terraced hillside, is another standout – although considerably more affordable. This Thai-style place is decorated with antiques and serves tasty Thai food. There's a street-side dining room if you don't want to sweat it.

Bluefin Tavern *(☎ 0 7633 0856; dishes 40-165B; open 3pm-11pm daily)* grills up Tex-Mex, pizza, burgers, steak and, of course, Thai food. The small front deck is nice and laid-back.

Thai Kitchen *(dishes 40-80B; open 9am-9pm Sun-Fri)* has basic Thai food in a casual, cafeteria-style setting. The food is good and cheap, and there are curries and other dishes to point to if you don't want to read the menu.

Omar *(☎ 0 7633 0611; dishes 100-300B; open 11am-11pm daily)*, behind Easy Riders Pub, isn't especially cheap – and the service is overly doting (to the point of being intrusive) – but it does a variety of Indian and other Central Asian dishes in a modern atmosphere.

Getting There & Around Săwngthăew and buses to both Kata and Karon leave frequently from the Th Ranong market in Phuket from 7am to 5pm for 20B per person. The main săwngthăew stop is in front of Kata Beach Resort.

Taxi destinations from Kata include Phuket town (200B), Patong (150B) and Karon (100B).

Motorcycle rentals are available at **Tuk's** *(☎ 0 7628 4049)*, near the Little Mermaid Guesthouse on Th Patak, for 150B to 1000B.

Nai Han
ในหาน

A few kilometres south of Kata, nearly at the southern tip of the island, this beach rims a picturesque bay and is similar to Kata and Karon (but not as developed). This is partly due to topography, but also to the presence of **Samnak Song Nai Han** – this monastic centre in the middle of the beach claims most of the beachfront land. The Meridien hotel occupies other prime sea-view property not owned by the monks, and developers have been forced to build further into the interior. Work seems to have slowed for the moment, and Nai Han is one of the less crowded beaches on the southern part of the island.

Hat Nai Han can be a dangerous place to swim during the monsoon season (May to

October), but it really varies according to daily or weekly weather changes – look for the red flag, which means dangerous swimming conditions. Beach chairs and umbrellas can be rented for 60B.

Places to Stay & Eat Except for the Yacht Club, there's not much accommodation with views of the beach.

Nai Han Beach Resort *(☎ 0 7638 1810, fax 0 7621 4687; rooms with fan/air-con Feb-Nov 500/800B, Dec & Jan 800/1000B)* has 20 tidy rooms with hot and cold showers. It's about 700m from the beach, near a small lagoon.

Orchid Bungalows *(☎/fax 0 7638 1396; rooms without/with kitchen 800/1000B)* is set behind an orchid nursery east of the lagoon. One of its three large, modern air-con rooms features an eat-in kitchenette with a sink, a small stove and utensils.

Le Royal Meridien Phuket Yacht Club *(☎ 0 7638 1156, fax 0 7638 1164; W www.lemeridien-yachtclub.com; rooms US$324-780)* sits on the northwestern end of Hat Nai Han. Originally built at the astronomical cost of 145 million baht, the hotel has given up on the idea of becoming a true yacht club, but still offers luxurious rooms. A few food carts and cheap eateries can be found above the beach a few hundred metres southeast of the Yacht Club.

Yanui Bayview Bungalows *(☎/fax 0 7623 8180; W www.phuketdir.com/yanuibayview; rooms with fan/air-con in low season 400/600B, in high season 600/800B)* is across the bay from the Yacht Club and around a small point, and features a set of plain cottages across the road from the beach. All rooms have hot water, good screens, firm beds and tile floors.

The Yanui serves food year-round. Across the road is a rustic restaurant, open only in the high season, that enjoys a beachfront location on its own small sandy cove. It's a very quiet and peaceful spot among coconut palms, mangroves and casuarina trees; the cape and grassy hills nearby have lots of hiking potential. You'll need your own transport to get here, however.

Getting There & Away Nai Han is 18km from Phuket and a sǎwngthǎew (leaving from the intersection of Th Ranong and the fountain circle) costs 25B per person. Túk-túk charters are 150B to 200B one way. Sǎwngthǎew between Nai Han and nearby Rawai charge a scandalous 20B.

Rawai

ราไวย์

Rawai, just a few kilometres from Nai Han, was one of the first coastal areas on Phuket

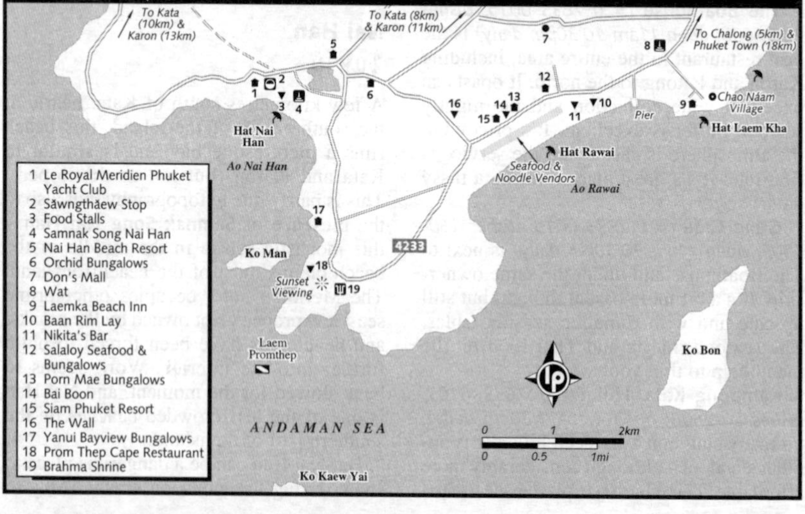

to be developed, simply because it was near Phuket and there was already a rather large fishing community here. It has lost popularity over the years with the 'discovery' of nicer beach areas such as Patong and Karon, but still attracts fair amounts of Thais and foreigners.

The beach is not so great, but there is a lot happening in or near Rawai: a **chao náam village** lies at the east side of town; boats leave from the beach to nearby islands for diving, snorkelling, day-tripping and overnight stays (see Nearby Islands later in this section); **Hat Laem Kha** (a better beach than Rawai) is just to the northeast; and there's good snorkelling off **Laem Phromthep** at the southern tip of Phuket island, less than 2km from Rawai. In fact, most of the visitors who stay at Rawai these days are divers who want to be near Phromthep or boat facilities for offshore diving trips.

Laem Phromthep is also a popular viewing point at sunset, when bus loads of Thai tourists come to pose for photos and enjoy the vistas. South of the viewpoint is a shrine to Phra Phrom (Brahma).

If you're looking for a physical challenge, **The Wall** restaurant, on the road from Rawai northwest to Nai Han, has a **rock-climbing wall** as well as massage, herbal saunas and a Jacuzzi.

Places to Stay The long-running **Salaloy Seafood & Bungalows** *(☎ 0 7638 1297; bungalows with fan/air-con 350/800B)* was remodelling when we visited; rates may be different when you arrive. Its seafood restaurant is one of the better – and more moderately priced – ones in the area. The bungalows close down for the low season.

Porn Mae Bungalows *(☎/fax 0 7638 1300; bungalows in low/high season 350/400B)* has simple and clean lodgings with fan, fridge, table and chairs.

Siam Phuket Resort *(☎ 0 7638 1346, fax 0 7638 1647; W www.siamphuketresort.com; rooms 1300-1800B)* is the most upscale place in town, with landscaped grounds, a pool and 50 air-con rooms. Prices rise by 300B per room from December 20 to January 20.

Laemka Beach Inn *(☎ 0 7638 1305, fax 0 7628 8547; bungalows with fan in low season 500-650B, in high season 650-800B, rooms with air-con in low/high season 900/1200B)* is more than 1km (by road) out of Rawai, on Hat Laem Kha. Its 30 thatched bungalows are spread among coconut groves above the beach and have screen doors and windows (a rare bonus in these parts). The shoreline along the rounded cape is an interesting mix of clean sand and large boulders, with good swimming. Many speedboats depart from here for nearby islands, and it's a favourite local picnic spot.

Places to Eat Besides the restaurants attached to the resorts in Rawai (of which Salaloy Seafood is the best), there are oodles of seafood and noodle vendors set up along the roadside near the beach. All the following listings are sit-down restaurants; the first three are on the main road through town (listed from northeast to southwest) and serve Thai and European food.

Baan Rim Lay *(☎ 0 7628 8067; dishes 70-190B; open 8am-10pm daily)* has good sea views and a small bakery/café next door.

Nikita's Bar *(☎ 0 7628 8703; dishes 80-225B; open 8am-10pm daily)* is interestingly decorated and very popular in the evenings; in addition to food and booze, it serves espresso drinks.

Bai Boon *(☎ 0 7628 8704; dishes 60-180B; open 8am-9pm daily)* has a menu that includes American, continental and German breakfasts.

The Wall *(☎ 0 7628 8908; dishes 50-600B; open 8am-late daily)*, on the road leading from Rawai northwest to Nai Han, offers French cuisine as well as a rock-climbing wall and herbal sauna.

Prom Thep Cape Restaurant *(☎ 0 1723 0059; dishes 80-150B; open 10am-10pm daily)* is just below the viewpoint for Laem Phromthep and has simple Thai meals.

Don's Mall *(☎ 0 7638 3100; 48-5 Soi Sai Yuan; dishes 100-650B; open 8am-10pm daily)* is a Texan-run food and entertainment complex whose varied menu stars hearty American meals of steak and ribs barbecued over a mesquite-wood fire. It also has an extensive wine list, fresh baked goods and much more. From Rawai, drive past The Wall and turn right at the next two main intersections (about 3.4km total from the beach). To get there from Phuket town (and many people make the trip just for the food), turn right onto Th Sai Yuan, just south of the Chalong roundabout, and proceed 3km; you can't miss it.

Getting There & Away Rawai is about 16km from Phuket and costs 20B by sǎwngthǎew from the circle at Th Ranong. Túk-túk charters cost at least 150B. Unscrupulous sǎwngthǎew drivers charge 20B for the much shorter trip from Rawai to Nai Han.

Ao Chalong

This large bay, on the northeast end of Phuket, is a pier area thronging with many dive shops and a few travel agencies, which can help you book trips to nearby islands (see following). It's not an especially good place to stay, but there are a couple good seafood restaurants on the beach – and Phuket's only official youth hostel is located nearby.

Places to Stay & Eat You'll find the **Phuket Youth Hostel** *(☎ 0 7628 1325, fax 0 2711 1986; W www.phukethostel.com; 73/11 Th Chao Fa west; dorm beds 180B, rooms with fan/air-con 360/440B)* 7km south of Phuket town (1km past Wat Chalong and on the same side) and 1.5km before Ao Chalong. It's a large, modern place with basic but good rooms. Package tours to nearby islands are offered, as well as land tours. All rates include breakfast.

Kan Eang 1 *(☎ 0 7638 1212; dishes 60-150B; open 11am-10pm daily)* is near the pier itself, boasting a great beachside location. It's a large, open-air restaurant with attentive staff and extensive menu; it specialises in seafood, which is good and reasonably priced.

Kan Eang 2 *(☎ 0 7638 1323; dishes 60-150B; open 11am-10pm daily)* has the same menu as its sister restaurant, but is farther north a kilometre or so. Both restaurants are popular with tour buses.

Nearby Islands

Ko Hae & Ko Raya Yai/Noi Ko Hae (also known as Coral Island), a few kilometres southeast of Ao Chalong, has good diving and snorkelling although jet skis and other pleasure craft can be an annoyance. The island gets lots of day-trippers from Phuket, but at night it's pretty quiet. The **Coral Island Resort** *(☎ 0 7628 1060, fax 0 7638 1957; W www.phuket.com/coralisland/index.htm; bungalows in low season 1800-2600B, in high season 2200-3000B)* has upmarket bungalows with air-con. The rates vary depending on proximity to the beach.

Two islands about 1½ hours by boat south of Phuket, Ko Raya Yai and Ko Raya Noi (also known as Ko Racha Yai/Noi), are highly favoured by divers and snorkellers for their hard coral reefs and crystal-clear water. Because the coral is found in both shallow and deep waters, it's a good area for novice scuba divers and snorkellers as well as accomplished divers. Visibility can reach 30m. The islands are inhabited by Muslim families who mainly farm coconuts and fish for a living.

On Ko Raya Yai, **Ban Raya** *(☎ 0 7635 4682, fax 0 7622 4439; W www.phuket.com/banraya; bungalows with fan/air-con in low season 1000/1400B, in high season 1300/1900B)* has sturdy, comfortable bungalows and offers diving instruction. Other places to stay include **Jungle Bungalow**, **Raya Resort** and **Raya Andaman Resort**.

Ao Chalong and Hat Rawai are the main departure points for these islands. A speedboat to Ko Hae costs about 150B per person one way (you may have to bargain hard), or you can hire an entire boat for 1000B to 1500B. If you're booking a room on Ko Raya, your host may arrange transport for around 400B per person via speedboat, or 1500B for an entire long-tail boat.

Aloha Tours *(☎ 0 7638 1215)*, just south of the main pier at Ao Chalong, is one of many agencies that book snorkelling tours to Ko Hae (700B) and Ko Raya (1100B). The tours include hotel pickup and transport to the pier, return speedboat ride, lunch and use of snorkelling gear. From Phuket town port, **Songserm Travel** *(☎ 0 7622 2570)* and **Pal Travel Service** *(☎ 0 7634 4920)* run daily passenger boats to Ko Raya. Both companies suspend service from May to October. Call for current prices and schedules.

Ko Yao

เกาะยาว

Ko Yao Yai (Big Long Island) and Ko Yao Noi (Little Long Island) are actually part of Ao Phang-Nga National Marine Park, but are more easily accessible from Phuket. Together they encompass 137 sq km of forest, beach, and rocky headland with views of the surrounding karst formations characteristic of Ao Phang-Nga.

In spite of being smaller, **Ko Yao Noi** is the main population centre of the two. Fishing sustains the locals, as does coconut, rice and rubber cultivation. **Hat Pa Sai** and **Hat Tha Khao**, both on Yao Noi, are the best beaches. **Ta Khai**, the largest settlement on the island, is a subdistrict seat and a source of minimal supplies. Bring a mountain bike to explore the dirt trails.

Ko Yao Yai is more isolated and rustic than its smaller sister island. Rubber farming takes place on the island, and just three bungalow operations have (so far) planted roots here. Please remember to respect the Muslim cultures on both these islands, especially by wearing modest clothing outside beach areas.

Boat trips to neighbouring islands, birdnest caves and *chao náam* funeral caves are possible. **Ko Bele**, a small island east of the twin Ko Yai, features a large tidal lagoon, three white-sand beaches, and easily accessible caves and coral reefs around the entire island.

Places to Stay Ko Yao Noi has a handful of places to stay.

Sabai Corner Bungalow *(☎ 0 1892 7827; bungalows with fan 350-550B)* offers eight sturdy thatch-and-wood bungalows with small verandas. The restaurant here is pretty good.

Long Beach Village *(☎ 0 7659 7472; bungalows 500-1500B)* is a friendly place with about 40 fan and air-con rooms and bungalows, crowded together in a tropical setting.

Tha Khao Bungalow *(☎ 0 1676 7726; bungalows with fan 500-1200B)*, on Hat Tha Khao, features five solid thatch-and-wood bungalows, including two family-size ones (with three bedrooms). The small restaurant does tasty food, and it also rents bikes and kayaks.

Koyao Island Resort *(☎ 0 1606 1517; w www.koyao.com; villas with air-con 2500-3500B)* has the most luxurious abodes of all, with elegantly rustic decor and amenities such as satellite TV and fridge.

On Ko Yao Yai there are three relatively new places with basic wood-and-thatch fan bungalows. These are **Halawee Bungalows** *(☎ 0 1607 3648; bungalows 400B)*, **Thiw Son** *(☎ 0 1956 7582; bungalows 350-500B)* and **Long Island Family Bungalows** *(☎ 0 1979 2273; bungalows 500B)*.

Getting There & Around Although both islands fall within the Phang-Nga Province boundaries, the easiest places to find boat transport to Ko Yao Noi are Phuket (Phuket Province), Ao Leuk and Ao Nang (both in Krabi Province). In Phuket town, catch a săwngthăew from in front of the day market to Bang Rong (on Ao Po) for 25B. From the public pier there are up to four boats daily, at 11am, noon, 2.30pm and 5pm. The fare is 50B per passenger and the trip takes just over an hour. Between departures or after hours you can charter a long-tail boat to the island for about 1000B one way. You can also charter boats from Ao Leuk and Ao Nang, in Krabi; these take a bit longer.

To go from Ko Yao Noi to Ko Yao Yai, catch a shuttle boat from the pier, Tha Manaw (20B, 15 minutes). Túk-túk on the islands provide transport for about 50B per ride.

Krabi Province

Krabi Province is blessed with some amazing scenic karst formations – similar to those in neighbouring Phang-Nga Province – along its coast and even in the middle of Mae Nam Krabi (Krabi River). These limestone cliffs add wonderful scenic beauty to the region, and have attracted international rock-climbers of all levels. But despite it having become a world-class climbing destination, Krabi Province mainly brings in travellers seeking sun, sand and some serious beach time. And, if you come from December to March, you can find all this – though hotels and bungalows tend to fill up with fellow tourists. This is not a problem during the rainy season (June to November), so if you visit during this time you'll have your choice of accommodation, and may even be lucky with windows of decent weather.

Krabi Province has some attractive islands as well as coastal beaches; over 150 of them offer excellent recreational opportunities. Many of the islands belong to the Hat Noppharat Thara/Ko Phi-Phi National Marine Park, including Ko Phi-Phi Don (probably the most poplar island in this region). In the high season boats head out regularly to the Ko Phi-Phi Archipelago as well as Ko Lanta, rapidly becoming the next 'in' destination.

Hundreds of years ago, Krabi's waters were a favourite hideout for Asian pirates

because of all these islands and water-filled caves. Latter-day pirates (some call them developers) now steal islands or parts of islands for other financial purposes – land encroachment is apparently taking place on Phi-Phi Don, Poda, Bubu, Jam (Pu), Po, Bilek (Hong), Kamyai and Kluang. About 40% of Krabi's provincial population is Muslim.

The interior of the province, noted for its tropical forests and the Phanom Bencha mountain range, has barely been explored. Bird-watchers come from far and wide to view Gurney's pitta (formerly thought to be extinct) and Nordmann's greenshank.

KRABI

กระบี่

postcode 81000 • pop 24,600

Nearly 1000km from Bangkok and 180km from Phuket, the fast-developing provincial capital of Krabi (gra-**bee**) has friendly people, delicious food and some local flavour – despite its popularity with foreigners. But travellers tend to breeze through town on their way to the wonderful destinations around Krabi, all of which offer memorable experiences: Ko Lanta to the south, Ko Phi-Phi to the southwest, and the nearby beaches of Ao Nang, Rai Leh and Tham Phra Nang to the west. Some travellers elect to stay in town and make day trips to the latter, however, as there are many good and affordable guesthouses here now as well as good options for dining. And it's not an unpleasant spot to hang around a couple of days…this place can grow on you.

Krabi sits on the mangrove-edged banks of Mae Nam Krabi right before it empties into the Andaman Sea. Across from town you can see Bird, Cat and Mouse Islands, named for their shapes. Although the town is essentially more Taoist-Confucianist and Muslim than Theravada Buddhist, **Wat Kaew** contains some older buildings from the early 20th century and lots of large old trees.

Information

Tourist Offices There's a small **TAT office** *(☎ 0 7561 2740; Th Utarakit; open 8.30am-4.30pm daily)* near the waterfront.

Immigration Offices Visas can easily be extended at the **immigration office** *(Th Chamai Anuson; open 8.30am-4.30pm Mon-Fri)* south of the main post office.

Post & Communications There is a **main post office** *(Th Utarakit; open 8.30am-4.30pm Mon-Fri, 9am-noon Sat & Sun)* with attached **telephone office**. The **CAT telephone office** *(open 8.30am-4.30pm daily)* is located 1.5km north of town on Th Utarakit.

You'll find there's no shortage of Internet cafés in Krabi.

Travel Agencies There are many travel agencies in Krabi, and most are fine, but you should still try to get recommendations whenever you can. Some good agencies include **Sweetland** *(☎ 0 7561 1146; 28 Th Khongkhla)*, **Ibris** *(☎ 0 7563 0276; 23 Th Issara)* and **Somporn** *(☎ 0 7563 0234; 72 Th Khongkhla)*; this last one is just a desk at the Star guesthouse. The restaurants **May & Mark** and **Café Europa** are also reliable places to buy transport tickets.

These agencies and dozens of others in town offer many tours that take in the surrounding areas of Krabi Province. These tours include exploring the large mangrove ecologies nearby, bird-watching tours, visiting rubber-tapping villages, and plenty of boat rides to idyllic uninhabited isles, some with coral reefs and luscious beaches set in tranquil sandy coves. Adventure activities are also offered and include snorkelling, kayaking, canoeing, river rafting, rock-climbing, cave tours and jungle treks.

Bookshops Phuket-based **The Books** *(☎ 0 7561 2693; 78-80 Th Maharat; open 8am-9pm daily)* has an outlet here. There's a good selection of English-language books, including Lonely Planet guidebooks, and plenty of area maps.

There are several **second-hand bookshops** around town that trade or sell books.

Medical Services You'll find **Krabi Hospital** *(☎ 0 7561 1210)* 1km north of town. If you have serious problems, however, you may want to go to the hospitals in Phuket instead.

Places to Stay

Guesthouses Krabi is now full of cheap guesthouses, including some excellent new choices that have popped up in the last year or two. Most have fan rooms only, though a few offer air-con. All prices rise in the high season from approximately November to April.

River View *(☎ 0 7561 2536, fax 0 7561 2536; 13 Th Khongkha; rooms with shared bath 80-120B)* is the cheapest in town, with just four barebones rooms. There's a roof patio with river views, and it's a friendly place.

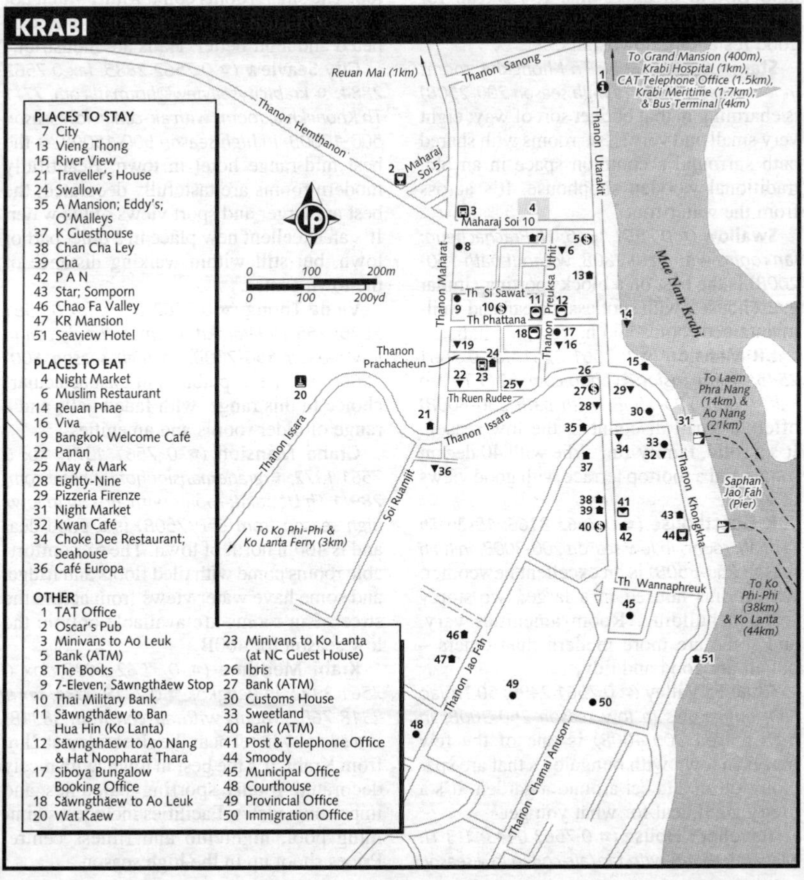

Cha (☎ 0 7562 1125; e chaguesthouse@hotmail.com; Th Utarakit; rooms in low season 80-200B, in high season 100-250B; rooms with air-con 400-450B) remains a friendly, family-run place with OK, semi modern budget rooms in a back patio area; there's a wide variety of choices and prices.

PAN (☎ 0 9866 4373; 182 Th Utarakit; rooms/bungalows in low season 100/200B, in high season 150/300B) is great for budget travellers who want rustic, cheap bamboo rooms and bungalows in an overgrown, weedy and hilly garden. There are some nice common bench areas in which to hang out.

Chan Cha Lay (☎ 0 7562 0952; w www.krabidir.com/chanchalay; 55 Th Utarakit; rooms in low season 150B, in high season 200-250B) is a beautiful new place with 15 modern and clean rooms. It's set up for travellers, with Internet connections and a good restaurant downstairs.

Star (☎ 0 7563 0234; Th Khongkha; rooms in low season 150B, in high season 200-250B) is charming in that budget sort of way; eight very small and very basic rooms with shared bath surround a common space in an old, traditional wooden shophouse. It's across from the waterfront.

Swallow (☎ 0 7561 1645; Th Prachacheun; fan rooms with bath 280B, without bath 150-200B) is the best on a block sporting similar guest houses, with spotlessly clean and well-maintained rooms and narrow, tile halls.

KR Mansion (☎ 0 7561 2761, fax 0 7561 2545; e krmansion@yahoo.com; 52/1 Th Jao Fah; rooms 200-250B, with bath 280-600B) offers a small discount in the low season. It's a solid, family-run oldie with 40 decent rooms and a rooftop terrace with good views of Krabi.

K Guesthouse (☎ 0 7562 3166; 15-25 Th Jao Fah; rooms in low season 200-300B, in high season 250-350B) is an excellent newcomer, with rooms housed in a large, two-storey wooden building. Room amenities vary, and some are more modern than others – but all are good and tidy.

Chao Fa Valley (☎ 0 7561 2499; 50 Th Jao Fah; bungalows in low season 250-300B, in high season 300-400B) is one of the few places in town with bungalows that are spacious, clean and set around a garden. It's a pretty good deal for what you get.

Traveller's House (☎ 0 7563 0443; 1-3 Th Maharat; rooms with fan/air-con in low season 300/400B, in high season 600/800B) is another good new guesthouse. It's on a busy corner, but the open lobby is still a pleasant hang-out spot. The 16 rooms are large and simple, and the furniture is especially nice.

A Mansion (☎ 0 7563 0511, fax 0 7563 0513; 12/6 Th Jao Fa; rooms with fan/air-con in low season 300/550B, in high season 350/700B) is yet another friendly, new place with modern, clean and beautiful rooms with TV. There's a café, bar and cheap laundry nearby.

Hotels It's not an especially good deal, and **City** (☎ 0 7561 1961; w www.city-riverside-hotel-group.com; 15/2-3 Th Sukhon; rooms with fan/air-con in low season 400/550B, in high season 450/700B) could use a new paint job. The small rooms come with TV and hot water; fan rooms are OK, air-con ones carpeted and a bit better. Halls are industrial.

City Seaview (☎ 0 7562 2885, fax 0 7562 2884; e krabicityseaview@hotmail.com; 77/1 Th Khongkhla; rooms with air-con in low season 500-1000B, in high season 500-1500B) is the best mid-range hotel in town. Beautifully modern rooms are tastefully decorated; the best are larger and sport views of the water. It's an excellent new place in a quiet part of town, but still within walking distance of the town centre.

Vieng Thong (☎ 0 7562 0020, fax 0 7561 2525; 155 Th Utarakit; rooms with air-con in low season 550-700B, in high season 800-1000B) is an acceptable (but unspectacular) choice in this range, with faded halls and a range of older rooms and amenities.

Grand Mansion (☎ 0 7561 1371, fax 0 7561 1372; e grandmansionhotel@hotel.com; 289/1 Th Utarakit; rooms with air-con in low/high season from 650/750B) is a good deal and is 400m north of town. The 58 comfortable rooms come with tiled floors and fridge, and some have water views from across the street. Fan rooms are available only in the low season for 400B.

Krabi Meritime (☎ 0 7562 0028, fax 0 7561 2992; in Bangkok ☎ 0 2719 0034, fax 0 2318 7687; rooms with air-con from 3831B) is a swanky hotel near the river, almost 2km from Krabi. It's the best in town, with nicely decorated rooms sporting balconies and impressive views. Facilities include a swimming pool, nightclub and fitness centre. Prices shoot up in the high season.

Places to Eat

Krabi gets a lot of foreign visitors, so many restaurant cater to homesick palates with either Western food or toned-down Thai food. For more authentic, inexpensive dishes, however, head out along Th Khongkha, near the long-tail boats. An atmospheric **night market** with good seafood sets up here, and there's a bigger **night market** on Th Sukhon as well.

May & Mark (☎ *0 7561 2562; Th Ruen Rudee; open 6.30am-9pm daily)* bake some great bread and serve an assortment of excellent Thai and Western food, such as pumpkin soup and homemade yogurt. Culinary surprises from Mexico and Germany pop up on the menu, too.

Bangkok Welcome Cafe *(Pe-pe; cnr Th Maharat & Th Prachacheun; dishes 25B; open 6am-4pm daily)* cooks up just eight inexpensive noodle and rice dishes. It's very popular at lunch time and probably the cheapest food in town that you can eat under a roof.

Muslim Restaurant *(open 7am-5pm daily)* serves *rotii kaeng*, the Malaysian-style breakfast of flat bread and curry. It's a local male hang-out.

Pizzeria Firenze (☎ *0 7562 1453; 10 Th Khongkha)* does 'simple but genuine Italian cooking', serving pizza, pasta, wine, gelato and Italian bread.

Eddy's (☎ *0 7562 3573; breakfast 35-70B; open 7am-11pm daily)* is a tiny café right under A Mansion. Very large and strong double espressos are brewed, along with other coffee drinks, breakfast items such as waffles, and some Thai dishes. There are nice bistro tables out front.

Kwan Café (☎ *0 7561 1706; 30 Th Khongkhla; dishes 35-120B; open 7.30am-9pm daily)* serves up lots of breakfast choices, sandwiches, pizza, tofu burgers, tiramisu and specialty coffees in a modern, clean and hip atmosphere. Service is cheerful and there are tables outside if you need to be seen.

Café Europa (☎ *0 7562 0407; 1/9 Soi Ruamjit; dishes 75-200B; open 8am-midnight daily)* is great for Western foods such as steak and potatoes, Danish meatballs or wine and cheese plates. The friendly proprietors give information on the area and have a mini-golf course across the way.

Viva (☎ *0 7563 0517; 29 Th Preuksa Uthit; dishes 100-180B, pizzas 130-340B; open 9am-midnight daily)* is a good, popular Italian restaurant with plenty of pasta, pizza and calzone selections. Also on tap are steaks, burgers, *lassi* and breakfast items – all served up in a modern space with bamboo furniture. Roving bands sometimes play here.

Reuan Phae *(no Roman-script sign; open 10am-10pm daily)* is an old floating restaurant on the river. The food here is not good, but the atmosphere can't be beat – sip a cold beer or rice whisky and feel the tides go up and down. Look for the restaurant's platform.

Choke Dee Restaurant (☎ *0 7563 0226; 226 Th Utarakit; dishes 50-100B; open 8am-11pm daily)* sits happily at its busy corner location, offering the usual range of travellers' grub along with wine, cocktails and movies.

Seahouse (☎ *0 7561 1325; 7/5 Th Jao Fah; dishes 50-150B; open 8am-11pm daily)* is around the corner from Choke Dee and also popular with travellers for its pizza, steak, cocktails and nice wood deck out front.

Eighty-Nine (☎ *0 7561 1245; 89 Th Utarakit; dishes 40-150B; open 7am-midnight daily)* sits right below its guesthouse and is popular for Western standbys such as spaghetti and pizza, though Thai food is also on the menu. There's a casual traveller's atmosphere here, enhanced by a travel agency and Internet access right in the dining area.

Panan *(cnr Th Ruen Rudee & Th Maharat; dishes 30-50B; open 8am-10pm daily)* has just a dozen inexpensive choices decorating the English menu on the wall. It's a simple, local corner place with a modern, clean atmosphere and a few sidewalk tables.

Reuan Mai *(no Roman-script sign;* ☎ *0 7563 1797; Th Maharat; dishes 60-150B; open 9.30am-10pm daily)* lies 1km north of town, hidden away in a gorgeous forest setting. Very good Thai food is professionally served at indoor and outdoor tables.

Entertainment

There are a few bars in town catering to *faràng*. **Smoody** *(open 9pm-2am daily)*, across from the old pier, offers 'slinky tunes and mellow vibes' in an eclectic space. Beers cost 40B to 80B. A branch of **O'Malley's**, next to Eddy's on Th Jao Fah, has an intimate atmosphere and a happy hour from 8pm to 9pm. It prides itself on being 'a booze bonanza for budget drinkers'.

Oscar's Pub, on Th Hemthanon towards the north of town, is a modern disco open

Bus Tickets in Krabi

Krabi town has become so popular with travelling foreigners that a few travel agencies have become adept at overcharging them for certain things like bus tickets. Departure times and bus conditions can also be unpredictable if you go with a private company. If you decide to buy a bus ticket from a travel agency in Krabi make sure you have a good idea of what you're getting: Shop around a little and do some comparisons.

If, however, you use the government terminal in nearby Talat Kao (4km north of town) you can be fairly sure bus conditions will be as you expected and that they'll leave as scheduled. Of course, travel agencies can also sell you bus tickets for buses leaving from the government terminal, but be aware these ticket prices may include a small commission.

Not all travel agencies are out to get you, though. The best way to find a reliable travel agency is to ask, ask, ask. Talk to fellow travellers (probably your best source), guesthouse employees (if you like and trust them), or just walk into a decent-looking agency and trust your instincts (after doing some homework). And remember, if some price sounds too good to be true, then it most likely is.

from 8pm to 2am nightly. A new entertainment area is supposed to be zoned north of town at Soi 5-7; some discos and bars may be situated here in the future.

Getting There & Away

Air Several airlines service Krabi. **THAI** has three daily flights to/from Bangkok, while **PB Air** has two a week. **Phuket Air** flies once or twice daily, depending on demand. **Air Andaman** may resume its flights to Phuket. **Silk Air** flies to Singapore four times weekly. There are no more flights to Ko Samui anymore, though this situation may change.

Tickets can be booked through any agency in town; see Travel agencies earlier.

Bus Krabi's government bus terminal, located 4km north of town at Talat Kao, features separate ticket booths for each line, a clean little restaurant, snacks and drinks for sale and clean toilets. There is no official TAT office here, but some travel agencies (with their own self-interests) may 'appear' to be one. Coming to this bus terminal is the best way to obtain the cheapest, most reliable bus tickets in Krabi (see boxed text 'Bus Tickets in Krabi').

Government buses to/from Bangkok include ordinary (255B), 2nd class air-con (357B), 1st class air-con (459B) and 24-seat VIP (710B). The trip takes 12 hours (14 hours ordinary). Buses leave Bangkok 6.30pm to 8pm; they leave Krabi 3.30pm to 7pm. See the 'Bus Destinations from Krabi' table on the following page for other destinations.

It's also possible to buy bus/boat combination tickets to Ko Samui (300B to 370B, 7½ hours, four daily) and Ko Pha-Ngan (450B, 8½ hours, four daily) from travel agencies in town. Note that new bus/boat services are constantly being introduced, however.

Săwngthăew Services to Ban Hua Hin (the ferry pier for Ko Lanta) leave from the intersection of Th Phattana and Th Preuksa Uthit. They run fairly frequently and cost 40B per person, taking 40 minutes.

Minivans These are booked through travel agencies in town. Prices can vary widely; shop around to get an idea of prices. Some sample (low-end) fares are: Ao Leuk (30B), Hat Yai (180B to 200B), Ko Lanta (150B), Trang (200B) and Surat Thani (120B).

Boat Krabi now has a new ferry terminal, located about 3km southwest of town, but as of publication it hadn't yet replaced Saphan Jao Fah (the pier in town). The following boat times and prices were based on current figures at the time of writing (when the terminal wasn't operating yet), so should be taken as a general guideline only.

The ferry to Ko Lanta (and Ko Jam) operates from October to April only (200B, two hours). There are two daily, at 10.30am and 1.30pm. The ferry to Ko Phi-Phi operates year-round (200B, 1½ hours). There are two daily, at 10am and 2.30pm.

See also Bus, earlier, for bus/boat combination tickets.

Getting Around

To/From the Airport The Krabi airport is 17km northeast of town. Minivans into town cost 80B, and taxis cost 400B if

Bus Destinations from Krabi

destination	fare (B)	duration (hrs)
Hat Yai		
ordinary	96	5
2nd-class	130	4
1st-class	173	4
Nakhon Si Thammarat		
ordinary	67	1½
Phuket		
ordinary	65	4
2nd-class	91	3
1st-class	117	3
Phang-Nga		
ordinary	46	2
2nd-class	64	2
1st-class	82	2
Ranong		
ordinary	106	5
Sungai Kolok		
1st-class	335	9
Surat Thani		
ordinary	61	3
2nd-class	126	2
Trang		
ordinary	50	2½
2nd-class	70	2
1st-class	90	2

boarded within the airport and 300B if you walk out of the airport (due to a taxi regulation). Getting *to* the airport, any travel agency sells tickets for minivans (80B). Alternatively, túk-túk/taxis cost 200/300B.

Bus Local red buses to the government bus terminal in Talat Kao cost 10B; board them in front of the 7-Eleven on Th Maharat. Local white buses to Ao Nang and Hat Noppharat Thara cost 20B and leave from Th Maharat.

Car Several travel agencies and guesthouses can arrange motorcycle rentals for 150B a day, with discounts in the low season. Jeep rentals range from 800B (open-top) to 1200B (air-con) per day. Café Europa arranges túk-túk charters to surrounding areas, with no commission.

Săwngthăew & Túk-Túk Săwngthăew to the government bus terminal cost 8B, while a motorcycle taxi costs 30B.

Túk-túk cruise around town like sharks. Destinations include the bus station (50B), Wat Tham Seua (100B) and the airport (200B); don't get charged per person.

Săwngthăew are probably the best option for getting around the Krabi area. Most leave from in front of the 7-Eleven on Th Maharat. Destinations include Ao Leuk (20B), Ao Nam Mao (40B), Ao Nang (20B, after 6pm 50B), Hat Noppharat Thara (20B) and Su-San Hoi (40B).

Boat Long-tail boats to East Hat Rai Leh run year-round for 70B and take 45 minutes; they leave when full, from Saphan Jao Fah pier. In low season, if the weather is bad these boats won't run – so instead you'll have to first take a săwngthăew to Ao Nam Mao (20B) and a long-tail boat from there. Long-tail boats from Ao Nam Mao to East Hat Rai Leh cost 30B during the day (50B at night) and run year-round in good or bad weather.

During low season, if you find that you're waiting too long at Saphan Jao Fah for a long-tail boat to fill (or if you don't like lengthy boat rides), you might consider taking a săwngthăew to Ao Nang (20B, 40 minutes) and a long-tail boat from there to West Hat Rai Leh (40B, 10 minutes). Of course, if the weather is bad enough, long-tail boats don't run from Ao Nang either.

From East Hat Rai Leh you can easily walk to Hat Tham Phra Nang or West Hat Rai Leh (and to Hat Ton Sai during low tide).

AROUND KRABI

Su-San Hoi

สุสานหอย

Nineteen kilometres west of Krabi, on Laem Pho, is the so-called Su-San Hoi (Shell Cemetery; pronounced sù-săan hăwy), a shell 'graveyard' where 75-million-year-old shell fossils have formed giant slabs jutting into the sea. This area is actually considered a national park, which means that you can officially be charged 200B entry as an adult foreigner. However, seeing these slabs – old as they are – is simply not worth 200B unless you are studying them for some future scholastic degree. Some foreigners have been charged just 20B, and in low season you may not be charged at all.

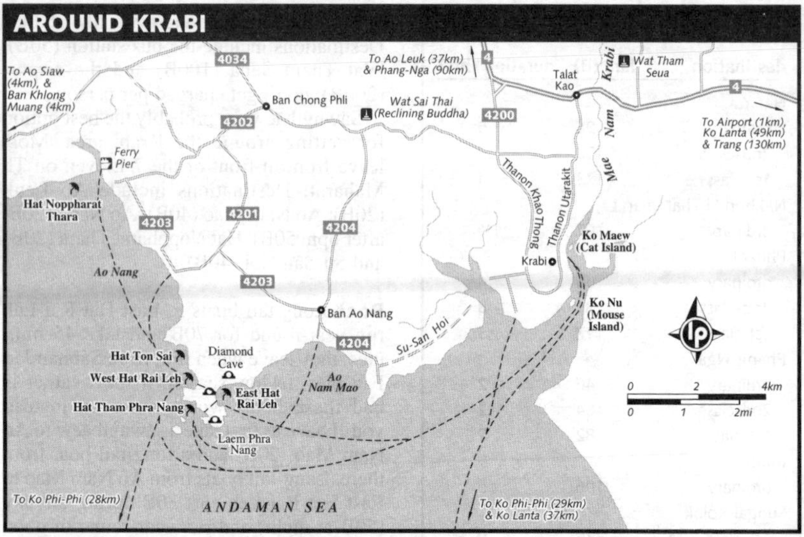

To get here, take a sǎwngthǎew from the 7-Eleven on Th Maharat (which also runs by the waterfront) for 40B – the trip takes 40 minutes.

Wat Tham Seua

วัดถ้ำเสือ

About 8km northeast of town, Wat Tham Seua (Tiger Cave Temple), is one of southern Thailand's most famous forest wát. The main *wíhǎan* (hall) is built into a long, shallow limestone cave, on either side of which dozens of *kùtì* (monastic cells) are built into various cliffs and caves. A troop of monkeys roam the grounds.

Wat Tham Seua's abbot is Ajahn Jamnien Silasettho, a Thai monk who has allowed a rather obvious personality cult to develop around him. In the large, main cave are large portraits of Ajahn Jamnien, who is well known as a teacher of *vipassana* (insight meditation) and *metta* (loving-kindness). It is said that he was apprenticed at an early age to a blind lay priest and astrologer who practised folk medicine and that he has been celibate his entire life. On the inside of his outer robe, and on an inner vest, hang scores of talismans presented to him by his followers – altogether they must weigh several kilograms, a weight Ajahn Jamnien bears to take on his followers' karma. Many young women come to Wat Tham Seua to practise as eight-precept nuns.

In the back of the main cave a set of marble stairs behind the altar leads up to a smaller cavern known as the Tiger Cave. At the back a Buddha footprint symbol sits on a gilded platform, locked behind a gate. Near one of the main cave entrances a life-size wax figure of Ajahn Jamnien sits in a glass case.

The best part of the temple grounds can be found in a little valley behind the ridge where the *bòt* is located. Walk beyond the main temple building keeping the cliff on your left, and you'll come to a pair of steep stairways. The first leads to a truly arduous climb of over 1200 steps – some of them extremely steep – to the top of a 600m karst peak. The fit and fearless will be rewarded with a Buddha statue, a gilded stupa and great views of the surrounding area; on a clear day you can see well out to sea.

The second stairway, next to a large statue of Kuan Yin (the Mahayana Buddhist Goddess of Mercy), leads over a gap in the ridge and into a valley of tall trees and limestone caves, 10 of which are named. Enter the caves on your left and look for light switches on the walls – the network of caves is wired so that you can light your way chamber by chamber through the labyrinth until you rejoin the path on the other side.

There are several *kùtì* in and around the caves. It's interesting to see the differences in interior decorating – some very spartan; others are outfitted like oriental bachelor pads.

A path winds through a grove of 1000-year-old dipterocarps surrounded by tall limestone cliffs covered with a patchwork of foliage; signs give the Latin names of several trees. If you continue to follow the path you'll eventually reach the stairway leading into the valley. If you go to the temple, please dress modestly: pants down to the ankles, shirts covering the shoulders and nothing too tight. Travellers in beachwear at Thai temples don't realise how offensive they are and how embarrassed they should be.

Getting There & Away To get to Wat Tham Seua, take a sǎwngthǎew from Krabi's Th Utarakit to the Talat Kao junction for 10B, then change to any bus or sǎwngthǎew going east on Hwy 4 towards Trang. Get off at the road on the left just past the small police station – tell the bus driver 'Wat Tham Seua'. Motorcycle taxis hang out here and charge 10B to the wát, or you can walk 2km straight up the road. In the morning a few sǎwngthǎew from Th Phattana in town pass the turnoff for Wat Tham Seua (12B) on their way to Ban Hua Hin. Also in the morning there is usually a sǎwngthǎew or two going direct to Wat Tham Seua from Talat Kao for around 20B. Private taxis to the wát cost 150B one way; túk-túk charge about 100B.

Wat Sai Thai
วัดสายไทย

A 15m reclining Buddha can be seen in a long rock shelter under a tall limestone cliff on the way to Ao Nang, about 7km from Krabi alongside Rte 4034. This is a wát in name only as there aren't enough monks in residence for official wát status (a few monks look after the place). You can see an old bell-less bell tower, some *thâat kràdùuk* (reliquary stupas) and the foundation for a former cremation hall remaining from when it was an active monastery.

AO NANG
อ่าวนาง

The coastal town of Ao Nang has become a full-blown resort destination of its own, a fast-developing strand of long, pleasant beach easily reached by road from Krabi. It's not a very large place though, and most services and hotels are crammed along either the main beach road or on short side streets. Basically, Hwy 4203 heads west into town, runs north along the beach about half a kilometre and then heads back inland for a bit before curving towards the coast again at Hat Noppharat Thara. For beach bums, Ao Nang is a much better choice of stay than Krabi, while having the easy access to highway roads that the Laem Phra Nang area (just to the south) doesn't have.

There are a couple of currency exchange booths in town, but for more extravagant services, you'll have to head to Krabi.

Activities
There are plenty of travel agencies in town that can book you on tours to surrounding attractions. You can explore mangroves, watch birds, take boat rides to idyllic islands and trek in the jungles. Two good agencies are **AP Resort** *(☎ 0 7563 7342; ⓦ www.aonang.com/aptravel)* and **Starlight** *(☎ 0 7563 7310; ⓔ poy_pont@yahoo.com)*.

Diving Many dive shops in town arrange day dives to nearby islands (such as Ko Poda Nai and Ko Poda Nok). At Ko Mae Urai, a kilometre west of Poda Nok, two submarine tunnels lined with soft and hard corals offer lots of tropical fish and are suitable for all levels of divers. Longer, live-aboard trips include Ko Bida Nok/Ko Bida Nai, the Maya Wall, Hin Daeng and Hin Muang. Going rates are 1600B to 3100B for day trips (including two dives) to nearby islands. Four-day open-water diving certification courses cost 10,500B.

Some good dive shops in town are **Blue Shark Divers** *(☎/fax 0 7563 7214; ⓔ bluesharkdivers@hotmail.com)*, **Kon-Tiki** *(☎ 0 7563 7675)* and **Coral Diving** *(☎ 0 7563 7662; ⓦ www.coral-diving.com)*.

Paddling Tours of the coast, islands and semisubmerged caves by inflatable canoe or kayak can be arranged through **Sea, Land & Trek** *(☎ 0 7563 7364; ⓔ seascaves@hotmail.com)* and **Sea Canoe Thailand** *(☎ 0 7569 5387; ⓦ www.seacanoe.net)*.

One of the best local paddles is the Tha Lin canyon river cruise, an estuary trip that

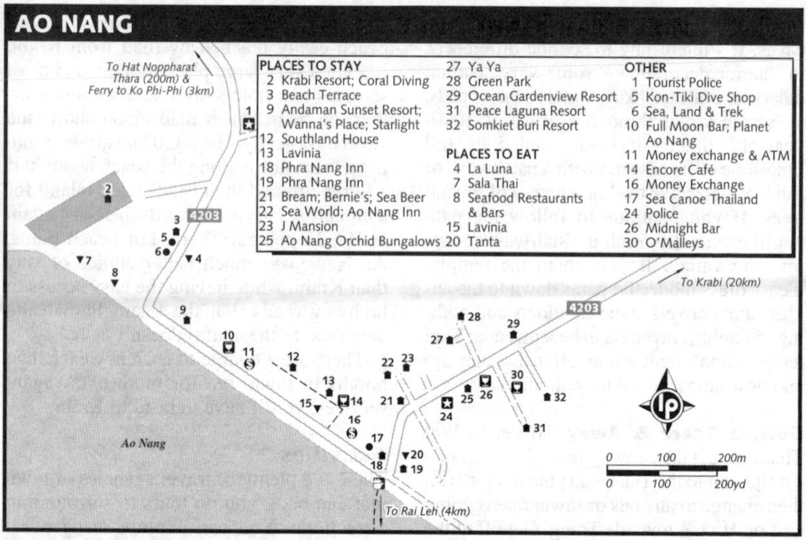

cuts through 200m-high foliaged limestone cliffs, mangrove channels and tidal lagoon tunnels. Birdwatching is great here. Birds frequently sighted include brown-winged kingfishers, Pacific reef egrets, Asian dowitchers and white-bellied sea eagles, while the most commonly seen mammals and reptiles are otters, macaques, gibbons and two-banded monitor lizards. Mudskippers and fiddler crabs abound.

Sea, Land & Trek does cavern explorations for 1500B (1200B in low season) and also has tours to Hong Island and Tha Lin Canyon. Sea Canoe Thailand charges 1700B to Tha Lin Canyon (1300B in low season) and also does cave trips.

Places to Stay

Except for the bungalows at Krabi Resort, you'll have to walk a bit to reach the hot sands. Also, note that low season is approximately May to October, while high season is November to April; not every place defines low or high season by the same dates. Some places tack on peak surcharges during the December to January holiday period.

Places to Stay – Budget & Mid-Range

There's a cluster of guesthouses inland about a block from the southern end of the beach. These have small, very basic and sometimes windowless fan rooms (some with shared bath) that cost 100B to 150B in the low season, 300B to 600B in the high season. Guesthouses here include **Bream**, **Bernie's** and **Sea Beer** and – unsurprisingly – they're popular with budget travellers.

Green Park (☎ *0 7563 7300; bungalows in low season 100-200B, in high season 300-600B)* is a bit farther inland on a side street and has small and shaky bamboo bungalows; the concrete ones are larger and newer. All surround a (scraggly) garden on a small hill, and it's quiet and friendly.

Ya Ya (☎ *0 7563 7176, 0 7563 7814;* W *www.yayaproperty.com; rooms & bungalows with fan in low/high season 150/650B)*, next to Green Park, offers good budget rooms and bungalows built of natural materials like bamboo. They come with private bath and are all surrounded by a jungle setting. Don't confuse these with Ya-Ya Bungalows on East Hat Rai Leh.

Ao Nang Orchid Bungalows (☎ *0 7563 7116, fax 0 7563 7116; bungalows with fan/air-con in low season 300/700B, in high season 800/1800B)* offers pleasant, comfortable, good-sized and newish bungalows surrounding a flowery garden. It's not a bad deal for the price.

Lavinia (☎ *0 7569 5405; rooms with fan in low season 200B, with air-con 500-700B,* *with fan in high season 600B, with air-con 1250-1800B)* has more of a homey and intimate feel than most other places in town. Six rooms come with a variety of amenities, and are nice, modern and central. Lavinia is located in an identical row of houses, behind the shopfronts across from the beach.

Southland House *(☎ 0 7563 7316; rooms with fan in low season 250-300B, with air-con 400-600B, with fan in high season 500-600B, with air-con 800-1200B)*, in the same row as Lavinia, has modern, comfortable and large rooms – the best one is huge and comes with sea views.

Sea World *(☎ 0 7563 7388; ⓔ seaworld_aonang@hotmail.com; rooms with fan in low season 300-350B, with air-con 500-700B, with fan in high season 500-700B, with air-con 800-1000B)* is similar to J Mansion but not quite as nice (and so a bit cheaper).

J Mansion *(☎ 0 7569 5128, fax 0 7569 5128; ⓔ j_mansion10@hotmail.com; rooms with fan/air-con in low season 400/600B, in high season 800/1000B)* is run by a friendly Thai family, offering great new modern rooms that are large and very clean. All have hot water, TV and fridge.

Peace Laguna Resort *(☎ 0 7563 7345, fax 0 7563 7347; ⓦ www.peacelagunaresort.com; rooms & bungalows with fan in low season 400B, with air-con 850-950B, with fan in high season 1000B, with air-con 1700-2200B)* looks like Eden for many visitors. Sweet, modern bungalows sit around a large lagoon on gorgeous, well-maintained grounds while a limestone cliff basks in the background. There's a nice pool next to the fish-filled lagoon, and a buffet breakfast (included in the price) is served nearby.

Places to Stay – Top-End

Ao Nang Inn *(☎ 0 7563 7607; ⓔ dutchkev@loxinfo.com; rooms & suites with air-con June-Sept 500-1200B, May & Oct 800-2500B, Feb-Apr & Nov 1200-3000B, Dec & Jan 1500-3500B)* has only four rooms and suites, but they're modern and beautiful. Two have kitchenettes; one has a loft and two bedrooms. All are large and tiled.

Andaman Sunset Resort *(Wanna's Place; ☎ 0 7563 7484; ⓦ www.wannasplace.com; rooms with fan in low season 500B, with air-con 700-800B, with fan in high season 1000B, with air-con 1700-2200B)* offers very pleasant rooms with a variety of amenities; some have sea views. Upscale bungalows are also available, and there's a small pool. The restaurant in front is reputedly pretty good.

Beach Terrace *(☎ 0 7563 7180, fax 0 7563 7184; rooms with air-con in low/high season 600/1800B)* is a modern apartment-style hotel where rooms have TV, fridge, small balcony and good baths. It's a better low season deal.

Somkiet Buri Resort *(☎ 0 7563 7320, fax 0 7563 7320; ⓔ info@somkietburi.com; rooms with air-con in low season 1200-1800B, in high season 2000-3000B)* could be the most paradise-like place in town. The lush jungle grounds are filled with ferns and orchids while lagoons, streams and meandering wooden walkways guide you to the 26 large and creatively-designed rooms. A great swimming pool sits amid it all – balconies either face this pool or a peaceful pond. The restaurant is good and sits under an open pavilion; the service everywhere is first-rate.

Krabi Resort *(☎ 0 7563 7030, fax 0 7563 7051; in Bangkok ☎ 0 2208 9165, fax 0 2208 9166; rooms & bungalows with air-con in low season 1200-2500B, in high season 3120-5470B)* was the original resort in the area, and offers very nice modern accommodation on landscaped grounds. The hotel rooms are in a two-storey building and sport pool views, while luxury bungalows sit in a leafy area right near the beach. Overall the place is very comfortable, and you should expect all the amenities.

Ocean Garden View Resort *(☎ 0 7563 7527, fax 0 7563 7211; ⓦ www.oceangardenview.com; rooms with air-con in low season 1300-1500B, in high season 2500-2800B)* is another good upscale choice, with comfortable, well-furnished and tasteful rooms (though the buildings are looking a bit piqued). Bungalows in the back garden are also great and have all the amenities, and the grounds are pretty lush. Breakfast is included.

Phra Nang Inn *(☎ 0 7563 7130, fax 0 7563 7134; ⓔ phranang@sun.phuket.ksc.co.th; rooms with air-con in low season 1500-2700B, in high season 3400-3900B)* has a unique bamboo theme to its decor. Eclectic designs in shell and tilework make this place look better inside than out. Rooms are clean and beautifully done (some have partial sea views) and there's a small pool. Breakfast is included.

A second, similarly designed branch is across the road from the original.

Places to Eat

Somkiat Buri Restaurant (*☎ 0 7563 7574; dishes 60-220B; open 7am-10pm daily*) cooks up great Thai food and has very attentive service, but the best reason to come here is the lush, open-sided pavilion you sit inside. Breakfast is also served for 60B to 120B.

Lavinia (*☎ 0 7569 5404; dishes 150-400B; open 5pm-11pm daily*) is one of the many Italian restaurants in Ao Nang. It's a popular place with modern furnishings.

Rialto (*dishes 150-320B*) is an Italian place next to Lavinia. Italian specialties along with Chinese and Thai food are served on long wooden benches best for large groups. The fruit shakes here are overpriced, but the pizza is OK.

Tanta (*☎ 0 7563 7118; dishes 60-250B; open 7.30am-10pm daily*) offers great Thai and international selections. It's a popular modern place, with a raised covered terrace and wood accents. Wine is also served.

Wanna's Restaurant (*dishes 45-110B; open 7am-10pm daily*) is popular for its variety of food: Burgers, cheese selections and Swiss specialities are on the menu along with Thai food and breakfast. Wanna's is a casual and inexpensive place.

La Luna (*dishes 130-220B; open 11am-11pm daily*) is another established Italian place serving pizza and panini, along with Greek salad and wine (95B per glass).

Sala Thai (*dishes 60-300B; open 10am-10pm daily*) is the last in a series of seafood restaurants on decks over the beach. Due to its reputation as the best one, it's the most popular. Crab, lobster, prawns and fish are on display for your selection. This restaurant – along with its neighbours – has wonderfully romantic atmosphere, with open wooden deck, sea breezes and great views.

Entertainment

Have a drink; there's no shortage of bars in Ao Nang.

O'Malley's (*beers 50-80B; open 6pm-2am daily*) pours cocktails for half price during its extended happy hour from 7pm to 11pm. It's on a calm side street and has great casual atmosphere, with wooden furniture and a free pool table. Guinness is available, but it's not cheap.

Midnight Bar (*☎ 0 7563 7210; open 5pm-late daily*) is run by a feisty German and sits above the street on its own laid-back, airy patio. It's the hang-out spot for certain local expats. The music tends towards hard rock, though it can vary depending on clientele moods.

Full Moon Bar (*☎ 0 7563 7548; beers 40-70B; open 3pm-2am daily*) serves cocktails with strange names in a very central, popular and generally good bar atmosphere.

Planet Ao Nang (*☎ 0 7563 7265; open 5pm-2am daily*) is near Full Moon Bar and is also a popular, happenin' spot to be caught drinking. The music, at time of writing, was good.

Encore Café (*pub food 50-80B; open 4pm-2am daily in high season*) has a modern air-con space, with pool table and live music on Friday at 10pm. Each night there's a different theme, such as ladies' night, speed pool, karaoke and sports viewing.

Getting There & Around

A ferry service to Ko Phi-Phi runs daily year-round at 9am (250B, two hours) and includes a ride to/from the pier in nearby Hat Noppharat Thara. In low season boats go via East Hat Rai Leh to pick up passengers; in high season they go via West Hat Rai Leh.

Long-tail boats to the Hat Rai Leh area run daily and cost 50B. These don't run in bad weather, so in this case take a săwngthăew to Ao Nam Mao (10B) and from there a long-tail boat (30B during the day, 50B at night). Long-tail boats from Ao Nam Mao run even in choppy weather. Long-tail boats from Ao Nang to Krabi run only in high season for 50B.

Săwngthăew are a good way to get around. Destinations include Krabi (20B during the day, 50B after 6pm), Hat Noppharat Thara (10B) and Ao Nam Mao (10B).

Taxis from Ao Nang *to* the airport cost 300B, but *from* the airport can cost up to 500B.

HAT NOPPHARAT THARA

หาดนพรัตน์ธารา

Starting just 200m north of Ao Nang and running a further 2km north is the shallow, scenic and relatively unspoilt beach of Hat Noppharat Thara (though it looks primed for development). Toward its northern end, right at the mouth of Khlong Haeng (a small canal) are some tall and very cool karst formations. During low tide it's possible to ford this canal, though it could be a muddy proposition.

Hat Noppharat Thara is part of the Hat Noppharat Thara/Ko Phi-Phi National Marine Park and a favourite spot for Thai picnickers. Along with a few scattered bungalow operations here are two government bungalows for rent, as well as a small park **visitors centre**, near the canal and ferry pier for boats to Ko Phi-Phi.

Beyond this canal and ferry pier is a more secluded section of Hat Noppharat Thara, a pleasant and shell-strewn strand that stretches a fair distance to the west. A bit farther from here some five-star hotels have been built. However, an isolated and almost island-like feel is still prevalent in this section of beach, with only a handful of bungalow operations having set up here. There *is* dirt road access from the north, but it can be rough riding.

Places to Stay & Eat The following places are listed from south to north. Those on the first section Hat Noppharat Thara are set back from the beach; all have their own restaurant, though a few other independent eateries are located here and there. There's an especially lively cluster of simple restaurants near the visitors centre area. Beyond the canal and ferry pier you'll have to rely on the local bungalows' restaurants unless you want to cross back over the canal.

The following places are on the first section of Hat Noppharat Thara.

Sabai Resort *(☎ 0 7563 7791; rooms with fan/air-con May-Oct 750/1200B, Nov-Apr 1100/1600B)* is a nice, new place away from the beach a bit, on a side street. On hand are some modern, clean bungalows, pleasant grounds, a decent pool and a restaurant.

Near Sabai Resort are a few cheaper places like **Cashew Nut** *(☎ 0 7563 7560; rooms with fan in low season 200-300B, in high season 400-600B)*, **Laughing Gecko** and **Family Bungalows** (the latter is farther down the street).

At the visitors centre, two **government bungalows** *(☎ 0 7563 7200)* are available for 400B (three people) and 1200B (nine people). They're quite OK, although on weekend the beach and visitors centre is thronged with local visitors. You can also rent **tents** for 200B (two people) to 300B (three people).

The following bungalows are past the canal and are ideal for travellers seeking some solitude.

Andaman Inn *(☎ 0 1893 2964; bungalows with fan in low season 200-300B, in high season 300-500B)* is first in line, a short walk along the beach. It offers 35 basic bungalows squared around a grassy area. Movies play at night in the restaurant; and electricity is available from 6pm to 6am. If you stay here, call ahead for a free boat ride.

Emerald *(☎ 0 1892 1072, fax 0 7563 1119; W www.come.to/emerald_krabi; bungalows with fan in low season 600B, with air-con 900-1200B, in high season 900-1800B)* is a much nicer place, with beautifully decorated and comfortable bungalows around a nice garden. Most have large, triangular verandas and there's a pleasant restaurant. It's only open October to June; call ahead for a free boat ride here.

Farther along the beach are the cheapies **Bamboo Bungalows**, **Sara Cove** and **Pine Bungalow**, with very basic accommodation from about 150B to 250B.

Getting There & Around A ferry runs to Ko Phi-Phi (250B, 1½ hours, daily at 9am) year-round and leaves from the ferry pier in Hat Noppharat Thara. Occasionally boats travel via West Hat Rai Leh to pick up passengers; in this case the trip takes two hours in total.

Hat Noppharat Thara can be reached by săwngthăew from Krabi (20B, 30 minutes). To reach nearby Ao Nang, săwngthăew charge 10B.

A long-tail boat plies across the canal to an isolated section of Hat Noppharat Thara for 10B per person; this same long-tail boat will take you farther down the beach to your bungalow for 20B to 30B. You can actually slog across the canal at low tide if you have no luggage, but it can get muddy.

LAEM PHRA NANG

แหลมพระนาง

South of Ao Nang a few kilometres is the jagged peninsula of Laem Phra Nang, which encompasses a series of spectacular clear bays with lush limestone cliffs that drop right into the blue sea. The beautiful beaches in this area include **Hat Ton Sai**, **West Hat Rai Leh**, **Hat Tham Phra Nang** and **East Hat Rai Leh**. All are separated by headlands and only accessible by boat from the Ao Nang or Krabi areas. You can easily walk from one bay and beach to another in just 10 minutes or so, except for Hat Ton Sai at high tide. It's a great idea to bring torches, since paths aren't lit up at night.

At the southern beach end of Hat Tham Phra Nang, under the tall limestone cliff, is **Tham Phra Nang Nok** – a cave with a story. Local legend claims that during the 3rd century BC a passing royal barque carrying a charismatic Indian princess named Sri Guladevi (Si Kunlathewi in Thai) foundered in a storm. The princess' spirit came to inhabit a large cave near the wreck, using power gained through many past lives to grant favours to all who came to pay respect. Local fisherfolk place carved wooden phalli in the cave as offerings to the Phra Nang (Holy Princess) so that she will provide plenty of fish for them.

Rock-Climbing

Limestone cliffs on the huge headland between Tham Phra Nang and East Rai Leh, and on nearby islands, offer world-class rock-climbing – with simply stunning views. Most surfaces provide high-quality limestone with steep, pocketed walls, overhangs, and the occasional hanging stalactite. About 700 sport routes have been bolted, many with mid- to high-difficulty ratings (the French rating system is used). Novices often begin with Muay Thai, a 50m wall with around 20 climbs at the southern end of East Hat Rai Leh. Certain areas are off-limits because they're part of Hat Noppharat Thara/Ko Phi-Phi National Marine Park, including the cliff next to the Rayavadee Premier resort and cliffs outside Tham Phra Nang Nai.

A half-day climb with guide, equipment and insurance costs about 800B, while an all-day climb costs 1500B and three days costs 5000B. You can also rent sport-climbing equipment for two people, which includes harnesses, shoes, a rope, 12 quickdraws, chalk and a guidebook for a half/full day (600/1000B).

It's not hard finding a climbing outfit; there are at least six in the area. A couple of the more established operators are **King Climbers** (*☎ 0 7563 7125, fax 0 7563 7849; e kingclimbers@iname.com*) and **Tex Rock Climbing** (*☎ 0 7563 1509; e texrock@loxinfo.co.th*). Most of these outfits shut down during the rainy season. For information on climbing in this area a good website is w www.simonfoley.com/climbing.

Diving & Snorkelling

Diving is possible in this area, though you'd have more choice of dive shops in Ao Nang. **Phra Nang Divers** (*☎ 0 7563 7064; w www.pndivers.com*) is at Railay Village. It offers day trips, instruction and live-aboards.

The islands off Laem Phra Nang are good areas for **snorkelling**. Besides Ko Poda and Ko Hua Khwan there is the nearer island of Ko Rang Nok (Bird Nest Island). Next to that is a larger, unnamed island (possibly part of the same island at low tide) with an undersea cave. Some of the bungalows do reasonably priced day trips to these as well as other islands in the area. Phra Nang Divers offers snorkelling trips for 500B to 900B for a half-day.

Hiking

On the cool little path from East Hat Rai Leh to Hat Tham Phra Nang is the trailhead to **Sa Phra Nang** (Holy Princess Pool), a hidden lagoon inside the cliff. This is not a hike for the weak or vertigo-prone; it's not long, but is very strenuous and at times dangerous. The trail starts ominously, with a slippery climb up a steep, lush hill covered in tree roots. Mouldy ropes guide you along the leafy mountain trails, with some 'free' (unprotected) rock-climbing down 15ft walls necessary at times. Windows along side trails reward you with astounding views of the West and East Hat Rai Leh double bays. The trailhead starts at the covered rest bench area.

Caves

On East Hat Rai Leh is **Diamond Cave** (*admission 20B*), consisting of three caverns. All three contain some of the most beautiful limestone formations in the country, including a golden 'stone waterfall' of sparkling quartz. Local mythology says that this cave is the grand palace of the sea princess, while Tham Phra Nang on the beach is her summer palace. To get here, just follow the signs.

Places to Stay & Eat

All the places listed here have their own restaurant, often located beachside. Low season runs approximately May to October, while high season is November to April (exact dates for each bungalow operator may vary, however). Many places increase their prices from late December to early January. Some even foist 'compulsory' (and expensive) dinners on guests for Christmas and New Year's Eve.

Hat Ton Sai Hat Ton Sai is the only beach in the area not easily accessible when the tide is high; during these times you'll either have to take a boat or do some rope-assisted rock scrambling. At low tide you can easily walk around the point to West Hat Rai Leh. Don't confuse this place with Hat Ton Sai on Ko Phi-Phi.

This beach has become the main rock-climbers' hang-out, mostly due to its isolation from the more upscale spots in the area but also because it has the cheapest digs around. Full-moon parties take place here (though not on Ko Pha-Ngan's scale, where the original full-moon parties started). Some places only have electricity at night.

Ton Sai Bungalows *(☎ 0 7562 2584; bungalows with fan in low season 50-250B, in high season 300-800B)* has 50 bungalows made of bamboo or concrete. They're well-spaced in a jungle setting, with the most expensive set closest to the beach. Kayaks are available for rent, and there's a bar and climbing school nearby.

Viking Village *(☎ 0 1970 4037; bungalows with fan in low season 500-100B, in high season 200-600B)* has simple bamboo and thatch- or tin-roofed bungalows with mosquito net; the cheapest have clean shared bath. The grounds aren't so tidy, though.

Green Valley Resort *(☎ 0 7562 1665; W www.krabidir.com/grvalleyresort; bungalows with fan in low/high season 400/600B)* has some cute white bungalows all lined up around leafy trees and a sparse garden. Inside they're fairly pleasant, with simple decor and tile floors.

Krabi Mountain View Resort *(☎ 0 7562 2610, fax 0 7562 2613; W www.krabimountainview.com; rooms with fan in low season 600-700B, with air-con 800-900B, with fan in high season 700-800B, with air-con 1200-1400B)* offers rows of tidy white bungalows set amid a shady forest. There's a big bar and restaurant area with satellite TV, plus a climbing shop.

Andaman Nature Resort *(☎/fax 0 7562 2585; bungalows with fan in low season 100-150B, in high season 550-800B)* is a climbers' hang-out, offering a variety of bamboo, wood or concrete bungalows. Some have newer amenities – and some are darker and older – so check a few before deciding.

West Hat Rai Leh This is where the more top-drawer places can be found in the area; the majority of rooms have air-con and modern facilities.

Railay Bay Resort *(☎ 0 7562 2571, fax 0 7562 2573; bungalows with air-con in low season 1200-1600B, in high season 2250-2400B)* commands a large lot, with renovated bungalows stretching to both bays. It's similar but not quite as nice as Sand Sea, though most are still comfortably modern. Breakfast and a splashy pool are included.

Sand Sea *(☎ 0 7562 2170, fax 0 7562 2608; W www.krabisandsea.com; bungalows with fan in low season 750B, with air-con 1600-1800B, with fan in high season 1450-1950B, with air-con 2850-3450B)* is beautifully located, with comfortable bungalows lining both sides of a flowery tropical garden. Brick paths meander to the beach, where a seaside restaurant awaits. Breakfast is included.

Railay Village Resort *(☎ 0 7562 2578, fax 0 7562 2579; e railayvillage@hotmail.com; bungalows with fan in low season 500B, with air-con 1200-1500B, with fan in high season 800B, with air-con 1800-2500B)*, next to Sand Sea, is a better deal, that is, if you like a rustic feel to your holiday. Good bungalows border a verdant, shrubby garden all the way seawards.

Railei Beach Club *(☎/fax 0 7562 2582, fax 0 7562 2596; e rbclub@phuket.ksc.co.th; homes 3,000-10,000B)* is a collection of private homes in an exclusive area. It's best to book these beautiful abodes at least two months in advance; there's a minimum stay of three nights. Electricity is available only from 6pm to 6am nightly.

BoBo Bar & Restaurant *(open 7am-10pm daily)*, next to Railay Village, is probably the only independent restaurant on the peninsula. Friendly, laid-back service in a casual dining area could be worth a try – nothing fancy should be expected here. Nearby is a coffee stand that is open 7am to noon.

Hat Tham Phra Nang The truly beautiful, five-star **Rayavadee** (*☎ 0 7562 0740, fax 0 7562 0630; w www.luxurycollection.com; rooms in low season 16,600-79,300B, in high season 30,092-145,994B*) monopolises 26 acres of this stunning beach area. Seven types of luxury bungalows dot the nicely landscaped grounds, each with 'basic' amenities like air-con, cable TV and refrigerator. All are two storey and are fabulously decorated in a traditional Thai style. Champagne breakfast, afternoon tea and dinner are included, as are water sports and airport transfers. Service charges and tax are not. There's a large pool and great security – guards won't let you enter the area to 'just have a look around'.

The Rayavadee is the only accommodation near Phra Nang beach, but the beach itself is public property. To get here, follow the trail from the south end of East Hat Rai Leh. From West Hat Rai Leh a footpath leads through the forest around to the beach. Take torches if you plan on watching the sunset; it gets dark very quickly next to the cliffs.

East Hat Rai Leh The northern part of this beach has mangroves and isn't the greatest; at high tide it disappears, and at low tide it turns into mudflats. This is where some of the more affordable accommodation in the area is located – though some bungalows have been upscaling.

Ya-Ya Bungalows (*☎ 0 7562 2593; rooms with fan in low season 200-600B, with air-con 900B, with fan in high season 550-1050B, with air-con 1500B*) is a renovated oldie that remains popular. Pleasant rooms made mostly of natural materials come in cute three-storey buildings with steep staircases and small wooden patios. They line a lush garden (mosquito repellent is crucial). Air-con rooms have fridge and TV.

Parkview Bungalow (*☎ 0 9908 4479; bungalows with fan in low season 100B, in high season 300-400B*) is set way inland past Diamond Cave (the actual cave, not the bungalows). It's a 10-minute walk around a perimeter wall from the beach to these very basic cheapies. There's little atmosphere in the rows of bungalows, but they're a definite consideration if you have a thin wallet.

Railay Hill Bungalow (*☎ 0 7562 1726; e railayhill@yahoo.com; camping in low/high season 50/100B, bungalows with fan in low season 200B, in high season 400-500B*) sits just past Parkview Bungalow. It's a much better place, with clean, large thatched A-frame bungalows built of logs. They're basic (just a mattress on the floor with a mosquito net) but comfortable enough, and sit among a thin forest. Wood-plank walkways connect the bungalows with the restaurant.

Diamond Cave Bungalows (*☎ 0 7562 2589; rooms with fan in low season 200-300B, with air-con 800B, with fan in high season 1300B, with air-con 2000-4000B*) is near the coastline and has a variety of modern, red-roofed and tiled-floor rooms in a pleasant setting up on a hill. Solid bungalows with a similar style are nearby.

Viewpoint Resort (*☎/fax 0 7562 1686; rooms & bungalows with fan in low season 300-400B, with air-con 600-800B, with fan in high season 600-800B, with air-con 1800-2000B*), near Diamond Cave, maintains 70 large, good and modern two-storey rooms and bungalows on a nice hillside setting. There's a pleasant pool on the premises.

Rapala (*☎ 0 7562 2586; bungalows with fan in low season 300-400B, in high season 1000-1200B*) is a good and friendly little place up a long wooden staircase at the northern end of this beach. A pleasant restaurant area greets you at reception, while out back are 28 simple but beautiful bungalows with hammocks and mosquito nets. Mattresses lie on the floor, but everything's done in a rustically elegant way, and the leafy garden paths feel intimate. There's even a tiny pool.

Coco Restaurant has a romantic atmosphere at night, when the lighting turns the shrubby garden into a mysterious jungle. It has a good reputation for its food.

Getting There & Away

It's possible to get to Ko Phi-Phi without leaving the Laem Phra Nang area. See Ao Nang's Getting There & Away section, earlier, for more information.

Getting Around

Hat Ton Sai, West and East Hat Rai Leh and Hat Tham Phra Nang are reachable only by long-tail boat. These run from three places: Krabi, Ao Nam Mao and Ao Nang.

PAUL BEINSSEN

Ko Lipe, Satun Province

DALLAS STRIBLEY

Ao Lo Dalam, Ko Phi-Phi Don, Krabi Province

KAREN TRIST

Hat Laem Thong, Ko Phi-Phi Don, Krabi Province

ANDERS BLOMQVIST

West Hat Rai Leh, Krabi Province

RICHARD NEBESKY

Hat Tham Phra Nang, Krabi Province

JOE CUMMINGS

Ko Panyi, Ao Phang Nga, Phang-Nga Province

RICH PROHASKA

Rock-climbing, Ko Phi-Phi Don, Krabi Province

From Krabi, year-round boats cost 70B and take up to an hour, depending on the beach. During the rainy season (May to September) these boats will not go past East Hat Rai Leh; this isn't a big problem because you can easily walk to the other beaches from here. If the weather is really bad, however, you should first take a săwngthăew to Ao Nam Mao (20B) and a long-tail boat from there (30B during the day, 50B at night). Also, the boat trip from Krabi to Hat Ton Sai is pretty long, so if you don't like lengthy boat trips take a săwngthăew to Ao Nang (20B) and a boat from there.

From Ao Nang, year-round boats cost 50B and take 15 to 30 minutes, depending on the beach. During the rainy season (May to September) these boats will not go past Tham Hat Phra Nang, but this isn't a serious problem (see earlier). Again, if the weather is really bad take a săwngthăew to Ao Nam Mao (10B) and a long-tail boat from there. When the weather really sucks Ao Nam Mao is the only place connecting the Laem Phra Nang area to the outside world, since it's the most sheltered bay.

THAN BOKKHARANI NATIONAL PARK

อุทยานแห่งชาติธารโบกขรณี

Than Bokkharani National Park *(admission 200B)* was established in 1991 and encompasses nine caves throughout the Ao Leuk area. It's located in northern Krabi Province.

The park is best visited just after the monsoons. At this time the park looks like something cooked up by Disney, but it's real and entirely natural. Emerald-green waters flow out of a narrow cave in a tall cliff and into a large lotus pool, which overflows into a wide stream and divides into many smaller rivulets in several stages. At each stage there's a pool and a little waterfall; the effect is magical.

Thais from Ao Leuk come to bathe here on weekends, when it's full of people playing in the streams and pools – and shampooing their hair, which seems to be a favourite activity here. During the week there are only a few people about; mostly kids fishing. Vendors sell noodles, excellent roast chicken, delicious battered squid and *sôm-tam* (green papaya salad) under a roofed area to one side.

Remember to bring insect repellent, and watch out for aggressive monkeys.

Caves

Among the protected caves scattered around the Ao Leuk district, one of the most interesting is **Tham Hua Kalok** (also called Tham Pee Hua Toe), set in a limestone hill in a seldom-visited bend of mangrove-lined Khlong Baw Thaw. Besides impressive stalactite formations, the cave features 2000- to 3000-year-old paintings of human and animal figures and geometric designs.

Nearby **Tham Lawt** (Tube Cave) is distinguished by a navigable stream flowing through it – it's longer than Phang-Nga's Tham Lawt.

There are seven other similar limestone caves in Ao Leuk district – Tham Waririn, Tham Khao Phra, Tham Khao Rang, Tham Phet, Tham Thalu Fah, Tham Sa Yuan Thong, Tham To Luang and Tham Chao Leh – most of which are difficult to find. Inquire at Than Bokkharani visitors centre for directions – you'll need your own transport to explore these caves.

Places to Stay

PN Mountain Resort (☎ *0 7568 1554; rooms with fan May-Oct 400B, with air-con 500-800B, with fan Nov-Apr 800B, with air-con 1000-1200B)* is in Ao Leuk on Hwy 4, 1km north of the park turnoff. It's a new place with modern rooms, though the pool is a bit murky. Behind the hotel is a dramatic backdrop: A lush limestone cliff wall with a hole in the middle.

Getting There & Away

Than Bok, as the locals call it, is near the town of Ao Leuk. The park entrance is on Rte 4039, 1.3km southwest of Hwy 4. Săwngthăew from Krabi cost 20B, but without your own transport it'll be hard to get around.

The best way to visit Tham Lawt and Tham Hua Kalok is to take kayak tours from the pier of Tha Baw Thaw. To get there from the visitors centre, drive southwest on Rte 4039 about 4km and turn right at the Tham Pee Hua Toe sign (there are various other signs here, too). Travel 1.8km and turn left at the cola sign; after 500m you'll come to the pier. Tours are run by **Choke Thara Travel** *(☎ 0 1272 2654)*. A two- to three-hour kayak trip costs 500B, while a four- to five-hour trip costs 1200B and includes lunch. Tours run along secluded Khlong Baw Thaw and through Tham Lawt before stopping at Tham Hua Kalok.

KHAO PHANOM BENCHA NATIONAL PARK

อุทยานแห่งชาติเขาพนมเบ็ญจา

This 50-sq-km park *(admission 200B)* is in the middle of virgin rainforest along the Phanom Bencha mountain range. The main scenic attractions are the three-level **Nam Tok Huay To, Tham Khao Pheung** and **Nam Tok Huay Sadeh**, all within 3km of the park office. You can discover other, lesser known streams and waterfalls, too. Clouded leopard, black panther, tiger, Asiatic black bear, barking deer, serow, Malayan tapir, leaf monkey, gibbons and various tropical birds – including the helmeted hornbill, argus pheasant and extremely rare Gurney's pitta – make their home here. Khao Phanom Bencha reaches 1350m in elevation, the highest point in Krabi Province. The name means Five-Point Prostration Mountain, a reference to the mountain's resemblance, in profile, to a man prostrating so that his knees, hands and head all touch the ground.

The park has a **camping ground** where you are welcome to pitch your own tent for a small fee.

Getting There & Away

Public transport direct to the park from Krabi or Talat Kao is rare. Two roads run to the park off Hwy 4. One is only about 500m from Talat Kao – you could walk to this junction and hitch, or hire a truck in Talat Kao all the way for 100B or so. The other road is about 10km north of Krabi off Hwy 4. You could get to this junction via sǎwngthǎew or a bus heading north to Ao Leuk.

It is cheaper to rent a motorcycle in Krabi for a day trip to Phanom Bencha than to charter a pick-up. Try to have someone at the park watch your bike while hiking to the falls – motorcycle theft at Phanom Bencha has been a bit of a problem in the past.

KO PHI-PHI

เกาะพีพี

Ko Phi-Phi is actually two islands about 40km from Krabi: Phi-Phi Leh and Phi-Phi Don. Both are part of Hat Noppharat Thara/Ko Phi-Phi National Marine Park, though only parts of Phi-Phi Don are actually under the administration of the Park Division of the Royal Forest Department.

After Phuket, this is the most popular tourist destination along the Andaman coast. During the high season from December to March, multitudes of travellers descend on the island and snatch up every available room and bungalow. The island still retains some of its original beauty, but to truly appreciate it you'll have to take a long hike to escape the crowds.

Ko Phi-Phi Leh

เกาะพีพีเล

Phi-Phi Leh is almost all sheer cliffs, with a few caves and a sea lake formed by a cleft between two cliffs that allows water to enter into a bowl-shaped canyon. The so-called **Viking Cave** (Tham Phaya Naak) contains prehistoric paintings of stylised human and animal figures alongside later paintings of ships (Asian junks) no more than 100 years old.

The cave is also a collection point for swiftlet nests. Swiftlets like to build their saliva nests high up in the caves between rocky hollows that are very difficult to reach. Agile collectors build vine-and-bamboo scaffolding to get at the nests but are occasionally injured or killed in falls. Before ascending the scaffolds, the collectors pray and make offerings of tobacco, incense and liquor to the cavern spirits.

Ao Maya and Lo Sama, scenic coves on the island's western and southeastern shores, are favourite stops for day-tripping snorkellers. Although once very pristine, the corals at these coves have been marred by bad anchoring and the beaches are somewhat littered with rubbish jettisoned by tour boats. In 1999 a Hollywood film company spent about two months shooting scenes for the motion picture *The Beach*, based on UK author Alex Garland's novel of the same name. See the boxed text 'Notes on *The Beach*', following, for details on the controversy that surrounded the filming here.

There are no bungalow operations on Ko Phi-Phi Leh, and it's not possible to spend the night on this island – day trips are the only way to see it.

Notes on *The Beach*

'There's no way you can keep it out of Lonely Planet, and once that happens it's countdown to doomsday.' So says one of the backpacking characters in *The Beach*, UK author Alex Garland's controversial novel set in Thailand. Published in 1997, the tale of a failed beach utopia slowly caught fire in the Gen X book market and in 1999 was transformed into a US$40 million motion picture.

The story traces a small, loosely-knit group of travellers who establish their own beach paradise on an island in Thailand's Ang Thong National Marine Park, not far from Ko Samui – though filming actually took place in Ao Maya (Maya Bay), on the Andaman Sea's Ko Phi-Phi Leh. The novel's selfish protagonist makes the mistake of passing on a map showing the beach's secret location to a pair of uninvited backpackers, whose island intrusion and subsequent confrontation with Thai dope growers brings the story to its climax.

When Twentieth Century Fox turned up in Thailand to begin filming, immediate controversy ensued; protestors were concerned that the production would turn Ao Maya into a wasteland. In reality, the production crew left the bay cleaner than it was before – after all, dynamite fishing, tour operators and plain old garbage had previously marred Maya's pristine waters and coastline. Just for the movie to start filming, the crew had to remove an estimated 3 to 4 tonnes of rubbish and even plant some new palm trees. This is hardly a surprise, given the abuse that so many of Thailand's tourist beaches often receive.

Despite the controversy, Ao Maya still remains beautiful and is one of Ko Phi-Phi's major tourist attractions. To see it you'll have to take a boat tour out from Ko Phi-Phi Don.

Ko Phi-Phi Don

เกาะพีพีดอน

Phi-Phi Don looks like two islands connected by a bridge of land only a few hundred metres long. This 'bridge' forms the beautiful double bays of **Ao Ton Sai** and **Ao Lo Dalam**, both of which have long, white-sand beaches. The mostly uninhabited western half of the island is called Ko Nok (Outer Island), and the larger eastern half is Ko Nai (Inner Island). At the north end of the Ko Nai is Laem Thong, where the island's *chao náam* population lives. The number of *chao náam* here varies from time to time, but there are generally about 100. Ko Phi-Phi's topography boasts scenic hills, awesome cliffs, long beaches, emerald waters and remarkable bird and sea life.

Beautiful Ao Ton Sai has become a noisy boat basin. Most of the island's services and bungalows are found here, in what is essentially a crowded tourist town – not unlike Hat Rin on Ko Pha-Ngan. Travellers in search of a lively social scene will find a wide choice of restaurants, beachfront bars and upmarket accommodation. Other parts of Phi-Phi Don aren't nearly this developed, although the once-brilliant coral reefs around the island are suffering from anchor drag and run-off from large beach developments. The least disturbed parts of the island so far are those still belonging to *chao náam*.

Hat Yao (Long Beach) faces south and has some of Phi-Phi Don's best coral reefs. North of Hat Yao is another beautiful beach, **Hat Ranti**, with decent surf. For several years the locals wouldn't allow any bungalows here out of respect for the large village mosque, situated in a coconut grove above the beach – but money talked, and the *chao náam* listened. Farther north of Hat Ranti is the sizeable bay **Ao Lo Bakao**, where there is a small resort, and near the tip of Laem Thong are a few more luxury resorts.

Park administrators had allowed development on Phi-Phi Don to continue fairly unchecked, although excessive building has stabilised to a significant degree over the last several years. It's actually doubtful the park ever had the power or influence to stop the construction. The rumour was that park officials wouldn't dare to even set foot on Ko Phi-Phi for fear of being attacked by village chiefs and bungalow developers profiting from tourism.

A small power plant has been built in the centre of the island, but it doesn't have sufficient capacity to supply all of the resorts – even in Ao Dalam and Ao Ton Sai. Many resorts on this part of the island are forced to use generators on certain days. Likewise, the single brackish reservoir on this island usually can't supply enough water, so some resorts have to turn their water supply off for certain hours of the day. In the past few years there have been serious water shortages due to a general lack of rain in southern Thailand; when this happens, your showers may taste a little salty. Also worth noting is that there are no cars on Ko Phi-Phi.

Orientation It's not hard to find your way around Ton Sai village, the maze of pedestrian walkways lined with travel agencies, dive shops, Internet cafés, restaurants and stores. It takes up most of the bridge of land between the two parts of Phi-Phi island. There are only two main walkways, with plenty of smaller interconnected alleys in between. You'll get to know the area after a couple hours of wandering.

Information In front of the Phi Phi Hotel is the **Siam Commercial Bank** *(open 9am-8pm daily)*, while **Krung Thai Bank** is near Reggae Bar. Many of the travel agents will also change money, although at poor rates. **Phi-Phi Health Centre** *(☎ 0 7562 2151; open 8am-midnight daily)* is in Ton Sai village.

Hiking Around the island are some hiking trails that can be explored. The one down south to Hat Yao starts after Andaman Beach Resort. This resort is private property, so it wouldn't do to start wandering around the grounds; simply go past the restaurant and up the blue-tile stairs – a dirt trail starts just to the right. There are poorly marked trails around the northern part of the island also; if you plan on exploring them

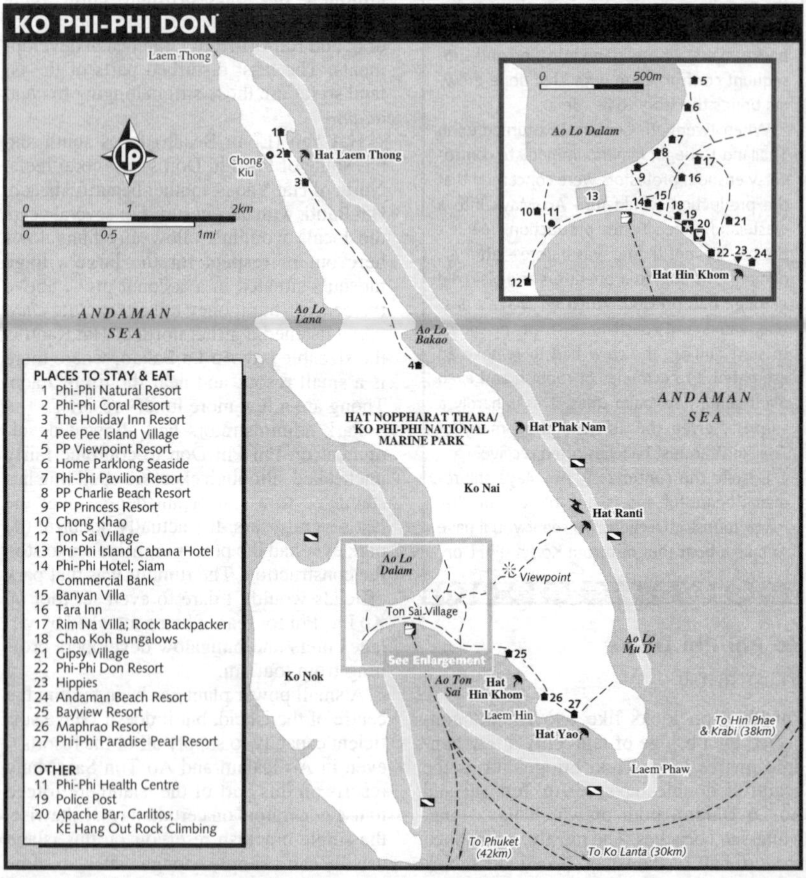

take a torch and water. At low tide you can use some beaches as walking trails.

Diving & Snorkelling The diving on Ko Phi-Phi is world-class and some think even better than Ko Tao. Over twenty dive shops compete for your business, and all can arrange diving and snorkelling trips around the island or to nearby islands. Some popular destinations within a 1½-hour boat ride include Ko Ha, Hin Daeng and Hin Muang. The ferry *King Cruiser* lies only 12m below the surface and is visited by dive operators from both Ko Phi-Phi and Phuket. Prices are fairly comparable at Phi-Phi's dive shops; guided dive trips start at 1100B for one dive and 1800B for two. An open-water certification course will set you back 9900B.

The best months for visibility are December to April, though certain other months (like June and July) see fewer divers and can be less hectic.

The typical all-day snorkelling trip includes lunch, water, fruit and equipment for 300B in a long-tail boat and 500B on a big boat. These usually stop at Ko Yung (Mosquito Island), Ko Mai Phai (Bamboo Island), Hin Pae (Goat Rock) and Ko Phi-Phi Leh.

Paddling You can rent kayaks at several places on the island for 300B per hour, 600B per half-day (700B a double) or all day for 800B (1000B a double).

Fishing All day fishing trips for marlin, sailfish, barracuda and other game fish in nearby waters are available aboard long-tail boats for 2000B per boat, including soft drinks, lunch and fishing tackle. A half-day trip (from 9am to 1pm or from 1pm to 5pm) costs 1600B. Fishing trips on big boats or speedboats cost significantly more than long-tail boats.

Rock-Climbing Yes, there are some good limestone cliffs to climb on Ko Phi-Phi, and the views from the top are spectacular. On the beach, near Carlitos is **KE Hang Out Rock Climbing** *(☎ 0 1979 2642; W www.kehangout.com)*, which charges 1000B for a half-day 'fun' climb and 1500B for a beginners' instruction course. Three-day advanced courses cost 5000B. All courses include a snack or lunch, plus equipment and insurance. Prices are a bit cheaper in low season.

Places to Stay During the high tourist months of December to February, July and August, nearly all the accommodation on Phi-Phi Don is booked out. Arrive early to stake out a place, and expect to pay a healthy peak surcharge if you're on the island during the Christmas and New Year's holidays. In the low season, though, rates are negotiable.

In the past there have been a few break-ins at bungalows along Ao Lo Dalam and Ao Ton Sai. It's not always a local thing – fellow travellers are often the culprits. Ko Phi-Phi is a major tourist destination, and common sense helps: Make sure your doors are locked, and don't leave valuables in your room. Some bungalow operations provide lockers for guests (bring your own padlock).

Ao Ton Sai A popular place at the end of the beach, **Ton Sai Village** *(☎/fax 0 7561 2434; bungalows with air-con in low/high season 1900/2800B)* has 50 attractive, comfortable and bamboo-walled bungalows. They are crowded together in tight rows though – almost claustrophobically so – but offer hot water, TV and fridge, and rates include breakfast.

Phi-Phi Island Cabana Hotel *(☎ 0 7562 0634, fax 0 7561 2132; W www.phiphicabana-hotel.com; rooms with air-con in low/high season 2000/3600B)* covers a huge swath of land stretching from bay to bay. It's a large, modern low-rise hotel with great beachside pool (complete with gaudy fountain) and pleasant, well-appointed rooms. It has the feel of a resort, with the expected list of sauna, fitness and entertainment facilities and services. Fan bungalows are also available for half the price of air-con rooms.

Banyan Villa *(☎ 0 7561 1233, fax 0 7562 0599; W www.phiphi-hotel.com; rooms with air-con in low season 1500-2200B, in high season 2200-2500B)* is a nice motel-like place and has beautifully decorated rooms, the best with balcony and sea or pool views. It's just past the really busy town area; look for the banyan tree shrine out front.

Phi-Phi Hotel *(☎ 0 7561 1233, fax 0 7562 0599; W www.phiphi-hotel.com; rooms with air-con in low/high season 800/1200B, with air-con & bath in low season 1500-1700B, in high season 1800-2000B)*, a short walk from the ferry piers, features well-appointed rooms in an unexciting four-storey building. Rates include breakfast.

Chao Koh Bungalows (*☎ 0 7561 1313, fax 0 7561 1313; rooms with fan in low season 200-600B, with air-con 900B, with fan in high season 700-1500B, with air-con 220B*) is a fair deal, offering modern, spacious and carpeted duplex-type rooms with large windows. The automatic scent sprayers can be a nuisance, however. The garden's a bit scraggly, but it's nicely located near the beach and just outside the crowded town area. There's Internet access in the lobby area.

Ao Lo Dalam You'll find **Chong Khao** (*☎ 0 1894 1233; rooms with fan in low season 150-500B, in high season 300-1200B*) inland on a rather unattractive lot with a few palm trees. A variety of bungalows, ranging from rickety and cheap to OK and modern, are lined up awaiting unfussy travellers.

PP Princess Resort (*☎/fax 0 7562 2079, fax 0 7561 2188; W www.ppprincess.com; bungalows with air-con in low season 1490-2190B, in high season 2890-3990B*) is an upscale place with small, modern and comfortable (though not luxurious) bungalows. This large place has an intimate feel, with plenty of greenery and garden paths surrounding the 90 wooden abodes. However, it still seems a bit overpriced as the buildings are looking a bit piqued. Facilities include a pool, dive shop and spa.

PP Charlie Beach Resort (*☎ 0 7562 0595, fax 0 7562 0615; W www.ppcharlie.com; rooms/bungalows with air-con in low season 1200/1500B, in high season 1500/1800B*) should look pretty spiffy when you arrive; it was remodelling at the time of writing. Simple and clean rooms and bungalows range in price depending on size and position on the beach. Pleasant restaurants and a beach bar offer an atmospheric seaside setting; rates include breakfast. Fan rooms are also available.

Phi-Phi Pavilion Resort (*☎/fax 0 7562 0633; bungalows with fan/air-con in low season 900/1200B, in high season 1800-2400B*) sits pleasantly in a coconut grove. Its well-spaced, well-decorated wood and thatched-roof bungalows boast large windows and high ceilings. Though it's not luxuriously upscale, it feels like 'paradise', with the beach not far away.

Home Parklong Seaside (*☎ 0 1229 2809; rooms with fan in low season 300-800B, in high season 600-1600B*) is next to the beach and has 14 rooms, the best facing seaside. These are housed in a large, one-storey wooden building shaded by trees. The rooms in the back are much too small and stuffy, but cheaper. The best features here are the permanently fixed wooden tables and chairs right next to the beach – great for playing cards, eating or just hanging around.

PP Viewpoint Resort (*☎ 0 1892 3150; e pp_viewpoint@hotmail.com; rooms & bungalows with fan in low season 450B, with air-con 800-1200B, with fan in high season 2000B, with air-con 2800-3000B*) is set on an open hillside with lots of stairs – the views are great, but you pay for them in leg muscles. The best rooms are huge, modern and really nice; the cheaper ones are huge and simple and require some serious stair-climbing. The restaurant is beachside and is casual and very relaxing. During the hot dry season from March to June, this hillside is hotter than most other locations.

Inland from the Beach Along the inland street maze of gift shops, scuba shops and cafés there are a few inexpensive places to stay, as well as an upmarket place or two.

Tara Inn (*☎ 0 7561 2402; W www.krabidir.com/tarainnbung; rooms with fan in low season 300-350B, in high season 600-700B*) has 12 pleasant rooms set in low-key buildings on a hillside. They're not new, but are OK for the price – especially in high season.

Rock Backpacker (*☎ 0 7561 2402; e therockbackpacker@hotmail.com; dorm beds with fan in low season 50-80B, in high season 250B, bungalows with fan in low season 100B, in high season 400-500B*) has a 16-bed dorm room – a rarity on Ko Phi-Phi. There are lockers for your stuff (bring a padlock). It's on a hill, beyond the interesting boat-shaped restaurant.

Rim Na Villa (*☎ 0 1894 2668; e tanu15@hotmail.com; rooms with fan in low/high season 300/500B*) maintains 50 basic bungalows on a hillside with rickety wooden walkways. There's a view of Ko Phi-Phi's reservoir. It's a friendly, pleasant enough budget choice.

Gipsy Village (*☎ 0 1229 0674; bungalows with fan in low/high season 250/700B*) lies on a grassy lot well inland from Hat Hin Khom. It has a tidy collection of basic but good tile-floor bungalows. The management is not terribly friendly, though at these prices you can deal with it.

Hat Hin Khom The **Phi-Phi Don Resort** (*☎ 0 1894 2511; e ppdonchukit@yahoo.com; bungalows with fan in low season 400B, with air-con 800-1500B, with fan in high season 1000B, with air-con 700-2700B)* commands a long stretch of beach. Identical small, pale-blue bungalows crowd the grassy grounds along paths, including the public beach trail (meaning little privacy for the most expensive seaside bungalows). Stuffy fan rooms with zero personality are available way inland in a small compound. Rates include breakfast at the seaside restaurant.

Andaman Beach Resort *(☎/fax 0 7562 1427; bungalows with fan in low season 500-600B, with air-con 1300-2900B, with fan in high season 1000-1200B, with air-con 2500-4000B)* features new, modern concrete bungalows. They're fairly decent, with amenities like TV and fridge, but otherwise nothing to write home about. The pleasant pool is a *faràng* magnet, however.

Bayview Resort *(☎ 0 7542 7500, fax 0 7542 7502; w www.phiphibayview.com; bungalows with air-con in low season 1300-2400, in high season 2700-4500B)* offers five kinds of modern-looking bungalows, some of which are very large and pleasant and have wooden floors. Decks sit overlooking the sea; prices depend on the view and amenities. The location is good and quiet and on a lush hillside away from Ton Sai village. An amenable Thai restaurant sits near the beach; rates include breakfast.

Maphrao Resort *(☎ 0 7562 2486; w www.maprao.com; bungalows with fan in low season 200-700B, in high season 300-1000B, villas with fan in low season 500-1100B, in high season 1200-1500B)* is a short, rather rough hike south of Hat Hin Khom. It offers a wide range of accommodation, including: cheap and simple triangular thatched bungalows with shared bath; more solid but still rickety boat-shaped structures; and large two-room villas. It has a very lush setting, and you'll have to pick your way along tree-root paths. Boat rides here cost 40B per person.

Hat Yao It's not easy getting here – you'll either have to take a boat (40B) or hike 45 minutes from Ton Sai village. And despite the distance from Ao Ton Sai, this beach is full of bungalows. It remains long and pretty, however, and you can follow a trail over to a secluded beach at Lo Mu Di.

Phi-Phi Paradise Pearl Resort *(☎/fax 0 7562 2100; e info@phiphiislands.com; bungalows with fan in low season 250-900B, with air-con 1400B, with fan in high season 600-1200B, with air-con 2200-2800B)* remains the most substantial place in the area, with almost 100 solid, decent bungalows spread in rows along the beach. It has a range of sizes and amenities – there is something for everyone. The grounds won't knock your socks off, and the huge restaurant/reception area is rather impersonal, but there *is* Internet access.

Hat Ranti Various members of a Muslim family living on this beach offer accommodation in clusters of simple, bamboo **bungalows** *(bungalows in low season 150-350B, in high season 200-450B)* on a hillside overlooking the beach. All beds have mosquito nets; prices vary with private or shared baths. Most places have a modest restaurant as well. It's all very low key. There's decent **snorkelling** right off the beach, and you can rent equipment to take advantage of it.

It can be hard to get boat pilots from Ao Ton Sai to bring you to Hat Ranti, since the family here refuses to pay commissions. You can walk via the lookout trail, however, once you get past the lookout the trail becomes overgrown and would be difficult with a large pack. Once you're on Hat Ranti the family can arrange boat trips anywhere around the island more cheaply than in Ton Sai. Note that the management at Phi-Phi Paradise Resort and other places on Hat Yao may tell you that there are no bungalows on Hat Ranti, or that they've been torn down. Come and see for yourself.

Ao Lo Bakao The only resort on this secluded beach, **Pee Pee Island Village** *(in Phuket ☎ 0 7621 5014, in Bangkok ☎ 0 2276 6056; w www.ppisland.com; bungalows with air-con in low season 2457-4660B, in high season 3807-6160B)* offers 84 luxurious bungalows with Thai-style decor, tropical furniture, thatched-roof and all the usual amenities. They sit in the shade of swaying palm trees on grassy grounds. The dining facilities are beautiful and relaxing, and views of limestone outcrops add a dramatic air.

Hat Laem Thong Between Phi-Phi Coral Resort and the Holiday Inn Resort is an area with beach chairs, a restaurant and a small dive centre with water-sports equipment for hire. A *chao náam* settlement of corrugated metal shacks is at the end of the beach.

Direct boats to Phuket leave in the afternoon from the pier here; prices can vary from place to place, so expect to pay around 300B to 450B for the 3½-hour trip. You can also take boats from here that meet up with the Krabi ferry.

All bungalows listed here come with air-con; service charges and taxes are extra. Most resorts charge a peak surcharge from mid-December to mid-January (or later).

Holiday Inn Resort (*☎ 0 7521 1334, fax 0 7562 0798; W www.holiday-inn.com; bungalows in low season 4750-5000B, in high season 6800-7550B*), at the southernmost point, consists of large Thai/Malay-style bungalows on 2m-high stilts spread over spacious, landscaped grounds with lots of coconut palms. Oceanfront units have big two-level decks while family cottages consist of two rooms with two bathrooms. On the grounds are a medium-size **swimming pool** and a well-equipped water sports centre.

Phi-Phi Coral Resort (*☎/fax 0 7562 3205, in Bangkok ☎ 0 2270 1520; W www.ppcoral.com; bungalows in low season 1900-2500B, in high season 2100-2800B*) has creative, comfortable and octagonal bungalows on the beach. Large tour groups often descend on this resort, however, making for a less-than-paradise experience.

Phi-Phi Natural Resort (*☎ 0 7561 3010, fax 0 7561 3000, in Bangkok ☎ 0 2982 7575; W www.phiphinatural.com; bungalows in low season 1200-3000B, in high season 1500-3800B*) has 70 modern and well-maintained but undistinguished (and even dingy) dark-wood bungalows on a large, grassy and also undistinguished lot. Most basic amenities (like fridge) are included. Family-size bungalows are also available. It's at the northern end of the beach, with views over a rocky cape.

Places to Eat Most of the resorts, hotels and bungalows around the island have their own restaurants. Cheaper and often better food is available at the restaurants and cafés in Ton Sai village, although virtually all of it is prepared for *faràng* palates, so the Thai dishes tend to be toned down to sub-hot levels.

Amico Resto (*☎ 0 7562 2066; dishes 70-250B; open 10am-11pm daily*) is a popular restaurant with a cosy back patio overlooking the busy pier area. Western favourites like steak, pizza and pasta are served along with more local Thai food. Toss it all down with some wine.

Thai Cuisine (*☎ 0 7563 1565; dishes 40-100B; open 10am-10.30pm daily*) lies across from Amico (east of the piers), a simple and casual place with natural decor and good ambience. The kitchen grills up Thai, seafood and breakfast.

Chao Koh (*dishes 60-120B; open 7am-10.30pm daily*), on the beach near Carlitos, is an open-air seafood place with displays of the freshly caught critters on ice. It's popular, well-priced and tasty food, served by either doting, confused or non-existent waitpersons – everything's great until it starts raining.

Hippies (*☎ 0 1970 5483; breakfast 40-75B; open 7am-6pm daily*) is a laid-back beachfront hang out spot serving Thai food. It's just past Phi-Phi Don Resort. There's also a bar that sometimes shows soccer on TV.

Pee Pee Bakery (*dishes 40-150B; open 7am-10pm daily*) is best for breakfast, when you'll be lucky to find an open table to sip your espresso. Also on tap are pizza, steak and Thai food. The atmosphere is modern and movies are shown on the tube. This is true of both branches of this bakery; one is on the main walkway east of the piers, while the other is farther inland near PP Pavilion Resort.

A row of **noodle shops** and barbecued-chicken stands, beyond Tin Tin's (down the lane and make a left), awaits those adventurous travellers who tire of pasta, schnitzel and banana pancakes. However, while many locals eat here, don't expect to get local prices – reckon on paying about 50B for a plate of curry and rice and a warm soft drink.

Entertainment There are some popular nightspots in town.

Tin-Tin's Bar (*☎ 0 1894 1097; cocktails 120-140B*) occasionally has live music in high season; if not, the beat tends towards hip hop, techno and other Western influences. Happy hour sees 50B beers. Tin-Tin's slogan is 'a night you won't remember…' and if you buy a whiskey bucket (and get one free) this will probably be the case.

JJs *(beers 50-60B; open 10am-midnight daily)* offers more of a pub-like atmosphere, complete with soccer on TV and English pub food such as steak and kidney pie (150B). It's inland a bit, before you hit Reggae Bar.

Reggae Bar is a monster place that opens at 10pm and doesn't really rock till midnight. Kickboxing provides some entertainment here. Nearby **Rolling Stoned Bar** *(open 6pm-2am daily)* often has nightly live music, and veers towards Rolling Stones, Pink Floyd and Led Zeppelin.

Cocktail Bar *(drinks 130B; open 2pm-midnight daily)* is above PP Scuba on the main walkway. This bar is modern and it has an open terrace.

Apache Bar is another large, open-air place terraced up from the beach and commanding an impressive view of Ao Ton Sai and the mountains – but you'll have to get there before dusk to enjoy it. Happy hour is from 6pm to 10pm.

Carlitos *(☎ 0 9927 3772)* can't be missed, literally: it puts on fire shows and dancing, and is lit up at night by fairy lights. Located next to the beach right on the path, it attracts more upscale *faràng* seeking hops.

Getting There & Away Ko Phi-Phi can be reached from Krabi, Phuket, Ao Nang and Ko Lanta. Most boats moor at Ao Ton Sai, though a few from Phuket use the isolated northern pier at Laem Thong (these would be best mostly for those guests staying on Hat Laem Thong). All of the following boat operate daily year-round, except for the Ko Lanta boats, which run October to April.

Boats depart from Krabi at 10.30am and 2.30pm, and return from Ko Phi-Phi at 9am and 1.30pm (250B, 1½ hours). Boats depart from Phuket at 8.30am, 1.30pm and 2.30pm, and return from Ko Phi-Phi at 9am, 2.30pm and 3pm (350B to 450B, 1¾ to two hours). Boats depart from Ko Lanta at 8am and 1pm, and return from Ko Phi-Phi at 11.30am and 2pm (200B to 250B, 1½ hours). Boats depart from Ao Nang at 9am and return from Ko Phi-Phi (via Rai Leh) at 3.30pm (250B, two hours). Prices and schedules are for the high season; in the low season tickets drop about 50B, and schedules will vary a bit.

Andaman Wave *(☎ 0 7522 2570)* runs the 40-minute *Jet Cruise*, which leaves Phuket at 8.30pm (Laem Thong at 3pm) and costs 400B one way.

Getting Around Transport on the island is mostly on foot, although fishing boats can be chartered at Ao Ton Sai for short hops around Ko Phi-Phi Don and Ko Phi-Phi Leh. Going anywhere in Ao Ton Sai, including Hat Yao (Long Beach), costs 40B per person. Be careful of boat drivers taking you short of your destination, then trying to extract more to reach your destination. Rates double at night.

Other boat charters around the island from the pier at Ton Sai include Laem Thong (400B), Lo Bakao (300B) and Viking Cave (200B). Chartering speedboats for six hours costs 6000B, while chartering long-tail boats costs 600B for three hours.

KO JAM (KO PU) & KO SI BOYA

เกาะจำ(ปู)/เกาะศรีบอยา

These large islands are inhabited by a small number of fishing families and are perfect for those seeking something other than the videos, *faràng* restaurants, beach bars and souvenir shops plaguing the adventure-seeking traveller. About the only entertainment is watching the local villagers load and unload their fishing boats or collect cashews and coconuts, or to swim and take long walks on the beach. But things are changing; over six bungalows exist here, and more are coming.

Joy Bungalow *(☎ 0 1464 6153; bungalows 150-700B)*, on the southwestern coast of Ko Jam, offers 44 attractive wood bungalows on grassy, palm-tree-shaded grounds. It's a popular place, but has gotten too big for some. There's a pleasant beachside restaurant, and Joy rents kayaks.

New Bungalows *(☎ 0 1464 4230; huts 150-600B)*, just south of Joy, features 17 bungalows, both basic huts and some nicer ones (plus a couple of cheap tree houses). During the rainy season the restaurant shuts down.

Woodland Lodge *(☎ 0 1893 5330; rayandsao@hotmail.com; bungalows 350-1000B)* is a new place with nine nicely decorated bungalows. Electricity is available from 6pm to 2am and there's a good seafood restaurant.

Golden Pearl *(☎ 0 7561 8131; goldenpearl@hotmail.com; with shared bath 50-150B, with private bath 250B)* is family-run and offers

19 bungalows and good service. You can rent bicycles, motorcycles and kayaks here, and tours to Ko Phi-Phi are organised.

Siboya Bungalow *(☎ 0 7563 0309, in Krabi ☎ 0 7561 2192; e siboyabungalow@hotmail.com; bungalows 150-1200B; open year-round)* is an atmospheric place on nearby Ko Si Boya. The 24 well-designed huts of bamboo, wood and thatch have verandas and hammocks, and are surrounded by rubber plantations. There are nearby trails to hike along.

Getting There & Away

Boats to both islands leave from Ban Laem Kruat, a village about 30km from Krabi, at the end of Rte 4036, off Hwy 4. From Krabi, take a local bus to Nua Khlon (25B), then another to Ban Laem Kraut (35B). There are three boats daily, at 12.30pm, 2pm and 4.30pm; passage costs 25B to Si Boya, 30B to Ban Ko Jam (45 minutes to one hour). These boats run all year.

Boats from Krabi run from October to April only. There are two daily, at 10.30am and 1.30pm. Boats back to Krabi leave at 8am and 1pm. There's usually a brief stop near Ko Jam (200B, 1½ hours) in each direction; long-tail boats go out to get passengers. From December to April, you may also be able to get a boat (100B, one a day at 8am) from the small pier on Th Utarakit, opposite Kasikornbank.

KO LANTA

เกาะลันตา

postcode 81150 • pop 20,000

When travellers refer to Ko Lanta, they're always referring to Ko Lanta Yai. There's also a Ko Lanta Noi – just off Yai's northeastern tip – but it holds no interest for travellers as it's ringed by mangroves rather than beaches.

Ko Lanta (Yai) has become a current sweetheart island for the intrepid backpacking crowd, though it's going upscale at an alarming rate. Beaches on Lanta's western shores are pleasantly soft, flat and sunny, and in isolated spots there's still some of that laid-back atmosphere that started attracting travellers in the first place. With popularity comes money-making possibilities, though, and Lanta holds prime real estate. Within the last few years many bungalow operators have either renovated old bungalows or built whole new operations, bringing air-con and round-the-clock electricity. The fact that much of Lanta is still owned by the local population of Muslim Thais and *chao náam* may save it from the mass development seen on Phuket or Ko Samui, but there are no guarantees – some of the poorer villages have already sold out.

Ko Lanta is a district of Krabi Province that consists of 52 islands, of which 12 are inhabited. The geography here is typified by stretches of mangrove interrupted by coral-rimmed beaches, rugged hills and huge umbrella trees. Other than tourism, the main livelihood for the local folk includes the cultivation of rubber, cashews and bananas, along with a little fishing.

Ban Sala Dan, a dusty two-street town at the northern tip of the island, is Ko Lanta's largest settlement with restaurants, minimarts, Internet cafés, souvenir stores, travel agencies, dive shops, motorcycle rentals and even a 7-Eleven. There's a petrol station just outside town. There are two ATMs; one at the bank *(open 9am-3pm Mon-Fri)* and the other at the 7-Eleven. However, it's still a good idea to bring money with you to the island.

There are more restaurants and Internet cafés along the island's main road, but there are no banks or ATMs outside Ban Sala Dan.

Ko Lanta National Marine Park

อุทยานแห่งชาติเกาะลันตา

In 1990, 15 islands in the Lanta group (covering an area of 134 sq km) were declared part of Ko Lanta National Marine Park *(admission 200B)* in an effort to protect the fragile coastal environment. **Ko Rok Nok** is especially beautiful, with a crescent-shaped bay featuring cliffs, a white-sand beach and a stand of banyan trees in the interior. The intact coral at **Ko Rok Nai** and limestone caves of **Ko Talang** are also worth seeing. Dive shops in Ban Sala Dan can arrange dives to these islands as well as coral-encrusted **Ko Ha**, **Ko Bida**, **Hin Bida** and **Hin Muang**. Camping is permitted on Ko Rok Nok.

Ko Lanta Yai itself is only partially protected since most of the island belongs to *chao náam*. As on Ko Phi-Phi, many bungalows have been built on shorelands under the nominal protection of the Royal Forest Department.

The interior of the island consists of rubber, cashew and fruit plantations, with a few stands of original forest here and there, mostly in the hilly southern section of the island. The park headquarters is at the southern tip of Ko Lanta Yai, and is closed in the off-season.

Tham Khao Mai Kaew
ถ้ำเขาไม้แก้ว

A great break from the beach is a trip to this complex of caves in the centre of Ko Lanta Yai. Even the hike in, through original forest, is quite pleasant. But the real fun begins when you descend through an indistinct hole in the rocks and enter the series of caverns. Some sections are as large as church halls, others require you to squeeze through on hands and knees. Sights en route include impressive stalactites and stalagmites, bats and even a cavern pool.

A Muslim family living near the trailhead guards access to the cave, giving two-hour **tours** for 150B per person. They also run a very basic restaurant where you can buy a variety of snacks and drinks.

The caves are located off the lower of the two cross-island roads, down a narrow, 1.5km dirt track through a rubber plantation. The best way to get there is by renting a motorcycle, although your bungalow may be willing to arrange transport.

Diving & Snorkelling

The uninhabited islands of Ko Rok Nai, Ko Rok Yai and Ko Ha, south of Ko Lanta Yai, offer plenty of coral along their western and southwestern shores. The undersea pinnacles of Hin Muang and Hin Daeng farther southwest are even better, with visibility of up to 30m in good weather, hard and soft corals, and plenty of large schooling fish such as sharks, tuna, manta ray and the occasional whale shark. The diving season extends from November to April.

There are a handful of dive operators on Ko Lanta. Most work out of Ban Sala Dan but can often be booked at beach bungalows. Two you could check out are **Lanta Diver** (*☎ 0 9867 7778; W www.lantadiver.com*) and **Ko Lanta Diving Center** (*☎ 0 7568 4065; W www.kolantadivingcenter.com*).

Places to Stay

Ko Lanta has quickly gone from being inhabited by simple, fan-cooled thatched bungalows with limited electricity to new or renovated air-conditioned, upscale and modern concrete resorts. There are still a few basic operations that won't upgrade, but most of what you'll now find runs towards the posher end of the scale; even four- and five-star resorts have started development on the island.

Many resorts now stay open year-round, and rates skyrocket from approximately mid-December to mid-January. The rates here don't reflect this month-long jump, so plan accordingly. During low season, you can try negotiating for better rates, especially if you stay a few days. Practically any resort will be happy to arrange island or snorkelling tours, massage sessions and transport rental. All are listed here more or less from north to south along the coast.

Ban Sala Dan & Laem Khaw Kwang

You've got a few choices if you need to be near the 'big' village.

Ru-Na (*Yut Hut; ☎ 0 9647 4706; rooms with fan in low/high season 300/600B*) is in Ban Sala Dan and has only three beautiful rooms with shared bath. The restaurant downstairs has a great deck overlooking the channel, and there's a pool table. It's at the western end of the main street.

Kaw Kwang Beach Bungalows (*☎ 0 7562 1373; bungalows with fan in low season 150-400B, with air-con 450-1250B, with fan in high season 300-800B, with air-con 900-2500B*), on Ko Lanta's northern curl of land, features around 50 good, modern bamboo and concrete bungalows in neat rows along shrubby paths. A large restaurant faces the bay, which has good snorkelling. There are other resorts being built along this bay that may be worth checking out.

Hat Khlong Dao The golden arc of Hat Khlong Dao holds a good concentration of bungalows. The long, wide and flat sands are great for walking and jogging. At the northern end, low tide takes the water way out.

Golden Bay Cottages (*☎ 0 7568 4161; e goldenbaylanta@yahoo.com; bungalows with fan May-Oct 300-400B, with air-con 500B, with fan Nov 400-500B, with air-con*

KO LANTA

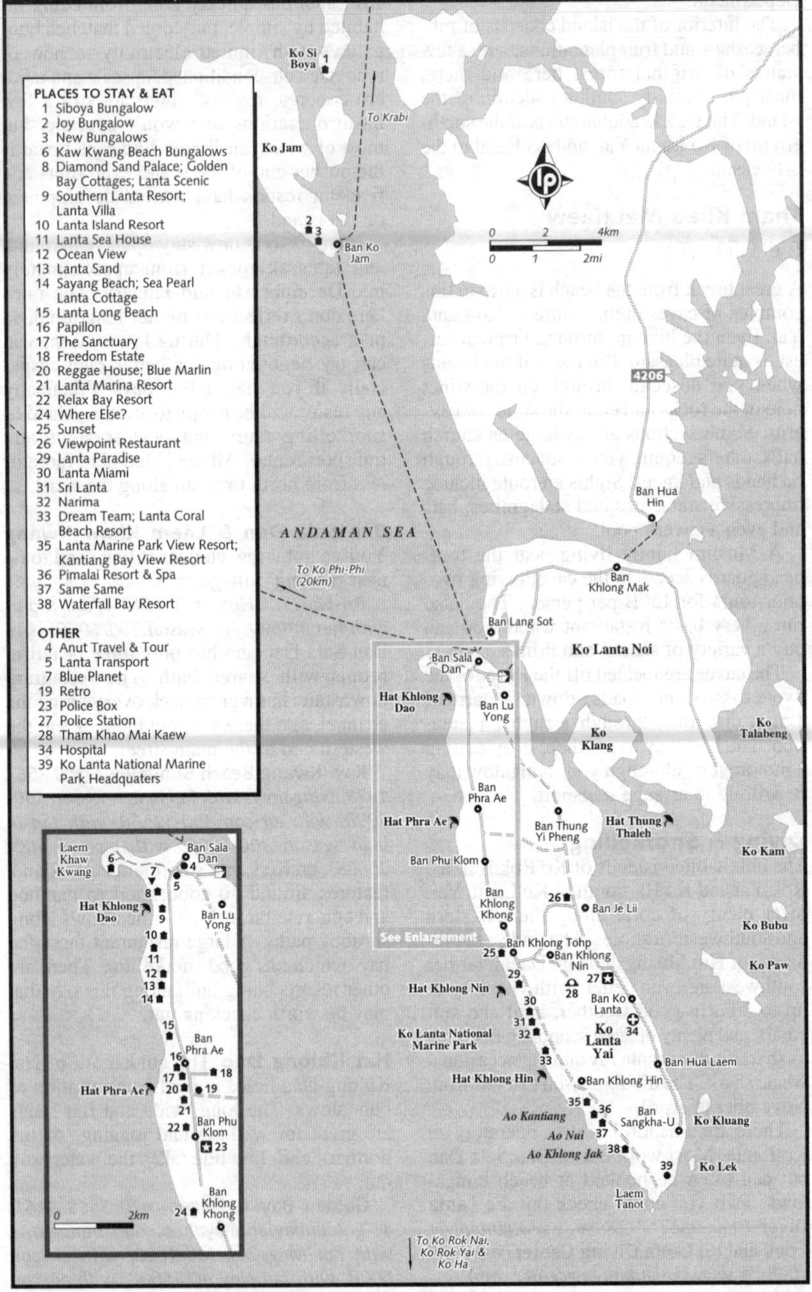
PLACES TO STAY & EAT
1 Siboya Bungalow
2 Joy Bungalow
3 New Bungalows
6 Kaw Kwang Beach Bungalows
8 Diamond Sand Palace; Golden Bay Cottages; Lanta Scenic
9 Southern Lanta Resort; Lanta Villa
10 Lanta Island Resort
11 Lanta Sea House
12 Ocean View
13 Lanta Sand
14 Sayang Beach; Sea Pearl Lanta Cottage
15 Lanta Long Beach
16 Papillon
17 The Sanctuary
18 Freedom Estate
20 Reggae House; Blue Marlin
21 Lanta Marina Resort
22 Relax Bay Resort
24 Where Else?
25 Sunset
26 Viewpoint Restaurant
29 Lanta Paradise
30 Lanta Miami
31 Sri Lanta
32 Narima
33 Dream Team; Lanta Coral Beach Resort
35 Lanta Marine Park View Resort; Kantiang Bay View Resort
36 Pimalai Resort & Spa
37 Same Same
38 Waterfall Bay Resort
OTHER
4 Anut Travel & Tour
5 Lanta Transport
7 Blue Planet
19 Retro
23 Police Box
27 Police Station
28 Tham Khao Mai Kaew
34 Hospital
39 Ko Lanta National Marine Park Headquaters
Ko Si Boya
To Krabi
Ko Jam
Ban Ko Jam
0 2 4km
0 1 2mi
4206
ANDAMAN SEA
To Ko Phi-Phi (20km)
Ban Hua Hin
Ban Khlong Mak
Ban Lang Sot
Ko Lanta Noi
Ban Sala Dan
Hat Khlong Dao
Ban Lu Yong
Ko Klang
Ko Talabeng
Ban Phra Ae
Hat Phra Ae
Ban Thung Yi Pheng
Hat Thung Thaleh
Ko Kam
Ban Phu Klom
Ban Khlong Khong
Ban Je Lii
Ko Bubu
See Enlargement
Ban Khlong Tohp
Ban Khlong Nin
Ko Paw
Hat Khlong Nin
Ban Ko Lanta
Ko Lanta Yai
Ko Lanta National Marine Park
Ban Hua Laem
Hat Khlong Hin
Ban Khlong Hin
Ao Kantiang
Ban Sangkha-U
Ko Kluang
Ao Nui
Ao Khlong Jak
Ko Lek
Laem Tanot
To Ko Rok Nai, Ko Rok Yai & Ko Ha
Laem Khaw Kwang
Ban Sala Dan
Hat Khlong Dao
Ban Lu Yong
Ban Phra Ae
Hat Phra Ae
Ban Phu Klom
Ban Khlong Khong
0 2km

700B, with fan Dec-Apr 500B, with air-con 600-1000B) is on the beach, with a range of bungalows in a scraggly garden – some claustrophobically crammed together. The bungalows with fans are small but OK, while the air-con ones are large, clean and decent. Across from here Royal Lanta Resort was being built at the time of writing, and promises elegant (and expensive) accommodation.

Diamond Sand Palace *(☎ 0 7568 4135; bungalows with fan/air-con Oct & Nov 300/500B, Mar & Apr 400/700B, 11 Jan-Feb 700-1000B, Dec-10 Jan 1500-1800B; closed May-Sept)* is on a small and cosy sandy lot. It has 20 attractive bungalows lining the main path to the beach, where the restaurant lies. Reach it via the paved road next to Lanta Scenic.

Lanta Scenic *(☎ 0 7568 4231; 🅦 www.lantascenic.com; air-con bungalows 400/600-700B in low season, 680-850/1000-1250B in high season)* is inland 50m from the beach. Cute bungalows are lined up neatly in a large grassy garden, with the fanciest sporting a fridge and TV.

Southern Lanta Resort *(☎/fax 0 7568 4174; 🅔 southlt@cscoms.com; bungalows with air-con in low season 800-2500B, in high season 1600-5000B)* boasts dozens of neatly lined bungalows of varying prices. It's another large, impersonal resort with a pool, huge restaurant and leafy paths. Rates include breakfast.

Lanta Villa *(☎ 0 7568 4129, fax 0 7568 4131; 🅦 www.lantavillaresort.com; bungalows with fan/air-con in low season 350/600B, in high season 1800/2300B)* is a good, comfortable mid-range choice. The fan bungalows have steeply-pitched roofs and are fine (though a bit musty), while air-con ones are large and come with fridge and TV. The grounds are thick and leafy, and there's a nice pool.

Lanta Sea House *(☎ 0 7568 4073, fax 0 7568 4113; 🅔 lantaseahouse@hotmail.com; bungalows with fan in low season 300-500B, with air-con 600-1500B, with fan in high season 500-1000B, with air-con 1000-3000B)* is an organised place with a beautiful garden and a variety of attractive bungalows (some of which are duplexes). The fan bungalows are simpler and made of wood. It's a good place for families, and there's a pool.

Ocean View *(☎/fax 0 7568 4089; 🅔 o_patiwat@hotmail.com; rooms with fan/air-con in low season 300/500B, in high season 500/800B)* is something different – hotel-style accommodation. It has 17 clean, modern and spacious rooms in a safe, friendly family atmosphere. It's affordable, but not right on the beach.

Hat Phra-Ae This place is another pleasant and peaceful long beach stocked with bungalow operations that are a bit more spread out than those further north.

Sayang Beach *(☎ 0 7568 4156; 🅔 sayangbeach@hotmail.com; bungalows with fan in low season 500-600B, with air-con 1300-1500B, with fan in high season 1000-1300B, with air-con 1800-2500B)* has pretty bungalows; even the smallest and cheapest ones are good. They sit in a grassy garden with palm trees.

Sea Pearl Lanta Cottage *(☎ 0 1737 0159, fax 0 7624 6051; 🅔 seapearllanta@hotmail.com; bungalows with fan in low season 100-150B, in high season 700-1000B)* has a line of decent thatch and bamboo bungalows under shady palms – despite facing a sandy parking lot they have a nice atmosphere. A cool restaurant sits by the beach.

Lanta Sand *(☎ 0 7568 4222, fax 0 7568 4034; 🅔 siriporn_ja@hotmail.com; bungalows with fan 600B, with air-con 1000-2500B; closed in low season)* harbours a well-tended grassy and palmy lot with beautiful, clean bungalows neatly lined around it. There's a pleasant restaurant/bar area on the beach.

Lanta Long Beach *(☎ 0 7568 4217, fax 0 7568 4215; 🅔 lantalongbeach@hotmail.com; bungalows with fan in low season 100-200B, in high season 200-400B)* is a motley collection of rustic bungalows, including three on extra-high stilts. It's got a great traveller vibe, and the restaurant serves tasty food. Tent rentals are available for 50B to 100B per night.

Papillon *(☎/fax 0 7568 4308; 🅦 www.papillonlanta.com; bungalows with fan in low season 200-400B, in high season 600-800B)* is new and has modest but good bungalows about 50m from the beach. There's a sandy garden area and a small pool, but everything (including the Thai/Scandinavian restaurant) is closer to the road than the water.

Freedom Estate *(☎ 0 7568 4251, fax 0 7568 4252; 🅔 freedomestate1@hotmail.com; rates 375-1125B depending on month)* is different in that it's inland and perched on a sparse, grassy hill – so you get views. Six air-con duplex bungalows come with big beds, kitchens and large patios. Reservations are recommended at any time.

The Sanctuary *(☎ 0 1891 3055; ⓔ sathaporn_yomphuk@yahoo.com; bungalows with fan in low season 250B, in high season 450-500B)* has over 20 simple thatched bungalows on a plain lot. The restaurant is a great hang-out for travellers, with weathered wooden benches and tables under a high thatched roof. It's often full, so reserve ahead.

Reggae House *(huts with shared bath in low season 100-150B, in high season 150-200B)* is as basic and cheap as you can get, with tiny thatched A-frames that could blow over in the next storm. It's best for hard-core backpackers who can deal with grungy bathrooms and would rather spend their time hanging out at the extremely laid back and cool bar, eclectically decorated with natural bits of sea detritus and Rasta colours. There are good wooden deck areas over the beach. Security isn't great here, so watch your valuables.

Blue Marlin *(huts in low season 100-150B, in high season 250-450B)*, near Reggae House, is a mishmash of 16 rattan and thatch huts.

Lanta Marina Resort *(0 7568 4168; fan huts in low season 250-500B, in high season 300-600B)*, just beyond Ban Phra Ae, gives you cheap and simple A-framed thatch huts. Rates vary according to demand; there's a large family bungalow also.

Relax Bay Resort *(☎ 0 7568 4194; ⓦ www.relaxbay.com; bungalows with fan in low season 300-700B, with air-con 900B, with fan in high season 700-1000B, with air-con 1300-2400B)* is a decent mid-range choice, with nice fan bungalows of differing sizes. The air-con ones are farther inland and not the best choice here. There are cheapie huts on the hillside for long-term tenants. An atmospheric restaurant, with great food cooked by a French chef, sits near the beach.

Where Else? *(☎ 0 1536 4870; ⓦ www.krabidir.com/whereelse; bungalows with fan in low season 100-200B, in high season 200-400B)* is funky and simple with very basic and rickety bungalows. It's in a grassy area and has a good backpacker vibe. The restaurant serves decent vegetarian Thai/Indian food.

Hat Khlong Nin & Beyond Another kilometre or so further south, the beach changes name again to Hat Khlong Nin – and here you'll find budget digs, along with the occasional ritzy place.

Sunset *(☎ 0 9973 1415; bungalows with fan in low/high season 150/400B)* is a nice, new place with large, crowded bungalows. The price is great, but it lacks atmosphere.

Lanta Paradise *(bungalows with fan/air-con in low season 200/400B, in high season 300/1200B)* offers 35 crowded bungalows in rows; unless you get a sea view, the atmosphere here just doesn't cut it. The restaurant is unique, however – a gaudy, concrete, pastel-coloured thing with two open floors of seating.

Lanta Miami *(☎ 0 1228 4506; bungalows with fan/air-con in low season 200/400B, in high season 250/700B)* is a friendly place featuring good, attractive wood and concrete bungalows set in a sparse garden. There's Internet access nearby.

Sri Lanta *(☎ 0 7569 7288, fax 0 7569 7289; ⓦ www.srilanta.com; bungalows with air-con in low season 2800-3000B, in high season 4500-5000B)* is new-age and upscale with simple but luxurious hillside bungalows decorated in natural materials. Most have breezy windows with sea views and creative indoor-outdoor baths. It has a small pool, spa, TV room, beachside restaurant and beautiful lounge areas. Included in the price are breakfast, Internet service and yoga.

Narima *(☎/fax 0 7560 7700; ⓦ www.narima-lanta.com; bungalows with air-con in low season 1000B, in high season 2000-3000B)*, on its own secluded beach, offers a lush leafy environment with tidy, upscale wood, thatch and bamboo bungalows.

Dream Team *(☎ 0 1228 4184; bungalows with fan in low season 100-300B, with air-con 300-600B, with fan in high season 300-700B, with air-con 1500-3000B)* starts with an unattractive entrance, but down the stairs are leafy garden paths and a pleasant beach area. Attractive bungalows surround a pool, and there's a large restaurant.

Lanta Coral Beach Resort *(☎ 0 7561 8273; bungalows with fan in low season 300-400B, in high season 400-600B)* sports a nice garden and 20 modern bungalows.

Lanta Marine Park View Resort *(☎ 0 1397 0793; ⓦ www.krabidir.com/lantampv; bungalows with fan in low season 150-300B, with air-con 800B, with fan in high season 250-1400B, with air-con 3000B)* occupies a hillside at the northern end of Ao Kantiang, with beautiful concrete bungalows sporting balconies with great views. Those farther back aren't as nice, but there are some good hang out tables and lounging platforms. A small and very laid-back bar is nearby.

Kantiang Bay View Resort *(☎ 0 1787 5192; rooms & bungalows with fan/air-con in low season 200/600B, in high season 300/2000B)* was remodelling at the time of writing, so prices may differ. There's a good traveller vibe here, with a restaurant and bar right on the beach. Accommodation is modern, concrete and comfortable enough.

Pimali Resort & Spa *(☎/fax 0 2551 9388; w www.pimali.com; rooms with air-con in low season 6000-13000B, in high season 8500-18000B)* is a gorgeous new four-star resort with 86 rooms spread over a landscaped hillside area – so large, in fact, that golf carts will transport you here and there. The rooms come with traditional Thai furniture, natural and artistic decor and private decks. There are foot showers at every room entrance. Facilities include a pool, spa, fitness room, dive shop, a library and three restaurants. Speedboat transfers are available (the road here isn't good).

Same Same *(☎ 0 7563 1797; bungalows in low/high season 250/300B)* has a driftwood bar that is excellent for watching sunsets. There are just three old and simple bungalows here, best for serious penny-pinchers.

Waterfall Bay Resort *(☎ 0 1836 4877; e waterfall@waterfallbay.com; bungalows with fan in low season 200-300B, with air-con 1000B, with fan in high season 800B, with air-con 1000-2500B)* is hard to reach because the road climbs up and down steeply at this end of Lanta. Here you'll find comfortable and modern air-con bungalows (some with loft) behind simpler fan ones of bamboo and wood, which face the sea. Renovations may change this, however. The namesake waterfall is a 30- to 40-minute walk. Call ahead and the staff will pick you up at Ban Sala Dan.

Places to Eat

There are a few decent places to eat in Ban Sala Dan and there is a **grocery store** *(open 7am-9pm daily)* on the road out of town.

Seaview *(dishes 30-70B; open 7.30am-9.30pm daily)* sits on a nice deck over the water, serving an extensive menu of seafood and Thai food, with breakfast in the morning.

Seaside *(☎ 0 7568 4184; dishes 30-60B; open 8am-10pm daily)* is similar to Seaview, with a very cool, funky back deck over the water.

Catfish *(☎ 0 7568 4185; dishes 30-90B; open 8am-9pm daily)* caters to backpackers, with Western food like burgers, baked potatoes and spaghetti, along with breakfasts and vegetarian food. It sells used books and is open in the high season only. Look for it at the eastern end of the main road.

Blue Planet *(☎ 0 9909 0529; dishes 40-100B; open 8am-10pm daily)* is a small, simple and friendly place with just seven tables. It's on the main road, but serves good Thai food, burgers/French fries, spaghetti and lots of pizza. Look for it next to Lanta Beer House.

Sayang Restaurant *(☎ 0 7568 4156; dishes 50-180B; open 7am-10.30pm daily)* is at the bungalow operation of the same name, and is popular for its Indian food, though vegetarian and Thai dishes are also served. It's near the beach but not on it, however.

Lanta Long Beach *(☎ 0 7568 4217; dishes 40-150B; open 7am-9pm daily in high season)* cooks up good Thai food (including vegetarian). Burgers, pasta and fish 'n' chips are also served, and the rustic restaurant sits over the beach.

The Sanctuary *(☎ 0 1891 3055; dishes 65-150B; open 9am-10.30pm daily)* is known for its vegetarian food, and also serves Indian, Thai and Western dishes (including breakfast). It's one of the best traveller restaurants on the island.

Retro *(☎ 0 9649 4842; open 7am-midnight in high season)* is a simple bamboo and thatched-roof place that serves international dishes like steak and pasta (fettucine, gnocchi and ravioli), just off the main road. Plans include adding a patio. Look for it across from **Ding Dong Restaurant**, which is also recommended.

Relax *(☎ 0 7568 4194)* is recommended for its French food (the chef is French); try the chocolate mousse for dessert. The restaurant itself has a pleasant ambience, and is on the beach (it's a bit of a hike from the parking lot).

View Point Restaurant *(☎ 0 1787 8697; dishes 40-150B; open 6am-midnight in high season)* is toward the other side of the island, just before you reach the village of Ban Je Lii. The view is unbeatable, taking in the surrounding countryside, sea and islands beyond – and a great terrace makes the most of it. The food is reasonably priced, but this is also a great spot for a drink. Try a fruit shake (30B), beer (40B to 110B) or coffee (25B to 50B).

Getting There & Away

Bus & Train If you're coming by train from Bangkok, get off in Trang (after 16 hours!), then take a bus (90B) or minivan (120B) to Ko Lanta. Avoid taking the train to Surat Thani if possible, as transport options can be more complicated from there.

Minivans leave from Krabi at 11am, 1pm and 4pm (180B to 200B, 1½ to 2½ hours). From Trang there are buses (90B) and minivans (120B). All prices include ferry crossings.

If you're heading back out from Ko Lanta, you have the choice of two bus companies. Both are located just outside Ban Sala Dan. **Anut Tour & Travel** has buses to Trang (180B, four daily at 7am, 7.30am, 8am and noon), Krabi (180B, three daily at 8am, 1pm and 7.15pm), Hat Yai (180B, two daily at 11am and 4pm) and Pak Bara (200B, one daily at 11am). **Lanta Transport**, a block away from Anut, has buses to Krabi (200B, three daily at 7.30am, 8am and noon), Phuket (350B, three daily at 7.30am, 8am and noon), Trang (200B, three daily at 7.30am, 8am and noon) and Bangkok (450B, one daily at 4pm in high season only).

Ferry There are frequent boat services to/from Ko Lanta.

Ban Hua Hin There are two short ferries connecting Ko Lanta to the mainland port of Ban Hua Hin. If you're driving a vehicle or taking a minivan to/from Ko Lanta, you'll be taking these two ferries. Each of these costs 50B for cars, 10B for motorcycles and 3B for pedestrians (prices are included if you've paid for minivan transport). Boats run half-hourly from 8am to 8pm daily. The pier on Ko Lanta is a bit south of Ban Sala Dan.

There's also a boat crossing between Ban Lang Sot and Ban Sala Dan (10B, many times a day from 7am to 8pm), but it's only for pedestrians and/or their motorcycles – and it involves long-tail boats, which aren't the best way to transport motorcycles anyway.

Krabi & Ko Phi-Phi Boats from Krabi operate October to April only. There are two daily, at 10.30am and 1.30pm (200B; two hours). Boats back to Krabi leave at 8am and 1pm. There's usually a brief stop near Ko Jam (200B, 1½ hours) in each direction.

Boats from Ko Phi-Phi run October to April only. There are two daily, at 11.30am and 2pm (200B to 250B, 1½ hours). Boats back to Ko Phi-Phi leave at 8am and 1pm.

Any travel agency or bungalow operation worth their salt will sell ferry tickets.

Getting Around

If it fits their schedule, some bungalow operators will provide free transport to/from Ban Sala Dan. There's talk of water taxis and săwngthăew coming into operation soon; considering the volume of travellers coming to Ko Lanta the past couple years, this would be a great addition. Until then, motorcycle taxis are available from Ban Sala Dan (the stand sits across from 7-Eleven) to almost anywhere along the beaches for 20B to 120B – rates are posted.

Motorcycles can also be rented from practically any bungalow operation, or in Ban Sala Dan, for 200B to 250B a day. Long-tail boat rentals are 4000B to 8000B per day; speedboats 12000B to 18000B

Trang Province

The province of Trang has similar geography to that of Krabi and Phang-Nga, with islands and beaches along the coast and limestone-buttressed mountains inland, but is much less frequented by tourists. Caves and waterfalls are the major attractions in the interior of the province, and Trang seems to have more than its share.

To the northwest of the provincial capital is Thaleh Song Hong (Sea of Two Rooms), a large lake surrounded by limestone hills. Hills in the middle of the lake nearly divide it in half, hence the name.

TRANG

อ.เมืองตรัง

postcode 92000 • pop 67,200

As a town Trang isn't the greatest of destinations, being your typical concrete, bustling mini-metropolis that on the surface doesn't hold much charm. As you get to know it, however, you start to see and experience things like the lively markets, tasty *ráan ko-píi* (coffee shops) and – at the right time of year – the Vegetarian Festival, made fervent by Trang's large Chinese population. Still, the main reason people come here is to access the nearby up-and-coming islands and beaches, and the city is full of travel agencies and resort offices that will help you achieve this.

Since at least the 1st century AD Trang has been an important trade centre. Between the 7th and 12th centuries it was a sea port for ocean-going sampans sailing between Trang and the Straits of Malacca. Nakhon Si Thammarat and Surat Thani were major centres for the Srivijaya empire at this time, and Trang served as a relay point for communications and shipping between the east coast of the Thai peninsula and Palembang, Sumatra.

During the Ayuthaya period, Trang was a common port of entry for seafaring Western visitors, who continued by land to Nakhon Si Thammarat or Ayuthaya. The town was then located at the mouth of Mae Nam Trang (Trang River), but later moved to its present location. Today Trang is still a point of exit for rubber from the province's many plantations.

Information

There are banks with ATMs on Th Phra Ram VI.

The **post office** *(cnr Th Phra Ram VI & Th Kantang; open 8.30am-4.30pm Mon-Fri,*

TRANG PROVINCE

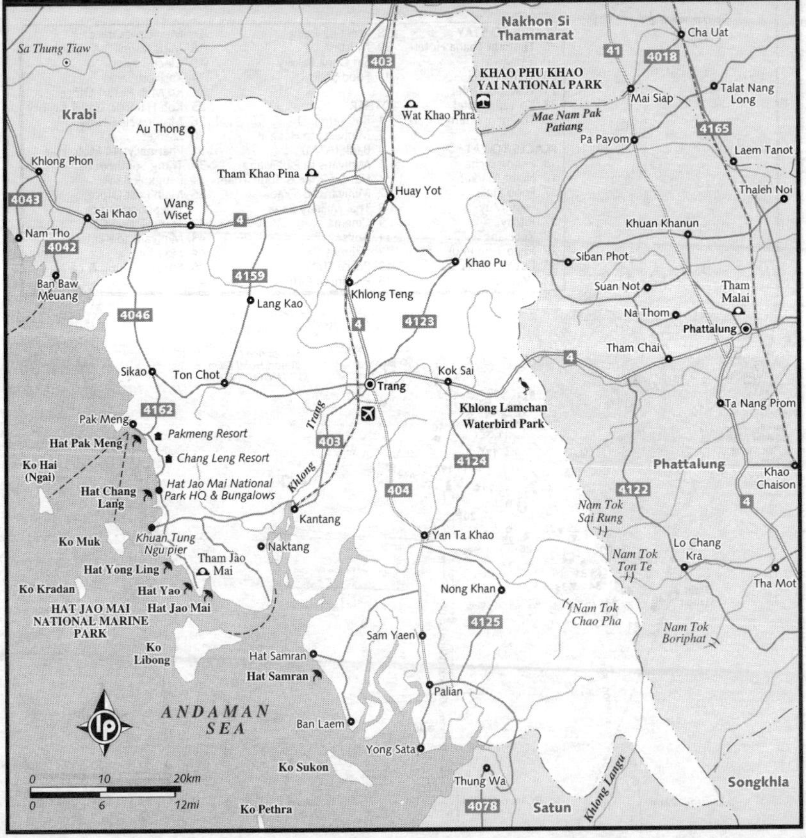

9am-noon Sat & Sun) and **telephone office** are in the same building.

There's an **Internet café** *(open 8am-2am daily)* on Th Visetkul near Th Ratchadamnoen; two others compete at the corners of Th Kantang and Th Phra Rama VI.

For medical service, head to **Wattanapat Hospital** *(☎ 0 7521 8585; 247/2 Th Phattalung)*, which has good facilities and some English-speaking staff.

Travel Agencies The staff at **Trang Travel Co** *(☎ 0 7521 9598; cnr Th Phra Rama VI & Th Kantang)* can speak English well and offer tours of the area's surrounding attractions. Day trips include the nearby islands (600B) and the waterfalls and caves (550B). It also provides airport shuttles for 30B per person.

Bookshops For English- and European-language titles, visit **Ani's** *(☎ 0 1397 4574; 285 Th Ratchadamnoen; open 9am-10pm daily)*. It's a decent second-hand bookshop and the owners are a good source of information on the area.

Mittasason *(no Roman-script sign; ☎ 0 7521 8811; 128/132 Th Visetkul; open 6am-9pm daily)* sells a few new books and magazines in English.

Places to Stay

Wattana Hotel *(☎ 0 7521 8184; rooms with fan 170-250B, with air-con 330B)*, not to be confused with the much fancier Wattana Park Hotel, has uninspired but decent-sized rooms. Most have charming views of a wall; TV is extra.

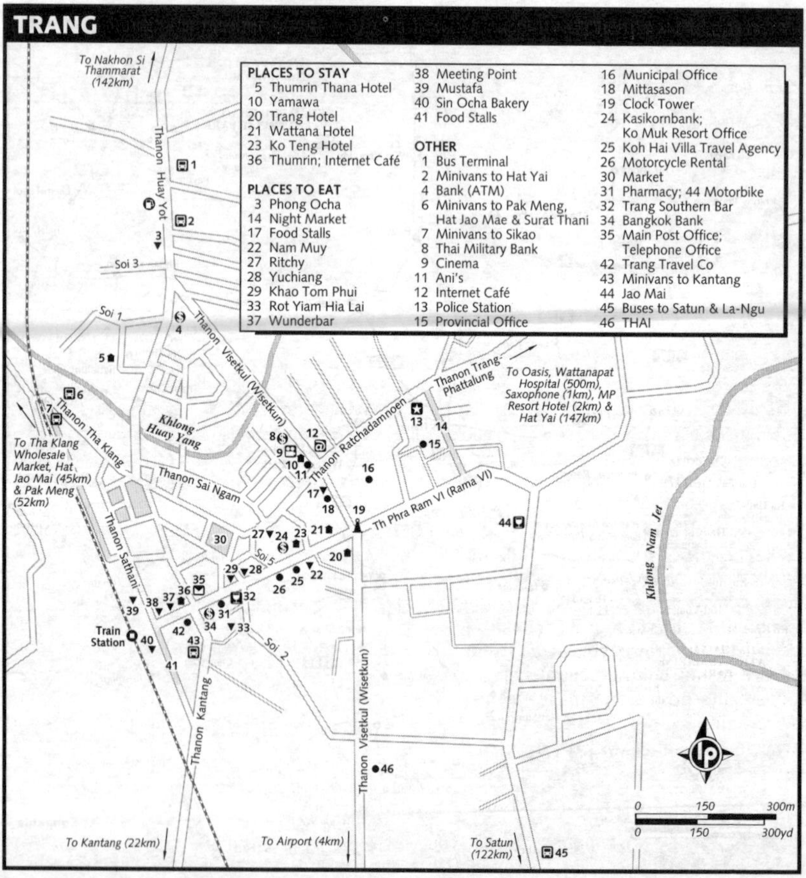

Yamawa *(☎ 0 7521 6617; ⓔ yamawa@cscoms.com; 94 Th Visetkul; rooms with fan per person 200B)* is heaven for the budget traveller. Beautifully decorated with natural materials, this pad offers good, clean rooms, a common TV area, a great rooftop bar (with excellent music), and a relaxing restaurant. It does tours to surrounding attractions and rents motorcycles for 200B per day. Practically every European language is spoken.

Ko Teng Hotel *(☎ 0 7521 8622; 77-79 Th Phra Ram VI; rooms with fan 180-380B)* is an old-timer, offering good, clean budget rooms. Ask for a room with a window.

Thumrin *(☎ 0 7521 1011, fax 0 7521 8057; Th Phra Rama VI; rooms with air-con 390-600B)* is a great deal if these prices stick. Deluxe rooms are naturally nicer, with carpeting, large windows and plenty of space. It's not luxurious – the furniture is marked – but the central location is great, and you can visit the Thumrin Thana to use its pool.

Trang Hotel *(☎ 0 7521 8944, fax 0 7521 8451; cnr Th Phra Rama VI & Th Visetkul; rooms with air-con 470-590B)* is not one of Trang's accommodation highlights. Rooms are decent, though not at all special, and the halls are downright dark and depressing. Amenities like TV and hot water cheer things up, and there's a lively coffee shop downstairs.

Thumrin Thana Hotel *(☎ 0 7521 1211, fax 0 7522 3288; ⓦ www.thumrin.co.th; 69/8 Th Trang Thana; rooms with air-con 1200-1600B)* is the best central hotel, boasting pretty spacious and clean rooms, though the lobby and halls are rather impersonal – and the convention wing doesn't make this monster of a hotel any more intimate. Rates include breakfast.

MP Resort Hotel *(☎ 0 7521 4230, fax 0 7521 1177; 184 Th Phattalung; rooms 1200-1400B, suites from 2500B)* can't be missed, and may even make you seasick; half of this behemoth is shaped like the Titanic. It's a great deal, though, if you make it out this far (we're not talking central here). Very comfortable, posh rooms make you feel like the captain, and the thick towels can wipe away any sea spray. All the expected facilities (as well as breakfast) are included.

Places to Eat

Trang is famous for *khànǒm jiin* that you douse in *náam yaa* (a spicy ground fish curry), *náam phrík* (a sweet and slightly spicy peanut sauce) and *kaeng tai plaa* (a very spicy mixture of green beans, fish, bamboo shoots and potato). To this you add fresh grated papaya, pickled vegies, cucumber and bean sprouts – all for just 10B per bowl. Look for it at the **night market**, just east of the provincial offices.

More food stalls sit next to the bookshop on Th Visetkul; the first one on the right is the best. A **day market** (with a few food stalls) convenes next to the train station.

Nam Muy *(no Roman-script sign; ☎ 0 7521 8514; 130/2 Th Phra Rama VI; dishes 60-200B; open 10am-10pm daily)* is a Chinese restaurant with a nice back patio. Look for the hot pot or shark sign amid the motorcycle dealers.

Khao Tom Phui *(no Roman-script sign; ☎ 0 7521 0122; Th Phra Ram VI; dishes 30-50B; open 4pm-2am daily)* takes up an airy, busy street corner and cooks good Thai, Chinese and seafood dishes. Look for the red sign with chopsticks.

Mustafa *(no Roman-script sign; ☎ 0 7521 4622; 59/6-8 Th Sathani; dishes 30-60B; open 7am-9pm daily)*, near the train station, is a large and casual place serving inexpensive Malay-style curries, *rotii kaeng*, *rotii khài* (roti with egg) and *mátàbà* (a flat, stuffed Indian pancake). Nearby are several smaller **food stalls** serving Muslim cuisine. Look for the green plastic chairs.

Meeting Point *(dishes 40-80B; open 8am-9pm daily)* caters to *faràng* waiting for their trains, with cable TV, wooden benches, a comfortable atmosphere and Western food like burgers and beer. Breakfast is served.

Wunderbar *(☎ 0 7521 4563; dishes 35-390B; open 10am-11pm daily; closed Sept–mid-Oct)* is a restaurant, not a bar. It serves Thai as well as food for homesick Westerners – pizza with beer, and wine with cheese. Travel services are also offered.

Also a bakery, **Richy** *(☎ 0 7521 1126; 52/9-10 Th Ratchadamnoen; dishes 45-350B; open 10am-11.30pm daily)* serves surprisingly good Western and Thai food ranging from steak, burgers and sandwiches to rice, noodle, curry and seafood.

Rot Yiam Hia Lai *(☎ 0 7522 4057; dim sum 10B; open 5pm-10pm Wed-Mon)* is an interesting little dim sum place with an intimate atmosphere tucked away down an alley. It has indoor and outdoor tables around a tiny garden, and tea and coffees are served. Look for the Chinese temple facade.

Coffee Shops Trang is famous for its *ráan kaa-fae* or *ráan ko-píi* (coffee shops), which are usually run by Hokkien Chinese. These shops serve real filtered coffee (called *kaafae thŭng* in the rest of the country) along with a variety of snacks, typically *paa-thâwng-kŏh*, *saalaapao* (Chinese buns), *khànŏm jìip* (dumplings), Trang-style sweets, *mŭu yâang* (barbecued pork) and sometimes noodles and *jók* (thick rice soup).

When you order coffee in these places, be sure to use the Hokkien word *ko-píi* rather than the Thai *kaa-fae*, otherwise you may end up with Nescafé or instant Khao Chong coffee – the proprietors often think this is what *faràng* want. Coffee is usually served with milk and sugar – ask for *ko-píi dam* for sweetened black coffee, *ko-píi dam, mâi sài náam-taan* for black coffee without sugar or *ko-píi mâi sài náam-taan* for coffee with milk but no sugar.

Sin Ocha Bakery *(Th Sathani; dishes 25-50B; open 7.30am-8.30pm daily)*, next to the train station, is the most convenient *ráan ko-píi* around and is very popular with travellers. Simple Thai dishes and breakfast are served, along with huge coffee drinks (10B to 40B) and teas. Decor is pleasantly non-pretentious, though the service could use a shot in the arm.

Yuchiang *(no Roman-script sign; Th Phra Ram VI; open 6am-8pm Mon-Sat)*, opposite Khao Tom Phui, is a beautiful, hard-core and classic Hokkien coffee shop with marble-topped round tables in an old wooden building. Food counters sit in front.

Phong Ocha *(☎ 0 7521 9918; Th Huay Yot; open 7am-10pm daily)*, north of the centre, sports four fake deer heads on the wall – very appetising. It's busy, though, serving locals traditional *ko-píi* along with *jók* and *mìi sŭa kài tŭun* (super thin rice noodles with herb-steamed chicken). Dim sum is also available.

Entertainment

Trang has it's share of entertainment venues; unfortunately, the best ones are a good ride away from the town centre. If you can't go that far, check out Yamawa's rooftop bar (see Places to Stay earlier); at the time of writing it was just getting started, and promised good drinks, music and atmosphere.

The following three places are north of town a few kilometres – a motorcycle taxi costs 10B to 20B, while túk-túk are 15B to 20B.

Oasis Pub & Restaurant *(☎ 0 1893 8474; open 7.30pm-1am daily)* is dotted with anorexic, tightly-clad waitresses who cater to males. There's a great leafy outdoor patio in front, and live Thai music inside. It's located north of Anusaowari (Monument Park) on Th Trang-Phattalung. If you get bored, head across the park to a huge ranch-style entertainment venue complete with stage.

Saxophone *(☎ 0 1273 9449; 65/5 Th Phloen Phitak; open 5pm-1am daily)* is an upscale bar/restaurant with nightly live music on an intimate stage. It's popular, cosy and romantic; the music is Western and played fairly well. Song requests are taken. Thai food is served, and Heineken draft is on tap for 150B.

Cha-Ngao *(no Roman-script sign; ☎ 0 7522 2469; 28/29-30 Th Phloen Phitak; open 11am-1am daily)* is two blocks away from Saxophone and even fancier, with a tasteful pub/restaurant atmosphere and brick, stone and wood decor. The air-con is heavy and the stage just big enough for a one-man band.

Jao Mai *(open 7pm-1am daily)* is just east of centre. It's a simple, airy and no-frills (almost funky) joint with eclectic decor and live Thai music – which if you're lucky will come from two jokester musicians who do a pretty good version of 'Hotel California'. Beers are cheap (60B) and basic Thai food is served (45B to 120B).

Trang Southern Bar *(Th Phra Rama VI; open 11am-1am daily)* has a great central location, but it's a bit haughty and the drinks are expensive. The space is clean and modern, with glowing green lights at night. Look for it on the corner; a few small tables sit outside.

Shopping

Trang is known for its wickerwork and, especially, mats woven of *bai toey* (pandanus leaves), which are called *sèua paa-nan*, or Panan mats. These are important bridal gifts in rural Trang, and are a common feature of rural households. The process of softening and drying the pandanus leaves before weaving takes many days. They can be purchased in Trang for about 100B to 200B.

The province also has its own distinctive cotton-weaving styles. The villages of Na Paw and Na Meun Si are the most highly regarded sources for these fabrics, especially the intricate diamond-shaped *lai lûuk kâew* pattern, once reserved for nobility.

The best place in town for good buys is the Tha Klang wholesale market, which is along Th Tha Klang.

Getting There & Away

Air The airport is 4km south of Trang. **THAI** *(☎ 0 7521 0804; 199/2 Th Visetkul)* operates one flight once or twice daily from Bangkok.

Bus & Share Taxi Buse services to/from Bangkok include VIP (750B, 12 hours, two daily), 1st-class (484B, 12 hours, two daily) and 2nd-class (377B, 13 hours, three daily).

Other long-distance bus destinations from Trang include Hat Yai (60B ordinary), Satun (101/55B 1st class/ordinary, two hours), Krabi (90/55B 1st class/ordinary), Ko Lanta (90B 1st class) and Phuket (105B ordinary).

A few destinations for share taxis are Hat Yai (70B), Satun (80B) and Krabi (80B). They leave from the train station. Minivans go to Hat Yai (80B), Surat Thani (130B), Ko Lanta (120B), Hat Jao Mai (50B), Pak Meng (50B) and Sikao (25B), among other places. They leave from different spots around town.

If you're coming from Ko Lanta, catch any north-bound vehicle and get off at Ban Huay Nam Khao, (the Hwy 4 junction) then get a bus south to Trang.

Ordinary buses to La-Ngu (for Pak Bara) cost 40B.

Train Only two trains travel all the way from Bangkok to Trang, the express No 83, which leaves Bangkok's Hualamphong station at 5.05pm and arrives in Trang at about 9am the next day, and the rapid No 167, which leaves Hualamphong station at 6.20pm, arriving in Trang at about 11am. Both trains offer 1st class (1240B), 2nd class (371B to 691B) and 3rd class (175B to 195B). From Thung Song in Nakhon Si Thammarat Province trains leave at 7am and 9am (two hours).

Getting Around

If you're heading to the airport, **Trang Travel Co** *(☎ 0 7521 9598; cnr Th Phra Rama VI & Th Kantang)* has shuttle services for 30B per person.

Motorcycle taxis around town cost 10B during the day and 20B at night. Loud túk-túk cost 15B. If you want to rent motorcycles, try the **pharmacy** *(44 Motorbike; ☎ 0 7521 8473; 42-44 Th Phra Rama VI)* at 200B per day; the Honda dealer across from Soi 5 (200B to 250B per day); **Yamawa** *(☎ 0 7521 6617; 94 Th Visetkul)* at 200B; and **Ani's** *(☎ 0 1397 4574; 285 Th Ratchadamnoen; open 9am-10pm daily)* at 150B.

TRANG BEACHES & ISLANDS

Trang's coast has a nice selection of sandy beaches, coves and islands, dotted here and there with the occasional limestone cliff. It's pleasantly relaxed, quite scenic at times and an up-and-coming area that has already attracted the attention of four- and five-star resorts – some currently being built along certain parts of the relatively undeveloped coastline. It'll be a while before overbuilding detracts from the natural charm of this region, however, but you should probably see it sooner rather than later.

The following beaches and islands are listed from north to south along the coast.

Hat Pak Meng
หาดปากเมง

Thirty-nine kilometres from Trang, in Sikao district, lies this long, broad, sandy beach near the small village of Pak Meng. The waters are usually shallow and calm, even in the rainy season. A couple of hundred metres offshore are several scenic limestone rock formations, including a very large one with caves. Several vendors and a few restaurants offer fresh seafood; you can use the sling-chairs and umbrellas on the beach, as long as you order something. A long promenade and sea wall runs along the middle and southern sections of the beach.

There are two places to stay here. Both run tours of nearby islands and rent motorcycles and bicycles.

Laytrang Resort *(☎ 0 7527 4227, fax 0 7527 4029; W www.laytrang.com; bungalows with air-con 800-1200B)* is a large place right in town, across from the beach. Its bungalows are farther inland, though, but they surround a large, pretty garden and are modern and clean, with large baths and pleasant decor. Its restaurant lies nearer to the sea, and serves good food.

Pakmeng Resort (*☎ 0 7520 3030, fax 0 7527 4111; bungalows with fan 300B, with air-con 500-700B*) is a few kilometres south of town and not as swank as Laytrang – it's also across the road from the beach. Basic fan bungalows come with concrete floors and bamboo furniture, while air-con ones have more amenities and are attractive, clean and polished. There's a neat canal out back.

Minivans from Trang go direct to Hat Pak Meng (50B). You can also take a minivan to nearby Sikao (25B), then a săwngthăew (15B) to Hat Pak Meng.

Ko Hai (Ngai)
เกาะไห(ไหง)

Ko Hai, also known as Ko Ngai, is actually part of Krabi Province to the north, but most accessible from Pak Meng. It's a fairly small island, covering not quite 5km, but the beaches are fine white sand, the water is clear, and virtually the whole island is ringed by coral.

Along Ko Hai's eastern shore are a few places of varying price and comfort. All should be able to provide inexpensive transport for you if you stay at their place. Chartering a long-tail boat to Ko Hai costs around 600B. These resorts on the island also operate half-day tours that take in nearby islands.

Koh Hai Villa (*☎ 0 1124 7631, in Trang ☎ 0 7521 0496; 112 Th Phra Rama VI; rooms & bungalows with fan 500-800B*) has accommodation ranging from small, colourful bamboo bungalows to nicer, more modern and concrete rooms and bungalows. They sit on a fairly pleasant grassy lot with palms. There's a restaurant, it's open all year, and the office in Trang can arrange cheap transfers here.

Ko Ngai Resort (*in Trang ☎ 0 7521 5923; w kohngai.com; bungalows with fan 800B, with air-con 1700-15000B*) is pretty plush. Fancy beachfront bungalows and houses have dark-wood walls, imaginative baths and romantic atmosphere. Less expensive bungalows are more modest. Grounds everywhere are palmy, prim and pleasant. Prices drop in the low season and rise during the holidays; rates include breakfast.

Fantasy Bungalow (*☎ 0 7521 6339, in Trang ☎ 0 7521 0317; e fantasy@kohngai.com; bungalows with air-con 2000-3000B*) lives up to its name, with 40 strangely shaped but good bungalows (in festive Caribbean-hues) that are priced according to view. Palm trees provide shade, and rates include breakfast.

Koh Ngai Paradise (*☎ 0 7521 6420; bungalows with fan 450B; closed in low season*) is one of the cheaper places on this island, offering simple huts. In Trang, contact it via the Meeting Point restaurant on Th Sathani, near the train station.

Hat Chang Lang
หาดฉางหลาง

Hat Chang Lang has a 2km-long beach that is very flat and shallow. At the northern end is Khlong Chang Lang, a stream that empties into the sea. The beach is part of the **Hat Jao Mai National Park** (*admission 200B*), and this is where the main park office is located. Nearby, there is a series of ancient rock art sketched in ochre on a cliff. National park **bungalows** (600B to 2000B) and **tents** (200B to 300B) are available to rent, and there's a grassy **camp site** beneath casuarina trees. Call ☎ 0 7521 3260 for reservations.

Chang Leng Resort (*bungalows with fan 400B, with air-con 500-600B*), about 4km north of the main park office, offers sturdy inland bungalows with TV and nice furniture. They line a gravel driveway around a garden. There's a nice restaurant in front, with views of the sea. Motorcycles and bicycles can be rented.

Ko Muk
เกาะมุก

Ko Muk is nearly opposite Hat Chang Lang on the mainland, and has several small beaches suitable for camping and swimming; there's also some lively coral around the island. The best beach, Hat Sai Yao (or Hat Farang), is on the opposite side of the island from the mainland. Near the northern end is **Tham Morakot** (Emerald Cave), a beautiful limestone tunnel that can be entered by boat during low tide. The tunnel stretches for 80m to emerge in an open pool of emerald hue, hence the cave's name. At the southern end of the island is pretty Ao Phangkha and the Muslim fishing village of Hua Laem.

Ko Muk Resort *(☎ 0 7521 2613, in Trang ☎ 0 7522 2296; 45 Th Sathani; bungalows with fan 250-300B)* is located near Hua Laem (a 10-minute walk north of the pier) and has simple but nicely designed wood and bamboo bungalows. The beach here turns to mud flats at low tide; the one in front of the Muslim village is slightly better (but cover up). The resort is open from November to June, and can organise boats to nearby islands. Contact its office in Trang to arrange transport here for 150B.

On pleasant Hat Farang are a few basic options, including **Charlie's Bungalows** *(bungalows with shared bath 350B)*, **Sabai Dee Resort** *(bungalows 350-400B)* and **Hat Farang Resort** *(rooms/bungalows with fan 150/300B)*.

The easiest place to get a boat to Ko Muk is from Khuan Tung Ngu pier, located between Hat Chang Lang and Hat Yong Ling (minivans from Trang cost 50B). Boats leave from 10am to noon and cost 35B (30 to 45 minutes). Private long-tail boats cost 800B.

Ko Kradan
เกาะกระดาน

Ko Kradan, southwest of Ko Muk, is the most beautiful of the islands that belong to Hat Jao Mai National Park. Actually, only five of six precincts on the island belong to the park – one is devoted to coconut and rubber plantations. The water is so clear in places that the bottom is clearly visible from the surface. This clear water permits the growth of corals and good healthy reefs along the northern side of the island, and the water is often shallow enough for snorkelling. There are fewer white-sand beaches on Ko Kradan than on Ko Muk, but the coral reef on the side facing Ko Muk is quite good for diving.

Ko Kradan Resort *(in Trang ☎ 0 7521 1391; rooms & bungalows 250-900B; open year-round)* has decent bungalows and cement rooms with fans and private bathroom. The beach isn't bad, and there's a coral reef out front. However, this resort has been given low marks in the past for serving expensive food and littering the area. Hopefully by the time you arrive things will have improved.

Unless you go with the resort's transport, the only way to reach Ko Kradan is to charter a long-tail boat (900B, one hour).

Hat Yong Ling & Hat Yao
หาดหยงหลิง/หาดยาว

Between Hat Chang Lang in the north, and Hat Jao Mai in the south are these two very long white-sand beaches separated by limestone cliffs riddled with caves. Hat Yong Ling is a short walk from the Hat Yong Ling park headquarters parking lot. It's a pretty bay lined with casuarina trees, and there are snack stands on weekends. Tidal pools sit off the beach at the base of the limestone cliffs, and you can camp nearby if you check in with the park officers first. Another curving beach nearby, **Hat San** can only be approached via a large cave that connects the two beaches. The striking karst formation that rises to the north of the beach resembles a shark's dorsal fin. The access road into Hat Yong Ling park is 2km long.

Hat Jao Mai & Hat Jao Mai National Park
หาดเจ้าไหมและ
อุทยานแห่งชาติหาดเจ้าไหม

Hat Jao Mai is in Kantang district, about 35km from Trang. It boasts a 5km-long, white-sand beach backed by casuarina trees and limestone hills with caves, some of which contain prehistoric human skeletal remains. Minibuses from Trang will bring you here for 50B.

This beach is part of the 231,000-sq-km **Hat Jao Mai National Park** *(admission 200B)*, which includes Hat Chang Lang farther north (where the main office is located) and the islands of Ko Muk, Ko Kradan, Ko Jao Mai, Ko Waen, Ko Cheuak, Ko Pling and Ko Meng. In this area the endangered dugong (also called manatee or sea cow) can sometimes be spotted, along with the rare black-necked stork. More common wildlife here includes macaques, langurs, wild pigs, pangolins, Pacific reef-egrets, white-bellied sea eagles and monitor lizards. The park is also rich in evergreen forest, mangrove forest, beach forest and limestone crag forest.

You can visit **Tham Jao Mai**, a large cave that boats can enter. It contains at least three levels and many side caverns with extensive stalactites, stalagmites, crystal curtains and fossils. In a small chamber at the top level is a beautiful small spring. To get here, you can charter a fisherman's long-tail boat for 400B from Ban Jao Mai Hat Yao.

There's no fancy accommodation at Hat Jao Mai.

Sinchai's Chaomai Resort (*☎ 0 7520 3034; tents 120B, bungalows with fan 200B, with air-con 300-500B*) features haphazardly built bungalows. The most basic are musty and have shared bath and mattresses on the floor, while air-con ones are more modern and also musty. At least the grounds are pleasant, and the squeaky white beach is just a few steps away. You can take a tour or rent a bicycle or motorcycle.

A short walk from Sinchai's is the village of **Ban Jao Mai Hat Yao**, where there's a local **coffee shop** and a **seafood restaurant** built on one of the village piers. Also here is **Had Yao Nature Resort** (*☎ 0 7520 3012; W www.thailandtrang.com; dorm beds 150B, rooms & bungalows with fan 300B, with air-con 500-600B*), which has a range of decent accommodation options. There's a wonderfully atmospheric restaurant located over the water. It does tours to surrounding islands and rents bicycles and kayaks; motorcycle rental can also be arranged.

Ko Libong

เกาะลิบง

Trang's largest island lies opposite Hat Jao Mai. There are three Muslim fishing villages on the island, so it's easy to get a boat from Ban Jao Mai Hat Yao for the 30-minute ride. Ko Libong has a few beaches and inlets, but it's mostly visited for its wildlife.

The island has its own wildlife sanctuary, a no-hunting zone located inland from Laem Ju Hoi, a cape that juts out from the island's east coast. Many species of birds from northern Asia and Siberia annually migrate here to pass the winter. Ko Libong is also surrounded by a veritable garden of seagrass, the main food of the dugong. Unfortunately, sightings are rare because this mammal is an endangered species that was hunted in the past – and boats have also caused fatal injuries to the animals.

The Botanical Department maintains **shelters** (*admission by donation*) on Laem Ju-Hoi, a cape on the eastern tip of the island. On the southwestern side of the island is a beach where camping is permitted.

Libong Nature Beach Resort (*☎ 0 1894 6936; W www.thailandtrang.com; bungalows with fan 500-700B*) has simple bamboo and thatch bungalows (and fancier brick ones) near the beach. Snorkelling and kayaking tours are organised, and there's a beachfront restaurant with reasonable prices. This place is run by the same family as Had Yao Nature Resort (on the mainland at Hat Jao Mai), so you can contact them there for transport here.

Libong Beach Resort (*☎ 0 7528 1160, reservations ☎ 0 7522 5205; bungalows with fan 400-600B*), to the north of Libong Nature Beach Resort, has decent A-frame bamboo bungalows sitting on a grassy lot. There's a cheap and simple restaurant also.

Boats to Ko Libong run throughout the day from Ban Jao Mai Hat Yao (30B, 30 minutes); for 60B you can get a ride to the resorts themselves. Chartering private long-tail boats costs 700B.

Ko Sukon

เกาะสุกร

This friendly and peaceful island is charmingly criss-crossed with a small network of paved roads and dirt trails that wind through water-buffalo-dotted rice fields, swaying coconut palms, shady rubber tree plantations and tiny villages. A small hilltop provides good views of the island, whose 2500 inhabitants subsist mainly on fishing and rubber cultivation. There's limited electricity, and just a handful of cars or trucks chug on the roads (most transport is by motorcycle). Because it's a mostly Muslim island, please remember to cover up as you're travelling inland; the locals will certainly appreciate this small gesture on your part.

Sukorn Beach Bungalows (*☎ 0 7520 7707, in Trang ☎ 0 7521 1457; W www.sukorn-island-trang.com; rooms with fan 450, bungalows with fan 750-950B*) offers beautiful bungalows in a grassy garden shaded by coconut palms. There's a relaxing restaurant, and the beach out front is golden brown. There are bicycles and motorcycles to be rented, and canoes that can be used for free. Rates drop by 60% from mid-May to November. Contact its Trang office, next to Wunderbar, for inexpensive transfers here.

Sukon Island Resort *(☎ 0 7521 1460, in Trang ☎ 0 7521 9679; bungalows with fan 300-800B)* is near Sukorn Beach Bungalows but is not as intimate, with over 40 white, modern concrete bungalows riding up a small inland hill (prices depend on the exact location). There's an attractive restaurant close to the beach.

Sowvanee Resort *(☎ 0 1082 5005; bungalows 200B)* is for hard-core budget travellers only, willing to share the area with a friendly Thai family who speak no English. The beach isn't great here (and you need to cover up anyway), so the only reason you'd stay is because it's 100m from the main village and pier. There are only two very basic bungalows, but more may be built. Next door to Sowvanee are five newer wood and bamboo bungalows with blue roofs; it was closed at the time of writing but may be operating when you arrive.

The best way to get to Ko Sukon is to go via your own resort's transport. The second best way is to take a minivan (25B) south to Yan Ta Khao, then a sǎwngthǎew to Ta Seh pier, where long-tail boats leave when full for 20B per person. Hiring the whole boat costs 200B. Motorcycles on Ko Sukon charge about 30B per ride.

Satun Province

Satun is the Andaman coast's southernmost province and borders the northernmost tip of Malaysia. Principal visitor attractions are the national parks of Ko Tarutao and Thaleh Ban, although the lush northern inland region of Satun Province is interesting to explore as well. The province gets its name from the Malay word *setul*, a type of fruit tree common in this area.

Before 1813 Satun was a district of the Malay state of Kedah, which at the time paid tribute to Siam along with Kelantan, Terengganu and Perlis. The Anglo-Siamese Treaty of 1909 released parts of these states to Britain, and they later became part of independent Malaysia. Satun didn't become a province of Siam until 1925.

Today an estimated 66% of the population is Muslim, most of whom speak Yawi (the language of the Malay Peninsula) or Malay as a first language; there are about a dozen mosques for every wát in the province. Main industries here include fishing, rubber and palm oil.

SATUN

อ.เมืองสตูล

postcode 91000 • pop 29,000

This modest little city may not appear very exciting at first, but there are a few interesting things to do in and around town, including checking out the good National Museum and climbing a scenic hill. You can rent bikes and pedal around the area, passing scenic agricultural lands and shrimp farms.

Within an hour's drive is the lush Thaleh Ban National Park and island-ridden Ko Phetra Marine National Park, and not far away is pristine Ko Tarutao National Marine Park. And since Satun is close to the coast and Malaysian border, you can enter or leave Thailand via land or sea.

As in the nearby provinces of Pattani and Narathiwat, you'll hear Yawi spoken in the streets of Satun. A few old Sino-Portuguese shophouses, some said to date back as far as 1839, lie along Th Buriwanit. There's also a modern, parachute-domed Bambang Mosque in the centre, constructed in 1979. Satun shuts down on Sunday.

Information

There are **banks** with ATMs in the centre of town, on Th Buriwanit. The **main post office** *(open 8.30am-4.30pm Mon-Fri, 9am-noon Sat & Sun)* and the **telephone office** are on Th Samanta Prasit. You can check your emails at **Satun Cybernet** *(134-136 Th Satun Thani; open 9am-10pm daily)* or try logging on at nearby **Turbo Internet** *(open 9am-9pm daily)*.

The **immigration office** *(☎ 0 7271 1080; open 8.30am-4.30pm Mon-Fri)* processes visa extensions for 500B. There's also an immigration office at Tha Tammalang (the pier), 7km south of town, but it doesn't extend visas. For cheaper visa extensions, however, you can cross out and back into Thailand via the Malaysia border. Either take a boat from Tha Tammalang to Kuala Perlis (100B return), or a sǎwngthǎew from Satun to Wang Prajan (the border town in Thale Ban National Park; 30B, one hour). These take longer but include interesting trips.

Organised Tours

For guided tours to Satun's surrounding attractions, contact **Pate Tours** *(☎ 0 7472 4085, 0 1910 2880; W www.patetour.com)*. A friendly couple organises biking, kayaking and trekking trips to Ko Tarutao, as well as nearby islands, caves and even inland destinations. The two-day, one-night Lidi Island rustic camping tour costs 1900B per person and includes snorkelling equipment, tent, transport and food; the one-day kayaking tour costs 700B per person (four person minimum) and includes transport, lunch and kayaking. There's also a trekking/kayaking trip with stays at jungle bungalows near Jed Cod cave, inland in Satun Province. English, Spanish, French and Thai are spoken.

National Museum

พิพิธพัณฑ์แห่งชาติสตูล

The Satun National Museum *(Soi 5, Th Satun Thani; admission 30B; open 9am-4pm Wed-Sun)* is actually an early 20th-century 'palace' that was built by a local prince to accommodate King Rama V during a royal visit. Unfortunately, the king never stayed here, but the handsome two-storey structure served as the provincial office of Satun and later, during WWII, was sequestered by the Japanese and used as a military headquarters.

Built in a pseudo-European style common in nearby Malaysia, the building has been restored and its rooms arranged to give a surprisingly thorough introduction to the traditions and folkways of the Thai Muslim

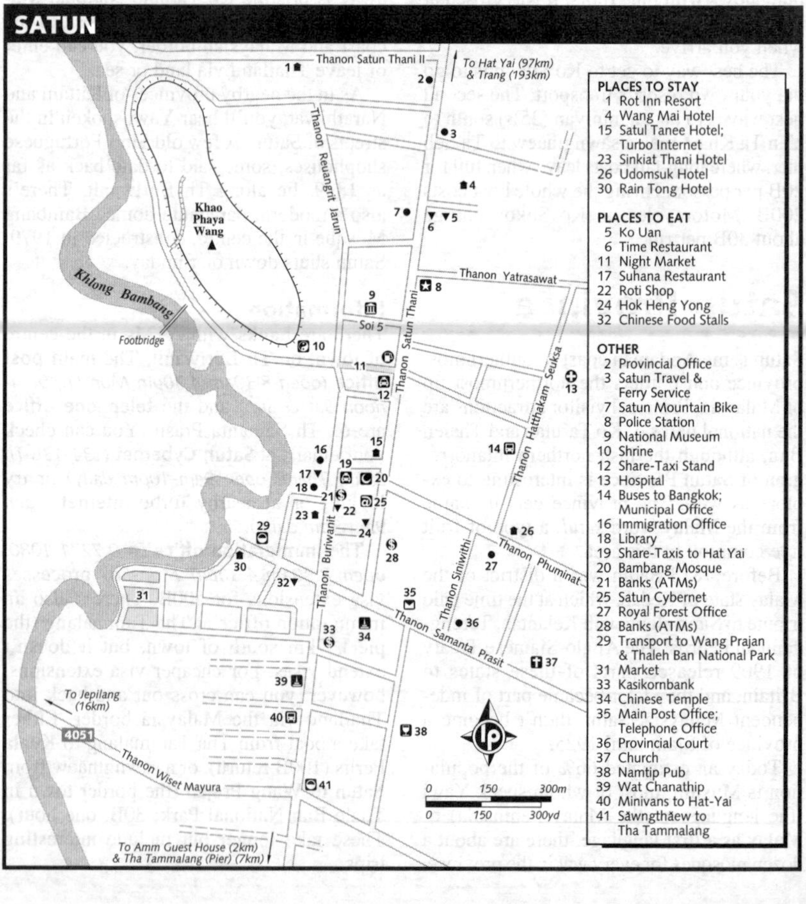

south. Most of the displays are miniature dioramas (with recorded narration in both Thai and English) that cover everything from southern mat weaving techniques to the traditional martial art called *silá*. Exhibits labelled in English also explain local marriage rites as well as male and female ritual circumcision. There are also narrated exhibits describing the Sakai, the tribal people who are believed to have inhabited the region long before the arrival of the Thai or Malay.

Khao Phaya Wang
เขาพญาวัง

Khao Phaya Wang is a limestone hill next to Khlong Bambang (or Mambang). Steps on the western side lead up the vine-choked cliff, and on top there are views of the winding green canal, rice fields and coconut plantations. You may see monkeys here. Below in the picnic area, vendors sell *sôm-tam*, *khâo nĭaw*, *kài thâwt*, *kûng thâwt* and *mîang kham* (pieces of ginger, onion, dried shrimp, toasted coconut, chilli, peanuts and lime placed into a wild tea leaf with a thick, sweet and salty tamarind sauce).

Places to Stay

Rain Tong Hotel *(☎ 0 7471 1036; Th Samanta Prasit; rooms with fan 140-180B)* is a friendly place with large, bright and pretty basic old rooms. Nearby is a share taxi stand, the river and the town's market.

Rot Inn Resort *(no Roman-script sign; ☎ 0 7472 4758; Th Satun Thani II; rooms with fan 150-200B, with air-con 260-350B)* is in a lush pastel orange building with a blue roof. Eight modern, large and spotless rooms have TVs and are a good deal. The only drawback is the long walk to centre.

Udomsuk Hotel *(☎ 0 7471 1006; Th Hatthakam Seuksa; rooms with fan 150B)*, on a corner lot, is an old place with simple, bright and worn rooms with Thai-style baths. They're basically OK, but those facing the street are noisy.

Satul Tanee Hotel *(Satun Thani; ☎ 0 7471 1010, fax 0 7471 1207; rooms with fan 210-270B, with air-con 370-470B)* starts with a painfully outdated lobby. The halls are industrial but the fan rooms are clean and tidy, and the air-con ones are surprisingly OK. All are large, but avoid the rooms facing the street.

Amm Guest House *(☎ 0 7472 4912, 0 6287 5730; 676 Mu 3 Th Sulakanukun; rooms with fan 300B)*, run by a Thai woman who speaks English and German, is 2km south of town and is a great place to stay for backpackers. Six rooms sit riverside, four right over the water and reached via a rickety wooden plank. The rooms are very basic and there's little privacy, but the atmosphere is special. To get here take the Tha Tammalang săwngthăew (10B).

Wang Mai Hotel *(☎ 0 7471 1607; 43 Th Satun Thani; rooms with air-con 600-700B)* is a landmark seven-storey building north of the town centre, offering good rooms with fridge, hot water and cable TV. There are good views from the upper floors.

Sinkiat Thani Hotel *(☎ 0 7472 1055, fax 0 7472 1059; 50 Th Buriwanit; rooms with air-con 665B)* is central and boasts good rooms with decent amenities, though the carpets can be spotty. It's similar to the Wang Mai but a better choice.

Places to Eat

Located right in the middle of town there is a good **night market**; many of the vendors here sell cheap Thai-Muslim treats and seafood. For cheaper eats, try the small group of **Chinese food stalls** on Th Samanta Prasit, near Th Buriwanit.

Suhana Restaurant *(Th Buriwanit; open 6am-6pm daily)* is an open, casual and reliable Muslim place with dishes you can point to out front. Across the street and three doors down from the corner, a popular **rotii shop** *(open 6am-noon daily)* with an olive awning serves excellent *mataba* – a vegetable rotii served with pickled side dish. Look for six tables with pale blue plastic chairs.

Time Restaurant *(☎ 0 7471 2286; 43/1-2 Th Surat Thani; dishes 45-90B; open 10.30am-midnight daily)*, near the Wang Mai Hotel, is the place to go for a modern, comfortable air-con environment. The Thai food is reasonably priced at this popular place.

Ko Uan *(no Roman-script sign; ☎ 0 7471 2103; 43/6-7 Th Surat Thani; dishes 30-60B; open 6pm-3am daily)*, around the corner from Time Restaurant, cooks up great Chinese food, especially vegie dishes. It's in a modern space with fan and air-con sections, and is closed the 7th and 8th of every month.

Hok Heng Yong *(Th Satun Thani; open 6am-4.30pm daily)* is a traditional Hokkien coffee shop with round marble-topped tables where older Chinese men hang around, eat a few snacks and chat about politics.

Entertainment

For a bit of excitement head over to **Namtip Pub** *(☎ 0 7271 1079; open 8am-1am Sun-Thur, 8am-2am Fri & Sat)* and ignore the coffee-shop sign, because this place is more of a modern lounge act. Locals visit to smoke and down their Heinekens (80B), while checking out the surprisingly good bands playing mostly Thai tunes along with Aerosmith, Scorpions and Clapton. Requests are taken, but charm them and they may let you sing on stage.

Getting There & Away

Bus, Share Taxi & Minivans Buses between Bangkok and Satun include VIP (865B, 13 hours, one daily), 1st class (556, 14 hours, one daily) and 2nd class (433B, 16 hours, two daily). It's a rather long trip, though – consider taking the train (see later).

Other bus destinations include Trang (200B, two hours), Krabi (350B, 4½ hours) and Phuket (450B, 6½ hours). One air-con bus covers these three destinations and leaves at 8.15am and 10.15am daily from Satun Travel and Ferry Service, across from the Wang Mai Hotel.

Local buses head to Trang (60B), Hat Yai (45B) and La-Ngu (20B). They run north along Th Satun Thani.

Share taxis go to Trang (80B), La-Ngu (30B), Pak Bara (50B), Hat Yai (50B) and Thaleh Ban/Wan Prajan (30B, one hour)

Minivans hop to Hat Yai and cost 60B.

Train If you want to take the train to Satun Province (about 15 hours), you can take the No 35, which leaves Bangkok at 2.20pm and gets to Padang Besar (60km from Satun) at 8am the following day (710B to 800B 2nd class). Taking the train to Hat Yai may give you more options, however; see Getting There & Away under Hat Yai in the Lower Southern Gulf chapter.

Boat Tha Tammalang is 7km south of town. It's a relatively pleasant area with a restaurant, souvenir and sundry shops, immigration office (that doesn't do visa extensions), a wandering money-changer, and boats to Malaysia and Ko Tarutao National Marine Park.

To buy tickets for Kuala Perlis in Malaysia, (50/100B one way/return, 45 minutes) look for a small desk opposite the restaurant, under a tree – this is such a loose location it may have changed. These boats leave when full. From Kuala Perlis back to Tha Tammalang, the boat ride costs RM10. You can also charter a boat to Perlis for 1400B.

To Pulau Langkawi (Langkawi Island) in Malaysia, boats leave at 8.45am, 10.30am, 2pm and 4pm (180B, 1½ to two hours). They return at 7.30am, 9.30am, 1pm and 3pm. If possible, bring Thai money from Langkawi, as there are limited moneychanging facilities at Tha Tammalang. There's also a service to Ko Tarutao (250/450B one way/return, one a day at 9am), which continues to Ko Adang (500/900B one way/return).

Getting Around

Săwngthăew to Tha Tammalang cost 20B per person; a motorcycle taxi costs 40B.

Pate Tours *(☎ 0 7472 4085, 0 1910 2880)* can arrange bicycle rentals in town, or try **Satun Mountain Bike** *(Th Surat Thani; open 9am-6.30pm daily)*, opposite the Wang Mai Hotel, which charges 300B per day for upscale mountain bikes.

PAK BARA

For tourists, this town exists only as a jumping-off point for Ko Tarutao National Park. Pak Bara is a one-street (Hwy 4052) kind of town, the main part of which runs for a kilometre or so along the shore before dead-ending at the pier. At the pier is an **information office** where you can book accommodation on Ko Tarutao.

Places to Stay & Eat

A few places in town offer accommodation for those spending the night before boarding the boat. Many have their own restaurants, but there are also a few eateries around town.

Best House Resort *(☎ 0 7478 3058, fax 0 7478 3417; rooms with air-con 490-590B)* is a pleasant choice only 200m from the pier, offering clean, spacious and modern rooms around a small murky lagoon. Amenities include TV and hot water, and there's a restaurant.

Bara Guest House *(rooms with fan 80-150B, bungalows 200-250B)* has decent but very basic budget rooms and a couple of bungalows out the back, which are closer to the beach. There's an **Internet café** a few doors down from here, towards the pier.

Grand Villa *(☎ 0 7478 3499; rooms with air-con 400B)* is a newer, nicer and more attractive place with off-street car parking.

Diamond Beach Bungalows *(☎ 0 7478 3138; bungalows with fan 200-350B)* offers rustically bleak thatched bungalows, along with some downright small and ugly concrete ones. It's about 1km from the pier. Other nearby places include **Garden Villa** and **Holiday Inn** (no relation).

Bara Resort *(☎ 0 7478 3333; bungalows with air-con 480B)* is 3km from the pier and features nine clean, large and modern bungalows well-spaced on a grassy lot. Amenities include such things as TV, hot water and fridge. This place is across the highway from the beach.

Getting There & Away

To get to Pak Bara from Satun, you must take a share taxi (30B) or bus (20B) to La-Ngu, then a sǎwngthǎew on to Pak Bara. Taxis to La-Ngu leave when full from near the night market on Th Satun Thani; buses run north along Th Satun Thani. You can also charter a taxi to Pak Bara for 300B.

Minivans connect Pak Bara to/from Hat Yai (60B). Buses (45B, 2½ hours) are much slower and less frequent.

KO TARUTAO NATIONAL MARINE PARK

อุทยานแห่งชาติหมู่เกาะตะรุเตา

This park *(☎ 0 7478 3485, 0 7472 9002; admission 200B)* protects a large archipelago of 51 islands, approximately 30km from Pak Bara and 60km northwest of Satun. Ko Tarutao, the biggest of the group, is only 5km from Pulau Langkawi in Malaysia. Only five of the islands (Tarutao, Adang, Lipe, Rawi and Klang) have any kind of regular boat service to them, and of these, only the first three are generally visited by tourists. Access to the other islands, which offer excellent beaches and coral reefs, can only be arranged by chartering long-tail boats.

Ko Tarutao National Marine Park remains one of the most beautifully isolated and pristine coastal areas in Thailand, in part because it requires a bit more effort to get there. This was probably a good reason it was chosen as location for the fifth 'Survivor' television series, broadcast in 2002. Accommodation on the islands is fairly basic, and the park is only officially open from around November to May, depending on the weather patterns.

Ko Tarutao

เกาะตะรุเตา

The park's 151-sq-km namesake features waterfalls, inland streams, beaches, caves and protected wildlife that includes dolphins, dugongs, sea turtles and lobster. Nobody lives here except for employees of the Royal Forest Department. The island was a place of exile for political prisoners between 1939 and 1947, and the remains of the prisons can be seen near Ao Talo Udang on the southern tip of the island, and at Ao Talo Wao on the middle of the east coast. There is also a graveyard, charcoal furnaces and fermentation tanks for making fish sauce. Pirates also once roamed these waters, and maybe still do.

Wildlife on the island includes dusky langur, mousedeer, wild pig, fishing cat and crab-eating macaque; dolphins and whales may be sighted offshore. Four types of sea turtle swim the surrounding waters – Pacific ridley, hawksbill, leatherback and green. All four species lay eggs on the beaches here between September and April.

Tarutao's largest stream, Khlong Phante Malaka, enters the sea towards the northern end of the island at Ao Phante Malaka; the brackish waters flow out of **Tham Jara-Khe** (Crocodile Cave – the stream here was once inhabited by crocodiles). The cave extends for at least a kilometre under a limestone mountain – no-one has yet followed the stream to the cave's end. The mangrove-lined watercourse should not be navigated at high tide, when the mouth of the cave fills.

The **park pier, headquarters and bungalows** are at Ao Phante Malaka, where there's also is a basic restaurant and small general store. For a view of the bays, climb Topu Hill, 500m north of the park office. A 23km road connects Ao Phante Malaka to Ao Talo Udang in the south; transport is available between these two bays (30B).

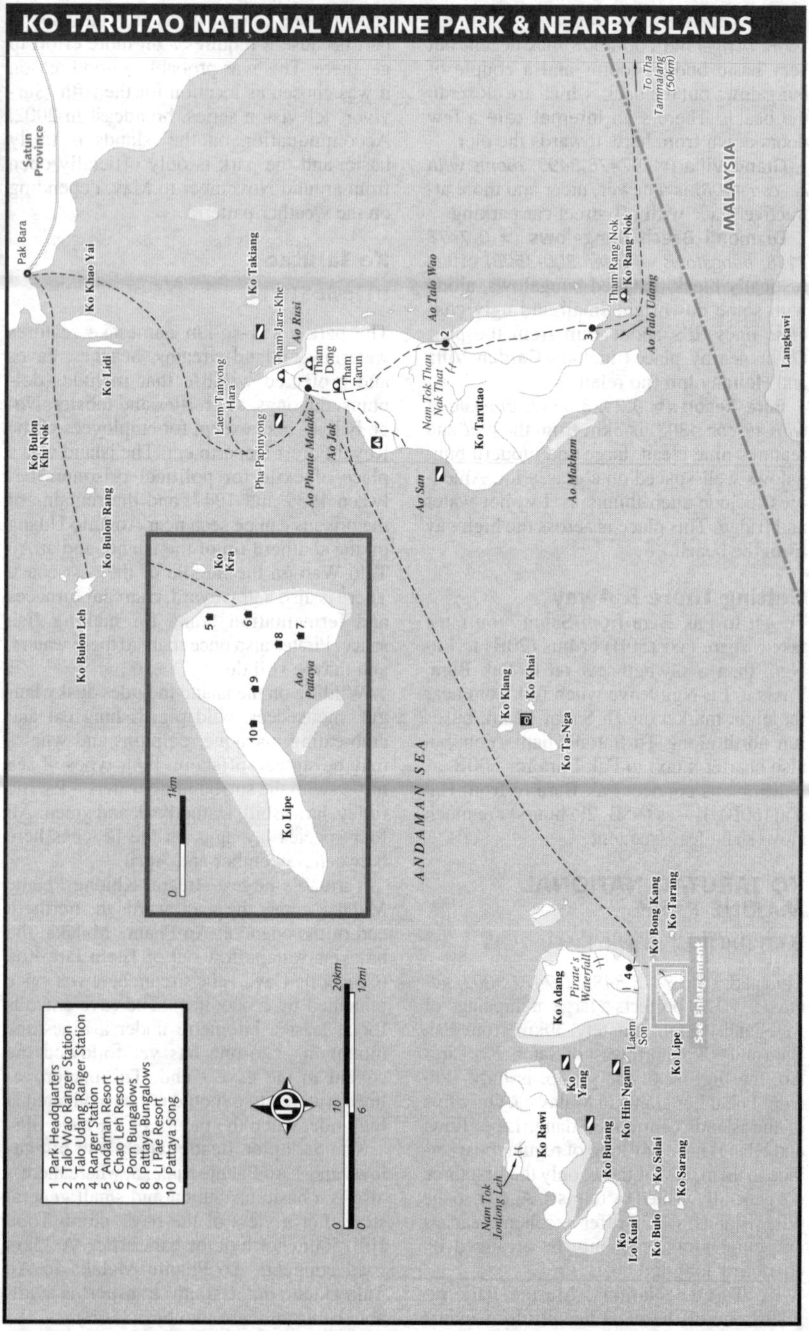
KO TARUTAO NATIONAL MARINE PARK & NEARBY ISLANDS
1 Park Headquarters
2 Talo Wao Ranger Station
3 Talo Udang Ranger Station
4 Ranger Station
5 Andaman Resort
6 Chao Leh Resort
7 Porn Bungalows
8 Pattaya Bungalows
9 Li Pae Resort
10 Pattaya Song
0
10
20km
0
6
12mi
Satun Province
Pak Bara
Ko Khao Yai
Ko Lidi
Ko Takiang
Ko Bulon Khi Nok
Ko Bulon Rang
Ko Bulon Leh
Laem Tanyong Hara
Pha Papinyong
Tham Jara-Khe
Ao Rusi
Tham Dong
Tham Tarun
Ao Phante Malaka
Ao Jak
Ao San
Nam Tok Than Nak That
Ko Tarutao
Ao Makham
Ao Talo Wao
Tham Rang Nok
Ko Rang Nok
Ao Talo Udang
To Tha Tammalang (50km)
MALAYSIA
Langkawi
Ko Kra
Ao Pattaya
Ko Lipe
0
1km
ANDAMAN SEA
Ko Klang
Ko Khai
Ko Ta-Nga
Ko Bong Kang
Ko Tarang
Pirate's Waterfall
Ko Adang
See Enlargement
Laem Son
Ko Lipe
Ko Yang
Ko Hin Ngam
Ko Rawi
Ko Butang
Ko Salai
Ko Sarang
Nam Tok Jonlong Leh
Ko Lo Kuai
Ko Bulo

The best **camping** is at the beaches of **Ao Jak** and **Ao San**, two bays south of the park headquarters; there's also camping at **Ao Makham** (Tamarind Bay), at the southwestern end of the island. Except for Ao Jak, these beaches are a long walk from the park headquarters; you may want to consider hiring a long-tail boat to take you there.

Ko Rang Nok (Bird Nest Island), off Ao Talo Udang, is another trove of the expensive swiftlet nests craved by Chinese diners around the world. Good coral reefs around the island include those near **Pha Papinyong** (Papillon Cliffs) and in the channel between Ko Tarutao and Ko Takiang; Ao San also has good reefs.

At park headquarters, you can pick up *Tarutao National Park; a Travellers Adventure Handbook* (20B), a paper booklet that details the park's facilities, flora, fauna and history.

Places to Stay Park **accommodation** *(in Pak Bara ☎ 0 7478 3485, 0 7472 9002, in Bangkok ☎ 0 2561 4292; tent sites 20B, beds in longhouse 100B, 2-person/4-person bungalows 600/1000B)* on Ko Tarutao is popular in the high season, so book ahead.

Getting There & Away Boats to Tarutao leave regularly between November and April, depending on the weather. During the rest of the year boat service is irregular, since the park is supposedly closed.

Boats from Pak Bara leave at 10.30am and 3pm daily (150/300B one way/return, 1½ hours); the 10.30am boat continues to Ko Adang (400/800B one way/return). Departures back to Pak Bara are at 9am and 1pm. It's best buying one-way tickets for each leg of your journey, as this would allow a choice of routes back.

There's also a comfortable boat service to Ko Tarutao from Tha Thammalang, 7km south of Satun. Boats leave at 11am and 2pm daily (250/450B one way/return, 1¼ hours); this boat continues to Ko Adang (500/900B one way/return, two hours). A long-tail boat from Adang to Lipe costs 20B.

Ko Khai & Ko Klang

เกาะไข่และเกาะกลาง

Between Ko Tarutao and Ko Adang is a small cluster of three islands called **Mu Ko Klang** (Middle Island Group), where there is good snorkelling. One of the islands, Ko Khai, also has a good white-sand beach. Boats from Ko Tarutao take about 40 minutes to reach Ko Khai. You can also charter long-tail boats from Ko Lipe out here for around 800B.

Ko Adang & Ko Rawi

เกาะอาดังและเกาะราวี

Ko Adang is 43km west of Tarutao and about 80km from Pak Bara. The 30-sq-km island is covered with forests and freshwater streams, which supply water year-round. Green sea turtles lay their eggs here between September and December. At the southern tip of the island, where the pier and park office are located, visitors can stay in a thatched **longhouse**. **Camping** is also allowed. The restaurant is a little expensive; try to order seafood rather than items that need to be brought in from the mainland. And as on Ko Tarutao, it's not a bad idea to bring some food of your own from the mainland.

An interesting hike can be undertaken along the island's eastern coast to a pretty beach 2km from the park ranger station. Inland a little way from the beach is a waterfall once – and perhaps still – used by passing pirate ships as a freshwater source. Around on the western coast, 3km from Laem Son, is another waterfall and the *chao náam* village of **Talo Puya**.

Laem Son has **longhouse** accommodation similar to that on Ko Tarutao for the same rates. A small **restaurant** provides basic meals and sundries; it's closed in the rainy season. You can pitch your own tent for 20B.

Getting There & Away The 10.30am boat from Pak Bara to Ko Tarutao continues to Ko Adang; it returns to Pak Bara (via Ko Tarutao) at 8am the next day (800B return).

There's also a comfortable boat service from Tha Thammalang, 7km south of Satun. Boats leave at 9am daily and stop in Ko Tarutao, continuing to Ko Adang (500/900B one way/return from Tha Tammalang; 250/450B from Ko Tarutao).

From Ko Adang, there's also a twice-weekly boat service to Langkawi Island, Malaysia.

Ko Lipe
เกาะหลีเป๊ะ

Ko Lipe is immediately south of Ko Adang and inhabited by about 500 *chao náam* who possibly originated on Ko Lanta. They subsist on fishing and some cultivation of vegetables and rice on the flatter parts of the island. For some reason the *chao náam* here prefer to be called *chao leh* – a term despised by other Moken on islands to the north. They also go by the term Thai Mai (New Thai), a nomenclature favoured by the Thai government.

This island has become the main place to stay in the park, and even has a dive shop (at Porn Resort). Several bungalows operations and a couple of simple restaurants and shops have set up in the main village along the eastern coast. The little island opposite the village, **Ko Kra**, has some fine snorkelling.

Hat Pattaya, on the southern side of the island, is the nicest of the two main beaches. There's also a coral reef here, along with small beach coves. Camping is possible.

You can walk overland between the village and Hat Pattaya in around 20 to 25 minutes, or take a long-tail boat for 20B. The *chao náam* can provide boat hire to nearby islets ringed by coral reefs.

Long-tail boats between Ko Lipe and Ko Adang also cost 20B.

Places to Stay & Eat Electricity is available from 6pm to midnight. There are only a few restaurants in Ko Lipe not associated with bungalows.

Andaman Resort *(in Satun ☎ 0 7471 1313; camping 20B, onsite tents 100B, bungalows 300-500B)*, at the northern side of the village, has a good range of 26 bungalows and some privacy. Less good is **Chao Leh Resort** *(☎ 0 7472 9201; bungalows 300-500B)*, at the other end of the village. The beach is also nicer in front of Andaman Resort than near Chao Leh Resort.

Li Pae Resort *(☎ 0 1896 5491; bungalows 300-700B)*, on Hat Pattaya, is the biggest operation with 30 spacious thatch-roof bungalows. Although it has more amenities than its competitors, this place also wins the prize for the least personality. **Pattaya Song** *(bungalows 300-700B)*, down at the western end of the beach, also has unpleasant bungalows on a hill.

Porn Bungalows *(☎ 0 1228 4566; bungalows 150-250B)* has a beautiful location on the adjacent hillside overlooking the bay. It's a friendly place that's often full, and the restaurant is good also.

Pattaya Bungalows *(bungalows 400-700B)*, also on the beach, has bamboo or concrete bungalows that are a little too crowded together. Beachfront ones are nice but book out early.

Ko Phetra National Marine Park
อุทยานแห่งชาติหมู่เกาะเภตรา

Twenty-two islands stretching between Pak Bara and the boundaries of Ko Tarutao belong to this little-visited, 495-sq-km park *(admission 200B)*. Uninhabited **Ko Khao Yai**, the largest in the group, boasts several pristine beaches suitable for camping, swimming and snorkelling. Crab-eating macaques are plentiful here, as local Muslims don't hunt them. There's a castle-shaped rock formation on one shore; during low tide boats can pass beneath a natural arch in the formation.

A park unit is on nearby **Ko Lidi** (or Lide), a Robinson Crusoe–type island which features a number of picturesque and unspoiled caves, coves, cliffs and beaches; camping facilities and kayak rentals are available. Between Ko Lidi and Ko Khao Yai is a channel bay known as **Ao Kam Pu**, a tranquil passage with cascading waters during certain tidal changes and some coral at shallow depths.

The park's mainland headquarters, visitors centre and pier is at **Ban Talo Sai**, down a 1.5km side road about 4km southeast of Pak Bara off Rte 4052 (between the 5km and 6km markers). There is a wonderfully located **seaside restaurant** *(open 8.30am-10pm daily)* and a short trail to a viewpoint, and you can also arrange boat transport to Ko Lidi here. If you want to stay here there are nice **seaside bungalows** *(☎ 0 7478 3008; bungalows 600-800B)*.

THALEH BAN NATIONAL PARK
อุทยานแห่งชาติทะเลบัน

This 196-sq-km park *(admission 200B)* lies on the Thailand-Malaysia border and encompasses the best-preserved section of white meranti rainforest (named for the dominant species of dipterocarp trees) in the region. Since the Malaysian side of the border has been deforested by agricultural development, this park is crucial to the forest's continued survival. The terrain is hilly, with a maximum elevation of 740m at Khao Chin. The area east of Rte 4184 is primary forest on granitic rock reaching up to 700m high, and there are many small streams around here.

The park **headquarters** *(☎ 0 7472 9202)*, situated on a lake in a lush valley formed by limestone outcrops, is only 2km from the border. Five kilometres north of the office and only 500m off Rte 4184 is **Nam Tok Yaroi**, a 700m, nine-tiered waterfall with pools suitable for **swimming**. Climb the limestone cliffs next to the park buildings for a view of the lake and surrounding area.

A network of trails leads to a number of other waterfalls and caves in the park, including **Nam Tok Rani**, **Nam Tok Chingrit**, **Tham Ton Din** and **Tham Lawt Pu Yu** (Pu Yu Tunnel Cave). A road also leads to **Nam Tok Ton Pliw**, cutting through secondary forest in the process of rehabilitation. There are vendor stands near the falls, which features several different levels with pools at the bottom of each. The turn-off for the falls comes 10km before the park entrance off Rte 4184 (10.5km from Rte 406).

Wildlife found within the park's boundaries tends to be of the Sundaic variety, which includes species generally found in Peninsular Malaysia, Sumatra, Borneo and Java. Common mammals include mouse deer, serow, tapir, chevrotain, chamois, various gibbons and macaques. Some of the rare bird species found here are the great argus hornbill, rhinoceros hornbill, helmeted hornbill, banded and bluewing pitta, masked finfoot, dusky crag martin and black Baza hawk. Honey bears and wild pigs are sometimes seen near park headquarters, and up in the limestone are 150cm monitor lizards and 40cm tree geckos. More elusive residents include the clouded leopard and dusky langur.

On Saturday and Sunday a **border market** where produce, clothing and homewares are sold, convenes along both sides of the border; you're permitted to cross free of visa formalities for this occasion.

The park entrance is about 37km northeast of Satun's provincial capital or 90km south of Hat Yai via Rte 406 and Rte 4184; coming from Malaysia it's about 75km from Alor Setar. The road to Thaleh Ban is rather pretty and winds through several villages, rubber plantations and banana plantations.

The best time to visit is from December to March, between seasonal monsoons. It can rain any time of the year here but the heaviest and longest rains generally fall in July, August, October and November. In January and February the nights can be quite cool.

Places to Stay & Eat

Near park headquarters and beside the pleasant lake are **bungalows** *(600B)* and **longhouses** *(1600B)*. Accommodation can be booked in advance by calling the **Royal Forest Department** *(in Bangkok ☎ 0 2561 2918; tent sites per person 20B)*. There's a Royal Forest Department office in Satun, but it doesn't book anything.

The park **restaurant** *(dishes from 30B; open 8am-8pm daily)* provides a nice view of the lake and simple Thai food. Next to the restaurant is a small shop selling a few toiletries and snacks.

Getting There & Away

The park is about 40km from Satun. It's best seen by private vehicle, since many of the sights are a bit of a distance from each other, and public transport around here is limited. The nearest places to rent cars are Hat Yai and Trang.

Hourly sǎwngthǎew (40B) run from the Rain Tong Hotel in Satun to Wang Prajan, just a few kilometres short of the park entrance. Sometimes these vehicles take you to the park gate, otherwise you can hitch or hop on one of the infrequent sǎwngthǎew from Wang Prajan into the park. If you're going from Hat Yai to Satun you can get off at Chalung to hop on these sǎwngthǎew. Sǎwngthǎew to Chalung and Hat Yai leave from the entrance nearly every hour from 8am until 1pm.

Language

Learning some Thai is indispensable for travelling in the kingdom; naturally, the more language you pick up, the closer you get to Thailand's culture and people. Foreigners who speak Thai are so rare in Thailand that it doesn't take much to impress most Thais with a few words in their own language.

Your first attempts to speak the language will probably meet with mixed success, but keep trying. When learning new words or phrases, listen closely to the way the Thais themselves use the various tones – you'll catch on quickly. Don't let laughter at your linguistic forays discourage you; this apparent amusement is an expression of appreciation. Travellers, both young and old, are particularly urged to make the effort to meet Thai college and university students. Thai students are, by and large, eager to meet visitors from other countries. They will often know some English, so communication is not as difficult as it may be with shop owners, civil servants etc, plus they are generally willing to teach you useful Thai words and phrases.

For a handy pocket-size guide to Thai, get a copy of Lonely Planet's excellent *Thai phrasebook*; it contains a section on basic grammar and a broad selection of useful words and phrases for travel in Thailand.

Many people have reported modest success with *Robertson's Practical English-Thai Dictionary* (Charles E Tuttle Co, Tokyo), which has a phonetic guide to pronunciation with tones and is compact in size. If you have difficulty finding it, write to the publisher at 2-6 Suido 1-chome, Bunkyo-ku, Tokyo, Japan.

More serious learners of the language should get Mary Haas' *Thai-English Student's Dictionary* (Stanford University Press, Stanford, California) and George McFarland's *Thai-English Dictionary* (also Stanford University Press) – the cream of the crop. Both of these require that you know the Thai script. The US State Department's *Thai Reference Grammar* by RB Noss (Foreign Service Institute, Washington, DC, 1964) is good for an in-depth look at Thai syntax.

Other learning texts worth seeking out include:

AUA Language Center Thai Course: Reading & Writing (two volumes) – AUA Language Center (Bangkok), 1979

AUA Language Center Thai Course (three volumes) – AUA Language Center (Bangkok), 1969

Foundations of Thai (two volumes) – by EM Anthony, University of Michigan Press, 1973

A Programmed Course in Reading Thai Syllables – by EM Anthony, University of Hawaii, 1979

Teaching Grammar of Thai – by William Kuo, University of California at Berkeley, 1982

Thai Basic Reader – by Gething & Bilmes, University of Hawaii, 1977

Thai Cultural Reader (two volumes) – by RB Jones, Cornell University, 1969

Thai Reader – by Mary Haas, American Council of Learned Societies, Program in Oriental Languages, 1954

The Thai System of Writing – by Mary Haas, American Council of Learned Societies, Program in Oriental Languages, 1954

A Workbook for Writing Thai – by William Kuo, University of California at Berkeley, 1979

An interactive CD-ROM called *Learning Thai Script* (Allen & Unwin, 1997) is also an excellent resource for teaching yourself to read and write the Thai script.

For information on language courses, see Language under Courses in the Facts for the Visitor chapter.

Dialects

Thailand's official language is Thai as spoken and written in central Thailand. This dialect has successfully become the lingua franca of all Thai and non-Thai ethnic groups in the kingdom. Of course, native Thai is spoken with differing tonal accents and with slightly differing vocabularies as you move from one part of the country to the next, especially in a north to south direction. But it is the central Thai dialect that is most widely understood.

All Thai dialects are members of the Thai half of the Thai-Kadai family of languages and are closely related to languages spoken in Laos (Lao, northern Thai, Thai Lü), northern Myanmar (Shan, northern Thai), north-western Vietnam (Nung, Tho), Assam (Ahom) and pockets of south China (Zhuang, Thai Lü). Modern Thai linguists recognise four basic dialects within Thailand: central Thai (spoken as a first dialect through central Thailand and throughout the country as a second dialect); northern-Thai (spoken from Tak Province north to the Myanmar border); north-eastern Thai (north-eastern provinces towards the Lao and Cambodian borders); and southern Thai (from Chumphon Province south to the Malaysian border). Each of these can be further divided into subdialects; north-eastern Thai, for example, has nine regional variations easily distinguished by those who know Thai well. There are also a number of Thai minority dialects such as those spoken by the Phu Thai, Thai Dam, Thai Daeng, Phu Noi, Phuan and other tribal Thai groups, most of whom reside in the north and north-east.

Vocabulary Differences

Like most languages, Thai distinguishes between 'polite' and 'informal' vocabulary, so that *thaan*, for example, is a more polite everyday word for 'eat' than *kin*, and *sĭi-sà* for 'head' is more polite than *hŭa*. When given a choice, it's better to use the polite terms, since these are less likely to lead to unconscious offence.

A special set of words, collectively called *kham raachaasàp* (royal vocabulary), is set aside for use with Thai royalty within the semantic fields of kinship, body parts, physical and mental actions, clothing and housing. For example, in everyday language Thais use the word *kin* or *thaan* for 'eat', while with reference to the royal family they say *sà wŏey*. For the most part these terms are used only when speaking to or referring to the king, queen and their children, hence as a foreigner you will have little need to learn them.

Script

The Thai script, a fairly recent development in comparison with the spoken language, consists of 44 consonants (but only 21 separate sounds) and 48 vowel and diphthong possibilities (32 separate signs). Experts disagree as to the exact origins of the script, but it was apparently developed around 800 years ago using Mon and possibly Khmer models, both of which were in turn inspired by south Indian scripts. Like these languages, written Thai proceeds from left to right, though vowel signs may be written before, after, above, below, *or* 'around' (before, after *and* above) consonants, depending on the sign.

Though learning the alphabet is not difficult, the writing system itself is fairly complex, so unless you're planning a lengthy stay in Thailand it should perhaps be foregone in favour of actually learning to speak the language. The names of major places included in this book are given in both Thai and Roman script, so that you can at least 'read' the names of destinations at a pinch, or point to them if necessary.

Tones & Pronunciation

In Thai the meaning of a single syllable may be altered by means of different tones – in standard Central Thai there are five: low tone, level or mid tone, falling tone, high tone and rising tone. For example, depending on the tone, the syllable *mai* can mean 'new', 'burn', 'wood', 'not?' or 'not'; ponder the phrase *mái mài mâi mâi măi* (New wood doesn't burn, does it?) and you begin to appreciate the importance of tones in spoken Thai. This makes it a rather tricky language to learn at first, especially for those of us unaccustomed to the concept of tones. Even when we 'know' what the correct tone in Thai should be, our tendency to denote emotion, verbal stress, the interrogative etc, through tone modulation often interferes with producing the correct tone. Therefore the first rule in learning to speak Thai is to divorce emotions from your speech, at least until you have learned the Thai way to express them without changing essential tone value.

The following is visual representation in chart form to show relative tone values:

Thai Tones

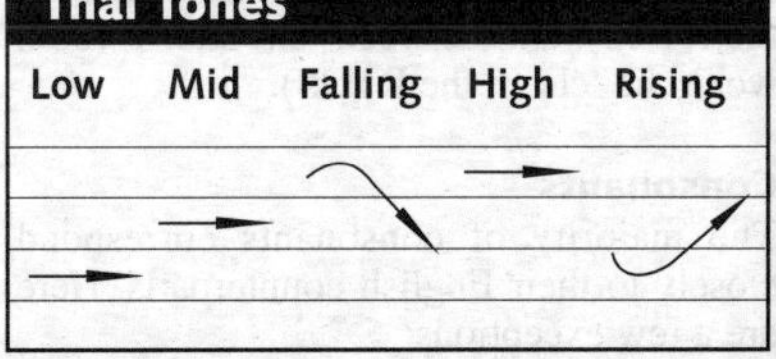

The following is a brief attempt to explain the tones. The only way to really understand the differences is by listening to a native or fluent non-native speaker. The range of all five tones is relative to each speaker's vocal range so there is no fixed 'pitch' intrinsic to the language.

1 The low tone is 'flat' like the mid tone, but pronounced at the relative *bottom* of one's vocal range. It is low, level and with no inflection, eg, *bàat* (baht – the Thai currency).
2 The level or mid tone is pronounced 'flat', at the relative middle of the speaker's vocal range, eg, *dii* (good); no tone mark used.
3 The falling tone is pronounced as if you were emphasising a word, or calling someone's name from afar, eg, *mâi* (no/not).
4 The high tone is usually the most difficult for westerners. It is pronounced near the relative top of the vocal range, as level as possible, eg, *máa* (horse).
5 The rising tone sounds like the inflection used by English speakers to imply a question – 'Yes?', eg, *sǎam* (three).

Words in Thai that appear to have more than one syllable are usually compounds made up of two or more word units, each with its own tone. They may be words taken directly from Sanskrit, Pali or English, in which case each syllable must still have its own tone.

The following is a guide to the phonetic system that has been used for the words and phrases included in this chapter (and throughout the rest of the book when transcribing directly from Thai). It's based on the Royal Thai General System (RTGS), except that it distinguishes: between short and long vowels (eg, 'i' and 'ii'; 'a' and 'aa'; 'e' and 'eh'; 'o' and 'oh'); between 'o' and 'aw' (both would be 'o' in the RTGS); between 'u' and 'eu' (both would be 'u' in the RTGS); and between 'ch' and 'j' (both would be 'ch' in the RTGS).

Consonants

The majority of consonants correspond closely to their English counterparts. Here are a few exceptions:

k	as the 'k' in 'skin'; similar to 'g' in 'good', but unaspirated (no accompanying puff of air) and unvoiced
p	as the 'p' in 'stopper', unvoiced and unaspirated (not like the 'p' in 'put'); actually sounds closer to an English 'b', its voiced equivalent
t	as the 't' in 'forty', unaspirated; similar to 'd' but unvoiced
kh	as the 'k' in 'kite'
ph	as the 'p' in 'put' (never as the 'ph' in 'phone')
th	as the 't' in 'tea'
ng	as the 'nging' in 'singing'; can occur as an initial consonant in (practise by saying 'singing' without the 'si')
r	similar to the 'r' in 'run' but flapped (tongue touches palate); in everyday speech often pronounced like 'l'

Vowels

i	as the 'i' in 'it'
ii	as the 'ee' in 'feet'
ai	as the 'i' in 'pipe'
aa	as the 'a' in 'father'
a	half as long as **aa**, as the 'a' in 'about'
ae	as the 'a' in 'bat' or 'tab'
e	as the 'e' in 'hen'
eh	as the 'a' in 'hate'
oe	as the 'er' in 'fern' (without the 'r' sound)
u	as the 'u' in 'flute'
uu	as the 'oo' in 'food', longer than **u**
eu	as the 'u' in 'fur'
ao	as the 'ow' in 'now'
aw	as the 'aw' in 'jaw' or 'prawn'
o	as the 'o' in 'bone'
oh	as the 'o' in 'toe'
eua	a combination of **eu** and **a**
ia	as 'ee-ya', or as the 'ie' in French *rien*
ua	as the 'ou' in 'tour'
uay	sounds like 'oo-way'
iu	as the 'ew' in 'yew'
iaw	as the 'io' in 'Rio' or Italian *mio*
aew	like a Cockney pronunciation of the 'ow' in 'now'
ehw	as 'air-ooh'
awy	as the 'oi' in 'coin'

Here are a few extra hints to help you with the alphabetic tangle:

- **ph** is never pronounced as the 'ph' in phone but like the 'p' in 'pound' (the 'h' is added to distinguish this consonant sound from the Thai 'p' which is closer to the English 'b'). This can be seen written as **p**, **ph**, and even **bh**.

- to some people, the Thai **k** sounds closer to the English 'g' than the English 'k'. The standard RTGS chooses to use 'k' to represent this sound to emphasise that it is not a 'voiced' sound, but more a glottal stop.
- there is no 'v' sound in Thai; *Sukhumvit* is pronounced Sukhumwit and *Viang* is really Wiang
- **l** and **r** are always pronounced as an 'n' when word-final, eg, *Satul* is pronounced as Satun, *Wihar* as Wihan. The exception to this is when 'er' or 'ur' are used to indicate the sound 'oe', as in 'ampher' *(amphoe)*. In the same way 'or' is sometimes used for the sound 'aw', as in 'Porn' *(phawn)*.
- **l** and **r** are often interchanged in speech and this shows up in some transliterations. For example, *naliga* (clock) may appear as 'nariga' and *râat nâa* (a type of noodle dish) might be rendered 'laat naa' or 'lat na'.
- **u** is often used to represent the short 'a' sound, as in *tam* or *nam*, which may appear as 'tum' and 'num'. It is also used to represent the 'eu' sound, as when *beung* (swamp) is spelt 'bung'.
- phonetically, all Thai words end in a vowel (**a**, **e**, **i**, **o**, **u**), semi-vowel (**w**, **y**), nasal (**m**, **n**, **ng**) or one of three stops (**p**, **t**, **k**). That's it. Words transcribed with 'ch', 'j', 's' or 'd' endings – like Panich, Raj, Chuanpis and Had – should be pronounced as if they end in 't', as in Panit, Rat, Chuanpit and Hat. Likewise 'g' becomes 'k' (Ralug is actually Raluk) and 'b' becomes 'p' (Thab becomes Thap).
- the 'r' in *sri* is always silent, so the word should be pronounced 'sii' (extended 'i' sound, too). Hence 'Sri Racha' really comes out 'Si Racha'.

Transliteration

Writing Thai in Roman script is a perennial problem – no wholly satisfactory system has yet been devised to assure both consistency and readability. The Thai government uses the Royal Thai General System of transcription for official government documents in English and for most highway signs. However, local variations crop up on hotel signs, city street signs, menus and so on in such a way that visitors often become confused. Add to this the fact that even the government system has its flaws. For example, 'o' is used for two very different sounds ('o' and the 'aw' in the Vowels section above), as is 'u' (for 'u' and 'eu' above). Likewise for 'ch', which is used to represent two different consonant sounds ('ch' and 'j'). The government transcription system also does not distinguish between short and long vowel sounds, which affect the tonal value of every word.

To top it off, many Thai words (especially names of people and place) have Sanskrit and Pali spellings but their actual pronunciation bears little relation to that spelling if Romanised strictly according to the original Sanskrit/Pali. Thus Nakhon Si Thammarat, if transliterated literally, becomes 'Nagara Sri Dhammaraja'. If you tried to pronounce it using this Pali transcription, very few Thais would be able to understand you.

Generally, names in this book follow the most common practice or, in the case of hotels for example, simply copy their Roman script name, no matter what devious process was used in its transliteration! When this transliteration is markedly different from actual pronunciation, the pronunciation is included (according to the system outlined in this section) in parentheses after the transliteration. Where no Roman model was available, names have been transliterated phonetically, directly from Thai. Of course, this will only be helpful to readers who bother to acquaint themselves with the language – and it's surprising how many people manage to stay for great lengths of time in Thailand without learning a word of Thai.

Problems often arise when a name is transliterated differently, even at the same location. 'Thawi', for example, can be seen as Tavi, Thawee, Thavi, Tavee or various other versions. Outside the International Phonetic Alphabet, there is no 'proper' (ie, accurate) way to transliterate Thai – only wrong ways. The Thais themselves are incredibly inconsistent in this matter, often using English letters that have no equivalent sound in Thai: Faisal for Phaisan, Bhumibol for Phumiphon, Vanich for Wanit, Vibhavadi for Wiphawadi. Sometimes they even mix literal Sanskrit transcription with Thai pronunciation, as in King Bhumibol (which is pronounced Phumiphon and if transliterated according to the Sanskrit would be Bhumibala).

Here are a few words that are often spelt in a way that encourages native English speakers to mispronounce them:

Common Spelling	Pronunciation	Meaning
bung	beung	pond or swamp
ko or *koh*	kàw	island
muang	meuang	city
nakhon or *nakorn*	nákhawn	large city
raja	usually râatchá if at the beginning of a word, râat at the end of a word	royal

Greetings & Civilities

When being polite, the speaker ends his or her sentence with *khráp* (for men) or *khâ* (for women). It is the gender of the speaker that is being expressed here; it is also the common way to answer 'yes' to a question or show agreement.

Greetings/Hello.
sàwàt-dii สวัสดี
(khráp/khâ) (ครับ/ค่ะ)

How are you?
sàbai dii rěu? สบายดีหรือ?

I'm fine.
sàbai dii สบายดี

Thank you.
khàwp khun ขอบคุณ

Excuse me.
khăw thôht ขอโทษ

I/me
phŏm ผม
(for men)
dì-chăn ดิฉัน
(for women)

you
khun คุณ
(for peers)
thâan ท่าน
(for elders and people in authority)

What's your name?
khun chêu àrai? คุณชื่ออะไร?

My name is ...
phŏm chêu ... ผมชื่อ...
(men)
dì-chăn chêu ... ดิฉันชื่อ...
(women)

Do you have ...?
mii ... măi?/ มี... ไหม/
... mii măi? ...มีไหม?

No.
mâi châi ไม่ใช่

No?
măi?/châi măi? ไหม?/ใช่ไหม?

(I) like ...
châwp ... ชอบ...

(I) don't like ...
mâi châwp ... ไม่ชอบ...

(I) would like ... (+ verb)
yàak jà ... อยากจะ...

(I) would like ... (+ noun)
yàak dâi ... อยากได้...

When?
mêua-rai? เมื่อไร?

It doesn't matter.
mâi pen rai ไม่เป็นไร

What is this?
nîi àrai? นี่อะไร?

go
pai ไป

come
maa มา

Language Difficulties

I understand.
khâo jai เข้าใจ

I don't understand.
mâi khâo jai ไม่เข้าใจ

Do you understand?
khâo jai măi? เข้าใจไหม?

A little.
nít nàwy นิดหน่อย

What do you call this in Thai?
nîi phaasăa thai นี่ภาษาไทย
rîak wâa àrai? เรียกว่าอะไร?

Getting Around

I'd like to go ...	
yàak jà pai ...	อยากจะไป...
Where is (the) ...?	
... yùu thîi năi?	...อยู่ที่ไหน?
airport	
sanăam bin	สนามบิน
bus station	
sathăanii khŏn sòng	สถานีขนส่ง
bus stop	
thîi jàwt rót pràjam thaang	ที่จอดรถประจำทาง
train station	
sathăanii rót fai	สถานีรถไฟ
taxi stand	
thîi jàwt rót tháek-sîi	ที่จอดรถแท็กซี่
I'd like a ticket.	
yàak dâi tŭa	อยากได้ตั๋ว
What time will the ... leave?	
... jà àwk kìi mohng ?	...จะออกกี่โมง?
bus	
rót meh/rót bát	รถเมล์/รถบัส
car	
rót yon	รถยนต์
motorcycle	
rót maw-toe-sai	รถมอเตอร์ไซค์
train	
rót fai	รถไฟ
straight ahead	
trong pai	ตรงไป
left	
sái	ซ้าย
right	
khwăa	ขวา
far/not far/near	
klai/mâi klai/klâi	ไกล/ไม่ไกล/ใกล้

Accommodation

hotel	
rohng raem	โรงแรม
guesthouse	
bâan phák (kèt háo)	บ้านพัก (เกสต์เฮาส์)
Do you have a room available?	
mii hâwng wâang măi?	มีห้องว่างไหม?
How much is it per night?	
kheun-lá thâo rai?	คืนละเท่าไร?
bathroom	
hâwng náam	ห้องน้ำ
toilet	
hâwng sûam	ห้องส้วม
room	
hâwng	ห้อง
hot	
ráwn	ร้อน
cold	
yen	เย็น
bath/shower	
àap náam	อาบน้ำ
towel	
phâa chét tua	ผ้าเช็ดตัว

Around Town

Can (I/we) change money here?
lâek ngoen thîi níi dâi măi?
แลกเงินที่นี้ได้ไหม?

What time does it open?
ráan pòet mêua rai?
ร้านเปิดเมื่อไร?

What time does it close?
ráan pìt mêua rai?
ร้านปิดเมื่อไร?

bank	
thánaakhaan	ธนาคาร
beach	
hàat	หาด
market	
tàlàat	ตลาด
museum	
phíphítháphan	พิพิธภัณฑ์
post office	
praisànii	ไปรษณีย์
restaurant	
ráan aahăan	ร้านอาหาร
tourist office	
sămnák ngaan thâwng thîaw	สำนักงานท่องเที่ยว

Shopping

How much?
thâo raí? เท่าไร?
too expensive
phaeng pai แพงไป
How much is this?
nîi thâo rai?/ kìi bàat? นี่เท่าไร?/ กี่บาท?
cheap, inexpensive
thùuk ถูก

Geographical features

beach
hàat sai หาดทราย
countryside
chonnábòt ชนบท
island
kàw เกาะ
lake
tháleh sàap ทะเลสาบ
map
phǎen thîi แผนที่
mountain/hill
phuu khǎo/khǎo ภูเขา/เขา
paddy (field)
(thûng) naa (ทุ่ง) นา
pond
nǎwng/beung หนอง/บึง
river
mâe náam แม่น้ำ
sea
tháleh ทะเล
town
meuang เมือง
track
thaang ทาง
village
(mùu) bâan (หมู่) บ้าน
waterfall
náam tòk น้ำตก

Health

chemist/pharmacy
ráan khǎi yaa ร้านขายยา
dentist
mǎw fan หมอฟัน
doctor
mǎw หมอ
hospital
rohng phàyaabaan โรงพยาบาล
aspirin (pain killer)
yaa kâe pùat ยาแก้ปวด
mosquito repellent
yaa kan yung ยากันยุง

Please call a doctor.
kàrúnaa rîak mǎw nòi
กรุณาเรียกหมอหน่อย
I'm allergic to penicillin.
pháe yaa phenísinlin
แพ้ยาเพนิซิลลิน
I'm pregnant.
tâng khan láew/mee tháwng
ตั้งครรภ์แล้ว/มีท้อง
It hurts here.
jèp trong née
เจ็บตรงนี้
I feel nauseous.
rúusèuk khlêun sâi
รู้สึกคลื่นไส้
I keep vomiting.
aajian bàwy bàwy
อาเจียนบ่อยๆ
I feel faint.
rúusèuk jà pen lom
รู้สึกจะเป็นลม
I have diarrhoea.
tháwng rûang
ท้องร่วง
I have a fever.
pen khâi
เป็นไข้
I have a stomachache.
pùat tháwng
ปวดท้อง
I have a headache.
pùat hǔa
ปวดหัว
I have a toothache.
pùat fan
ปวดฟัน

Time, Days & Numbers

What's the time?	
kìi mohng láew?	กี่โมงแล้ว?
today	
wan níi	วันนี้
tomorrow	
phrûng níi	พรุ่งนี้
yesterday	
mêua waan	เมื่อวาน
Sunday	
wan aathít	วันอาทิตย์
Monday	
wan jan	วันจันทร์
Tuesday	
wan angkhaan	วันอังคาร
Wednesday	
wan phút	วันพุธ
Thursday	
wan phréuhàt	วันพฤหัสฯ
Friday	
wan sùk	วันศุกร์
Saturday	
wan săo	วันเสาร์

0	*sŭun*	ศูนย์
1	*nèung*	หนึ่ง
2	*săwng*	สอง
3	*săam*	สาม
4	*sìi*	สี่
5	*hâa*	ห้า
6	*hòk*	หก
7	*jèt*	เจ็ด
8	*pàet*	แปด
9	*kâo*	เก้า
10	*sìp*	สิบ
11	*sìp-èt*	สิบเอ็ด
12	*sìp-săwng*	สิบสอง
13	*sìp-săam*	สิบสาม
20	*yîi-sìp*	ยี่สิบ
21	*yîi-sìp-èt*	ยี่สิบเอ็ด
22	*yîi-sìp-săwng*	ยี่สิบสอง
30	*săam-sìp*	สามสิบ
40	*sìi-sìp*	สี่สิบ
50	*hâa-sìp*	ห้าสิบ
100	*ráwy*	ร้อย
200	*săwng ráwy*	สองร้อย
300	*săam ráwy*	สามร้อย
1000	*phan*	พัน
10,000	*mèun*	หมื่น
100,000	*săen*	แสน
one million	*láan*	ล้าน
one billion	*phan láan*	พันล้าน

Emergencies

I need a doctor.	
tâwng-kaan măw	ต้องการหมอ
Help!	
chûay dûay!	ช่วยด้วย
Stop!	
yùt!	หยุด
Go away!	
pai sí!	ไปซิ
I'm lost.	
chăn lŏng thaang	ฉันหลงทาง

Glossary

aahăan – food
aahăan pàa – 'jungle food', usually referring to dishes made with wild game
ajahn – *(aajaan)* respectful title for teacher; from the Sanskrit term *acarya*
amphoe – district, the next subdivision down from province; also written *amphur*; see also *tambon*
amphoe meuang – provincial capital
ao – bay or gulf

baarámii – charisma or personal power; from the Pali-Sanskrit term *parami*, meaning 'perfections'
bàat – a unit of weight equal to 15 grams
baht – *(bàat)* the Thai unit of currency
bai sĭi – sacred thread used by monks or shamans in certain religious ceremonies
bai toey – pandanus leaf; used in cooking and mat making
ban – *(bâan)* house or village
bàw náam ráwn – hot springs
benjarong – traditional five-coloured Thai ceramics
Bodhisattva – in Theravada Buddhism, the term used to refer to the Buddha during the period before he became the Buddha, including his previous lives
bòt – central sanctuary in a Thai temple used for official business of the Order *(sangha)* of monks, such as ordinations; from the Pali term *uposatha*; see also *wíhăan*
Brahman – pertaining to Brahmanism, an ancient religious tradition in India and the predecessor of both Hinduism and Buddhism; not to be confused with 'Brahmin', the priestly class in India's caste system

chaa – tea
chaihàat – *(hàat)* beach; also *hat*
chao bâan – villager
chao leh – sea gypsies; also *chao náam*
chao naa – farmer
chao náam – sea gypsies; also *chao leh*
chedi – (from the Pali *cetiya*) stupa; monument erected to house a Buddha relic

doi – (in the northern regions) mountain

fàràng – Western, a Westerner

ganja – *(kanchaa)* marijuana leaves, sometimes used as a condiment in dishes of *kŭaytĭaw*
gopura – entrance pavilion in traditional Hindu temple architecture, often seen in Angkor-period temple complexes

hat – *(hàat)* beach; also *chaihàat*
hàw mòk – fish or seafood steamed in banana leaves
hăw phĭi – spirit shrine in a Buddhist monastery compound
hăw rákhang – bell tower
hăw trai – a tripitaka (Buddhist scripture) hall
hâwng – see *hong*
hâwng thăew – two- or three-storey shophouses arranged side by side along a city street
hèt khîi khwai – psilocybin mushrooms; literally 'buffalo-shit mushrooms'; also called *hèt mao*
hĭn – stone
hong – *(hâwng)* room; in southern Thailand this word may refer to the island caves semisubmerged in the sea

Isan – *(ìsăan)* general term used for northeastern Thailand; from the Sanskrit name for the medieval kingdom Isana, which encompassed parts of Cambodia and northeastern Thailand

jangwàt – province
jâo meuang – political office in traditional Thai societies throughout Southeast Asia; literally 'principality chief'
jataka – *(chaadòk)* stories of the Buddha's previous lives
jiin – Chinese
jík-kŏh – Thai hoodlum
jók – broken-rice congee

kaafae – coffee
kâew – crystal, jewel, glass, or gem
kaafae thŭng – filtered coffee; sometimes called *ko-píi* in southern Thailand
kài yâang – grilled spiced chicken
kamnan – precinct officer, the next higher official after a *phuu yài bâan,* or village chief
kàp klâem – (literally, 'with the bottle') drinking food

kàthoey – transvestites and transsexuals; often translated to 'lady-boy' in Thai English
kaw-lae – traditional fishing boats of southern Thailand
khaen – reed instrument common in northeastern Thailand
khăo – hill or mountain
khâo – rice
khâo lăam – sticky rice soaked in coconut milk and baked in a length of bamboo
khâo mòk – spiced rice steamed with chicken, beef or mutton; a Muslim-Thai speciality
khâo tôm – boiled rice soup
khlong – *(khlawng)* canal
khŏhn – masked dance-drama based on stories from the *Ramakian*
khon isăan – the people of northeastern Thailand
king-amphoe – subdistrict
klawng – Thai drums
ko – *(kàw)* island; also *koh*
ko-píi – term for filtered coffee in southern Thailand; also *kaafae thŭng*
kràbìi-kràbawng – a traditional Thai martial art employing short swords and staves
ku – small chedi that is partially hollow and open
kŭaytĭaw – a noodle soup with fish or pork balls, herbs and spices
kúay hâeng – Chinese-style work shirt
kùtì – meditation hut; a monk's dwelling
kun siang – a kind of sweetened sausage

lâap – spicy meat or fish salad with mint leaves
lăem – cape (in the geographical sense)
lákhon – classical Thai dance-drama
làk meuang – city pillar/phallus
láksànà – characteristic, feature
langsat – *(laangsàat)* small, round fruit grown in Thailand
lâo khăo – 'white spirit', an often home-made brew
lâo thèuan – home-made (ie, illegal) liquor
lék – little, small (in size); see also *noi*
lí-keh – Thai folk dance-drama
loi kràthong – the ceremony celebrated on the full moon of the end of the rainy season
longyi – Burmese sarong

mâe chii – Thai Buddhist nun
mâe náam – river; literally 'water mother'
Mahanikai – the larger of the two sects of Theravada Buddhism in Thailand
maha that – common name for temples containing Buddha relics; from the Sanskrit-Pali term *mahadhatu*; literally 'great element'
mâi sànùk – not fun
málaeng tháp – type of beetle, the wings of which are used in certain handicrafts
mánohraa – southern Thailand's most popular traditional dance-drama
masjid – *(mátsàyít)* a mosque
mátàbà – an Indian pancake stuffed with savouries
mát-mìi – technique of tie-dyeing silk or cotton threads and then weaving them into complex patterns, similar to Indonesian *ikat*; the term also refers to the patterns themselves
mâw hâwm – Thai work shirt
măwn khwăan – wedge-shaped pillow popular in northern and northeastern Thailand; literally 'axe pillow'
metta – *(mêt-taa)* Buddhist practice of loving-kindness
meuang – city or principality
mondòp – small square, spired building in a *wát*; from Sanskrit *mandapa*
muay thai – Thai boxing
mùu-bâan – village
mŭu yaw – white pork sausage

náam – water
náam ngíaw – sweet, spicy sauce (literally 'Shan sauce'); used in northern Thai dishes
náam phrík – chilli sauce
náam plaa – fish sauce
náam tòk – waterfall
năem –pickled pork sausage
naga – *(nâak)* a mythical serpent-like being with magical powers
nákhon – city; from the Sanskrit-Pali *nagara*; also spelt *nakhorn*
năng – Thai shadow play
nĕua – north
ngaan sòp – funeral ceremony
ngaan wát – temple fair
ngâwp – traditional Khmer rice farmer's hat
nirvana – (Pali, *nibbana,* Thai *níp-phaan*) in Buddhist teachings, the state of enlightenment; escape from the realm of rebirth
noen – hill
noi – *(nâwy)* little, small (amount); also *noy*; see also *lék*
nok – *(nâwk)* outside; outer

pàak náam – estuary
paa-té – batik
paathâwngkŏ – Chinese 'doughnut', a common breakfast food
pàk tâi – southern Thai
phâakhamáa – piece of cotton cloth worn as a wraparound by men
phâa mát-mìi – thick cotton or silk fabric woven from tie-dyed threads
phâasîn – same as above for women
phansăa – 'rains retreat' or Buddhist Lent; a period of three months during the rainy season that is traditionally a time of stricter moral observance for monks and Buddhist lay followers
phĭi – ghost, spirit
phík-sù – a Buddhist monk; from the Sanskrit *bhikshu*, Pali *bhikkhu*
phin – small, three-stringed lute played with a large plectrum
phleng khorâat – Khorat folk song
phleng phêua chii-wít – 'songs for life', modern Thai folk music
phrá – an honorific term used for monks, nobility and Buddha images; from the Pali *vara*, meaning 'excellent'
phrá khrêuang – amulets of monks, Buddhas or deities worn around the neck for spiritual protection; also called *phrá phim*
phrá phuum – earth spirits
phrá sàksìt – monk or amulet believed to have spiritual power
phuu khăo – 'mountain' in central Thai
phuu yài bâan – village chief; see also *kamnan*
pìi-phâat – classical Thai orchestra
plaa thuu – popular type of mackerel
ponglang – *(pong-laang)* northeastern Thai marimba (percussion instrument) made of short logs
prang – *(praang)* Khmer-style tower on temples
prasada – blessed food offered to Hindu or Sikh temple attendees
prasat – *(praasaat)* small ornate building with a cruciform ground plan and needlelike spire, used for religious purposes, located on *wát* grounds; any of a number of different kinds of halls or residences with religious or royal significance; from the Sanskrit *prasada*

râi – an area of land measurement equal to 1600 sq metres
reua hăang yao – long-tailed boat
reuan thăew – longhouse
reusĭi – an ascetic, hermit or sage (Hindi *rishi)*
rót kàsèt – farm truck
rót pràp aakàat – air-con vehicle
rót thammádaa – ordinary bus (non air-con) or ordinary train (not rapid or express)
rót tûu – a minivan
rotii – *(roti)* round flat bread, common street food often found in Muslim restaurants

săalaa – open-sided, covered meeting hall or resting place; from Portuguese term *sala*, literally 'room'
saalaapao – Chinese dough dumplings
săamláw – (also written *samlor)* three-wheeled pedicab; see also *túk-túk*
sămnák sŏng – monastic centre
sămnák wípàtsànaa – meditation centre
samsara – in Buddhist teachings, the realm of rebirth and delusion
sàtàang – Thai unit of currency; 100 sàtàang equals 1 *baht*
săwngthăew – (literally 'two rows') common name for small pick-up trucks with two benches in the back, used as buses/taxis; also written *songthaew*
sĕmaa – boundary stones used to consecrate ground used for monastic ordinations; from the Sanskrit-Pali term *sima*
serow – Asian mountain goat
sêua mâw hâwm – blue cotton farmer's shirt
soi – lane or small street
sôm-tam – spicy green papaya salad
Songkran – *(sŏngkraan)* Thai New Year, held in mid-April
sŭan aahăan – outdoor restaurant with any bit of foliage nearby; literally 'food garden'
sùkhăaphíbaan – sanitation district, a political division lower than *thêtsàbaan*
sù-săan – cemetery

tâi – south
tàlàat náam – floating market
tambon – precinct, next subdivision below *amphoe*; also written *tambol*
thâat – four-sided, curvilinear Buddhist reliquary, common in northeastern Thailand; also *that*
thâat kràdùuk – bone reliquary, a small stupa containing remains of a Buddhist devotee
tháleh sàap – inland sea or large lake

tha – *(thâa)* pier, landing
thâm – cave
thammájàk – Buddhist wheel of law; from the Pali *dhammacakka*
tham bun – to make merit
Thammayutika – one of the two sects of Theravada Buddhism in Thailand; founded by King Rama IV while he was still a monk
thâm reusĭi – hermit cave
thànŏn – street
thêp – angel or divine being; from Sanskrit term *deva*; also *thewádaa*
thêtsàbaan– a division in towns or cities much like 'municipality'
thewádaa – see *thêp*
thúdong – a series of 13 ascetic practices, for example eating one meal a day, living at the foot of a tree, undertaken by Buddhist monks; a monk who undertakes such practices; a period of wandering on foot from place to place undertaken by monks
thŭng yaang ànaamai – condom
tràwk – alley; also *trok*
trimurti – collocation of the three principal Hindu deities, Brahma, Shiva and Vishnu
Tripitaka – Theravada Buddhist scriptures
túk-túk – motorised *săamláw*

vipassana – *(wípàtsànaa)* Buddhist insight meditation

wâi – palms-together Thai greeting
wan phrá – Buddhist holy days, falling on the days of the main phases of the moon (full, new and half) each month
wang – palace
wát – temple-monastery; from the Pali term *avasa* meaning 'monk's dwelling'
wát pàa – forest monastery
wáthánátham – culture
wíhăan – any large hall in a Thai temple, but not the *bòt*; from the Sanskrit term *vihara*, meaning 'dwelling'; also *wihan* or *viharn*

yaa dawng – herbal liquor; also the herbs inserted in *lâo khăo*
yâam – shoulder bag
yài – big
yam – spicy Thai-style salad; usually made with meat or seafood
Yawi – the traditional language of Java, Sumatra and the Malay Peninsula, widely spoken in the most southern provinces of Thailand; the written form uses the classic Arabic script plus five additional letters

ACRONYMS

AUA – American University Alumni
BMA – Bangkok Metropolitan Authority
CAT – Communications Authority of Thailand
CPT – Communist Party of Thailand
KMT – Kuomintang
KNU – Karen National Union
NGO – Nongovernmental Organisation
PLAT – People's Liberation Army of Thailand
SRT – State Railway of Thailand
TAT – Tourism Authority of Thailand
THAI – Thai Airways International

Thanks

Many thanks to the travellers who used the last edition and wrote to us with helpful hints, useful advice and interesting anecdotes:

Gep Aadriaanse, Lee Abbott, Tommy Aberg, Sander Abruti, Wayne Adams, Jackie Addenbrooke, Jackman Adi, Cat Adler, Paul Adshead, Liz Ainslie, Jim Aird, Husain Akbar, Chelsea Albucher, Neil Aldred, David Alexander, Sue & Bader Alhajji, Michelle & Pomy Ali, Cecile Alizon, Katherine Allen, Chris & Betta Allman, Curt Allred, Patricia Almond, Jorge Alves, Thomas Amend, Gretchen Amerongen, Henrik Yde Andersen, C Robert Anderson, Lane Anderson, Michael Anderson, Nick Anderson, Ray Anderson, Walter Andrea, Baumann Andreas, Jessica Andrews, Phil Andrews, Johan Angberg, Patrik Aqvist, Malcom Archard, Carole Arnaud-Battabdier, Wayne Arondus, Sean Arrowsmith, Arne Augedal, Grety & Boaz Avramovich, Deborah Axam, Hirokazu Azuma, Ilone Baake, Ismail Baba, Alexander Babiak, Eric Bacci, Chris Bain, Peter Baker, Alexandre Balcer, Mark Balfe, Peter Ball, Svenne Balucci, Warren Bane, A Bannock, Fabien Barbazan, Herve Barbazange, Kristina Barbera, Rene & Katrine Barendsz, Will Barker, Wayen Barley, John Barnett, Nina Barnett, Chris Baroni, Thomas Barron, Summer Bartholomew, Lee Bartlett, Michael & Rosemary Bartlett, Nigel Bartlett, Izzy Bartley, Kieron Barton, Doug Bast, Giovanni Battista Bernardi, Garry & Mireille Batzel, Andreas Baumann, Catherine Baynes, Jane Beattie, Jacques Beaudry, Janet Beccaloni, Guenther Beckermann, John Beckwell, Chloe Beesley, Jeremy Begalke, Carol Belding, Petr Benda, Maria & Tony Benfield, A Bennett, Christian Berberski, Simon Beresford, Jessica Bergman, Edward A Berkovich, Aubrey Berry, Walter Bertschinger, Kees Beukelman, Markus Bhnert, John Biale, Darin Bielby, Elise Bigelow, Gordon Biggar, Matthew Glen Bigham, Lennard Bijl, Dean & Kate Biskupovich, Frank Black, Veronica Blackbourn, Charlie Blackwell, Tamzin Blair, Karen Blanchard, Marc Blehert, Wayne Bleier, Catherine Block, Jonny Block, Nadine Blokker, Johanna Bloomberg, Yoni Blum, Jon Boagey, Gkanya Boasakul, Patricia Bohle, John Boley, Sue Bollans, Michael Boller, Vernon Bolton, Gertjan Bon, Mike & Jan Bond, Julia Bonn, Maria Bonnevie, Richard Borenstein, Nick Borg, Nicole Borner, Diederik Borst, Prue Borthwick, Marcio Boruchowski, Anne Bos, Kent Bostrom, Bruce Bougourd, Stephanie Bourgeois-Fend, Catherine Bourne, Gerrit Bouwhuis, Paul Bowes, Sean Bowman, Jim Boyd, Katie Boylan, Nichola Bradbury, Rob Bradley, Stefan Braunewell, James Bravant, Tim Brazier, Damian Brennan, Thomas Brennan, Siobhan Breslin, Greg Brett, Bert Brilleman, Joanna Brittain, Mary D Broderick, Tom Broderick, David Brodtmann, Stephen Brookes, Marc Brookhuis, Gordon Brosadair, Jim Broughton, Andrew Brown, Chris Brown, David Brown, Jackum Brown, Kevin Brown, Tristan Brown, C A Browning, Jeremy Brugmans, York Bruijn, Julian Brunt, Herman Bruyninx, Jeroen Bruyns, Tom Bryce, Lisa Buchanan, Karin Buchberger, Richard Buck, Gemma Buckle, Ger Buckley, Sarah Buckley, Sarah Budd, Karin Buehler, Kristy Buesnel, Larry Buickel, Sebastian Buks, Susanne Bulten, Birgit Bungeroth, Jantien Bunk, Ralf Burgert, Alex Burgess, Anna Burgess, Linda Burgin, Gloria Burnet, Katherine Burnie, Helene Bustad-Johannessen, Ben Buston, Kelly Busuttil, Karen Buswell, Cynthia Butler, Hans Buyl, Philip Caballero, Aine Cadavona, Douglas & Kelly Cadot, Fionnuala Callaghan, Peter Callaghan, Dick Calvert, Fergy Campbell, Jared Cantlon, Lynn Canzano, Angela Cheng Caplan, Norm Cappell, Pierluigi Caramellino, Eva Carleberg, Mette & Henrik Carlsen, Adam Carlson, Christine Carriou, Alister Carroll, E Sean Carter, Jenne Casarotto, Romelle Castle, Stuart Cavaliero, Erik Cederquist, Radek Cerny, John Chadwick, Steve Chambers, Aimee Chan, Eddie K L Chan, Gilbert Chan, Rebecca Chan, Georgia Chandler, Jean-Luc & Doris Chapatte, Wendy Chau, David Chen, Lawrence T Cheung, Carl Chin, Alessandro Cioni, Nick Chomonter, Agnes Chong, Kong Thau Chong, Michael Christoffersen, Arthur Chuang, Suwat Chumsri, Jesse Church, Matthew Churchward, David Clark, Jen Clarke, Rachel Clarke, Steve Clarke, Robin Claye, Martin Cleland, Thierry Clerc, Roy Clogstoun, Michelle Coates, David Cohen, Robin Cohen, Yaron Cohen, Hazel Colbert, Susannah May Colbert, Stephen Colbourn, Dennis Collins, Tony Colonello, Christine Coman, Herb Con, Chris Condin, Martin Conway, Kay Louise Cook, Marilyn Cook, Trevor Cook, Claudia Cool, Bryan Cooper, Peter Cooper, Ruby Cooper, Ashleigh Copeland, Daniel Corey, Rob Cormack, Ursula Cornu, Robert Correa, Paul Costa, John Cotton, Darragh Courtney, Alex Cousins, Scott Cowin, Nick Cox, Stephanie Cox, Giles Craig, Elizabeth Crane, Sonia Cribley, Nadia & Pino Criminelli,

Andrea Crisp, Juy Croager, Holly Crofton, Jocasta Crofts, Tim & Marika Crosby, Fred Cross, Terry Crossley, Ian Cruickshank, Carla Cudini, Patrick Cuff, Daniele Cuminale, Rene Curley, Jon Curry, Alex N Custer, Betti Czarl, Amanda D Normanville, Amanda da Cunha Gelfant, Guy Dahan, Natasha Dahanayake, Felix Dahm, Willem & Sandra Damen, Rainer Dangelmaier, Bryun Daniels, Jennifer Danning, Nicola Danslow, Sue D'Arcy, Alan Dare, Kate Darley, Sonja Darlington, Eleena Darlow, Mireille Dauphinais, Daniela Daute, Julian Davey, Alun Davies, Charlotte Davies, David R Davies, Geoff Davies, Fred Davis, Julie Davis, Sue Davis, Peter Day, David Dayton, Joon de Berg, Astrid de Boer, Han de Bont, Walter de Bruijn, Maaike de Meyer, Rob & Melanie de Raad, Katrien De Voldere, Claire Deacon, Steve Deadman, Trine Degner, Kees Dehl, Cato Delanda-Carthago, Amanda Delaney, Thomas Delorjn, Liz DeLoughrey, Joeri Demey, Serkan Demiral, Jillian Dempster, Sandy Denize, Peter Denton, Jim D'Enyar, Olivier Deparis, Caroline Dereymaeker, Rena Derezin, Arne Deussen, Nora Devai, Anna Di Bartolo, Elio Di Mauro, Johnny Diamond, Dianne Daley, David Dickson, Larry M Diebel, Lies Dieben, Greg Diefenbach, Anke Dijkstra, Dick Dijkstra, Sabine Dinges, Matina Dishes, Mark Distler, Graham Dix, Dan Dixon, Jamie Dixon, Jenni Dixon, Daniel Dizcola, Tracy Docheff, Ron Doering, Ineke Dohrmann, Mathew Doidge, Dr Lendvai Domonkos, Daniel Donnelly, Marie Donnelly, Cheryl Donohoe, Amy Donovan, Lou Douillard, Tim Dowdall, Anne Doyle, Marcel Driessen, Emma Drinkwater, Kev & Dot Drinnen, Matt Dufort, Jo Duggan, Winai Dulyavidh, Rachel Duncan, Celia Dunn, D Dunne, Dominic Dunne, Siobhan Dunne, Leandro H Duran, Mark Duvall, Katarzyna Dziewulska, Philip Eastwood, Peter Edan, Norman Edge, Roger Paul Edmonds, Per Edstrom, Simone Egger, John Elliott, Angie Eng, Anna & Lisa Eng, Jesse Engdahl, Bob Ennis, John Ensor, Michelle Enticknap, Achara & Don Entz, Hakan Eriksson, Ben Ernst, Matt & Eileen Erskine, Ceri Eskins, Carmen Estermann, Caroline Evans, Lucy Evans, Peter Evans, Brian Fagan, Caryll Fagan, James Farley, David Farrell, D'Arcy Faulkner, Janus Vest Fausing, Raphael Favre, David Fearn, Evan Fearn, Jon Fearon, Stale Fedgaard, Magdalena & Krysztof Fedorowicz, Crists Fedryna, Roger Feller, Darryl Ferguson, Neil Ferguson, Elisa Helena Fernandes, Tom Ferrington, Poul Fersling, Luci Ferspal, Thomas Fessler, Ryan Filteau, Geraldine Finch, Jonathan Finegold, Davida Finger, Jon Fischer, Juliane Fischer, Mark Fitchett, Graham Fitzgerald, Harry Fitzherbert, Tim Fitzsimmons, Gavin Fitzsimmous, Bryce Flannery, Gebhard Flatz, Sarah Fletcher, Sharon & Alison Fogarty, Oyvin Fonnes, Greg Ford, Kendall Ford, Sari Fordham, Tim Forster, Ryan Forsythe, Duncan Fortune, Alan Foster, John Foster, Joanna Foster, Barry & Trish Fox, Charlotte Fox, John Francis, Marilyn Francis, De Segonzac Francoise, Sarah Franklin, Tomas Fransson, Gerdy Frantzke, Anni Frederiksen, Stale Fredgaard, Alan Freeman, Heather Freeman, Sarah Freeman, Tim Freeman, Betti Frenkiel, Mark Freshney, Annette Freude, Kristin Frey, Felix Frie, Hannah Friedrich, Katrin Friedrich, Roger Friedrich, Richard Frost, Shin Fujieda, Anthony Fulford, Petra & Dirk Funhoff, Anthony Gage, Helen Gail, Shevaun Gallwey, Ann Galvin, Paula Galvin, Rhiannon Gambold, Robert Gangi, Gwen Garcelon, Russell Gardner, Anna Garling, Lynsey Garner, Dana Garrison, Fabian Garro, Steohanie Gauducheau, Ben Gaum, Mickael Gaupillat, Roger Gebhardt, Ramon Geenen, Martine Geijsels, Michael Geisthor, Helen Georghiou, Emma Gibson, Alice Gifford, Mark Gilbey, Kai Gildhorn, Martin Gill, Stephen Gill, Steve Gill, Bill Gilliam, Catrina Gilliam, Richard Gillingham, Renee Gillioz, Jen Gintzler, Katia Giraud, J Girdler, Stan Glantz, Brad Gledhill, Gail Goehrig, Bob & Eunice Goetz, Bernie Goldman, Tom Goldsmith, Omar Gonzalez, Keith Gore, Sile Gorman, Paul F Gorringe, Tony Gough, Sylvain Goupil, Sidsel Graae, Steve Grant, Sandra Grasso, Jon Gray, Tamy Green, Justine Gregson, Jim Greenhill, Nick Greening, Mike P Gregoire, Helen Gregory, Alex Griffin, Mari Griffin, Eva-Marie Griffiths, A Groesbeck, Tanja Grussendorf, David Guest, Gandalf Guzendorf, Eric Haanstad, Marion Haas, Jasmine Haere, Renee Hagell, Alyce Hager, R J Hahn, R E Haines, Tamara Hale, Derek Hall, Ellenise Hall, Tina Hall, Roz Hallard, Tom Halliday, Dave Halse, Tomm Hammer, Stefan Hammond, V Hammond, David Hampshaw, Gary & Luke Hampson, Bernard Hanneke, Paul Hannon, Anette Hansen, Marieta Hansen, Rene Hansen, Stinne & Flemming Hansen, Tracy Hanson, Johann Hanzy, Ian Harbison, Wendy Hardman, Ed Hardy, Eddie Hardy, Darren Hare, Noel T Hargreaves, James Harmen, Jan Harmsen, Toni Harmsen, Audrey & Dennis Harper, Graham Harrell, Deb & Tony Harrip, Patrick Harris, Tye Hartall, Jonathan Harth, David Hartington, Jane Hartley, Christoffer Hartmann, Holger Jan Hartmann, Andreas Hartung, Oliver Harwood, Eric Haskell, Mikkel Hass, Noel Hathorn, Christian Hawkins, Tracy Hay, Allan Healy, Janis Hearn, David Hecht, Paul Hecht,

Janos Hee, Kieran Hegarty, Jonas Heide Munck, Paul Heinrich, Michael Helder, Andy Helmrich, Rene Helsloot, Carola Helwig, Ross Henderson, Anastasia Hendley, Esther Hendrik, Patrik Henriksson, Karen Herman, Julian Hernandez, Vincente Hernandez, Amelia Hess, Nicole Hess, Jon Hewson, Mechtild & Freek Hielckert, E Hiensch, Wayne Higgins, Daz Highway, Belinda Hill, Chloe Hill, Lol Hind, David Hirzel, Lisa Ho, Megan Ho, Susan Hobson, Rob Hocking, Simon Hodge, Rob & Lene Hodgkins, Geoff & Carol Hodgson, Kathleen Hodgson, Nicola Hogg, Neal Hollands, Steve Hollins, Adrian Holman, Will Holme, Britt Holmen, Uvo Holscher, Sander Mossing Holsteijn, Inge-Bjorn Mossige-Norheim, Lyn Holt, Peter Holt, Tara Holt, Andy Homan, H Hood, Rob Hoogenbos, Niels Hooiveld, Nathaniel Hope, David Hopkinson, Dawn Horridge, Anne Horsley, Danielle Horwich, Kew Hose, Clive Hosking, Kieran Howe, Lee Hubbard, Robin Hudson, Den Hughes, Laura Hughes, Samatha Hughes, Jurgen Hugli, Hannu Huhta, Erik Huiberts, Paul & Karen Hull, Remko Hulst, Alice Humlova, Martyn Humphreys, Devin Hunt, Mark Hunter, James Hutchinson, Michael Hvidtfeldt, Blanche Iberg, Rune Iglebak, Anthony Iglesias, Corinna Ilg, Atle Ingebrigtsen, Christine Ingemorsen, Jenny Ingerson, Jen Innes, Susan Irwin, Lindsay Isherwood, Sheryl Ishizaki, Shamim Islam, Andre Iwaszkiewicz, Tereska Iwinska, David Jackson, Jan Jacobs, Kenneth Jademo, Miles Jaffe, Barry Jaggers, Maneesita Jaidee, Taskeshi Jaiean, Lena Jakobsson, Viola Janbroers, Leclaire James, Jennifer Jameson, Ms Jane, Alain Janssens, Heleen Janszen, Alexandra Jarvis, Massoud Javadi, Kanittha Jeanpetch, Mark Jeffery, Phillip & De Jeffries, Neil Jenkins, Amelia Jenkinson, Tilen Jenko, Nicolas Jerez Capdeville, Paul Jerkenstam, Jose Jimeenez, Jose Jimenez, Michael Johannes, Ian Johnson, Michele Johnson, Nigel Johnson, Stewart Johnston, Andrew Johnstone, Destinee Jones, Fred Jones, Leigh Jones, Richard Jones, Wally Jones, Sandy Jordan, Tom Joseph, Naegeli Jost, Aneta & Djordje Jovovic, Patrick Joyce, Guido Jung, Ole Jungmann, Tony Jurica, Laurie Jutras, Boris Kaeller, Line Kallstad, Dan Kalmar, Lulu Kamlah, Risto Kantola, Hiren Kapadia, Janina Karr, Jennifer Kavanagh, Terry Kaye, Ross Keane, Matt Keen, Chad Keenan, Megan Keir, Alison & Daniel Kelly, Jeltsje Kemerink, Thomas Kemmere, Brenda Kemp, Robert Kemp, Tomas Kempe, Karlijn Kempen, Jim Kendall, Jay & Sophie Kenny, Dan Kent, Mary Rose Kent, Elise Keppler, Raymond Kerr, Carool Kersten, Arina & Marcel Kettenis, Chung Khoon, Pattarit Khunkitti, Domnal Kidney, Ratanaporn Kidsanayotin, Kathy Kieffer, Hilde Kievit, Dave King, Martyn King, Ryan King, Ester van Kippersluis, Susannah Kinley, Louise Kiss, Ruri Kitadai, Krin Kitiyos, Danne Kjellin, Corne Klaassen, Janica Kleiman, Cees Kleinveld, Michael Klepper, Cornelius Kluessien, Geoffrey Knoell, Jossie Knorr, Deborah Koch, Charles Koehl, Estelle Koh, Rasmus Kold, Louise Kolind-Andersen, Pieter Korst, Kimmo Kosonen, Volker Koss, Dr Damir Kovac, Petra Kowal, Len Kowalik, Jochem Kramer, Gerhard Kratz, Julia Kresmann, Joshua Krist, Thomas Krogh, Daniela Kronseder, Johannes Kruth, Joerg Kuehne, Joe Kuhn, Benedikt Kuipers, Jacob & Corina Kuipers, George Kullmann, Yoshikazu Kunugi, Eva Kylberg, Donald R La Mere, Justin La Sala, Justin Lacombe, K K Lahiri, Judie Lam, Clare & Colin Lamb, Curtis Lambrecht, Betty Lamet, Chris & Dawn Landes, Rosalie Landstra, Astrid Lang, Craig Langford, Bo Lanner, Silvija Lapadatovic, Ulrike Lapper, Hanna Lasson, Ryan Latimer, Shoham Latz, Hind & Lol Laurent, John Law, Anna Lawley, John Lawlor, Alan Lawson, Keith Lawson, Anne Le Blanc, Damien Le Gal, Gary Leahy, Carol Leaman, Andrea Lederer, Emma Lee, Gina Lee, S Leece, Julie Leech, Pauline Lees, Michele Legge, Thomas Lehne, Delphine Lelievre, Pierre Lemasson, Benedikte Lensberg, Miki Lentin, Lucas & Vanessa Leonardi, David L'Estrange, Annabel Lewis, Shania Lewis, Anna Liden, Siang Lie Yeu, Lisa Liebich, Trina Lightbody, Margo Linehan, Harm Linssen, Sarah Linton, Shirley Linton, Julia Lippold, Geoff Lipscomb, Adrian Liston, V Liu, Kevin Livermore, Andrew & Gina Livingstone, Marta Llorente, Christine Loft, Steven Logan, Iris Lohrengel, Sue Long, Beatriz Lorente, Lou Lonsdale, Ramon Lopez, Dirk Louwers, Michelle Lowings, Renate & Patrick Lubben, Jérôme Lucas, Deborah Ludlam, Carolyn Lui, Lynn & Bill Luke, Joanne Lumb, Per Lundevall, Becky Lunn, Coral Lyddon, Allison M, Rachel M, Liselotte Maas, Anneloes Maas-Geesteranus, Duncan Macdonald, Matt & Donna Maciejewski, Maik Macho, Anthony Mack, Jason MacKenzie, John Maclaren, Robert MacRiner, Elizabeth Madden, Andreas Magnusson, Annette Mainka, Malcolm Mair, Andrea Malcouronne, Heather Mallette, M H Mallory, Mike Manley, Erin Mangurten, Dikla Mantin, Ariel Maor, Larry Marechal, Catelijne Markenstein, Allegra Marshall, Judy & Kelvin Marshall, Andrew Martin, Carla Martin, David Martin, Emma Martin, Lina Martin, Tom Jorgen Martinussen, Volker Maschmann, Steven Mathers, Zoe Matthews, Lisa Matthiesen, Olivier

Mauron, Sevgi Mavi, John Mayall, Roland Mayer, Liat Mazor, Tammy M Mazzullo, Tom McAuliff, Eoin McCarney, Colleen McClure, Victoria McColm, Calli McCrae, Jamie McCrory, Kathleen McCrory, Chris McCullough, Ray & Rosemary McCully, Ciaran McGarrigle, Fiona McGarva, Stephen McGhee, Declan McGinley, Bill McGinn, Lorraine McGrath, Dennis McGregor, Allison Mcguire, Charles McIntyre, Natalie McIntyre, Sarah McIntyre, Frances McKay, Jand McLardie, Margaret McLaughlin, Celia McLean, Ian McLeod, Karen McLinton, Tammy McMinn, Hilary McNamara, Peter McNamara, Simon McNiff, Jalela McQueen, Tracey McTernan, Michael McWhirter, Elizabeth McZeo, Henry Meester, Anand Mehta, Jeroen Meijden, David Meiklejohn, Mark Mellor, Ineke Mertens, Tony Messenger, Rogan Mexted, Ceciel Meys, Wesley Mezzone, Omtzigt Michiel, Andrew Middleton, Fred Midtgaard, Paloma Mignini, Anne Militello, Beverly A Miller, Karral Miller, Lynda Miller, Paul Miller, Laura Millman, Christina Mills, Michelle Mills, Sumalee Milne, John & Amelia Milsom, Bonnie Miners, Olivia Mirodone, Angie Mishkin, Kunal Misra, Ian Mitchell, Riz & Nina Mithani, Tomae Miura, Kazuya Miyashita, Dennis Mogerman, Anna Mohn, Myrthe Mohr, Lars Molin, Claire & Claudio Molinario, Camilla Moller, David Moller, Chad Montabon, Gavin Mooney, Tom Mooney, Annalee Moore, Garry Moore, Neal Moore, Zoe Moore, Nnenna Morah, Khadine Morcom, Annabella Morelos-Chan, Jean-Claude Moret, Bill Morgan, Sauro Morganti, Sarah Morlok, Frank Morris, Steve Morrison, Steve Morrissey, Ann Mortensen, George Moschis, Eugene Mosier, Bob Moulang, Moira Mount, Sky Mowen, Andreas Mueller, Roland Mueller, Sandeep Mukerji, Nicki Mulhall, Eliza Muller, Eric Muller, Julie Murnaghan, Niamh Murphy, R H Murray-Philipson, Katherine Murrin, Beth Murzyn, Mark Naftalin, Christina Nagel, Tali & Jud Naim, Maria Natoli, Magnus Neergaard, Roderick Neilsen, Ciaran Neligan, Michael Nepia, Raquel Neto, Elaine Ng, Henry Nguyen, Brent Nicholas, Teresa Nicholls, Tony Nicholls, Trine Maria Nielsen, Horst Niemert, Paul Nikitopoulos, Alex & Diane Nikolic, Christian Nilsen, Julia Niven, Andrea Nordenstreng, Kim Norgrove, Andrzej Nowak, Dr Sheila Nunn, Bente Nyland, Evan Obercian, Megan O'Brien, Shane O'Brien, Suzanne O'Brien, Ryan O'Byrne, Rolando Ochoa, Sean O'Connell, Shula O'Dowd, James Oehlcke, Ivan Oerum, Sabine Oesselke, Patricia Oey, Jessica Ogilvy-Stuart, Chia-Yen Oh, Francoise Ohayon, Hitoshi Oi, Shannon O'Laughlin, Xavier Op De Laak, Wendy Opperman, Sherman & Brenda Oraas, Billy O'Reilly, Brendan O'Rourke, John Orsler, Lee O'Shea, Eric Osmond, Barbara Ostergaard, Pjotr Ostrica, John O'Sullivan, Ronnie Otten, Jenny Ovaere, Patrick Overwijk, David Oxley-Oxland, Jill Oxner, Hanna Pace-O'Shea, Orkay Padam, R K Padam, Julie Page, Graham Paisley, Goran Palmgren, Walter Paoli, Jim Parisi, Eleanore Park, Dennis Parlevliet, Nicholas Park, Colin Parsons, Tim Parsons, Frank Paschold, John Pasley, Komal Patel, Penny Patmore, Trent Paton, Amanda Patterson, Carol & Robert Patton, Pauline Patton, John Paulsen, Nick Payton, Zoar Paz, Andy Peck, Garry Peck, Martin Peek, John Peene, Scott Peerenboom, Lucille & Paul Peeters, Peter Peirson, Annette Pelgrim, Ruth Pendry, Gualberto Perez, Owen Perkins, Patrik Persson, Emmanuel Perve, Tim Peters, Soren B Petersen, Vivian Petersen, Henning Petersen, Daniel Peterson, Larry Peterson, Mariska Petri, Nils Pettersson, Hans Juergen Pfaffenhofen, Edith Pfister, Huong Lam Pham, Ng Keng Phoy, Hannah Pike, Custodio Pintado, Alexandra Pitman, Karin Pizzinini, Nico Plat, Inesa Pleskacheuskaya, Rolf Poelman, Sven Poguntke, Michal Polat, Adriana Poli, Alberto Poli, Florian Poltz, Ben Posener, Kira Posewitz, Robert Pospiech, Katherine Potter, Caroline Potterton, Craig Powell, Daniel Preda, Juergen Preimesberger, John Prendergast, Richard Prendergast, Clare Prenton, Ansula Press, Andy Price, Daniel & Catherine Price, Julie Price, Michael Price, David Priest, Lorna & Ben Pritchard, Morten Pritzkow, Lynaia Pulido, N L Pulman, Andrea Purdekova, Shahreen Quazi, Gabriel Quoirin, Deki Radha, Jo Rae, Kerin Raistrick, Binhma Rajsombath, Prasad Ramachandran, Jose Ramon, Alana Ramos, Herb & Marg Ramseldar, Leif Dodrh Rasmussen, Nipon Ratana-Arporn, Gary Rathbone, Thomas Rau, Michael Rausch, Titti Ravaid, Paolo Ravazzano, Mark Rebuck, Kristin Redfern, Non Reed, Ann Reeves, Sofia Rehn, Dietrich Rehnert, Denise Reich, Nicole Reichenbach, David Reid, Marleen Reinders, Abe Remmo, William Rendle, Felix Reychman, Sue Reynolds, Duncan Rhodes, Aileen & Tim Rich, Garry & Carol Richens, Amy Richter, Andrew Ridler, Andreas Rieck, Matthew A Rifkin, Phillip Rigby, Liz Rinker, Michell & Jessica Rishe, Anita Ritchie, Milagros Rivera, Arden Rivers, James Rixon, John Robarge, Joyce Robarge, Judith Robertson, Emma Robinson, Julian Robov, Chris Rockett, Marco Roebers, Andrea Rogge, Anusorn Rojvatunyu, Tom Rom, Lars Romsvik, Rie Aleksandra Rorstrand, Doug Rose, Jonny Rose, Simon Rose, Chris Rosher, Georgina

Ross, Eric Roth, Dave Rouelett, Diana Rowat, Jim Rowe, Nicholas Rowell, Karen Rowland, Mark Rowlatt, Steve Rudman, Simon Rufus, Kristian Rumble, Stephanie Rummel, Glenn Runcie, Frances Runnalls, Greg Rushbury, Angie Russell, Jim Ryan, Kevin Ryan, Mary Ryan, Richard Ryan, David & Marilyn Sabold, Stefan Sagel, Willem Saher, Paola Salis, Erika Salloux, Victor D Samper, Jeremy & Sara Sampson, Mak Mun San, Aase & Magne Sand, Felicia Sanders, Christian Sano, Mario Saraceni, Val Sarver, Lliane & Manfred Satlot, Louis & Martha Savelkoul, Xandra Savelkouls, James Savidge, Richard Sayers, Fernanda Baeza Scagliusi, Ken Scallon, Peter Scarborough, David Scarry, Jack & Joan Schafer, Jorn Schakenraad, Antoinette Schapper, Nina Schemainda, Joachim Schessl, Caddie Schintler, Adrian Schmid, Hansi Schmid, Mathias Schmid, Martin Schmidt, Martin Schneider, Michel Schneider, Patrice Schneider, Stefan Schnellbacher, Helmet Schoenenberger, Sandra Scholze, Siw Schroder, Johanna Schroeder, Walbert Schulpen, J Schwartz, Emanuele Scianca, John G Scott, Stephen Scott, Martin Searle, Charlene Searle, Martin Searle, Richard Sevicke-Jones, Noah Shaikh, Frederick Shannon, Victor Shao, Paul Sharman, Karen Sharpe, Bill & Wannee Shaw, Ira Shaw, Norman Shepherd, Tory Shepherd, Michael Sheridan, Matt Sheriff, Rotem Shkolnik, Katz Shoham, Neville Shortt, Eddie Shroff, David Shum, S S Sidhu, Laura Sikstrom, Natsa Silar, Marjorie Silva, Don Silver, Ken Silver, Pierre Simard, Martina Simbuerger, Sharon Simha, Wouter Simonse, David & Christina Simpson, Sarathip Sirivibulya, Irene Sitskoorn, Ed Skebe, Ingvar & Ewa Skeppstedt, Jan-Christian Skjaeggerud, Nick Skrobot, Ingrid Skulstad, Mark Slade, Petr Slechta, Sharon Sloman, Matthew Smedley, Valentina Smirnios, Bill Smith, David J Smith, J Smith, Kathryn Smith, Martyn & Lynne Smith, Matin Sobek, Gary Soden, Olle Sodergren, Anna Solero, John Solt, Lorenzo Sonelli, May Soo Thoo, Reshma Sood, Todd Sorel, Eskil Sorensen, Finn Sorensen, James Sorrell, Jude Sowden, Lucy Sparks, Brett & Khem Spearman, Sarah Spence, Lauren Spencer, Seana Sperling, Mark Sperry, Sabine Springweiler, Chris Sprotte, Nienhe Spruijt, Chusri Srichuwong, Isabelle Staehli, Devet Stan, Fiona Standfield, Douglas Stasinowsky, John Statham, Rachael Stead, Ulrike Steinbrenner, Bo Stenberg, Daniel Stephan, Matt Stephenson, Emma Stevens, Jo Stilges, Andrew Stillman, Valentine Stockdale, Lynn Stone, Carol Stoner, Dr John Stonham, Rob Street, Abigail Strong, Paul Strong, Antje Struewing, Stian Bjaroy Stubbrud, Michelle Sturman, Donruedee Suchartwudhi, Marie Sule, Amy Sullivan, Razia Sultana, Ninni Suni, Joe Sura, Martin Svenningsen, Anders Svensson, Ivan Swater, Catherine Sweatman, John & Moy Sweetman, Christine Sydneysmith, Don Tait, Nick Talwar, Janice Tan, Leslie Tan, T K Tan, Anna Tapp, Alex Tarrant, Stephane Taulaigo, Anne Marie Taylor, Graham Taylor, Rachael Taylor, Holly Te, Ruud Teeuwen, Henri Teitler, Anna Templeton, Anne-Louise Ten Houten, Lisa Tenuta, Kris Terauds, Ray Teuten, John Tha, Jeff Thaldorf, M Thanasakdi, Christina Themar, Laurent Thery, Julie Thewlis, Les Thompson, David Thomson, David Thorne, Steve Thorp, Brian Tiernan, Justin Tilbury, P A Tillman, Rupert Tipler, Stan Tkachenko, Gregory T'Kint, Bea Toews, M Tolenaars, Arthur Torrence, Carla Treasure, Lisa Trencher, Harry S Truman, Bobby Tse, Pracha Tuangpernsub, Tara Tulley, Ellen Tullo, David Turner, Jeff Turner, Margaret & Tony Twemlow, Derry Tyrrell, Paul Tzimas, Monica Ueltschi, Lele & Tom Uhl, Fabio Umehara, Samuel Urech, Tero Vaananen, Jacob Valdez, Stephanie Valido, Andrew Valls, Jeroen van Aar, Loes van Beest, Verne van Berkel, Christel van Hout, Radboud & Nancy Van de Ven-Geerts, Irma van den Berg, Alexandra van den Bos, Michel van den Braak, Michel & Derk van den Braak, H van den Broek, Ellen van den Haak, Marieke van den Ham, Peter van der Burgh, Max van der Hoeven, Henk van der Horst, Paulien van der Linden, Jan van der Sanden, Julie van der Vrecken, Richard van Dijk, Martijn van Elzakker, Hiske van Haren, Wilmar van Hengel, Chris Van Hooft, Wanida Van Houtte, Martin van Huijstee, Anneke van Kollenburg, Henk van Kuijk, Els van Lavieren, An Van Looveren, Teun van Metelen, Ingrid van Ommen, Patrick van Roest, Joost van Schooten, Peter van Spall, Geert Van Steyvoort, Astrid van Thienen, Lara van Turnhout, Luit van Velzen, Jeroen van Vliet, Pieter Van Waeyenberge, M Van Wier, Juliet van Wijngaarden, Darryl & Tania Vance, Sofie Vandewoestijne, Peter Van't Westeinde, Al & Trudy Veenstra, Jacques Et Gi Veit, Berend Veldhoen, Carol Venable, Amanda Vennables, Andrea Vera, Kim Verbon, Margriet Verhagen, Jacoline Verheul, Mieke Verkerk, Norma Vernon, Olga Vernooij, Pim Vernooij, Martien & Hanneke Versteeg-van Adrichem, Bart Verwilligen, Michaela Veverkova, Kevin Vickers, Joanna Vince, Filip Vincke, Jyrki Virtanen, Frank Visakay, Arlinde Vletter, Cees Vletter, Patrick Vogt, Sandra & Yakeer Volotzki, Hans J Von Der Pfordten, Kai Vonk, Maike Voorhuis, Jeroen Vos, Nicholas Vreeland, Janet Vulevich, Terhi & Juha-Pekka Vuorio, Zita

Wachsmann, Reto Wagner, Clive Walker, Roger Walker, Tim Walker, Gillian Wallace, Jennie Wallace, Colin Waller, Valerie Wallis, Dawn Walsh, Philip & Ann Walters, Kate Walton, Michael Ward, Rebecca Ward, Terry Ward, Carl Warren, Liz, Jeff & Oliver Warrener, Jessica Watson, Rosie Watson, Emma Watt, Jane Weber, W G M Webers, Angie Webster, Ben Wee, Sandy Weed, Gerard Weeverink, Ross Wehner, Helmut Wehowsky, Wolfram Weidemann, Yael Weiss, Michael Weissbluth, Viktor Weisshaeupl, J C Welch, Mark Wellington, Bertil Wendel, Hauke Wendt, Jo Werelds, Asher & Noi Werty, Barney West, Lara Westgeest, Ian Westley, Rachel & Andy Westnidge, T J M Weston, Frank Wheby, Jenny Wheeler, David Whetter, Caroline White, Norah White, Melanie Whittle, James Whyte, Carol Wicking, Larry Wiechern, Melanie Wielens, Suzanne Wild, Dr Dennis Wiley, Oliver Wilkinson, Latt Willatts, Rebecca Williams, Reg Williams, Ross Williams, Terry Williams, Terry Williams-Yeephat, Timothy Willis, Doc Wilsey, Steve Wilson, Max Wiman, Jackie Winter, Otto Wintzell, Alison Winward, Nichol Wiseman, Paula Wiseman, Erwin Wisman, Mijke Witbraad, Mark Withers, Shonagh Withey, Liesbeth Witteman, Andrea Woelke, Brendt Wohlberg, Judy Wolf, Kori Wolfard, H Wolff, Rossmeier Wolfgang, Adrian Wong, Joyce Wong, Julie Wong, Vincent Woo, Kyle Wood, Rebecca J Wood, Sarah Wood, Tonia & Daniel Wood, Geoffrey Woodruff, Andrew Woods, Carol Woods, Christian Woodyatt, Zoey Worsfold, Ali Worsley, Joyce Wouters, C Wrentmore, Lauren Wright, Markus Wunderlich, Jeroen Wynen, Kevin Yamaguchi, Kazub Yamazueki, Jaehoon Yang, Vaknin Yaniv, Asoka Yapa, Henrik Yde-Andersen, Mike Yeomans, Siang Lie Yeu, Jade York, Alvin Yoshinaga, John Yu, Dawn Yule, Debbie Zauder, Nicholas Zdenkowski, Urs Zellweger, Joe Zettl, Maike Ziesemer, Martin Zillger, Allison Zinder, Gaby Zollner, Anat Zve

LONELY PLANET

Guides by Region

Lonely Planet is known worldwide for publishing practical, reliable and no-nonsense travel information in our guides and on our Web site. The Lonely Planet list covers just about every accessible part of the world. Currently there are 16 series: Travel guides, Shoestring guides, Condensed guides, Phrasebooks, Read This First, Healthy Travel, Walking guides, Cycling guides, Watching Wildlife guides, Pisces Diving & Snorkeling guides, City Maps, Road Atlases, Out to Eat, World Food, Journeys travel literature and Pictorials.

AFRICA Africa on a shoestring • Botswana • Cairo • Cairo City Map • Cape Town • Cape Town City Map • East Africa • Egypt • Egyptian Arabic phrasebook • Ethiopia, Eritrea & Djibouti • Ethiopian Amharic phrasebook • The Gambia & Senegal • Healthy Travel Africa • Kenya • Malawi • Morocco • Moroccan Arabic phrasebook • Mozambique • Namibia • Read This First: Africa • South Africa, Lesotho & Swaziland • Southern Africa • Southern Africa Road Atlas • Swahili phrasebook • Tanzania, Zanzibar & Pemba • Trekking in East Africa • Tunisia • Watching Wildlife East Africa • Watching Wildlife Southern Africa • West Africa • World Food Morocco • Zambia • Zimbabwe, Botswana & Namibia
Travel Literature: Mali Blues: Traveling to an African Beat • The Rainbird: A Central African Journey • Songs to an African Sunset: A Zimbabwean Story

AUSTRALIA & THE PACIFIC Aboriginal Australia & the Torres Strait Islands •Auckland • Australia • Australian phrasebook • Australia Road Atlas • Cycling Australia • Cycling New Zealand • Fiji • Fijian phrasebook • Healthy Travel Australia, NZ & the Pacific • Islands of Australia's Great Barrier Reef • Melbourne • Melbourne City Map • Micronesia • New Caledonia • New South Wales • New Zealand • Northern Territory • Outback Australia • Out to Eat – Melbourne • Out to Eat – Sydney • Papua New Guinea • Pidgin phrasebook • Queensland • Rarotonga & the Cook Islands • Samoa • Solomon Islands • South Australia • South Pacific • South Pacific phrasebook • Sydney • Sydney City Map • Sydney Condensed • Tahiti & French Polynesia • Tasmania • Tonga • Tramping in New Zealand • Vanuatu • Victoria • Walking in Australia • Watching Wildlife Australia • Western Australia
Travel Literature: Islands in the Clouds: Travels in the Highlands of New Guinea • Kiwi Tracks: A New Zealand Journey • Sean & David's Long Drive

CENTRAL AMERICA & THE CARIBBEAN Bahamas, Turks & Caicos • Baja California • Belize, Guatemala & Yucatán • Bermuda • Central America on a shoestring • Costa Rica • Costa Rica Spanish phrasebook • Cuba • Cycling Cuba • Dominican Republic & Haiti • Eastern Caribbean • Guatemala • Havana • Healthy Travel Central & South America • Jamaica • Mexico • Mexico City • Panama • Puerto Rico • Read This First: Central & South America • Virgin Islands • World Food Caribbean • World Food Mexico • Yucatán
Travel Literature: Green Dreams: Travels in Central America

EUROPE Amsterdam • Amsterdam City Map • Amsterdam Condensed • Andalucía • Athens • Austria • Baltic States phrasebook • Barcelona • Barcelona City Map • Belgium & Luxembourg • Berlin • Berlin City Map • Britain • British phrasebook • Brussels, Bruges & Antwerp • Brussels City Map • Budapest • Budapest City Map • Canary Islands • Catalunya & the Costa Brava • Central Europe • Central Europe phrasebook • Copenhagen • Corfu & the Ionians • Corsica • Crete • Crete Condensed • Croatia • Cycling Britain • Cycling France • Cyprus • Czech & Slovak Republics • Czech phrasebook • Denmark • Dublin • Dublin City Map • Dublin Condensed • Eastern Europe • Eastern Europe phrasebook • Edinburgh • Edinburgh City Map • England • Estonia, Latvia & Lithuania • Europe on a shoestring • Europe phrasebook • Finland • Florence • Florence City Map • France • Frankfurt City Map • Frankfurt Condensed • French phrasebook • Georgia, Armenia & Azerbaijan • Germany • German phrasebook • Greece • Greek Islands • Greek phrasebook • Hungary • Iceland, Greenland & the Faroe Islands • Ireland • Italian phrasebook • Italy • Kraków • Lisbon • The Loire • London • London City Map • London Condensed • Madrid • Madrid City Map • Malta • Mediterranean Europe • Milan, Turin & Genoa • Moscow • Munich • Netherlands • Normandy • Norway • Out to Eat – London • Out to Eat – Paris • Paris • Paris City Map • Paris Condensed • Poland • Polish phrasebook • Portugal • Portuguese phrasebook • Prague • Prague City Map • Provence & the Côte d'Azur • Read This First: Europe • Rhodes & the Dodecanese • Romania & Moldova • Rome • Rome City Map • Rome Condensed • Russia, Ukraine & Belarus • Russian phrasebook • Scandinavian & Baltic Europe • Scandinavian phrasebook • Scotland • Sicily • Slovenia • South-West France • Spain • Spanish phrasebook • Stockholm • St Petersburg • St Petersburg City Map • Sweden • Switzerland • Tuscany • Ukrainian phrasebook • Venice • Vienna • Wales • Walking in Britain • Walking in France • Walking in Ireland • Walking in Italy • Walking in Scotland • Walking in Spain • Walking in Switzerland • Western Europe • World Food France • World Food Greece • World Food Ireland • World Food Italy • World Food Spain **Travel Literature:** After Yugoslavia • Love and War in the Apennines • The Olive Grove: Travels in Greece • On the Shores of the Mediterranean • Round Ireland in Low Gear • A Small Place in Italy

LONELY PLANET

You already know that Lonely Planet produces more than this one guidebook, but you might not be aware of the other products we have on this region. Here is a selection of titles that you may want to check out as well:

Thailand's Islands & Beaches
ISBN 1 74059 500 9
US$19.99 • UK£11.99

Thai Phrasebook
ISBN 0 86442 658 5
US$6.95 • UK£4.50

Healthy Travel Asia & India
ISBN 1 86450 051 4
US$5.95 • UK£3.99

Bangkok Map
ISBN 1 74059 101 1
US$5.99 • UK£3.99

Chiang Mai & Northern Thailand
ISBN 1 74059 064 3
US$17.99 • UK£11.99

South East Asia Phrasebook
ISBN 0 86442 435 3
US$8.95 • UK£5.99

South East Asia on a Shoestring
ISBN 1 74104 164 3
US$24.99 • UK£14.99

Bangkok
ISBN 1 74059 460 6
US$16.99 • UK£11.99

Bangkok Condensed
ISBN 1 74059 351 0
US$11.99 • UK£6.99

Buddhist Stupas in Asia: The Shape of Perfection
ISBN 1 86450 120 0
US$34.99 • UK£24.99

Diving & Snorkeling Thailand
ISBN 1 86450 201 0
US$16.99 • UK£10.99

Available wherever books are sold

Index

Abbreviations

HP Historical Park
NP National Park
NMP National Marine Park
TH Thailand's Highlights

Text

Bold indicates maps.

Bold indicates maps.

Bold indicates maps.

I

Bold indicates maps.

Bold indicates maps.

Q

R

Bold indicates maps.

Bold indicates maps.

Y

Z

Boxed Text

MAP LEGEND

CITY ROUTES

- Freeway — Freeway
- Highway — Primary Road
- Road — Secondary Road
- Street — Street
- Lane — Lane
- On/Off Ramp
- Unsealed Road
- One Way Street
- Pedestrian Street
- Stepped Street
- Tunnel
- Footbridge

REGIONAL ROUTES

- Freeway
- Primary Road
- Secondary Road
- Minor Road

BOUNDARIES

- International
- Provincial
- Disputed
- Wall

HYDROGRAPHY

- River, Creek
- Canal
- Lake
- Spring; Waterfalls

TRANSPORT ROUTES & STATIONS

- Train
- Underground Train
- Skytrain
- Ferry
- Walking Trail
- Walking Tour
- Path
- Pier or Jetty

AREA FEATURES

- Building
- Park, Gardens
- Market
- Sports Ground
- Beach
- Cemetery
- Campus
- Plaza

POPULATION SYMBOLS

- CAPITAL — National Capital
- CAPITAL — Provincial Capital
- CITY — City
- Town — Town
- Village — Village
- Urban Area

MAP SYMBOLS

- Place to Stay
- Place to Eat
- Point of Interest

Airport/Airstrip-field	Cinema/Theatre	Museum	Stately Home
Archaeological Site	Dive Site/Snorkelling	National Park/Tree	Surfing/Swimming Pool
Bank/Border Crossing	Elephant Kraal	Parking/Petrol Station	Taxi or Tuk-Tuk
Bird Sanctuary/Zoo	Embassy/Hospital	Police/Post Office	Telephone
Bus Terminal/Stop	Fountain, Golf Course	Pub or Bar/Toilet	Temple (Buddhist)
Camping Area/Fort	Internet Cafe	Sǎwngthǎew	Temple (Hindu)/Shrine
Cave/Lighthouse	Lookout/Mountain	Shopping Centre	Temple (Sikh)
Cathedral, Church	Monument/Mosque	Shrine (Chinese)	Tourist Information

Note: not all symbols displayed above appear in this book

LONELY PLANET OFFICES

Australia
Locked Bag 1, Footscray, Victoria 3011
☎ 03 8379 8000 fax 03 8379 8111
email: talk2us@lonelyplanet.com.au

USA
150 Linden St, Oakland, CA 94607
☎ 510 893 8555 TOLL FREE: 800 275 8555
fax 510 893 8572
email: info@lonelyplanet.com

UK
72-82 Rosebery Ave, London EC1R 4RW
☎ 020 7841 9000 fax 020 7841 9001
email: go@lonelyplanet.co.uk

France
1 rue du Dahomey, 75011 Paris
☎ 01 55 25 33 00 fax 01 55 25 33 01
email: bip@lonelyplanet.fr
www.lonelyplanet.fr

World Wide Web: www.lonelyplanet.com *or* AOL keyword: lp
Lonely Planet Images: www.lonelyplanetimages.com